ARTS AND CULTURE

An Introduction to the Humanities

Combined Volume

ARTS AND CULTURE

An Introduction to the Humanities

Fourth Edition

Janetta Rebold Benton
Pace University, New York

Robert DiYanni
New York University

Prentice Hall
Boston Columbus Indianapolis New York San Francisco Upper Saddle River
Amsterdam Cape Town Dubai London Madrid Milan Munich Paris Montreal
Toronto Delhi Mexico City São Paulo Sydney Hong Kong Seoul Singapore Taipei Tokyo

President, SSA: *Yolanda de Rooy*
Editorial Director: *Craig Campanella*
Editor-in-Chief: *Sarah Touborg*
Acquisitions Editor: *Billy Grieco*
Editorial Assistant: *Jessica Parrotta*
Director of Marketing: *Brandy Dawson*
Executive Marketing Manager: *Kate Mitchell*
Marketing Assistant: *Lisa Kirlick*
Editorial Project Manager: *David Nitti*
Senior Managing Editor: *Ann Marie McCarthy*
Assistant Managing Editor: *Melissa Feimer*
Production Liaison: *Joe Scordato*
Full-Service Management: *S4Carlisle Publishing Services*
Photo Researcher: *Bill Smith Group*
Senior Manufacturing Manager for Arts & Sciences: *Mary Fischer*
Senior Operations Specialist: *Brian Mackey*
Senior Art Director: *Pat Smythe*
Cover Design: *Jill Lehan*
Cover Image: *Giovanni Paolo Panini (Roman, 1691–1765), "Interior of the Pantheon, Rome," c. 1734. Oil on Canvas. 1.280 × .990. (50 1/2 × 39); framed, 1.441 × 1.143 (56 3/4 × 45). Samuel H. Kress Collection. Photograph © 2001 Board of Trustees, National Gallery of Art, Washington. 1939.1.24.(135)/PA. Photo by Richard Carafelli.*
Senior Digital Media Editor: *David Alick*
Pearson Imaging Center: *Corin Skidds*
Media Project Manager: *Rich Barnes*
Image Permissions Coordinator: *Beth Brenzel*
Composition: *S4Carlisle Publishing Services*
Printer/Binder: *The Courier Companies*
Cover Printer: *Lehigh-Phoenix Color*

For our children:
Alexandra, Ethan, Meredith, and Leland;
Karen and Michael.

Credits and acknowledgments borrowed from other sources and reproduced, with permission, in this textbook appear on appropriate page within text or on pages 623–625.

Library of Congress Cataloging-in-Publication Data

Benton, Janetta Rebold
Arts and culture : an introduction to the humanities / Janetta Rebold Benton Robert DiYanni. — 4th ed.
p. cm.
"Combined volume/Volume I/Volume II."
Includes bibliographical references and index.
ISBN-13: 978-0-205-81667-5 (combined vol., ch. 1-ch. 24 : alk. paper)
ISBN-10: 0-205-81667-3
ISBN-13: 978-0-205-81660-6 (v. 1, ch. 1-ch. 12 : alk. paper)
ISBN-10: 0-205-81660-6
[etc.]
1. Arts—History. I. DiYanni, Robert. II. Title. III. Title: Introduction to the humanities.
NX440.B46 2010
700.9—dc22

2010039648

10 9 8 7 6 5 4 3 2 1

Prentice Hall
is an imprint of

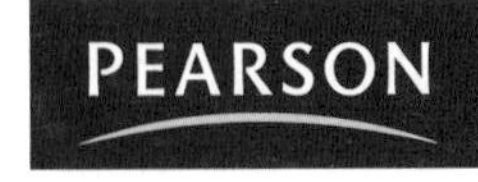

www.pearsonhighered.com

Student Edition
ISBN-10: 0-205-81667-3
ISBN-13: 978-0-205-81667-5

Examination Copy
ISBN-10: 0-205-82941-4
ISBN-13: 978-0-205-82941-5

Contents Overview

VOLUME I

VOLUME II

Contents

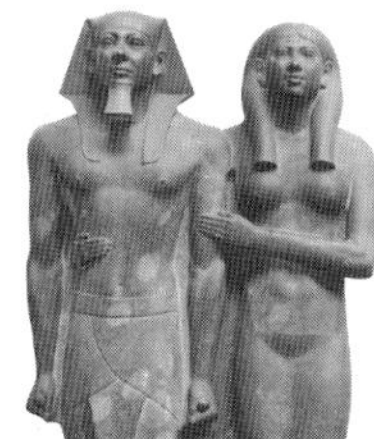

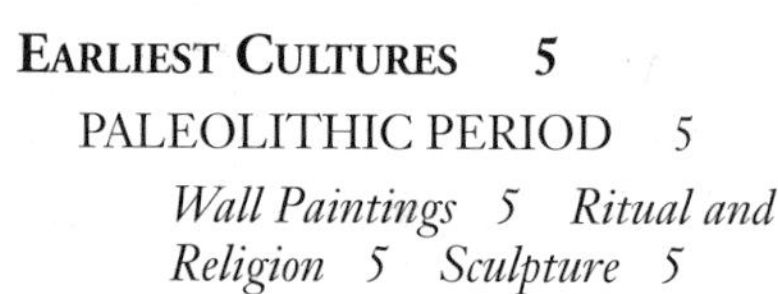

CHAPTER 2

Aegean Culture and Early Greece 39

CHAPTER 3

Classical and Hellenistic Greece 59

CHAPTER 4

Roman Civilization 87

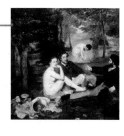

CHAPTER 10

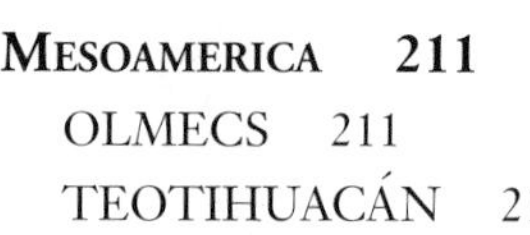

Early Civilizations of the Americas and Africa 209

CHAPTER 11

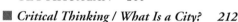

Early Middle Ages and the Romanesque 235

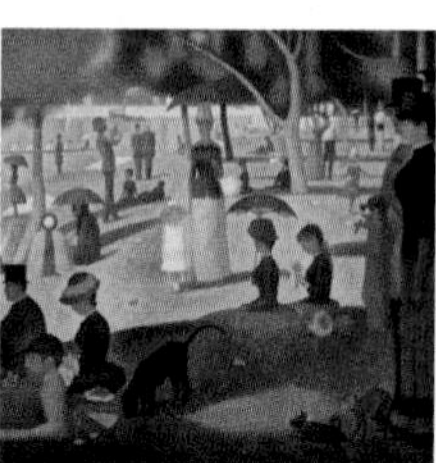

CHAPTER 19

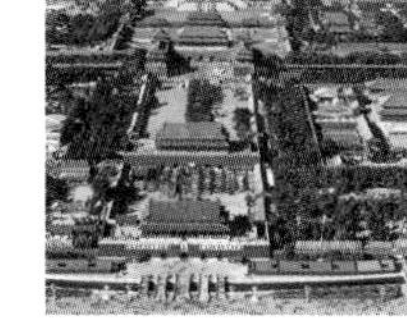

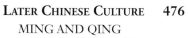

Later Chinese Civilization 475

CHAPTER 20

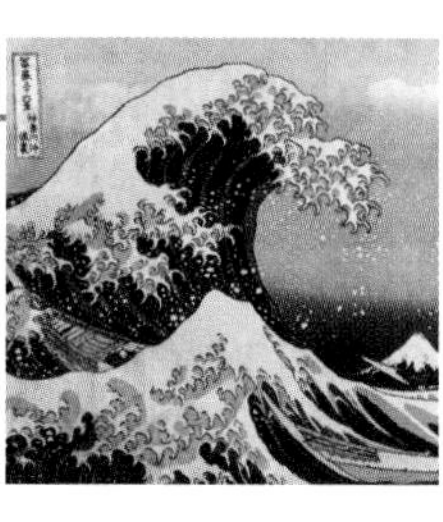

Later Japanese Civilization 493

CHAPTER 21

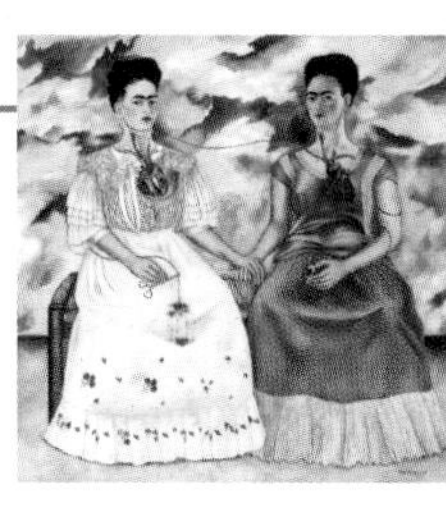

Later Africa and Latin America 511

CHAPTER 22

Early Twentieth Century 529

CHAPTER 23

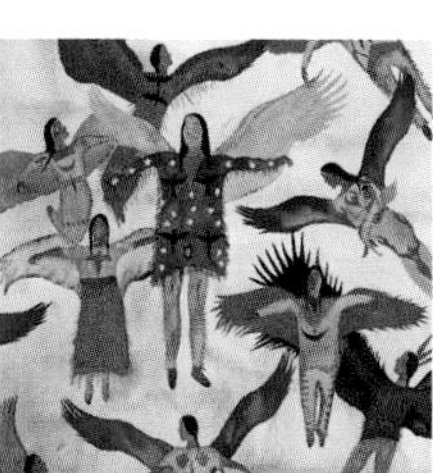

Mid-Twentieth Century and Later 565

CHAPTER 24

Diversity in Contemporary Life 589

PREFACE

As in our first three editions of *Arts and Culture*, we provide in this Fourth Edition an introduction to the world's major civilizations—to their artistic achievements, their history, and their cultures. Through an integrated approach to the humanities, *Arts and Culture* offers an opportunity to view works of art, read literature, and listen to music in historical and cultural contexts.

Works of art from different cultures reveal common human experiences of birth and death, love and loss, pleasure and pain, hope and frustration, elation and despair. Study of the humanities—literature, philosophy, history, religion, and the arts—reveals what others value and believe, inviting each of us to consider our personal, social, and cultural values in relation to those of others.

In studying the humanities, we focus our attention on works of art that reflect and embody the central values and beliefs of particular cultures and specific historical moments. In our approach we consider the following questions:

1. *What kind of artwork is it? To what artistic category does it belong?* These questions lead us to consider a work's type.
2. *Why was the artwork made? What was its function, purpose, or use? Who was responsible for producing it? Who paid for or commissioned it?* These questions lead us to consider the context of a work.
3. *What does the work express or convey? What does it reveal about its creator? What does it reveal about its historical and social context?* These questions lead us to considerations of a work's meaning.
4. *How was the artwork made or constructed?* This question leads us to consider materials and techniques.
5. *What are the parts or elements of a work of art? How are these parts related to create a unified artwork?* These questions lead us to considerations of formal analysis, understanding the ways the artwork satisfies aesthetically.
6. *What social, cultural, and moral values does the work express, reflect, or embody?* This question leads us to consider the social, cultural, and moral values of an artwork.

In *Arts and Culture*, we highlight the individual artistic qualities of numerous works, always in view of the cultural worlds in which they were created. We discuss each work's significance in conjunction with the social attitudes and cultural values it embodies, without losing sight of its individual expression and artistic achievement.

Two important questions underlie our choice of works in *Arts and Culture:* (1) What makes a work a masterpiece of its type? (2) What qualities of a work of art enable it to be appreciated over time? These questions imply that certain qualities appeal to something fundamental and universal in all of us, no matter where or when we may live. These are the aesthetic principles and predilections that link all of us together.

MAKING CONNECTIONS

We believe that a study of the humanities involves more than an examination of the artistic monuments of civilizations past and present. In our view, it also involves a consideration of how forms of human achievement in many times and places echo and reinforce, as well as alter and modify each other. An important aspect of humanities study involves seeing connections among the arts and ideas of a given culture and discovering relationships between the arts and ideas of different cultures. We have highlighted four forms of connections that are especially important:

1. *Interdisciplinary connections* among artworks of an individual culture
2. *Cross currents* among artworks of different cultures
3. Transhistorical links between past and present, *then and now*
4. The *cultural impact* or influence of one culture on later cultures

These forms of connection invite our readers to locate relationships among various humanities disciplines and to identify links between the achievements of diverse cultures. Discovering such connections can be intellectually stimulating and emotionally stirring since the forms of human experience reflected in the works of art of many cultures resonate with common human concerns. These artworks address social questions about who we are, philosophical questions about why we exist at all, and religious questions concerning what awaits us after death. These and other perennial questions and the varying perspectives taken on them have been central to many cultures, and find expression in their arts. To highlight these questions, we have included the following features throughout the text.

■ INTERDISCIPLINARY CONNECTIONS

For example, one type of interdisciplinary connection appears in the ways the music and architecture of Renaissance Florence were influenced by mathematical proportion and ancient notions of "harmony." Mathematics played a crucial role in all the arts of the Renaissance. Architects were guided in the design of their buildings by mathematical ratios and proportions; composers likewise wrote music that reflected mathematical ratios in both its melody and harmony.

■ CULTURAL CROSS CURRENTS

These reflect the ways artistic ideals, literary movements, and historical events influence the arts of other cultures. For example, Turkish military music found its way into the symphonies and piano compositions of Viennese composers, such as Mozart and Beethoven. Japanese woodblock prints influenced the art of the Impressionist painter Claude Monet and the Post-Impressionist painter Vincent van Gogh. And the dynamic cybernetic sculpture of contemporary artist Wen-Ying Tsai weds Western technology with ancient Chinese aesthetic principles.

■ THEN & NOW

Also considered are connections between the past and present. *Then & Now* offers discussions of a wide range of subjects that form various types of historical bridges.

■ CULTURAL IMPACT

This feature appears at the end of each chapter. It explains the influence of one culture or civilization on later ones, showing how the essential, broad themes explored in the chapter continue to impact today's world.

■ CRITICAL THINKING

This Critical Thinking boxed feature invites students to do just that—think critically about an aspect of culture relevant to each chapter.

GLOBAL COVERAGE

Arts and Culture includes a wide-ranging overview of the world's civilizations. In addition to Western culture, we examine the civilizations of Africa, China, India, Japan, Latin America, and Mesoamerica. We emphasize the contributions of women, from the eleventh-century writings of the Japanese Murasaki Shikibu, the twelfth-century music of the German Hildegard of Bingen, and the fourteenth-century writings of the Italian Christine de Pizan, to the Renaissance painting of the Italian Properzia de'Rossi, or the Baroque still lifes by the Flemish Clara Peeters, to the Rococo art of the French painter Marie-Louise-Elisabeth Vigée-Le Brun and the numerous women writers, painters, sculptors, architects, and photographers of the nineteenth and twentieth centuries from many parts of our world. In the final chapter of *Arts and Culture* we bring together a broad spectrum of styles, voices, and perspectives, which, although focusing on contemporary multicultural America, reflects trends and influences from around the globe. We highlight a number of current issues in the arts including how technology has globalized the arts. The numerous and varied contributions of artists and writers include works by Native American artists, Latina/Latino writers, and Australian Aborigine artists.

Throughout the book, we have tried to present the arts and cultures of the world to suggest their richness, variety, and humanity. As a reader of *Arts and Culture*, you can find in these pages the background necessary to understand the artistic achievements of many civilizations and the representation of human experience in all its complexity. In a time of rapid social change when the world's cultures are becoming increasingly globalized, it has become necessary to understand the values of human beings around the world, as they have been recorded, inscribed, and celebrated in the arts and achievements of all cultures.

LEARNING TOOLS FOR STUDENTS

Arts and Culture offers a number of learning tools for students. A helpful starter kit appears at the beginning of the book, giving readers a brief introduction to the study of the visual arts, literature, music, history, and philosophy. Each chapter begins with a full-page timeline and Chapter Overview to introduce the chapter's content. Maps and tables appear within each chapter to further illustrate and organize important information. Each chapter ends with a list of key terms as well as suggested websites for further study. A glossary appears at the end of the book; terms in the glossary are highlighted in boldface in the text.

BOOK FORMAT

For flexibility in teaching, *Arts and Culture* is available in three volumes: Volume I contains Chapters 1–12, Volume II contains Chapters 13–24, and the Combined Volume contains Chapters 1–24. Additionally, reading selections appear at the end of each chapter in Volumes I and II, but not in the Combined Volume; instructors preferring a single volume text without readings may select the Combined Volume.

NEW IN THE FOURTH EDITION

In this Fourth Edition of *Arts and Culture*, we have preserved the book's key features but have made important adjustments and necessary corrections of fact and perspective throughout. We have also expanded and contracted various discussions to create a better balance among the arts and humanities and to improve the historical contexts. In doing so, we have added many new photographs to accompany new discussions, in addition to replacing numerous photographs from the previous edition with images that better reflect the original artwork.

EXPANDED COVERAGE OF HUMANITIES FROM AROUND THE GLOBE

We have responded to requests to expand coverage of humanities from around the globe. Works of art have been added from China, Japan, Turkey, Nigeria, and Peru.

INCREASED FOCUS ON WOMEN ARTISTS

The Fourth Edition of *Arts and Culture* places greater emphasis on the accomplishments of women than is found in any other book on global humanities.

NEW SECTIONS

Two new sections have been added to the final chapter: New Uses of Old Media, and Recent Trends in International Architecture.

NEW TOPICS FOR CONNECTIONS, CROSS CURRENTS, AND THEN & NOW BOXES

We have updated several of the boxed features, providing new topics: Then & Now and Critical Thinking boxes.

NEW READINGS

A number of the reading selections at the end of each chapter in Volumes I and II are new. Some longer works have been scaled back to make space for a greater variety of selections.

FACULTY AND STUDENT RESOURCES TO ACCOMPANY *ARTS AND CULTURE*

***Music for the Humanities* CD**—This music CD is available with the text and its musical selections represent important works from a broad variety of time periods and styles.

Volume 1 with music CD: ISBN 0205816606
Volume 2 with music CD: ISBN 0205169236
Combined Volume with music CD: ISBN 0205170781

MyHumanitiesKit—This dynamic online resource provides opportunities for practice, assessment, and instruction—including digital flashcards of every image of the text. Easy to use and easy to integrate into the classroom, it engages students as it builds confidence and enhances students' learning experience. Visit www.myhumanitieskit.com to begin.

Instructor's Manual with Tests—An invaluable professional resource and reference for new and experienced instructors, providing chapter summaries, further topics for discussion, activities, and hundreds of sample test questions, these resources are carefully organized to make preparation, classroom instructions, and student testing smoother and more effective. ISBN: 0205019560.

MyTest—This flexible online test-generating program includes all questions found in the printed Test Item File. Instructors can quickly and easily create customized tests with MyTest. Visit www.pearsonmytest.com to begin.

BOOKS *À LA CARTE*

Give your students flexibility and savings with the new Books *à la carte* edition of *Arts and Culture*. This edition features exactly the same content as the traditional textbook in a convenient three-hole-punched, loose-leaf version—allowing students to take only what they need to class. The Books *à la carte* editions for both Volumes I and II cost less than a used text—which helps students save about 35% over the cost of a new book.

Volume 1 *à la carte* edition: ISBN 0205034691
Volume 2 *à la carte* edition: ISBN 0205034713

CUSTOM PUBLISHING OPPORTUNITIES

Arts and Culture is available in a custom version specifically tailored to meet your needs. You may select the content that you would like to include or add your own original material. See your local publisher's representative for further information.

ACKNOWLEDGMENTS

Arts and Culture represents the cooperative efforts of many people. The book originated with a suggestion fifteen years ago by Tony English, then of Macmillan Publishing. Work on the project began with Tony and his Macmillan colleagues and continued with Prentice Hall when Simon & Schuster acquired Macmillan in 1993. At Prentice Hall we had the good fortune to work with Bud Therien, Publisher, who oversaw the book's development in every respect, and Clare Payton, Development Editor, who helped shape the first edition.

Also deserving of particular mention for their work on the first edition are Sylvia Moore for her contribution to the introductory materials, Jenny Moss for her work on the timelines and glossary, and Ailsa Heritage and Andrea Fairbrass for their imaginative work on the maps.

We owe thanks to Henry Sayre, without whom we could not have completed the first edition of *Arts and Culture* on schedule. Professor Sayre helped us shape the drafts of our chapters, melding our styles and recommending organizational changes that have resulted, we believe, in an integrated and compelling overview of the humanities.

For the Fourth Edition, our thanks go to Sarah Touborg, Editor-in-Chief; Kate Mitchell, Executive Marketing Manager; Tiffany Timmerman, Production Editor; Joe Scordato, Production Liaison; and Jessica Parrotta, Editorial Assistant.

We would like to thank the following reviewers, who offered us wise counsel: Jane Anderson Jones, Manatee Community College; Richard Mahon, Riverside Community College; Brian A. Pavlac, King's College; Danney Ursery, St. Edward's University; Richard A. Voeltz, Cameron University; Katherine Wyly, Hillsborough Community College; Lynn Spencer, Brevard Community College; Richard A. Voeltz, Cameron University; Scott H. Boyd, College of DuPage; Richard Mahon, Riverside Community College; and Jane Anderson Jones, Manatee Community College.

We want to thank Margaret Manos for her excellent work on early versions of the manuscript, and for her wise and extremely helpful advice in making decisions on what to cut and what to add for the previous edition. In addition, we would like to extend our appreciation to A. Daniel Frankforter of Pennsylvania State University, for his many helpful corrections and suggestions on the history portions; to Jane Pyle of Miami Dade College for expanding our music coverage; to Stephen Addiss of the University of Richmond for his work revising and expanding our Asian chapters; to Jonathan T. Reynolds of Northern Kentucky University for his expansion of the African chapters; and, finally, to Bill Christy of Ohio University for his work on the timelines, key terms, and web links.

We also wish to thank our reviewers for this Fourth Edition. Their comments and suggestions helped us in many ways. Thanks to: Cynthia Andreas, Lynn University; Sarah Clunis, Cornell College; Lisa Hochtritt, Rocky Mountain College of Art and Design; Nathan Poage, Houston Community College; Aditi Samarth, Richland College; and Susan Taylor, University of Central Oklahoma.

We would also like to thank each other for offering mutual support, encouragement, advice, and help throughout a long and sometimes arduous process of writing, revising, and editing. Our families, too, deserve our thanks, for without their patience and understanding we could not have completed our work with equanimity and good humor. In particular, the encouragement and loving support of our spouses, Elliot Benton and Mary DiYanni, enabled us to do our work on *Arts and Culture* with a minimum of anxiety and a maximum of pleasure.

INTRODUCTION

Arts and Culture is an introduction to the humanities, from the earliest times to the present day. The goal of the book is to familiarize readers with a fundamental body of art, history, and ideas as a basis for understanding Western and non-Western cultures. In demonstrating the interrelationships between the creators of art and the historical and social forces at work in various cultures, the text fosters an understanding of the creative process and the uses of the arts.

THE HUMANITIES AND THE ARTS

The humanities are those areas of thought and creation whose subject is human experience. They include history, philosophy, religion, and the arts. Broadly speaking, the arts are objects or experiences created by human beings. The role of the human creator, therefore, is central to any study of the arts since, ultimately, the arts and humanities are a record of human experience and concerns. The arts convey information—a lyric poem or a watercolor can describe or portray a summer's day, for example—yet this is not their primary function. More importantly, the arts give form to what is imagined, express human beliefs and emotions, create beauty, move, persuade, and entertain their audiences.

The arts include visual art and architecture, drama, music, and literature, and photography and film. Seeing the arts within their historical and social context is necessary for understanding their development. For example, the figure of the biblical giant-killer, David, was popular during the Renaissance in the Italian city-state of Florence. Michelangelo's *David* was commissioned by the Florentine city officials (see fig. 13.18). Florence had recently fought off an attempt at annexation by the much larger city-state of Milan. Thus, the biblical David slaying the giant, Goliath, became a symbol of Florentine cleverness and courage in defense of independence. It is a theme particular to its time and place, yet one that has been used throughout history to express the success of the "little" person against powerful exploiters.

RECORDS OF CULTURE

We study what survives, which is not necessarily all that once existed. Not all arts survive the passage of time. Art can be divided into the durable and the ephemeral, or short-lived. Surviving objects tend to be large (the Pyramids) or hidden (the contents of tombs). Until human beings created the means of capturing moving images and sounds, the ephemeral arts such as music and dance could be described but not reexperienced. Therefore, some of the oldest arts—music and dance of the ancient world, for example—are lost. With the development of writing, humans began the long process of liberating themselves from the tyranny of time. They began to communicate across space and time, leaving a record of their lives. In our own century, we have seen our recording abilities explode from sound recording and silent movies at the turn of the century into the digitized world of the CD-ROM and the Internet today. The result has been an unprecedented expansion in the humanities.

ROLE OF THE ARTIST

The functions of the artist and the artwork have varied widely during the past five thousand years. In our time, the artist is seen as an independent worker, dedicated to the expression of a unique subjective experience. Often the artist's role is that of the outsider, a critical or rebellious figure. He or she is a specialist who has usually undergone advanced training in a university department of art or theater, or a school with a particular focus, such as a music conservatory. In our societies, works of art are presented in specialized settings: theaters, concert halls, performance spaces, galleries, and museums. There is usually a sharp division between the artist and her or his audience of nonartists. We also associate works of art with money: art auctions in which paintings sell for millions of dollars, ticket sales to the ballet, or fundraising for the local symphony.

In other societies and in parts of our own society, now and in the past, the arts are closer to the lives of ordinary people. For the majority of their history, artists have expressed the dominant beliefs of a culture, rather than rebelling against them. In place of our emphasis on the development of a personal or original style, artists were trained to conform to the conventions of their art form. Nor have artists always been specialists; in some societies and periods, all members of a society participated in art. The modern Western economic mode, which treats art as a commodity for sale, is not universal. In societies such as that of the Navajo, the concept of selling or creating a salable version of a sand painting would be completely incomprehensible. Selling Navajo sand paintings created as part of a ritual would profane a sacred experience.

Artists' identities are rarely known before the Renaissance, with the exception of the period of Classical Greece, when artists were highly regarded for their individual talents and styles. Among artists who were known, there were fewer women than men. In the twentieth century, many female artists in all the disciplines have been recognized.

Their absence in prior centuries does not indicate lack of talent, but reflects lack of opportunity. The necessary social, educational, and economic conditions to create art rarely existed for women in the past.

Artists of color have also been recognized in the West only recently. The reasons for this absence range from the simple—there were few Asians in America and Europe prior to the middle of the nineteenth century—to the complexities surrounding the African diaspora. The art of indigenous peoples, while far older than that of the West, did not share the same expressive methods or aims as Western art. Until recently, such art was ignored or dismissed in Western society by the dominant cultural gatekeepers.

CONTEXTS AND AESTHETICS

Our understanding of the arts depends in part on our knowledge of the historical and social context surrounding a work. For instance, for whom was a particular work intended—a private or a public audience? What was or is its setting—public, private, accessible, or hidden? How is the work related to the economic workings of its time: for example, was it commissioned by a ruler, a religious organization, a group of guildspeople, a corporation? Was it created by nuns or monks, by peasants, or by specially-trained craftspersons? Each of these considerations expands our understanding of a given work, even when we cannot know all the answers.

The branch of philosophy devoted to thinking about the arts is called "aesthetics." Aesthetic knowledge is both intuitive and intellectual; that is, we can grasp a work of art on an emotional level while at the same time analyzing it. There is no single, unquestionable body of aesthetic knowledge, although philosophers have tried to create universal systems. Each culture has its own aesthetic preferences. In addition, different disciplines and different styles within a culture reflect different aesthetic values.

FORM AND CONTENT

When discussing works of art, it is useful to distinguish between the form of the artwork and its content. The form of a work of art is its structural or organizing principle—the shape of its content. A work's content is what it is about—its subject matter. At its most basic, formal analysis provides a description of the apparent properties of an artwork. Artists use these properties to engineer our perception and response. In music, for example, a formal analysis would discuss the melody, the harmony, and the structure. In visual art, comparable elements would be line, color, and composition. The goal of formal analysis is to understand how an artwork's form expresses its content.

Contextual approaches to the arts seek to situate artworks within the circumstances of their creation. Historians of the arts conduct research aimed at recreating the context of a given work. Armed with this information, the historian interprets the work in light of that context. Knowing, for example, that *Guernica* (see fig. 22.25), Pablo Picasso's anti-war painting, depicts an aerial bombing of a small village of unarmed civilians in the Spanish Civil War, drives its brutal images of pain and death home to viewers. Picasso chose black, white, and grey for this painting because he learned of the attack through the black and white photojournalism of the newspapers. Knowing the reason for this choice, which may otherwise have seemed arbitrary to modern viewers of the work, adds to the meaning of the image. Picasso's choice of black and white also intensifies the horrors he depicts.

CRITICAL THINKING

Among the most important purposes of any study of the arts and humanities is to develop habits of mind, including critical thinking. By critical thinking, we do not mean "being critical" of something in the ordinary sense. Rather, we mean developing a capacity to analyze and synthesize, compare and contrast, understand causes and effects, understand, appreciate, and evaluate the cultural productions—the architecture, sculpture, painting, photography, film, literature, music, philosophy, and other arts of all civilizations, whether ancient or modern, and whether similar to or radically different from our own.

Critical Thinking in this sense involves asking questions, making observations and connections, drawing inferences and provisional interpretive conclusions about the meaning of artworks and considering their importance to the civilizations in which they were created. It also involves considering basic issues, such as: What does it mean to live in a society as an individual human being? To what extent does living in one kind of society, in a particular civilization at a particular historical moment, affect one's thoughts, perceptions, attitudes, and feelings? How does the world view of ancient Africans, Babylonians, Chinese, Egyptians, Greeks, Romans, Sumerians, and others compare and contrast with one another and with those of people living in different cultures around the world today?

Each chapter of *Arts and Culture* contains much information and analysis that invites such considerations. And, although the book does not contain study questions or review assignments (those can be found in supplements to *Arts and Culture*), it does contain, in each chapter, a highlighted brief discussion labeled "Critical Thinking." You are invited to think about the issues raised in each of those discussions, as for example, why cows are considered sacred in India, a Hindu civilization, along with the effects of treating cows as sacred animals, as well as considering what "sacred cows," in a metaphorical sense, exist in your own culture.

An additional thought about such critical thinking questions is that when we study civilizations of the past, we are not just studying cultural artifacts and learning about historical events. Additionally, we are learning about people, human beings, who, like us, experience joy and sorrow, frustration and elation, pleasure and pain. And, finally, here we will use the word "critical" in still another sense, for the study of the humanities disciplines through history is critical to understanding ourselves in today's world. We put before you for critical consideration the notion that studying the humanities not only adds to your stock of knowledge, while enriching your own life and imaginatively extending its possibilities, but also deepens your appreciation of other peoples and their values. In addition, studying the arts and humanities of many cultures critically challenges what we believe and think we know to be true.

STARTER KIT

HUMANITIES

This Starter Kit provides you with a brief reference guide to key terms and concepts for studying the humanities. The following section will give you a basis for analyzing, understanding, and describing art forms.

COMMONALITIES

We refer to the different branches of humanities—art and architecture, music, literature, philosophy, history—as **disciplines.** The various humanistic disciplines have many key terms in common. However, each discipline has defining characteristics, a distinct vocabulary, and its own conventions, so that the same word may mean different things in different disciplines.

Every work of art has two core components: form and content. **Form** refers to the arrangement, pattern, or structure of a work, how a work is presented to our senses. **Content** is what a work is about, its meaning or substance. The form might be a Tang Dynasty painting; the content might be the beauty of nature in a particular place. To comprehend how the form expresses the content is one of the keys to understanding a work of art, music, or literature.

The term **artist** is used for the producer of artworks in any discipline. All artworks have a **composition,** the arrangement of its constituent parts. **Technique** refers to the process or method that produced the art. The **medium** is the physical material that makes up the work, such as oil paint on canvas.

STYLE

We use the term **style** to mean several different things. Most simply, style refers to the manner in which something is done. Many elements form a style. Artists working at the same time and place are often trained in the same style. When mentioned in a text, historical styles are usually capitalized, as in *Classical Greek* art, referring to the arts of that particular time and place, which shared distinct characteristics. If used with lowercase letters, such as *classical* style, the term refers to works which, although not from Classical Greece, are similar in character to Classical Greek art, or to Roman art, which was largely derived from Greek forms.

Conventions are accepted practices, such as the use of a frontal eye in a profile face, found in the art of the ancient Egyptians, or the use of the sonnet form by Shakespeare and his contemporaries.

FUNCTIONS AND GENRES

In the most general terms, the functions of the arts can be divided into religious and secular art. **Religious** or liturgical art, music, or drama is used as part of the ritual of a given religion. Art that is not religious art is termed **secular** art. Secular art is primarily used to provide pleasure and entertainment, but among other functions has been its use in the service of political or propaganda ends.

Each discipline has subsets, called **genres.** In music, for example, we have the symphony, a large, complex work for orchestra, in contrast to a quartet, written for only four instruments. In literature we might contrast the novel, with its extended narrative and complexities of character, with the compression of a short story. From the seventeenth to the nineteenth centuries, certain subjects were assigned higher or lower rank by the academies that controlled the arts in most European countries. Portrait painting, for example, was considered lower than history painting. That practice has been abandoned; today the genres are usually accorded equal respect and valued for their distinctive qualities.

VISUAL ARTS

The visual arts are first experienced by sight, yet they often evoke other senses such as touch or smell. Because human beings are such visual creatures, our world is saturated with visual art, in advertising, on objects from CD covers to billboards, on TV and the Internet. The visual arts occur in many varieties of two-dimensional and three-dimensional forms, from painting, printmaking, and photography, to sculpture and architecture.

As is the case with other arts, the origins of the visual arts are now lost. However, their development represents a milestone in human civilization. Drawing, the representation of three-dimensional forms (real or imagined) on a two-dimensional surface, is an inherent human ability, and failure to draw by a certain stage in a child's growth is a sign of serious trouble. The creation and manipulation of images was and is a first step toward mastery of the physical world itself.

The visual arts use different methods. **Representation** is an ancient function of visual art, in which a likeness of an object or life form is produced. Artists use different methods to represent a subject (what is actually depicted, such as a portrait of a person, a still life, a landscape, a historical event, etc.). If the work is realistic, the subject is accurately depicted and readily recognizable. If the work is abstracted, the subject, although not photographically

Visual Arts

Line: A mark on a surface. Lines may be continuous or broken. They are used to create patterns and textures, to imply three dimensions, and to direct visual movement.

Shape: An area with identifiable boundaries. Shapes may be **organic,** based on natural forms and thus rounded or irregular, or they may be **geometric,** based on measured forms.

Mass: The solid parts of a three-dimensional object. An area of space devoid of mass is called **negative space;** while **positive space** is an area occupied by mass.

Form: The shape and structure of something. In discussion of art, form refers to visual aspects such as line, shape, color, texture, and composition.

Color: The sensation produced by various wavelengths of light. Also called **hue.** Red, blue, and yellow are the **primary colors,** which cannot be made from mixing other colors. **Secondary colors** (orange, green, and purple) are hues produced by mixing two primary colors.

Value: The lightness or darkness of an area of color, or as measured between black and white. The lighter, the higher in value it is; the **darker,** the lower in value.

Texture: The appearance or feel of a surface, basically smooth or rough. Texture may be actual, as the surface of a polished steel sculpture, or implied, as in a painting of human flesh or the fur of an animal.

Composition: The arrangement of the formal components of a work, most frequently used to describe the organization of elements in a drawing or painting.

horizon line

One-point perspective

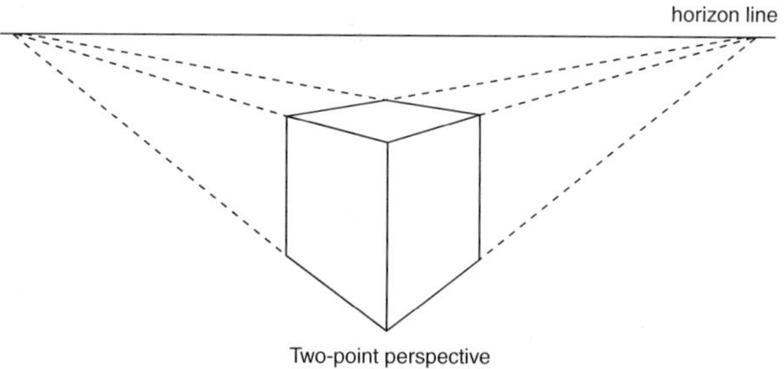

Two-point perspective

Perspective: A system of portraying three-dimensional space on a two-dimensional surface. In **one-point** linear perspective, lines recede toward a single **vanishing point** on the horizon line. In **two-point** perspective there are two vanishing points. **Atmospheric** or **aerial** perspective uses properties of light and air, in which objects become less distinct and cooler in color as they recede into distance.

recorded, is nevertheless identifiable. If the work is nonobjective there is no longer a recognizable subject.

Realistic paintings, drawings, and prints often create an illusion of pictorial space (an illusion of three dimensions on a two-dimensional surface) by using perspective. There are two types: 1) atmospheric perspective, and 2) linear perspective, both defined in the box above. These are characteristic of Western art, whereas Eastern art tends to emphasize the picture plane. Landscapes, as Zho Jan's *Seeking the Tao in the Autumn Mountains* (Figure 8.8), does not employ Western methods of creating illusions of space. Inscriptions, as in Shitao's *Searching for the Past*, by stressing the picture plane, further compress the sense of space. Abstract and nonobjective art, arising in the twentieth century, are more concerned with the elements on the picture plane (the surface of the paper or canvas) rather than in creating an illusion of depth.

Formal Analysis

To analyze a work of visual art formally, its visual elements are considered without reference to the content, whereas moving to more sophisticated levels involves the content as well. At its simplest, the content is what is represented, the subject matter, whether a person, an orange, or a flag. However, the image may not stop with the representation; there may be a symbolic element. It is useful to distinguish between signs and symbols. **Signs** convey visual information

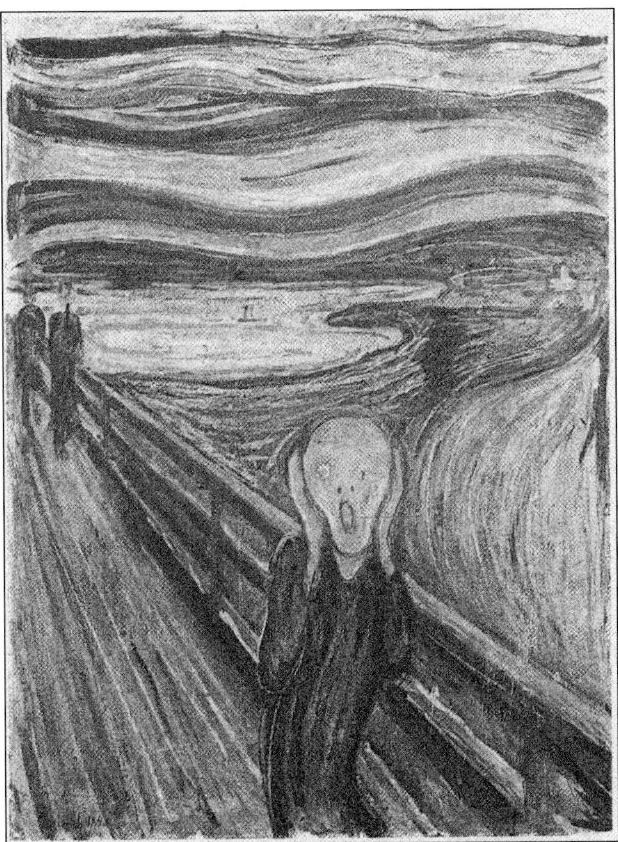

FIGURE 0.1 Edvard Munch, *The Scream*, 1893, tempera and casein on cardboard, 36 × 29″ (91.3 × 73.7 cm), Nasjonalgalleriet, Oslo. © 2003 The Munch Museum/The Munch-Ellingson Group/Artists Rights Society (ARS), New York/ADAGP, Paris. J. Lathion/© Nasjionalgalleriet 02.

economically by means of images or words. **Symbols** are images that have resonance, or additional meaning. Works of visual art may use both signs and symbols. Artists use symbolic systems, part of the visual language of their time. Like all languages, these must be learned. Sometimes artists create their own symbols.

Iconography is the language of symbols. The **iconography** of a work of art is often religious in nature. For example, different representations of Jesus derive from incidents in his life. To understand the deeper levels of the work, it is necessary to understand the iconography. The use of personal iconography by an artist is a relatively recent development of the past few centuries.

The following analysis of *The Scream* by Edvard Munch (fig. 0.1) will serve as an example of this process. Viewed formally, the major visual elements used by Munch in this painting are line and color. There are two kinds of lines: the geometric lines that form the sharply receding bridge contrast with the swirling organic lines of the main figure and the landscape, sea, and sky. There is little or no modelling or shading. The colors contrast bright red and yellow with rich blue, offset by neutral tones. *The Scream* is a painting executed on cardboard with rapid, loose brushstrokes. The composition is dynamic; the artist has used exaggerated diagonals to suggest a dramatic perspective for the bridge. The figure at the front is the focal point. The craft is secondary to the expressive purpose of the work.

It should be obvious that in *The Scream* more is going on than the preceding analysis indicates. Three people are on a bridge at sunset. Two are walking away; one stands transfixed with his hands over his ears. The expression on his face functions as a sign to convey shock or horror. To understand the significance of his expression, we turn to the historical context and the artist's life. Munch, a Norwegian artist who worked in the late-nineteenth and early-twentieth centuries, was one of the artists who rejected conventions and created personal symbolic systems, based largely on his experience. *The Scream* is usually interpreted as representing a screaming person. This is not correct. As we know from the artist's diary, the work refers to the "scream of nature." The image captured is a powerful evocation of a sensitive man overwhelmed by nature's power, which his companions cannot sense. The swirling lines suggest the impact of screaming nature on this person. The blood-red sky resonates as a symbol of savage nature oblivious to the puny humans below.

COMPONENTS OF THE VISUAL ARTS

The basic elements used to construct a work of visual art are line, shape, mass, form, color, value, texture, and composition. While many drawings are executed in black mediums, such as pencil and charcoal, on a white ground, color is a vital ingredient of art, especially important in conveying information as well as emotion to the viewer. Color affects us both physically and psychologically and has significance to us both in our personal lives and in our cultural traditions.

There can be no color without light. In the seventeenth century, Sir Isaac Newton observed that when sunlight passed through a glass prism it was broken up, or **refracted,** into rainbow colors. Our perception of color depends upon reflected light rays of various wavelengths. Theorists have arranged colors on a **color wheel** (fig. 0.2) that is well-known to students of painting and even young schoolchildren. On it are the **primary colors**—red, yellow, and blue—and **secondary colors**—orange, green, and purple. Some wheels show **tertiary colors** such as yellow-green and red-purple. The primary colors cannot be created by mixing other colors, but secondary and tertiary colors are made, respectively, by mixing two primaries, or primaries and secondaries, together. **Complementary** colors are those opposite each other on the wheel, so that red is opposite from green, orange from blue, and yellow from purple. Many artists have studied and worked with the **optical effects** of color, especially the French Impressionist Claude Monet and the Post-Impressionist Georges Seurat.

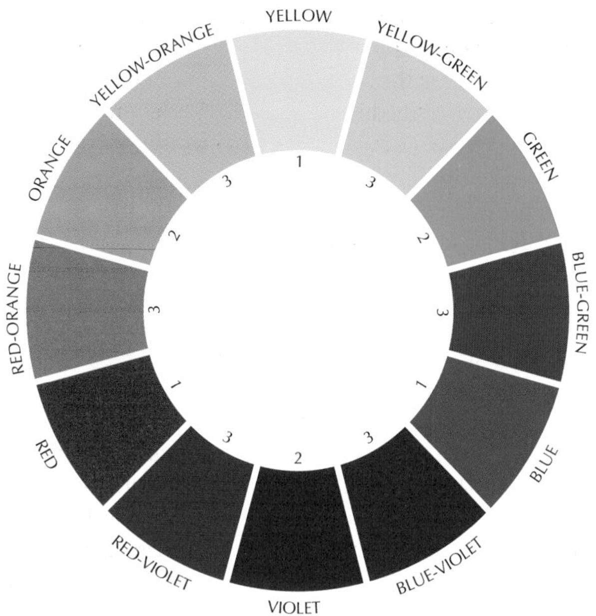

FIGURE 0.2 Color wheel.

SCULPTURE

A sculpture is a three-dimensional form made by carving, modeling, or assembling. Unlike paintings, drawings, and prints, which have two dimensions (height and width), sculptures have three dimensions (height, width, and depth).

Subtractive Sculpture. Using materials that have natural solid mass, such as stone, wood, or ivory, the sculptor shapes the work of art by removing material, cutting it away, usually with a hammer and chisel. The finished work must fit within the dimensions of, for example, the block of marble. Obviously, the work must be planned carefully in advance, for if a major error is made in carving, such as breaking off an extremity of a figure, correction is virtually impossible.

Physical strength may be required to carve in stone, as the *Seated Buddha* (Figure 7.5) of schist. However, greater control is required to carve in wood, as the Yoruba mask from the Republic of Benin (Figure 21.1), due to the varying resistance offered by the wood, depending upon whether the sculptor cuts with or against the grain.

Marble is the traditional medium for sculpture. Marble, limestone, and sandstone are all essentially calcium carbonate, the difference being the size and density of the crystalline structure of the stone. Limestone and sandstone are grainier, softer, and more easily worked than marble. They have a mat surface, whereas marble can be polished to a shine.

Additive Sculpture. Using materials that have no natural mass, shape, or dimensions, such as plaster, clay, or wax, the sculptor gradually builds up the desired form by modeling it. The scale of the sculpture is not limited, as it would be by the size of a block of stone or piece of wood. Because the material is soft, an **armature** (a rigid structure, usually of metal) may be needed for support. The artist can continually revise the form while working, and can easily make changes. For this reason, wax and clay are often used to make small studies for sculpture to be carved on a larger scale in stone.

Alternatively, a work modeled in clay or wax, which are rather impermanent materials, may be cast in metal—traditionally, bronze is used. A small **statuette** can be cast solid, as the tiny bronze horse shown in Figure 2.11, but a large piece, as the huge statue of Marcus Aurelius shown in Figure 4.17, must be hollow. This is not only because of the expense and weight, but because, were it solid, the bronze, which must be heated to make it molten for the casting process, would crack as it gradually cooled.

The material selected by the sculptor affects the form of the finished work, or, conversely, the sculptor selects the material according to the form he or she wishes to create. For example, bronze is very strong—a figure made of bronze could be posed as if balancing on one toe, whereas the same figure, if carved of stone, would be likely to break.

Assembled Sculpture. A modern type of sculpture is the **mobile,** invented by the American **Alexander Calder.** As the name suggests, the sculpture, which is usually suspended from the ceiling, actually moves with every breeze. As Figure 23.11 shows, the colored shapes are linked together, and a delicate balance carefully achieved. Calder also created **stabiles,** which used the same brightly colored metal shapes, but rest on the ground and do not move.

Another modern form of sculpture is the **assemblage** made of **found objects,** sometimes called **ready-mades.** As the term "assemblage" suggests, the mixed-media sculpture is created by assembling or compiling various bits, pieces, and objects, as was done by **Robert Rauschenberg** in Figure 23.13.

ARCHITECTURE

Architecture is a branch of the visual arts that combines practical function and artistic expression; it is art to inhabit. The function served by a building usually determines its form. In addition to the purely useful purpose of providing shelter, architecture answers prevailing social needs. The use of architects to design and erect public and religious structures has given rise to many innovative forms throughout history. Architecture reflects the society in which it is built. Structural systems depend upon the available building materials, technological advancements, the intended function of the building, and aesthetics of the culture. The relationship between a building and its **site,** or location, is integral to architecture. The Greek Parthenon (fig. 0.3), for example, crowns a hill overlooking Athens. The elevated location indicates its importance, and the pathway one must ascend to reach the Parthenon is part of the experience. A striking example of the adaptation of architecture to the natural environment is seen in homes of the Anasazi culture at Mesa Verde, Colorado, built into the cliff (fig. 10.14).

LITERATURE

SPEECH, WRITING, AND LITERATURE

Literature differs from the visual arts since it is not built from physical elements, such as paint and stone; nor is it composed of sound as is music, but from words, the basic elements of language. Paint and sound have no intrinsic meaning; words do. Speech depends on meaningful units of sound—words, which are the building blocks of communication in language. Literature presupposes language, with its multitudes of meaning (content), its **grammar** (rules for construction), and its **syntax,** the arrangement of words.

Language, essentially communicative, has many functions. We use language to make emotional contact with others: for example, a parent using baby talk to a child too young to understand the meaning of words. Through language we convey information to each other, as in the classroom, where a dialogue between teacher and student is part of the educational process. All literature is language, but not all language is literature. Distinguishing between literature and other forms of language is sometimes difficult, but refinement in language and careful structure or form typically characterize literature.

Literature, in the broadest sense, is widely apparent in everyday life. Popular songs, magazine essays, greeting card verse, hymns, and prayers are all forms of literature. One meaning of the word ***literature,*** in fact, is what is written. Generally, however, the term "literature" is reserved for those works that exhibit "the best that has been thought and said," works that represent a culture's highest literary achievements.

FIGURE 0.3 Ictinus and Callicrates, Parthenon, Acropolis, Athens, 448–432 B.C.E.

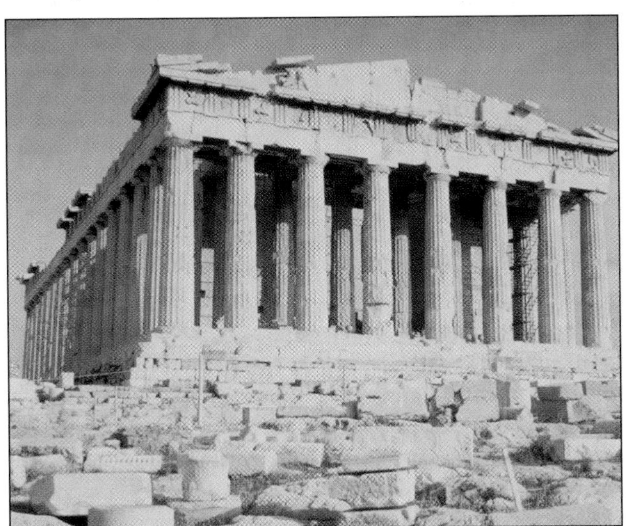

LITERACY AND LITERATURE

The Development of Literature. Literature predates literacy. Ancient literature was **oral**—spoken—rather than written. To make it easier to remember and recite, much of this was in the form of song or poetry. The invention of writing enabled people to communicate across space and time. It was with this invention that recorded history was born. The earliest writings of the ancient world are businesslike records of laws, prayers, and commerce—informative but not expressive. When mechanical methods of printing were developed, literacy spread. Today, universal literacy is a goal in all civilized countries.

The Functions of Literature. Literature serves a variety of social functions. One of its most ancient functions is as **religious literature,** the prayers and mythology of a given culture. The myths of the Greeks and Romans have exerted a powerful influence on Western culture; their origins lie deep in the history of Egypt and Mesopotamia. **Epic literature,** such as the African Epic of Son-Jara, or the sagas from Norway and Iceland, were passed down by oral tradition. Literature distinct from liturgical or epic forms was invented by the ancient Greeks, and, broadly speaking included history, philosophy, drama, and poetry. Novels and short stories as we know them today were a much later development. The novel in its modern form was named for tales popular in Italy in the late-thirteenth century, though the novel is generally identified with prose narratives that developed in the eighteenth century in Europe.

Since literature is a communicative act, it is important to consider the audience and setting. Silent reading is a recent development, alien to the oral roots of literature. Most literature through the ages was meant to be recited, sung, or read aloud in groups ranging from general public gatherings to the intimate setting of the private home. Authors today may give readings from their work in libraries, bookstores, and educational institutions.

FORMS OF LITERATURE

Literature can be divided into fiction and nonfiction, poetry and prose.

Poetry is distinguished by its concentrated and precise language, "the best words in the best order," as one poet defined it. **Diction** is the poet's selection of words, and **syntax** the ordering of those words in sentences. Other poetic elements include images—details that evoke sense perception—along with metaphor and other forms

Architecture

Architect: One who designs and supervises the construction of buildings. Ideally, the architect is part builder with a sound knowledge of engineering principles, materials, structural systems, and other such practical necessities, as well as part artist who works with form, space, scale, light, and other aesthetic properties.

Scale: The relative size of one thing compared to another. The relationship of a building to another element, often the height of a human being.

Site: The location of an object or building. Care must be taken to choose a solid, attractive, and appropriate building site.

Structural System: The engineering principles used to create a structure. Two basic kinds of structural system are the **shell** system, where one or more building materials such as stone or brick provide both support and covering, and the **skeleton and skin** system, as in modern skyscrapers with steel skeletons and glass skin.

Column: A supporting pillar consisting of a base, a cylindrical shaft, and a decorative capital at the top. Three Classical orders, established in ancient Greece, are the **Doric, Ionic,** or **Corinthian,** identified by the capital.

Post and Lintel: A basic structural system dating from ancient times that uses paired vertical elements (posts) to support a horizontal element (lintel).

Arch, Dome, and Vault: An arch consists of a series of wedged-shaped stones, called **voussoirs,** locked in place by a **keystone** at the top center. In principle, an arch rotated 180 degrees creates a **dome.** A series of arches forms a **barrel** or **tunnel vault.** When two such vaults are constructed so that they intersect at right angles, a **cross** or **groin vault** is created. Roman and Romanesque masons used semi-circular arches, whereas Gothic masons built with pointed arches to create vaults that were reinforced with **ribs,** permitting large openings in the walls. The true arch, dome, and vault are dynamic systems—the lateral thrust that they exert must be buttressed externally to prevent collapse.

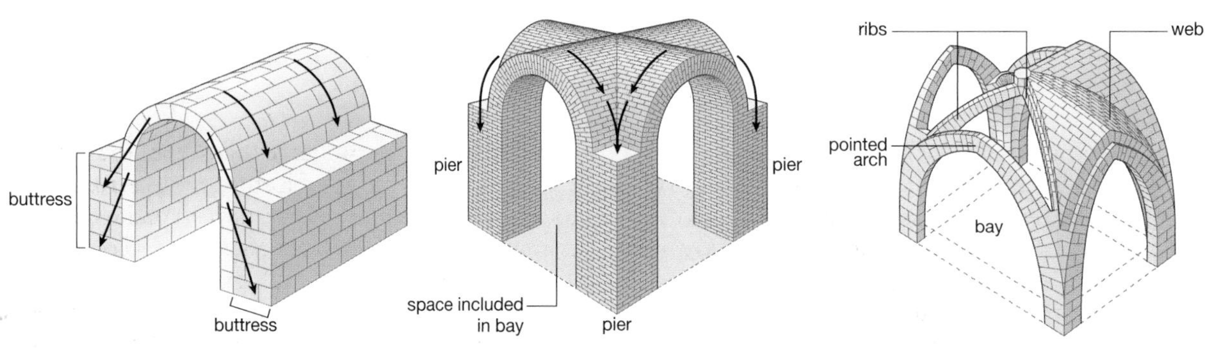

barrel or tunnel vault   groin or cross vault with rounded arches   groin or cross vault with pointed arches and ribs

of comparison. With its roots in song, poetry of many eras and places exhibits rhyme and other types of sound play as well as rhythm and meter, the measured pattern of accent in poetic lines. Drama, plays intended for performance, are sometimes written in verse, rhymed or unrhymed, as, for example, in **blank verse.**

Language that is not poetry is **prose.** Not all prose is literature; some, such as journalism or technical writing, is purely descriptive or informative, as some visual art is purely representational. Literature can be fiction or nonfiction, or a combination of both. Fiction is a work of the imagination. Fictional forms can be long and complex, as in a novel or play, or short and concise, as in a novella or short story. Nonfiction, which deals with actual events or persons, includes expressions of opinion, such as political essays. Functions of nonfiction include explanation, persuasion, commentary, exposition, or any blend of these. Sometimes philosophic essays and works of history are included in the category of literature.

Fiction and drama, and much nonfiction as well, create their effects through elements such as the plot, or story line, characters, description of the setting, dialogue between the characters, and exposition, or explanation. The latter is presented in the voice of a narrator, who may represent the author using the third-person perspective, or may instead be a character expressing a first-person point of view.

Literature

Fiction: Literature that is imaginative, rather than descriptive of actual events. Typical fictional forms are the short story and the novel, which has greater length and complexity.

Nonfiction: An account of actual events and people. Forms of nonfiction include essays, biography and autobiography, and journalistic writing, as for newspapers and magazines.

Narrative: The telling of a story; a structured account of events.

Narrator: The storyteller from whose **point of view** the story is told. The point of view can be **first-person** or **third-person,** and may shift within the work. The narrator can be **omniscient,** knowing everything, or limited to what she or he can know personally or be told by others.

Plot: The plan or story line. To plot a story is to conceive and arrange the action of the characters and the sequence of events. Plots typically involve **rising action,** events that complicate the plot and move it forward to a **climax,** the moment of greatest intensity. This is followed by the **denouement,** the resolution of the plot.

Characters: The people in a literary work. The leading character is known as the **protagonist,** a word stemming from ancient Greek drama in which the protagonist was opposed by an **antagonist.**

Dialogue: Conversation between two or more characters. Drama is mainly rendered through dialogue; it is used in fiction to a lesser extent.

Setting: Where the events take place; includes location, time, and situation. In theatrical productions, a **set** is the scenery, sometimes very elaborate, constructed for a stage performance. In films the set is the sound stage or the enclosure where a scene is filmed.

Exposition: Explanatory material, which, especially in drama, often lays out the current situation as it arises from the past.

In common with visual art and music, literature has **themes,** or overarching ideas that are expressed by all the elements working together. The structure of a work of literature is analogous to the composition of a symphony or a painting. Writers use symbolism, much as visual artists do. A successful work of literature will likely establish a mood, hold the reader's interest through a variety of incidents or ideas with evident focus, yet possess an overall sense of unity.

Autobiography, as a separate literary and historical endeavor, began with the *Confessions* of St. Augustine (354–430 C.E.), in which he told the story of his life and the progress of his religious convictions. Autobiography is history written from a subjective point of view. The memoir, so popular in recent years, is descended from this first, spiritual autobiography.

Biography is a branch of both literature and history. The author's role is complicated because a biographer must check the facts of the subject's life, usually by interviewing both the subject and many other people. Deciding the major theme of a person's life, the relationship between that person and his or her time, and considering what is true as well as what is germane are the biographer's responsibility. Different biographers may offer quite different interpretations of a subject's life.

History is a powerful force that shapes the humanities as a whole. The writing of history varies across cultures, and as cultures change, history itself is continuously under revision. The leaders of some societies would never allow the publication of versions of history that vary from their orthodox beliefs, no matter what the facts might be. Because history is an interpretative discipline, several versions of events may coexist, with scholars arguing and defending the merits of each. This is particularly true in our multicultural and pluralist era.

MUSIC

We are surrounded by sounds at all times. The art that derives from our sense of hearing is music, order given to sounds by human intent. A temporal art, one that exists in time, music is the least material of the arts, its basic elements being sound and silence. Silence in music is analogous to a painter's, sculptor's, or architect's use of negative space: unoccupied but important, so that the intervals between the notes are necessary parts of a musical piece. Music permeates our daily lives—in the movies, on radio and television, in elevators and stores. The success of the Apple ipod and other music players and of music and video streamed from the Internet, reflects our human desire to surround ourselves with music.

Until the development of sound recording, music was one of the **ephemeral** arts, like dance and live theater, which exist only for the duration of their performances. Until the late Middle Ages, music in the West was not written down, or **notated.** It was taught by ear, passed on from one generation to the next.

SOCIAL AND RITUAL ROLES

Music has many different functions. It has been and remains a major element in religious ritual. It is also used frequently in collective labor; the regular rhythm that characterizes work songs keeps the pace steady and makes the work more fun. For example, aerobics classes and workout tapes depend on music to motivate exercisers and help them keep the pace. On the other hand, parents use lullabies to lull their babies to sleep.

Since the late Middle Ages, Western music has developed many conventional types. These genres vary with the audience, the instruments, and the musical structures. **Liturgical** music was designed for churches, used sacred texts, and took advantage of church acoustics. The soaring vaults of Gothic cathedrals were perfect for the music of the Middle Ages. Music known as **chant** or **plainsong** is simply the human voice singing a religious text without instrumental accompaniment. When the voice is unaccompanied, it is known as **a cappella.** When the sound is made by specialized devices, called **instruments,** the music is termed **instrumental.**

Secular, that is nonreligious, music brought about other forms. **Chamber music,** instrumental music that was originally played in palaces for royalty and nobility, calls for more intimate spaces, a small ensemble of players, and small audiences. **Orchestral music** is the most public and complex form, involving a full orchestra and a concert hall, where the acoustics, or quality of sound, is very important. **Popular music,** often shortened to **pop,** appeals to a wide audience. It includes rock, folk, country, rap, and other types of music. **Jazz** is an improvisational form that arose in the United States from blues and ragtime. **Musical theater,** as the name implies, is a combination of drama and music. Its songs often enter the pop repertoire as **show tunes. Opera,** a narrative in which both dialogue and exposition is sung, combines music with literature and drama.

INSTRUMENTS

Musical instruments, which vary widely across cultures, can nevertheless be grouped in families. Probably most ancient are the **percussion** instruments, which make noise as they are struck. Drums, blocks, cymbals, and tambourines are percussion instruments. **Stringed** instruments, deriving from the hunting bow, have strings stretched between two points; sounds are produced when they are plucked, strummed, bowed, or struck. **Woodwinds** are hollow instruments that were originally made of wood, such as the flute, recorder, and panpipes. **Reed** instruments, such as the oboe, are woodwinds that use a mouthpiece created from a compressed reed. **Brasses** are metal horns like the tuba, trumpet, and cornet. In addition to their musical function, brasses were long used by the military to communicate over distances in battle or in camp. Using a prearranged trumpet call, the commander could sound "retreat" or "charge."

MUSICAL QUALITIES AND STRUCTURE

Musical structure ranges from a simple tune or rhythm to the intricacy of a symphony or an opera. The tone, or sound of a specific quality, is the basis of all music, using varieties of high or low pitches and timbres with varying intensity and tempos. Music appeals to our emotions through tempo, musical color or timbre, and harmonic structure. We associate different emotions with different timbres. The harp, for example, evokes gentleness or calm, whereas brasses evoke more stirring emotions.

Musical structure can be simple, such as Ravel's *Bolero,* which uses the repetition of a single melody with increased tempo and volume to build to a climax. Increases in tempo generate excitement, literally increasing the listener's heart rate and breathing speed. These qualities were used to good advantage in Blake Edwards's film *10.* Composers of movie music manipulate our emotions expertly, heightening the appeal of the action.

The comparatively uncomplicated pop songs we sing are based on melodies, a succession of notes, with accompanying words. We are also familiar with the 32-bar structure of most pop and rock music, in which **verses** alternate with repeated **choruses.** To appreciate and enjoy more complex music, some understanding of structure is important. The simple song "Row, Row, Row Your Boat," familiar to many of us from childhood, is a **round** or **canon;** the same melody is sung by each voice, but voices enter one after the other, creating overlapping notes, or **chords.** More elaborate forms stemming from such simple structures are found in **classical** music, beginning with European music of the eighteenth and nineteenth centuries.

Harmonic structure is a complex topic. Western music is written in **keys,** a system of notes based on one central note, such as the key of C Major. The different keys have their own emotional connotations. A **minor key** is often associated with sadness; a **major key** seems happier or more forceful. Notes that seem to fit together are consonant, while clashing notes are dissonant. Generally, consonance seems peaceful or happy to most people, while dissonance may be unsettling.

Music

Acoustics: The qualities of sound, often used to describe the relationship between sound and architecture, as in a concert hall.

Vibrations: Trembling or oscillating motions that produce sound. When singers or stringed instruments produce a wavering sound, causing a fluctuation in pitch, it is termed **vibrato.**

Pitch: The sound produced by vibrations. The speed of vibrations controls the pitch: slow vibrations produce low pitches; fast vibrations produce high pitches.

Tempo: The speed at which music is played or sung. This is shown on sheet music, usually in Italian terms, by **tempo marks** that indicate the desired speed. A device called a **metronome** can indicate tempo with precision.

Timbre: The characteristic sound or tonal quality of an instrument or voice. Also termed **color,** it can refer to the combination produced by more than one instrument's timbres, as **orchestral color.**

Tone: A sound of specific pitch and quality, the basic building material of music. Its properties are pitch, timbre, duration, and intensity.

Note: The written symbol for a tone, shown as **whole notes, half notes,** etc. These indicate the time a note is held, with a corresponding **rest** sign. **Notation** is the use of a set of symbols to record music in written form.

Melody: The succession of notes or pitches played or sung. Music with a single melodic line is called **monophony,** while music with more than one melodic line is **polyphony.**

Texture: In music, this refers to the number of diffent melodic lines; the greater the number, the thicker the texture.

Harmony: The combination of notes sung or played at one time, or **chords;** applies to homophonic music. **Consonance** refers to the sound of notes that are agreeable together; **dissonance** to the sound of notes that are discordant.

NON-WESTERN MUSIC

Music of the non-Western world shares with Western music a tradition of early oral transmission and an affiliation with the values and beliefs of its originating culture. Like Western music, too, music of non-Western traditions has undergone change and reflects the influence of musical traditions with which it has had contact over the centuries.

Nonetheless, there are distinctive differences among the world's many and varied musical traditions, and a number of differences between Western and non-Western musical forms, textures, and harmonic, melodic, and rhythmic systems. Pentatonic scales, for example (the 5-note scales illustrated by the black piano keys), are of non-Western origin. Micro-tones, pitches that exist between the half-tone steps of traditional Western musical scales, are another non-Western influence. So too are the intricate rhythmic patterns of Indian music, as performed by tabla players as they accompany master musicians performing on the sitar, an instrument that produces sounds, pitches, and harmonies beyond the scope of those common to Western music.

The best way to learn about and listen to music from other times, places, and traditions, is to understand it within its cultural context and to approach differences with an open mind and an attentive ear. Whether you are listening to Japanese shakuhachi music, which has a ceremonial quality, or to Indonesian gamelan music, with its uniquely orchestral combination of xylophone, bronze bowls, gongs, flutes, percussive and plucked instruments, or to African Mbira music, with its repetitive melodies and strong dance connections, the route to understanding and enjoyment is to be willing to entertain new sounds, new combinations of instruments, and new musical experiences.

HISTORY, RELIGION, AND PHILOSOPHY

History, the recording and explanation of events, and philosophy, the search for truth, have both influenced the arts. These subjects have themselves evolved as humanistic disciplines. **Aesthetics,** the branch of philosophy concerned with the functions, practice, and appreciation of the arts, along with their role in society, is an important part of this book and of cultural studies in general.

History

Until the Greek historian Herodotus, traveling in the Mediterranean lands of the sixth century B.C.E., turned his questioning and skeptical eye on the received beliefs and tales of peoples he met, history was inseparable from religious faith and folk memory. Herodotus began as a kind of cultural anthropologist, and he deliberately distinguished his historical writing from the epic tradition by writing prose rather than poetry.

History is the study of the human past and involves an inquiry into and report upon real events and people. That encompasses quite a diverse lot, including plagues, invasions, emigrations, wars, revolutions, cultural and religious changes and developments, constitutional and political developments, providential history, and more. Among related genres and lines of inquiry are myth and epic, biography, memoir, drama, ethnography, novels, inquests, and yet-to-be combined and discovered genres.

History is a field of research and investigation into the causes and effects of past events. Often these events are chronicled by historians in a set of linked stories or narratives that focus on various kinds of human activities, from war, politics, and diplomacy, to economic, social, religious, artistic, and other cultural developments. Historians also discuss the study of their discipline as an end in itself and as a way of providing perspective on problems of the present.

Historians have developed methods of inquiry, questioning the likelihood of stories and delving into the motives of their informants. They learned to consider nonhistorical accounts and records and checks on their official versions. They began to consider the psychological motives of the people they chronicled. The artistry of historians' presentation has since become part of the discipline of history.

Traditionally, historians have reported and recorded past events, usually in writing, relying for their evidence on written documents, oral accounts, and other materials, such as pictures, inscriptions, and monuments. From what has been said, what has been written, and what has been physically preserved, historians attempt to understand the past—on what happened, on why and how it happened, and on how events of one time affected or influenced those of subsequent times.

The study of history has been classified as part of the humanities, and also as a branch of the social sciences. It is useful to consider history as a kind of bridge between them, as history uses methodologies of both the humanities and the social sciences. In *Arts and Culture*, we discuss history as background and context—social, cultural, political, religious, economic—for understanding the development of architectural, artistic, kinetic, literary, musical, photographic, and other types of arts and humanities endeavors. By studying paintings, drawings, carvings, and other artifacts, information can be recovered even in the absence of a written record.

The study of "pre-history," in fact, refers to the period before the existence of written records. In recent decades the study of prehistory has become essential to avoid excluding certain civilizations, such as those of sub-Saharan Africa and pre-Columbian America.

Religion

Religion involves a set of beliefs concerning the origins, purpose, and nature of the universe and the place of human beings within it. In religious terms, the universe is seen as the creation of a supernatural being or agency. A moral code and a set of rituals and devotional practices are a response to a civilization's understanding of its relationship to the creator(s) of the universe. Linked with religion in this sense are social and political beliefs, philosophical claims, laws, rituals, and behaviors that are encoded in or suggested by scriptures, or sacred religious texts.

Religions are associated with myths, or traditional stories that convey the worldview of a people. "Myth" has both pejorative, or negative, and nonpejorative, or neutral, meanings. We use the term here to suggest that the myths associated with the religion of any people or civilization express its ideals, beliefs, and values, whether the mythic stories are based on actual historical events or not. Among the religions of the world whose myths convey such beliefs, ideals, and values are those of African, Australian Aboriginal, and Native American civilizations, as well as the religious traditions of the East and West. The Asian religions include those of Hinduism, Buddhism, Sikhism, and Jainism, along with the religious philosophies of China, especially Confucianism and Taoism. The Western religions of the Abrahamic tradition include Judaism, Christianity, and Islam.

Religion as a way of life is captured in the arts, music, and cultural practices of a civilization or a people. Religion has played a crucial role in the development of the arts, which provide images, sounds, and words for use in worship, prayers, and religious stories. Theology, the study of the nature of the divine, prescribes religious practices, moral beliefs, and rules for social behavior. The dominant religion in a culture often controls the art, either directly by training artists and commissioning art, or indirectly through influencing beliefs and values. The medieval Catholic belief in the efficacy of relics to heal or give aid, for example, led to the practice of pilgrimage, and from that to the creation of churches and cathedrals. As religious orders acquired holy relics, they housed them in shrines within the churches, to which pilgrims came to seek aid and to pay homage. Problems arose when the many pilgrims who came to be healed and blessed disrupted services for the local population. Romanesque architects, in response, developed the ambulatory, or walkway, that allowed pilgrims to see the relics without interrupting worshipers at a service, thereby altering religious architecture.

Different religions hold very different aesthetic ideas and celebrate varying images of beauty, such that nudity was acceptable in the temple statues of Classical Greece and Hindu India, but not in Christian churches or cathedrals. Islam prohibits any figurative images in places of worship, and thus Islamic mosques are decorated with geometric designs. And some Native American peoples believe that a permanent house of worship is inappropriate in and of itself, preferring instead to worship and communicate with divinity in nature.

In many cultures, religion is intertwined with philosophy. Confucianism, Taoism, Hinduism, and Buddhism, for example, are all based on intricate philosophical systems that are allied with various beliefs and social practices. And as with philosophy, religion is concerned with the development of moral and ethical principles for living.

PHILOSOPHY

Philosophy is the study of fundamental or essential questions about the nature of existence, knowledge, values, reason, mind, and language. Philosophy, which means "love of wisdom" in Greek, differs from other approaches to fundamental questions by its reliance on rational argument.

Some of the kinds of questions philosophers ask and explore include "What is the meaning of life?" a question also at the heart of religion. "How should I live my life?" "What is the meaning of it all—what's the purpose of life, not just my own, but of all life?" "How do I know that I exist, and how can I prove it?"

Metaphysics, the study of the nature of being, tackles the questions: "What is being; what is the nature of reality?" "Do we have free will?" Epistemology, the study of the nature of knowledge, is concerned with the possibility and scope of knowledge, and inquires into how we know what we know or what we think we know. Among the concerns of epistemology are the relationships between truth and belief—and the justifications for what we believe and think to be true.

Ethics, or moral philosophy, is concerned with good and evil, right and wrong, action and behavior. Among the concerns of ethics are questions of morality, whether there are absolute or universal ethical principles and values, or whether ethically based behavior is situational or contextual. The famous idea of the "golden rule" (to treat others as you want to be treated) is an example of a guiding ethical principle of behavior.

Logic is the study of argument and valid forms of argument. The heart of logic is rationality, reasoning carefully via valid premises to sound and valid conclusions. The syllogism is one of the foundations of logic, as in this example: "Dogs are always ready to eat. My dog Fido has just come in from playing outside. I better get his food ready now." Logicians are concerned with fallacious or incorrect reasoning, and to that end have identified a series of classic mistaken forms of argument called logical errors in reasoning, which include such fallacies as circular argument, attacking a person rather than his ideas, and accepting that something that happens after something else is caused by what happened before.

Other branches of philosophy include aesthetics, which deals with beauty, art, perception, taste, and sentiment; and the philosophy of mind, which deals with the nature of the mind and its relationship to the body. Developments in cognitive science, a melding of philosophy, psychology, and neurology, have complicated and enhanced the philosophy of mind. In addition, the philosophy of language inquires into the nature, origins, and use of language; the philosophy of religions considers questions about religion, as the philosophy of science and the philosophy of history do the same for those domains of knowledge. Related to the last of these is political philosophy, the study of government and the relationship of individuals and communities to the state. Political philosophy focuses on questions of justice, law, and the rights and obligations of citizens.

In addition to these ways of identifying the concerns and interests of philosophical inquiry, we can also divide the study of philosophy into geographical areas and chronological periods, such as the philosophies of China and India, on one hand, and Western philosophy, on the other; or ancient, medieval modern and contemporary philosophy, for example. Within and among these categories, we can place various philosophical traditions, such as those of skepticism and stoicism, Neoplatonism and Thomism, rationalism, empiricism, and existentialism, to name a few. These various kinds of philosophy are explained briefly throughout this book, in the chapters devoted to the times and places of their development.

ARTS AND CULTURE

An Introduction to the Humanities

Chapter 1

History

ca. 35,000–10,000 B.C.E.	*Homo sapiens* begins supplanting Neanderthal in Europe
ca. 8000–3000 B.C.E.	Farming replaces hunting
ca. 3100 B.C.E.	King Narmer unites Upper and Lower Egypt
ca. 3000 B.C.E.	Bronze Age begins in Mesopotamia and Egypt
ca. 2700 B.C.E.	King Gilgamesh reigns in Sumer
ca. 2332–2279 B.C.E.	King Sargon I rules Akkad
1792–1750 B.C.E.	King Hammurabi reigns in Babylon, unites Sumer and Akkad
1674 B.C.E.	Hyksos invade northern Egypt
1478–1458 B.C.E.	Queen Hatshepsut rules
1479–1425 B.C.E.	King Thutmose III, first pharaoh, rules
1352–1336 B.C.E.	King Amenhotep IV (Akhenaten) rules
ca. 1336–1327 B.C.E.	King Tutankhamen rules
689 B.C.E., 648 B.C.E.	Assyrians sack Babylon
669–627 B.C.E.	Ashurbanipal reigns in Assyria
525 B.C.E.	Persia conquers Egypt

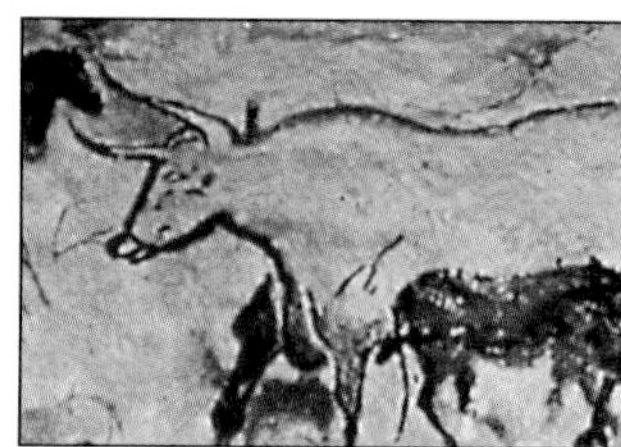

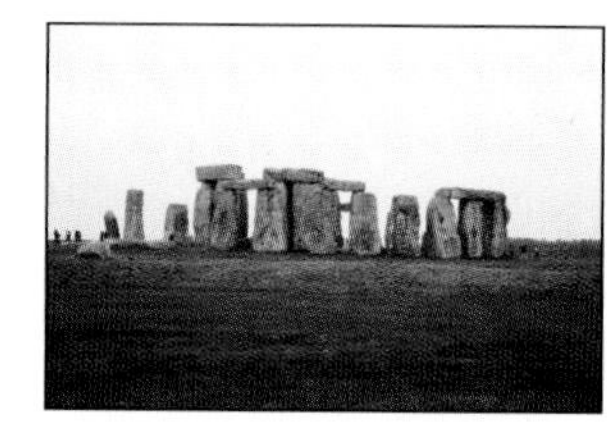

Art and Architecture

ca. 25,000–20,000 B.C.E.	*Woman of Willendorf*
ca. 15,000–10,000 B.C.E.	Wall paintings at Lascaux
ca. 8000–3000 B.C.E.	Wall paintings in the Valtorta Gorge
ca. 3100 B.C.E.	*Palette of Narmer*
ca. 2600 B.C.E.	Stepped Pyramid of Zoser
ca. 2530–2470 B.C.E.	Great Pyramids at Giza
ca. 2500 B.C.E.	Great Sphinx
ca. 2500–2050 B.C.E.	Ziggurat of King Urnammu
ca. 2470 B.C.E.	Statue of Mycernius and Khamerernebty
ca. 2300–2200 B.C.E.	*Victory Stele of Naram-Sin*
ca. 2000 B.C.E.	Stonehenge
ca. 1478–1458 B.C.E.	Temple of Queen Hatshepsut
ca. 1400 B.C.E.	*Nobleman Hunting in the Marshes*
1352–1336 B.C.E.	Portrait of Queen Nefertiti
1260 B.C.E.	Temple of Amen-Mut-Khonsu
	Temple of Ramesses II
ca. 650 B.C.E.	Limestone relief of *Sack of the City of Hamanu by Ashurbanipal*

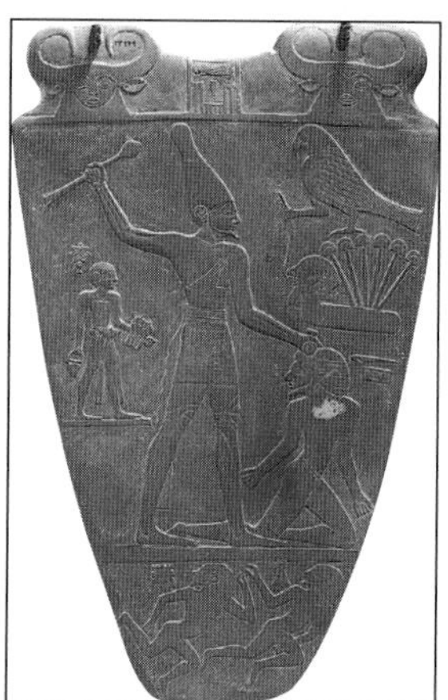

Literature and Philosophy

ca. 100,000 B.C.E.	Evidence of religious practice
ca. 3300 B.C.E.	Earliest preserved tablets with pictographs
ca. 3000 B.C.E.	Writing begins in Mesopotamia
ca. 2500 B.C.E.	Papyrus in use in Egypt
2040–1786 B.C.E.	Hieratic (cursive) writing develops during the Middle Kingdom
ca. 1900–1600 B.C.E.	*The Epic of Gilgamesh,* first written down by Akkadians
ca. 1760 B.C.E.	Stele inscribed with the Law Code of Hammurabi
196 B.C.E.	Rosetta Stone

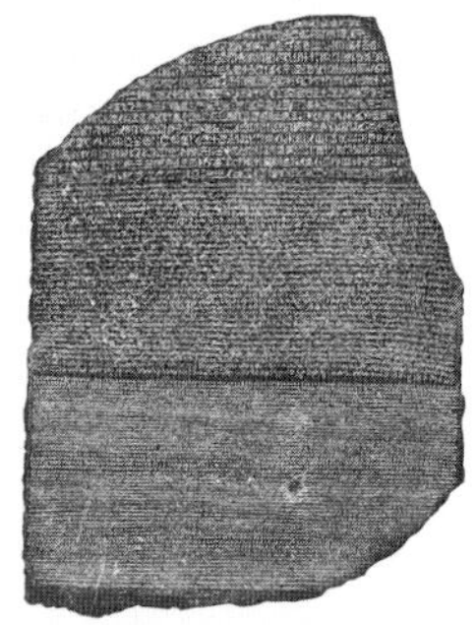

Prehistoric, Mesopotamian, and Egyptian Civilizations

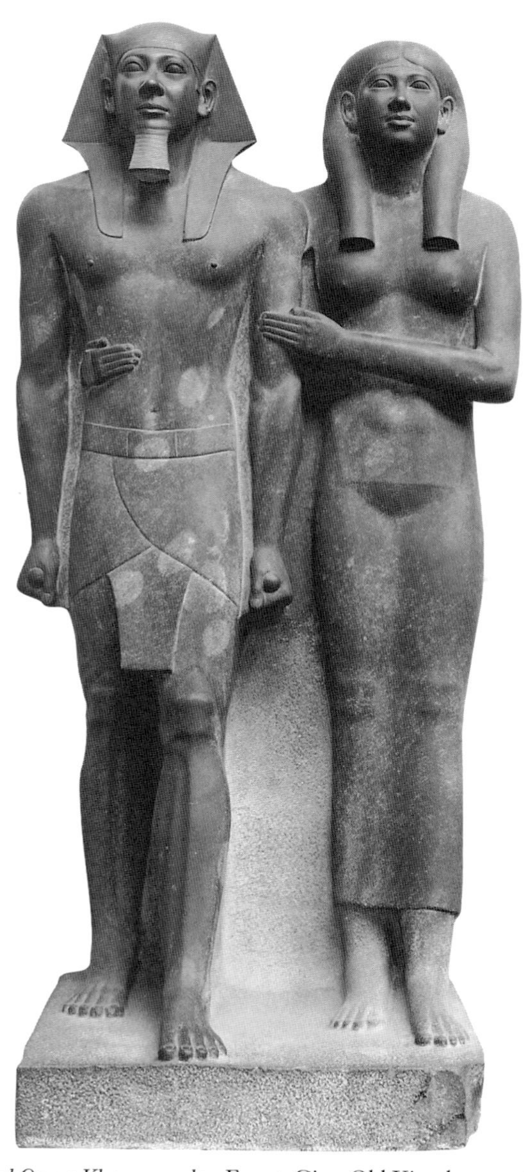

Pharaoh Mycerinus and Queen Khamerernebty. Egypt, Giza. Old Kingdom, ca. 2490–2472 B.C.E., Fourth Dynasty, greywacke, height 56″ × 22$\frac{1}{2}$″ × 21$\frac{3}{4}$″ (142.2 × 57.1 × 56.2 cm). Harvard University-Boston Museum of Fine Arts. Expedition, 11.1738 Courtesy, Museum of Fine Arts, Boston. Reproduced with permission. © 2008 Museum of Fine Arts, Boston. All Rights Reserved.

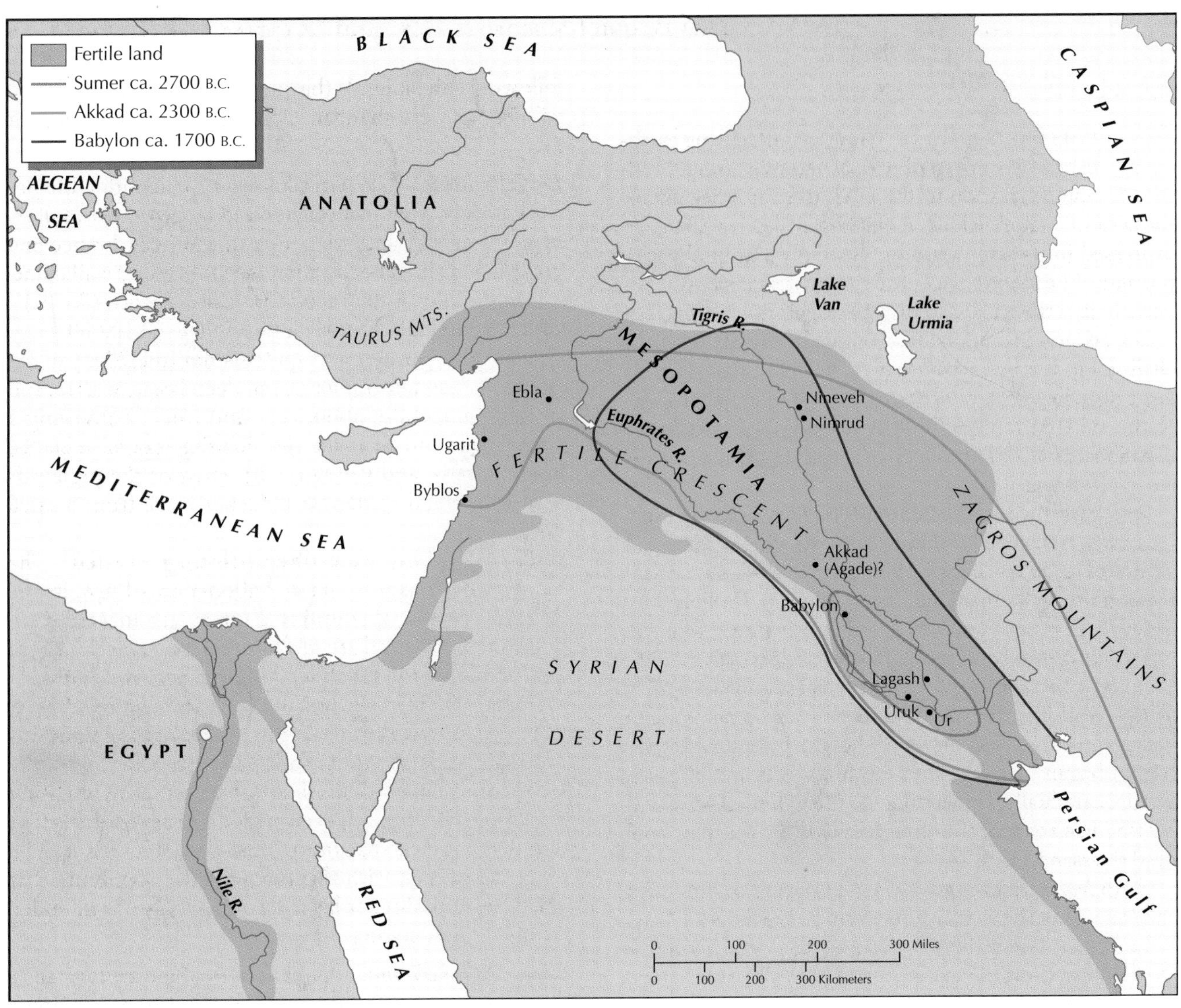

MAP 1.1 The Ancient Near East and the Fertile Crescent.

CHAPTER OVERVIEW

EARLIEST CULTURES

Prehistoric society and the birth of the visual arts

MESOPOTAMIA: THE CRADLE OF CIVILIZATION

The expansion of agrarian peoples' borders and ideas in the ancient Near East

CIVILIZATION OF THE NILE

A divided Egypt comes together through a shared culture and religion

OLD KINGDOM

Dynasties 3–6: The rise of the pyramids, sculpture, and relief painting

MIDDLE KINGDOM

Dynasties 11–14: Egypt prospers

NEW KINGDOM

Dynasties 18–20: A mature and powerful Egypt rules in art and world politics

EARLIEST CULTURES

A CULTURE IS A WAY OF THINKING AND living established by a group of people and transmitted from one generation to the next. It is, in other words, the basis of communal life. A culture's collective values are expressed in its arts, writings, customs, and intellectual pursuits. The ability of a culture to express itself well, especially in writing, and to organize itself thoroughly, as a social, economic, and political entity, distinguishes it as a civilization. It is important to note, however, that some aspects of civilizations predate writing—monumental architecture and urban organization, for example. Further, an occasional civilization, such as that of the Inca, never developed writing.

Just when the earliest cultures took form, and then subsequently transformed themselves into civilizations, is a matter of some conjecture among anthropologists, scientists who study humankind's institutions and beliefs from the earliest times. The first historical evidence of a culture coming into being can be found in the artifacts of the earliest *homo sapiens*, or "the one who knows." About 35,000 years ago, the hominid species *homo sapiens*, which had come into being about 200,000 B.C.E., probably in Africa, began to assert itself in the forests and plains of Europe, gradually supplanting the Neanderthal *homo erectus* who had roamed the same areas for the previous hundred thousand years.

Both *homo sapiens* and *homo erectus* were tool makers, as even our earliest ancestors seem to have been. *Kenya pithecus* (the "Kenya ape"), for instance, which lived in the Olduvai Gorge in east-central Africa between nineteen and fourteen million years ago, made crude stone weapons or tools. *Homo sapiens* and the Neanderthals both cooked with fire, wore skins as clothing, and used tools. They evidently buried their dead in ritual ceremonies, which provide the earliest indications of religious beliefs and practices. These activities suggest the transmission of knowledge and patterns of social behavior from one generation to the next. But between 35,000 and 10,000 B.C.E.—the last part of the period known as the **Paleolithic,** or Old Stone Age, when *homo sapiens* became more and more dominant and the Neanderthal line died out—the first objects that can be considered works of art began to appear, objects that seem to express the values and beliefs of the Paleolithic people. The Paleolithic period thus represents the very earliest cultural era.

PALEOLITHIC PERIOD

The Paleolithic period corresponds to the geological Pleistocene era, or Ice Age. Periodically, glaciers moved south over the European and Asian continents, forcing the inhabitants of the areas to move south, around the Mediterranean and into Africa. These people lived nomadic lives, following animal herds (bison, mammoths, reindeer, and wild horses were abundant), on which they depended for food.

Wall Paintings. What is known of Paleolithic life derives largely from paintings found in caves, particularly in the Franco-Cantabrian area of southern France and northern Spain. The most famous prehistoric wall paintings are those in the cave at Lascaux, France (fig. 1.1), which were created between ca. 15,000 and 10,000 B.C.E. The Lascaux paintings are quite naturalistic. Many of the animals—bison, mammoths, reindeer, boars, wolves, and horses—gracefully jump, run, and romp, conveying a remarkable sense of animation. Painting is done in blacks, browns, reds, and yellows, with most of the pigments used of mineral oxides, with deeper black from burned bones.

How and why were these paintings created? The paintings at Lascaux and at Vallon-Pont-d'Arc, in the Ardèche region of southern France, are located deep within the caves and are often very hard to reach. There is no evidence of human habitation where the paintings are located—instead, people seem to have lived at or near the entrances to the caves, where natural light was available. It is thought that the artists worked by the light of oil lamps. One theory holds that by creating these animals in paint, deep within the caves, the artists may have hoped that more animals would actually be born. Associated with this theory is the possibility that the superimposing, or layering, of animals was intended to show them mating.

Ritual and Religion. Unlike much of the art created in later eras, prehistoric art is thought to be related to ritual, linked with prayer to placate the powers of nature. In a form of sympathetic magic, power could be gained over elements of nature. For example, the theory that hunting rituals were performed in the caves to gain control over the animals depicted there is strongly supported not only by the painting of spears on the animals, but also by actual spearheads found driven into some of the painted animals, which are shown to bleed as a result of their injuries. Thus, in order to ensure a successful hunt, the animal may have been killed in effigy before the hunt.

Art, religion, and ritual were bound together as images, words, and physical movement were combined to achieve success in the hunt. Religion and ritual were critically important for prehistoric cultures in which some measure of control over nature was necessary for survival.

Sculpture. Only a fraction of the sculpture made in prehistoric times of durable materials such as ivory, bone, horn, stone, and clay is known today, and still fewer sculptures made of a perishable material, such as wood, remain.

Depictions of the human figure are rare in Paleolithic sculpture, and the few known are mostly female figures. The most famous example of prehistoric sculpture is the

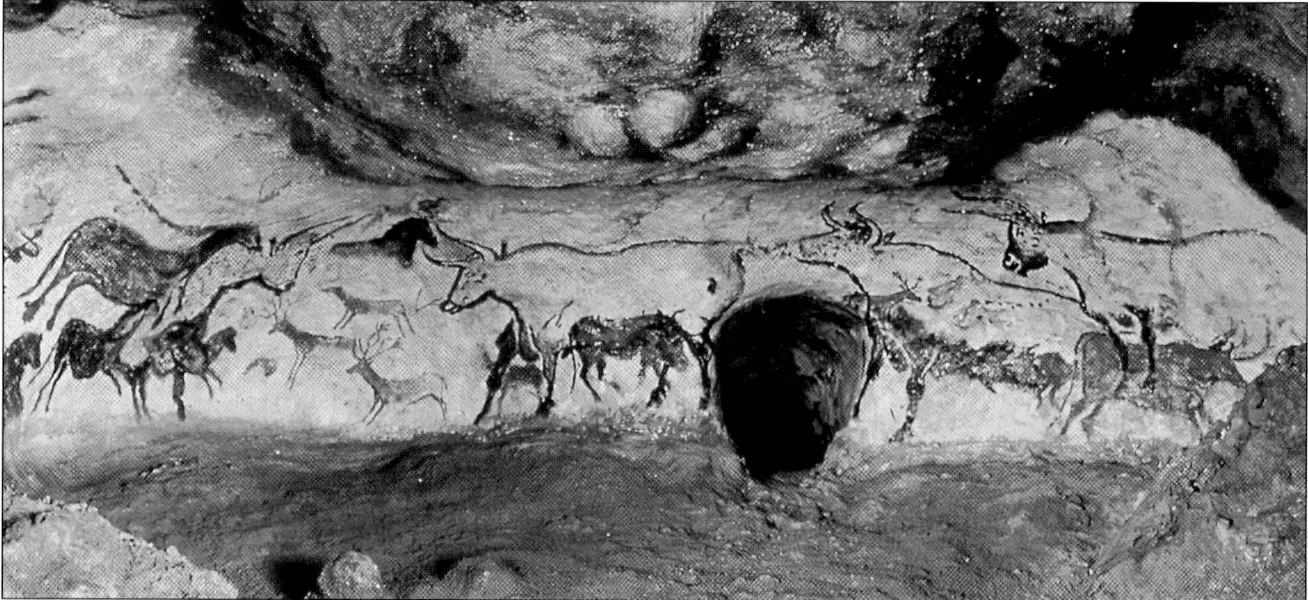

FIGURE 1.1 Overview of the Hall of the Bulls, Lascaux, Dordogne, France, ca. 15,000–10,000 B.C.E., cave painting. Prehistoric artists depicted with notable realism the animals on which they depended for food. With very few exceptions, the animals represented in such paintings are identifiable.

so-called *Woman* (or *Venus*) *of Willendorf* (fig. 1.2), a stone figure small enough to be held in a hand, dated to about 25,000–20,000 B.C.E., and named for the place where it was found in western Austria near the Danube River.

The *Woman of Willendorf* is highly stylized. The greatly enlarged breasts and abdomen—which suggest pregnancy—indicate the work's possible connection to human fertility. In fact, prior to the Neolithic period, almost no other human types are known. Perhaps such figures were a type of idol and were intended to promote human fertility, much as the cave paintings of animals might have been intended to "create" animals for the hunters.

NEOLITHIC PERIOD

By 8000 B.C.E., possibly the most important transformation in the history of human civilization took place: Around the world, in the Near East, in South and Central America, and in Southeast Asia, human beings ceased to hunt and began instead to farm, plowing and planting seeds, growing crops, and domesticating animals, using them not only as a reliable source of food and clothing but also as beasts of burden, inaugurating what is known as the **Neolithic** period, or New Stone Age. Hunters and gatherers became herders and farmers, and more permanent societies began to develop.

This transformation from a nomadic life of hunting to a more settled life of herding and agriculture revolutionized life for prehistoric peoples. One historian has characterized the Neolithic era as the matrix from which civilization appears and provides the preconditions on which it rests. These preconditions include the ability to grow wheat, maize, rice, and barley, along with the capability of domesticating formerly wild pigs, goats, sheep, and cattle. These developments radically altered the conditions of human existence.

Wall Paintings. In the Valtorta Gorge (fig. 1.3) on the southeast coast of Spain, paintings that date from sometime after 8000 B.C.E. and possibly as late as 3000 B.C.E. suggest that hunting remained the chief preoccupation of these peoples. But changes and advances are evident. Unlike the paintings of the Franco-Cantabrian area that are located deep in caves, the Valtorta Gorge paintings are on the smooth limestone walls in rock shelters and beneath cliff overhangs. The subjects portrayed differ significantly also, for here the human figure is given prominence, with people shown hunting animals, fighting, and dancing together, as a group or community.

A degree of narrative is evident in the Valtorta wall paintings as the hunters, running from the left, attack the herd crossing a stream from the right. The composition is organized with a definite flow to the chase, a sense of action and movement conveyed by the lively postures of the figures—indeed, this appears to be a record of an actual event. A superb document of early hunting techniques, the scene shows hunters using the bow and arrow, a weapon not seen in Franco-Cantabrian art.

Architecture. Prehistoric architecture survives only from the Neolithic period, and very little survives at all. Structures made of wood, other plant material, or mud brick decayed and disappeared long ago.

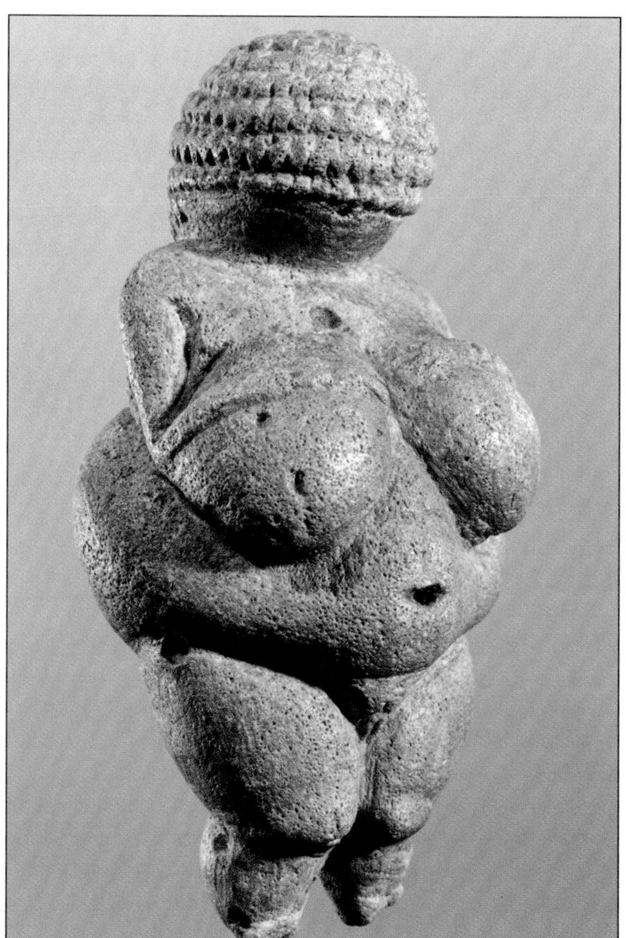

FIGURE 1.2 *Woman of Willendorf*, found at Willendorf, Austria, ca. 25,000–20,000 B.C.E., limestone, height $4\frac{3}{8}''$ (11 cm), Naturhistorisches Museum, Vienna. The so-called *Venus of Willendorf* is the most famous (but not the most physically distorted) of several extant female figurines thought to be associated with prehistoric beliefs about human fertility, or, alternatively, fat as a sign of physical beauty in an era when food was scarce.

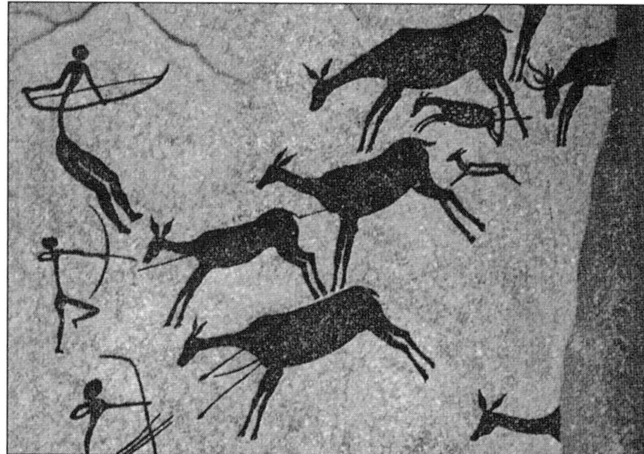

FIGURE 1.3 Herd crossing river, hunters with bows and arrows, Valtorta Gorge, Levant, Spain, ca. 8000–3000 B.C.E., rock painting. Because humans are prominently depicted, are shown using weapons, and because this scene has a definite composition, the Valtorta Gorge paintings are believed to date later than those at Lascaux.

The most famous example of prehistoric architecture is surely the **cromlech,** or circle of stones having a religious purpose, known as Stonehenge (fig. 1.4), located on the Salisbury Plain in Wiltshire, England, and completed ca. 2000 B.C.E. A **henge** is a circle of stones or posts. Stonehenge is not the only prehistoric cromlech to have survived, but it is the most impressive and best preserved. The outer trench is approximately 150 feet in diameter, and the individual stones approximately 20 feet high. There is a definite entranceway, as well as four mounds evenly placed on the outer trench, and a central stone referred to as the altar stone. The huge upright stones form an outer circle and two inner circles or U shapes. Some of the stones are shaped into rectangles, and some also have patterns cut into them. Stonehenge is constructed using the **post and lintel** system—in its simplest form, two vertical posts support a horizontal lintel. At Stonehenge, the vertical posts have dowel pins carved into their uppermost end, which fit into circular depressions carved on the underside of the lintels at both ends, thereby locking the posts and lintels together.

What can the purpose or function of so monumental an undertaking have been? The answer seems to be connected with several "correspondences." If you stand in the center of Stonehenge and look to the so-called heelstone, you see that the top aligns with the horizon. The sun rises directly over the heelstone at the summer solstice, the longest day of the year. On each of the four mounds were other stones at horizon level—the one to the southwest is

FIGURE 1.4 Stonehenge, Salisbury Plain, Wiltshire, England, completed ca. 2000 B.C.E., bluestone and sarsen, height of stones of outer circle 20′ (6.09 m). This enigmatic remnant of prehistoric architecture is believed to have been a monumental clock, laid out so the stones relate to the position of the sun at the summer and winter solstices.

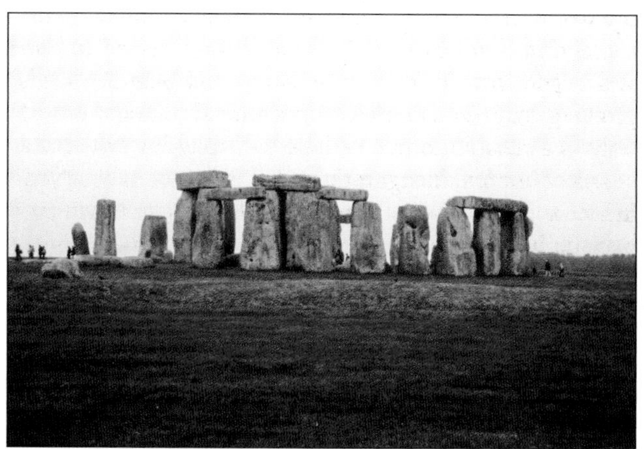

at the point of the setting sun at the winter solstice, the shortest day of the year. Stonehenge, therefore, seems to be an enormous sun clock or calendar, based on the rising and setting sun at the summer and winter solstices.

MESOPOTAMIA: THE CRADLE OF CIVILIZATION

Even before Stonehenge was built in England, two far more advanced civilizations were developing in the Near East: that of Mesopotamia and that of Egypt. Mesopotamian civilization developed in the valley between the Tigris and Euphrates Rivers: Mesopotamia is a Greek word meaning literally "the land between two rivers." Consisting of the eastern part of what is known as the Fertile Crescent, which extends northward along the eastern coast of the Mediterranean through what is today Israel and Lebanon, eastward into present-day Syria and Iraq, and south down the Tigris and Euphrates valleys to the Persian Gulf, Mesopotamia was the most fertile and arable land in the Near East, and perhaps, at the dawn of the Neolithic Age, the most fertile in the world. It was here, at any rate, that around 9000 B.C.E. agriculture—literally, from the Latin *cultura*, or cultivation, of the *ager*, land—was first fully developed.

By about 3000 B.C.E., two further developments had taken place that had a decisive influence on the course of civilization. Sometime after 6000 B.C.E. people learned to mine and use copper; by 3000 B.C.E., they had discovered that by combining tin with copper they could produce a much stronger alloy, bronze, which allowed tremendous innovations in the production of weapons, tools, and jewelry. This marked the beginning of the Bronze Age.

The second development marks the move from prehistory into the first historical period—that is, a period for which written records exist. By about 3000 B.C.E., the people of ancient Mesopotamia were using written language, known today largely from clay tablets that were first unearthed in the mid-nineteenth century. Chiefly the province of the upper class and priests, this writing was accomplished in wedge-shaped **cuneiform** characters (from the Latin *cuneus*, meaning "wedge") made with a stylus that was itself wedge shaped and that was pressed into wet clay tablets. The original purpose of this writing seems to have been to keep agricultural records. Among the oldest examples of cuneiform writing, for instance, is a tablet from a temple complex at Uruk that lists sacks of grains and heads of cattle. Cuneiform writing began as a **pictographic** system. In its earliest form, the symbol for "cow" was an abstract "picture" of a cow's head:

But the pictographs were quickly abstracted even further, presumably in no small part because it was difficult to draw a curve with a reed stylus in wet clay. Between 2500 and 1800 B.C.E., the sign for "cow" was first turned ninety degrees sideways and then converted into a series of quickly imprinted wedges:

By combining pictograms, more complex ideas—or **ideograms**—and even abstract ideas could be represented. A bird next to an egg meant "fertility." Two crossed lines meant "hatred" or "enmity," and parallel lines signified "friendship":

Sometime around 2000 B.C.E., another important development occurred, when pictograms began to represent not only objects but sounds—the birth of phonetic writing.

Assisted by these technical advances, three successive civilizations—those of Sumer, Akkad, and Babylon—blossomed in Mesopotamia over the following 1,500 years.

Table 1–1 DEVELOPMENT OF WRITING
Cuneiform (Mesopotamian): wedge-shaped images incised in clay
Pictographic: pictures of objects as "words"—cow =
Ideographic: combinations of pictures as ideograms—hatred =
Hieroglyphic (Egyptian): pictures and sounds together
Phonetic (Phoenician): sounds as syllables
Alphabetic (Greek): letters as sounds

SUMER

The Sumerians, who lived at the southern end of the Tigris and Euphrates Rivers, founded the Mesopotamian cvilization between 3500 and 3000 B.C.E., contemporary with the beginning of Egyptian civilization. Sumerian culture reached its zenith by approximately 2800–2700 B.C.E. It was at this time that Sumer's most famous king, GILGAMESH [GIL-gah-mesh] (ca. 2700 B.C.E.), ruled Uruk, one of the many independent city-states that grew up in Mesopotamia.

Each Sumerian city-state had its own local god and its own local ruler. The kings were not thought of as gods—rather, the god was considered the owner of the city-state, with the king as an intermediary between the god and the people. In each city-state, the buildings were clustered around the temple of the city's god. Religion focused on seasonal fertility. Agricultural mythology included the Bull of Heaven, whose fiery breath could burn crops, and Imdugud, a lion-headed eagle whose wings covered the heavens in dark clouds, a good creature who brought rain and ended droughts brought on by the Bull of Heaven.

Like most early religions, Sumerian and later Mesopotamian religions were **polytheistic**—that is, there were many gods and goddesses, who often competed with one another for the attention of worshipers. The gods were human in form, and possessed human personalities and foibles—that is, they were **anthropomorphic.** The four chief gods were Anu, the heaven god; Ninhursag, the mother goddess; Enlil, the god of air; and Enki, the god of water. As human as the behavior of these gods might be, they were nonetheless clearly superior to humans, particularly by their immortality. The cuneiform sign for god is a star, which also means "on high," or "elevated," as well as "in the heavens."

Architecture. Sumerian domestic architecture seems to have consisted largely of houses that were square or rectangular in plan and built of mud brick. Archaeologists have not been able to work out the precise layouts of Mesopotamian cities, but it seems certain that at the heart of the settlement would have been the temple. Sumerian temples were built on raised platforms known as **ziggurats,** an example of which is the Ziggurat of King Urnammu at Ur, in Iraq (fig. 1.5), constructed ca. 2500–2050 B.C.E. of sun-baked mud brick and, consequently, now greatly disintegrated. The lowest level is fifty feet high. The walls are **battered,** that is, sloping, making them stronger than vertical walls because they are self-buttressing. The walls are constructed with **weeper holes** to allow water that collects in the masonry to run out through these small, regularly placed openings. The ziggurat at Ur demonstrates the use of specific orientation in architecture, for the corners point north, south, east, and west.

The actual temple was atop the ziggurat. Within the temple, a statue of the god stood in the sanctuary, a long room running the entire length of the temple. The lower levels of the ziggurat were covered with dirt and planted with trees, thus creating the effect of a mountain with a temple on top. This practice is explained by the belief that the gods lived on the mountain tops, so ziggurats brought worshipers closer to heaven.

Sculpture. Although Sumerian sculpture includes occasional secular subjects, most examples appear to be religious or commemorative in purpose, and to have been made for temples. The human figure is represented in a distinctive manner unique to Sumerian sculpture. The style is one of formal simplification, geometric and symmetrical. The figure type is squat in proportions, with broad hips and heavy legs.

A statue formerly thought to represent Abu (Abu means "father" in Arabic languages), the god of vegetation (fig. 1.6), comes from a group of similar statues dated ca. 2600 B.C.E., carved of white gypsum, with black limestone and white shell insets, found in the Abu temple at Tell Asmar. Some of these statues may represent gods. Others may represent worshipers. Curiously, it appears that Sumerian people might have a statue carved to represent themselves and do their worshiping for them—in their place, as a stand-in. An inscription on one such statue translates, "It offers prayers." Another inscription says, "Statue, say unto my king (god) . . ."

FIGURE 1.5 Ziggurat of King Urnammu (Nanna), Ur (El Muqeiyar), Iraq, ca. 2500–2050 B.C.E., sun-baked mud brick. The Sumerians built their temples atop ziggurats—rectangular mountains constructed of mud brick, with battered (sloping) walls.

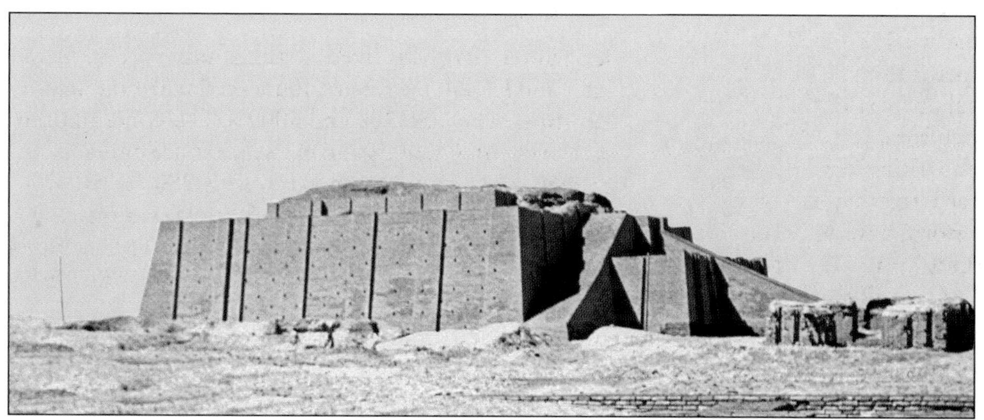

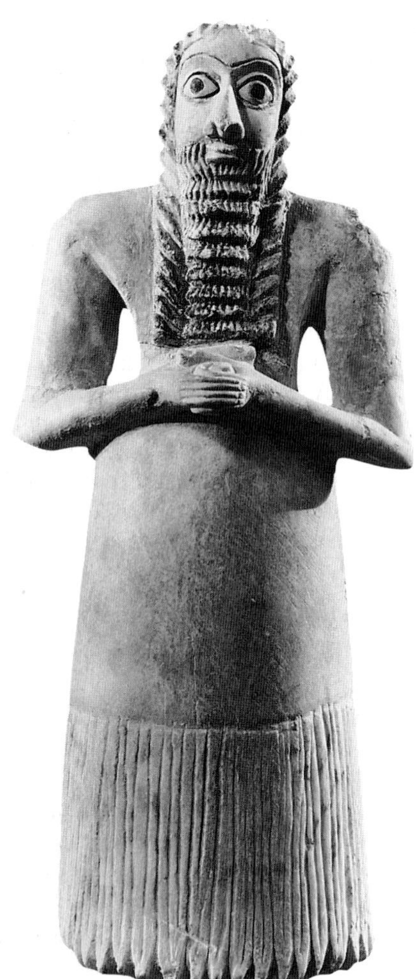

FIGURE 1.6 Standing man, formerly thought to represent Abu, the god of vegetation. From Tell Asmar, ca. 2600 B.C.E. White gypsum, insets of black limestone and white shell, height ca. $11\frac{3}{4}''$ (29.8 cm), Fletcher Fund, 1940 (40.156). The Metropolitan Museum of Art, New York, NY, U.S.A. Image copyright © The Metropolitan Museum of Art/Art Resource, NY. Sumerian statues are easily recognized by their large eyes, single eyebrow, and seemingly astonished facial expression.

Literature. The oldest known major literary work in the world is *The Epic of Gilgamesh*, the earliest elements of which date from about 1900 B.C.E., when Gilgamesh reigned in the Euphrates city-state of Uruk. Legends about Gilgamesh were told but not recorded until hundreds of years after his death. Before about 2000 B.C.E., these stories were recorded on cuneiform tablets. From around 1900–1600 B.C.E. onward, the Gilgamesh stories were written down by the Akkadians, a people who spoke an early Semitic language related to both Hebrew and Arabic. The earliest known version of the epic was discovered in the seventh century B.C.E. in the library of the Assyrian king Ashurbanipal (669–627 B.C.E.).

Like other ancient epics such as those of Homer (see Chapter 2), *The Epic of Gilgamesh* includes elements of folklore, legend, and myth that accrued over time. The work is compiled of originally separate stories concerning Gilgamesh; Enkidu, a primeval human figure; Utnapishtim [OOT-nah-PISH-tim], a Babylonian counterpart of Noah; and a number of other figures.

The epic begins with a kind of prologue that emphasizes Gilgamesh's wisdom as a ruler and his importance to recorded history. The prologue also characterizes him as a semidivine figure, who, though not immortal, is courageous, strong, and beautiful. He is also described as an arrogant and oppressive ruler. When his people cry out for help to their gods for assistance, the god Anu creates Enkidu, a primitive combination of man and wild animal, a figure related to those depicted on the lyre from the tomb of Queen Puabi in Ur.

The story of the mutually positive influences Gilgamesh and Enkidu exert upon each other, of their developing friendship, and their heroic adventures occupies the bulk of the epic. An additional segment concerning Gilgamesh in the Underworld forms a kind of epilogue. In their first adventure, Gilgamesh and Enkidu confront and kill the giant Humbaba. When the goddess Ishtar proposes that Gilgamesh become her lover, he refuses, which precipitates the goddess sending the Bull of Heaven to destroy the city of Uruk by famine.

The second adventure of Gilgamesh and Enkidu involves the slaying of the destructive Bull, the punishment for which is Enkidu's death through illness. After losing his companion, Gilgamesh journeys to visit Utnapishtim, the only human ever granted immortality, but fails to learn the secret of everlasting life, though he does return home having gleaned much else from the wisdom of Utnapishtim. With this knowledge he rules as a wise king. Gilgamesh's adventures are occasions for writers to explore questions that will be raised again in later epics. What is the relationship between human beings and their deities? How are human beings linked with the world of nature and animals? What are the obligations of friendship, family, and public duty? How should we live in the face of mortality?

The earliest known poet, from Mesopotamia, is the poet-priestess Enheduanna, who wrote in the Sumerian language. Daughter of the Akkadian king Sargon, Enheduanna wrote works that in part assisted her father in his attempt to unite Akkadia and Sumeria. Her best-known poems are hymns to Akkadian and Sumerian gods and goddesses, most notably to Inanna, the Sumerian goddess of love.

AKKAD

Under the leadership of King SARGON I, who ruled ca. 2332–2279 B.C.E., and his grandson and successor NARAM-SIN [NA-ram-sin], the Semitic people of Akkad conquered all of the city-states of Sumer. Subsequently, the governors of these cities were "slaves" to the king of Akkad, and he himself was a god to them.

Cross Currents

Sumerian Myth and the Bible

There are strong parallels between Sumerian mythology and the stories in the biblical book of Genesis. For instance, surviving Sumerian texts parallel the story of Noah and the flood, including an episode in The Epic of Gilgamesh—a huge flood did indeed inundate Mesopotamia about 2900 B.C.E. In another Sumerian myth, the story of Enki and Ninhursag, which is some three hundred verses long, Enki, the great Sumerian god of water, creates a garden paradise in Dilmun by bringing water up from the earth. In Genesis 2:6, a similar event occurs: "But there went up a mist from the earth, and watered the whole face of the ground." Ninhursag, the mother-goddess of the Sumerians, causes eight plants to sprout in this proto-Garden of Eden, and Enki, wanting to taste the plants, has another lesser god pick them. Ninhursag is furious and pronounces the curse of death upon Enki. This is a moment in the story that anticipates the biblical God's fury at Adam and Eve for eating the apple that Satan has tempted them with and their expulsion from the garden into a fallen world in which they must confront their mortality. Unlike Adam and Eve, however, Enki is eventually restored to immortality by Ninhursag, but the parallels between the two stories are striking.

Also close in spirit to the biblical Creation story is the *Poem of the Supersage*, an Akkadian text written down about 1700 B.C.E. Like most Akkadian texts, it is probably based on Sumerian legend. The story begins in a divine society where the gods, in order to satisfy their material needs, had to work. Some gods, the leaders, called Anunnaki, were pure consumers, but the rest were laborers. These last, called Igigu, finally revolted, creating the prospect of famine among the Anunnaki. It was Enki who resolved the crisis by proposing that the gods create a substitute labor force out of the clay of the earth, whose destiny it would be to work and whose life would have a limited duration. Thus, as in Genesis, humankind is created out of clay, must labor, and is mortal.

The most celebrated example of Akkadian art is the *Victory Stele of Naram-Sin* (fig. 1.7), ca. 2300–2200 B.C.E. A **stele** is a vertical slab of stone that serves as a marker. The *Victory Stele of Naram-Sin*, which is six and a half feet high, is carved on one side only. At the top of the scene is a set of stars—the sign for Naram-Sin's protecting gods—and below, Naram-Sin and his army victoriously climb a mountain, as if to place themselves in closer proximity to the gods, the defeated lying slaughtered or begging for mercy at their feet. Naram-Sin himself, taller than the rest, as is always the case in Akkadian depictions of royalty, wearing the horned helmet used to identify the gods, and, standing at the very top of the battle, on the bodies of two victims, strides confidently to his place as the leader of all Mesopotamia.

Figure 1.7 *Victory Stele of Naram-Sin*, ca. 2300–2200 B.C.E., limestone, height 6′ 6″ (1.98 m), Musée du Louvre, Paris. This stone slab carved in relief served as a public monument to commemorate the military accomplishments of Naram-Sin. In this, it deserves comparison to the palette of the Egyptian pharaoh Narmer (see fig. 1.14).

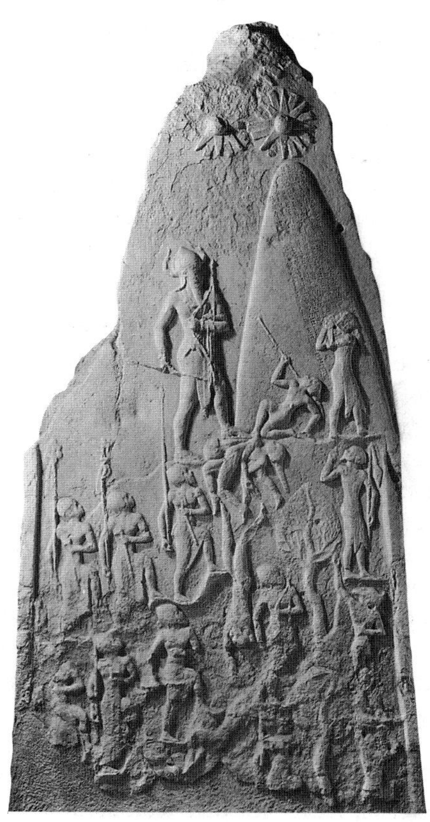

Babylon

However powerful Sargon I and Naram-Sin might have been, the Akkad kingdom lasted under two hundred years. For the next three hundred years, until about 1900 B.C.E., Mesopotamia was subject to constant division and conflict among its various city-states. Then a tribe of nomads, originally known as the Amorites, invaded the region from the Arab peninsula and established a royal city in Babylon. In 1792 B.C.E., when HAMMURABI [hamooh-RAH-bee] (r. 1792–1750 B.C.E.), the first great king of Babylon, took power, the Sumerian and Akkadian city-states were unified as a single kingdom under his rule.

Then & Now

Expressions of Love

On display at the Istanbul Museum of the Ancient Orient is a 4,000-year-old cuneiform tablet that contains a Sumerian love poem, possibly the oldest written text that expresses sexual love. An excerpt from the tablet translates as, "Bridegroom dear to my heart, goodly is your beauty, honeysweet. You have captivated me, let me stand trembling before you; Bridegroom, I would be taken to the bedchamber." In the Sumerian community, such lovemaking between a king and his priestess, which the groom and bride represent, was a symbolic act, designed to ensure the fertility of the Sumerian land and thus the community's well-being. Today, such expressions of love and sexual desire lack any relationship to the fertility of the earth. What has remained constant, however, is the lovers' expressions of desire for one another, the ancient cuneiform tablet's text as dramatically overt a statement of sexual desire as might be expressed today.

Sculpture. One of Hammurabi's great accomplishments was to codify the laws of the region. The stele inscribed with the Law Code of Hammurabi (fig. 1.8), carved of basalt ca. 1760 B.C.E., which stands seven feet high, is both a work of art and a historic legal document. Hammurabi's law code is the earliest known written body of laws. The code consists of 282 laws arranged in six chapters: 1. Personal property; 2. Land; 3. Trade and commerce (this chapter seems strikingly modern, for it includes fixing of prices, contracts, rates of interest, promissory notes, and credit); 4. Family; 5. Maltreatment; and 6. Labor (including the fixing of wages). The penalties, which included death, varied according to the social class of the harmed person and were based on an eye-for-an-eye, tooth-for-a-tooth approach to law.

The relief at the top of the Law Code of Hammurabi shows Shamash, the sun god who controlled plant life and weather, dispelled evil spirits of disease, and personified righteousness and justice—the appropriate god for a law code. (Shamash is also represented in the *Stele of Naram-Sin* as one of the stars overlooking the scene.) Hammurabi appears to converse with Shamash, from whom he receives the laws. The difference in importance between the two figures is made clear, the king standing while Shamash is shown larger, elevated, and enthroned.

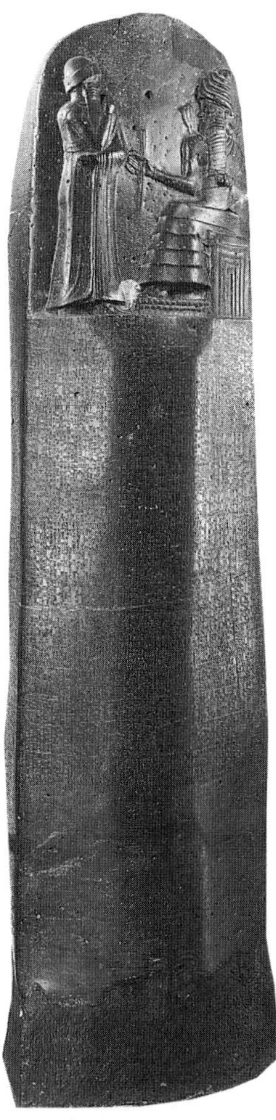

FIGURE 1.8 Stele inscribed with the *Law Code of Hammurabi*, ca. 1760 B.C.E., basalt, height of stele ca. 7′ (2.13 m), height of relief ca. 28″ (71.1 cm), Musée du Louvre, Paris. The significance of this legal document was made clear to the Babylonian people by the relief at the top of the stele that depicts the sun god Shamash giving these laws directly to Hammurabi, king of Babylon.

Assyria

Babylon fell to the nomadic Kassite people in about 1550 B.C.E. This was followed by a period of relative cultural decline, before the great ancient Mesopotamian civilization was developed by the Assyrians. The Assyrian culture began in the middle of the second millennium B.C.E., achieved significant power around 900 B.C.E., and lasted until 612 B.C.E. when Nineveh and Syria fell. The ideals of an imperialistic culture mobilized for conquest are reflected in the emphasis on fortifications and military subjects in art.

Sculpture. Stone was abundant in the northern region of the Tigris and Euphrates valleys where the Assyrians originated, permitting them to produce large-scale sculpture. Between the ninth and seventh centuries B.C.E., stone guardian monsters were placed at gateways and defined an Assyrian style; several examples survive, including those from the palace of ASHURNASIRPAL II [ash-er-na-SEER-pal] (r. 883–859 B.C.E.) at Nimrud (fig. 1.9). The headdress is peculiar to Mesopotamian deities and is similar to that worn by Shamash on the Babylonian stele with the Law Code of Hammurabi. With the body of a lion, wings of a bird, and head of a human, such guardian figures were perhaps intended to combine human intelligence with animal strength. Perhaps they were intended to be frightening as well or to impress people with the king's power. Alternatively, they have been said to represent the Assyrian god Nergal, whose emblem is a winged lion.

Seen from the front, only the two front legs of these creatures are visible. Seen from the side, four legs are visible and the creature appears to be walking. To make this monster appear correct both from the front and the side, the sculptor has generously given him five legs!

Other than gateway guardians, Assyrian sculpture consists mostly of **reliefs**—figures cut from a flat, two-dimensional background. **Statues in the round**—sculptures that are freestanding and can be seen from all sides—are extremely rare. Assyrian reliefs were part of the architecture; the carved panels were set into the walls of the palaces.

The limestone relief depicting the *Sack of the City of Hamanu by Ashurbanipal* (fig. 1.10), from the palace of ASHURBANIPAL [ash-er-BAN-ee-pul] (r. 669–ca. 627 B.C.E.) at Nineveh, was carved in approximately 650 B.C.E. The carving illustrated is one of a series of historical reliefs that records the defeat of the Elamites by Ashurbanipal. Here, the story of the Assyrian sack of Hamanu is clearly told. Buildings are burned; Ashurbanipal's

FIGURE 1.9 *Human-Headed Winged Lion* (lamassu), from the northwest palace of Ashurnasirpal II at Numrud (Calah), ca. 883–859 B.C.E., limestone, height 10′ $2\frac{1}{2}$″ (3.11 m), length 9′ $1\frac{1}{2}$″ (2.78 m), Metropolitan Museum of Art, New York. Part human and part animal, the five-legged Assyrian gate monsters are among a vast population of early imaginary composite creatures. Later artists, in various cultures, created generations of descendants with a remarkable range of implausible physiognomies.

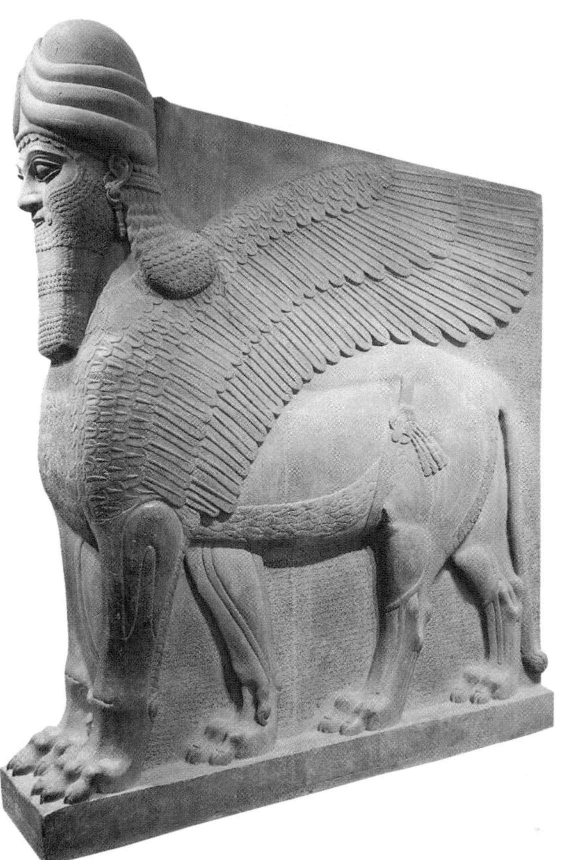

FIGURE 1.10 *Sack of the City of Hamanu by Ashurbanipal,* from the palace of Ashurbanipal Nineveh (Kuyunjik), Iraq, ca. 650 B.C.E., limestone relief, 36″ × $24\frac{1}{2}$″ (92.7 × 62.2 cm), British Museum, London. Assyrian emphasis on narration and documentation permitted disregard for relative scale and spatial logic. Realistic representation of a military campaign in stone relief first appears on the Column of Trajan (see figs. 4.15 and 4.16) in the second century C.E.

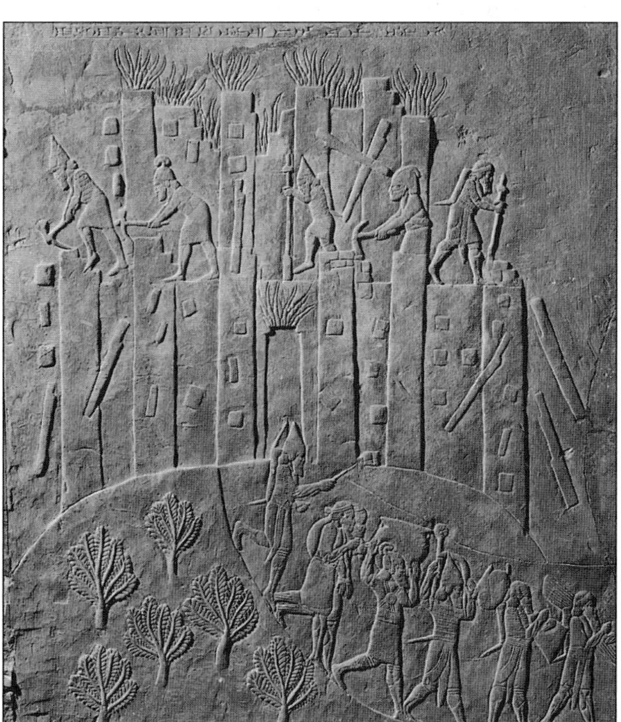

Connections

FUNDAMENTALS OF CIVILIZATION

Civilization requires many different components to function. The study of early cultures indicates what some of these things are: technology, or tools and special technical skills that give rise to trade; laws, for the regulation of society; governmental structures; cities, or permanent settlements; and writing, through which culture is transmitted.

One Sumerian text outlines the knowledge necessary to live as civilized people. An extraordinary tale, narrated by Berossos, a Babylonian scholar who, around 300 B.C.E., recorded in Greek the history and traditions of his country, it recalls a time when the people of Chaldea, on the Persian Gulf, in Lower Mesopotamia, "lived an irreligious life, similar to that of animals":

> In the first year an extraordinary monster appeared . . . on the shore of the Red Sea, and its name was Oannes. Its entire body was that of a fish, and underneath his head was a second one, as well as feet similar to those of a man—an image that is still remembered and that is still depicted up to today. This being lived among the people without eating anything and taught them writing, science, and technology of all types, the foundation of cities, the building of temples, jurisprudence, and geometry. He also revealed to them [how to cultivate] grains and how to harvest fruits. In short, he revealed to them all that constitutes civilized life. He did it so well that ever since one has found nothing exceptional in it. When the sun set, the monster Oannes plunged back into the sea to pass the night in the water, because he was amphibious. Later similar creatures appeared . . .

The story is not meant to be interpreted literally. Like many of the adventures in *The Epic of Gilgamesh*, it is a **myth,** a story involving legendary heroes, gods, and creatures that explains important cultural practices or beliefs. However "true" or otherwise the story may be, the lesson is clear: No one thing guarantees civilization. It is the combination of science, technology, agriculture, mathematics, law, literature, architecture, and the arts that constitutes civilized life.

soldiers tear down buildings with pickaxes; pieces of the structures fall through the air; soldiers carry contraband down the hill. This matter-of-fact record was no doubt intended to glorify Ashurbanipal's military achievements and to intimidate enemies wanting to challenge his authority. It should be added that the Assyrians had a reputation for ferocity, which they earned, in part, by their practice of impaling the heads of their enemies on spikes.

NEBUCHADNEZZAR'S BABYLON

The description of Rome in the book of Revelation in the New Testament of the Bible includes the following description of the great sixth-century B.C.E. Mesopotamian city of Babylon: "What city is like unto this great city . . . that great city that was clothed in fine linen and purple and scarlet and decked with gold and precious stones and pearls! . . . Babylon, the Great, the Mother of Harlots and of the Abominations of the Earth." The biblical prophet tells us as much about his own Judeo-Christian morality as he does about Babylon's decadence, but of Babylon's great wealth and position in the sixth century B.C.E. there can be no doubt.

The Assyrians undertook a major rebuilding of the original city that Hammurabi had built a thousand years earlier, after sacking and destroying it in 689 B.C.E. Only forty years later, in 648 B.C.E., its population had once again become sufficiently irritating to the Assyrian kings to cause Ashurbanipal to attack it again, killing all those who opposed him. "I fed their corpses to the dogs, pigs, *zibu*-birds, vultures, the birds of the sky and the fish of the ocean," Ashurbanipal bragged.

After the death of Ashurbanipal, when Assyrian dominance in the region collapsed, the city again rose to prominence. Referred to by scholars as Neo-Babylon, to distinguish it from the Babylon of Hammurabi, and sometimes called Chaldea as well, it was rebuilt by the architects of NEBUCHADNEZZAR II [ney-book-ad-NEZ-zahr] (r. 604–562 B.C.E.) to become the greatest city in the Near East. It was graced by its famous Hanging Gardens, one of the so-called Seven Wonders of the World. Rising high above the flat plain of the valley floor was its Marduk ziggurat—sometimes believed to be the biblical Tower of Babel, since Bab-il was an early form of the city's name.

The richness of the city is embodied in the most remarkable of its surviving parts, the Ishtar Gate (fig. 1.11), built ca. 575 B.C.E. by Nebuchadnezzar himself and today housed in the Berlin State Museum. Ishtar is the Sumerian goddess of love and war. Her gate is ornamented with bulls, lions, and dragons—all emblematic of her power—arranged in tiers, on a blue background, in brown, yellow, and white. The gate rose over the Processional Way, known in Babylonian as *Aibur-shabu*, the place "the enemy shall never pass." Leading up to the gate was a broad paved road lined with high walls that were decorated with the figures of 120 lions, symbols of Ishtar. The animals on both the Ishtar Gate and the wall of the Processional Way are made in relief of **glazed** (painted and fired) **brick,** the technique for making them probably invented in Mesopotamia during Nebuchadnezzar's reign. The glaze made the mud bricks waterproof, which accounts for their survival.

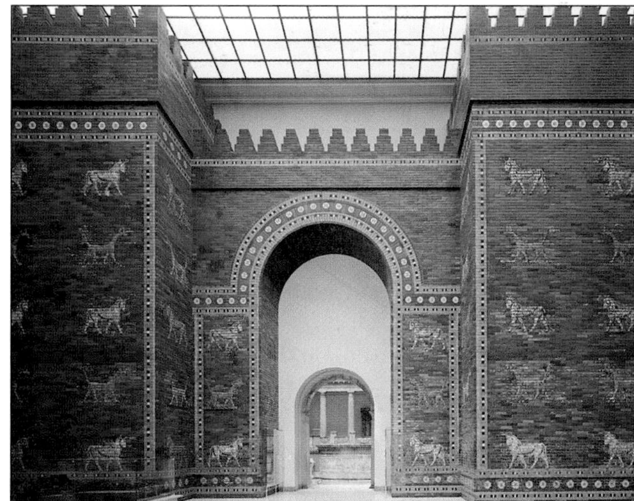

FIGURE 1.11 Ishtar Gate, from Babylon, ca. 575 B.C.E., glazed brick, Staatliche Museen zu Berlin, Preussischer Kulturbesitz, Vorderasiatisches Museum, Berlin. The appeal of animals as architectural ornaments to the Babylonians is evident on this gate to Nebuchadnezzar's sacred precinct.

PERSIA

In 539 B.C.E., the King of Persia, CYRUS II [SI-rus] (r. 559–530 B.C.E.), entered Babylon without significant resistance and took over the city, forbidding looting and appointing a Persian governor. Cyrus offered peace and friendship to the Babylonians, and he allowed them to continue worshiping their own gods. In fact, legend quickly had it that as he advanced on the city, the Babylonian god Marduk was at his side.

The Persians originated from Elam, in modern-day western Iran. Although some sites date back to around 5000 B.C.E., the Persians had begun to rise to power by the sixth century B.C.E. and by 480 B.C.E. their empire extended from the Indus River in the east to the Danube in the north. Moreover, in the same period that Cyrus overran Mesopotamia, the other great Near Eastern civilization, Egypt, lost its independence to the Persians. Persian art is found across this large geographical area.

Religion. Perhaps the most lasting innovation made by Persian culture was in religion. The prophet Zoroaster, or Zarathustra, who lived around 600 B.C.E., rejected the polytheism of earlier Mesopotamian cultures and instead developed a **dualistic religion,** in which the universe is divided between two forces, one good and one evil. According to Zoroaster, Ahuramazda, the god of light, was caught up in an eternal struggle with Ahriman, the god of darkness. As noted earlier, the Christian Bible may have been influenced in some of its stories by *The Epic of Gilgamesh.* Similarly, some ideas in Zoroastrianism may have influenced later religions, such as the idea of a "Prince of Darkness" (Satan) and a Last Judgment.

Architecture. Because the ancient Persian religion centered on fire altars in the open air, no religious architecture was needed. However, huge palaces with many rooms, halls, and courts were constructed. The visitor to the palace at Persepolis (fig. 1.12), built 518–ca. 460 B.C.E. by DARIUS [DAR-ee-uss] (r. 521–486 B.C.E.) and XERXES I (r. 485–465 B.C.E.) who were the successors of Cyrus, is met by huge guardian monsters at the entrance towers of the Porch of Xerxes, reminiscent of the Assyrian

FIGURE 1.12 Palace of Darius and Xerxes, Persepolis, Iran, 518–ca. 460 B.C.E., overview. Constructed on a raised platform and impressive in its enormous scale, the palace includes large rooms filled with forests of columns. The plan—axial, formal, and repetitious—appears to have been laid out on a grid.

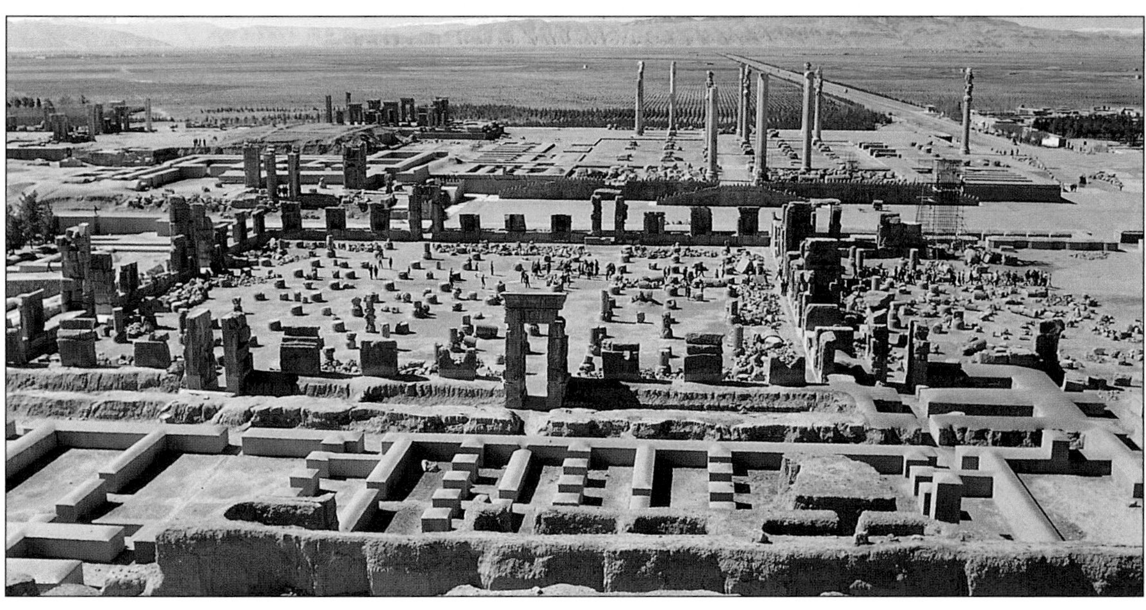

Then & Now

BEER

The beer people drink today is an alcoholic beverage made by fermenting grains and usually incorporating hops, but the process of making it was discovered nearly 8,000 years ago, around 6000 B.C.E., in Sumeria. The Sumerians made beer out of *bappir*, or half-baked, crusty loaves of bread, which they crumbled into water, fermented, and then filtered through a basket. Surviving records indicate that as much as 50 percent of each grain harvest went into the production of beer and that in Ur, around 3000 B.C.E., needy persons were allotted one gallon of beer each day as part of a general social welfare program.

Literally hundreds of surviving cuneiform tablets contain recipes for beer, including *kassi* (a black beer), *kassag* (fine black beer), and *kassagsaan* (the finest premium beer). There were wheat beers, white beers, and red beers as well. One surviving tablet, which is rather reminiscent of modern advertising slogans, reads "Drink Ebla—the beer with the heart of a lion." Kings were buried with elaborate straws made of gold and lapis lazuli, designed for sipping beer. There was even a goddess, Ninkasi—"she who fills the mouth"—who looked over the production and distribution of the drink. "I feel wonderful, drinking beer," wrote one poet, about 3000 B.C.E., "in a blissful mood with joy in my heart and a happy liver." But the Law Code of Hammurabi specifically banned the selling of beer for money. It could be bartered only for barley: "If a beer seller do not receive barley as the price for beer, but if she receive money or make the beer a measure smaller than the barley measure received, they shall throw her into the water."

Today there are over six hundred breweries making beer in the United States alone, each with its own unique process, producing perhaps ten times that many beers, each with its own unique flavor and color. The tradition, clearly, is as long and venerable as civilization itself.

guardian monsters. The palace of Persepolis is also similar to Assyrian palaces in being set on a raised platform. At Persepolis the palace stands on a rock-cut terrace, 545 by 330 yards, approached by a broad stairway of 106 shallow steps. Beyond were the main courtyards and the Throne Hall of Xerxes, known as the Hall of One Hundred Columns. This room was a forest of pillars, filled by ten rows of ten columns, each column rising forty feet. This was a new style for Mesopotamia, based on the use of tall columns.

Relief Sculpture. The palace at Persepolis was decorated with stone reliefs, including that of *Tribute Bearers Bringing Offerings* (fig. 1.13), flanking the stairway and carved ca. 490 B.C.E. Such ceremonial sculpture is concentrated almost exclusively along the staircases, giving a decorative

FIGURE 1.13 *Tribute Bearers Bringing Offerings*, flanking stairway, Palace of Darius and Xerxes, Persepolis, Iran, ca. 490 B.C.E., limestone relief, height 8′ 4″ (2.54 m). Courtesy of the Oriental Institute of the University of Chicago. The message conveyed by these stiff, formal, and generous gift-bearing figures, passed by the visitor when entering the palace, is hardly subtle.

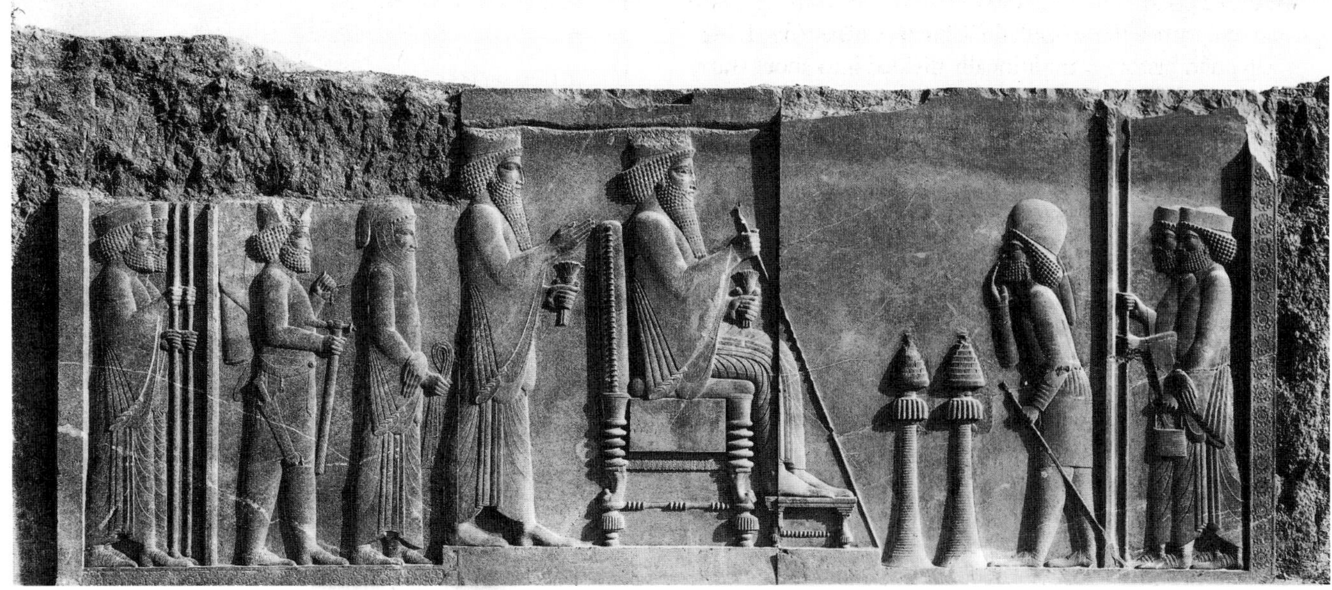

Critical Thinking

THE CONCEPT OF "CIVILIZATION"

The words "civil," "civilization," and "civilized" denote the elements of an organized society with a structured set of behaviors. These words are often set off against the words "barbaric," "barbarous," and "barbarian," which suggest the absence of civilized elements. Consider the extent to which civilized societies can exhibit barbaric qualities and the extent to which groups characterized as barbarians might exhibit aspects of civilized behavior. To what extent do these words continue to identify useful and valid distinctions? To what extent have they lost that function?

emphasis to the main approaches. Three to six figures are used to represent each of twenty-three different nations of the empire. The repetition of stylized figures—in attendance, as servants, and in processions—may be said to become monotonous. These figures are stiff, if not frozen; representations of animals in Persian art have greater life and personality than representations of humans.

CIVILIZATION OF THE NILE

LIKE ITS MESOPOTAMIAN COUNTERPART, ancient Egyptian civilization developed slowly from about 5000 B.C.E. to approximately 3100 B.C.E. with no united or central government. There were in essence two independent Egypts: Upper Egypt and Lower Egypt ("Lower" Egypt actually lies north of "Upper" Egypt). Upper Egypt was a narrow strip of land on either side of the Nile River, extending seven hundred miles from the first cataract, or waterfall, in the south to the Nile Delta. Lower Egypt was situated in the northern lands of the fertile Nile Delta where the river branches out and runs into the Mediterranean. Then, around 3100 B.C.E., the two Egypts were united by the king of Upper Egypt, NARMER, also known as MENES [ME-neez], and it is with this event that Egyptian history is usually said to begin. The event is celebrated in one of the earliest surviving Egyptian stone sculptures, the so-called *Palette of Narmer* (fig. 1.14).

Egyptian history is traditionally divided into about thirty dynasties. We know very little of the first two **dynasties,** but beginning with the third, the Egyptian dynasties are grouped into several major periods distinguished by their stability and achievement: the Old Kingdom (2686–2181 B.C.E., consisting of dynasties 3–6), the Middle Kingdom (2040–1786 B.C.E., consisting of dynasties 11–14), and the New Kingdom, or Empire (1552–1069 B.C.E., consisting of dynasties 18–20). So-called "Intermediate" periods of relative instability intervened between each of the "Kingdoms," and the last, "New" Kingdom was followed by a Late Period that concludes around 525 B.C.E. when Egypt finally lost its independence and was absorbed into the Persian Empire.

Despite times of relative disruption, life was unusually secure in ancient Egypt. The fertility of the Nile Valley, which was due to the huge amounts of topsoil swept each summer into the Nile River delta from far upstream in the African lake region and the Ethiopian plateau, supported the establishment of a permanent agricultural society. Moreover, the surrounding deserts largely eliminated the fear of invasion. The king, later called "pharaoh," which means "great house," was the absolute ruler and considered divine. Beneath him was a large class of priests and government

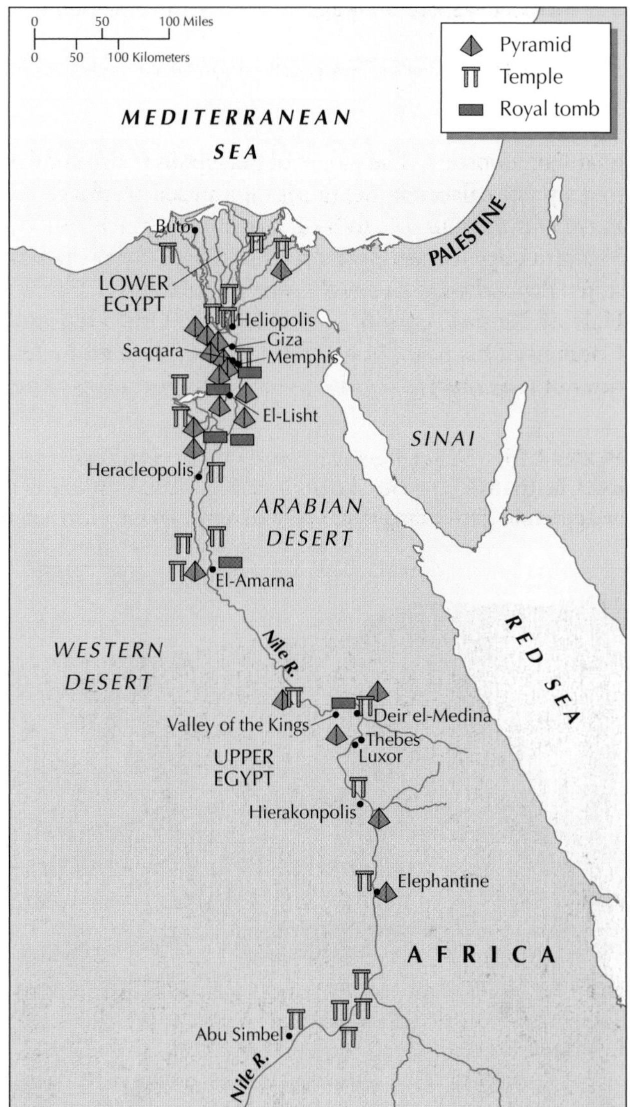

MAP 1.2 Ancient Egypt.

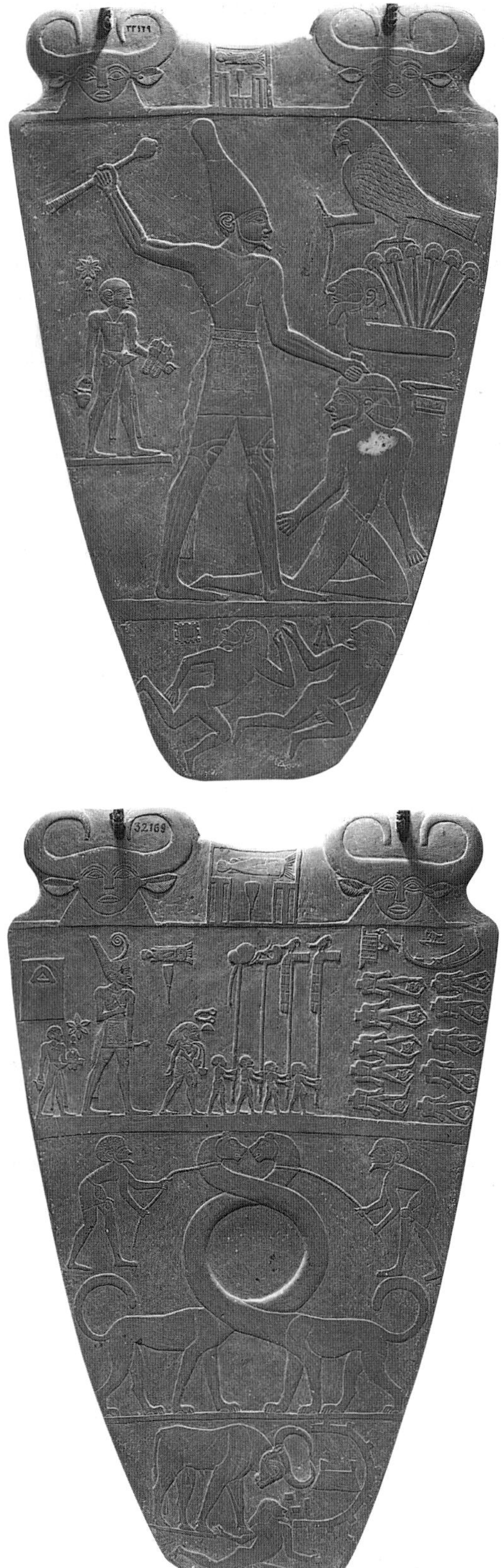

FIGURE 1.14 *Palette of Narmer*, front and back, from Hierakonpolis, ca. 3100 B.C.E., First Dynasty, slate, height 25″ (63.5 cm), Egyptian Museum, Cairo. This celebrated work is simultaneously a functional palette, an exquisite relief carving, and an historical document of the uniting of Lower and Upper Egypt by Narmer, the first pharaoh of the first Egyptian dynasty.

bureaucrats. The permanence and stability of life and the highly centralized organization of ancient Egyptian society is reflected in the monumental and essentially permanent architecture of the pyramids. In fact, with few exceptions the art of Egypt remained remarkably consistent in style over three millennia. The unquestioning acceptance of convention is a major characteristic of ancient Egyptian culture. As a result, a sense of order and continuity pervades the history of ancient Egyptian life and art.

HIEROGLYPHICS

The Egyptians had developed a calendar, used irrigation systems, discovered the use of basic metals, and started using **hieroglyphics,** their writing system, all before 3000 B.C.E. For centuries scholars thought that the "glyphs" or characters used in hieroglyphics all represented complete ideas rather than individual units of sound. Indeed, until 1822 the actual meaning of the hieroglyphics was unknown. In that year, however, a Frenchman, Jean François Champollion, deciphered the Rosetta Stone (fig. 1.15). This was a large fragment of basalt that had been found during Napoleon's military

FIGURE 1.15 Rosetta Stone, 196 B.C.E., basalt, British Museum, London. The same information is inscribed in three languages: (1) Greek; (2) demotic script, a simplified form of hieroglyphic (the common language of Egypt); and (3) hieroglyphic, a pictographic script. By comparing the languages, hieroglyphics were finally translated in the early nineteenth century. © The Trustees of the British Museum/Art Resource, NY.

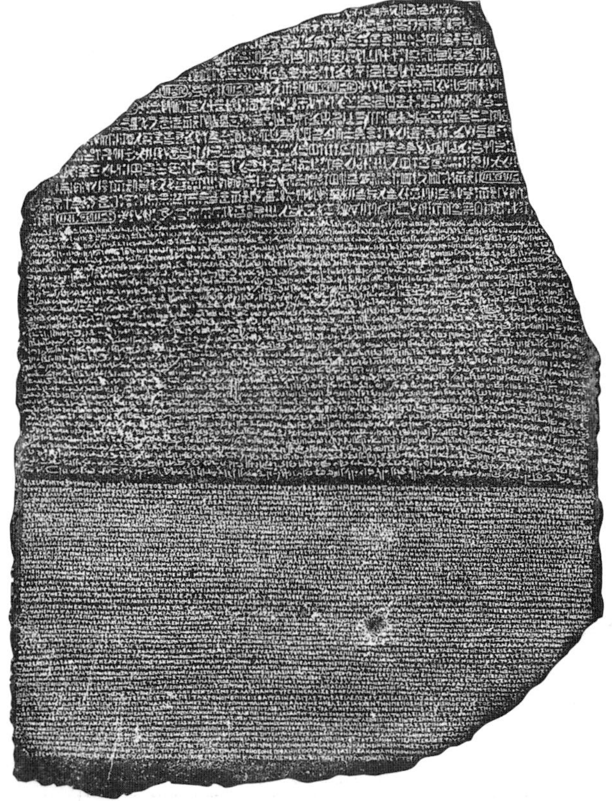

campaign in Egypt near the town of Rosetta in the Nile Delta. When it became apparent that the three languages on the Rosetta Stone expressed almost the same thing—a decree in honor of Ptolemy V (196 B.C.E.), Champollion was able to establish that the corresponding Egyptian symbols were meant, as in Sumerian, to be read not just symbolically but phonetically as well. Thus, although a pictograph of a fish did indeed represent a "fish," combined with other pictographs it represented the sound of the word "fish," which is pronounced "nar." For instance, the name of the king of a united Egypt, Narmer, consists of the sign for a fish, "nar," and the sign for a chisel, which is pronounced "mer."

RELIGIOUS BELIEFS

Ancient Egyptian religion was polytheistic, involving belief in a profusion of gods. Among the most important gods in Egypt were the cosmic forces, including the sun, earth, sky, air, and water. The Nile was also worshiped as a deity, not surprisingly given its importance to Egyptian life. These forces and aspects of nature were depicted in various forms, often as animals, humans, or as hybrids. For example, the sun was sometimes pictured as a falcon, other times as a falcon-headed man wearing a sun disk as a crown. The animal attributes of the gods were often a shorthand for their qualities. For example, Hathor, who was the goddess of joy and love—attributes which the Egyptians viewed the cow as possessing—was depicted as a cow.

Among the most important of the Egyptian gods was Osiris, originally a local god of Lower Egypt, whose worship eventually spread throughout the country. The legend of Osiris's death at the hands of his brother Set, and the search for the corpse by Isis, Osiris's wife, plays an important part in Egyptian mythology, and is connected with Egyptian belief in the afterlife. According to the myth,

Table 1–2 MAJOR ANCIENT EGYPTIAN GODS AND GODDESSES

Amen/Amon	creation deity; linked to the god Ra as Amen-Ra/Amon-Ra
Anubis	god of embalming, of preserving the dead
Apis	god of fertility
Aten	sun god
Bast	a cat goddess; protects cats as well as people who care for cats
Bes	helps women in childbirth; protects children
Hapi/Hapy	god of the Nile River flood
Hathor	goddess of fertility; goddess of the sky; protectress of the dead and of the royal palace; Ra's mother, wife, and daughter
Horus	originally the god of the sky; associated with the pharaoh; son of Osiris and Isis
Imhotep	architect of the stepped pyramid of the pharaoh Zoser; deified as the god of medicine and patron of scribes
Isis	the divine mother goddess; guardian of the dead; healed the sick; a skilled magician; sister and wife of Osiris and mother of Horus
Khons	god of the moon
Maat	goddess of truth, right, and proper behavior; the ostrich feather in her hair was weighed against the heart of the dead person to determine whether they had led a pure life
Min	god of virility; consort of Qetesh
Mut	"mother"; wife/consort of Amon
Neith	goddess of war and of wisdom
Nephthys	with her sister Isis, a protectress of the dead
Nut	goddess of the sky
Osiris	god of the dead, of the afterlife, of the underworld
Ptah	patron god of craftsmen; creator of the universe
Qetesh	goddess of love and beauty; consort of Min
Ra/Re	the sun god
Selket	a goddess whose scorpion killed wicked people; aided women in childbirth
Set/Seth	god of storms and violence; brother and murderer of Osiris; rival of Horus
Shu	god of air and wind
Tefnut	goddess of mist and clouds
Thoth	god of writing; of wisdom; messenger of the gods
Thoueris	goddess of fertility; protected women in childbirth

Then & Now

THE NILE

"Egypt," the Greek historian Herodotus wrote, "is a gift of the Nile." In ancient Egypt, the Nile flooded every summer, from July to October. The floods began when the rain in the central Sudan raised the level of the White Nile, one of its tributaries, followed by the summer monsoon in the Ethiopian highlands raising the level of the Blue Nile, another of its tributaries. By August, these waters reached Egypt proper, flooding the entire basin except for the highest ground, where villages and temples were built, and depositing a deep layer of silt over the fields.

If rainfall came short of expectations, the next season's crops could be dramatically affected; and, sometimes just as disastrous, if rainfall was excessive, villages and farms had to be evacuated. To combat this, gauges, or "Nilometers," were placed upstream on the Nile, and river levels could be compared with records kept over the centuries, so those downstream might know what to expect each August. In fact, annual taxes were levied according to the height of the river in any particular year.

In 1899, in order to gain greater control over the Nile and help local agriculture, the British financed a dam project on the Nile at Aswan, 550 miles upstream from Cairo. At Aswan, the Nile pours rapidly through steep cliffs and gorges, and it seemed a perfect spot for a dam. When the dam was finished in 1902, it regulated the flow of the river and allowed for an extra 10 to 15 percent of land to be farmed.

Originally 98 feet high, the dam was raised to 138 feet in 1933. By then a giant lake, 140 miles long, stretched behind it, submerging Nubian villages and a large number of monuments for part of the year, most famously the Temple of Isis. In the 1950s, President Nasser proposed another dam, the Aswan High Dam. The endangered Temples of Isis and Hathor were removed to higher ground for safety.

Designed to provide Egypt with predictable and sufficient water resources, as well as providing for the country's electrical needs, the Aswan High Dam has had foreseeable negative impacts as well as beneficial ones. Even the early British dam had stopped the natural flow of silt down the Nile, forcing farmers to rely on chemical fertilizers instead. But worse, perhaps, is the fact that Lake Nasser, behind the Aswan High Dam, has changed rainfall patterns in the region and significantly raised the level of the underground water table far downstream, threatening even the temples of Luxor 133 miles to the north. The Nile today never floods, but this victory has had its costs.

after Isis discovered her husband's dead body in Phoenicia, she brought it back to Egypt and buried it there. Set came upon the buried body and, enraged, tore the dead Osiris limb from limb, scattering the pieces throughout the country. Again Isis found her dead husband's body parts and buried each where it lay.

The son of Isis and Osiris avenged his father's death by engaging Set in battle and defeating him. However, when Set was brought to Isis, instead of killing him, she set him free. According to some versions of the myth, Osiris was restored to life and became king of the underworld. This myth of Osiris's resurrection later became an important element of the cult of Isis, the most important mother goddess in Egyptian religion, and a significant influence on Egyptian belief in life after death.

The Afterlife. Much of Egyptian life appears to have been oriented toward preparing for the hereafter. The Old Kingdom Egyptians believed that the body of the deceased must be preserved if the ***ka***, the indestructible essence or vital principle of each person, roughly equivalent to the Christian concept of a soul, were to live on. This is why the Egyptians embalmed and bound their dead. This process of mummification was a complex procedure that involved emptying the bodily cavities of their organs, refilling them with spices and Arabic gums, and then wrapping the body in layers of bandages. This took seventy days to complete, after which the mummified body was ready for the hereafter, where it would rejoin its *ka*. To be doubly sure of the survival of the *ka*, a likeness of the dead person was made in a hard stone, intended to serve as a backup, should anything happen to the mummy. One Egyptian word for sculptor translates literally as "he who keeps alive." Members of the noble class were mummified and accompanied by their personal likeness; common people were merely buried in holes, though Egyptian religion does appear to have offered them the hope of life in an afterworld, too. The belief in the necessity of housing the dead in a tomb that would endure forever, for the benefit of the *ka* of the deceased, gave rise to Egypt's monumental conception of architecture, exemplified most spectacularly in the pyramids.

OLD KINGDOM

The Old Kingdom (2686–2181 B.C.E.) was a time of political and social stability in Egypt, a stability reflected in its grandest achievements, the great pyramids. Although tradition long held that slaves built these giant funerary monuments to the kings, it now seems clear that an entire class of artisans, sculptors, and builders was responsible for them. That a culture could organize such mammoth undertakings and accomplish them with what appears to be the willing cooperation of its people emphasizes the unity of the society as a whole.

ARCHITECTURE

The ancient Egyptian architecture extant today is made of stone. Many kinds of stone were abundantly available, and this availability must in part explain the giant proportions of these surviving buildings. Limestone and sandstone were easily quarried in nearby locations along the Nile cliffs. Harder stones, such as granite, basalt, and quartzite, were obtained from more remote regions.

Although Egypt lacked timber, other plant materials could be employed instead. For instance, lotus and papyrus reeds, bundled together and matted with clay, were used as building materials. Mud brick, made by mixing mud from the Nile River with straw, shaping the resulting substance into bricks, and then allowing them to dry in the sun, was also used. Mud-brick buildings were cool in the summer, warm in the winter, and, because Egypt has little rainfall, lasted quite well. Homes of peasants were made in this way. The pharaoh's home was also made of mud brick, but was larger, lime washed, and painted.

Mastabas. The earliest burial places of the Old Kingdom Egyptian nobility were ***mastabas,*** flat-topped one-story rectangular buildings with slanted walls. Faced with brick or stone, the *mastabas* were oriented very specifically, with the four sides facing north, south, east, and west. Surviving *mastabas* vary in length from 15 to 170 feet, and vary in height from 10 to 30 feet. The interiors have different layouts, but all include the following: (1) a chapel or offering room, used to make offerings to the spirit of the dead person (there are two doors to this room, one real, the other false—to be used by the spirit to collect what was offered); (2) the ***serdab*** or cellar, a tiny secret room in the center of the *mastaba,* containing a statue of the dead person (the *ka* statue) and treasure; and (3) a shaft running from the *mastaba* down through the earth, and into the actual burial chamber located perhaps over a hundred feet below ground level. The plan of the *mastaba* is believed to be an adaptation of a house plan, for the tomb was regarded as the house of the soul.

The Great Pyramids. The Great Pyramids at Giza (fig. 1.16) on the west bank of the Nile were built in the Fourth Dynasty of the Old Kingdom. The three pyramids were built by the pharaohs CHEOPS [KEE-ops], ca. 2530 B.C.E.; CHEFREN [KEF-run], ca. 2500 B.C.E.; and MYCERINUS [MIK-ur-EE-nus], ca. 2470 B.C.E. Because the pharaoh was considered divine and would consequently return to the gods when he died, the pyramids were designed to soar to heaven. Inscribed on the walls of later pyramids are descriptions of kings climbing the sides of the pyramids to join the sun god Ra, and the triangular shape may itself symbolize the falling rays of the sun.

FIGURE 1.16 Great Pyramids, Giza, built for the Old Kingdom pharaohs Cheops, ca. 2530 B.C.E., Chefren, ca. 2500 B.C.E., and Mycerinus, ca. 2470 B.C.E., Fourth Dynasty, limestone and granite. The permanence of the pyramids, built to last forever, was related to the Egyptian concept of an afterlife and the mummification of their dead.

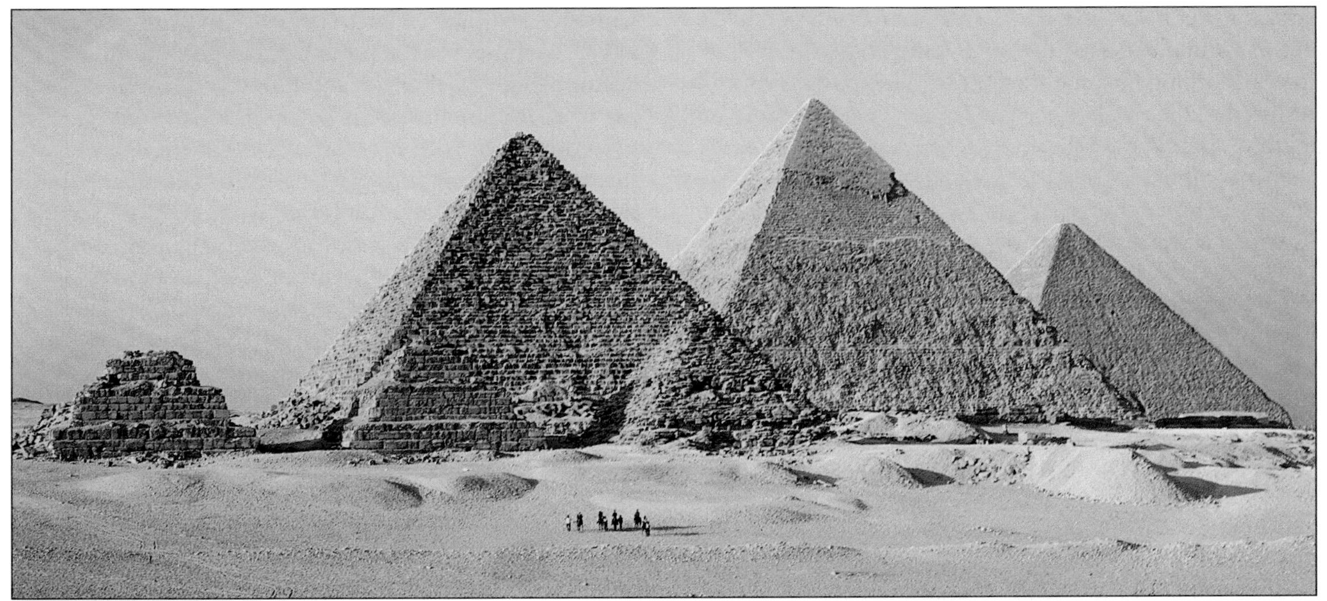

The Great Pyramids are extraordinary accomplishments of engineering. Satisfying the Egyptian craving for permanence, the pyramid is one of the most stable geometric forms. The Great Pyramids are built of solid limestone masonry. The blocks were cut with metal tools in the eastern Nile cliffs, marked by the stone masons with red ink to indicate their eventual location, floated across the river during the seasonal floods, and then dragged up temporary ramps and moved into their final position. The largest and oldest pyramid, that of Cheops, covers 13 acres and is made up of approximately 2.3 million blocks, each averaging 2.5 tons in weight. When the polished, pearly white limestone encasement stones were still intact, it is believed to have soared skyward approximately 480 feet.

With characteristic Egyptian mathematical precision, the three Great Pyramids are aligned, their corners oriented north, south, east, and west. The proportions of the base width to the height of the pyramids are eleven to seven, a proportion that modern research has shown is inherently pleasing to many people. Inside, the pyramids have systems of corridors that lead to the burial chamber, where the mummified body of the pharaoh was placed, along with the rich possessions that were to accompany him to the afterlife.

The Book of the Dead

The expectation of life after death colored all aspects of Egyptian culture. Among the objects found in the coffins of the dead were papyrus scrolls containing prayers and incantations, or spells, to guide the soul in the afterlife. *The Book of the Dead*, which the Egyptians referred to as *The Book of Coming Forth by Day*, spells out the procedures through which the deceased had to pass before being admitted to the Field of Reeds, the eternal realm of the god Osiris. There the deceased soul's heart was weighed against how well he or she had treated others and respected the gods. A favorable judgment could be rendered for those able to recite a confession like the following[1]:

> I have not inflicted pain. I have not caused anyone to go hungry. I have not made any man to weep. I have not committed murder. I have not given the order for murder to be committed. I have not caused calamities to befall men and women. I have not plundered the offerings in the temples. I have not defrauded the gods of their cake-offerings. I have not carried off the fenkhu cakes [offered] to Spirits. I have not committed fornication. . . . I have not filched [land from my neighbor's estate] or added it to my own acre. I have not encroached upon the fields [of others].
>
> I have not committed sin. . . . I have not committed robbery with violence . . . I have not stolen. . . . I have not slain men and women. . . . I have not stolen grain. . . . I have not purloined offerings. . . . I have not uttered lies. . . . I have not uttered curses. . . . I have not committed adultery. . . . I have not attacked any man. . . . I have not blasphemed. . . . I have wronged none, I have done no evil.

A favorable judgment meant the soul would join other living souls in a realm of peace and joy. An unfavorable judgment meant the soul's heart would be devoured by the monster Ament. For those who could not claim to have led a good life, *The Book of the Dead* contained incantations that might protect against an unfavorable judgment.

Sculpture

The Great Sphinx. Most extant Egyptian sculpture is religious or political in purpose, and either reflects the characteristic Egyptian desire for immortality and belief in an afterlife or demonstrates the pharaoh's power and divinity. The Great Sphinx (fig. 1.17), which guards the pyramid of Chefren at Giza, is a majestic and monumental symbol of the king's strength created by combining a human head (probably an idealized portrait of Chefren himself, the face of which is now damaged) with the body of a lion. The Great Sphinx is 65 feet high, the scale indicative not only of the power of the pharaoh, but also of the Egyptian love of enormous proportions. The Sphinx reappears in Classical Greek mythology, in particular in the story of Oedipus (see Chapter 3).

FIGURE 1.17 Great Sphinx, Giza, ca. 2500 B.C.E., Fourth Dynasty, sandstone, height 65′ (19.81 m). Although similar to the Assyrian guardian monsters in combining a human head and an animal body (see fig. 1.9), here the facial features are those of the pharaoh, and the monumental dimensions are intended to impress the viewer with his power.

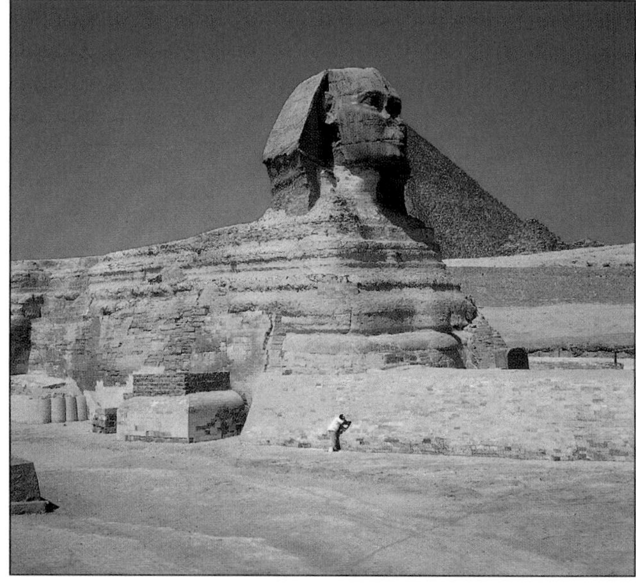

[1]Adapted from *The Book of the Dead*, ed. E. A. Wallis Budge (New York: Gramercy/Random House, 1999), 574–579.

The Human Figure. Egyptian sculptors depicted the human figure in a very limited number of poses: sitting on a block, standing with one foot forward, sitting cross-legged on the floor (a less common pose), or kneeling on both knees (quite rare). Further, each of these poses is shown in a specific way and according to certain conventions. These standard poses were established in the Old Kingdom and continued largely unchanged through the three millennia of ancient Egyptian culture. To be original and innovative was not a goal for ancient Egyptian artists.

The Pharaoh Chefren (fig. 1.18), for whom the second of the three Great Pyramids of Giza was built, represents the type that sits on a block. He is idealized, his individual characteristics minimized, and his features carved in general terms to suggest power and immortality. Sitting stiffly erect, he is shown to be a majestic, serene ruler. Although his clothing consists of a simple kilt and a linen headdress, the hawk or falcon with its wings protecting his head is a sign of the sun god Horus, or Ra, indicating that Chefren is the divine son of the god and is under this god's protection. The false ceremonial beard derives from the idea of a pastoral chieftain wearing a goat-beard from his flock. Chefren probably held a scepter, symbol of divine royalty, in his right hand. This ceremonial royal attire is seen on the earliest kings and was perpetuated by generations of later rulers.

The double statue of the royal couple, Pharaoh Mycerinus and his wife, Queen Khamerernebty (fig. 1.19), carved of stone, ca. 2470 B.C.E., demonstrates the

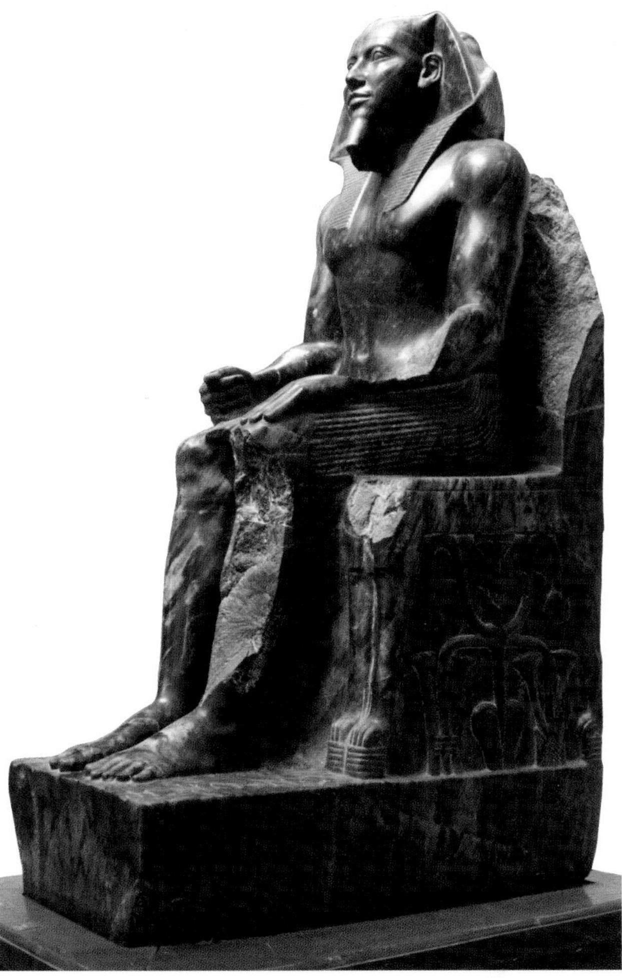

FIGURE 1.18 *Pharaoh Chefren*, from Giza, ca. 2500 B.C.E., Fourth Dynasty, diorite, height 66″ (1.68 cm). Egyptian Museum, Cairo. The two poses in which the human figure was most often depicted by Egyptian sculptors of the Old Kingdom were sitting on a block, as here, or standing as seen in Figure 1.19.

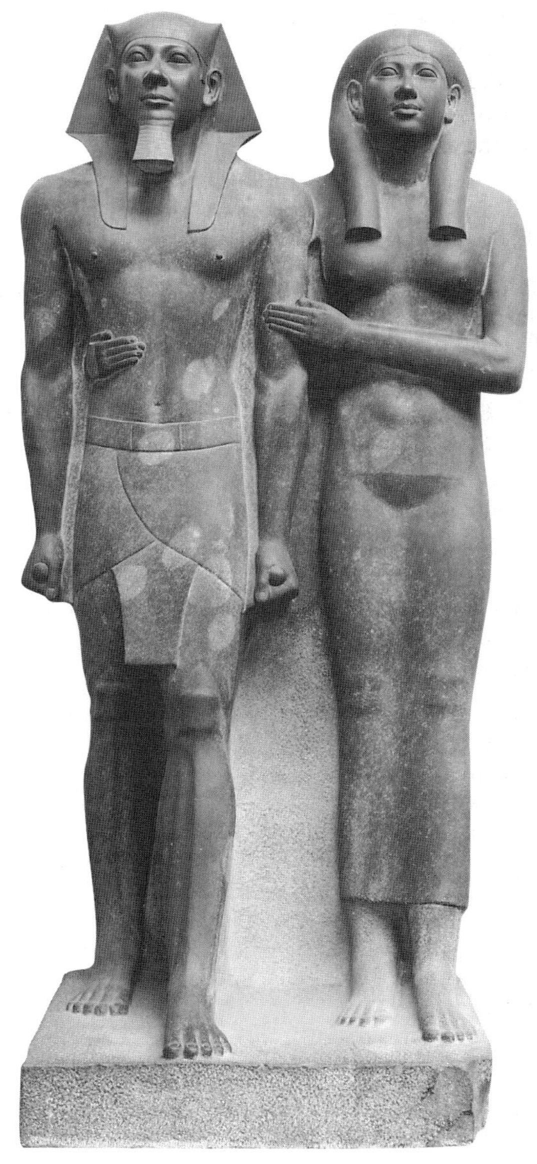

FIGURE 1.19 *Pharaoh Mycerinus and Queen Khamerernebty.* Egypt, Giza. Old Kingdom, ca. 2490–2472 B.C.E., Fourth Dynasty, greywacke, height 56″ × $22\frac{1}{2}$″ × $21\frac{3}{4}$″ (142.2 × 57.1 × 56.2 cm). Harvard University-Boston Museum of Fine Arts. Expedition, 11.1738 Courtesy, Museum of Fine Arts, Boston. Reproduced with permission. © 2008 Museum of Fine Arts, Boston. All Rights Reserved. In this common pose, the figures stand with one leg forward, yet are rigidly erect, weight equally distributed on both feet, and therefore appear immobile.

conventions of representing the standing figure. This is believed to have been the first double statue of its kind; it set a fashion for showing the pharaoh embraced by, or supported by, the queen. The queen's revealing dress clings to her contours. The king, in addition to a wrapped linen skirt, wears a ceremonial false beard and headdress, both symbols of rank.

Certain features seen here are characteristic of all Egyptian standing figures: the frontality, the erect stance with the left foot forward and the arms rigidly against the body, and the sense of vigor and dignity. In spite of both having a foot forward, these stiff figures do not appear to be walking, for weight is equally distributed on both feet. This is not a natural stance; people normally stand with their weight equally on both feet only when side by side, or, more frequently, stand with their weight supported on one foot.

Because such sculpture was funerary in purpose and was placed in the tomb as a precaution against having no home for the *ka* if the mummy were destroyed, permanence was of great importance—the web of stone between the queen and king is intended to prevent breakage. (This statue was actually buried with Mycerinus in his pyramid at Giza.)

The seated scribe (fig. 1.20) represents the type that sits on the floor, legs crossed—a pose used especially for depictions of scribes. Carved of limestone, with inlaid eyes, he appears very alert, ready to take dictation. He once held a writing implement in his right hand, poised above the scroll unrolled across his lap and stabilized by his left hand. While members of the nobility were routinely idealized and shown in their physical prime, those who *served* the nobility were evidently permitted by artists to age, to be physically imperfect, and to be individualized.

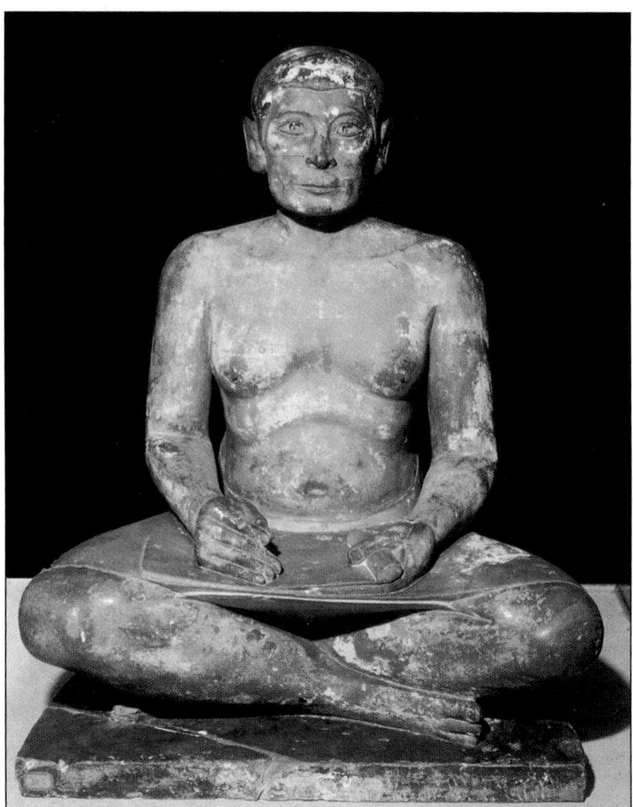

FIGURE 1.20 *Seated Scribe*, from Saqqara, ca. 2400 B.C.E., Fifth Dynasty, painted limestone, eyes inlaid with quartz, rock crystal, ebony, and bronze, height 21″ (54 cm). Musée du Louvre, Paris. In contrast to generalized depictions of the Egyptian noble class, this scribe is portrayed with greater individuality and realism, even permitted to age and acquire rolls of flesh around his waist.

RELIEF SCULPTURE AND PAINTING

Relief sculpture and painting were closely linked in ancient Egyptian art, and reliefs were often painted. Clarity in storytelling seems to have been more important to the artist than naturalistic representation. The style, which includes few nonessentials, is condensed and abbreviated. Figures are shown predominantly from the side, although the eye and shoulders are shown from the front. Clearly, these nonanatomical figures are not drawn directly from models but are instead memory images of a composite view of the human body, each part of the body shown from its most characteristic point of view. Egyptian art does not portray what the eye sees, but what the mind knows is there.

Ti Watching a Hippopotamus Hunt. An engaging depiction known as *Ti Watching a Hippopotamus Hunt* (fig. 1.21) was painted on the wall of Ti's tomb in Saqqara, dated ca. 2500–2400 B.C.E. in the Fifth Dynasty. Ti does not actually participate in the killing; instead, he stands on a small boat and directs his servants, who hold harpoons. As is traditional, Ti is distinguished from his social inferiors by being made bigger, and his pose combines both frontal and profile views. The water of the Nile River is shown as wavy lines, with fish, hippopotami, and a crocodile shown in profile. The ribbed background represents the papyrus plants along the banks of the Nile. At the top of the painting, where Egyptian artists often put background detail, there are buds and flowers, and birds of various kinds, some of which are being stalked by foxes.

A tomb painting such as this was meant to be seen only by the *ka* of the deceased—in this case the *ka* of Ti, whose position was that of "Curator of Monuments." His own final monument, like those of other high-ranking Egyptians, was painted with murals showing him in the afterlife. However, because the afterlife was believed to be a more blissful continuation of real life, it may be assumed that such tomb paintings documented daily life in ancient Egypt—at least in its more pleasant aspects.

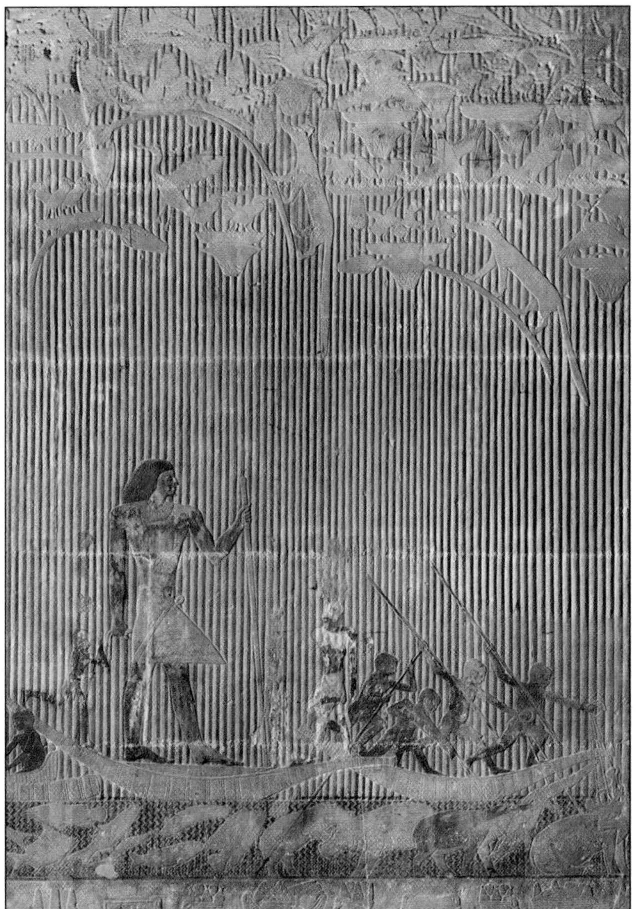

FIGURE 1.21 *Ti Watching a Hippopotamus Hunt*, Tomb of Ti, Saqqara, ca. 2500–2400 B.C.E., Fifth Dynasty, painted limestone wall relief, height ca. 3 9″ (1.14 m). Standard conventions of mixed perspective in ancient Egyptian art include depiction of the eye from the front, though the head is shown in profile, and the shoulders from the front, though the legs are shown from the side.

MIDDLE KINGDOM

After the collapse of the Old Kingdom, a period of political and social turmoil ensued—the first of the so-called intermediate periods of Egyptian history. For over 150 years no single dynasty could reunite the country as Narmer had done a thousand years earlier. Finally, in about 2040 B.C.E., a prince by the name of Mentuhotep II, from Thebes, managed to subdue both upper and lower parts, inaugurating the Middle Kingdom. The subsequent government was far less centralized than that of the Old Kingdom, with only affairs of national import being left to the king, while much more authority was given to regional governors. Under these new conditions, the country prospered as never before. Large-scale waterworks were undertaken to irrigate higher ground in the Nile basin, and farming yields, which were already higher than anywhere else in the world, increased dramatically.

ARCHITECTURE

Few monuments of the Middle Kingdom can be seen today, for they were replaced by grander structures during the New Kingdom or were built of mud brick and, consequently, have largely disappeared. A few traces of pyramids remain—they appear to have been similar to those of the Old Kingdom but smaller, and a number of rock-cut tombs, burial places hollowed out of the faces of cliffs, survive. These are to be found at Beni Hasan, located 125 miles up the river from Giza, and were built ca. 2100–1800 B.C.E., during the Eleventh Dynasty.

The basic plan of these tombs is believed to be similar to that of an Egyptian home of the time. Each tomb consists of a vestibule or portico, a hall with pillars, a private sacred chamber, and a small room at the rear to contain a statue of the dead person. The interior has certain elements that appear to be stone versions of structures originally made of other materials. Thus, although the columns are of stone, the form is that of a bundle of reeds tied together. The ceiling is painted with a diapered and checkered pattern that looks much like the woven matting used to cover houses. The walls are also often painted, though there is a change from Old Kingdom subjects discernible here. Instead of military exploits, the paintings now feature depictions of domestic and farm life.

NEW KINGDOM

After the Middle Kingdom collapsed and a second intermediate period had begun, an eastern Mediterranean tribe called the Hyksos invaded northern Egypt in 1674 B.C.E., bringing with them bronze weapons and horsedrawn chariots. For over two hundred years, Egypt was again divided. But beginning in 1552 B.C.E., the old order was reestablished, perhaps by means of the new technology that the Hyksos tribes had introduced to their unwilling hosts. Certainly, it was through contact with the Hyksos that Egypt entered the Bronze Age. The New Kingdom or Empire that resulted was the most brilliant period in Egyptian history. It was a Theban king, AHMOSE I [AR-mohz], who first pushed back the Hyksos into Palestine, conquering foreign peoples along the way and bringing into being the first Egyptian empire. During the reign of THUTMOSE III [thoot-MOS-uh] (r. 1479–1425 B.C.E.), the first Egyptian king to be called "pharaoh," Egypt controlled not only the entire Nile basin but the entire eastern Mediterranean coast as far as present-day Syria. The great empire only fell into decline after about 1200 B.C.E., when it came under the successive influence of Assyria and Libya, and finally lost its independence to Persia in about 525 B.C.E.

ARCHITECTURE

The New Kingdom established its capital at Thebes, and a great amount of building was done there as well as up and down the length of the Nile. Much art was produced in an exuberant display of wealth and sophistication. Burial was still carried out with great care during the New Kingdom, but the futility of pyramids as places of safe preservation was now fully recognized. Pyramids, monumental advertisements of the treasures contained within, were irresistibly attractive to robbers and looters. Consequently, nobility and royalty were now buried in chambers hollowed deep into the cliffs on the west bank of the Nile River in the Valley of the Kings at Thebes. Here, rock-cut tombs were approached by corridors up to 500 feet long hollowed straight into the hillside. The entrances were carefully hidden, and rocks were arranged over the entrances to look as if they had fallen there. Many clever tricks and precautions were used by the ancient Egyptians to protect their tombs. In one case, their success lasted until 1922, when the shaft tomb of Tutankhamen (sometimes referred to popularly today as King Tut) was found nearly intact. All other known tombs were looted in antiquity.

Temple of Queen Hatshepsut. The Old Kingdom has been called the period of the pyramids; the New Kingdom is the time of the temples. The concern for concealment brought about the end of monumental memorial architecture. A mortuary temple of the queen or king would now be built far from the actual tomb. The funerary Temple of Queen Hatshepsut (fig. 1.22), for instance, was built against a cliff at Deir el-Bahari, Thebes, ca. 1478–1458 B.C.E., early in the Eighteenth Dynasty, by the architect SENMUT [SEN-mut].

In a culture dominated by male kings, HATSHEPSUT [hat-SHEP-sut] (r. 1478–1458 B.C.E.) is a figure of some significance. At the death of her husband, Thutmose II, she became regent of Thutmose III, her son-in-law. For the next twenty years, Thutmose III, who would later conquer so much of the Mediterranean, was at best something like her prime minister, carrying out her will. The size and magnificence of her temple reflect her political importance.

FIGURE 1.22 Senmut, Funerary Temple of Queen Hatshepsut, Deir el-Bahari, Thebes, ca. 1478–1458 B.C.E., early Eighteenth Dynasty. In the New Kingdom, the body of the queen or pharaoh was buried in a different location from the mortuary temple. That of Queen Hatshepsut was built with terraces, ramps, sculptures, and hanging gardens.

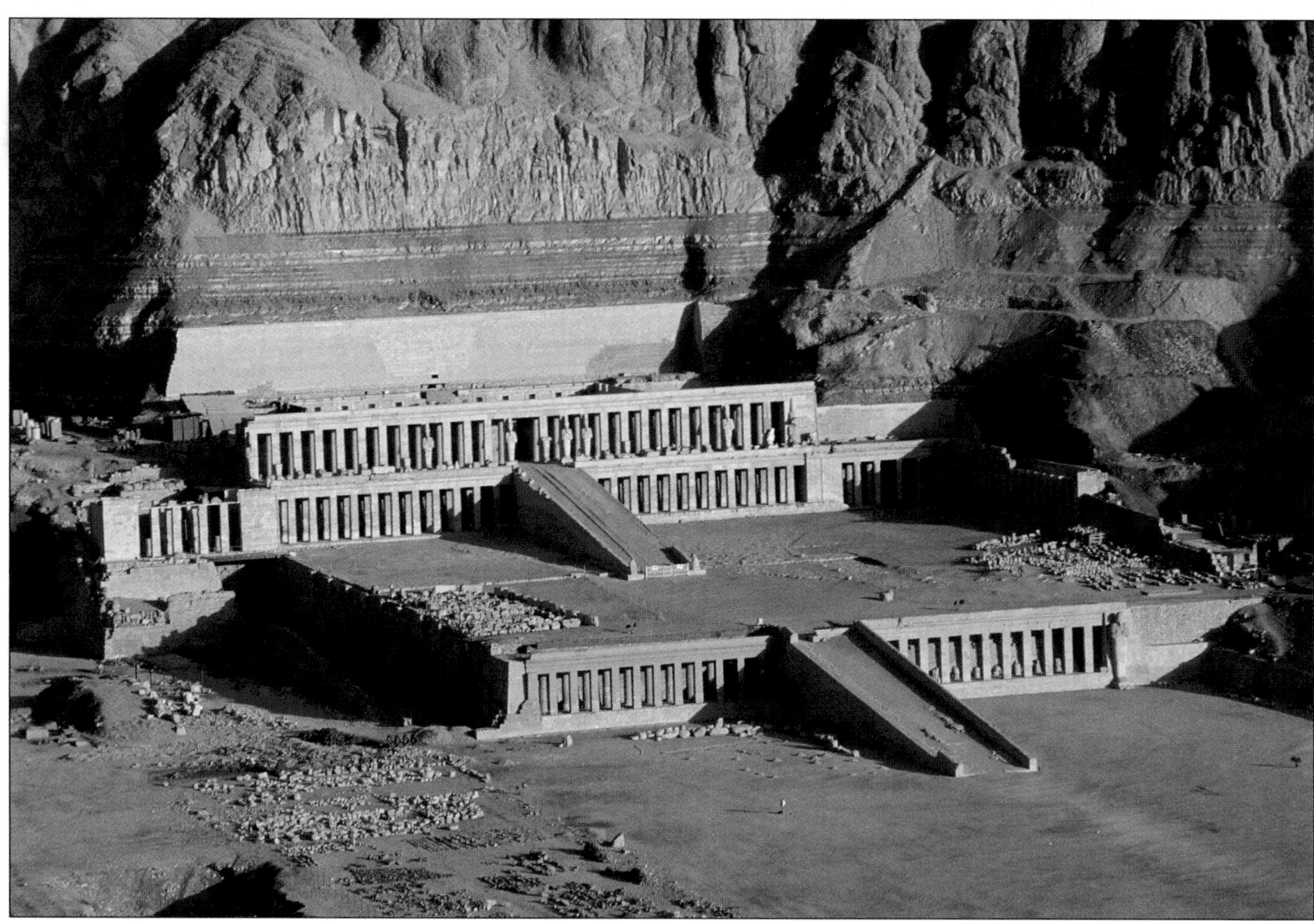

The huge temple is constructed of repeated elements—colonnaded terraces with columnar porticoes (covered walkways), halls, and private chambers. The three terraces are connected by ramps to the cliff, and chambers are cut into the cliff. These chambers are chapels to the god Amen; to the cow-headed goddess Hathor, who protects the city of the dead; to Anubis, the god of embalming, who protects the dead; and to the queen herself.

Typical of Egyptian buildings, the Temple of Hatshepsut was roofed with stone. As a result, the rooms are dense forests of statues and square or sixteen-sided support columns—the distance between these supports had to be small enough to span with a stone lintel. Sculpture was used lavishly; there were perhaps two hundred statues in Hatshepsut's funerary temple. The walls were covered with brightly painted low relief. The terraces, now bare, were once filled with gardens.

Temple of Amen-Mut-Khonsu. In the New Kingdom, many temples dedicated to the gods were built, and the priesthood remained powerful. The Temple of Amen-Mut-Khonsu (the god Amen, and his wife Mut, the goddess of heaven, were the parents of Khonsu) at Luxor (fig. 1.23) is one of the largest Egyptian temples. It was built over a long time period, with major construction under Amenhotep III (r. 1390–1352 B.C.E.), and under Ramesses II (r. ca. 1279–1212 B.C.E.). The temple, which was considered the home of the god, was based on house plans, but made larger and more permanent. The entire temple complex, like many other Egyptian temple complexes, is organized around a longitudinal axis and is essentially symmetrical.

Family Homes. Much of what is known today about the ancient Egyptians derives from the study of royal tombs; consequently, knowledge of Egyptian life is largely limited

FIGURE 1.23 Temple of Amen-Mut-Khonsu, Luxor, major construction under Amenhotep III, ca. 1390 B.C.E., and Ramesses II, ca. 1260 B.C.E. Like all ancient Egyptian temples, this is constructed on the post and lintel system. Columns and capitals look like plant stalks and buds—perishable forms have been made permanent in stone.

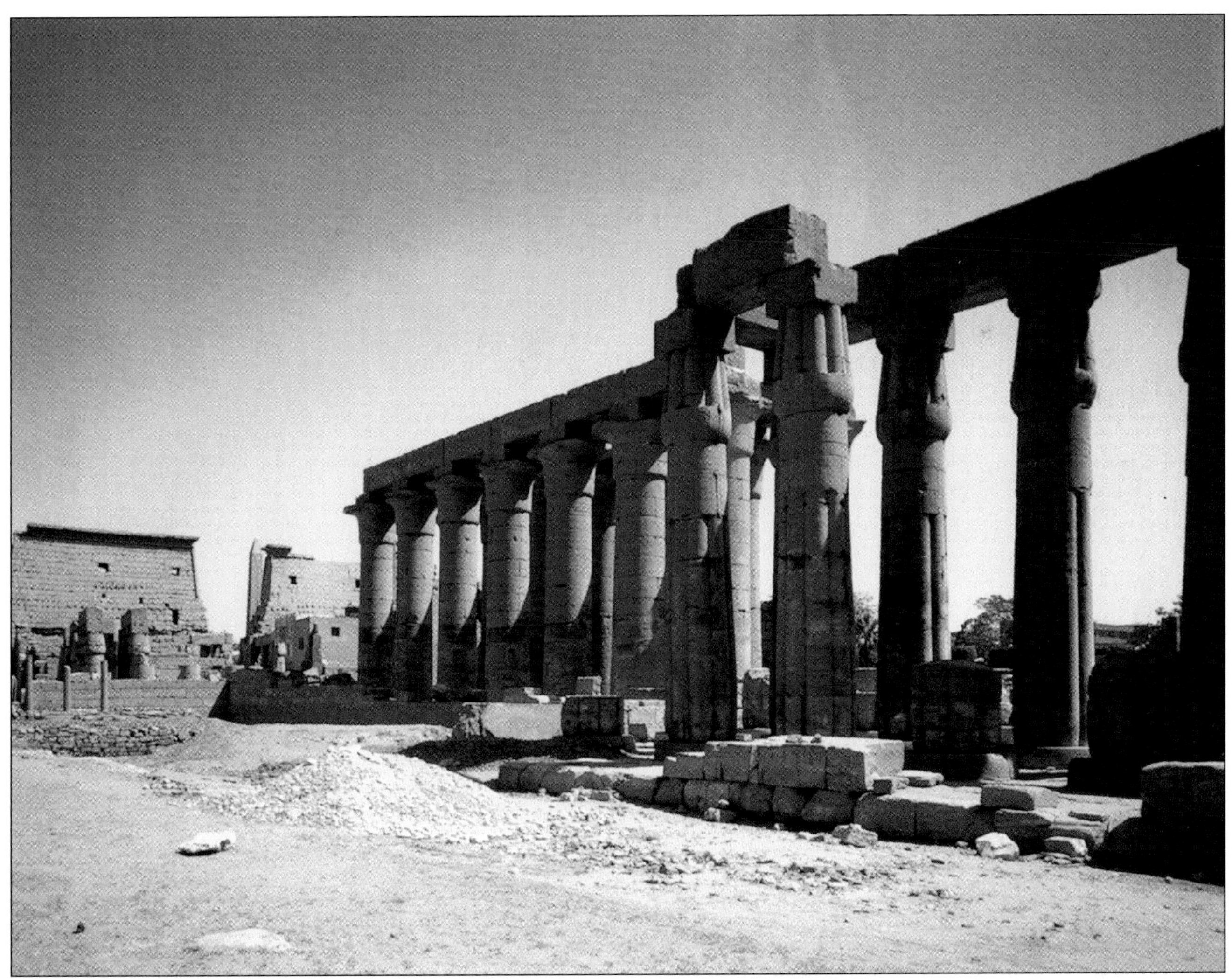

to the uppermost levels of society. But at a few sites the homes of everyday people have been unearthed, and much can be learned about the lifestyle of average Egyptians from these excavations.

One such site is Deir el-Medina, a village that first came into being in the Eighteenth Dynasty as the permanent residence of the tomb builders and artisans who worked across the Nile at Luxor. The city existed for nearly four centuries, through the Twentieth Dynasty, and grew to contain about seventy homes within its walls and fifty outside. The interior layout of each of the houses is relatively uniform. The entrance room, which opened onto the street, was the household chapel, with niches for offerings and an image of the god Bes, a family deity associated with childbirth. Behind this was the main room, with a high roof supported by one or more columns. A raised platform on one wall served as both an eating area and bed. Beneath this was a cellar. One or two smaller rooms for sleeping or storage led off the main room. At the back of the house was a walled garden, which also served as the kitchen, with an oven in one corner and, nearby, a grain silo and grinding equipment. A staircase led from this courtyard to the roof of the house, where the cool evening breezes of the Nile could be enjoyed. Furniture might have included stools, tables, wooden beds, and lamps made of pottery, containing oil and a wick.

More lavish homes, with large gardens and pools, were built by Egyptians of higher standing. A painting of the home and garden of the royal scribe Nakte (fig. 1.24), from the Eighteenth Dynasty, shows him with his wife, standing before their home, giving praise to the king and queen. Their garden pool is surrounded by trees, including a grape arbor. The house is whitewashed to reflect the heat. High up on the wall are windows into the main room, and on the roof are two triangular vents designed to catch the evening breezes. The house is elevated on a platform to protect its mud brick from moisture and flood.

SCULPTURE

Temple of Ramesses II. The perpetuation of Old Kingdom types into the New Kingdom is demonstrated at the Temple of Ramesses II at Abu Simbel (fig. 1.25), built ca. 1260 B.C.E., during the Nineteenth Dynasty. The facade and inner rooms are cut into the sandstone on the west bank of the Nile. In theory, the temple was built in honor of the sun; there is a statue of the sun god in a niche in the center of the facade. At the top of this facade is a row of dog-headed apes, sacred to the worship of the rising sun. Reliefs and hieroglyphs on the facade also have to do with the pharaoh Ramesses II's respect for the sun god. But all this is overshadowed by the four enormous statues of Ramesses II, each 65 feet high. (The much smaller figures around and between the legs of these statues are members of his family.)

Despite their giant scale, however, these four statues look very much like statues carved more than a millennium earlier during the Old Kingdom in the pose, physical type, and attire. When they are compared closely, differences between sculpture of the Old, Middle, and New Kingdoms do become apparent: Old Kingdom sculpture is relatively realistic; New Kingdom sculpture is more elegant. But, in view of the enormous time span, the differences are minor. Once again, Egyptian art is seen to be characterized by remarkable uniformity.

FIGURE 1.24 *House and Garden of the Scribe Nakte*, from Nakte's *Book of the Dead*, Eighteenth Dynasty, British Museum, London. In the New Kingdom, papyrus scrolls that would assist the dead in successfully passing their last test before Osiris prior to enjoying the afterlife were often placed among the wrappings of mummified bodies. Called *Books of the Dead*, these scrolls were often beautifully decorated. © The Trustees of the British Museum/Art Resource, NY.

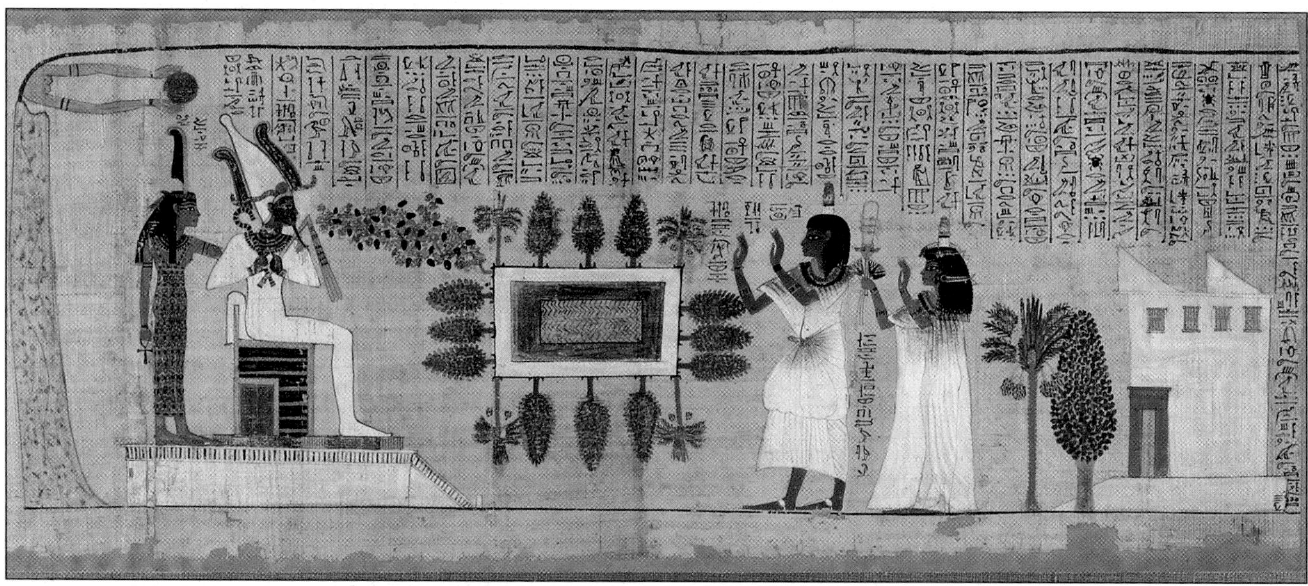

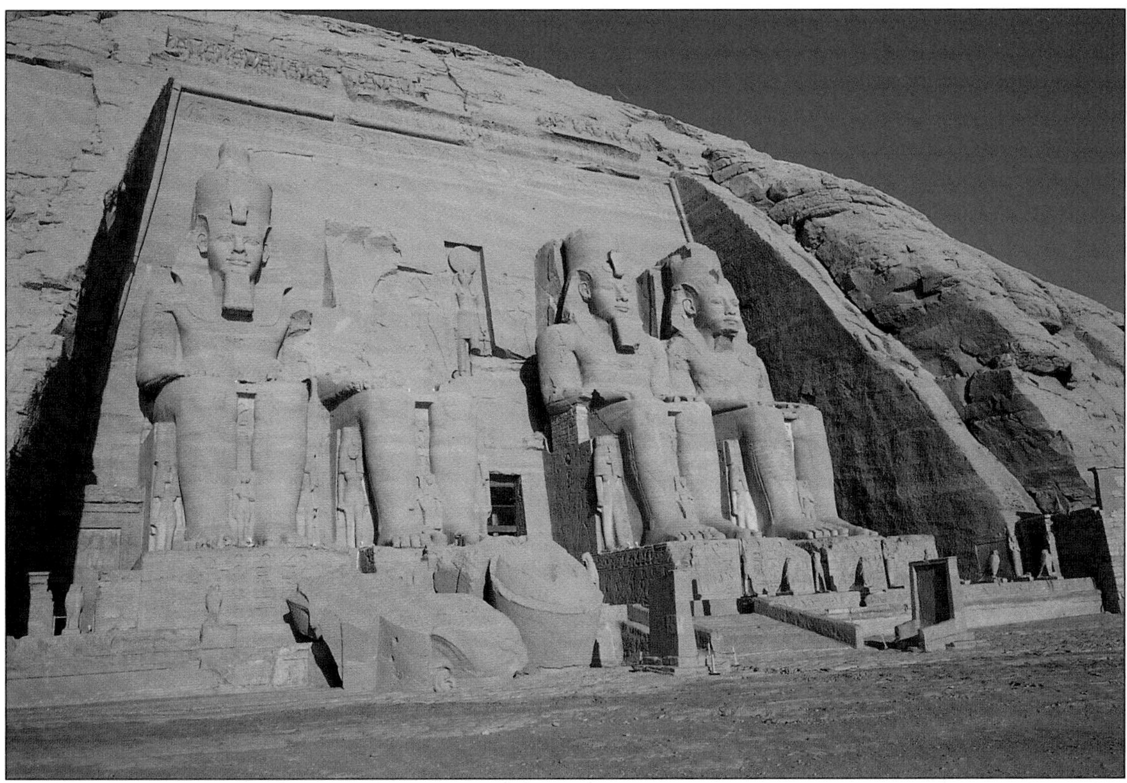

FIGURE 1.25 *Four Seated Figures of Ramesses II,* Temple of Ramesses II, Abu Simbel, facade, ca. 1260 B.C.E., Nineteenth Dynasty. So completely governed by tradition and convention was Egyptian art and culture that, more than 1,200 years after Chefren was carved, these figures of Ramesses II demonstrate that the seated figure continued to be depicted in almost exactly the same way.

RELIEF SCULPTURE AND PAINTING

As in the Old and Middle Kingdoms, New Kingdom temples and tombs were decorated with reliefs and paintings. There were some innovations, however. For instance, greater freedom of pose, wider variety of movement, more complex figure groupings, and a more flowing line are seen in the New Kingdom than in the Old Kingdom. But the basic conventions endure, such as the profile head with frontal eye, the impossible poses, and the arrangement of figures in zones of the register system.

Nobleman Hunting in the Marshes. Painted around 1400 B.C.E., in the Eighteenth Dynasty, in a tomb at Thebes, the *Nobleman Hunting in the Marshes* (fig. 1.26) illustrates this new freedom, as well as the perpetuation of long-established tradition in New Kingdom painting. Active and agile, the nobleman holds three birds in one hand and a wand in the other. Equally impressive is the acrobatic accomplishment of the cat sitting on the bending lotus stems, for she catches one bird with her teeth, another with her claws, and a third with her tail. One bird is catching a butterfly. All people, birds, animals, and fish are shown in profile. The birds neatly form a series of overlapping profiles.

Nobleman Hunting in the Marshes deserves comparison with *Ti Watching a Hippopotamus Hunt* (see fig. 1.21),

FIGURE 1.26 *Nobleman Hunting in the Marshes,* from a tomb at Thebes, ca. 1400 B.C.E., Eighteenth Dynasty, wall painting on dry plaster, British Museum, London. Created a millennium after the painting of *Ti Watching a Hippopotamus Hunt,* (fig. 1.21) the painting *Nobleman Hunting in the Marshes* demonstrates the remarkable consistency of ancient Egyptian style. Emphasis continued to be placed on the clarity with which information was conveyed rather than on realistic representation.

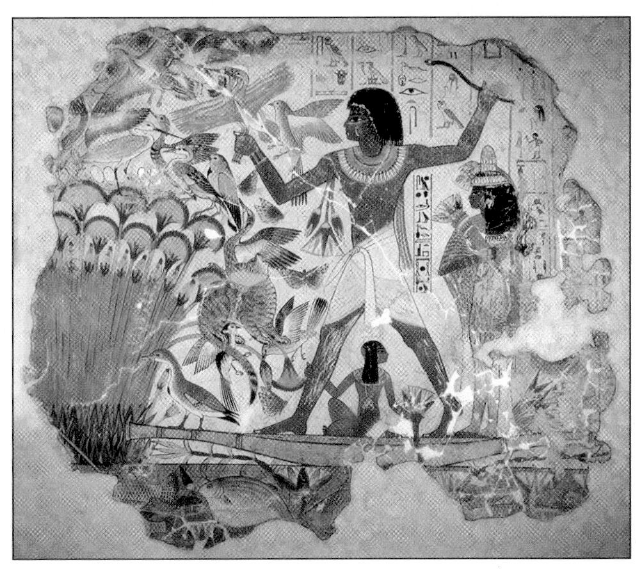

Connections

DANCE AND MUSIC IN ANCIENT EGYPT

What we know of music and dance in ancient Egypt depends on two very different kinds of evidence: the visual record of dancers and musicians we find in surviving reliefs and paintings; and, more problematic, present musical and dance forms that appear to have survived since ancient times. Of the first, we have, for instance, a detail of a wall painting from the tomb of Nebamun at Thebes, dating from about 1400 B.C.E. (fig. 1.27). It shows four seated women, three of whom are watching and apparently clapping along with music played on a double oboe by the fourth. Two nude figures dance to the music. So relaxed is the scene that most of the conventions of traditional Egyptian representation have been abandoned.

In addition to the double oboe seen here, Egyptian music made special use of harps, lutes, and lyres. Surviving paintings often show a blind man playing the harp, but lutes and lyres were apparently played predominantly by women. Single oboes, flutes, and clarinets were also popular, and trumpets were used in military and religious ceremonies. Religious festivals appear to have been primarily musical occasions, and participants routinely danced throughout the celebration.

Many modern Egyptians, as well as scholars, believe that contemporary belly dancing derives from dances such as that seen in the wall painting on the tomb of Nebamun. The belly dance, called the *baladi*, probably originated in Egypt as part of both fertility and funeral rituals. Like the contemporary belly dance, the original dances may well have been designed to create a sense of physical and emotional rhapsody, and they probably utilized many of the same musical effects, particularly ever-increasing rhythmic pace and provocative physical movement.

FIGURE 1.27 *Musicians and Dancers*, detail of a wall painting from the tomb of Nebamun, Thebes, ca. 1400 B.C.E., fragment, $11\frac{3}{4} \times 27\frac{1}{4}''$ (29.9 × 69.2 cm), British Museum, London. The two central figures, the one playing the reeds and the seated figure next to her, are remarkable in the way that they face the viewer, a point of view rarely seen in Egyptian painting. © The Trustees of the British Museum/Art Resource, NY.

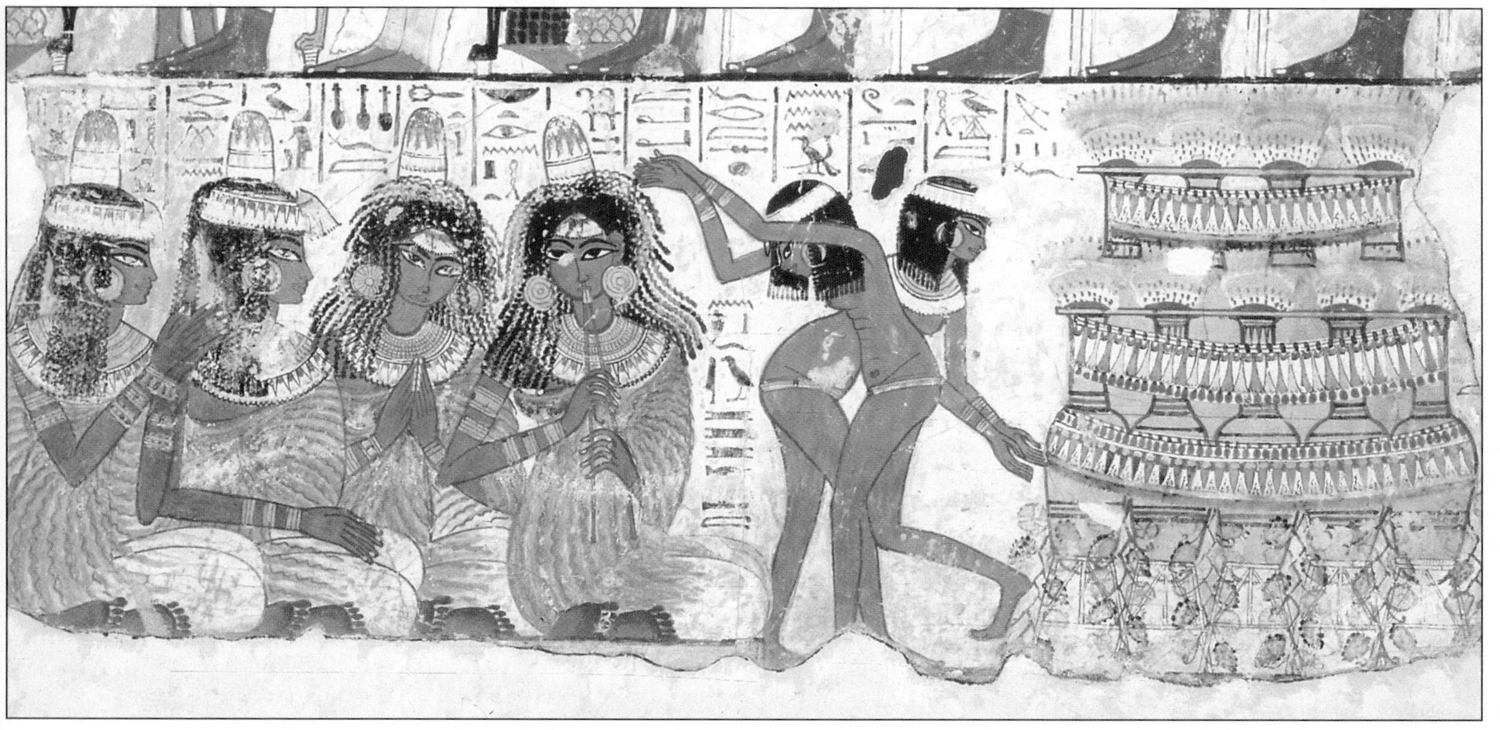

painted a thousand years earlier in the Fifth Dynasty. The similarities are striking. Both men are longhaired and wear white skirts. Both stand *on* their boats, rather than *in*. Both of their boats are *on* rather than *in* the water. In both, people are drawn with the heads and legs seen from the sides, but eyes and chest from the front. The continued use of relative size to indicate importance is shown by the small figure between the nobleman's legs; she cannot be interpreted as being in the distant background, for she grasps his shin.

AKHENATEN AND TUTANKHAMEN

The sole significant challenge—and it proved only a temporary deviation—to Egypt's consistency of attitude and approach to representation and design came in the Eighteenth Dynasty under Amenhotep IV [am-EN-oh-TEP] (r. 1352–1336 B.C.E.). He closed the Amen temples, displaced the sun god Amen-Ra, officially dispensed with the pantheon of other Egyptian gods, and replaced them all with a monotheistic system, worshiping the single god Aten, the sun disk. He moved the capital from Thebes to a new city far to the north that he called Akhetaten, "the horizon of Aten," modern day Tell el-Amarna. He then changed his name to Akhenaten [AK-uhn-AH-tan], too, which means "He who is effective on behalf of Aten." Just as significantly he transformed the art of Egypt, liberating it from convention.

Akhenaten, Nefertiti, and Their Children Worshiping the Sun. This painted limestone relief (fig. 1.28), dated ca. 1348–1336 B.C.E., represents an extraordinary change

FIGURE 1.28 *Akhenaten, Nefertiti, and Their Children Worshiping the Sun*, ca. 1348–1336 B.C.E., Eighteenth Dynasty, painted limestone relief, $12\frac{1}{4}'' \times 15\frac{1}{4}''$ (31.1 × 8.7 cm), Staatliche Museen zu Berlin, Preussischer Kulturbesitz, Agyptisches Museum. The only notable break in the continuity of Egyptian life were the changes—political, religious, and artistic—instituted by the pharaoh Akhenaten in the Eighteenth Dynasty.

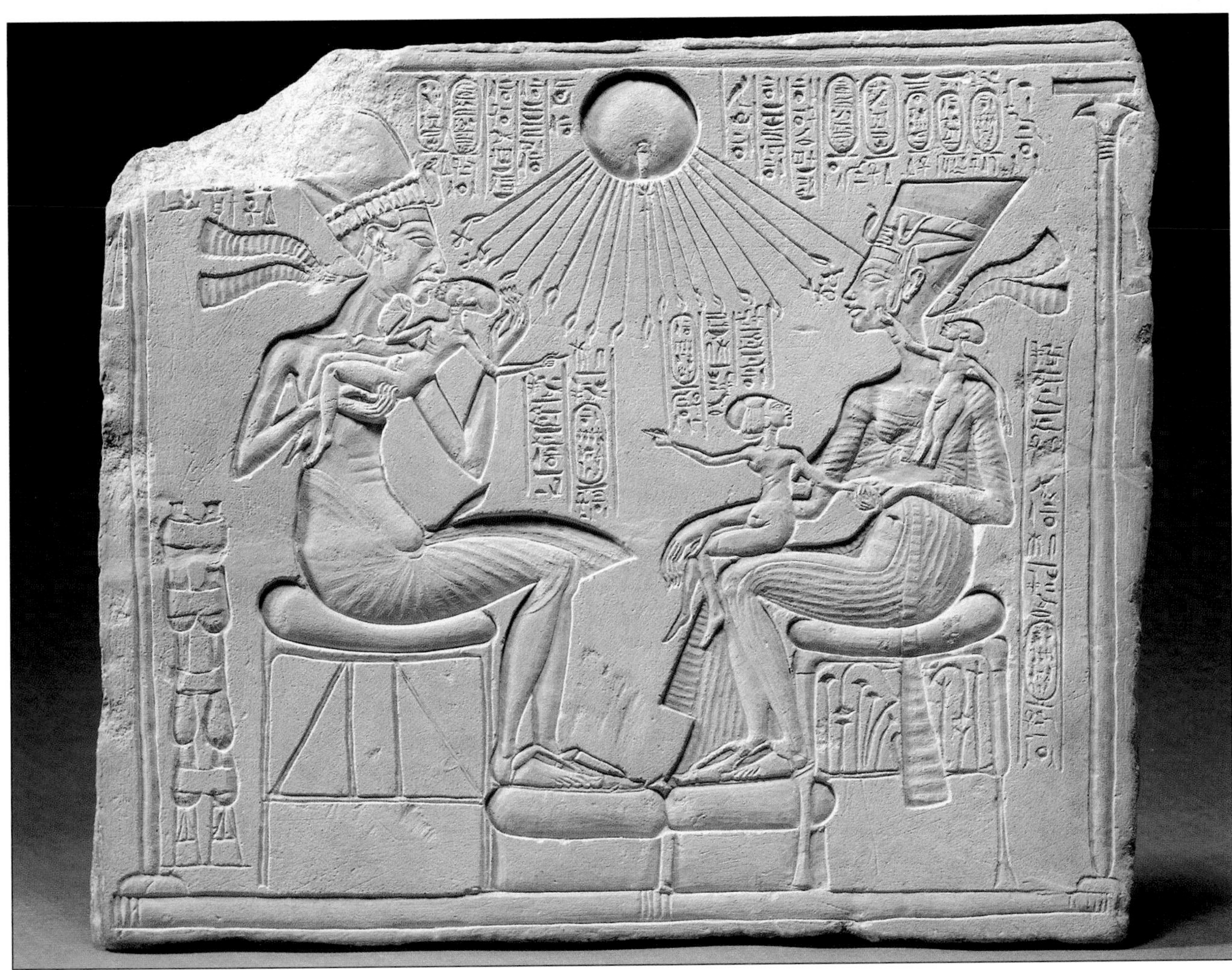

from traditional Egyptian art. Akhenaten and his Queen, Nefertiti, play with their three daughters, who are shown as miniature adults. Akhenaten even kisses one of his children, a rare display of affection in Egyptian art. These people are shown in casual poses. More notable, however, are their physical distortions—long necks and skulls, protruding abdomens, and large hips, presumably shown to create a likeness. Although royalty, Akhenaten and his family are not idealized, perfect physical types. Royalty is now depicted in domestic situations, casually, intimately. Rather than stressing dignity, this art is playful and informal.

Queen Nefertiti. Akhenaten's wife, the beautiful Queen Nefertiti (fig. 1.29), was recorded in a life-size portrait in ca. 1348–1336 B.C.E., carved of limestone and painted, the eyes inlaid with rock crystal. Discovered in 1912 in the studio of Thutmosis, Akhenaten's chief sculptor, this individualized portrait is characteristic of the more informal, relaxed style of Akhenaten's reign. The carving of this charming portrait is sensitive and refined, and its beauty is probably not exaggerated. Surviving texts refer to the Queen as "Fair of Face," "Great of Love," and "Endowed with Favors."

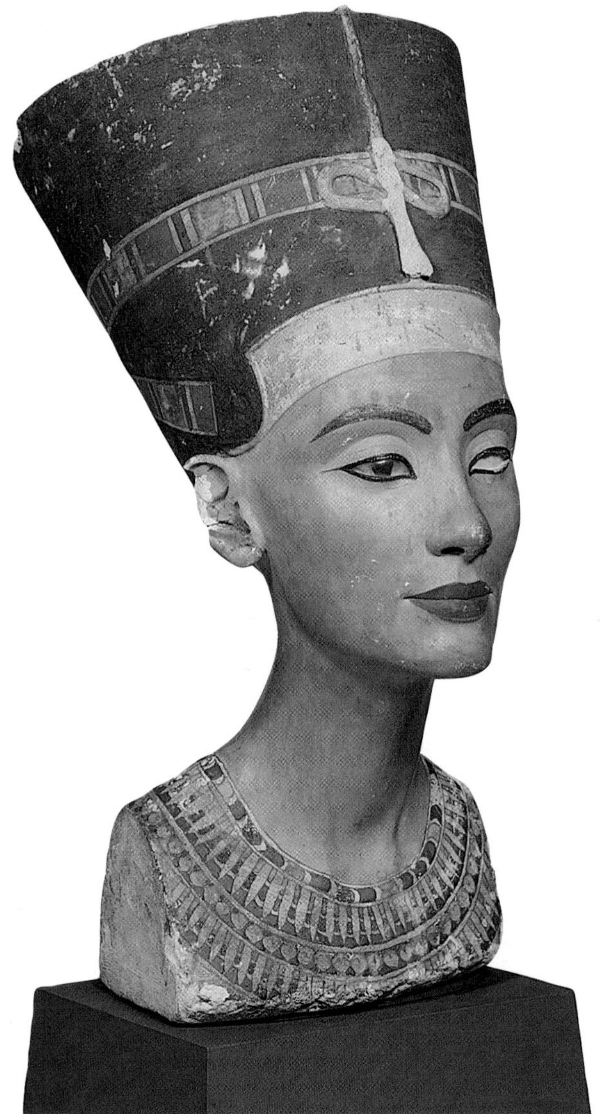

FIGURE 1.29 *Queen Nefertiti,* ca. 1348–1336 B.C.E., Eighteenth Dynasty, painted limestone, rock crystal eyes, height 20″ (50.8 cm), Staatliche Museen zu Berlin, Preussischer Kulturbesitz, Agyptisches Museum. Although ideals of beauty have changed greatly throughout time, the appeal of Nefertiti, elegant wife of Akhenaten, endures.

Tomb of Tutankhamen. Akhenaten's successor was TUTANKHAMEN [too-tan-KAH-moon] (r. ca. 1336–1327 B.C.E.), at the end of the Eighteenth Dynasty. Tutankhamen was married to one of the daughters of Akhenaten and Nefertiti. However, as king, Tutankhamen disavowed his parents-in-law and returned to the worship of Amen, reestablishing the capital at Thebes. Tutankhamen's fame today derives from the discovery of his tomb, nearly intact and containing an extraordinary treasure, in the early 1920s by the British archaeologist Howard Carter. Tutankhamen's tomb, which was uncovered in the Valley of the Kings near Thebes, consisted of a corridorlike shaft leading to four decorated rooms.

From this tomb comes the death mask of Tutankhamen (fig. 1.30), which was found over the head of the mummified pharaoh. Made of polished gold and inlaid with colored glass and semiprecious stones, weighing 24.2 pounds, this alone makes clear why tombs were sacked. The vulture and cobra on his forehead are protective symbols. Additionally, the vulture represents Upper Egypt and the cobra represents Lower Egypt. On the shoulders are falcon heads. He wears a false ceremonial beard.

Tutankhamen was probably between eighteen and twenty years old when he died of gangrene after breaking his leg. Despite the brevity of his reign, this minor ruler was buried in a sarcophagus that contained three coffins, one inside another, the outer two of wood covered with gold sheets, and the innermost one made of solid gold.

EGYPTIAN MUSIC

Because historians have found no Egyptian musical notation to speak of, we can only speculate about the sound of the music itself; however, thanks to the pictorial

Cross Currents

NUBIA

Far up the Nile River, near Khartoum, Nubia was the first complex hierarchical society south of the Sahara desert. Egypt maintained extended contact with Nubia, which was famed for its reserves of iron, copper, and gold. Nubia, in fact, means "gold" in the Egyptian language. In exchange for these valued metals, Egypt sent pottery, wine, honey, and finely woven textiles to Nubia.

By about 2500 B.C.E., Nubian leaders had established the kingdom of Kush, a wealthy state that came to dominate the upper reaches of the Nile. Around 2300 B.C.E., the Egyptian pharaohs sent a prince of Aswam named Harkuf on three journeys to Nubia to trade and to recruit Nubian mercenaries to fight in Egypt's armies.

During the Middle Kingdom, Nubia came under Egyptian rule, but during the ninth century B.C.E., the Nubian kingdom of Kush ruled southern Egypt. By the eighth century B.C.E., Kush had five of its kings reign as Egyptian pharaohs, known as the twenty-fifth or "Ethiopian" dynasty.

FIGURE 1.30 Death Mask of Pharaoh Tutankhamen, from his innermost mummy case, ca. 1336–1327 B.C.E., gold inlaid with colored glass and semiprecious stones, height 21" (54 cm), weight 24.2 lbs. (11 kg). Egyptian Museum, Cairo.

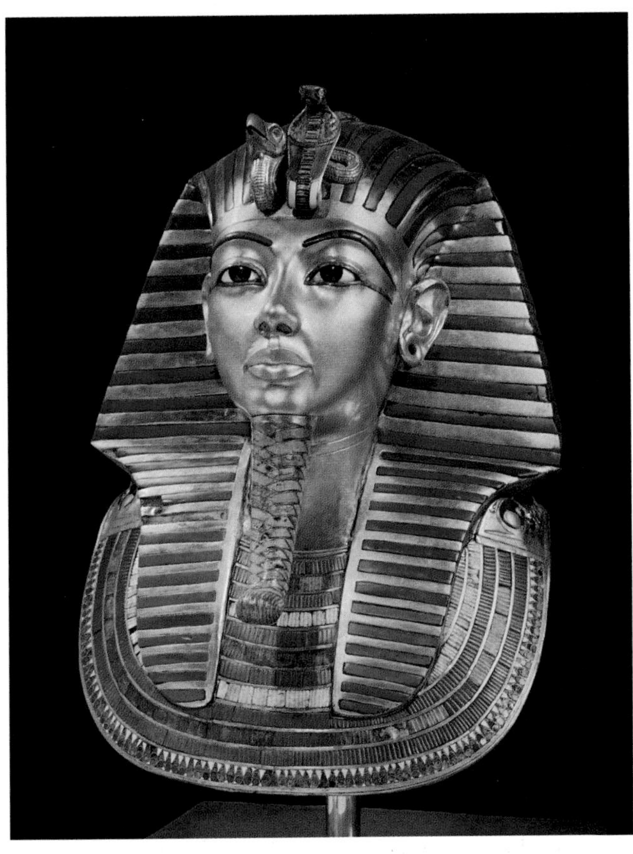

characteristics of hieroglyphics, we do know of the widespread use of music in Egyptian culture. Drawings of both secular and sacred rituals, plus actual instruments found in tombs, suggest that music formed an important part of life for the ancient Egyptians. Like so many of the arts of this ancient time, music was spread by the aural tradition, passed down from generation to generation. Although vocal music was probably the most prominent musical genre, because it is the most natural means of expression, instrumental music accompanied Egyptian poems, making them into songs of celebration, mourning, or declarations of love. Small ensembles performed at the many rituals of harvest, birth, and death.

A closer look at music instruments gives us the best clue as to the importance and function of music in this era. The harp seems to be the most prominent Egyptian instrument. It consisted of a bent piece of wood much like the bow of a bow and arrow, but with many gut strings of varying lengths producing a variety of pitches. Pictures showing several strings being plucked at the same time indicate there was probably harmony in the music, which contradicts the common historical claim that one melody was the only texture of music for the ancients. A melody with harmony might have been possible, or even two different melodies played simultaneously. Modes or scales were obviously used imitating melodic lines because the structures of string instruments indicate a gradation from low pitches to high.

Pictures of percussion instruments also indicate that music was used for walking, chanting, and dancing. Such

Cross Currents

Ancient Egypt in the European Imagination

Of the "Seven Wonders of the World" first listed by Greek authors in the second century B.C.E., only the pyramids at Giza survive. Perhaps because of this, they have come to symbolize in Western consciousness what is perhaps the closest thing to eternity on earth. As a twelfth-century Arab historian put it: "All things fear time, but time fears the pyramids." When Napoleon Bonaparte attacked Egypt in 1798, in order to cut off England's lifeline to India, he inspired his troops on the day of one of the most famous battles in history, the Battle of the Pyramids, with the words: "Soldiers, forty centuries look down upon you."

The Frenchman Hubert Robert's 1760 painting *The Pyramid* (fig. 1.31) captures another of its aspects: Not only was it eternal, it was colossal. Robert's painting overstates its scale: The figures that approach it are minuscule and the pyramid itself disappears off the canvas into the clouds and airy mists, like a Himalayan peak, as if the painting cannot contain it. But Robert does capture something of its emotional power. Unable to perceive its bounds, we realize we are in the presence of something that approaches, imaginatively at least, the infinite—what eighteenth-century writers would call the "sublime."

The sublime is both spiritual—an earthly manifestation of God—and terrifying, because it makes our own being seem so insignificant and ephemeral. Probably no writer in the nineteenth century summed up the ability of Egyptian art to so move us better than the English poet Percy Bysshe Shelley, whose poem "Ozymandias" is based on a statue in the mortuary temple of Ramesses II:

I met a traveler from an antique land,
Who said: Two vast and trunkless legs of stone
Stand in the desert . . . Near them, on the sand,
Half sunk, a shattered visage lies, whose frown,
And wrinkled lip, and sneer of cold command,
Tell that its sculptor well those passions read
Which yet survive, stamped on these lifeless things,
The hand that mocked them, and the heart that fed,
And on the pedestal these words appear:
"My name is Ozymandias, king of kings:
Look on my works, ye Mighty, and despair!"
Nothing beside remains, Round the decay
Of that colossal wreck, boundless and bare
The lone and level sands stretch far away.

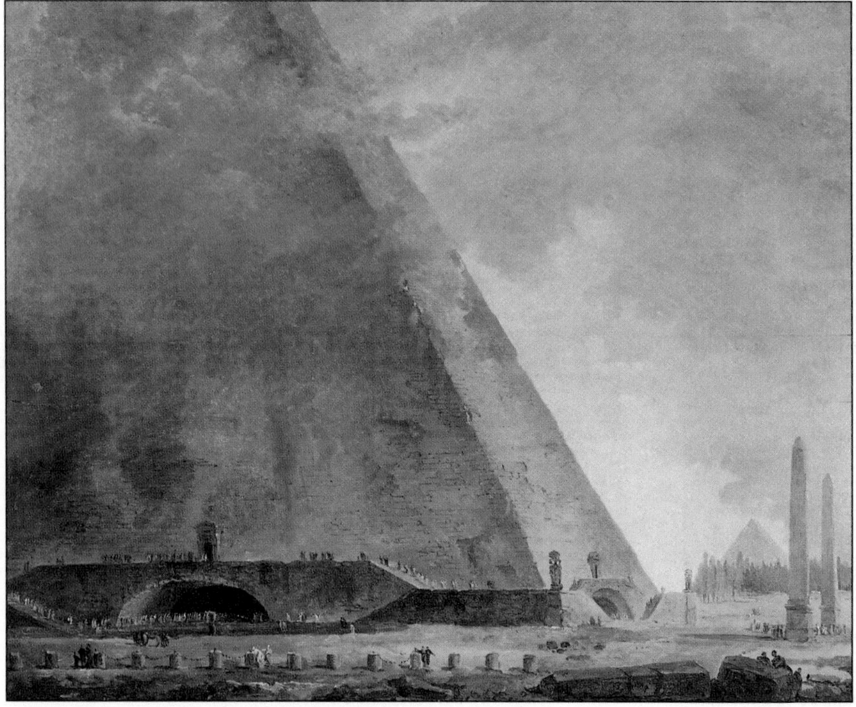

FIGURE 1.31 Hubert Robert, *The Pyramid*, 1760, oil on wood, 4′ × 4′ × $2\frac{1}{4}''$ (1.22 × 1.28 m), Smith College Museum of Art, Northampton, Massachusetts. Robert's work was painted amidst a general revival in France of monumental Egyptian architecture, particularly of funerary monuments, many of which were proposed in competitions organized by the French government, but none of which was ever built.

Cultural Impact

Ideas implicit in prehistoric art reappear in later eras, evidence of a continuum of human creativity and concerns through the ages. Certain depictions of animals, as seen in the cave paintings at Lascaux and the sculptures at Le Tuc d'Audoubert, suggest that the ability to recreate an image has a long history. The greater realism in the depictions of animals than of humans, evidenced by the *Woman of Willendorf*, indicates that artistic distortion was already a conscious choice in prehistoric times. Intentional deviation from absolute visual reality is evident as early as the steles that record the victory of Naram-Sin and the laws of Hammurabi. Indeed, the entire history of art may be regarded as a series of fluctuations between degrees of realism and abstraction.

Early cultures developed at very different times in various parts of the globe. Certain cultures regarded as prehistoric, due to absence of extant documentation, actually postdate othercultures. For example, prehistoric Stonehenge was constructed ca. 2000 B.C.E., making it a relatively new structure when compared to the great pyramids of Egypt, built between ca. 2530 and ca. 2470 B.C.E. The simple static post and lintel seen at Stonehenge was used as a basic construction method throughout the centuries—it is seen in buildings as disparate as the Parthenon, a temple of the fifth century B.C.E. (fig. 3.3), and Le Corbusier's Savoye House, a private home of 1929–30 (fig. 23.9).

Ancient Egypt, one of the most structured societies of all times, created art of correspondingly extreme stylistic consistency over thousands of years. Nowhere else is the apparent avoidance of innovation and disinterest in experimentation found. Yet we may wonder if the same qualities were characteristic of art produced for people other than royalty, and for purposes other than political or funereal.

The appeal of ancient Egypt's pyramids persists, the form perpetuated in our own time most notably by the architect I. M. Pei in his 1988 design for the entry to the Louvre Museum in Paris. Although the pyramidal form is repeated, rather than emphasizing its permanence by building in stone like the ancient Egyptians, Pei's pyramid, constructed of glass, assumes a sense of fragility. The ancient Egyptian pyramid functioned as a tomb to protect the remains of the pharaoh and the accompanying treasure from the public, whereas its Parisian descendant serves to promote public access to the Louvre's artistic treasures.

Use of large-scale sculpture both to immortalize and to glorify political leaders seen in the images of the pharaoh and his family, as of Ramesses II on the facade of his temple at Abu Simbel, begins in ancient Egypt. We see how very effectively art was employed to convey a political message in later cultures, for example, in the sculpture of the ancient Roman emperor Augustus of ca. 20 B.C.E. (fig. 4.13) and in Jean-Antoine Houdon's portrait of George Washington of 1788–92 (fig. 16.14).

evidence of a beat suggests the music had a more complicated rhythm and was much more musically advanced than that of the early Western church (see Chapter 5). The Egyptians' poetic language itself would have influenced the rhythm and as a means of expression, inflections in the voice would have had an automatic transference into the rhythm. Pictures of metal instruments being struck by dancing girls or actual wood and brass instruments preserved in tombs give us an idea of the tone color of Egyptian music.

Certainly, wind instruments evolved from an ample supply of reeds and other water plants growing beside the Nile River. Wind blowing through these vibrating sources would have produced sounds of nature that were copied and adapted to a mode of expression for this culture so closely connected to the land. Instruments similar to the shofar (ram's horn) of the Hebrew people were abundant and used as a means of communication.

Performances were given by professionals. There was a variety of social levels, with the highest belonging to those musicians of the temple that were both male and female. Lower on the social scale were musicians who acted as entertainers for various festivals or who accompanied dancers or workers in action.

LITERATURE: LYRIC POETRY

The literature of the ancient Egyptians is not readily available: Most of what remains exists only in scattered fragments. The oldest Egyptian poems, dating from ca. 2650 to 2050 B.C.E., are religious. Most are incantations and invocations to the gods to aid the departed Egyptian kings. But one of the most important Egyptian religious poems is the pharaoh Akhenaten's "Hymn to the Sun." In this poem, Akhenaten presents himself as the son of Aten, and then describes the sun's rising: "At dawn you rise shining in the horizon, you shine as Aten in the sky and drive away darkness by sending forth your rays. The Two Lands [Lower and Upper Egypt] awake in festivity, and people stand on their feet, for you have raised them up. They wash their bodies, they take their garments, and their arms are raised to praise your rising. The whole world does its work."

Other ancient Egyptian poems of interest include a series of lyrics composed between ca. 2000 and 1000 B.C.E., especially the love poems written during the late Rameside period (ca. 1300–1100 B.C.E.). As with later Greek and Roman love poetry, and the nearly equally ancient love poetry of the Hebrews (the biblical Song of Songs), ancient Egyptian love poems display a wide range of mood and feeling. Written on limestone as well as on papyrus, these ancient love poems reflect attitudes that appear strikingly modern.

KEY TERMS

culture
Paleolithic
Neolithic
cromlech
henge
post and lintel
cuneiform
pictographic
ideograms
polytheism
anthropomorphism
ziggurat
battered
weeper holes
stele
relief sculpture
statues in the round
myth
glazed brick
dualistic religion
dynasties
hieroglyphics
ka
mastaba
serdab

WWW. WEBSITES FOR FURTHER STUDY

http://www.culture.gouv.fr/culture/arcnat/chauvet/en/
(Explores the cave at Chauvet.)

http://www.greatbuildings.com/buildings/Stonehenge.html
(Excellent images and commentary concerning Stonehenge.)

http://www.usc.edu/schools/annenberg/asc/projects/comm544/library/images/828.html
(Takes a look at the Victory Stele of Naram-Sin.)

http://oi.uchicago.edu/OI/MUS/HIGH/OI_Museum_Assyria.html
(Assyrian art museum.)

http://www.metmuseum.org/works_of_art/department.asp?dep-3
(Metropolitan Museum of Art, Ancient Near East collection.)

http://logos.uoregon.edu/explore/orthography/egypt.html
(Examines Egyptian hieroglyphs.)

http://greatpyramid.org/aip/index.htm
(The American Institute of Pyramidology.)

http://touregypt.net/egyptantiquities/
(Site on Egyptian antiquities.)

http://academic.memphis.edu/egypt/index.html
(Institute of Egyptian Art and Archeology.)

http://touregypt.net/museum/index.htm
(A virtual museum concerning the dynasties.)

http://www.Mesopotamia.co.uk
(All things Mesopotamian.)

http://www.musiced.about.com/od/ancientmusic
(Music of ancient cultures and civilizations.)

http://www.Ancient-egypt-online.com/egyptian_music
(Ancient Egyptian Music.)

http://www.williamsound.com/gold_lyre_music_info.html
(The Gold lyre of Ur and music in Mesopotamia.)

Chapter 2

History

ca. 1800 B.C.E.	Mycenaeans arrive on Greek peninsula
1623 B.C.E.	Volcanic eruption on the island of Thera
ca. 1460 B.C.E.	Mycenaeans conquer Crete
ca. 1400 B.C.E.	Knossos destroyed by Greeks
ca. 1250 B.C.E.	Trojan War; Mycenaean sack of Troy
ca. 1100 B.C.E.	Dorian invasions
776 B.C.E.	Olympic games begin
594–593 B.C.E.	Solon reforms Athenian government
507 B.C.E.	Cleisthenes divides Athens into demes
490 B.C.E.	Battle of Marathon

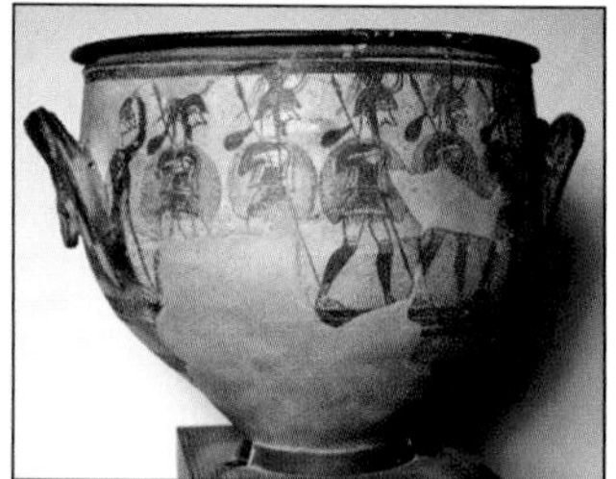

Art and Architecture

third millennium B.C.E.	Statuette of a woman
ca. 1700–1500 B.C.E.	*Snake Goddess* statuette
1700–1300 B.C.E.	Palace of Minos, built and modified
1630–1500 B.C.E.	*Landscape*, wall painting
ca. 1550–1500 B.C.E.	Gold mask from tomb V
ca. 1550–1450 B.C.E.	*Toreador Fresco*
ca. 1300–1200 B.C.E.	Lion Gate
	Treasury of Atreus
ca. 1200 B.C.E.	*Warrior Vase*
750 B.C.E.	Geometric style Dipylon krater
ca. 590–580 B.C.E.	Kouros
550–525 B.C.E.	Exekias, amphora
ca. 515 B.C.E.	Euxitheos and Euphronios, calyx krater

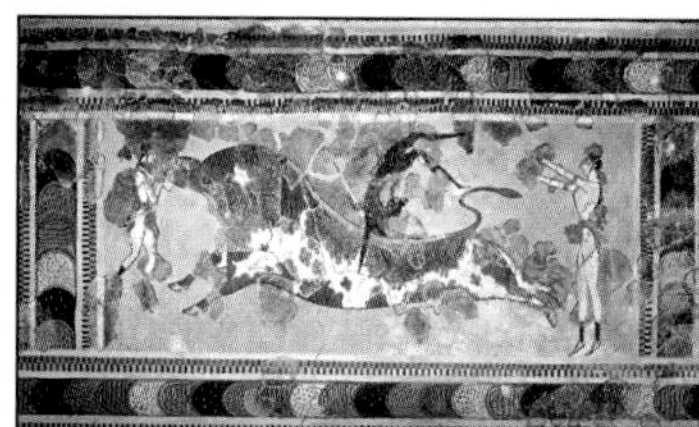

Literature and Philosophy

ca. 800 B.C.E.	Homer, *Iliad and Odyssey*
mid-seventh century B.C.E.	Alphabetic writing derived from Phoenicians, begins
621 B.C.E.	Draco publishes Athenian code of laws
(ca. 610–580 B.C.E.)	Sappho, *He Is More than a Hero*
seventh century B.C.E.	Hesiod's *Theogony*
sixth and fifth centuries B.C.E.	Herakleitos' materialist philosophy
560–550 B.C.E.	Democritus' atomist philosophy
550–525 B.C.E.	Pythagoras' number philosophy

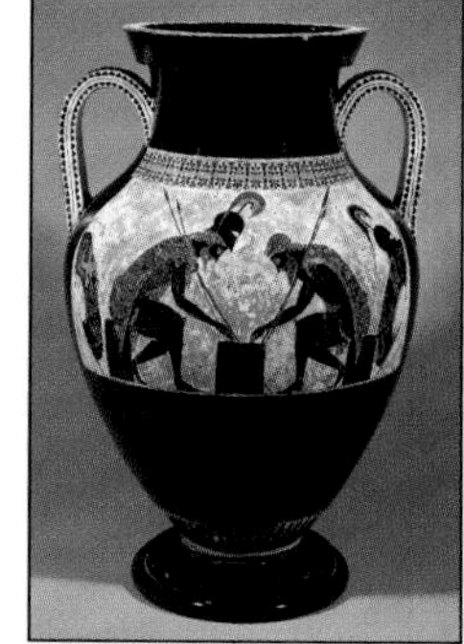

Aegean Culture and Early Greece

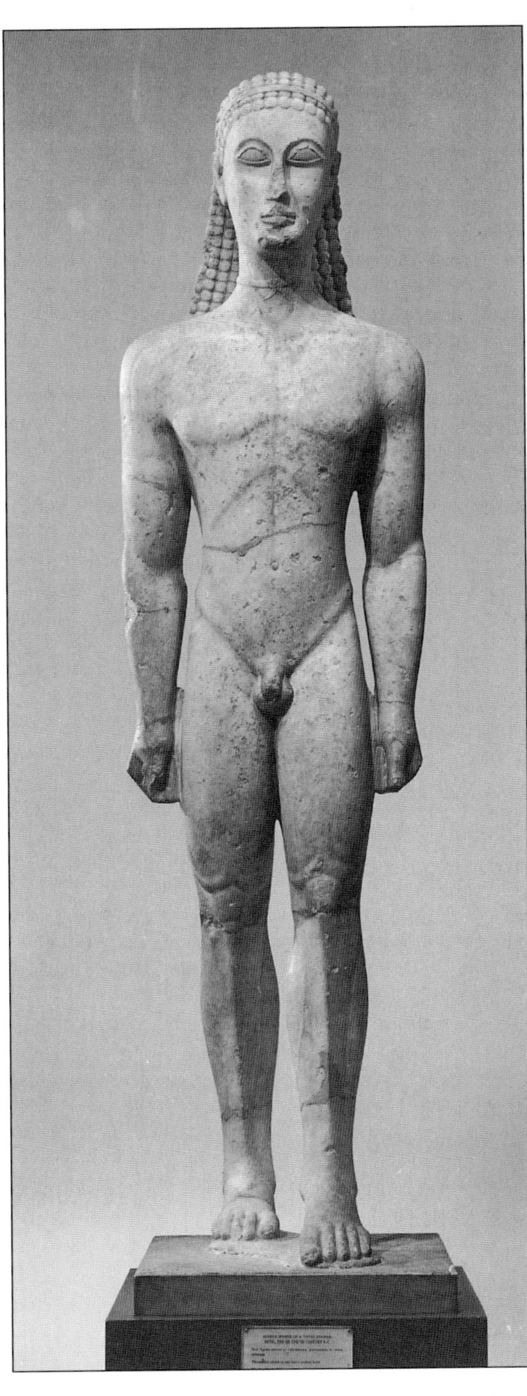

Kouros, ca. 590–580 B.C.E., marble, height 6′4″ (1.93 m), Fletcher Fund, 1932, Metropolitan Museum of Art, New York.

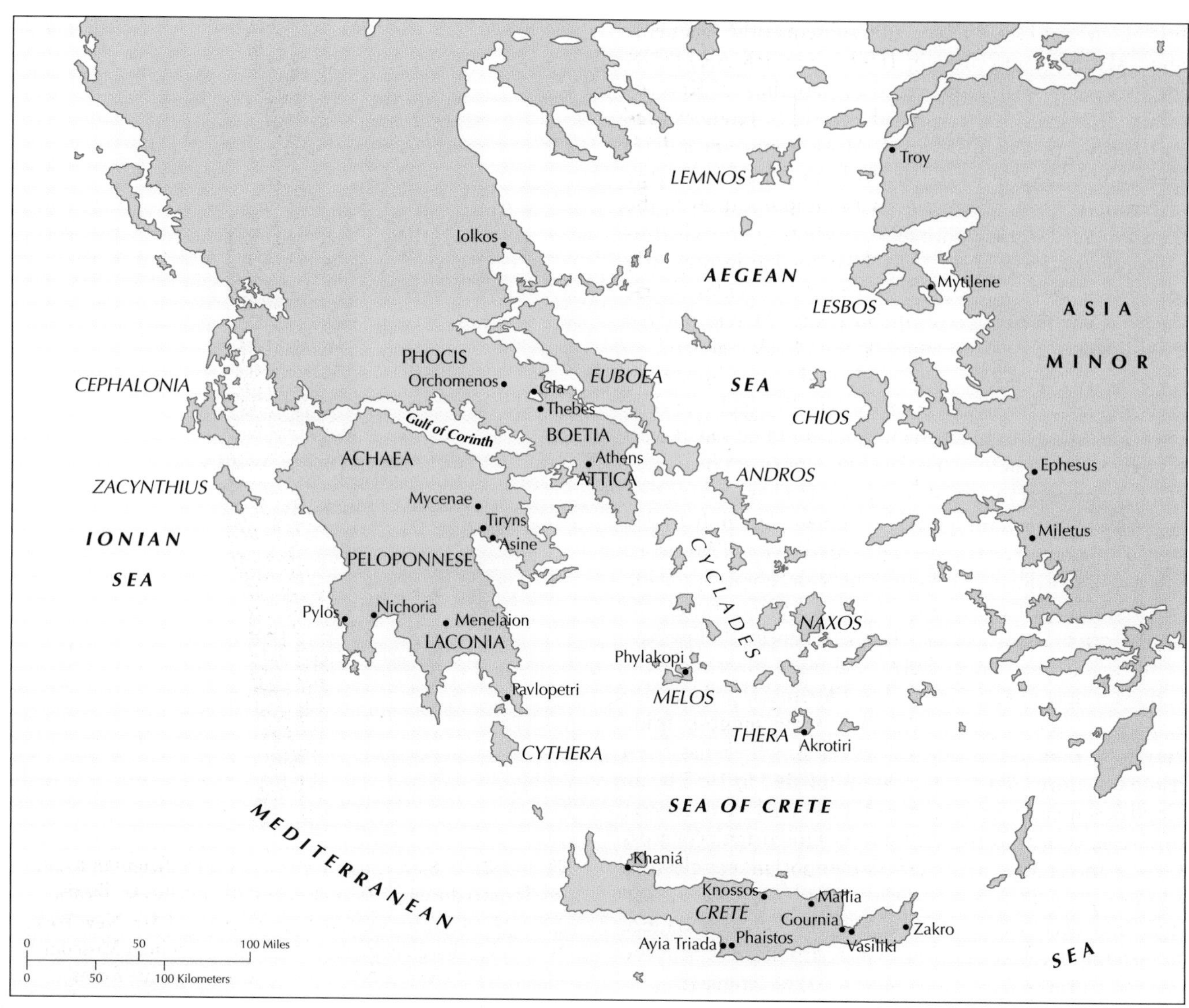

MAP 2.1 The Aegean world.

CHAPTER OVERVIEW

AEGEAN CULTURES

Early Mediterranean people, mythology, and the arts

RISE OF ANCIENT GREECE

Western civilization takes root

AEGEAN CULTURES

We now know that between approximately 3000 and 1100 B.C.E., prior to the rise of the Greek city-states, a number of cultures flourished along the coasts of the eastern Mediterranean and on the islands in the Aegean Sea. However, until about 1870, the existence of these cultures—Troy in Anatolia, Mycenae on mainland Greece, and Knossos on Crete—was considered more likely than not the creation of one poet's imagination. For the principal evidence for these great early cultures was to be found in Homer's Greek epics, *The Iliad* and *The Odyssey*. But when the archaeologist HEINRICH SCHLIEMANN [SHLEE-man] (1822–1890) first uncovered Helen's Troy and, subsequently, Agamemnon's Mycenae, and then, in 1899, when SIR ARTHUR EVANS (1851–1941) uncovered the labyrinth of Knossos on Crete, it became clear that the world of Homer's *Iliad* and *Odyssey* had really existed. More important still, it seemed that the stories and myths from these Bronze Age civilizations were, at some deep and important level, the basis of later Greek traditions and beliefs. Three civilizations rose to dominance in quick succession in this early Aegean period: the Cycladic culture on the Cyclades islands, the Minoan culture centered on the island of Crete, and the Mycenaean or Helladic culture on the Greek mainland.

Early Aegean culture was dominated by one important geographical factor, the Aegean Sea itself, which was dotted with over a thousand islands and could be sailed with confidence long before the development of sophisticated navigational equipment. What appears to have been a rich maritime culture developed. The Minoans certainly traded with mainland Greece, especially with the city of Mycenae. There is also evidence of commerce with Egypt. Surviving tablets found at Knossos on Crete are written in two different scripts known as Linear A and Linear B. The first of these remains undeciphered, although there are indications it may have originated in Phoenicia, present-day Lebanon. Such linguistic influence again suggests trade contacts. The second script, Linear B, which has been dated to before 1460 B.C.E., was deciphered in 1952 by an English scholar, who discovered it to be an early version of Greek. It has also been found on similar tablets across Greece and at Mycenae itself. Two important conclusions can be drawn from this. In the first place, Mycenaeans must have occupied Crete by 1460 B.C.E. Second, and more important, is the suggestion that by around this date the Aegean cultures shared a common, Greek language.

CYCLADIC CULTURE

The most ancient of the Aegean civilizations developed in the Cyclades in the second half of the third millennium B.C.E. (2500–2000 B.C.E.). It continued to thrive, probably under the influence of the Minoan civilization in Crete, to the south, until the middle of the second millennium B.C.E.

Many statuettes found in tombs in the Cyclades were carved of marble in workshops there during the third and second millennia B.C.E. They range in size from a few inches to lifesize. The marble statuette of a nude female with her arms crossed over her body (fig. 2.1) is characteristic of most extant examples of Cycladic art. The only indication of attire or jewelry are lines incised at the neck. Although the legs are together and straight, the figure was not made to stand up. These Cycladic figures are presumed in general to represent the Mother Goddess, bringer of fertility and the major deity in the ancient Aegean. Since they were often buried with people, they are also presumed to have had a part in the funeral ritual.

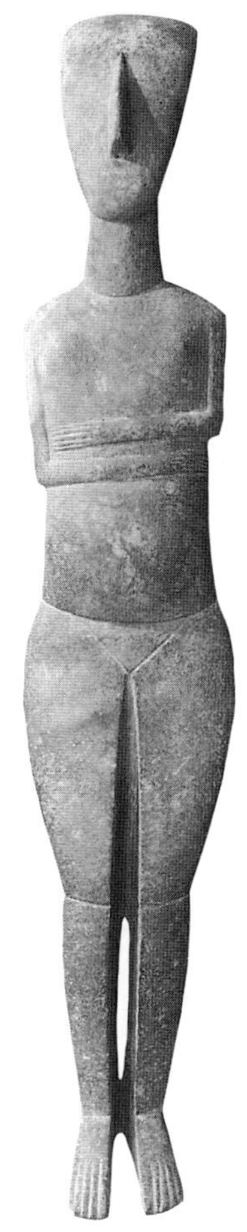

FIGURE 2.1 Statuette of a woman, third millennium B.C.E., marble, height $24\frac{3}{4}$″ (62.9 cm), Gift of Christos G. Bastis, 1968 (68.148). The Metropolitan Museum of Art, New York, NY, U.S.A. Image copyright © The Metropolitan Museum of Art/Art Resource, NY. This flattened physique forms a striking contrast to the bulbous body of the prehistoric *Woman of Willendorf* (see fig. 1.2). Yet this Cycladic figure, and others like it, are also thought to have been connected with early beliefs about human fertility.

The non-naturalistic anatomy of the carving is characteristically Cycladic. An angular torso is flattened and two dimensional; a cylindrical neck supports an oval head, flattened on top, with receding forehead. The eyes would probably have been painted on, and lips and ears may have been carved in relief. But the most notable facial feature is the particularly prominent nose. The proportions of the Cycladic figures vary somewhat—some are rounder, others more angular, the shoulders and hips broader or narrower. The pose, however, is almost unvarying.

A number of wall paintings discovered at Akrotiri on Thera include a landscape unlike any other known to have survived from antiquity (fig. 2.2). Swallows fly above a landscape consisting of a series of jagged peaks, with giant plumes of red lilies erupting from their tops and sides. It is thought that the art of wall painting was probably brought to the Cyclades from

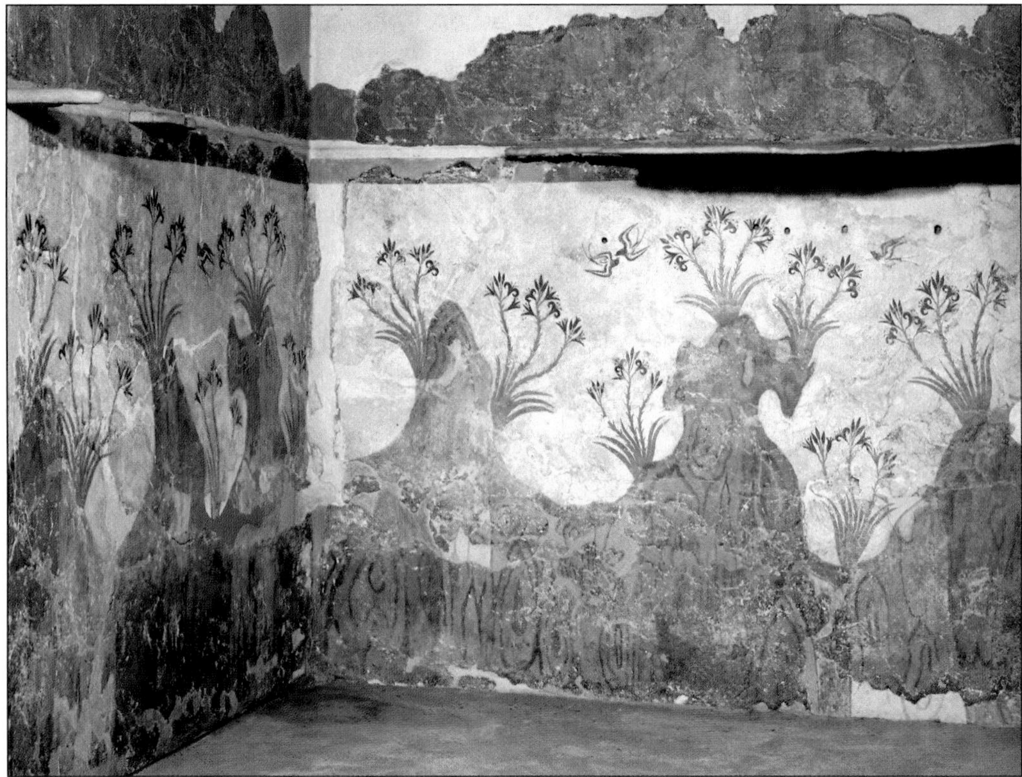

FIGURE 2.2 *Landscape*, from Akrotiri, Thera, Cyclades, before 1630–1500 B.C.E., wall painting with areas of modern reconstruction, Museum of Prehistoric Thera. Recently discovered, these murals show an affection for nature, though the subjects are by no means copied literally. Rather, nature's forms have been translated by the painters into a colorful, rhythmic decoration. The result is quite unlike anything else known from antiquity.

Crete soon after 1700 B.C.E., but nothing like this work is found in Minoan culture.

MINOAN CULTURE

According to later Greek myth, the Minoan civilization on the island of Crete was created by an offspring of Zeus, the chief deity in the Greek pantheon of the gods. Zeus's main characteristics include his ability to change his physical form and his attraction to mortal women. On one occasion, Zeus is said to have fallen in love with Europa, a Phoenician princess. He, therefore, transformed himself into a beautiful white bull and approached Europa who, entranced by the creature, climbed onto its back. Zeus immediately flew up into the sky with his prey. According to the myth, the product of their union was King Minos, the founder of the civilization on Crete. It was after this king that the archaeologist Sir Arthur Evans later named Minoan civilization. Evans's archaeological work established that life had flourished on the island between around 2800 B.C.E. and 1400 B.C.E., a period that Evans subdivided into three main phases—Early Minoan, Middle Minoan, and Late Minoan. It was with the beginning of the Middle Minoan phase, ca. 2000 B.C.E., that the civilization appeared to have developed significantly, at which time a series of large urban centers grew up on the island at Knossos, Phaistos, Mallia, and Zakro.

The Minoans were sailors and traders. Crete, which is the largest of the Aegean islands, nearly 150 miles in length, was provided with natural protection by the sea; life was secure on this idyllic island. Consequently military subjects are rarely found in Minoan painting and sculpture, and Minoan architecture is not fortified. Moreover, the extant Minoan architecture is largely domestic and secular, for although religion appears to have played an important cultural role, temples do not seem to have been a part of it. The most significant architectural remains are generally referred to as palaces, although they appear to have served a wide variety of functions beyond simply housing the ruling families.

Palace of Minos. The major surviving Minoan architectural monument is the so-called Palace of Minos at Knossos, built between 1700 and 1300 B.C.E. The palace was continually modified—parts were added, demolished, and reconstructed, until the arrangement seemed to be without a plan. It was also enormous, once covering six acres and including 1,300 rooms. Built around a central courtyard and several smaller courtyards, the palace is a seemingly arbitrary accumulation of rooms linked together by corridors, highly irregular and confused in layout. The Greeks later referred to it as the "Labyrinth," meaning literally the House of the Double Axes (from the Greek *labyrs*, "double ax"). Over time, however, the word **labyrinth** has taken on the meaning of "maze."

Open and airy, the palace was constructed with many porticoes, staircases, airshafts, and lightwells (uncovered vertical shafts in buildings allowing light into the lower stories), and built on several levels and in several stories—up to five stories in some areas. But the room ceilings were low and, consequently, the palace never rose very high. The wall surfaces were stuccoed and covered with **murals.**

The Minoans built with an unusual and distinctive type of column. The Minoan column is referred to as an "inverted" column because, unlike the later Greek column, it tapers downward, the diameter being smaller at the bottom than at the top. The columns were made of wood rather than stone and were painted bright red. They stood on simple stone bases and were topped by bulging cushion-shaped capitals (fig. 2.3). Replicas now line the Great Staircase of the palace at Knossos. This impressive staircase once served as a lightwell and gave access to all five stories of the palace.

FIGURE 2.3 Palace of Minos, Knossos, Crete, ca. 1700–1300 B.C.E., staircase in east wing with inverted columns. Structurally as sound as the usual column shape that tapers to the top (compare the columns on the ancient Greek Parthenon, fig. 3.3), this inverted shape, which tapers toward the bottom, is a characteristic of Minoan architecture.

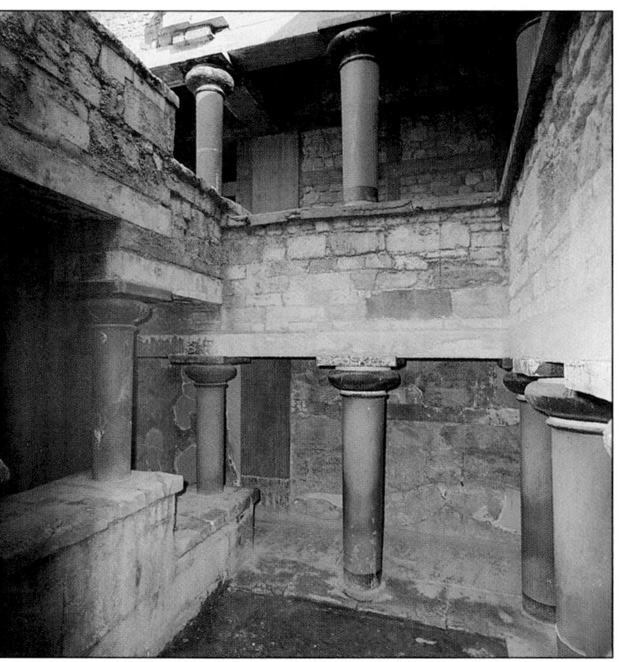

The basement of the palace was the storage area for food, supplies, and valuables. Some of the earthenware storage vases remain in place. These huge **pithoi** (singular, **pithos**) were used to store oil, grain, dried fish, beans, and olives. The palace was a self-sufficient unit that included oil and wine presses as well as grain mills. Highly valued items, such as those made of gold and other precious materials, were stored beneath the floor of the basement. These objects were placed in carefully cut holes lined with stone slabs.

Because of today's tendency to judge other cultures on the basis of their plumbing and level of sanitation, it may also be worth mentioning that the palace had fine bathrooms with decorated **terra cotta** bathtubs, as well as good plumbing and an effective sewage system.

Toreador Fresco. The Minoans made lavish use of wall paintings. The most famous example features the bull, known to have been a sacred animal on Crete. Known as the *Toreador Fresco* (fig. 2.4), it was painted around 1550–1450 B.C.E. in the Palace of Minos at Knossos. The dark areas are original; the rest is restoration. The activity depicted here is bull-vaulting, in which a person jumps over a running bull's back. As the painting illustrates, when the bull charges, the jumper must "take the bull by the horns," so to speak, vault onto its back, and hope to land standing up like the figure on the far right of this painting. Despite the fact that there are other representations of this activity, the purpose of bull-vaulting remains unclear. It may have been a means of sacrificing people or it may have been an early form of bullfighting; whether this was a ritual or a sport remains uncertain. It has even been questioned if the

FIGURE 2.4 *Toreador Fresco*, from the Palace of Minos at Knossos, Crete, ca. 1550–1450 B.C.E., wall painting, height with border ca. $24\frac{1}{2}''$ (62.2 cm), Archaeological Museum, Herakleion (Iraklion), Crete. The importance of the bull in Minoan culture is evidenced by this display of bull vaulting. In spite of extensive restoration, the delicacy and lively animation typical of Minoan wall painting remains evident.

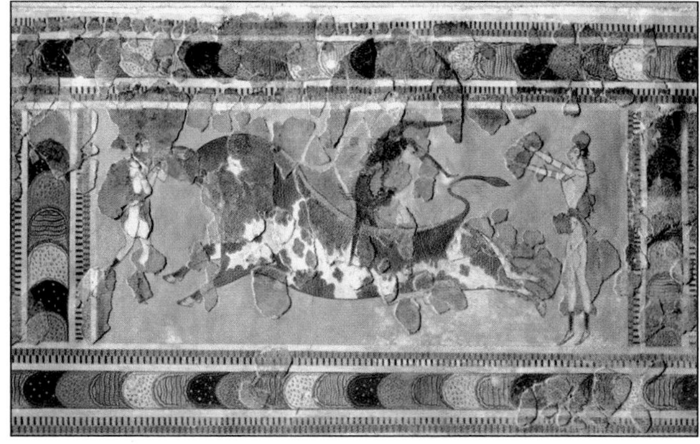

Then & Now

SNAKE GODDESS

The efforts of the Feminist movement in the United States and Europe in the late 1960s and early 1970s gave rise not only to a vast array of social and political reforms but to revisions of historical interpretation as well. Most art history texts before the early 1970s, reflecting the social balance within the society that produced them, paid little or no attention to art by women, and most works of art were viewed from a particularly male perspective. Attempting to redress the balance, Feminist historians became especially interested in the art of Aegean civilizations because it seemed that artifacts such as the Minoan *Snake Goddess* (fig. 2.5) were the products of a matriarchal culture in which women, rather than men, played the dominant roles.

Key to this theory is a 1976 book by Merlin Stone entitled *When God Was a Woman.* "It was quite apparent," Stone wrote, describing her research into Aegean culture, "that the myths and legends that grew from, and were propagated by, a religion in which the deity was female, and revered as wise, valiant, powerful and just, provided very different images from those which are offered by the male-oriented religions of today." If it were a male, King Minos, for example, who exercised governmental authority, it was perhaps the female goddess who exercised spiritual and moral authority in Crete.

The demonization of woman has had a long tradition in Western culture dating from the Ancient Sumerian epic of Gilgamesh with its snakes and dangerously seductive women. This demonization is reflected in the Greek transformation of the Minoan Snake Goddess into the mythic figure of the Medusa, whose hair is a nest of vipers and whose gaze turns men into stone, as well as in the Christian story of Eve's seduction by the Devil, who, significantly, takes the form of a snake, bringing about humankind's expulsion from Paradise.

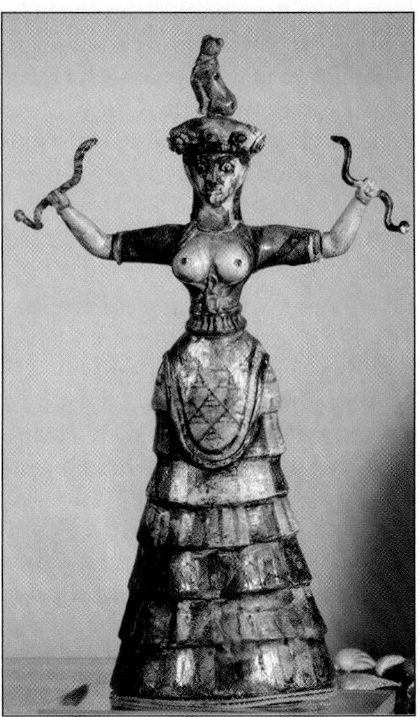

FIGURE 2.5 *Snake Goddess,* ca. 1700–1500 B.C.E., faience, height $11\frac{5}{8}''$ (29.5 cm), Archaeological Museum of Herakleion, Crete, Greece. Minoan religion focused on female deities. In Minoan art, both women and men were depicted with unusually tiny waists and long flowing hair.

acrobatic feat depicted is actually possible, but no one has come forward with an offer to prove it one way or the other.

Snake Goddess. Although the Minoans produced no large-scale sculpture in the round, they did create small-scale figures. The best known example of Minoan sculpture is the *Snake Goddess,* or *Snake Priestess,* a statuette made of **faience,** a lustrous glazed ceramic, ca. 1700–1500 B.C.E. (see fig. 2.5). The physical type of the statuette, with its rounded limbs and body and pinched waist, is typically Minoan. The chief deities of the Minoan religion were female—mother or fertility goddesses. The goddess portrayed here holds a snake in each hand. In many religions snakes were associated with earth deities and with male fertility. Snakes were believed to be in direct contact with the gods of the lower world and therefore supposed to be able to cure disease and restore life. The snakes, combined with the goddess's frankly female form and bared breasts, suggest fertility.

MYCENAEAN CULTURE

Beginning about 2000 B.C.E., Greek-speaking peoples began to invade the Greek mainland, inaugurating the Mycenaean or Helladic Age (*Hellas* is the Greek word for "Greece"). After about 1500 B.C.E., when Minoan culture began to decline, these mainland peoples started to have increasing influence throughout the region. As opposed to the islanders, who relied on the sea for protection and whose palaces were, as a result, open and airy, the mainland Greeks built strong fortresses and, under continual threat of invasion from the north, were evidently much more concerned with things military. Most of these strongholds—such as Mycenae and Tiryns—were in southern Greece, the Peloponnese, although there were also settlements in the north, in particular at Athens and Thebes. Among these, Mycenae was the most powerful and richest center; as a result, the entire culture takes its name from this city.

In Homer's *Iliad*, the Trojan War begins when the king of Mycenae, Agamemnon, leads the Greeks against the city of Troy. In legend, the battle was said to have been precipitated when the Trojan prince Paris abducted Helen, the wife of Agamemnon's brother. Homer's story seems to have had a basis in history, although it is more plausible that the Greeks were prompted in their aggression by their predilection for plunder. The Mycenaeans also conquered other territories in the Mediterranean area, including Cyprus, Rhodes, and Crete, assimilating many aspects of the defeated people's art, especially that of the Minoan civilization.

The Palace at Mycenae. The main gateway to the fortified hilltop city of Mycenae was the famous Lion Gate (fig. 2.6), built ca. 1300–1200 B.C.E. The Lion Gate is constructed of huge stones, with the horizontal **lintel** above the doorway estimated to weigh twenty tons. Above the lintel is a **relieving triangle,** an opening that serves to relieve the weight on the lintel. The relieving triangle is filled by a relatively thin slab of limestone on which lions are carved in relief. Symmetrical rampant guardian lions, muscular and powerful, flank a Minoan column—an "inverted" column that tapers downward and has a cushion-like capital. This relief is the oldest piece of monumental sculpture in Europe.

The Lion Gate leads to, among other structures extant at Mycenae, the so-called Treasury of Atreus (fig. 2.7), built ca. 1300–1200 B.C.E. Atreus was the father of Agamemnon. The building was given its name by the archaeologist Heinrich Schliemann, who had a fanatical interest in Homer's heroes. It is, however, a little misleading, since it was neither a treasury nor was it associated with Atreus. It was actually a tomb.

The **dromos,** or entranceway, was cut into the hillside, and the walls were lined with **ashlar masonry,** in which each stone is carefully cut with right-angle corners. At the end of the dromos, the doorway to the tomb is surmounted by a lintel and a relieving triangle. Originally the doorway facade was elaborately decorated with carved reliefs of various colored stones, and the doorway was flanked by slender columns carved with ornamental relief, the columns tapering downward in the Minoan manner. The tomb itself is a **tholos** (plural, **tholoi**), the term for any round building, in this case a domed circular tomb shaped like a beehive about 43 feet high. The technical name for this kind of structure is a **corbeled dome.** Such a building is constructed by first digging a circular pit in the earth. Courses of ashlar masonry are then laid in a circle around the circumference of this space, each successive course slightly overhanging the one below, gradually diminishing the diameter of the circle, until a single stone, the "capstone," covers the small remaining opening. The projecting corners of the masonry blocks are then cut off and smoothed to create a continuous curving surface.

FIGURE 2.6 Lion Gate, entrance to Mycenae, Greece, ca. 1300–1200 B.C.E., limestone, height of relief ca. 9′6″ (2.89 m). The lion, the animal most frequently depicted throughout the history of art, was often used as a guardian figure.

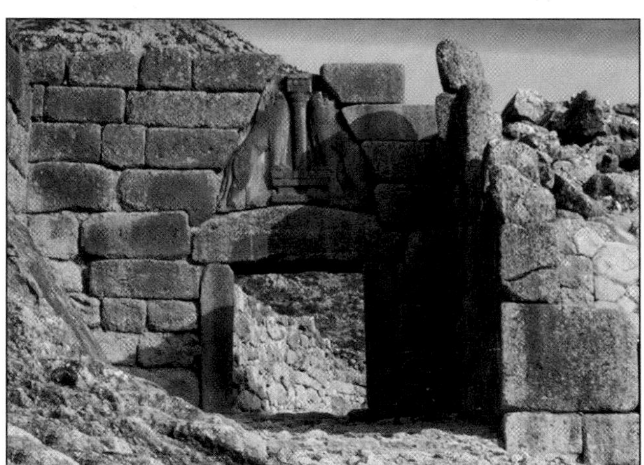

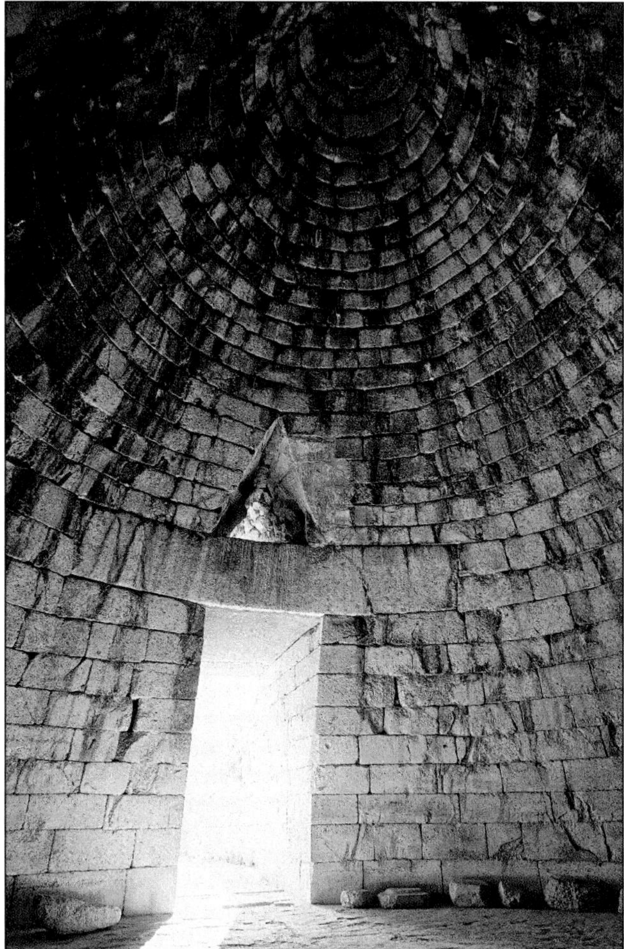

FIGURE 2.7 Interior, Treasury of Atreus, Mycenae, Greece, ca. 1300–1200 B.C.E., stone, height of vault ca. 43′ (13.11 m), diameter 47′6″ (14.48 m). The final step in the construction of a corbeled dome was to cut off all projecting edges and smooth the stone surface into a continuous curve.

Then & Now

Heinrich Schliemann and the Modern Discovery of Troy

Born into a poor German family, Heinrich Schliemann (d. 1890) was a linguistic genius who learned Russian in six weeks, became involved in the indigo trade in Moscow, cornered the market, and became very rich while still a young man. He amassed more wealth by establishing a banking and loan business in California. He divorced his first wife because she was not interested in archaeology; among his second wife's attractions was the fact that she knew *The Iliad* in Greek by heart—the new couple entertained themselves by reciting passages in turn.

Schliemann was convinced Homer's *Iliad* was factual and the location of Troy could be determined from descriptions in the story. Excavation began in 1870. In 1873, Schliemann found walls and believed he had discovered ancient Troy. However, he was having difficulty obtaining permission to excavate from the Turkish government, which feared Schliemann would steal any treasure he might find. These fears were well founded, for when Schliemann came upon a few gold objects, he dismissed the workmen and dug out these objects with the aid of his wife. The Schliemanns concealed their finds, probably hiding them in Greece.

The city of Troy was in nine levels. Although Schliemann believed Homer's Troy was at the second level from the bottom, Troy Two, it was, in fact, Troy Six or Seven; Homer's Troy was about a millennium more recent than Schliemann thought. Yet Schliemann did prove the Trojan War was fact, and his finds provided great impetus to the study of archaeology, a new field in the 1870s. Considered the founder of modern archaeology, Heinrich Schliemann excavated at Troy, Mycenae, Tiryns, and Orchomenos.

Just inside the Lion Gate at Mycenae is Royal Grave Circle A (there is also a second—Grave Circle B), dated 1600–1500 B.C.E., which was excavated by Schliemann in 1876. Schliemann found that this double circle of stone slabs enclosed six shaft graves. In these graves Schliemann found golden treasure. Many of the bodies buried here had been literally laden with gold. Two children were found wrapped in sheets of gold. Among the objects unearthed here were a magnificent gold diadem embossed with geometric patterns, small individual ornaments of gold plate sewn or stuck onto the clothing, a **rhyton** (drinking vessel) in the shape of a lion's head, gold cups, bronze dagger blades inlaid with gold, silver, and copper, a gold breast plate, and gold masks (fig. 2.8), some of which were found placed over the faces of the dead. These last were made of thin sheet gold and hammered into shape over a wooden core.

The objects found in the excavations of Grave Circle A make it easy to understand why Homer referred to the city of Mycenae as *polychrysos*—"rich in gold." These are the graves of the nobility—the Mycenaean ruling system was one of family dynasties—but they are not the graves of Atreus and Agamemnon, even though the mask illustrated here is often referred to as the "mask of Agamemnon." In fact, the mask predates any possible Mycenaean invasion of Troy by nearly three hundred years (the Trojan War is now dated to ca. 1250 B.C.E.).

The Warrior Vase. Probably no surviving artifact better embodies the warlike character of the Mycenaeans than the famed Warrior Vase (fig. 2.9), made ca. 1200 B.C.E. Between bands of decoration, soldiers march, seemingly in single file. At the far left, a woman raises her arm to bid farewell to the troops. The execution of the painting is careless, the figures are caricatures, and the vase itself is crudely constructed. The base is significantly smaller than the opening, making the shape unstable and impractical. The Warrior Vase dates from the end of the

FIGURE 2.8 Gold mask, from tomb V of Grave Circle A, Mycenae, Greece, ca. 1550–1500 B.C.E., gold, height ca. 12″ (30.5 cm), National Archaeological Museum, Athens/Hirmer Fotoarchiv, Munich, Germany. The rich burials of Mycenaean nobility included a variety of sheet gold objects. Homer described Mycenae as "rich in gold."

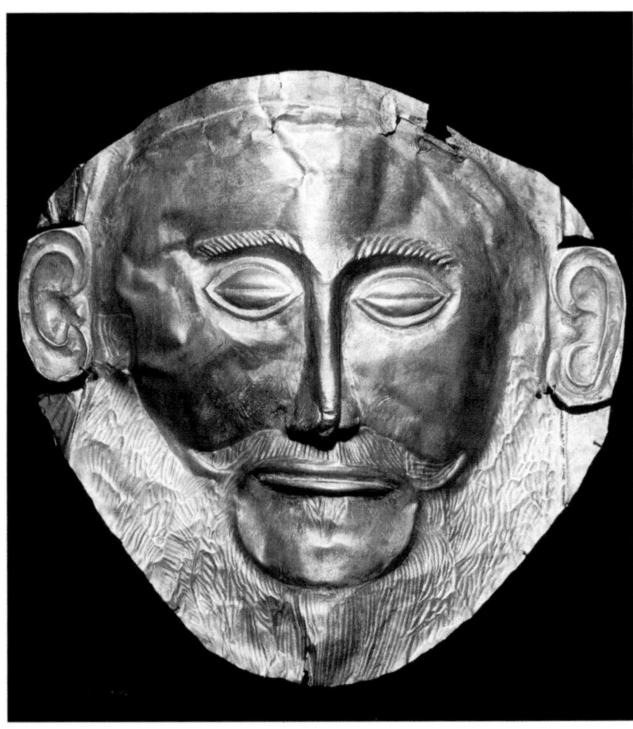

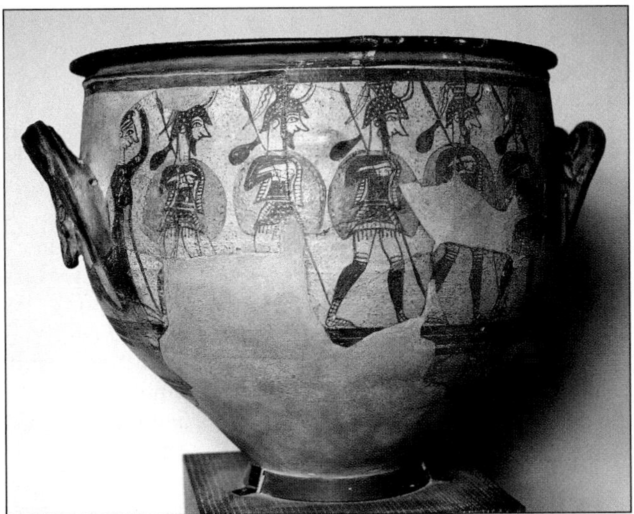

FIGURE 2.9 *Warrior Vase*, from Mycenae, Greece, ca. 1200 B.C.E., terra cotta, height ca. 16″ (40.6 cm), National Archaeological Museum, Athens. Differing from the characteristic flora-and-fauna decoration of the Minoans, whose safety was ensured by their island location, the war motifs of this vase reflect the more military aspect of Mycenaean life. Although not realistically drawn, the decoration of the Warrior Vase provides a document of early defensive arms and armor.

Mycenaean civilization and, in its unrefined execution and decoration, can be seen to portend the destruction of social order in Mycenae. Around 1100 B.C.E. the Aegean civilization died out, resulting in a period of decline in which writing seems to have disappeared, and art-making ground to a halt. Faced with Dorian invaders from the north, whose weapons were made of iron instead of bronze—perhaps the very invaders the soldiers depicted on the Warrior Vase are marching to meet—Mycenaean civilization collapsed.

RISE OF ANCIENT GREECE

Mycenaean civilization, and with it the Bronze Age in the Aegean, came to an abrupt end around 1100 B.C.E. During the following century, many of the accomplishments of the previous millennia appear to have been forgotten. Not until around 1000 B.C.E. did the Greeks of the mainland begin to forge a new civilization that would culminate in the fifth century B.C.E. in the achievements of Classical Athens. The history of Greece in the intervening centuries is usually subdivided into several phases: the Geometric period, ca. 1000–700 B.C.E.; the Orientalizing period, a period of Greek colonization and contact with the East, ca. 700–600 B.C.E.; and the Archaic period, ca. 600–480 B.C.E. It was owing to the achievements of these five hundred years that Greek culture was able to flourish so spectacularly after 480 B.C.E. and that the artistic, cultural, and political foundations of modern Western civilization were laid.

PANTHEON OF GREEK GODS

According to Greek **mythology,** before the world was created, before the division into earth, water, and sky, there was Chaos. From this Chaos there emerged a god named URANOS [YOOR-ah-noss], representing the heavens, and a goddess named GAEA [JEE-ah], representing the earth. Their union produced a race of giants called the Titans. One of these, KRONOS [KROH-nos], overthrew his father, Uranos, and married his sister RHEA [REE-ah]. Their offspring were the Olympian gods. However, there was a prophecy that Kronos himself would be overthrown by one of his own children, and so to forestall this he decided to eat all his own progency. Only ZEUS [ZOOSS] survived, saved by Rhea. When Zeus ultimately and inevitably revolted against his father, Kronos regurgitated all the other children—DEMETER [du-MEE-ter], the goddess of agriculture and fertility; HERA [HEAR-ah], goddess of marriage and stability; HADES [HAY-deez], god of the underworld; POSEIDON [pu-SIGH-dun], god of the sea; and HESTIA [HESS-tiah], goddess of the hearth and home. Zeus married Hera, and from them emerged a second order of gods and goddesses: APOLLO [a-POLL-oh], who as god of the sun and light represents intellectual beauty; DIONYSOS [die-oh-KNEE-see-us], god of wine and revelry; APHRODITE [ah-fro-DI-tee], goddess of love, who represents physical beauty; ARES [AIR-ease], god of war; and ARTEMIS [AR-tum-iss], goddess of the moon and the hunt. ATHENA [a-THEE-nuh], goddess of wisdom, and of the arts and crafts, and patron goddess of Athens, sprang full grown from the brow of Zeus himself—a pure idea.

It was Prometheus, a Titan, who first took earth, mixed it with water, and fashioned human beings out of the resulting mud, forming them in the image of the gods. His brother fashioned the animals, bestowing on them the various gifts of courage, strength, swiftness, and wisdom, together with the claws, shells, and wings that distinguish them from one another. The first woman was Pandora, a joint creation of all the gods. According to one version of the story, each of the gods gave her something—Aphrodite gave her beauty, Hermes the gift of persuasion, Apollo musical skill. Zeus presented her to Prometheus's brother, and she brought with her a box containing all her marriage presents. When she opened the box, all the blessings escaped—except hope! In another, darker version, Pandora was given to humankind as a punishment, and the jar she carried contained curses that plague humans.

Unlike the gods of the ancient Hebrews and of India, those of ancient Greece could rarely be counted on for help. Exceptions are Prometheus, who gave humans fire, and Athena, who helped Odysseus in many ways. Traditionally inhabiting the top of Mount Olympus, in northeastern Greece, the Greek pantheon, the family headed by Zeus, supervises human society. Unlike the Christian system, there is no god who represents complete good or complete evil.

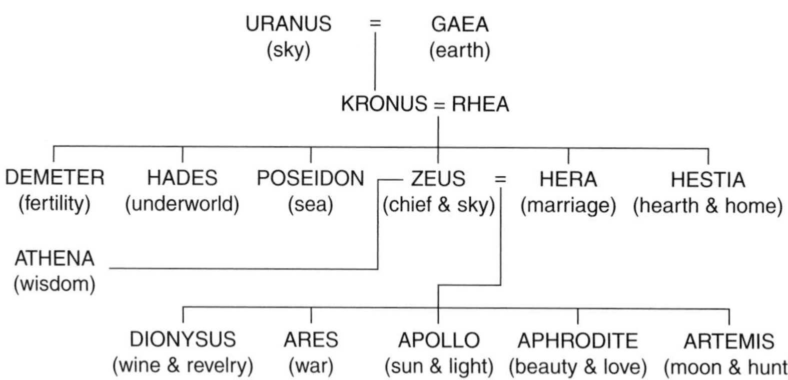

Zeus is a patriarch, a father, in some sense a model for the tyrant of the Greek polis, but frequently an adulterous husband. His wife, Hera, is often jealous with good cause. Their marital relationship reflects the weakness of human relationships, and their monumental jealousies and rages were reflected not only in the devastating wars that disrupted Greek life but also in the petty animosities that spoiled civic harmony.

Fate, however, was a reality that transcended the power of the gods. And although there was no single "God" with absolute power, there was a coherence to the Greek mythological universe that set limits to the power of the gods. The ancient Greek attitude toward their gods embodied their skeptical view of human nature, and many of the more famous Greek myths reflect this. However, unlike Christianity and Judaism, Greek culture never developed a single unified account of these myths, which exist instead in many varying forms.

Mystery Cults. As with other cultural traditions, Greek myths served as the basis for religious cults, which created a sense of community among disparate groups that comprised the Greek populace. Cults, such as the Eleusinian mystery cult, conducted special rituals open only to initiates or cult members. The Eleusinians emphasized strong moral standards, and they held a ritual meal. Other cults, such as the fertility cult of the goddess Demeter, admitted only women. Such cults provided women, who were excluded from political life, with roles outside the home. Demeter cult members would gather on a hill for three days, offer sacrifices to the goddess, and hold a communal feast of celebration.

Perhaps the best known of the Greek cults was the cult of Dionysus, the god of wine and revelry, whose mysteries were celebrated in the spring. Dionysian revelers would stream into the mountains to dance and sing to frenzied music, which drove the celebrants to rip apart sacrificial victims, usually a goat, but on occasion a human being.

Oracles. Oracles were religious professionals who interpreted the will of the gods. The most famous of the Greek oracles was the oracle of Apollo at Delphi. This oracle was a woman who was reputed to receive cryptic messages from the god while she was in a trance. Messages relayed to the oracles typically took the form of riddles, which demanded careful analysis and interpretation. One inquiry of the Delphic oracle was made by King Croesus of Lydia, who asked whether he should wage war against the Persians. The oracle's answer was that if Croesus did war against Persia, a mighty empire would be destroyed. Croesus thought that the prophecy referred to the destruction of Persia; however, it was his own empire that fell at the hands of the Persian king Cyrus. Another famous inquiry was brought by Oedipus, who sought the oracle's help in identifying the murderer of King Laius, who, unbeknown to Oedipus, was his biological father. What the oracle said, how it was interpreted, and what consequences resulted are described in Sophocles's play *Oedipus the King*.

THE GEOMETRIC PERIOD

The Geometric period (ca. 1000–700 B.C.E.) is sometimes referred to as the Heroic Age, since it was during this time that Homer created his poetic epics, *The Iliad* and *The Odyssey*, centered on the figures of the great heroes Achilles and Odysseus. The other arts are less well preserved for us now. There is very little trace of architecture and not much sculpture. Most of the evidence for the visual art of the period is derived from pottery.

Cultural development in this period appears to have been slow. After the destruction of the Mycenaean empire, mainland Greece lacked a political center. When communities began to emerge, as at Athens in Attica and at Sparta in Laconia, they took the form of independent city-states, **poleis** (singular, **polis**).

The development of the Greek polis, which provided the focus for political, artistic, and religious activities in the region, is central to the later Western ideal of democracy. However, in this early period, each polis was ruled by a council of aristocrats. It is also important to note that the polis, with its tradition of fierce independence, meant that even at its artistic and cultural

Cross Currents

HESIOD'S *THEOGONY* AND MESOPOTAMIAN CREATION MYTHS

In his *Theogony*, HESIOD [HEH-see-ud] (ca. seventh century B.C.E.) presents a poetic account of the origins of the Greek gods. The *Theogony* identifies Gaia as the original divine being. Gaia is both the physical earth and a giant humanlike deity who produces her own mate, Uranos, the sky. This primal couple then spawns the first beings, the Titans, whom Uranos tries to eliminate by stuffing them back into the recesses of their mother. One of these children, the Titan Kronos, slays his father and replaces him as Gaia's consort.

Like his father Uranos, Kronos disposes of his offspring. However, one child, Zeus, is saved by Gaia and grows in safety until he can liberate the other devoured children, battle with the Titans, and displace his father as the chief male deity.

The Greek account of the origin of the gods is indebted to various Mesopotamian creation accounts. From Mesopotamia, Greece derived the idea of projecting a magnified version of human power onto the divine realm. Greece also borrowed the idea of the universe as a city governed by a succession of rulers, each displaced by the next in a power struggle. Moreover, with its lists of succeeding gods, Hesiod's *Theogony* echoes Mesopotamian lists of kings, which are traced back genealogically to the gods. Both Mesopotamian and ancient Greek poetry account for the order and hierarchy of the universe.

Like Homer's epics, Hesiod's works had a profound effect on succeeding generations of Greek culture. Hesiod's poems were considered repositories of wisdom and technical knowledge about a host of matters, including farming and war. The works of both Homer and Hesiod went on to form the foundation of classical Athenian education in the fifth century B.C.E.

height in the fifth century B.C.E., Greece remained politically fragmented and always on the verge of violent self-destruction. Athens and Sparta, for instance, remained hostile neighbors. Their temporary alliance in the early fifth century B.C.E. managed to beat off Persian invaders, but Greek civilization was delivered a fatal blow later in the same century by the Peloponnesian War between these same two city-states.

Ceramics. There was undoubtedly some cultural continuity between Mycenaean Greece and the civilization that reemerged after 1000 B.C.E. However, the distinctive style of art that appears around the latter date was probably influenced by the Dorian invaders. Known as the **Geometric style** and characterized by geometric forms, it soon dominated the art of the Greek mainland.

Geometric pottery is distinguished by decoration in bands that cover the entire surface, the decoration adapted to the zones or divisions of the vase. In contrast, the decoration on earlier Aegean pottery flows over the entire surface of the object.

A characteristic example of the Geometric style is the eighth-century B.C.E. terra cotta **krater,** a large vase with a wide mouth, seen in fig. 2.10. The subject depicted on this vase, used to mark a burial, is a common one: mourners lamenting the deceased, who is shown lying on a funeral bier. Funerary processions are pictured going from the home of the deceased to the cemetery. Other Dipylon vases include depictions of funeral processions, horse-drawn chariots, animals to be eaten at the funeral banquet, and funeral games—it was customary to have games at funerals in honor of the deceased. Significant to the future course of vase painting is the beginning of narrative. Greek potters would increasingly decorate a greater percentage of the surface with larger and more representational figures that relate a tale.

FIGURE 2.10 *Funerary Crater*, attributed to the Hirschfeld Workshop. Terra cotta, height $42\frac{5}{8}''$ (108.3 cm.), dia. at mount $28\frac{1}{2}''$ (72.4 cm). The Metropolitan Museum of Art, Rogers Fund, 1914 (14.130.14). Photograph © 1996 The Metropolitan Museum of Art. Geometric-style vases are, as the term indicates, decorated with precisely drawn, simple geometric forms. Each of the several shapes of Greek vases has a name and was used for a specific purpose; this very large krater was used as a burial marker.

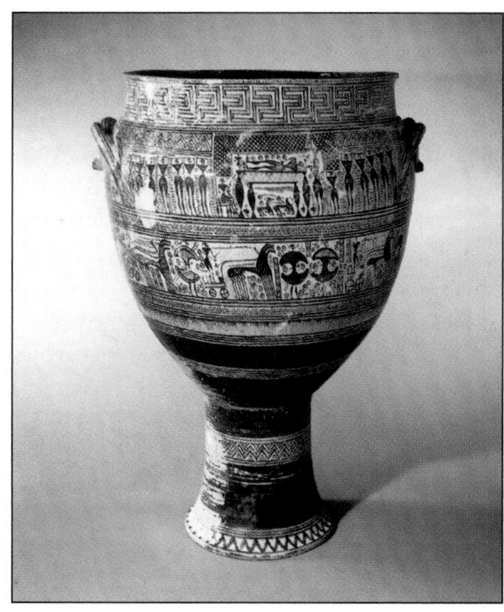

Sculpture. Prior to the mid-seventh century B.C.E., Greek sculptors restricted their work to small-scale pieces in wood, clay, ivory, and bronze (bronze casting of sculpture seems to have started in Greece in the ninth century B.C.E.). All work in perishable materials has been lost, but there are a few extant ivory pieces and many fine bronzes.

The surviving examples, found in tombs and sanctuaries, are statuettes of humans and animals. Bronze cows and rams were used as votive offerings to the gods in place of actual sacrificial animals. Because horses were associated with certain goddesses and gods, they received special attention and may have been used as votive offerings to the deities. The example shown here (fig. 2.11) dates to the second half of the eighth century B.C.E. This late Geometric horse is simplified, abstracted, and highly sophisticated. It is representative of a physical type found in sculpture and in painting—the horse looks like those on contemporary Geometric vases. The pinched waist, moreover, is common to both horses and humans in Geometric art, be it in sculpture or in painting.

***Homer's* Iliad *and* Odyssey.** Greek poetry in written form begins with the two most famous epics in Western literature, *The Iliad* and *The Odyssey.* Tradition credits the authorship of these poems to Homer, about whom nothing is known with certainty except his name. Early Greeks believed Homer to have been blind, and many scholars think he lived in Ionia, in Asia Minor, but none of this is certain. Both *The Iliad* and *The Odyssey* were first put in writing during the seventh century B.C.E., although they are based on a long oral tradition predating their written versions by hundreds of years. Despite their long genesis, each epic bears the stylistic imprint and imaginative vision of a single resourceful poet.

FIGURE 2.11 Horse, second half of the eighth century B.C.E., bronze, height ca. $6\frac{3}{8}''$ (16 cm), Staatliche Museum, Berlin. In the Geometric period, forms of nature were simplified and made literally geometric; torsos of horses and humans (as on the Geometric vase in fig. 2.10) turned into triangles.

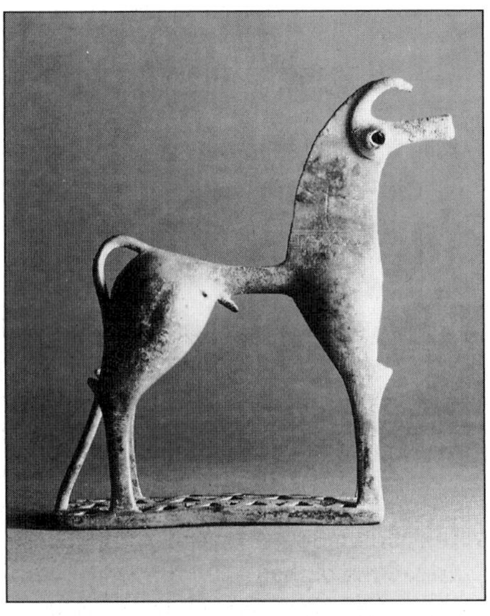

Both *The Iliad* and *The Odyssey* reflect their social context, a warring aristocratic society in which honor, courage, heroism, and cunning are the prime human virtues. The gods and goddesses of the Greek pantheon figure prominently in the Homeric epics. Each of the poems centers on a single heroic figure. *The Iliad* describes the wrath of Achilles and its consequences for himself and his comrades. *The Odyssey* tells the story of Odysseus, who, after long years spent wandering, returns to reclaim what is his own from a group of Greek princes who have more or less laid siege to his wife and home. Homer's *Iliad* and *Odyssey* have been enormously influential in the history of Western poetry. The Roman poet Virgil's *Aeneid* (see Chapter 4) and John Milton's *Paradise Lost* (see Chapter 14) both imitate Homer's epics in their different ways, to cite only two famous examples.

The Iliad describes a short period toward the end of the Trojan War (ca. 1250 B.C.E.), the ten-year siege that a band of ancient Greek military adventurers laid against the city of Troy. The work focuses on the anger and exploits of its hero, Achilles, renowned as the greatest of all soldiers. The epic begins with a quarrel between Achilles and the Greek king and military commander, Agamemnon, over the beautiful Trojan woman, Briseis. Agamemnon had taken Briseis as his royal right, even though Achilles believed he had earned her as his share of the battle spoils. Achilles expresses his disgust with Agamemnon by withdrawing sulkily and refusing to do battle with the enemy. Without Achilles' help, the Greeks are repeatedly defeated by the Trojans. Achilles returns to battle only after his friend Patroclus is killed. He kills Hector, the son of the Trojan king Priam, and abuses his corpse out of frustration and guilt at having let his friend Patroclus die through his anger. The source of the quarrel, the reason for Achilles' return to battle, and the military exploits Homer describes in vivid detail all reflect the warrior world *The Iliad* celebrates. Though the gods are present throughout to comment on the action, at the center of Homer's world are his human actors. The poet is concerned with human responsibility and motivation, and for these reasons his work stands at the very beginning of the Western literary tradition.

Although *The Iliad* glorifies great deeds performed on the battlefield, the poem also conveys a sense of war's terrible consequences. Homer vividly describes battles, with armies arrayed against one another in deadly combat. He describes with equal drama the conflicting loyalties of heroes on both sides as they take leave of their wives and families to kill one another in defense of honor and in pursuit of military glory. These heroic values are honored

Critical Thinking

THE ODYSSEY ON FILM

The Odyssey of Homer was made into a television film in 1997. Directed by Andrei Konchalovsky, it was later released in theaters and is now available on DVD. Whether or not you have seen the film version of Homer's epic, you can consider the following questions, if you have read it.

1. What do you think the director should emphasize in filming the story? Why?
2. To what extent do you think the director should include references to the Trojan War? Why?
3. What actors would you cast in the following roles: Odysseus, Penelope, Athena, Telemachus, Circe (Kirke), Calypso, Cyclops?
4. How might the gods on Mount Olympus be portrayed? Explain.

consistently throughout the epic, though *The Iliad*'s worldview is occasionally tempered by scenes that portray other, less military virtues. For example, kindheartedness and forgiveness are exemplified in the scenes between the Trojan warrior Hector and his family, and in the scene describing Achilles' meeting with the old Trojan king Priam, who comes to ask Achilles for the body of his son Hector.

Perhaps the most famous adventure story in Western literature, Homer's *Odyssey* contains a number of memorable episodes. Two of the most famous concern dangerous escapes. In one episode, Odysseus is captured by the giant one-eyed Cyclops. Odysseus gets the Cyclops drunk, blinds him with a stake, and escapes from the monster's cave by clinging to the belly of a sheep so the Cyclops cannot feel him. In a second adventure, Odysseus and his men have to sail through the dangerous seas inhabited by the Sirens, whose enchanting singing causes sailors to crash their boats on the rocky shores of their island. To avoid this fate, Odysseus plugs his men's ears with wax and then has them tie him to the mast of their ship.

These and other exotic events make *The Odyssey* different in spirit from *The Iliad.* Other differences concern *The Odyssey*'s hero, Odysseus, who after a twenty-year absence from home, returns to his wife, Penelope, and his son, Telemachos. Whereas Achilles' strength in *The Iliad* is purely physical, Odysseus also has mental fortitude. Odysseus' cunning and wit enable him to escape numerous dangerous predicaments, and he also pursues self-knowledge. Odysseus seems much more modern than Achilles, and his journeys toward understanding and toward "home" and all that means take place in a world much closer to our own than the more primitive world of *The Iliad.* Moreover, where the focus of *The Iliad* is narrowly trained on the military world, the vision of *The Odyssey* is much wider. Its values are those of home and hearth, of patience and fidelity, of filial piety, of the wisdom gained through suffering. The range and depth of its depiction of women far surpasses *The Iliad*'s image of women as the mere property of men. In addition to the clever and faithful Penelope, *The Odyssey*'s female characters include the intelligent and beautiful princess Nausicaa; the dangerously seductive witch Circe; the goddess Calypso, who offers Odysseus immortality; Athena, who serves as Odysseus' guide and protector; and Odysseus' nurse, Euryclea. Moreover, when Odysseus visits the Land of the Dead, he sees not only his mother, Anticleia, who had died in his absence, but other famous women of heroic times.

Odysseus' journey home is interrupted by his one-year stay with Circe and by the eight years he remains on Calypso's island. In total, he is absent from Penelope and home for twenty years, ten for the long siege of Troy and ten for his voyage. This long delay is due partly to Odysseus' unalterable fate and partly to his temperament. Warring within him are two contrary impulses: a wish to return to the peaceful kingdom of Ithaca, where he reigns as prince, and a desire to experience adventure and test himself against dangerous challenges. This split is echoed by the clash between Odysseus' temptation to forget his identity as husband, father, and king in his adventures, and his responsibility to resume these less exotic and more stable roles.

The Odyssey makes reference at a number of points to characters and events of *The Iliad,* most notably to the death of Achilles. In an important scene near the middle of *The Odyssey,* Homer has his hero descend to the underworld, where he meets the spirit of Achilles. Odysseus also encounters the shade of Agamemnon, whose murder by his wife serves as a warning of the fate that could befall a man who has been away too long. Homer uses the tragic story of the house of Atreus in thematic counterpoint to the duties and responsibilities of husband, wife, and son that *The Odyssey* endorses.

Insofar as they reflect an entire culture's values, the Homeric poems became the basis of Greek education. The human characters in *The Iliad* and *The Odyssey* served as models of conduct—of heroism and pride, of cunning and loyalty—for later generations. The Homeric gods, however, were less models of ideal behavior than influences on human events. Homer gives them a secondary importance, choosing instead to emphasize men and women living out mysterious destinies. Moreover, Homer reveals the gods as subject to the same implacable fate as humans. Although they are honored and worshipped by the characters, the gods are also portrayed as worthy of blame as well as praise, of laughter as well as fear.

Sappho and the Lyric Poem. As with epic poetry, there was an oral tradition of lyric poetry long before the first verse was written down. Unlike epic, which was chanted, lyric poetry was originally sung, accompanied by the lyre, the stringed instrument from which the name *lyric* derives. Also unlike epic, which flourished in Ionia, lyric flourished on the island of Lesbos, especially in the sixth century B.C.E. with the lyric poetry of Sappho [SAFF-oh] (ca. 610–580 B.C.E.). Where epic provides a somewhat distant and communal perspective on human experience in narrative, lyric offers a poetic, personal voice, an intimate expression of subjective feeling and sensation.

Sappho's fame as a poet was acclaimed by Plato, who described her as "the tenth Muse." The Early Christian Church, however, did not appreciate the sensuality of the poems, nor the lesbian subject matter of many of them. Much of Sappho's work was destroyed during the Middle Ages, with manuscripts of her poetry consigned to fires during the fourth century C.E. in Constantinople and during the eleventh century in Rome. Only a few poems remain in their entirety along with a series of fragments of others.

Little is known of Sappho's life, except she was married and had a daughter, Cleis. Even from what little survives of Sappho's works, readers can appreciate the intensity of emotion they express and the direct and graceful way they celebrate female experience.

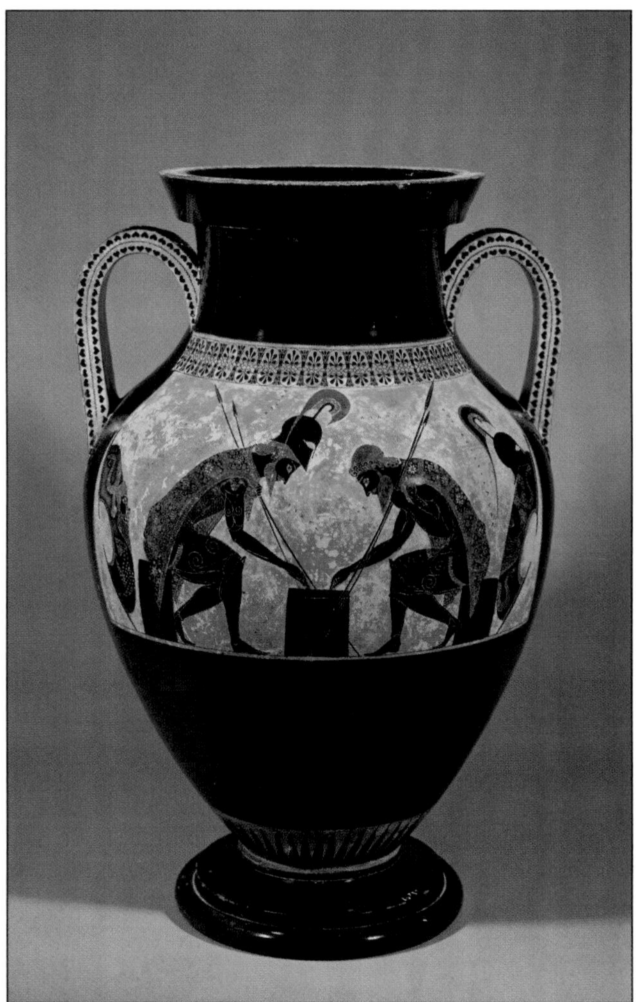

FIGURE 2.12 Exekias, *Ajax and Achilles*, amphora, black-figure style, 550–525 B.C.E., terra cotta, height $26\frac{3}{8}$″ (67 cm), Vatican Museums, Rome. Narrative became progressively more popular on vases, the subjects often taken from mythology. Exekias, master of the black-figure style, is especially noted for his carefully composed scenes.

THE ARCHAIC PERIOD

The Archaic period, ca. 600–480 B.C.E., saw the emergence of the two most important types of Greek vase painting, known as black-figure and red-figure, both focusing in Athens, which took the lead in vase manufacturing from Corinth.

Black-Figure Ceramics. The black-figure style was refined in the second half of the seventh century B.C.E. and reached its peak between 600 and 500 B.C.E. In the **black-figure style,** painting is done with a black glaze on a natural orange clay background. The artist draws the outlines and then fills in the color. Details are created by scraping through the black glaze to reveal the orange clay beneath. Because the artist must exert considerable pressure to make these details, the lines do not tend to flow readily.

The **amphora,** a two-handled vessel, by EXEKIAS [egg-ZEEK-yas], dated 550–525 B.C.E. (fig. 2.12), is a mature example of the black-figure style. On it are depicted Achilles and Ajax from Homer's epic *The Iliad.* The figures stand on a baseline, suggesting some concept of a three-dimensional space. The composition is a perfect balance of verticals, horizontals, and diagonals, the figures' poses conforming to the shape of the vase. Exekias paints perfect profile portraits yet the eye is seen from the front in the Egyptian manner; not until around 470 B.C.E. would artists depict the eye in profile. Narratives dominate vase decoration over the next centuries, the subjects frequently derived from mythology as well as daily life.

Red-Figure Ceramics. Around 530 B.C.E., under pressure from the Persians, a flood of Ionian Greek refugees came to Greece from Asia Minor, introducing Oriental and Ionic influences to mainland art. At the same time, **red-figure style** vase painting started in Athens. As this style took hold, the black-figure style gradually disappeared. Red-figure finally replaced black-figure around 500 B.C.E.

The red-figure technique is essentially an inversion of the black-figure technique, for now the figures are left the color of the clay and the background is painted black.

Connections

LANDSCAPE AND ARCHITECTURE

According to Vincent Scully, an architectural historian, the great Greek temples can best be understood by exploring their relation to the landscape around them. Characteristically, the Greek landscape is formed by mountains of moderate size, which surround very clearly defined areas of valley and plain, and by islands, clearly demarcated land surfaces surrounded by flat blue sea. Unlike the deserts of Asia Minor and northern Africa or the Alps of central Europe, the Greek landscape is of a scale and clarity that can be contained, so to speak, by the human eye.

With this in mind, Scully notes that each of the Minoan palaces possesses the same relation to the landscape. The palace is set in an enclosed valley on a north–south axis; there is, nearby, a gently mounded or conical hill; beyond this, on the same axis, is a higher, double-peaked or cleft mountain.

The two Greek temples of Hera at Paestum have an analogous relation to the landscape. Hera is not only the wife of Zeus, and thus the goddess of marriage and domestic stability, but also the earth mother. The temples at Paestum were built side by side, on the same axis, oriented toward a conical notched mountain to the east. Standing beside them, at their western end, the direction from which the viewer would naturally approach them, the perspective created by their sides points toward the mountain itself. "Once seen together," Scully writes, "both landscape and temple will seem forever incomplete without the other. Each ennobles its opposite, and their relationship brings the universe of nature and man into a new stable order."

Details within the contours of the figures are painted with a brush and are consequently more fluid than when incised in the black-figure technique.

Signed by EUXITHEOS [yoog-SITH-ios] as potter and EUPHRONIOS [yoo-FRO-nios] as painter is a **calyx krater** (fig. 2.13), dating from about 515 B.C.E., on which is depicted the *Death of Sarpedon* from the story of the Trojan War. In this scene, Sarpedon is lifted by the twin brothers Sleep and Death in the presence of Hermes and two Trojans. The narrative element is highly developed, as is the refined style. Sarpedon is shown from the front, the anatomy realistically rendered, details of the muscles, tendons, and beards finely depicted.

Sculpture. The history of ancient Greek sculpture is dominated by images of the human figure, particularly the **kouros** (plural, **kouroi**) [COO-ross; COO-roy] (fig. 2.14), a lifesize representation of a nude male youth, seen standing with one foot forward and arms to his sides, and the **koré** (plural, **korai**) [CO-ray], the female equivalent, but clothed.

The characteristic pose of the kouros is believed to have derived from Egyptian sculpture. The marble kouros

FIGURE 2.13 Euxitheos and Euphronios, *Death of Sarpedon*, calyx krater, red-figure style, ca. 515 B.C.E., terra cotta, height 18″ (45.7 cm), Purchase, Bequest of Joseph H. Durkee, Gift of Darius Ogden Mills and Gift of C. Ruston Love, by exchange, 1972. Metropolitan Museum of Art, New York. Art Resource, NY. Whereas in the black-figure technique details must be scraped through the black glaze, in the red-figure technique details are painted on with a tiny brush. Details are therefore achieved more easily, and greater fluidity of line is possible.

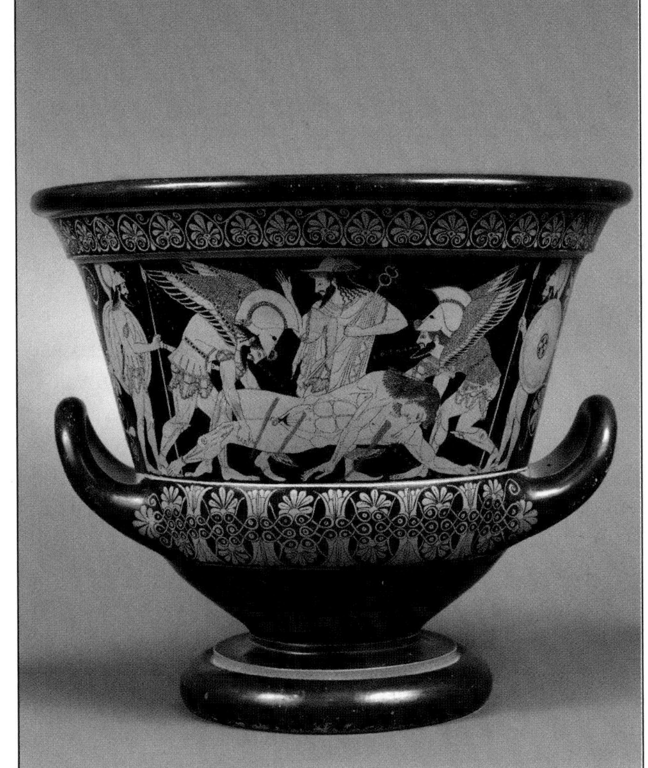

Table 2–1	TIME PERIODS IN ANCIENT GREEK CULTURE
Geometric	ca. 1000–ca. 700 B.C.E.
Orientalizing	ca. 700–ca. 600 B.C.E.
Archaic	ca. 600–ca. 480 B.C.E.
Classical	ca. 480 B.C.E.–323 B.C.E. (death of Alexander the Great)
Hellenistic	323 B.C.E.–30 B.C.E. (death of Cleopatra)

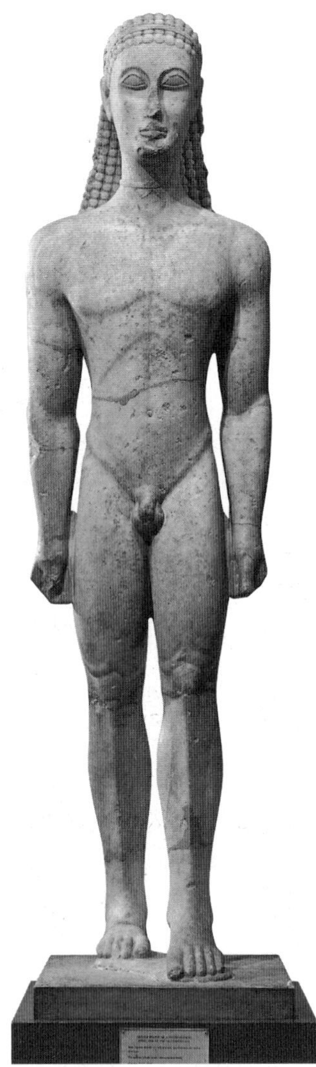

FIGURE 2.14 Kouros, ca. 590–580 B.C.E., marble, height 6′4″ (1.93 m), Fletcher Fund, 1932, Metropolitan Museum of Art, New York. A Greek kouros is a statue of a standing nude male. Details of the anatomy form a decorative surface pattern. The pose, with one foot forward yet the weight of the body equally distributed on both feet, comes from Egypt.

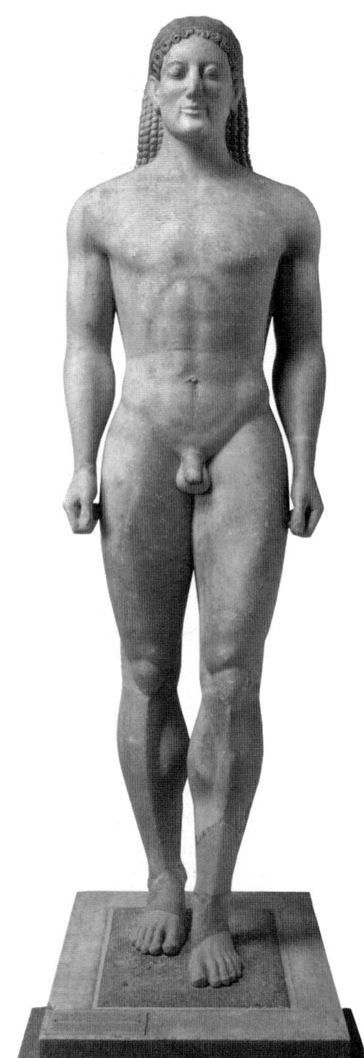

FIGURE 2.15 Kouros, known as *Kroisos*, from Anavyos cemetery near Athens, ca. 525 B.C.E, marble with remnants of paint, height 6′4″ (1.93 m). National Archaeological Museum, Athens. Over time, kouros figures gradually became more naturalistic in their proportions. Because these changes are well-documented, it is possible to use them to assign approximate dates to the many extant kouroi.

(fig. 2.14), carved ca. 590–580 B.C.E., shares many of its features with Egyptian figures (see fig. 1.19): the rigid frontality, erect stance, and pose with left foot forward. However, the Greek figure is nude and has been carved to be free-standing. There are thus no webs of stone between the arms and body and between the legs, and no supporting back pillars.

The kouros reproduced here was originally painted—sculpture was customarily colored with reds, yellows, blues, and greens. Some pieces still retain some of their original color; touches of red pigment remain on this kouros's hair and elsewhere.

Early kouros figures are highly stylized and characteristically have an enigmatic expression, which is often referred to as an **Archaic smile.** The eyes are abnormally large, and the hair forms a decorative beadlike pattern. The anatomy is arranged for design rather than in strict imitation of nature; thus the abdominal muscles and kneecaps become surface decoration. The figures are not portraits of individuals and there is no evidence that they were done from models.

Compare the kouros made ca. 590–580 B.C.E. to another, dated ca. 525 B.C.E., known as *Kroisos* (fig. 2.15), representing the mature Archaic period. A funerary inscription on the base gives the name of the deceased as Kroisos—but the base may not be original to this figure. Kouros figures are not individualized; there is no evidence they were made from live models. The pupose of

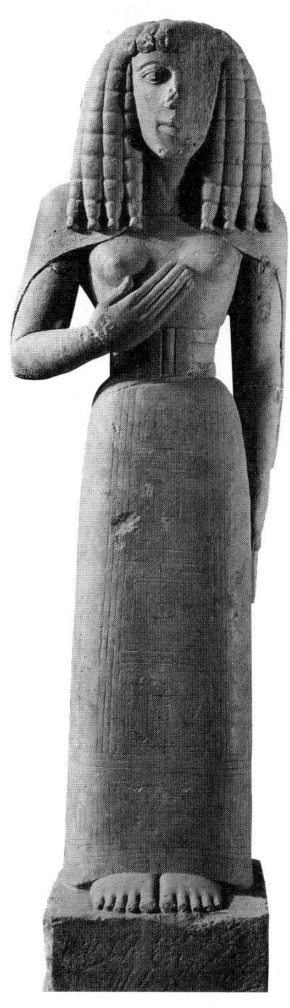

FIGURE 2.16 Koré, wearing a Doric peplos, known as the Lady of Auxerre, ca. 650–625 B.C.E., limestone and paint, height $29\frac{1}{2}''$ (75 cm). Musée du Louvre, Paris. The Doric peplos, made of thick heavy fabric, although belted at the waist, obscures the shape of the lower body. The proportions of the figure are still awkward and inaccurate.

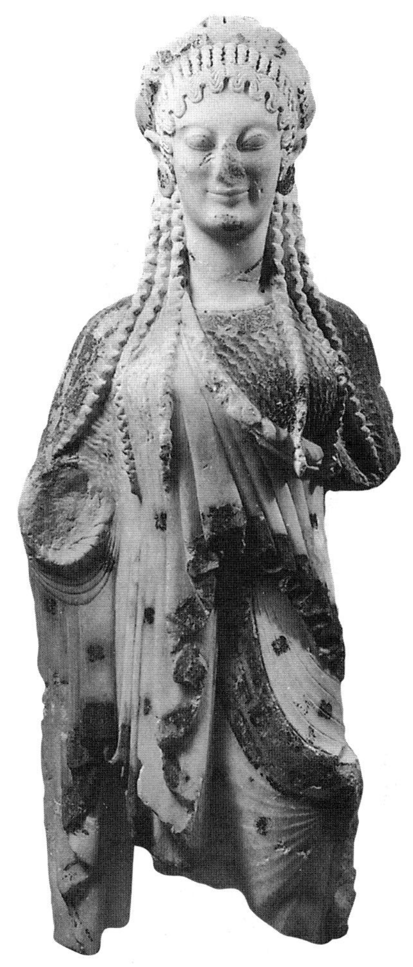

FIGURE 2.17 Koré, wearing an Ionic chiton, ca. 520 B.C.E., marble, height $22\frac{1}{8}''$ (56.3 cm), Acropolis Museum, Athens. The decorative chiton, made of soft thin fabric, clings to the body. The Archaic smile is still evident here.

the many kouroi is not clear, for although they are presumed to be votive offerings, whether they represent the donor, the deity, or someone else remains uncertain. Those that were placed on graves may represent the deceased. As yet, Kroisos retains the Archaic smile, and his hair still twirls into a schematized decorative pattern of curls around the face, hanging in bead-like coils. The pose is unchanged: frontal, with the left foot forward, and the arms close to the body. However, over time, kouros figures became more naturalistic in their proportions as the narrow waist gradually expanded, and less stylized in their appearance as the lines cut into the surface were replaced by three-dimensional curves.

Equal time for female figures, korai. A *koré* (fig. 2.16) carved ca. 650–625 B.C.E. is now known as the "Lady of Auxerre" because she had been used as decoration in a theater in that French city. She is typical of Archaic figures: Her hair forms a symmetrical pattern, her forehead is minimized, the eyes are not recessed, and she exhibits the "Archaic smile"—although this is not likely to have been the intended interpretation of the expression. Standing straight and rigid, her right hand is raised to her chest. She wears the then-current fashion for women, the Doric peplos, made of heavy fabric that hung from the shoulders without shaping, her pinched waistline emphasized by a broad belt. Other than the toes that barely emerge beneath her long skirt, no indication that she has two legs is given, for the clothing masks the body beneath.

The changes that were gradually taking place are demonstrated by a late Archaic koré (fig. 2.17), carved ca. 520 B.C.E. Made of marble, this particular koré was elaborately painted. Figures like this with one hand extended may represent a goddess or donor. Exquisitely sculpted, this delicate and dainty figure appears soft and sensual. The face still has an "Archaic smile," but the eyes are smaller than they were before, and the slanting eyes, hairstyle, and decorative treatment of the costume suggest an Eastern origin for this figure in the Ionian islands—perhaps the island of Chios.

She wears an Ionic chiton, a belted single-piece garment for women, which was imported to Athens from eastern Ionia just before the middle of the sixth century B.C.E. Much attention is given to this costume. The fabric is thin and clings to the body, the folds and draping are complex, the cut of the garment is asymmetrical, and the hemlines are emphasized with colored bands. The cloak, worn over the chiton, ties on one shoulder, creating diagonal patterns and curved lines. The simplicity of earlier sculpture has given way to more refined subtleties as Greek culture was becoming more sophisticated.

Philosophy. Perhaps nothing distinguishes the rise of ancient Greece as a civilization more than its love of pure thought. The Greeks were the first to practice **philosophy,** literally the "love of wisdom," in a systematic way, categorizing the various aspects of the world and their relation to it in terms that were based not on faith or emotion but on logic and reasoning.

Before the ascendancy of Socrates and his pupil Plato in the late fifth century B.C.E. a group of early Greek thinkers, called the Presocratics, hotly debated the nature of the world and their place in it. The Presocratic philosophers located near the Ionian city of Miletus in Asia Minor changed the way the world can be understood. Instead of an approach based on mythological tradition, Milesian thinkers such as THALES [THAY-lees] (624–526 B.C.E.) and HERACLITUS [hair-a-CLITE-us] (ca. 537–475 B.C.E.) offered more abstract conceptual explanations based on their observations and their sense that the universe was governed by impersonal and uniform laws. These forces and laws the earliest Greek philosophers attempted to identify and explain. For Thales, the source of the universe and its primal material was water, which, he reasoned, could explain both the changing and the more stable qualities of the universe. Thales brings to his thinking a more naturalistic, even empirical outlook than had been in evidence previously.

For Heraclitus, the primary material of the universe was fire, which also exists in constantly fluctuating forms. Heraclitus saw the world as being in a state of constant flux, and especially in a state of strife, in which opposites constantly conflict. Nothing *is*, he claimed; rather all is in a constant state of *becoming.* "One can never step into the same river twice," he wrote. And perhaps equally enigmatically, he suggested that human beings should seek to understand the order of the universe, which he called its Logos, and live their lives in conjunction with its spirit.

Heraclitus is believed to have flourished in Ephesus around 500 B.C.E. Like the other pre-Socretic thinkers, very little remains of his writings: just a series of brief fragments, many of them riddled with paradox, such as his idea that there is a unity of opposite things—cold and hot, dry and moist, waking and sleeping, youth and age, life and death. Heraclitus held that these opposites change into one another, that they are united through such change, and that change is the fundamental reality of the universe. Among modern thinkers who found inspiration in Heraclitus' ideas was the German philosopher Hegel, who took Heraclitus' notion of the unity of opposites and built his historical materialism out of it, seeing the battle between thesis and antithesis as yielding a synthesis. Another modern thinker who paid tribute to Heraclitus was the physicist Werner Heisenberg, the inventor of the "uncertainty principle." Heisenberg wrote that Heraclitus' idea that all of life is in a state of flux reflects an early understanding of the concept of energy, which he saw as the fundamental cause for all change in the physical world, making Heraclitus something of an honorary proto-quantum physicist.

Another group of thinkers, the **atomists,** led by DEMOCRITUS [dih-MAH-crih-tus] (ca. 460 B.C.E.), conceived of the world as being made up of two basic elements: atoms—small, invisible particles that cannot be divided into smaller units—and the void, the empty space between atoms. Atomism survived in a changed form in the later philosophy of the Epicureans (see Chapter 3) and had a dramatic influence on the thinking of the scientists who evolved modern atomic theory and quantum mechanics.

Perhaps the most important of these Presocratic thinkers was PYTHAGORAS [pih-THAY-guh-rus] (582–507 B.C.E.). For him, "number" was at the heart of all things. Today he is most often remembered for his theorem in geometry—in right-angle triangles, the square of the hypotenuse is equal to the sum of the square of the other two sides. These triangles are unified by number, a principle Pythagoras also applied to music. He knew that a string of a certain length, when plucked, made a certain sound; divided in half, it played the same note, only an octave higher. Mathematical ratios, he reasoned, determined musical sound relationships. The entire natural world, including the movement of the planets, depended on these same ratios, he believed. According to Pythagoras, there was, underlying all things, a "harmony of the spheres."

Pythagoras believed that the universe consisted primarily and fundamentally of numbers, which were for him the ultimate reality. Numbers were accorded symbolic, even mystical properties, with the first ten numbers of particular importance. The number one, indicated by a point, represents "unity," the source of everything in the universe. The number two, two points on a line, is considered imperfect because it can create division. The number three, represented by a triangle, combines the first two numbers and allows for a beginning, middle, and end. The number four, symbolized by the square, is considered a perfect number, and a powerful one since the three-dimensional figure of a pyramid can be created from four points. Each of the remaining numbers through ten has analogous symbolic properties, with ten being representative of the world because it can be created from lower

Cultural Impact

Ideals of physical beauty—male and female—vary greatly from one culture and time period to another. That of the slender Cycladic woman (Fig. 2.1) contrasts strikingly with the curves of the Greek feminine ideal seen in the koré of ca. 520 B.C.E. These early female figures may be compared with later versions of female beauty as seen in Botticelli's sensuously fluid *Venus* (fig. 13.13), Rubens' fleshy mermaids (fig. 15.18), Ingres's languidly linear *Odalisque*, and Rodin's solidly and realistically sculpted woman in *The Kiss* (fig. 18.15). Curiously, the angular, segmented, two-dimensional body of the Cycladic female figure has less in common with these substantial feminine images than with more modern figures, such as the faceted females in Picasso's 1907 *Demoiselles d'Avignon* (Fig. 22.2), and more recently, with contemporary fashion models, whose slim bodies and angular features adorn the covers of popular women's magazines.

Ancient Greece has also had a significant influence on the literature of subsequent civilizations. Homeric epic continued in a line through Virgil's first-century *Aeneid*, to Dante's fourteenth-century *Divine Comedy* and Milton's seventeenth-century *Paradise Lost*. And although epic is no longer a popular literary genre, the epic similes or extended comparisons found in *The Iliad* and *The Odyssey* remain a staple of contemporary poetry. One literary genre, however, that has flourished from ancient Greek times until today is the lyric poem, the earliest major recorded exemplar of which is Sappho, whose passionate love lyrics directly influenced the Roman poet Catullus and numerous Renaissance poets, including Shakespeare's contemporary, Ben Jonson. Love poems, which trace their lineage to Sappho, are among the most popular literary genres, as evidenced by new editions of love poems by earlier authors, such as Shakespeare, and by numerous anthologies of love poems in the twenty-first century, one of which, *To Woo and to Wed*, was edited by Robert Pinsky, an American poet laureate.

prime numbers and because it contains musical and arithmetical proportions. Ten can be created by adding the first four numbers and by cubing the numbers one and three then adding them. The Pythagoreans deified the number ten. Medieval catholic thought was influenced by such notions of numbers, as evidenced in the special value accorded numbers in Christian theological thought, which extended to the way number and proportion were reflected in the great medieval cathedrals (see p. 260, Numerology at Chartres.)

KEY TERMS

labyrinth
mural
pithos (pl. pithoi)
terra cotta
faience
lintel
relieving triangle
dromos
ashlar masonry
tholos (pl. tholoi)
corbeled dome
rhyton
mythology
polis (pl. poleis)
Geometric style
krater
black-figure style
amphora
red-figure style
calyx krater
kouros (pl. kouroi)
koré (pl. korai)
Archaic smile
philosophy
atomist

www. WEBSITES FOR FURTHER STUDY

http://www.getty.edu/art/collections/objects/o15054.html
(This site contains a brief description and image of Cycladic sculpture.)

http://www.perseus.tufts.edu/cache/perscoll Greco-Roman.html
(A good general site on all things Greek and Roman, including ancient written works.)

http://www.varchive.org/schorr/warvase.htm
(An excellent discussion of the Warrior Vase can be found here.)

http://metmuseum.org/TOAH/HD/ecyc/hd_ecyc.htm
(Early Cycladic art and culture.)

http://cycladic.gr/frontoffice/portal.asp?cpage=node
(Museum of Cycladic art.)

Chapter 3

History

480 B.C.E.	Athens destroyed by Persians
479 B.C.E.	Athenians defeat Persians
461–429 B.C.E.	Perikles rules Athens
431–404 B.C.E.	Peloponnesian War
430–429 B.C.E.	Plague kills Perikles
404 B.C.E.	Athens falls to Sparta
359–336 B.C.E.	Philip of Macedon reigns
338 B.C.E.	Philip of Macedon conquers Greece
336–323 B.C.E.	Alexander the Great reigns

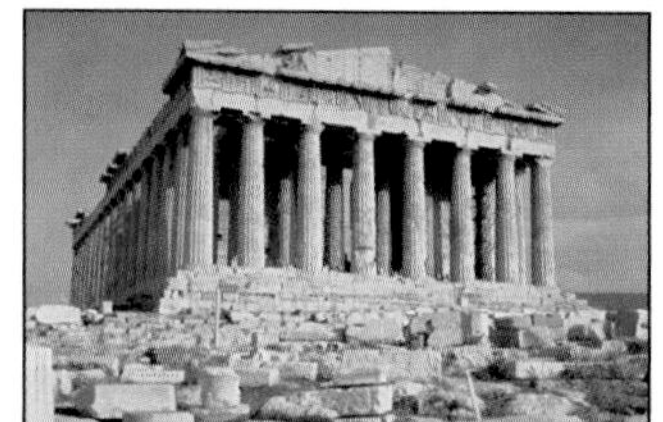

Art and Architecture

480 B.C.E.	*Kritios Boy*
ca. 450–440 B.C.E.	Polykleitos, *Doryphoros*
448/447–438/432 B.C.E.	Iktinos and Kallikrates, Parthenon
ca. 445–430 B.C.E.	Achilles Painter, *Muse and Maiden*
437–432 B.C.E.	Mnesikles, Propylaia
431–404 B.C.E.	Polykleitos the Younger, theatre Epidauros
ca. 350–300 B.C.E.	Praxiteles, *Aphrodite of Knidos*
ca. 200–190 B.C.E.	*Nike of Samothrace*
ca. 180–160 B.C.E.	Altar of Zeus
ca. 150 B.C.E.–first century C.E.	Hagesandros, Athanodoros, Polydoros of Rhodes, *Laocoön and His Sons*

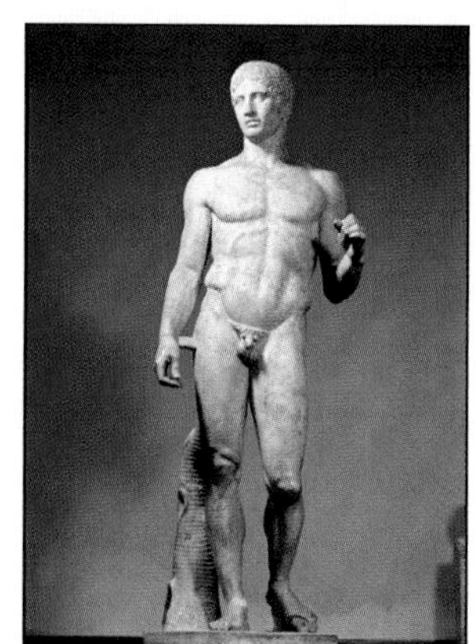

Literature and Philosophy

469–399 B.C.E.	Socrates
458 B.C.E.	Aeschylus, the *Oresteia*
ca. 441 B.C.E.	Sophocles, *Antigone*
430–429 B.C.E.	Sophocles, *Oedipus the King*
415 B.C.E.	Euripides, *The Trojan Women*
411 B.C.E.	Aristophanes, *Lysistrata*
407 B.C.E.	Plato becomes Socrates' student
387 B.C.E.	Plato founds Academy at Athens
367–347 B.C.E.	Aristotle studies at Academy under Plato
360 B.C.E.	Plato, *The Republic*
ca. 350–300 B.C.E.	Aristotle, *The Poetics*
343–336 B.C.E.	Aristotle serves as tutor to Alexander the Great
335 B.C.E.	Aristotle founds Lyceum in Athens

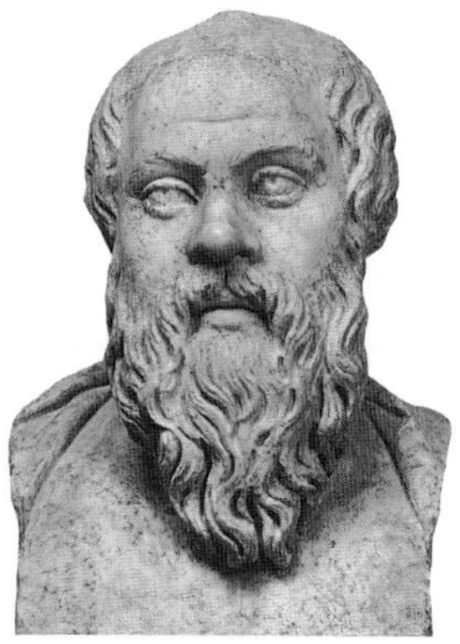

Classical and Hellenistic Greece

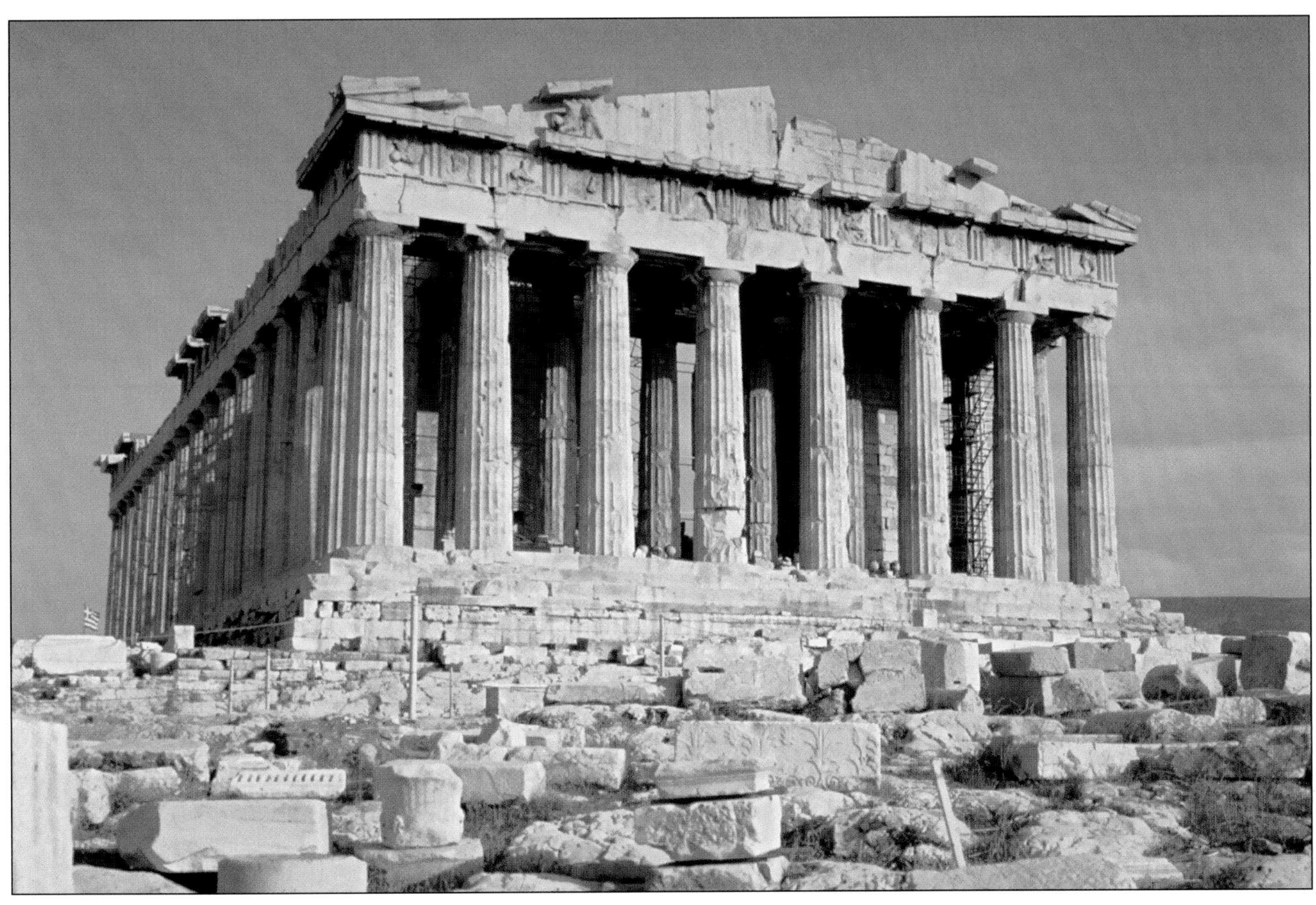

Iktinos and Kallikrates, Parthenon, Acropolis, Athens, 448–432 B.C.E., marble.

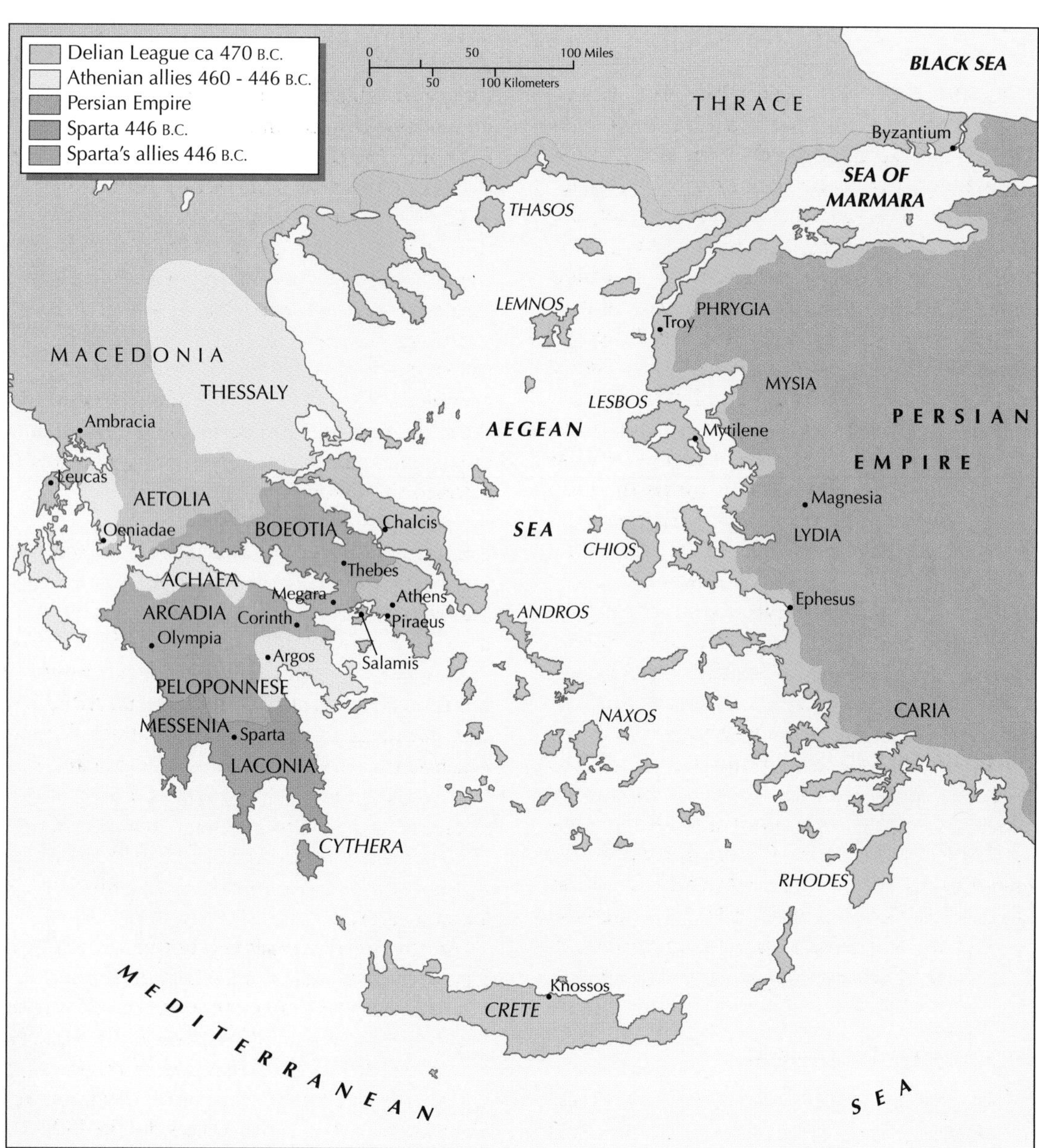

MAP 3.1 Classical Greece.

CHAPTER OVERVIEW

CLASSICAL GREECE
The golden age of the arts

HELLENISTIC GREECE
A geographic expansion of the empire and a scholarly exploration of the past

CLASSICAL GREECE

IN THE DECADE BETWEEN 490 AND 480 B.C.E., something remarkable happened in Greece, and in Athens in particular, that resulted in one of the most culturally productive eras in the history of humankind. Before 490 B.C.E., as we explored in the last chapter, the Greeks had developed a highly sophisticated culture, but it pales by comparison to developments in the so-called Athenian Golden Age, a period of unsurpassed cultural achievement that can be said to begin with the Athenian defeat of the Persians in 479 B.C.E. and end nearly eighty years later, in 404 B.C.E., when Athens fell to Sparta. But the cultural achievement of the era was by no means exhausted with Athens's fall. This Golden Age had sparked a **Classical** period in Greece—"classical" because it forms the very basis of Western tradition down to this day—that would extend nearly another century until the death of Alexander the Great in 323 B.C.E. Even as the political power of Greece waned, its cultural preeminence carried on, through a **Hellenistic** period (from the verb "to Hellenize," or spread the influence of Greek culture), in which the basic tenets of Greek thought were perpetuated by the three dynasties that emerged after Alexander's death—the Ptolemies in Egypt, the Seleucids in Syria and Mesopotamia, and the Antigonids in Macedon—despite the competition for political dominance among them. Only after Rome captured Corinth in 146 B.C.E., making Greece into a province of the Roman Empire, did Greek culture begin to be absorbed into the new "Romanized" world. Even then the Hellenistic period was not truly at an end, continuing in Egypt until the death of Queen Cleopatra in 30 B.C.E.

FROM ARCHAIC TO CLASSICAL

Political Reform. Many things contributed to the astonishing rise of Athens as the cultural center of the world in the fifth century B.C.E. Chief among them is the century of political reform that preceded the Golden Age. As early as 621 B.C.E., the benevolent ruler DRACO [DRAY-koh] published what is thought to be the first comprehensive code of laws in Athens. This offered a single standard of justice to all Athenians, whether the landed aristocracy, the growing commercial class, or poor farmers.

Just as important to this process of change was SOLON [SOH-lon] (ca. 640–558 B.C.E.), who reformed the civil administration of Athens. He divided the citizens into four classes, all of whom had the right to take part in the debates in the political Assembly. Though Solon limited the highest offices to members of the nobility, he did allow the lower classes to sit on juries, and jury duty became a civic responsibility. He ended debt slavery (the practice of paying off a debt by becoming the creditor's slave), employed large numbers of artisans, and promoted trade, particularly trade in pottery. PISIS-TRATOS [pi-SIS-truh-tus] (ca. 605–527 B.C.E.) went even further, redistributing the large estates of some nobility to landless farmers, who, as a result of their improved economic status, suddenly found themselves able to vote. Like Solon, Pisistratos also championed the arts, commissioning the first editions of *The Iliad* and *The Odyssey* for students and scholars, and encouraging the development of Greek theater.

Shortly prior to 508 B.C.E., CLEISTHENES [KLICE-thuh-nees] (d. 508 B.C.E.) divided Athens into **demes** (neighborhoods), representing what he had labeled the ten "tribes" of Athens. Each "tribe" was allotted fifty seats on a Council of Five Hundred. The fifty representatives for each neighborhood were selected at random from a list of nominees. The Council elected ten generals yearly to run the city, and at the head of them was a commander in chief, also elected yearly. Thus, out of the demes of Athens, developed the first democracy.

The Persian Threat. This democracy was put to the test beginning in 490 B.C.E. when the same Darius who built the palace at Persepolis in Persia (see fig. 1.12) invaded the Greek mainland. On the plain of Marathon, north of Athens, Darius' mighty army was confronted by a mere ten thousand Greeks, led by General MILTIADES [mil-TIE-uh-dees]. In a surprise dawn attack, Miltiades' troops crushed the Persians, killing an estimated six thousand; the Greeks suffered only minimal losses. Victory was announced to the waiting citizens of Athens by a messenger who ran many miles from Marathon to Athens with the news, an early form of what would, centuries later, become a marathon run.

But the Persian giant was not yet tamed. A rebellion in Egypt and the death of Darius in 486 B.C.E., following which his son Xerxes ascended the throne, preoccupied the Persians temporarily. But all the while the Athenian general THEMISTOCLES [thih-MIS-tu-klees] was preparing for what he believed to be the inevitable return of the Persian army. And come Xerxes did, in 480 B.C.E., with an army so large that reports had it drinking rivers dry.

It is to HERODOTUS [heh-ROD-ut-us] (484–420 B.C.E.), the first writer to devote himself solely to history and who is therefore known as the Father of History, that we are indebted for much of our knowledge of the Persian Wars. He estimated the Persian army at five million men, surely an exaggeration, but certainly the Persians far outnumbered the Greeks. Although a Greek allied army fought most of the battle, a small force of three hundred Spartan soldiers has gone down in history. Led by LEONIDES [lee-ON-ih-dees], they went north from Athens to Thermopylai [thur-MOP-uh-lye], a narrow pass between the sea and the mountains, where they held off the Persian advance for days, buying time for the Greek army to retreat and set up a second line of defense. Betrayed by a local guide, who showed Xerxes a path around the pass, the Spartans were finally surrounded, but continued fighting until all were dead. Athens was destroyed by the Persians, and Themistocles retreated to the island of Salamis [SAL-ah-miss]. This was a trick, however, for when the Persians sailed after him, they were unable to maneuver in the narrow bay, and the Persian fleet was entirely destroyed. Within a year, the Persian land forces were also driven from the mainland, and Greece was free.

GOLDEN AGE OF ATHENS

Over the centuries Athens had grown and prospered, a city within strong stone walls, protected by a vast citadel on an **acropolis** (literally, the high point of the city, from *akros*, meaning "high," and *polis*, "city"). There, temples were erected, law courts and shrines were built, and a forum for the Pan-Athenaic Games was constructed. The Persians destroyed all this and more in 480 B.C.E. The whole of Athens had to be rebuilt.

The entire population was put to work restoring the city's walls. When the walls were completed, the Athenians turned their attention to the **agora,** or marketplace, in which shopkeepers and craftspeople made, displayed, and sold their wares. Here, at the foot of the Acropolis, they built a council chamber, a court house, several long **stoas,** or roofed colonnades, to house shops, and a smaller royal stoa in which the "Laws of Solon" were carved on stone and could be viewed by all citizens.

No attempt was made to rebuild the temples on the Acropolis. Their foundations were left bare as a reminder of the Persian aggression. But by mid-century, the restoration of the site seemed a matter of civic responsibility, an act of homage to Athena who had helped the Greeks defeat the Persians, and it was taken on by the great Athenian leader PERIKLES [PAIR-ih-klees] (ca. 500–429 B.C.E.). Perikles was first elected general-in-chief in 461 B.C.E., and, except for two years when he was voted out of office, remained in command until his death in 429 B.C.E. Under the artistic and administrative supervision of PHIDIAS [FI-dee-us], the best artists and artisans were hired, over 22,000 tons of marble were transported from quarries ten miles away, and vast numbers of workers were employed in a construction project that lasted until the end of the century. The acropolis embodied, for Perikles, the Athenians' "love of beauty," as he put it in an oration delivered in 430 B.C.E. at a state funeral for Athenian citizens who had died in battle. Its buildings were "things of the mind," he said, embodiments of the greatness of Athens itself (fig. 3.1). And it is true that when work on the citadel was completed, the Acropolis at Athens was, with the possible exception of the Egyptian pyramids, probably the most impressive visual spectacle in the world.

It is often said that the Greeks' characteristic pursuit of balance and order in their art was a reaction to the extreme disorder of the world around them. Two major disasters struck Athens in the late fifth century B.C.E. The first, a devastating plague, occurred in 430–429 B.C.E., its most important victim being Perikles himself. The Greek historian THUCYDIDES [thyou-SID-id-ease] (ca. 460–ca. 400 B.C.E.) described how the "bodies of the dying were heaped upon one another" as "half-dead creatures" were "staggering about in the streets or flocking around the fountains in their desire for water." A year earlier, the long-standing Spartan resentment of Athenian power had erupted in the Peloponnesian War, which ended with Athens's defeat at the hands of the Spartans in 404 B.C.E. The war brought an end to Athenian supremacy and to the Greek golden age. It also signaled the breakdown in the city-state structure that had prevailed for centuries.

FIGURE 3.1 General view of the Acropolis. Even in relative ruin, the Athenian Acropolis remains a breathtaking sight and a poignant reminder of past accomplishments.

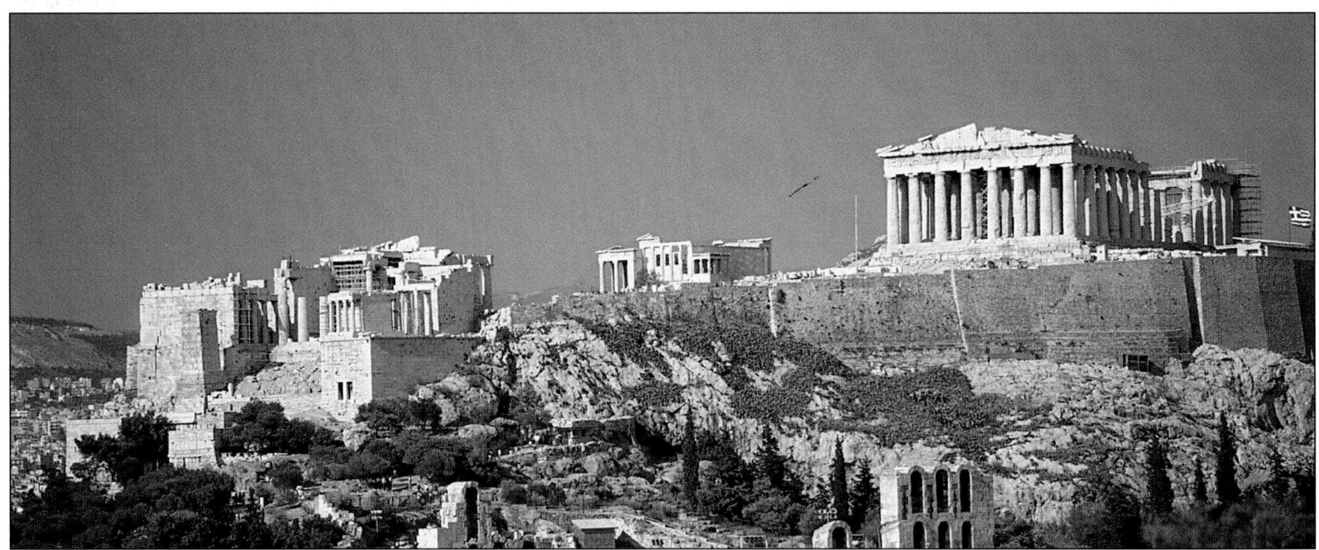

ARCHITECTURE AND ARCHITECTURAL SCULPTURE ON THE ACROPOLIS

The Greek Orders. The ancient Greeks developed the three **orders** or arrangements of architecture—the Doric order, the Ionic order, and the Corinthian order (fig. 3.2). Although there are differences in the entablature, shaft, and base, the column capital is the easiest way to determine whether the order used in the construction of a building is Doric, Ionic, or Corinthian.

The **Doric** is the oldest and simplest of the three orders and was the order most frequently employed by the ancient Greek architects. By the Golden Age it had been perfected. Its capital is characterized by the square block of the **abacus** and the cushion-shaped **echinus,** usually cut from the same piece of stone. There is no base beneath the Doric column, whereas there is a base beneath the Ionic and Corinthian columns. The Doric **frieze** consists of alternating **triglyphs,** so called because they have three sections, and **metopes,** square or rectangular areas that may be decorated.

The **Ionic** order is characterized by the scroll/volute capital—graceful and curling. The Ionic was Eastern in origin and was especially popular in Asia Minor and the Greek islands. The **entablature** has a frieze of continous decoration.

The **Corinthian** order, a development of the Hellenistic age, is characterized by the large curling acanthus leaves that ornament the capital. The Corinthian is the most ornamental and delicate of the three orders. It was the order least used by the Greeks but most favored later by the Romans.

The Parthenon. Built by Perikles with funds intended for the defense of Athens, the Parthenon [PAR-theeh-none] (fig. 3.3) is the only Acropolis building that was actually finished—construction of the rest was halted by the Peloponnesian War. The Parthenon is considered the ultimate example of ancient Greek architecture, the paradigm of perfection. Dated by inscriptions to between 448/447 and 438 or 432 B.C.E., it is the perfect example of the Classical Doric temple and is dedicated to the goddess Athena. Located at the highest point on the Acropolis, the Parthenon is the largest building there and is also the largest Doric building on the Greek mainland. The architects were IKTINOS [ik-TIE-nus] and KALLIKRATES [ka-LIK-kra-tees]. Phidias took on the task of its sculptural decoration, and he made a gold and ivory cult image of Athena Parthenos, dedicated in 437 B.C.E.

The beauty of the Parthenon derives largely from the perfection of its proportions. The facade is based on the so-called **Golden Section:** the width of the building is 1.618 times the height, a ratio of approximately 8:5. Plato regarded this ratio as the key to understanding the cosmos. Additionally the Parthenon possesses all of the "refinements"—the deviations from absolute regularity and rigidity—used by ancient Greek

FIGURE 3.2 Diagram of the Doric, Ionic, and Corinthian orders. The three orders of Greek architecture were developed in antiquity and continue to be used even today.

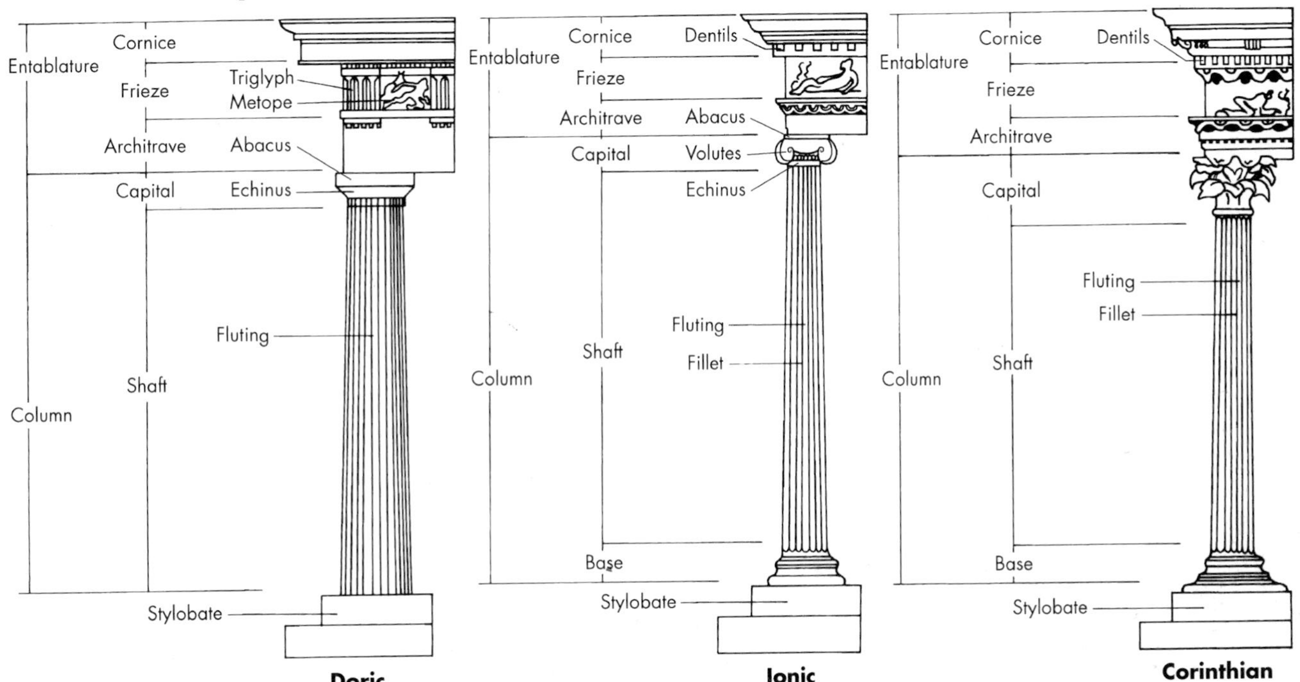

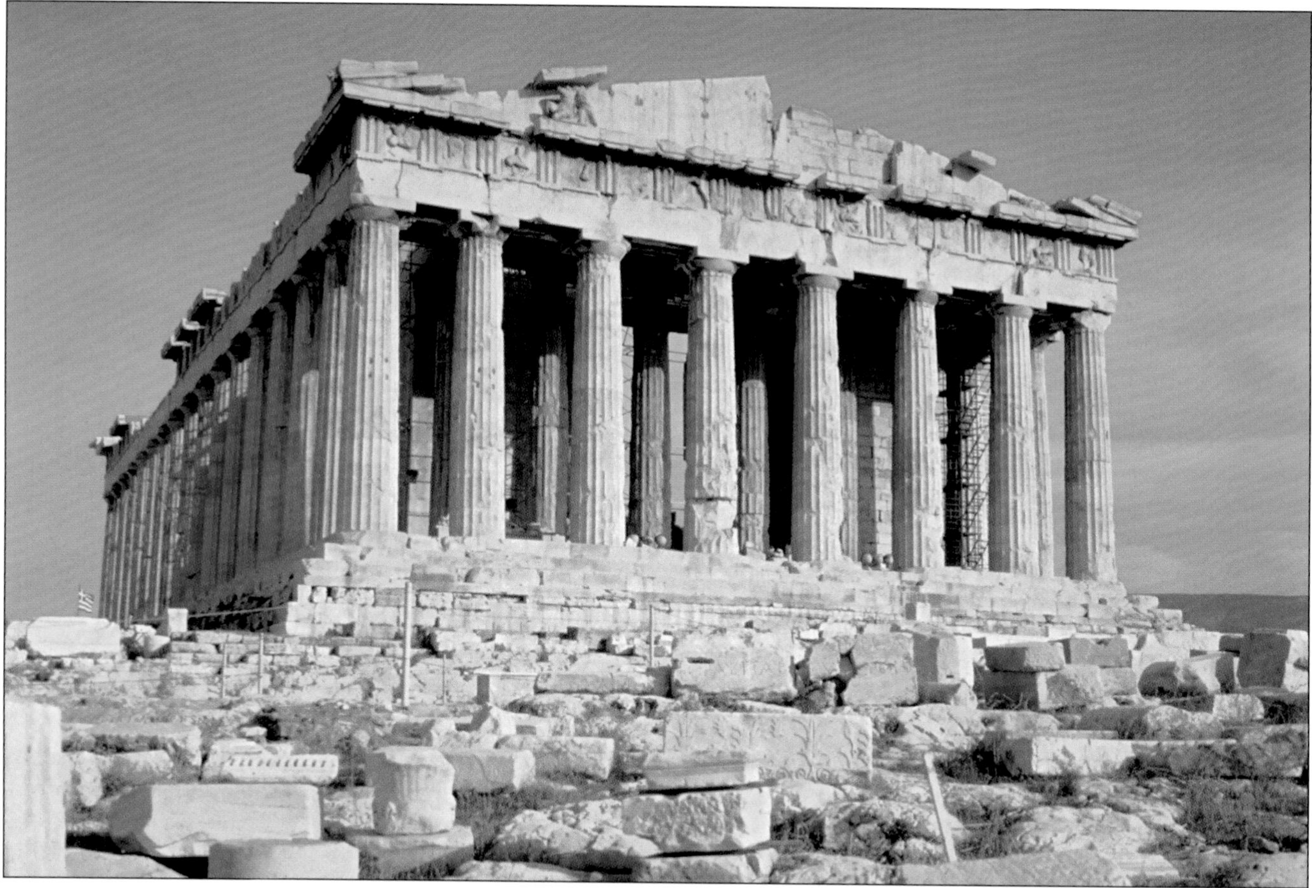

FIGURE 3.3 Iktinos and Kallikrates, Parthenon, Acropolis, Athens, 448–432 B.C.E., marble. The epitome of Classical Greek architecture, the Parthenon is a regular Doric temple. All major lines actually curve slightly. Such refinements are now believed to have been intended to add to the beauty of the building rather than to correct for optical distortion.

architects. Despite appearances, there are no straight lines to the Parthenon. The steps and the entablature both form convex curves. Each block of marble is a rectangular prism with precisely cut right-angle corners, but when the courses were laid, the blocks were positioned so as to be faceted in relation to one another. The columns have **entasis,** the slight bulge in the column shaft, and they taper to the top—that is, their diameter is less at the top than at the bottom. Further, the columns at the corners are wider and are placed closer together than elsewhere.

Parthenon Sculpture. There are three categories of surviving Parthenon sculpture: ninety-two squarish metopes on the entablature, carved in high relief—most of those that survive have as their subject the mythological battle between the Lapiths and centaurs; the frieze on the upper wall of the cella, carved in low relief; and the huge figures that filled the east and west pediments, carved in the round.

The west pediment depicts the competition between Athena and Poseidon for the land of Attica. The east pediment depicts the birth of Athena from the head of Zeus. The figures are badly damaged, but nonetheless

Table 3-1 BUILDINGS ON THE ACROPOLIS, ATHENS, GREECE

Building	Architect	Date of Construction
Propylaia	Mnesikles	437–432 B.C.E.
Parthenon	Iktinos and Kallikrates	448–432 B.C.E.
Erechtheion	Mnesikles	437 or 421–406/405 B.C.E.
Temple of Athena Nike	probably Kallikrates or Mnesikles	427–424 B.C.E.

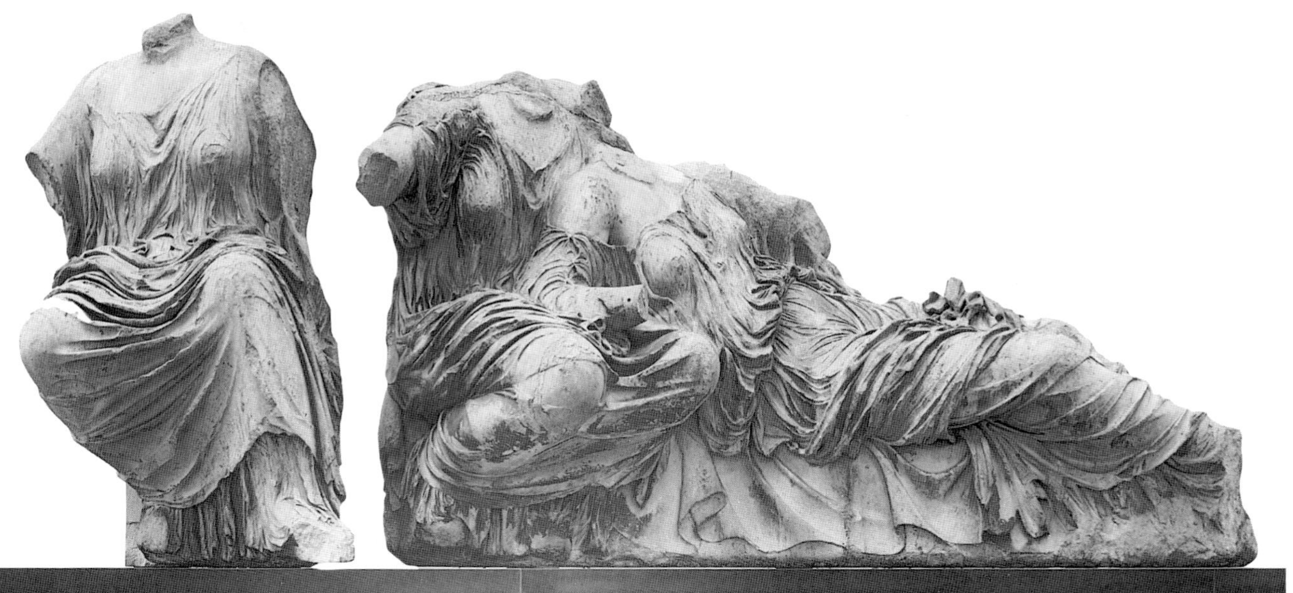

Figure 3.4 Three seated goddesses, east pediment, Parthenon, 438–432 B.C.E., marble. Far from their stiff ancestors, the movements of these casual figures seem to flow easily. The drapery is contrived to reveal the body and appears almost wet.

demonstrate the Classical balance between idealism and naturalism. Perfectly and powerfully proportioned bodies are revealed by naturalistic drapery folds (fig. 3.4).

The frieze (fig. 3.5) was carved ca. 440 B.C.E., also of marble. The background of the frieze was painted and so were details of the horses' bridles and reins. Other accessories were made of bronze and riveted on. A recent interpretation suggests that the Parthenon frieze is a version of one of the foundation myths of Athens, that of King Erechtheus and his daughters.

Figure 3.5 *Procession of Figures*, relief, from the Parthenon, Acropolis, Athens, ca. 440 B.C.E., marble, height of relief frieze 3′6″ (1.07 m), Musée du Louvre, Paris. Herve Lewandowski/ Reunion des Musées National/Art Resource, New York. The aesthetic principle of unity and variety is demonstrated here: The figures have enough in common to appear unified, yet sufficient variety to avoid monotony. The physical type favored in the Classical period was strong and young, idealized rather than individualized.

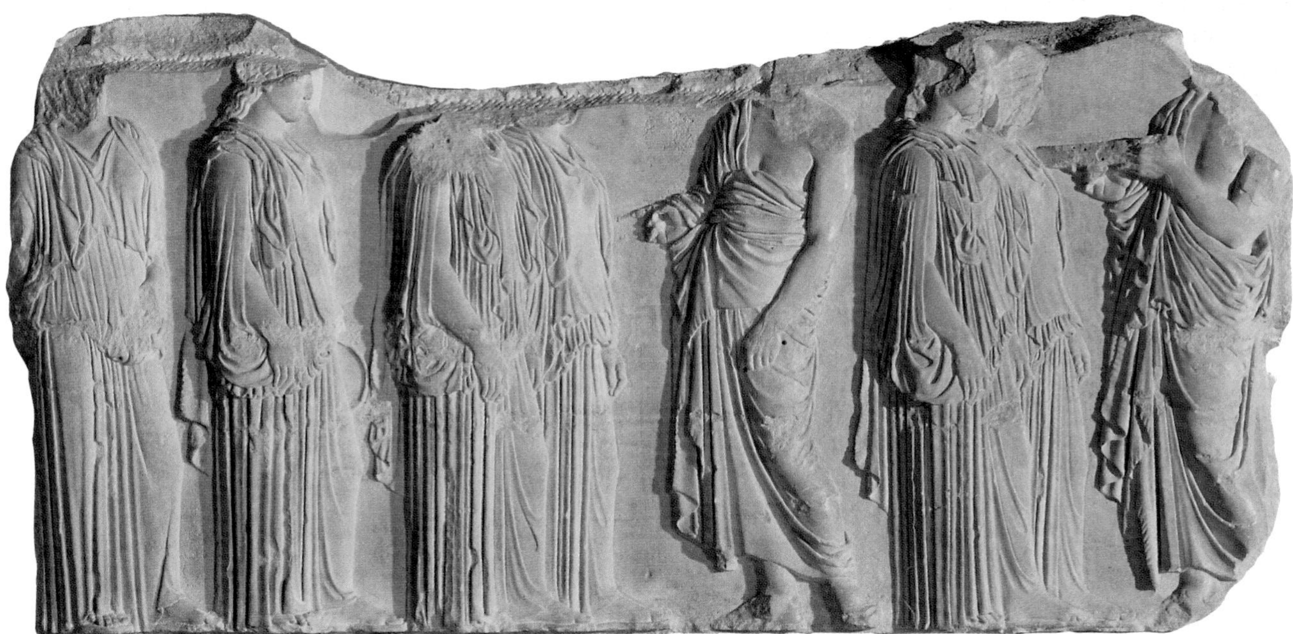

The Erechtheion. The most architecturally complex building on the Acropolis, the Erechtheion [er-EK-thee-on] (fig. 3.6), was begun either in 437 B.C.E., the same year as the Propylaia, or in 421 B.C.E., after the death of Perikles. Work continued until 406/405 B.C.E., but the building was never finished. The architect may have been Mnesikles, the architect of the Propylaia.

The most famous part of the Erechtheion is the Porch of the Maidens on the south side. Here are six **caryatids**—female figures used as architectural supports (male figures that function in the same way are called **atlantes**). The structural use of sculpture in architecture is a rarity in ancient Greece. These statues blend with the building, the curls of their hair flowing into the capitals. They stand in the *contrapposto* pose (see next section), the supporting leg hidden by the drapery of their dress that falls in folds simulating the fluting of a column, emphasizing their architectural role. The figures form an obvious group, yet each of the six is slightly different—an example of the Greek aesthetic principle of "unity and variety."

The Temple of Athena Nike. The Temple of Athena Nike (fig. 3.7), dated between 427 and 424 B.C.E., was probably built from a plan by either Kallikrates or Mnesikles. This miniature temple has four Ionic columns on the front and four on the back. The continuous sculpted frieze on the entablature is also an Ionic feature. Between 410 and 407 B.C.E. a surrounding wall covered with low-relief sculpted panels depicting Athena as she prepared for her victory celebration was added—*Nike* is Greek for "victory."

FIGURE 3.6 Mnesikles, Erechtheion, Acropolis, Athens, 437 or 421–406/405 B.C.E., marble. The most complex of the Acropolis buildings, the highly irregular plan of the Erechtheion covers several areas sacred to the early history of Athens. On the Porch of the Maidens, female figures (caryatids) perform the structural role of columns.

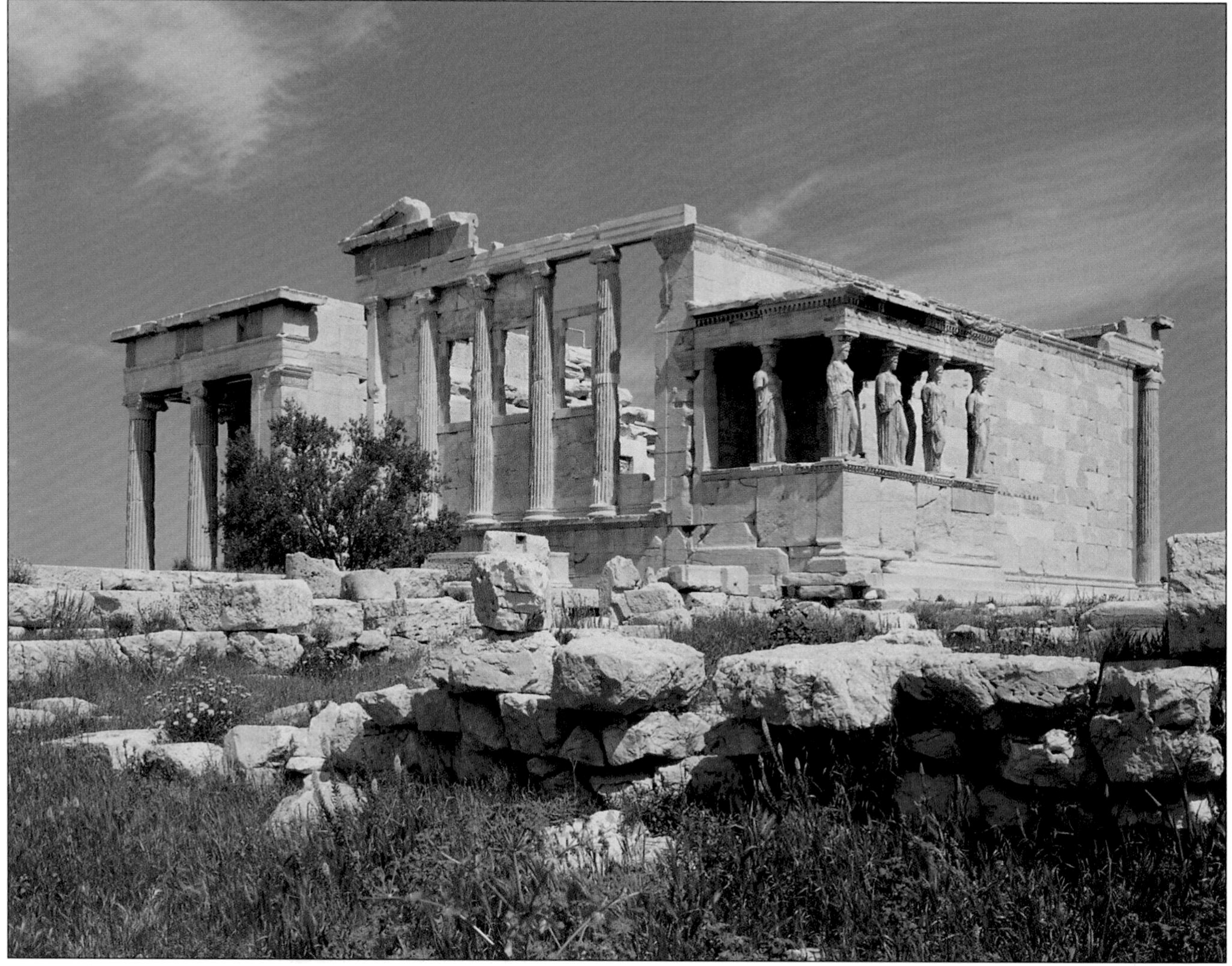

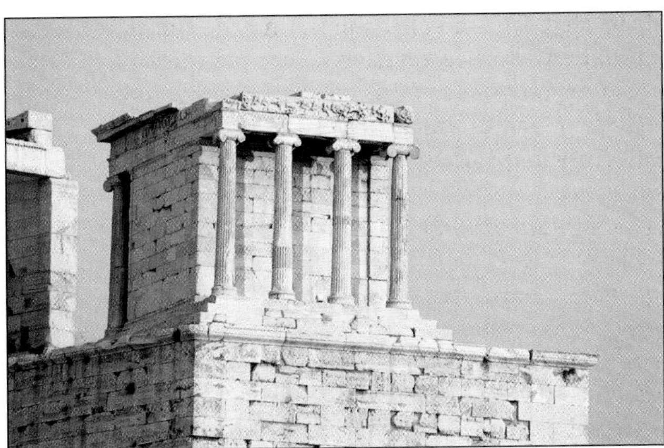

FIGURE 3.7 Probably Kallikrates or Mnesikles, Temple of Athena Nike, Acropolis, Athens, 427–424 B.C.E., marble. Dedicated to Nike, the winged goddess of victory, this tiny Ionic temple was largely dismantled and has now been reconstructed.

SCULPTURE

The chief subject of the sculpture on the Acropolis, characteristically Greek, is the human figure. Just as the design of the temples was determined by carefully conceived orders as well as mathematically precise notions of proper proportion and scale, the human figure was portrayed according to equally formalized ideal standards.

Kritios Boy. The kouros called the "Kritios Boy" (fig. 3.8) was executed in a style associated with that of the sculptor KRITIOS [CRIT-i-os] of Athens, whose work is otherwise known only from Roman copies. The *Kritios Boy* differs from earlier kouroi significantly in terms of pose. The spine forms a gentle S curve; one hip is raised slightly in apparent response to the displacement of weight onto one leg. This is the **contrapposto** (counterpoise) pose, introduced by the ancient Greeks at the beginning of the transition to the Classical period. The head is turned slightly to the side, the pose is relaxed and natural. The body is carved with accurate anatomical detail, and the Archaic smile has gone. A new sense of movement appears, in large part a result of his weight falling on a single leg. Although the arms are broken off, it is apparent that they were not placed rigidly at the sides as in earlier figures. The *Kritios Boy* indicates a growing anatomical understanding of bone, muscles, tendons, fat, flesh, and skin, and the way in which they work together.

Polykleitos. The sense of naturalness and perfection hinted at in the *Kritios Boy* is fully realized in the *Doryphoros (Spear-Bearer)* (fig. 3.9). This was originally made in bronze, ca. 450–440 B.C.E., by POLYKLEITOS [pohl-ee-KLYE-tus], but now survives only in a marble Roman copy. At about the same time as he was working on *The Spear-Bearer*, Polykleitos developed a set of written

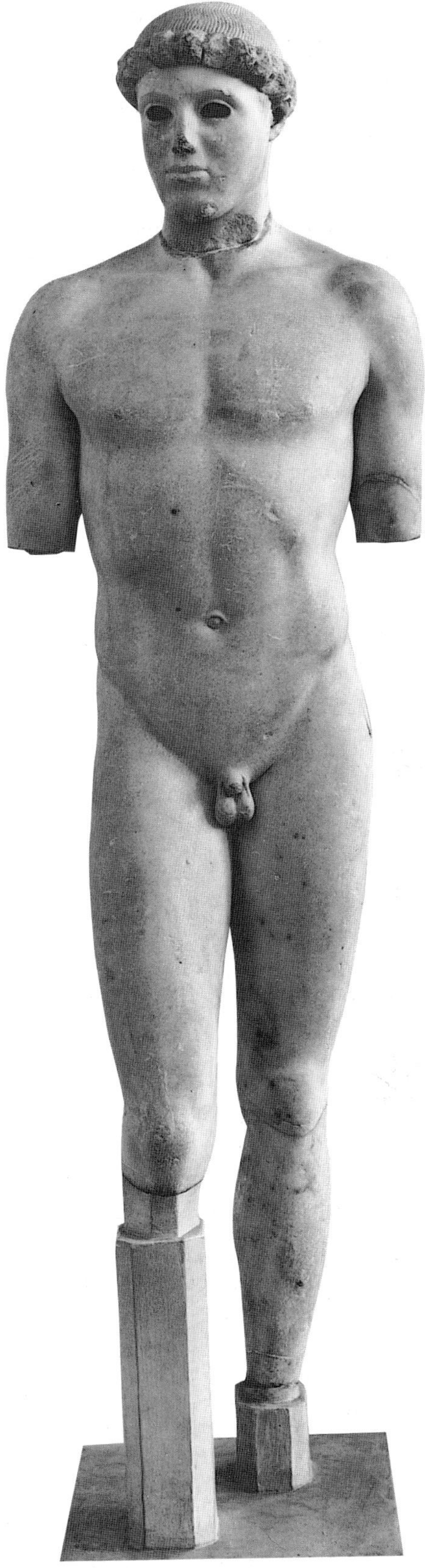

FIGURE 3.8 *Kritios Boy*, ca. 480 B.C.E., marble, height 3′10″ (1.17 m), Acropolis Museum, Athens. This figure is transitional between the Archaic and Classical periods. The rigid frontality of the Archaic era is broken by the gentle turn of the head and the slight movement in the torso.

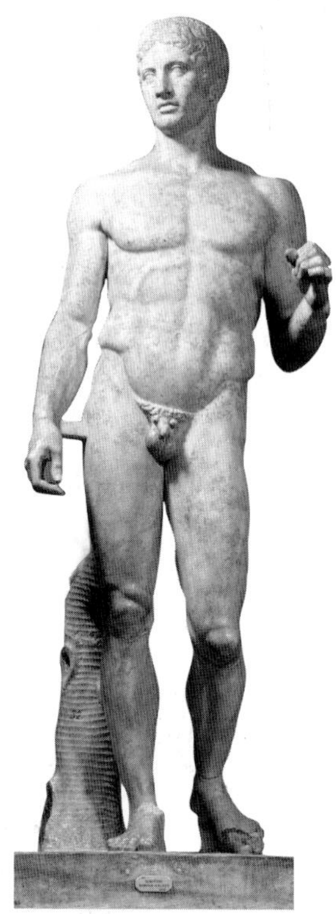

FIGURE 3.9 Polykleitos of Argos, *Doryphoros (Spear-Bearer)*, Roman copy of a Greek original ca. 440 B.C.E. Height 6′6″ (1.98 m). Museo Archeologico Nazionale, Naples, Italy, Scala/Art Resource, New York. In the Classical period, the relaxed and natural *contrapposto* (counterpoise) pose, with the weight on one leg, hips and shoulders no longer parallel, and spine in a gentle S curve, became the norm.

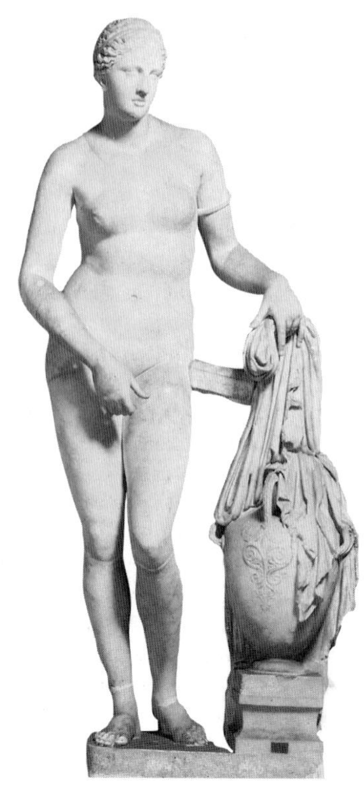

FIGURE 3.10 Praxiteles, *Aphrodite of Knidos*, Roman marble copy of a Greek original of ca. 350–300 B.C.E., height 6′8″ (2.03 m), Museo Pio Clementino, Musei Vaticani, Rome, Scala/Art Resource, New York. The female nude became a popular subject in the Hellenistic period. An illusion of warm soft flesh is created from cold hard stone.

rules for sculpting the ideal human form. By careful study of copies of Polykleitos' work, the basics of *The Canon* can be discerned. All parts of the body were considered. The height of the head was used as the unit of measurement for determining the overall height of the body—*The Spear-Bearer* is eight heads tall. This statue was viewed in antiquity as the definitive word on perfect proportions and was copied many times.

The Spear-Bearer stands in a fully developed *contrapposto* pose. Because only one leg is weight-bearing, the two sides are not identical. The pelvis and shoulders are tilted in opposite directions. The spine forms a gentle S shape. The pose is natural, relaxed, and perfectly balanced. With complete understanding of the human body, Polykleitos recorded everything—down to the veins in the backs of the hands.

Praxiteles. The sculptor PRAXITELES [prac-SIT-el-ease] is known especially for Aphrodite (Venus) figures, represented by the *Aphrodite of Knidos* (fig. 3.10), another Roman copy after an original of ca. 350–300 B.C.E. Aphrodite is the goddess of love, born from the sea. In the sixth and fifth centuries B.C.E., male nudes were commonplace, as we have seen, but the female nude was a rarity. However, due to the influence of Praxiteles, whose work was highly praised in ancient times, the female nude became a major subject for late Classical and Hellenistic artists. The subject here is the modest Aphrodite—she covers herself—yet sensuality is not suppressed in the slightest. She stands in a slight S curve, weight on one foot, turning her head, in a relaxed and easy pose.

VASE PAINTING

White-Ground Ceramics. In the first half of the fifth century B.C.E., a new technique was introduced into Greek ceramic production. In this **white-ground technique,** the vase is made of the same reddish Attic clay that was used for earlier black- and red-figure pottery. However, here a white slip is painted over the surface of the vase. The figures are not then filled in, as they were in the black-figure technique, nor is the background filled in, as in the red-figure technique. Instead, the central picture and surrounding decorative patterns are painted on with a fine brush. The style is characterized by free and spontaneous lines. The white-ground technique presents the

Then & Now

THE OLYMPIAD

The ancient Greeks had a prescription for good living that is still popular today: "*mens sana in corpore sano,*" as the Romans translated it, "A sound mind in a sound body." The Greeks celebrated the human body and physical accomplishment as no other culture had before, particularly in sporting contests. These events were an important part of the Pan-Athenaic festival in Athens, but the most enduring of all sporting contests was the Olympiad, begun in 776 B.C.E. at Olympia on the Greek Peloponnese (fig. 3.11). These Olympic Games were held every four years until 394 C.E., when the Roman Emperor Theodosius abolished all non-Christian events in the empire.

From the outset, the short foot race, or *stade*, was the most important event. Held in honor of Zeus, the course was six hundred feet in length (the length of the *stadium* at Olympia), about equivalent to a modern-day two-hundred meter race. Legend has it that at the first Olympics, Herakles paced off the length himself by placing one foot in front of the other six hundred times.

The first thirteen Olympic Games consisted solely of this race, but soon the *diaulos* was added, consisting of two lengths of the stadium (or about one time around a modern track), as well as the *dolichos*, a long-distance race consisting of either twenty or twenty-four lengths of the stadium, perhaps two and a half miles. An athlete who won all three races was known as a *triastes*, or "tripler." The greatest tripler of them all was Leonidas of Rhodes, who won all three events in four successive Olympiads between 164 and 152 B.C.E.

Over the years, other events were added, including, in 708 B.C.E., the *pentathlon*, consisting of five events—discus, long-jump, javelin, running, and wrestling—all contested in the course of a single afternoon. Only two measurements of the early long-jumps survive, from the mid-fifth century B.C.E., both of which are over sixteen meters in length. Since the current world long-jump record is just under nine meters, it is probable that the Greek long-jump was a multiple jump event, comparable to the modern triple-jump (the modern record of which is just over seventeen meters). By the mid-fifth century B.C.E. the games had become a five-day event and had been expanded to include a chariot race and even sculpture exhibitions.

Centuries after their suppression by Theodosius, the Olympic Games were reinitiated in Athens in 1896. At this first modern Olympiad, the organizers celebrated the return of the games by introducing a new running event, the "marathon," to celebrate Phidippides's legendary run in 490 B.C.E. from the plain of Marathon to Athens with news of the stunning Greek defeat of the Persians.

Today the Olympic Games have become more than just an athletic contest. They are big business. The United States Olympic Committee has an annual operating budget of $388 million for funding the training and preparation of U.S. athletes. They are also usually a major economic boon to the community that hosts the games. When Atlanta hosted the 1996 Summer Games, the cost of 73,000 hotel rooms pumped over $5.1 billion into the local economy. After more than a century of being held outside Greece, the Olympics returned to Athens in the Summer of 2004.

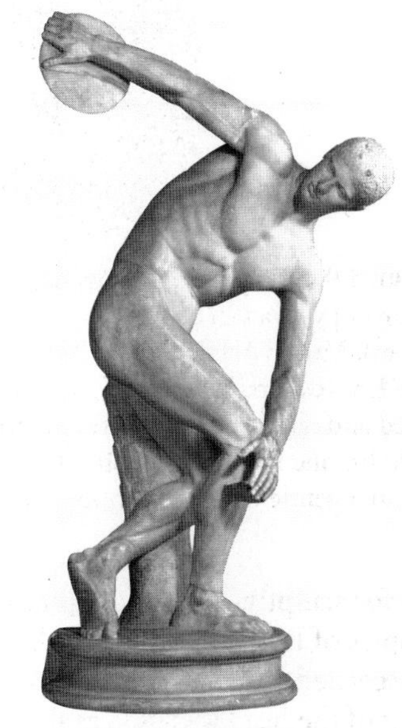

FIGURE 3.11 Myron of Athens, *Discobolus (Discus Thrower)*, Roman marble copy after a bronze original of ca. 450 B.C.E., lifesize, Museo Nazionale Romano delle Terme, Rome, Italy. Scala/Art Resource New York.

painter with no more technical problems than working on the equivalent of a white piece of paper—except that the surface of the vase curves.

The white-ground technique is associated in particular with **lekythoi** (singular, **lekythos**), small cylindrical oil jugs with a single handle, used as funerary monuments and offerings. A lekythos (fig. 3.12) by the Achilles Painter, painted ca. 445–430 B.C.E. in a mature Classical style, shows a muse and maiden on Mount Helikon playing a kithara, a stringed musical instrument. Mount Helikon is the mountain of the muses; muses, goddesses of the arts, excelled in song.

EMERGENCE OF DRAMA

Aeschylus. Greek drama developed from choral celebrations honoring Dionysos, the Greek god of wine and fertility. These celebrations included dancing as part of the religious ritual. Legend has it that the poet Thespis introduced a speaker who was separate from the chorus

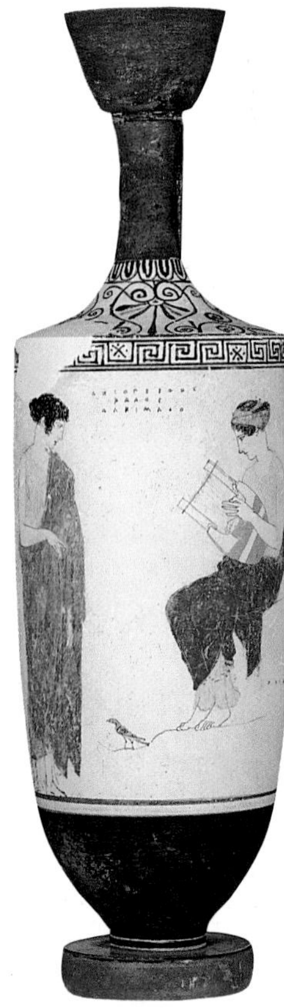

FIGURE 3.12 Achilles Painter, *Muse and Maiden*, lekythos, white-ground style, ca. 445–430 B.C.E., terra cotta, height 16″ (40.7 cm), Staatliche Antikensammlungen und Glyptothek, Munich, Germany. One of the great advantages of working in the white-ground technique is that technical restrictions are reduced to a minimum. Neither the figures (as in the black-figure style) nor the background (as in the red-figure style) need to be filled in.

but who engaged in dialogue with it. From this dialogue drama emerged. A second actor was then added to this first speaker and the chorus by AESCHYLUS [ESS-kuh-luss] (ca. 524–456 B.C.E.), who is today acknowledged as the "creator of tragedy."

Greek plays were performed in huge outdoor amphitheaters capable of seating upward of fifteen thousand people. The theater at Epidauros, for example, accommodated sixteen thousand (fig. 3.13). The audience sat in tiers of seats built into the slope of the hillside. The hills echoed the sound of the actors' voices, which were projected through large masks that further amplified them. The words appear to have been mostly sung to music, and music accompanied the dances performed by the chorus.

Ancient Greek plays were performed on an elevated platform. Behind the acting area was a building (*skene*) that functioned as both dressing room and scenic background. Below the stage was the orchestra, or dancing place for the chorus. Standing between the actors and the audience, the chorus had an important part in the drama, often representing the communal perspective. One of the chorus's principal functions was to mark the divisions between the scenes of a play, by dancing and chanting poetry. These lyrical choral interludes typically comment on the action and interpret it while providing the author's perspective on the mythic sources of the plays.

Aeschylus is the earliest dramatist whose works have survived. Seven of his nineteen plays are still extant. His plays, like those of his successors Sophocles and Euripides, were all written for the twice-annual festivals for Dionysos held at Athens. Each dramatist had to submit three tragedies and a lighthearted "satyr" play for performance together at the festival. The work for which Aeschylus is best known—the trilogy called the *Oresteia* [oar-es-TIE-uh], after the central character, Orestes [oar-ES-tees]—won first prize in the festival at Athens of 458 B.C.E. The first play in the trilogy, *Agamemnon*, dramatizes the story of the murder of the Greek king, Agamemnon, who upon returning from the Trojan War is slain by his wife, Clytemnestra [clie-tem-NES-tra], and her lover Aegisthus [aye-GISS-this]. The second play, *The Libation Bearers*, describes the return of Agamemnon and Clytemnestra's son, Orestes, who kills his mother and her lover to avenge the death of his father. The concluding play, *The Eumenides* [you-MEN-ih-dees], describes the pursuit of Orestes by the Furies for his act of vengeance and Orestes' ultimate exoneration in an Athenian court of law.

Taken together, the three plays dramatize the growth of Greek civilization—the movement from a Homeric tribal society system, in which vengeance was the rule and individuals felt obligated to exact private vengeance, to a modern society ruled by law. The third play of the trilogy describes the establishment in Athens, under the jurisdiction of the goddess Athena, the city's patron, of a court of law to decide Orestes' case. Athena herself must render the verdict as the jury of citizens is unable to decide Orestes' guilt or innocence. Symbolically, with the establishment of the court of law in the last part of the trilogy, the old order passes and a new order emerges. Communal justice rather than the pursuit of individual vengeance comes to regulate civil society.

Sophocles. Of the Greek tragic dramatists, SOPHOCLES [SAH-fuh-clees] (496–406 B.C.E.) is perhaps the most widely read and performed today. Unlike those of his forebear Aeschylus, Sophocles' plays focus on individual human, rather than broad civil and religious, concerns. His most famous plays—*Oedipus the King* and *Antigone*—center on private crises and portray characters under extreme duress. *Antigone*, which takes place in Thebes, a city prostrated by war, turns on the difficult decisions that Antigone, Oedipus' daughter, and King Creon, his brother-in-law, must make. In *Oedipus the King*, set against a background of a plague-stricken city, Sophocles examines the behavior of

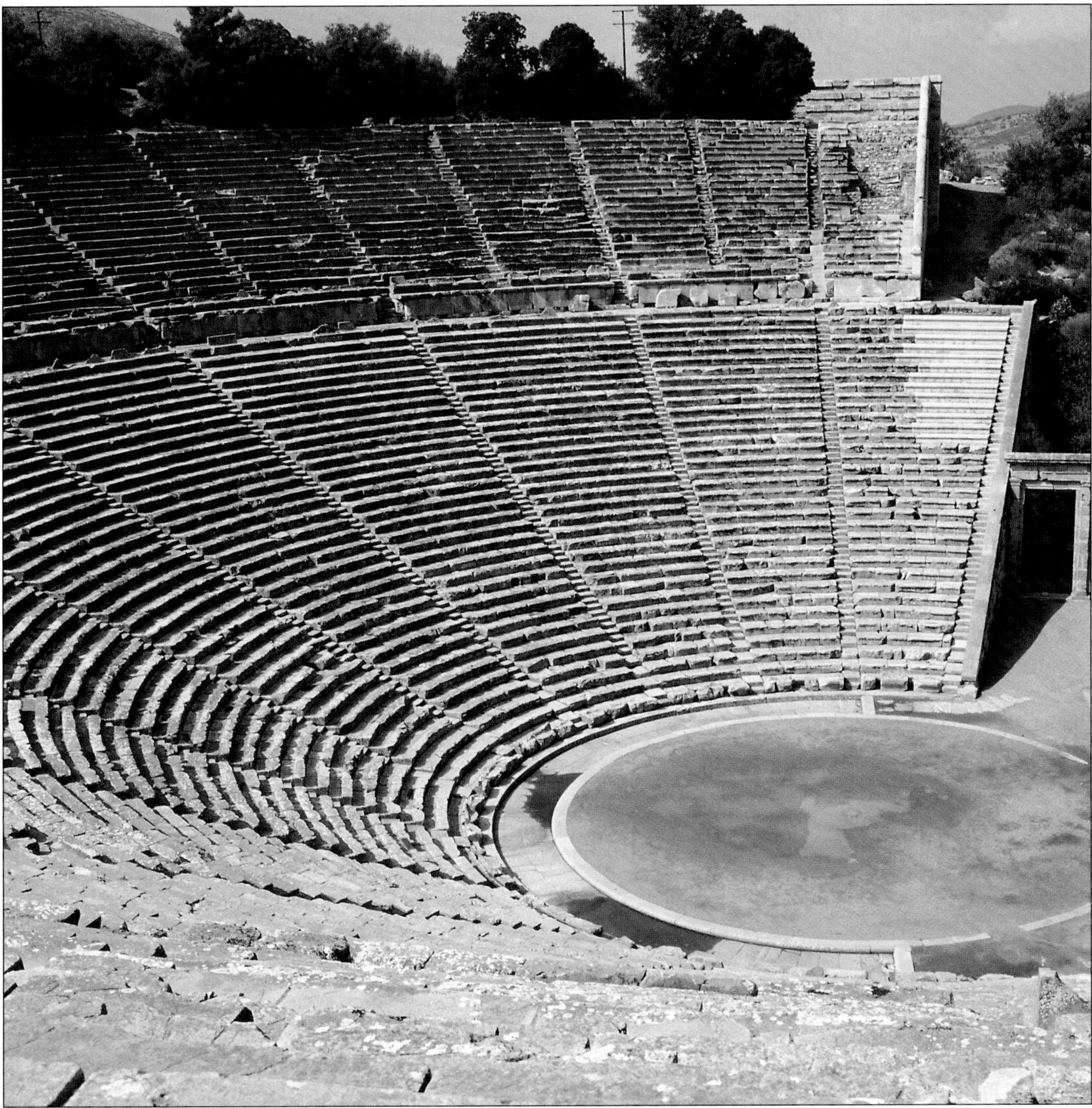

FIGURE 3.13 Polykleitos the Younger, theater, Epidauros, ca. 350 B.C.E., later modified. Alinari, Art Resource, New York. Ancient Greek theaters were built into a hillside that provided support for the tiers of seats. Ancient Roman theaters, in contrast, were built freestanding.

Oedipus, who has been destined before birth to murder his father and marry his mother.

Athenian audiences watching performances of *Oedipus the King* would have been familiar with Oedipus' story from sources such as Homer's *Odyssey*. Oedipus' parents, King Laius and Queen Jocasta of Thebes, had been foretold of their son's terrible fate and therefore left him as a baby in the wilderness to die. This plan went awry when the child was taken by a shepherd to Corinth, where he was adopted by a childless couple, King Polybus and Queen Merope. Upon hearing an oracle pronounce his fate, and believing Polybus and Merope to be his natural parents, Oedipus then left Corinth to get far away from the king and queen. Ironically, however, en route to his true birthplace, Thebes, Oedipus kills an old man who gets in his way. This old man, Oedipus only much later discovers, was his true father, Laius.

Sophocles' version of the story, *Oedipus the King*, begins at the point when Thebes has been suffering a series of catastrophes, the most terrible of which is a devastating plague. Oedipus had previously saved Thebes from the Sphinx, a winged creature with the body of a lion and the head of a woman. The Sphinx had terrorized the city by devouring anyone who crossed its path and was unable to answer its riddle correctly—"What goes on four legs in the morning, two legs in the afternoon, and three legs in the evening?" Oedipus solved the riddle by answering "Man." After slaying the Sphinx, Oedipus was given the kingship of Thebes and the hand of its recently widowed queen, Jocasta, in reward. Unknown to Oedipus, but known to the Athenian audience, was the fact that Jocasta was his mother and her recently slain husband, Laius, had been killed by Oedipus himself. All this and more Oedipus soon discovers as he comes to self-knowledge.

Sophocles' *Oedipus the King* is one of the greatest tragedies in theatrical history—one of the definitions of **tragedy** is the representation of the downfall of a great hero. It also provides one of the best examples of **dramatic irony,** where speeches have different meanings for the audience and the speaker: The audience knows much more than the speaker. Thematically, the play raises questions about fate and human responsibility, particularly the extent to which Oedipus is responsible for his own tragic destiny. Sophocles portrays his tragic protagonists heroically. These tragic heroes suffer the consequences of their actions nobly and with grandeur.

In the twentieth century, Sigmund Freud used the Oedipus story as the basis for his theory of the **Oedipus complex.** According to Freud's theory, a boy grows up competing with his father for his mother's attention and affection, so much so that the boy at times hates his rival father enough to wish him dead. Conversely, his feelings for his mother are rooted in his unresolved desire for sexual gratification with her.

Euripides. One of the greatest and most disturbing of Greek tragic dramatists is EURIPIDES [you-RIP-idease] (ca. 480–406 B.C.E.). As Aristotle put it, where Sophocles depicts people as they ought to be, Euripides depicts them as they really are. His plays were written under the shadow of the Peloponnesian War, and they spare no one, showing humankind at its worst. Although ostensibly about the enslavement of the female survivors of Troy, *The Trojan Women*, first staged in 415 B.C.E., is a barely disguised indictment of the women of Melos after the Athenian defeat of that city. In *The Bacchae*, Euripides depicts a civilization gone mad, as followers of Dionysos kill the king of Thebes under the drunken belief that he is a wild animal. Dionysos' followers, perhaps in part a portrait of the Athenian people, are unwilling to think for themselves and hence liable to be led blindly into the most senseless of acts.

In *Electra*, a play that somewhat parallels *Oedipus the King*, Euripides creates a female counterpart to Sophocles' tragic hero. With the help of her brother, Orestes, Electra murders her mother, Clytemnestra, thus avenging the death of her father, Agamemnon, at the hands of Clytemnestra and her lover. Euripides emphasizes Electra's haunted mind after her just but morally horrifying act.

Aristophanes. All was not tragedy on the Greek stage, however. Comedy was very popular, and the master of the medium was ARISTOPHANES [air-ihs-TOF-fannees] (ca. 445–388 B.C.E.). His plays satirized contemporary politics and political personalities, poking fun at Greek society and ridiculing the rich in particular. Aristophanes even took on Socrates, depicting him as a hopeless dreamer. In *Lysistrata*, produced in 411 B.C.E. in the midst of the same Peloponnesian War that so outraged Euripides, Aristophanes' title character persuades her fellow Athenian women to withhold sexual favors from their husbands until peace is declared. They carry out their plans with merriment, teasing their husbands and even occupying the Acropolis. The women win the day, judging their husbands' priorities acutely, and at the end of the play Spartans and Athenians are reconciled and dance together in joy.

ATHENS AND SPARTA

Athens	Sparta
Literate society; poetry and drama	Militaristic society; no poetry and no drama
Democracy	Oligarchy
Scientific/philosophical	No science or philosophy
Girls not educated	Girls educated
Women excluded from athletic contests	Women competed in athletic contests
Women prevented from owning property	Women allowed to own property

PHILOSOPHY

Of all the legacies of Greece, its philosophical tradition is one of the most enduring. The Greeks believed that what distinguished human beings was their ability to reason, and thus the philosopher held a special place in their society.

Socrates. SOCRATES [SOC-ra-tees] (469–399 B.C.E.), the most famous of Western philosophers, is known primarily through his characterization in Plato's dialogues. In Plato's writings, Socrates (fig. 3.14) appears as a figure whose goal is self-knowledge and truth. Best known for questioning others' beliefs and eliciting their assumptions in a form of dialectical inquiry known as the "Socratic method," Socrates is a model of intellectual honesty. He was sentenced to death in 399 B.C.E. after being put on trial for impiety and corruption of the young. The authorities offered Socrates the chance to escape, but the philosopher chose death over exile.

Known as the "Father of Ethics," Socrates pursued wisdom so as to know the good, the just, and the beautiful.

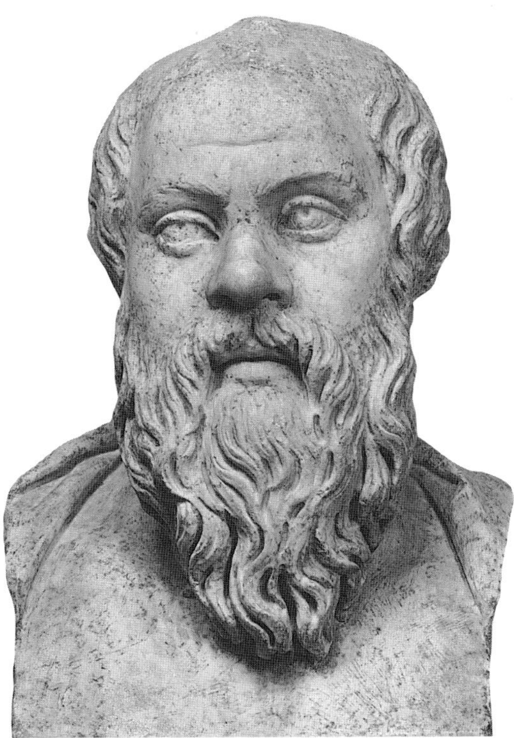

FIGURE 3.14 Lysippos, *portrait bust of Socrates*, Roman copy of an original bronze of ca. 350 B.C.E., marble, lifesize, Museo Nazionale Romano, Rome. At his trial in 399 B.C.E., for impropriety toward the gods and corruption of the young, Socrates cheerfully admitted to causing unrest and insisted it was his duty to seek the truth.

His pursuit of right living was governed by his famous maxim "Know thyself." Socrates urged self-examination and questioning of one's own and others' ideas and assumptions. Socrates believed that such discourse was necessary for the moral life and happiness.

Socrates was active at a time when **Sophists** taught philosophy for practical and opportunistic ends. Although Sophist philosophers shared Socrates' emphasis on the concerns of life in the world, their aims and practices differed from his. In place of eternal truths, the Sophists believed that morals and ethics were matters of convention and that no such thing as truth existed. Knowledge, the Sophists said, was relative, based on individual experience, and hence could be reduced to opinion. Unlike Socrates, the Sophists would argue either side of an issue with the sole goal of being persuasive. The phrase "mere rhetoric" and the term "sophistry" to mean specious reasoning refer to the practices of the Greek Sophists.

For Socrates, as expressed in his maxim "The unexamined life is not worth living," self-awareness through reason determines how to master passion and appetite. Living a virtuous life directed by a reasoned pursuit of moral perfection leads to happiness.

Socrates provided Western thought with a new philosophical direction. By living according to his principles, by making philosophy a lifelong process, Socrates also provided a model and ideal of one who loves wisdom, the literal meaning, in Greek, of the word "philosopher."

Socrates is the philosopher *par excellence*, the most influential philosopher of them all, though, paradoxically, hardly anything is known about him, and he wrote nothing at all. The real Socrates remains an elusive figure, available to us through some bits and pieces in Plato's dialogues. In fact, it is largely through Plato's writings that we come to know Socrates—the Socrates who is quoted by Plato in his *Phaedo* as saying, "To be afraid of death is only another form of thinking that one is wise when one is not. It is to think that one knows what one does not know." We know Socrates as the philosopher who reminds us that the more we know, the less we know; as the thinker who encourages us to be humble about what we think we know; as the saintly prophet who lives and breathes wisdom every moment of his waking life, and when he comes to die, does so with a dignity and lightness of being that takes our breath away.

Plato. PLATO [PLAY-toh] (427–347 B.C.E.), a pupil of Socrates, and Socrates are frequently spoken of in the same breath because so many of Plato's dialogues present Socrates as a character and speaker. As a result, it is not easy to determine where Socrates leaves off and Plato begins. It is perhaps best to consider Plato's idealist philosophy as extending key elements of Socratic thought. In dialogues such as *The Symposium* and *The Republic*, Plato (fig. 3.15) developed the perspective implicit in his mentor's life and teaching.

Plato believed that truth could be found in mathematical perfection. Plato argued, for instance, that the *idea* of a circle, rather than any actual example of one, was true and perfect. Any example of a circle only approximated the perfect idea which existed in a special realm that transcended all particular manifestations. Plato identified this realm as the realm of Perfect Forms or Ideas.

To understand what philosophy is, among the best advice is simply to read Plato. It was Plato who introduced the word "philosophy" into general currency, and it was Plato who practiced the kind of study and analysis which we understand as "philosophy." Plato was born, lived, worked, philosophized, and died in Athens. The name Platon, which means "broad" in Greek, was given him in his school days because of his broad shoulders, though his given name was Aristocles. Although Plato was trained in poetry and warfare, the normal preparation for an aristocrat of his time, he was more interested in politics and philosophy. At the heart of his philosophical investigations was a search for truth.

Plato postulated that ideal Goodness, Truth, and Beauty were all One, in the realm of Ideal Forms. Thus all actions can be measured against an ideal, and that ideal standard can be used as a goal toward which human beings might strive. According to Plato, human beings should be less concerned with the material world of impermanence and change and more concerned with the spiritual realm of Perfect Forms. Thus the highest

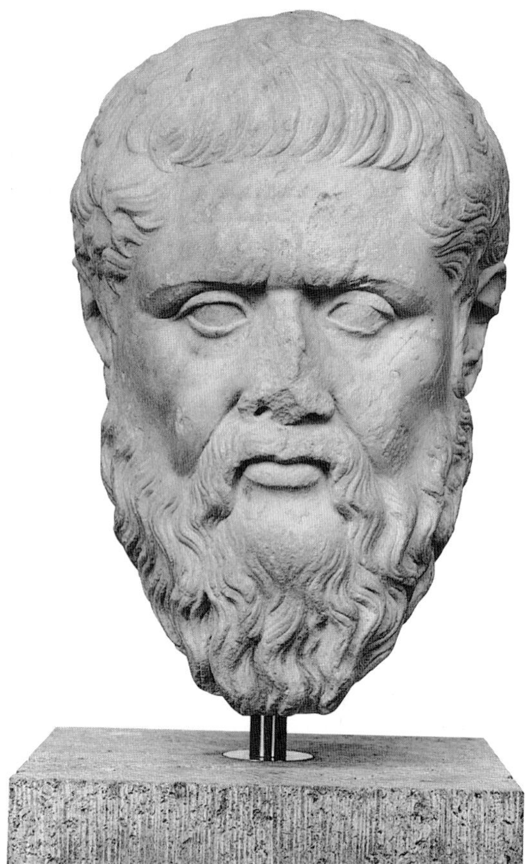

FIGURE 3.15 Silanion (?), *portrait bust of Plato*, 350–340 B.C.E., Roman copy of an original bronze of ca. 427–347 B.C.E., marble, Staatliche Antikensammlungen und Glyptothek, Munich, Germany. Although his real name was Arsitocles, Plato went by his nickname, which means "the broad one," a physical trait evident even in this portrait bust.

spiritual principle, reason, should be used to control emotion, or spirit, and desire.

Both ideas are advanced in Plato's best-known work, *The Republic*, a complex and ambitious book concerned primarily with justice and how to achieve a just society. Plato proposes the division of society into three layers, each of which reflects one of the three aspects of the soul. Plato argues that people whose impulse is toward satisfying their desires are not capable of making judgments in accordance with reason and should therefore occupy the lowest position in society, that of servitude. Above these workers are the soldiers, whose primary force is that of emotion, spiritedness. The soldiers and the workers in Plato's republic work together at their allotted tasks under the directorship of the highest social group, the philosophers, whose decisions govern the republic by reason.

For Plato, as noted in his *Republic*, "the state is the soul writ large." And the reason that guides the Philosopher Kings of his ideal state corresponds to the wisdom espoused when a person demonstrates an understanding of his Ideal of the Good.

A humorous story can serve to illustrate how one person's good differs from another's, and thus how the ideal is not easy to reach.

> *At a college faculty meeting, an angel appears and addresses the chair of the philosophy department with these words: "I will grant you one of the following blessings: Wisdom, Beauty—or a million dollars," The professor, right away says, "I wish for wisdom." After a flash of lightning, the professor appears transformed, but remains sitting and staring down at the table. One of his colleagues whispers, "Say something." And the professor says, "I should have taken the money."*

In Book 7 of *The Republic*, Plato uses two analogies to explain his idea about different levels of knowledge or understanding. One, the analogy of the Divided Line, presents a vertical line divided into four segments, with the upper two representing the intellectual world and the lower two the visible world. The lowest part represents shadows and reflections (explained below in the Allegory of the Cave); the one above that represents material and natural things. The two lower parts are complemented by the upper segments, which represent reasoning about the world and its objects (the lower segment of the upper line), and philosophical principles arrived at without reference to objects (abstract thought, the uppermost portion of the line).

Plato supplements this image about the nature of knowledge with his famous Allegory of the Cave. In this, he describes a cave in which human beings are chained to a wall. The only light visible is that reflected from a fire behind and above them. When objects are cast as shadows on the wall, the cave inhabitants take these shadows for reality. Only the one freed from the cave can see that what he had previously considered real are simply shadowy reflections of their actual counterparts. Instead of being a prisoner of illusion like those still chained in the cave, the escapee has a true knowledge of reality.

For Plato, such a revelation reflects the difference between ignorance and knowledge of truth, between the world of material objects and the realm of Ideal Essences, the true forms of those things. This division between the higher spiritual forms and the lower material world is echoed by other dualisms in Plato's philosophy. Foremost among the divisions are those between the philosopher and the common people, the perfect and the imperfect, and the spiritual life and the physical life.

Aristotle. Born in Stageira, in Thrace, ARISTOTLE [air-iss-TOT-ul] (384–322 B.C.E.) studied in Plato's school, the Academy, in Athens. He remained there for twenty years until Plato's death in 347 B.C.E., when he left to establish his own school, first in Assos and later in Lesbos. Aristotle's most famous pupil was Alexander the Great, whom the philosopher served as private tutor from 343 until 336 B.C.E., when Alexander succeeded to the Macedonian throne.

Connections

LITERARY ELEMENTS OF PLATO'S *DIALOGUES*

Plato's *Philosophical Dialogues* have long been regarded as a literary as well as a philosophic masterpiece. In addition to their engaging conversational style, Plato's writings exhibit the following characteristics:

- The *Dialogues* individually are cast as intellectual dramas. They dramatize a conflict of ideas, typically represented by Socrates and one or more other speakers.
- The *Dialogues* collectively present a quest or epic journey in search of wisdom. An additional epic dimension is evident in the character of Socrates, who is unafraid of the unjust death to which he is condemned by the Athenian authorities. The neoclassical French painter, David, portrayed Socrates as he was preparing to drink the hemlock that would kill him.
- The *Dialogues* employ various forms of metaphorical thinking and analogy, the most famous of which is Plato's Allegory of the Cave in Book 7 of *The Republic*.
- The *Dialogues* contain various repeating images, the most important of which, light, symbolizes the highest form of knowledge, a form of divinely intuited illumination.

In 335 B.C.E. Aristotle, known as the "Father of Science," returned to Athens to establish his own school at the Lyceum, where lectures and discussions took place under a covered walkway. Lecturers moved about among their audiences, thereby acquiring the designation "Peripatetics" (walkers). Like Socrates, Aristotle was charged with impiety and condemned by the Athenian tribunal of judges. Upon leaving Athens before a sentence of death could be carried out, Aristotle is reputed to have remarked that he would not allow Athens to commit a second crime against philosophy.

Aristotle was fascinated by plant and animal life. One-quarter of his writings, in fact, is concerned with categorizing nature. He identified more than five hundred animal species and dissected as many as fifty. And while he was an observant student of life both on sea and land, he declared incorrectly that plants reproduce only asexually, that the heart was the center of human consciousness, and that there was an empty space in the back of our heads where our souls reside. In what is surely insulting to women, Aristotle believed that women are defective by nature, primarily because they can't produce male fluid, or semen, which the Greeks believed to contain the little seeds into which full human beings develop. Thus, it can be said that as a primitive scientist, Aristotle was often mistaken, though as a logician, ethicist, and dramatic theorist he exerted an enduring influence.

Aristotle's logic provides a framework for scientific and philosophical thinking still in use today. The basis of Aristotle's logic is an analysis of argument. Its central feature is the **syllogism.** In syllogistic reasoning, one proposition or statement follows from another by necessity, when the premises are true. In such a case the syllogism is considered valid, as in the following example:

All philosophers are mortal.
Aristotle is a philosopher.
Aristotle is moral.

In the next example, the syllogism is invalid even though the conclusion is true, because one of the propositions—the first—is untrue:

All philosophers are men.
Aristotle was a philosopher.
Aristotle was a man.

Aristotle's logic also includes an analysis of the basic categories used to describe the natural world. According to Aristotle, things possess substance (their primary reality) and incidental qualities. Aristotle's distinction is sometimes classified as one between "essential" and "accidental" properties, such that the essential properties make a thing what it is, whereas the accidental ones determine how it is what it is, but not what it is *per se*. For example, Aristotle believed that rationality was essential for all human beings; it is what makes us human rather than members of another species. And since Socrates was a human being, his rationality defined him as being Socrates. For Socrates, moreover, rationality was not only an essential property of his being; it was his singular defining and most compelling quality. Without the property or essential characteristic of rationality, Socrates would not have been Socrates. In contrast to this essential quality of rationality, Aristotle considered Socrates' physical appearance, his snub-nose, for example, as accidental, nonessential. Socrates' snub-nose was not essential to who Socrates was; it was, rather, an incidental or accidental feature of how Socrates was who and what he was. And if Socrates had lived in the plastic surgery era and had a nose job, he would still have been Socrates, Aristotle's and our model of a rational thinker.

Aristotle disagreed with his teacher Plato on a number of important issues. For Aristotle, an object's matter and form are inseparable. Even though we can think of the "whiteness" of a dog and its "dogness," those concepts do not have independent existence outside of the things they embody.

Unlike Plato, who posited a realm where the perfect idea of a dog exists independent of actual dogs, for Aristotle the idea of a dog can only exist in relation to an actual canine quadruped. By insisting on the link between form and matter, Aristotle brought Platonic ideas down to earth.

Similarly, Aristotle emphasized the way the substance of a thing becomes itself in a *process* of growth and development. With his early study of biology as an influence, Aristotle's thinking takes account of development and process in ways that Plato's more mathematically influenced philosophy does not. For example, Aristotle describes the *potential* of a seed to become a flower or a fruit, of an embryo to become a living human or animal.

Aristotle's philosophy is grounded in the notion of teleology, which views the end or goal of an object or being as more important than its starting point or beginning. His teleological mind explains the way all material things are designed to achieve their purpose and attain their end. This end or goal of each thing is the fulfillment of the potential it embodies from the beginning of its existence.

An acorn is meant to become an oak tree; an egg is meant to hatch into a bird. Bees and beans and bananas all have their own telos, or inner end-goal, to become what they are meant to be. The following humorous story might help anchor this notion:

> *A woman was walking down the street with her grandchildren. A friend stopped to ask how old they were. She replied, "The dentist is four and the surgeon is six."*

Clearly, the woman had the end in sight for both of her grandchildren.

Aristotle arrives at a conviction about the nature of God from logic rather than from ethics or religious faith. In his *Physics*, Aristotle argues that everything is in motion toward realizing its potential. Because everything is in motion, there must be something that provided the first impulse (the prime mover) and that itself is not in motion. For to be in motion is to be in a potential state, and the prime mover must be in a state of completeness and thus not in motion. The prime mover, therfore, must be immaterial as well as unchanging.

Finally, Aristotle differed from his Greek predecessors significantly in his approach to ethics. For Aristotle, there were no absolutely unchanging ethical norms to guide behavior and determine conduct. Instead, there were only approximations based on the principle of the mean between extremes. Courage thus exists as a balance between cowardice and rash behavior, and temperance as a balance between deprivation and overindulgence. Virtue consists of negotiating between extremes, the balance point changing according to circumstances.

Aristotle's ethics is grounded in the realities and contingencies of this world. Aristotle consistently emphasized concrete, tangible, everyday experience and thus provided a necessary empirical counterpoint to the idealism espoused by his teacher and predecessor, Plato. Together their complementary philosophies have spurred theological and philosophical speculation for more than two thousand years. If, as one modern philosopher put it, "All philosophy is but a footnote to Plato," Aristotle's has been the richest, most complex, and most influential "footnote" of all.

Of his many achievements, Aristotle's work as the first Western literary theorist has been among his most influential. Aristotle's literary ideas are developed in his *Poetics*, a treatise on the nature of literature, focusing particularly on Sophocles' *Oedipus the King*. *The Poetics* offers a provocative and enduring set of ideas about the literary experience. Aristotle, in fact, is concerned in *The Poetics* not only with literature but with art in general.

An important idea derived from *The Poetics* concerns Aristotle's notion of "catharsis." Aristotle explains catharsis as a purging of the passions of pity and fear aroused in an audience during the tragic action of a play. Aristotle considers this catharsis the goal or end of tragedy. Aristotle's reasoning reverses conventional wisdom, suggesting that an audience's experience of pity and fear at, for example, Oedipus' tragic fate, would provide pleasure and not pain. The reason is that the emotions built up during the course of the tragic dramatic action are "purged" by the end of the performance. In Aristotle's view, the purging includes both physical purging through the excitement generated and released, and a spiritual purgation analogous to the release or cleansing of the soul for religious purposes. Such purging thus contributes to the health of the society beyond the theater.

Aristotle's insights into literary language and dramatic structure have remained influential for more than two thousand years. Throughout the Renaissance, and well into the eighteenth and nineteenth centuries, Aristotle was recognized as having set the standards for literary appreciation. At the end of the second millennium, nearly 2,500 years after Aristotle wrote *The Poetics*, literary historians and critics continue to employ Aristotle's categories and terminology.

PLATO AND ARISTOTLE CONTRASTED

1. Plato separated Ideal Forms from material things. Aristotle insisted on the inseparability of form and matter.
2. Plato celebrated mathematics as the model of pure thought. Aristotle grounded his philosophical system in biology.
3. For Plato the highest form of knowledge was knowledge of the pure Forms or Ideals—Platonic Idealism. For Aristotle, knowledge was grounded in empirical reality—Aristotelian Empiricism.
4. Plato favored intuition over logic. Aristotle made logic the basis of his philosophy.
5. Plato used reason to overcome the physical world. Aristotle used reason to discover the order of the world.
6. Plato's philosophy influenced Augustine's theology. Aristotle's philosophy influenced Aquinas's theology.

Connections

MUSIC AND MATHEMATICS IN ANCIENT GREECE

Music, for the ancient Greeks, was not an isolated art. The basic elements of Greek music derived from mathematics, which served as the foundation of ancient Greek philosophy and astronomy. Music thus became associated with these other Hellenic achievements, largely through ideas about number, especially numerical relationships expressed as ratios. The most important early Greek theorist of music was PYTHAGORAS [Pi-THAY-go-rus] (ca. 580–507 B.C.E.). Pythagoras' influence extended into the Middle Ages and beyond, largely through the *De Musica* of BOETHIUS [BEE-thee-us] (ca. 480–524 C.E.), a Christian philosopher who once described music as "number made audible." Pythagoras and Boethius believed all things beautiful are subject to number, an idea Boethius expressed in his formulation that "music demonstrates in sound the pure world of number and derives its beauty from that world."

More is known about Greek musical theory than about its practice, largely because few music manuscripts have survived. Treatises such as *The Section of the Canon*, attributed to Euclid (fl. ca. 300 B.C.E.), the Greek mathematician who invented geometry, provide the earliest full account of Pythagoras' acoustical theory.

For Pythagoras, numbers provided the key to understanding the universe. He believed music and arithmetic function as a single unit, with the system of musical sounds governed by mathematical laws. Pythagoras argued that because music embodies number in ratios and proportions, music exemplifies the harmony of the universe.

Pythagoras studied the relationships between two or more given notes and represented them in numerical equations. (The ratios 12:6, 9:6, 12:9, and 9:8 represent the proportions between musical intervals, and these ratios have remained the basis of the tonal system of Western music since ca. 500–1500 C.E.)

Pythagoras' concern with beautiful numerical ratios is echoed not only in the sounds described in ancient Greek musical treatises but also in the proportions Greek architects used to design buildings and Greek sculptors employed in modeling the human figure. It finds further expression in ancient Greek astronomy.

Although musical analysis has undergone considerable change since Pythagoras' time, his basic ideas about tonal relationships remain an important element of music theory today. Moreover, his connection between music and mathematics and its later adaptations in philosophy and astronomy reveal his continued influence well beyond the bounds of his famous geometrical theorem. To take only one example, the medieval quadrivium's inclusion of music, along with arithmetic, geometry, and astronomy, suggests both the importance of music in the medieval curriculum and its close relationship with mathematics. Finally, Pythagoras' belief in the fundamental unity of the world, grounded in number, has served as a powerful influence for scientists, mathematicians, and philosophers seeking to understand the laws of the universe.

MUSIC AND GREEK SOCIETY

Music is mentioned in ancient Greece as early as Homer's *Iliad*, which includes a reference to Achilles playing a lyre in his tent. It was not uncommon for a warrior to soothe his spirits with the charms of music, much as in ancient Israel David played the harp to assuage the anxieties of King Saul.

An integral part of Greek life, music was associated with festivals and banquets, religion and social ritual, including marriages, funerals, and harvest rites. It was associated with Greek drama, for which a special place, the orchestra, was set aside for dancers. Music was an essential part of the Homeric epics, which were chanted to the accompaniment of the lyre. In addition, music formed a significant part of the Olympic athletic contests. At the festivals, the ancient Greeks held contests for musicians equal to those of the athletes, awarding prizes and honors of similar measure.

The **lyre** appears on numerous Greek vases. Its tortoise-shell bowl provided the resonance, much as the body of an acoustic guitar does today. The strings were plucked with the fingers or with a plectrum (the quill of a feather). The aulos was a double-piped wind instrument with a double reed that vibrated with an aggressive and strident tone much like that of a modern oboe. It was probably the aulos that supported choruses of Greek plays by duplicating the melodic line.

Music was so important to the ancient Greeks that all philosophers, including Plato and Aristotle, made a point of discussing it. Plato, for example, believed music could influence human emotion and character. He argued that only music that encouraged bravery and emotional stability should be taught to the young. Aristotle also believed in the importance of music for building character. Like Plato, Aristotle wrote about music's power to affect the development of the inner person, particularly the power of music to affect the soul. Other ancient philosophers commented on music's ethical influence. Like Plato and Aristotle, they associated certain musical modes with virtue and vice, spiritual development and spiritual danger.

The Musical Modes. Greek music was primarily a music of melody, with little concern for harmony. For the ancient Greeks, musical scales, or **modes,** on which melodies were based, had particular ethical effects associated with them. Each mode used a particular sequence of intervals that established its modality. The Greek system, still in use today, divides the octave into twelve equal-sounding smaller intervals, each called a **half step.** In a musical mode or scale, there are eight tones with seven intervals between them, five of which are half steps and two **whole steps.** The position of the whole and half steps in the scale or mode affects the specific character or quality of the scale or mode. Some scales or modes sound "happy" or "bright"; others sound "mournful" or "dark." Strings on lyres were often tuned to one of the "calming scales" as dictated by the doctrine of *ethos.*

Each of the Greek musical modes was considered to have a specific ethical effect on hearers, thus resulting in the various strictures placed on them by Plato and Aristotle. The best of the modes, the one most conducive to virtue, was thought to be the Dorian mode, which, for Aristotle, represented the golden mean of music, comparable to the golden mean of his ethics.

Although ancient Greek instruments, such as the lyre, can be recognized from their depiction in painting and sculpture, the melodies played on them are virtually extinct. The scraps of melody inscribed on papyrus or incised in stone do not provide much help in understanding what ancient Greek music sounded like. The best available examples of ancient Greek musical manuscripts date from the second century B.C.E. and are tributes to the god Apollo.

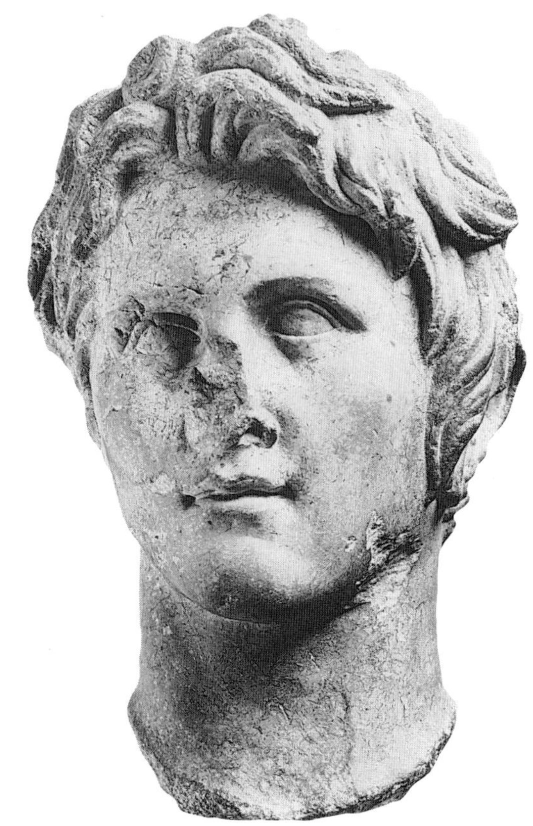

FIGURE 3.16 *Portrait bust of Alexander the Great,* Roman copy of a Greek original of ca. 330 B.C.E., marble, Staatliche Kuntsammlungen, Dresden Museum, Germany. Although a womanizer, an excessive drinker, and perhaps a megalomaniac, Alexander was nevertheless a great general who astonished the world with his stunning succession of military triumphs, which gave the word "empire" a new meaning.

HELLENISTIC GREECE

After the fall of Athens in 404 B.C.E., Sparta controlled the Greek mainland, until Thebes ended Spartan hegemony. In 359 B.C.E., Macedonia, a minor Greek state on the northern end of the Aegean, beyond Mount Olympus, began to assert itself when Philip II became ruler. In 338 B.C.E., Macedonia defeated the Greeks decisively at Chaeronea. Ambassadors were dispatched to Athens and Thebes with terms for peace. Among the ambassadors to Athens was Philip's eighteen-year-old son, Alexander—Alexander the Great (356–323 B.C.E.), as he would come to be known (fig. 3.16). Raised to rule, Alexander came to enjoy the enthusiastic support of almost all Greek intellectuals. When Philip II was assassinated in 336 B.C.E.—possibly at Alexander's behest, since Philip had divorced his mother and removed his son from substantive roles in the government—Alexander took control.

On his accession, he crushed a rebellion in Thebes, destroying the city and selling the entire population into slavery. He then set out to expand the Macedonian empire and control the world. By 334 B.C.E., he had defeated the Persians. Prior to entering Egypt, Alexander controlled only the coast of the eastern Mediterranean. By 332 B.C.E., he had conquered Egypt, where he founded the great port city of Alexandria in the Nile Delta. Marching back into Mesopotamia, he entered Babylon and made a sacrifice to the local god, Marduk. Then he marched on Persepolis and burned it. Convinced India was small, and that beyond it lay Ocean, as he called it, by which route he could return to Europe by sea, he set out to conquer present-day Pakistan. However, his troops were exhausted and met unexpected resistance in the form of war elephants; Alexander was thus forced to sail down the Indus River to the Indian Ocean. Along this route he founded present-day Karachi—at the time named Alexandria, after himself. Returning finally to Babylon, in 323 B.C.E., Alexander caught a fever and died.

The Hellenistic era begins with Alexander's death at the age of thirty-three. Alexander had brought about a mingling of Eastern and Western cultures through his policies and conquests. For instance, he encouraged

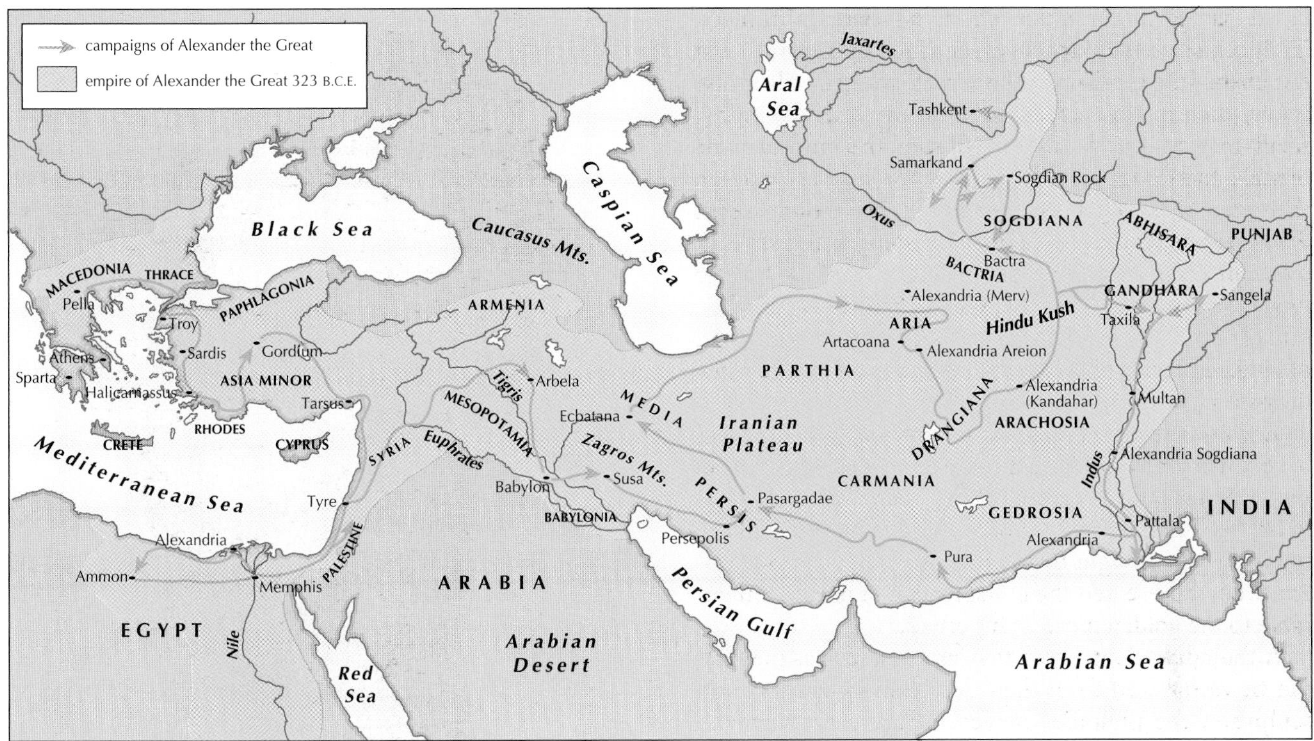

MAP 3.2 Alexander's empire.

marriages between his soldiers and Middle Eastern women by providing large wedding gifts and by marrying two Persian women himself. But culturally the Greek army had a greater impact on the Middle East than the Middle East had on it. In fact, the term "Hellenistic," first used in 1833 by the historian Johann Gustav Droysen, was coined to describe the impact of Greece on the Middle East—its "Hellenization"—after Alexander's death. The generals Alexander had installed as governors of the different territories in his empire set themselves up as kings. Political, artistic, social, and economic dominance shifted from the mainland of Greece to the new Hellenistic kingdoms such as those of the Seleucids in Syria and the Ptolemies in Egypt. The cities of Pergamon in Turkey and Alexandria in Egypt in particular were great centers of learning. The massive library at Alexandria contained over 700,000 papyri and scrolls, and Pergamon's library rivaled it. As if inspired by the dramatic successes of Alexander himself, the art such Hellenistic cities spawned was itself highly dramatic. Where Classical Greek art was concerned with balance and order and idealized its subjects, Hellenistic art focused on the individual, in all the individual's unidealized particularity, and on emotional states. Even the dominant philosophies of the day reflect this tendency.

More important for the future of Western thought were the acts of preservation and dispersion performed by Hellenistic scholars as they collected, edited, analyzed, and interpreted the philosophical works of the past. This work of humanistic scholarship included preserving not only the works of ancient Greek philosophy and literature, especially those of Plato and Homer, for example, but the Greek translation of the Hebrew Bible as well. Moreover, the emergence of humanistic scholarship was accompanied by educational institutions established for its continued development. In the spectacular libraries at Alexandria and Pergamon, and in Athens, which was home to a great academy of its own, Greek intellectual achievements endured.

ARCHITECTURE AND SCULPTURE

Altar of Zeus at Pergamon. Perhaps nothing better embodies the extravagant Hellenistic attitude to architecture and the visual arts in general than the upper city of Pergamon in Asia Minor, built by KING ATTALOS [ah-TAL-us] (r. 241–197 B.C.E.) and almost finished by EUMENES II [you-MEN-ease] (197–159 B.C.E.). This Hellenistic city was grand in vision, designed on a large scale and embellished with a profusion of ornament. Essentially a large complex of architecture and sculpture built in the slope of a hill, Pergamon appears as if nature has been sculpted into several terraces occupied by splendid structures. The upper city included the celebrated Altar of Zeus built 180–160 B.C.E. under

Eumenes II, a demonstration of the dramatic theatricality and large scale favored in the Hellenistic era. In 278 B.C.E., the Gauls came sweeping into Asia Minor, to be conquered by Attalos I of Pergamon in 241 B.C.E. This monument was erected to commemorate the victory over the Gauls.

On the sides of the podium of the altar was the relief frieze of the *Battle of the Gods and the Giants* (fig. 3.17), four hundred feet in length. Known as **gigantomachy,** the subject of the revolt of the giants—the Titans of Greek mythology—against the gods was popular with Hellenistic artists. On the Altar of Zeus its treatment can be interpreted symbolically. Here the gods' triumph over the giants symbolizes the victories of Attalos I—art and politics working together for propagandistic ends. The style of this work—its action, violence, display of emotion, and windblown drapery—also defines the Hellenistic age in the arts. All restraint is gone,

FIGURE 3.17 *Battle of the Gods and the Giants,* Altar of Zeus, Pergamon, ca. 180–160 B.C.E., height 7′6″ (2.34 m), Staatliche Museen, Berlin. Here Athena has grabbed the hair of a winged monster who writhes in agony. His mother, identifiable by her "monstrous" curled locks, rises to help him.

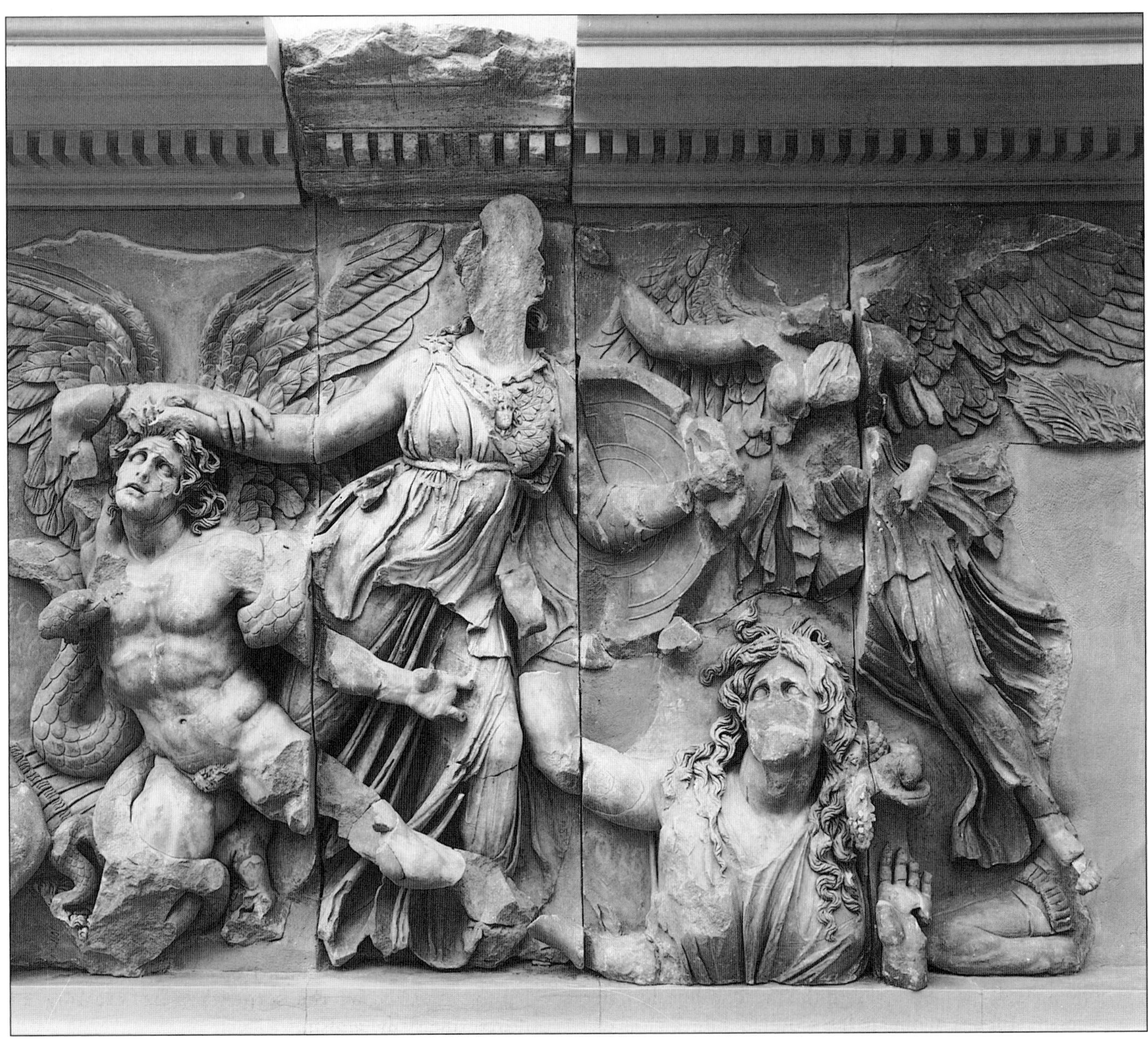

Cross Currents

THE HELLENIZATION OF INDIA

By 326 B.C.E., Alexander the Great's forces had pushed as far east as the Punjab in northwest India. It was there that they confronted, for the first time, war elephants, two hundred strong. Although Alexander's troops defeated the Indian troops, it was rumored that the army of the Ganges, further east, was equipped with five thousand such beasts, and thus the Greek troops refused to go on. But the connection between the Greek world and India had been established.

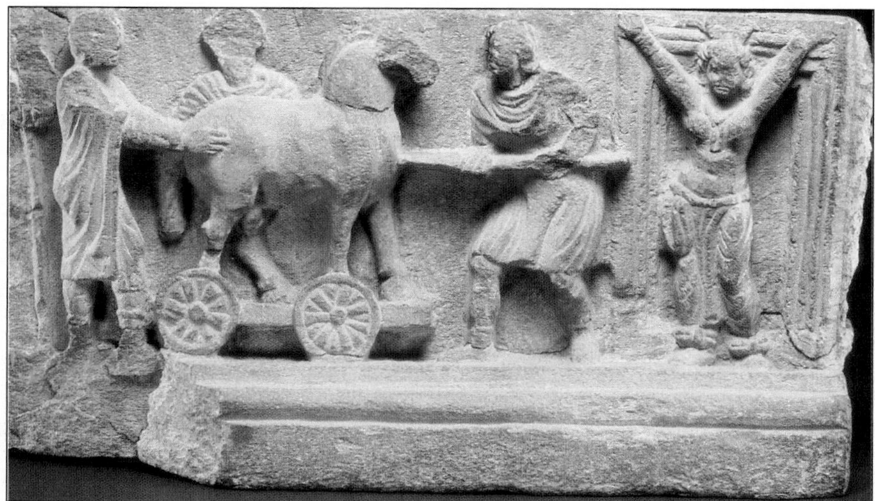

FIGURE 3.18 Trojan horse frieze, Gandhara, second to third century C.E. Although the style shows local influences, the subject matter here is most definitely Greek as the Trojan prophetess Cassandra and the priest Laocoön (see fig. 3.20) attempt to block the entry of the Greek gift-horse into Troy.

Remnants of Alexander's forces settled in Bactria, between the Oxus River and the Hindu Kush mountains. Excavations at the Bactrian Greek city of Al Khanum have revealed Corinthian capitals and fragments of statues of various gods and goddesses. Coins with images of Herakles, Apollo, and Zeus were produced. There were portraits of the Bactrian kings on the other sides: Euthydemus, Demetrius, and Menander. However, it was not always Greek ideas that triumphed over Indian cultural traditions. Around 150 B.C.E., King Menander was converted to Buddhism by the monk Nagasena. The monk's conversation with the king is preserved as *The Questions of Melinda* (Melinda was the Indian version of Menander's name).

At Gandhara, on the north end of the Indus River, across the Khyber Pass from Bactria, Greek influence was especially strong. Although Gandharan art is mostly Buddhist in content, it has a Hellenistic style. In Taxila, a temple resembling the Parthenon in structure was constructed between 50 B.C.E. and 65 C.E. There is even evidence that the Homeric legend of the Trojan horse was known here (fig. 3.18).

much as Alexander had abandoned it politically at the era's outset.

Nike of Samothrace. The splendid Hellenistic *Nike of Samothrace* (fig. 3.19), also known as the *Winged Victory*, is related to the figures in the Pergamon frieze in the great sweeping gesture of the body, in the suggestion of movement through space, and in the revealing treatment of the drapery. The date of the Nike of Samothrace is debated, but it was probably created between 200 and 190 B.C.E. The statue was originally placed on the prow of a stone ship located in a niche cut into the mountainside above the Sanctuary of the Great Gods at Samothrace. The head was turned to face the sea. The composition was designed to give the impression that the goddess had just descended to the prow of the ship, her garments still responding to her movement through space.

Laocoön and His Sons. An expenditure of still greater energy, induced by agony, is seen in the *Laocoön* group (fig. 3.20), sculpted by Hagesandros, Athanodoros, and Polydoros of Rhodes according to ancient sources. The date of this statue is debated, the possibilities ranging from 150 B.C.E. to the first century C.E. It was rediscovered only in 1506 in Rome.

The subject of the sculpture is taken from Homer's *Iliad.* Laocoön was a priest of Apollo of Troy. He and his sons were strangled by snakes sent from the sea by Apollo when Laocoön tried to warn the Trojans against accepting the wooden horse, seemingly left as a gift to them by the retreating Greeks. In the sculpture the figures writhe violently, but all in one plane, like a relief. Laocoön and his two sons try to move apart, but are bound together by the serpent's coils, creating an extraordinary dynamism.

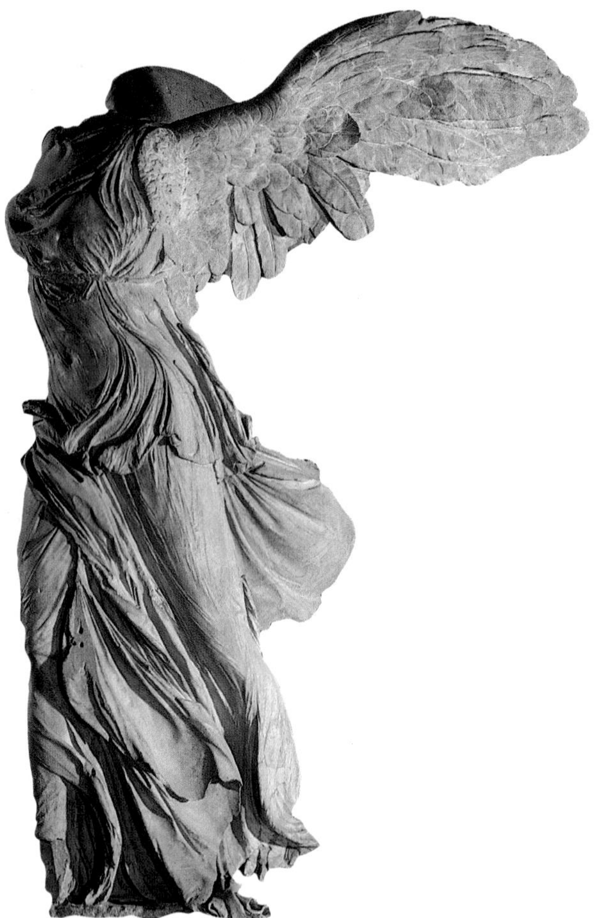

FIGURE 3.19 *Nike of Samothrace*, ca. 200–190 B.C.E., marble, height 8′ (2.44 m), Musée du Louvre, Paris. Stone seemingly brought to life, this dynamic figure of Victory moves through space, the drapery blown against her body by her rapid movement.

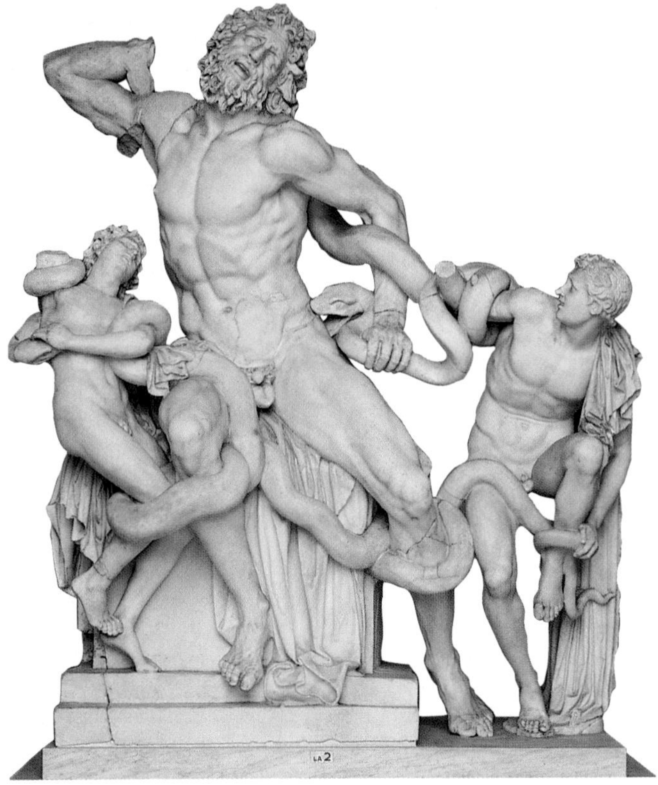

FIGURE 3.20 *Laocoön and His Sons*, perhaps a Roman marble copy after a Greek original by Hagesandros, Athanodoros, and Polydoros of Rhodes, variously dated between the second century B.C.E. and the first century C.E., height 7′ (2.10 m), Museo Pio Clementino, Musei Vaticani, Rome. Reunion de Musées Nationaux (RMN), Art Resource, New York. In the Hellenistic period, drama replaced the emotional restraint of the Classical period. Laocoön and his sons, attacked by serpents, make obvious their torment through straining poses and agonized facial expressions.

PHILOSOPHY

The English words "stoic," "skeptic," "epicurean," and "cynic" derive from schools of Greek philosophy—Stoicism, Skepticism, Epicureanism, and Cynicism. Although none of these philosophical systems has had the long-term impact of Platonism or Aristotelianism, Stoicism and Epicureanism dominated Greek philosophy during the Hellenistic period. In addition, all four philosophies were embraced by the Romans, with Stoicism also later finding a home in Christian philosophy.

Stoicism. **Stoicism** was less concerned with formulating a systematic philosophy than with providing an approach to everyday living. Primarily ethical in impulse, it offered a basis for conduct in responding to life's misfortunes. According to the Stoic view, an intelligent spiritual force resembling reason, the *Logos*, pervades the universe. Human beings can achieve happiness only by bringing their wills into harmony with this pervasive universal reason. The individual must accept whatever fortune brings; all the individual can do is exercise control over her or his own will. Characteristic Stoic virtues are serenity, self-discipline, and courage in the face of suffering and affliction.

Stoicism is less a fatalistic acceptance of what is than an attitude toward life that values apathy, or disengagement, as a virtue. The Stoic response to life is akin to that of Buddhism, which encourages nonattachment, not becoming invested in the outcome of things. The Stoics sacrificed some kinds of pleasure, such as pleasures of the senses and of acquisition of material things, for other satisfactions, such as maintaining their composure, their sense of equilibrium, no matter what happened to them. The Stoics recognized that they could not control external circumstances, but they could control their response to those circumstances.

Epicureanism. **Epicureanism** is frequently thought of as a philosophy of self-indulgence and pleasure

Cultural Impact

Classical Greek civilization, especially that of Golden Age Athens, was crucial to the development of Western civilization as we know it today. The Greeks of antiquity developed a rich and vibrant culture, whose achievements consisted of preeminent masterpieces of pottery, sculpture, and architecture, poetry and drama. Their achievements also included expertise in the practical arts of commerce and seafaring; metalwork, coining, and engraving, medicine and athletics; and philosophy, education, and government—many of which continue to exert a significant influence on the contemporary Western world.

PROTAGORAS [proh-TA-go-rus] (ca. 485–415 B.C.E.) wrote, "People are the measure of all things," a phrase that heralded the enterprise first undertaken in Classical Greece but has been central to Western culture ever since. Classical Greek civilization thoroughly explored the human condition, recognizing the realities and constraints of human life, yet constantly striving to realize ideals. The Greeks invented democracy and left it as a legacy for nations to emulate two millennia after Athens's decline. The Greek ideal of political freedom also served as the basis for the pursuit of other ideals, such as justice, truth, and beauty. Political freedom was one aspect of the culture's belief in individual expression.

Another important legacy left by Classical Greece was its system of *paideia*, or learning, which was grounded in respect for individual thought and emphasized logic, dialectic, debate, and elegance of expression. The philosophy of Plato and Aristotle continued to be influential through the Middle Ages and into the Renaissance. In some areas of thought—logic, poetics, and rhetoric—Aristotelian principles remain influential today, as for example in the rhetoric of Stephen Toulmin. The Greek philosophical tradition continues as contemporary philosophers, such as Robert Nozick and Marth Nussbaum, analyze intellectual problems. Greek educational ideals are reflected in the contemporary university.

The impact of Classical and Hellenistic Greek civilization has been so pervasive and so extensive that the public buildings of many cities in Europe and America reflect Greek architectural style. The influence of Greek sculpture can be seen in grand public buildings and in palatial private residences. Above all, against the backdrop of a warring mainland Greece in the fifth century B.C.E., the Greeks provided the Western world with a sense of the value of harmony and balance in all things—in art and architecture, literature and philosophy, politics and everyday life.

seeking. Its primary practical impulse, however, is to escape fear and pain. The founder, EPICURUS [ep-ee-CURE-us] (341–271 B.C.E.), taught that fear, especially the fear of death and punishment after death, is responsible for human misery. As an antidote to what he considered religious and mythological superstition, Epicurus argued that the gods lack interest in the affairs of human beings, and death utterly extinguishes pain. Thus, according to Epicurus, human beings have nothing to fear from it.

A materialist, Epicurus believed the soul, like the body, was a physical substance, composed of tiny particles in motion. As such, for Epicurus the only path to knowledge was through physical sensation; consequently, the way to achieve happiness was to enhance physical pleasure and to limit physical pain. Epicurus argued that the way to achieve lasting pleasure was to avoid what he called "kinetic" pleasure in favor of "static" pleasure, which creates a state of equilibrium. For example, Epicurus recommended rejecting the pleasure of indulging in spicy or rich food for a simpler diet that prevented the pain of hunger while avoiding the dangers of indigestion. Similarly, Epicurus preferred the stability of friendship over the shifting pleasure and pain afforded by romantic passion.

Skepticism. The English word "skeptic" derives from the Greek *skeptikos*, which means "inquirer." **Skepticism** is not necessarily a negative perspective; rather it requires an attitude of questioning. Two early and important exponents of Skepticism were SEXTUS EMPIRICUS [em-PIR-i-cuss], who lived in the mid-second century B.C.E., and his intellectual ancestor, PYRRHO [PIE-roh] (ca. 360–270 B.C.E.). As with Stoicism and Epicureanism, Skepticism was less a philosophical system than a perspective on experience anchored in practical advice about how to live an unperturbed life. The aim of the Skeptic, like that of the Stoic and the Epicurean, was to establish and preserve a state of physical and mental composure, a condition of psychological stability and emotional equilibrium.

What distinguishes Skepticism from Stoicism and Epicureanism is its emphasis on achieving this state of unperturbed equilibrium through suspending judgment about nearly everything. The reason for this suspension of judgment is that we cannot know anything with certainty, because for every assertion there can be a counterassertion, and all evidence is inconclusive in itself. The conflict between opposing assertions—for example, "the gods exist" and "the gods do not exist"—can only be settled by an appeal to an additional criterion, in this case, a belief. But because the criterion can be similarly called

Critical Thinking

BLACK ATHENA

In his book *Black Athena: The Afroasiatic Roots of Classical Civilization*, Martin Bernal argues that ancient Greek culture derived from Egypt and Phoenicia. Bernal contends, moreover, that European scholars have consistently failed to acknowledge the African and Asian roots of Classical civilization. In response, Mary Lefkowitz has rebutted Bernal's arguments in her book *Not Out of Africa*. Two questions underscore the disagreement: (1) whether the Egyptians were a black African people; (2) whether the Greeks were indebted to Egyptian learning. How would you go about deciding with whom to agree on these issues? What steps would you take in evaluating Bernal's claims and Lefkowitz's counterarguments?

into question, there is nothing on which finally to base knowledge. Thus, according to the Skeptics, peace of mind can only be achieved by abandoning the search for knowledge and accepting uncertainty.

Cynicism. **Cynicism** was a school of thought founded by ANTISTHENES [An-TIS-the-nees] (ca. 455–360 B.C.E.), a pupil of Socrates. Anticipating the Epicurean thinkers, Antisthenes argued that happiness can be attained only by freeing oneself from desires. (This notion is also central to classical Buddhism.) Perhaps the best known exemplar of the philosophy of Cynicism was Diogenes (ca. 404–323 B.C.E.), who influenced later Stoic thinkers. Little is known of Diogenes beyond some anecdotes, including one about how he wished hunger could be as easily gratified and satisfied as masturbation satisfied the need for sex.

The Cynics, however, are important largely for their sense of detachment from desire. Like the Stoics, who came after and were influenced by them, the Cynics advocated the absence of desire rather than a lust for life. The Cynics' rule, as it were, was to pursue the more laborious path of virtue rather than the easier road of pleasure. Although the meaning of the term "cynic" is allied with "one who lives a dog's life," shamelessly and without a secure sense of humor, the philosophical overtones of the Cynics' writings suggest one who distrusts all easy claims to altruism and comfort.

KEY TERMS

Classical
Hellenistic
demes
acropolis
agora
stoa
orders
Doric
abacus
echinus
frieze
triglyphs
metopes
Ionic
entablature
Corinthian
Golden Section
entasis
caryatids
atlantes
contrapposto
white-ground technique
lekythos (pl., lekythoi)
tragedy
dramatic irony
Oedipus complex
Sophists
syllogism
lyre
modes
half step
whole step
gigantomachy
Stoicism
Epicureanism
Skepticism
Cynicism

www. WEBSITES FOR FURTHER STUDY

http://www.hyperhistory.com/online_n2/maptext_n2/greece_pers.html
(A basic map of the Persian wars, including links to the wars themselves.)

http://www.culture.gr/2/21/211/21101a/e211aa01.html
(A good discussion of the architecture of the Acropolis.)

http://www.arwhead.com/Greeks/
(A basic general site on all things Greek, including architecture, theatre, war, and pottery.)

http://classics.mit.edu/Browse/browse-Sophocles.html
(A good site devoted to the works of Sophocles with discussion boards.)

http://www.wsu.edu_delahoyd/greekmusic
(Ancient Greek music.)

http://classics.uc.edu/music
(Ancient Greek music on papyrus.)

Chapter 4

History

287 B.C.E.	Equal citizenship granted to plebeians
264–146 B.C.E.	Punic Wars
241 B.C.E.	Conquest of Sicily
238 B.C.E.	Conquest of Sardinia, Corsica
218–216 B.C.E.	Hannibal's invasion of Italy
146 B.C.E.	Conquest of Carthage, Macedonia, Greece
133 B.C.E.	Conquest of Pergamum
63 B.C.E.	Conquest of Judaea
63 B.C.E.–C.E. 14	Octavian Caesar Augustus, establishes *Pax Romana* during his rule
58–50 B.C.E.	Conquest of Gaul
31 B.C.E.	Conquest of Egypt
C.E. 64	Fire destroys Rome
C.E. 79	Vesuvius erupts, destroying Pompeii and Herculaneum
C.E. 98–117	Trajan rules
C.E. 180	Roman Empire is at its largest: 1,750,000 square miles of land and 50 million people
C.E. 284	Diocletian divides Roman Empire
C.E. 330	Constantine moves seat of Roman Empire from Rome to Byzantium

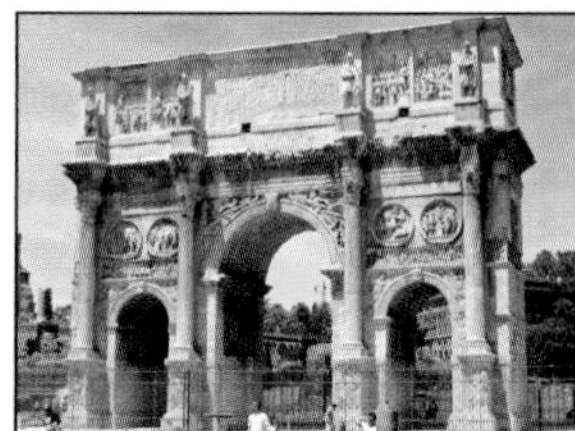

Arts and Architecture

ca. 520 B.C.E.	Tomb of Hunting and Fishing
	Wife and Husband Sarcophagus
500 B.C.E.	*Capitoline She-Wolf*
first century B.C.E.	*A Roman Patrician with Busts of His Ancestors*
ca. 80 B.C.E. late second–mid-first century B.C.E.	*Portrait of a Roman;* Temple of "Fortuna Virilis"
late first century B.C.E.–early first century C.E.	Pont du Gard
ca. 20 B.C.E.	*Augustus of Primaporta*
13–9 B.C.E.	Ara Pacis
C.E. 63–79	Ixion Room, House of the Vettii
C.E. 80	Colosseum
C.E. 106–13	Apollodorus of Damascus, Column of Trajan
C.E. 118–25	Apollodorus of Damascus, Pantheon
C.E. 164–66	Equestrian statue of Marcus Aurelius
C.E. 213–17	Baths of Caracalla
C.E. 315	Arch of Constantine
C.E. 325–26	Head of Constantine the Great

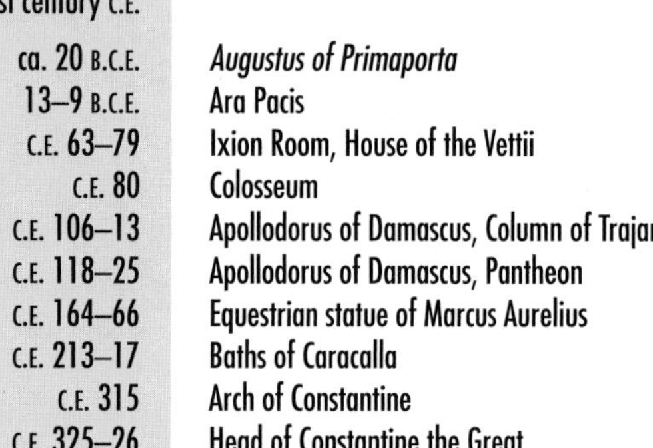

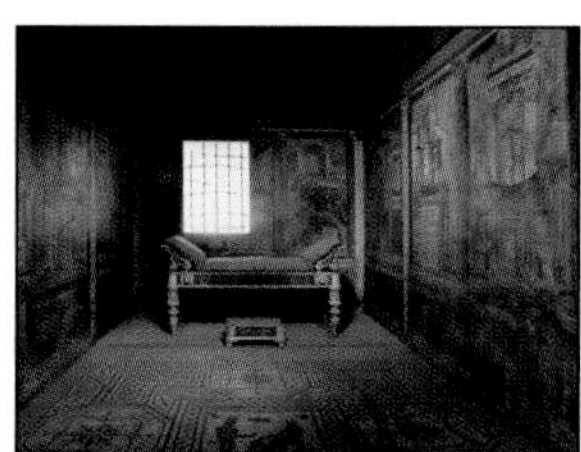

Literature and Philosophy

ca. 254–184 B.C.E.	Plautus, *The Haunted House*
first century B.C.E.	Lucretius' *De Rerum Natura* Cicero, Horace, Ovid, Petronius
ca. 30–19 B.C.E.	Virgil, *The Aeneid*
19 B.C.E.	Horace, *Odes*
46–44 B.C.E.	Cicero, *Orations*
	Marcus Aurelius, *Meditations*
first century B.C.E.	Epictetus and Stoicism
ca. 60 B.C.E.	Catullus, *Love Poems*

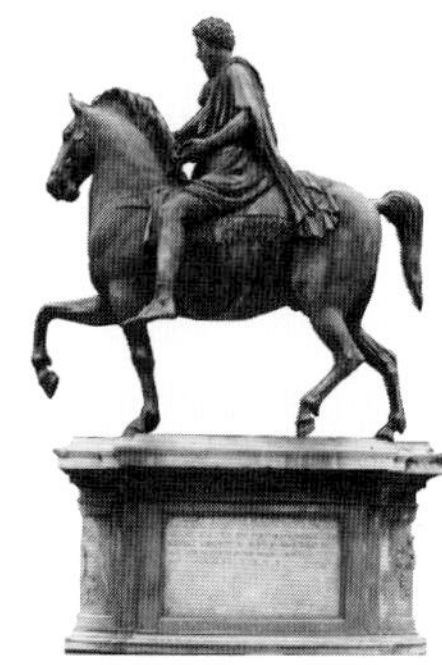

Roman Civilization

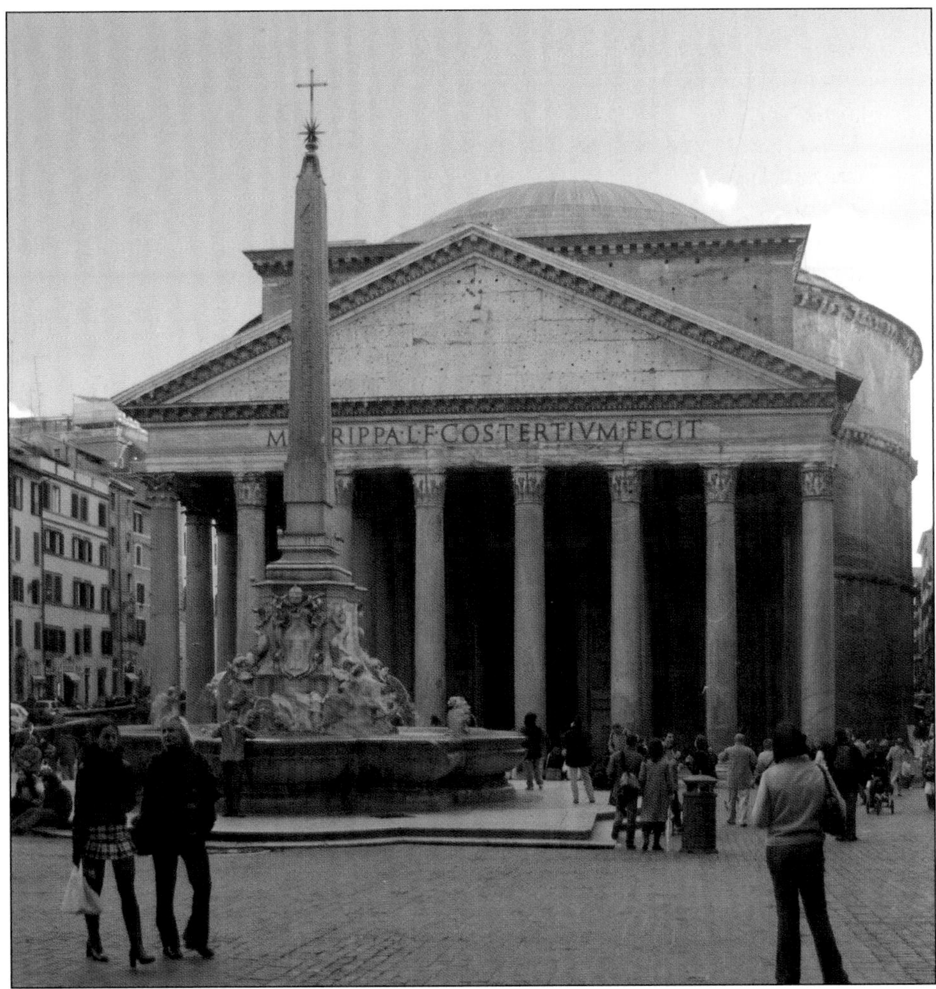

Apollodorus of Damascus, Pantheon, Rome, 118–25 C.E., exterior.

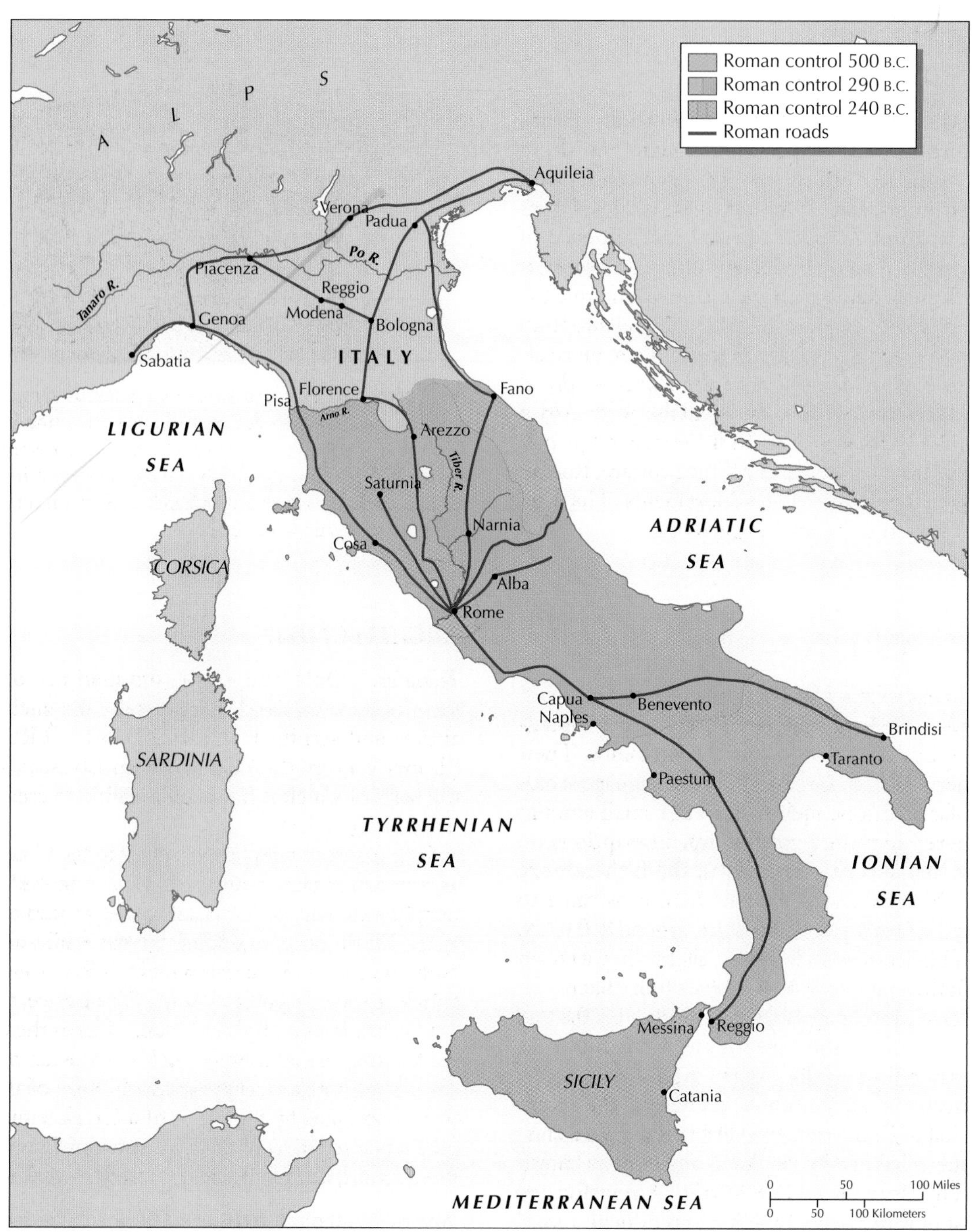

Map 4.1 The expansion of Roman rule to 200 B.C.E.

Chapter Overview

ETRUSCAN CIVILIZATION

Rome's ancestors set the stage for greatness

THE ROMAN REPUBLIC

Conquest, feats of engineering, and portrait sculpture

THE EMPIRE

All roads lead to Rome—Augustus builds, Constantine converts to Christianity

The Greek Legacy and the Roman Ideal

In many ways, Rome inherited its culture—its art, its literature, its philosophical and religious life—from Greece. By the seventh century B.C.E., and along with the Latins, Etruscans, and Celts, the Greeks occupied parts of the Italian peninsula. This ensured the influence of Greek ways on the developing Italian culture. However, it was the later Roman determination to control and rule the entire Western world that consolidated the Hellenization of the West and much of the Eastern world. Even more effectively than Alexander the Great, the Romans spread Greek art and literature as far as Britain in the north, Africa in the south, the Euphrates River in the east, and Spain in the west. Apart from disseminating Greek culture, Roman civilization produced remarkable achievements of its own, in the fields of politics, law, and engineering.

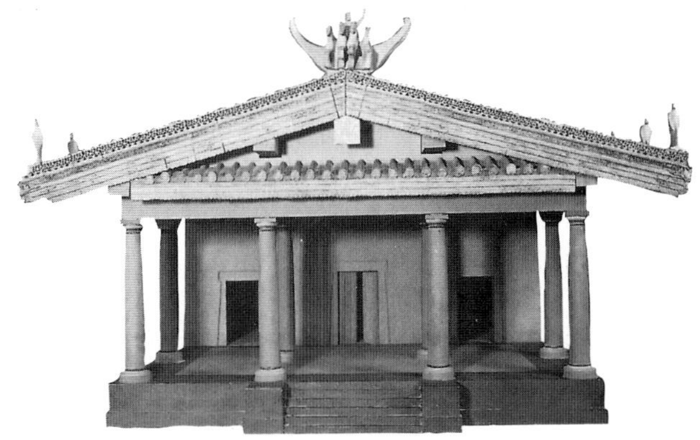

Figure 4.1 Reconstruction of an Etruscan temple according to Vitruvius, Instituto di Etruscologia e Antichità Italiche, University of Rome. To a great extent, the Etruscan temple form was a modification of the Greek. Different from the Greek, however, are the high flight of stairs on one side only, deeper porch, and wider cella.

ETRUSCAN CIVILIZATION

While the Greeks were settling in southern Italy and Sicily, another people—the Etruscans—inhabited the central Italian mainland. Little is known about the Etruscans. Their alphabet is derived from Greek, but their language seems unique, insofar as can be judged from the small amount of undeciphered literature and the few inscriptions on works of art that survive. Herodotus, the fifth-century B.C.E. Greek historian, said that the Etruscans came to Italy from Lydia (Turkey) in Asia Minor around 800 B.C.E. Dionysius of Halicarnassus, however, claims they were an indigenous Italian people, which appears more likely.

Etruscan civilization proper dates from about 700 B.C.E. and was at its peak in the seventh and sixth centuries B.C.E.—the same time as the Archaic period in Greece. While Etruscan civilization was at its height, the future imperial capital of Rome remained little more than a cluster of mud huts inhabited by shepherds and farmers known as Latins. Why Rome would eventually be transformed into the most powerful city in the world is difficult to say, except that, positioned on the south bank of the Tiber River in central Italy, it was midway between the Etruscan settlements to the north and the Greek colonies in the south of the peninsula. Rome thus lay on the trade route between the two civilizations. The Etruscans were influenced by the Greeks and came to know them literally "through" Rome. They sent skillfully manufactured bronze household utensils down the Tiber through Rome and on to the Greeks in the south in return for Greek vases, many of which have been found in Etruscan tombs. Greek heroes and deities were incorporated into the Etruscan pantheon, and their temples reflected Greek influence. In turn, the Etruscans exerted an important civilizing influence over the Latins in Rome.

Architecture

Temples. Only the stone foundations of Etruscan temples have survived. Fortunately, the ancient Roman author and architect VITRUVIUS [vi-TROO-vee-us] (fl. first century C.E.) described an Etruscan temple, on the basis of which it has been possible to create a reconstruction (fig. 4.1).

The Etruscan temple was similar to the Greek temple in its rectangular plan, raised podium, and peaked roof. Some temples were built with columns of the **Tuscan order,** which is the Doric order modified by the addition of a base. Nonetheless, the Etruscan temple differs from the Greek temple in several significant ways. For instance, the Etruscan temple has steps on only one side, whereas the Greek temple has steps on all four sides. The Etruscan temple has a deep front porch, occupying much more of the platform than is occupied by the porch of a Greek temple. And the cella (enclosed part) of the Etruscan temple is divided into three rooms, further differing from the Greek temple plan.

Tombs. Although Etruscan temples have disappeared, a significant number of tombs remain. Etruscan tombs were rich with weapons, gold work, and vases. As a result, like their Egyptian and Mycenaean counterparts, they were the targets of grave robbers. Scientific excavation of Etruscan tombs began only in the mid-nineteenth century.

The tombs are of two types: corbeled domes covered with mounds of earth, and rock-cut chambers with rectangular rooms. The most famous and most impressive of the rock-cut tombs at the ancient site of Cerveteri is the so-called Tomb of the Reliefs (fig. 4.2), of the third century B.C.E. The tomb is made of **tufa,** a type of stone that is soft when cut, but hardens when exposed to the air and tends to remain white. Such tombs were used for families; this one has places for over forty bodies. The interior of the

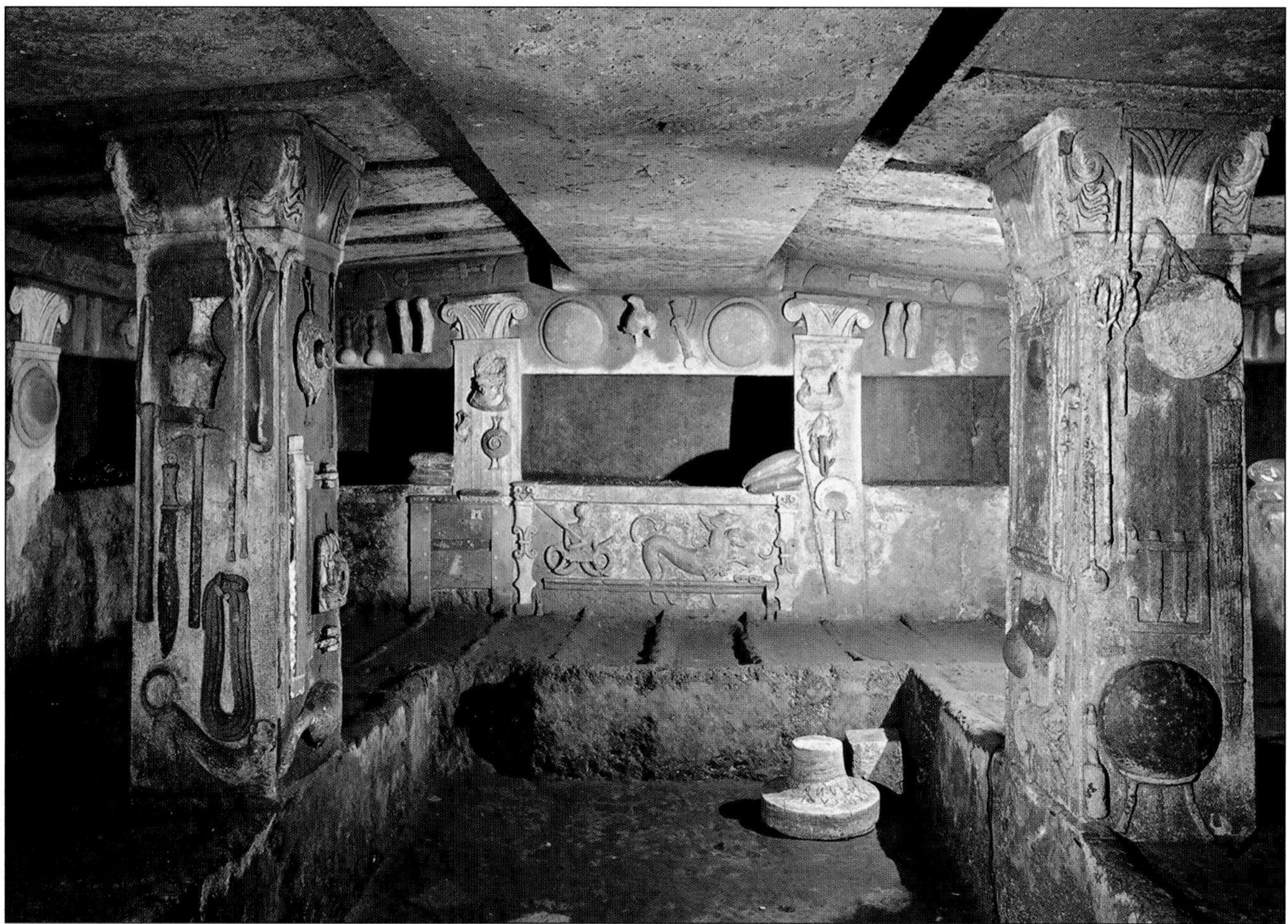

FIGURE 4.2 Tomb of the Reliefs, Cerveteri, third century B.C.E., interior. This exceptional tomb is believed to duplicate an actual Etruscan home in stone, even including pillows and pets. An entire family was buried here.

Tomb of the Reliefs replicates a home and provides a document of Etruscan life. The beds even have stone pillows! Roof beams are carved, and on the walls are depictions of weapons, armor, household items, and busts of the dead. The column capitals are similar to an early Ionic type brought to Greece from Asia Minor, which supports Herodotus' theory that the Etruscans originated in Lydia.

Other tombs were painted with scenes from everyday life. Particularly fine examples have been found at Tarquinia, where the subjects include scenes of hunting and fishing, banquets, musicians, dancers, athletic competitions, and religious ceremonies. The paintings in the Tomb of Hunting and Fishing (fig. 4.3), of ca. 520 B.C.E., in which fish jump out of the water in front of a man who attempts to catch them, and birds fly around a man who attempts to shoot one with a sling shot, convey a sense of energy and even humor.

This wall painting is presumably a view of the afterlife. Its optimism is also seen in Etruscan sculpture. An early example is offered by a wife and husband sarcophagus, from Cerveteri (fig. 4.4), ca. 520 B.C.E. The sarcophagus, modeled in clay and once brightly painted, is shaped like a couch, with the deceased couple shown to recline on top; women and men were social equals. Like contemporary Greek statues, the pair have Archaic smiles (see Chapter 2). They are shown as if alive, comfortable, healthy, and happy, although they do not seem to be individualized portraits.

SCULPTURE

The Etruscans were celebrated in antiquity for their ability to work in metal. Their homeland of Tuscany (which is named for the Etruscans) is rich in copper and iron and provided ample raw materials. From 600 B.C.E. onward, the Etruscans produced many bronze statuettes and utensils, some of which they exported. The most famous Etruscan bronze sculpture is the so-called *Capitoline She-Wolf* (fig. 4.5), of ca. 500 B.C.E. The two suckling babes, the legendary twin founders of the city, Romulus and Remus, were added in the Renaissance. However, the she-wolf is authentic and has the energy and vitality

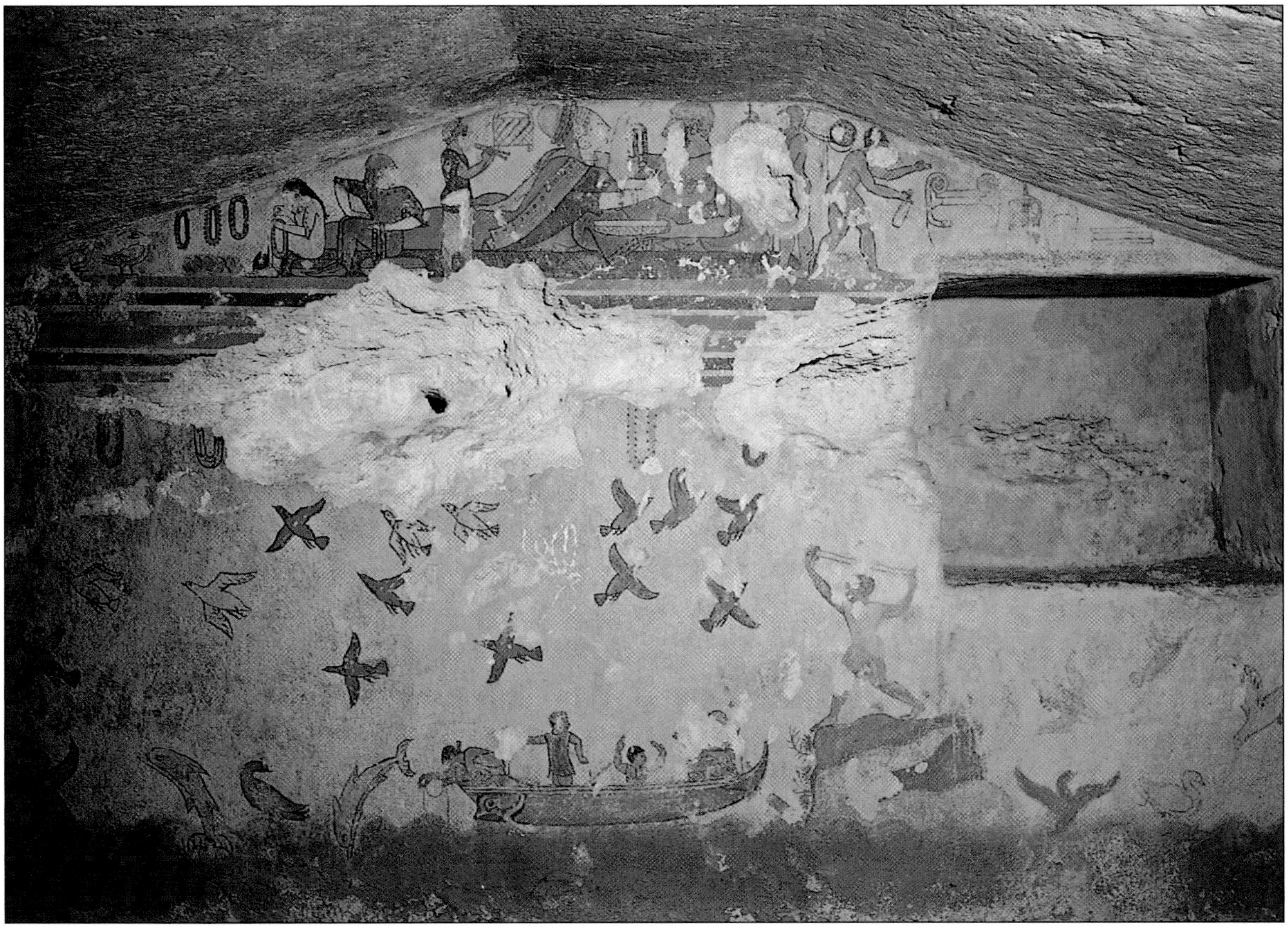

FIGURE 4.3 Tomb of Hunting and Fishing, Tarquinia, wall painting, ca. 520 B.C.E. This and other tomb paintings record the good life when Etruria prospered in the sixth century B.C.E. Later, as the economic situation declined, the outlook on the afterlife was less optimistic.

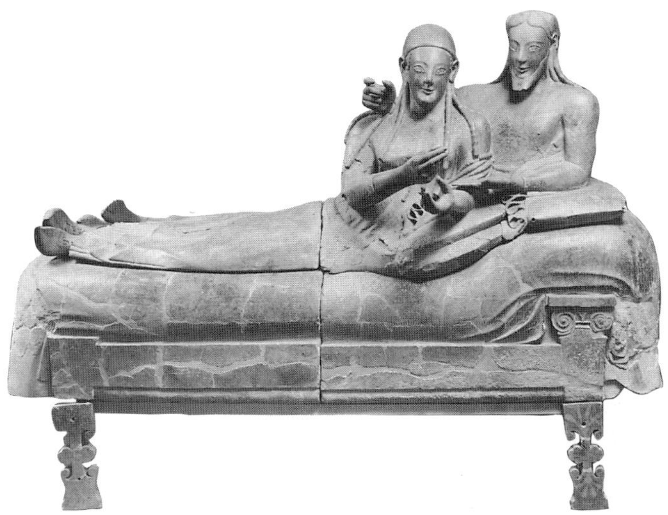

FIGURE 4.4 Wife and Husband Sarcophagus, from Cerveteri, ca. 520 B.C.E., terra cotta, length 6′7″ (2.01 m), Museo Nazionale di Villa Giulia, Rome. The deceased couple is shown as if alive, healthy, and enjoying themselves. The rounded forms are readily achieved in malleable terra cotta, unlike hard stone.

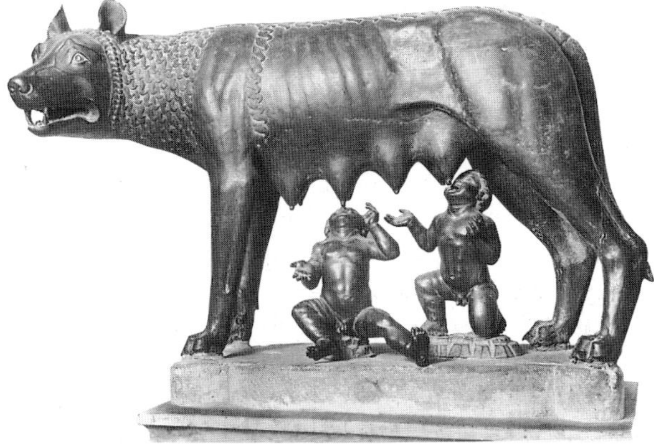

FIGURE 4.5 *Capitoline She-Wolf,* ca. 500 B.C.E., bronze, height $33\frac{1}{2}''$ (85.1 cm), Museo Capitolino, Rome. The Etruscans were famed in antiquity for their fine metalwork. With the twin infants, added in the Renaissance, this Etruscan bronze has become the symbol of Rome.

characteristic of Etruscan art. A beautiful decorative surface is achieved by contrasting the crisp, curving patterns of the neck fur with the wolf's sleek, smooth body.

THE ROMAN REPUBLIC

Beginning with Romulus, Rome was ruled first by a succession of kings and then, in 509 B.C.E., constituted itself a republic, which lasted until 27 B.C.E. Romulus himself is said to have established the traditional Roman distinction between the **patricians,** the land-owning aristocrats who served as priests and magistrates, lawyers and judges, and the **plebeians,** the poorer class who tilled the land, herded livestock, and worked for wages as craftspeople, tradespeople, and laborers. To complicate this traditional distinction, however, there is evidence of wealthy plebeian families and poor patricians. In fact, the distinction between these Roman social strata may very well have been one of "first" families versus later immigrants.

Initially, the plebeians depended on the patricians for support. According to one ancient historian, each plebeian in Romulus' Rome could choose for himself any patrician as a patron, initiating the system known as **patronage.**

The essentially paternalistic relationship of patrician to plebeian reflects the family's central role in Roman society. At the head of the family was the *pater*, the father, and it was his duty to protect not only his wife and children, but also his clients, those who had submitted to his patronage. In return for the *pater*'s protection, his family and his clients were obligated to give him their total obedience and to defer to him in all things—an attitude the Romans referred to as ***pietas.*** The patrician males led the state as they led the family, contributing to the state's well-being in return for the people's gratitude and veneration. So fundamental was this attitude that by imperial times, the Roman emperor was referred to as the *pater patriae*, "the father of the fatherland."

From the outset, the republic was plagued by conflict between the patricians and the plebeians. There was obvious political inequality. The Senate, the political assembly responsible for formulating new law, was almost exclusively patrician. Thus the plebeians formed their own legislative assembly, the Consilium Plebis, electing their own officers, called tribunes, to protect them from the patrician magistrates. Initially, patricians were not subject to legislation passed by the plebeian assembly—the plebiscite. Finally, in 287 B.C.E., however, the plebiscite became binding legislation on all citizens, whether plebeian or patrician, and something resembling equal citizenship was established for all.

At about the same time, Rome began a series of military campaigns that would, eventually, result in its control of the largest and most powerful empire ever created. By the middle of the third century B.C.E., Rome had established dominion over the Italian peninsula. Beginning in 264 B.C.E., the city inaugurated a series of campaigns against Carthage, a Phoenician state in North Africa. The Punic Wars ensued (from the Latin *poeni*, meaning "Phoenician"). When they ended, in 146 B.C.E., Carthage had been razed, and Rome had established an overseas empire, with control over the islands of Sicily, Corsica, and Sardinia.

The Roman army had traditionally been made up of citizen property owners, but in about 107 B.C.E., a general named Gaius Marius began to enroll men in the army who did not meet the property or citizenship qualification. These men saw military service as a career, and a professional army was soon in place. Each soldier served for twenty years and, when not involved in combat, was occupied by the construction of roads, bridges, and aqueducts. At the end of their service, they were given land in the province where they had served, as well as Roman citizenship.

The financial opportunities afforded by imperial conquest stimulated the growth of a new "class" of Roman citizen. Born into families that could pursue senatorial status, these men instead chose careers in business and finance. They called themselves *equites* ("equestrians"), probably because they served in the cavalry in the military—only the wealthy could afford horses—and they embraced a commercial world that their patrician brothers (sometimes quite literally their brothers) found crass and demeaning. By the first century B.C.E., these *equites* were openly in conflict with the Senate, pressing for greater and greater rights for both themselves and the plebeians.

Civil war among Roman political factions soon erupted. The general LUCIUS CORNELIUS SULLA [SOO-lah] ruled as dictator from 82 to 79 B.C.E., murdering thousands of his opponents and introducing a new constitution, that placed power firmly in the hands of the Senate. But all he finally succeeded in doing was exacerbating the situation. Struggles for power between Gaeus Pompeius Magnus—Pompey the Great—and GAIUS JULIUS CAESAR [SEE-zar] (fig. 4.6) finally ended in 48 B.C.E. with Caesar's defeat of Pompey. Caesar became dictator of an empire that included Italy, Spain, Greece, Syria, Egypt, and North Africa. In 45 B.C.E., on the Ides of March—March 15—Caesar himself was assassinated. The civil wars that followed brought the republic to a definitive end, and Caesar's adopted grand-nephew and heir, Octavian, became the sole power in Rome, the *pater patriae*, "father of the fatherland." Renaming himself Augustus, "the revered one," Caesar Augustus reigned as emperor from 27 B.C.E. until 14 C.E.

ART OF THE ROMAN REPUBLIC

Although the Romans conquered the Greeks militarily and politically, the Greeks conquered the Romans artistically and culturally. As the first-century B.C.E. poet Horace put it, "*Graecia capta ferum victorem cepit*" ("Captive Greece conquered her wild conqueror"). Roman writers rarely make reference to Roman artists. Instead, they write about

Cross Currents

THE ROMAN PANTHEON

The major gods of the Romans were essentially the same as those of the Greeks. In adopting the Greek gods, the Romans demonstrated in yet another way how the great military conquerors were themselves conquered by Greek culture. The accompanying chart identifies the deities of Rome with their Greek counterparts and their corresponding roles and responsibilities:

Greek	Roman	Role/Function
Zeus	Jupiter/Jove	chief god/sky
Hera	Juno	wife of Zeus/Jove
Eros	Cupid	god of love
Dionysos	Bacchus	god of wine/revelry
Demeter	Ceres	earth goddess/grain
Persephone	Proserpina	queen of the underworld
Aphrodite	Venus	goddess of love and beauty
Ares	Mars	god of war
Apollo	Apollo	god of sun, music, and the arts
Artemis	Diana	goddess of the hunt
Hermes	Mercury	messenger of the gods
Poseidon	Neptune	god of the sea
Hades	Pluto	god of the underworld
Athena	Minerva	goddess of wisdom
Hephaistos	Vulcan	god of metalwork

There were, nonetheless, some important differences in the way the Romans viewed their gods. The Roman pantheon reflected the culture's political rather than spiritual values, and Roman gods tended to be less embodiments of various human virtues and foibles and more personifications of abstract ideas—love, war, and fortune, for instance.

The Romans also had a vast array of other, local gods. Every place, tree, stream, meadow, and wood had its own spirit. Unlike the gods of Greek origin, anthropomorphic, or human, characteristics were rarely attributed to these spirits. However, it was essential for, say, a farmer to keep on good terms with the spirit of his fields. Because so much depended on annual water flow, the sources of rivers were especially venerated spots and often decorated with numerous shrines.

the Greek masters—Polykleitos, Phidias, Praxiteles, Lysippos. Roman authors refer to the Greeks as the "ancients"; Greek art already had the authority of antiquity for the Romans. The Romans not only imported Greek vases, marbles, and bronzes, but Greek artists as well, many of whom they then put to work copying Greek originals.

Yet Roman art is not solely a continuation of Greek art. The Romans were very different from the Greeks, and their art is accordingly different in emphasis and focus. The Romans were impressed with great size—the size of their empire, of their buildings, of their sculptures. Above all, the Romans were a practical people. They were superb engineers. Their sculpture and painting is realistic, with an emphasis on particulars—specific people, places, and times—a trend that continued until the second century C.E., when Christianity began to foster a more abstract and mystical direction.

Architecture. The Romans adopted the Greek orders—the Doric, Ionic, and Corinthian—but made modifications. Directly influenced by the Tuscan order of Etruscan architecture, the Romans made Doric columns taller and slimmer and gave them a base. The acanthus leaves of the Corinthian order were combined with the volutes of the Ionic order to create the **composite order.** The Romans used the orders with greater freedom than the Greeks, often taking elements from each for use on a single building. The Romans used the Corinthian order most, the Doric least—the opposite of the Greeks. Unlike Greek architects, Roman architects often used **engaged columns** (columns that are attached to the wall) on the inside and outside of buildings.

Much Roman building, like Greek building, was done with ashlar masonry, using carefully cut stone blocks laid in horizontal courses. But in the late second century B.C.E., the Romans developed a type of wall made by setting small broken stones in cement. Such walls were very strong and could be faced with different types of patterned stonework. This construction method opened new directions in architecture, including construction using **concrete,** which consists of cement mixed with small pieces of stone. Concrete is strong, can be cast into any shape, and is far less costly than stone construction. Although the Romans did not invent concrete, they developed its potential.

The rectangular Ionic Temple of "Fortuna Virilis" in Rome (fig. 4.7) was built late second to mid-first century B.C.E. and was probably dedicated to Portunus, the Roman god of harbors and rivers. Etruscan elements include the raised platform or podium, the entry on one end only by ascending a flight of stairs, a front porch that takes up

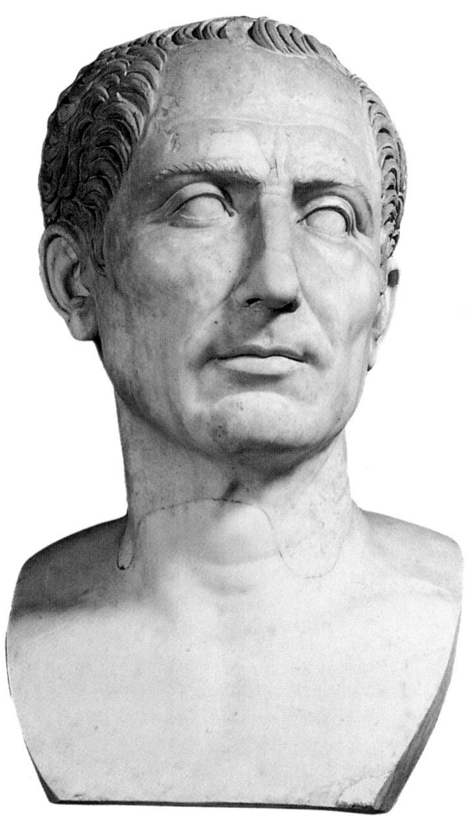

FIGURE 4.6 Portrait bust of Julius Caesar, first century B.C.E., marble, height 38″ (96.5 cm), Museo Archeologico Nazionale, Naples. Like all Roman portrait sculpture of the time, the bust is stunningly realistic. Every anomaly of the facial terrain has been observed and recorded.

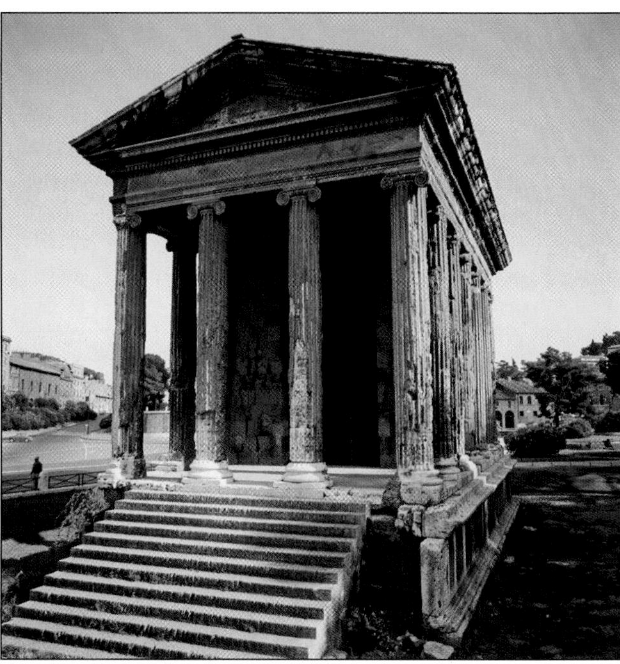

FIGURE 4.7 Temple of "Fortuna Virilis," Rome, late second to mid-first century B.C.E. The rectangular Roman temple form is essentially a combination of the Greek and Etruscan temple forms—compare to the Greek Parthenon (see fig. 3.3) and the Etruscan temple (see fig. 4.1).

about one-third of the whole podium area, and a cella nearly as wide as the podium.

Aqueducts. The Romans constructed an extensive network of **aqueducts** throughout their territories. Some of the aqueducts were many miles long, crossing valleys, spanning rivers, going over mountains and even passing underground. In Rome itself, beginning in 144 B.C.E., a system of aqueducts brought water to all seven of the city's hills, paid for by spoils from the victory in Carthage.

The most famous and best preserved of the ancient Roman aqueducts is the Pont du Gard (bridge over the Gard River) at Nîmes, in southern France (fig. 4.8), built first century B.C.E.–first century C.E. The Pont du Gard is based on a series of arches, each arch buttressed by the arches on either side of it. The water channel is at the very top and is lined with cement. Flat stone slabs were placed over the top to keep out leaves and debris.

Sculpture. The ancient Romans made extensive use of sculpture—on both the inside and outside of public and private buildings, on columns, arches, tombs, and elsewhere.

The Romans imported and copied Greek statues, and they modeled their own sculpture on that of the Greeks. But whereas the Greeks made statues of deities and idealized heroes, Roman sculpture focused on individual people, particularly political figures.

A Roman Patrician with Busts of His Ancestors (fig. 4.9), from the late first century B.C.E., also makes clear the great emphasis placed on lineage by the ancient Romans. The high level of realism may have been assisted by the custom of making deathmasks, called *imagines* by the Romans. Shortly after death, a wax mask was modeled on the face of the deceased and was then sometimes transferred to stone. Masks of the ancestors of the deceased were carried or worn in funeral processions, and portrait busts and *imagines* of ancestors were generally displayed in homes. This man wears the toga, a garment fashionable in the Republican era.

LITERATURE

Like their counterparts in the visual arts, Roman writers owe an immense debt to the Greeks. For the most part, Roman poets used Greek genres, although satire appears to have been a Roman invention. Roman playwrights sometimes adapted Greek plays, with varying degrees of ingenuity.

Catullus. Like the Greek lyric poet Sappho, CATULLUS [ka-TUL-us] (84–54 B.C.E.) wrote passionate

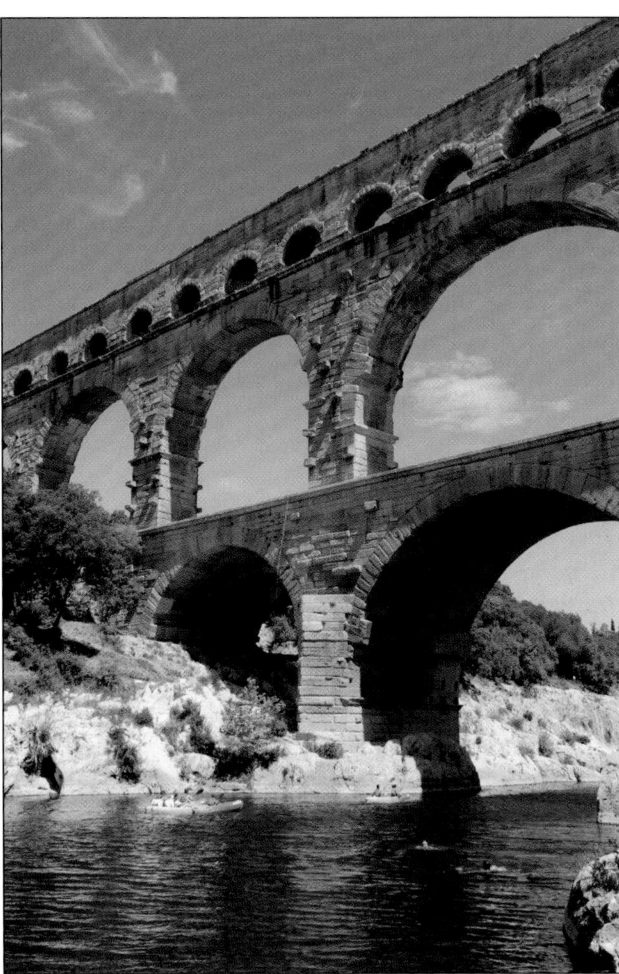

FIGURE 4.8 Pont du Gard, Nîmes, France, late first century B.C.E.–early first century C.E., height 180′ (54.9 m), current length approx. 900′ (275 m). Between 8,000 and 12,000 gallons of water were delivered to Nîmes per day through this aqueduct, which extended for thirty-one miles.

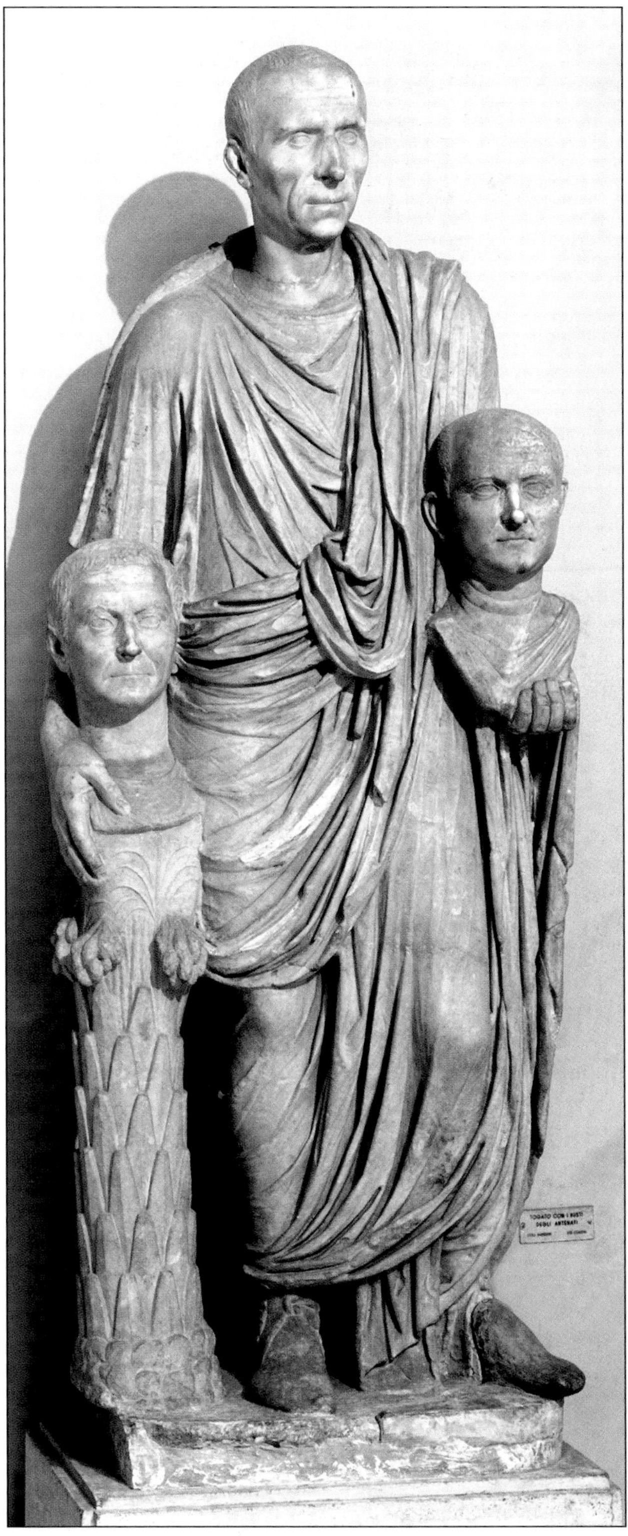

FIGURE 4.9 A Roman man holding busts of his ancestors. Late first century B.C.E., marble, lifesize, Musei Capitolino, Rome, Italy. Photograph © Scala/Art Resource, NY. The great importance Romans attached to family and lineage, exemplified here in this austere sculpture, is one of the motivating forces in the development of highly realistic portraiture during the Republican era.

love poems, one of which is, in fact, a translation into Latin of one of Sappho's most celebrated lyrics, "Seizure."

Reflecting daily life in first-century B.C.E. Rome, many of Catullus' poems are written in a racy colloquial style. Catullus also wrote twenty-five poems about his love affair with Lesbia. These demonstrate his range and show him at his passionate best. Catullus can also be moving in expressing grief, as his lament for the death of his brother demonstrates.

Roman Drama: Plautus and Terence. Although Greek theater excelled in the grandeur of tragedy, the theatrical glory of Rome is its comedy. The two most important Roman comic dramatists are PLAUTUS [PLOW-tus] (ca. 254–184 B.C.E.) and Terence (195–159 B.C.E.). Terence's plays were aimed at an aristocratic audience, by whom he was subsidized; Plautus wrote for the common people. Not surprisingly, Plautus is the more robust and ribald of the two. Although the plays of both dramatists are humorous, Terence's wit is more cerebral than Plautus', which more often elicits a belly laugh. Despite these differences, the works of both playwrights are adaptations of Greek comedy.

Terence offers subtlety of plot for Plautus' farce; he provides character development and interplay for Plautus' stock figures; and he presents economical dialogue in place of Plautus' colorful wordplay. Terence more obviously exhibits tolerance for his characters and appreciation for their mixed motives and muddled but often good intentions. He is more sympathetic toward the elderly, particularly the old fathers that Plautus ridicules. Terence is also more interested in women than Plautus, generally making them more complex and interesting characters.

Plautus's chief characters, those who run the dramatic engine of his plots, are typically slaves and parasites who turn the tables on their masters. With a notable lack of respect for authority, Plautus' characters flout social regulations, especially by undermining figures of authority—masters, fathers, and husbands. In Plautine comedy, slaves outwit their masters, sons fool their fathers, and wives dupe their husbands.

THE ROMAN EMPIRE

When Octavian, Caesar Augustus (63 B.C.E.–14 C.E.), as he was soon known, assumed power in 27 B.C.E., he claimed to have restored the Republic. In reality, however, he had complete authority over not only the Senate but over all of Roman life. By 12 C.E. he had been given the title *Pontifex Maximus*, or "High Priest," and when he died, two years later, the Senate ordered that he be venerated henceforth as a god. Together with his wife Livia, who was herself a skilled administrator, he created the conditions for a period of peace and stability in the empire that lasted for two hundred years. Known as the *Pax Romana*, the "Roman Peace," it was made possible in large part by Augustus' sensitivity to the people that Rome had conquered. Inclusion in the Roman empire was not limited by ethnic identity; Roman citizenship was available to conquered people in other lands. This universalist tendency paralleled Christianity's missionary impulse to spread the Christian message throughout the world. (See Chapter 5.)

In fact, the *Pax Romana*, or Roman peace, which extended throughout the Roman empire, made possible the rapid spread of Christianity.

Augustus dispatched governors to all the provinces with armies to maintain law and order. But these armies, freed of the need to conduct wars, turned to building great public works—aqueducts, theaters, libraries, marketplaces, and roads. Trade was greatly facilitated, and economic prosperity spread throughout the empire. Rome, however, remained at the heart of this trade network. After nearly a century of political turmoil, Augustus' rule ushered in a new Golden Age. The art and literature of the Augustan period are regarded as the pinnacle of Roman cultural accomplishment.

The empire was so strong by the end of Augustus' reign that even a series of debauched and decadent emperors, such as CALIGULA [cal-IG-you-lah] (12–41 C.E.) and NERO [NEAR-oh] (37–68 C.E.), could not destroy it.

There were also some very able emperors, including the so-called "Five Good Emperors"—NERVA [NER-vah] (r. 96–98 C.E.), TRAJAN [TRAY-jan] (r. 98–117 C.E.), HADRIAN [HAY-dree-an] (r. 117–138 C.E.), ANTONINUS PIUS [PIE-us] (r. 138–161 C.E.), and MARCUS AURELIUS [OW-REE-lee-us] (r. 161–180 C.E.). These five ruled for eighty-four consecutive years, during which Rome flourished as never before. By 180 C.E. the Roman empire had grown to enormous proportions, extending from Spain in the west to the Persian Gulf in the Middle East, and from Britain and the Rhine River in the north to Egypt and the Sahara Desert in the south. It encompassed some 1,750,000 square miles and about fifty million people.

However, beginning with the rule of Marcus Aurelius' son COMMODUS [coh-MODE-us] (r. 180–192 C.E.), the empire started to flounder. His murder inaugurated a series of civil wars. Of the twenty-six emperors to rule between 235 and 284 C.E., twenty-five were murdered, as various military factions vied for power. In addition, plague ravaged Rome—between 251 and 266 C.E. many thousands of Romans died from it. And, perhaps most ominously, the empire's borders began to be seriously threatened by barbarian hordes.

In 284 C.E., DIOCLETIAN [DI-oh-CLEE-shun] briefly restored order by dividing the empire into four portions—the **tetrarchy**—and assumed personal control of Asia Minor, Syria, and Egypt. His counterpart in the West, also designated "Augustus," was MAXIMIAN [mac-SIM-ee-an].

After the abdication of Diocletian and Maximian in 305 C.E., the tetrarchy briefly continued until CONSTANTINE [CON-stan-tine] seized control of the entire empire in 324, ruling until his death in 337. In 330, Constantine moved the seat of government from Rome to the port city of Byzantium, which he renamed Constantinople after himself—humility was not part of the job description of the Roman emperor (today the city, known as Istanbul, is in Turkey). Rome's long ascendancy as the cultural center of the Western world was at an end (see Chapter 6).

One invaluable source for our knowledge of the Roman empire was provided by a natural disaster. In 79, the volcano Vesuvius, located about 150 miles south of Rome near the bay of Naples, erupted, engulfing a number of small Roman towns, including the fashionable suburban residences of Herculaneum and Pompeii. Most inhabitants escaped—but with only their lives. Everything else was left in place, food literally still on the tables. Vesuvius

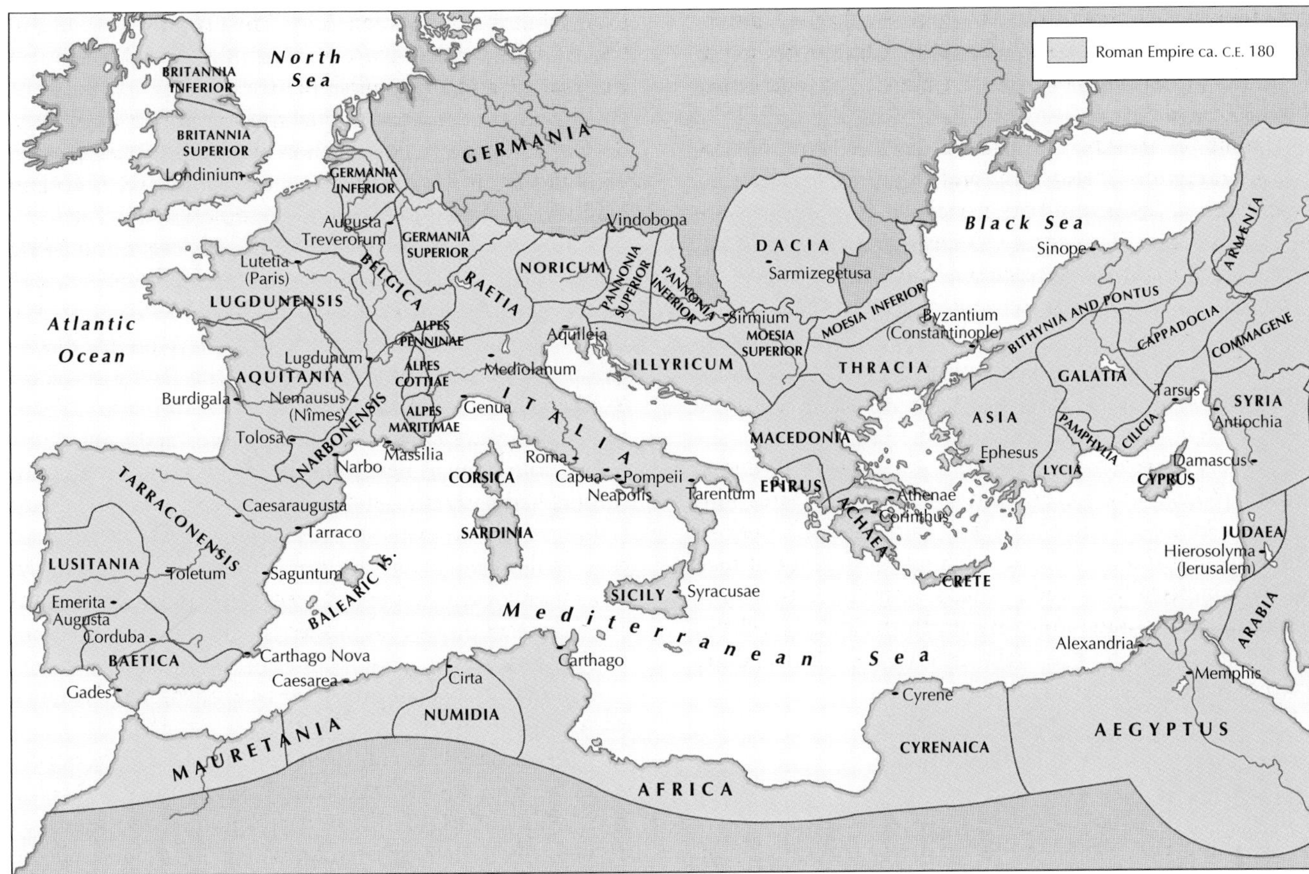

MAP 4.2 The Roman Empire at its greatest extent, ca. 180 C.E.

buried Herculaneum in hot mud and lava that hardened like stone thirty-five to eighty feet deep. Pompeii was covered in twenty to thirty feet of pumice stone and ash. Excavation was begun at both sites in the mid-eighteenth century—a process that has been far easier at Pompeii, but which today is still not complete at either site and has provided a great deal of information on first-century C.E. life in the Roman empire. Our knowledge of Roman painting, for instance, would be immeasurably poorer without the evidence of these towns.

MUSIC

Our knowledge of Roman music is based on what we can learn from mosaics, sculpture, and the remains of brass instruments found on ancient battlefields. Just as Romans adopted much of Greek architecture, sculpture, poetry, and philosophy, so too Greek music was absorbed. Roman music differed, however. Whereas Greek music was basically contemplative and served as a background to plays and poetry, Roman music was loud and aggressive and featured in open-air games, festival parades, and military attacks.

Brass instruments such as the cornu (a "G"-shaped instrument) and the tuba (a long straight trumpet) played accompaniment through raging wars. These instruments were also used to communicate field orders and to announce important visitors. Applying their engineering skills, the Romans used the flow of water to power an organ that could be heard for miles. This instrument, called the hydraulos, was used in the Circus Maximus and the Colosseum to rouse the crowd, much like the organ at today's baseball games. This instrumental music, a painful reminder of Christians killed for sport, was banned from the early Christian church.

Roman pipers played a flutelike instrument at funerals and between acts at plays. Guests at a dinner party might be entertained by vocal and instrumental dinner music. Theater music evolved from interludes between acts to longer pieces that frequently appealed to the audience as much as the drama itself.

ARCHITECTURE

An active builder, Augustus once claimed to have restored eighty-two temples in a single year. Suetonius' *Lives of the Caesars* says that Augustus boasted, "I found Rome a city of brick, and left it a city of marble," although he did so largely by putting a marble veneer over the brick.

Roman Forum. One of Augustus' most ambitious projects was his forum, dedicated in 2 B.C.E. Augustus, a skilled manipulator of public opinion, gave political significance to this forum by dedicating its temple to Mars the Avenger. It was intended to serve as a reminder of the revenge he had taken on the murderers of his uncle, Julius Caesar, and the temple, with eight columns across its front, was one of the largest in the city, rivaling the Athenian Parthenon in size. The Forum of Augustus is actually one of many fora traditionally referred to collectively in the singular as "the forum." The Roman forum consists of nineteen fora—those of Julius Caesar, Augustus, Trajan, Nerva, a forum of peace, and so on—all abutting one another. The original use of the forum was similar to that of the Greek agora. The forum was the center of city life, the public area where assemblies were held, justice was administered, and markets were located. There were also a number of temples, such as two dedicated to Vesta, the Temple of Saturn, the Temple of Castor and Pollux, and the Temple of Antoninus Pius and Faustina. Although each forum was symmetrical in plan, the different fora were combined chaotically.

Colosseum. The celebrated Colosseum in Rome (fig. 4.10), so called because of its association with a colossal statue of the emperor Nero, was dedicated in 80 C.E. The Colosseum is an **amphitheater,** a type of building developed by the Romans. The word "theater" refers to the semicircular form. The prefix "amphi" means "both"; an amphitheater is a theater at both ends and therefore circular or oval in plan. The seating area of the Colosseum accommodated over fifty thousand people, each of whom had a clear view of the arena. To protect the audience from the brilliant Roman sunshine, an awning could be stretched over part of the Colosseum.

The supporting structure of the Colosseum is made of concrete, but the exterior was covered with a stone facing of **travertine** (a form of limestone) and tufa. Holes can now be seen in the stone where people dug to get at the bronze clamps that held the facing in place. These stones hide the supporting structure. This is fundamentally different from the Greek approach to architecture, where the structure was not hidden but, rather, emphasized.

On the exterior, entablatures separate the stories and engaged columns separate the arches. The three architectural orders are combined. On the lowest level is the Tuscan variation on the Doric order; above is the Ionic; and the third level is Corinthian. These columns, engaged to the wall, have no structural function; their only purpose is as surface decoration.

The practical Roman designers combined the use of concrete with another extremely important architectural development—the arch. The visitor to the Colosseum can enter or exit through any of eighty arches around the Colosseum at street level. Each of these arches is buttressed by its neighbors and buttresses its neighbors in

FIGURE 4.10 Colosseum, Rome, dedicated 80 C.E. The freestanding amphitheater, developed by the Romans, was made possible by the use of concrete and the arch principle. Compare this to the Greek theater of Epidauros where support for the seats is provided by the hillside (see fig. 3.13).

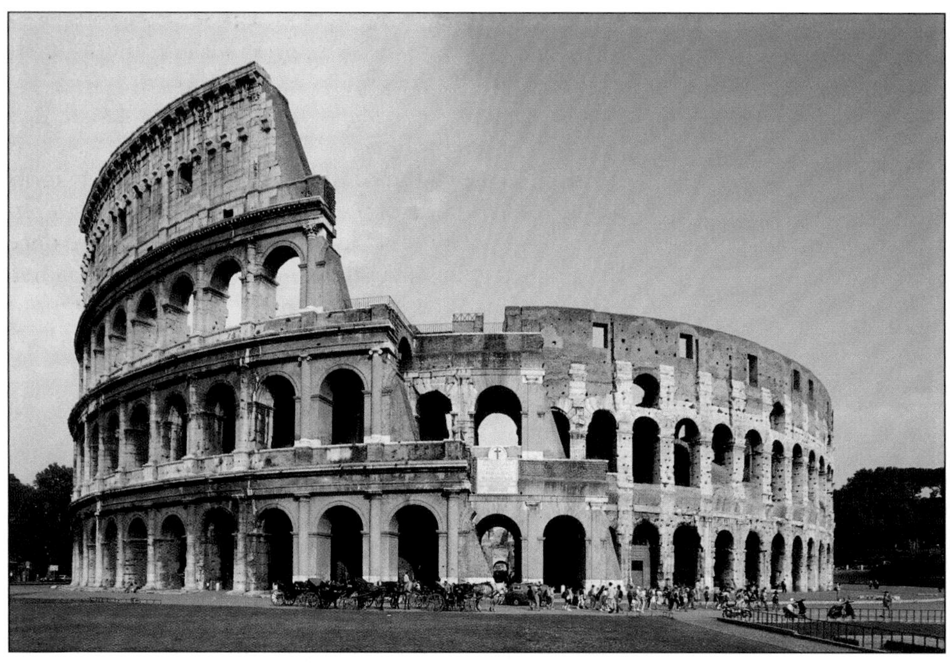

turn, as is true of the Pont du Gard. The interior is constructed with vaulted corridors and many staircases to permit the free movement of a large number of people.

A tremendous number of amphitheaters were built throughout the empire because it was official policy that the state should provide entertainment for the public. This entertainment included several categories of bloody combat: human versus human; human versus animal; animal versus animal; and naval battles—the Colosseum could be flooded to accommodate warships. The quality of this "entertainment" soon turned into a political issue, but the displays nonetheless became progressively more extravagant.

Pantheon. Built between 118 and 125 C.E. during the reign of Emperor Hadrian and designed by the architect Apollodorus of Damascus, the magnificent Roman Pantheon (fig. 4.11) is a large circular temple dedicated to "all the gods" (the literal meaning of the word *pantheon*). Originally, steps led up to the entrance, but over the centuries the level of the street has been raised, and once there was also more to the porch. Otherwise, the Pantheon is very well preserved. In contrast to the Greek emphasis on the exterior of temples, the most important part of the Pantheon is the interior. Inside, the enormous dome that crowns this building is the focus of attention. The space is not interrupted by interior supports, creating a feeling of vast spaciousness (fig. 4.12). The Pantheon was considered the most harmonious interior of antiquity.

The dome, based upon the arch principle, is another of the great innovations of Roman architecture. A series of arches forms a **vault.** An arch rotated 180 degrees forms a **dome.**

FIGURE 4.11 Apollodorus of Damascus, Pantheon, Rome, 118–25 C.E., exterior. A superb display of Roman engineering skill, the Pantheon includes a variety of ingenious devices to deal with the lateral thrust exerted by the dome. The paradigm of circular temples, the Pantheon would prove to be the model for many buildings in the following centuries.

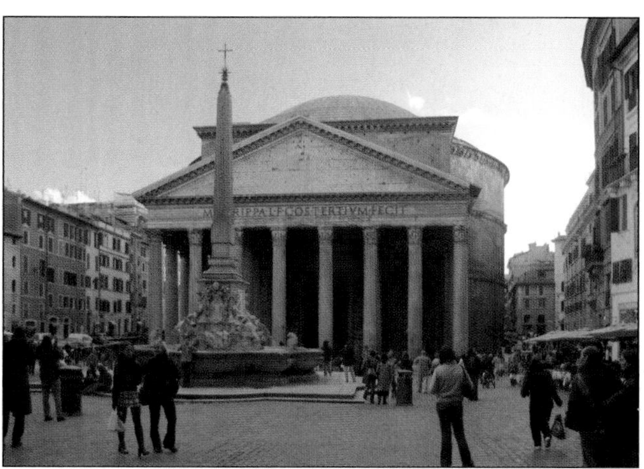

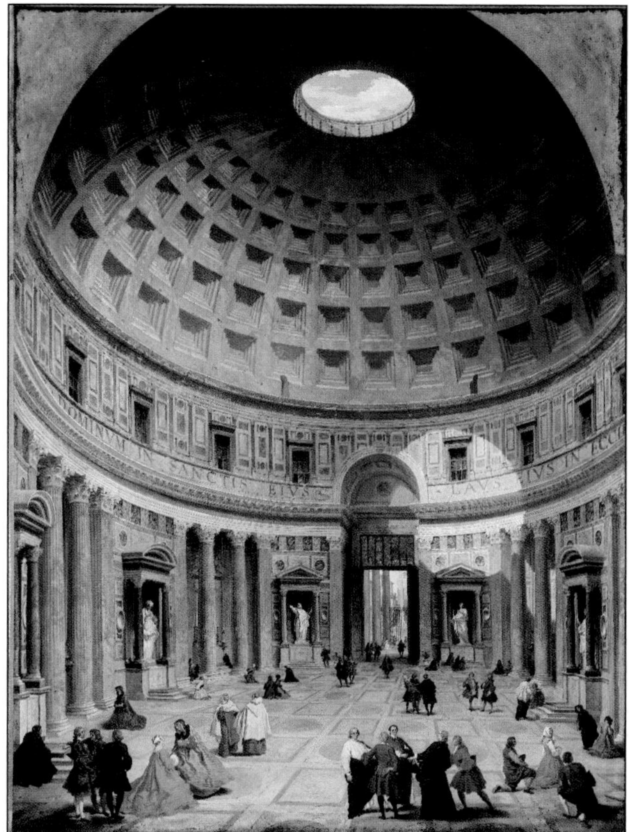

FIGURE 4.12 Giovanni Paolo Panini (Roman, 1691–1765), *Interior of the Pantheon, Rome*, ca. 1734, oil on canvas $50\frac{1}{2}'' \times 39''$ (1.28 × .99 m), Samuel H. Kress Collection. Photograph © 2001 Board of Trustees, National Gallery of Art, Washington, 1939. 1.24(135)/PA. Photo by Richard Carafelli.

The Pantheon's dome is raised on a high base, making the height and diameter of the dome the same—144 feet. The Pantheon was the largest dome until the twentieth century. The dome is made of concrete, the weight of which is concentrated on eight pillars distributed around its circumference. The **oculus,** the "eye" or opening in the center of the ceiling, is thirty feet across and the sole source of light in the building. The squarish indentations in the dome, called **coffers,** were once plated with gold and each had a bronze rosette fastened in the center. The effect, with the brilliant sunlight of Rome coming from the central oculus above, must have been dazzling.

SCULPTURE

With Augustus' rise to power in 27 B.C.E., sculpture changed its style. Depictions of realistically rendered aging Republicans were jettisoned in favor of more idealized versions of youth and an increased taste for things Greek. This change in taste was in part the result of Augustus'

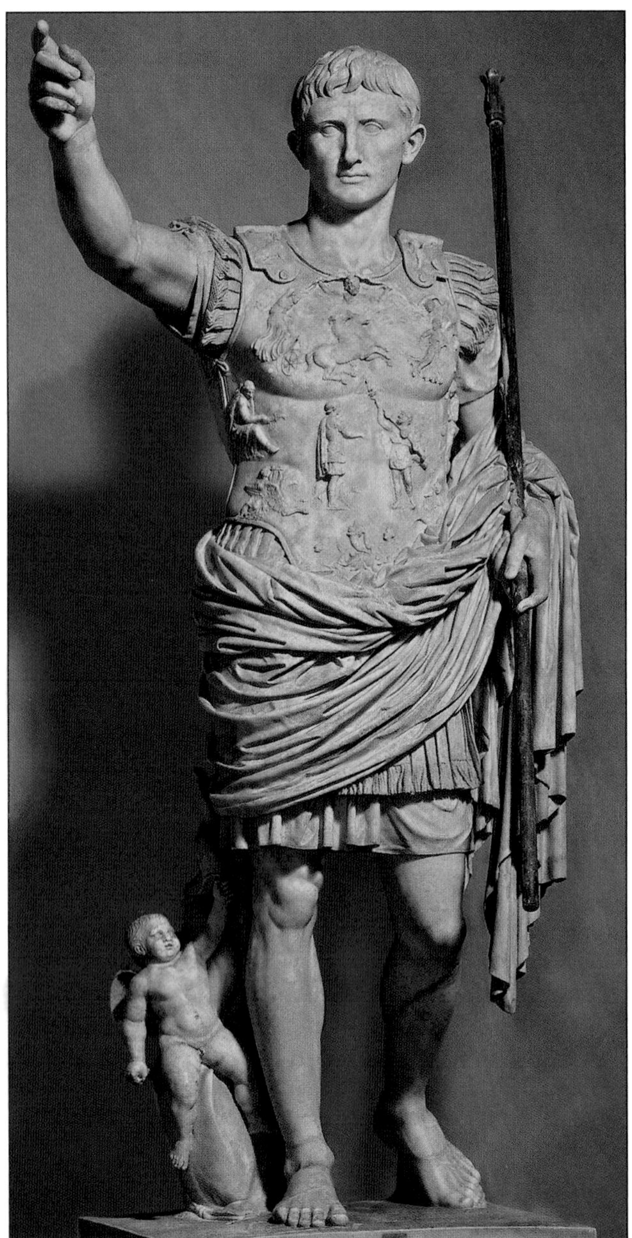

FIGURE 4.13 *Augustus of Primaporta*, ca. 20 B.C.E., marble, height 6′8″ (2.03 m), Braccio Nuovo, Musei Vaticani, Rome. Although this statue does record the appearance of Emperor Augustus, under his reign harsh Roman republican realism was somewhat softened by Greek idealism.

efforts to import Greek craftspeople and artists. In the new Augustan style, Greek idealism was combined with Roman realism.

Augustus of Primaporta. The statue known as *Augustus of Primaporta* (fig. 4.13), ca. 20 B.C.E., is a slightly over-lifesize marble figure intended to glorify the emperor and Roman peace under his rule. The face of the statue is recognizably that of Augustus; the same features are seen on other portraits of the emperor, although here somewhat idealized. Augustus is shown to be heroic, aloof, self-contained. A prototype is seen in figures such as the *Doryphoros* (*Spear-Bearer*) of Polykleitos (see fig. 3.9); indeed, Augustus probably held a spear in his left hand originally, but it has since been restored as a scepter. There is perhaps even a concession to traditional Greek nudity in showing the emperor barefoot. The grand gesture with one arm extended—as if addressing his troops—was a common pose. The cupid riding on a dolphin beside Augustus' right leg is an allusion to Aeneas' mother, Venus, in Virgil's heroic poem, *The Aeneid*, suggesting Augustus' own supposed divine heritage. The relief on Augustus' cuirass (breastplate) is symbolic and refers to the *Pax Romana*, the peace and harmony that prevailed under his reign.

Ara Pacis. At times the distinction between architecture and sculpture is blurred, for a building that is totally covered with relief sculpture, as is the *Ara Pacis* (*Altar of Peace*), built 13–9 B.C.E. by Augustus. Whether it is sculpture or architecture, however, it is undoubtedly the greatest artistic work of the Augustan age. Augustus billed himself as the "Prince of Peace," and this altar is an example of art used as political propaganda.

The *Ara Pacis* is a small rectangular building. Among the extensive reliefs that adorn its sides is an imperial procession including Augustus and Livia (fig. 4.14). Accompanying them is the imperial household, including children, priests, and dignitaries. These figures move along both of the side walls of the altar, converging toward the entrance. The degree of naturalism achieved in this marble relief is striking. The depictions of people are varied—some stand still, others talk with their neighbors, or form groups, or look off in different directions; figures are seen from the front, from the side,

FIGURE 4.14 *Ara Pacis*, relief of procession of figures, 13–9 B.C.E., height ca. 5′3″ (1.6 m). Augustus, now older, is depicted with his wife, Livia. Unlike the timeless, generalized, idealized Greek relief from the Parthenon (see fig. 3.5), the Roman relief shows specific people at a specific event.

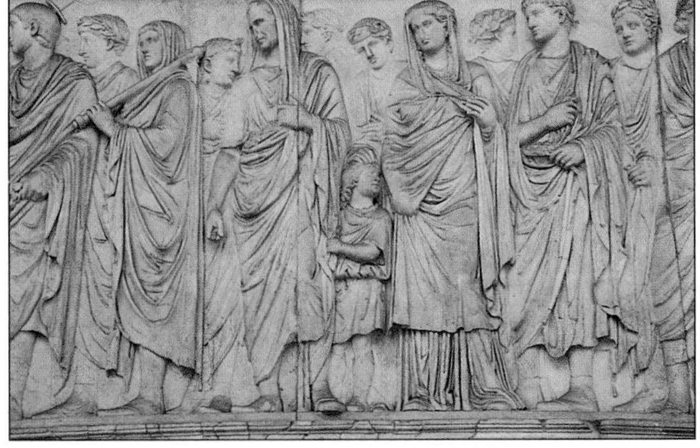

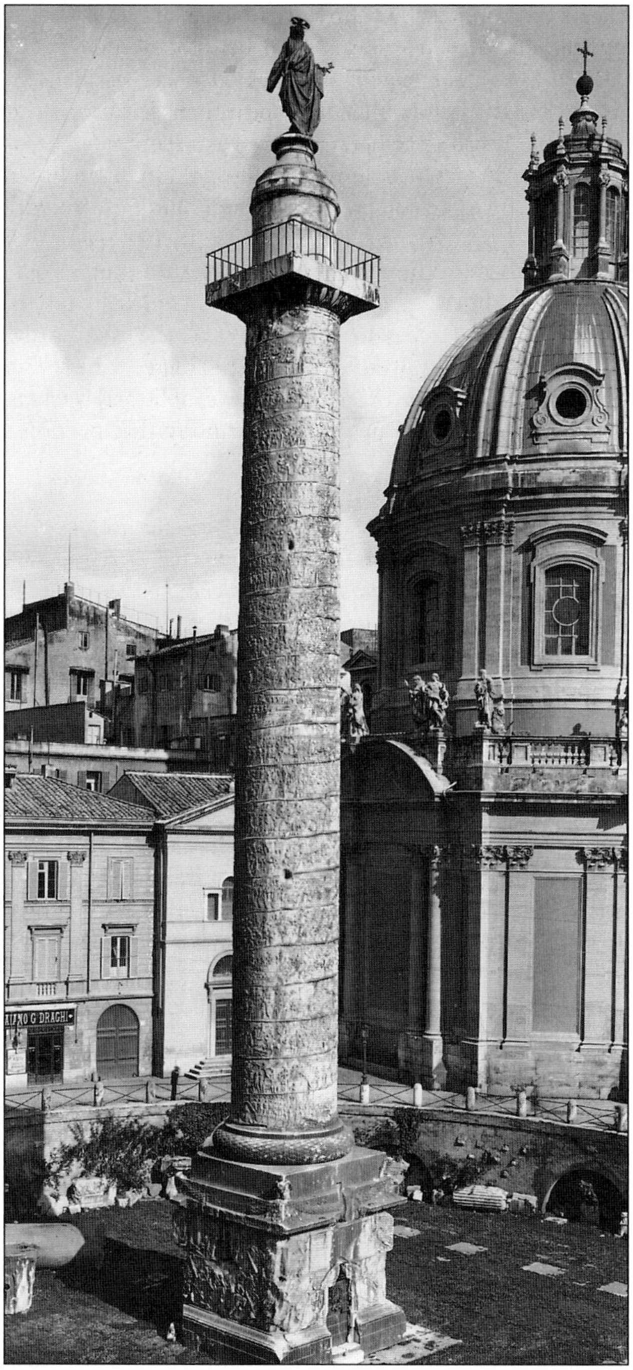

FIGURE 4.15 Apollodorus of Damascus, Column of Trajan, Rome, 106–13 C.E., marble, height with base 125′ (38.1 m). In spite of the obvious difficulty the viewer encounters in following a story told in a relief that spirals around a column rising high above, this was not the only such commemorative column erected by the Romans.

and in three-quarter views. Drapery is skillfully rendered so that fabric falls naturalistically, yet also forms a pleasing rhythmic pattern of loops and curves across the whole relief.

An illusion of spatial recession has been created in stone relief. Figures in the front are a little larger than those in the back and are carved in higher relief. Because the different levels of relief create an illusion of space, blank areas between the figures no longer look like a solid wall but rather read as actual space into and from which figures recede and emerge. A particularly clever illusionistic touch is the positioning of toes so they protrude over the ledge on which the figures stand. It is as if the figures are genuinely three dimensional and capable of stepping out of their space and into ours, adding to the immediacy of the work.

Column of Trajan. Columns, usually erected to celebrate a military victory, are another distinctively Roman form of movement. The emperor Trajan (r. 98–117 C.E.) erected the Column of Trajan (fig. 4.15) in the Forum of Trajan in Rome in 106–113 C.E. The creator of the Pantheon, Apollodorus of Damascus, designed the column.

The base is made of huge blocks with a square stairway inside, while a circular stairway consisting of 182 steps winds around the interior of the actual column. The surface of the column is covered with a continuous band of relief 656 feet long that makes twenty-three turns as it spirals upward like a twisting tapestry. The relief consists of about 150 scenes and 2,500 figures.

The reliefs (fig. 4.16), reading from the bottom to the top, document an actual event—the military campaign of 101–03 C.E. to subdue the forces of Decebalus, prince of Dacia, present-day Romania. This was the first of Rome's wars against the Dacians. In the second, in 105–07 C.E., Trajan completely destroyed his enemy.

FIGURE 4.16 Apollodorus of Damascus, Column of Trajan, Rome, 106–13 C.E., relief, detail of fig. 4.15. The long band of reliefs records Trajan's victories over the Dacians with documentary accuracy. Details of setting, armor, weapons, and even military tactics are included.

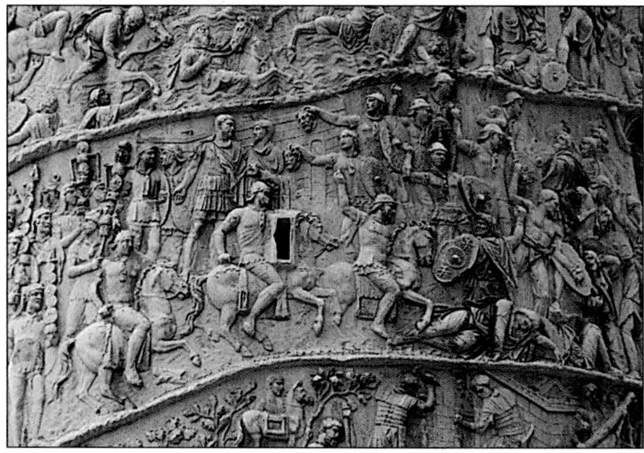

Then & Now

PLAUTUS AND THE CONTEMPORARY BROADWAY THEATER

Plautus has been called "the father of musical comedy." This designation applies not only because his plays include numerous and extensive song passages, but also because of his enormous influence on subsequent drama, including the contemporary Broadway stage. Unfortunately, the music for the songs in Plautus' plays has long been lost. Only the lyrics remain.

Nevertheless, Plautus is alive and well in modern American theater. In the 1930s, and again in the 1990s, his popular *Menaechmi (The Menaechmi Twins)* was turned into an American musical entitled *The Boys from Syracuse* (referring to the city in Sicily). The *Menaechmi* had earlier been transformed by Shakespeare into *The Comedy of Errors*, which, like Plautus' original, revolves around the mistaken identities of identical twins. In the mid-1990s, Broadway was home to a revival of *A Funny Thing Happened on the Way to the Forum*, which had an original Broadway run in 1962. This modern adaptation of Plautus mines the vein of comic gold found in three of Plautus' plays.

Why does Plautus' dramatic and comic genius speak to a contemporary American audience? Essentially for the same reasons it spoke to his Roman contemporaries: It pokes fun at sober pieties; it mocks conventional wisdom; and it expresses an irreverent attitude toward what is fashionable and important. It makes people laugh both at themselves and at their society, even while they remain obliged to live within it.

Equestrian Statue of Marcus Aurelius. The over-lifesize equestrian statue of Emperor Marcus Aurelius (fig. 4.17), of 164–66 C.E., became a favorite type of commemorative sculpture. This statue has survived to the present only because it was long mistaken for a portrait of Constantine, the first Christian emperor, and was thus spared the fate of being melted down as so many other "pagan" Roman bronzes were (for instance, the statue of Trajan on top of his column—see fig. 4.15). A philosopher-emperor, gentle and wise, who held Stoic beliefs, Marcus Aurelius is garbed in the traditional robes of the Republican philosophers. He subdues his enemies without weapons or armor—originally, a barbarian lay beneath the horse's upraised hoof—and in victory brings with him the promise of peace.

FIGURE 4.17 *Equestrian Statue of Marcus Aurelius*, 164–66 C.E., gilded bronze, height 11′6″ (3.51 m), Piazza del Campidoglio, Rome. This equestrian image became a model for future representations of military leaders.

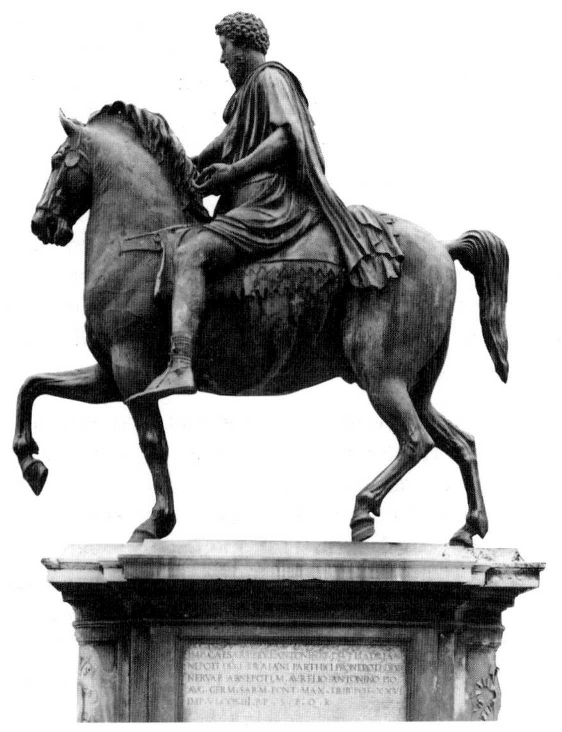

Head of Caracalla. A time of political revolution and social change, the violence of the third century in Rome is embodied in the portrait head of Caracalla (fig. 4.18). The emperor's real name was Antoninus; his *Constitutio Antoniniana* gave everyone living in the Roman empire civil rights.

Yet he was also a brutal soldier who consolidated his hold on the throne by murdering his brother, and it is this aspect of his character that is portrayed in sculpture. How has the sculptor accomplished this? His facial expression is stressed, the eyes emphasized by carving out the pupils and engraving the irises. Caracalla gazes into the distance, seemingly focusing on a definite point. His forehead is furrowed, his brow contracted, as if in anxiety.

Many copies of the bust survive—Caracalla must have approved of this image himself. It is as if brutality has become the very sign of power and authority. The portrait set a style for the third century, which emphasizes such animated facial expression. The skillful carving, creating a vivid contrast between flesh and hair, is descriptive rather than decorative.

Connections

THE *ARA PACIS* AND THE POLITICS OF FAMILY LIFE

Three generations of Augustus' family appear in the section of the *Ara Pacis* illustrated in fig. 4.14. On the left, his head covered by his robe, is Marcus Agrippa. At the time of the carving he was married to Augustus' daughter Julia and was next in line to be emperor after Augustus, but he died in 12 C.E., two years before Augustus himself. Next to him in the relief is his eldest son, Gaius Caesar, who clings to Agrippa's robe. Augustus was particularly fond of Gaius and his younger brother Lucius. The two boys often traveled with the emperor, and he took on important aspects of their education, teaching them to swim, to read, and to imitate his own handwriting. The proud grandmother, Augustus' wife Livia, stands beside Marcus Agrippa and Gaius Caesar. Behind her is her own son Tiberius, who would in fact succeed Augustus as emperor. Behind Tiberius is Antonia, Augustus' niece and the wife of Tiberius' brother Drusus, at whom she is looking. Antonia holds the hand of her and Drusus' son, Germanicus. Drusus' nephew Gnaeus clings to his uncle's robe.

In the period before the *Ara Pacis*, there are very few examples of depictions of children in Roman public sculpture, a fact that raises an important question: What moved Augustus to include children so conspicuously in this monument? By the time Augustus took control of Rome, slaves and freed slaves threatened to outnumber Roman citizens in Rome itself, and they clearly outnumbered the Roman nobility. Augustus took this seriously and saw it as the result of a crisis in Roman family life. Adultery and divorce had become commonplace. Furthermore, the cost of maintaining a family was increasing. Consequently Roman families were becoming smaller and smaller.

Augustus introduced a series of measures to combat this decline in the traditional Roman family. He criminalized adultery and passed a number of laws designed to promote marriage as an institution and encourage larger families. Men between the ages of twenty-five and sixty and women between the ages of twenty and fifty were required to marry. A divorced woman was required to remarry within six months, a widow within a year. A childless woman, married or not, was required to pay large taxes on her property. A childless man was denied any inheritance. And the nobility were granted political advantages in line with the size of their families.

The *Ara Pacis* can be seen as part of Augustus' general program to revitalize the institution of marriage in Roman life. His own family, so prominently displayed in the frieze, was intended to serve as a model for all Roman families.

FIGURE 4.18 *Caracalla*, ca. 215 C.E., marble, lifesize. Samuel D. Lee Fund. Metropolitan Museum of Art, New York. Art Resource, NY. This bust records Emperor Caracalla's physical appearance, but goes beyond the superficial representation of the subject's facial terrain to reveal his personality—which was described as often angry.

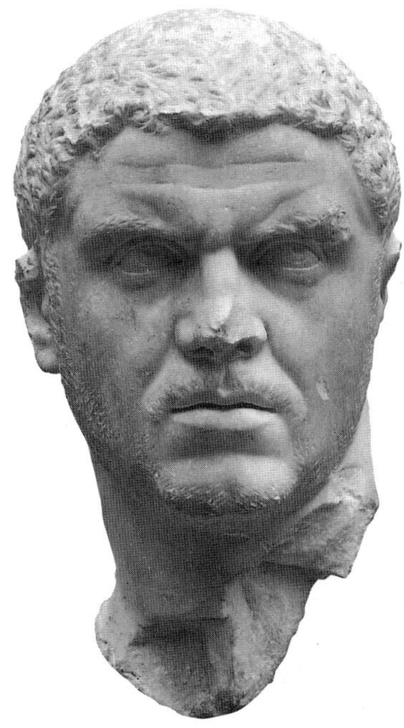

Head of Constantine. The eyes of this head of Constantine the Great (fig. 4.19), the first Christian emperor, who ruled 306–37, gaze out into the distance like Caracalla's, but Constantine no longer seems to focus on anything in particular. Instead, in keeping with the spirituality of the times, he appears to be in a kind of trance. The head itself, over eight feet high, was originally part of an enormous thirty-foot-high seated sculpture of the emperor, of which only a few marble fragments survive, among them a giant hand that points heavenward. Placed behind the altar of the Basilica Nova in Rome, it dominated the interior space. Constantine is both mystical and majestic. He is shown to be calm, capable, and composed by an image that is self-glorifying and self-exalting.

The Arch of Constantine. Constantine had come to power after defeating the emperor Maxentius. To celebrate his victory, the Senate erected a giant triple arch next to the Colosseum in Rome (fig. 4.20). Much of the decoration was taken from second-century C.E. monuments, and the figures changed to look like Constantine. The medallions decorating the arch were carved 128–38 C.E. during the time of Hadrian. The frieze below, carved in the early fourth century, originally had Constantine in the center, later replaced by a figure of Jesus.

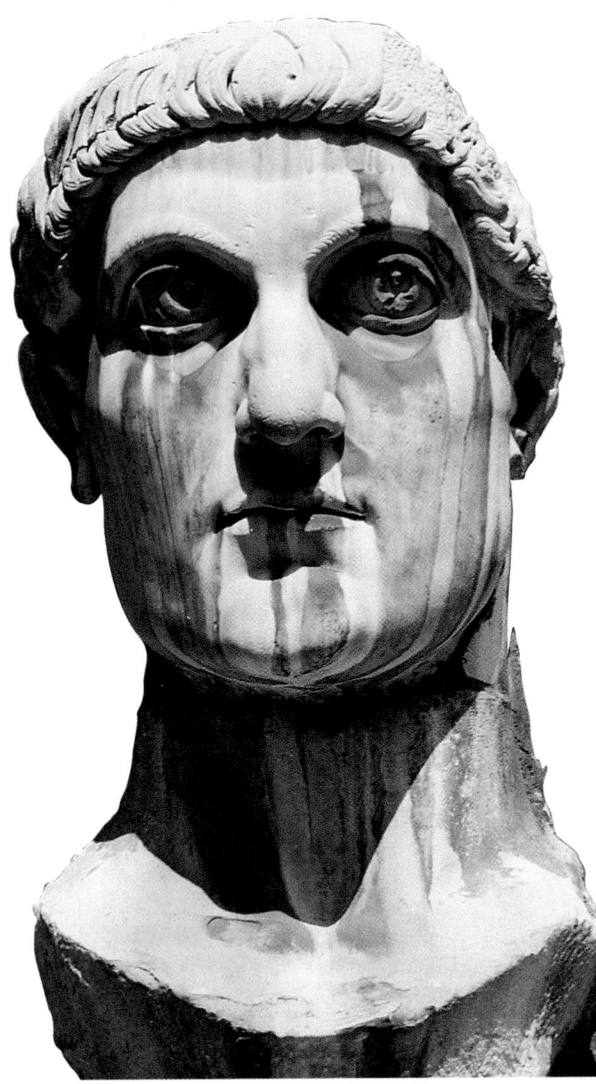

FIGURE 4.19 *Constantine the Great*, head from a huge statue, 325–26 C.E., marble, height 8′5″ (2.58 m), Palazzo dei Conservatori, Rome. This image of Constantine, the first Christian emperor, impresses through enormous scale rather than photographic realism. With the spread of Christianity came a turn away from the factual and toward the spiritual.

PAINTING

Only a fraction of the paintings produced by ancient Roman artists remain. The small-scale portable paintings on ivory, stone, and wood are now almost entirely gone, although it is known that such paintings sold for high prices. Almost the only Roman painting to survive is found on walls in the form of **murals.**

The walls of private homes were frequently painted. The best extant examples of ancient Roman wall painting are those that were preserved in Pompeii and Herculaneum by the eruption of the volcano Vesuvius in 79 C.E. A few later examples have survived in Rome, Ostia, and the provinces.

The German historian August Mau classified ancient Roman wall painting into four styles in 1882. Although Mau's system continues to be used today, there is disagreement among art historians as to precisely when one style ends and the next begins.

First Style. The First Style starts in the second century B.C.E. and continues until ca. 80 B.C.E. It is referred to as the "incrustation" or "masonry" style, since the paintings of this period attempt to imitate the appearance of colored marble slabs. The wall surface from the Casa di Sallustio at Pompeii (fig. 4.21), of the mid-second century B.C.E., is divided into squares and rectangles which are painted to look like costly marble wall-facing. There are no figures and no attempt to create the illusion of three-dimensional space—the only illusion is that of marble created in paint.

Second Style. The Second Style begins about 80 B.C.E. and lasts until 30 or 20 B.C.E. It is often referred to as the "architectonic," "architectural," or "illusionistic" style. In this period actual architectural structures, which were themselves colored, were copied in paint. A characteristic example of the Second Style is the *cubiculum* (fig. 4.22) from the Villa at Boscoreale, a mile north of Pompeii, built shortly after the mid–first century B.C.E. The bedroom of a wealthy Roman by the name of Publius Fannius Synistor, this room was at the northwest corner of a colonnaded court of the house. It was buried by the eruption of Mount Vesuvius in 79 C.E. and was only rediscovered in the late nineteenth century.

The walls of the room are painted with illusionistic architecture that creates open vistas into space. The painter has extended the dimensions of the room; the solid wall is obliterated. It has been suggested that this was inspired by stage painting—there are theater masks at the top of the wall, and Vitruvius refers to the use of stage scenery as house decoration. Or perhaps this reflects actual contemporary architecture. Might this be a portrayal of an ideal villa? Could this be a visual retreat—the idea of escaping from daily cares into this fantastic architectural realm?

The painter uses perspective, but not scientifically or consistently. It is not possible to make a logical groundplan of this cityscape. What do the buildings stand on? Yet the light falls as if from an actual window in the back wall.

Both the First and Second Styles evidence the Roman delight in fooling the viewer's eyes. Such realism was admired in antiquity. In his *Natural History*, Pliny says a certain painted decoration was praised "because some crows, deceived by a painted representation of roof-tiles, tried to alight on them." With different textures, with marble columns that appear round, with painted colonnades on a projecting base, a fairly convincing illusion of three dimensions is created on a two-dimensional surface. The Boscoreale *cubiculum* is intended to trick the eye on a grand scale. The murals may be indicative of the villa owner's desire to amuse, to entertain, and, especially, to impress his guests.

Third Style. The Third Style dates from the late-first century B.C.E. to the mid-first century C.E. The Third Style is variously known as the "ornamental/ornamented,"

Table 4–1 EMPERORS OF ANCIENT ROME

The most significant Roman emperors and the dates they reigned:

Augustus	27 B.C.E.–14 C.E.	Septimius Severus	193–211
Tiberius	14–37	Caracalla	211–217
Caligula	37–41	Alexander Severus	222–235
Claudius	41–54	Maximinus Thrax	235–238
Nero	54–68	Philip the Arab	244–249
Vespasion	69–79	Gallienus	253–268
Titus	79–81	Aurelian	270–275
Domitian	81–96	Diocletian	284–305
Nerva	96–98	Maximian	286–305
Trajan	98–117	Constantius Chlorus	305–306
Hadrian	117–138	Galerius	305–311
Antonius Pius	138–161	Maxentius	306–312
Lucius Verus	161–169	Licinius	311–324
Marcus Aurelius	161–180	Constantine the Great	307–337
Commodus	180–193		

FIGURE 4.20 Arch of Constantine, 312–15 C.E., Rome. The simple type of ancient Roman triumphal arch has a single opening; the more complex type like the Arch of Constantine has three openings. Typically Roman is the nonstructural use of columns as surface decoration.

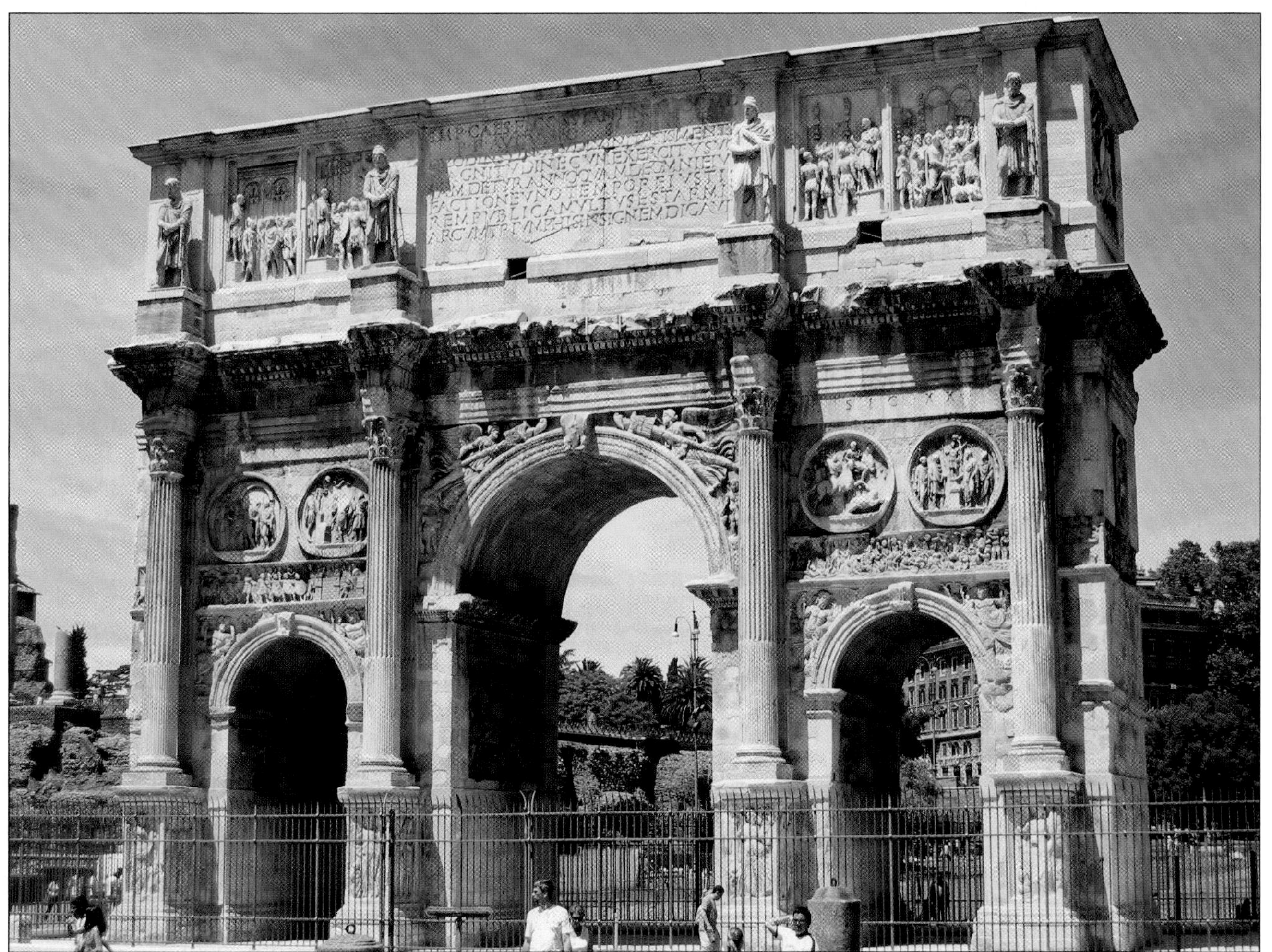

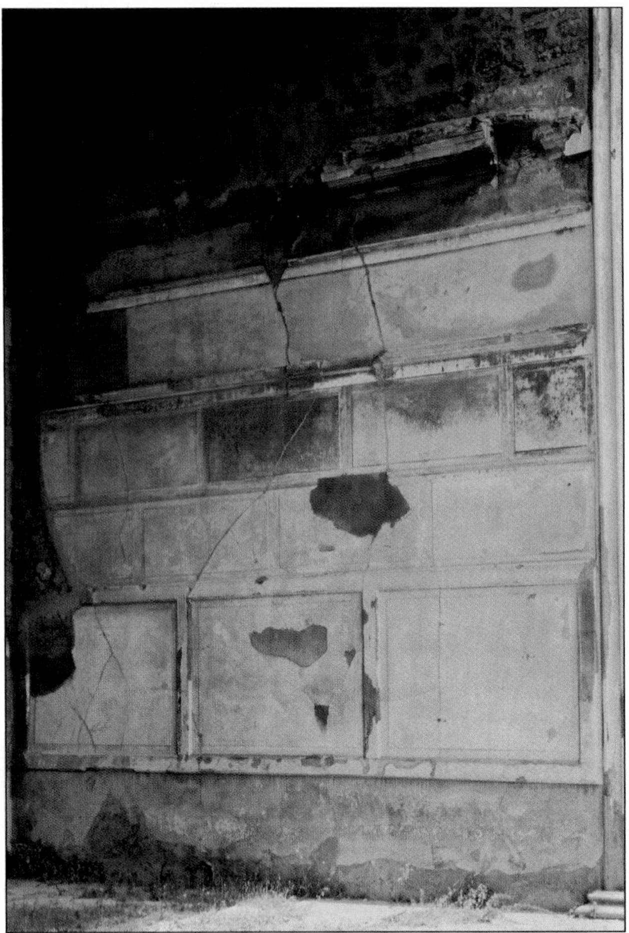

FIGURE 4.21 Casa di Sallustio, Pompeii, second century B.C.E. The first of the four styles of ancient Roman wall painting (a system of classification developed not by the ancient Romans but by a nineteenth-century historian) is readily recognizable. Also known as the "incrustation" style, the First Style consists of painted imitations of marble slabs.

"capricious," "ornate," "candelabra," or "classic" style. There is a new concern with decorative detail. The abrupt shift evident in the Third Style coincides with the reign of Augustus.

The Third Style places an emphasis on the wall surface rather than on illusions of depth (fig. 4.23). Walls are now often almost monochromatic, the range of colors restricted to red, black, or white. These large areas of monochrome emphasize the wall's two-dimensionality. Landscapes are no longer spread over the wall to create spatial illusions, but are instead treated as framed pictures on the wall, as vignettes, not located in depth behind the wall surface but on the surface. The surrounding flat fields of colors are painted with elaborate details of architecture, plant forms, and figures, delicate and decorative. The massive columns and architectural framework of the Second Style have given way to spindly nonstructural columns.

Fourth Style. The Fourth, and final, Style largely dates from the mid-first century C.E. or from the earthquake in 62 C.E. until the eruption of the volcano Vesuvius in 79 C.E., although extant examples postdate the eruption of Vesuvius. The Fourth Style is the most elaborate of all and is known as the "composite," "fantasy," or "intricate" style. The painting technique is somewhat freer, sketchier, more impressionistic than in the First, Second, or Third Styles. There is greater use of still life, mythological, and landscape subjects.

The Ixion Room of the House of the Vettii in Pompeii (fig. 4.24), painted 63–79 C.E., is typical. Within the Fourth Style are returns to "false" earlier styles. This example combines the simulated marble inlay of the First Style on the lower wall, the illusionistic architecture of the Second Style on the upper wall, and the framed vignette surrounded by a flat area of solid color of the Third Style. A completely painted fantasy is achieved. Figures and architecture are combined. What more could possibly be added to this playful and decorative ornament?

PHILOSOPHY

Stoicism. Like so much else in the artistic and philosophical traditions of Greece, Stoicism migrated to Rome (see Chapter 3). From the second century B.C.E. through the period of the Roman empire, Stoicism was the dominant Roman philosophy. The great Roman orator MARCUS TULLIUS CICERO [SIS-ur-oh] (106–43 B.C.E.) commented on it, but Stoicism's two best known adherents and practitioners were EPICTETUS [eh-pic-TEE-tus] (ca. 60–110 C.E.), a Greek slave and secretary in the imperial administration, and Epictetus' student Marcus Aurelius, who reigned as emperor some years after Nero.

Like the Greek philosophers who came after Aristotle, Epictetus was a practical philosopher. His interest lay less in elaborating a metaphysical system than in providing guidance for living a life of virtue and equanimity. Epictetus exemplified the Stoic ideal in his own life, living simply and avoiding the temptations and distractions of the world as much as possible. He urged his followers, in his *Discourses*, to control what elements of their lives they could and to avoid worrying about those they could not. Epictetus accepted, for example, that he could not change the fact he was a slave. What he could control, however, was his attitude toward his situation. It was this attitude, according to Epictetus, that determined one's moral worth, not one's external circumstances.

Unlike Epictetus, Marcus Aurelius was born into a wealthy Roman family. He succeeded his uncle, Antoninus Pius, to the imperial throne in 161 C.E. This was a time of great difficulty for Rome, which had suffered a devastating plague as well as incursions into its territories by barbarians. As emperor, Marcus Aurelius spent nearly half his life on military campaigns. It was during his military duties that he composed his *Meditations*, a series of reflections on the proper conduct of life.

The Meditations are more attentive to religious questions than Epictetus's *Discourses*. Like his Greek Stoic predecessors, Marcus Aurelius described the divine less in terms of a personal god in the Judeo-Christian tradition and more as an indwelling spirit of rationality. Marcus Aurelius considered the entire universe to be governed by reason, and he accepted the world as fundamentally good. It is the ethical

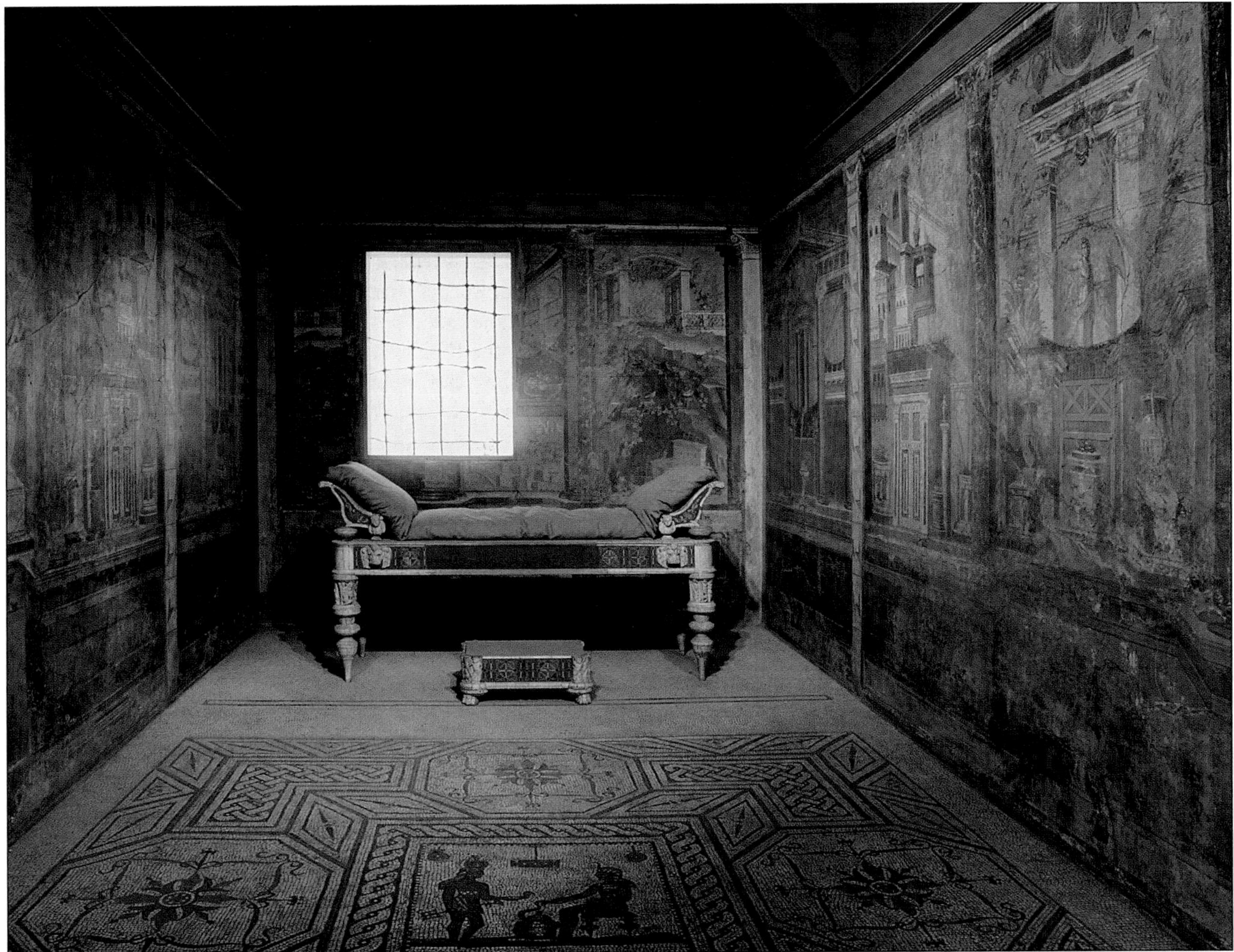

FIGURE 4.22 Roman paintings. Pompeian, Villa at Boscoreale. Bedroom (*cubiculum, nocturnum*) overview, first century B.C.E. Rogers Fund, 1903 Metropolitan Museum of Art, New York. In this example of the Second Style, also known as the "architectonic" style, an entire bedroom is painted with illusionistic architecture and distant cityscapes.

dimension of *The Meditations*, however, that has determined their popularity and influence. In preaching a doctrine of acceptance, Marcus Aurelius recommended that a person not return evil for evil, but rather ignore the evil that others did to one, since what happened to an individual's person and possessions was insignificant. According to Marcus Aurelius, only the soul, the inner self, counted.

ROMAN HISTORIANS

Gaius Sallustus Crispis, Sallust (ca. 86–34 B.C.E.), began writing about 43 B.C.E. Sallust's birth during a time of civil war, and his maturation during a period of foreign war and political strife, likely contributed to his preoccupation with violence and political conflict. Sallust's historical writing deals with corruption in Roman politics, the origins of party struggles, and the history of Rome from 78 to 67 B.C.E.

Titus Livius, or Livy (59 B.C.E.–17 C.E.), wrote an extensive history of Rome, from the mythological founding of the city to the year 9 C.E. Livy's history was written in 142 books, of which only about 36 have been preserved. His work differs from Sallust's in its emphasis on individual historical figures and their influence, rather than on conflicting political forces. Livy wrote history to provide his countrymen with a panoramic account of their past, to celebrate its glories, and to encourage them to abandon decadent behavior. His varied and flexible writing style, although sometimes factually inaccurate, is particularly well suited to the analysis of historical characters and to recreating the rhetorical brilliance of their speeches.

Like Livy, much of the work of GAIUS CORNELIUS TACITUS [TASS-i-tus] (ca. 56–120 C.E.) has been lost. About a third of his important works, the *Histories* and the *Annals*, have survived. The *Histories* provide an account of Tacitus' own time, from 69 to 96 C.E., whereas the *Annals* cover an earlier period from the death of Augustus and the succession of Tiberius in 14 C.E. to the end of Nero's reign in 68 C.E. Tacitus' work analyzes the decline of political

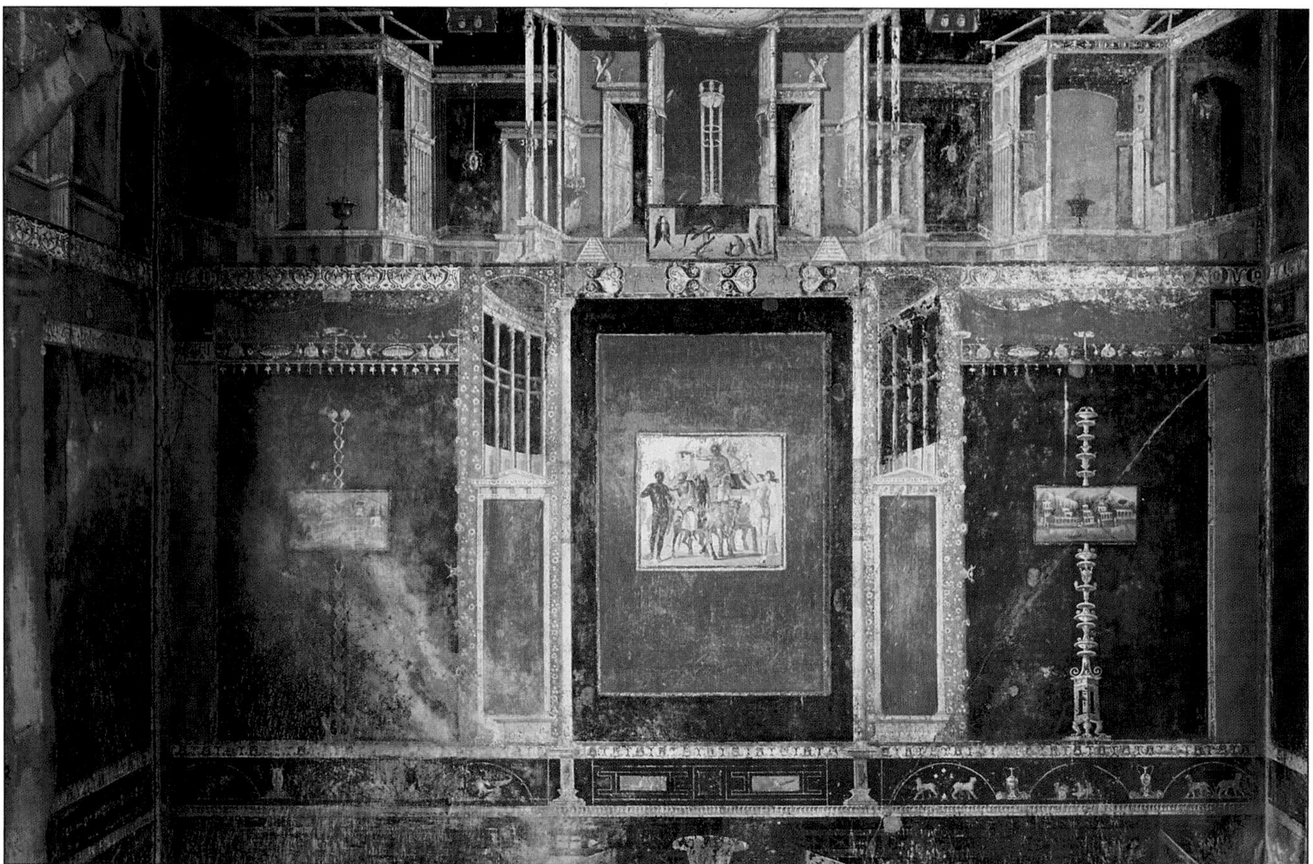

FIGURE 4.23 House of M. Lucretius Fronto, Pompeii, mid-first century C.E. In the Third Style, also known as the "ornamental" style, there is a return to a flatter effect with large areas of solid color and scenes treated as framed pictures hanging on the wall.

freedom in Rome and criticizes dynastic power. Tacitus found Tiberius false, Claudius weak, Nero unstable, and the imperial wives dangerous.

Just how false, weak, unstable, and dangerous the Roman emperors were is taken up in considerable detail in the *Lives of the Caesars* by GAIUS SUETONIUS [Sway-TONE-ee-us] (ca. 69–122 C.E.). A biographer as well as a historian, Suetonius' *Of Famous Men* includes short biographies of Roman orators, rhetoricians, philosophers, and poets, including lives of Horace, Terence, and Virgil. His *Lives of the Caesars*, which covers the first twelve emperors from Julius Caesar to Domitian, presents a vivid picture of Roman society, particularly the political corruption and moral decadence of its leaders.

LITERATURE

Poetry in the Roman empire flourished as never before under the rule of Augustus. Augustus himself appears to have been a significant patron of the literary arts and he encouraged writers to glorify the themes of his reign—peace and the imperial destiny of Rome.

Virgil. Latin poets celebrated Roman culture while emulating the cultural achievements of their Greek predecessors. The poet who best harmonized these two cultural and literary strains was Publius Vergilius Maro, known simply as VIRGIL [VER-jil] (70–19 B.C.E.), whose poem *The Aeneid* [ee-NEE-id] rivals the Homeric epics in literary splendor and cultural significance.

Virgil was almost certainly commissioned by the emperor himself to write his great epic. Much in the poem is Augustan in theme.

The Aeneid is a heroic account of the events that led to the founding of the city of Rome and the Roman empire, especially the misfortunes and deprivations that accompany heroic deeds. The poem concerns the Trojan prince AENEAS [ee-NEE-as], who flees his home as it is being destroyed at the end of the Trojan War and sails away to found a new city in Italy—the successor to the great Trojan civilization. Clearly Aeneas' new city is the forerunner of Rome, and the person of Aeneas in the poem is obviously in some degree intended to honor Augustus himself—the links between Augustus and Aeneas were alluded to by other artists.

The first of the *Aeneid*'s twelve books begins *in medias res* (in the middle of things), as Aeneas and his men are caught in a storm and shipwrecked at Carthage on the north African coast. Dido, the Carthaginian queen, provides food and shelter, and Aeneas describes the destruction of Troy at the hands of the Greeks (Book II) and his journey to Carthage (Book III). Enamored of Aeneas, Dido urges him to remain at her court

Then & Now

GRAFFITI

The urge to write on walls is apparently as old as civilization itself. Before the invention of writing, for instance, prehistoric people outlined their hands on cave walls, as if to say, "I was here." In contemporary society, our national parks and monuments are plagued by this apparently basic human need to announce our presence, as generation after generation have inscribed their names and dates of visit on canyon walls and giant redwoods. One of the earliest records of the Spanish conquest of the American Southwest is preserved on Inscription Rock at El Morro National Monument in New Mexico. It reads, "Passed by here the Adelantado Don Juan de Oñate, from the discovery of the Sea of the South, the 16th April of 1605." It is the first of a long legacy of such inscriptions, culminating in the graffiti that today "decorates" so much of the local landscape—the so-called "tags," or names, of graffiti "writers" that vie for prominence on many walls of urban America.

The Romans, it seems, were themselves great practitioners of the "art" of graffiti. In Pompeii alone over 3,500 graffiti have been found. Among them is the normal fare: "Successus was here;" "Publius Comicius Restitutus stood here with his brother;" "We are here, two dear friends, comrades forever. If you want to know our names, they are Gaius and Aulus;" and "Gaius Julius Primigenius was here. Why are you late?" But the Romans were also adept at the kind of graffiti we normally associate today with "bathroom humor": One wit apparently paraphrases Julius Caesar's famous boast "I came, I saw, I conquered," transforming it into "I came here, I screwed, I returned home." There are as well many graffiti of the "Marcus loves Spendusa" and "Serena hates Isidore" variety. But one writer sums up the feelings of future generations of graffiti readers: "I am amazed, O wall, that you have not collapsed and fallen, since you must bear the tedious stupidities of so many scrawlers."

rather than travel to Italy to establish a new home for his people. When Aeneas instead leaves her to fulfill his destiny, the queen commits suicide by throwing herself on a funeral pyre, the spiking flames of which are visible to Aeneas as he sails away (Book IV). Books V and VI describe Aeneas' arrival in Italy and his journey to the underworld—a characteristic feature of epic poems. In the second half of the poem (Books VII–XII), Virgil describes Aeneas' arrival at the Tiber River, which will be the site of the future city of Rome, and the Battle of the Trojans with the Latin people who live there, a battle ultimately won by the Trojans.

FIGURE 4.24 Ixion Room, House of the Vettii, Pompeii, 63–79 C.E., The Fourth Style, also known as the "composite" style, combines aspects of the earlier styles: imitation marble incrustation; illusionistic architecture; and areas of flat color with small framed scenes.

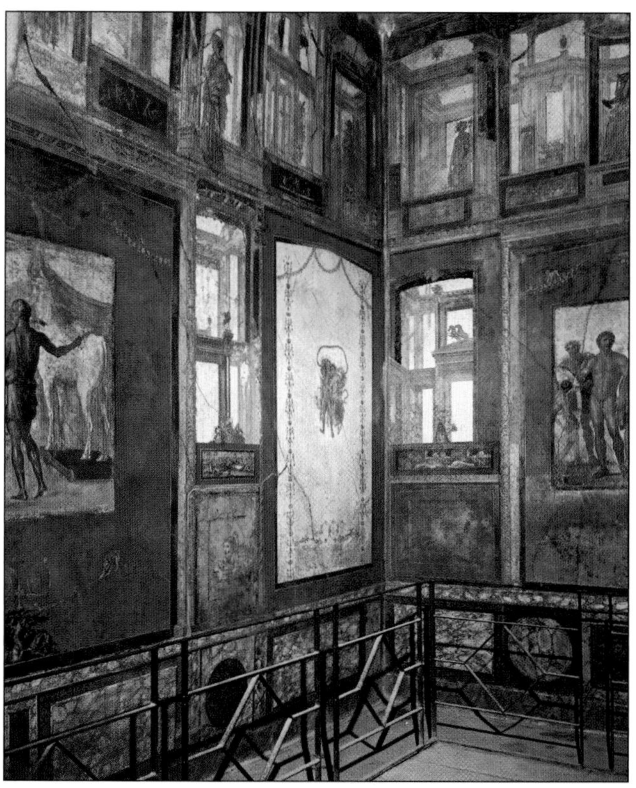

Aeneas struggles with both his destiny and his conscience. He experiences danger and suffering in his arduous journeys and battles; and he experiences anguish over his harsh treatment of Queen Dido. While celebrating Aeneas' victory and heroism and highlighting his courage and filial piety, Virgil also expresses sympathy and compassion for all human beings, whose existence is characterized by suffering and sorrow, an experience beautifully captured in Virgil's words from Book II, *lacrimae rerum*, "the tears of things."

It is probable that Augustus felt that his great empire should have a literary work to rival Homer. Like Homer's *Iliad*, Virgil's epic depicts the horrors and the glories of war. Like Homer's *Odyssey*, Virgil's poem describes its hero's adventures, both dangerous and amorous. In spite of Virgil's debt to Greek epic, however, *The Aeneid* is a thoroughly Roman poem. It is saturated in Roman traditions and marked at every turn by its respect for family and country, characterized by *pietas*, or piety, a devotion to duty, especially love and honor of one's family and country.

Roman Satire. Although Latin literature, like much Roman art and architecture, was based closely on Greek models, the Romans developed one literary genre almost exclusively as their own—**satire.** It is true that a few Greek poets wrote satirical verse, most notably, Arkilokhos in the seventh century B.C.E., but the Greeks did not have a name for satire and

Cultural Impact

The Roman genius for organization and problem solving is among its most significant cultural legacies. The Romans were superb engineers.

Their roads, bridges, baths, aqueducts, theaters, forums, walls, palaces, and monuments can be found in more than thirty modern nations. These numerous feats of engineering are massive in scale, technically sophisticated, extraordinarily practical, and built with a meticulous attention to the craft of surveying.

The road system they put in place across Europe is, in part, still in use today. The Romans built bridges and aqueducts that crossed rivers and valleys and carried fresh water to houses and public baths. Roman town architecture was also eminently practical. Great amphitheaters like the Colosseum in Rome were designed to accommodate vast crowds and to let them enter and exit quickly and efficiently. Today's sports fans attend football games and soccer matches at similarly sized stadiums that owe much to their Roman antecedents.

Romans' love for the efficient and practical is also seen in their political structure. The Romans invented the field of civil law—the branch of law that deals with property rights—which became the foundation of legal systems in many Western countries. The Romans were also responsible for the idea of natural law, which emerged from the philosophy of Stoicism. Natural law postulated a set of rights beyond those described in civil (or property) law and became the basis for the "inalienable rights" promised by the framers of the American Declaration of Independence many centuries later (see Chapter 17).

The idea of civility in social conduct and civilized discourse in public life is another of Rome's cultural legacies (although we must remember that Rome had slaves, and women had few rights). But perhaps the Romans' greatest impact was in their language, Latin, which is the ancestor language for the Romance languages—Italian, Spanish, French, and Romansh all descend from it. And although English is Germanic in root, it nonetheless contains thousands of Latin loan words, so much so that studying Latin in school provides the basis for developing an extensive English vocabulary. And finally, the Romans, who inherited their alphabet from the Greeks through the Phoeneicians, but who also made changes in it, left in the Roman alphabet an even more pervasive cultural legacy.

did not recognize it as a distinct literary genre. Arkilokhos' poems were called *elegies*, not satires. It was left to the imagination of Gaius Lucillius (ca. 180–102 B.C.E.) to devise a poetic form and manner called *satura*, or *satira*, and to write more than thirty books of satires, in which he laments the triviality of the world and the greed and stupidity of people. What would become popular and typical targets of satire first appear in his poems: bores, cuckolds, gluttons, misers, politicians, thieves, and whores, among others.

Horace. The most important writer of **odes**—lyric poems on particular subjects made up of lines of varying lengths—was Quintus Horatius Flaccus, known simply as Horace (65–8 B.C.E.). Of humble origins, Horace was freed from economic worry when he was befriended by Virgil, who helped him secure the support of Maecenas, a wealthy patron of the arts. Like Virgil, Horace was also encouraged to write poetry by Augustus. Horace's odes espouse a philosophy of moderation, which derives from earlier Greek culture. Horace's influence on English poetry was perhaps greatest from the sixteenth to eighteenth centuries. One of his most famous poems, "Ars Poetica" ("The Art of Poetry"), was especially valued as a guide to poetic practice during the Renaissance and the eighteenth century.

Horace was fully aware of his genius, boasting that "not all of me shall die," and "I have raised a monument more lasting than bronze." His odes celebrate wine, women, and song, while also recounting the glories of Roman history. And though Horace's fame rests most squarely on his four books of Odes, he is also recognized as a consummate satirist, inspired by Lucillus, but more urbane in style and tone and more tempered in his satirical indictments. Unlike Lucillus, Horace satirized general types rather than specific individuals, thus becoming a major influence on the satirical traditions that developed in seventeenth century Europe, especially in England and France.

Ovid. Augustan Rome's successor to Catullus, OVID [O-vid] (43 B.C.E.–17 C.E.) wrote witty and ironic poems. The titles of Ovid's books reveal his persistent interest in the erotic—the *Amores* (*Loves*) and the *Ars Amatoria* (*The Art of Love*). His most famous work, the *Metamorphoses* [meh-tah-MOR-foh-sees], is based on a series of stories about transformation, many derived from Greek mythology. These are often related with an erotic twist. Ovid's poetry combines skillful narrative with elegance and grace. In addition, Ovid is generally recognized as a subtle analyst of the human heart. Though ironic, Ovid's poetry is not cruel or sarcastic; rather, Ovid seems almost compassionate toward the characters whose experiences he describes.

Seneca. LUCIUS ANNAEUS SENECA [SEN-uh-kuh] (4 B.C.E.–65 C.E.) was a Stoic thinker, a statesman, and a dramatist. Seneca was the tutor to the Roman emperor Nero and, when the young prince ascended to the throne, he served as a trusted adviser. Eventually he fell out of favor, however, and after being implicated in a conspiracy to assassinate the emperor, he was ordered to kill himself. Stoic to the end, Seneca opened his veins and bled to death.

Critical Thinking

ANCIENT ROME IN THE MOVIES: *GLADIATOR*

Many films have been made in which Rome has been depicted at different historical stages. Among the most popular is the recent movie *Gladiator*, starring Russell Crowe, a film that won a number of major film awards, including the Oscars for best actor and best film of 2000.

Why do you think *Gladiator* became a hit? What accounts for its popularity?

To what extent is the film historically accurate? And how would you go about evaluating its historical accuracy?

Would it matter greatly if the plot were fiction while the general spirit of the times was accurately depicted? Explain.

How would you characterize the film's treatment of Commodus, Marcus Aurelius, Maximus, and Lucilla? To what extent have they been portrayed with reasonable historical accuracy?

Seneca's plays, written more to be recited than performed, are deeply indebted to his Greek precursors: Sophocles, Aeschylus, and Euripides. In fact, the titles of a number of his plays are identical to those of the Greek dramatists—*Medea*, *Agamemnon*, and *Oedipus*, for example. Characterized by violence and bloodshed, Seneca's plays had an important influence on Renaissance drama, particularly on the development of revenge tragedy in Elizabethan England, including Shakespeare's *Hamlet*.

Petronius. First-century C.E. Rome was saturated in material rather than spiritual values. The Roman emperor Nero set the tone with elaborate banquets, orgiastic feastings, and bloody entertainments. During Nero's reign, the satirist PETRONIUS [peh-TROHN-ee-us] provided a sharply realistic picture of the manners, luxuries, and vices of the age. The *Satyricon* [sah-TIR-ih-con], usually attributed to Petronius, depicts the pragmatic materialism of first-century C.E. Rome. Although only fragments of the work survive, the *Satyricon* nonetheless vividly conveys early Rome's veneration of material wealth and infatuation with physical pleasure.

In the longest extant section of the work, "Dinner with Trimalchio," an aristocratic narrator describes a meal he and his friends share with the slave-turned-millionaire, Trimalchio. The dinner conversation reflects the temper of early Roman civilization in the characters' selfishness, their anti-intellectualism, and their obsession with cheating one another. The satire is enhanced by numerous echoes of the Greek heroic traditions with references to Homer's *Iliad* and *Odyssey*. The ironic references reflect the Roman characters' distance from the heroic ideal—they live only for themselves and only for the moment. Already the idealism of Augustan Rome seems very distant.

KEY TERMS

Tuscan order	*pietas*	tetrarchy	oculus
tufa	composite order	amphitheater	coffer
patrician	engaged column	travertine	mural
plebeian	concrete	vault	satire
patronage	aqueduct	dome	ode

www. WEBSITES FOR FURTHER STUDY

http://www.initaly.com/regions/classic/etruscan.html
(An introductory site on Etruscan art, culture, and architecture with links.)

http://classics.mit.edu/Carus/nature_things.html
(This site discusses Lucretius's On the Nature of Things, *including commentary.)*

http://www.alnpete.co.uk/lepcis/plans/tour.html
(This is a tour of the major sights of the site of Lepcis Magna.)

http://harpy.uccs.edu/roman/html/romptg.html
(The Four Pompeiian painting styles are presented in various Roman villas.)

http://www.experiencefestival.com/culture_of_ancient_rome
(All things Roman, includes Roman music.)

http://www.bbc.co.uk/history/ancient/romans
(British broadcasting site covers broad swath of ancient Roman culture.)

Chapter 5

History

ca. 2000 B.C.E.	Abraham is called from Mesopotamia to Canaan
ca. 1600 B.C.E.	Hebrews leave Canaan for Egypt
ca. 1250 B.C.E.	Moses and Hebrews wander in Sinai desert, reach Canaan
ca. 1000 B.C.E.	Israelites establish monarchy
ca. 1000–961 B.C.E.	David reigns
ca. 961–922 B.C.E.	Solomon reigns
ca. 922 B.C.E.	Monarchy split into kingdoms of Israel and Judah
722 B.C.E.	Israel falls to Assyrians and its people scatter
587 B.C.E.	Judah falls to Nebuchadnezzar II; hostages sent to Babylon
539 B.C.E.	Babylonian Captivity ends when Persians defeat Babylon
34 C.E.	Stephen, first martyr, is stoned to death
35 C.E.	Paul converts to Christianity
200 C.E.	Rome is center of Christianity
313 C.E.	Constantine the Great legalizes Christianity
325 C.E.	First Council of Nicaea develops Nicene Creed
330 C.E.	Constantine names Constantinople new capital of Roman Empire
391 C.E.	Theodosius I declares Christianity the official religion of the Roman Empire
395 C.E.	Roman Empire split into East and West
527–65 C.E.	Justinian reigns
1054 C.E.	Schism between Eastern and Western Churches
1071 C.E.	Conquest of eastern Byzantine provinces by Seljuk Turks
1204 C.E.	Crusaders pillage Constantinople
1453 C.E.	Constantinople falls to Turks

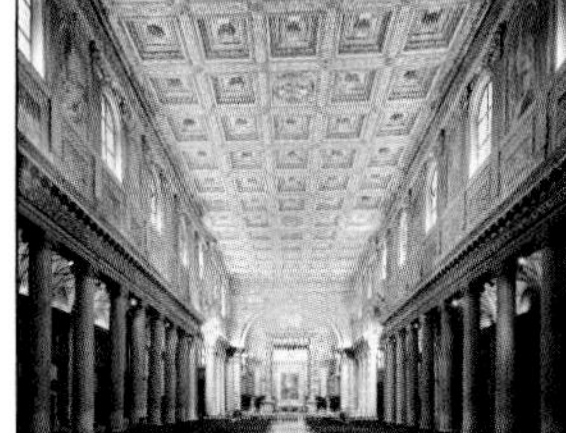

Arts and Architecture

ca. 333 C.E.	Old St. Peter's
391 C.E.	Sarcophagus of Junius Bassus
fourth century C.E.	Catacomb of Santi Pietro e Marcellino, Dome of Heaven
526–47 C.E.	San Vitale
532–37 C.E.	Anthemius of Tralles and Isidorus of Miletus, Hagia Saphia
ca. 547 C.E.	Emperor Justinian and Empress Theodora mosaics
begun 1063 C.E.	Saint Mark's, Venice
ca. 1200 C.E.	Creation Dome mosaic
late thirteenth century C.E.	*Madonna and Child Enthroned*

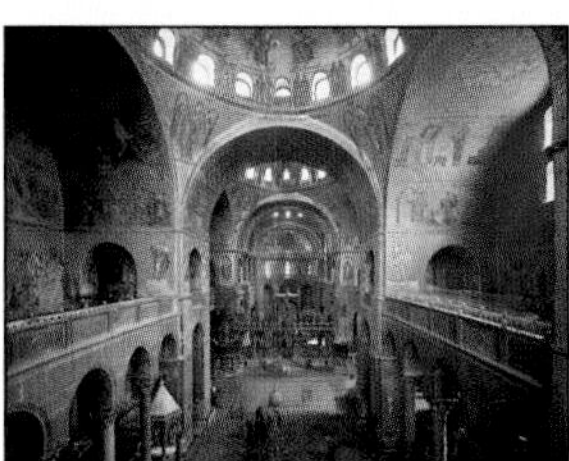

Literature and Philosophy

ca. 3000 B.C.E.	Portions from book of Genesis circulated orally
ca. twelfth–tenth centuries B.C.E.	Book of Genesis recorded
early first century C.E.	Books of Ezra and Nehemiah written
ca. 70–100 C.E.	Gospels written
75–95 C.E.	Book of Revelation written
397 C.E.	Augustine, *Confessions*

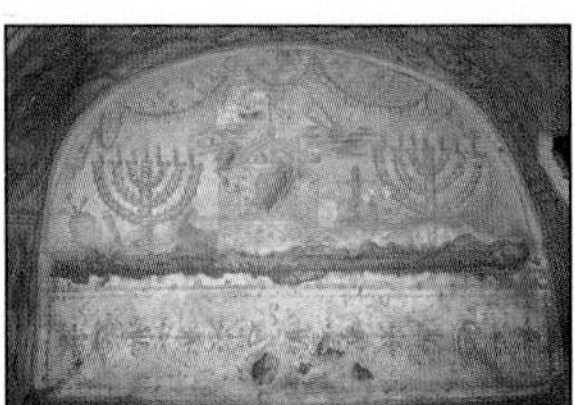

Judaism, Early Christianity, and Byzantine Civilization

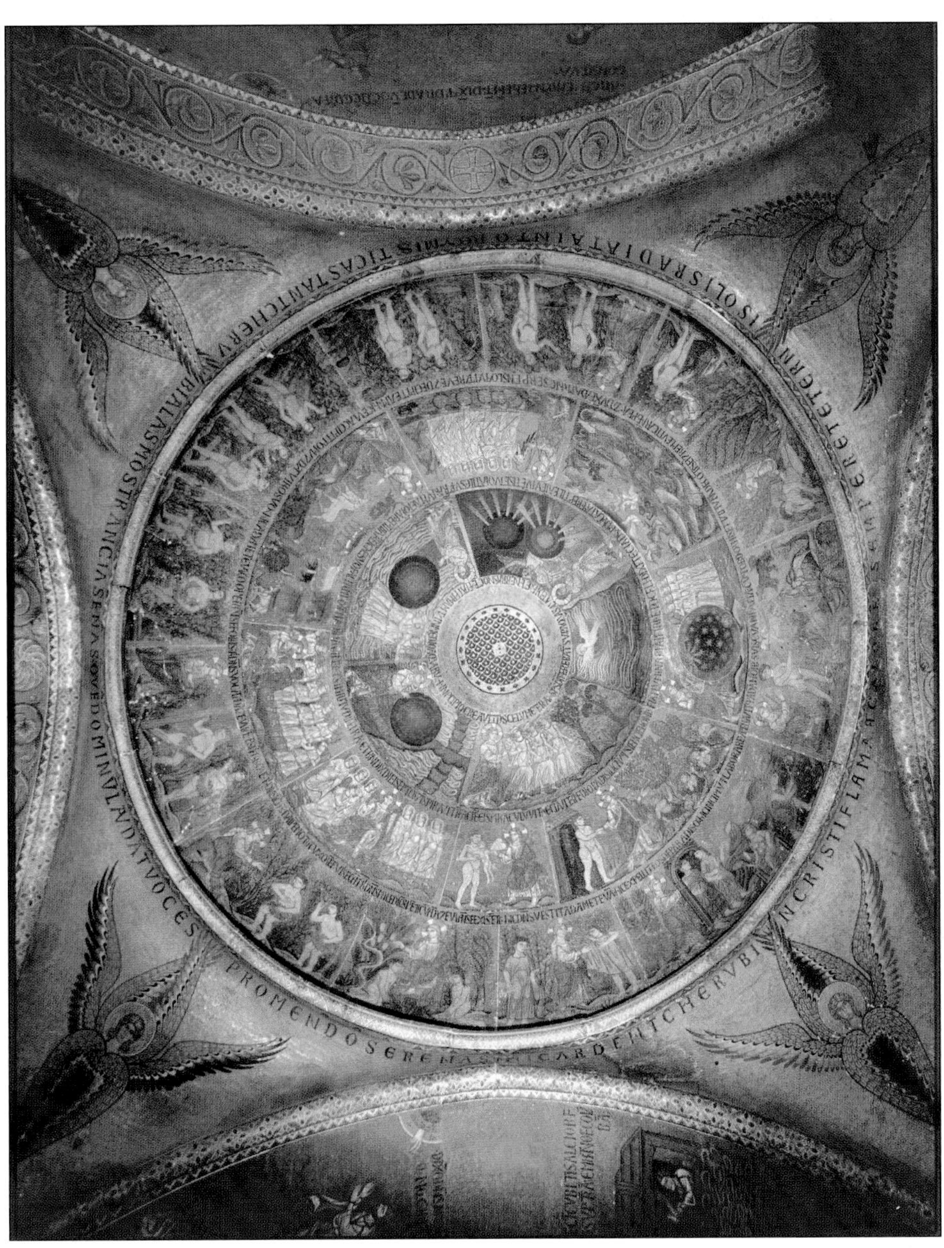

Creation Dome, narthex of St. Mark's, Venice, ca. 1200, mosaic.

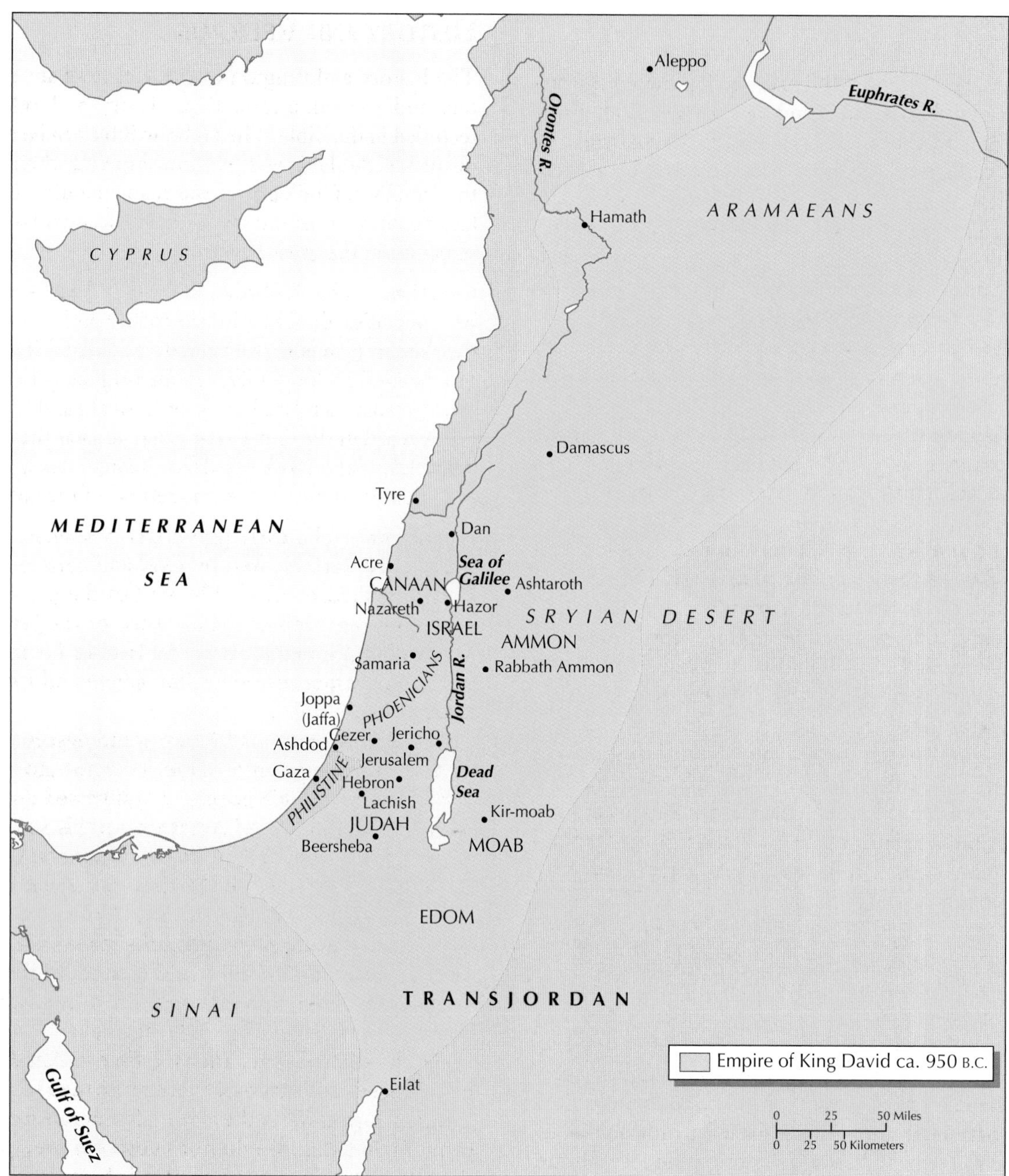

Map 5.1 Ancient Israel.

Chapter Overview

JUDAISM

The Hebraic faith establishes its history and tradition with the Bible

EARLY CHRISTIANITY

The arts nurture and transmit the beliefs of the Christian faith

BYZANTINE CIVILIZATION

The schism of the church forges the way for Byzantium in the East

JUDAISM

THE GREEKS AND THE ROMANS dominated the ancient world politically and socially, but another tradition, although not as significant artistically or politically, came to influence Western civilization as well. The founders of this tradition called themselves the "Children of Israel," the Israelites, or Hebrews (from *Habiru*, meaning "nomad" or "outcast"). Later they became known as Jews, a name derived from their place of habitation, the area around Jerusalem known as Judaea.

Whereas the Greco-Roman tradition was rational, practical, and dedicated to the arts, the Hebrew tradition was spiritual, mystical, and founded on faith. The Jews produced a "religion of the book," what Christians regard as the Old Testament portion of the Bible, providing a spiritual and moral foundation for Western culture. Judaism itself sought no converts—the Hebrew scriptures represented God's words to his "Chosen People." These scriptures emphasized a special national destiny, privilege, and responsibility. Christianity, which grew out of Judaism, did seek converts, and was from its earliest days in the first century C.E. a missionary religion, seeking to attract as many followers as possible. It spread the word of God through **evangelists,** from the Greek *euangelos,* meaning "bearer of good news"—*eu* means "good" and *angelos* "messenger." The missionary zeal of the Early Christians ultimately united the Greco-Roman and biblical traditions. In 313 C.E., the Roman emperor Constantine granted toleration to Christians, and then received Christian baptism on his deathbed in 337 himself.

The nomadic Hebrew people were forced out of the Mesopotamian basin about 2000 B.C.E. by the warlike Akkadians and the ascendancy of the Babylonians. Led by the patriarch Abraham, the Hebrews settled in Canaan, the hilly country between the Jordan River and the eastern Mediterranean coast. Canaan became their homeland and was, the Hebrews believed, promised to them by their god. **Monotheistic** (meaning the belief in only one God), as opposed to the polytheistic religions of Greece, Rome, and other Near Eastern peoples, the Hebrew religion had but one God—Yahweh, a name so sacred that the pious never speak or write it.

In contrast, other Near Eastern tribes worshiped multiple divine beings. The Babylonians, for instance, paid homage to, among others, a storm god and a rain god. Where the gods of Egypt and Mesopotamia were immanent, or present in nature, Yahweh was transcendent, apart from nature, which he also controlled. Thus the sun, which the Egyptians worshiped as a god, was for the Hebrews subject to the power of their god, who had created it. Moreover, they considered the figures of other religions subordinate to the God of Israel.

HISTORY AND RELIGION

The history and religion of the Hebrews are essentially one and the same, and that history and religion are recorded in the Bible. The Hebrew Bible can be read as the history of the Hebrews' relationship with their god. For the Israelites, God's power was made manifest in particular events, such as the creation of the world and its destruction in the great flood.

Creation. The Hebrews believed that God created heaven and earth. The Bible describes both the world and the human beings that originally populated it as "good." Humankind no longer lives in the original paradise, however, because, as related in Genesis, Adam and Eve disobey God's word in the Garden of Eden and eat the forbidden fruit. Adam and Eve's expulsion inaugurates a pattern of exile that continues in the wanderings of the patriarchs.

Patriarchs. The early patriarchs of ancient Israel believed they were favored by God and consequently led lives that honored God. The first of the patriarchs was Abraham, regarded as the ancestor of the Jews. When God called Abraham out of the land of Ur to Canaan, Abraham's response was an immediate and total acceptance of God's will.

To Abraham and his followers and descendants God made the solemn promise of the **covenant.** An agreement between God and his people, it was passed down to the patriarchs who followed Abraham—to his son Isaac and his grandson Jacob, or Israel. In the covenant, God agrees to be the Hebrew deity if the Hebrews agree, in turn, to be his people and to follow his will. With each patriarch, God renews the covenant originally made with Abraham. This covenant is referred to many times in the first five books of the Bible, which are called the Law, or the *Torah* (Hebrew for "instruction" or "teaching").

Seven hundred years after the time of Abraham, a renewal of the covenant took place while the Hebrews were living in Egypt. Why they had left Canaan for Egypt in about 1600 B.C.E., we do not know, but they prospered there until the Egyptians enslaved them. In about 1250 B.C.E., the patriarch Moses defied the pharaoh, and led his people out of Egypt (the Exodus) into the Sinai desert, which lies on the peninsula between Egypt and Canaan. There, on top of Mt. Sinai, God is said to have given Moses the Decalogue, or Ten Commandments.

1. You shall have no other gods before me.
2. You shall not make for yourself a graven image, or any likeness of any thing that is in heaven above, or that is on the earth beneath, or that is in the water under the earth.
3. You shall not take the name of the Lord your God in vain.

4. Observe the sabbath day, to keep it holy, as the Lord your God commanded you.
5. Honor your father and your mother.
6. You shall not kill.
7. Neither shall you commit adultery.
8. Neither shall you steal.
9. Neither shall you bear false witness against your neighbor.
10. Neither shall you covet your neighbor's wife, or anything that is your neighbor's.

The Hebrews carried the Decalogue with them, carved into stone tablets kept in a sacred chest called the Ark of the Covenant (fig. 5.1). Other sacred objects were also kept in the Ark such as the menorahs (seven-branched candelabra), which had been described by God to Moses, and which originally lit the Ark in its portable tabernacle. Although they do not cover every aspect of the wide-ranging ethical thinking of the Biblical authors, the Ten Commandments contain the essence of the religious law of the ancient Judeo-Christian world. Their influence has been enormous. Beginning with the six hundred and more laws recorded in the book of Leviticus, and continuing with the exploration of morality in the time of Jesus, the Commandments provide a basis for moral reflection and analysis.

For the ancient Hebrews, divine acts like the conferring of the Ten Commandments were acknowledgements of their status as God's Chosen People. And though the Hebrews wandered for forty years "in the wilderness" of the Sinai, they were delivered to the Promised Land, the land of "milk and honey," by the patriarch Joshua, who led them across the Jordan River and into Canaan once again. Over the next two hundred years, they gained control of the entire region, calling themselves Israelites, after the patriarch Jacob, who had named himself Israel.

Prophets. Despite the imperative of God's covenant, the ancient Hebrews believed human beings were ultimately responsible for their own actions and for doing whatever was necessary to improve their lot. When something was wrong in the social order, the onus was on believers to correct it. This would become the central message of the biblical prophets from the eighth through the sixth century B.C.E.

The Israelite prophets spoke for God. They were not "prophetic" in the sense that they foretold the future. Instead they functioned as mouthpieces, preaching what they had been instructed by God in vision or through ecstasy. They taught the importance of living according to the Ten Commandments. In many cases, the prophets operated as voices of conscience, confronting the Israelite kings with their wrongdoings. The most important biblical prophets were Isaiah, Jeremiah, and Ezekiel, although there were another twelve whose books are included in the Hebrew Bible.

Isaiah called for social justice and for an end to war. A verse from the book of Isaiah adorns the United Nations building in New York City: "And they shall beat their swords into ploughshares, and their spears into pruning hooks; nation shall not lift up sword against nation, neither shall they learn war any more" (Isa. 2:4).

FIGURE 5.1 *Menorahs and Ark of the Covenant*, wall painting in a Jewish catacomb, third century C.E., 3′11″ × 5′9″ (1.19 × 1.8 m), Villa Torlonia, Rome. The form of the menorah probably derives from the Tree of Life, an ancient Mesopotamian symbol.

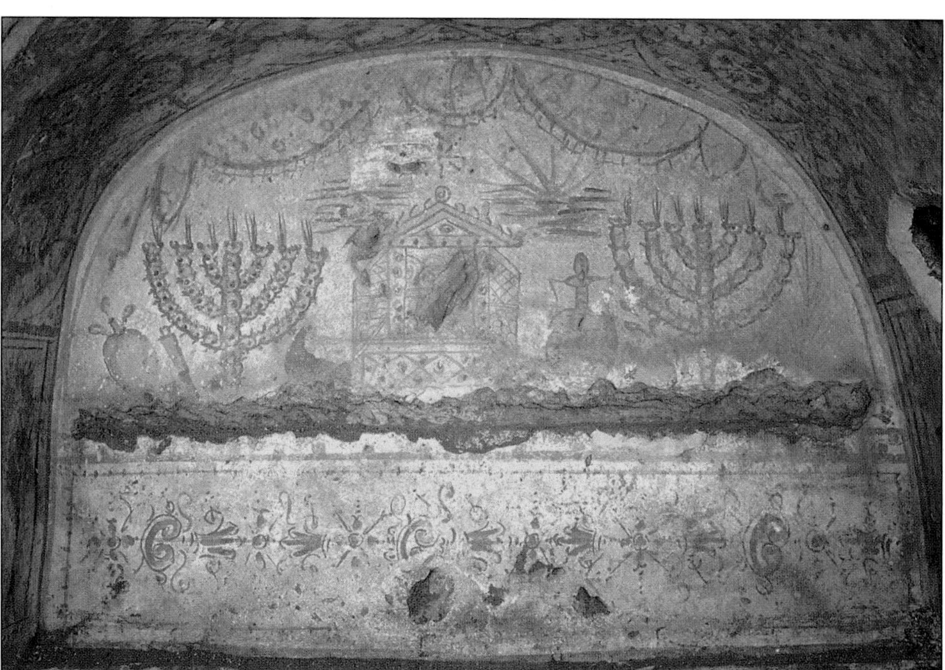

Then & Now

THE BIBLE

The books of the Hebrew Bible were composed over a period of nearly fifteen hundred years, from approximately 3000 B.C.E., from the earliest Genesis materials until near the beginning of the second century B.C.E., when the book of Daniel was written. Original manuscripts of the biblical books have not survived. The earliest extant passages are those found in caves in Qumran—the "Dead Sea Scrolls"—which include parchment scrolls of the prophetic book of Isaiah (fig. 5.2).

Originally written in Hebrew, with brief sections in Aramaic, a Near Eastern Semitic language, the present-day Bible in English has been influenced by a series of different translations: Greek (the Septuagint); Latin (the Vulgate—translated by St. Jerome); and Renaissance English, initially translated by John Wycliffe and William Tyndale. The most important early English translation, however, was that undertaken by a committee established by King James I. Known as the "King James translation" or the "Authorized Version" or "AV," this rendering has exerted profound influence on English and American literature for nearly four hundred years.

During the 1940s and 1950s, the King James translation was updated and corrected, taking account of archaeological discoveries made in the late nineteenth and early twentieth centuries, and reflecting developments in historical and linguistic scholarship. The resulting Revised Standard Version (RSV) was revised once more and published as the New Revised Standard Version (NRSV) in the 1990s.

FIGURE 5.2 The Dead Sea Isaiah Scroll (detail), first century B.C.E.–first century C.E. The Scrolls are copies of the Hebrew Bible made by a radical Jewish sect that disavowed the leadership of Jerusalem. The Scroll contains all sixty-six chapters of the Bible's longest book.

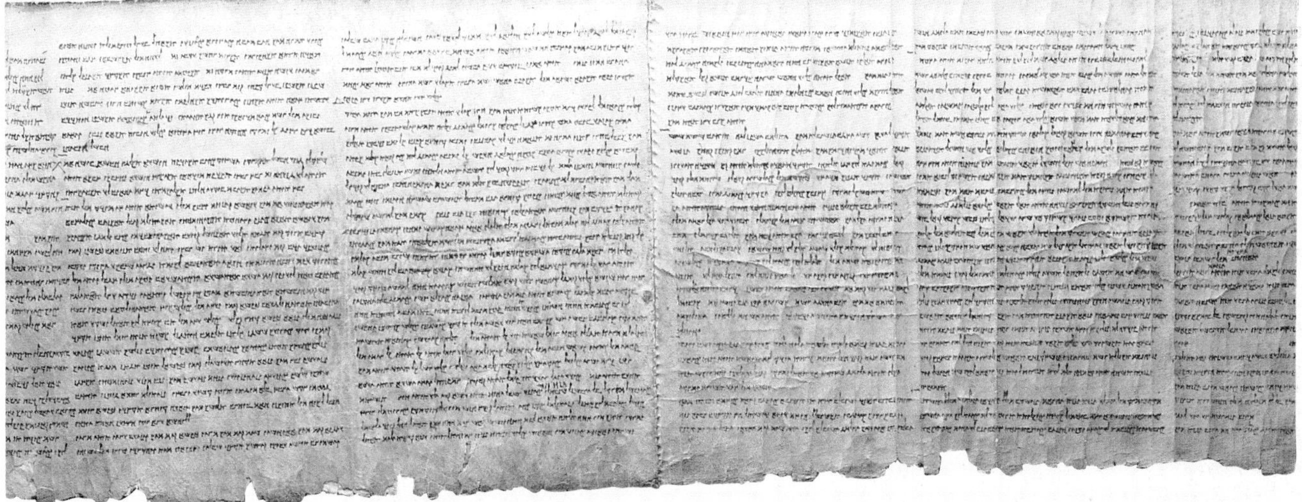

Kings. By 1000 B.C.E., the kingdom of Israel was established, with SAUL (r. ca. 1040–1000 B.C.E.) as its first king. The first book of Samuel describes Saul's kingship and the arrival of David, who saves the Israelites from their enemy, the Philistines, by slaying the giant Goliath with a stone from a slingshot.

DAVID (r. ca. 1000–961 B.C.E.) was Israel's greatest king. His reign lasted about forty years and was a time of military success, a period that included the capture of Jerusalem, which David made the capital of his kingdom. David's rule did not prevent him from composing poetry and music, including, as is traditionally held, though doubted by some scholars, some of the biblical Psalms. Perhaps the most interesting aspect of David, however, is his imperfection, for the Bible depicts him as a person who was both a sinner and a penitent. His transgressions include having one of his soldiers, Uriah, dispatched to the front line where he would undoubtedly be killed, so David could marry his widow, Bathsheba. Yet David was also to suffer the death of his son Absalom, who mounted a military rebellion against

Cross Currents

THE BIBLE AND ASIAN RELIGIONS

The Golden Rule

When Jesus said, "You shall love your neighbor as yourself" (Mark 12:29–31), he was expanding on a text from the book of Deuteronomy in the Old Testament, in which the biblical writer presents what Jesus called the first great commandment: to "love the Lord your God with all your heart, with all your mind, and with all your strength" (Deut. 6:4–5). Allied with this statement is a version of it that has come to be known as the Golden Rule: "Do unto others as you would have them do unto you" (Matthew 7:12).

More than five hundred years before Christ, however, Confucius had said something similar: "What you do not wish done to yourself, do not do to others" *(Analects)*. Another version of this teaching was voiced by the Jewish rabbi Hillel, around the time of Christ as: "What you yourself hate, don't do to your neighbor. This is the whole Law; the rest is commentary."

The essence of this message is also anticipated in Taoist and Buddhist texts. Here are Lao-Tzu and Buddha offering still other versions of the command to love all beings:

> To those who are good to me, I am good; and to those who are not good to me, I am also good, and thus all get to be good.
>
> Lao-Tzu, *Tao Te Ching*

> Hatred is never appeased by hatred in this world; it is appeased by love. This is an eternal Law.
>
> Buddha, *Dhammapada*

Islamic, Jain, and Hindu traditions record similar advice:

> Hindu: Do naught unto others which would cause pain if done to you.
>
> Mahābhārata

> Islamic: No one of you is a believer until he desires for his brother that which he desires for himself.
>
> Hadith

> Jain: We should regard all creatures as we regard our own self.
>
> Tirthonkara

him. The books of Samuel reveal political intrigues and complex familial dynamics with great subtlety and literary artistry.

The last important Israelite king was David's son, SOLOMON [SOL-oh-mun] (r. ca. 961–922 B.C.E.). Famous for his wisdom, Solomon is also associated with the Temple he had built in Jerusalem. Like his father, Solomon was a poet. He is the reputed author of the biblical Song of Songs, a sensual love poem that has been read by later critics as a metaphor for the love between God and his people.

Following the death of Solomon, the kingdom of Israel was split in two. The Northern Kingdom retained the name Israel; the Southern Kingdom was called Judah. The Northern Kingdom fell to the Assyrians in 722 B.C.E.; the Southern Kingdom was overrun in 587 B.C.E. by the Babylonians under the command of NEBUCHADNEZZAR [ne-BYUK-ad-NEZ-ah], who destroyed Solomon's magnificent temple. The Southern Kingdom Hebrews were carried off into exile, which inaugurated a period known as the Babylonian Captivity.

Jerusalem in the Time of David and Solomon. King David chose Jerusalem as the seat of political power. In neutral territory, midway between the northern and southern kingdom power centers, Jerusalem straddles the crest of a mountain range, between the sea and the river Jordan.

During David's reign, the city defenses were strengthened, largely through the extension of the city's walls and the erection of defensive towers. A royal palace was constructed and houses were built for David's wives and concubines, for his many court officials, and for his bodyguards and mercenary soldiers. In addition, after planning an elaborate temple that could be constructed later, during the reign of David's successor, his son, Solomon, David arranged to have the Ark of the Covenant brought to Jerusalem and housed in a special tent.

From his newly established capital, David extended his control over the neighboring tribes, conquering territory ranging from the Red Sea north to Damascus and from the Mediterranean into the desert beyond the Jordan River. David failed, however, to unite the kingdoms of Judah in the north and Israel in the south, and after having his rule challenged by his son Absalom, David eventually turned over his kingdoms and his capital city to Solomon, son of David and Bathsheba.

Politically astute, Solomon aligned himself with neighboring territories by taking wives from competing tribes. Also an astute businessman, he increased his country's foreign trade and exploited its natural resources of copper and iron. He used slave labor to fortify the city and then to build a magnificent palace and an elaborate temple to house the Ark of the Covenant.

Solomon's reign was peaceful; riches accumulated but morals began to decay. Solomon's many foreign wives brought their foreign gods with them to Jerusalem, introducing idolatry. With Solomon's death, the country split, and the Babylonian king, Nebuchadnezzar, captured the city, inaugurating a period known as the Babylonian captivity. The golden age of Israel ended.

Return from Exile. The Hebrews remained in exile for over sixty years. Those returning to their homeland around 539 B.C.E., rebuilt their Temple. The period from the rebuilding of the Temple to 70 C.E. was one of almost continuous foreign occupation. The Roman destruction of Jerusalem marked the end of Jewish power in the region until the middle of the twentieth century.

However, after rebuilding the Temple, the Jews established a theocracy (a religiously governed state). Although many exiles returned to Judah, many others remained dispersed outside Judah and were known as Jews of the Diaspora, or Dispersion. During the post-exilic period, Jewish beliefs began to include new features, very likely influenced by the Persian religion of Zoroastrianism, especially the idea that the world was divided into two competing and contrasting forces of Good and Evil, imaged as forces of Light and Darkness, respectively. From this period also derive a number of concepts that would later prove of importance to Christianity—an apocalyptic day of judgment and a Messiah, or Anointed One, who would create a time of peace.

THE BIBLE AS LITERATURE

The Hebrew Bible (from the Greek name for the city of Byblos, the major exporter of papyrus, the material used for making books in the ancient world) consists of the canon of books accepted and officially sanctioned by Judaism. These include three major groupings: the Law, the Prophets, and the Writings. The Law comprises the first five books: Genesis, Exodus, Leviticus, Numbers, and Deuteronomy. (Authorship of these books is ascribed to Moses.) The Prophets include those mentioned and, in addition, the books of Joel, Obadiah, Jonah, Micah, Nahum, Habakkuk, Zephaniah, Haggai, Zechariah, and Malachi, as well as six historical books: Joshua, Judges, Samuel (two books), and Kings (two books). The remaining books, known as the Writings, include the narrative books of Ruth, Esther, and Daniel; the poetic books of Psalms and the Song of Songs; and the wisdom books of Proverbs, Job, and Ecclesiastes. Also part of the Writings are Chronicles, Lamentations, Ezra, and Nehemiah.

Some of the biblical books ascribed to the time of Solomon are actually products of the Hellenic age. Ecclesiastes and The Song of Songs, for example, include concepts such as philosophy, chance, and wisdom that would have been foreign to Jews in Solomon's time. These ideas, however, were eventually assimilated into Jewish thought.

The stories about David in the book of Samuel, and those of Daniel and Jonah, the poetry of the Song of Songs and the Psalms, and the wisdom of Ecclesiastes are significant literary achievements. Two books of the Hebrew Bible, however, tower above the rest: Genesis and Job—Genesis for its fascinating narratives, and Job for its sublime philosophical poetry. Both Genesis and Job, moreover, reflect the ideals of ancient Israel.

History and Fiction. The narratives in the book of Genesis can be read as being literally true. However, if they are looked at from a literary perspective, they may be divided into two categories: prehistoric myths and historicized fiction. The stories of the Creation and the Fall, of the Great Flood, and of the Tower of Babel are myths explaining the origin of the universe and its creatures, the reason human beings suffer pain and death, and the emergence of the world's languages. These **etiological stories,** or stories about the origins and causes of things, occupy the first eleven chapters of Genesis.

The second category of narrative—historicized fiction—includes the stories of the patriarchs Abraham, Isaac, and Jacob. These stories passed down through oral tradition, and achieved written form around the twelfth to the tenth centuries B.C.E. The patriarchal stories have the character of history, as accounts of deeds performed

Table 5–1 BOOKS OF THE BIBLE

Hebrew Scriptures (Old Testament) In order of appearance		
Genesis	2 Chronicles	Daniel
Exodus	Ezra	Hosea
Leviticus	Nehemiah	Joel
Numbers	Esther	Amos
Deuteronomy	Job	Obadiah
Joshua	Psalms	Jonah
Judges	Proverbs	Micah
Ruth	Ecclesiastes	Nahum
1 Samuel	Song of Solomon	Habakkuk
2 Samuel	Isaiah	Zephaniah
1 Kings	Jeremiah	Haggai
2 Kings	Lamentations	Zechariah
1 Chronicles	Ezekiel	Malachi
Greek Scriptures (New Testament) In order of appearance		
Matthew	Ephesians	Hebrews
Mark	Phillipians	James
Luke	Collosians	1 Peter
John	1 Thessalonians	2 Peter
Acts	2 Thessalonians	1 John
Romans	1 Timothy	2 John
1 Corinthians	2 Timothy	3 John
2 Corinthians	Titus	Jude
Galatians	Philemon	Revelation

by particular individuals. However, they differ from later biblical narratives, such as the books of Samuel, which have been termed "fictionalized history."

The stories about David in the book of Samuel use techniques of fiction and take liberties with the historical facts on which they are based. The earlier patriarchal stories describe characters and situations to convey theological ideas and to account for events, such as how the Hebrews found themselves in Egypt (which is explained in the stories about Joseph and his brothers [Gen. 37–50]).

Biblical Poetry. As with other ancient civilizations, Hebraic poetry was bound up with the religious, social, and military life of the Hebrews. War victories were celebrated in verse, as were other achievements, such as the liberation of the Hebrew slaves from their Egyptian masters. Indeed, the two oldest recorded Hebrew poems are celebrations of great accomplishments. The Bible's oldest poem, the Song of Deborah (Judges 5:1–31), describes how its heroine, Jael, saves the Hebrew people by killing the Canaanite military leader Sisera. Better known is the "Song of the Sea," which celebrates the destruction of the Egyptian pharaoh's army, along with his chariots and horsemen, in the Red Sea.

Religious faith is the consistent concern of ancient Hebrew poetry, such as the poetry of the Psalms, the prophecies of Isaiah, and the wisdom of Job. Complementing these religious works are other biblical poems in a more secular vein (although they, too, have been interpreted allegorically as religious). The most beautiful of these are the Song of Songs (also known as the Song of Solomon) and the book of Ecclesiastes.

EARLY CHRISTIANITY

With its belief that a Messiah would come into the world to save humankind, thereby fulfilling God's promises, Judaism was fundamental to the emergence of Christianity and to the formulation of the new religion's central tenets. Many apocalyptic Hebrew writings, including chapters 7–10 of the book of Daniel, predicted the coming of a Savior. John the Baptist further prepared the way for Jesus' ministry by preaching that a Messiah was at hand. Those who believed Jesus when he preached the Kingdom of God was imminent, and who saw that Kingdom as represented in Jesus, became the first Christians.

Just as Jews believe they are God's Chosen People and Muslims their holy book, the Quran, is the word of God, Christians believe Jesus is God and Savior. Moreover, they maintain that by accepting Jesus as their Savior, they will share eternal life with him in heaven. One element of their faith is the belief that Jesus rose from the dead after being crucified by the Romans. Their faith gave rise to a revision of the Messianic prophecy, which converted a hope for an earthly king into a belief in a divine king, whose coming to earth signaled new hope in human redemption. Jesus' kingdom would be a kingdom of the next world, the afterlife, to which the redeemed Christian soul would be taken after death.

JESUS AND HIS MESSAGE

Jesus was Jewish. His followers, who identified him as the Christ—which means "Messiah" or "Anointed One"—were the first Christians. Jesus was born in Judaea, a land under the political control of the Romans, during the reign of the emperor Augustus.

The public ministry of Jesus began when he was thirty years old, with the performance of his first miracle, the changing of water into wine, at the marriage feast of Cana, a small village north of Nazareth, where Jesus was born. This first miracle is recorded in the New Testament Gospel of John.

Yet it is Jesus' teaching, rather than his miracles, that is central to Christian beliefs and values. He delivered his message in simple and direct language that common people could understand: Believe in him and be saved; beware of false prophets; do not get lost in the intricacies of religious ritual observance; stick to the essentials of faith in God, love of humanity, and hope for the future. He taught through stories, or **parables,** such as that of the Good Samaritan. Parables illustrate an essential Christian principle: in the case of the Good Samaritan, that believing Christians should love their "neighbors"—and that their neighbors include all human beings.

Jesus's teaching can be reduced to two essentials: to love God above all, and to love others as one loves oneself. Jesus' ideals are summed up in the Sermon on the Mount, the fullest version of which is in the Gospel of Matthew.

CHRISTIAN ANTECEDENTS

The antecedents of Christianity take three basic forms: cult antecedents, philosophical antecedents, and Jewish antecedents. Christian cult antecedents involve specific symbolic rituals that influenced later Christian practices; Christian philosophical antecedents involve particular ideas that came to influence Christian beliefs. Jewish antecedents of Christianity were largely scriptural, although common bonds linked Jewish and Christian rituals as well.

Cult Antecedents. Christianity did not spring fully formed from the teachings of Jesus, or from the writings of Paul. The special form of individualized immortality associated with Christianity had been a feature of the mystery cults that flourished in Egypt, Persia, and Greece. Besides postulating a form of personal immortality, many mystery cults performed symbolic rituals to enact the birth, death, and rebirth of deities. The Isis cult of Egypt, for example, as well as the cults of Mithra in Persia and Dionysius in Greece, included such symbolic reenactments. As the god of wine and revelry, Dionysus inspired initiates to partake of wine, symbolizing the blood of the deity. Cult members were typically initiated into the mysteries or secrets of the cult by participating in symbolic rituals that included fasting, on the one hand, and eating a symbolic meal, on the other. Such symbolic rituals would influence later Christian rituals.

Another background to and source from which early Christianity derived rituals and borrowed traditions was that of Roman paganism, itself a blend of local and borrowed traditions and religious practices. Among these was the recognition of Roman gods and goddesses as protectors with specialized functions. The household gods, for example, protected the home; Vesta protected the hearth; the locus genii protected the outside areas of a place. Among the specialized functions of Mars, god of war, was the protection of soldiers. It is not far from these Roman beliefs and practices to later Christian traditions that honor saints, as it is not far from the Near Eastern cult practices to later Christian symbolic communal celebrations of a shared communion meal and an emphasis on spiritual purification through fasting.

Philosophical Antecedents. Additional background to and influences on early Christianity include Greek philosophical ideas, especially those of Stoicism and Neoplatonism. Stoicism emphasized self-control and human brotherhood, both of which became hallmarks of Christian thinking. Neoplatonism emphasized the refined spiritual nature of reality, with a special emphasis on the spiritual union of the individual soul with the "One" or ultimate reality that underlay physical appearances. The Neoplatonist philosopher Plotinus was perhaps the most significant influence, especially his notion of a soul's ascent through ever higher levels of spiritual purification and perfection, an idea found in Christian mysticism and one that found expression in Dante's *Paradiso*.

Jewish Influences. In addition to Roman, Greek, and Near Eastern influences on the development of Christianity, there was also a strong Jewish influence. As a religion that would share a large part of its scriptures with Judaism, Christianity leaned heavily on Jewish traditions and beliefs. Most important among these were a shared vision of a personal universal deity, a God who made moral demands on his subjects. Also central were the strong ethical standards at the heart of Judaism and Christianity. In addition, Christian rhetorical and literary practice was influenced by Jewish prophetic and apocalyptic writings.

Strong bonds linked Jewish and Christian ritualistic traditions, most notably perhaps the connection between Jewish Passover and Christian Easter, which celebrates Jesus' resurrection from the dead, a ritual and belief influenced as well by death and resurrection elements in the mystery cults. On a smaller scale, both religions embrace the idea of a weekly holy day, the Jewish Sabbath (observed on Saturday) and the later Christian day devoted to churchgoing and worship of God on Sunday.

EARLY CHRISTIAN HISTORY

Christianity spread throughout the Mediterranean due to the efforts of martyrs and missionaries. Stephen, the first Christian martyr, was stoned to death in 34 C.E. for preaching blasphemy against the Jewish god; Sebastian was tied to a tree and shot full of arrows, martyred for refusing to acknowledge the Roman gods.

Paul was the most important of the first-century Christian missionaries. Born Saul, at first he was strongly opposed to Christianity until he underwent conversion on the road to Damascus in 35 C.E. (the so-called Damascene conversion). From then until his execution ca. 62 C.E., he proselytized tirelessly for Christianity, formulating doctrine, writing to other Christian communities, and traveling at least as far west as Rome.

The next centuries were a period of slow growth for Christianity and of continual persecution at the hands of the Romans. For instance, in 64 C.E. Nero blamed the Christians for a fire that burned down the imperial capital. Two hundred years later, the emperor Decius expelled the Christians from Rome. Such persecution was unusual in the Roman empire, where other sects and religions were usually tolerated. The problem for the Roman authorities appears to have been the Christians' refusal to worship the Roman gods alongside their own God. The first great turning point came in 313 C.E., when the emperor Constantine issued the Edict of Milan, which granted Christianity toleration as a religion. Constantine convened councils concerned with matters of faith, such as the trinitarian nature of the godhead. The First Council of Nicaea developed the Nicene Creed, the conventional recitation of Christian belief in Jesus as both the son of God and as God incarnate. After Constantine's death, Julian attempted to restore paganism, but in 391 Theodosius I declared Christianity the Roman state religion, banning all pagan cults.

The Christian church, however, united in name only. In spreading across the Mediterranean from Jerusalem, Christianity encompassed varying practices and factions, resulting in separate Christian churches in the Roman and Greek worlds. Finally, the Christian church split into two branches in the Great Schism of 1054. The Eastern Church, with a patriarchal leader in Constantinople, formerly Byzantium (currently Istanbul), challenged the supremacy of the Roman leader, the bishop of Rome, the pope. Each leader excommunicated the other. The different languages of the two churches and their differing perspectives on issues, including the legitimacy of a married clergy, led to the development of widely differing institutions.

EARLY CHRISTIAN ART

There is no such thing as an "Early Christian style" of art. In fact, at first Christianity was averse to art because it served the worship of idols. However, Christians recognized that art could help illustrate the Bible's teachings to illiterate followers. No longer the object of worship but a means to worship, art became an important instrument of theology.

Architecture. When Christianity was made an official state religion, the need for churches arose. Derived from the Roman basilica, the Early Christian basilica was well established by the fourth century. Old St. Peter's in Rome (fig. 5.3) is the quintessential example. Erected by Constantine over the tomb of St. Peter, it was destroyed in the fifteenth century to make way for the present St. Peter's (see Chapter 13).

When entering an Early Christian basilica like Old St. Peter's (fig. 5.3), the visitor first came into the **atrium,** a rectangular forecourt, open in the center to the sky, surrounded on all four sides by columnar arcades. The atrium was the area for people not yet baptized. Next, the visitor passed through the **narthex,** an entrance hall or vestibule. Having now reached the actual church, the visitor entered the **nave,** a large rectangular space for the masses of people, and flanked on both sides by one or two **aisles,** separated from the nave by colonnades. The **transept** provided additional space. The **apse** is a semicircular space at the end of the church. The visitor had to walk from one end of the church to the other to reach the altar located just in front of the apse.

The reconstruction drawing of the exterior (fig. 5.4) shows the nave with **clerestory** windows, that is, a row of windows on an upper story. Because the nave ceiling was of lightweight wood, it was easy to support, windows could be made in the walls, and sunlight admitted. The disadvantage of wood was the danger of fire.

In addition to the basilica plan with its longitudinal axis, as used in Old St. Peter's, round or polygonal buildings with domed roofs were also built in the Early Christian era. The finest example is Santa Costanza in Rome (fig. 5.5 and fig. 5.6), built ca. 350 C.E. This mausoleum, constructed for the emperor Constantine's daughter Constantia, was once part of a larger church.

The exterior, made of unadorned brick, is plain and simple, but the interior is ornate with rich materials, textures, colors, and designs. Light comes in through the clerestory windows. The surrounding circular aisle, or

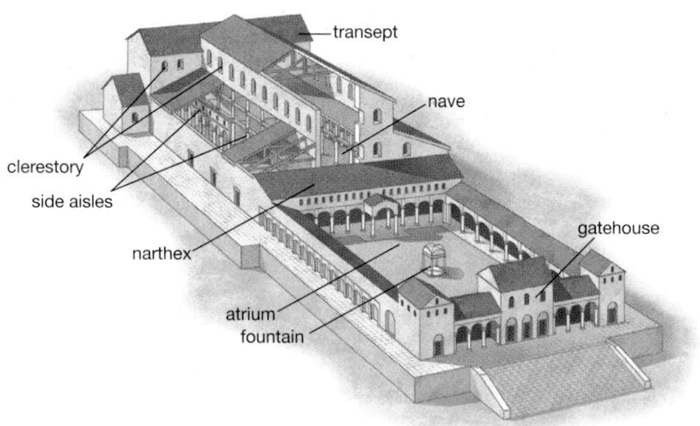

FIGURE 5.4 Old St. Peter's, Rome, begun ca. 333 C.E., reconstruction drawing. Based on the Roman basilica, which would house, in the apse, a statue of the emperor, the new Christian church placed a *cathedra* or "chair of the bishop" in the emperor's place—hence the origin of the word "cathedral."

FIGURE 5.3 Old St. Peter's, Rome, begun ca. 333 C.E., plan. The type of church established here, known as the early Christian basilica, would be the basis for later churches built with a longitudinal axis—the Latin-cross plan.

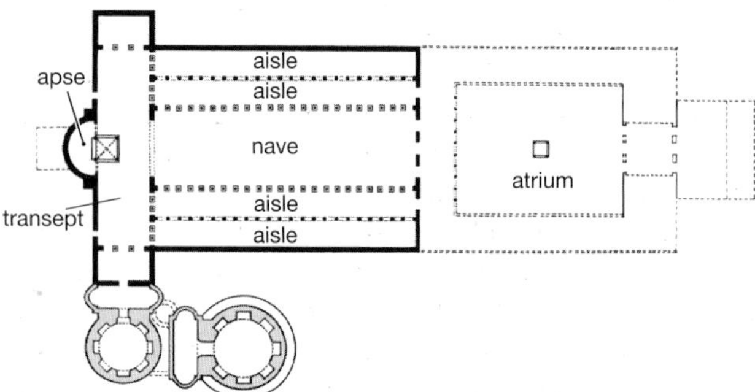

FIGURE 5.5 Santa Costanza, Rome, ca. 350 C.E., plan. A central plan (circular or polygonal) building, when roofed with a dome, as here, offers an uninterrupted interior space.

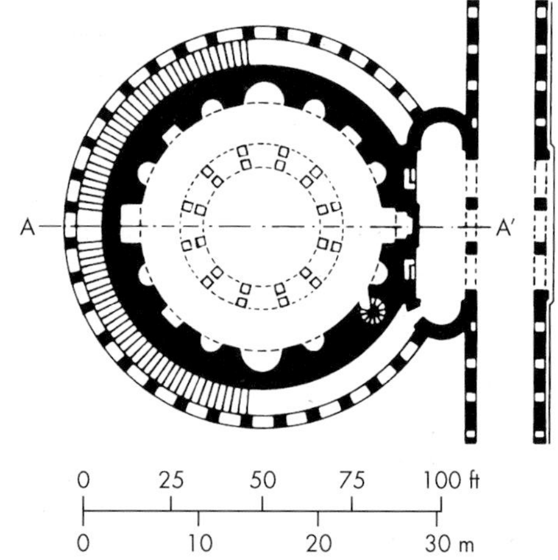

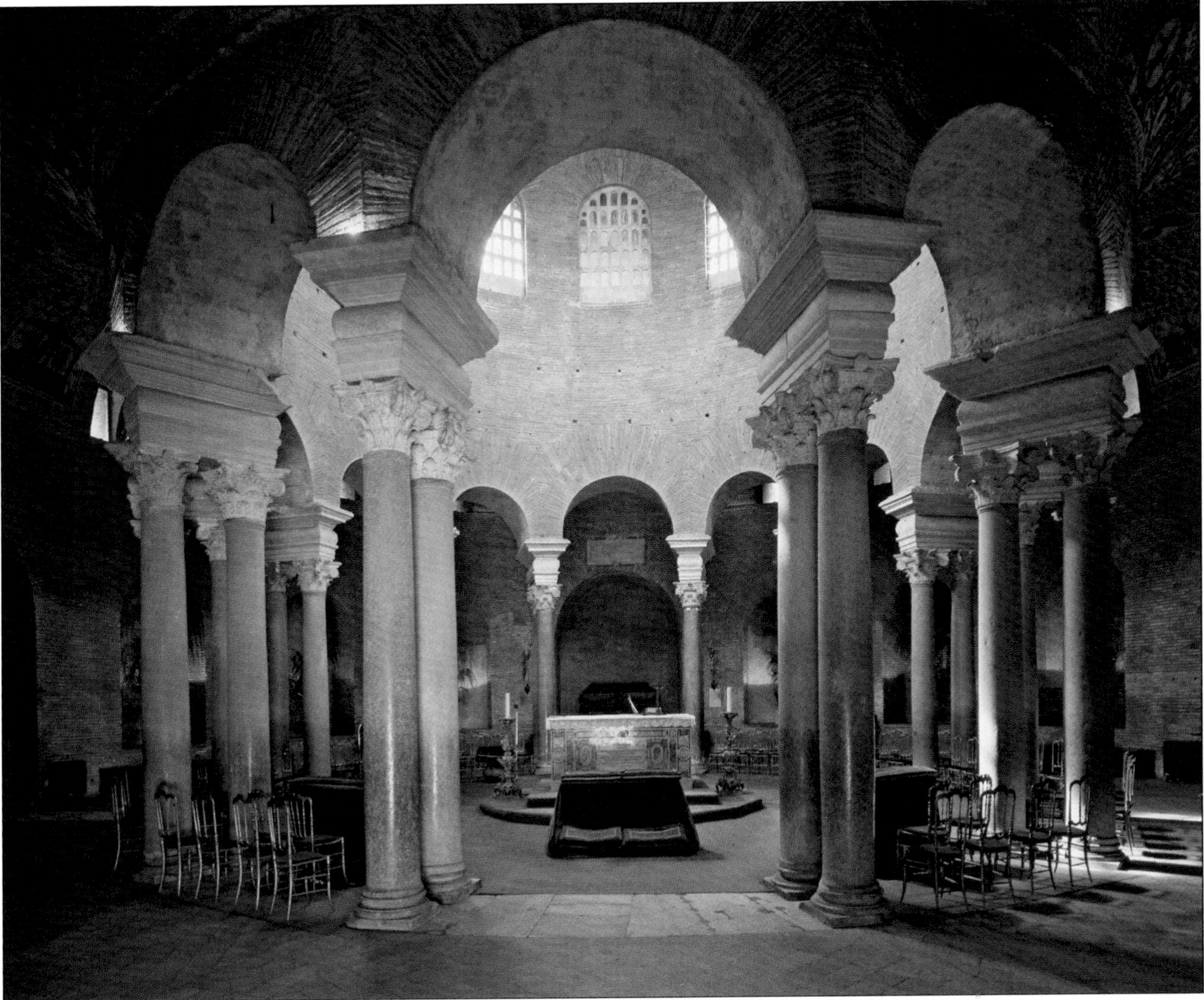

FIGURE 5.6 Santa Costanza, Rome, ca. 350 C.E., interior. The basic scheme of Santa Costanza would later be used by Byzantine architects and would also serve as the model for the baptisteries connected to Christian churches.

ambulatory, is covered with a barrel vault, which is ornamented with mosaics (fig. 5.7).

These mosaics consist of a vine pattern with small scenes along the sides. Laborers are shown picking grapes, putting them into carts, and transporting the grapes to a press, where three men crush them underfoot. This subject, common on tavern floor mosaics, may seem out of place here. But because wine plays an important part in the Christian liturgy, it was possible to adopt and adapt a pagan subject to Christian needs.

Sculpture. In the Early Christian era, due to Christianity's disdain for idol worship, sculpture was secondary to painting and mosaic. For the most part, sculptors turned to small-scale relief work on stone **sarcophagi** (coffins) and ivory panels. Marble sarcophagi, the fronts and occasionally the lids of which were carved with figures in high relief, are among the earliest works of Christian sculptors, with examples dating from the early third century C.E. onward. The *Sarcophagus of Junius Bassus*, a prefect of Rome (a high position similar to that of a governor or administrator), is among the most notable of these (fig. 5.8). Bassus converted to Christianity shortly before his death in 359. The front of his sarcophagus is divided by two tiers of columns into ten areas. The subjects depicted in these panels are drawn from the Old and New Testaments of the Bible. The upper row, left to right, shows the sacrifice of Isaac; St. Peter taken prisoner; Jesus enthroned with Saints Peter and Paul; and, in two separate sections, Jesus before Pontius Pilate. The lower row, left to right, shows the misery of Job; Adam and Eve after eating from the Tree of Knowledge; Jesus entering Jerusalem; Daniel in

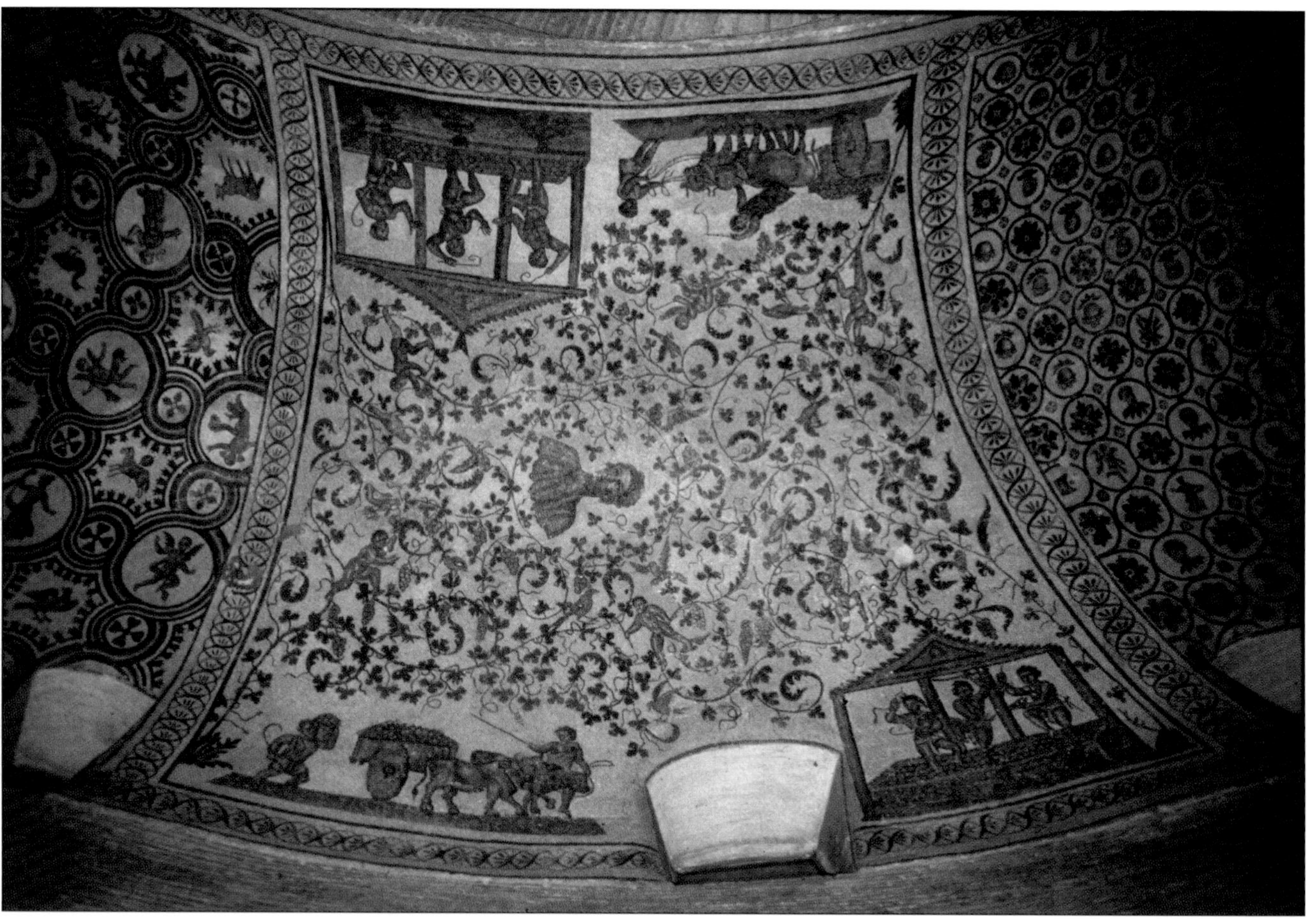

FIGURE 5.7 *Wine-Making Scene*, ambulatory vault of Santa Costanza, Rome, ca. 350 C.E., mosaic. Demonstrating the Christian adaptation of pagan subjects, the vine here represents the words of Jesus, "I am the true vine." The grapes came to symbolize the eucharistic wine and, therefore, the blood of Jesus.

the lions' den; and St. Paul being led to his death. The proportions of the figures are far from Classical and reflect a late Roman style, as also seen in the fourth-century reliefs on the Arch of Constantine in Rome (see fig. 4.20). Large heads are supported on doll-like bodies. Background setting is almost entirely eliminated in these crowded scenes, action or drama kept to a minimum, and the figures, even when the story suggests they should be animated, are passive and calm. These little vignettes are not intended to provide the viewer with a detailed narrative, for they are only required to bring to mind a story that the viewer is expected to know already.

Painting. The earliest Christian art is found in the **catacombs**—the underground cemeteries of the Christians in and around Rome. The catacombs were practically underground towns of sepulchers and funeral chapels, miles of subterranean passageways cut into the rock.

A painted ceiling in the Catacomb of Santi Pietro e Marcellino in Rome (fig. 5.9), from the fourth century, is a well-preserved example. The walls of catacombs were decorated with **frescoes,** paintings made quickly on freshly applied lime plaster. The subjects depicted were generally related to the soul's future life. Especially common was the subject of *Jesus the Good Shepherd*, seen also in sculpture. Filling the center of the ceiling, the painting embodies the idea that the Christian people make up Jesus' flock and, as the Good Shepherd, Jesus watches over and cares for them. The arrangement painted here represents the dome of heaven, with the decoration positioned to form a cross. The story of Jonah is shown in the surrounding semicircles. Jonah is thrown overboard into the mouth of the waiting whale (the curly serpent-dog makes clear that whales were not known from firsthand experience in fourth-century Rome). Jonah emerges from the whale and then relaxes in safety under the vines. The figures that stand between the semicircles have assumed a common early prayer pose—the *orans* (from the Latin word for "praying"), with hands raised to heaven.

Popular Old Testament subjects for catacomb paintings were Noah and the Ark, Moses, Jonah and the whale, Daniel in the lions' den, and the story of Susanna. Popular New Testament themes were taken from the life of Jesus,

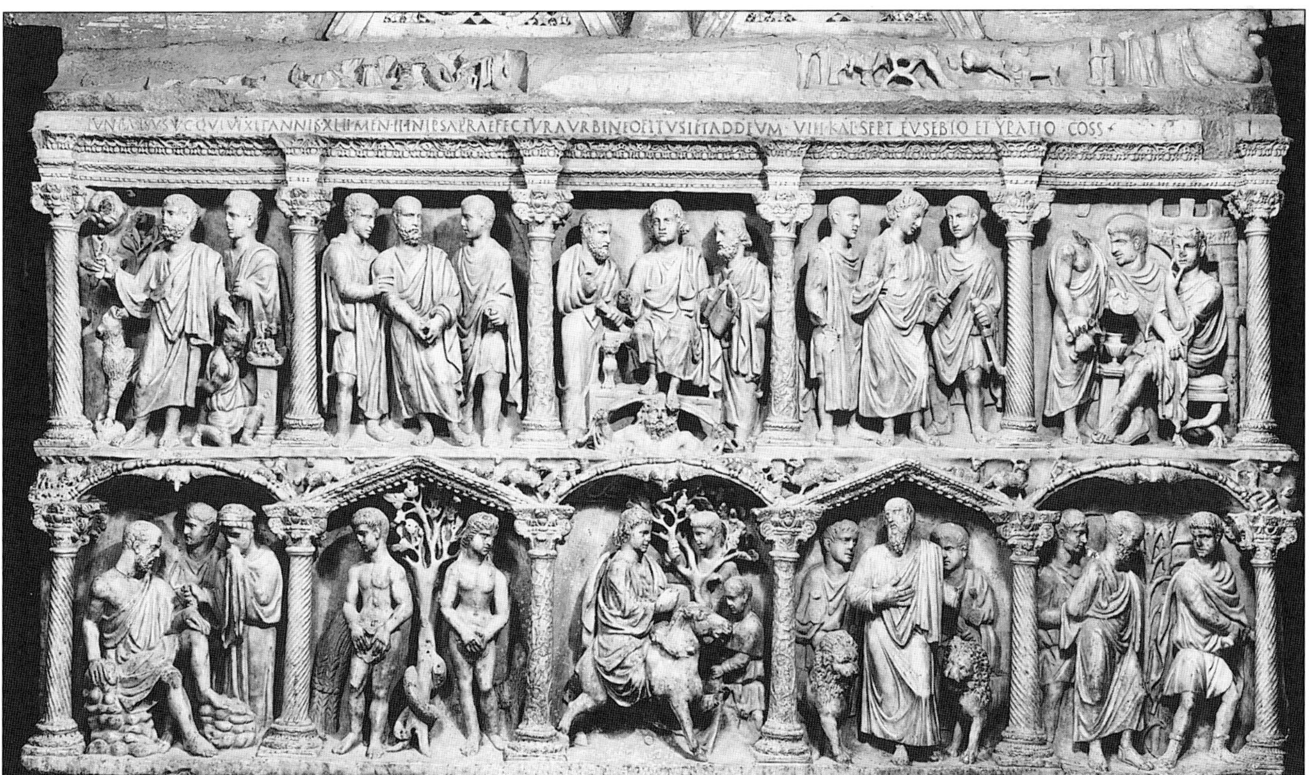

FIGURE 5.8 *Sarcophagus of Junius Bassus*, ca. 359 C.E. marble, $3'10\frac{1}{2}'' \times 8'$ (1.18 × 2.44 m), Museo Petriano, St. Peter's, Rome. Early Christian sculpture consists primarily of reliefs carved on sarcophagi and small ivory plaques. Greater importance was attached to the recognition of the subjects than to realistic representation of the human body.

especially the miracles, such as the healing of the paralytic and the resurrection of Lazarus. These subjects illustrate how God is merciful and will intervene to save the faithful. The rewards of prayer are emphasized. Depictions of Jesus' passion (his suffering at the end of his life) are entirely omitted; the earliest known representations of the passion are fifth-century carvings. The catacomb paintings do not treat the subject of Jesus' death and resurrection, which was a popular subject in the Renaissance (see Chapters 13 and 14).

THE NEW TESTAMENT AS LITERATURE

The New Testament is for Christianity what the Hebrew scriptures are for Judaism and the Quran is for Islam: the repository of revealed religious truth. The New Testament, written in Greek, records and interprets the acts and words of the Christian Savior, Jesus Christ. The New Testament contains four distinct types of writing: the gospels, or accounts of Jesus' life and ministry; the epistles, or letters to the early Christian churches; the Acts of the Apostles, a history of the spread of Christianity during the thirty years after Jesus' death and resurrection; and Revelation, or the Apocalypse, the last biblical book, which is concerned with the end of the world.

Gospels. Apart from Paul's letters, the gospels are the earliest books of the New Testament. Written from about forty to around one hundred years after the death of Jesus, the New Testament is far closer in time of composition to the events it describes than is the Old Testament to the events it describes. None, however, is an eyewitness account of Jesus' life and work.

Of the surviving gospels, the Gospel of Mark is the earliest, composed around 70 C.E. It portrays Jesus as a miracle worker as well as a dynamic and vibrant social reformer. The Gospel of Mark is action centered, moving quickly from one event to the next, describing Jesus' life, ministry, passion, and death.

The Gospel of Matthew, written ten to twenty years after that of Mark, emphasizes Jesus as the Messiah referred to in Old Testament prophecies, the one who would complete the Jewish community's destiny. Luke's gospel is the only one that describes Jesus' birth in a manger in Bethlehem. Luke's gospel also focuses more on women—from Mary the mother of Jesus, to Mary Magdalene, a sinner Jesus forgives, to Jainus' daughter whose illness he cures, to the sinful woman who washes and anoints Jesus' feet.

The Gospel of John differs radically from the three synoptic gospels, even as those three gospels differ from one

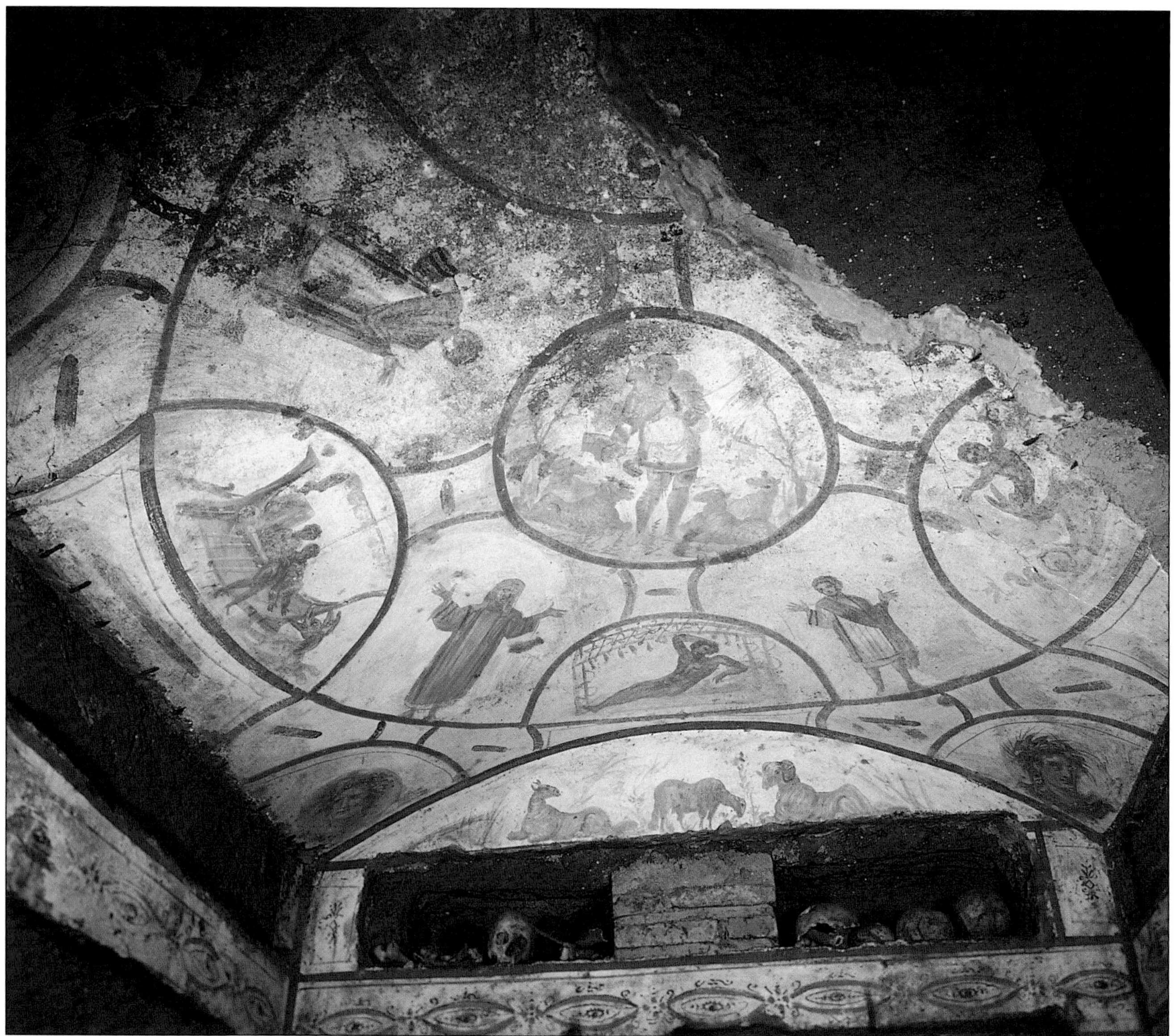

FIGURE 5.9 *Dome of Heaven,* painted ceiling in the catacomb of Santi Pietro e Marcellino, Rome, fourth century C.E. Catacombs, the underground burial areas of the Early Christians, were painted with symbolic subjects. Jesus was repeatedly shown as the good shepherd with his flock of followers.

another in focus, emphasis, and degree of sophistication. John's is the most theological of the gospels, the one most attuned to the religious and philosophical implications of Jesus' work and words.

John's gospel begins, for example, with an idea inherited from Greek thought: Jesus is the *Logos,* the divine word that came into the world as a light into darkness. Another image that pervades John's gospel is that of water. John describes Jesus as the living water who quenches the spiritual thirst of those unable to find satisfaction in their lives. This image is closely tied to Jesus' emphasis on being reborn into the kingdom of heaven through the agency of baptism in water and a spiritual and methaphorical baptism of the spirit.

Epistles. The New Testament contains twenty-one epistles addressed to Early Christian communities. Fourteen of these letters are traditionally ascribed to the apostle Paul. The titles of the Pauline epistles are derived from their recipients: Romans, Corinthians, Ephesians, and so on. They were written as a means of explaining points of doctrine, clarifying misunderstandings, and exhorting various communities to remain committed to their faith in Jesus. The importance of Paul to the spread of Christianity in the first century C.E. and his influence in formulating Christian doctrine can hardly be exaggerated. Along with his travels, Paul's epistles served his missionary vocation, to spread Christianity throughout the Greco-Roman world.

Cross Currents

CHRISTIAN AND PAGAN GODS

From the beginning, Christianity was at odds with pagan religions and their multiple deities. From the standpoint of Christian monotheism, the pagan gods were false idols, and the myths associated with them, fictions.

And yet, as different as Christianity was, it nonetheless absorbed elements of pagan myths and belief. Pagan elements had counterparts in a number of features of Christianity. These similarities included belief in a god who died and was reborn; communal worship; celebration of ritual ceremonies commemorating the deity; pilgrimages, processions, fasting; and initiates taking new names upon entrance into the religious community.

This connection was most evident, however, with regard to the pagan and Christian deities. The accommodation of the pagan gods into Christianity was one of reinterpretation. For although the characteristics of the pagan deities were retained, their qualities were given a new Christian meaning. The Greek god Apollo, for example, became a precursor of the Son of God; Apollo's prophetic power affiliated him with the Holy Spirit. Similarly, Prometheus' sacrificial effort to liberate humanity was seen in light of Christ's sacrifice; Prometheus' transgression—his exceeding his human state by interfering with the gods—linked him with Lucifer, the angel who rebelled against God, and when hurled into hell, became known as Satan.

In the same way that pagan deities such as Apollo, Prometheus, and Orpheus were reinterpreted in connection with Christ, God the Father subsumed elements and characteristics associated with pagan deities such as Zeus and Kronos. The Virgin Mary assumed qualities linked with those of Aphrodite, Persephone, and Artemis. This absorption of the pagan deities into Christianity, moreover, extended to the Christian saints. Saint Michael, for example, absorbed the militant qualities of Mars. And Saint Christopher, who as legend has it, bore the Christ child on his shoulders to ford a stream, was linked with Atlas, who bore the world on his shoulders.

Paul's epistles expound the Christian doctrines of the Incarnation and the Atonement, or Redemption. The Incarnation refers to the birth of God in human form as Jesus. As a co-equal member of the Holy Trinity (the union of Father, Son, and Holy Ghost in a single godhead), Jesus is divine. In taking on a human form, in the flesh and living and dying like any mortal, Jesus revealed his love for humankind. Paul also wrote that Jesus became human so he could suffer and die for the sins of humankind; his suffering atones for human beings' sins and redeems humankind.

The theology in the Pauline epistles is intricate and complex. In developing theories to explain Christian beliefs, such as the resurrection of the body and the immortality of the soul, Paul relied both on Greek philosophical ideas and on the Old Testament, which he interpreted in light of the new teaching. Paul's ideas have influenced Christian teaching for nearly two thousand years and are reflected in many works of Western literature, including Chaucer's *Canterbury Tales*, Dante's *Divine Comedy*, Shakespeare's plays, and Milton's *Paradise Lost*.

Revelation. Also known as "The Apocalypse," the Greek word for "unveiling," Revelation presents a visionary account of the Last Judgment and the end of the world. Written sometime near the end of the first century C.E., ca. 75–95, this final book of the Bible presents a symbolic vision of the future. The symbols used include the seven seals, the seven lamps, the Great Beast, the seven bowls, and the woman, child, and dragon. The meaning of this symbolism has spawned numerous conflicting interpretations through the centuries.

EARLY CHRISTIAN MUSIC

The music of the Early Christian church had its roots in Jewish worship. Jewish religious rites were accompanied by chanting of sacred texts, with an instrumental doubling on the harp or lyre. Essentially, two different kinds of singing developed in Christian services: **responsorial** and **antiphonal.** In Christian services, the congregation sang simple responses to cantors and choirs, which sang the more complex parts. In singing a psalm, for example, the cantor or choir would sing the verses and the congregation the standard response of "Amen" or "Alleluia."

This responsorial type of chanting was complemented by antiphonal singing, in which either a cantor and the congregation or different parts of the congregation alternated in singing verses of the psalm. In some cases the congregation would be divided into parts, usually positioned on opposite sides of the church, to enhance the effectiveness of this alternation of the chant.

Early Christianity, unlike Judaism, prohibited instrumental accompaniment of any kind, which was considered pagan. Up until the fourth century, early Christian

Connections

GREEK AND ROMAN INFLUENCES ON CHRISTIANITY

Aspects of Platonism harmonized with Christian thought and were absorbed during the early history of the church. The major Platonic tenets taken over include the following:

1. the existence of a perfect transcendental reality outside of the world of materiality and time;
2. the immortality of the soul;
3. the priority of spirit over matter;
4. an emphasis on self-knowledge;
5. the subjection of the passions to reason;
6. a view of death as a release from the bonds of the body;
7. an emphasis on goodness, beauty, and truth.

These elements of Platonic thought were synthesized with the Judeo-Christian emphasis on a personal god acting with providential design in effecting the divine plan for history.

Yet however much early Christianity absorbed elements of Greek philosophy differences remained. Most important among these differences are these:

1. Judaism and Christianity imagined divinity to be singular, unique, and historically present.
2. The Judeo-Christian concept of history was progressive and linear, moving forward to the grand culmination of the Messianic kingdom (Judaism) and the Parousia (Presence and Return of Christ at the end of the world—Christianity).

Ironically, Rome, which had been the great persecutor of early Christianity, became the center of Christianity in the West. The administration of Roman law was displaced by the Catholic Church with its institutional hierarchy and its spreading empire. Rome became Christianized; Christianity became Romanized.

Critical Thinking

CHRISTIANITY'S INFLUENCES

Although Christianity was a new and different religion from the religions that predated and preceded it, it also has been associated with beliefs and practices of Hebraic Roman religious traditions as well as Greek philosophical traditions. Why do you think these earlier religious and philosophical traditions impacted Christianity so strongly? What do you think the early leaders of Christianity thought of those influences? To what extent do you think the theologians of the early Christian Church would have found such influences congenial and to what extent dangerous? Why?

liturgical music (music used in religious ritual) was based exclusively on sacred texts. Starting in the fifth century, some nonscriptural hymns supplemented these scripture-based chants.

Musical practice differed somewhat in churches that followed the Byzantine liturgy rather than that of St. Ambrose. The Western liturgy of Ambrose made accommodations for active musical participation by the congregation. This required the music to be kept relatively simple, with a single note sung to each syllable. In contrast, Byzantine liturgical music was more complex, with many notes sung to a syllable in a florid style. These sixth-century Byzantine liturgical musical practices were modified, however, by the seventh-century reforms toward less complex chant melodies.

PHILOSOPHY: AUGUSTINE AND THE NEOPLATONIC INHERITANCE

The spread of Christianity during the early centuries was accompanied by a need to explain and systematize Christian thought. After Paul, the single most important expounder of Christian doctrine was Augustine (354–430) from Hippo (near present-day Algeria), in northern Africa.

Augustine achieved a synthesis of the Platonic philosophical tradition and the Judeo-Christian emphasis on divine revelation. For Augustine, human beings can only know true ideas when they are illuminated in the soul by God. Augustine dismissed knowledge derived from sense experience as unreliable. Such empirical knowledge was

Connections

GNOSTICISM AND CHRISTIANITY

Alternative, suppressed forms of quasi-Christian belief existed alongside orthodox Christianity in the early church. One influential form of early Christianity was Gnosticism, central to which was a belief that redemption could be achieved through possessing special secret knowledge. Gnostics believed they had access to secret wisdom (*gnosis* is the Greek word for "knowledge"). This special knowledge was restricted to small groups of Gnostic adherents who pursued lives of asceticism and who observed strict dietary practices, refraining from sensual indulgence and removing themselves from temptation.

Gnosticism was a dualist philosophy, which, like Zoroastrianism and Manicheism, divided the world into good and evil. The evil part, which was material rather than spiritual, was created by a demonic spirit. It was this demonic spirit that was said to be responsible for the fall of humanity. Second century C.E. Gnostics believed humankind predates the fall and that, before that event, all human beings contained a spark of divinity within them.

Gnosticism shocked the followers of early orthodox Christianity, who were dismayed by Gnostic beliefs in reincarnation and equality for women. Gnosticism nonetheless managed to establish itself as an alternative form of Christianity. Suppressed Gnostic texts coexisted with the canonical Christian scriptures, the Gospel of Thomas, dating from the second century perhaps being the best known and most widely disseminated, and the Gospel of Judas Iscariot, the betrayer of Jesus, the latest to stir controversy among Christians.

suspect due to humanity's fall from grace. To Plato's emphasis on pure ideas, Augustine added divinely revealed truth as recorded in scripture and interpreted by church tradition.

In his early adulthood, Augustine had lived a life of self-indulgence and debauchery. His *Confessions* describe his dissatisfaction with this way of life, his search for spiritual fulfillment, and, finally, his conversion to Christianity.

As the first Western autobiography, Augustine's *Confessions* was enormously influential. Throughout the Middle Ages the book was read, copied, and imitated. The book's image of the spiritual journey influenced medieval poems of pilgrimage, such as William Langland's *Piers Ploughman* and Dante's *Divine Comedy.* As well as providing a framework for these and other forms of spiritual autobiography, the *Confessions* paved the way for the Renaissance rediscovery of the self.

In addition to his *Confessions*, Augustine wrote *On Christian Doctrine*, which analyzes and explains the central tenets of Christian teaching, and the *City of God*, in which he explores the relationship between faith and reason, and the cause of history as a movement toward the clash of two opposite visions of life, represented by two contrasting cities, an earthly city and a heavenly one, the city of God.

One of Augustine's central ideas is that evil does not possess reality in the same sense that good does. According to Augustine, evil is a deficiency in good rather than something that exists in its own right. God did not create evil; rather, evil entered the world through incorrect choices made by human beings, as when Adam chose to disobey God's injunction not to eat the forbidden fruit (Genesis 1). Regardless of the source of sin, however, Augustine follows St. Paul in explaining how Christ redeemed humanity, and how life is a spiritual pilgrimage toward God, in whom human beings find their salvation and their eternal rest.

Like Paul, whose epistles he echoes frequently, Augustine distrusted the fleshly body, which he held accountable for humankind's fall from grace. Augustine, in fact, described the original sin as "concupiscence," or lust, to which he had himself succumbed during his early adulthood. This distrust of the physical body and his subordination of it to the faculties of the spiritual soul were to affect church teaching for many centuries.

Another influential Augustinian idea was that of humankind's inability to obtain salvation on its own. Augustine argued that only God could freely grant this grace. Because human beings were unable to save themselves, their only hope for salvation lay in accepting God's truth as revealed in sacred scripture, including the New Testament. Furthermore, since human beings were prone to error, misunderstanding, and sin due to the corruption they inherited from Adam and Eve's original sin, they were not in a position to understand the complexities of divine revelation on their own. For that, they needed the authoritative teaching of the church.

Augustine wrote voluminously in support of church authority and unity in matters of doctrine. He made vigorous attacks on the doctrines that circulated around the church in the early centuries. He also defended Christianity against charges that the new religion was responsible for the decline of Roman civilization. Instead, Augustine saw the fall of

Rome as part of God's providential plan for the progressive development of human history toward its fulfillment in the Parousia—the return of Jesus to earth at the end of the world.

BYZANTINE CIVILIZATION

In 330 C.E., with the Roman empire in severe economic and political decline, the emperor Constantine established the trading city of Byzantium as his new Eastern capital, renaming it Constantinople in the process.

From this time on, power and influence increasingly deserted Rome, which became a favorite target for invading barbarian hordes from the north. In 410, a barbarian tribe from Germany, the Visigoths, laid siege to the former capital and, when the Senate refused to pay the invaders tribute, Rome was sacked for the first time in eight hundred years. Another group, the Vandals, sacked the city again in 455.

Meanwhile, the Western empire was crumbling. Successive waves of Saxons, Angles, and Jutes attacked and occupied Britain; Burgundians wrested large parts of France from the Romans, and the Vandals came to control North Africa and Spain. By the end of the fifth century, Roman power had disintegrated, and the empire had been replaced by a patchwork of barbarian kingdoms.

In the East, however, imperial life flourished in the capital of Constantinople. There, a new and influential Christian civilization took root, usually known as BYZANTIUM [bi-ZAN-tee-um] after Constantinople's original name. Christian Byzantium continued to thrive for hundreds of years, although after the seventh century it had to compete with the rising civilization of Islam for control of the Mediterranean basin. Finally, in the fifteenth century, Constantinople itself was occupied by Muslim forces.

Of the early Byzantine emperors, JUSTINIAN [jus-TIN-ee-an] (r. 527–565) exerted the greatest cultural and political influence. His armies defeated Germanic tribes in Italy, Spain, and North Africa. Most important, however, was his rebuilding program in Constantinople itself. It was Justinian's wife and empress, THEODORA [THEE-oh-DOOR-ah], who persuaded her husband not to abandon Constantinople. Together, Justinian and Theodora sought to restore the grandeur of the empire and of their capital, Constantinople.

BYZANTINE ART

So generously did Justinian patronize the arts that his reign is referred to as the First Golden Age of Byzantine art, with Constantinople as its artistic capital. However, much of the art created during this First Golden Age survives only outside Constantinople, in particular in the city of Ravenna and in the monastery of St. Catherine built by Justinian at Mount Sinai.

San Vitale, Ravenna. The architecture and mosaics of the church of San Vitale in Ravenna (fig. 5.10), dated

FIGURE 5.10 San Vitale, Ravenna, 526–47. Exterior view and floor plan. Copyright Alinari/Art Resource, NY. A central-planned building is either circular, like Santa Costanza (see figs. 5.5–5.6), or polygonal, like San Vitale. An advantage of the central dome is the large space covered; a potential disadvantage is that the visitor's eyes tend to be attracted up into the dome rather than toward the altar.

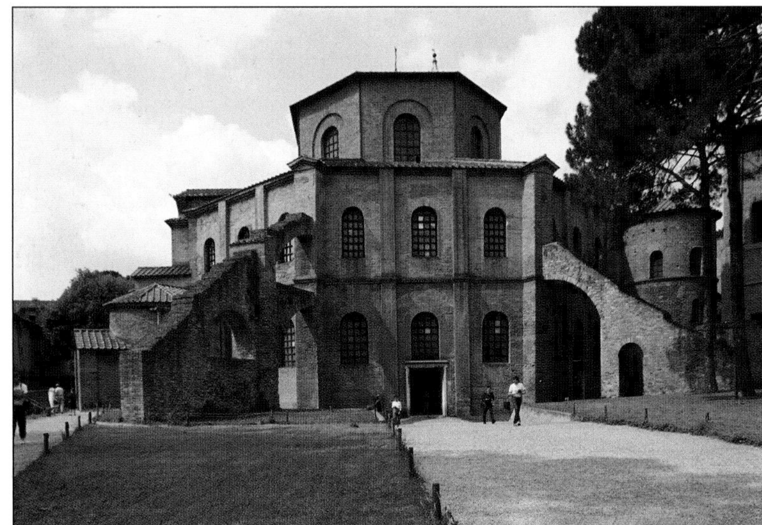

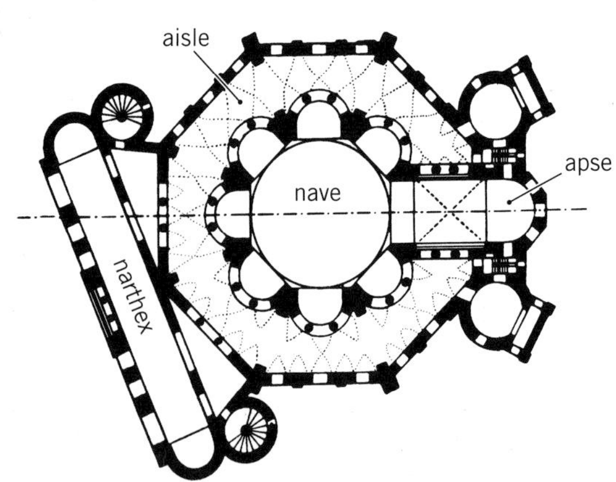

526–47, are especially important accomplishments of the First Golden Age. Though begun by Bishop Maximian in 526, San Vitale bears the imprint of the influence of Constantinople and Justinian. It is octagonal in plan, a shape favored in Constantinople. Light is admitted to the interior by windows on the lower levels. However, this light is filtered through the aisles, which are two stories high, before reaching the nave. The only direct light, and therefore the strongest and most dramatic, enters the nave from the third-story clerestory above.

Like the circular church of Santa Costanza in Rome (see figs. 5.5–5.6) the polygonal San Vitale has no longitudinal axis and is therefore referred to as having a central plan. Unlike the Early Christian churches of the basilica type that have a longitudinal axis (see figs. 5.3–5.4), such structures have no need of rows of columns to hold up their ceilings and are capped with domes, which are supported by the walls and external buttresses instead. The result is that the interior feels light and spacious. However, two focal points compete for the visitor's attention. Whereas on entering a church with a longitudinal axis, the worshiper is naturally directed toward the altar, the center of the ritual, this is less obviously the case at San Vitale, where the worshiper's eyes are also drawn up to the dome.

In striking contrast to its drab exterior, the interior of San Vitale (fig. 5.11) is opulent in its ornament, made colorful by mosaics that cover all the upper portions (the angels on clouds are later additions), by thin slabs of marble veneer, and by marble columns with carved and painted capitals. Seemingly insubstantial, the lacy delicacy of the surface decoration belies the underlying strength of the structure.

Flanking the altar at San Vitale and drawing the worshiper's gaze down from the dome are the celebrated mosaics of the emperor Justinian and the empress Theodora (fig. 5.12) of ca. 547. Justinian and Theodora, each accompanied by attendants, are shown as good Christian rulers, ever to be in attendance at the religious service. The figures are not necessarily intended to be

FIGURE 5.11 San Vitale, Ravenna, 526–47, interior. This view only begins to indicate the complexity of San Vitale's interior space. Light enters on three levels, playing over the polished marble surfaces and glittering glass mosaics.

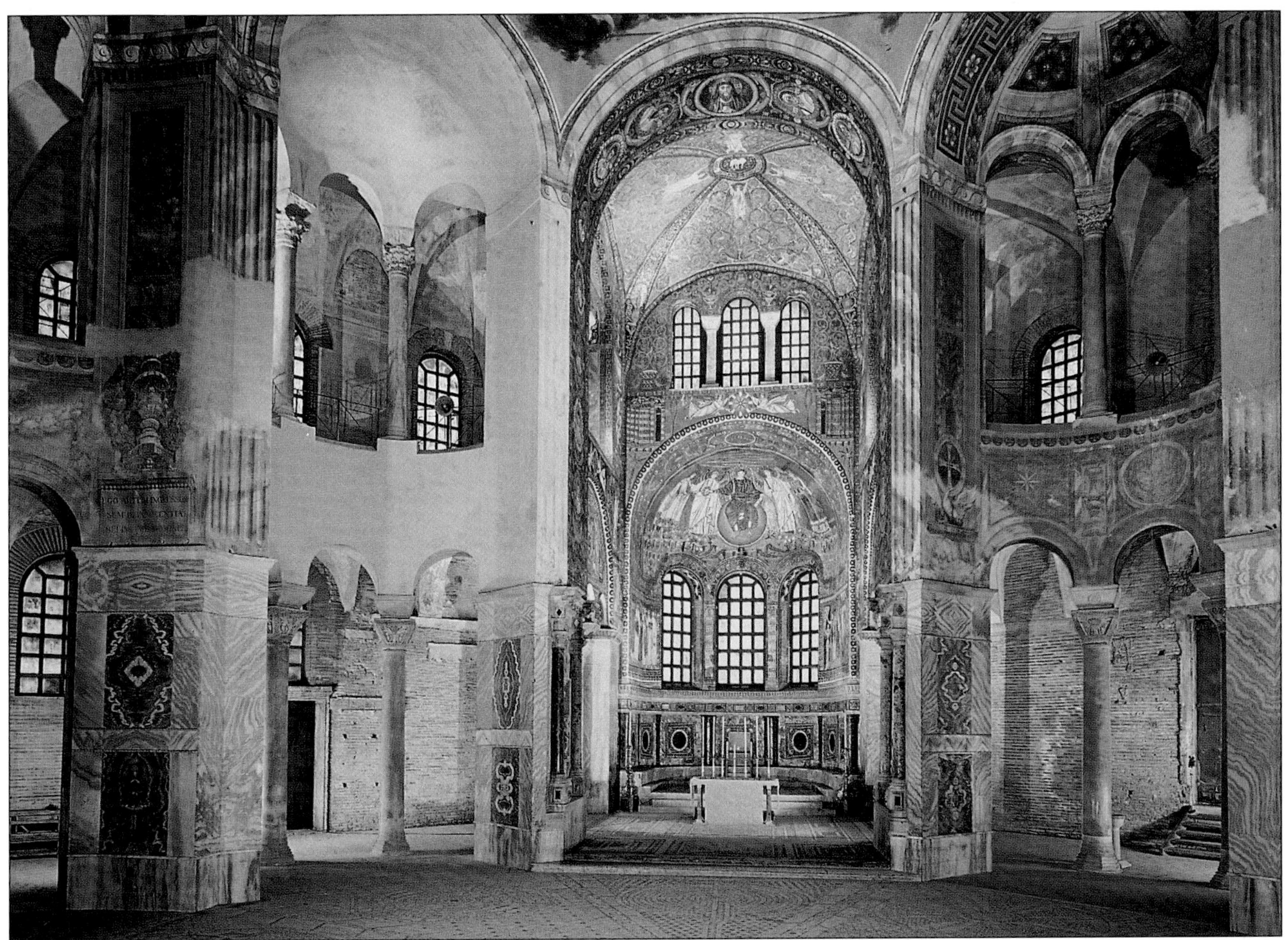

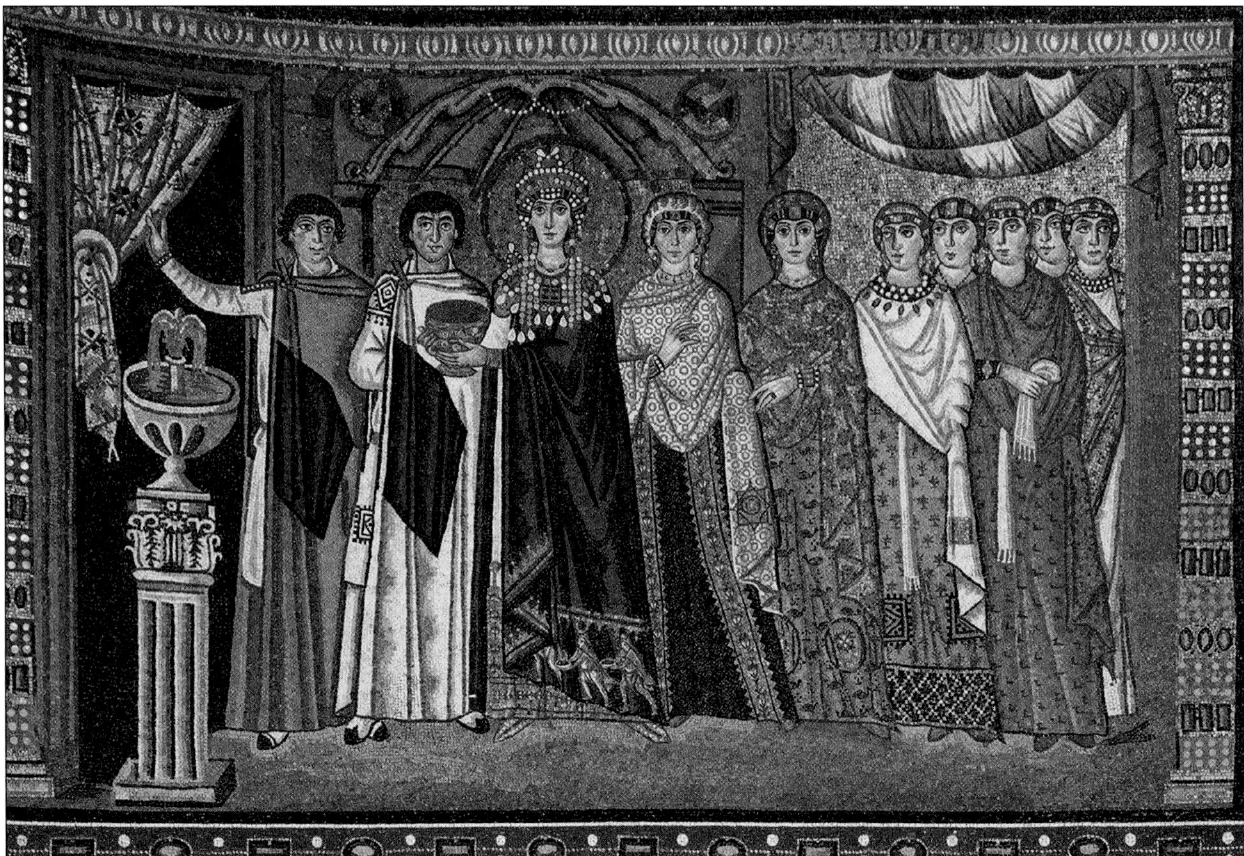

FIGURE 5.12 *Theodora and her Attendants,* San Vitale, Ravenna, ca. 547, mosaic. The typical Byzantine face is shown to have large eyes, a long nose, and a tiny mouth. The body is characteristically slender and weightless—or so we might hope, since the figures appear to step on one another's feet.

recognizable portraits of specific individuals. Instead, everyone looks much alike, with big dark eyes, curved eyebrows, long noses, and small mouths—the characteristic Byzantine facial type. Their drapery gives no suggestion of a body beneath; the only indication that these people have legs is the appearance of feet below the hem of their garments. Their elongated bodies seem insubstantial, ethereal and immaterial, motionless, their gestures frozen.

The flat frontal figures form a rhythmic pattern across the surface of the mosaic. Three-quarter views, which suggest a degree of movement and dimension, are avoided. The Byzantine lack of concern for realistic or even consistent representation of space is illustrated by the doorway on the left, the top and bottom of which are seen from two different vantage points. The ancient Roman interests in specific details and spatial illusion are gone. Yet whatever this architectural decoration may lose in realism, it gains in splendor. Realism is not the goal here. Glittering mosaic is an ideal medium with which to enhance the image of divine power promoted by the Byzantine emperor and empress while simultaneously increasing the splendor of San Vitale.

GOLDEN AGE OF CONSTANTINOPLE

Constantinople (known as Istanbul after 1930) lies on the straits of Bosphorus, at the confluence of the Black Sea and the Sea of Marmara. The city has a fine harbor, controlling the land route from Europe to Asia and the waterways that lead to the ports on the Black Sea, the Aegean, and the Mediterranean. Fortified by walls on three sides and the straits on the other, it withstood attacks for a thousand years, until the Turks captured it in 1453, after which it became a Muslim city.

Life in Constantinople at the time of Justinian was rich in pleasures. The well-to-do enjoyed a level of hygiene and health unknown in Europe at the time. Entertainments included chariot races at the amphitheater and theatrical productions notorious for their indecency. The empress Theodora had been an actress before marrying Justinian and had a somewhat unsavory reputation as a result. This, however, was only one aspect of the city. Constantinople was also a place of elegance and splendor, with one of the most magnificent religious buildings ever constructed, the Church of the Holy Wisdom, or Hagia Sophia, built by Justinian and Theodora after the revolt in 532. The great domed structure stands as testimony to their ambitions (fig. 5.13).

Well into the ninth and tenth centuries Constantinople remained the largest, richest, and most sophisticated city in the world. The immense city walls with their 37 gates and 486 towers—not to mention Constantinople's hundreds of churches and chapels and the monumental Hagia Sophia, which sailors could use as a landmark twenty miles out at sea—gave the impression of indomitable power.

The wealth of Constantinople was legendary. The city produced manuscripts and jewelry of every description, as well as rich fabrics in cotton, linen, and silk, embroidered with gold. Valuable metals, ivory, and precious stones were abundant, as were spices, including ginger and cloves, pepper, and saffron. So too were medicinal drugs and ingredients for dyeing fabric.

As the world's richest and largest market, Constantinople was tightly controlled; its customs duties were high and restrictive. Demand for its goods was maintained by limiting their supply and by keeping prices high. Although commerce with cities throughout western Europe developed, only Venice was given privileged trading status.

By virtue of its easy access to land and sea trade routes, Constantinople was well situated to transport goods between East and West. Yet despite this abundant mercantile exchange, there was still mutual mistrust between Constantinople and the West.

Most important of all were the deep-rooted differences between the Christian churches of the West and East. Latin was the language of the Roman church, Greek that of the Byzantine church. In Rome, the early church

FIGURE 5.13 Anthemius of Tralles and Isidorus of Miletus, Hagia Sophia, Istanbul, 532–37. The towers surrounding Hagia Sophia are a later, Ottoman addition. The central dome is buttressed by smaller half domes, in turn buttressed by smaller half domes, creating a structurally sound and visually striking church.

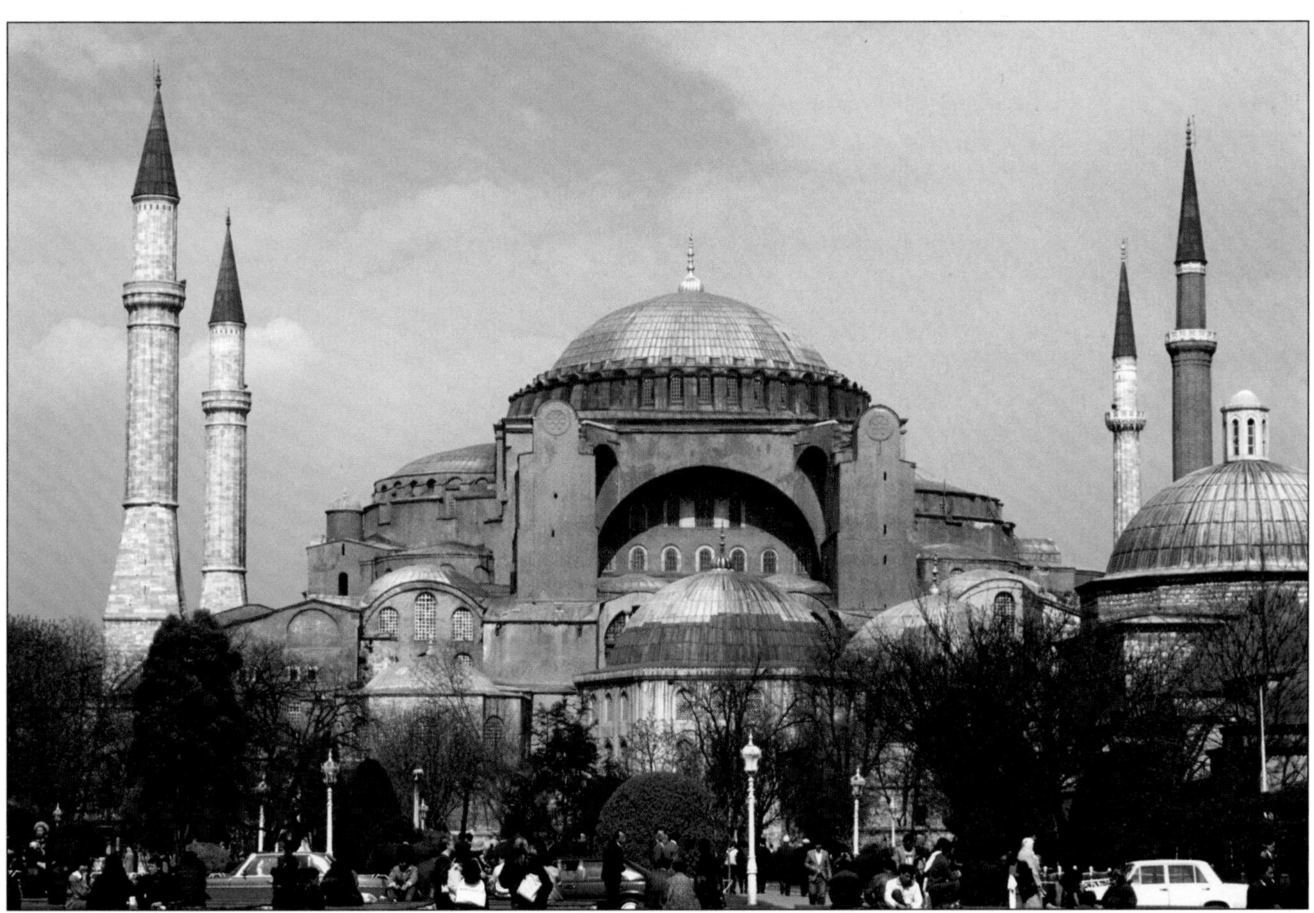

was ruled by local bishops, one of whom was elevated by Rome's lay Christians. In Constantinople, the church was controlled by a patriarch who was appointed, and often disposed of, by the emperor. In the West, priests were encouraged to be celibate and in 1139 celibacy became compulsory; in the East, priests could and often did marry. These differences were exacerbated when the Eastern patriarch refused to submit to the authority of the Roman pope in 1054, precipitating a final and permanent **schism,** or split, between the Eastern and Western churches.

Hagia Sophia. Hagia Sophia, the Church of the Holy Wisdom in Constantinople (fig. 5.13), was built for Justinian and Theodora between 532 and 537 by the architects Anthemius of Tralles and Isidorus of Miletus. There is little exterior decoration (the four minarets, or towers, are later Ottoman additions). Seen from the outside, Hagia Sophia appears to be a solid structure, building up by waves to the huge central dome.

The plan (fig. 5.14) shows the arrangement around the central dome, with half domes on opposite sides, which are in turn flanked by smaller half domes. Thus Hagia Sophia, although domed, is not a pure central-plan church like San Vitale, because a longitudinal axis is created by the oval nave. Hagia Sophia's ingenious plan has a single focus of attention as well as a great open space, combining the advantages of the longitudinal basilica plan with those of the domed central plan.

Unlike the dome of the Roman Pantheon (see fig. 4.11), which rests on a circular base, the dome of Hagia Sophia is supported by a square base formed by four huge piers. Transition from circle to square is achieved through the use of four **pendentives,** pieces of triangular supporting masonry. In effect, the dome rests on a larger dome from which segments have been removed. Hagia Sophia is one of the earliest examples of a dome on pendentives.

The interior (fig. 5.15) is an extremely lofty, light-filled, unobstructed space. From the inside, the dome seems to billow or to float—as if it were suspended from above rather than supported from below. Because the dome is made of lightweight tiles, it was possible for the architects to puncture the base of the dome with a band of forty windows. The light that streams through these windows is used as an artistic element, for it is reflected in the mosaics and the marbles. A rich polychromatic scheme is created by the red and green porphyry columns, the polished marble slabs on the lower walls, and the mosaics on the upper walls. Like San Vitale, the elaborate surface decoration conceals the strength of the underlying structure.

St. Mark's, Venice. The First Golden Age of Byzantine art ended with the "iconoclastic controversy." Yet when in 843 the **iconophiles**—the lovers of artistic images—triumphed over the iconoclasts, a Second Golden Age of Byzantine art began, lasting until the beginning of the thirteenth century. The biggest and most elaborate church of the Second Golden Age is St. Mark's in Venice, begun in 1063. Its location on one side of a large **piazza** (open public area) is particularly impressive. The original facade has since been modified.

The plan is a **Greek cross**—that is, a cross with four arms of equal length. There is a dome over the center, plus a dome over each arm (fig. 5.16). All five domes are covered with wood and gilt copper, making them very striking and giving St. Mark's a distinctive silhouette.

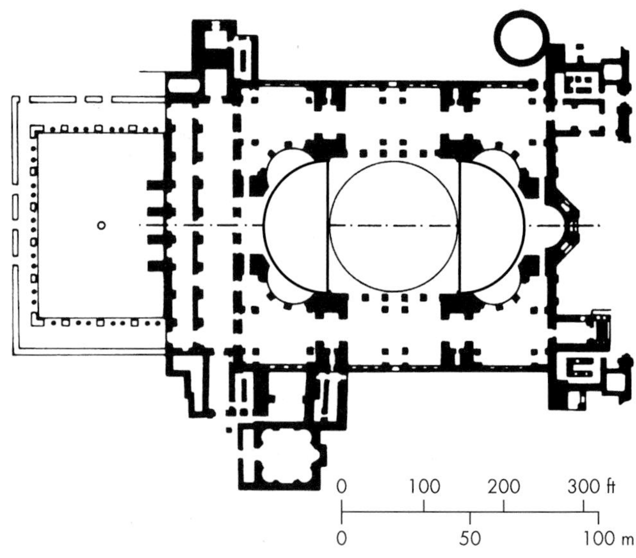

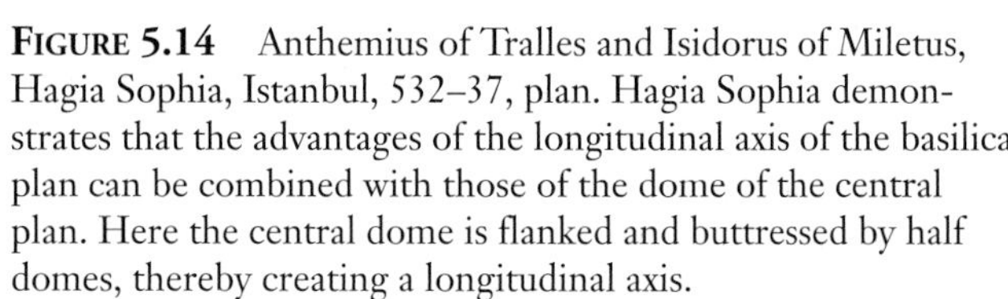
FIGURE 5.14 Anthemius of Tralles and Isidorus of Miletus, Hagia Sophia, Istanbul, 532–37, plan. Hagia Sophia demonstrates that the advantages of the longitudinal axis of the basilica plan can be combined with those of the dome of the central plan. Here the central dome is flanked and buttressed by half domes, thereby creating a longitudinal axis.

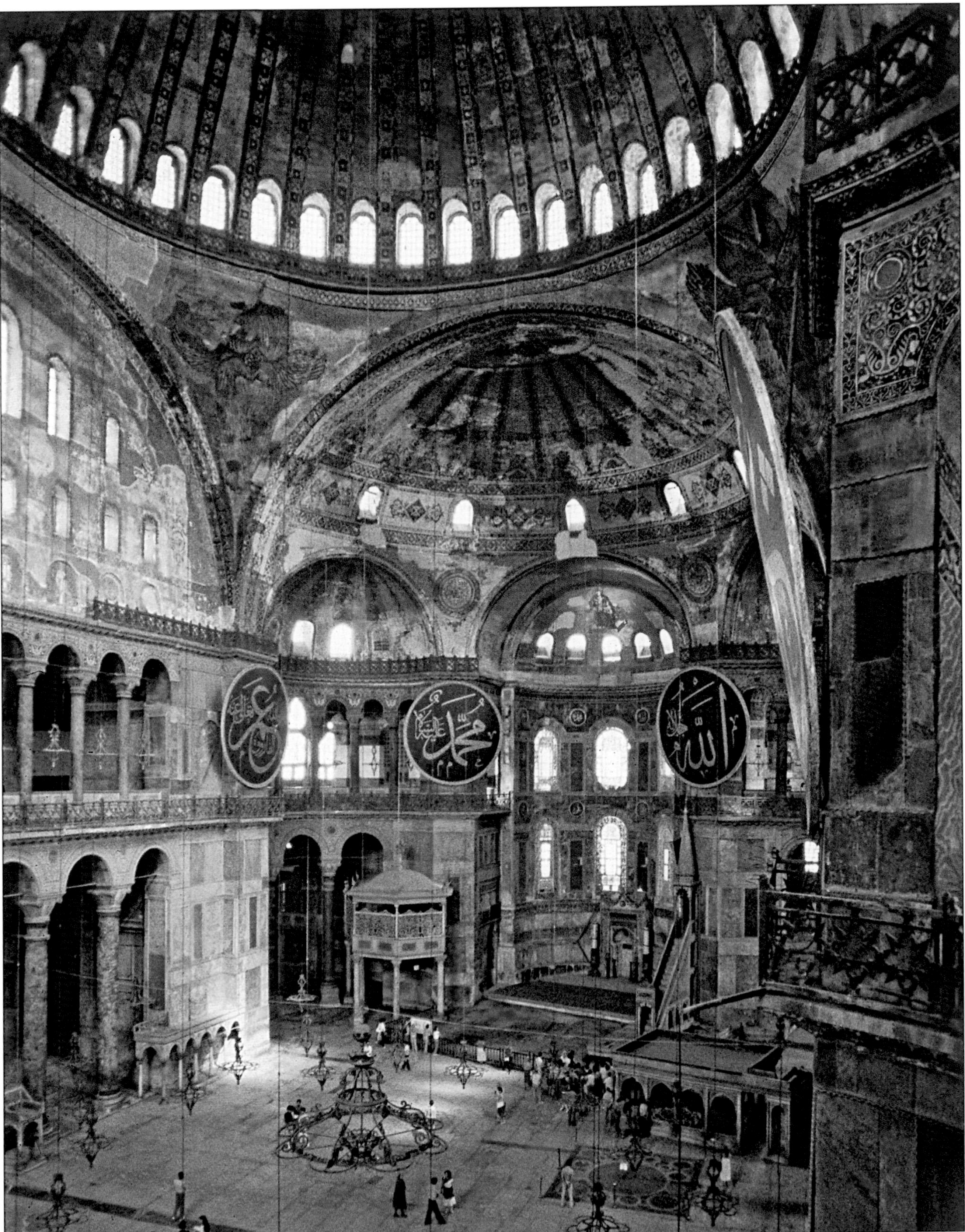

FIGURE 5.15 Anthemius of Tralles and Isidorus of Miletus, Hagia Sophia, Istanbul, 532–37, interior. Triangular pendentives provide the transition between the circular dome and the square base on which it rests. The closely spaced windows at the base of the dome create a ring of light that makes the dome appear to float.

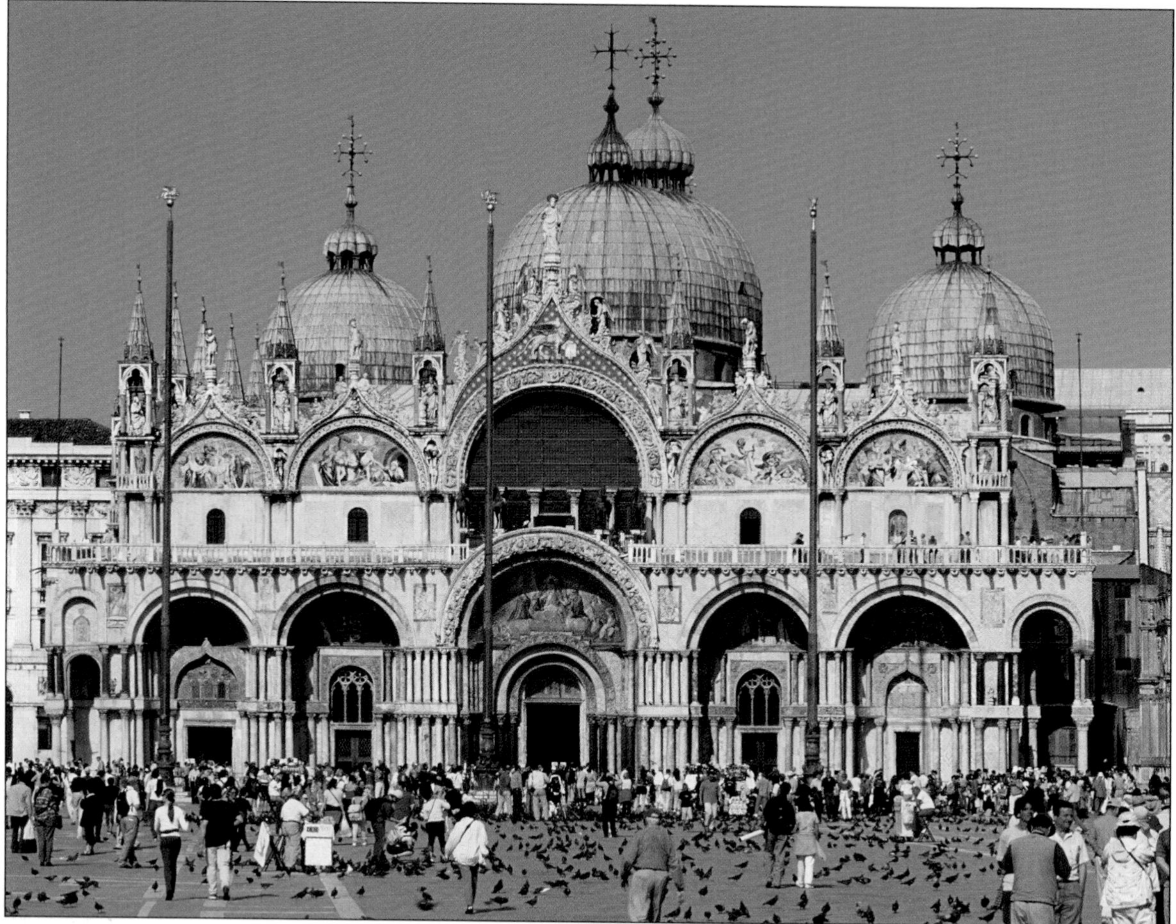

FIGURE 5.16 St. Mark's, Venice, begun 1063, exterior. A dramatic silhouette is created by the five domes. St. Mark's Greek-cross plan, with four equal arms, differs from the Latin-cross plan with one dominant axis, represented by Old St. Peter's (see fig. 5.3).

The interior of St. Mark's (fig. 5.17) offers the visitor an experience in ultimate splendor. The vast space is quite dark, originally illuminated only by windows in the bases of the domes and by the flickering light of countless candles. Yet all the surfaces glitter, for they are covered with mosaics, many of which are made with gold **tesserae** (the small cubes of color material that are pressed into wet plaster to make a mosaic).

Among the celebrated mosaics of St. Mark's, the most famous is the Creation Dome in the narthex, made about 1200. The story of Genesis is told in a series of scenes arranged in three concentric circles. The narrative begins in the innermost circle with the creation of heaven and earth. The story of Adam and Eve occupies part of the second circle and the outermost circle (fig. 5.18). In the scene shown here, God is pictured creating Eve from Adam's rib. Among the other memorable scenes is that in which God is shown giving Adam his soul, usually represented by a tiny winged figure entering Adam's mouth.

These mosaic figures hardly appear to have been taken from live models. Instead, the figures—doll-like and stocky with big heads—are intended to express the superhuman nature of the subject portrayed. The setting is symbolic only and represented in the simplest manner possible to convey the ideas. To elucidate the narrative, aids, such as bands of lettering and symbols, are employed. Emphasis is on design, decoration, and on the didactic message.

Madonna and Child Enthroned. Characteristic of this Byzantine style is the *Madonna and Child Enthroned* (fig. 5.19), a late-thirteenth-century egg tempera painting on a wooden panel. Egg tempera (pigment mixed with egg yolk) was the standard medium used to paint on wood throughout the Middle Ages.

Madonna and Child Enthroned represents a type repeated over and over according to strict rules. It is an **icon,** a painted image of a religious figure or religious scene used in worship. In this *Madonna and Child Enthroned,* Mary's

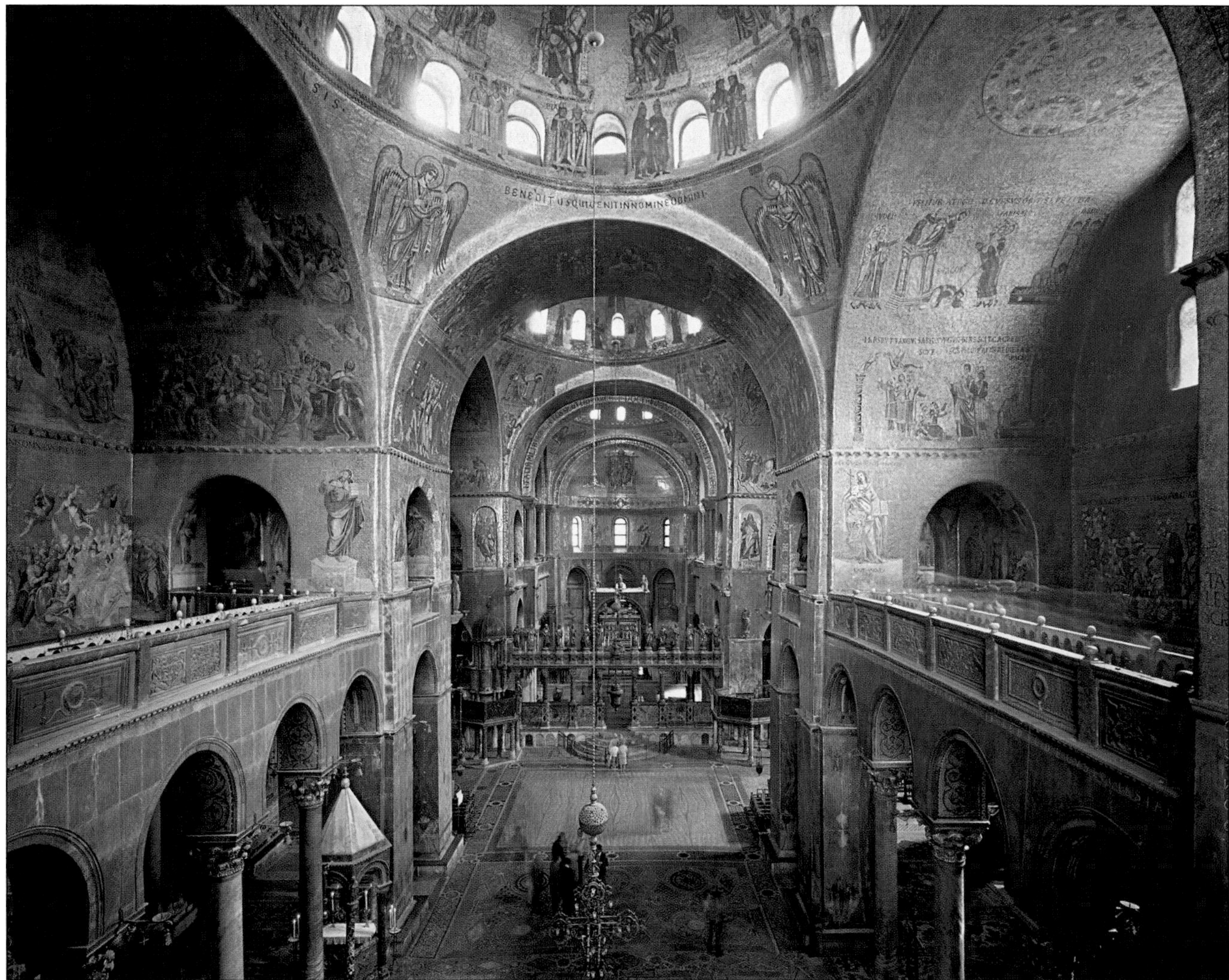

FIGURE 5.17 St. Mark's, Venice, begun 1063, interior. Glittering gold mosaics covering the walls and vaults successfully transport the visitor from the crowded streets of the island city of Venice to an extraordinary otherworldly environment.

typically Byzantine face has a somewhat wistful or melancholy expression. She is gentle and graceful, her bodily proportions elongated. Jesus' proportions are those of a tiny adult. Moreover, he acts as an adult, holding the scroll of law in one hand and blessing with the other.

Mary is traditionally shown wearing garments of red and blue—both primary colors. Jesus wears orange and green—two secondary colors. Byzantine drapery is characterized by elaborate and unrealistic folds, seemingly having a life of their own, independent of the body beneath. The hard ornamental highlights contrast with the soft skin of the figures.

These figures, barely of our species, do not inhabit our earthly realm. Compression of space is emphasized by the flat decorative designs. The throne, which has been compared to the Colosseum in Rome, is drawn in such a way that the interior and exterior do not correspond. Similarly, the footstool does not obey the rules of **linear perspective,** which require objects to diminish in scale as they recede into space. The artist does not seek to portray our earthly world; instead, this is God's heavenly domain.

Floating in this golden realm are two half angels. Each carries a staff, a symbol of Jesus' passion, and an orb or globe with a cross, which signifies Jesus' domination over the world. These are examples of **iconography,** the language of symbols, which was especially useful in an era when few people were literate. It was intended that the audience would be able to recognize the subject immediately. Consistency in the use of symbols, therefore, was important. The quest for innovation, for the novel, for things unique, had no place in Byzantine religious art.

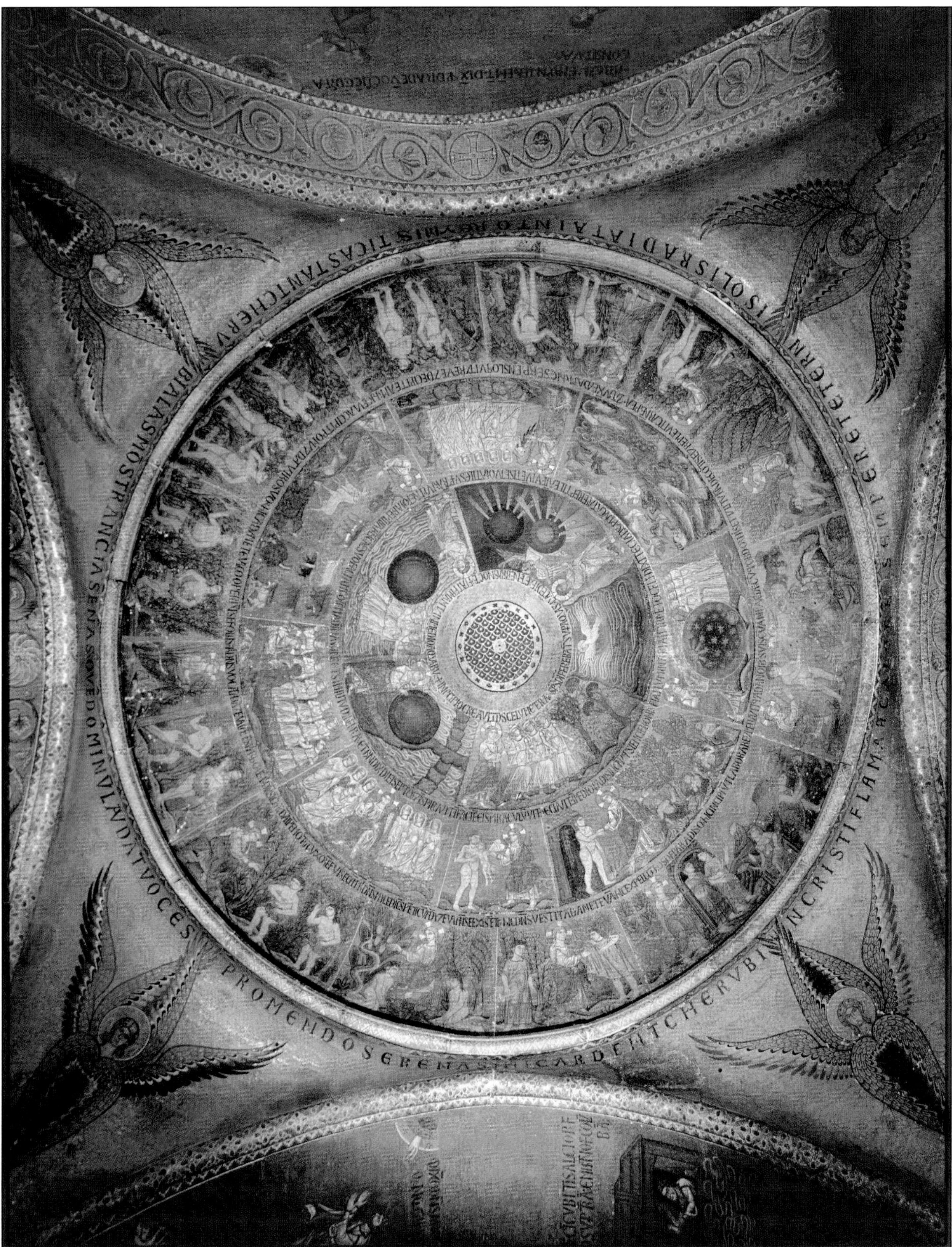

FIGURE 5.18 Creation Dome, narthex of St. Mark's, Venice, ca. 1200, mosaic. Engaging narrative is more important than realism in these mosaics. The intended audience was assumed to be familiar with the biblical stories told here, which, therefore, could be depicted in summary rather than in detail.

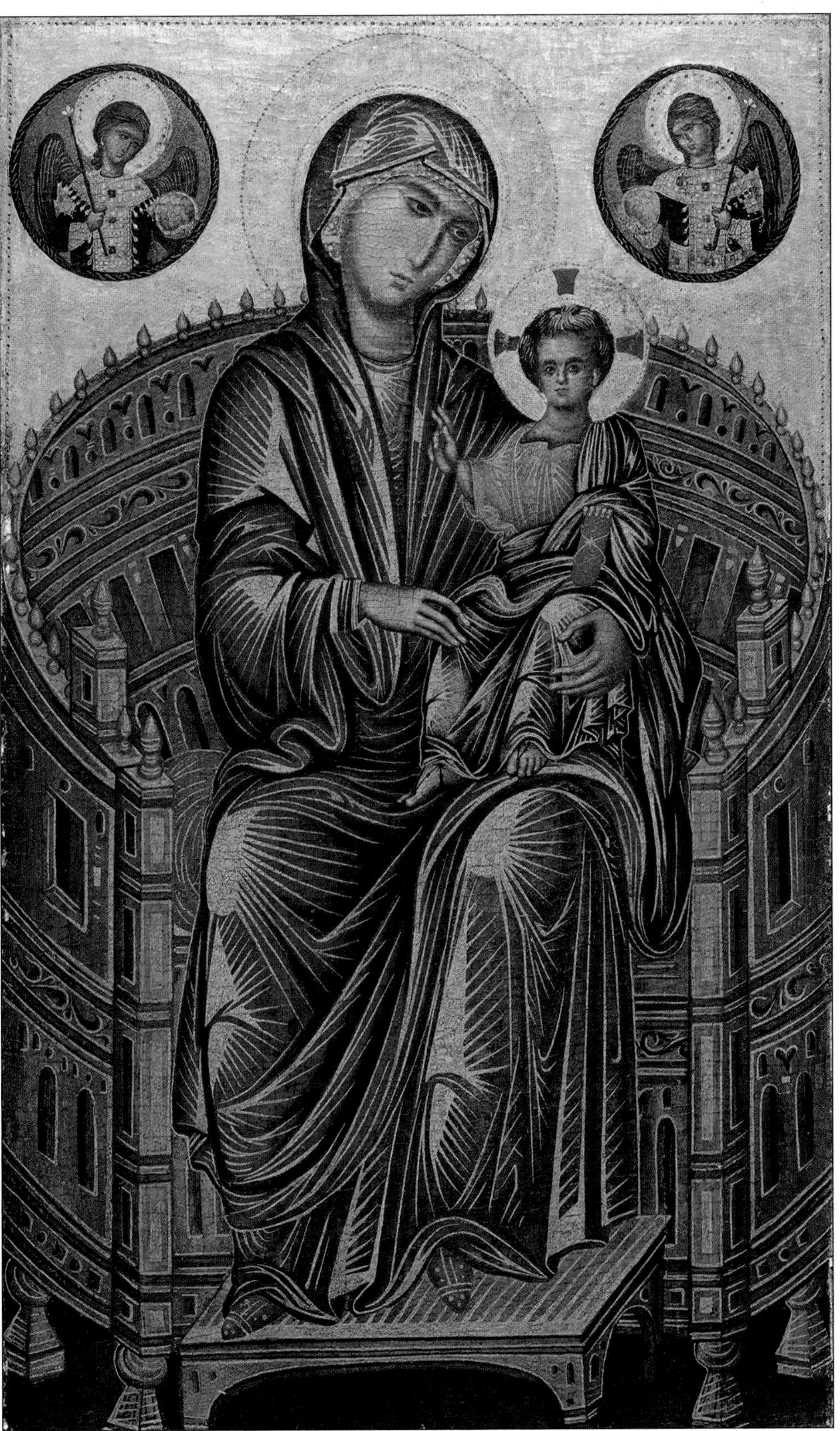

FIGURE 5.19 *Madonna and Child Enthroned*, ca. 1270. Tempera on panel, $38\frac{1}{8}'' \times 19\frac{1}{2}''$ (.970 × .495 m). Framed: $40\frac{1}{4}'' \times 22\frac{3}{4}''$ (1.022 × .578 m). Andrew W. Mellon Collection Photograph © 2001 Board of Trustees, National Gallery of Art, Washington. 1937.1.1.(1)/PA. The characteristic Byzantine figure type is slender and delicate. The drapery that forms angular folds is typically Byzantine.

Cultural Impact

Judaism's legacy centers on ethics and social justice. From the beginning, the ancient Hebrews emphasized the importance of ethical principles, which they read in the Ten Commandments, the book of Deuteronomy, and the teachings of the Hebrew prophets. To this day, the Jewish concern for social justice is expressed in countless Jewish philanthropic programs. Like their Jewish predecessors, Christians, too, have a long tradition of social service, running schools, shelters, hospices, and hospitals.

A powerful missionary impulse spread Christianity throughout the world, disseminating the philosophical thought of the early church fathers. Like their Jewish counterparts, Christian thinkers developed elaborate interpretations of the Bible; finely discriminating textual analysis characterizes both traditions and persists to this day.

Painting, sculpture, and architecture in medieval western Europe were almost exclusively Christian in inspiration. Medieval music, philosophy, and literature also reveal a strong Christian influence. And though the modern and contemporary worlds have become decidedly more secular, the influence of Judaism and Christianity persists in Jewish and Christian religious beliefs and practices of peoples around the world.

Byzantine civilization has also left a legacy. Throughout the Middle Ages, the Code of Justinian was the standard legal text in universities. Byzantine trade enabled the patronage of the arts in Renaissance Italian cities. Like their Western monastic predecessors, Byzantine scholars preserved ancient Greek texts, which were ultimately disseminated throughout Europe in the fifteenth century. Moreover, Orthodox Eastern Christianity continues to be practiced today in both Greece and Russia.

KEY TERMS

evangelist
monotheistic
covenant
etiological story
parable
atrium
narthex
nave
aisle
transept
apse
clerestory
ambulatory
sarcophagus
catacomb
fresco
responsorial
antiphonal
liturgical
schism
pendentive
iconophile
piazza
Greek cross
tesserae
icon
linear perspective
iconography

www. WEBSITES FOR FURTHER STUDY

http://www.ibiblio.org/expo/deadsea.scrolls.exhibit/intro.html
(The exhibition of Scrolls from the Dead Sea at the Ancient Library of Qumran and Modern Scholarship exhibit at the Library of Congress, Washington, D.C.)

http://www.religioustolerance.org/chr_otb4.htm
(The books of the Hebrew Scriptures [Old Testament] of the major prophets.)

http://www.ntcanon.org/places.shtml
(This table summarizes a few of the important places, and their important witnesses, in the development of the canon of the New Testament and links to some early images of various figures.)

http://www.metmuseum.org/explore/Byzantium/byz_1.html
(A Brief Summary of Byzantine History—this is a full site of many links and images, sponsored by the Metropolitan Museum of New York.)

http://www.jmi.org.ok/jewish/music.html
(A history of Jewish music from ancient prayer chants of 3000 years ago.)

http://www.religiousstudies.once.edu/jdtabor/judaism.html
(Overview of recent Judaism, including archeology and The Dead Sea Scrolls.)

http://www.iclnet.org/pub/resources/christian_history.html
(Links to Internet Accessible Files relating to the early church, including canonical documents and creeds.)

http://www.pbs.org/wgbh/pages/frontline/shows
(From Jesus to Christ, the first Christians.)

http://www.isthmia.osu.edu/teg/50501/chron.htm
(A chronology of early Byzantine history.)

http://www.huntfor.com/arthistory/medieval/byzantine.htm
(Byzantine icons.)

http://www.Monachos.net/.../108_early_christian_and_byzantine_music_history_and_performance
(Early Christian and Byzantine music.)

Chapter 6

History

610	Muhammad founds Islam
637	Arabs conquer Persia
656–661	Civil War
734	Martel defeats Muslims at Poitiers
762–766	New capital built at Baghdad
1037–1194	Anatolian Seljuk dynasty
1232–1492	Spanish Nasirid dynasty
1258	Mongol armies destroy Baghdad

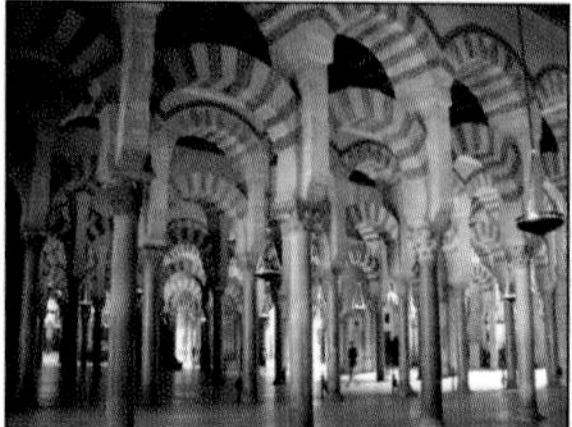

Arts and Architecture

786	Mosque at Cordova begun
early fourteenth century	Alhambra Palace begun
1354–91	Court of the Lions, Alhambra
1550–57	Sinan, Mosque of Sultan Sulayman
1556–65	*A Sheik Meditating in a Pavilion*

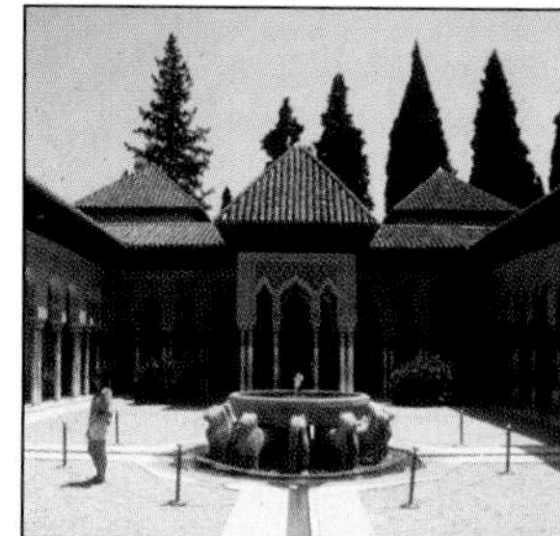

Literature and Philosophy

575–646	Al-Khansa, Poems
610	Muhammad establishes Islam
ca. 650	Text of Quran created
ninth century	Hadith recorded
tenth century	*Thousand and One Nights* first recorded in Arabic
980–1037	Avicenna
eleventh century	Firdawsi
1126–1198	Averroes
thirteenth century	Jalaloddin Rumi, Poems

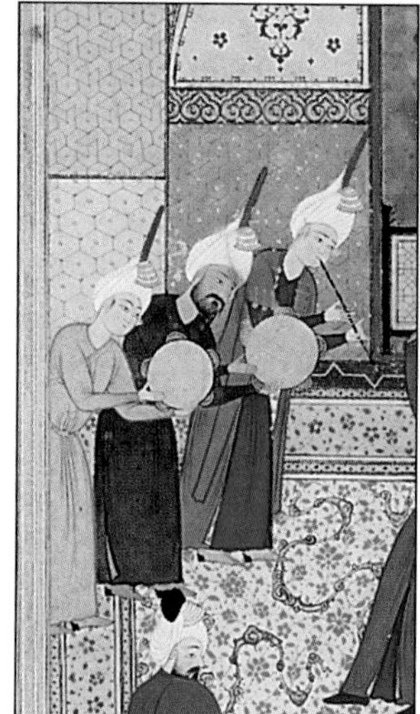

Islamic Civilization

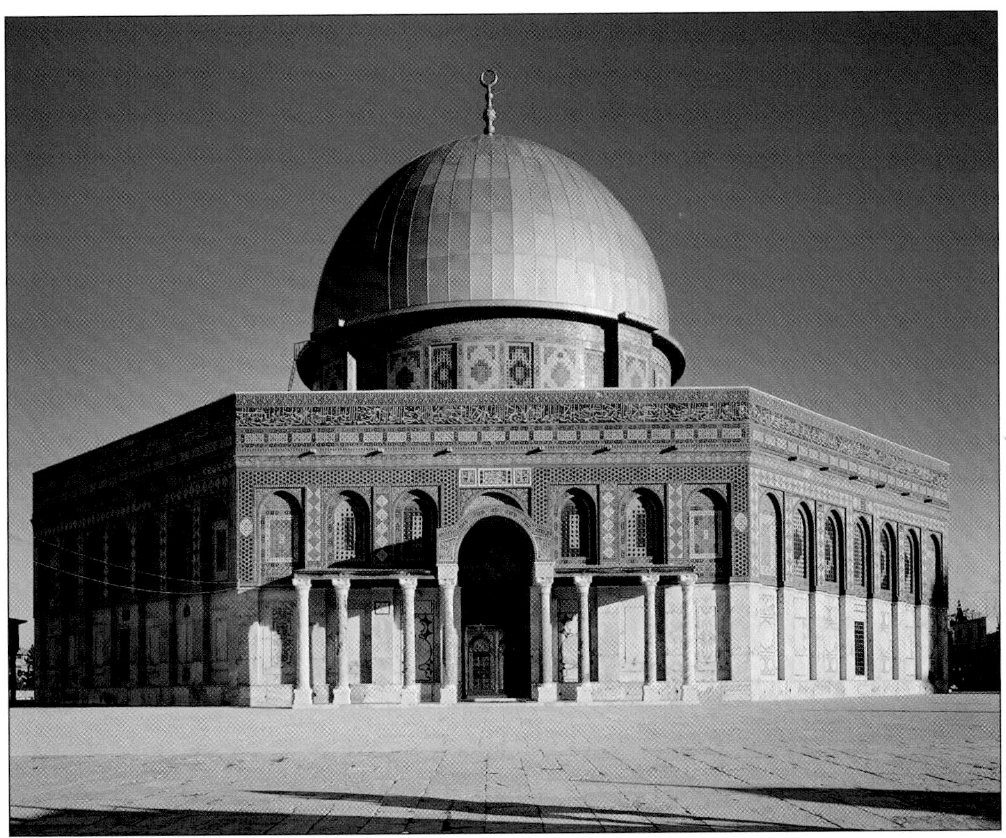

Dome of the Rock, Jerusalem, Late 680s–692.

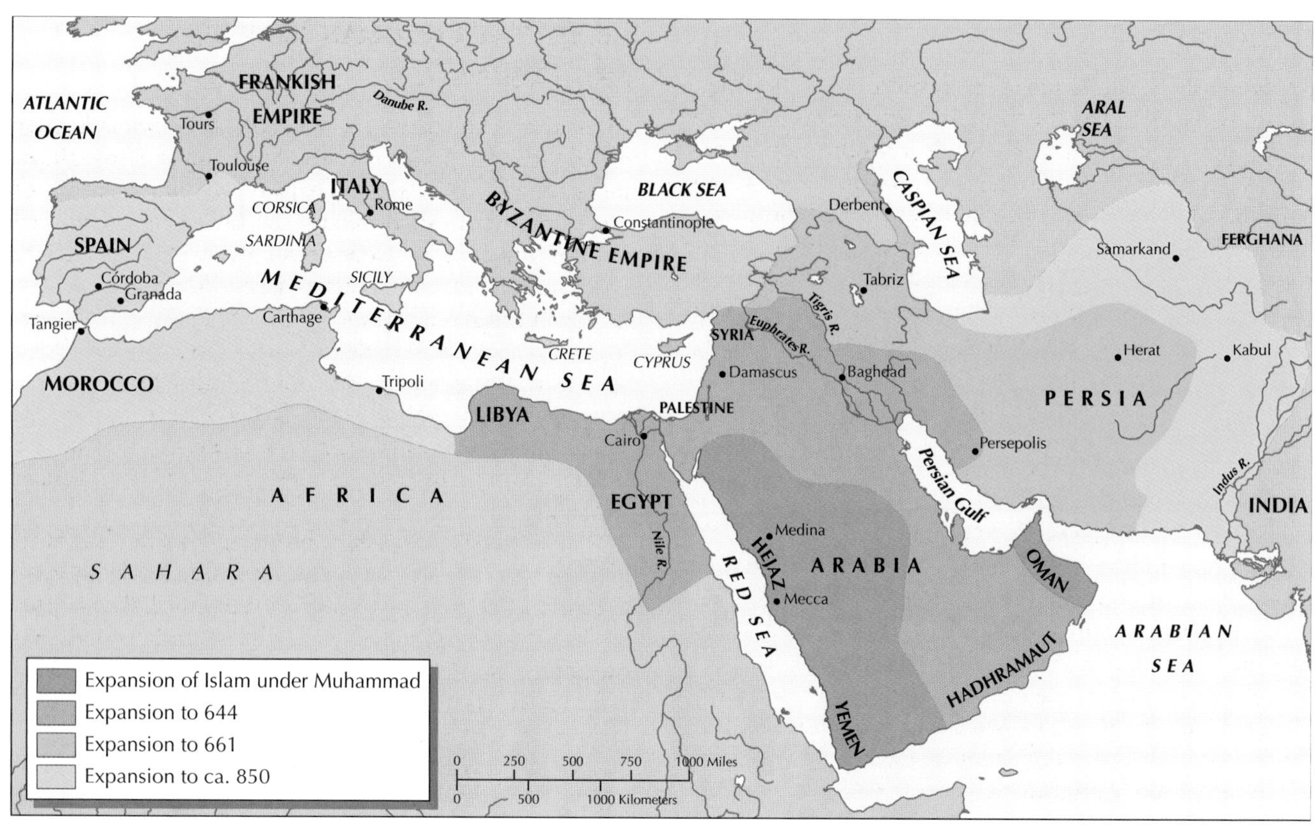

MAP 6.1 The expansion of Islam to ca. 850 C.E.

CHAPTER OVERVIEW

ISLAMIC CIVILIZATION

A new religion emerges from the Middle East

ISLAMIC CIVILIZATION

ISLAM IS THE YOUNGEST OF THE WORLD'S major religions. It was first proclaimed by MUHAMMAD (ca. 570–632) in the town of Mecca, in Arabia, in about the year 610. The followers of Islam, Muslims, consider their faith to be the third and final revelation of God's truth—the first and second manifestations being Judaism and Christianity. Islam, from the Muslim perspective, is seen as a fulfillment of Judaism and Christianity, and thus Muslims accept the sanctity of significant portions of Hebrew and Christian scripture. All three religions share a belief in a single God and are thus monotheistic. In Islam, God is called "Allah."

Islam absorbed foreign influences from both East and West, and served as a bridge between them. Initially, after its founding by Muhammed, Islam provided a unifying function, bringing together under one spiritual banner a multitude of Arabic tribes with varied customs, speaking different languages. As Islam grew, it absorbed aspects of the cultures it conquered. Islam today is the religion of a billion and a half people spread around the globe, one testimony among many to its continued importance spiritually and culturally.

What accounts for the rapid spread of Islam? One explanation is the simplicity of its basic teachings—its five pillars of faith, prayer, charity, fasting, and pilgrimage. Another is the convergence of its religious, political, and military objectives in a messianic mission. And once conquered by Islam, foreign populations were offered economic opportunities, which won as many converts to Islam as did militarism. It spread in part through spiritual appeal, in part through commercial magnetism, and in part through military subjugation. Thus, Islam grew rapidly throughout the world—through Arabia, Egypt, Syria, Iraq, and North Africa, and then on to southern Spain and east Asia to the borders of China.

Religion

Muhammad. Muhammad is revered as a prophet. Muslims consider him the "seal," or final culmination, of the prophetic tradition that extends from the biblical patriarch Abraham through Moses and on to Jesus, whom Muslims also revere as a prophet but do not consider a divinity. The word *Muslim* literally means "one who surrenders"; *Islam* means "submission to God." In the first place, Muslims surrender themselves to the prophet Muhammad and through him to Allah, by obeying Muhammad's instructions for living.

A merchant by profession, Muhammad received, at about the age of forty, what he described as a call to become God's messenger and prophet. According to Islamic tradition, Muhammad heard a voice enjoining him to "recite," to which he responded, "What shall I recite?" The answer came to him in the form of a series of revelations from Allah that lasted more than twenty years, beginning at Mecca and continuing in Medina, a city north of Mecca, to which Muhammad fled in 622 because of hostility to his religious message. He died in Medina ten years later. Muhammad's flight to Medina is known as the *Hijrah* or *Hegira*, and marks the beginning of the Muslim calendar (622 C.E. = 1 for Muslims).

Upon Muhammad's death, a succession of caliphs took his place, which led to a division among the Islamic faithful. In 656 C.E., those who favored choosing only a member of Muhammad's family as caliph, rallied around ALI [AH-lee], Muhammad's cousin. They called themselves SHI'ITES [SHE-ites]. But when Ali was chosen caliph, civil war broke out, Ali was murdered, and the UMAYYAD [OO-MY-ad] dynasty, which bore no family relation to Muhammad, took control. The ninety-year Umayyad rule was marked by prosperity, but Shi'ite resentment remained. In 750, led by the great-grandson of a cousin of Muhammad, Abūl Abbas, the Shi'ites overthrew the Umayyad caliphs, and the capital of Islam was moved east from Damascus to Baghdad, under the ABASSID [a-BAA-sid] dynasty.

The consequences of this transfer of power and change in capital city were significant, shifting the center of gravity from the Mediterranean to Mesopotamia, where many trade routes intersected. Culturally, it meant a transfer of power from a Byzantine world to a Middle Eastern one, in which traditional influences were important. The Caliphate was also transformed, becoming the seat of divine authority with a military force and a salaried bureaucracy to sustain and support it. The Abbasids created significant economic changes as well, improving commerce and banking systems and developing a vast network of trade that encompassed India, China, Ceylon, the East Indies, and reaching to the Baltic via the Caspian and Baltic Seas. It extended on to Russia and then to Africa, the chief trade commodities being gold and slaves.

Islam, the Ottoman Empire, and Europe

In the thirteenth century, a group of Asiatic nomads, later called Ottoman Turks, converted to Islam and brought an increased energy to Muslim expansion. Under a series of powerful rulers, called sultans, the Ottomans conquered the Byzantine city of Constantinople in 1453. A century later, under Sultan Suleyman I (the Magnificent), the Ottoman Empire was at the height of its power. However, by 1700, the Ottoman sultans had lost control over Egypt and Lebanon, and by the early nineteenth century had lost control of Serbia and Greece. Fueled by the fires of nationalism, other Eastern European states, including the Balkans, swept themselves out from under Ottoman control.

The seeds of destruction of Ottoman rule, however, had been sown centuries before. First came a deterioration in the quality of imperial leadership, with the two immediate successors to Suleyman the Magnificent—Selim the Sot and Ibrahim the Crazy—notoriously weak and ineffectual rulers. Second, religious tensions and political factions exacerbated the problem.

Equally important was a military decline occasioned in part by the high cost of maintaining increasingly expensive land and naval forces. In addition, unproductive wars fought against European enemies sapped Ottoman economic strength. And, finally, the advances in science and technology that were fueled by capitalist expansion in Europe did not occur at a similar rate and to the same degree in the Ottoman Empire. As a result, European Christendom increased, Turkish Islam decreased, and the center of economic and military power shifted westward in the mid-nineteenth century.

Nevertheless, the influence of Islam on the West remained considerable, especially on the art, music, and architecture of the Iberian Peninsula. But perhaps the Ottoman empire's greatest achievement was less its influence on the West or its military conquests than its unification of Arab peoples under the banner of Islam and its continuing spread as the world's fastest growing religion.

The Quran. Despite this political strife, Islam remained strong. At the center of the religion is the Quran (or Koran), the scripture of Islam. The word *Quran* means "recitation" and reflects the Muslim belief that the book is a recitation of God's words to Muhammad. Muhammad memorized the messages he received and dictated them to various scribes. Unlike the Hebrew scriptures, which were composed over a period of more than twelve hundred years and which for a long time remained in many different versions, the text of the Quran was definitively established after Muhammad's death by the third caliph, Uthman, around 650.

Slightly shorter than the New Testament, the Quran is divided into 114 **Surahs,** or chapters, which become

Cross Currents

THE SILK TRADE

As early as the first century B.C.E., silk from China began to reach Rome, where it was received with astonishment and admiration. Here was the lightest and most beautiful cloth ever seen, but the secrets of its production remained closely guarded by the Chinese.

The trade route that linked China to the West, and most importantly to Rome, was called the "Silk Road." Less a direct land route than a shifting network of caravan trails between remote kingdoms and trading posts, the Silk Road traversed China from the Han capital of Xi'an, north and west across the Taklamakan Desert, and on to the oasis city of Kashgar. From there, caravans carrying Chinese silk proceeded across the mountain passes of northern India, and on into the ancient Persian cities of Samarkand and Bukhara. Eventually the land route would come to an end at Constantinople, or at the Mediterranean ports of Antioch or Tyre, after which ships would complete the journey to Rome.

Although silk was the primary commodity traded with the West, eastern merchants also loaded camels with ceramics, fur, and lacquered goods. In exchange, they received gold, wool, ivory, amber, and glass from the West. It was Chinese silk, however, that captured the imagination of Rome, so much so that the Romans, who had learned about the Chinese from the Greeks, called the material *serica,* from the Greek word for the Chinese, *Seres.* For the Romans, China was synonymous with silk.

Until the sixth century C.E., silk was regularly supplied to the Romans by the Persians, who monopolized the silk trade and charged high prices. It was the Byzantine emperor Justinian who eventually broke this monopoly in the sixth century. According to the historian Procopius (died C.E. 562), "certain monks from India, knowing with what zeal the emperor Justinian endeavored to prevent the Romans from buying silk from the Persians (who were his enemy), came to visit the emperor and promised him that they would undertake the manufacture of silk." These monks explained to Justinian that silk was made by silkworms fed on mulberry leaves; Justinian promised them "great favors" if they would smuggle the requisite worms and mulberry trees back to Constantinople and begin to cultivate them there for him. This they did, and Justinian initiated a flourishing silk trade that was to become one of the chief sources of his vast wealth.

shorter as the Quran progresses. The first Surah contains 287 **ayas,** or verses; the last contains only three. Each Surah begins with the words, "In the name of Allah, the Beneficent, the Merciful."

The words of the Quran are the first Muslims hear when they are born and the last many hear before death. The Quran forms the core of Muslim education and serves as a textbook for the study of Arabic. Moreover, verses from it are inscribed on the walls of Muslim homes and mosques as decoration and as a reminder of their faith.

An additional important source of Islamic teaching, the **hadith** ("narrative" or "report"), consists of the sayings of Muhammad and anecdotes about him, which were initially passed on orally, but in the ninth century were collected and written down by scholars. Six canonical collections of hadith are used to determine points of Islamic theology and doctrine.

Basic Tenets and the Five Pillars of Islam. The basic tenets of Islam concern the nature of God, creation, humankind, and the afterlife. According to Islam, God is one, immaterial, invisible, and omnipotent. This single God dominates the entire universe with his power and his mercy. He is also the creator of the universe, which, because it is his creation, is also beautiful and good.

The supreme creation of Allah, however, is humankind. As in the Judeo-Christian scriptures, human beings, made in the image of God, are viewed as the culmination of creation. Women and men possess distinct, individual souls, which are immortal, and can live eternally with God—provided individuals live their earthly lives according to Islamic teaching.

To achieve heaven, Muslims must accept belief in Allah as the supreme being and the only God. They must also practice their religion by fulfilling the obligations characterized as the "five pillars" of Islam. These are repetition of the creed, daily prayer, almsgiving, fasting during Ramadan, and pilgrimage to Mecca.

The Islamic creed (*shahadah*) consists of a single sentence: *La ilaha illa Allah; Muhammad rasul Allah* ("There is no God but Allah; Muhammad is the messenger of Allah"). All Muslims must say this creed slowly, thoughtfully, and with conviction at least once during their lives, though many practicing Muslims recite it several times each day.

Daily prayer (*salat*) is recited five times: at dawn, midday, midafternoon, sunset, and nightfall. In Muslim communities, *muezzins* call the faithful to prayer from mosque towers. Whether the people pray where they are or go to the mosque, they must cleanse themselves of impurities before praying. During prayer, Muslims face Mecca and perform a series of ritual gestures that includes bowing and prostration.

Charity or almsgiving (*zakat*) is the third pillar of Islam. In addition to ad hoc giving to the poor, Islam instructs its followers to contribute one-fortieth of their income and assets to the needy. Originally a form of tax, today the *zakat* is a respected form of holy offering.

The fourth pillar is the fast (*sawm*) during the holy month of Ramadan, the ninth month of the Muslim lunar calendar. The fast includes abstaining from food, drink, medicine, tobacco, and sexual intercourse from sunrise to sundown. Moreover, during the month of fasting, Muslims are expected to recite the entire Quran at least once. Ramadan is considered the Islamic holy month because it was during Ramadan that Muhammad received his initial call as a prophet and during Ramadan that he made his historic flight from Mecca to Medina ten years later.

The final pillar of Islam is the pilgrimage (*hajj*) to Mecca, which all healthy adult Muslims are expected to complete at least once (fig. 6.1).

Islamic Mysticism: The Sufis. Like all other major religions, Islam has its mystics. Because it developed in Byzantium, where there was a strong Jewish and Christian mystical tradition, and also in India, which had its own ascetic tradition, Islam was influenced to find its own mystical path. This path was followed most powerfully by the **Sufis.** The word *sufi* means "woolen" and refers to the coarse woolen clothing the Sufis wear as a sign of their rejection of worldly comforts.

Table 6–1 FIVE PILLARS OF ISLAM
1. Repetition of the creed (***shahadah***): There is no God but Allah; Muhammad is the messenger of Allah.
2. Daily prayer (***salat***): Dawn, midday, midafternoon, sunset, nightfall
3. Almsgiving (charity): One-fortieth of income and assets (***zakat***)
4. Fasting during Ramadan (***sawm***): Abstention from food, drink, medicine, tobacco, sex from sunrise to sundown
5. Pilgrimage (***hajj***): Once in a lifetime pilgrimage to Mecca, the Muslim holy city

FIGURE 6.1 *Jesus Watching Muhammad Leave Mecca,* from a medieval Persian manuscript, from Al-Biruni, "Chronicle of Ancient Nations." ORMS. 161.f.10v. Courtesy of Edinburgh University Library. Muhammad leaves Mecca on camelback in the *hijrah* or emigration in the year 622 that became the founding moment of Islam, escaping the wrath of the polytheistic Meccans who rejected his message of faith in the one true God. Regarded in Islam as one of Muhammad's prophetic predecessors, Jesus is shown looking on approvingly, in an image that both suggests continuity and also shows Muhammad about to go beyond the religious understandings of his day.

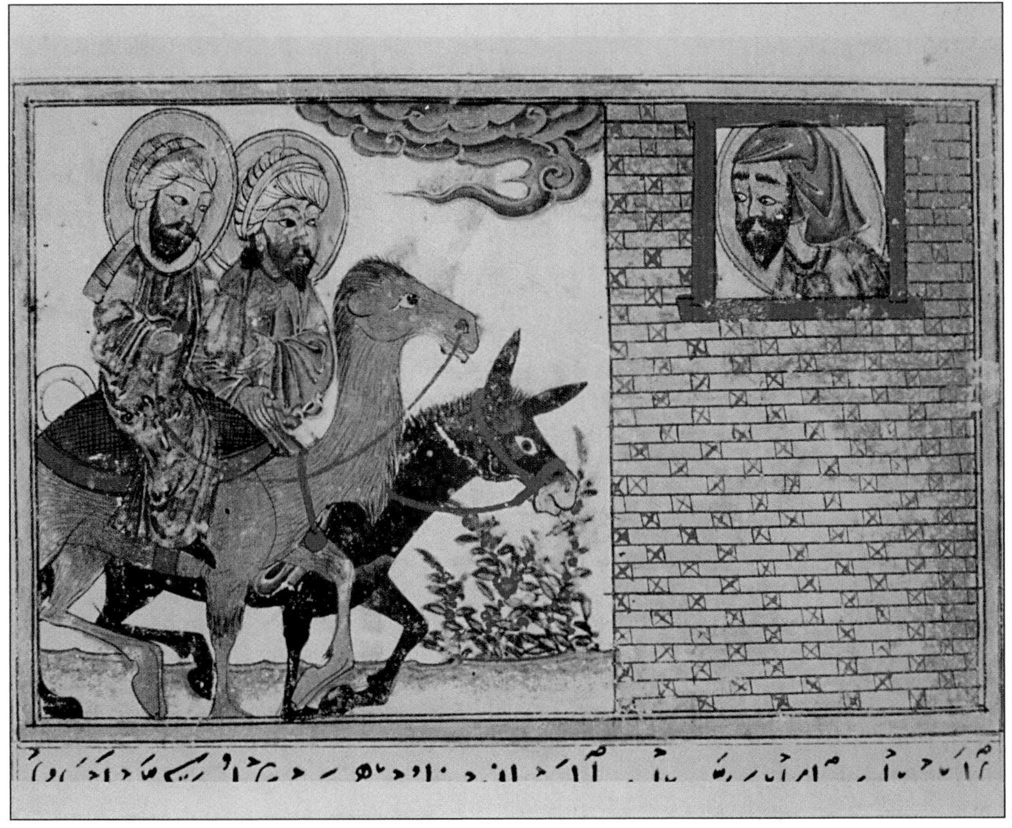

Table 6–2 ISLAMIC AND CHRISTIAN BELIEFS

Although Islam shares many beliefs with Christianity, there are important differences between the doctrines of these Western faiths. The table lists some of the fundamental ones.

Muslims	Christians
Revere Jesus as a great prophet.	Worship Jesus as God.
Believe Jesus ascended into heaven but did not die on the cross.	Believe in the resurrection and ascension of Jesus.
Believe in the sin of Adam and Eve, but not the idea of inherited sin for all.	Believe all humanity inherited the original sin of Adam and Eve.
Accept the Torah, Psalms, and Gospels as sacred scripture, but do not accept the rest of the Hebrew or Christian scriptures.	Accept as sacred scripture a larger biblical canon than Muslims, one that includes historical and prophetic books as well as poetic and wisdom literature.

Although the Sufis trace their lineage back to the seventh century, it is more likely the movement began in earnest in the ninth century, when there was an increase in materialism; the Sufis' choice of austerity was a direct response to this. During the twelfth century, the Sufis organized themselves into monastic orders, much like the monks of medieval Christendom. A convert to a Sufi order was called a *fakir* ("poor man") or *dervish* ("beggar"), terms intended to indicate the monk's experience of poverty and begging. Although the monastic practices of the Sufis varied, they generally included strict discipline along with abstinence, poverty, and sometimes celibacy.

One of the more notable features of Sufism in early Islam is that it recognized women as fully equal to men. A woman could become a Sufi leader or *shaykh* (feminine *shaykha*). Among the most prominent of *shaykhas* was RABIA AL-ADAWIYYA [RAA-be-ah] (d. 801), who preached an intensely devotional love of God with a corresponding withdrawal from the ordinary world. Her emphasis on worshiping God out of pure love, rather than for either temporal or eternal reward, served as both an inspiration and a model for other Sufis.

Prominent among Sufi ideas is the soul's yearning and perpetual search for God, since God is the ultimate source of all life. This notion is expressed in the poetry of the thirteenth-century Persian mystic JALALODDIN RUMI [ROO-me] (1207–73), whose poems often feature a lover seeking his beloved as a metaphor for the soul's seeking of God.

PHILOSOPHY

Avicenna and Averroes. If the Quran expresses Islamic theology and the Sufis the mystical element of Islamic thought, Islam's philosophical bent is best figured by AVICENNA [ah-vee-SEN-ah] (980–1037) and AVERROES [a-VER-o-ease] (1126–1198).

Better known as a doctor than as a philosopher, Avicenna articulated the beliefs of Islam in terms drawn from Aristotle and Plato, wedding two divergent Greek philosophical traditions as well as linking Greek philosophy with Islamic beliefs. Following Aristotle, Avicenna argued that God was the creator, or Prime Cause, of all that exists, a necessary being whose existence and essence were one and the same.

The second major voice of Islamic philosophy was raised not in Arabia but in Spain by Averroes, another physician-philosopher. Like Avicenna, Averroes attempted to build a bridge between the philosophy of Aristotle and the more Neoplatonically based theology of Islamic thinkers.

By following Aristotle's lead in paying renewed attention to the natural world, Averroes paved the way for Thomas Aquinas (see Chapter 12) to develop his scholastic philosophical system, which was also indebted to Aristotle and which, like the philosophy of Averroes, privileged reason above faith. Both Aquinas and Averroes, for example, argue that the existence of God can be proved by reason without the aid of revelation.

Averroes and Avicenna helped preserve the Western intellectual tradition through their reverence for education, books, and philosophy. The libraries acquired by Islamic rulers and philosophers continued the philosophic tradition that began in the West with the Greeks and found renewed expression in the religious thought of the Middle Ages and the scientific spirit of later centuries.

MATH, SCIENCE, AND SCHOLARSHIP

Among the most important contributions of Islamic culture to the West was Arabic numbers and the concept of zero, a discovery of Al-Khwaizmi (780–850), arguably the greatest of Muslim scholars. Among his achievements was the invention of algebra. Before his introduction of the nine numbers we know today and the placeholder, zero, the West made do with Roman numerals, a cumbersome system, far inferior to the elegance of the Arabic numeric system. A further numerical refinement was made by Al Uglidisi in the next century—the concept of decimal fractions, as for example, in the value of Pi: 3.1416.

In addition to their mathematical inventions, Muslim scholars made a number of key scientific discoveries and contributions. Muslim chemists invented the process of distillation and created the distillate, alkuhl (alcohol), which is forbidden to Muslims. Islamic astronomers made more precise instruments such as the astrolabe, which is used to measure the altitude of stars above the horizon. The Egyptian Muslim scientist, Al Hazen (d. 1038) advanced the field of optics and improved the technology for making and grinding lenses. Muslim physicians wrote books on diseases such as rabies, measles, and smallpox, among them Rhazes (d. 932), director of a Baghdad hospital. Moreover, the famous Jewish doctor, Moses Maimonides, was trained in Arabic medicine. Maimonides

Critical Thinking

THE PROBLEM OF HEADSCARVES

With the influx of Muslim immigrants from northern Africa into France in the past few decades, a number of social and cultural issues have arisen. One of them involves the wearing of headscarves in public by girls and women. On the one hand, this would seem to be a simple matter of freedom of expression—choosing what to wear is a basic right. On the other hand, wearing the headscarf is seen as expressing allegiance to Islam, and France prohibits public expressions of religious affiliation. What do you think should be done about this issue? Why?

and other Arabic-trained Jewish physicians were consulted by the sultan of Baghdad and by the Pope in their respective centuries.

In addition to such practical mathematical and scientific contributions to knowledge, Islamic scholars, following the admonition of Muhammad to "seek knowledge," preserved numerous Greek manuscripts of Plato, Aristotle, Gales, Ptolemy, and others. These scholars copied, edited, and translated the Greek texts into Arabic. They also provided commentaries on Aristotle's works and preserved much knowledge of botany, astrology, and medicine among Greek-influenced Mediterranean peoples. All of this scholarship and practical knowledge became enormously influential in the development of medieval European universities.

SCHOLARLY CROSS FERTILIZATION

During the early Middle Ages, when Islam was born in the seventh century, there was little contact between Europe and the Arab world. While Arab power consolidated and Islam spread over the next centuries, Arab scholars picked up where the Greeks had left off. Arab mathematicians, for example, became masters of algebra and trigonometry, adding to the Greek invention of geometry. Translation was the crux, as Arabic scholars translated Greek and Indian texts into Arabic, and then translated these and other Arabic works into Latin and Hebrew. Medieval Arab scholars, thus, served as a bridge linking ancient and medieval scholarship of the world, centuries before the European Renaissance.

ISLAMIC ART AND ARCHITECTURE

Islamic art is not the art of one particular group of people, nor that of one country. Rather, it is the art associated with the life of one person, Muhammad, and the teachings of one book, the Quran. It is therefore a fusion of many different cultures, the most influential of which are Turkish, Persian, and, particularly and originally, Arabic.

Mosques. There is little evidence of art in Arabia before Islam and, at first, Islam did not encourage art. Islam opposes idol worship—Muhammad had all pagan idols destroyed. Furthermore, a Muslim could pray anywhere without the need of religious architecture. Nonetheless, in the late seventh century, Muslim rulers started to build palaces and **mosques**—the buildings in which Muslims assemble for religious purposes. In an attempt to compete with Byzantium, the caliphs built with materials and on a scale to rival Christian churches. Typically, a mosque is rectangular in plan, with an open court, and a fountain in the center used for purification. Covered walkways, with flat roofs supported on columns and arches, lead to the side, on which is located the **mihrab,** a small niche indicating the side facing Mecca. All mosques are oriented toward Mecca, Muhammad's place of birth, and it is the direction in which Muslims turn when praying. **Minarets** are towers beside mosques from which the faithful are called to prayer by the **muezzin,** the person who ascends a spiral staircase to a platform at the top.

Construction of the mosque at Cordova in Spain was started in 786. The plan (fig. 6.2) is simple, making it easy to enlarge the mosque by adding more aisles, as was done

FIGURE 6.2 Mosque, Cordova, begun 786, plan. Although the original structure was enlarged four times, the traditional plan continued to be organized and precise, as if laid out on a grid. The mosque includes a court, prayer hall, and arcades.

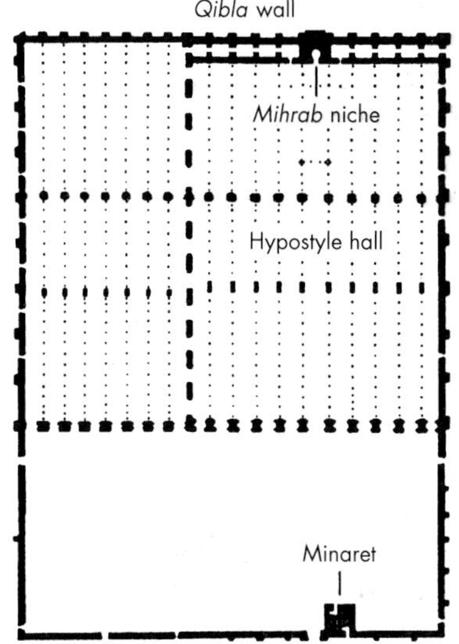

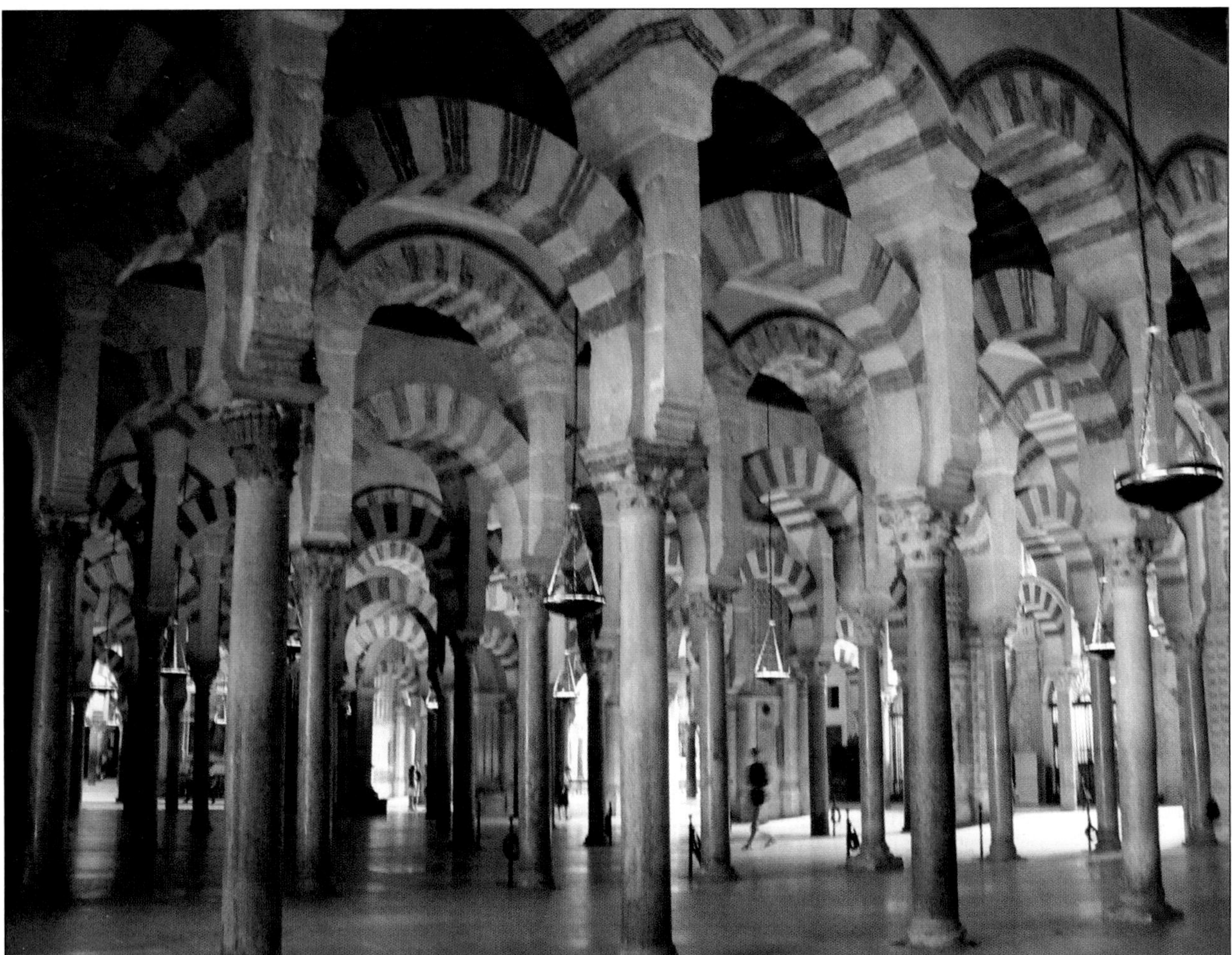

FIGURE 6.3 Mosque, Cordova, begun 786, interior. Decoration in plaster and marble creates an effect of delicacy and lightness, of the material made immaterial. Walls have not one plane but many, and the layers of space overlap, becoming meshlike.

on several occasions. The interior (fig. 6.3) contains hundreds of columns. A visitor must follow the aisles through this forest to reach the mihrab side. There are two tiers of arches, which create a light and airy interior, an impression enhanced by the contrasting stripes of the **voussoirs**—the wedge-shaped stones that make up the arches. The individual arches are the characteristically Muslim horseshoe shape. The result is a fluid, almost mystical space.

The Mosque of Sultan Sulayman (Suleiman) (fig. 6.4), built 1550–57, is the main mosque of Istanbul in Turkey, an enormous complex including tombs, hospitals, and facilities for traveling merchants that symbolizes the city's importance as the center of Western Islamic civilization. The architect of the mosque was SINAN [sin-AHN], the greatest master of his day. The mosque appears to build up in waves, as does Hagia Sophia (see Chapter 5), which was built a thousand years earlier in the same city: The Muslims were clearly attempting to rival the Byzantines. The very tall minarets give emphasis to the vertical; those at Hagia Sophia are later Muslim additions. The similarity between the buildings continues with the domes for, like Hagia Sophia, the mosque has a large dome, two big half domes, and several smaller ones. The surface decoration of the facade is so light and lacy that it makes the building appear delicate and fragile. The courtyard is constructed with columns and arches but, rather than a flat roof, there is a series of domes—the same roofing system employed in the mosque itself, creating a sense of unity between inside and out.

The interior of the mosque (fig. 6.5) has a ring of windows at the base of the dome, which makes the dome appear weightless and floating, and a large number of windows in the walls, turning them into airy screens. The shimmering tile decoration has the effect of separating the surface from its underlying structural function. Ornamental patterns and inscriptions are found

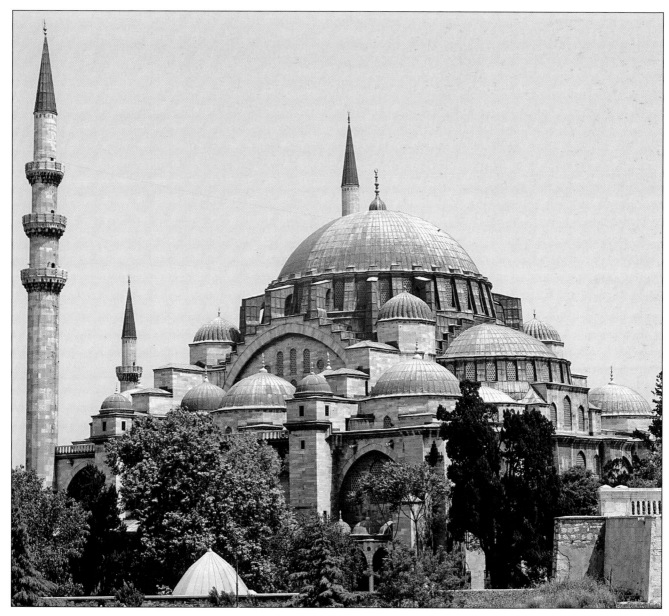

FIGURE 6.4 Sinan, Mosque of Sultan Sulayman, Istanbul, 1550–57, exterior. Like Hagia Sophia, built in the same city by the Christian Byzantines a millennium earlier (see fig. 5.13), this Islamic mosque consists of a large central dome with abutting half domes and smaller semi domes.

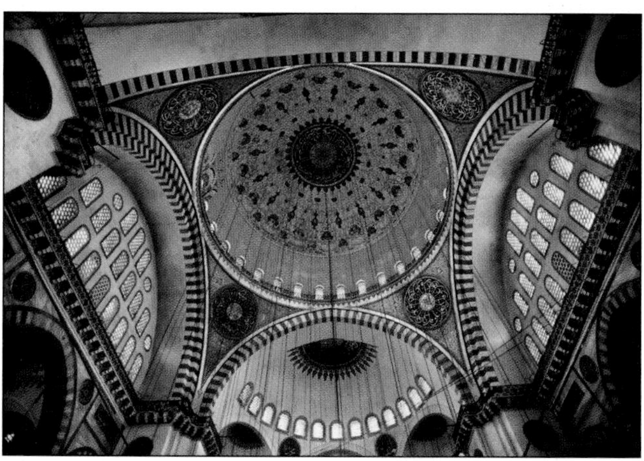

FIGURE 6.5 Sinan, Mosque of Sultan Sulayman, Istanbul, 1550–57, interior. The interior of this Islamic mosque, with a ring of windows at the base of the dome, is worthy of comparison with the interiors of the Byzantine churches of Hagia Sophia and St. Mark's (see figs. 5.15 and 5.17).

Then & Now

JERUSALEM

The possession of the city of Jerusalem has historically been contested by three major world faiths: Judaism, Christianity, and Islam. The city's history is one of warring religious factions, all claiming its holy ground for themselves. Today, within a space of five hundred yards, sometimes in peaceful coexistence, sometimes not, lie the western wall of ancient Israel's Temple of Solomon, the rock marking the place of Jesus' tomb, and the Muslim shrine designating the site where Muhammad is believed to have ascended to heaven.

Archaeological evidence indicates that Jerusalem began in the Bronze Age as a mere nine-acre settlement at the edge of the Judaean desert. The Hebrew king David made Jerusalem the capital of the unified country of ancient Israel during the early tenth century B.C.E. He extended the city limits, building towers and battlements throughout. The city's most glorious years, however, occurred during the reign of King Solomon, David's successor. Solomon built a magnificent temple to house the holy Ark of the Covenant. To this temple he attached an equally magnificent palace while also extending the city walls and further enlarging its defenses.

Numerous times in its history, Jerusalem has been captured or destroyed. Alexander the Great took the city without resistance in 332 B.C.E. In 250 B.C.E., Ptolemy the Great destroyed the city walls. In 168 B.C.E., the Syrian king Antiochus Epiphanes enslaved Jerusalem's inhabitants. The Roman leader Pompey captured the city in the first century B.C.E., and the Roman general Titus crushed a rebellion a century later, leveling the city in the process. A thousand years later, the Crusaders conquered the city, taking it from the Muslims, and leaving it little more than a military outpost, dispersing those citizens who were spared from death.

Muslims, Jews, and Christians all lay claim to the Temple Mount, the site of Solomon's Temple. For Muslims, the Temple Mount and the magnificent mosque constructed on it, the Dome of the Rock (fig. 6.6), are second only to Mecca and Medina as holy sites. For Jews and Christians, this was the site of the patriarch Abraham's aborted sacrifice of his son Isaac. For members of all three faiths, Solomon's Temple was the site of Jesus's debate with the rabbis and a place where he preached.

The city of Jerusalem is constructed out of the history and cultures of many peoples. Roman vaults are coupled with Christian convents; an Arab arch cannot be separated from a Jewish wall. This complex mix of religions and cultures makes Jerusalem a truly multicultural city, whose bedrock is a faith in God, albeit a God called by various names, and conceived under a variety of identities.

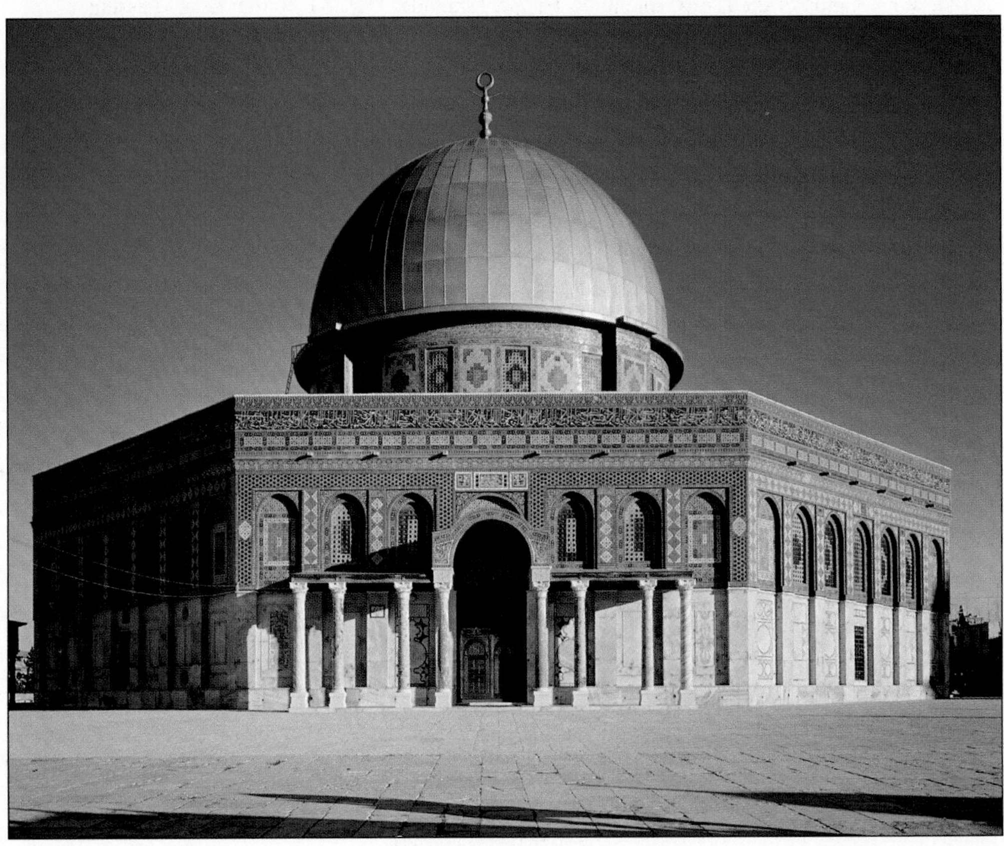

FIGURE 6.6 Dome of the Rock, Jerusalem, late 680s–692.

everywhere. The tiles are often floral and polychromatic; ceramicists and architects worked together to create an effect whereby visitors feel surrounded by gardens of luxurious flowers.

Alhambra Palace. The Alhambra Palace in Granada, Spain, is one of the finest examples of Islamic architecture. A palace fortress, the Alhambra is the most remarkable legacy of the Nasirid dynasty, which ruled southern Spain from 1232 until the united armies of Catholic Spain under the leadership of Ferdinand and Isabella chased the last Muslim rulers out of the country in 1492.

The Alhambra is built on top of a hill overlooking the city of Granada, providing spectacular views and a cool respite from the heat of southern Spain. Surrounded by gardens built in terraces, the palace is irregular in plan, with several courts and a number of towers added by successive rulers.

Here, architectural function is obscured. Walls become lacelike webs. Surfaces are decorated with intricate patterns that disguise and seem to dissolve material substance. The solidity of stone is eclipsed as domes filled with designs seem to become floating lace canopies. The dissolution of matter is a fundamental principle of Islamic art. This style is unlike any other in the history of art.

Decoration is made of tile and stucco, which is either modeled in low relief or is built up in layers that are then cut away to create the effect of stalactites. Surfaces are covered with a seemingly infinite variety of complex geometric patterns. Decoration is exquisite, achieving the height of sophistication, refinement, and richness. Ornament is profuse, yet the whole is controlled by a predilection for symmetry and repeated rhythms. Much use is made of calligraphic designs, including decorative Cufic writing, floral patterns, and purely abstract linear elements. Arabic **calligraphy**—fine handwriting—pervades Islamic art, appearing not only in manuscripts, but also on buildings, textiles, pottery, and elsewhere. The popularity of calligraphy is in part a result of traditional Muslim iconoclasm. Because the figurative arts were discouraged, artists elaborated the abstract beauty of handwriting.

The Court of the Lions (fig. 6.7), built 1354–91 by Mohammed V, is probably the most famous part of the Alhambra. It is named for the stone lions that form the base of a fountain in the middle of the court. The Court of the Lions is considered the quintessence of the Moorish style.

FIGURE 6.7 Court of the Lions, Alhambra Palace, Granada, 1354–91. Rather than stressing the supporting structure, emphasis is on the decorative surfaces, the slender columns, and the extreme sophistication with which all surfaces are ornamented.

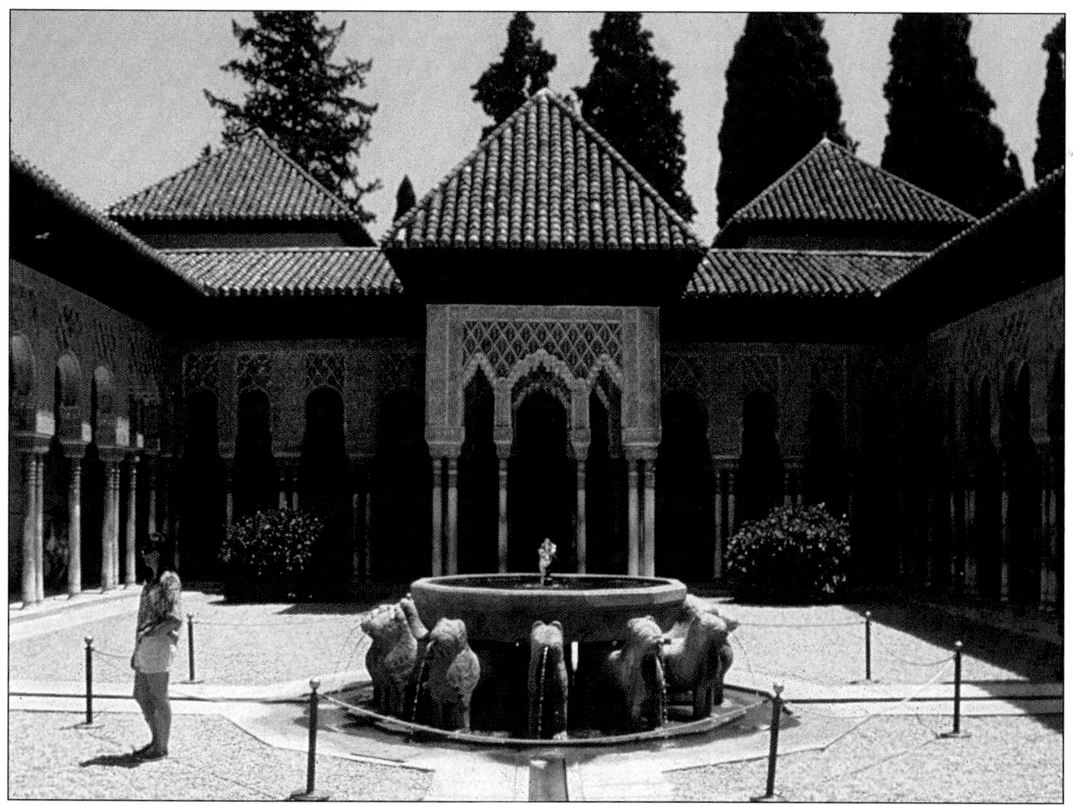

Slender columns surround the courtyard, arranged singly or in pairs, and support a series of arches of fantastic shapes.

Another palace that accommodated a different way of life is Topkapi Palace in Istanbul, the vast complex of buildings and courtyards covering acres of land. Topkapi means "Cannon Gate." The Ottoman Turks conquered Istanbul (then called Constantinople) in 1453; Sultan Mehmet II began construction of the palace in 1459. The Ottoman Empire, which centered in today's Turkey, was at its peak of power during the sixteenth and seventeenth centuries. From 1465 until 1856, Topkapi Palace was the official residence of the Ottoman Sultans.

Each of the four courts of the palace was used for a different function. Ceremonies and festivals were held by the rulers in the Second Court. The sultans actually lived in the smaller Third Court, which includes the Audience Hall of the Sultans, built under Mehmet II. The harem area (fig. 6.8), constructed in the late sixteenth century, was comprised of almost 400 rooms, including a hospital, kitchen, laundry, several bathrooms, and a suite of forty rooms and a courtyard for the Sultan's mother, the most powerful woman in the harem. Within the harem area is the Imperial Hall, also called the Festival or Throne Room. Housing the throne of the Sultan, it is the largest and grandest room in the harem.

Topkapi Palace has three separate kitchens (one of which was used specifically for preparing desserts). Annual consumption is recorded to have included approximately 30,000 chickens and 23,000 sheep to feed the approximately 4,000 people who lived here when Topkapi Palace was at its peak.

Ceramics and Miniature Painting. Islamic pictorial arts were curtailed by Muhammad's opposition to idolatry. The Quran's view that statues are the work of the devil largely eliminated sculpture. The lions in the Court of the Lions at the Alhambra Palace are rare examples, and, moreover, they serve a functional purpose, acting as supports for the water basin of the fountain. Although the Quran does not mention painting or any other artistic medium, the argument against the portrayal of human figures or animals—or, indeed, anything living—is that only God can create life and the artist must not try to imitate God. Thus mosques contain no figurative representations; geometric and plant designs were preferred. Nonetheless, Islamic art does include some images of living things, but they are not large scale, nor made for public display. Instead, such images are usually restricted to small-scale paintings or functional objects, such as textiles and vessels (fig. 6.9). Thus, despite this ban on figurative images, a rich

FIGURE 6.8 Harem Courtyard, late sixteenth century, Topkapi Palace, Istanbul, built 1459f. The palace consists of a series of rectangular spaces with four open courtyards, a harem section, fountains, pavilions, mosques, and domes.

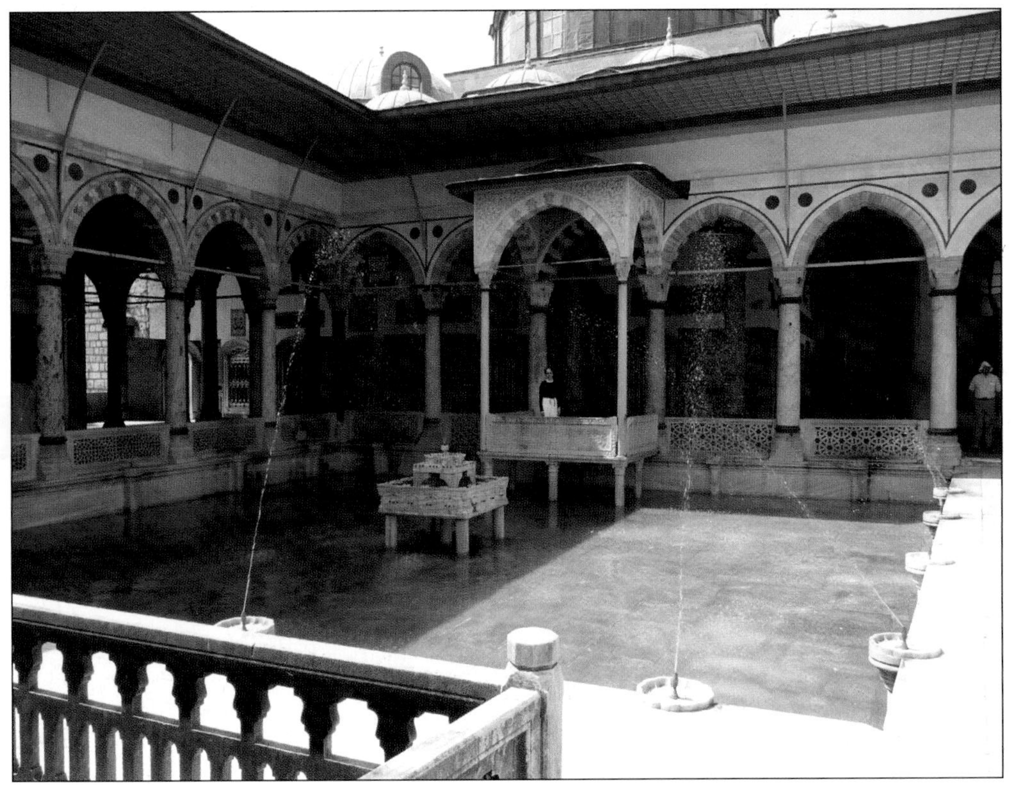

Cross Currents

Paper: Islam's Gift to the West

The paper on which the words you are reading are printed owes a great deal to Islamic civilization. Although paper was invented in China during the first century C.E., it was Muslim merchants traveling the Silk Road routes in the eighth century who first brought it to the West. Moreover, it was through Islamic culture in North Africa that paper found its way to Europe during the early Middle Ages. Islamic civilization thus provides the link between the invention of paper in ancient China and its extensive distribution after the invention of printing in fifteenth-century Germany. In both Islamic and European civilizations, paper became an effective medium for conveying religious beliefs—through many beautifully calligraphied versions of the Quran and handsomely printed versions of the Bible, both of which reached a vast audience of readers. And though digital images and electronic transmission of information comprise the most recent mass communications technology, paper remains a vital medium for communicating ideas and expressing artistic visions.

tradition of figurative miniature painting extends from the thirteenth to the late seventeenth century, depicting the hadith, or traditional legends appended to the Quran, as well as the poetry of religious mystics. For example, *A Sheik Meditating in a Pavilion* (fig. 6.10) illustrates a scene from the poem *Haft Aurang* (*The Seven Thrones*), written by the Persian poet JAMI [JAR-me] (1414–1492).

Figure 6.9 Bowl, from Iran, twelfth or thirteenth century, ceramic, diameter $8\frac{1}{2}''$ (21.7 cm), Khalili Collection, London. The Naser D. Khalili Collection of Islamic Art (POT 12), Photograph © NOUR Foundation. © Copyright The British Museum. The figurative design showing a couple in a garden was popular in the period. The decorative bands of script that are around the rim of the plate repeat two words: "Glory" and "Piety."

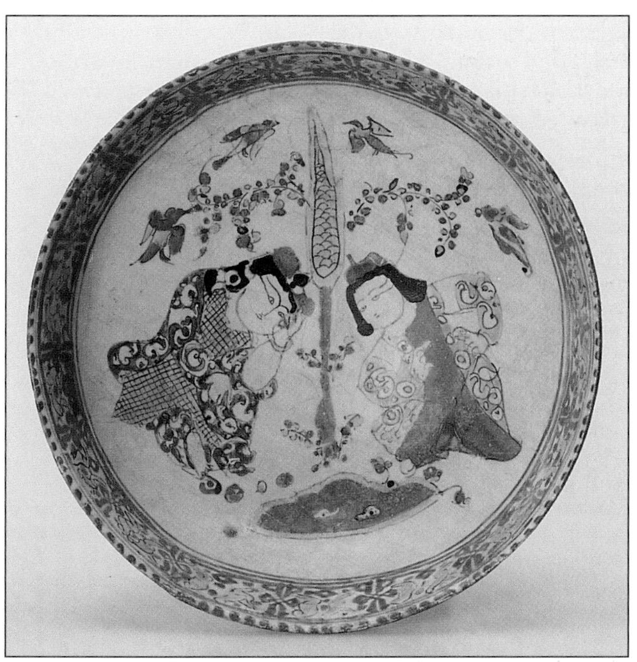

Literature

Arabic and Persian Poetry. Like English poetry, Arabic poetry appeared in written form around 700 C.E. as Arab lexicographers and philologists began to collect and record poems that had survived orally in various Arab tribal traditions. These poems had long been chanted by *rawi*, professional reciters, who kept the verse alive.

Figure 6.10 *A Sheik Meditating in a Pavilion*, illustrating the poem *Haft Aurang* (*The Seven Thrones*), by Jami, 1556–65, $13\frac{1}{2}'' \times 9\frac{1}{8}''$ (34.3 × 23.9 cm). Courtesy of the Freer Gallery of Art, Smithsonian Institution, Washington, DC. The delicacy of the technique and the decoratively patterned two-dimensional quality of Islamic painting is similar to Chinese painting (see Chapter 8).

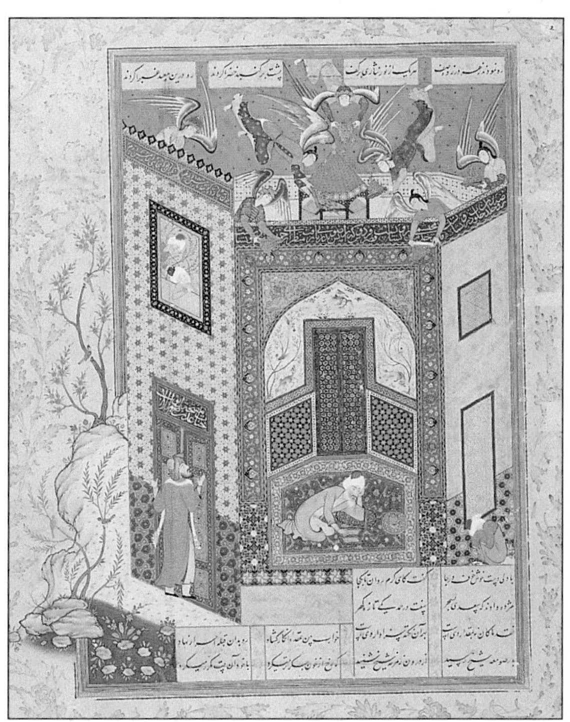

One of the oldest forms of Arabic poetry is the *qasidah*, a highly formalized ode. The *qasidah* has three parts: (1) a visit to an abandoned encampment to find the beloved, whose departure the poet laments; (2) the poet's journey to find her, replete with descriptions of flowers and animals, especially his camel, which he eulogizes; and (3) a eulogy on a neighbor or tribe that often includes a tribute to the poet's own ancestry. The *qasidah* ranges from 30 to 120 lines in length, each line ending with the same rhyme. Central to any *qasidah* is the image, or rather a series of juxtaposed images, that vividly expresses what the poet has observed.

When Arabs invaded and conquered Persia in 637 C.E., they brought with them Islam and their Arabic script, which the Persians adopted in place of their complicated ideograms. Many Arabic words passed into Persian and some literary forms underwent modification. With the adoption of the Arabic script came an explosion of Persian poetry, including work by the early Persian poet FIRDAWSI [fear-DOW-see] (late tenth–early eleventh century). Like other Persian poets of his time and later, Firdawsi wrote in both Arabic and Persian, translating poems readily from one language to the other. The first major Persian poet and one of the greatest, Firdawsi wrote the epic *Shahnamah* (*Book of Kings*), a work of sixty thousand couplets (fig. 6.11).

One consequence of translating Persian poems into Arabic was the introduction into Arabic poetry of the quatrain (*ruba'i*, plural *ruba'iyat*), a Persian form of four lines with rhyming pattern of AABA. The *ruba'i* is familiar to readers of English through Edward Fitzgerald's translation of *The Ruba'iyat of Omar Khayyam*. The influence of the two poetic traditions, however, was reciprocal, and the Arabic *qasidah* was taken into Persian. The exchange of forms also includes the *ghazal*, a short Arabic love lyric of five to fifteen couplets believed to be of Persian origin.

Persian poetry is almost always lyrical, and its most frequent subject is love. Common features include the distraught lover, who, anguished over imagined slights, is completely at the mercy of a haughty and indifferent beloved. Some scholars have suggested the relationship of sorrowful lover to paramour is a metaphor for the relationship between the believer and God. In fact, there is a school of Persian poetry, influenced by the mystical ideas of Sufism, that uses many of the same images as love poetry. The ambiguity of subject found in some Persian love poetry can also be found in the biblical Song of Songs. In addition, the technique of using the language of physical love to describe the love of divinity is analogous to that of certain Western poets, such as John Donne and Emily Dickinson. Persian writers, moreover, have a long history of using mysticism and symbolism to veil meaning in politically perilous times.

A further characteristic of Persian poetry is its celebration of spring, a time of renewal and hope. Seasonal celebration has a prominence in Persian poetry for a number

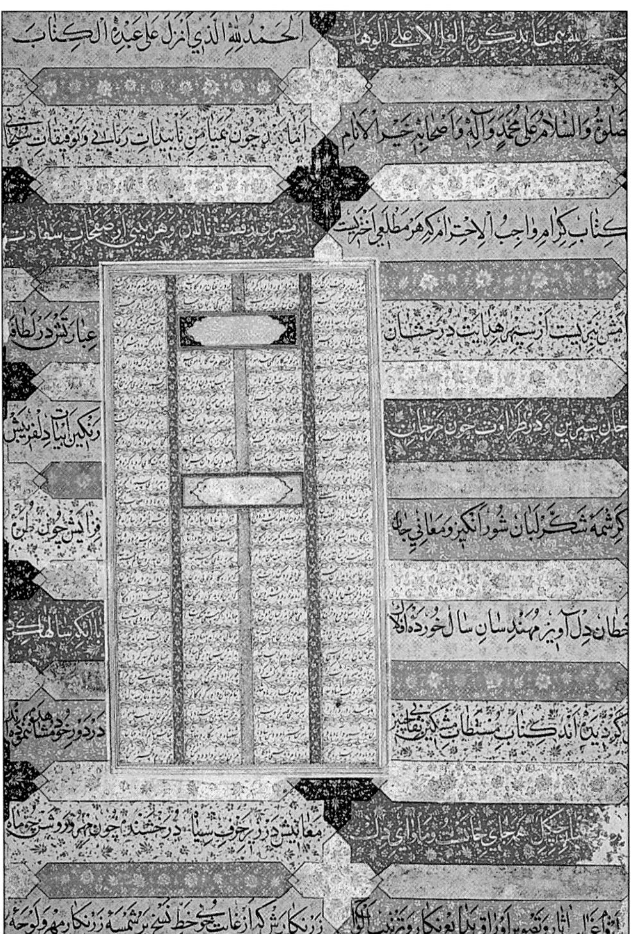

FIGURE 6.11 Persian, Safavid, page from a manuscript of the *Shahnamah of Firdawsi*, Shiraz, Iran. 1562–83, opaque watercolor, ink, and gold on paper, 13″ × $18\frac{11}{16}$ (3 × 43 cm). Francis Bartlett Donation and Picture Fund (14.692). Reproduced with permission. © 2005 Museum of Fine Arts, Boston. All Rights Reserved. Until recent times, every Muslim text began with the phrase "In the name of Allah." Called the *bismillah*, the phrase opens the Quran. Here it is at the top right hand corner (Arabic texts read right to left). To write the *bismillah* as beautifully as possible is the highest form of Islamic art.

of reasons. One reason has to do with the climate and topography of Persia, an area that is largely desert, in which the blossoming of flowers in the spring is an especially welcome sight. Another is that, since Persians celebrate their solar New Year on March 21, the first day of spring, the season is associated with gift-giving and a renewal of hope. In addition, Persian poets often celebrate the transience of the flowers of spring as emblems of the transience of earthly joy.

Arabic Prose: The Thousand and One Nights. One of the most famous of all Arabic works of literature is *The Thousand and One Nights*, better known in the West as *The Arabian Nights*. Of Indo-Persian origin, the stories recounted in *The Thousand and One Nights* were introduced

Connections

Sufism, Dancing, and Music

Sufism attempted to achieve direct contact with God through mystical trance. One method of achieving trance and thus connection with the divine was through dance, especially the spinning circular form of dance that became associated with the "whirling dervishes." Dance provided the Sufi with an outlet for emotion and an opportunity to achieve ecstasy through psychic illumination in trance.

The music that accompanied such dancing would probably have been primarily percussive, for example, a drum beat, that pounded out a steady rhythm, or would perhaps have included wooden flutes, tambourines, or even a stringed instrument, such as an *ud*, or Arabic lute.

The painting reproduced here (fig. 6.12) appears in a Turkish manuscript dating from the sixteenth century. The dancers in the center raise their hands in ecstatic celebration, while the figures in the foreground may have succumbed to dizziness. Music and dancing were disapproved of by some Muslims, but they were nonetheless practiced by many Sufi orders, for whom the dance may be seen as representing the soul's movement toward God.

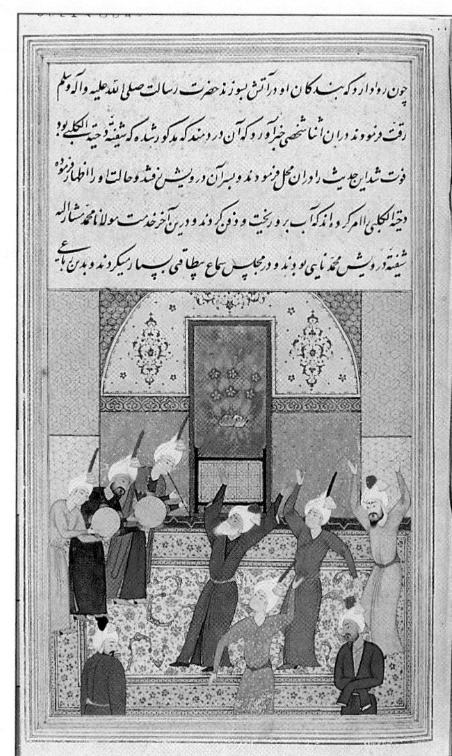

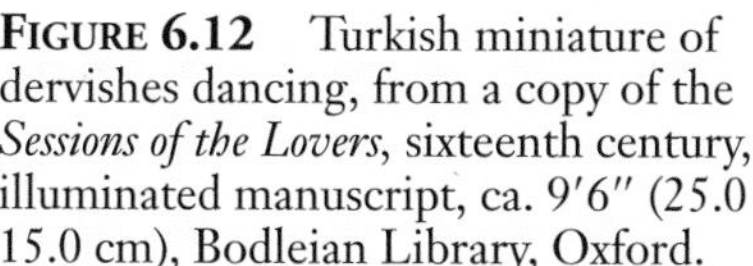

Figure 6.12 Turkish miniature of dervishes dancing, from a copy of the *Sessions of the Lovers*, sixteenth century, illuminated manuscript, ca. 9′6″ (25.0 15.0 cm), Bodleian Library, Oxford.

into written Arabic some time during the tenth century and subsequently embellished, polished, and expanded. Different as their ethnic origins may be—Persian, Indian, Arabic—the stories of *The Thousand and One Nights* became assimilated to reflect the cultural and artistic history of the Arabic Islamic tradition.

The stories cast a romantic glow of Eastern enchantment, and, although they do not chronicle the adventures of a single hero as do medieval narratives such as the *Song of Roland* or the *Divine Comedy*, they are linked by the device of a single narrator, Shahrazad, the wife of the Persian king Shahrayar, who is entertained night after night by her storytelling, which prolongs her life and cures his hatred of women. The stories are remarkable for their blending of the marvelous with the everyday.

Music

During the period of the four orthodox caliphs, or representatives of Muhammad, who reigned from the prophet's death in 632 until 661, music was classed as one of the *malahi*, or forbidden pleasures. Associated with frivolity, sensuality, and luxury, it was deemed to be at odds with the religious values of Islam. With the advent of the Umayyad dynasty (661–750), however, music began to find a favorable audience throughout the Islamic world. The Umayyads held a lively court in Damascus, one that encouraged the development of the arts and sciences.

Persian music had an influence on Arabic music, and vice versa. Moreover, in the same way that Islam influenced poetry in southern Spain, so the Cordovan Islamic community supported the development of a new and distinctive musical style in Andalusian Spain. Music, especially Arabic music, flourished most, however, during the Abbasid dynasty (750–1258), the period immediately following the reign of the Umayyads. During the reign of the Abbasids, music became an obligatory accomplishment for every educated person, much as it did later at the courts of Renaissance Europe. Yet with the collapse of the Abbasid dynasty and the destruction of Baghdad by the Mongol armies in 1258, music declined during a period of general intellectual and cultural stagnation.

Cultural Impact

During the two centuries following Muhammad's death, Arab conquerors introduced Islam throughout Asia and North Africa, India, southern Spain, and the Mediterranean islands. Diplomats, merchants, and other travelers exchanged news and goods, and an extensive trade and communications network emerged. As Islam spread, it encountered Hinduism, Judaism, and Christianity, as well as with Greek philosophy, science, and political thought. Absorbing and adapting these and other traditions, the Muslim empire prospered.

One important legacy of Islamic civilization is its architecture, particularly in southern Spain in Andalusia. Examples of Moorish-style architecture can be found in southern Europe and in the southern United States, especially in Florida and Texas, where Spanish influence is strong. Muslim artists also introduced the institution of courtly love poetry and music, in which poets sang to their mistresses, accompanied by a lute, tambourine, or guitar.

Islamic civilization also left us the tradition of the prayer rug, a small carpet or portion of a carpet used by devout Muslims when they pray. Each small rug or section of a larger carpet is just the right size for an individual supplicant.

Finally, the tales in *The Thousand and One Nights* captured the imagination of European readers from their first publication. Although these tales did not reach the West until after Chaucer and Boccaccio had written their comic masterpieces, Chaucer's "Squire's Tale" from his *Canterbury Tales* and some of the tales from Boccaccio's *Decameron* were of Arabian origin. The exotic tales of *The Thousand and One Nights* continue to delight today, both in their written form and in their cinematic transformations.

Medieval Arabic music was influenced to a significant degree by ancient Greek musical theory, which reached Near Eastern scholars in the ninth century when the works of Ptolemy, Pythagoras, and other Greek theorists were translated into Arabic. One Arabic theorist in particular who was influenced by Greek musical theory was AL-KINDI [al-KIN-dee] (790–874), who, like his Greek precursors, was interested in the effects of music on people's feelings and behavior.

Although much Islamic music was court music, which served either as vocal entertainment or as an accompaniment for dancing by professional dancers in palaces and private residences, religion also made use of music. Music was, and still is, used in calling Muslims to prayer, in chanting verses of the Quran, in hymns for special occasions and holy days, and in the *dhikr*, in which music accompanies the solemn repetition of the name of God.

KEY TERMS

Surah
ayas
hadith
Sufi
mosque
mihrab
minaret
muezzin
voussoirs
calligraphy

www. Websites for Further Study

http://www.fordham.edu/halsall/source/arab-y67s11.html
(Islamic political philosophy: Al-Farabi, Avicenna, Averroes—good information for comparison.)

http://archnet.org/library/sites/one-site.tcl?site_id=3005
(Sinan, Mosque of Sultan Sulayman, Instanbul, 1550–57. Click on thumbnail image to select from five views of the mosque: interior, exterior, and detail.)

http://www.Islamic civilization.net
(Overview of various aspects of Islamic civilization.)

http://www.cyberislam.org
(Muslim contributions to science, mathematics, astronomy, medicine, and philosophy, in the Middle Ages.)

http://www.Angelfire.com/ca2/mysticalpathwaynurhu/
(History of music in Islam.)

http://www.metmuseum.org/toah/hd/oma/hd_oma.htm
(The Nature of Islamic art.)

Chapter 7

History

ca. 326 B.C.E.	Alexander the Great invades north India
324–301 B.C.E.	Chandragupta Maurya reigns
ca. 250 B.C.E.	Sarnath Capital
269–232 B.C.E.	Ashoka reigns
375–415 C.E.	Chandra Gupta II reigns
710 C.E.	First Muslim invasion of India
ca. twelfth century C.E.	Mahadeviyakka active
1192 C.E.	Delhi Sultanate, first Muslim kingdom Buddhism declines
1526	Mogul empire established

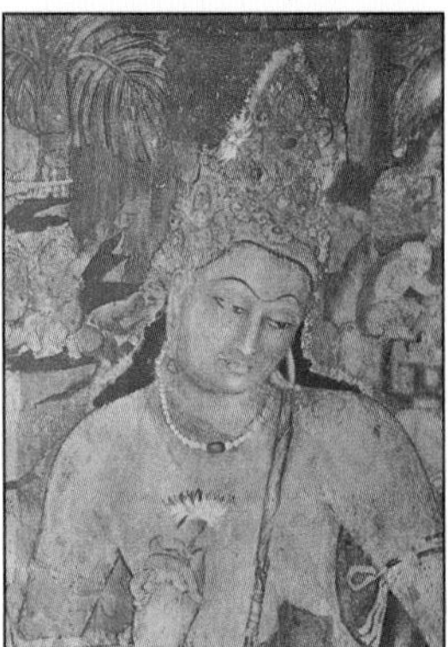

Arts and Architecture

ca. 530 B.C.E.	Vishnu Narayana on the Cosmic Waters
third B.C.E.–first century C.E.	Great Stupa at Sanchi
fourth–fifth century C.E.	Standing Buddha
fifth century C.E.	Ajanta cave paintings
1025–50 C.E.	Kandariya Mahadeo temple
eleventh–twelfth century C.E.	Shiva Nataraja
1630–48 C.E.	Taj Mahal

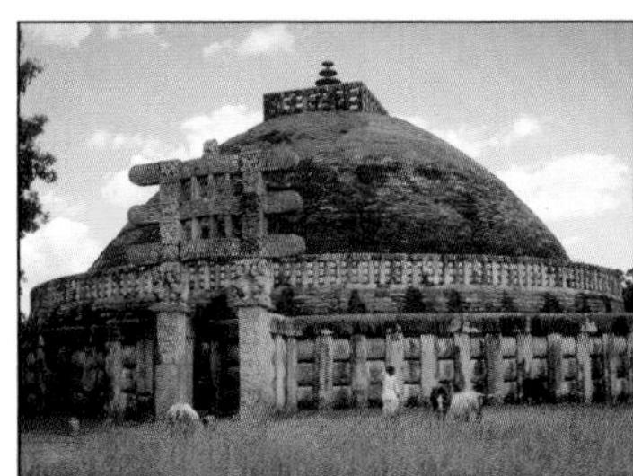

Literature and Philosophy

1500 B.C.E.	Hinduism evolves from Aryan religious beliefs
1500–1000 B.C.E.	*Vedas* first recorded by Aryans
ca. 550 B.C.E.	Valmiki's *Ramayana* first recorded
ca. fourth century B.C.E.	*Jataka* tales
ca. 260 B.C.E.	Ashoka establishes Buddhism as state religion
ca. first century B.C.E.	*Bhagavad Gita*

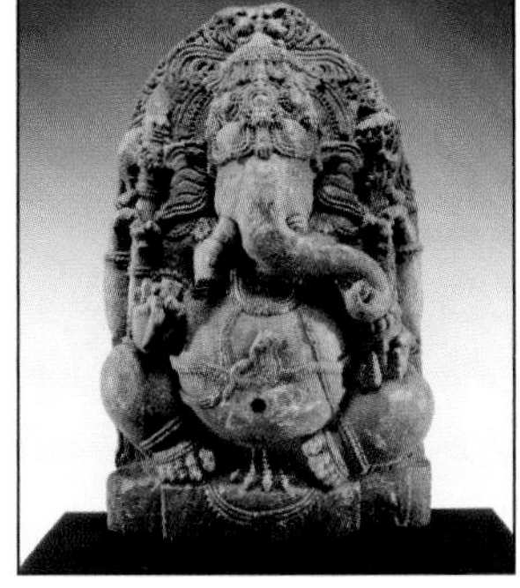

Indian Civilization

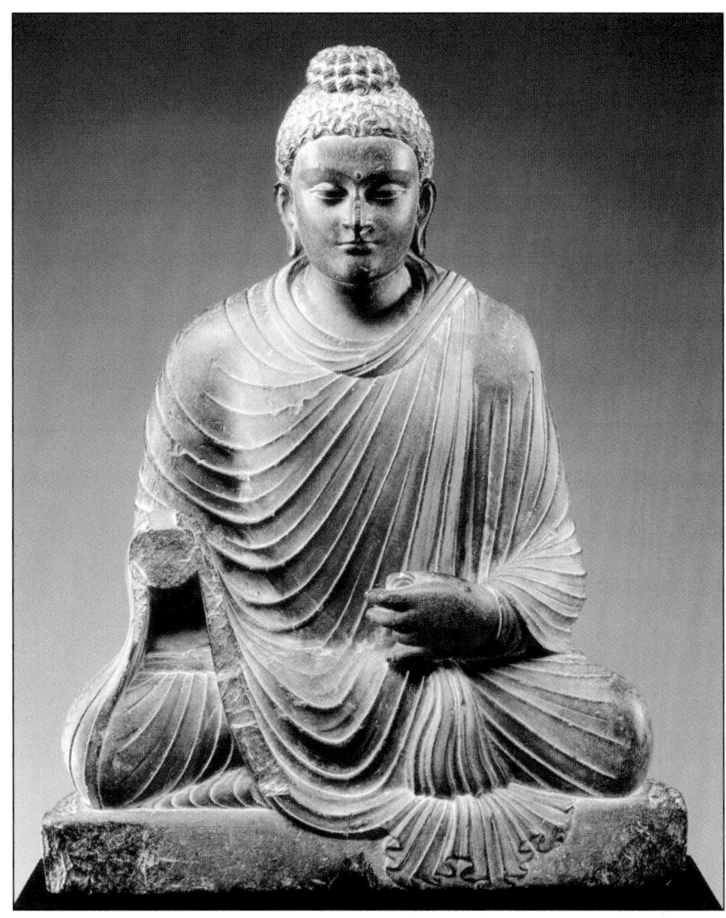

Seated Buddha, from Gandhara, Peshawar District (Pakistan), Kushan, second–third century C.E., dark gray schist. The Adolph D. and Wilkins C. Williams Fund. Katherine Wetzel/Virginia Museum of Fine Arts, Richmond.

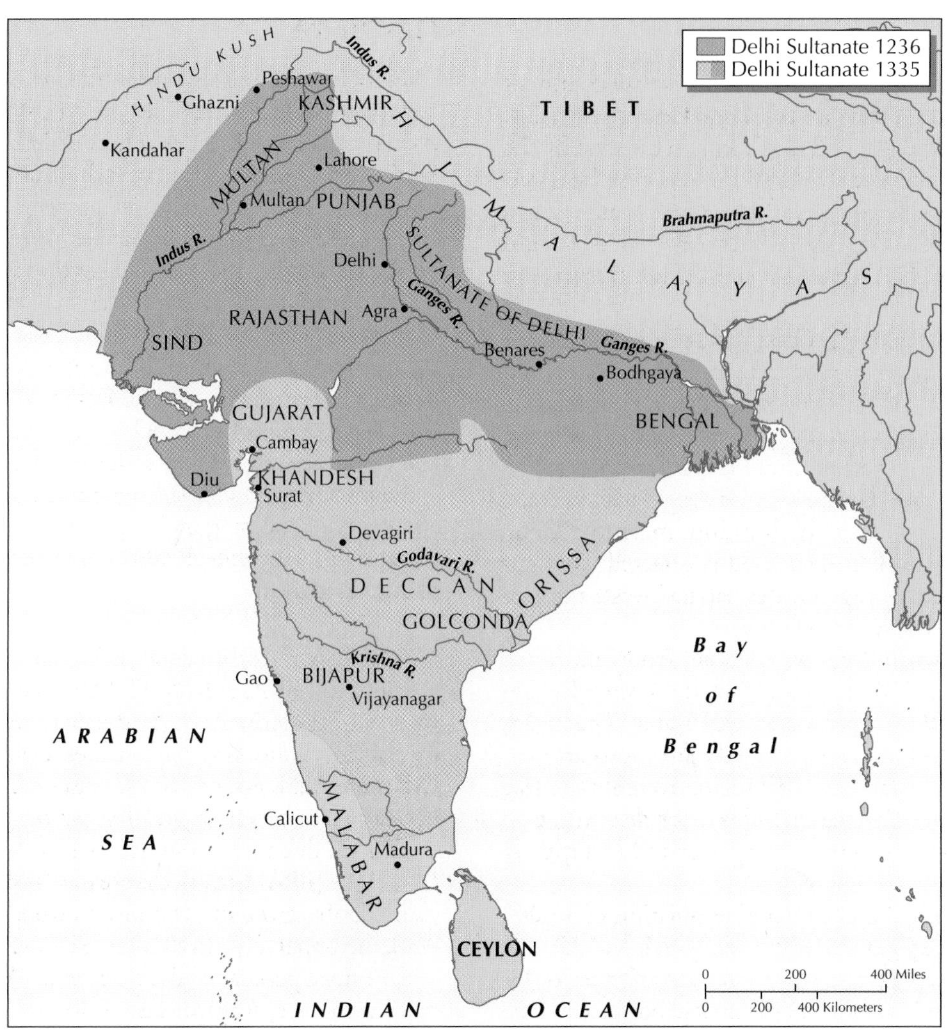

Map 7.1 Muslim India under the Delhi Sultanate.

Chapter Overview

VEDIC PERIOD

Hinduism takes root

MAURYA PERIOD

Buddhism rises in political and religious prominence

MAURYAN TO BACTRIAN TO KUSHAN

Greco-Roman artistic influences meet Buddhism

GUPTA ERA

Flourishing culture and commerce

HINDU DYNASTIES

Southern Indian arts prosper despite constant war

VEDIC PERIOD

INDIA, AS WE KNOW IT TODAY, is a distinct subcontinent bordered on the north by the Himalayan mountains, on the east by the Bay of Bengal, and on the west by the Arabian Sea. The only land routes into or out of the country are the northwestern passes through the Hindu Kush, the mountains separating India from Iran, and eastward past the mouth of the Ganges River, through Burma into China.

But despite its relative geographic isolation, India has long been the center of trade between East and West, on both land and sea. In his *Geography*, the ancient author Ptolemy records the visits of Western traders to stations on the Silk Road in the second century C.E. Between the fifth and ninth centuries C.E., the Chinese regularly traveled along Indian trade routes. In addition, maritime trade routes up and down the Indian coast connected China to the West long after Mongol hordes had laid waste the Silk Road itself in the thirteenth century.

The first known indigenous people, from the Indus Valley civilization (2500 B.C.E.–1500 B.C.E.), were known as the Dasas, or Pre-Aryan culture of India. The Indus Valley people developed an extremely advanced and sophisticated culture that covered a region roughly the size of western Europe. The major Indus cities discovered so far are Mohenjo-daro on the Indus River and Harappa in the Punjab.

Mohenjo-daro had an estimated population of 35,000 to 40,000 people, larger than Pompei, which had 25,000. Excavations of the site reveal a civilization of great organization and centralization; cities were laid out in grid patterns, reflecting a high degree of civil planning. Moreover, a centralized drainage system ran through the city, and seven hundred wells supplied water to its inhabitants. Workshops for dyeing, pottery, and metalwork have also been found.

Sometime around 1500 B.C.E. light-skinned **nomadic** Aryan tribes from the Russian steppes and Central Asia brought horses and chariots and settled in northern India. In many ways they were much less advanced—technologically and intellectually—than the native Indian population; however, they brought with them early forms of a language—**Sanskrit**—and of a religion—Hinduism—that would evolve to become very important to Indian cultural life. This era is referred to as the Vedic period (1500 B.C.E.–300 B.C.E.), named after the oldest surviving sacred Indian writings, the **Vedas,** and represents a time of cultural assimilation that proved critical to India's subsequent development.

It would take over a thousand years for the Aryans and Dasas to become fully integrated. During this period, in response to the growing complexity and social rigidity of Hinduism, various alternative religions emerged—most notably Buddhism and Jainism, both of which challenged the Hindu hereditary class structure.

HINDUISM

The origins of Hinduism are unknown, although they are believed to date to around the sixth century B.C.E., perhaps even as early as 1500 B.C.E. The word **Hindu** derives from *Sindhu,* the Sanskrit name for the Indus River. Like the Ganges, another important Indian river, the Indus was used for religious ceremonies, especially for rites of purification.

Hindu worship focuses on a pantheon of gods who personify natural forces, not on a historical teacher or prophet. In Hinduism the ideal life has four basic goals: (1) *dharma:* the pursuit of human righteousness, duty, and cosmic order; (2) *artha:* the accumulation of worldly success; (3) *kama:* pursuit of spiritual love; and (4) *moksha:* release from empty pleasures and suffering in the world. Moksha is the most important goal; by breaking bonds with daily existence and focusing on integrating the self with the universal truth (Absolute Reality), one can escape the cycle of birth and death.

Hindu Gods. At the center of Hindu religious thought is the idea of BRAHMAN [BRAH-man], the indivisible essence of all spiritual reality, the divine source of all being. In ancient Hinduism (sometimes called Brahmanism), **Brahman** is the essence of the universe, manifesting itself in creation, preservation, and destruction. In later Hinduism, Brahman's three functions are divided among three gods: BRAHMA [BRAH-mah], the creator (as distinct from Brahman, the ubiquitous spirit of the universe); VISHNU [VISH-noo], the preserver; and SHIVA [SHE-vah], the destroyer.

The most popular of the three gods, **Vishnu,** is the god of benevolence, forgiveness, and love. He enjoys games and pranks. His consort, or companion, is **LAKSHMI** [LACK-shmee], with whom he is often depicted. Because of his great love for humankind, Vishnu is said to have appeared on earth many times in various forms, including that of a man. Among his **avatars,** or appearances in earthly form, is his incarnation as KRISHNA [KRISH-nah], a charioteer who advises the warrior Arjuna about his military responsibilities. **Krishna** is also believed by some Hindus to have been reincarnated as the Buddha.

Shiva represents and reflects life's processes and paradoxes. He is both the creative and destructive flow of life: motion and calm, male and female, dark and light,

Table 7–1 MAJOR HINDU GODS AND THEIR FUNCTIONS

God	Role or Function
Brahma	Creator: source of being
Vishnu	Preserver: benevolence, forgiveness, love
Shiva	Destroyer: disease and death
Lakshmi	Consort of Vishnu: sexuality and reproduction
Kali	Consort of Shiva: sexuality and reproduction

everything and its opposite. Shiva is an ambivalent god who embodies, defies, and reconciles himself with all aspects of life. He is also the god of dance, an extremely important aspect of Indian culture and expression. His most frequent consort is Parvati, with whom he has several sons; the most popular is Ganesha, the elephant-headed deity who bestows prosperity. Parvati's fierce, destructive manifestation is KALI [KAH-lee], often depicted with a necklace of human skulls. Because for Hindus, death is a prelude to rebirth, Shiva and Kali are also gods of sexuality and reproduction. According to one tradition, there are 330 million Hindu gods, and a single god can be worshiped under a variety of manifestations. Hindus accept and worship numerous gods because they are able to accept many varying perspectives on existence. Gods and goddesses often are depicted with multiple heads and arms as a way of conveying their immense power and ability to be all seeing.

Ganesha (fig. 7.1) is one of the more lovable of the Hindu gods. The son of Shiva and Parvati, he is associated with playfulness and prosperity. According to one legend, his mother Parvati was taking a bath and created a boy from the dirt of her own body. She then asked the boy to stand guard while she finished bathing. In the meantime, Shiva returned home to find a stranger blocking the door to his wife's room. Shiva became angry and cut off the boy's head. Parvati, learning of this, was grief stricken. In order to console her, Shiva ordered his troops to fetch the head of anyone found sleeping with his head pointing north. The troops found an elephant sleeping and brought back its head. Shiva attached the elephant head to the body of the boy and revived him.

Ganesha is usually shown with his favorite round sweets in his hand that represent the seeds of the universe and are offered by other gods and devotees. He wears a snake tied around his middle because when riding on his rat vehicle one day, the rat tripped on a snake and Ganesha tumbled to the ground. His belly ripped open in the process, and the sweets he had already eaten fell out. The sweets were put back into his belly, which was then tied closed with the snake.

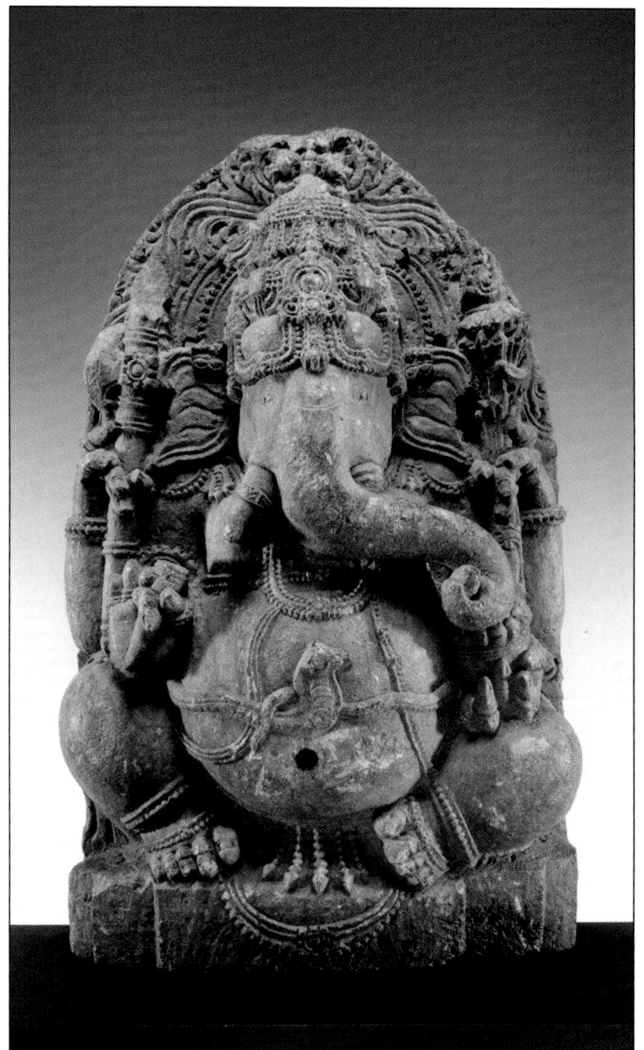

FIGURE 7.1 *Ganesha*, Southern Deccan Karnataka, Hoyshala Period, ca. early twelfth century. Gray chloritic schist. 33″ × $20\frac{1}{4}$″ × 10″ (83.8 × 51.4 × 25.4 cm). The Nasli and Alice Heeramaneck Collection, gift of Paul Mellon. Katherine Wetzel/Virginia Museum of Fine Arts, Richmond. Ganesha, god of overcoming obstacles, is among the most popular of Hindu gods.

Samsara. Both Hinduism and Buddhism, the two major religions that emerged in India, revolve around the idea of **samsara**, the transmigration of the soul, or reincarnation. The goal of both religions is to escape the continuous cycle of death and rebirth through enlightenment (*nirvana* in Buddhism, or *moksha* in Hinduism).

Karma. The idea of **karma** is central to Hindu thought. *Karma* (which means "action") involves a kind of moral cause and effect, in which people's actions affect their moral development. An individual's actions and the accumulation of merit through these actions determine the form in which he or she will be reincarnated; it places responsibility for one's thoughts and actions on oneself. The law of karma suggests that the present condition of a person's life has been determined by actions in previous existences.

Hindu Class Structure. The social structure of ancient Indian society derives from and reflects these religious concepts and beliefs, and it is based on the division of society into four distinct classes, or castes.

At the top of the social order, the Brahmins serve as Hindu society's priests, leaders, seers, and religious authorities. Next in rank are the Kshatriyas, who in ancient times were Hindu society's kings and aristocratic warriors, but more recently have been its administrators, politicians, and civil authorities. Beneath the Kshatriyas are the Vaishyas, the society's entrepreneurs: in ancient times merchants and traders, in more recent times also its professionals, such as doctors, lawyers, and teachers. The Shudras are Hindu society's laborers, its servant class. **Dalits,** or **outcastes,** who fall outside the four main castes, are considered "untouchable" and therefore avoided by members of other castes. Outcastes are either non-Aryan by birth or were originally members of the other castes but violated caste laws, such as those regarding work or marriage.

This hierarchical model of society was later challenged by certain communities that were based on different religious ideals, such as the Jains and the Buddhists. The caste system, however, has continued to be the governing principle of Indian society for two thousand years.

LITERATURE: THE HINDU CLASSICS

The Vedas. The earliest Indian literature was composed by the Aryans, the nomads who migrated to India around 1500 B.C.E. Composed between 1500 and 1000 B.C.E. in Sanskrit, *The Vedas* consist of a set of hymns which praise the Hindu gods. All later works ultimately derive from these Vedic songs, and most are a commentary on them. Transmitted orally at first, *The Vedas* were chanted during religious rituals, accompanied by various instruments. The Vedic religion and text emphasized social hierarchy and ritual sacrifice to obtain the favor of the gods.

The Upanishads. *The Upanishads*, an anthology of philosophical poems and discourses, were later added to *The Vedas*. Although not as popular with ordinary people as the hymns and prayers of *The Vedas*, *The Upanishads* have been influential in Indian philosophy. They contain discussion and teachings that, although at odds with the polytheism of Vedic myth and legend, explain key Hindu ideas such as **maya** (illusion) and **karma** (action). *The Upanishads* were largely a reaction against the ritualistic, sacrificial religious practices of the Vedics as well as the increasingly powerful priest group.

According to *The Upanishads*, human beings do not realize that what appears real to the senses is entirely illusory, and that what counts eternally is the spiritual essence of life (Brahman), of which they are a part. The idea of unity and oneness with the universe becomes central to Upanishad thought.

The Upanishads typically illustrate the idea of maya and ignorance with a story about a tiger that had been orphaned as a cub and raised among goats. Believing itself to be a goat, the cub ate grass and made goat noises. One day, another tiger came upon it and took the confused tiger to a pool in which his tiger image was reflected. It was then that the cub realized his true nature. In the same way, human beings need to realize their true nature, the divinity that resides within all.

The Ramayana. The oldest of Hindu epics, *The Ramayana (The Way of Rama)* by VALMIKI [val-MIH-kee] (sixth century B.C.E.) is also the most popular work of Indian literature, and among the most influential literary works in the world. The story of Prince Rama and his queen, Sita, has its narrative origins in Indian folk traditions that go back to as early as the seventh century B.C.E. *The Ramayana* itself is dated approximately 550 B.C.E., when Valmiki, much like Homer in ancient Greece, gathered the various strands of the story into a cohesive work of literature organized in seven **kanda,** or books. Blending historical sagas, myths, legends, and moral tales with religious and social teaching, *The Ramayana* has long been the single most important repository of Indian social, moral, and ethical values.

Devout Hindus believe Rama is one of the two most important avatars, or incarnations, of the god Vishnu, who assumed human form to save humankind. Reading or witnessing a performance of episodes from *The Ramayana* is thus considered a religious exercise, as is repeating the name of Rama.

The Ramayana stands, moreover, as an enduring monument and a living guide to political, social, and family life in Vedic India. The behavior of its hero, Prince Rama, serves as a model for the behavior of the ideal son, brother, husband, warrior, and king. Rama's respect for his father and love for his wife, along with his regal bearing and self-control, represent the paradigm for Indian males to emulate. Rama's behavior is also closely linked to the religious values embodied in the epic. His wife Sita loves, honors, and serves her husband with absolute fidelity. In being governed by dharma ("truth" or "law") rather than self-interest, Rama and Sita stand as models for Hindu life.

The story of *The Ramayana* is complex and intricate. One of its central motifs concerns Rama's disinheritance, which is instigated by the jealous queen, Rama's stepmother Kaikeyi, who wants her own son, Bharatha, to become king instead of Rama. The king, Rama's father, reluctantly has his son exiled, but thereafter soon dies, desolate over Rama's departure. With his wife, Sita, and his brother, Lakshmana, Rama lives in the wilderness of central India. After fourteen years of living in the jungle, Sita is abducted by the king of the demons, Ravana, who holds Sita captive for several years before she is rescued by Rama with the help of Hanamun and his monkey army. However, because Sita has dwelled in another man's house, Rama must reject her. Once her innocence is proven, however, Sita is hailed as the embodiment of chasity and fidelity. She represents the ideal Indian female beauty, and Rama goes on to rule as a wise and compassionate king.

The Mahabharata. The second great Indian epic is *The Mahabharata*, which was composed over a period of more than eight hundred years, between 400 B.C.E. and 400 C.E. Unlike *The Ramayana*, which focuses on the adventures of one central hero, *The Mahabharata* chronicles the story of a pair of rival warring families, the Pandavas and the Kauravas. The warlike world of *The Mahabharata* is more akin to that of *The Iliad*, whereas the adventure-filled quest of *The Ramayana* has more of the character of Homer's other great epic, *The Odyssey*. With its hundred thousand verses, *The Mahabharata* is four times the length of *The Ramayana*, and more than eight times that of *The Iliad* and *The Odyssey* combined. What *The Mahabharata* lacks in

Connections

THE LOGIC OF JAINISM

Jainism, which arose at the same time as Buddhism, was also a reaction to Hinduism, particularly the caste system and the claims of the Brahmins to social superiority. Its founder was MAHAVIRA [ma-ha-VEE-rah] (599–527 B.C.E.), which means "Great Man." His early life resembles that of Sakyamuni, the founder of Buddhism. Born a prince, who, as legend has it, was attended by five nurses, "a wet-nurse, a nurse to bathe him, one to dress him, one to play with him, and one to carry him," Mahavira was raised in luxury. But as he grew older, he tired of this life, and at the age of thirty he joined a band of monks who practiced an ascetic existence. But even the monks had too indulgent a lifestyle for his taste, and so Mahavira set out on his own, wandering the Indian countryside entirely naked, maintaining that salvation is possible only through severe deprivation of the pleasures of life and the practice of *ahimsa*, not causing harm to any living thing.

The ultimate goal in Jainism is also release from the cycle of samsara, but more than any other Indian religion, it emphasizes self-reliance and responsibility for one's own fate. The individual must control personal passions in order to purify and perfect the soul. The soul is hindered by karma, which to the Jains is not actions, but imperceptible particles of matter that fill the whole cosmos. These bits of karma penetrate the soul through one's actions of the mind, body, and speech and wrap themselves around the soul, which must be released from this mass of particles by annihilating both old and new karma. The individual can prevent the penetration of karma particles through total isolation, fasting, meditation, self-control, and renunciation of the ego. Once free of karma particles, the soul is released from the cycle of rebirth. Jainism is a profoundly ethical faith emphasizing virtue, self-control, and nonviolence against all life forms.

Jainism has gained a wide following in India, and today the Jains number about two million, with an especially large community in Bombay, where MAHATMA GANDHI [GAHN-dee] (1869–1948), the great twentieth-century pacifist leader, was influenced by its tenets. One of the most distinctive features of the Jain philosophy is a special sensitivity to the relativity of all things. A favorite Jain parable is the story of the six blind men, each of whom puts his hands on a different part of an elephant and describes what he feels in totally different terms—it is like a fan, a wall, a snake, a rope, and so on. In Jainist thought, each description is satisfactory given each person's limited knowledge of the whole of the elephant. In one sense, an elephant is like a snake, but only in a very limited way. By extension, all knowledge is, from one point of view, true, and from another, false or incomplete.

unity and focus, however, it makes up for in multiplicity of incident, breadth of social panorama, and philosophical discursiveness.

Forming part of the sixth book of *The Mahabharata* is the *Bhagavad Gita*, the section most familiar to Western readers. It is also the epic's most important source of spiritual teaching. Written early in the first century B.C.E., the *Bhagavad Gita* centers on the moral conflict experienced by Arjuna, a warrior who struggles with his duty to kill his kinsmen during the war between the Pandavas and Kauravas, a great battle that ends in the destruction of both armies.

When Arjuna sees his relatives ready to do battle against one another, he puts down his weapons and refuses to fight. His charioteer, Krishna, an avatar of the god Vishnu, explains it is Arjuna's duty to fight: Even though the Hindu religion generally prohibits killing, the sanction is lifted for members of Arjuna's warrior class, the Kshatriyas. He also tells Arjuna that fighting can break the karmic cycle of samsara, the endless cycle of birth, death, and reincarnation to which mortal beings are subject, and move him toward spiritual liberation. Arjuna learns that the spirit in which an act is performed counts more than the act itself. Because Arjuna is not fighting to achieve any particular goal but only to fulfill his duty, his behavior is irreproachable.

MAURYA PERIOD

In ancient India, each region was politically autonomous. These regions were governed by small dynasties that remained relatively immune from outside influences and challenges. From time to time, however, the governments of individual regions would join together in loose federations to create empires. One of the earliest and most important of these was the empire of the Maurya, which emerged in response to a power vacuum created by Alexander the Great's conquest of northern India around 326 B.C.E.

CHANDRAGUPTA MAURYA [MOW-ya], effectively the first emperor of India, reigned from 324 to 301 B.C.E. His empire extended from the Ganges River to the Indus and into the northern mountains. After Chandragupta's death, and following the reign of his son Bindusara, came the most important of Mauryan emperors, ASHOKA [a-SHOW-ka], who assumed the throne in 269 B.C.E. Lasting nearly forty years (269–232 B.C.E.), Ashoka's reign marked a critical turning point in Indian history—the emergence of Buddhism as a political force in India. Regretting the terrible destruction his armies had wrought in a victorious battle with the armies of a neighboring region, Ashoka became a champion of nonviolence and embraced **Buddhism,** which had begun to displace the more worldly Hinduism three centuries earlier.

The connection between political power and religious idealism continued throughout Ashoka's life and for half a century after his death. The emperor sent missionaries, including his daughter and son, throughout India to spread the Buddhist faith. He also had sites marked that were of religious and historical significance to Buddhists, and monuments to house the possessions and remains of the Buddha.

BUDDHISM

The historical Buddha was born Siddhartha Gautama Sakya (ca. 563–483 B.C.E.), a prince in a kingdom in the foothills of the Himalayas, in present-day Nepal. He is also known as Sakyamuni, meaning "the sage or silent one of the Sakya." At his birth, it was prophesied that Sakyamuni would be either a king or a world redeemer. He was raised in a princely household, and so as a young man was sheltered from pain and suffering. Wanting to experience the world beyond the palace walls, he asked his father to allow him to see the city. His father arranged an excursion befitting the young prince. The king ordered that all commoners and those afflicted with ailments be kept out of sight so as not to distress the prince. The sick, old, and maimed were also cleared from the prince's path.

Seeing that the city was joyful and the people content, the prince was delighted. But the gods, in an attempt to incite the prince's renunciation of the world, led him to an old man, then a sick man, and then a corpse. Encountering all these conditions of human existence caused the prince to meditate on his experiences. As he pondered what he had seen, a mendicant monk appeared and explained his life as an ascetic. Sakyamuni's experiences with old age, disease, death, and the monk are referred to as the Four Encounters. The prince decided he would leave his father's palace and live the life of an ascetic, searching for a way to relieve human suffering.

Upon leaving the palace, Sakyamuni wandered the countryside and meditated with a group of ascetics for six years. When he realized asceticism would not lead to salvation, he rejected this path. Instead, he determined there must be some path to enlightenment that would not exhaust one's body and mind. He sat under a pipal tree (known as the Bodhi tree or tree of wisdom) where he vowed not to move until he attained enlightenment. Sakyamuni mediated for forty-nine days and nights and was subject to numerous distractions by Mara the Tempter, who sought to destroy Sakyamuni's concentration and resolve.

Finally, on the night of the full moon, Sakyamuni achieved enlightenment. He then set out to help and educate others in this path. He gave his first sermon at Deer Park in India, setting into motion the dharma (religious truth or law) represented in the Four Noble Truths and the Eightfold Path (listed later).

The Buddha also reiterated the importance of the **Middle Path,** rejecting the extremes of both asceticism, which only weakens the body and mind, and indulgence, which obstructs wisdom. After forty-five years of preaching and dedicating himself to others, the Buddha (a word derived from the name of the tree under which he first achieved enlightenment—the Bo tree, short for **Bodhi,** meaning "wisdom" or "enlightenment") died at the age of eighty.

Buddhism versus Hinduism. Unlike Hinduism, which developed over many centuries, Buddhism seemed to arise overnight, even if it took many centuries for a political leader to adopt it. Buddhists challenged Hindu religious practice in a number of ways. Sakyamuni's followers argued that the caste of Brahmins was granted too much power and given too many privileges. The forms of ritual had become, they believed, devoid of meaning, and were debased by being linked with commercial transactions. Hindu philosophical thought had become excessively intricate and arcane, and consequently increasingly disconnected from everyday spiritual life. Religious mystery had degenerated into mystification and magic. Superstition and divination had replaced miracle and true mysticism. Perhaps worst of all, too many people had come to believe their actions did not matter, that whatever they believed they would be caught up in samsara, the endless cycle of rebirth, from which escape was impossible.

Buddhists responded to this by providing an alternative religious practice in which each individual had to find her or his own way to enlightenment. So devoid of the notion of higher authority is Buddhism that it was originally a religion without a god. There is only enlightenment. Furthermore, ritual is an irrelevant diversion from the real work of achieving enlightenment. The Buddha taught that it need not take hundreds of lifetimes or thousands of reincarnations to break out of the round of existence. A determined individual could achieve enlightenment in a single lifetime and so attain **nirvana,** that is, liberation from the limitations of existence and rebirth in the cycle of samsara.

As a result of these new objectives, early Buddhism had few of the characteristics of traditional religions. It posited no creation or last judgment. It presented no revelation from a god. Instead, it emphasized the here and now.

The Four Noble Truths and the Eightfold Path. Buddhist thought is based on an analysis of the human condition founded on four basic axioms or truths. These principles have come to be known as the Four Noble Truths:

1. Life consists of suffering, impermanence, imperfection, incompleteness.
2. The cause of life's suffering is selfishness.
3. Suffering and selfishness can be brought to an end.
4. The answer to life's problems of suffering is the Eightfold Path.

	Hinduism	Jainism	Buddhism
Founder	unknown	Mahavira	Sakyamuni (Buddha)
Gods	Brahma/Shiva Vishnu, etc.	none	none
Goals	dharma artha moksha	ahimsa	nirvana satori
Texts	Upanishads Vedas Mahabharata	Angas Upangas	Sutras Shastras Pitakas

The Eightfold Path itself consists of knowledge of these Four Noble Truths, the first step on the path, followed by seven other steps: right aspiration toward the goal of enlightenment; right speech that is honest and charitable; right conduct—no drinking, killing, lying, or lust; right living according to the goals of Buddhism; right effort; right thinking with an emphasis on self-awareness; and the right use of meditation to achieve enlightenment.

MAURYA ART

The earliest large and significant body of Indian art extant today dates from the Maurya period, chiefly from the reign of the emperor Ashoka. Much of this work was created to celebrate Ashoka's conversion to Buddhism. Ashoka ordered the construction of numerous **stupas,** or memorial buildings, that enshrined relics of the Buddha, marking sites sacred to his memory. Many of the eighty thousand or more stupas erected during Ashoka's reign were dedicated to the Buddha and his miracles. Later, stupas were used for burial of the remains of sacred monks.

Sarnath Capital. Ashoka also had a large number of stone columns built to memorialize significant events in the Buddha's life. Carved into many of these, as well as into rocks and caves, were edicts that promoted various aspects of the Buddhist creed. The stone pillars usually had capitals, often carved in the forms of animals, usually lions. One of the most magnificent of these is a beautifully preserved lion capital (fig. 7.2) from a pillar at Sarnath that dates from about 250 B.C.E.

The Sarnath capital consists of three elements. On top of a Persian-style fluted bell are four animals, bull, horse, elephant, and lion, walking around in a clockwise direction, and four wheels carved in relief. The animals may have directional significance, and they appear to be keeping the wheels in motion, turning around the pillar. Above these elements are four lions carved back to back all the way around the capital. The stylization of the lions' facial features and claws, along with the decorative handling of their manes and upper torsos, is similar to that of the lion sculptures at Persepolis, a city destroyed by Alexander the Great before his invasion of northern India. As described in Chapter 3, Alexander's forces made an enduring cultural impression on the region. It is highly likely therefore that either Persian sculptors or Persian-trained Greek sculptors created this capital, which marks a dramatic growth in the style, complexity, and beauty of Indian sculpture.

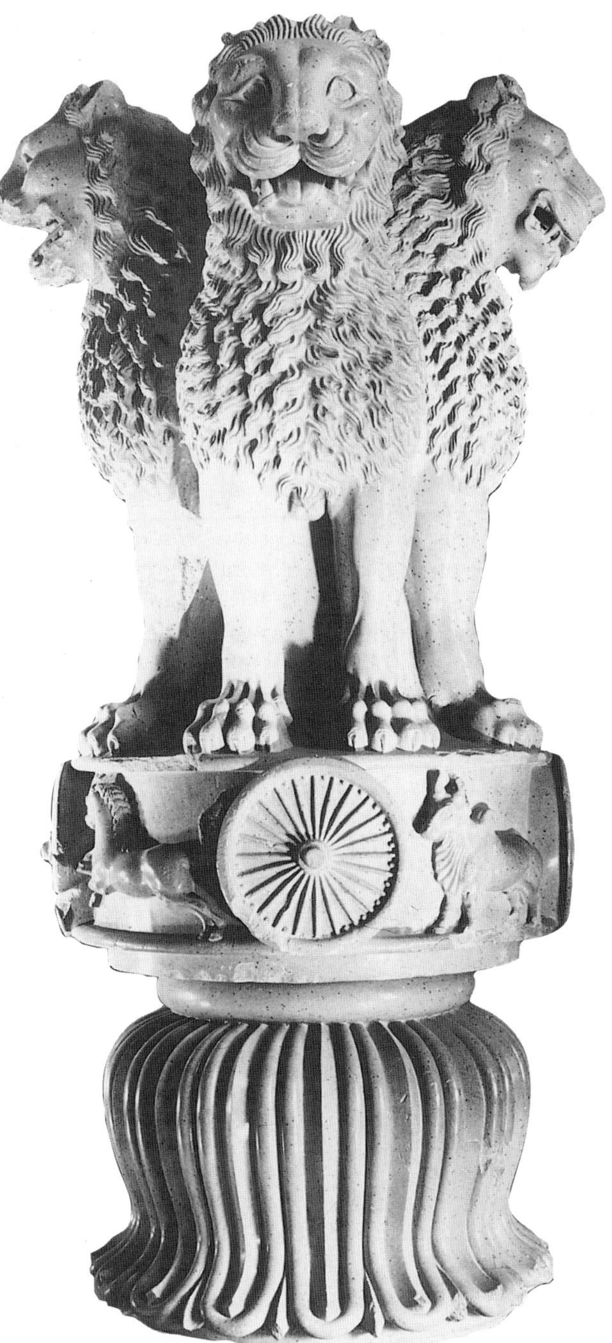

FIGURE 7.2 Lion capital of a pillar erected by Ashoka at Sarnath, Mauryan, ca. 250 B.C.E., Chunar sandstone, height $7'\frac{1}{2}''$ (2.15 m), Archaeological Museum, Sarnath, India. This lion capital reveres the lion as king of the animal world while honoring the Buddha as king lion among religious teachers.

The seven-foot sculpture was originally surmounted by a large stone wheel on the lions' shoulders. This capital (now used as the emblem of the modern Republic of India) is highly symbolic. Hailing from a period during which Buddhist art avoided representing the Buddha directly, the Sarnath lion capital suggests his presence in other ways. The wheel symbolizes the wheel of the law (the dharma) and the Buddha's sermon at Deer Park in Sarnath where this capital was located. The wheel is also a symbol of cosmic order in Upanishad thought, representing the flow of life and all that is possible. The lion itself is the Persian symbol of royalty and may have been borrowed in this context to represent Ashoka. The lion is also a symbol of Sakyamuni's clan, and the Buddha is often referred to as having a "lion's roar." Thus Ashoka's edicts carved on the pillars, and the lions roaring, proclaim the Buddha's words concretely and symbolically.

Great Stupa at Sanchi. Many of the stupas (burial mounds containing the relics of the Buddha) erected by Ashoka were enlarged by subsequent dynasties in the second and first centuries B.C.E. For instance, at Sanchi in central India, Ashoka had built a stupa sixty feet in diameter and twenty-five feet high. The Andhras, who ruled in the region toward the end of the first century B.C.E., doubled its size (fig. 7.3). They replaced Ashoka's wooden railings with new stone ones nine feet high. A sixteen-foot-high passage encircling the stupa was also added. At the very top of the stupa are three umbrellas (**chattras**) that symbolize protection of the objects below. The umbrellas are positioned on a central axis (**yasti**), which is the most important symbol of the stupa because it represents the world axis, a concept similar to Ashoka's pillars.

However, the architectural glories of the Sanchi stupa are four carved stone gates, each of which is more than thirty feet high (fig. 7.4). Begun during the first century B.C.E., but only completed during the first century C.E., the gates are adorned with symbols associated with the Buddha, including the wheel of the law, stories from his life, and tales of his animal incarnations. Additional figures include elephants, peacocks, and **yakshis,** or protective female earth spirits.

The Sanchi stupa symbolizes the cosmos, its four gates representing the four corners of the universe. Its umbrella points toward the sky, linking heaven with earth and a life of bliss with that of pain and suffering below. Entering the eastern gate of the stupa, a visitor would move clockwise in a circle around it on a path especially constructed for that purpose. Even though the stupa can not be entered directly, like Hindu temples it invites worshipers to enter into a spiritual state of mind.

FIGURE 7.3 Great Stupa, Sanchi, from the east, third century B.C.E.–early first century C.E. For the increasing numbers of Buddhist faithful, the stupa became a central symbol of religious faith.

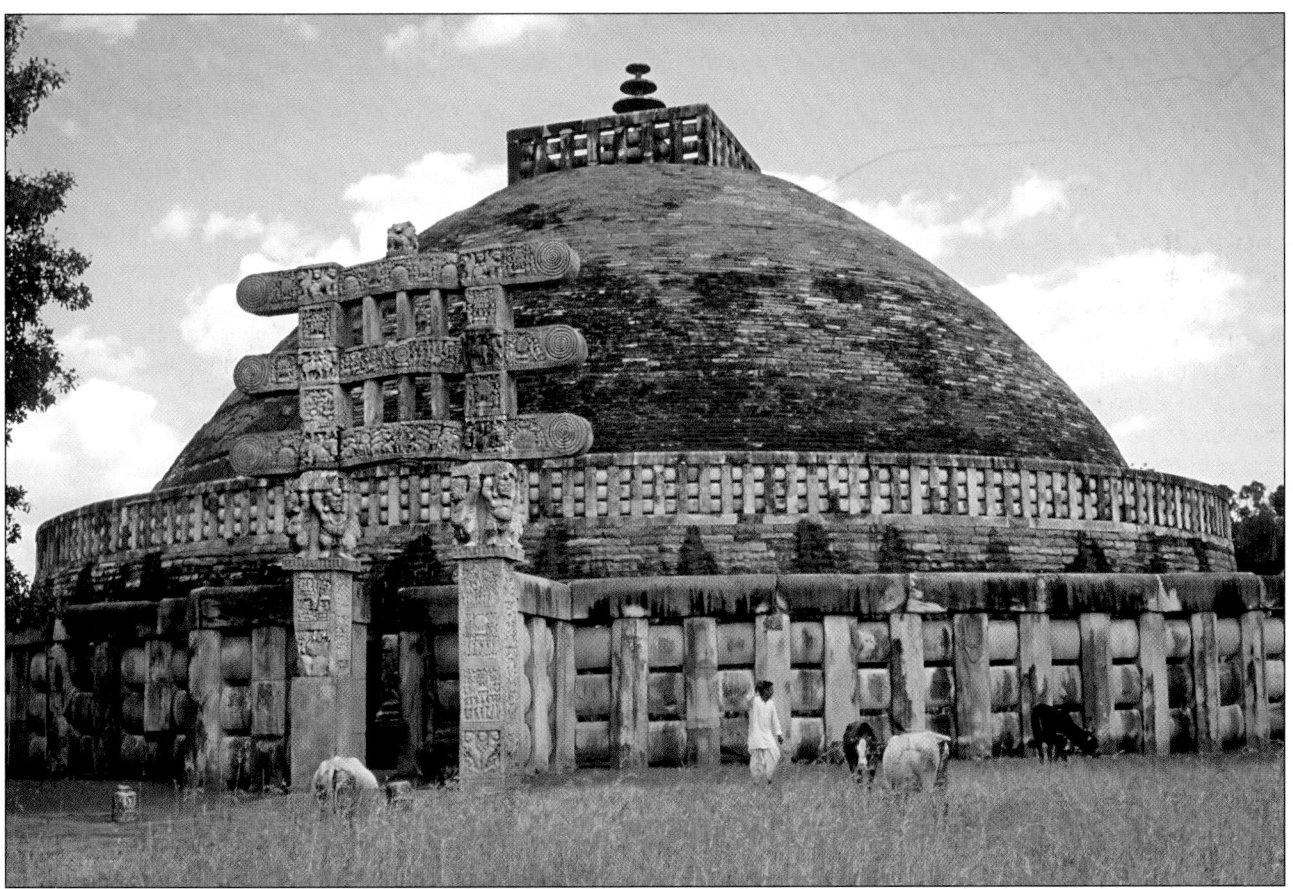

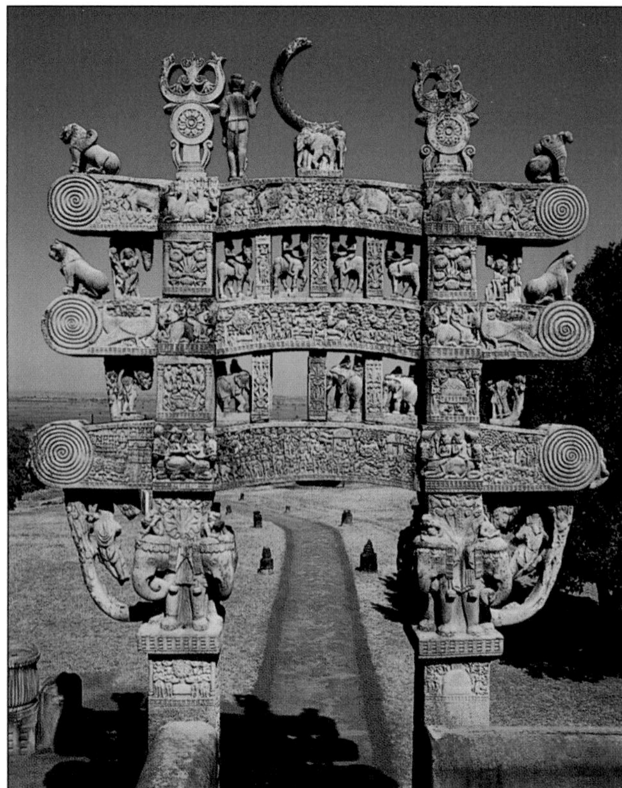

FIGURE 7.4 Gate of the Great Stupa, Sanchi, inner facade of the north gate, third century B.C.E.– early first century C.E., stone, height 34′ (10.35 m). Depicted on the columns and cross beams of this large stone gate are events in the life of the Buddha and stories from the *Jataka* tales.

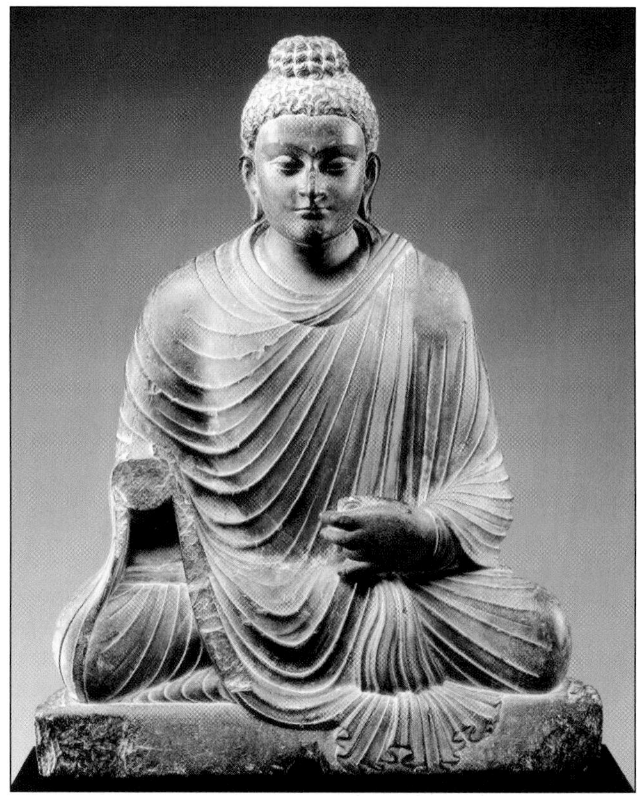

FIGURE 7.5 *Seated Buddha*, from Gandhara, Peshawar District (Pakistan), Kushan, second–third century C.E., dark gray schist. $55\frac{1}{4}'' \times 27\frac{3}{8}'' \times 6\frac{1}{4}''$ (89.53 × 68.67 × 15.88 cm). The Adolph D. and Wilkins C. Williams Fund. Katherine Wetzel/ Virginia Museum of Fine Arts, Richmond. This Buddha figure exhibits grace, calm, and elegance.

MAURYAN TO BACTRIAN TO KUSHAN

During its decline, the Mauryan empire suffered from acute economic difficulties attributable to its large and salaried core of administrators. By about 185 B.C.E., the Mauryan empire had disappeared, and yet India's local rulers maintained order in various large regions of the Indian subcontinent. Among the most important of these was the Bactrian kingdom of northwest India, which came under the rule of the imperial heirs of Alexander of Macedon, who had blended with local populations and who had invaded northern India in the early second century B.C.E. Bactria was a vibrant center of trade that had commercial links with China to the east and the Mediterranean to the west. The northern region of Gandhara became a center of both commercial and cultural exchange, promoting cross-cultural East–West interaction.

By the end of the first century B.C.E., nomadic conquerors from central Asia defeated the Indo-Greek kingdom in Bactria. Rule was established by the Kushan emperors, whose kingdom spread from modern-day Pakistan and Afghanistan, across northern India to Gujurat and the central part of the Ganges River valley. Like their Bactrian predecessors, the Kushan rulers contributed to the silk road commercial network, in large part by ensuring peace in the region between Persia and China.

As nomads, the Kushan had no artistic legacy of their own, so once they were settled in the northern frontier of Afghanistan they adopted foreign traditions, most notably Greco-Roman forms of sculpture. As they gained power, they entered Northwest India and adopted Buddhism, building monasteries and stupas. Most significantly, however, they applied the Greco-Roman sculptural aesthetic to Buddhist imagery and they are often credited with commissioning the first iconic (anthropomorphic) images of the Buddha (fig. 7.5).

Instead of a spiritually inspirational mortal never depicted artistically in human form, the Buddha was now a deity on which followers could focus their devotion. These iconographic images appear as translations of Greco-Roman sculpture, their traditional monks' robes resembling Roman togas with deep ridges and their faces revealing Apollo-like features. However, these early artists made sure these figures could be clearly identified as the Buddha. He can be distinguished by thirty-two physical characteristics (**laksana**), the three most identifiable being:

Ushnishna: the cranial protuberance signifying symbolic omniscient power.
Urna: the round mark in the center of his forehead symbolizing the power to illuminate the world.
Elongated ears: the result of the heavy earrings worn during his princely days. The removal of the earrings symbolizes his renunciation of the material world.

The Kushan are also credited with the creation of the first bodhisattva figures. **Bodhisattvas** are regal, elegant beings with princely bearing who have attained enlightenment but who choose to remain in this world in order to help others on their path to enlightenment. Bodhisattvas represent fully compassionate beings. Popular mainly in northern India, this new Mahayana form of Buddhism spread rapidly to China, Japan, and Korea, along the trade routes that ran through India's mountain passes.

GUPTA ERA

Of the ancient Indian empires that developed from this period, the most important was that of the Gupta, which lasted from the fourth to the sixth century C.E. During the reign of the Guptas, India flourished culturally and commercially. Significant scientific discoveries were made; important developments occurred in literature, music, sculpture, and painting. In terms of Indian cultural achievements, the Gupta era is comparable to Periklean Athens, Han China, and Augustan Rome. It was during the reign of Chandra Gupta II (r. 375–415 C.E.), for example, that the cave paintings at Ajanta were undertaken.

The Gupta empire eventually collapsed under repeated onslaughts by the Huns, who had previously invaded and conquered the Roman world. Regional autonomy was reestablished as the empire became increasingly fractured. From early in the eighth century, Islamic influences began to appear in India, culminating five hundred years later when northern India and the Ganges area fell directly under Turkish Islamic control. Buddhism was eclipsed to a large extent, and as Hinduism gradually reasserted itself, it became mixed with Muslim influences.

GUPTA ART

Gupta art has become associated with the deeply spiritual figure of the Buddha, standing with equanimity, eyes half closed in meditation. Whether standing or seated, Buddhas sculpted in the Gupta Buddhist style appear calm, their worldly cares replaced by an inner tranquillity that suggests otherworldliness. Purely Indian ideals of spirituality were never more fully expressed than in Gupta sculpture. India was no longer under the aesthetic influence of the Roman empire, and native artists were free to develop forms featuring native aesthetics and spiritual richness. Gupta-period sculpture is described as "classical" in terms of its perfection of beauty and expression. The spiritual ideals of the Buddha are now fully balanced and harmonized with the physical manifestations of the Buddha figure.

In the "Standing Buddha" (fig. 7.6), the heavy Greco-Roman–style robe of the Kushan period piece, with its deeply carved drapery folds, is replaced by a sheer robe with drapery abstracted into thin strings cascading rhythmically down the body. The face is softer, more serene, and the compassion of the figure shows through with a lightness and spiritual dignity indicative of Gupta sculpture. There is also an emphasis on the body beneath the robe, which is a very Indian aesthetic, creating a sense of life breath (**prana**) that is important in Indian culture.

As in all sculptural representations of the Buddha, the hands are highly symbolic. Different hand gestures (**mudra**) are used to convey different messages to the viewer. This figure reaches forward with his right hand (now missing) in the *abhaya* mudra, a sign of reassurance, blessing, and protection. His left hand drops to his side in the *varada* mudra, signifying charity and the fulfillment of all wishes. Other mudra include the *dharmachakra* mudra, a sign of teaching in which the hands make a circle with the thumb and forefinger, a reference to the wheel of dharma and the Buddha's first sermon at Deer Park. The mudra most familiar to Westerners is the *dhyana* mudra, in which the hands rest on the Buddha's lap, palms facing upward. A gesture of meditation and harmony, it symbolizes the path to enlightenment.

The political and cultural unity of the Gupta era gave rise to a luxurious aristocratic culture that culminated in the rich aesthetic at Ajanta, where a series of about thirty caves were cut into the side of a 80-meter cliff running from east to west for 600 meters. At Ajanta, the sensuous physical beauty associated with Indian art now symbolizes spiritual beauty as well. The main cave was originally covered with paintings, including the ceiling. The paintings describe the various lives and incarnations of the Buddha as narrated in the ***Jataka*** tales. The central Buddha sculpture is flanked by two painted bodhisattva figures forming a trinity. The facial features of the bodhisattvas Padmapani and Avalokitesvera are serene, reflecting the embodiment of compassion. Padmapani is shown holding a blue lotus and standing in the classic **tribhanga** sculptural pose (fig. 7.7), in which the figure stands, his body in a slight S-curve, with his weight on one leg. Gupta-period Buddhist images were to influence the development of Buddhist art throughout Southeast Asia and the Far East.

THE *JATAKA* AND THE *PANCATANTRA*

Ancient Indian literature contains many folktales and animal stories. One of the most important collections of early stories is the *Jataka*, which means "the story of a birth," consisting of 547 tales that describe the lives the Buddha passed through before achieving enlightenment. The ***Pancatantra*** is a group of didactic stories, designed with the practical aim of providing advice about getting on in the world.

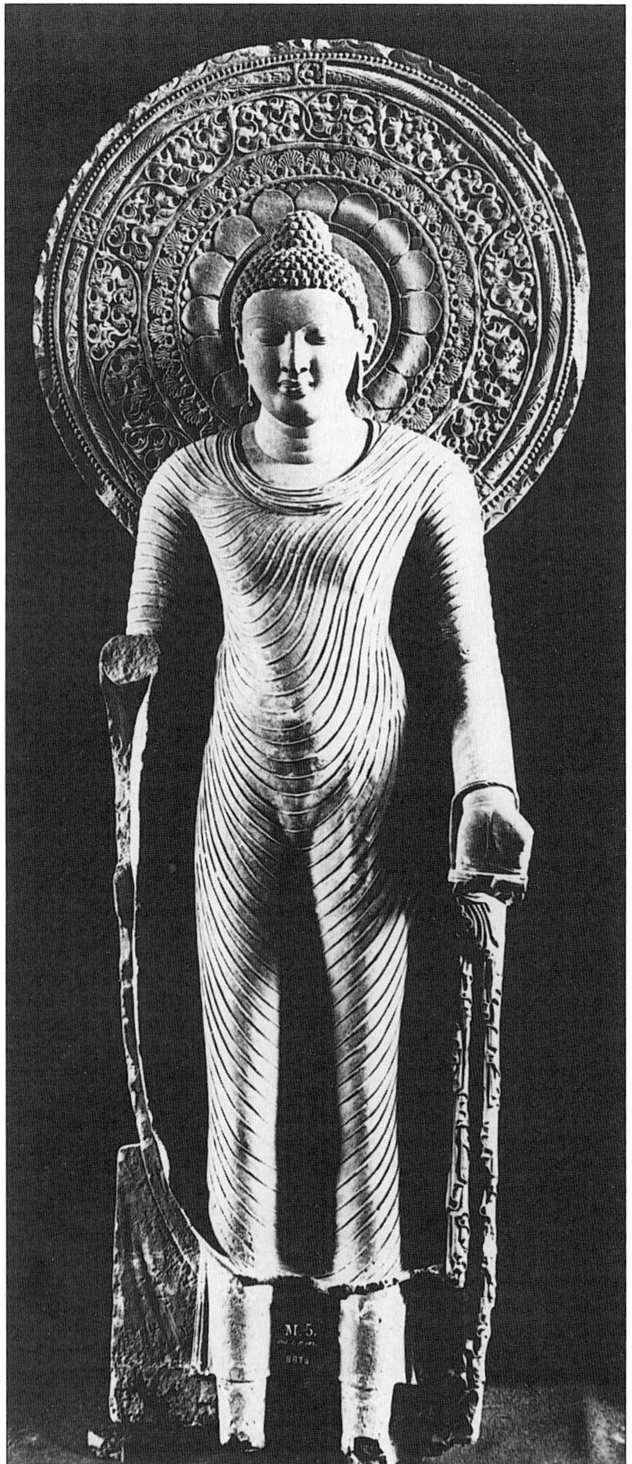

FIGURE 7.6 *Standing Buddha*, from Mathura, Gupta, late fourth–early fifth century C.E., red sandstone, height 7′$\frac{3}{8}$″ (2.17 m), National Museum, New Delhi. The elegance of this standing figure, especially its calm serenity, characterizes the Gupta Buddhist style of sculpture.

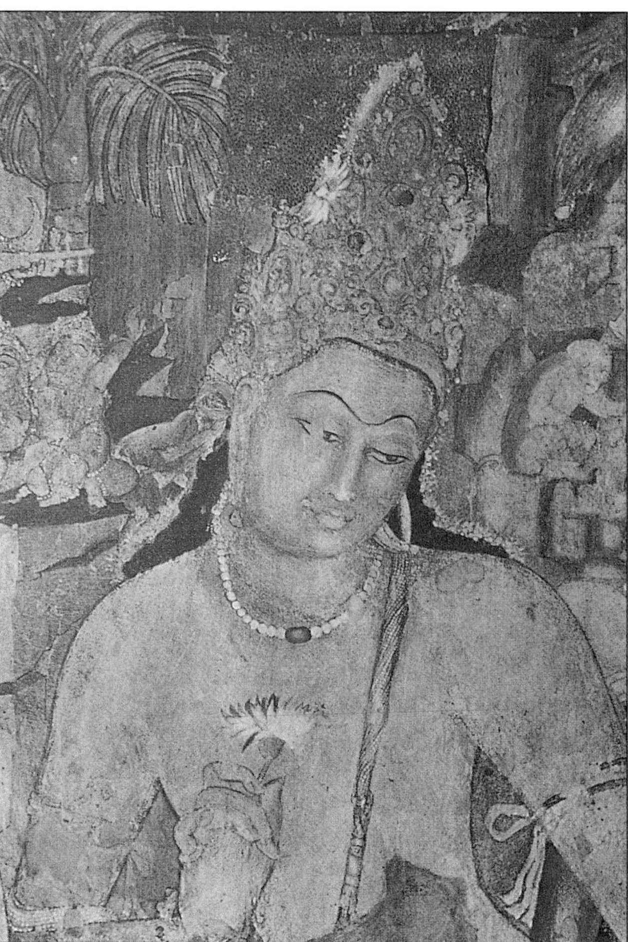

FIGURE 7.7 *Bodhisattva Padmapani*, Ajanta caves, Gupta, late fifth century C.E., wall painting. Didactic stories about the Buddha's life and teachings are illustrated here. In this detail, a serene facial expression indicates this bodhisattva's compassion.

One of the most famous tales of the fourth century B.C.E., *Jataka* describes a hare who sacrifices itself to feed a hungry brahmin. The tale's action reveals the hare to be a bodhisattva in the form of an animal. Like another *Jataka* hero, a monkey who gives up his life for others, the hare displays the perfection of spiritual being in a completely selfless act.

This is quite different from the spirit and flavor of the *Pancatantra*, in which the behavior of its animal heroes is more self-serving and pragmatic. *Pancatantra*, which means "the five strategies," suggests the book's pragmatic inclination. Composed during the second or third century C.E., the stories are linked so one story is joined to another in a continuous chain. This is similar to the connected stories of *The Thousand and One Nights* (see Chapter 6), which may have been influenced by the *Pancatantra*. The authors of the *Jataka* and the *Pancatantra* provide fast-moving action, witty dialogue, and memorable counsel in stories that entertain as they instruct, be that in Buddhist spirituality or in more worldly wisdom.

HINDU DYNASTIES

Although Buddhism flourished during the Gupta era, the Gupta monarchs themselves were increasingly attracted to Hinduism. Temples and sculptures of Hindu gods began to appear, and they continued to proliferate well into the fifteenth and sixteenth centuries, when Muslim kings from Persia took control of most of the subcontinent. Particularly in the south, where the warring Hindu dynasties of the Pallavas and the Cholas vied for power, a long period of great artistic production was set in motion, marked both by decorated temples, rich in stone sculpture, and by the rise of bronze as a favored medium for sculpture.

HINDU TEMPLES

The structures and designs of Hindu temples were established in the series of ancient texts called **shastras.** These function as guides to many different activities, not just temple building, and include advice on cooking, warfare, love-making, poetry, and music. The guides to architecture, especially those concerning temple architecture, do not always concur in every detail with actual temple construction.

Temples in the south are better preserved than northern temples, since the Muslim incursion into India was most destructive in the north. One of the most magnificent and largest of medieval Hindu temples and one in an exceptional state of preservation is the Kandariya Mahadeo temple at Khajuraho, dating from the eleventh century (fig. 7.8). As with many temples of that period, it forms part of a cluster of temples in the area.

The Kandariya Mahadeo temple is situated on a high masonry platform that emphasizes height and verticality; the **sikhara** (tower) rises over 98 feet (30 m) from the base of the temple. The temple's profile reveals its symbolism as a mountain with intricate domelike roofs that rise in a crescendo of grandeur. Equally compelling is the vibrancy and richness of their surface ornamentation. The richly decorated walls include over six hundred sculptures on the exterior and two hundred on the interior, dominating the overall aesthetic. Niches and screens, pillars and openings, pavilions and courtyards enhance the splendor of the edifice. Adorning the temple is a wealth of sculpture that depicts historical and mythological subjects, such as the monarchs who reigned during the temple's construction; the ***Surasundaris,*** or divine nymphs, in amatory poses; figures of dancers and musicians; mothers with children; lovers; women adjusting their hair; and a vast array of other images.

SCULPTURE

Bronze was the medium most favored by the southern Indian Chola dynasties from the tenth to the twelfth centuries. Chola sculptors employed the ***cire perdue,*** or **lost-wax process.** In this technique, a model of the subject was first made in wax, which is easy to mold. The wax model was then encased in clay and heated; the wax melted but the clay did not. Holes were made in the clay surround before it was heated, however, to permit the wax to run out. The hollow clay case was then filled with molten bronze. When the bronze cooled and hardened, the clay was broken away, leaving a finished bronze cast.

FIGURE 7.8 Kandariya Mahadeo temple, Khajuraho, Chandella, ca. 1025–50. This temple's tower soars more than a hundred feet into the air, its eighty-four subordinate towers providing a visual display of majestic grandeur.

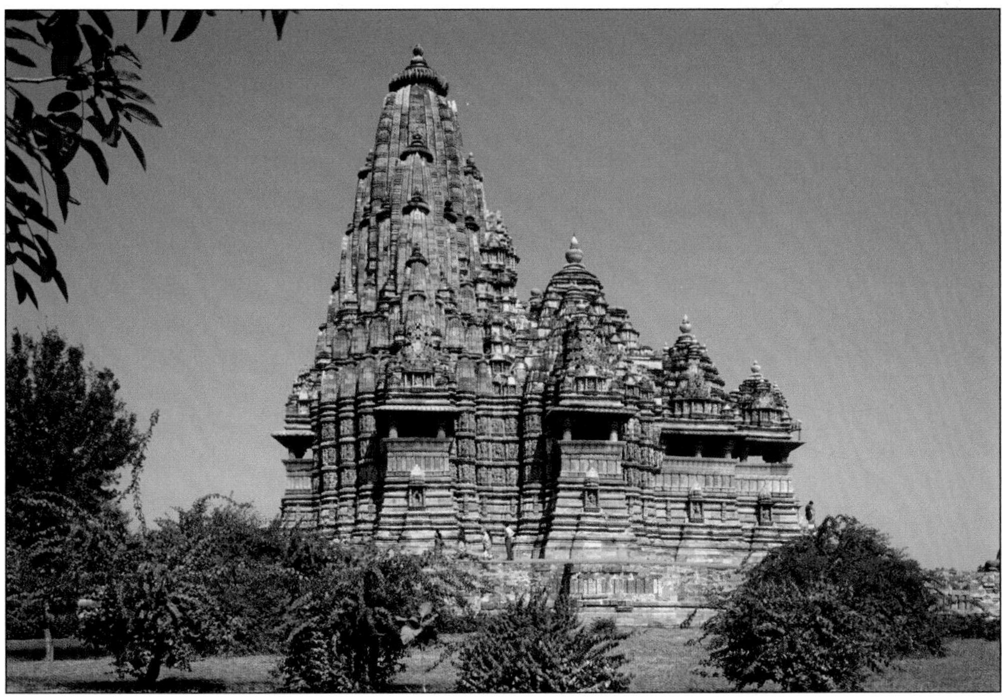

Then & Now

MUSLIM INDIA

Islam arrived in India as early as the eighth century, but it was not until the twelfth century that it began to have a powerful impact on the subcontinent. In 1192, the Afghan king Muhammad of Ghur, invading from the north by land, defeated the Hindus. After initial fighting, a spirit of peaceful coexistence lasted for several centuries. But no two religions could be more different than Hinduism and Islam. Hinduism is sufficiently loose in its religious structure to allow great divergences in spiritual beliefs and practices, whereas Islam controls almost every aspect of daily life. But where Hinduism is intellectually liberal and Islam conservative, the opposite is true socially. The social restrictions of Hinduism's caste system, in contrast to the possibilities of social mobility and equality offered by Islam, may have led many Indians to adopt the Islamic faith. Especially around Delhi and Agra, where the Muslim rulers held sway, Islam took firm hold and was responsible for creating some of the greatest monuments of Indian culture.

The most famous building in India is the Taj Mahal (fig. 7.9), in Agra, built 1630–48 by the Muslim Shah Jahan as a mausoleum for his wife, Mumtaz Mahal. Some 20,000 workers took nearly twenty years to build the Taj, including transporting thousands of white marble blocks 120 miles.

The Taj Mahal's white marble walls are deeply cut with arched recesses that catch shadows, creating a three-dimensional facade. The building appears to be weightless, the dome floating like a balloon. Decoration includes floral relief carving and gray stone inlay. Jade and crystal from China, lapis lazuli from Afghanistan, and coral and mother of pearl from the Indian Ocean were used in its lavish detail. The landscape setting continues the formal concern with symmetry: The building is reflected in a long pool flanked by rows of small trees and shrubs. The Taj Mahal is celebrated for its exquisite refinement and enchanting elegance.

By the twentieth century, relations between India's Hindus and Muslims had reached a crisis point, and in 1947, after a violent and bloody partition, the independent Muslim state of Pakistan was born, consisting of two separate areas: West Pakistan, with its capital at Islamabad near the Khyber Pass on the Indus River, and East Pakistan (which seceded from the union in 1971 to become Bangladesh), with its capital at Dacca. The fifty million Muslims who were left in India became an official minority with the right to be represented in the Indian parliament.

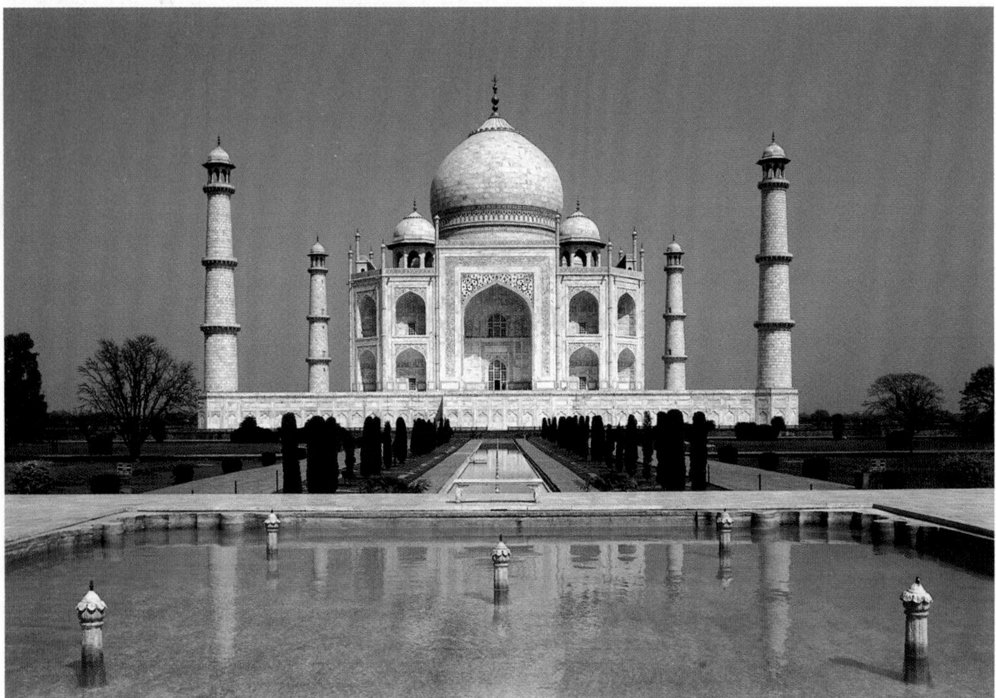

FIGURE 7.9 Taj Mahal, Agra, 1630–48. This mausoleum was built by Shah Jahan for his wife, Mumtaz Mahal. The white marble domes seem to reach heavenward while they are reflected in the long pool of water.

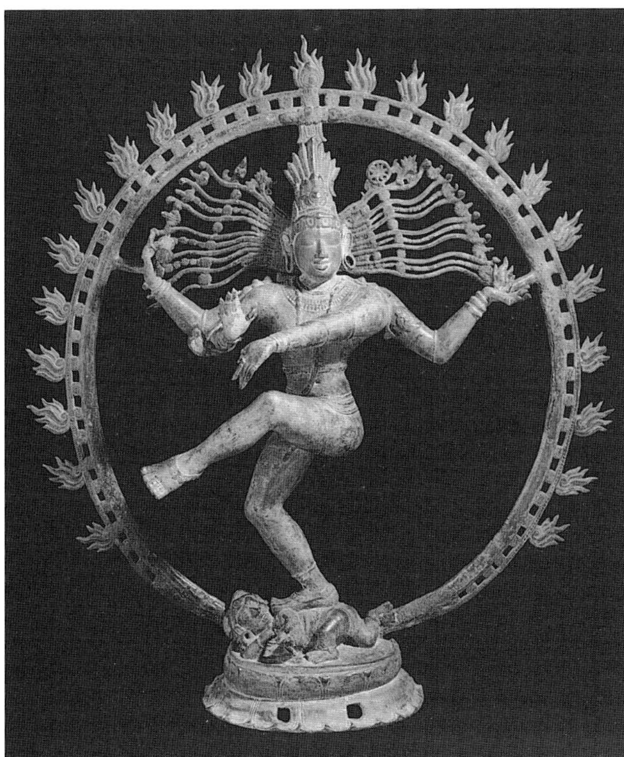

FIGURE 7.10 *Shiva Nataraja (Lord of the Dance)*, Chola, eleventh-twelfth centuries, bronze, height $32\frac{1}{2}''$ (82 cm), Von der Heydt Collection, Museum Rietherg, Zurich. The most famous of Hindu icons, the dancing Shiva is both the creator and destroyer of the universe.

The *Shiva Nataraja (Lord of the Dance)* (fig. 7.10) is perhaps the most famous of Hindu icons. Numerous examples of this icon exist—strict rules governing its production have resulted in a remarkable consistency across individual instances—and it continues to be produced in southern India to this day. The icon depicts the dancing Shiva as creator and destroyer of the universe, symbolized by the ring of flames around him. With his hair flying out in two directions, and his arms and legs seemingly in motion, the dancing Shiva crushes Apasmarapurusha, the demon of ignorance, promising relief from life's illusoriness, and also offering reassurance and blessing in the *abhaya* mudra of his front right hand. This dance is said to herald the last night of the world, when all the stars fall from the sky and the universe is reduced to ashes. But the dance promises the renewal of creation itself.

HINDU LYRIC POETRY

The poetry of the twelfth-century mystic MAHADEVIYAKKA [ma-ha-de-VEE-ha-ka], the foremost Indian woman poet before the modern era, represents the quintessential medieval genre of **bhakti,** or devotional religious poetry. Bhakti poetry was part of a larger movement in which the poets were recognized as saints and celebrated as models of religious devotion. Their poems honored the chief Hindu gods Shiva and Vishnu, especially the latter's major avatars Krishna and Rama.

Bhakti devotional poetry is rooted in deeply felt emotion. As with the mystical and devotional poetry of other cultures, it uses colloquial language and draws on imagery from everyday experience in an attempt to convey a sense of earthly longing for the divine. Like the poems of the English Renaissance poet John Donne (see Chapter 14), those of Mahadeviyakka employ images of physical love and experience to convey a sense of spirituality. Mahadeviyakka's poetry also exhibits a carefree, daredevil attitude that is, perhaps surprisingly, not at odds with a deep longing for communion with the godhead.

INDIAN DRAMA: KALIDASA'S *SAKUNTALA*

Kalidasa (fourth to fifth centuries C.E.) is best known as the author of *Sakuntala and the Ring of Recollection*, usually referred to by its short title, *Sakuntala*. Kalidasa flourished during the classical era of the Guptas, between 390 and 470. The plot of this most beloved of Indian plays was adapted from the *Mahabharata*. The play tells the story of the beautiful maiden Sakuntala, who is first seen in the woodland hermitage of the King Dusyanta, who falls in love with her. The ring of the title figures in the plot as it is first lost, then found, and serves, with the aid of gods and sages, to reunite the lovers in a happy ending.

Like all Sanskrit plays, *Sakuntala* ends happily because that is what the dramatic tradition requires. Ancient Sanskrit drama thus differs strongly from ancient Greek drama, which often ends tragically. Tragedy, however, is alien to the Hindu conception of the universe, in which history is cyclical and in which human action is based on karma rather than on character and destiny, as in Greek drama.

MUSIC

Indian music is essentially melodic. Harmony is present only as a backdrop, in the form of the continuous sounding of a single tone; the complex melody is elaborated over the top. Indian music is rarely written out formally as a score. This independence from notation offers performers great interpretive latitude, allowing them the opportunity to improvise creatively and develop the mood of the pieces they play. The music is typically performed by a soloist, who plays or sings the melody; a drummer, who supplies the rhythm; and a third player, who provides the drone chord, which is a single three-note chord sounded continuously throughout the piece, usually on the lutelike **tambura.**

Although also serving a purpose as entertainment, Indian music is rich in religious associations. Hindu deities, for example, are frequently evoked in classical dance and songs. Moreover, it is not uncommon for musicians to consider their performance an act of religious devotion.

The most important instrument in the performance of Indian music is the human voice. With its great flexibility and expressiveness, the voice provides a model for other instruments. As in the Western classical tradition, singers of Indian music are trained to perform an extensive range of

Cross Currents

RAVI SHANKAR AND PHILIP GLASS

Born in Baltimore in 1937, American composer Philip Glass was trained at the Juilliard School of Music in New York. He was frustrated with the state of contemporary music until, in the 1960s, he was hired to work on the soundtrack for *Chappaqua*, a now-forgotten alternative film. His job was to take the improvised Indian ragas of Indian musician RAVI SHANKAR [SHAN-kah] (b. 1920) (fig. 7.11) and transcribe them into Western musical notation so Western musicians could perform them on the soundtrack. Glass was particularly impressed with the background drone chord of the raga. He thought it was made up of units of two and three notes that formed long chains of modular rhythmic patterns. He was in fact entirely wrong in terms of musicology, but it led him, as misreadings so often can, to invent his own distinct musical style. He traveled to India many times and gradually developed an almost hypnotic rhythmic style of his own. The music he began to compose consisted of the rhythmic units he had heard in Shankar's work, with simple and apparently arbitrarily chosen notes or pitches strung together in cyclical groups. The repetitiveness of the musical form suggests the drone chord of the raga.

The culmination of the Indian connection in Glass's music was his opera *Satyagraha*, first performed in Rotterdam, Holland, in 1980. The work consists of several stories from the life of the young Mahatma Gandhi, the great pacifist and political and spiritual leader who led the campaign to free India from British rule. The work's title, *Satyagraha*, means "holding fast to the truth" and refers to Gandhi's nonviolent method of noncooperation and civil disobedience. Slow and meditative in its rhythm, the music evokes the image of Gandhi sitting in protest as he fasted and meditated, in full confidence that India would eventually triumph.

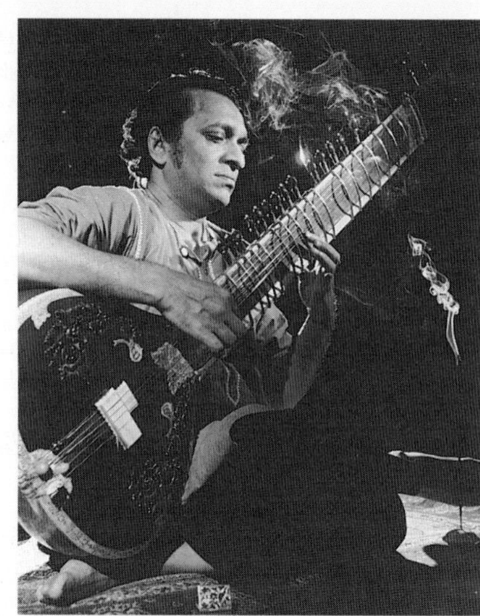

FIGURE 7.11 Ravi Shankar playing the sitar, *Life* magazine, 1958. The sitar is a lute-shaped instrument with an extended neck and moveable frets that enable performers to produce a wide range of scale tones.

Critical Thinking

SACRED COWS

According to Hinduism, cows are sacred and thus not to be killed for their meat. Cows wander the streets of Indian towns and villages unharmed. The expression "a sacred cow" has come to refer to an idea or concept in a culture that is not permitted to be harmed or tampered with. In the United States, for example, the concept of social security, a system in which workers make monetary contributions during their working lives so that they can collect a modest monthly stipend when they retire, is considered a metaphorical sacred cow. In France, the idea of a guaranteed job from which it is almost impossible to be fired is another example of such a conceptual sacred cow. Politicians in both countries are reluctant to change these policies. What are some other sacred cows? You might think of social, political, economic, religious, or other cultural beliefs and behaviors that through tradition have become solidified such that it is difficult if not impossible to challenge or change them. What are some benefits and drawbacks of such sacred cows?

vocal intricacies. These vocal acrobatics include modulations of pitch involving many more tones than those of standard Western musical scales.

The **sitar** is a lute-shaped instrument with an extended neck and movable frets that enable performers to produce an enormous number of tones. The standard sitar has five melody strings, two drone strings, and a dozen or more sympathetic strings beneath them. These lower strings are not struck with the fingers or a plectrum like the others. Instead, they vibrate in sympathy with those actually played, lending the music an enriched shimmering sound.

The sitar is the chief instrument used in playing **ragas,** musical compositions based on one of the eight primary **rasas**—moods or flavors—of Indian aesthetics: love, courage, hatred, anger, mirth, terror, pity, and surprise, all of which are balanced in tranquility. Ragas can also be expressed in painting and poetry. A raga, then, is a work of art that conveys a distinct impression (the word *raga* means "passion" or "feeling"). Because of their highly specific character, ragas are typically associated with a particular Hindu deity, a particular time of day or season of the year, or a particular religious festival.

Cultural Impact

Unlike the Chinese Tang and Song dynasties and the Islamic Umayyad and Abbasid dynasties, India's political organization was not centralized. India's traditions, although centered on Hinduism, found room for other religious developments such as Buddhism. Like other societies, India experienced cultural change, with Indian traditions influencing and being influenced by cultural and religious developments in other lands. Like Islam, Hinduism emerged as an important popular religious faith within the Indian subcontinent. In addition, Indian merchants helped establish not only Hinduism, but Buddhism and Islam as well in Southeast Asia.

The most significant legacy of ancient India is its Hindu religious heritage. The *Bhagavad Gita*, for example, has become famous well beyond the borders of India. This ancient text had a decisive influence on the American transcendentalist writer Henry David Thoreau, who alludes to it in his book *Walden*. The *Bhagavad Gita*, moreover, has also served as inspiration for political and social action as well as a stimulus for the practice of nonviolent resistance, made famous in the twentieth century by Mahatma Gandhi in India, and by Martin Luther King, Jr., in the United States during the civil rights struggle in the 1960s.

A standard musical raga form includes an improvised prelude or introductory section called an **alap,** played in a free tempo. The purpose of the alap is to introduce the spirit and mood of the raga. The alap is followed by a formally composed musical section for a solo instrument with a percussion accompaniment. The final section is an improvisation on the composed music with many returns of the theme, in a form loosely comparable to the rondo (or returning theme) of Western music. Toward the end of a raga performance, the emphasis shifts from melodic elaboration to a display of the performer's own virtuosity.

KEY TERMS

nomad
Sanskrit
Vedas
Hindu
Brahman
Vishnu
Lakshmi
avatar
Krishna
Shiva
samsara
karma
dalits (outcastes)
maya
kanda
Jainism
Buddhism
Middle Path
Bodhi
nirvana
stupa
chattras
yasti
yakshis
laksana
ushnishna
urna
bodhisattva
prana
mudra
Jataka
tribhanga
Pancatantra
shastras
sikhara
Surasundaris
cire perdue (lost-wax process)
bhakti
tambura
sitar
ragas
rasas
alap

www. WEBSITES FOR FURTHER STUDY

http://www.gosai.com/links/india-links.html
(This is a good source for the Vedic culture, with many links.)

http://mcel.pacificu.edu/as/students/cgono/siddhartha.html
(This site has an excellent history of Buddhism.)

http://www.indiantravelportal.com/temples//index.html
(This site covers many general topics of all things Indian.)

http://www.mnsu.edu/emuseum/prehistory/india
(Very early Indian culture and civilization.)

http://www.rhapsody.com/album/shankar-sitar-concertos-ragas
(Ravi Shankar performs Indian ragas.)

http://www.crystallinks.com/indiaculture.html
(Music, painting, dance, theatre, and more, with representative images.)

http://wsu.edu/~dee/ANCINDIA/CONTENTS.HTM
(Jainism compared with Buddhism, visual cultures, Indian music, women in ancient India, and more.)

Chapter 8

History

ca. 1050–221 B.C.E.	Zhou dynasty
604 B.C.E.	Laozi born
551–479 B.C.E.	Confucius lives
221 B.C.E.	Qin dynasty (221–206 B.C.E.) first unites China
206 B.C.E.–220 C.E.	Han dynasty
ca. 220–590 C.E.	Buddhism spreads
ca. 350 C.E.	Six Dynasties
460–470 C.E.	Buddha of Yun Kang
sixth century C.E.	Buddhism introduced to Japan from China
618–907 C.E.	Tang dynasty
907–960 C.E.	Civil war
960–1279 C.E.	Song dynasty
1271 C.E.	Marco Polo arrives in Hangzhou
1274 C.E., 1281 C.E.	Mongol attacks under Kublai Khan

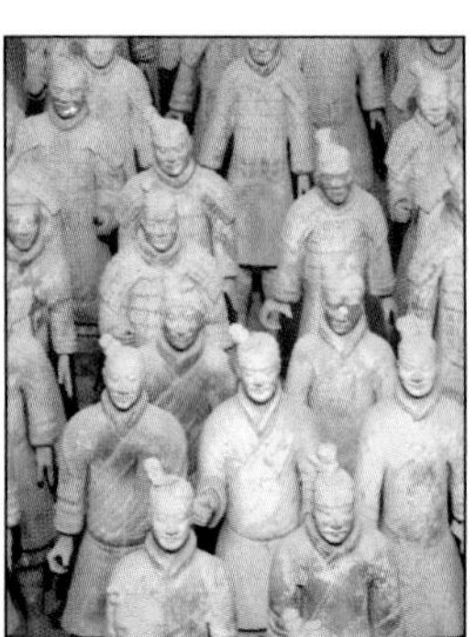

Arts and Architecture

twelfth century B.C.E.	*Fang ding*
433 B.C.E.	Bronze bells
ca. 970 C.E.	Zhu Jan, *Seeking the Tao in the Autumn Mountains*
1072 C.E.	Guo Xi, *Early Spring*

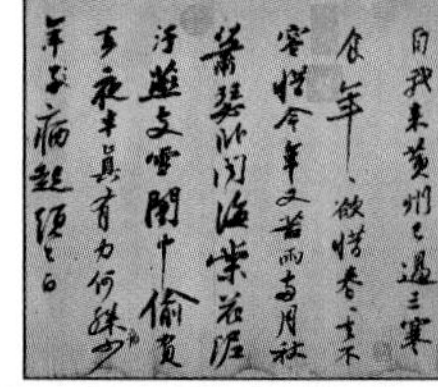

Literature and Philosophy

604 B.C.E.	*Tao Te Ching* composed
551–479 B.C.E.	*Analects* composed
sixth century B.C.E.	*Book of Songs* compiled
ca. 220–590 C.E.	Midnight Songs composed
365–427 C.E.	Tao Qian lives and writes poems
699–761 C.E.	Wang Wei lives and writes poems
701–762 C.E.	Li Bai lives and writes poems
712–770 C.E.	Du Fu lives and writes poems

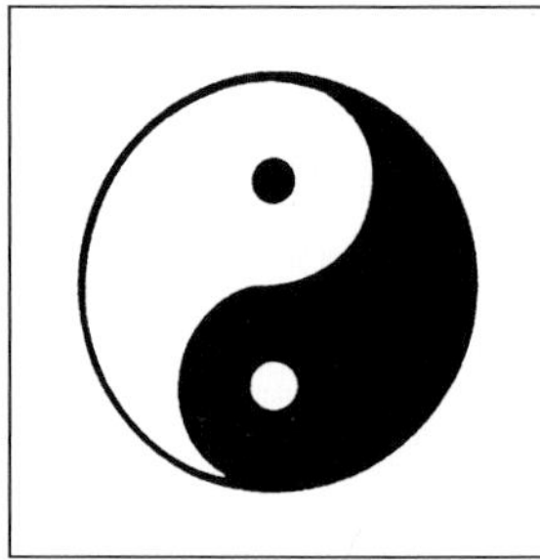

Early Chinese Civilization

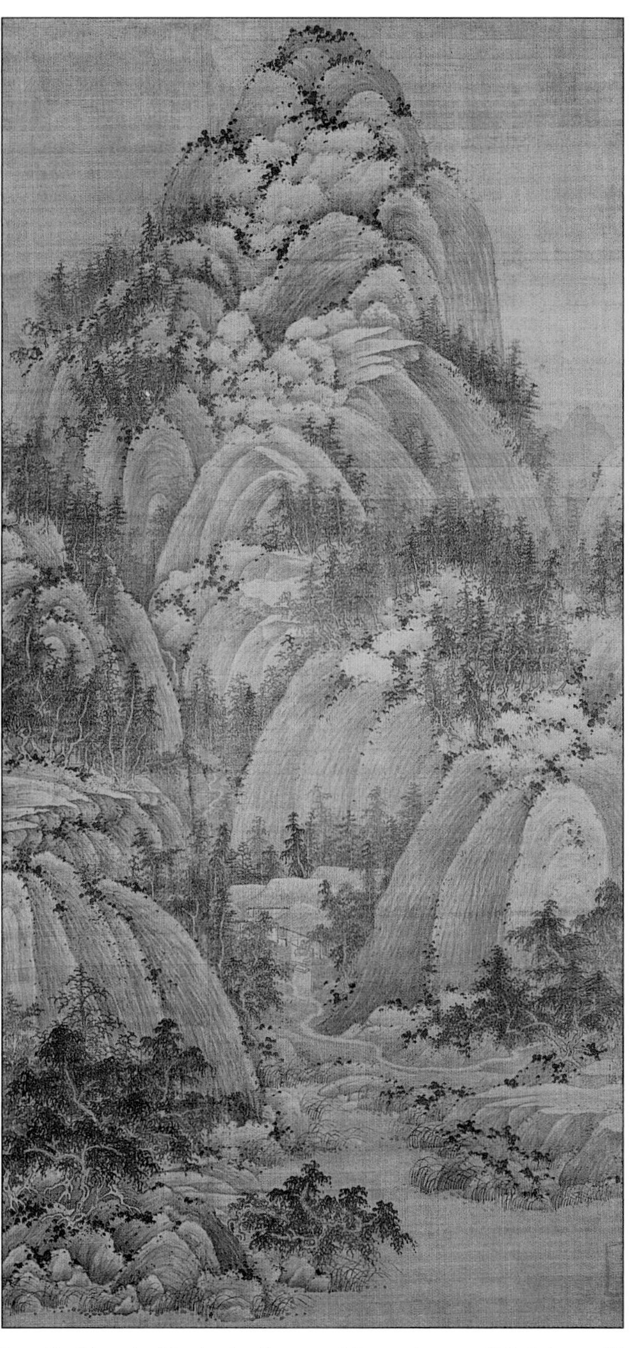

Zhu Jan, *Seeking the Tao in the Autumn Mountains*, ca. 970, ink on silk, 61 × 30″ (156.2 × 78.1 cm), National Palace Museum, Taipei, Taiwan.

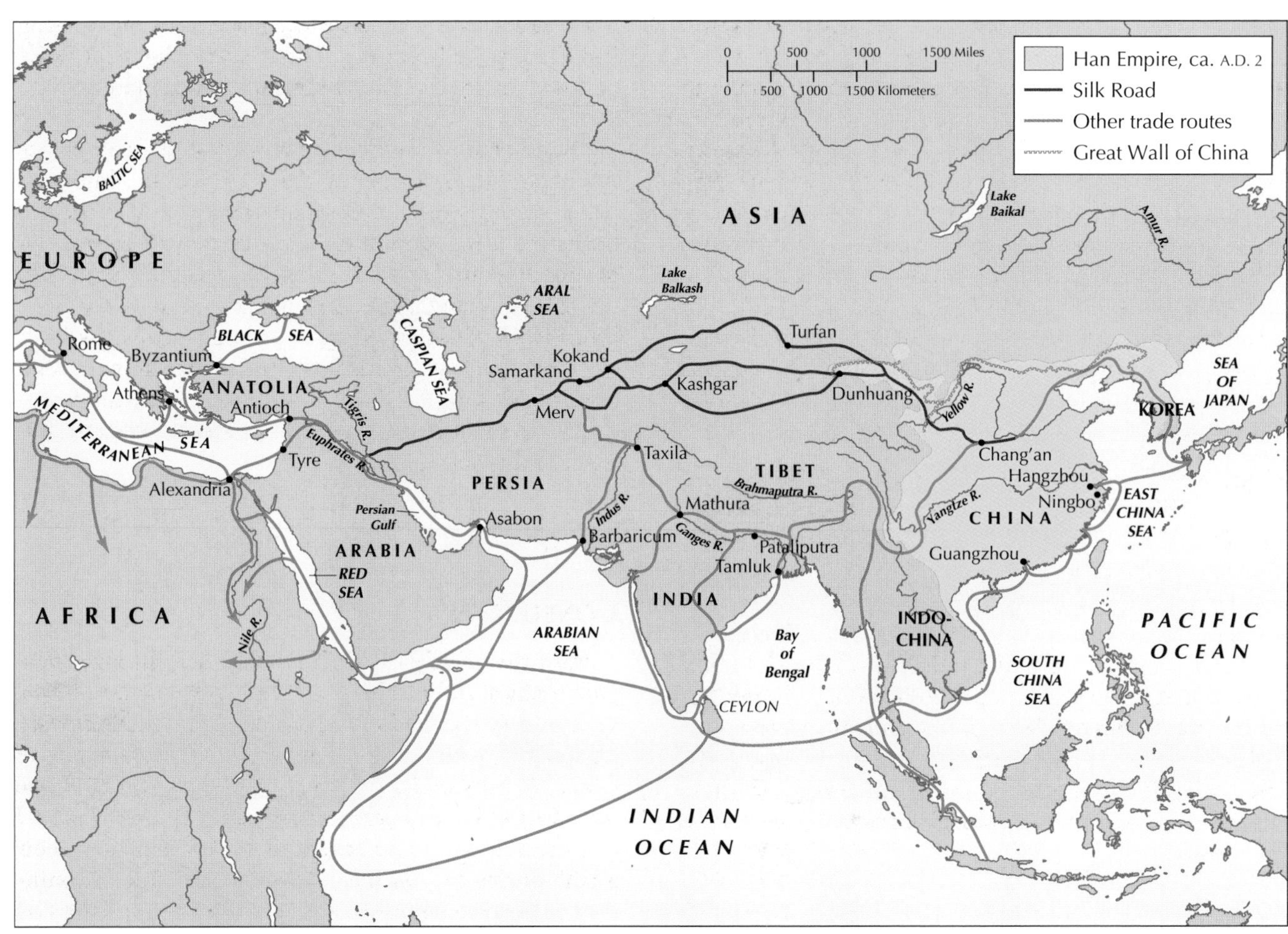

MAP 8.1 Han China and the Silk Road.

CHAPTER OVERVIEW

EARLY DYNASTIES

EARLY DYNASTIES

SHANG AND ZHOU DYNASTIES

CHINA IS THE WORLD'S OLDEST CIVILIZATION, tracing its roots back as far as the fifth millennium B.C.E., although the earliest of the Chinese eras for which archaeological evidence has been found is that of the Shang dynasty, dating from ca. 1600 B.C.E. The Shang dynasty itself was long believed to be only legend and myth, until its existence was verified through twentieth-century excavations. These have yielded not only ancient artifacts but also the oldest examples of Chinese writing, utilizing a separate graph (character) for each word. This written language has remained virtually unchanged for centuries, uniting a country about the size of the United States, where the spoken form of the language has varied so much that it cannot be understood from region to region.

The ancient Shang people inhabited the central Yellow River Valley area of China and developed the most advanced technology of the Chinese Bronze Age. The ruler of the Shang state had a quasi-divine status, which was honored by the people in ritual ceremonies and through serving the ruler in war. The talents of Shang craftworkers were also deployed in honoring their god-king rulers.

Although the oldest Shang cities discovered so far were at Erlitou (2000 B.C.E.) and ZHENGZHOU [Zheng-JOE] (1600 B.C.E.), it is the later city site of Anyang (ca. 1384–1111 B.C.E.) that has yielded the majority of Shang artifacts. At Anyang, archaeologists have found rich burial sites, but no city walls or dwellings, leading them to believe Anyang may have been a royal burial site for another city.

The Shang kings ruled until about eleventh century B.C.E., when the Zhou people came from the northwest and conquered them. The new Zhou dynasty (ca. eleventh century–221 B.C.E.) then introduced organized agriculture, which replaced the Shang emphasis on hunting. The Zhou established a feudal society—in which land was granted to someone by the king or an overlord in return for support in war and loyalty—with the Zhou king ruling as a "T'ien," or "Son of Heaven." The principles of societal relationships that the Zhou formulated were to influence later Chinese civilization, and they can be found in such Chinese classics as the *Book of Odes* and the *Book of Ritual.* Yet although the Zhou modified the social and religious practices of the Shang, they adopted other aspects of Shang culture, in particular the Shang use of bronze casting and their decorative techniques.

Shang and Zhou Bronzes. Although jade and glazed pottery artifacts dating from the Shang dynasty have been found, by far the most numerous and important Shang artifacts are made of bronze. These, buried with the dead, were presumably meant to serve the king or nobleman in his future life. The *fang ding* (fig. 8.1) was used for storing food and wine for social and religious ceremonial functions. The emphasis on animal motifs, which is typical of the intricate ornamental design found in Shang bronze artifacts, suggests the importance of hunting in Shang culture. The most important and numerous of these mysterious motifs is the T'ao-t'ieh mask, which can be found hidden within the surface patterns of most Shang and Zhou period bronzes. The creature can most easily be found by locating its two eyes, then deciphering the rest of its facial features.

FIGURE 8.1 *Fang ding*, Tomb 1004, Houjiazhang, Anyang, Henan, Shang dynasty, bronze, twelfth century B.C.E., © The British Museum. The ornate design on this square vessel was typical for Shang bronze artifacts, suggesting both animals and more mysterious forms of life.

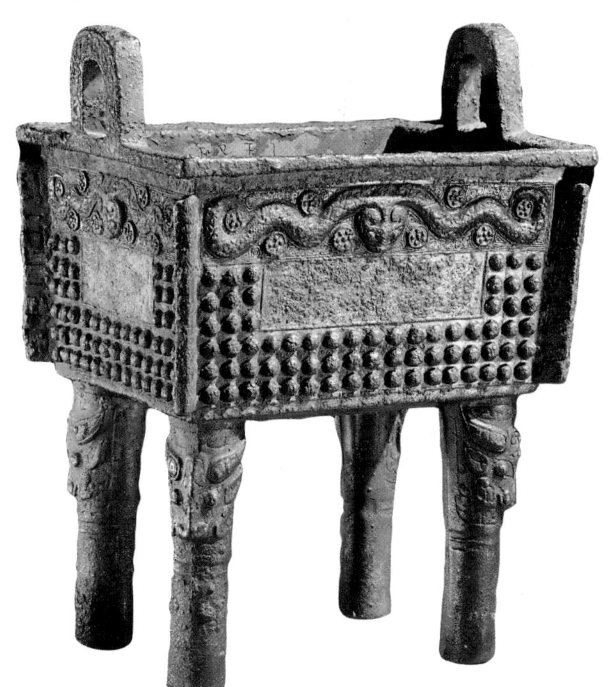

Such bronze objects remained of great importance throughout the Zhou period that followed. In addition to being buried in graves, bronzes were now also used to honor the living, as inscriptions carved in their bases indicate. One indication of the great wealth of the Zhou rulers is the monumental carillon, consisting of sixty-five bronze bells, discovered in the tomb of Marquis Yi of Zheng (fig. 8.2). Each of the bells, believed to have been used in rituals to communicate with the supernatural, produces two quite distinct tones when struck near the center or at the rim.

CHINESE PHILOSOPHY

CONFUCIANISM

Toward the middle of the Zhou dynasty, the two great philosophical and religious traditions indigenous to China took hold: Confucianism and Taoism. Like Buddhism (see Chapter 7), which would later have its own impact on China, **Confucianism** is based on the teachings of one man. CONFUCIUS [con-FYOU-shus] (551–479 B.C.E.) was the son of aristocratic parents who had lost their wealth during the decline of feudalism in China. Confucius' father died before he was born, and he was raised by his mother in poverty. He received an education from the village tutor, studying poetry, history, music, hunting, fishing, and archery, the traditional educational disciplines of the time. After a brief stint as a government official, Confucius embarked on a career as a teacher. He wandered from place to place, offering his services as an adviser on human conduct and on government. After many years as a successful and famous teacher, Confucius spent the last part of his life quietly teaching at home.

After his death, Confucius' sayings, along with those of his followers, were collected together during the fifth century in a volume called *The Analects.* Drawing on cultural values anchored in ancient Chinese tradition, these eminently practical sayings focus on this world rather than the next. Although Confucius deeply respected the Chinese cultural heritage, valuing its best aspects, he adapted ancient traditions to the circumstances of his own time. Living in a period of political chaos and moral confusion, Confucius emphasized the importance of the traditional values of self-control, propriety, and filial piety to maintain a productive and good society. It was through such virtues that Confucius believed anarchy could be overcome and social cohesion restored.

Confucius' point of departure was the individual rather than society. He believed that if each individual could be virtuous, the family would live in harmony. Similarly, if each family lived according to certain moral principles,

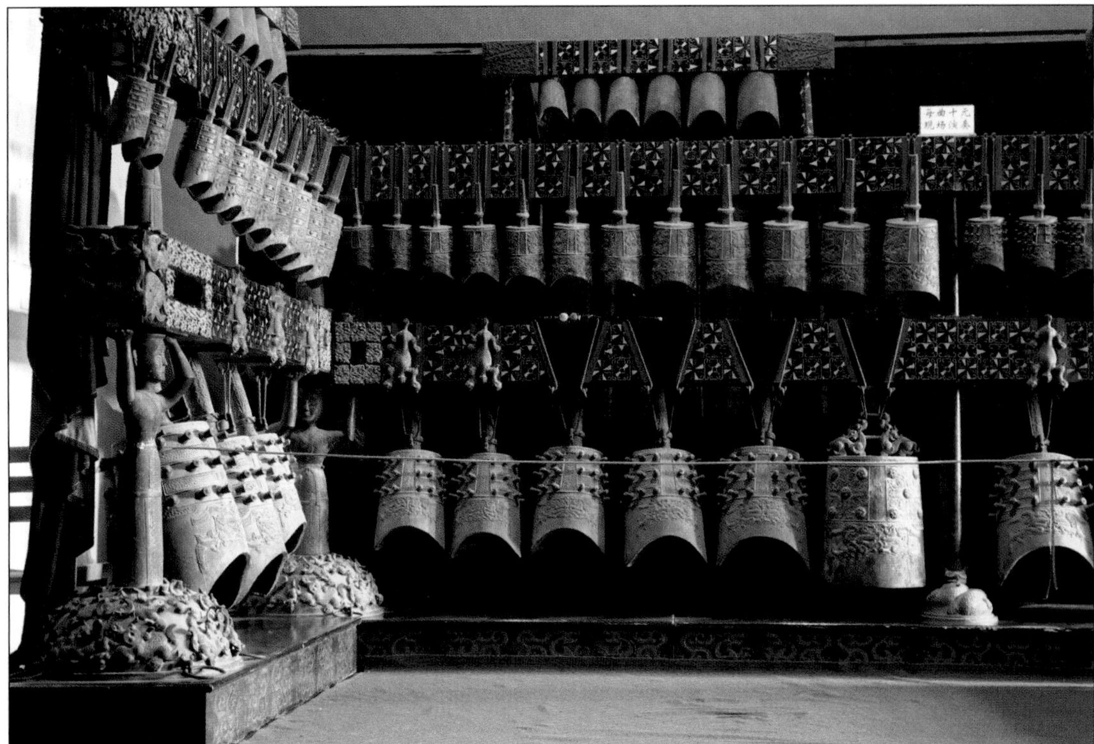

FIGURE 8.2 A unitary ensemble of 65 Chinese bronze Zhong bells, in Qingfeng Tower, Hefei, Anhui province, China. © NRT-Travel/Alamy. Not only a major feat of bronze casting, these bells are also a musical marvel, with two different notes available from each bell.

the village would be harmonious. Village harmony, in turn, would lead to a country focused on moral values, coupled with an aesthetic sensibility that would allow life to be lived to its fullest creative potential.

Four qualities in particular—***li***, ***jen***, ***te***, and ***wen***—were valued in Confucian teaching. *Li* equates to propriety, ceremony, and civility, and it requires the development of proper attitudes and a due respect for established forms of conduct. At its heart are the four basic social rules of human relationships: courtesy, politeness, good manners, and respect, especially a reverence for age. These are supplemented by a fifth rule or concept, that of ***yi***, or duty, a sense of the obligation one has to others. These five key rules strongly underpin the centrality of the family in Chinese life. Children's duty to their parents is the root from which moral and social virtues grow. In talking to an older person, for example, the younger person responds only after the elder has spoken. The younger person also listens with due deference and does not interrupt or contradict.

Jen, sometimes translated as benevolence, refers to the ideal relationship that should exist between people. Based on respect for oneself, *jen* extends this respect to others and manifests itself in acts of charity and courtesy. According to the Confucian ideal, *jen* and *li* together make for a superior human being.

Te refers to virtue. Originally it referred to the quality of greatness that enabled an individual to subdue enemies, inspire respect, and influence others. However, in Confucian teaching it came to signify a different kind of power—that of moral example rather than that of physical strength or might. A strong leader who guides by example exhibits *te*. So do the forces of nature, as the following saying from *The Analects* illustrates:

> Asked by the ruler whether the lawless should be executed, Confucius answered: "What need is there of the death penalty in government? If you showed a sincere desire to be good, your people would likewise be good. The virtue of the prince is like the wind; the virtue of the people is like grass. It is the nature of grass to bend when the wind blows upon it."

The final characteristic of Confucian tradition, *wen*, refers to the arts of peace, that is, to music, poetry, art, and other cultural activities. Confucius considered the arts a form of moral education. He saw music as especially conducive to order and harmony, and he believed the greatest painting and poetry function in the same way as an excellent leader, since they provide a model of excellence.

Ultimately, Confucius was an empiricist, justifying the value of his moral prescriptions by an appeal to experience. His teachings were designed to help his followers live a better individual and communal life in the present rather than to achieve an eternal reward after death. Morality, moreover, depended on context. There was no inflexible "thou shalt not." Instead, any moral decision was guided by the circumstances of a particular problem.

Today we can find a significant Confucian influence in China, Taiwan, and Korea, and a corresponding Taoist influence in Vietnam, Laos, and Cambodia. It is important, however, to acknowledge how these two influential traditions overlap in all these cultures.

TAOISM

Like Confucianism, TAOISM [DOW-ism] is principally concerned with morality and ethical behavior insofar as they benefit people in the present world. Thus it is often considered a philosophy rather than a religion. Its founder was LAOZI [LOW-ZEE] (b. 604 B.C.E.), whose name means "the Old Master." Little is known about him, although a number of legends exist to explain how he came to write the *Tao Te Ching (The Way and Its Power)*, which summarizes Taoist teaching. In the most popular of these legends, Laozi, having retired from court life, was journeying out of China when a guard at a mountain pass recognized him and insisted he write down the sum of his wisdom before leaving the country.

The Tao (or Dao) is the ultimate reality behind existence, a transcendent and eternal spiritual essence. Mysterious and mystical, it is finally impossible to define in words. As the *Tao Te Ching* states, "Tao called Tao is not Tao, names can name no lasting name. . . . Tao is the mysterious center of all things."

At the same time, however, the Tao is immanent, existing in nature and manifesting its ordering principle in the cycle of the seasons, the flowing of rivers, and the singing of birds. In this sense, Tao is the governing order of life represented by the rhythm and force of nature. "Tao in action: vague and intangible, shadowy and obscure, but within it there is life, life so real that within it there is trust. Look—you won't see it; listen—you won't hear it; use it—you will never use it up."

Taoism is also a way of ordering one's life so as to achieve peace and harmony with the rest of creation.

> The ancients who followed Tao were dark, wondrous, profound, penetrating, deep beyond knowing. Because they cannot be known, they can only be described: cautious, like crossing a winter stream; hesitant, like respecting one's neighbors; polite, like a guest; yielding, like ice about to melt; blank, like uncarved wood; open, like a valley; mixing freely, like muddy water. Calm the muddy water, it becomes clear; move the inert, it comes to life.

Like Confucianism, Taoism values *te*, or power: "Great te appears flowing from Tao." In Taoism, however, *te* is the sense of essential identity and integrity. The characteristic nature of each thing is its *te;* for a person it is integrity or genuineness—one's authentic self at its best. Instead of competition, *te* proposes cooperation; instead of insistent willfulness, patient attentiveness. "Knowing others is intelligent, knowing oneself is profound; therefore the sage desires no desires, prizes no prizes, but helps all beings find their own nature."

Along with *te*, Taoists encourage ***wu-wei*** (nonaction), a kind of creative calm without excessive purposefulness, involving relaxing the conscious mind. Like the Buddhist and Hindu ascetic ideals, *wu-wei* seeks the denial of the personal and the dissolution of the conscious individual self. "Those highest in *te* take no action, and don't need to act. Those lowest in *te* take action, and do need to act. . . . Tao bears them and *te* nurses them, rears them, supports them, shelters them, nurtures them, supports them, protects them."

Taoism further illustrates the concept of *wu-wei* with examples from nature, especially water. Supple yet strong, water adapts itself to its surroundings, flowing over or filling what it encounters. "Best to be like water, which benefits the ten thousand things and does not contend. It pools where humans disdain to dwell, close to the Tao."

The Taoist ideal of ***p'u***, which literally means "unpainted wood," stresses simplicity. The Taoist prefers unvarnished wood, and thus Taoist architecture employs wood in its natural state, leaving gilt and lacquer to the Confucians, along with ceremonialism and the intricate forms and formulas of civilized life. Taoist painting uses only simple lines, suggesting much in little. Human figures in such paintings are kept small in relation to the vastness of nature.

Taoism and Confucianism together represent the yin and yang of Chinese religious philosophy. They are complementary sides of a complex and intricate system of belief and behavior. The table below identifies the contrasting yet complementary features of these two systems of thought.

CONFUCIANISM AND TAOISM

Confucianism represents the classical; Taoism represents the romantic.

Confucianism stresses social responsibility; Taoism stresses responsibility toward nature.

Confucianism emphasizes humans; Taoism emphasizes nature.

Confucianism is practical; Taoism is mystical.

Confucianism is influential in China, Korea, and Taiwan; Taoism is influential in Cambodia, Laos, and Vietnam.

The Chinese say that Confucius roams with society, whereas Laozi roams beyond it. They also tell a story about a Confucian and a Taoist that reflects the difference in tone and style between the two approaches to life.

The Taoist Zhuangzi and the Confucianist Huizi were walking together over a bridge when Zhuangzi said, "Look how the minnows dart here and there at will. Such is the pleasure fish enjoy." "You are not a fish," retorted Huizi. "How do you know what pleasures fish experience?" "You are not I," responded Zhuangzi. "How do you know I do not know what gives pleasure to fish?"

Yin and Yang. One of the best known of all Chinese images is that of the yin and yang (fig. 8.3). **Yin and yang** represent contrasting but complementary principles that sum up life's basic opposing elements—pain and pleasure, good and evil, light and dark, male and female, and so on. Instead of seeing these contrasting elements as contradictory, the Chinese emphasize the way in which they interact with and complement one another.

Illustrating the philosophical ideal of harmonious integration, the two forms, yin and yang, coexist peacefully within a larger circle. Each form provides the border for its opposite, partly defining it. In the very center of each form, there is the defining aspect of the complementary form: The dark teardrop contains a spot of white; the white teardrop includes a small dark circle. One cannot exist without the other.

Yin is the negative form, associated with earth, darkness, and passivity. Conversely, the yang form is positive and associated with heaven, light, and the constructive impulse. Yin and yang represent the perpetual interplay and mutual relation of all things.

Lyric Poetry. Unlike most national literatures, which typically have their origins in prose tales, epic poetry, or other narrative forms, the earliest known Chinese literature is lyric poetry. Lyrics are usually written to be set to music and are personal in nature. Educated Chinese were expected not only to understand and appreciate poetry, but also to compose it.

The Book of Songs, which contains material passed down orally from as far back as the tenth century B.C.E., was first written down in the sixth century B.C.E. in Confucius' time. It is one of the five ancient Confucian classics, and some scholars have suggested that Confucius himself edited the collection. The poems are variously concerned with love and war, lamentation and celebration, and reflect the perspectives of all strata of ancient Chinese society, from peasants to kings.

As suggested by its title, *The Book of Songs* contains poems meant to be accompanied by music. More than half of the 305 poems are classified as folk songs; the remainder were either written for performance at court or as part of a ritual. The individualism and occasional rebelliousness of the speakers in the poems sometimes make them seem at odds with the Confucian ideal. However, the depth of feeling they express and the richness of the experience they draw on have ensured that *The Book of Songs* remains not only popular but also essential reading for educated Chinese to the present day.

FIGURE 8.3 The yin/yang symbol. Yin and yang represent the complementary negative and positive principles of the universe.

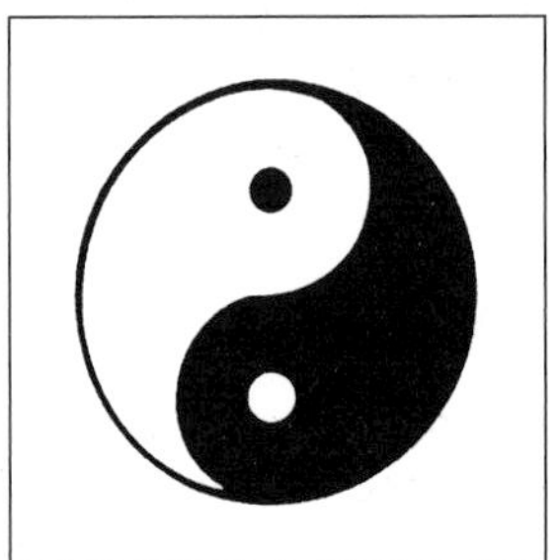

Music. During the time of Confucius and Laozi, music was categorized according to its social functions. Particular types of music played on certain instruments in specified tonalities were designated for use in accompanying the chanting of poetry, the worship of ancestors, as well as at court banquets, country feasts, archery contests, military parades, and the like. Confucius, like Plato, believed music should be used to educate. Music was meant to display the qualities of moderation and harmony, mirroring the emphasis that Confucius placed on those virtues in social and political life. Certain dangerous aspects of music were to be avoided, such as its ability to induce excited states of emotion.

EMPIRE: QIN AND HAN DYNASTIES

Both Confucianism and Taoism developed in response to the political instability of the Zhou dynasty, which began to be undermined by invasions from the west in 771 B.C.E. Political fragmentation continued until the QIN [CHIN—the origin of the name China] dynasty (221–206 B.C.E.) unified the country for the first time.

Although the Qin dynasty's rule was brief, it introduced many measures to ensure that the empire could be ruled efficiently and would remain unified, which indeed it has been almost always to the present day. The Qin rulers established a central bureaucracy, divided the country into administrative units, and standardized the writing system, as well as the currency, weights, and measures. All citizens were made subject to Qin laws, and everyone had to pay taxes to the Qin emperor.

The Qin initiated major building projects—networks of roads and canals that would link the different parts of the empire. It was also the Qin who created most of the 1,400-mile-long Great Wall as a defense for their empire against invaders from the northwest. The Great Wall (fig. 8.4) was made in part by joining together the border walls of the formerly independent regions, and it remains one of the world's most remarkable structures, visible from high in space.

There was a downside to this great imperial ambition, however. In order to maintain control, the Qin suppressed free speech, persecuting scholars and destroying classical literary and philosophical texts, which were only preserved by the ingenuity of those who memorized and later reconstructed them. Confucianism was temporarily supplanted with a new philosophical system called *Legalism* created by Qin intellectuals.

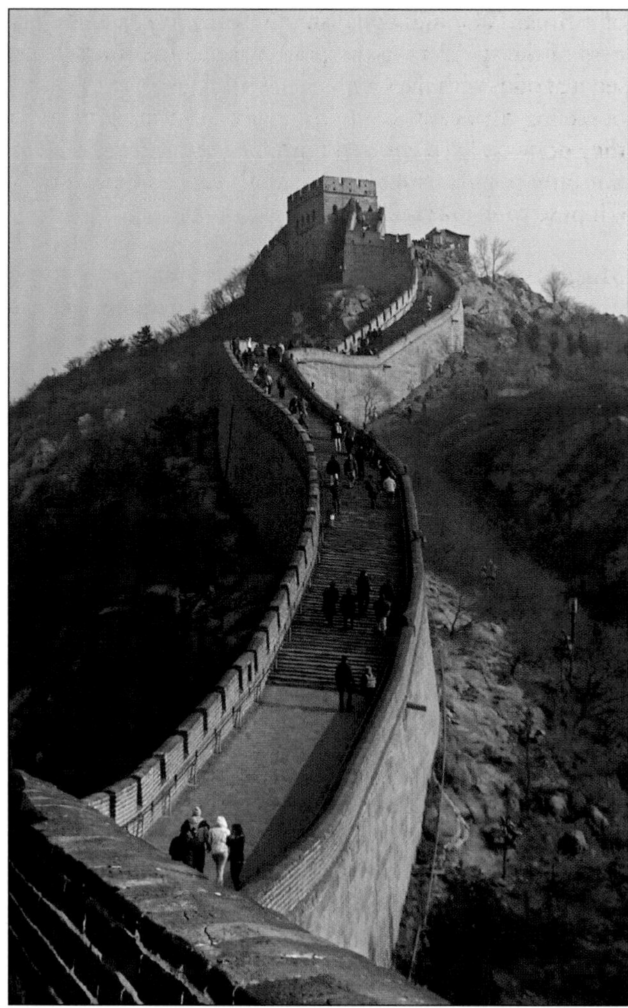

FIGURE 8.4 *Great Wall of China,* section near Beijing. The king of Qin, who proclaimed himself the first Chinese emperor and later came to be known as **Emperor Qin Shi Huangdi,** was powerful, effective, and ruthless as he unified the vast Qin empire. Among his accomplishments was the Great Wall of China, as it has come to be known. Although defensive in purpose, the skill and beauty of the stone construction of this wall, with crenellated fortifications and towers at regular intervals, make this a work of art.

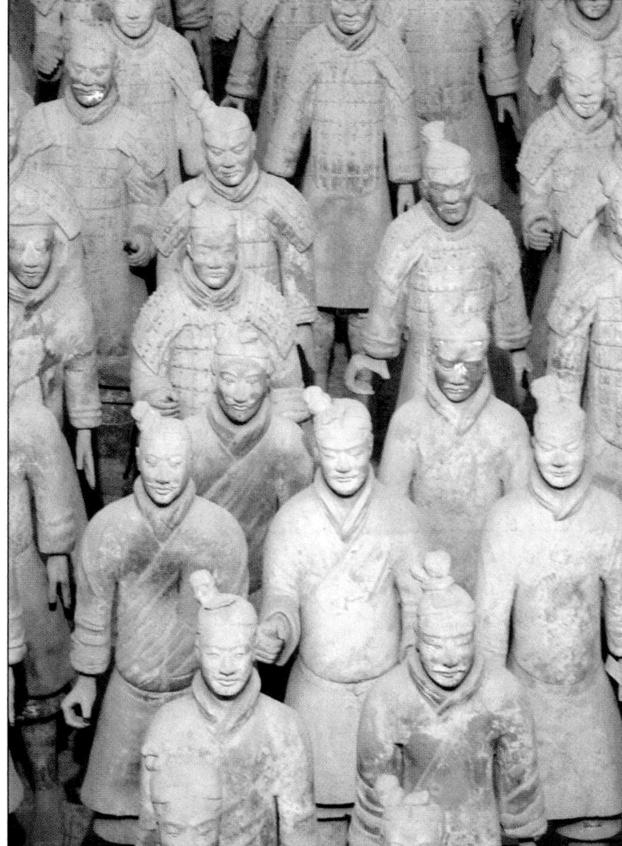

FIGURE 8.5 Tomb figures, from the mausoleum of the first Qin emperor, Shaanxi. Qin Dynasty, ca. 210 B.C.E., terra cotta, lifesize. This army of soldiers, found buried near the mausoleum of the first Qin emperor, was meant to serve him in the afterlife.

Reflecting a belief in the absolute power of the emperor, Qin rule proved so harsh that rebellions soon broke out, and the dynasty was overthrown after only fifteen years in power.

Some idea of the aspirations of grandeur of the Qin dynasty can be gained from viewing the tomb of the first Qin emperor, QIN SHI HUANGDI [CHIN-SHEE-HUANG-DI] (r. 221–206 B.C.E.) (fig. 8.5). Excavators working in Shaanxi province inadvertently uncovered thousands of lifesize terra cotta figures, that had been buried in the emperor's tomb to accompany and serve him in the afterlife. The emperor's burial ground was also richly stocked with furniture, as well as with wooden chariots, and even contained a model of the Qin universe, with representations of rivers and constellations of stars and planets.

With the advent of the Han dynasty (206 B.C.E.–220 C.E.), Chinese culture found its most characteristic and defining forms. Han emperors restored Confucianism to favor, making it the state philosophy, established a national academy to train civil servants, and reinvigorated classical learning by honoring scholars and employing them in the national bureaucracy.

It was under the Han dynasty that the Silk Road trade route was established. It was along this route that goods traveled from China to India, and on to Greece and finally Rome. It was also on the Silk Road that religious missionaries from the West brought Christianity to India and Persia, and even more significantly, that Buddhism spread from India into China, where it soon flourished.

THE SIX DYNASTIES

Intrigue and rebellion led to political and social disunity during the period of the "Six Dynasties" (220–589 C.E.), which followed the Han dynasty. Warring factions fought

Then & Now

EAST/WEST TRADE

Trade between Asia and the West has an ancient history, with the Silk Road its earliest and most important route. In the early twenty-first century, trade between East and West continues to flourish. Now, however, the goods travel by boat and plane rather than by camel. Communication occurs via phone, fax, and computer. And the international language of communication is, for the most part, English.

The northwest coast of the United States trades vigorously with the Asian countries of the Pacific Rim. These include but are not limited to China, Korea, Indonesia, and Japan. Western Europe has long carried on significant trade with Japan, and now with China's membership in the World Trade Organization, with China as well. Throughout the United States, trade with Southeast Asia, especially Vietnam, has increased dramatically with the normalization of U.S.–Vietnamese relations twenty years after the end of the Vietnam War.

Many U.S. and Western European companies anticipate a long and financially rewarding relationship as countries such as China and Vietnam enter the world of telecommunications and computing. One thing is virtually certain. As long as political stability exists in Asia, and as long as Asian governments are receptive to open markets, trade between East and West will increase dramatically in the twenty-first century.

for control of the country, with six successive dynasties gaining power for a brief time. From this period of political turmoil there survives a series of monumental stone sculptures cut into caves at Yun Kang (Yungang, Shanxi), testifying to the fervor with which many Chinese accepted Buddhism. The most colossal of these is a forty-five-foot-high image of the Buddha (fig. 8.6), made around 460–470 C.E. The statue is carved directly into the rock cave, in the manner of Indian monumental sculpture, from which the figure clearly derives (compare fig. 7.5). This earliest of Buddhist styles of sculpture in China has been termed "archaic," and, as in ancient Greece (see fig. 2.14), the figures characteristically wear what has been called an "archaic smile."

TANG DYNASTY

At the end of the Six Dynasties period, the Sui rulers (581–618 C.E.) reunited China. The Sui, the last of the six dynasties, were quickly overcome, however, by the Tang dynasty, who went on to reestablish China as a world power during nearly three hundred years of prosperity and cultural enrichment (618–907 C.E.).

The Tang emperors restored the Silk Road, which had fallen into disuse during the Six Dynasties period, forging trade and cultural links with other countries, especially Persia, India, and, by sea, Japan. During the Tang dynastic period, literature and the other arts were held in high esteem, with civil servants and gentry required to master calligraphy, as well as the Confucian classics, and to compose poetry of their own.

Li Bai and Du Fu. Much early Chinese poetry was composed according to ancient folk-song models. These poems were called ***shih***. Two of the great practitioners of shih were Li Bai, previously known as Li Po (701–762) and DU FU [DOO FOO] (712–770). Both poets have long been associated with Confucianism and Taoism. Du Fu is often described as a Confucian poet, since his poems stress the importance of love of family and of harmonious social relationships. They also celebrate the Confucian ideals of self-discipline and serenity.

The poems of Li Bai are written in a more open style and take greater liberties with the formal poetic conventions of the time than the poems of Du Fu. Li Bai (fig. 8.7) has been described as a poetic individualist and a precursor of the Western Romantic poets (see Chapter 18). His verse has been profoundly influential in China and also in Japan, where he is known as Rihaku. Through the translations of Ezra Pound and the sinologist Arthur Waley, he has also had a strong impact on modern American poetry.

SONG DYNASTY

When the Tang dynasty came to an end in 907, China was thrown into a half century of civil war. The empire was reunified in 960 under the Song rulers, who inaugurated a period of great technological advancement. During the Song dynasty (960–1279), China saw within its borders the invention of the navigational compass, paper currency, gunpowder, and printing, well before Gutenberg's invention of movable type in fifteenth-century Germany. The

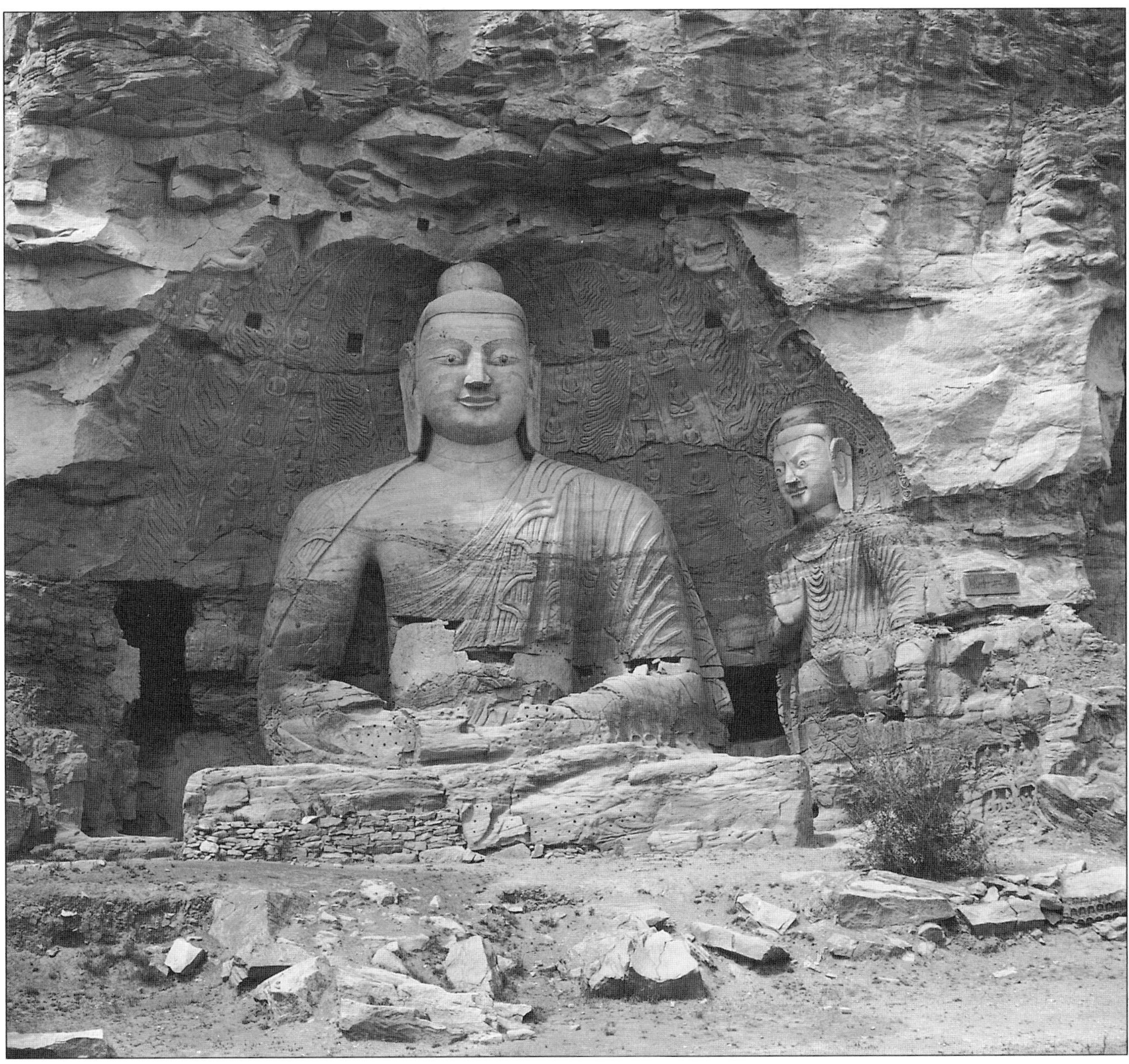

FIGURE 8.6 Colossal Buddha, cave 20, Yungang, Shanxi province, 460–470 C.E., stone, height 45′ (13.72 m). Carved out of living rock, this huge image demonstrates the importance of Buddhism in China during a time of nearly incessant warfare.

rule of the Song emperors created two conditions necessary for artistic development: first, an abundance of leisure time, which allowed for intellectual pursuits, including a reformulation of Confucian ideals; second, the availability of patronage, which helped bring about a resurgence in the art of painting and, with it, elaborations of art theory.

Painting. The art of painting flourished during the Song period. *Seeking the Tao in the Autumn Mountains* (fig. 8.8), by ZHU JAN [JOO JAN] (active. ca. 960–980), is, as its title suggests, representative of the Taoist-influenced artistic tradition. Huge mountains evoke a sense of the remote and the eternal; rising dramatically and powerfully in the center of the painting, they suggest the modest position of humanity in the grand scale of the natural world.

Neo-Confucianism, which developed during the Song dynasty, unified Taoism and Buddhism into a single system of thought. *Early Spring* (fig. 8.9), by

Connections

THE SEVEN SAGES OF THE BAMBOO GROVE

According to semi-legendary tradition, early in the Six Dynasties period seven Taoist poet-philosophers, seeking relief from the formalities of Confucianism, began to hold meetings in a bamboo grove. There, these "Seven Sages" gathered to consider the spiritual side of their life, write and discuss poetry, play musical instruments, play chess, contemplate nature, and, perhaps above all, drink wine. The latter, they felt, released the spirit from all constraint. As one famous saying of the Sages had it,

Brief indeed is a man's life!
So, let's sing over our wine.

Ruan Ji was said to have given up a high official post in order to live near a brewery. In one of his famous poems, entitled "Singing from My Heart," he remembers his seriousness as a youth and comments that now "I mock myself for my past gloom." Liu Ling, another sage, wrote the "Hymn to the Virtue of Wine" and is notorious for having tricked his teetotaling wife by telling her he too had decided to give up alcohol and having her prepare a feast for the gods, and then drinking all the wine intended for the gods himself.

The Seven Sages inaugurated a tradition that would last for many centuries in China. During the Tang dynasty, the poet Li Bai took his followers on a similar retreat to a garden of peach and plum trees on a moonlit spring night. There, they too drank wine and, having liberated themselves from the constraints of their everyday lives, composed their poems. Both the gathering of the Seven Sages in the bamboo grove and Li Bai's conclave in the orchard would be a subject for painters for generations to come (fig. 8.7).

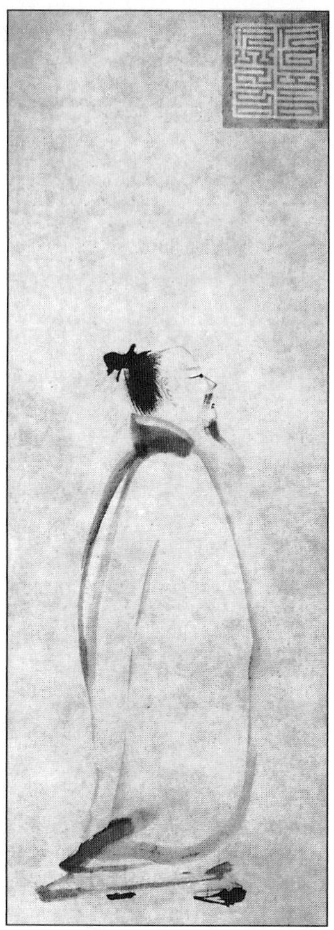

FIGURE 8.7 Liang Kai, *The Poet Li Bai Walking and Chanting a Poem*, Southern Song dynasty, ca. 1200, hanging scroll, ink on paper, 31″ × 11$\frac{7}{8}$″ (80.6 × 30.2 cm), Tokyo National Museum, Japan. This depiction of Li Bai, considered Zen in style, juxtaposes the quick brushstrokes used to describe the robe with the precise and detailed work on his face.

Critical Thinking

MARCO POLO

The most famous medieval Westerner believed to have contact with medieval China is Marco Polo (1254–1324) of Venice. His *Travels* describes his journey through China, Burma, and Tibet, and includes his description of the city of Hangzhou, famed for its bridges and canals, as well as of the palace and kingdom of Kublai Khan in Mongolia. Some scholars, however, have cast doubt on the authenticity of Marco Polo's descriptions. They argue, for example, that he exaggerated what he saw to attract readers, and that his not mentioning perhaps one of the greatest and most awesome of sights—the Great Wall of China—indicates that he may not have actually been in China at all. Suspicion about his book has arisen also because Polo himself is absent from his *Travels.* His book, some say, is more of a medieval bestiary that describes strange (and wildly imaginary) creatures. Others contend that much of the geography, history, and anthropology included in Polo's book are authentic.

How would you go about deciding which of these scholars to believe? What kinds of evidence would you look for to confirm, refute, or qualify Marco Polo's descriptions of what he saw on his travels through medieval China? And how might you explain his absence from the *Travels* and his neglect of the Great Wall?

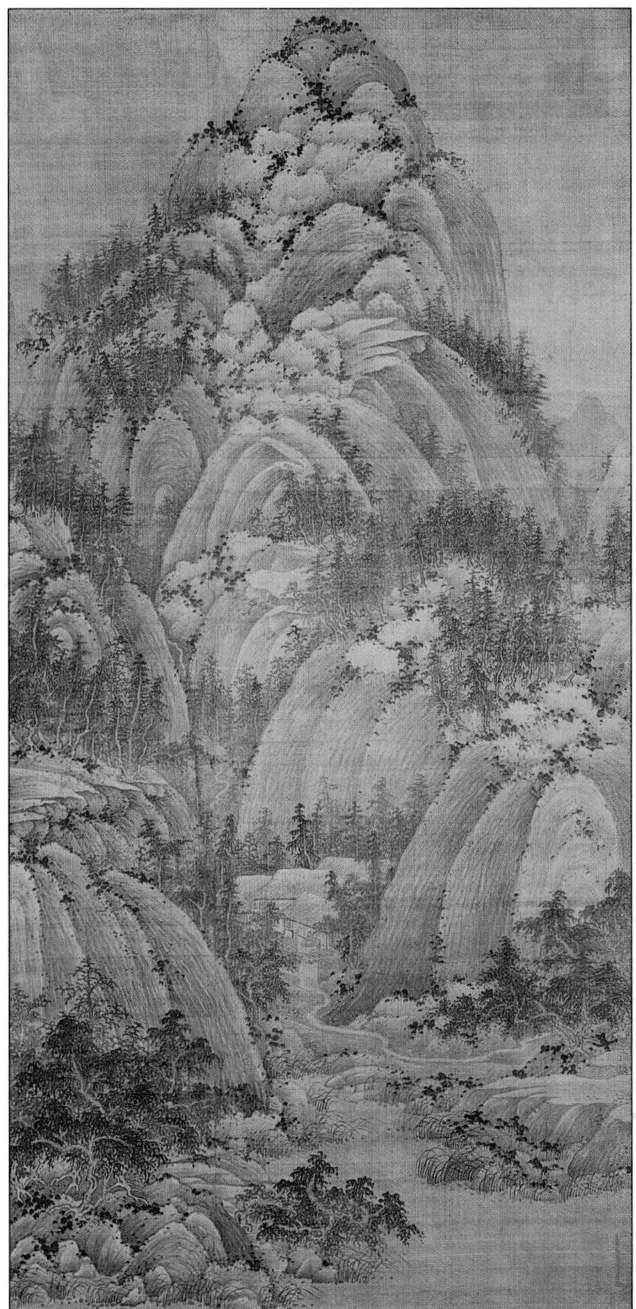

FIGURE 8.8 Zhu Jan, *Seeking the Tao in the Autumn Mountains*, ca. 970, ink on silk, 61 × 30″ (156.2 × 78.1 cm), National Palace Museum, Taipei, Taiwan. Long, sweeping brushstrokes complemented by carefully placed dots of dark ink accentuate the mountain's grandeur as they guide the viewer's gaze upward.

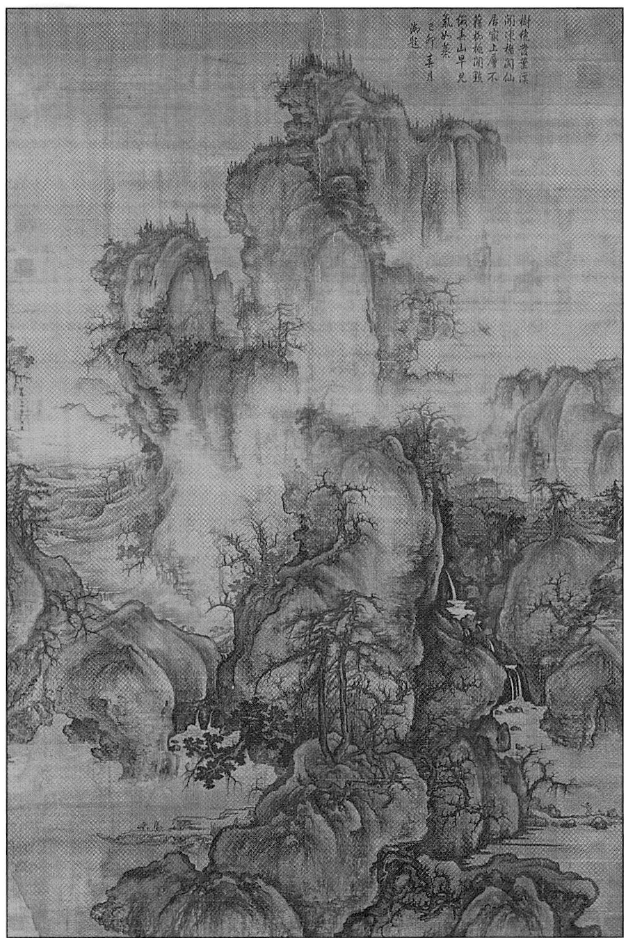

FIGURE 8.9 Guo Xi, *Early Spring*, Northern Song dynasty, 1072, hanging scroll, ink and slight color on silk, height 5′ (1.52 m), National Palace Museum, Taipei, Taiwan. This landscape represents the integration of three different forms of perspective: high distance (looking up at the main peak), deep distance (looking down into valleys), and level distance (looking across marshes).

GUO XI [GOO-OH SEE] (after 1000–ca. 1090), embodies the Confucian ideal of *li*, which is the principle at the heart of nature. As in Zhu Jan's painting, the human presence in this landscape passes almost unnoticed, so vast is the scale of the central mountain. Small figures can be identified in the lower foreground on both the left and right, and in the middle distance on the right a village is tucked between the hills. The mountain, representing nature, is a powerful symbol of eternity that dwarfs human existence.

A court painter during the reign of Emperor Shenzong (r. 1068–1085), Guo Xi was given the task of painting all the murals in the Forbidden City, the imperial compound in Beijing that foreigners were prohibited from entering. His ideas about painting were recorded by his son in a book entitled *The Lofty Message of the Forests and Streams.* According to this interpretation, the central peak in *Early Spring* symbolizes the emperor himself, its tall pines the gentlemanly ideals of the court. Here Guo Xi has painted the ideal Confucian and Buddhist world; the emperor, like the Buddha surrounded by his bodhisattvas, gathers all around him, just as in *Early Spring* the mountain, the trees, and the hills suggest the proper order and rhythm of the universe.

Another form of painting also began in the Song dynasty, practiced by and for the scholar-poet-artists who served as officials, and therefore could practice their art as amateurs. This became known as the literati school, which was to become the single most important tradition in Chinese art in succeeding dynasties. One of the leading figures in this movement was the poet-calligrapher Su Shi (1036–1101), who wrote that painting merely to depict outer reality was like the work of a child, and true painters became so totally immersed that their art came from within themselves. For example, he wrote that his friend Wen Tong (1018–1079), when he painted bamboo, "forgot himself and became a bamboo."

In his two prose poems written in 1082 on the "Red Cliff" (fig. 8.10) where a famous battle had been fought centuries earlier, Su Shi gave voice to fundamental literati views of humans and nature, with a Buddhist sense of human impermanence. He has been out boating with a companion, and soon his friend becomes melancholy at the fleeting nature of life and fame, saying, "we are no more than the flies of summer, grains of millet on the ocean vastness—it grieves me that life is so short." Su Shi replies that the river flows and the moon waxes and wanes, but they are always the same river and moon. "If we look at things from the eyes of change, there's not an instant of stillness in the universe. But if we observe the changelessness of things, then we, and all beings, have no end. . . . The clear breeze over the river, the bright moon over the hills, these we may enjoy and they will never be exhausted."

FIGURE 8.10 Li Song (active 1190–1230), *The Red Cliff*, Southern Song dynasty. Album leaf mounted as a hanging scroll, ink and color on silk, ivory roller. $9\frac{3}{4} \times 10\frac{1}{4}''$ (24.76 × 26.03 cm). The Nelson-Atkins Museum of Art, Kansas City, Missouri. Purchase: William Rockhill Nelson Trust, 49-79. The small but nevertheless significant figures, viewing the cliff from the boat, are a visualization of the prose poetry of Su Shi, in which feelings of unity with nature can dispel human unhappiness.

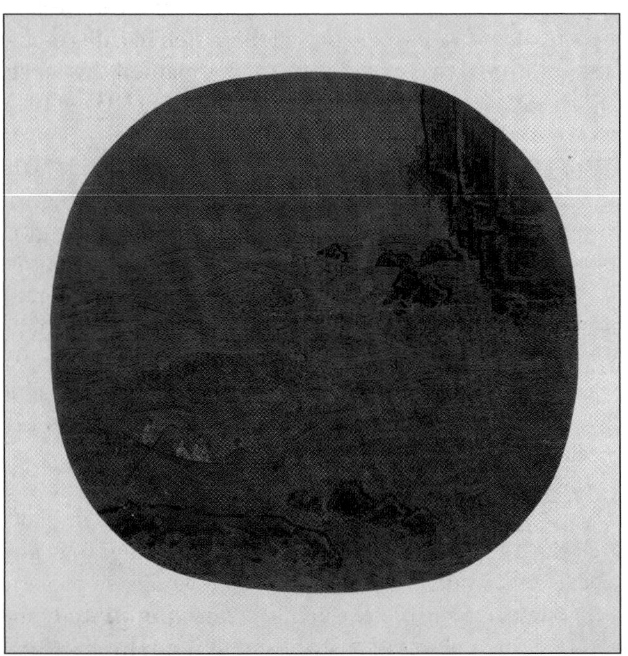

Ceramics. Among the most important of China's contributions is the development of a highly refined art of ceramics. For over 3,000 years, Chinese potters have produced masterpieces of ceramics in an amazing variety of shapes, colors, and decorative styles.

Typical of many Tang Dynasty ceramic figurines is the polychrome glazed equestrian seen in fig. 8.11. Curiously, the horse is rendered with greater realism than the seemingly boneless rider. Complex shapes such as horses and camels were cast in molds, in separate sections that were joined with clay slip. The white clay was painted with a glaze containing copper, iron cobalt, and manganese that was fired at a low temperature. Figurines, which include animals and people, as well as vessels and plates made in this Tang polychrome technique, were buried in tombs.

FIGURE 8.11 ***Horse and Rider***, Tang Dynasty (618–907), "three-color" ceramics. The Art Archive\Picture Desk, Inc./Kobal Collection. The dripping glazes are characteristic of Tang ceramics called ***Tangsancai***, meaning "Tang three colors," although there are actually more than three.

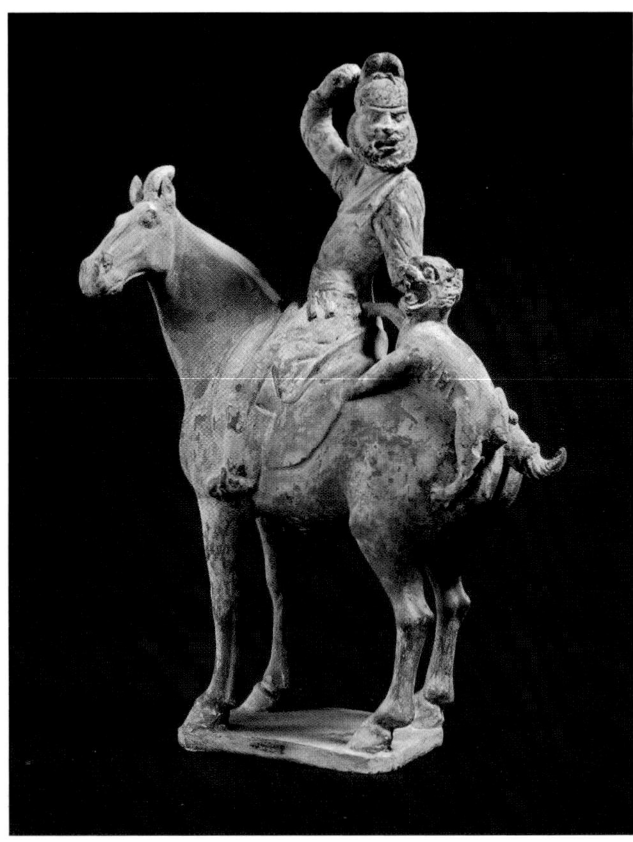

Cross Currents

MARCO POLO'S HANGZHOU

Little was known about China and the Far East in the West before the nineteenth century. One of the most important sources was the account written by the Venetian traveler Marco Polo (ca. 1254–1324). His description of the Song capital, Hangzhou, is particularly vivid.

Hangzhou, formerly called Kinsai, or the "City of Heaven," might also have been called the "City of Bridges," since twelve thousand wood and stone bridges cross its wide waterways. Described by Polo, who arrived in the city in 1271, as, "without doubt the finest and most splendid city in the world," Hangzhou in the Song dynasty was an important commercial center as well as the imperial capital of China. Its population—of more than a million people—was then the largest in the world. Thirty-foot-high crenelated walls, studded with towers, protected the city against enemy attack. Guards stationed strategically at the bridges to repulse invaders also served as timekeepers, striking a gong and drum to mark the passing of the hours.

On the city's streets, porters carried goods suspended from long poles in baskets and jars. On its canals, boats and ships of many sizes transported food and building materials. Its markets, open three days a week in the city's squares, were crammed with food and spices, books and flowers, cloth and gemstones, in addition to a huge variety of meats and game. Dress, as in the West, was a mark of social and financial status for both women and men. The rank of **mandarins** (government officials) was indicated by robes and headgear. On special occasions, these mandarins wore silk robes embroidered with flowers, animals, and symbols. Their belt buckles were made of jade or rhinoceros horn, and their caps were adorned with buttons, again signaling the officials' importance.

Among the places people congregated were parks and lakes, especially the great West Lake, often filled with boats, barges, and floating teahouses, from which passengers could view the numerous palaces, temples, pagodas, and pavilions that dotted the surrounding landscape. On land, the wealthy congregated in clubs and centers to read poems, enjoy plays, song, and dance, as well as to practice calligraphy and painting. It was especially important for young men with the ambition to become scholar officials to become well versed in the Chinese classics in preparation for the civil service examinations. Young women were also expected to take lessons, with classes in music, dancing, spinning, embroidery, and social etiquette preparing them for the good marriages they hoped to contract.

Equally prized are the fine designs of flowers and animals enlivened by special effects of "partridge feather," "hare's fur," and "oil spot," used on white, ivory, willow, celadon, and shades of blue porcelain produced during the Song dynasty. The Chinese were able to create such astonishing ceramic and porcelain works due to their understanding of how to control kiln temperatures and to their extensive knowledge of glazes, including how to mix them to create unusual effects of color.

Song Dynasty ceramics are valued for their superb integration of shape, glaze, and decoration, evidencing an outstanding command of the technical aspects of potting, firing, and glazing techniques. The shape of Song ceramic ware tends toward the simple and elegant (fig. 8.12). Unlike Tang dynasty ceramic pieces, in which a clear distinction is evident among the neck, body, and foot, Song ceramic ware blends these three parts in a unified and flowing harmony. When decoration is used (and it is used only sparingly in Song ceramics), it serves to enhance the form of the piece rather than to attract attention to itself.

Calligraphy and Writing. Unlike the West, where calligraphy, or beautiful writing, is considered a minor art, in China the art of calligraphy has long enjoyed a high status among the arts. At the heart of the higher forms of Chinese culture and one of the three perfections or gentlemanly arts, calligraphy is linked with its companion arts of poetry and painting. All three—poetry, painting, and calligraphy—were considered aspects of the same aesthetic expression since poems were written in calligraphy and paintings were typically accompanied by such calligraphied poems. An example by Su Shi (1037–1101) is seen in figure 8.13.

Because writing and calligraphy were held in such high esteem, the brushes used in their creation were highly valued, some considered works of art in their own right, much as a violin bow might be so considered. In recording the movements of hand, wrist, and arm, the calligraphy brush acts like a kind of seismograph, through which a person's calligraphy conveys something essential about the calligrapher. In producing calligraphy according to the ancient rules and guidelines, the writer reveals his character and spirit as well as his or her intentions.

Finally, it should be remembered that Chinese art forms a continuum with religion, politics, philosophy, and everyday life. Just as painting, poetry, and calligraphy are aspects of a single harmonious artistic whole, so too are the related aspects of creating art, collecting it, studying it, and writing about its history and philosophy.

Cultural Impact

Among the many legacies left by ancient Chinese culture has been the influence of its Tang dynasty poets, especially Li Bai (Li Po). The American modernist poet Ezra Pound, with the help of the Asian scholar Ernest Fenellosa, made a series of translations or adaptations of Li Bai's poems, the most famous of which is *The River-Merchant's Wife: A Letter.* More important than any single poem, however, was the adoption of a modernist literary aesthetic that emphasizes the importance of the image to convey a poem's meaning and feeling. This Pound and other modernist poets derived from their reading of Li Bai and Tang dynasty poets.

The ethical and philosophical legacy of Confucianism remains a major influence, particularly in its Neo-Confucianist form, which incorporates Buddhist thought within a Confucian value system. Neo-Confucianism has influenced East Asian thought over a long period of time, and remains today a dominant factor in Korea, and Japan, where it has shaped moral thought and traditional cultural values. In addition, Chinese commodities such as silk, porcelain, and lacquerware remain highly prized. And, of course, the Chinese inventions of gunpowder, paper, and the magnetic compass have had an enormous impact throughout history.

FIGURE 8.12 Celadon vase. Height 11″ (28 cm). China. Song dynasty. Song ceramics pieces were often glazed with various shades of green.

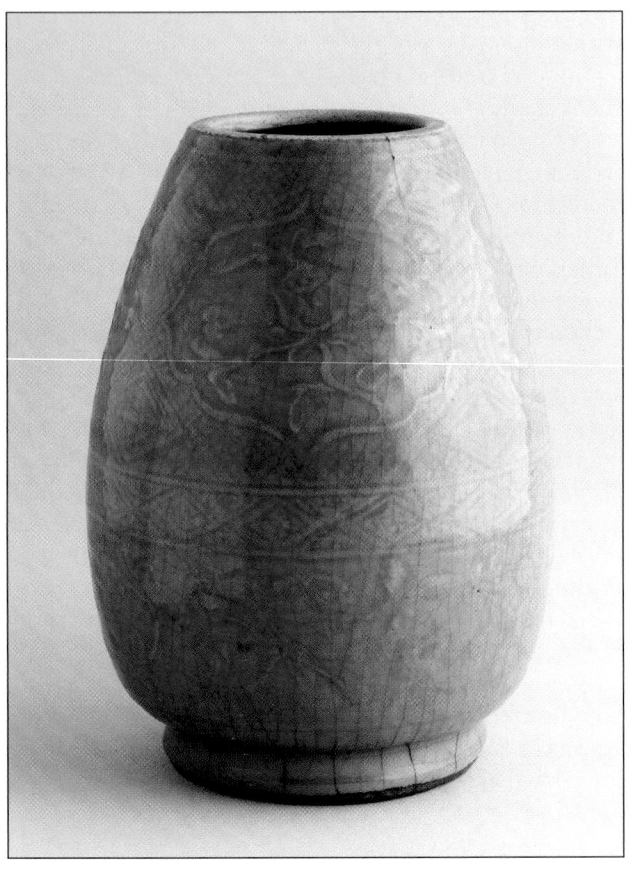

FIGURE 8.13 Fragment of calligraphy by Su Shi (1036–1101) of his poem "Cold Provisions Day." Su Shi was a fine scholar, poet, and calligrapher, and a noted painter of bamboo.

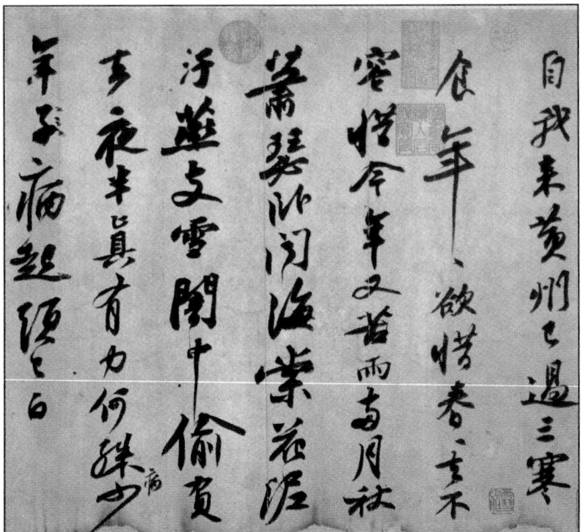

KEY TERMS

Confucianism
li
jen
te
wen
yi
Taoism
wu-wei
p'u
yin and yang
shih
Neo-Confucianism
mandarins

www. WEBSITES FOR FURTHER STUDY

http://www.friesian.com/confuci.htm
(This is a worthwhile site on Confucian philosophy.)

http://www.wsu.edu/~dee/CHIINRES.HTM #Philosophy
(Visit this site for a thorough explanation of yin and yang and Chinese philosophy.)

http://www.chinavista.com/experience/shijing/shijing.html
(Shijing [The Book of Songs] is the earliest collection of Chinese poems including 305 poems of the Zhou dynasty (1122–256 B.C.E.). The page has one of the poems in translation, but the whole page can be converted to two forms of Chinese.)

http://www.archeolink.com/ancient_chinese_civilization.htm
(A general site about ancient Chinese civilization, illustrated.)

http://www.crystallinks.com/china.html
(General site on all things ancient Chinese, from archeology and anthology to dragons and mythology, the silk road, and the terracotta army – and more.)

http://worldmusic.nationalgeographic.com
(Ancient Chinese music.)

Chapter 9

History

330–352 C.E.	Yomoto rule (Warlords)
sixth century C.E.	Buddhism introduced into Japan from China
552–646 C.E.	Asuka born and dies
712 C.E.	Kojiki, record of ancient matters
794–1185	Heian Period
1147–99	Minamoto Yoritomo born and dies
1185–1392	Kamakura Period
1192	Minomoto Yoritomo declared first Shogun
1392–1523	Ashikaga Period

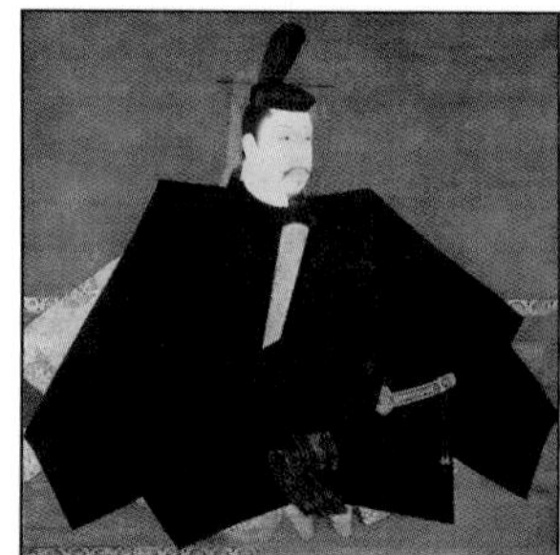

Arts and Architecture

623 C.E.	Tori Busshi, *Shaka Triad*
670 C.E.	Horyu-ji temple compound
1120	Hand scrolls
fifteenth century	Tea ceremony
1480s	Ryoan-ji temple, dry garden

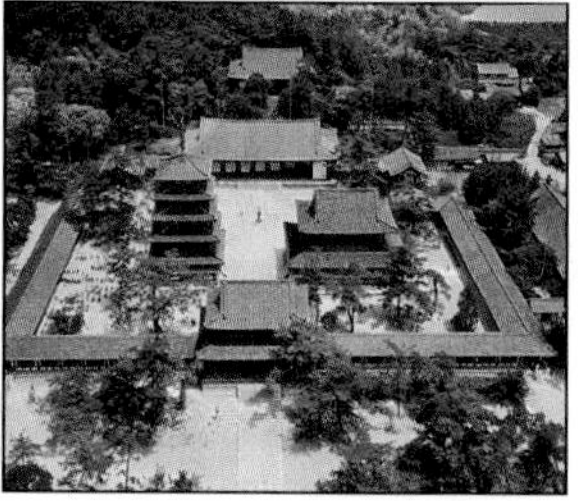

Literature and Philosophy

eighth century	Manyoshu, poetry collection
689–700	Kokinoto no Hitomoro, poet active
834–?	Ono no Komachi lives and writes poems
966–1017	Sei Shonogan, *Pillow Book*
ca. 1021	Murasaki Shikibu, *The Tale of Genji*
1283–1350	Yoshida Kenko, *Essays in Idleness*

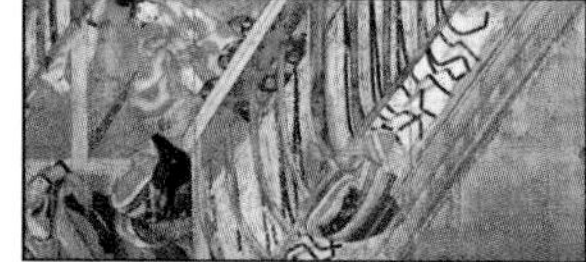

Early Japanese Civilization

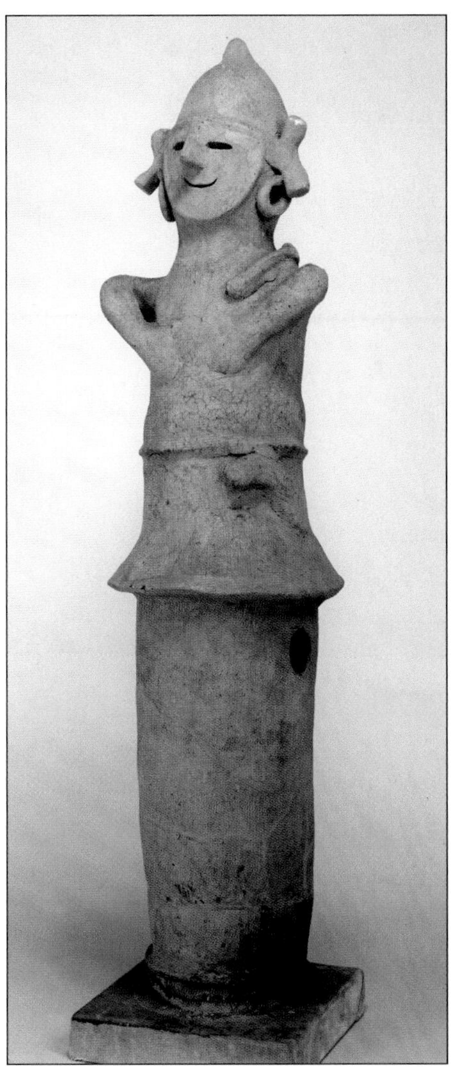

Haniwa Figure, from the Akabori Site, Gumma Prefecture, Japan, fourth–fifth centuries B.C.E., earthenware, $36\frac{1}{4}''$ (92 cm) tall, Tokyo National Museum. TNM Image Archives. Source: http://TnmArchives.jp/

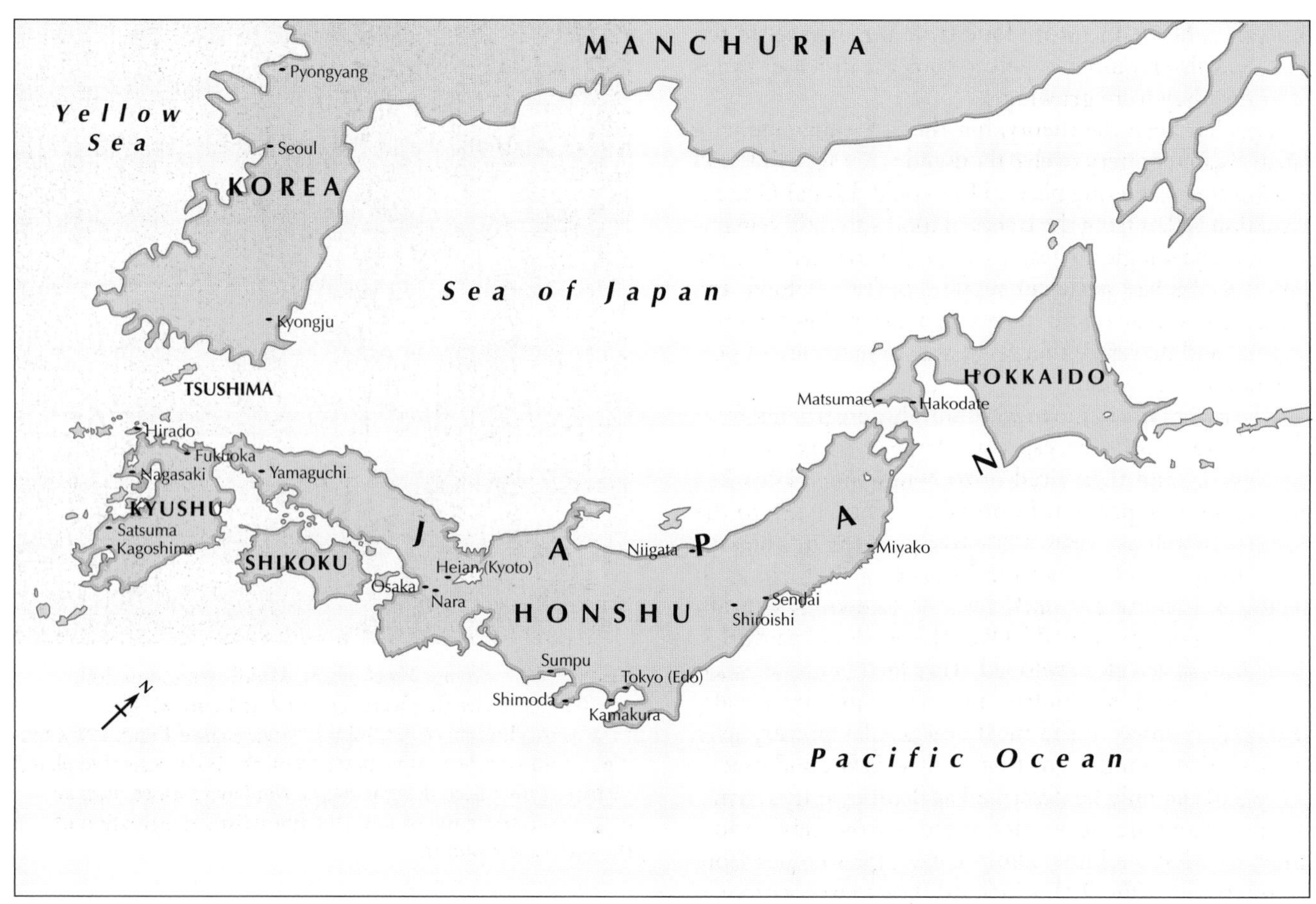

MAP 9.1 Japan before the fifteenth century.

CHAPTER OVERVIEW

JAPAN BEFORE THE TWELFTH CENTURY

JAPAN FROM THE TWELFTH TO THE FIFTEENTH CENTURY

JAPAN BEFORE THE TWELFTH CENTURY

PREHISTORIC JAPAN

IN 1960, THE FIELD OF ARCHAEOLOGY WAS GIVEN a shock when scientific carbon dating showed that the world's first pottery was created in Japan. Recent tests have pushed back the dating to 10,000 B.C.E., well before any other cultures developed their own ceramic traditions. Because it has generally been believed Japan followed the lead of China in cultural development, scholars at first doubted the tests, and since then they have debated how Japan could have led the world in creating pottery.

The general theory is that human societies can be grouped into the few basic divisions of hunting-gathering, agricultural, and urban. These are most easily understood by knowing where people obtain their food; they hunt or find it, they grow it, or they buy it at the store. Pottery, being heavy and cumbersome, was not developed by hunting-gathering peoples, who moved from place to place over the course of a year and did not store food for very long. When cultures developed to agricultural phases, however, people tended to stay in one place, needed to store food from one harvest to the next, and also required vessels to cook the different forms of grains they were growing.

This has been the theory, but the early inhabitants of Japan created pottery twelve thousand years ago while still in a hunting-gathering phase. How could this be? One explanation is that from the traces of foodstuffs still remaining in archaeological sites, it can be determined that the early peoples had sufficient supplies of fish, seafood, and plants to live year round in certain areas, rather than migrating, and therefore they were able to make use of pottery in their daily lives.

The early pots in Japan were simply constructed from clay into various forms, especially large cooking and storage vessels, and then fired in trenches, since kilns had not been developed yet. In order to add strength to the pottery as well as create attractive patterns on the surface, many vessel walls were impressed with ropes or cords, and so the era itself became known as **Jomon**, meaning "cord patterned." Over the course of centuries, these Jomon vessels developed, were further embellished with coils and geometric patterns, and eventually emerged as some of the most spectacular pottery ever created, with rim designs that went well beyond practicality and can only be described as flamboyantly artistic. Because there are no written records from this period, much of what we know about early Japan comes from Jomon pottery (fig. 9.1), which exhibits a great variety of both shape and decoration, suggesting a society that was bold and confident in its way of life.

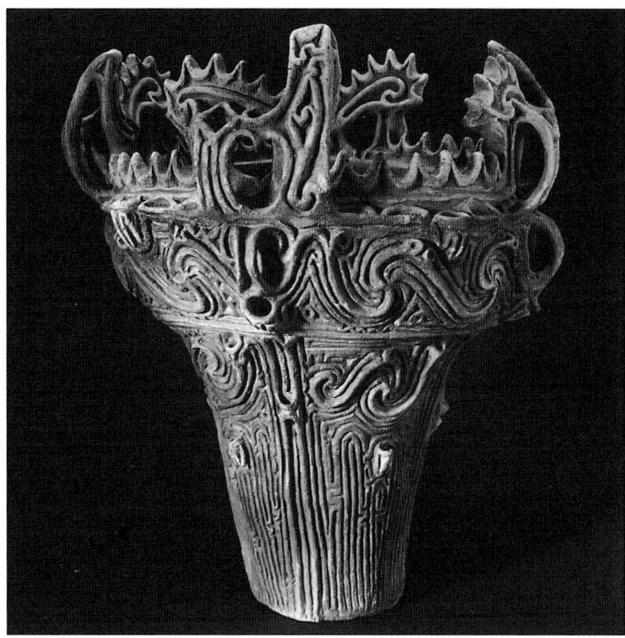

FIGURE 9.1 *Storage Vessel,* Japan, Middle Jomon period, ca. 2000 B.C.E., earthenware, height 2′ (61 cm). © The Cleveland Museum of Art, John L. Severenance Fund, 1984. 68. The geometric decorative patterns on the body resemble plates of armor; the raised designs on the rim have a more organic expression, testifying to the dramatic artistic imagination of the prehistoric potter.

Around the year 300 C.E. a new wave of people came from the Korean peninsula, bringing elements of culture that led to great changes in Japan. Agriculture, which had begun in a rudimentary way during the Jomon period, now was greatly advanced, particularly rice cultivation, which meant that larger-scale groupings of people were now possible, leading to Japan's first emperors. The Jomon people, who were racially Caucasian, were gradually pushed to the north and formed the basis of the Ainu peoples, who still live on the island of Hokkaido.

The new peoples, racially the same as present-day Japanese, built huge graves for their leaders, some with artificial hills surrounded by moats. Upon these graves they began to erect ceramic tubes, perhaps to help the earth stay in place. Before long these cylinders, called ***haniwa*** [hah-nee-wah], were decorated with models of boats, houses, and animals. The final forms to emerge were human figures (fig. 9.2), who were shown in many different guises and activities.

There is some debate as to the purpose of these ceramic *haniwa*. In China as in other early cultures, sculptures were placed inside tombs to assist the dead in their next lives, but in Japan they were placed on top of the graves. Were these figures meant to be guardians? If so, why are there birds and animals, mothers nursing babies, falconers, shamans, and people doing ordinary everyday tasks? Again, without written records, we can only speculate, but it seems these *haniwa* formed some kind of link between the living, who could view them atop the grave mounds from across the moats, and the dead, over whom they stood.

The next major change in Japan took place beginning in the fifth and sixth centuries, when a new wave of influence came over from Korea and China. This brought many things that were to become vital parts of Japanese culture, including a writing system, Buddhism, advances in medicine, more complex governmental systems, new forms of poetry, music and architecture, and the arts of brush painting and calligraphy.

RELIGION

Buddhism and Shinto. Of the influences Japan received from China and Korea, perhaps the most significant was Buddhism, which China had itself imported from India. After an initial reluctance, Japan embraced the new religion with great fervor, copying sacred texts (which was also a way to practice the written language that was now learned from China), building temples, and ordaining monastics—the first of whom were three women.

Japan, however, already had its own religious practices, later designated as **Shinto** to distinguish them from the

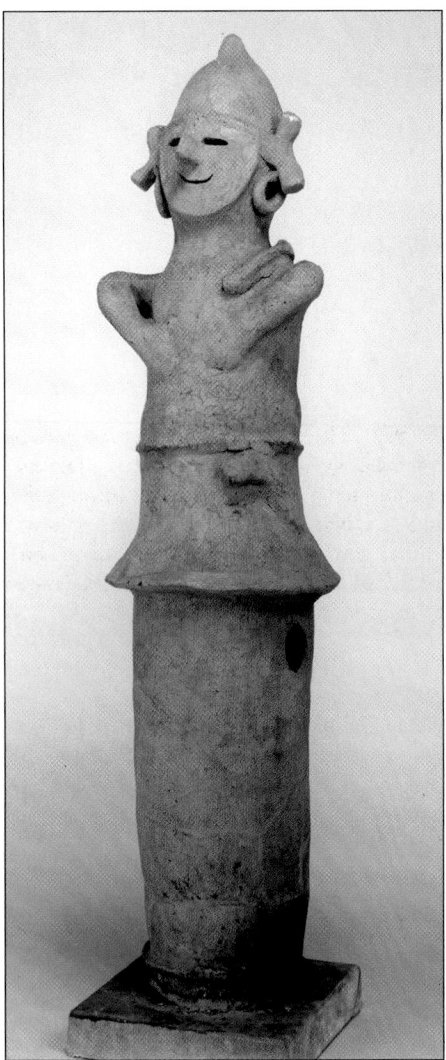

FIGURE 9.2 *Haniwa Figure*, from the Akabori Site, Gumma Prefecture, Japan, fourth–fifth centuries B.C.E., earthenware, height $36\frac{1}{4}''$ (92 cm), Tokyo National Museum. TNM Image Archives. Source: http://TnmArchives.jp/. This figure is believed to represent a farmer holding a plow blade on his shoulder, evidence of the agricultural society that had developed by this time in central Japan.

imported forms of Buddhism. Over many centuries, Shinto developed from a kind of nature worship into a state religion of patriotic appreciation of the Japanese land. Shinto came to require a commemoration of Japanese heroes and significant events from the nation's history. Later, Shinto could also include earlier aspects of animism, nature worship, and ancestor worship, and Shinto rituals could be carried out in private homes as well as in Shinto temples.

To some extent, the formal development of Shinto was a reaction against Chinese religious and cultural influence. In addition, during the seventh and eighth centuries, the Japanese collected their native myths in the ***Kojiki***, "Chronicles of Ancient Events." In explaining the origin of Japanese culture, the *Kojiki* describe the creation of the Japanese islands by two Shinto ***kami***, or gods, Izanagi and his consort Izanami. All other gods descend from these two, of whom the most important is Ameterasu, the sun goddess, who is considered the ancestor of the Japanese emperors.

Table 9–1 EARLY JAPANESE HISTORICAL PERIODS AND THEIR MAJOR ACHIEVEMENTS

Period	Achievement
Kofun (300–552)	Yamoto rule (warlords)
Asuka (552–646)	Shaka Triad (ca. 623)
Nara (646–794)	Horyu-ji temple (ca. 670), oldest wooden temple in the world
Heian (794–1185)	*The Tale of Genji* (ca. 1000)
Kamakura (1185–1392)	Hand scrolls (twelfth century)
Ashikaga (1392–1523)	Tea ceremony

COURTLY JAPAN: ASUKA AND NARA PERIODS

Art and Architecture. The earliest surviving wooden Japanese sculptures and architecture, those of the Asuka period, 552–646 C.E., are closely identified with Buddhism. One of the best preserved and most important Japanese temples is Horyu-ji, the oldest wooden temple in the world (ca. 670) (fig. 9.3). Horyu-ji's architectural design reveals how Buddhist-inspired Chinese architecture influenced early Japanese temple building, although its asymmetrical relationship of structures is a typically Japanese aesthetic trait.

Among the many treasures housed in the buildings of Horyu-ji is a sculpture known as the *Shaka Triad* (fig. 9.4). This triple image shows the Buddha, whose Japanese name is Shaka or Shakyamuni, with attending bodhisattvas on either side. The large figures, especially the Buddha sitting in the center, reveal the sculptor TORI BUSSHI's [BOOSH-yi] awareness of the Chinese sculptural tradition from the pre-Tang period, including the focus of attention on the large head and hands. The expert use of gilt bronze demonstrates how quickly and successfully the international sculptural tradition was adopted in Japan.

From the late seventh century on, Japanese rulers were true monarchs, no longer merely aristocratic warlords. Around the same time, Nara became Japan's first true capital. Although the rulers of ancient Japan are often referred to as emperors, these rulers are best thought of as sovereigns. The distinction is important because it signals a shift from the military authority of the earlier warlords to a genuine pursuit of political and cultural cohesion. The patronage of Buddhism became one of the most important facets of court life, and many temples were built within and without the city of Nara that were much larger than Horyu-ji and featured outpouring of sculptures and paintings of Buddhist dieties.

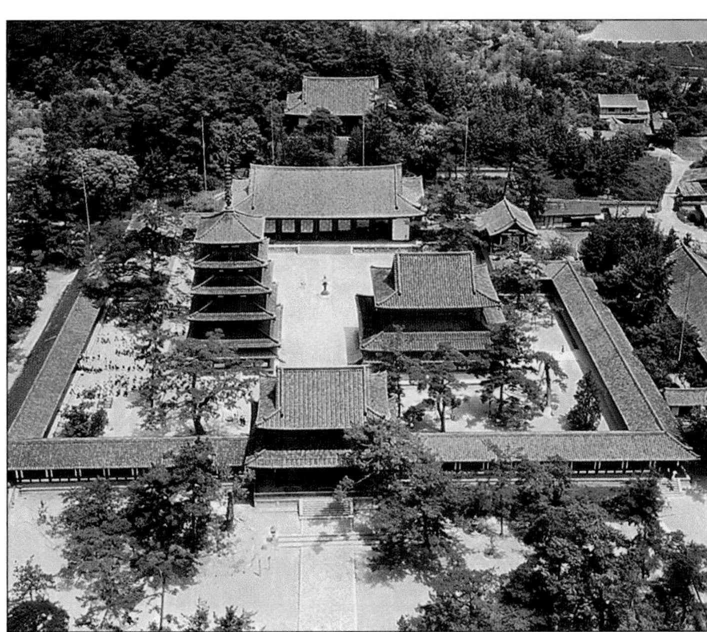

FIGURE 9.3 Horyu-ji compound, with pagoda and Golden Hall, Nara, Japan, ca. 670 C.E., aerial view. Visitors entering this temple compound move through the first building and then must take a turn to the right or the left rather than moving in a straight line from one building to the next. This favoring of lateral over linear movement is a characteristic of Japanese artistic style.

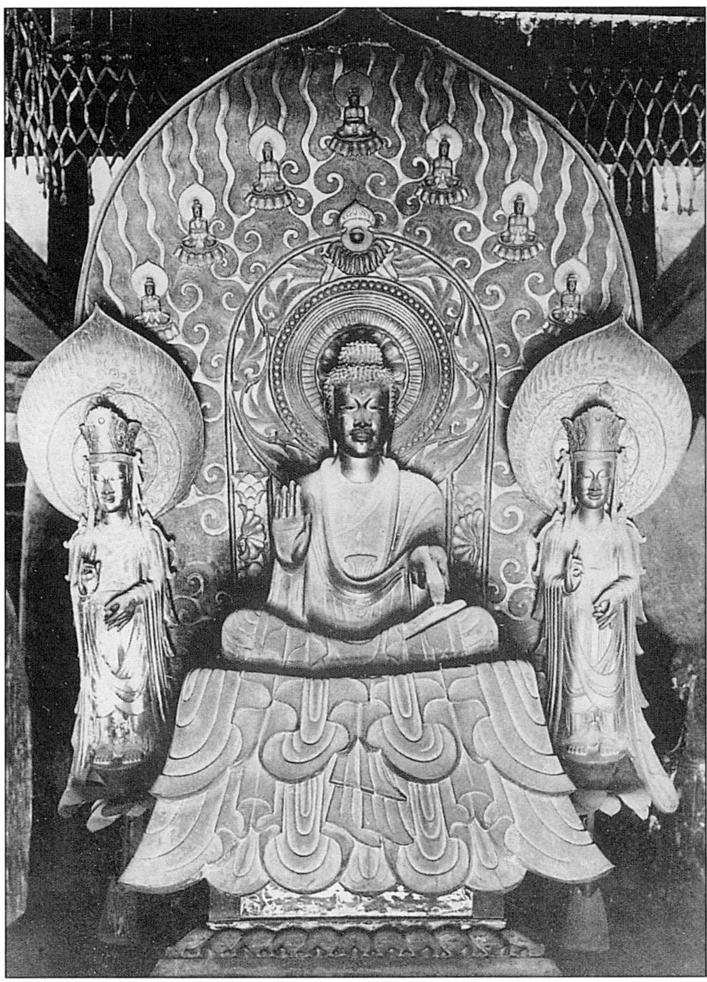

FIGURE 9.4 Tori Busshi, *Shaka Triad*, Nara Prefecture, Asuka period, 623, bronze, height 5′ 9′ (1.76 m), Horyu-ji. The Buddha, flanked by attendant bodhisattvas, sits on a simple throne against a decorative background that testifies to his sacred status.

Kojiki and Nihongi. Kojiki, or the Records of Ancient Matters, is the oldest volume of Japanese ancient history. It begins with the creation of the world by the Kami, or deities, Izanagi and Izanami; it concludes with the period of Empress Suiko, Japan's first empress, who reigned from 592–628 C.E.

Divided into three major parts, the Kojiki contains songs and poems along with myths and historical records. The myths and records are written in a mixture of Chinese and Japanese, whereas the songs are written strictly in Chinese characters.

The first part of the Kojiki, the Kamitsumaki or "upper roll," focuses on the creation of the world and of various deities. The second part, the Nakatsumaki, or "middle roll," covers the period between the first Japanese emperor, Jimmu, and the fifteenth, Emperor Ojin. The third part, the Shimosutsumaki, or "lower roll," covers the period from the sixteenth to the thirty-third emperors.

The Nihongi, or Nihonshoki, or the "Chronicles of Japan," picks up where the Kojiki leaves off and catalogs the descent of the Yamato rulers through the end of the seventh century. In combination with the Kojiki, the Nihongi has been an influential document in Japan, including its naming of the country "Nippon."

COURTLY JAPAN: HEIAN PERIOD

In 794, the Japanese capital was moved to Heian (now Kyoto), which became one of the most densely populated cities in the world. The Heian period was a period of rich productivity and peace, with the Japanese sovereign strongly supported by aristocratic families. Court culture during the Heian era became extremely refined and elegant, and the secular as well as sacred arts flourished.

Courtiers of both sexes, if they wanted to inspire respect among their peers, were expected to be able to write poetry in the classical five-line ***waka*** form, with syllables of 5-7-5-7-7 (the haiku was later to develop from the first three lines of a *waka*). Featuring *mono no aware* ("the emotion of things" or "the sadness of things"), court poetry expressed the feelings that lay under the surface of elegant court life. For example, Lady Akazome Emon (eleventh century) wrote this verse after her lover failed to appear:

> I should not have waited—
> it would have been wiser
> to sleep and dream
> than to see the night pass
> and watch this moon slowly sink

Many *waka* are about romantic love, but one poem by the ninth-century courtier Narihira might apply to any of us at crucial moments of our lives:

> I have always known
> someday I must take this road—
> but just yesterday
> I did not realize that
> it would be today

Although both men and women wrote classical poetry, it was women who wrote most of the prose fiction of the time, including the world's first novel, *The Tale of Genji (Genji Monogatari).* The most enduring and influential of all works of Japanese literature, *The Tale of Genji* is a sprawling narrative of court life, spanning many generations and featuring the hero, Prince Genji, among a host of other characters. This novel was written by MURASAKI SHIKIBU [moo-rah-sah-key] (ca. 976–ca. 1026), a member of the Japanese aristocracy. Her work is highly regarded for its psychological sublety and its rich portrayal of character, and it tells us a great deal about the exquisite refinement of court life during Japan's most elegant era.

The Heian era was a time of cultural sophistication, during which Japanese painters and poets broke away from the Chinese aesthetic influence of previous periods. To some extent, the novel romanticizes courtly life as the author experienced it, although without idealizing the characters so much that they lose their credibility. According to an eighteenth-century Japanese scholar, Matoori Noringa, the greatness of *The Tale of Genji* lies in the way it conveys the sorrow of human existence as reflected in the behavior of its hero, Genji. Although he sometimes violates the injunctions of Confucianism and Buddhism, Genji nonetheless "combines in himself all good things." Like the author who created him, Genji exhibits great sensitivity to the people who cross his path, especially the many women who share his love.

Heian Hand Scrolls. The art of the Heian period includes both religious and secular subjects, all done with great refinement. The works of this era also reflect the development of more distinctively indigenous Japanese styles. Landscape painting, for example, began to depart from Chinese depictions of majestic mountains, replacing them with representations of softer rolling hills, maple trees, and cherry blossoms. In general, Japanese landscapes of this period are utilized as the backgrounds to narrative tales, which often evoke the sense of transience and poignant sadness also found in Japanese poetry.

One of the most distinctive of secular Japanese painting style is exhibited in the painting of narrative hand scrolls, or ***emaki-mano***, associated with religions or court life. Some of the most celebrated hand scrolls depict *The Tale of Genji* (fig. 9.5). The oldest illustrations of this work, dating from ca. 1120, survive only in self-contained sections, along with short pieces of the handwritten text.

The highly decorative *Genji* illustrations emphasize the placement of figures, their costumes, and the use of color. The artist breaks up the composition by using screens, walls, and the sliding panels found in traditional Japanese palaces. Figures are usually shown at an angle, with the viewpoint from above. Women are depicted in broadly draped garments that hide their figures, leaving only their heads and hands visible. They are engaged in calm activity, one combing another's hair while others read and look at picture scrolls. The overall effect is to convey a sense of court life quietly, with little overt dramatic action, but the

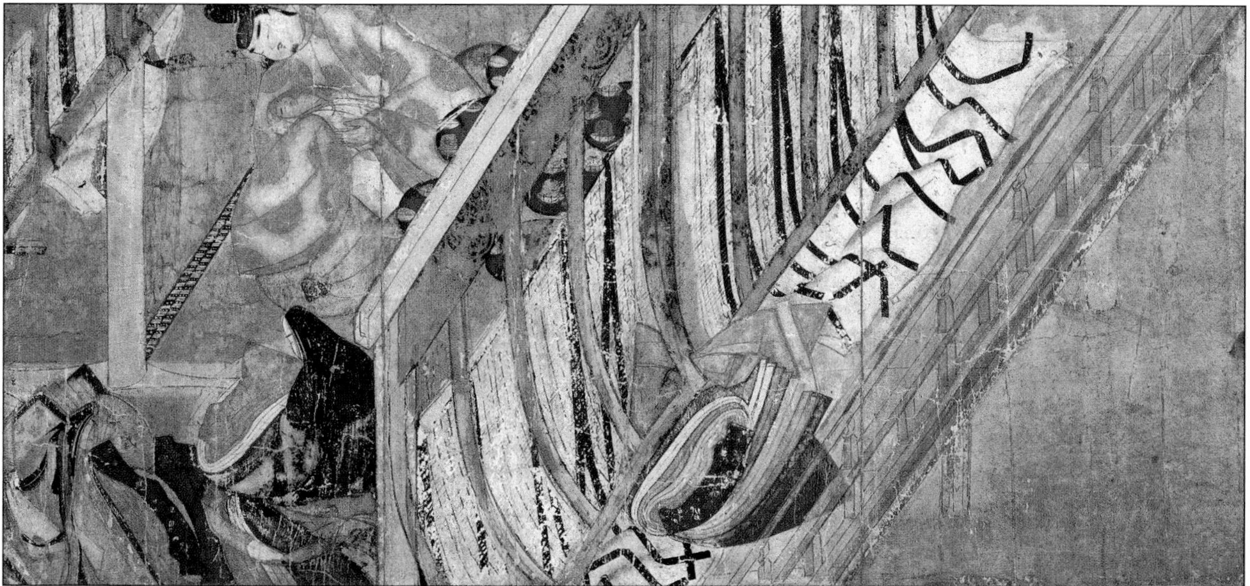

FIGURE 9.5 Illustration to the Azumaya chapter of *The Tale of Genji*, late Heian period, twelfth century, hand scroll, ink and color on paper, height 8′ (21.6 cm), Tokugawa Art Museum, Nagoya. This hand scroll section illustrates a scene in which Prince Genji holds the baby he knows is not his while his wife looks down in sadness. Despite their lofty positions, they are unable to find happiness, as shown by the way they huddle into a corner of the painting.

figures placed in strong assymetrical compositions convey a sense of deep emotion.

Noh Theatre. Masked dance forms came into use in Japan during the sixth century C.E., functioning as religious and secular ritual and as entertainment. Noh masks (fig. 9.6) are smaller than those used for Bugaku, which reached its peak during the Heian period, and which was performed initially at court and later at local shrines. Each Bugaku dance had a mask associated with it.

Noh plays are virtuoso performances that combine chant, mime, and dance. They are accompanied by music, masks, and elaborate costumes. Influenced by Buddhist spirituality, the Noh play's subjects are taken from history, legend, and magic. Traditionally performed in sets of five plays—a play each for a god, warrior, woman, and demon followed by a contemporary or other miscellaneous play, Noh dramas are performed with minimal props and scenery. As with classical Greek tragedy, the audience for Noh plays usually already knows the plot. Costumes and masks make the actors heroic and heighten the force of their gestures and words—much as in ancient Greek drama. The Noh actors' anonymity contributes to the play's mystery and power.

WARRIOR JAPAN: KAMAKURA PERIOD

During the later Heian era, rulers began to see their power diminish at the hands of the **samurai,** regional warriors in the service of the governing nobility. Because these warriors were at the disposal of families competing for power, they were instrumental in the change during the twelfth century from court rule to that of military leaders who effectively controlled Japan while the court retained only its cultural and symbolic meaning.

The era from 1185 to 1333 is known as the Kamakura period because the capital was now moved to Kamakura, in part to escape the effete influence of the court. In a tradition inaugurated by MINAMOTO YORITOMO [MI-na-MO-to] (1147–99), these warriors began to give themselves the title of **shogun** (general in chief) of the samurai (fig. 9.7). They continued to pay lip service to the official sovereign, but it was the shogun who exercised authority until 1868, when imperial rule was restored. The shogun and his samurai prided themselves on their self-reliance, and they were particularly attracted to Zen, a form of Buddhism that promoted self-sufficiency.

Zen Buddhism. By the ninth century, Buddhism and Shinto had converged, to a certain extent, with the boundaries between the two religions becoming blurred. Shinto kami and Buddhist deities, for example, gradually became conflated, Buddhist priests used Shinto temples for meditation and worship, and Shinto temples assumed elements of the Buddhist architectural style. New forms of Buddhism, however, began to assume prominence, including esoteric sects with a galaxy of deities and complex ceremonies that appealed to courtiers, and in response, the Pure Land sect, which became popular with everyday people. In **Pure Land Buddhism,** the believer had only to repeat the mantra "Namu Amida Butsu" (NAH-MOO-AH-MEE-DAH-BOOT-TZU, Praise to Amida Buddha), to be reborn in Amida's Western Paradise.

Connections

COURTS, CULTURE, AND WOMEN

One of the most unusual aspects of medieval Japanese court culture was the importance and position it accorded women writers. The most renowned works of early Japanese literature were written by women: *The Tale of Genji*, *The Pillowbook*, *The Sarashina Diary*, and many poems of the Manyoshu, an eighth-century collection of Japanese poems. The women who wrote these important literary works were either situated at the imperial court or were closely associated with it.

Two major reasons account for the prominence of women writers in Japan at this time. The first relates to the Japanese writing system. Fujiwara leaders engaged in competition to have their daughters married to the emperor. They thus educated them well in Japanese script although writing in Chinese was mostly reserved for men. When successful, these women became the emperor's consorts or his empresses. Even when not quite this successful, women like Sei Shonogan and Murasaki Shikibu became ladies in waiting to aristocratic royalty and wrote works that were highly valued in circles of power and influence.

FIGURE 9.6 *Noh Mask: Ko-omote*. Japan. Ashikaga period, fifteenth century C.E. Painted wood, height about 10″ (25.4 cm). Kongo Family Collection, Tokyo. Such masks were used in Noh dramas, which served religious and secular ritualistic and entertainment functions.

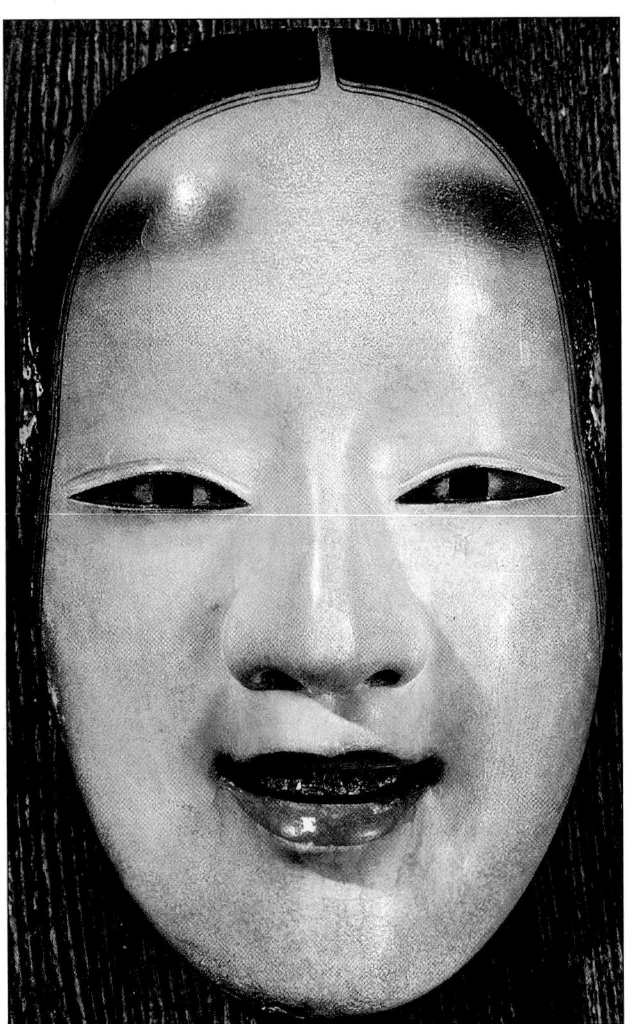

In the Kamakura period, however, a new form of Buddhism arrived from China that especially appealed to warriors for its focus on self-discipline and inner strength. That form, known as **Chan** (Meditation) in China, in Japan became **Zen Buddhism.** Although it had always been a form of counterculture in China, for those who did not feel satisfied with Confucian society, in Japan it became a major religious and cultural force, with a strong influence on the aesthetics of various arts from ink painting to the tea ceremony.

FIGURE 9.7 Fujiwara Takanobu (1142–1205), *Minamoto no Yoritomo*, hanging scroll, ink, and color on silk. In the twelfth century, Minamoto No Yoritomo, depicted here in a traditional formal portrait, rose from a warrior official to become the first shogun, a title used by the military rulers of Japan until 1868.

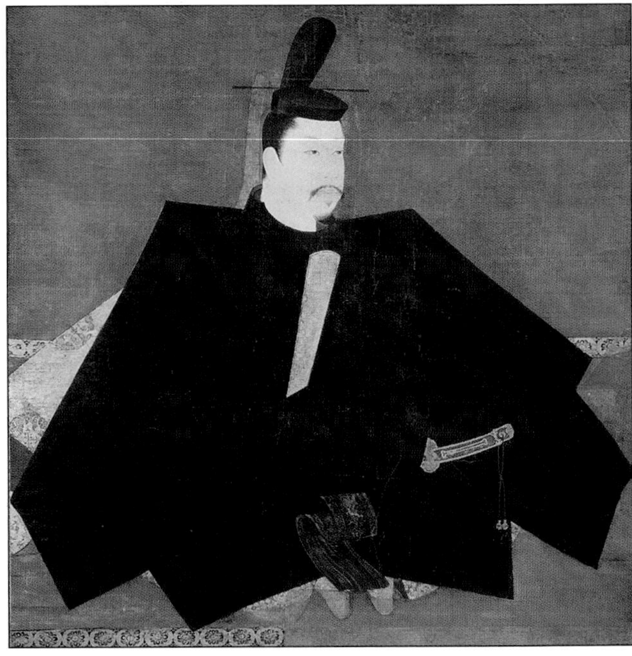

Cross Currents

JAPAN AND CHINA

Many main elements of Japanese culture derive from China, as do the central elements of other East Asian countries, including Korea and Vietnam. China has served for East Asian countries as cultural stimulus, source, and inspiration. From China, Japan inherited a major religion, Buddhism, which had come to China from India. Japan also borrowed Chinese characters for writing until developing its own vernacular writing system, Kana, in the ninth century.

Prior to using the Kana system, Japanese literature and history were recorded using Chinese characters to represent the sounds of Japanese (the Kojiki, for example), or Chinese characters for the Chinese language (the Nihonji, for example). Yet while these and other areas of Japanese culture, such as the tea ceremony and landscape painting, owe much to Chinese influence, the Japanese people over the centuries have made them their own, putting their distinctive cultural stamp upon them.

Zen has been defined as "the art of seeing into the nature of one's own being." It is less a religion or a philosophy than a way of life, an attitude, an active stance toward everyday experience. A unique combination of Taoism and Buddhism, Zen emphasizes meditation to discover the Buddha within each one of us. Nor is Zen concerned with the afterlife—with heaven or hell—or with the immortality of the soul. Its focus instead is on living in the world around us. When a Zen master was asked about life after death, he replied, "Leave that to Buddha, it is no business of ours."

When another Zen master was questioned as to how one could escape the reality of cold and heat, the pangs of hunger and the parching of thirst, he answered, "In winter you shiver, in summer you sweat. When you are hungry eat, and drink when you are thirsty." One does not try to escape physical reality. In Zen, one accepts it for what it is. Life is to be lived right here and now, attentively and appreciatively, and so Zen meditation can permeate everything from getting dressed and eating, to reading, working, and relaxing.

LATER WARRIOR JAPAN: ASHIKAGA PERIOD

One great problem with warrior culture was that the samurai were in the service of feudal lords, rather than a central government. The Kamakura period ended in civil war in 1333, and insurrections of one kind or another continued to plague Japan almost continuously until 1573. During this era, known as the Ashikaga period, Japan was ruled by shoguns and their samurai warriors, and as a result Zen influence dominated Japanese culture.

Tea Ceremony. One of the major cultural practices of Japan, founded on Zen thinking, is the tea ceremony or ***cha-no-yu.*** According to Rikyu, one of its founders, "The tea ceremony is nothing more than boiling water, making tea, and drinking it." Yet the tea ceremony rose to prominence in the 1470s when the Ashikaga ruler Yoshimasa retreated from the conflicts that dominated urban life to collect Chinese paintings and ceramics at his villa on the island of Higashiyama. The Zen monk Murata Juko suggested to him that by drinking tea in a small hut, with only a few companions, he could experience ***wabi,*** "lonely seclusion." This requires a heightened sense of awareness, in which the practitioner experiences, for instance, "the cold winter wind on his skin." Murata also insisted in selflessness, writing that "nothing holds back the way of tea more than attachment to oneself and feelings of self-satisfaction; we must always be aware of our own shortcomings."

In the tea ceremony proper, the iron kettle, the pottery tea bowls made in China or, later, in local Japanese kilns, the small jars for holding powdered tea, and even the bamboo tea scoops were objects to be contemplated and appreciated for their humble practicality. In time, the most celebrated of these items came to be worth astonishing amounts of money and prestige, and were used as major gifts between feudal lords, but they generally expressed a spirit of natural simplicity. The tea hut was decorated with a hanging scroll of a painting or calligraphy, preferably by a Chinese or Japanese Zen monk, and a flower arrangement appropriate for the time of year might also be displayed. The hut itself was built of natural materials in a carefully designed garden through which visitors would arrive and later depart, clearing their minds of worldy concerns. As Rikyu stated, in the act of drinking tea together, "here the Buddha-mind reveals itself."

In most cultures, there has been a trend over the centuries toward ever more refined and technically complex forms of art. In Japan this can be seen in the developments from the Asuka and Nara eras to the Heian period, as court culture favored increasingly richly decorative styles and techniques in calligraphy, painting, architecture, and other arts. The tea ceremony, strongly influenced by Zen, turned these aesthetics upside-down. Rikyu taught that in the tearoom it is best if every object is less than perfect, and he saw the beauty of utensils that had been broken or otherwise damaged. Therefore in the *wabi* sensibility of Rikyu and his followers, a rough pot from the Japanese countryside or a mended Korean bowl could be as highly admired as a delicate Chinese

Then & Now

SUMO WRESTLING

One of Japan's most distinctive sports is *sumo*, or Japanese wrestling, which originated during the Heian period, when it became a popular spectator sport. Sumo differs from Western-style wrestling, which originated in Greece. Unlike Western wrestling, where the object is to pin one's opponent to the mat by his shoulders, in sumo the object is to push one's opponent out of the competition ring or to throw him down within it. Sumo wrestlers confront each other much like two football linemen trying to block each other or knock each other off balance. One similarity between Western wrestling and sumo is the ritual in which the wrestlers parade into the ring wearing, in the case of sumo wrestlers, long, decorated skirts, and Western wrestlers, a kind of robe that bears the wrestler's name. Both Western and sumo wrestlers then strip down to a more basic attire, trunks or trunks and tank top for the Western wrestler and loin cloth for their sumo counterparts. Sumo involves more ritual, including the wrestlers tossing salt to purify the ring, squatting across from and glaring at each other, and performing a series of standardized gestures. Today some of these rituals have been reduced, though they continue in attenuated form to link Japanese sumo past and present.

porcelain, and unglazed ceramics were often preferred to, or mixed with, elaborately decorated ones. There were exceptions to this rule of modesty and sparseness; one shogun even commissioned a tea hut covered with gold leaf. Nevertheless, the virtues of natural rusticity and unpretentious functionality as seen in the tea ceremony have continued to influence Japanese design and taste to this day.

LANDSCAPE PAINTING

The respect for the land that distinguishes the Shinto religion, combined with literati and Zen Chinese **ink-style painting** traditions, were developed in the landscape painting of the Muromachi period (1392–1568), which shows reverence for the grace and grandeur of nature and the humble place of human beings within it. Japanese painting suggests less a naturalistically rendered scene than an extension of unseen vistas beyond the explicity depicted view. This pictorial tradition characterizes the Zen ideal of "capturing the principle of things as they move on."

Sesshu. Of Japanese Muromachi artists, the priest/painter SESSHU [SES-SHU] (1420–1506), more than anyone else, took Chinese ink-style painting and made it Japanese. In 1467–69, he traveled to China, where examples of landscape painting greatly influenced his work. However, Sesshu was to put a distinctive, Zenlike mark upon the tradition, writing on his return that he had learned more from viewing China's mountains than from its painters, and the Japanese monk-artists of the past were his true teachers.

His *Winter Landscape* (fig. 9.8) suggests the cold, brittle mood that the season inspires. Sesshu's bold brushstrokes and diagonal lines suggest the power of nature, as patches of blank paper signify snow and depict winter's starkness. In striking contrasts of black and white, the painting's bold angular outlines convey a chilly strength; the tiny figure travels through this dynamic scene as a pilgrim through the world.

FIGURE 9.8 Sesshu, *Winter Landscape*, Japan, Ashikaga period, ca. 1470s, hanging scroll, ink and slight color on paper, $18\frac{1}{4} \times 11\frac{1}{2}''$ (46.3 × 29.3 cm), Tokyo National Museum, Tokyo. TNM Image Archives Source:http//TNMArchives.jp/. The harshness of the pictorial style, seen in this unsentimental representation of a wintry world, is characteristic of Sesshu.

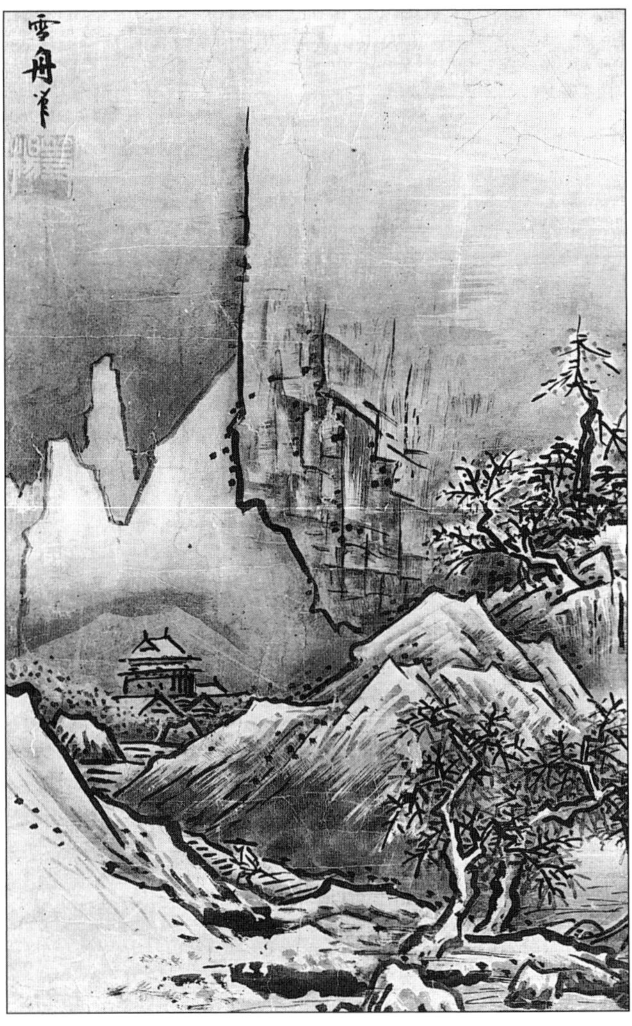

Critical Thinking

ZEN AND EVERYDAY LIFE

Although Zen is firmly linked with Japanese culture, it has become a deeply entrenched U.S. cultural import. Among the numerous contemporary books about Zen one might find in a decent-sized bookstore are the following: *Zen Miracles: Find Peace in an Insane World; Zen Training; Zen Living; Zen Commitments; Voices of Insight; Song of Mind; Waking Up to What You Do; The Companion of Zen;* and *Zen 24/7.*

Why do you think Zen continues to exert such an influence today—not only in Japan, but in other countries, especially in the United States? What aspects of the Zen approach to living do you think are particularly influential? Why?

Sesshu's landscape scrolls possess some of the boldness of his Chinese contemporary, Shen Zhou. Sesshu's work, however, emphasizes strong lines. His extended vistas are consistently subordinated to visual drama and experience, reflecting the Zen qualities of immediate apprehension and intuitive understanding.

In Sesshu's era, the shogunate favored Zen painting, just as they favored Zen monks as advisers and teachers. After 1600, however, the government turned to neo-Confucianists to be their advisers and teachers, and Zen became less dominant as a cultural force, although it was still significant. Instead of painter-monks, the leading Zen masters now created paintings and calligraphy for their followers, rather than to decorate palaces, mansions, and castles.

TEMPLE OF THE GOLDEN PAVILION (KINKAKUJI)

One of the most interesting and elegant buildings constructed during the Muromachi period is the Kyoto landmark, Kinkakuji, known as the Temple of the Golden Pavilion (fig. 9.9). Erected in 1397 under the shogun Yoshimitsu (1358–1408), the Golden Pavilion, so named

FIGURE 9.9 Temple of the Golden Pavilion (Kinkakuji), Kyoto, Muromachi period, 1397.The building was constructed for the shogun as a retreat and converted to a temple after his retirement.

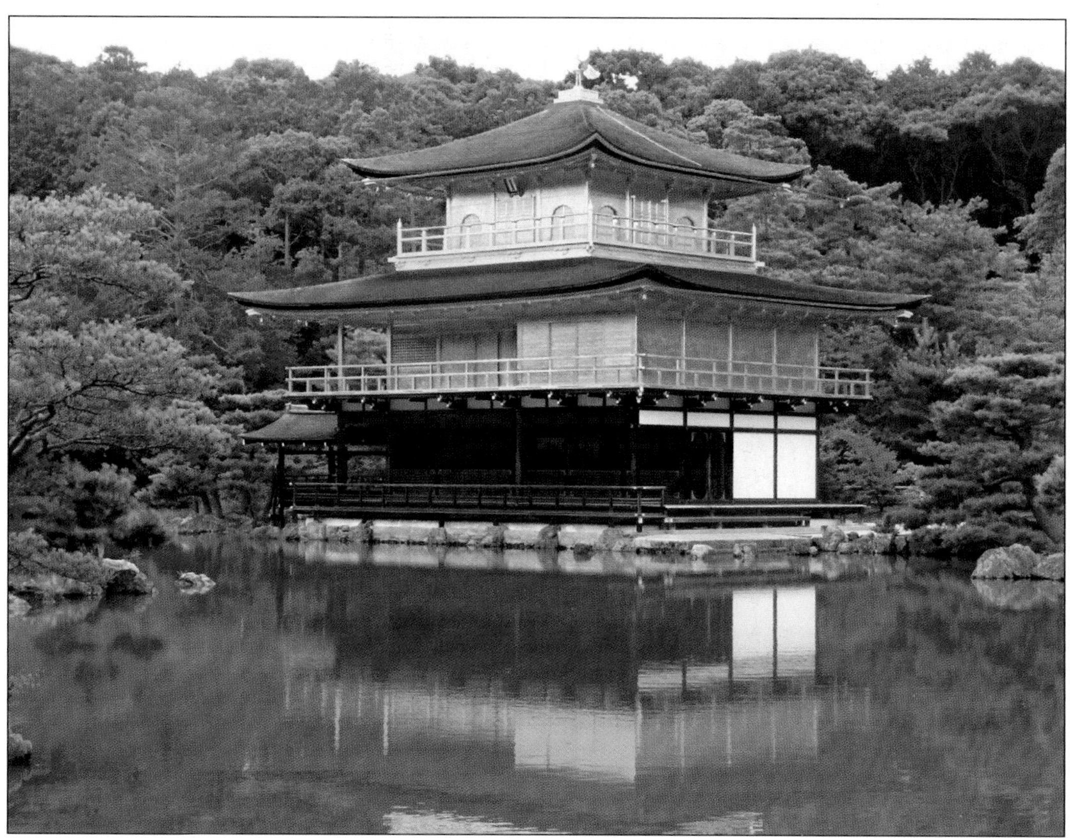

because parts of the exterior are covered with gold leaf, was originally a private chapel designed for Yoshimitsu's villa. After his death, it was converted into a Buddhist temple and monastery, with a Zen meditation hall and rooms for contemplating the landscape and the moon. Its three stories culminate in a curving Chinese-pyramidal and Japanese-shingled roof. The pavilion is set on a platform that juts into a pond surrounded by trees, which are carefully planted to create a look of natural variety and profusion. The structure seems simultaneously set off from and into the landscape in a harmonious blending of nature and civilization. The overall effect is one of spontaneous simplicity.

JAPANESE GARDENS

Japanese gardeners created two fundamentally different types of gardens, seen in figs. 9.10 and 9.11, both at the Zen Buddhist **Ryoan-ji Temple**, in Kyoto, known as the Temple of the Peaceful Dragon (the dragon refers to the power of the emperor). The land was a private Fujiwara residence in the eleventh and twelfth centuries, and became a Zen temple in the late fifteenth cenury.

The Kyoyochi Pond garden includes the five traditional requirements for a Japanese garden: a pond, a waterfall, a bridge, rocks, and trees. This style of garden was favored by the nobility. The large pond with lily pads and lush surrounding plantings produce an enchanting environment.

FIGURE 9.10 Kyoyochi Pond, twelfth century, Ryoan-ji Temple, Kyoto. This large pond is part of an extensive garden that appears so casual as to almost be nature's work, yet, in fact, was skillfully designed to achieve this effect.

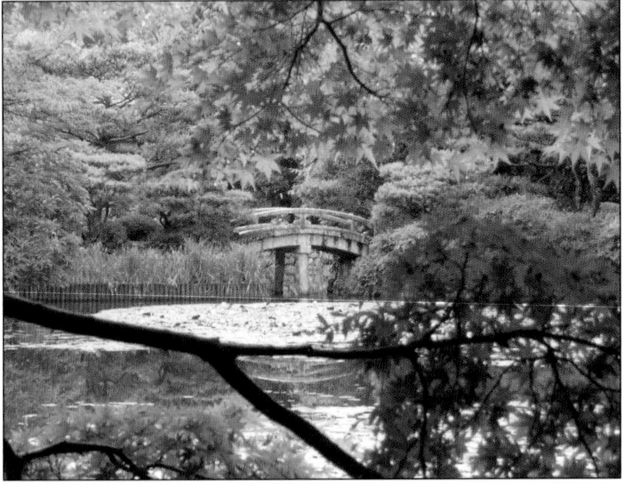

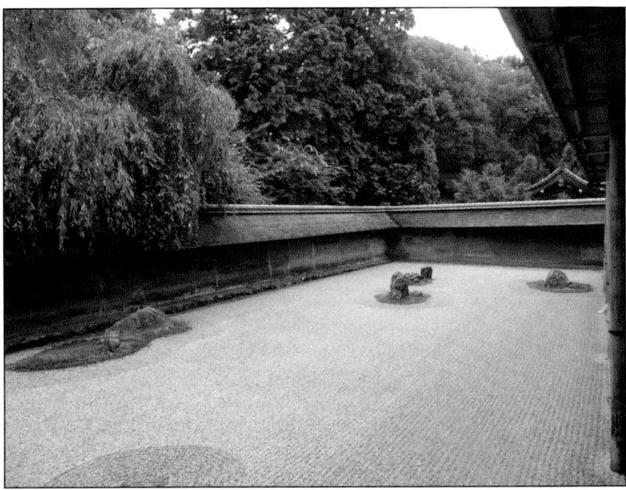

FIGURE 9.11 Dry landscape garden, late fifteenth or early sixteenth century, Ryoan-ji Temple, Kyoto. This rectangular Zen garden consists of fifteen rocks surrounded by moss and white gravel. Limited elements have been carefully chosen and placed, creating a pure and peaceful environment intended to foster meditation and contemplation.

This type of green garden co-existed in Japan with a very different type: The most famous garden at the Ryoan-ji Temple is the "dry rock garden," or "dry landscape garden," also known as a "withered landscape," and called **Kare-sansui** in Japanese. This is believed to be the original garden of this type, and to have been created in the late fifteenth or early sixteenth century. The most important dry gardens were constructed at Zen temples. At Ryoan-ji, in a flat, rectangular space, white gravel that is raked daily surrounds fifteen stones of varying sizes and shapes and their encircling moss. The viewer is intended to observe the garden, but not physically enter it. As one walks around the garden, no matter where one stands, only fourteen of the fifteen rocks may ever be seen at a time. It is said that only those who achieve enlightenment are able to see all fifteen simultaneously, as the invisible becomes visible. Simple and subtle, this is meant to express and to elicit emotions and thoughts, to allow for contemplation and communication. The absence of materialistic display is related to Zen philosophy; Zen has been described as "the art of the void," as evidenced here.

Cultural Impact

The influence of early Japanese civilization on later periods and in countries in both Asia and the West has been considerable. Among the cultural legacies of ancient and medieval Japan are swordsmanship, flower arranging, and the tea ceremony. Associated with the warrior culture of the Japanese samurai, swordsmanship and swordcraft, or the making of swords, have continued well into the twentieth century, but exist today mostly as relics of a bygone era. Japanese flower arranging and the tea ceremony, also of medieval origin, retain their cultural significance not only in Japan, but in countries in which Japan has had cultural contact.

The impact of Zen on modern Japanese culture has been noted, but not to be overlooked is the influence of the books by D.T. Suzuki, one of the world's most renowned scholar/practitioners of Zen. His book *Zen and Japanese Culture* reveals the extent to which Zen continues to pervade everyday life in Japan. Suzuki's works have influenced and inspired others who have written their own accounts that reveal Zen's influence in Germany through the art of *Zen in the Art of Archery* by Eugene Herrigel and in the United States with *Zen and the Art of Motorcycle Maintenance* by Robert Pirsig.

Herrigel's book describes his attempt to learn archery Zen style while in Japan. Herrigel learned the Zen lessons of replacing fear of failure with an expectation of fulfillment. He also learned how "not to shoot," but to "let the shot fall from him," like ripe fruit falling naturally from a tree. Pirsig's book applies Zen principles to the author's life as a teacher and as a father who is developing a relationship with his teenage son. Like Herrigel, Pirsig uses the skills associated with a mechanical art, in his case, motorcycle maintenance, to develop Zen values and ideals by which to live.

KEY TERMS

Jomon
haniwa
Shinto
Kojiki
kami
waka
emaki-mano
samurai
shogun
Pure Land Buddhism
Chan
Zen Buddhism
cha-no-yu
wabi
ink-style painting
Ryoan-ji Temple
Kare-sansui

www. WEBSITES FOR FURTHER STUDY

http://www.japan-guide.com/e/e2055.html
(General information about Buddhism and its importation and development in Japan. Important dates and names are hyperlinked to other sections.)

http://www.city.kasugai.aichi.jp/world/english/tofu.html
(Tofu Ono [894–966] is one of the most best-known calligraphers in Japan. During the Heian period there was a movement to create culture indigenous to the Japanese people and not the prevailing influence of Chinese culture.)

http://www.lyrichord.com/nohmusic
(Japanese Noh theatre music.)

http://www.archeolink.com/ancient_japan.htm
(Outline of the major developments between the Jomom and Nara periods.)

http://www.crystallinks.com/japan1.html
(Images and articles on representative objects from ancient Japan.)

Chapter 10

History

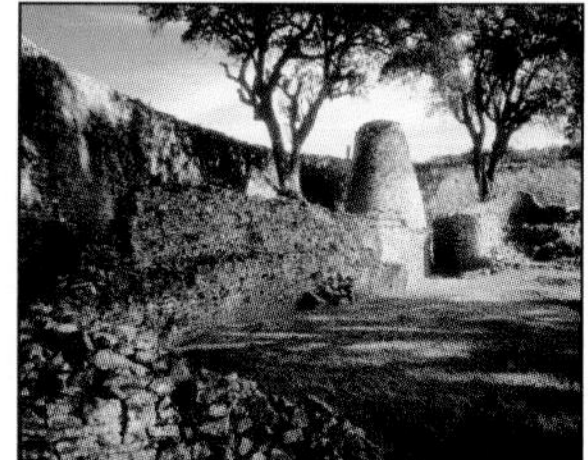

5000 B.C.E.	Sedentary agriculture in West African savannahs
3000 B.C.E.	Bantu Migration
700 B.C.E.	Iron working in northern Tanzania
500 B.C.E.	Iron working in West Africa
third century B.C.E.	Jenne-Jeno and Gao settled in fertile inland delta of Niger river
first century B.C.E.	Traders from Mediterranean and India sail to East African coast
early centuries C.E.	Romans unify Mediterranean region, including North Africa; Christianity spreads
219–38 C.E.	Yax Moch Xoc rules over Tikal
431 C.E.	Bahlum Kuk founds Palenque
650–700 C.E.	Earthquake in Andes
651 C.E.	Defeat of Muslim forces by Christian Nubians at the battle of Dongala
ca. 750 C.E.	Teotihuacán sacked and burned
eighth century C.E.	Islamic state firmly entrenched in North Africa
ninth century C.E.	Igbo-Ukwu developed in forest region of Southeastern Nigeria
thirteenth century C.E.	Benin, one of the largest and longest-lived forest states strengthens
ca. 1325 C.E.	Aztecs build city of Tenochtitlán
fifteenth century C.E.	Portuguese establish trading posts at El Mina (modern day Ghana) and with Kongo
ca. 1502–20 C.E.	Moctezuma II reigns as Aztec emperor
1519 C.E.	Cortés arrives in Mexico
1532 C.E.	Pizarro encounters and overthrows Inca empire

Arts and Architecture

70,000 B.C.E.	Cave artifacts at Blombos in South Africa
4800 B.C.E.	Rock paintings in Sahara and South Africa regions
ca. 900–500 B.C.E.	Colossal Head
ca. 100 B.C.E.–500 C.E.	*Moche Lord with a Feline*
ca. 150 C.E.	Pyramid of the Sun
451 C.E.	Coptic (Egyptian) and Nestorian (Middle Eastern) Christian churches break with Roman church
ca. 500 C.E.	Huaca del Sol (Pyramid of the Sun)
seventh century C.E.	Temple of Inscriptions
thirteenth century C.E.	Benin region develops sophisticated state-sponsored art program built around the casting of bronze sculptures using "lost wax" casting
fifteenth century C.E.	Coatlicue
ca. 1450 C.E.	Machu Picchu built

Literature and Philosophy

sixteenth century C.E.	*Popol Vuh*
	Cantares Mexicanes
	Epic of Son-Jara
1558 C.E.	Legend of the Suns

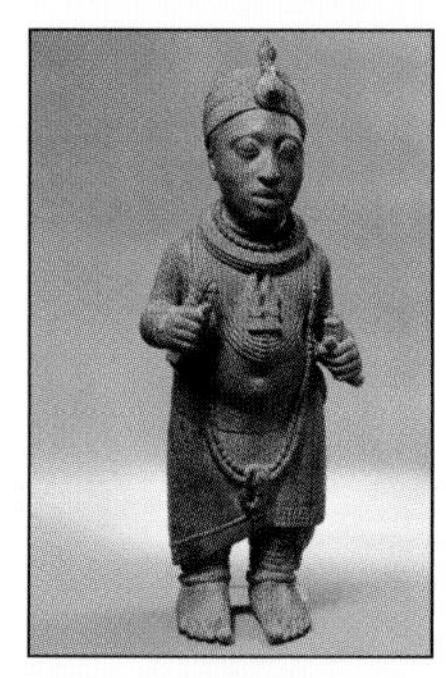

Early Civilizations of the Americas and Africa

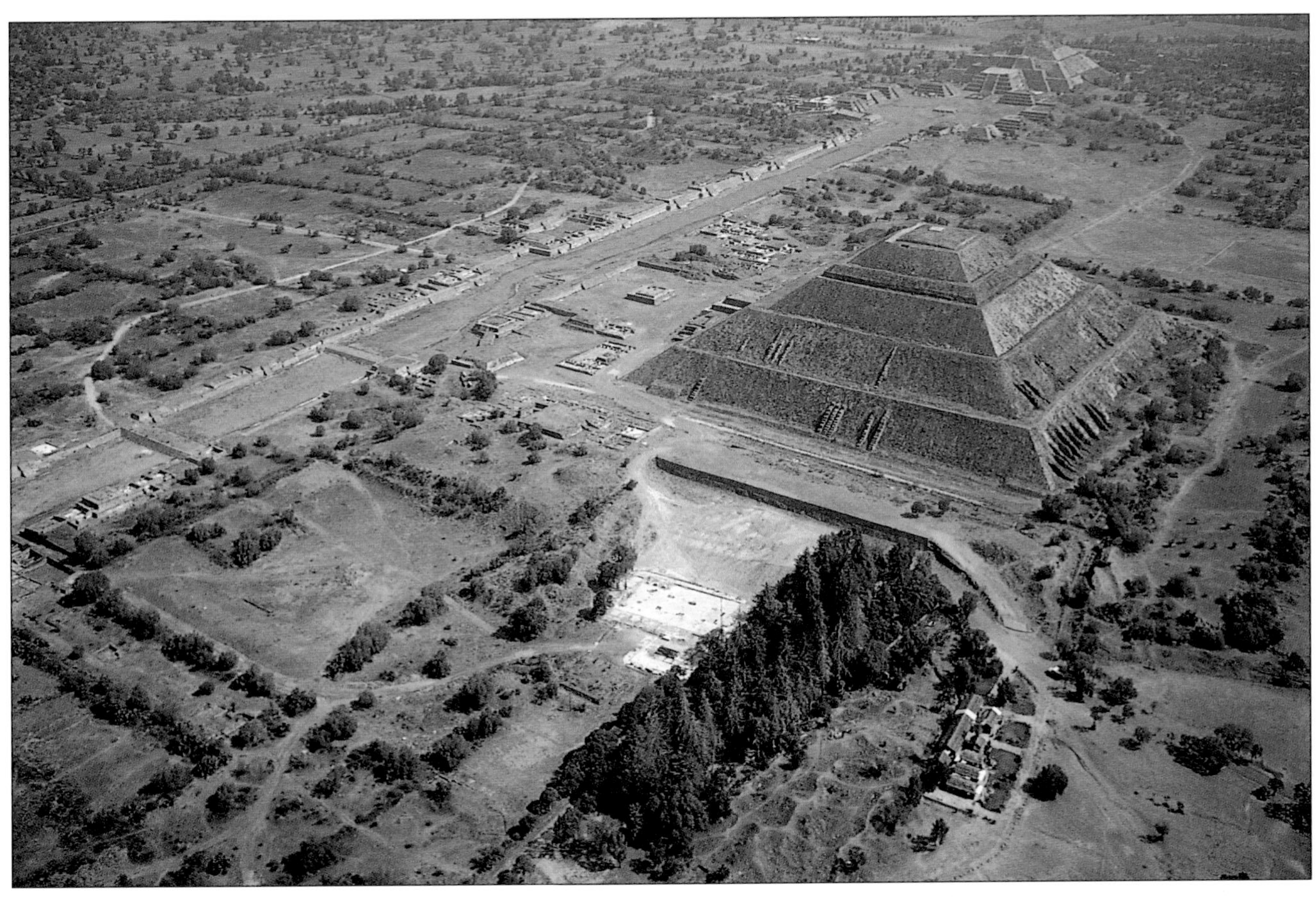

Teotihuacán, Mexico, Teotihuacán culture, 350–650 C.E.

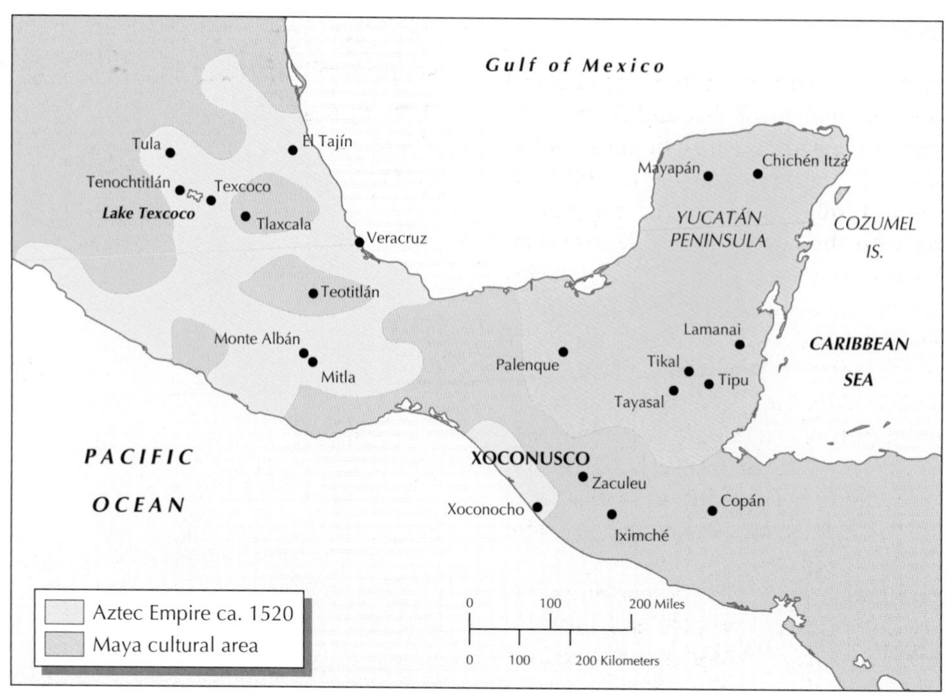

Map 10.1 Mesoamerica on the eve of the Spanish Conquest.

Chapter Overview

MESOAMERICA

"Middle America" establishes itself as a cultural mecca

CULTURES OF PERU

Geographical constraints fail to hinder civilizations unique to the world

NORTH AMERICA

Vast lands and opportunities provide the basis for rich cultural heritages from coast to coast

CIVILIZATION OF EARLY AFRICA

Multiple cultures thrive and evolve

Sometime between 30,000 and 12,000 years ago, at the height of the Ice Age, tribal hunters began to migrate from Asia into the Americas across a land bridge that extended for perhaps a thousand miles south of the present-day Bering Straits. This giant plain was rich in grass and animal life, and the tribes were naturally drawn on further across it, and then on southward, in pursuit of game. By 11,000 B.C.E., they had reached the tip of South America and the Atlantic coast of North America.

As the ice melted and the oceans rose at the close of the Ice Age, the tribes in the Americas were cut off from Asia and Europe. This isolation lasted until October 12, 1492, when Christopher Columbus landed on San Salvador in the Bahamas. Thinking he was on the east coast of Asia, near India, Columbus called the people who met him "Indios," Indians. These Native Americans seemed simple and uncivilized to Columbus, but they were in fact the descendants of ancient and often quite magnificent civilizations, some of which dated back to the first millennium B.C.E.

MESOAMERICA

Mesoamerica is a cultural area extending from central Mexico to Honduras, and includes Belize and Guatemala. The ancient Mesoamerican cultures include those of the Olmecs (1300–600 B.C.E.), the Maya (250 B.C.E.–900 C.E.), and the Toltecs (900–1200), precursors of the Aztecs (1350–1521), along with the civilization of Teotihuacán (100–800). The Mesoamericans spoke many languages. Among these was the Nahua family of languages, which includes the language of the Aztecs and the Maya, dialects of which survive to this day in southern Mexico and Guatemala. The diverse early Mesoamerican civilizations shared other cultural features, including hieroglyphic writing, an applied knowledge of astronomy, early cultivation of maize, the use of calendars, and a form of monarchical government intimately linked with religious ideas and practices.

Prior to the arrival of Europeans in Mesoamerica, the various complex civilizations that sprouted and withered influenced one another and were interconnected. The high level of interaction among these ancient Mesoamerican societies included trading in raw materials, such as obsidian, and products such as carved jade. Over the roughly 2,500 years from the rise of the Olmecs to the decline of the Aztecs, ideas and inventions, such as writing and the calendar, were exchanged along with the trade in goods.

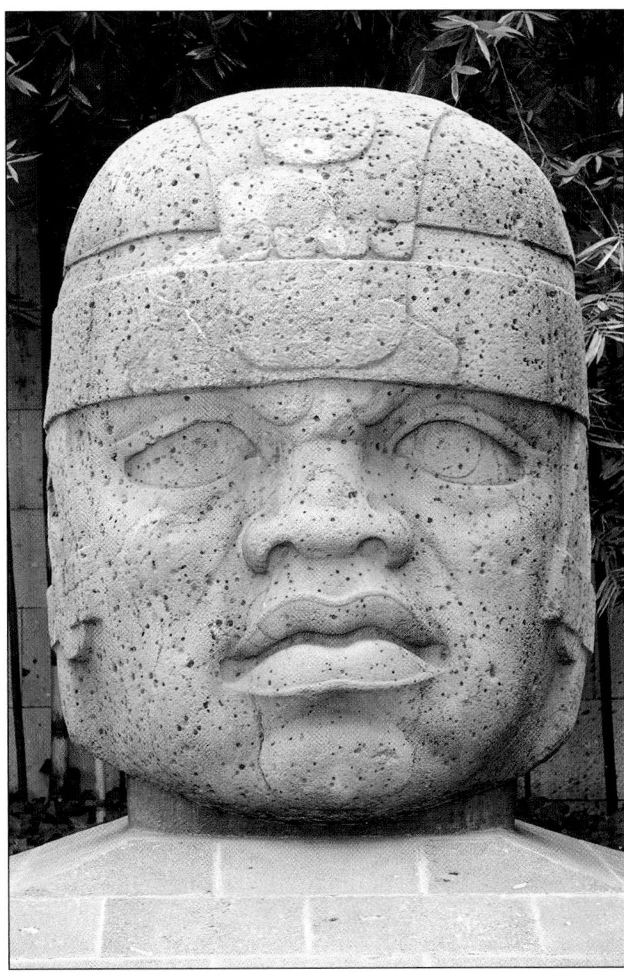

Figure 10.1 Colossal Head, from La Venta, Mexico, Olmec culture, ca. 900–500 B.C.E., basalt, height 7′ 5″ (2.26 m), La Venta Park, Villahermosa, Tabasco, Mexico. This example of a giant carved stone head represents the height of sculptural achievement among the ancient Olmecs.

Olmecs

The earliest Mesoamerican art dates from about 1300 B.C.E. when the Olmecs inhabited the southern coast of the Gulf of Mexico, especially the area between Veracruz and Tabasco. There is some question whether the Olmecs were a distinct people and culture or whether the term "Olmec," which derives from a word for rubber, refers to an artistic style that prevailed throughout ancient Central America.

Whoever they were, the Olmecs were outstanding stone carvers. The most remarkable carvings that have survived to the present day are a series of sixteen colossal stone heads up to twelve feet high (fig. 10.1). Eight of these heads were found in San Lorenzo, Veracruz, where they were placed facing outward on the circumference of a ceremonial area. They are carved of basalt. Because the nearest basalt quarry is fifty miles away in the Tuxtla Mountains, the enormous stones from which the heads were carved had, apparently, to be dragged down from the mountains, loaded onto rafts, floated down to the Gulf of Mexico, then up river to San Lorenzo, and finally dragged up and positioned on the ceremonial plateau.

Believed to be portraits of Olmec rulers, the heads share similar facial features, including flattened noses, thick lips, and puffy cheeks. They all are capped with headgear similar to old-style American football helmets. This is believed to have served as protection in war and in a type of ceremonial ball game played throughout Mesoamerica. Among other discoveries at San Lorenzo are stone figurines of ball players and a ball court. (See Then & Now p. 213 and fig. 10.2.)

Teotihuacán

Among the most splendid of all Mesoamerican sites must be the ancient city of TEOTIHUÁCAN [te-oh-te-wu-KAN], which means "where one becomes a god." **Teotihuacán** (fig. 10.3) grew to dominance after 300 B.C.E. By the time it reached the height of its political and cultural influence, between ca. 350–650 C.E., its population numbered between 100,000 and 200,000, making it one of the largest cities on earth at the time.

Critical Thinking

WHAT IS A CITY?

Scholars have debated the issue of what constitutes a "city," or an urban center, in the ancient world. Much of the debate has centered on whether writing is an essential characteristic. Other potential characteristics include formal organization, diverse populations, and interdependence. Which of these traits do you think is most important in deciding on whether a place might be defined as a city? Why? And what other traits could or should be considered as elements that would qualify a site as a city?

The people of Teotihuacán were great pyramid builders. The city is laid out in a grid pattern with a giant avenue (the Avenue of the Dead) at its center. This central artery links two great pyramids, the Pyramids of the Moon and of the Sun, which are the focal points of six hundred smaller pyramids, five hundred workshop areas, nearly two thousand apartment compounds, numerous plazas, and a giant market area. Built in about 150 C.E. over a natural cave (but only rediscovered in 1971), the Pyramid of the Sun is oriented to mark the passage of the sun from east to west and the rising of the stellar constellation the Pleiades on the days of the equinox. Thus it links the underworld to the heavens, the forces of life and death.

Along the Avenue of the Dead are a series of ziggurat-like structures with numerous steps leading to an elevated platform, which originally supported a temple. After the Pyramids of the Sun and the Moon, the most important structure in Teotihuacán was the Temple of Quetzalcoatl, the god of priestly wisdom. This temple contains elaborate relief carvings, which include the heads of feathered serpents and fire serpents.

The overall design and layout of Teotihuacán suggests its role as an astronomical and ritualistic center. The relation of the Pyramid of the Sun to the others suggests the order of the universe, a cosmological order that influenced all aspects of life, including political organization, social behavior, and religious ritual. Even time was represented. Each of the two staircases of the Pyramid of the Sun, for example, contains 182 steps, which, when the platform at the apex is added, together total 365. This spatial representation of the solar calendar is echoed in the Temple of Quetzalcoatl, which has 364 serpent fangs.

By about 700, Teotihuacán's influence had waned, and the city was sacked and burned in about 750. We can only speculate about what finally led to its demise, but an ecological explanation is possible. The surrounding countryside had been pillaged to provide lime for the mortar used to build Teotihuacán. As the city's population grew, adequate provision of food became a problem. Coupled with the effects of drought, the environmental catastrophe wreaked on the countryside probably made it impossible to maintain a stable civilization.

FIGURE 10.2 An ancient ball court at Monte Alban in the Mexican valley of Oaxaca. © Danny Lehman/CORBIS, NY. All Rights Reserved. Various types of ball games were played in Mexico for more than two thousand years.

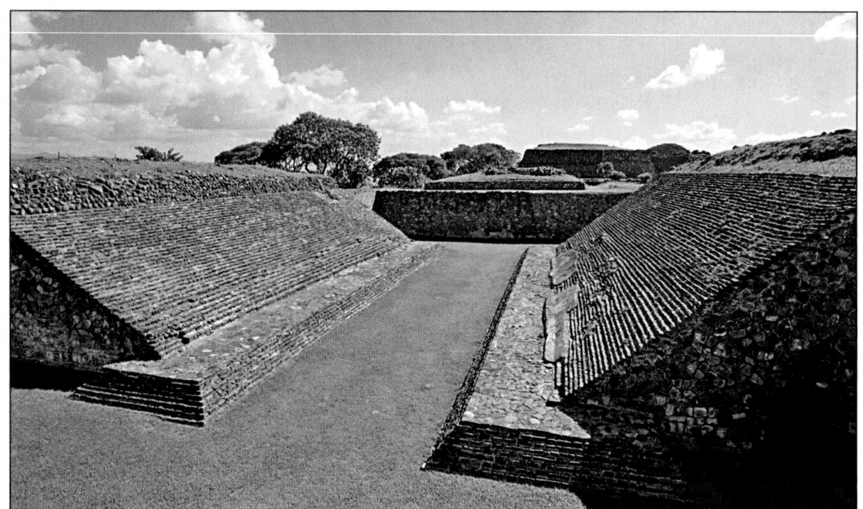

Then & Now

MESOAMERICAN BALL GAMES

Ancient Americans played a variety of games using balls of various sizes. In one of them the Hachtli players tried to shoot a rubber ball through a stone ring. The Olmecs left ball courts made around 1500 B.C.E., and colossal Olmec stone heads are sometimes shown wearing helmets presumed to have been used in their ancient ball games.

Much more than a mere sport, in which onlookers sometimes made bets, Ancient Mesoamerican ball games were rituals of religious significance. They were also a matter of life and death. The Mayan epic *Popol Vuh* describes a ball game in which Hero Twins descend into the underworld to defeat the Lords of Death and thereby save humanity.

Unlike modern-day basketball, which tends to be a high-scoring affair, with many baskets made by both teams, ancient ball games were rough defensive contests in which scoring was difficult, since use of the hands was not allowed.

A more serious difference between contemporary basketball and the ancient version is that modern players, when they fail at a crucial shot at game's end, come back to play another day, whereas members of losing teams in ancient Mesoamerica often found themselves offered as a ritual sacrifice.

FIGURE 10.3 Teotihuacán, Mexico, Teotihuacán culture, 350–650 C.E. The city of Teotihuacán covered an area nine miles square and contained between 100,000 and 200,000 people, an enormous scale and population for a culture of its time.

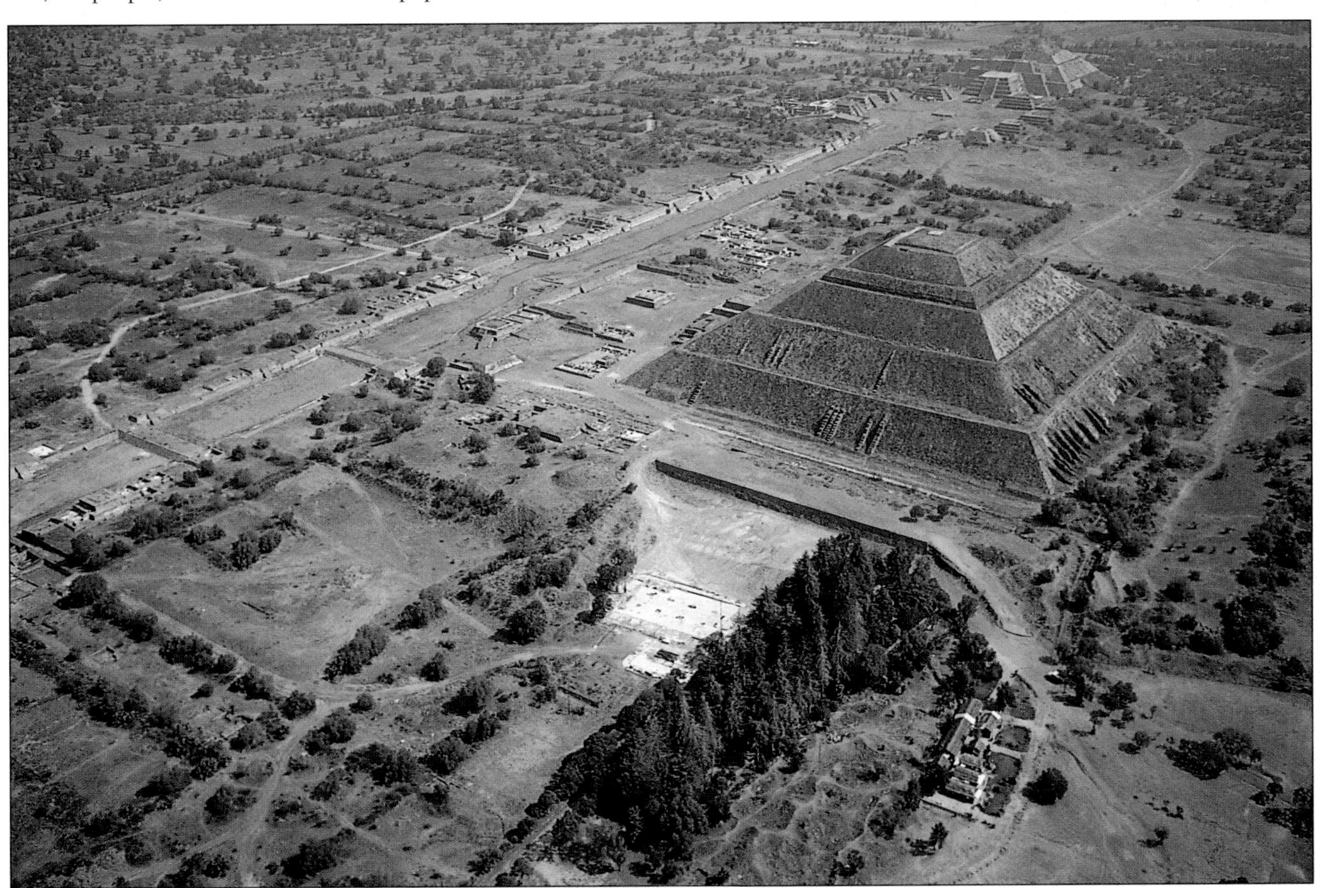

Connections

MAYAN WRITING AND WALL PAINTING

Recently, archaeologists have made a number of stunning discoveries amidst ancient ruins in San Barto, Guatemala. Among the most important of these finds is the earliest known Mayan writing, a column of hieroglyphs that pushes back the date of a developed writing system hundreds of years. One problem, however, is that the archaeologists have had great difficulty translating these newly discovered hieroglyphs. They are expected to be helped, though, by another discovery nearby of murals in vivid colors depicting the Mayan myth of creation and kingship. Scholars will analyze the murals seeking clues to breaking the code of the ancient preclassical period writing. They will also use Mayan writing of a millennium later to find connections with the earlier hieroglyphs. In addition, the discovery of additional examples of the ancient writing at other sites is also expected to aid in their decoding efforts.

MAYAN CULTURE

The ancient Maya inhabited the Yucatán peninsula, which extends into Belize and Guatemala, parts of the Mexican states of Chiapas and Tabasco, and the western part of Honduras and El Salvador. The culture appears to have lasted from about 250 B.C.E. to 900 C.E. Although the Maya possessed their own form of hieroglyphic writing, they shared with other Mesoamerican peoples the use of books made of fig-bark paper or deerskin that unfolded into screens.

The ancient Maya are set apart from their ancient Mesoamerican neighbors, however, in their arithmetical and astronomical knowledge, which rivaled that of the ancient Babylonians. The Maya possessed a profound understanding of the regularity and continuity of the heavenly bodies, which they saw as a metaphor for the ruler's consistent safeguarding of his people.

Mayan writing is the most expressive and complex in the Native American world. Mayan writing survived in part because it was carved into stone and thus was able to withstand destruction and decay. Mayan writing falls into two main categories: (1) dynastic records, including the genealogies of rulers and records of their victories, sacrifices, and communion with their ancestors; (2) astronomical records and priestly timekeeping records. Interestingly and paradoxically, the Mayan writing system was designed less to communicate than to keep information secret, one reason that its esoteric code took so long for scholars to crack and interpret.

Mayan Universe. For the Maya, the universe consisted of three layers—the Upperworld of the heavens, the Middleworld of human civilization, and the Underworld below—linked by a great tree, the **Wacah Chan** which grew from the center of the Middleworld and from which the cardinal directions flowed. Each direction possessed its own symbolic significance and was represented by its own color, bird, and gods. East was the principal direction, since the sun rose there, and its color was red. North was the direction of the dead, and its color was white. The king was the personification of the Wacah Chan. When he stood at the top of a pyramid in ritual activity, he was seen to link the three layers of the universe in his own person. During such rituals, the king would let his own blood in order to give sustenance to the spiritual world. Although ritual bloodletting seems to many people to be a barbaric or at least an exotic practice, we should remember that Christians symbolically drink the blood of Jesus when they celebrate Holy Communion. The role of blood in Mayan ritual is similar.

To the Maya, time was not linear, as we conceive it, but cyclical. They used two calendars. The first was a 365-day farming calendar that consisted of eighteen "months" of twenty days each and one short month of just five days. The second was a sacred calendar of 260 days, which probably relates to the average length of human gestation from the first missed menstrual flow to birth (actually 266 days). It is clear that this second calendar possesses a close connection to Mayan bloodletting rituals. The Mayans combined the two calendars to create a long cycle of fifty-two years, or 18,980 days (a particular day in one calendar will fall on the same day in the other calendar every fifty-two years), at the end of which time repeated itself.

Mayan Literature and Myth. The great work of Mayan myth and literature is the *Popol Vuh*, an epic narrative that describes the creation of the world. Written in the Quiche language around 1500, but regarded as extant during the Mayan classic era, the *Popol Vuh* outlines traditional Mayan views on human beings as well as the origins of the world. According to the story, the gods wished to create intelligent beings who would praise them. They made three unsuccessful attempts, using mud, wood, and animals as materials, before they decided to use water and maize, critically important substances in Mesoamerican culture. Like the Homeric epics for ancient Greece and the Mahabharata of ancient India, the *Popol Vuh* serves Mesoamerica as a repository of its cultural ideals and values.

Tikal. Among the most important sites of classic Mayan culture is that of TIKAL [te-KAL], in present-day Guatemala. There, one of the great "ancestors" of Mayan civilization, Yax Moch Xoc (r. 219–238 C.E.), ruled over a city that contained in an area of just over six square miles six giant temple-pyramids used for the celebration of religious rituals of the kind just described.

The meticulously ordered layout of Teotihuacán is not characteristic of Mayan cities. Tikal and other Mayan urban centers seem instead to have grown by accretion, undergoing rebuilding and modification over centuries. Most striking among the remains of Tikal's buildings are six enormous temple-pyramids (fig. 10.4). Two of these are unusually steep, rising to a height of nearly 230 feet, and face each other across a large grassy square. Each is topped by an extension that resembles the comb of a rooster, called a **roof comb,** and gives the impression of an elevated throne on an enormously high dais.

FIGURE 10.4 Tikal, Guatemala, Mayan culture, ca. 700 C.E. University of Pennsylvania Museum. Because Mayan rituals were conducted in the open air, temple architecture atop pyramids emphasized external features.

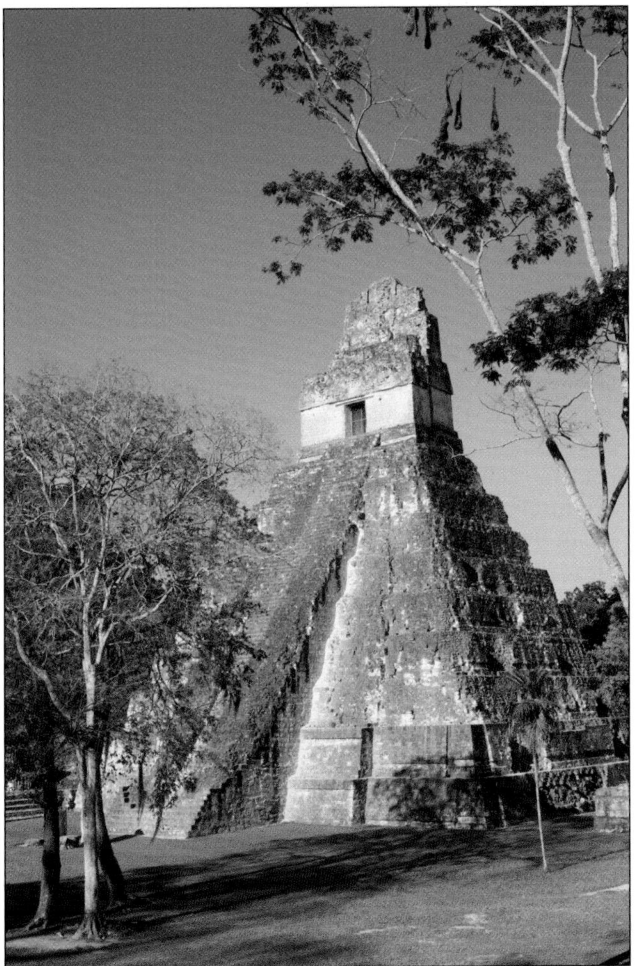

War dominated Tikal life. For two hundred years after 300 C.E., Tikal exercised power over the southeastern region of Mesoamerica. Its patron and protector was the Jaguar God, whose strength and hunting ability were likened to the power of the king himself and the warlike ferocity of the Tikal people. Like the king, the jaguar can adapt to every environment, hunting with equal facility on land, in water, and even in the Upperworld of the trees. That it hunts at night, with eyesight that penetrates the darkness, suggests its magical powers.

The Jaguar Kings of Palenque. The Jaguar God is common to all Mesoamerican cultures, from the Olmecs to the Aztecs. At Palenque, the Mayan kings called themselves Bahlum, "Jaguar," and their history is recorded on the Temple of Inscriptions (fig. 10.5). According to king lists carved in the temple's corridors, the first king was Bahlum Kuk ("Jaguar Quetzal"), who founded the city on March 11, 431 C.E.

These king lists, which record a dynasty of some twelve kings, were commissioned by two rulers: Pacal ("Shield") and his oldest son Chan **Bahlum** ("Snake Jaguar"). Pacal ruled for sixty-seven years, beginning in 615, and the Temple of Inscriptions was erected as his tomb. In 1952, the Mexican archaeologist Alberto Ruz discovered a hidden staircase at the heart of the temple, and at its bottom Pacal's body, adorned with a jade collar and green headband, lying in a red-painted stone sarcophagus. The outside of the sarcophagus is decorated with a magnificent stone relief carving (fig. 10.6), which depicts Pacal's fall down the Wacah Chan, the great tree at the center of the world. Pacal lands at the bottom on an altarlike image that represents the setting sun.

TOLTECS AND AZTECS

Among the best known of the Mesoamerican civilizations is that of the Aztecs (or Mexica, as they referred to themselves). This civilization flourished relatively late, after approximately 1350, and continued until it was overcome by the Spaniards in 1521.

The greatest Aztec families claimed descent from the Toltecs, who were said to have invented the calendar and who were the mightiest of warriors. The Toltecs came to power in Tula in Hidalgo Province around 900 C.E. after Teotihuacán's power had diminished. In the twelfth century, the militaristic Toltecs came to a violent end, when Tula was burned and its inhabitants scattered. Among the escaping tribes were the Mexica, who wandered into the Valley of Mexico around 1325 and built a village on the shores of Lake Texcoco. There they dug canals, draining high areas of the lake and converting them into fertile fields, and also built the magnificent city of Tenochtitlán. By 1440, when MOCTEZUMA ILHUICAMINA [muck-tay-ZOO-mah] (r. 1440–1486) assumed power, they considered themselves masters of the entire world.

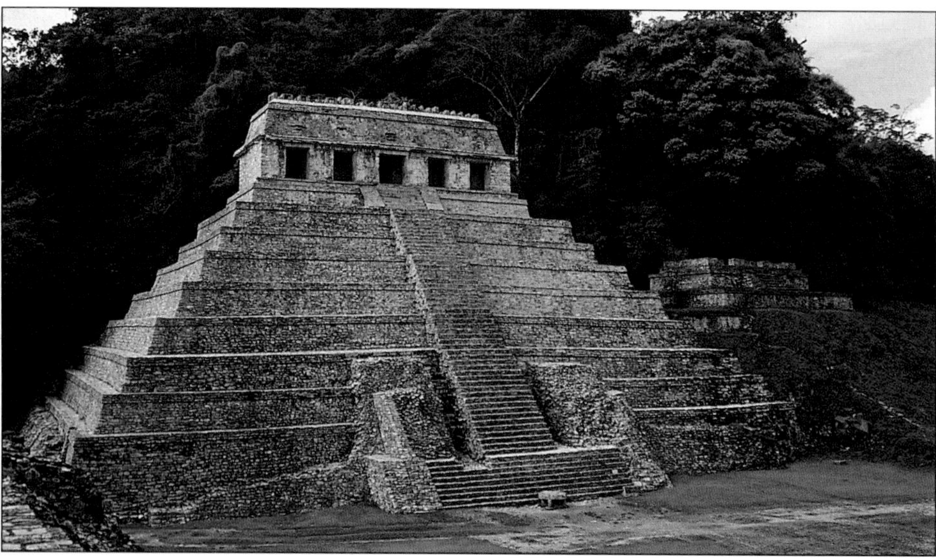

FIGURE 10.5 Temple of Inscriptions, Palenque, Mexico, Mayan culture, seventh century C.E. Rising in nine steps, like the temples at Tikal, the temple is inscribed with the history of the Palenque kings and rests over the grave of Pacal, one of its greatest leaders.

FIGURE 10.6 Sarcophagus lid, tomb of Pacal, Temple of Inscriptions, Palenque, Mexico, Mayan culture, ca. 683 C.E., limestone, ca. 12′ 6″ × 7′(3.80 × 2.14 m). The lid represents Pacal's fall in death from the sacred tree of the Maya, whose roots are in the earth and whose branches are in the heavens.

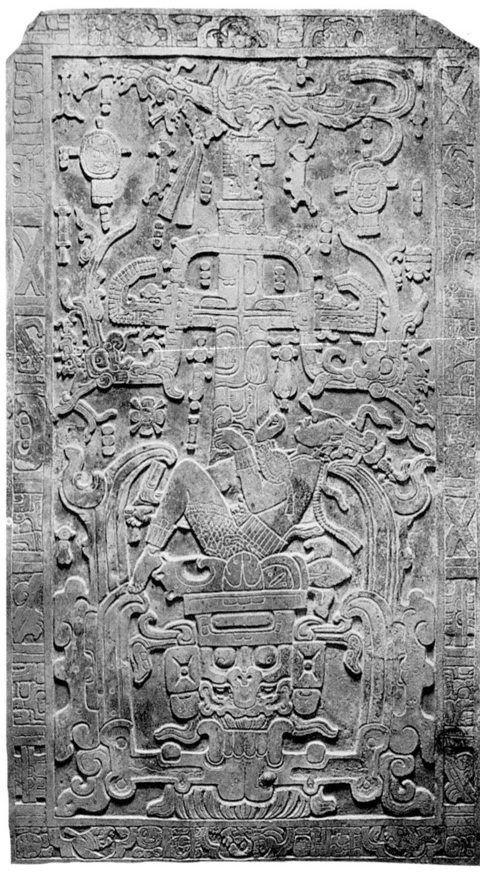

Perhaps the most frequently cited aspect of Aztec culture is human sacrifice, which was linked with religious ritual. As in Mayan culture, the shedding of human blood was seen as necessary for the continuance of the earth's fertility. The sun, moon, earth, and vegetation gods required human blood for their sustenance and the continuance of human life. During the reign of Moctezuma Ilhuicamina's successor, Ahuitzotl (r. 1486–1501), no fewer than twenty thousand captives were sacrificed in the city.

The central activity of the Aztec state was war, with the primary goal to secure enough captives for sacrifice. Young men were prepared for war from their birth. A newborn male was greeted with war cries by his midwife, who took him from the mother and dedicated him to the sun and to battle. His umbilical cord was buried by a veteran warrior in a place of battle. Following soon upon birth was the naming ceremony, during which the baby boy's hand was closed around a tiny bow, arrows, and shield. Shortly after this ceremony, priests fitted the child with the decorative lip plug worn by Aztec warriors.

At puberty most commoner (i.e., nonroyal) boys, with the exception of those destined to become priests, were placed under the jurisdiction of the youth house, which was associated with a local warrior house. Although young boys were trained for war, they were also taught various horticultural, mercantile, hunting, and fishing skills. Nonetheless, the way a young man secured prestige and fame was in war rather than in the pursuit of a vocation, with success measured in the number of enemy captured alive for later ritual killing on ceremonial occasions.

Then & Now

THE MAYANS

Like Pacal himself, Palenque and the other Mayan states would eventually fall. Some time in the ninth century, the Maya abandoned their cities and returned to the countryside to farm, where their descendants work the fields to this day. Scattered across the southern Mexican state of Chiapas and throughout Guatemala, the contemporary Mayans speak twenty different dialects of their original language and engage in distinctly different cultural practices, sometimes in villages separated by no more than ten or twelve miles. In Chiapas, for instance, the Mayan inhabitants of the village of Zinacantán characteristically dress in bright red and purple and celebrate fiestas with loud bands and fireworks; in nearby Chamula the men wear white or black wool serapes, carry large, intimidating sticks, and practice a stern, mystical brand of Catholicism that blends Mayan interest in the spirit world of animals with a part-Christian, part-Mayan sense of self-sacrifice.

Many traditional Mayan practices survive in contemporary culture. Not only do the beautiful embroidery and weaving of the contemporary Mayans contain references to ancient Mayan hieroglyphics, but Mayan women still associate giving birth with the ancient 260-day calendar. In fact, children born on particular days are still esteemed by contemporary Mayans as **daykeepers,** persons able to receive messages from the external world, both natural and supernatural, through their bodies. These daykeepers describe a sensation in their bodies as if air were rapidly moving over it in a flickering manner, similar to sheet lightning moving over a lake at night. The daykeepers learn to interpret these tremblings and eventually become the head **mother-fathers,** or priest-shamans, of their respective families.

Blood also continues to play a significant role in contemporary Mayan culture. Throughout Guatemala and Chiapas, blood is still considered an animate object, capable of speaking. Shamans can receive messages from a patient's blood by "pulsing," or touching a patient's body at various pressure points. An ancient poem, which continues to be recited among contemporary Mayan peoples who no longer practice the ritual, describes the dance of the bowman, who sharpens his arrows and dances around the victims in preparation for their sacrifice. The song recalls and memorializes the staging of the sacrificial action, and testifies to the importance of memory as an aspect of Mayan culture.

For Aztec men, dying in battle was considered a great honor, as is evident in the following Nahuatl song:

> There is nothing like death in war,
> nothing like the flowery death
> so precious to Him who gives life:
> far off I see it: my heart yearns for it!

Aztec art typically reflects the fierceness of the culture. A colossal statue of Coatlicue, the "Serpent Skirt" (fig. 10.7), goddess of the earth, shows a face with two serpent heads set on a thick powerful body. The serpents may represent blood jetting from the heads of ritually sacrificed women. Coatlicue's necklace is made up of human hearts and hands, with a human skull dangling at its base. Her skirt, which consists of writhing snakes, suggests sexual activity and its aftermath, birth.

Coatlicue is said to embody the Aztecs' belief in the creative principle, an attitude reflected in their love of poetry. For the Aztecs, poetic speech, chanted or sung, was a creative force, one that not only conveyed their vision of the world but simultaneously enacted it. This power of the poetic spoken word was further displayed in the Aztec emphasis on systematic memorizing of poems and songs to preserve Aztec cultural traditions. Poetry was called **flower song.** In Aztec painted scrolls, poetry is represented as a flowered scroll emanating from an open mouth. This use of images—of flower and song together—was characteristic of **Nahuatl** metaphor, standing for poetry specifically, and more generally for the symbolic dimension of art.

Aztec Gods. Among the most important Aztec gods are Huitzilopochtli and Quetzalcoatl. To a considerable degree, the Aztec predilection for human sacrifice derived from their devotion to Huitzilopochtli. Warriors took the god as their patron deity when conquering neighboring peoples. When Aztec wars were successful, the god's priests demanded human sacrificial victims for his appeasement. At the dedication of a large temple honoring Huitzilopochtli, the god's priests are reputed to have sacrificed eighty thousand victims, some of whom were Aztec criminals, while others were neighboring peoples who had come under Aztec subjugation.

Quetzalcoatl, the feathered serpent god, was honored under different names by earlier Mesoamerican peoples, including those of Teotihuacán. A more peaceful god than Huitzilopochtli and Coatlicue, Quetzalcoatl was honored as patron of agriculture as well as patron of arts and crafts. Images of Quetzalcoatl can be found in Aztec codices, sheets of parchment that could be folded into long strips in book-like form (fig. 10.8).

Then & Now

CHOCOLATE

Chocolate has long been a popular food in the Americas and in Europe, especially in Belgium, France, Spain, and Switzerland. The origins of chocolate go deep into ancient Mesoamerica. Centuries before the Maya used chocolate as currency and the Aztecs consumed it in unsweetened liquid form, chocolate seeds of the *Theobroma* cacao tree were transformed into an edible treat. The Aztecs declared *xocaltl*, or chocolate, to be a gift from their god Quetzalcoatl and served it as a drink to members of the court. The Toltecs staged rituals in which chocolate-colored dogs were sacrificed. According to Hernando Cortez's account of Aztec life, Montezuma's court drank two thousand pitchers of chocolate a day. And when the conquistadors searched his palace, looking for gold and silver, they found enormous quantities of cocoa beans instead.

The Maya were also chocolate lovers and served a spicy, bittersweet fermented drink made from the seeds of cocoa beans and mixed with maize and chili peppers. With the Spanish conquest of the Maya in central America, chocolate was introduced into Europe, where its bitterness was tempered by mixing in sugar and vanilla, and where it became the stimulating drink of kings and aristocrats, and later, a popular dessert treat for the masses (the Hershey bar), prior to its more recent status as a luxury item (the truffles of Godiva). Its popularity today remains unabated as a component of "sinful" desserts (what restaurant omits chocolate from its desserts?), as a hot drink for adults when mixed with coffee in café mocha, as a cold sweetened drink for children, as a supposed aphrodisiac, as a stimulus with purported medical benefits, and, of course, as the main ingredient in the most decadent of desserts, including the chocolate bombe and a mousse called Chocolate Suicide, offered by a restaurant in St. Louis.

FIGURE 10.7 Coatlicue, Aztec, fifteenth century, stone, height 8′ 6″ (2.65 m), Museo Nacional de Antropologia, Mexico City. With her two rattlesnake heads and her skirt of serpents, along with large serpent fangs and necklace of human body parts, this Aztec deity induces awe in some and amazement in others who stand in her presence.

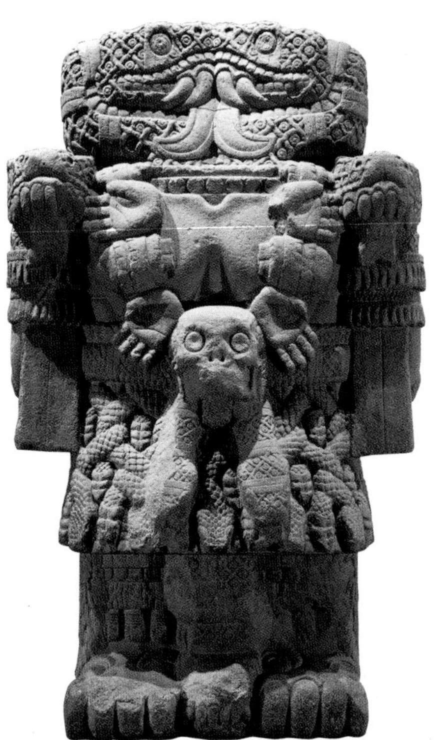

Aztec Language. The primary Aztec language during the time of the Spanish conquest in the sixteenth century was Nahuatl (NA-watl). Nahuatl continues to be spoken by nearly two million Nahua-Mexicans who live in a broad swath of central Mexico. Referred to today as "Mexicano," Nahuatl, which exists in two dozen dialect variants, is among the more than fifty native Indian languages of Mexico that are in danger of disappearing.

Nahuatl is an agglutinative language, one that strings together prefixes, word roots, and suffixes into very long words. Among them is an eighteen-syllable Nahuatl word that reputedly means "you honorable people might have come along banging your noses, so as to make them bleed, but in fact, you didn't." Other words are simple, such as "chocolatl" and "tomatl," from which English has derived "chocolate" and "tomato." Efforts to preserve Nahuatl, along with other Native Mexican Indian languages, are underway with the building of new dictionaries to supplant those made by missionaries centuries ago. Among the techniques being used is having elder Nahuatl native speakers recite traditional stories, which are then scoured for words to include in the dictionary.

CULTURES OF PERU

Peru is a land of dramatic geographical contrasts. Along the Pacific coast is one of the driest deserts in the world, where the rivers that descend out of the Andes mountains to the east form strips of oases. The Andes themselves are mammoth mountains, steep and high. Beyond them, to the east, lies the jungle, the tropical rain forest of the Amazon basin. These various terrains were home to a series of

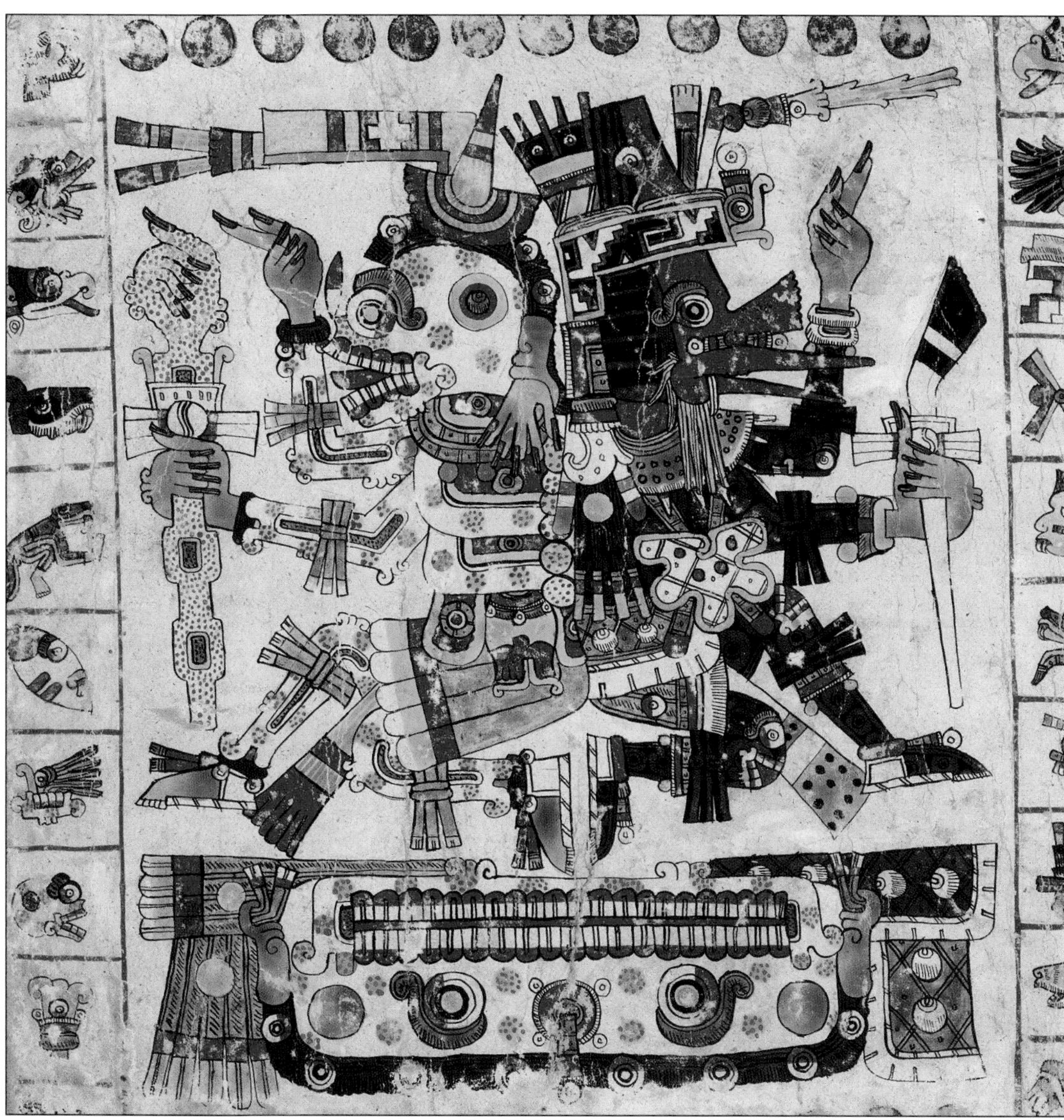

FIGURE 10.8 Aztec peoples, *Mictlantecuhtli and Quetzalcoatl.* Manuscript illumination. Vatican Library, Rome. Biblioteca Apostolica Vaticana.

cultures, in particular the Moche and the Inca, before the arrival of Spanish colonists.

THE MOCHE

Among the early cultures to develop in Peru was that of the Moche, who controlled the area along the Peruvian north coast from 200 to 700 C.E. They lived around great **huacas,** pyramids made of sun-dried bricks, that rose high above the river floodplains. The largest was Huaca del Sol, the Pyramid of the Sun (fig. 10.9), which is 135 feet high—about two-thirds the height of the Pyramid of the Sun at Teotihuacán. Its truncated summit, however, is much vaster than Teotihuacán's. At least two-thirds of the pyramid was destroyed in the seventeenth century when Spanish colonists, searching for gold, diverted the Moche River into it and used the river's fast current to erode the mound. The colonists did indeed discover many gold artifacts buried with the dead in the sides of the structure. Unfortunately, they melted these artifacts down for bullion. What they left, however, is a record of the pyramid's construction. The sliced-away mound reveals at least eight stages of construction, and we can extrapolate to conclude that around 143 million bricks, made in rectangular molds from river silt, were used to build it.

The Moche were gifted metalsmiths, and they employed the same lost-wax technique used by the Romans. They adorned their copper sculptures with gold by binding liquid gold to the copper surface at temperatures reaching as high as 1472°F (800°C). Further decorated with turquoise and shells, the results were often astonishingly beautiful. But the Moche were, above all, the most gifted ceramic artists in the Americas. In addition to working with potter's wheels, they also produced clay objects from molds,

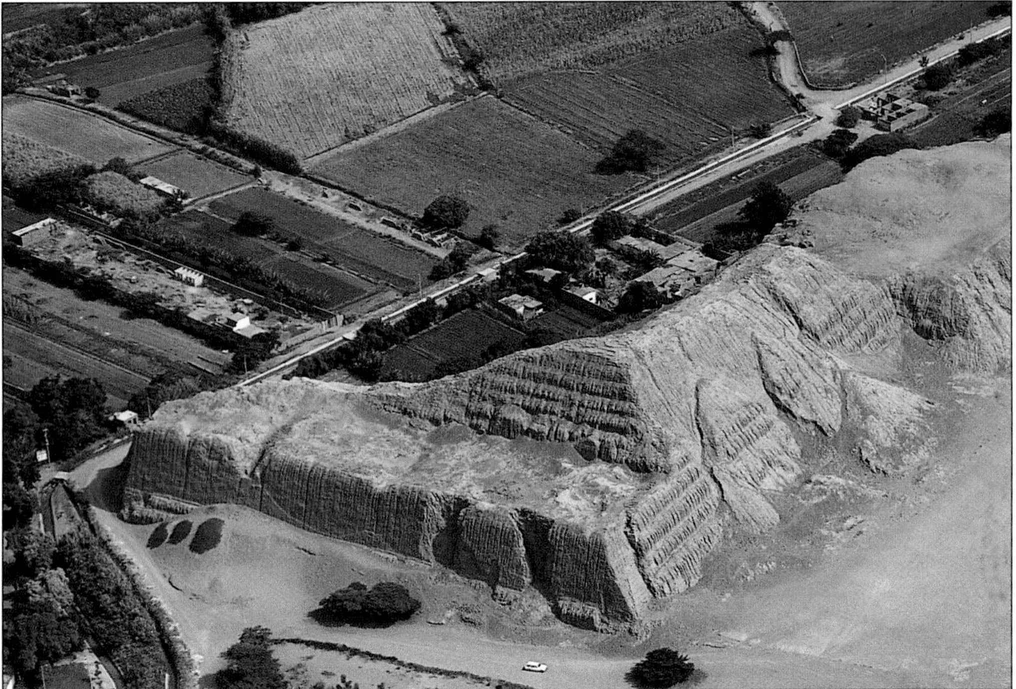

FIGURE 10.9 Huaca del Sol (Pyramid of the Sun), Moche culture, Moche Valley, Peru, ca. 500 C.E., height 135′ (41.1 m). Destroyed by Spanish colonizers seeking gold, this giant pyramid was built of more than 143 million sun-dried bricks.

allowing them to reproduce the same objects again and again. Their most distinctive designs are found on bottles with stirrup-shaped spouts that curve out from the body of the vessel. Bottles might be decorated with images of anything from the king or high official—as illustrated here (fig. 10.10), in ceremonial headdress and stroking a jaguar cub—to strange part-animal/part-human deities, and to everyday scenes such as a design for a typical Moche house.

FIGURE 10.10 *Moche Lord with a Feline*, Moche culture, Moche valley, Peru, ca. 100 B.C.E.–500 C.E., painted ceramic, height $7\frac{1}{2}''$ (19 cm), Buckingham Fund, 1955. 2281. Photograph © 2005, Art Institute of Chicago. All Rights Reserved. Vessels such as this one were buried in large quantities with people of high rank.

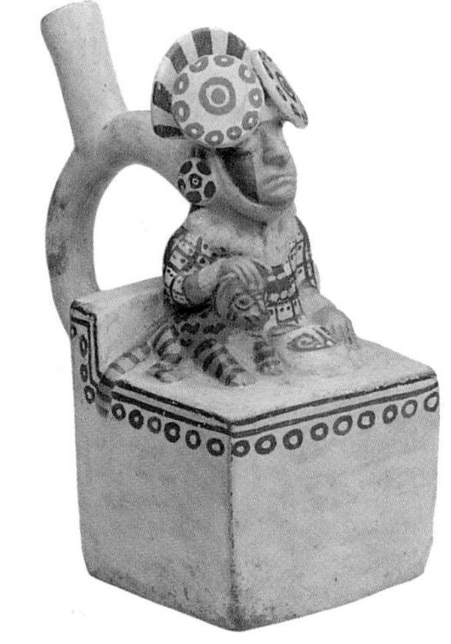

Warriors do battle on some of the vessels, prisoners are decapitated and dismembered on others, and on another famous example, a ruler in a giant feather headdress looks on as a line of naked prisoners passes before him.

Around 800, Moche society vanished. Evidence suggests that some time between 650 and 700 a great earthquake rattled the Andes, causing massive landslides, filling the rivers with debris, and blocking the normal channels to the ocean. As the sand washed ashore, huge dunes were formed, and the coastal plain was suddenly subject to vast, blinding sandstorms. It seems clear as well that **El Niño,** the warm current that slides up and down the Pacific coast of the Americas, changed the climate, destroying the fisheries and bringing torrential floods to the normally dry desert plain. It was all apparently too much, and the Moche disappeared.

THE INCA

Roughly contemporaneous with the rise of the Aztecs in Tenochtitlán was the emergence of the Inca civilization in Peru around 1300. The Incas inhabited the central Andes in what is today primarily Bolivia and Peru. They became a dominant military force around 1500 and appear also to have developed an organizational capacity to rival the engineering genius of the Romans. The Inca capital was at Cuzco, a city of 100,000 inhabitants at its height, built on a broad open valley between the Andes mountains north of Lake Titicaca. They called their empire ***Tawantinsuyu,*** "Land of Four Quarters," and, in fact, four highways emanated from Cuzco's central plaza, dividing the kingdom into quadrants. The 19,000 miles of roads and tracks that extended throughout their empire provide some indication of their engineering skill. The Incas understood the need for a functional communications system in a territory as large as theirs. Along these roadways, official runners could carry messages as far as 125 to 150 miles per day. And along them as well llamas carried goods and products for trade.

One of the most impressive of all Inca accomplishments is the fortified town of Machu Picchu (fig. 10.11), built around 1450. Located high in the Andes mountains, Machu Picchu was built perhaps as a refuge for Inca monarchs, perhaps as a place of religious retreat. Terraced fields adorn the slopes of the mountain that rises from the valley thousands of feet below. The stones for the walls and buildings were hoisted without benefit of carts or any wheeled contrivance, because the wheel was not used in either the Andes or Mesoamerica before the arrival of the Spaniards. Tools used for fitting the stones together snugly were primitive—mostly stone hammers, since neither the Andean nor Mesoamerican civilizations had developed metal implements at this time.

Machu Picchu was abandoned shortly after the arrival of Francisco Pizarro and the Spanish conquistadores. The Spaniards destroyed Inca civilization with technologically advanced weapons by enlisting the allied assistance of Inca enemies, and through the agency of contagious diseases, especially smallpox. Just a dozen years after Moctezuma and the Aztecs had been defeated by the Spanish under Hernán Cortés, the Andean Inca civilization suffered an equally ignoble demise. Machu Picchu was overlooked by the Spaniards, perhaps in part because it was a small village of five hundred inhabitants. To this day it remains one of the architectural wonders of the world.

Inca Society and Religion. Inca society was organized into four main classes: rulers, aristocrats, priests, and peasants. The Incas honored their chief rulers as deities descended from the sun. Their rule was absolute, and they retained their exalted position after death. Royal remains, which were mummified, were considered sacred, as dead rulers were believed to serve as intermediaries with the gods. On certain festivals, rulers would dress the remains of their ancestors, adorn them with jewelry, and present them with food and drink both to honor them and to remain on good terms with them.

FIGURE 10.11 Machu Picchu, Inca culture, Peru, ca. 1450. This beautiful mountain habitation escaped destruction when the Spaniards overwhelmed the Inca civilization in 1532, partly because of its remote location high in the Andes mountains, and partly because it was not a large city like the Inca capital of Cuzco.

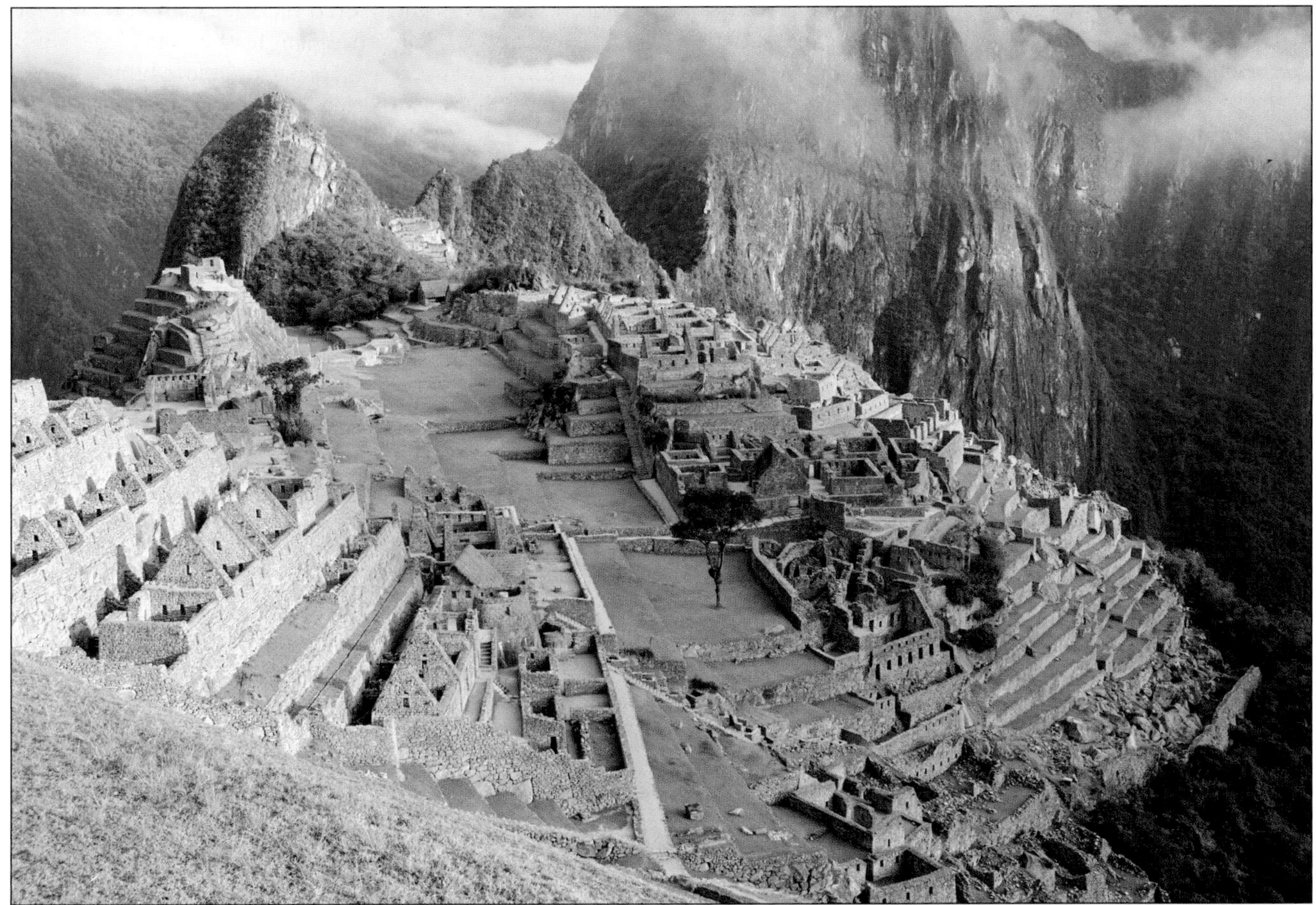

Connections

MYSTERY OF THE NAZCA LINES

Perhaps no phenomenon better underscores the intimate connection between art, archaeology, and science than the mystery of the famous **Nazca lines.** These are giant drawings made on the plains of the south Peruvian coast where the earth is covered by a topsoil of fine sand and pebbles that, when dug away, reveals white alluvium. A culture that traded with the Moche to the north and thrived from 100 B.C.E. to 700 C.E., the Nazca dug away this top soil to create a web of lines, some running straight for as long as five miles, others forming complex geometric designs in the shape, for instance, of a monkey with a coiled tail or, as illustrated here, a hummingbird (fig. 10.12).

Ever since the German-born mathematician and astronomer Maria Reiche became obsessed by the lines in 1932, they have been the center of controversy. Reiche single-handedly surveyed all of the lines over the course of her career and concluded that the straight lines point to celestial activity on the horizon and the animals represent ancient constellations. In 1963, Nazca was visited by Gerald Hawkins of Boston University, whose computer calculations of Stonehenge had helped reveal its astronomical relations, but he was unable to link many of the lines to the configuration of the heavens in the Nazca period. In the early 1970s, Erich von Däniken theorized that the lines were guidance patterns for alien spacecraft, a proposal that soon gained a wide and vocal following.

More recently, archaeologists have proposed that these **geogylphs,** as they are called, are actually depictions of giant gods whose job it is to guarantee both the availability of water and the fertility of the Nazca valleys. This theory is supported by the fact that in several sites, the straight lines point, not at aspects on the horizon, but directly at natural springs and water sources.

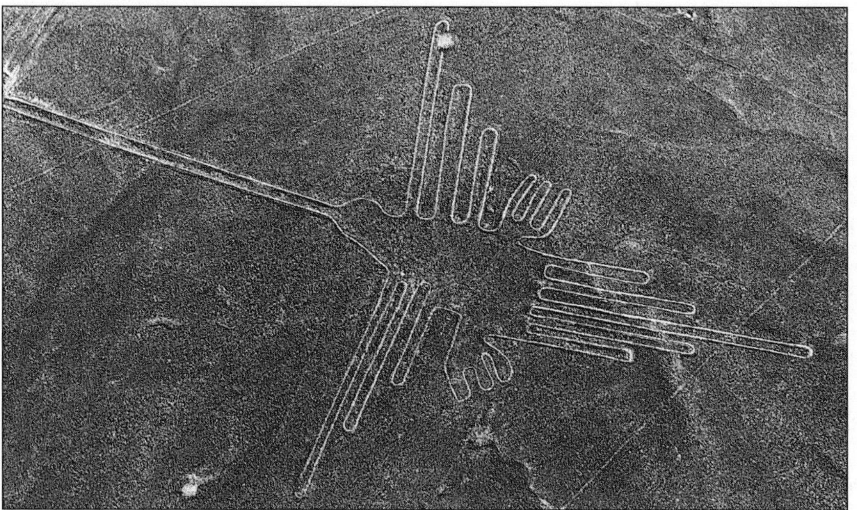

FIGURE 10.12 Earth drawing of a hummingbird, Nazca Plain, southwest Peru, Nazca culture, ca. 200 B.C.E.–200 C.E., length ca. 450′ (138 m), wingspan ca. 200′ (60.5 m). Aerial photographs and satellite images have revealed not only figurative designs such as this one, but over eight hundred miles of straight lines.

Inca rulers, who technically owned everything in the realm, including the land, supervised the aristocrats, who allocated land for the peasants to cultivate. Like the priests, aristocrats led privileged lives, including the right to wear large ear spools, which created "big ears." The priests, who descended from royal and aristocratic families, were well educated and influenced Inca society through their oversight of religious ritual, which included veneration of the sun god, Inti, as well as other astral deities. In Cuzco alone, four thousand priests and attendants served Inti, whose temple attracted pilgrims from the farthest reaches of the Inca empire.

Andean Music, Music of the Incas. For the Incas, music was part of ritual. They knew how to cast metals and to work with stone, and they used that knowledge to make

Table 10–1 ANCIENT AMERICAN CULTURES AND WORKS

Olmec	1300 B.C.E.–600 B.C.E.	Colossal heads
Mayan	250 B.C.E.–1000 C.E.	Tikal pyramids/Cyclical calendars
Nazca	200 B.C.E.–200 C.E.	Hummingbird earth drawing
Moche	200 B.C.E.–700 C.E.	Sun-dried brick pyramids
Toltec	900 C.E.–1200 C.E.	Aztec ancestors
Inca	1300 C.E.–1537 C.E.	Machu Picchu
Aztec	1350 C.E.–1521 C.E.	Coatlicue, the "Serpent Skirt"

musical instruments, such as bells and trumpets, out of brass and stone. They made wind instruments (such as horns and flutes) and percussion instruments (such as bells and drums) out of reeds, pottery, bones, and shells. They also made a unique wind instrument called a panpipe, which is a series of flutes made of cane or pottery, and tied together in a row.

Inca music often accompanied ritualized religious dancing. Repetitive rhythms were used to induce a kind of hypnotic trance in the dancers. Among the most famous of Andean musical dances is "El Condor Pasa," which is based on folk melodies. Its melody was noted in 1916 by the Peruvian composer Daniel Alomia Robles, and became the basis for the "El Condor Pasa" song, "If I Could, I Surely Would," popularized by the folk/pop singing duo of Simon and Garfunkel.

NORTH AMERICA

The Native American populations in North America were far less densely concentrated than those in Meso- and South America. The peoples of the region lived primarily nomadic lives, hunting and fishing, until around 1200 B.C.E., when the production of maize spread from Mexico into the southwest region of the present-day United States, inaugurating agricultural production in the north thousands of years after its introduction in the south. The climate of North America was not, in fact, conducive to raising corn, and the practice was slow to take hold. As a result, the organized and complex civilizations that have usually accompanied agricultural development were also slow to form. Indeed, down to the time of the European colonization of the region at the end of the fifteenth century, many native peoples continued to live as they had since the time of the extinction of the vast herds of mammoth, mastodon, and other species that inhabited the continent at the end of the Ice Age, ca. 6000 B.C.E.

NORTHWEST COAST

One of the oldest cultures of the north developed along the northwest coast of the continent, in present-day Oregon, Washington State, British Columbia, and Alaska. Reaching back to approximately 3500 B.C.E., when the world's oceans had more or less stabilized at their current levels, rich fishing grounds developed in the region, with vast quantities of salmon and steelhead migrating inland up the rivers annually to spawn. One of the richest habitats on earth in natural resources, the northwest was home to over three hundred edible animal species.

Here the native peoples—among them the Tlingit, the Haida, and the Kwakiutl—gathered wild berries and nuts, fished the streams and inlets, and hunted game. In the winters, they came together in plank houses, made with wood from the abundant forests, and engaged in a rich ceremonial life. By 450 B.C.E., they had become expert woodworkers,

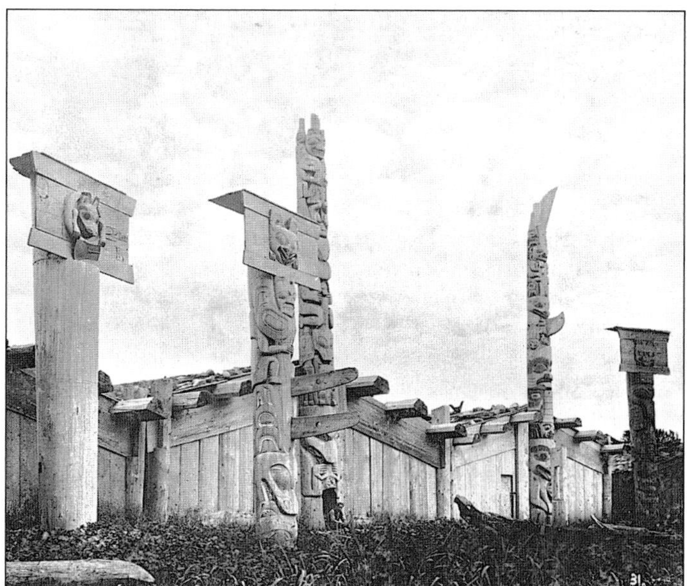

FIGURE 10.13 Haida mortuary poles and house frontal poles at Skedans Village, British Columbia, 1878, National Archives, Canada. Totem poles were traditionally carved to honor the leader of a clan upon his death, and they also stood in front of homes, serving a spiritual function.

not only building their winter homes out of timber and rough-sawn planks, but also carving out canoes and making elaborate decorative sculpture. The most famous form of this decorative sculpture is the so-called **totem pole** (fig. 10.13). These mortuary poles, erected to memorialize dead chiefs, consist of animal and spirit emblems or totems stacked one upon the other, for which the poles are named.

The kinship ties of the extended family tribe were celebrated at elaborate ceremonies called **potlatches,** hosted by the chief. Guests arrived in ceremonial dress, formal speeches of welcome followed, and gifts were distributed. Then dancing would follow long into the night. The potlatch was intended to confirm the chief's authority and ensure the loyalty of his tribal group.

SOUTHWEST

The native populations of the desert southwest faced severe difficulties in adapting to conditions following the end of the Ice Age. Like the Moche in Peru who lived in similar desert conditions, tribes gathered around rivers, streams, and springs that brought precious water from the mountains. However, water in the North American desert was far less abundant than in the South American river oases. Nonetheless, the inhabitants of the region, called the Anasazi (meaning "ancient ones"), slowly learned to recognize good moisture-bearing soil, to plant on north- and east-facing slopes protected from the direct sunlight of late day, and to take advantage of the natural irrigation of floodplains.

Small farming communities developed in the canyons and on the mesas of the region. In the thirty-two square miles of Chaco Canyon, in the northeastern region of

Cross Currents

CONQUEST AND DISEASE

The end of the great buffalo herds was not the only devastation the conquering Europeans brought with them. In 1519, in Veracruz, Mexico, one of the invading Spanish soldiers came ashore with smallpox. The Native Americans had no natural immunity. Of the approximately 11 million people living in Mexico before the arrival of the Spaniards, only 6.4 million remained by 1540. By 1607, perhaps 2 million indigenous people remained. When the Spanish arrived in California in 1679, the population was approximately 310,000. By 1900, there were only 20,000 Native Americans in the region. Along the eastern seaboard of the United States, through the Ohio Valley and the Midwest, entire populations were exterminated by disease. In the matter of a month or two, an entire village might lose 90 percent of its people.

The destruction of Native American peoples, and with them their traditions and cultures, is movingly stated by the Wanapum prophet Smohalla, many of whose people died not long after the 1844 arrival of Marcus Whitman to establish a mission in the Walla Walla Valley of Washington State:

The whites have caused us great suffering. Dr. Whitman many years ago made a journey to the east to get a bottle of poison for us. He was gone about a year, and after he came back, strong and terrible diseases broke out among us. The Indians killed Dr. Whitman, but it was too late. He had uncorked his bottle and all the air was poisoned. Before there was little sickness among us, but since then many of us have died. I have had children and grandchildren, but they are all dead. . . . We are now so few and weak that we can offer no resistance, and their preachers have persuaded them to let a few of us live, so as to claim credit with the Great Spirit for being generous and humane.

present-day Arizona, thirteen separate towns, centered around circular underground ceremonial rooms called **kivas,** had begun to take shape by 700 C.E. In the kiva, the community celebrated its connection to the earth, from which all things were said to emanate and to which all things return—not just humans, but, importantly, water as well. Connected to other sites in the area by a network of wide, straight roads, the largest of these towns was Pueblo Benito, which was constructed between 900 and 1250. Shaped like a massive letter "D," its outer perimeter was 1,300 feet long. At the center of the "D" was a giant plaza, built on top of the two largest kivas (there are thirty other kivas at Pueblo Benito).

Perhaps the most famous Anasazi site is Mesa Verde (fig. 10.14) in southwestern Colorado, near the Four Corners where Colorado, Utah, Arizona, and New Mexico all meet. Discovered in 1888 by two cowboys, Richard Wetherill and Richard Morgan, searching for stray cattle, Mesa Verde consists of a series of cliff dwellings built into the cavelike overhangs of the small canyons and arroyos that descend from the mesa top. As many as 30,000 people lived in the Montezuma Valley below, but probably no more than 2,500 people ever lived on the mesa itself. On the mesa these inhabitants developed an elaborate irrigation system consisting of a series of small ditches that filled a mesatop reservoir capable of holding nearly half a million gallons of water.

In about 1150, severe drought struck the Four Corners region, and the Anasazi at both Chaco and Mesa Verde abandoned their communities. They migrated into the Rio Grande Valley of New Mexico, where they were absorbed into the later native societies of the southwest, particularly the Hopi and the Zuni.

FIGURE 10.14 Spruce Tree House, Mesa Verde, Colorado, Anasazi culture, 1200–1300 C.E. Visible in front of the buildings to the right are three round kivas. Originally, these would have been roofed, and the roofs would have formed a common plaza in front of the buildings. The Anasazi farmed on the mesatop above.

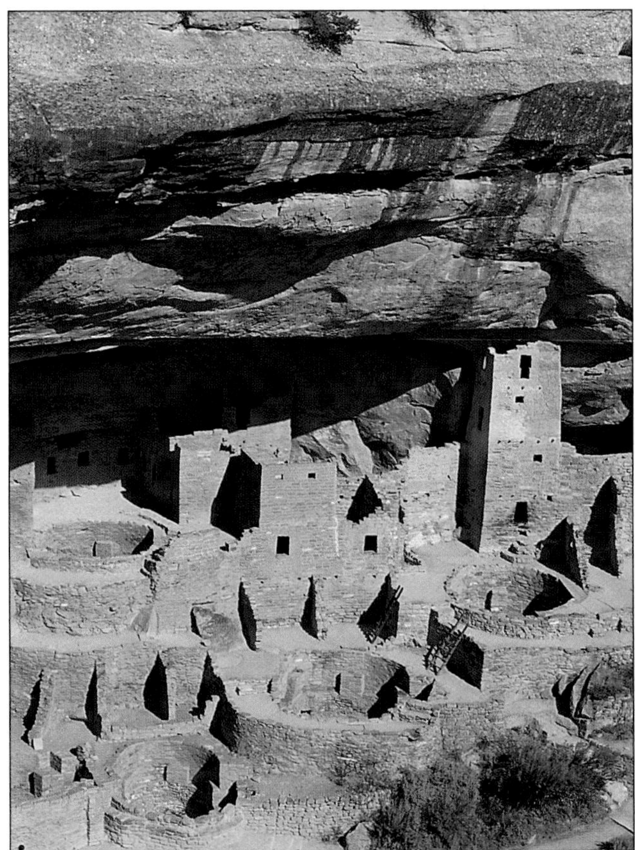

MOUNDBUILDERS

Throughout the Mississippi and Ohio River basins, beginning in about 1000 B.C.E. with the arrival of **maize** from Mesoamerica, small farming villages began building monumental earthworks in which to bury their dead. By far the largest of these was at Cahokia, in present-day East St. Louis, Illinois, where as many as 30,000 people lived between 1050 and 1250 C.E. The so-called Monk's Mound, the biggest earthwork ever constructed in North America, rises in four stages to a height of nearly one hundred feet and extends over sixteen acres.

The **moundbuilders** had begun by burying their dead in low ridges overlooking river valleys. The sites were apparently sacred, and as more and more burials were added, the mounds became increasingly large, especially as large burial chambers started to be constructed, at about the time of Jesus, to contain important tribal leaders. Sheets of mica, copper ornaments, and carved stone pipes were buried with these chiefs and shamans, and the mounds became increasingly elaborate. One of the most famous is the Great Serpent Mound (fig. 10.15), built by the Adena culture between 600 B.C.E. and 200 C.E. Overlooking a small stream, it rises from its coiled tail as if to strike a giant oval form which its mouth has already encircled. What it symbolizes is as mysterious as the forms of the Nazca lines in Peru.

BUFFALO HUNTERS

It remains unclear what led to the extinction of the great game species at the end of the Ice Age—perhaps a combination of over hunting and climatic change. But one large pre-extinction mammal continued to thrive—the bison, commonly known as the buffalo. The species survived because it learned to eat the grasses that soon spread across the Great Plains of North America, where it roamed. Hunting it became the chief occupation of the peoples who inhabited the region.

Archaeological evidence suggests that as many as 8,500 years ago a group of Native Americans who lived southeast of Kit Carson, Colorado, stampeded an entire herd of buffalo off a cliff. The fall killed about 152 of the animals, and they were butchered where they lay for their hides and meat. The practice of stampeding continued, essentially unchanged, down to the time of the Spanish conquest, when horses were reintroduced to the Americas—the native variety had grown extinct by 600 C.E.—and with the horse, the rifle.

FIGURE 10.15 Great Serpent Mound, Adams County, Ohio, Adena culture, 600 B.C.E.–200 C.E., length ca. 1254′5″ (382.5 m). Although the Great Serpent Mound in Adams County is perhaps the most spectacular example, there are between three and five hundred such mounds in the Ohio Valley alone.

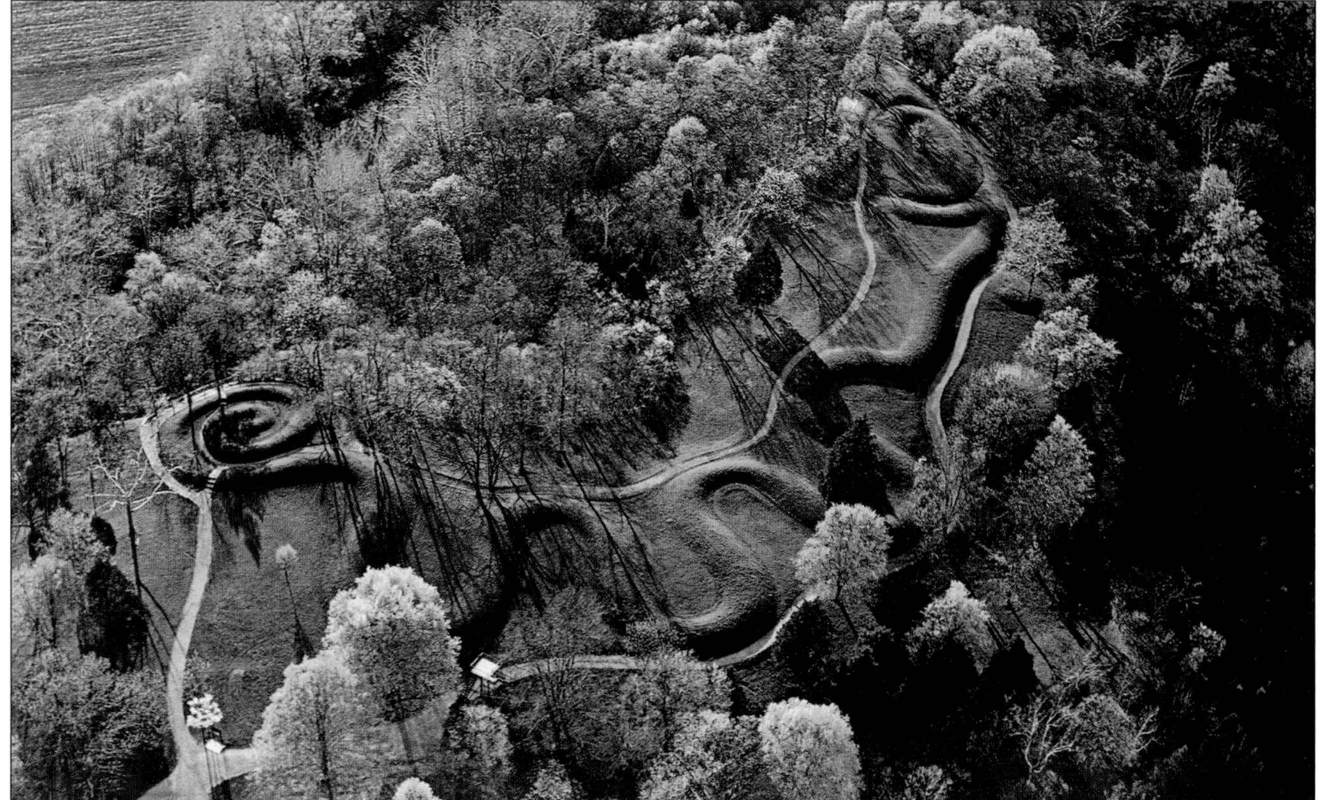

But perhaps the most devastating change as far as the buffalo were concerned was the coming of the Europeans themselves. The great herds that roamed the continent quickly disappeared. Between 1830 and 1870, the buffalo population in the West dropped from around thirty million to an estimated eight million. Between 1872 and 1874, hunters killed an estimated 4,374,000 buffalo on the Great Plains. As the railroad builder Granville Dodge reported in the late summer of 1873: "The vast plain, which only a short twelvemonth before teemed with animal life, was a dead, solitary, putrid desert." The Crow warrior, Two Legs, put it this way: "Nothing happened after that. We just lived. There were no more war parties, no capturing horses from the Piegan and the Sioux, no buffalo to hunt. There is nothing more to tell."

AFRICA

To discuss the diversity of African art and culture in a small space is a great challenge for a variety of reasons. First, Africa is a big place, much bigger than you might think just from looking at a map. Indeed, the continent is more than three times as large as the continental United States. The Sahara desert alone is nearly as large as the United States. Further, Africa is home to a multitude of societies and cultures. Complementing such cultural diversity is also a wide range of economic and political variation. As such, it is difficult to talk about groups as different as the Hausa (a West African people famous for large cities and long-distance trade) and the San (South African hunter-gatherers) in the same breath. Finally, there is the unfortunate reality that most Americans grow up unconsciously accepting a great variety of stereotypes and myths about Africans. For example, despite what we might gather from a host of nature shows, most Africans have never even seen an elephant. Moreover, stereotypes of African so-called primitivism lead many to underestimate the complexity and quality of African achievements.

PHYSICAL ENVIRONMENT

The African continent contains a variety of ecological and physical environments. Africa is neither a giant desert nor a huge jungle. Africa has both of these, of course, and a number of other climates as well. The southern tip of Africa, for example, is home to penguins, and Mount Kilimanjaro, in Tanzania, is capped with a permanent glacier. Africa's climates center on the equator, which runs roughly through the middle of the continent. Here, in the region known as the Congo Basin, is found one of the world's largest rain forests. The rain forests also extend along much of the West African coast, stretching westward to Guinea. North and south of these rain forests the weather becomes increasingly dry. The rain forests give way to more typical forests, then to savannah grasslands, and eventually to deserts, with the Sahara in the north and the Kalahari and Namib in the south. The weather in all these regions is determined by what is known as the **Intertropical Convergence Zone (ITCZ),** a climatic border where the cool wet air of the south Atlantic meets the warm dry air from the Sahara Desert. The ITCZ moves north from roughly May to September and south from roughly October to April—taking rain to wherever it goes. Rather than having four seasons, these regions of Africa have only two: wet and dry. In the wet season it may well rain every day, but in the dry season rain is absent for months on end. Such weather patterns have had significant impact on African agricultural practices. However, in the northern and southern extremes of the continent, the weather is what is often described as "Mediterranean," with four distinct seasons and a fairly cool, wet winter.

Also important to African history and culture is the nature of the soil itself. Geologically speaking, Africa is what is known as a *shield* surface. It has been exposed to the elements, with very little volcanic, glacial, or otherwise significant geological activity for millions of years. This is critical because it means African soils have had little chance to be renewed or replenished. As a result, most African soils are **lateritic:** high in salt and iron content and notoriously short on nutrients and vulnerable to erosion. Compounding this problem is the general warmth of the regions between the Mediterranean climates of the north and south. It is often thought that warm weather is good for agriculture, but it really is not. The year-round warmth means that decomposition continues even in the dry season when nothing can be grown, resulting in an absence of **humus,** the nutrient-rich decaying matter that enriches the soil. Agriculture in Africa is not impossible, but it is much more difficult than in temperate zones. There is a very good reason that North America and Eurasia are the world's breadbaskets and that Africa, South America, and Australia are not. Notably, the exception to this rule is the **rift valley** of East Africa. Running from Ethiopia to Zimbabwe, this chain of volcanic mountains is one of the world's richest farming areas, producing some of the world's best coffee as a result. The wealth of the Nile, discussed in Chapter 1, is the result of these rich soils being carried from the Ethiopian highlands to the floodplains of ancient Egypt.

EARLY AFRICAN CULTURES AND INNOVATIONS

As indicated in Chapter 1, Africans in Egypt helped found one of the world's most impressive and long-lasting cultures. The remarkable achievements of Egypt, however, are complemented by other impressive developments elsewhere on the continent. Indeed, the fertility provided by the Nile floods made Egypt a fairly easy place to create a state. Hunting and gathering societies (which predated ancient Egypt) not only succeeded in flourishing in the

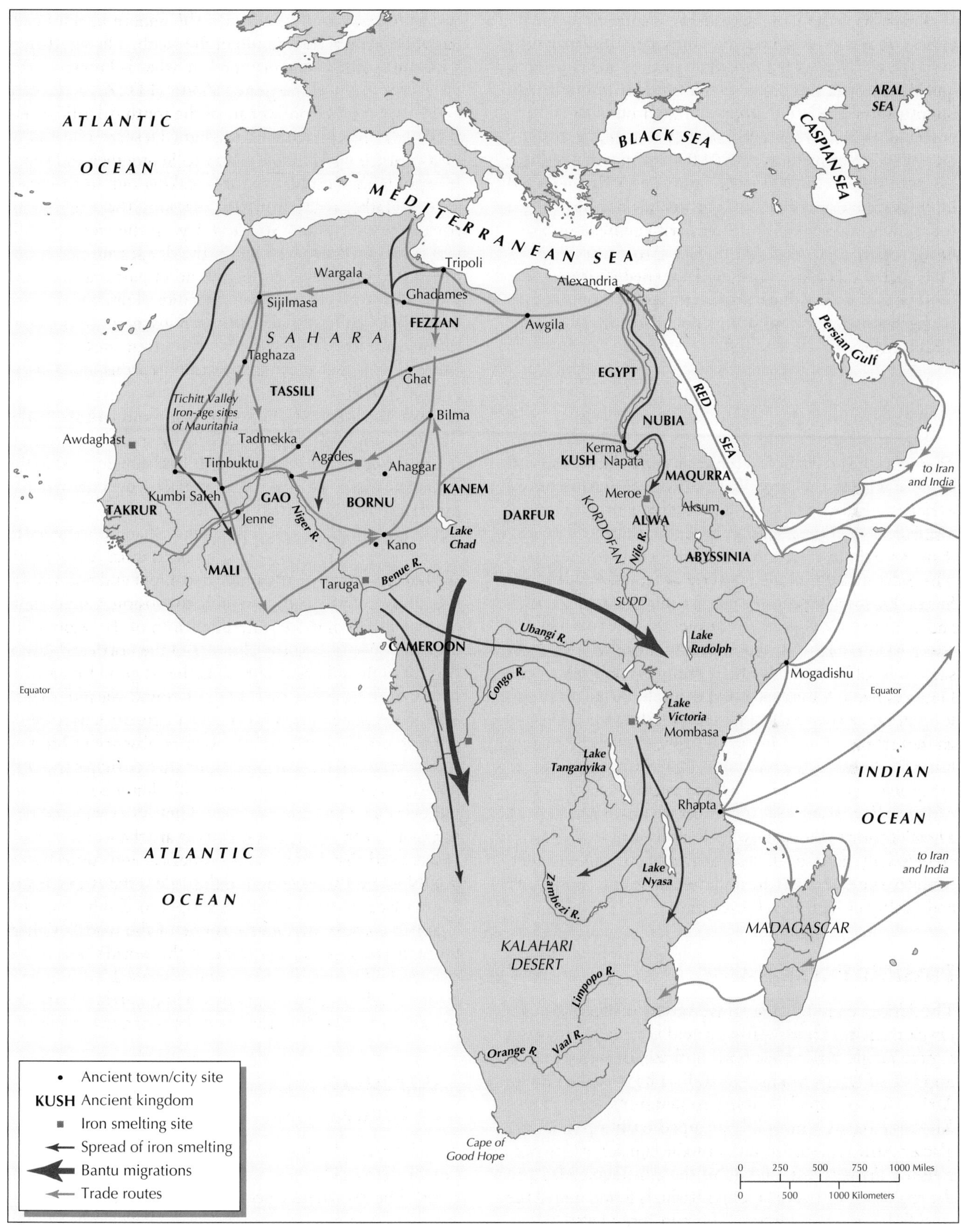

Map 10.2 Africa before 1300 C.E.

West African savannahs, but also in the forests and southern savannahs (which were for a time geographically isolated from agricultural innovations in the north and east). Hunters and gatherers relied on a complex and thorough understanding of their physical floral and faunal surroundings to survive. Indeed, many today might envy the quality of life of such early societies. Hunters and gatherers, it turns out, have to work only a few hours a day to provide a nutritious diet. Such a situation left them ample free time to undertake crafts such as stone working (for tools) and even artwork. Although artworks of wood or other perishables do not remain, areas of Africa such as the Sahara and southern Africa are home to numerous **rock paintings** remarkable not only for their artistic qualities, but also for the wealth of information they provide us about the ancient environment. It is how we know that the Sahara was once wet, and what species of plants and animals lived there (fig. 10.16).

Not all Africans remained hunters and gatherers, however. As early as 5000 B.C.E., sedentary agriculture was also being developed in the West African savannahs—built around the farming of millet and sorghum, two grains well adapted to the region's drought-prone climate. Rice also became important along the inland delta of the Niger River. Similarly, agriculture also developed in the highlands of Ethiopia, where local crops such as **t'eff** (among the world's smallest grains) allowed early farmers to take advantage of rich soils but also harsh high-elevation weather. Elsewhere in the savannahs and desert fringes, many Africans developed complex pastoralist lifeways around the herding of cattle, goats, and camels. Such animals could feed on plants inedible to humans. By extracting food from the animals in the form of meat, blood, and milk, humans were able to live in the otherwise inhospitable environments.

Beginning from the region of modern-day eastern Nigeria and western Cameroun, perhaps as early as 3000 B.C.E. the Bantu migration occurred. This migration, which was to continue over the next four thousand years, saw the introduction of sedentary agriculture into the forests of central Africa—largely thanks to two forest crops: the oil palm and the yam (*not* the sweet potato). **Bantu** is itself a word that means "the people" in a subfamily of the Niger-Congo language group. Although once the Bantu migrations were thought to be a rapid conquest by superior iron-wielding agriculturalists, who displaced inferior hunters and gatherers, it is increasingly apparent that the process was slow and relatively peaceful. Linguistic and archaeological evidence suggests that Bantu speakers learned many critical skills not only from forest peoples such as the **Batwa** (pygmies), but also from **Cushitic**-speaking savannah agriculturalists millennia later. Ironworking does seem to have been a factor, but it came fairly late in the game (around 500 B.C.E. in West Africa). Similarly, archaeological evidence suggests that ironworking was developed independently in the region of northern Tanzania around 700 B.C.E.

FIGURE 10.16 A rock painting from Tassili, in the central Sahara. Dating to around 10,000 B.C.E., this painting reflects both a keen artistic eye and a remarkable knowledge of the environment.

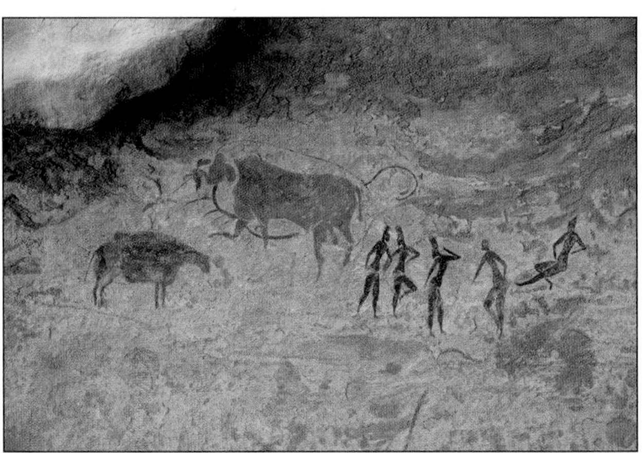

EARLY AFRICAN POLITICAL AND RELIGIOUS CULTURE

Although there are a great variety of African political and religious systems, many African societies, especially in the ancient era, lived in what are often termed *stateless societies*. Such communities, often pastoralists or forest dwellers, had no single individual or group (such as a king or aristocracy) whose job it was to tell other people what to do. This does not mean, however, that such societies lacked *authority*. Rather, institutions of kinship and seniority, and the recognition of knowledge and personal achievement, provided certain individuals with influence. Similarly, the relatively small size of local communities allowed groups to discuss problems and develop solutions through debate and consensus. Such a system is very similar to our modern notion of democracy, in that power rests in the entire community rather than with a few privileged individuals.

Further, such societies were often quite aware of other political alternatives. The Igbo of southeastern Nigeria, for example, have long had a motto that states "the Igbo have no kings." Clearly, the Igbo knew what kings were, but decided they did not want them. Stateless societies became less common over time, however, as many African societies and states expanded to the point where more centralized systems of authority and bureaucracy became necessary.

Religious authority, too, played an important part in African community life. Although possibly thousands of indigenous African religious systems exist, certain commonalities provide an introduction to these complex systems of cosmology and belief. Perhaps one of the key characteristics of African religions is the concept of **pantheism.** Thus, rather than seeing a single all-powerful God (such as in Judaism or Islam), African religions tend to see divine power as diffuse. There may be a single High God, but that divine being is both too distant and incomprehensible for humans to interact with. Rather, this High God has myriad manifestations (all sharing the single divine spirit) that are more accessible to human needs. For example, among the Yoruba (who have inhabited the southwestern region of what is now Nigeria for at least one thousand years) the High God **OLUDUMARE** (oh-lu-DU-mah-ray) created the world and humanity, but numerous "lesser" gods, known as the **ORISA** (ohr-ISH-ah), interact with humans. For example, **OGUN** (oh-GOON), the orisa of iron, has long served as the patron of soldiers and has more recently become the patron of auto mechanics. Notably, most African traditional religions have little or no notion of the sort of conflict between good and evil that so permeates religions originating from the Middle East. Similarly, African religions generally do not have a concept of an end to time, in the form of a judgment day or apocalypse.

The diffuse nature of political and religious authority in many African societies is also reflected in the nature of artistic expression. Art was not something that belonged only to the rich. Even the most mundane of items could be lavishly decorated. Similarly, African musical traditions make little distinction between performers and audience. Rather than politely sitting and listening, the audience is as much a part of the performance as the musicians themselves, expected to clap, sing, and dance right along with the professionals.

REGIONAL DEVELOPMENTS IN AFRICA BEFORE 1800

North and Northeastern Africa. From very early on, North and northeastern Africans interacted closely with populations in the Mediterranean and Arabia. This should hardly be a surprise, since it is often easier for long-distance trade to take place across oceans and seas than across land. As such, the ancient Egyptians interacted extensively with populations in Mesopotamia and, later, Greece—just as they carried on extensive relations with Nubia and Ethiopia via the Nile River. Culture is always a two-way street, and these interactions led to mutual influence and exchange. Herodotus, the Greek father of history, for example, credited the Egyptians as the source of mathematics and Greek religion. Contacts with the wider Mediterranean world and Red Sea worlds would be a constant source of influence for North and northeastern Africa. The Phoenician settlement at Carthage intermingled with local Berber-speaking populations to create a unique culture known as **Punic** and grew as a trading power that would dominate the western Mediterranean until the rise of Rome (discussed in Chapter 4). The unification of the circum-Mediterranean world under the Roman empire in the early centuries C.E. encouraged an increased level of interaction around the region (although often unwillingly for those who chafed at Roman rule). Latin and Greek became languages of government and high society.

Following Roman lines of trade and communication, Christianity spread rapidly from the Middle East into North Africa and also into Europe. The new religion spread not only as a unique message of salvation that appealed to the poor and powerless, but also as a rejection of Roman authority. Early Christians drew the ire of the Roman state largely because they refused to make sacrifices to the emperor, who was considered a god. Notably, North Africa and the Nile Valley stretching through Nubia to Ethiopia would become influential parts of the expanding Christian world. Alexandria in Egypt was home to one of the first Christian catechetical schools, called the **Didascalia.** Here early Christian texts were collected, discussed, and translated. Saint Jerome, who first translated the Bible into Latin, is believed to have first studied at the Didascalia. North African Christians would play a central role in debating and defining exactly what it meant to be Christian. Debates over Neo-Platonism and Gnosticism (discussed in Chapter 5) and Arianism and Monophysitism took place among North African Christians. **Arianism,** named for Arius, a priest from Alexandria, argued that Jesus is not the son of God, but rather an angel-like creation sent to provide a new gospel. Arianism would later be spread by missionaries to the Germanic tribes of Europe. Thus the first western European Christians had doctrinal roots in Egyptian Arianism. The Monophysite position, held by the **Coptic** (Egyptian) and Nestorian (Middle Eastern) churches, was that Jesus' divinity outweighed his humanity, which was an anathema to the Roman church's claim that Jesus possesses both human and divine characters in equal measure. In 451, these churches broke with the Roman church. The Coptic church would continue to grow and thrive in the Nile Valley, eventually developing a close relationship with the Ethiopian state. In the twelfth century, King Lalibela of Ethiopia commissioned the creation of churches that were hewn from solid rock, a unique feat in Christian architecture (fig. 10.17). Like the churches themselves, Ethiopian Christianity would prove very durable, weathering challenges from Islam and local religions to survive into the modern era.

The rise of Islam in the seventh century also had a substantial impact in North Africa. The Islamic state spread rapidly across the North African coast, although the defeat of Muslim forces by Christian Nubians at the Battle of Dongala in 651 greatly slowed the expansion of Islam in the upper Nile region. In North Africa, a woman named Al-Kahina (the Soothsayer) led a spirited Berber resistance to Islamic armies until her defeat in 698. Despite such opposition, by the early eighth century, the Islamic state was firmly entrenched in North Africa, although the bulk of the population would not convert to Islam until the tenth and eleventh centuries. Notably, however, North Africa became a refuge for Muslims, particularly **Shi'ites** and KHARIJITES (Car-IH-jites), who were at doctrinal

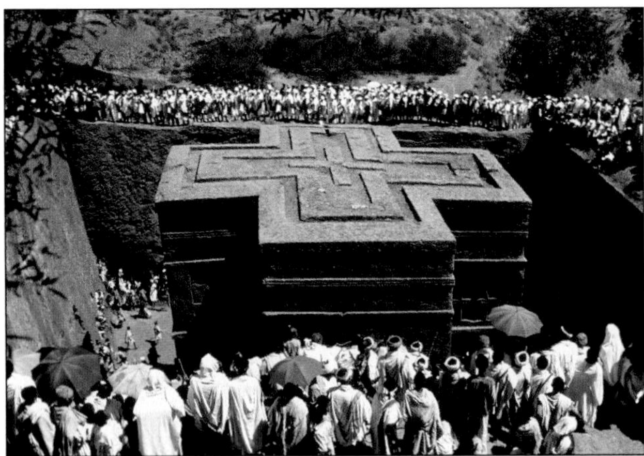

FIGURE 10.17 A rock-hewn church in Ethiopia. Constructed in the twelfth century C.E., these churches are a testimony to the power of the Ethiopian church and state.

odds with Sunni orthodoxy. In the tenth century, the Shi'ites would found the Fatimid dynasty, expanding from modern Tunisia to a capital in Egypt. This state would dominate the region for over two centuries, and at times challenge the Baghdad-based Abbasid Caliphate for leadership of the Islamic world. Despite such internal conflicts, the expansion of Islam encouraged trade and cultural exchange between North Africa and the Middle East. From poetry to architecture, Islamic artistic elements became deeply entrenched in North Africa.

Savannahs and Forests of Western and Central Africa. The West African savannahs and forests were home not only to important human innovations in agriculture, such as the domestication of millet and oil palms, respectively, but also to complex urban societies and states. Beginning perhaps as early as the third century B.C.E., cities such as Jenne-Jeno and Gao began to be settled in the fertile inland delta of the Niger River. Several factors encouraged this development. The savannahs themselves were fertile, and the growing of rice, millet, and sorghum produced a large surplus of grain for trade both into the desert to the north and the forests to the south. In exchange, the savannah cities received forest products, such as ivory, palm oil, kola nuts, and gold, and desert products, such as salt and cloth, from North Africa. The position as intermediaries between the forests and North Africa allowed the residents of the savannah cities to grow wealthy not only from production, but also from the taxation of trade moving across their boundaries. From the early period C.E. to the sixteenth century, this volume of trade continued to increase, and savannah states such as Ghana, Mali, and Songhai grew rich from control over the trade. Close economic ties to North Africa also led to a gradual conversion of these states' rulers and traders to Islam, although rural and agricultural populations would continue to practice traditional African religions well into the nineteenth century. Mali and Songhai were among the richest empires of the era. When MANSA MUSA (MAHN-sah MOO-sah), a Muslim ruler of Mali, performed the Hajj (pilgrimage) to Mecca in 1324 and 1325, he spent so much gold during a stopover in Alexandria that the local economy was temporarily debased by inflation. Such images convinced Europeans of the time that Africa was a land of great wealth and achievement.

Timbuktu has long been a center of the Muslim religion in west Africa. Settled in 1087 by the Tuareg, its fame as a center of trade in gold spread as far as Europe. Under the Songhai emperor Mohammed Askia I (ca. 1494–1527), the Muslim university of Sankore reached its height and preserved an extensive library of native African literature.

The forests of West and Central Africa proved a greater challenge to the creation of cities and states. By the end of the first millennium C.E., Africans in the region had developed technological, social, and political frameworks that allowed for the creation of larger-scale societies in the forests. As early as the ninth century C.E., a state developed in the forest region of what is now southeastern Nigeria. Named Igbo-Ukwu after a nearby modern town, archaeological evidence from the site shows not only a concentration of wealth and authority in the hands of a kinglike figure, but also metal-working technology. In Nigeria, the king of Ife, known as the *Ooni*, was depicted in his coronation costume (fig. 10.18). The horn in his left hand contains strong medicine, while in his right is a wooden staff that will be replaced, upon coronation, by a beaded cow-tail fly whisk, indicative of authority. The carefully crafted figure is chubby and child-like in his proportions. He wears beaded collars and necklaces and beaded badges hanging on his chest, as well as beaded cuffs on his forearms and lower legs.

Just to the east in Nigeria would develop Benin, one of the largest and longest lived forest states. Growing in power by the thirteenth century, Benin is a testimony to the ability of humans to develop complex economic and political systems despite environmental challenges. Benin not only dominated the region, but also developed a sophisticated state-sponsored art program built around the casting of bronze sculptures. By using a sophisticated system called lost wax casting, full-size models of sculptures were made of beeswax, and then a ceramic mold was built around them. Then molten bronze was poured into the mold, melting away the wax. Each such sculpture (some of which could be quite large) was unique (fig. 10.19). Similar metal-working techniques would later be adopted in ASANTE (Ah-SHAHN-tay), a state that would rise up in the early eighteenth century in what is modern-day Ghana. Asante grew wealthy in part as a major producer of gold. The Asantehene (king) of Asante and his royal court carried and wore a stunning amount of gold during public appearances. The "throne" of Asante was the Golden Stool, which reputedly appeared from heaven to show the divine support of the first Asantehene, Osei Tutu.

East and South Africa. East Africa is in part unique because of its connection to the Indian Ocean. Unlike the Atlantic to the west, the Indian Ocean is friendly to sailing

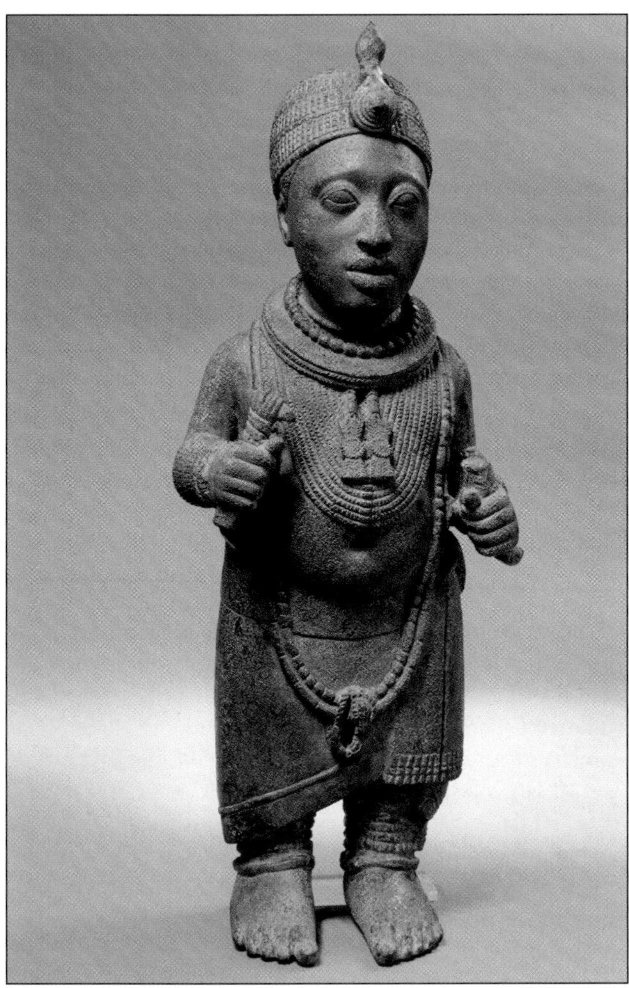

FIGURE 10.18 A standing figure of an *Ooni*, Yoruba, Ife, Nigeria, twelfth–fifteenth century, zinc-brass, $18\frac{1}{2} \times 6\frac{13}{16} \times 6\frac{7}{16}''$ (47.1 × 17.3 × 16.3 cm), The National Commission for Museums and Monuments, Lagos (79.R.12). In addition to being a work of art that documents both custom and costume, this statuette evidences advanced techniques of metal working.

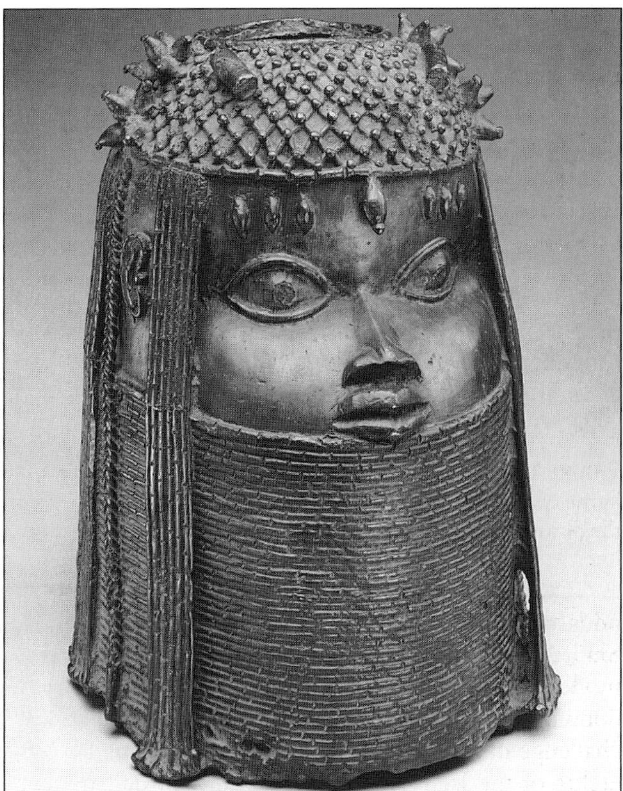

FIGURE 10.19 Head of an Iyoba, Edo, Court of Benin, Nigeria, eighteenth century, brass, iron, height $13\frac{1}{8}''$ (33 cm), gift of Klaus G. Perls, 1991. Metropolitan Museum of Art, New York. The Iyoba is the mother of the Oba, the Benin King. Great importance, prestige, and power was accorded the Iyoba for, as she protects her son, she protects the kingdom. All Iyoba heads include representations of broad coral-bead necklaces which cover the entire neck—a part of the royal costume to this day.

voyages and greatly facilitated long-distance trade. As early as the first century B.C.E. it is clear that traders from the Mediterranean and India were sailing to the East African coast. As such, East Africa was from ancient days very cosmopolitan. In this setting developed a unique culture known as the **Swahili,** (which translates as "people of the coast"). The Swahili language reflects both African and Middle Eastern linguistic elements, and the Swahili themselves reflect genetic and cultural ties that are more Indian Ocean than purely African or Arab. As intermediaries in a highly valuable trade, the Swahili grew wealthy, especially as the growth of Islamic states in the Middle East and India fostered even greater demand for trade. Swahili towns featured multistory homes built of coral blocks. Although the outsides were austere, the interiors were lavishly decorated with trade goods from Africa, the Middle East, and Asia. Interestingly, however, as Islam became increasingly influential among the Swahili during the ninth and tenth centuries, it did not spread into the interior of East Africa. Thus, although Islam followed trade routes into West Africa, it did not do so in the east.

One key source of trade goods for the Swahili was Great Zimbabwe. Located in the modern country that shares its name, this state grew to prominence during the thirteenth and fourteenth centuries. Although gold was a major good traded east to the coast, most of Zimbabwe's wealth seems to have been based in a mixed farming and cattle-herding economy. The capital city's huge drystone walls stand even today (fig. 10.20).

AFRICA AND THE TRANSATLANTIC SLAVE TRADE

When advances in European maritime transport first began to facilitate increased interaction between Africans and Europeans, the initial exchanges tended to be peaceful. The Portuguese established trading posts at El Mina (in modern-day Ghana) and with the Kongo Kingdom at Luanda in the fifteenth century, for example. Trade in these early decades focused on items such as ivory, gold, and spices. However,

Cultural Impact

Sub-Saharan African societies entered into commercial relationships with Muslim peoples in Southwest Asia and in North Africa. The states that the African peoples established in West Africa and coastal East Africa extended the influence of the sub-Saharan African peoples through extensive trade, particularly in gold, ivory, and slaves. Trade facilitated the introduction of Islam into African society. Mosques were built, as were Islamic schools. By around 1500 C.E., African traditions had blended with Islamic institutions in sub-Saharan African societies.

The original inhabitants of Mesoamerica lived in smaller societies than those in India, China, and Japan. Ancient American peoples lacked an advanced transportation technology that facilitated an extensive trade and communications network among peoples of the Eastern Hemisphere. This, however, did not prevent them from developing complex societies with sophisticated cultural and religious traditions, long before they had contact with European and other peoples. The Aztecs and Incas, in particular, built powerful imperial states organized around agricultural production in widely varying climactic conditions.

Native American peoples of the northwest coast and the midwest and southwest have left legacies of various kinds. The peoples of the northwest have left a respect for the waters and have handed down their skills in canoe building and in fishing. Peoples of the southwest have long had a tradition of outstanding textile weaving, which they share with the Andean peoples. In addition, Native Americans of the southwest remain expert in creating pottery and jewelry, particularly with semiprecious stones and gold and silver. The techniques they developed for hammering, embossing, soldering, welding, casting, and gilding remain in use today.

Africans worked not only as agricultural laborers, but also as mining engineers, cowboys, cooks, and household servants. They often had a far greater degree of cultural influence than they are generally given credit for. In particular, African foods, notions of religion, and styles of music and artwork made deep impressions on the societies of the American South, Latin America, and the Carribean. Gumbo, deep-fried foods, and barbeque are examples of African contributions to the cuisines of the Americas. Similarly, we need only listen to the music of these regions to hear the significant African influence. Finally, African notions of the divine syncretized with Catholicism in many regions to form new religions such as Voudou, Candomble, Santeria, and Macumba. Thus, even what we tend to characterize as "American" or "Latin American" is in many ways African as well. The impact of these African cultural elements in the Americas is discussed in greater detail in Chapter 22.

as profits from sugar plantations in the Atlantic islands and Brazil grew in significance, the nature of trade between Africans and Europeans began to change. Africans possessed both a resistance to Old World infectious diseases and tropical parasitic diseases, which allowed them to somewhat better endure the harsh conditions of plantation labor than Native Americans and Europeans. Whereas the life expectancy of European or Native American slaves on sugar plantations was often less than a year, enslaved Africans might live as long as seven. Further, Africans often possessed a knowledge of tropical crops and soils that could enhance the productivity of the plantations. Ironically, for Africans it was strengths, not weaknesses, that made them the victims of the Atlantic slave trade.

FIGURE 10.20 A view of the inside wall of the stone enclosure at Great Zimbabwe. Constructed around the thirteenth century, this structure is remarkable in that it was built without the use of mortar in a technique known as drystone architecture.

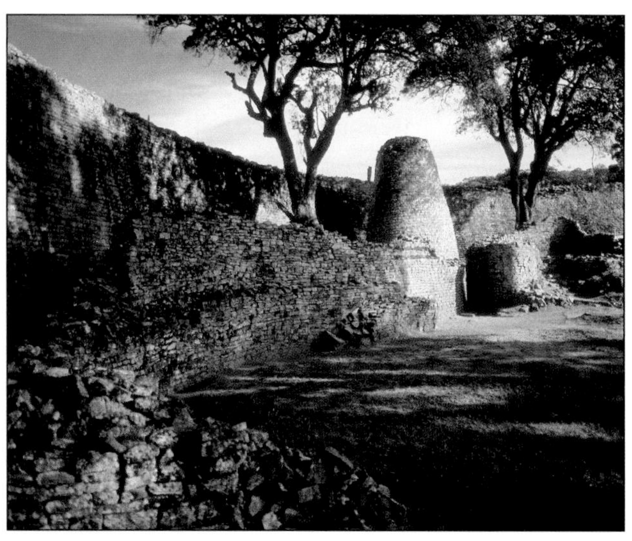

Thus, as the value of Africans as slaves increased, so did European demand for slave labor from Africa. Over the course of the next three centuries, the slave trade would grow from a few thousand individuals per year to a peak of nearly 100,000 per year in the latter eighteenth century. Overall, some eleven million enslaved Africans would be exported to the New World, and millions more would die either in wars of conquest fought to acquire captives in Africa or during the torturous continental passage to the coast and middle passage to the Americas. European and African slave traders grew wealthy from this human trade, as did plantation owners and factory owners in the Americas and Europe, who benefited from cheap slave labor. In Africa, wars to capture slaves and the increasing role of slave trading as a source of wealth likely served to disrupt local economies and systems of political legitimacy.

KEY TERMS

Mesoamerica
Teotihuacán
Wacah Chan
roof comb
Bahlum
daykeeper
mother-fathers
flower song
Nahuatl
huacas
El Niño
Tawantinsuyu
Nazca lines
geoglyphs
totem pole
potlach
kiva
maize
moundbuilder
Intertropical Convergence Zone (ITCZ)
lateritic
humus
rift valley
rock paintings
t'eff
Bantu
Batwa
Cushitic
pantheism
Oludumare
orisa
Ogun
Punic
Didascalia
Arianism
Coptic
Shi'ites
Swahili

www. WEBSITES FOR FURTHER STUDY

http://www.mesoweb.com/welcome.html
(MesoWeb is a site with several components and can be viewed either in html or with animations using Shockwave Flash plugin. It has many images and descriptions of Mesoamerican cultures.)

http://www.raingod.com/angus/Gallery/Photos/SouthAmerica/Peru/IncaTrail/MachuPicchu1.html
(Several images of Machu Picchu, Inca culture, ca. 1450.)

http://www.civilization.ca/aborig/haida/hvske01e.html
(An extensive discussion of Northwest Native American Indian cultures such as the Skedans.)

http://www-learning.berkeley.edu/wciv/ugis55a/readings/earlyafrica.html
(A good introductory site for early African cultures.)

http://witcombe.sbc.edu/ARTHafrica.html#africa
(Art history resources on the web by Chris Witcombe; a good site for early African art.)

http://www.ancientmexico.com
(An interactive map of Mexico showing pre-Columbian archaeological sites.)

http://www.ancientmesoamerica.org
(Prehistoric Mesoamerican material culture and investigative archaeological techniques.)

http://www.archeolink.com/ancient_african_civilizations.htm
(A good introduction to ancient African civilizations with excellent links.)

http://www.lyrichord.com/africa
(African music.)

http://www.andeannation.com/hist
(Cultures of peoples of the Andes.)

http://www.mnsu.edu/emuseum/cultural/music/south_america.shtml
(Music of the Andes, and more.)

http://www.andes.org/bookmark.html
(Andean folk music.)

Chapter 11

History

sixth century	Pope Gregory the Great
768–814	Charlemagne rules as king of the Franks
800	Pope Leo III crowns Charlemagne emperor creating Holy Roman Empire
843	Treaty of Verdun breaks up the Carolingian Empire
987–1328	Capetians rule in France
eleventh –thirteenth centuries	Crusades
1066	Norman conquest of England
ca. 1140–1170	"Court of Love" established in Poitiers
1200	University of Paris granted royal charter
1215	Magna Carta

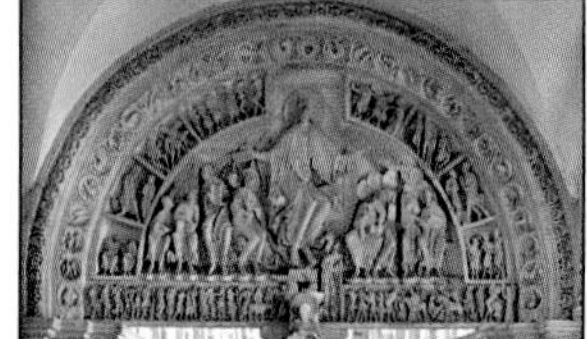

Arts and Architecture

792–805	Palatine Chapel, Aachen
ca. 800–10	*Gospel Book of Charlemagne*
ca. 817–20	Plan for ideal monastery
ca. 1025	Guido D'Arezzo, musical notation
ca. 1066–82	Bayeux "tapestry"
begun ca. 1070 or 1077	Saint-Sernin, Toulouse
1120–32	Sainte-Madeleine, Vézelay
1120–32	*Mission of the Apostles,* Sainte-Madeleine, Vézelay
ca. 1140–70	Hildegard of Bingen, liturgical music
begun 1174	Bonanno Pisano, campanile, Pisa
1181	Nicholas of Verdun, *Klosterneuburg Abbey altarpiece*

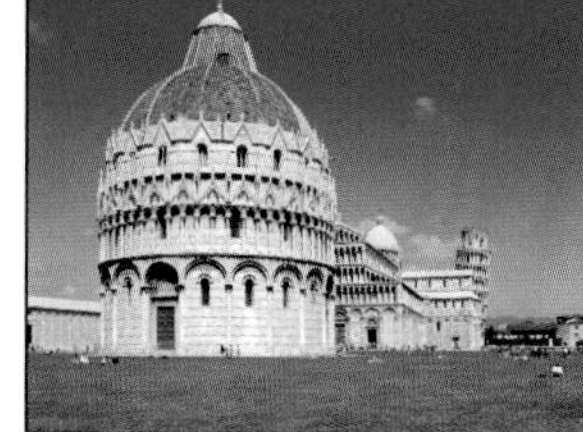

Literature and Philosophy

eighth century	*Beowulf*
mid-eleventh century	*Song of Roland*
1170–74	Cappelanus, *Art of Courtly Love*

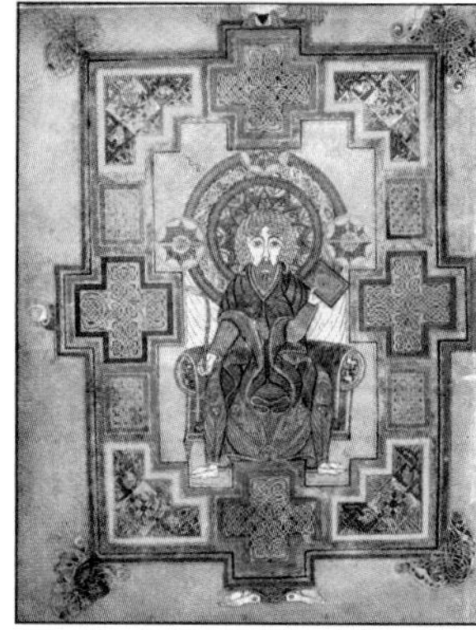

Early Middle Ages and the Romanesque

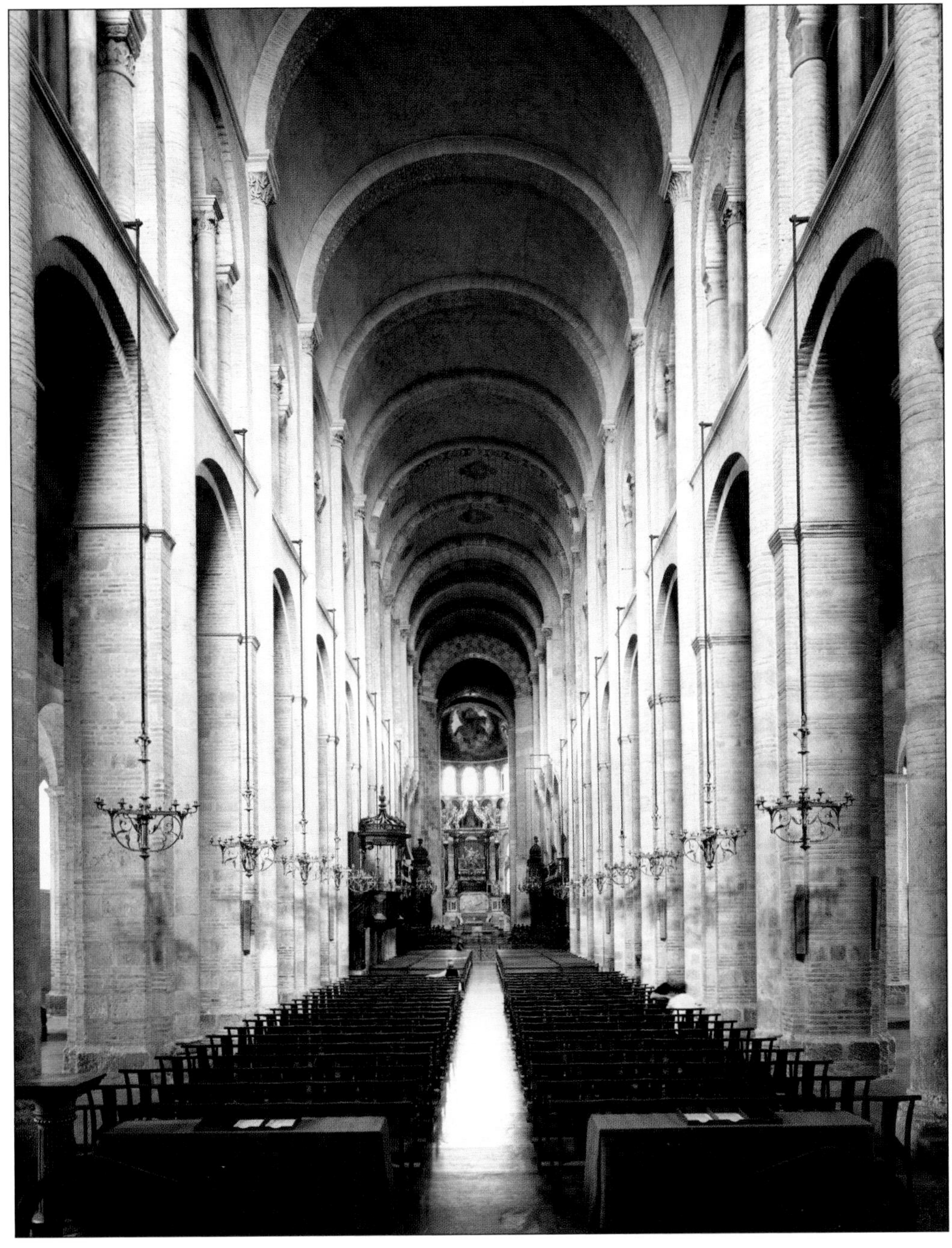

Saint-Sernin, Toulouse, begun ca. 1070 or 1077, nave looking toward altar.

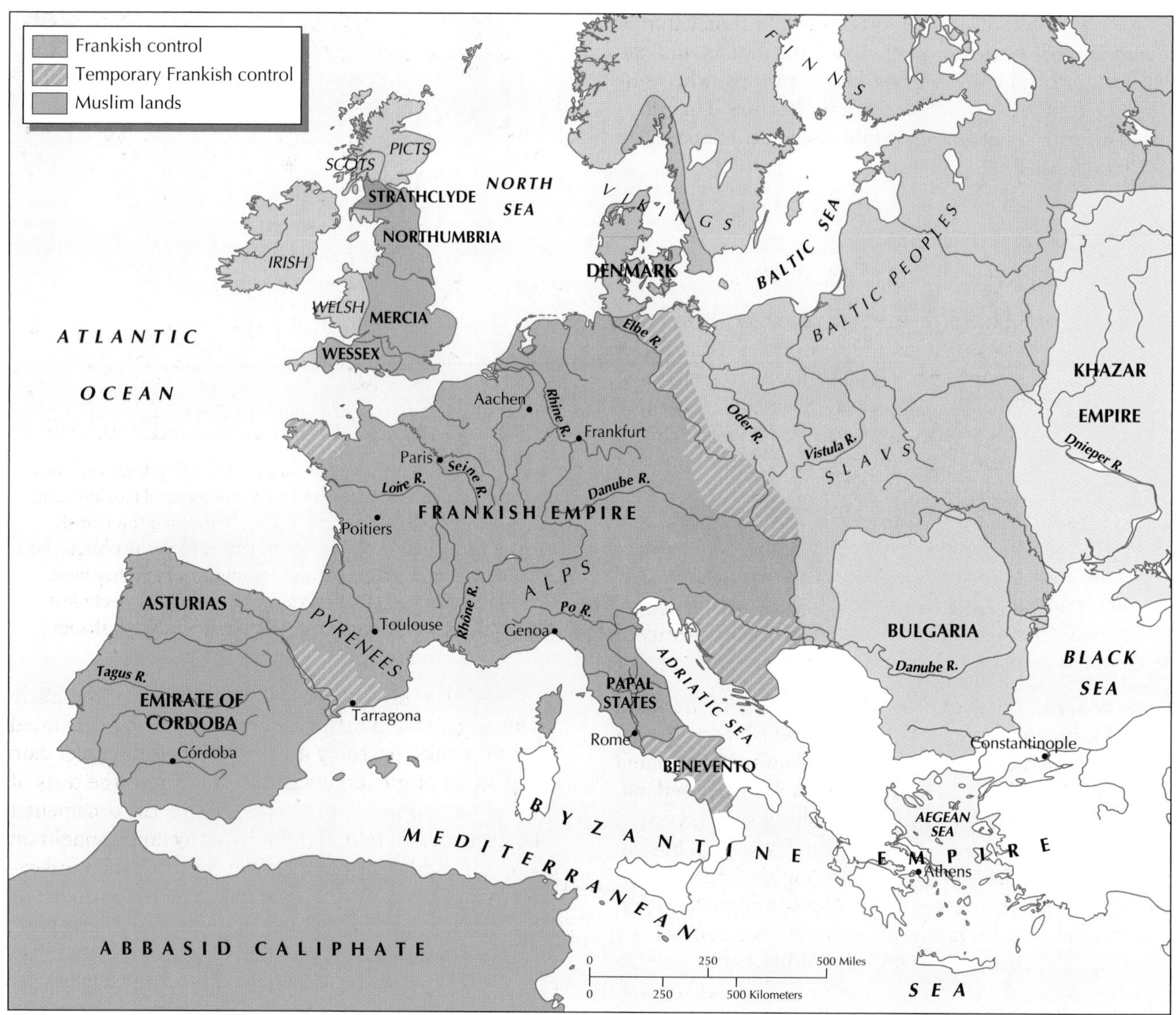

Map 11.1 The Carolingian world, ca. 814.

Chapter Overview

EARLY MEDIEVAL CULTURE

Charlemagne and Pope Gregory exert their influence on politics and culture

ROMANESQUE CULTURE

The rise of France and England along with their church architecture and sculpture

EARLY MEDIEVAL CULTURE

The Early Middle Ages generally refers to culture in western Europe from ca. 500 to ca. 1000—that is, the second half of the first millenium C.E. The period referred to as the "Dark Ages" stretched only from the sixth to the eighth century, and can be considered "dark" only in that so few documents survive to shed light on this era. The Early Middle Ages were a period of tremendous cultural accomplishment. The fifteenth-century flowering of Western civilization that we call the Renaissance, or "rebirth," was only possible because of what took place in the thousand years that preceded it. The beginning of this period was marked by the collision of two very different cultural forces: the Christian Church, which gradually spread northward from Rome, and the Germanic tribes and other barbarian groups, who controlled civic and social life in northern Europe. Their mutual cultural assimilation would come to shape early medieval life.

MERGING OF CHRISTIAN AND CELTO-GERMANIC TRADITIONS

In the first half of the fifth century C.E., Anglo-Saxons invaded Britain from northeastern Europe as part of the vast migration of Germanic tribes into the former territories of the Roman empire. The Anglo-Saxons were actually three different tribes, the Angles, the Saxons, and the Jutes, who, though distinct, shared the same ancestors, traditions, and language. In Britain, they quickly suppressed the indigenous Christian inhabitants, the Celts. By 550, Christianity had disappeared from all but the most remote corners of Britain, and the culture of the country had become distinctly Germanic. Although by 675 Britain was again predominantly Christian, there is little trace of Christianity in some of the earliest artifacts from this period.

Animal Style. Some of the finest examples of the art of these Germanic tribes are the exquisite objects discovered in the rich burial ship of an East Anglian king, dated between 625 and 633, at Sutton Hoo in Suffolk, England. As part of the king's funeral rite, the ship was lifted out of the water, dragged some distance inland, and then buried. The site was excavated in 1939. Among the artifacts discovered was a purse cover (fig. 11.1) made of gold, garnet, and enamel (the background has been restored) with a clasp made of enamel on gold. This **animal style** pattern consists of distorted creatures, their bodies twisted and stretched. Some are made up of parts from different animals. Interlaced with these bestial forms are purely abstract patterns. But this is by no means wild, undisciplined design. On the contrary, the symmetrical compositions are meticulously compiled of smaller units that are, in themselves, symmetrical. The unifying aesthetic suggests a preference for vigorous, ornamental patterns. The swirling lines and animal interlace seen here are the two basic forms that later appear in Irish Anglo-Saxon manuscript illumination.

Christian Gospel Books. The only paintings that survive in good condition from the early medieval era are in illuminated manuscripts produced in monasteries in northern England and Ireland after the mid-seventh century. **Illuminated manuscripts** are books written by hand on **parchment** (animal skin; the finest quality is called **vellum**) and elaborately decorated with paintings. Each separate page is referred to as a **folio.** Early examples are usually copies of the four Christian gospels of Matthew, Mark, Luke, and John. The paintings show the Christian assimilation of the Anglo-Saxon animal style.

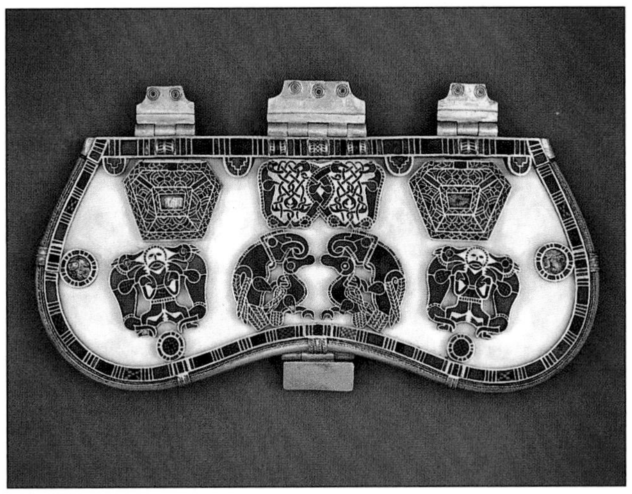

FIGURE 11.1 Purse cover, from the burial ship found at Sutton Hoo, England, 625–33, gold, garnets, and enamel (background restored), length 8″ (20.3 cm), ©The Trustees of the British Museum/Art Resource, NY. This and other exquisite objects show how inappropriate it is to call the era during which they were created the "Dark Ages." Working with the highest technical skill, artists created symmetrical patterns from animal shapes.

The *Book of Kells*, the finest gospel book of the Early Middle Ages still in existence, was written and decorated by Irish monks, probably around 800, but the exact date and place of origin are uncertain. It contains the texts of the four gospels in Latin. As is clear from the ornamental folio depicting St. John (fig. 11.2), perfection is sought on the smallest scale humanly possible. The fine technical execution is accompanied by a lack of concern for the accurate representation of the human body. John is seen from the front yet appears flat, no more three dimensional than the surface on which he is painted. The intentionally stylized human figure is treated as a pattern of lines. The curvilinear drapery falls in impossible folds, forming a two-dimensional decorative design that gives little hint of a solid body beneath. This Celtic style of manuscript illumination, like its Byzantine counterpart (see Chapter 5), takes us far from nature and the Classical tradition's allegiance to portraying the visible world. Such a move from the physical to the spiritual reflects a shift in a patronage from secular to religious and the growing power of the medieval Church.

The Beowulf Epic and the Christian Poem. The greatest of the Anglo-Saxon Germanic epics is *Beowulf.* It was probably composed in the first half of the eighth century, although the only version of it that survives dates from the tenth century, and much of the poem has been lost.

Beowulf is an almost completely Germanic tale. Set in Denmark, its action exemplifies the values of a warrior society. As a good king Beowulf is referred to as "ring giver," or "dispenser of treasure," and his duty is to take care of his loyal thanes or noblemen. Yet the act of giving has a spiritual side as well—out of generosity, unity and

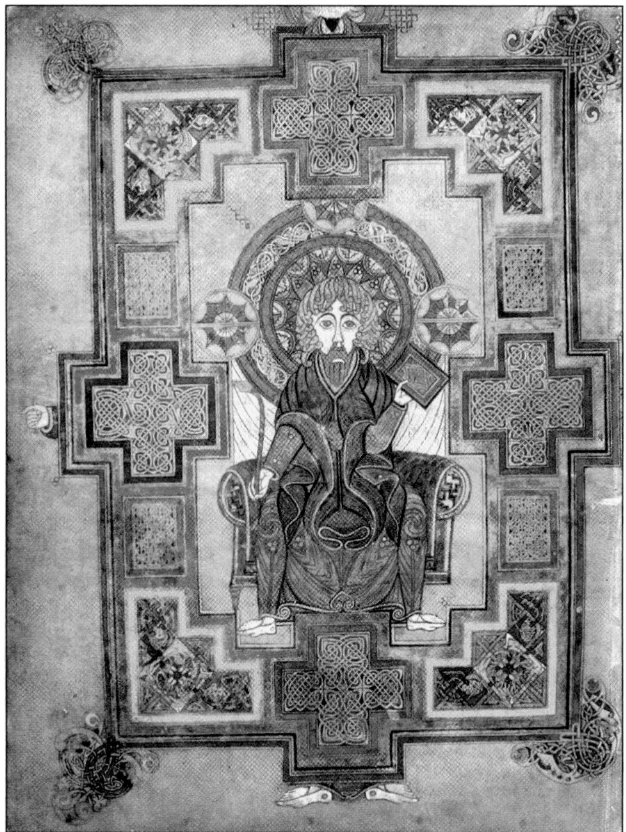

FIGURE 11.2 *St. John*, folio from the *Book of Kells*, ca. 800, manuscript illumination, 13 × $9\frac{1}{2}$" (33 × 24.1 cm), Trinity College Library, Dublin. The human body is treated as if it is as flat as the folio's surface and is incorporated into the two-dimensional design. The Classical tradition of realism and pictorial illusionism is no longer identifiable here. A person seems to stand behind the painted decoration, seen most clearly at the "foot of the page."

brotherhood emerge. This bonding, called *comitatus*, is balanced by the omnipresent threat of death.

There are hints of a Christian perspective in *Beowulf*, though these are submerged and are supplied by the narrator, rather than the characters. Jesus is never mentioned (there are no allusions to the New Testament at all), and Beowulf's funeral, in a burial ship like that found at Sutton Hoo, is entirely pagan. The immortality that is his reward is the pagan form of immortality—the celebration of his memory in the poem itself.

In contrast to *Beowulf*, the short *Caedmon's Hymn*, the oldest extant Old English poem, composed between 658 and 680, employs the language of Anglo-Saxon heroic verse in an explicitly Christian context. Like a heroic king, God is referred to as the *Weard*, or Guardian, of his kingdom.

CHARLEMAGNE AND THE CAROLINGIAN ERA

The convergence of Christian and Germanic cultures, which occurred long before the eighth century, culminates in the rule of Charles the Great or CHARLEMAGNE [SHAR-lu-main] (742–814), king of the Franks. His rule is generally considered to have inaugurated a period of cultural reawakening in western Europe. Accordingly, this period is known as the Carolingian era. Often credited with the major achievements of the so-called Carolingian Renaissance, Charlemagne saw himself as a successor to the great Roman emperors, and his court at Aachen was a focal point for the promotion of literacy.

Feudal Society. Charlemagne's government was essentially an early version of **feudalism,** a legal and social system that developed in western Europe in the eighth century. Under feudalism a lord would offer protection and land to his vassals, or servants, in return for an oath of fealty, or loyalty, and military support. Charlemagne divided his enormous empire into approximately three hundred counties, each governed by a count who was given authority to rule over it. Such a land grant was called a *feudum*, a fief, from which the term "feudal" derives. A fiefdom was hereditary, that is, passed on at the death of the vassal to his heir.

Feudalism involved a provision or grant of land for military service. In exchange of the fief or property, a vassal owed his lord a certain number of military service days. The feudal system included other reciprocal obligations of lords and vassals, such as hospitality. Aristocratic vassals were known as chevaliers in France and as knights in Germany and England. Much medieval literature features their exploits, from the French *Song of Roland* to the German *Tristan and Iseult* and the English *Canterbury Tales*, which includes a tale told by a knight.

Architecture. To match his imperial ambitions, Charlemagne created at Aachen in Germany a sumptuous palace and a magnificent royal chapel (fig. 11.3), designed by ODO OF METZ [OH-doh]. Apart from this chapel, little Carolingian architecture has survived. Nonetheless, it is clear that Carolingian ideas influenced later medieval styles.

Literature: The Song of Roland. One of the most famous of all early medieval French literary works is the *Song of Roland*, a ***chanson de geste,*** or "song of deeds," which dates from the mid-eleventh century in Brittany. It consists of more than four thousand lines, which are given their regularity and shape by the use of **assonance,** or the repetition of vowel and consonantal sounds, rather than by pure rhyme. The poem is based on a historical incident from the year 778, and tells the story of the Christian army of Charlemagne doing battle against the Muslim Saracens.

The poem is noted for its clarity and for the elegance of its language, the simplicity of its narrative, and the masterful precision of its detail. The feudal code of honor serves as a foundation for, and standard against which to measure, the actions of its major characters. Celebrating loyalty over treachery, courage over cowardice, good judgment over foolishness, the *Song of Roland* exemplifies the values of French feudal society. Roland is at once a valiant warrior, an obedient and faithful servant of his king, and a warm and affectionate friend, whose behavior is governed by a Christian sense of moral rectitude.

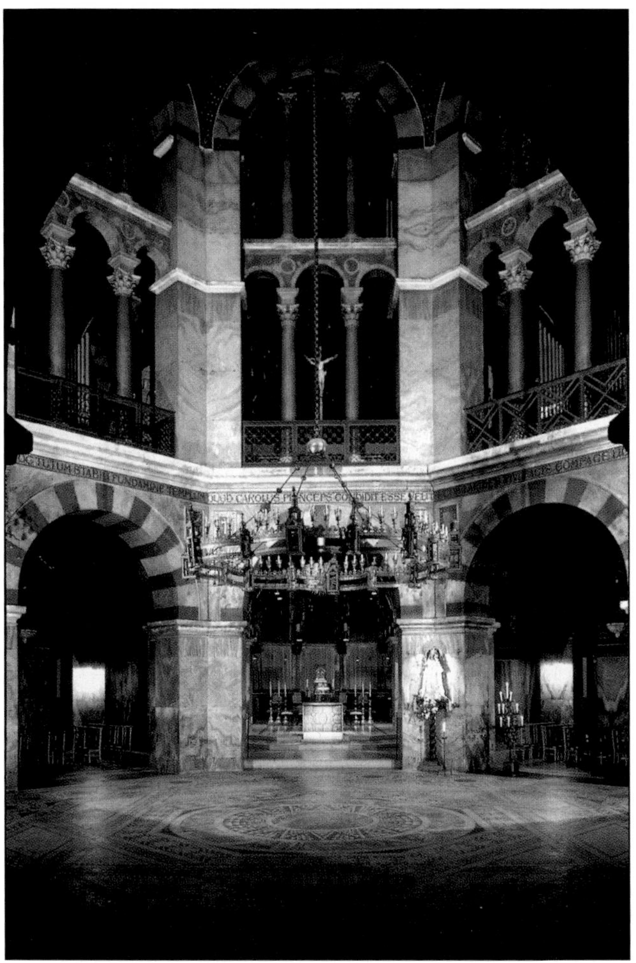

FIGURE 11.3 Odo of Metz, Palatine Chapel, Aachen, Germany, 792–805. © Achim Bednorz, Koln. Charlemagne was determined to make his chapel worthy of his piety, and so had materials brought from Rome and Ravenna to enrich it. The massive proportions and semicircular arches recall the architecture of ancient Rome.

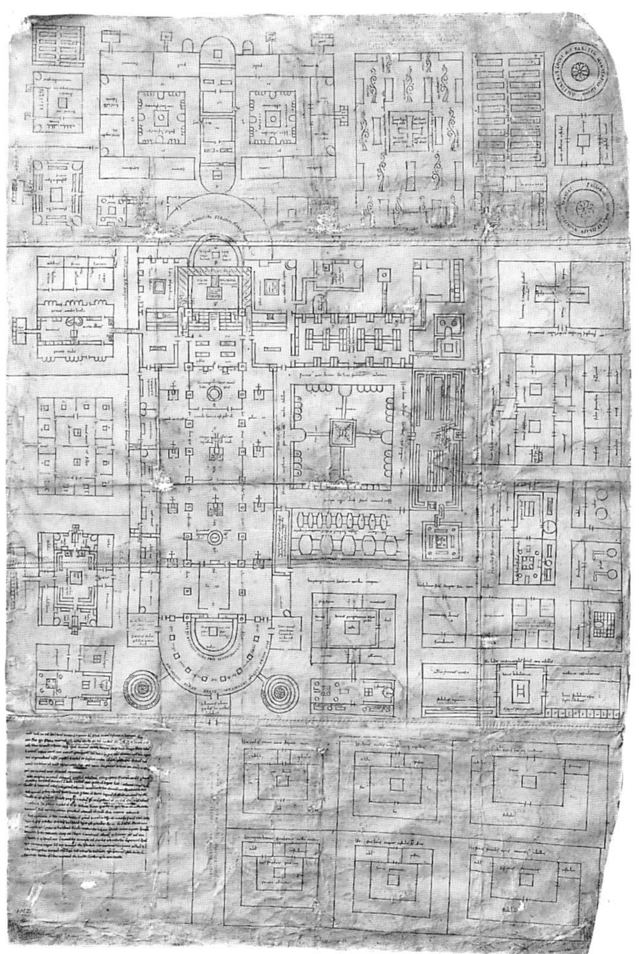

FIGURE 11.4 Plan for a monastery, ca. 817–20, red ink on parchment, 2′4 × 3′8$\frac{1}{8}$″ (71.1 × 112.1 cm), Stiftsbibliothek, St. Gallen, Switzerland. This plan for a prototype monastery was intended to be adopted and adapted to the specific needs of each monastic community—no monastery was ever built that precisely matched its layout. However, the drawing illustrates the basic ideal, which was that the monastery should provide for all the monks' needs.

MONASTICISM

Monasticism, a term derived from the Greek word *monos*, meaning "alone," had been an integral part of Christian life since the third century. During the Middle Ages, monasticism developed rapidly, resulting in an increasing number of monasteries and religious orders of monks and nuns. However, the observance of rules was anything but strict, and the lifestyle enjoyed in many monasteries was often quite relaxed. Among the earliest monastic guidelines were those provided by St. Benedict (480–543), who established a monastery at Monte Cassino, south of Rome, and created the Benedictine order. Dividing their day into organized periods of prayer, work, and study, the Benedictines had a life that was summed up in the motto "Pray and work." Their lives were based on four vows: They were to possess nothing (poverty); live in one place their entire life (stability); follow the abbot's direction (obedience); and remain unmarried (chastity).

Another order, established at Cluny, France, instead fostered art and music. The Cluniacs soon spread beyond their original monastery to establish monastic houses throughout Europe. The Cistercian order rebelled against the wealth and luxury of the Cluniacs. Established at Cîteaux in 1098, the Cistercian was a far more ascetic order than the Benedictines. For example, they simplified their religious services, stripping them of elaborate ceremony and complex ritual, as well as removing much religious art from their surroundings. The Cistercians also fasted and prayed longer and more frequently than the Benedictines.

Monasteries. The original plan for an ideal Carolingian monastery that was never built (fig. 11.4) gives a good idea of what a medieval monastery was like. The monastery was intended to be self-contained and self-sufficient. The largest building is the church. To the south of the church is the cloister, which is a standard part of the medieval

Cross Currents

VIKINGS

The term Viking was used originally for seafarers from Vik in southern Norway who raided the British Isles. Later, Viking referred to Norse raiders of Eastern Europe and the Mediterranean. Still later, Viking came to refer to all medieval Scandinavian seafarers, whether or not they plundered.

The Vikings, who sailed in sleek vessels often decorated with a dragon-headed prow, were the first to establish settlements in Scandinavia, Russia, and Ireland. In 1000 C.E. they established a colony in Newfoundland in modern Canada and others as far south as Maine. Although some of the Viking settlements were short lived, others remained for centuries.

The more peaceful Viking seafarers developed a trade network with other Europeans. The more militant Vikings pushed the British ruler King Alfred (r. 871–899) to establish fortified kingdoms for protection and then merge those kingdoms into a larger realm of England and Scotland. The Vikings also influenced the future history of England and France by creating the duchy of Normandy.

monastery. The **cloister** is a square or rectangular space, open to the sky, usually with a source of water such as a fountain or well in the center, surrounded on all four sides by covered walkways. In the cloister garden, or **garth**, the monks might read, study, meditate, talk, and have contact with nature within the confines of the cloistered life. Also on the south side are the **refectory,** where meals were taken, the dormitory, baths, latrines, and various workshops. To the west are places where animals could be kept. To the north are the guest house, school (monasteries played an important part in the revival of learning, for it was here that education was available), and abbot's house. To the east are the physician's quarters (with bloodletting mentioned on the plan), and the infirmary, a short distance from the cemetery. The plan shows several kitchens, located throughout the monastery. It is worth noting that the

Connections

MYSTERY PLAYS AND THE GUILDS

Between the years 1000 and 1300, the population of Europe nearly doubled (to roughly seventy million), and urban areas began to grow as people gathered together in the interest of trade and commerce. The populations of these newly developing towns, which tended to form around old Roman settlements, along trade routes, and near the castles of great landowners, were, at least to a degree, free of feudal control, a fact that made them also free of organized government.

One of the chief means of establishing order in the growing towns and cities was the guild system. **Guilds** were associations of artisans and craftspeople (and soon merchants and bankers too) that regulated the quality of work produced in their own trade and the prices that an individual shopkeeper or tradesperson could charge. The guilds also controlled the training of apprentices and craftspeople, set wages, supervised contracts, and approved new businesses. They built guild halls around the central square of the town, usually in front of the church. They also provided insurance and burial services for their members.

The guilds actively participated in the presentation of the so-called **mystery plays**—an early English corruption of the Latin word *ministerium*, or "occupation," referring to the guilds—a form of liturgical drama that began to develop in the ninth century. The mystery plays were dramatizations of narratives in the Old and New Testaments, usually composed in cycles containing as many as forty-eight individual plays. Typically, they would begin with the Creation, then recount the Fall of Adam and Eve, the Flood and Noah's Ark, David and Goliath, and so on, through the Old Testament to the Nativity, the events of Jesus's life, the Crucifixion, and the Last Judgment.

Each guild was responsible for an individual play, which was sometimes connected with its own trade. The shipwrights' guild might present the story of Noah's Ark, for instance, and the bankers the story of Jesus and the moneylenders. These dramas were performed in the open air at different places around the town. In some towns, each guild would have its own wagon that served as a stage, and the wagons would proceed from one location to another, with the actors performing at each stop, so the audience could see the whole cycle without moving. In other towns, the plays were probably acted out on a single stage or platform in the main city square.

The mystery plays were performed every summer, either at Whitsuntide, the week following the seventh Sunday after Easter, or at Corpus Christi, a week later. They served as both entertainment and education for their largely illiterate audience. They also functioned as festive celebrations that brought together every aspect of medieval life—social, political, economic, and religious—for the entire community.

plan includes more than one building for servants. However, little if any heating was part of the plan, and winters must have been extremely difficult to endure.

Manuscript Illumination. Much of the work carried out by the monks consisted of revising, copying, and illustrating liturgical books. Due to the classical revival encouraged by Charlemagne, the human figure again became important in the visual arts. An image of St. John (fig. 11.5) is included in the *Gospel Book of Charlemagne*, also known as the *Coronation Gospels*, dated ca. 800–810. The manuscript is said to have been found in Charlemagne's tomb at his court in Aachen. St. John is portrayed in the Roman tradition—the style is similar to wall paintings found at Pompeii and Herculaneum (see figs. 4.21–4.23). A frame has been painted onto the vellum folio, creating the impression that the viewer is looking through a window to see John outside. The legs of John's footstool overlap the frame, as if the frame were genuinely three dimensional. The proportions of John's body are accurate and he wears a garment much like a Roman toga.

FIGURE 11.5 *St. John*, from the *Gospel Book of Charlemagne* (*Coronation Gospels*), ca. 800–810, manuscript illumination, $12\frac{3}{4} \times 9\frac{7}{8}''$ (32.4 × 25.1 cm), Schatzkammer, Kunsthistorisches Museum, Vienna. Emperor Charlemagne encouraged a revival of the antique—in part for political purposes. The impact of the antique is evident in this depiction of St. John, which is more realistic than that in the *Book of Kells* (see fig. 11.2).

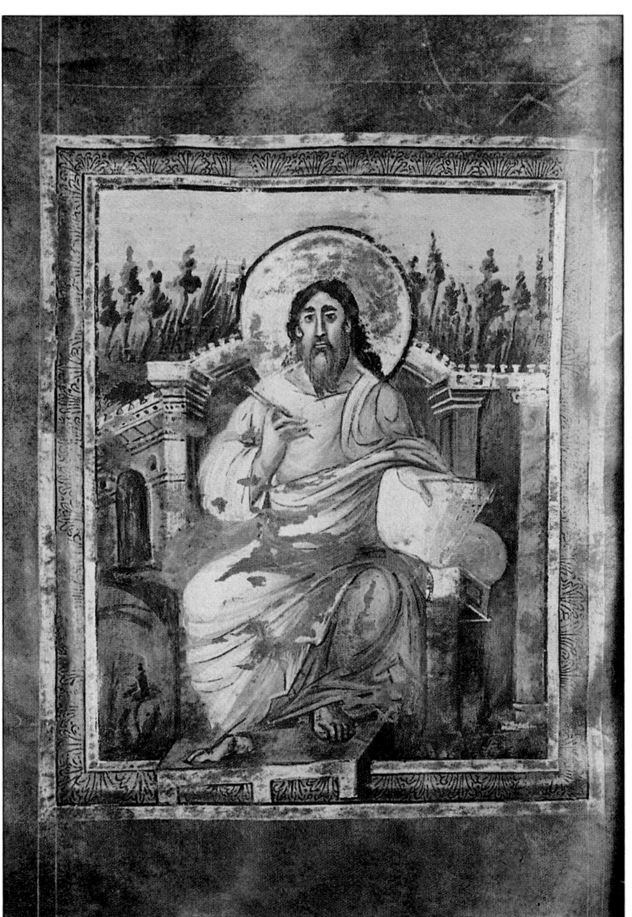

Music: Gregorian Chant. Music, which in the Middle Ages was largely linked to religion, was a particular passion of Charlemagne's, who brought monks to his kingdom from Rome to standardize ecclesiastical music. In church services for the laity (nonclergy) and in worship in the monasteries, the predominant form of music was **plainchant,** in which Latin liturgical texts were sung to a single melody line (**monophony**) without harmonic instrumental accompaniment.

The monks from Rome brought with them a particular tradition of Church music. This was **Gregorian chant,** which took its name from Pope Gregory the Great (540–604), who by legend is connected with the development of this form of music. A distinctly Frankish chant remained popular in Charlemagne's time too. During the centuries that followed, many new types of chant were composed, some of which were elaborated with **tropes,** or turns, in which other texts or melodies were introduced. Chants became more complex as the development of **polyphony** took place, in which two or more voice lines are sung simultaneously.

The basic chants have a serene, otherworldly quality with their flexible rhythms and melodic lines that typically move in tandem within a narrow range of pitch. Part of this quality comes from the use of church modes rather than major-minor scales. It also derives from the lack of harmonic accompaniment, as well as from the large resonating space of the cathedrals or monastery churches in which chants are frequently sung. The free-floating rhythms of the chant, with a lack of a steady beat or pattern of rhythmic accents, contribute to its solemnity, so much so that chant is sometimes described as "prayer on pitch."

During the reign of Charlemagne, Gregorian chants, which had formerly been passed down orally, were codified and written down in a rudimentary form of musical notation that used small curved strokes called **neumes** to indicate the up-and-down movement of the chant melody. This early notation scheme was ill suited to indicate actual melodies of tropes, which were ornamental in structure and often elaborate in their melodic contours. In the eleventh century, an Italian monk, GUIDO D'AREZZO [da-RET-zoh] (ca. 997–1050), created a musical graph, or set of lines, on which to mark the various chanted musical pitches. Guido colored the lines to set a "relative pitch" for each color; eventually the lines and spaces between grew in number as melodies evolved to meet composers' desires for expression. Used primarily for sacred music, this Guidonian graph used colored lines to make the representation of the musical pitches easy to read. It took two more centuries for the musical staff to develop, and until the sixteenth and seventeenth centuries before notes were written in the rounded forms common today.

Problems of rhythmic notation were not solved until Franco of Cologne explained in his treatise, *Ars Cantus Mensurabilis*, that different note shapes could be used to give different rhythmic values to those pitches previously notated in the square-note style of the Gregorian chant. Although there were only four basic shapes, Franco's system gave a definite relationship of time to each note. It was this musical notation that gave both order of performance and freedom of expression to musicians of the Middle Ages.

ROMANESQUE CULTURE

After Charlemagne's death in 814, the personal bonds that held the Holy Roman Empire together weakened. After two centuries of political fragmentation, however, around the year 1000, a few powerful feudal families began to extend their influence, conquering weaker feudal rulers and cementing their gains by intermarriage. These families soon developed into full-fledged monarchies. Two in particular—in France and in England—rose to real and lasting prominence.

THE FEUDAL MONARCHS

The Capetians. When HUGH CAPET [CA-pay] (ca. 938–996) ascended to the French throne, he established a dynasty of kings that would rule for nearly 350 years. Because of the strategic location of his barony—it was the best place to position defenses against invading Viking forces—he was accepted by the feudal lords of France as their king in 987. Throughout the subsequent CAPETIAN [ca-PEA-shun] era, the dukes of Normandy quarreled with their king. Nevertheless, the Capetian monarchs gradually consolidated power around themselves, and Paris became the political and intellectual center of Europe.

The Norman Conquest. Although servants to the Capetian kings in France, the dukes of Normandy claimed England for themselves and ruled as kings in their own right. The story of their conquest of England is recounted in the Bayeux Tapestry, dated ca. 1066–82 (fig. 11.6). The **tapestry** (actually a giant embroidery) tells how William, duke of Normandy (ca. 1027–87), conquered King Harold of England in 1066 and was crowned king of England. William became the first Norman king of England and was known thereafter as William the Conqueror.

William divided England up into fiefs for his Norman barons, ruling as a feudal monarch. And although he maintained some Anglo-Saxon customs and laws, Norman culture proved influential in England. For instance, the Latin-influenced French language spoken by the Norman invaders gradually began to mix with the native Anglo-Saxon, and the English language as we know it today started to emerge.

FIGURE 11.6 *King Edward Sends Harold of Wessex to Normandy*, detail of the Bayeux Tapestry, ca. 1066–82, wool embroidery on linen, height approximately $19\frac{1}{2}''$ (49.5 cm), total length ca. 231′ (70.41 m), Centre Guillaume le Conquérant, Bayeux, France. The entire story of the invasion of England by William of Normandy, thereafter known as William the Conqueror, is told on this so-called tapestry. A document of military tactics and weaponry, the various parts of the narrative show the soldiers in battle, preparing for combat, traveling, and eating.

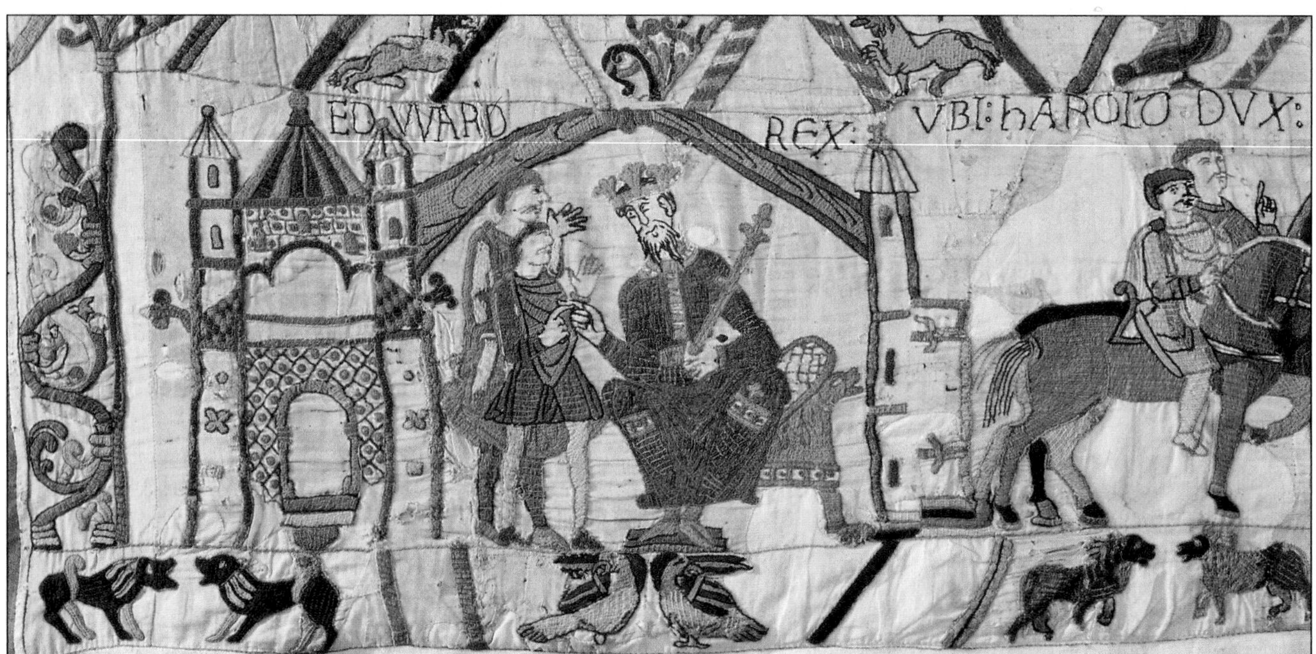

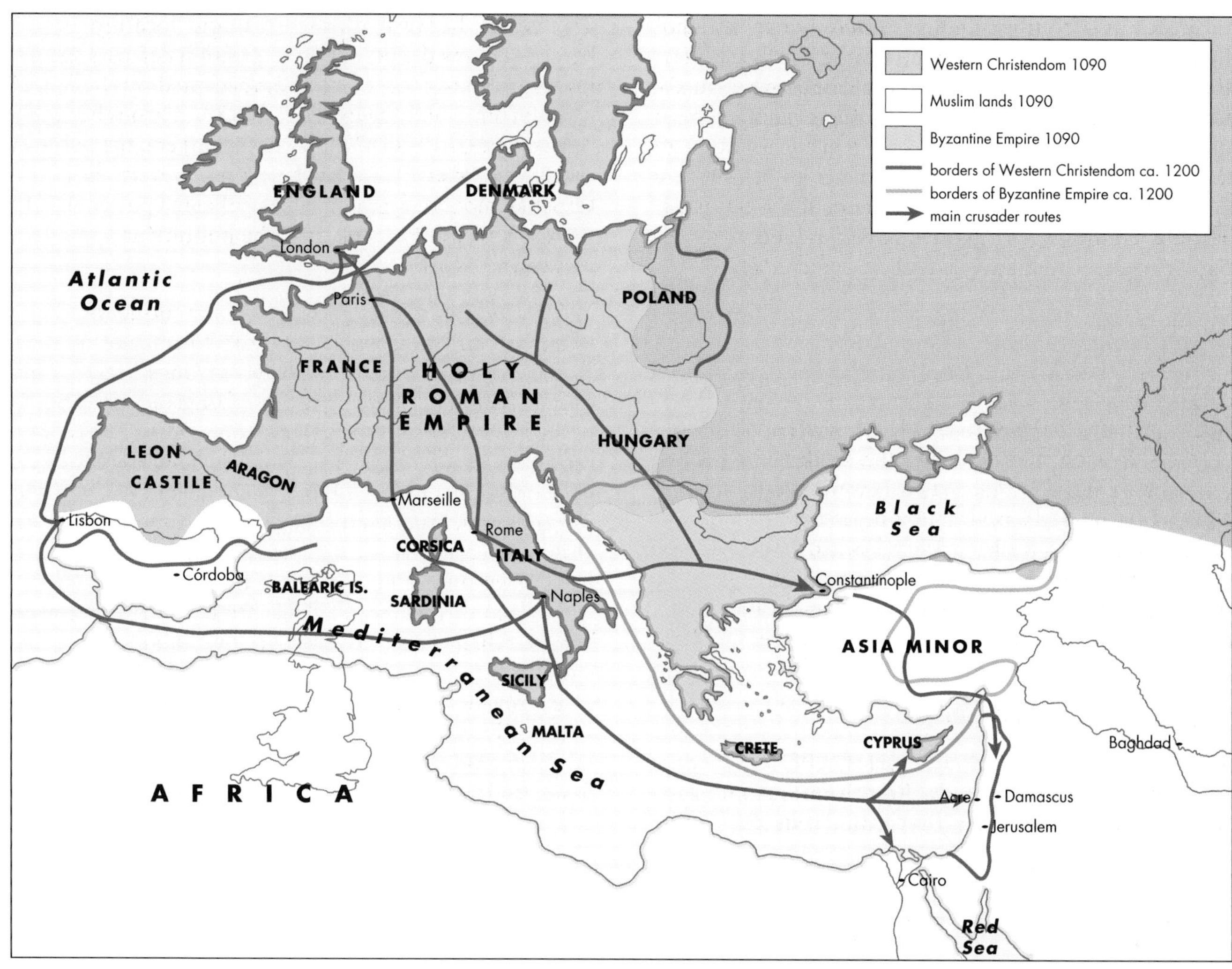

MAP 11.2 The Crusades.

Magna Carta. Relations between the rulers of England and France remained difficult. In 1199, King Philip Augustus (r. 1180–1223) succeeded in expelling the English from France north of the Loire River. The English barons, outraged at the expense of King John's continued campaign against France, drew up a list of demands that John was forced to sign on June 15, 1215. Called the Magna Carta, or "Great Charter," the document was among the first to set a limit on royal authority. It also gave freemen certain rights, such as trial by jury. The Magna Carta is often seen as a crucial political document that paved the way for constitutional monarchy and the development of democracy in western Europe.

Crusades. The term **crusade,** derived from the Latin word *crux,* meaning cross, refers to a holy war. The crusaders, who organized a series of military expeditions to recover the Holy Land in Palestine from Muslim occupiers, wore strips of cloth in the form of a cross on the backs of their garments. In doing so, they were allying themselves with Jesus, who was executed by the Roman authorities, who had him nailed to a wooden cross.

The first Crusade was launched in 1095 by Pope Urban II, who called for Christian knights to seize from the Turks the holy city of Jerusalem. The response to the Pope's call was enthusiastic, as an army of peasants and knights set out shortly afterward for Palestine, though without adequate planning, weapons, or discipline.

After the first crusade experienced disastrous results with few crusaders reaching the Holy Land and fewer still returning to Europe, French and Norman nobles organized a better planned and armed second crusade, which succeeded in capturing Jerusalem in 1099. This military success, along with others that followed, spurred Turks, Egyptians, and others to settle their differences and expel the Christian invaders. Under the Muslim leader Saladin, the Turks recaptured Jerusalem in 1187.

Other crusades followed, crusades which were largely failures militarily, religiously, and politically. But the crusades did aid in stimulating East–West trade and in accelerating the exchange of ideas. European scholars and missionaries encountered Muslim philosophers and theologians, and Muslim merchants traded with their European counterparts. The extensive exchange of goods, ideas, and technologies greatly influenced European development.

Romanesque Architecture

Pilgrimages and Churches. **Pilgrimages** were a social phenomenon of medieval life. Their chief purpose was to worship **relics** (objects believed to be associated with saints and especially with Jesus and Mary, or parts of their bodies), especially relics that were claimed to have miraculous powers. Pilgrimages were an important expression of religious faith, but they also represented a social opportunity to meet people from different cultures, having different customs.

For the many people who traveled great distances along the pilgrimage routes, facilities were available at abbeys, priories, monasteries, and hospices. Some of these were built specifically for pilgrims at intervals of twenty or so miles, not a difficult distance to cover in a day. People slept in big open halls, and there were special chapels for religious services. Charities were set up to aid the sick and the destitute and to take care of the dead.

Churches visited in this way by medieval pilgrims are referred to as "pilgrimage churches." All have the same basic plan and certain similarities of construction. Their style is called **Romanesque,** and indeed the architecture relies on the basic Roman elements of the **basilica** plan (see fig. 5.3), employing rounded arches, vaulted ceilings, piers and columns for support, and thick, sturdy walls. However, the style is not called Romanesque for this reason but because it was associated with the romance languages. All pilgrimage churches had large naves with flanking aisles, a transept, choir, ambulatory, and radiating chapels on the east end.

Saint-Sernin, Toulouse. Among the most important buildings constructed in the eleventh century is Saint-Sernin in Toulouse (fig. 11.7), the best known of the great pilgrimage churches. Saint-Sernin was started ca. 1070 or 1077 but never finished. The west **facade,** which underwent restoration in 1855, has been generously described as an "awkward bulk." The builders' original intent (and the Romanesque norm) was to have two facade towers, but they were never completed. The apse end was completed by about 1098, with many different roof levels that reflect the interior plan. Each chapel is seen as a separate bulge from the outside; above the ambulatory, the apse protrudes; and the levels build up to the crossing tower. Each space is separate, as is typical of Romanesque architecture.

Saint-Sernin, like the other great pilgrimage churches, has a Latin-cross plan (fig. 11.8)—with one long arm—as opposed to the Greek-cross plan, which has four arms of equal length. The proportions of Saint-Sernin are mathematically determined: The aisles are composed of a series of square **bays** that serve as the basic unit; the nave and transept bays are twice as large; the crossing

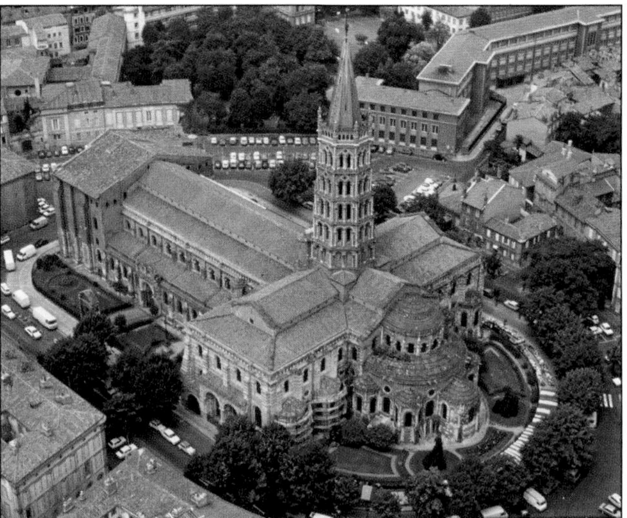

FIGURE 11.7 Saint-Sernin, Toulouse, begun ca. 1070 or 1077, aerial view from the southwest. The exterior of the building reflects the interior. Each section of space is clearly defined and neatly separated, unlike the flowing spaces that will characterize Gothic architecture.

FIGURE 11.8 Saint-Sernin, Toulouse, begun ca. 1070 or 1077, plan. This Latin-cross plan with ambulatory and radiating chapels is typical of churches located along the pilgrimage route leading to Santiago de Compostela. In the many chapels, pilgrims venerated relics, especially if a relic were believed to be able to create miracles.

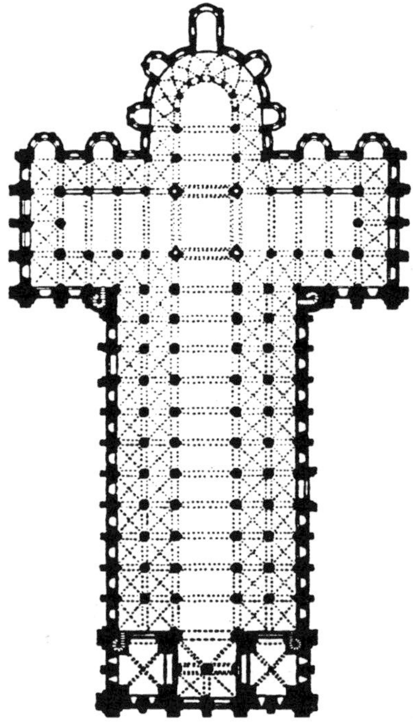

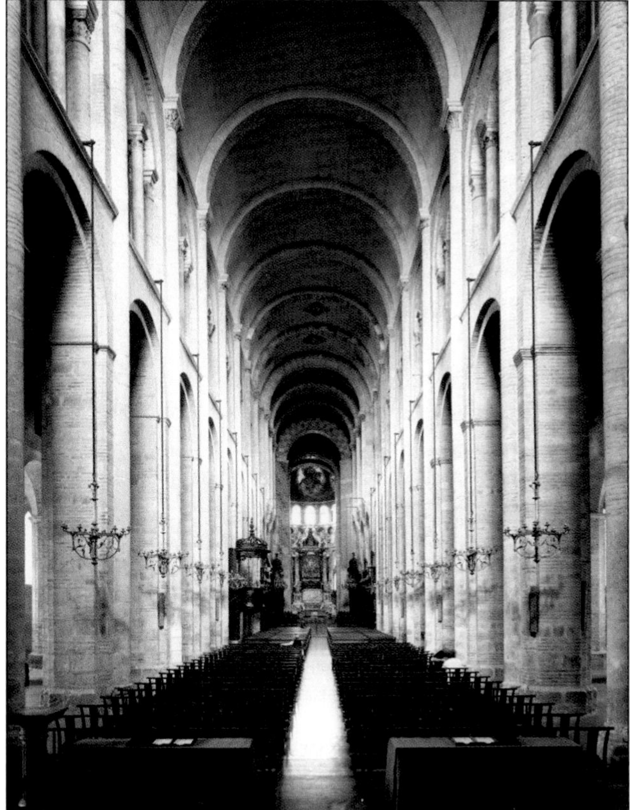

FIGURE 11.9 Saint-Sernin, Toulouse, begun ca. 1070 or 1077, nave looking toward altar. Romanesque masons experimented with various vaulting methods, using most frequently the barrel (tunnel) vault based on the semicircular arch. Advantages of this stone vault, compared to the wooden ceiling of the Early Christian basilica, include superb acoustics and minimized risk of fire; disadvantages include lack of direct light into the nave.

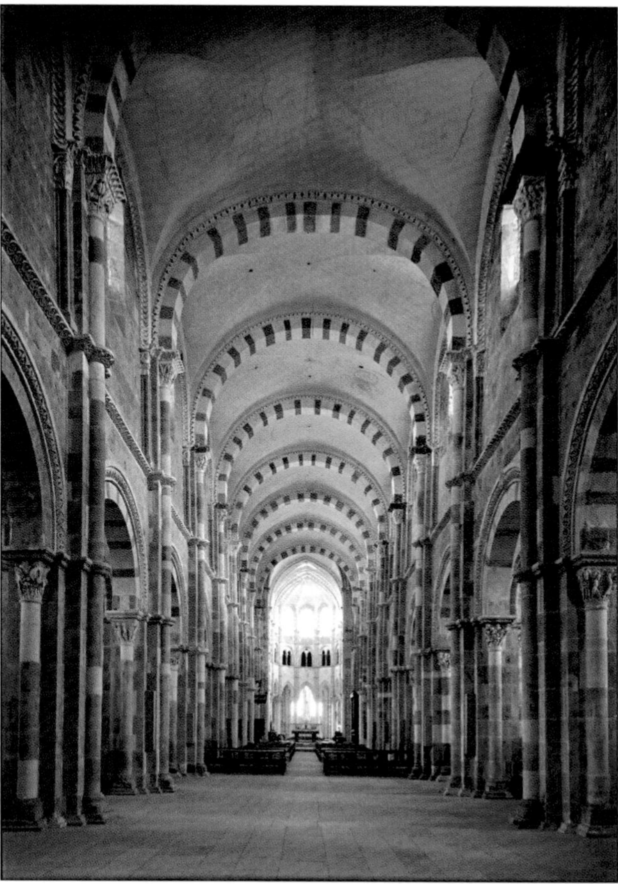

FIGURE 11.10 Sainte-Madeleine, Vézelay, nave looking toward altar, built 1120–32. A solution to the problem of obtaining direct light in the nave is found in the use of cross (groin) vaults, which provide a space for windows on the nave walls.

tower is four times the basic unit, as are the bases of the intended facade towers. Certain ancient Greek temples had similar numerical ratios between their different parts.

The nave of Saint-Sernin (fig. 11.9) is typically Romanesque, with thick walls, closely spaced piers, engaged columns on the walls, and a stone vault. The **barrel vault** (also called a **tunnel vault**) covering the nave is a structural system that offers several advantages. Here, the acoustics are superb, with voices reverberating through the vaulted space. The threat of fire is reduced—a constant danger in the Middle Ages, especially to structures with wooden ceilings. The large interior is open, free of the intrusive posts necessary to the post and lintel system. Yet the barrel vault also has its disadvantages. An extension of the arch principle, it exerts a constant lateral thrust that must be buttressed. This is accomplished largely by the great thickness of the walls, which means any opening in the supporting walls weakens the system. Consequently the windows in Romanesque churches are few and small, and the interiors are often very dark.

Sainte-Madeleine, Vézelay. The pilgrimage church of Sainte-Madeleine in Vézelay was built between 1096 and 1132. At its peak, Vézelay had eight hundred monks and lay brothers living in its monastery.

The nave (fig. 11.10), built between 1120 and 1132, is very light for a Romanesque church. It is also very harmonious, as simple mathematics determine the proportions of the interior. The alternating light and dark **voussoirs** (wedge-shaped blocks of stone that make up the arches) are inconsistent in size, resulting in irregular stripes. The supports are massive. The nave elevation is two stories high, as at Saint-Sernin, which is customary for pilgrimage churches. At Vézelay, however, the upper level is a clerestory with a row of windows. This is made possible because the nave bays are covered by **cross vaults** (also called **groin vaults**)—two tunnel (barrel) vaults intersecting at right angles, which automatically create a flat space on the wall where a window can be constructed. Vézelay's interior therefore offers a solution to the problem of obtaining direct light in the nave. However, the structure was neither well built nor adequately buttressed—problems developed and the walls began to lean. Flying buttresses were added in the Gothic era and then rebuilt in the nineteenth century. The walls now lean outward by about twenty inches.

Cathedral Group, Pisa. Of all the Romanesque cathedrals constructed outside the pilgrimage routes, perhaps one of the most striking is that in Pisa, Italy. The "cathedral group" in Pisa (fig. 11.11) consists of the cathedral, begun in 1063; the baptistery, begun in 1153; and the ***campanile*** (the bell tower), of 1174, the famous "leaning tower of Pisa." All three buildings are covered in white marble, inlaid with dark green marble, a technique used by the ancient Romans.

The baptistery is circular and domed. The first two floors are Romanesque, with marble panels and arcades. The pointy gables are fourteenth-century Gothic. The architect of the cathedral was Buscheto, although the facade was designed by Rainaldo. The marble arcades are a Pisan hallmark. **Blind arcades** create a lacy effect, with colorful light and shade patterns. The five stories of arcades on the facade match the interior: The bottom corresponds to the nave arcade; the first open arcade reflects the galleries; the second open arcade the roof of the galleries; the third the clerestory; and the last the roof. Simple mathematical ratios determine the dimensions, for the blind arcade is one-third the height of the facade, whereas each open arcade is one-sixth the height.

Pisa's most famous monument is undoubtedly the "leaning tower." The bell tower is usually a separate building in Italy, whereas in other countries there are normally two bell towers on the facade of a Romanesque church. The designer of the campanile was Bonanno Pisano. The campanile leans because the foundations were poorly laid and offer uneven resistance. Most Italian towers of the Middle Ages leaned, but rarely to this degree. The tower is 179 feet tall and is now approximately sixteen feet out of plumb.

SCULPTURE

The vast majority of people living in western Europe during the Middle Ages were illiterate—a portion of the clergy included. Sermons were therefore, literally, carved in stone, with sculptors creating the equivalent of picture books for those who could not read.

Romanesque architectural sculpture is concentrated on church portals, especially on **tympana** (the **tympanum** is the semicircular section above the doorway, with a horizontal lintel at the bottom, supported by a central **trumeau,** or post) and column capitals. This kind of sculpture was once painted with bright colors.

The typical Romanesque tympanum has a figure of Jesus in the center, in majesty. He is surrounded by a **mandorla,** a glory of light in the shape of a pointed oval. Outside the mandorla, the subjects of different tympana vary.

FIGURE 11.11 Cathedral group, Pisa: baptistery, begun 1153; cathedral, begun 1063; campanile, begun 1174. In addition to marble incrustation, the architecture of Romanesque Pisa is characterized by tiers of arcades. The "leaning tower of Pisa" owes its fame to foundations that were not made properly.

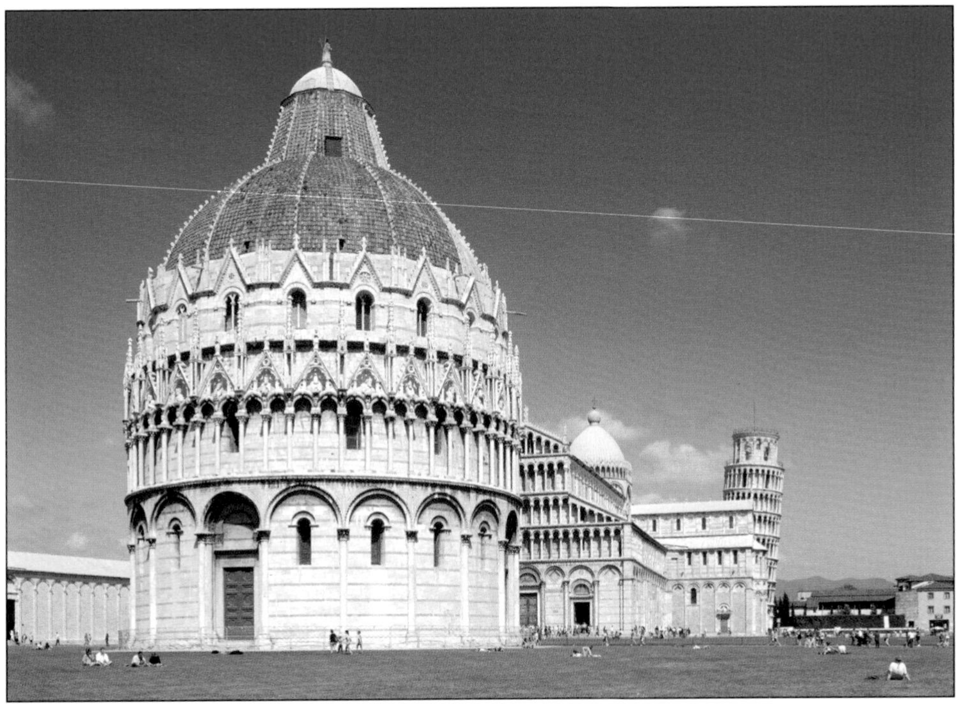

Cross Currents

The Pisa Griffin

From 1100 until 1828, a three-and-a-half-foot-high Islamic bronze griffin (fig. 11.12) (a mythological creature, half eagle, half lion) stood on top of the cathedral in Pisa. This griffin may have originally been a fountain spout, but how it came to Pisa is unknown. Scholars have suggested that its provenance might be Persia, in the east, or perhaps Spain, in the west. But whatever its origins, placed on top of the cathedral that was itself built to celebrate Pisa's 1063 victory over Muslim forces in the western Mediterranean, it soon came to symbolize the city's place at the very center of Mediterranean trade.

The griffin is decorated with incised feathers on its wings, and the carving of its back suggests silk drapery, linking it with Asia. A favorite symbol of both the Assyrians and Persians, the griffin was said to guard the gold of India, and the Greeks believed these creatures watched over the gold of the Scythians. For Muslims, the eaglelike qualities of the beast signified vigilance, and its lionlike qualities, courage. By the time it was placed on Pisa cathedral, Christians had appropriated the beast to their own iconological ends, where it came to signify the dual nature of Jesus, his divinity (the eagle) and his humanity (the lion).

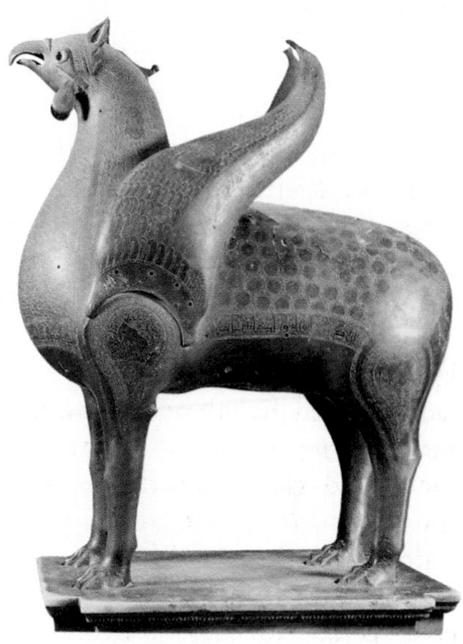

Figure 11.12 Griffin, from the Islamic Mediterranean, eleventh century, bronze, height 3′6$\frac{1}{8}$″ (1.07 m), Museo dell'Opera del Duomo, Pisa. The griffin, an invention of ancient mythology created by amalgamating a lion and an eagle, has been interpreted symbolically by various cultures. This griffin stood atop Pisa cathedral until it was moved to the cathedral museum in 1828.

Vézelay, Mission of the Apostles. An extraordinary tympanum can be found in the narthex of the church of Sainte-Madeleine in Vézelay (fig. 11.13), carved 1120–32. The subject depicted here is the *Mission of the Apostles*, presented as an allegory of the congregation's own mission to spread the Christian message continually to all the peoples of the earth. To show Jesus' thoughts passing into the minds of the apostles, rays emanate from Jesus' hands as he touches the head of each of them. To show that the message must be spread at all times, the second **archivolt** (arch above the tympanum) depicts the signs of the zodiac and the labors of the months. The innermost archivolt and the lintel depict the various types of people believed to inhabit the distant regions of the earth. Shown there, as described in fanciful travelers' tales of the time, are people with dog heads, who communicate by barking—the Cynocephali—and a pig-snouted tribe. Such figures continue on the lintel where the different races approach Peter and Paul. Last are the Panotii,

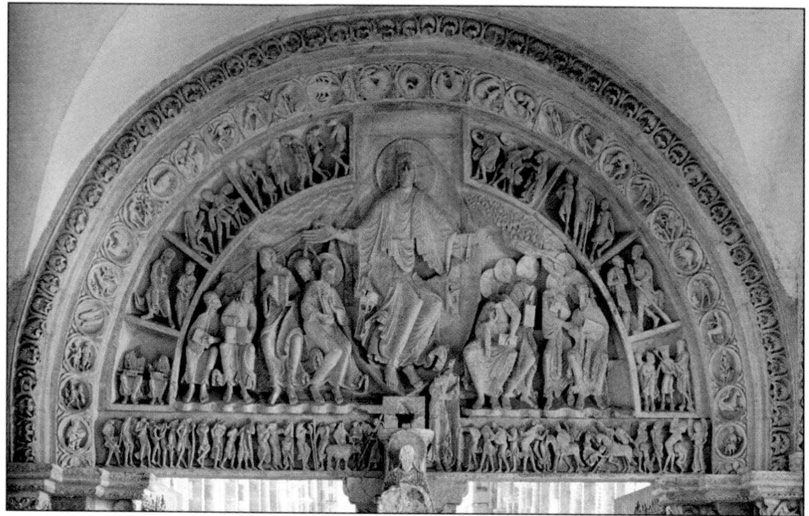

Figure 11.13 *Mission of the Apostles*, tympanum, Sainte-Madeleine, Vézelay, 1120–32. This tympanum (the semicircle above the entry) contains relief sculpture that is simultaneously decorative and didactic. The message is that Jesus' ideas, shown to travel from his fingertips to the heads of the apostles, are to be conveyed to all parts of the world at all times of the year, as represented symbolically around the tympanum by the signs of the zodiac.

whose ears are so large they can be used to envelop the body like a blanket if it is cold, or to fly away if their owner is in danger. The diminutive stature of the pygmies is indicated by their use of ladders to mount their horses. Vézelay's tympanum provides the modern visitor with a revealing insight into the twelfth-century view of the world, which was based largely on ancient literary sources, rather than on contemporary and accurate accounts of actual travel and contact with other peoples.

PAINTING

Images of the Madonna and Child. Frequently depicted in Romanesque art, especially during the twelfth century, in all geographic areas in which the Romanesque style was found and created in a variety of media, was the subject of Mary enthroned, holding her young son Jesus in her lap, referred to as the *Madonna and Child* (fig. 11.14). Characteristically stiff and rigid, both stare at the viewer rather than interacting with one another. The family resemblance between mother and child is evident. Jesus has the proportions of a miniature man rather than of a child. Typically Romanesque is the treatment of drapery, as if pressed and pleated into parallel ridges. Although the drapery obeys the laws of gravity on Mary's legs, the folds falling downward, the same is not true for the drapery folds on her upper arms. Indeed, the style turns away from the visible world in favor of the spiritual world. The subject of the Madonna and Child retained its popularity in the following Gothic era, but changed to a warmer relationship between a mother and child who have normally proportioned bodies and are garbed in flowing drapery. See fig. 12.15, Notre-Dame-de-Paris, carved of marble in the early fourteenth century.

FIGURE 11.14 *Virgin and Child in Majesty.* Oak, Linen, gesso and polychromy on walnut. H: $31\frac{5}{16}'' \times 12\frac{1}{2} \times 11\frac{1}{2}''$ (79.5 × 31.7 × 29.2 cm). The Metropolitan Museum of Art, Gift of J. Pierpont Morgan, 1916. (1632.194) Photograph © 1999 The Metropolitan Museum of Art. Typical of this popular subject in Romanesque art are the formal stiffness of the figures' poses and the gravity-defying, perfectly pressed pleats of their drapery.

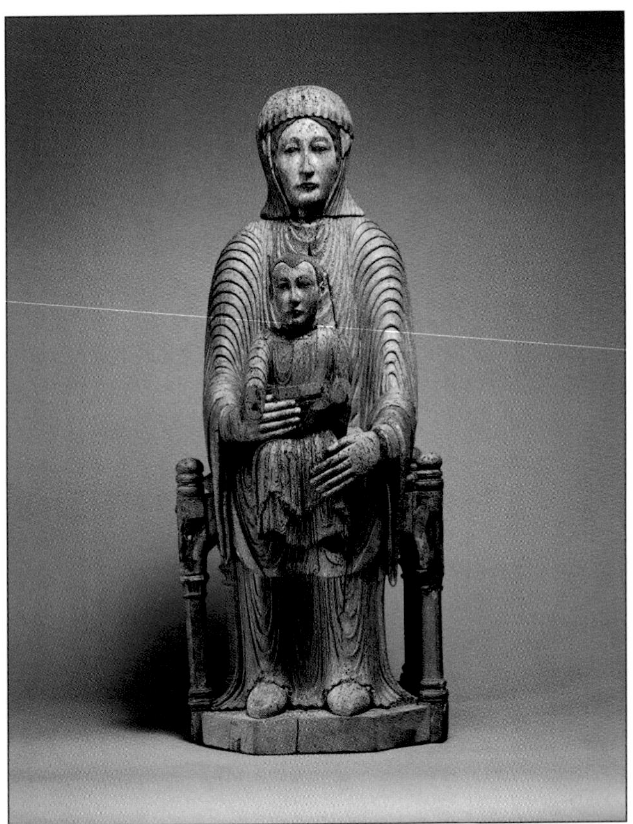

DECORATIVE ARTS

Reliquaries and Enamels. The relics venerated by pilgrims were kept in containers called **reliquaries.** The reliquary coffer shown in fig. 11.15 was made in the French city of Limoges in the twelfth century. Limoges was one of the two major areas in western Europe where enamel work was manufactured, the other being the Mosan area, today part of Belgium. An example of Mosan work is Nicholas of Verdun's masterpiece, the altarpiece at Klosterneuburg Abbey, near Vienna. The original altarpiece had forty-five plaques, each depicting a different scene, the figures engraved and gilded on separate enamel plaques. The *Birth of Jesus* (fig. 11.16) shows the infant on

FIGURE 11.15 Reliquary coffer, twelfth century, enamel, French, Limoges, now in Saint-Sernin, Toulouse. Elaborate coffers such as this were used to house precious relics such as a piece of Jesus' cross, a piece of silk worn by his mother Mary, a drop of her milk, or a strand of a saint's hair. Some relics were thought to be endowed with magical powers.

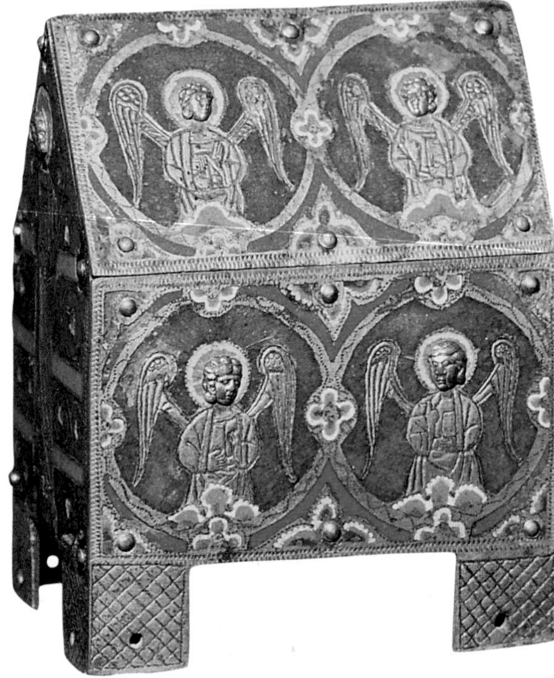

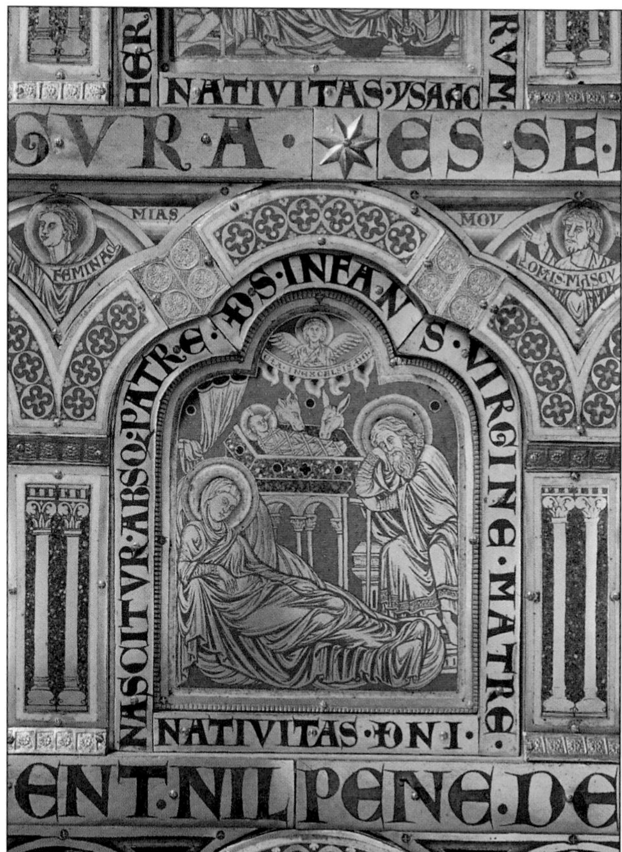

FIGURE 11.16 Nicholas of Verdun, *Birth of Jesus*, detail of the *Klosterneuburg Abbey Altarpiece*, 1181, enamel on gold, height of each plaque $5\frac{1}{2}''$ (14 cm), Klosterneuburg Abbey, Austria. By the late twelfth century, the Romanesque was being superseded by the Gothic, and evidence of greater interest in recording the visible world appeared. The drapery now reveals the form beneath, clinging and seemingly wet—unlike the flat folds unrelated to the body found in earlier Romanesque art.

an altar, a reference to his future sacrifice. He is wrapped in swaddling clothes, as babies customarily were in the Middle Ages. The ox and the ass are traditional inclusions, derived from Isaiah, intended to indicate that even these humble animals recognized Jesus' divinity. There is a sense of a three-dimensional body beneath the drapery, a return to the classical manner of depicting the relationship between the figure and the fabric that covers it. Artistic representation changed after the mid-twelfth century to accommodate a growing interest in the human figure, in nature, and in the world in general. The art of Nicholas of Verdun, located at this turning point, is moving out of the Romanesque era and into the Gothic.

CHIVALRIC TRADITION IN LITERATURE

With their men off fighting in the crusades, medieval women began to play a powerful role in everyday life. Many women of the noble class ran their family estates in their husbands' absence, and, though they had little official or legal status, they promoted a chivalric ideal in which their own position was elevated and the feudal code of stern courage and valiant warfare was displaced in favor of more genteel and refined patterns of behavior.

Troubadours. Among the most influential proponents of this new chivalric code were the **troubadours,** poet-musicians who were active in the area of Provence in southern France. Writing in Occitan, the language of southern France at that time, they wrote words to sing to original melodies (as opposed to church composers, who used chant melodies handed down from the past). Troubadours were especially active in aristocratic circles, and they sometimes had kings and queens as their

Table 11–1 SYMBOLS IN MEDIEVAL CHRISTIAN ART: ANIMALS

Medieval art makes extensive use of symbols. Virtually every animal, object, color, or number conveyed a meaning. The interpretation of the symbols may vary depending on the context in which they appear.

Ape / monkey	Symbol of sin, lust, and the devil. Monkeys are known for their ability to ape human behavior.
Bee	Symbol of industry, as in "busy as a bee."
Cat	Symbol of laziness and lust.
Centaur	A composite creature invented in antiquity, having the head of a man and the body of a horse, thus combining the human's intelligence with the horse's strength and lust; fond of wine and women.
Dog	Symbol of fidelity.
Dragon	In Western art, the dragon symbolizes the devil, sin, and evil in general; in Eastern art, in contrast, the dragon has positive connotations.
Fish	Because the initial letters of "Jesus Christ, God's son, savior" in Greek spell "fish," the fish is a symbol of Jesus.
Lamb	A sacrificial animal and therefore a symbol of Jesus.
Lion	Usually a symbol of Jesus, long regarded as "king of the beasts."
Unicorn	A composite creature invented in antiquity. Unicorns have white fur and the form of a small horse with a single horn in the middle of the forehead. The unicorn can be caught only by a virgin woman and is thus a symbol both of Jesus and of purity.

Critical Thinking

THE ART OF LOVE

In the ancient Rome of the Latin poet Ovid, love and sex were synonymous, and the goal of a man was the seduction of the beloved. As a counter to this pagan emphasis on the physical aspects of love, Christians emphasized spiritual love based on sacrifice for the beloved. In the Middle Ages, a period in which religion governed every aspect of life, court poets had to find ways to come to terms with both the physical and spiritual dimensions of love the following advice in the form of a list is offered by Andreas Capellanus from his medieval book *The Art of Courtly Love*. To what extent do you think that Capellanus has been successful in accommodating love's physical and spiritual dimensions? Does Capellanus introduce any other important aspects of love? To what extent do you think his ideas are relevant today? Explain.

1. The pretext of marriage is no proper excuse against love.
2. No one who is not jealous can love.
3. No one can have two loves at once.
4. Love is always growing or diminishing.
5. There is no savour in anything obtained by the lover against the beloved's will.
6. It is not customary for a man to love before puberty.
7. It is right that the lover should remain unmarried for two years after the death of the beloved.
8. No one should be deprived of his love without very good reason.
9. No one can love unless driven on by the prospect of love.
10. Love is always banished from the home of avarice.
11. It is not right to love women one would be ashamed to take to wife.
12. A love divulged rarely lasts.
13. The true lover desires no embraces from any other than the beloved.
14. An easy conquest makes love worthless; a difficult one gives it value.
15. Every lover grows pale at the sight of the beloved.
16. At the sudden sight of the beloved, the lover's heart quakes.
17. A new love drives out the old.
18. Honesty alone makes a person worthy of love.
19. If love grows less, its decline is swift and it seldom recovers.
20. A man in love is always fearful.
21. True jealousy always increases love's ardour.
22. A suspicion concerning the beloved increases jealousy and love's ardour.
23. A man perturbed by thoughts of love sleeps and eats less.
24. The beloved's every act ends in thoughts of the lover.
25. The true lover esteems nothing good except what he thinks will please the beloved.
26. Love can deny nothing to love.
27. The lover cannot be sated with the solace of the lover alone.
28. A slight presumption forces the lover to suspect the worst of the beloved.
29. He who is fired by too much lust is not likely to love.
30. The true lover is at all times continually absorbed in imagining the beloved.
31. Nothing prevents a woman from being loved by two men or a man from being loved by two women.

patrons. Members of the court themselves composed works too.

The chivalric values were promoted especially by Eleanor of Aquitaine, her daughter Marie of Champagne, and her granddaughter Blanche of Castille. Eleanor was herself the granddaughter of one of the first such poets, Duke William IX of Aquitaine, and together with Marie she established a "Court of Love" in Poitiers in 1170. The court was governed by a code of etiquette, which was given written form in *The Art of Courtly Love* (1170–74) by Andreas Cappelanus. Marie commissioned Cappelanus to write, and she clearly intended the book to be an accurate portrayal of life in Eleanor's court.

In fact, the court of love was first developed by Eleanor in England before she left Henry II to live with her daughter in Poitiers. Among the poets who wrote for her in England, evidence suggests, was Marie de France (twelfth century), the first woman to write verse in French. Marie de France is best known for her ***lais*** **(lays),** narratives of moderate length, which typically involve one or more miraculous or marvelous incidents and adventures concerning romantic love. A number of her *lais* concern the stories of Arthurian legend, including that of Sir Launfal. Marie's treatment of the action is less heroic than it is romantic, the characters less noble than human, the plot less concerned with grave matters of history and state than with the intimate affairs and feelings of a few people.

One of Eleanor's most gifted troubadour poets was BERNART DE VENTADORN [VEN-tuh-DOR] (d. 1195). The following stanza, from a poem apparently addressed to Eleanor herself, gives the modern reader

Then & Now

CHANT

For most of its history, chant was the official music of the Catholic Church, just as Latin was its official language. With the Vatican reforms of 1965, however, both the Church's official language and its official music were changed.

The earliest chants were transmitted orally; they were first written down in the ninth century. One explanation for the consistency of these early melodies is that they were the responsibility of a single individual—St. Gregory, who was often depicted with a dove (symbol of divine inspiration) on his shoulder.

Chant suffered a first challenge to its authority as the dominant liturgical musical form in the Reformation of the sixteenth century. Then it was supplanted in Protestant worship by hymns and cantatas such as those composed by J.S. Bach (see Chapters 14 and 15). Catholic church music during the same time developed a rich tradition of polyphony that coexisted with monophonic chant. In the 1960s, chant gave way, even in Catholic worship, to alternative forms of music, including melodies and hymn tunes in popular styles, such as gospel and folk music.

At the end of the twentieth century, however, chant had a surprising resurgence, less as a form of Catholic liturgy than as a reflection of popular musical taste. In the mid-1990s the CDs *Chant* and *Chant II* exhibited crossover power by heading both the popular and classical music charts. Sung by Spanish monks from the Benedictine abbey of Solesmes, *Chant* inangurated and reflected a renewed interest in spirituality. The mystical otherworldly character of this early music has brought a bit of the Middle Ages into the contemporary world.

some idea of the freedom of expression the troubadour poet was given:

Evil she is if she doesn't call me
To come where she undresses alone
So that I can wait her bidding
Beside the bed, along the edge,
Where I can pull off her close-fitting shoes
Down on my knees, my head bent down:
If only she'll offer me her foot.

There is no direct reference to sexual consummation, though it is implied. Adultery was strictly forbidden by the chivalric code, and though the passions expressed here are strong, they are carefully controlled. Even if in actual court life nobles succumbed to temptation, in poetry at least the notion of *courtoisie*, "courtesy," was always upheld. In the end, much of the pleasure of the poetry of courtly love is derived from the clever word play. The poetry celebrates, in its purest form, the ennobling power of friendship between man and woman.

Chrétien de Troyes. An especially popular literary form depicting the chivalric relations between knights and their ladies was the **romance,** a long narrative form taking its subject matter generally from stories surrounding King Arthur and his Knights of the Round Table. Among the very first writers to popularize the romance was CHRÉTIEN DE TROYES [CRE-tee-EN] (ca. 1148–ca. 1190), whose account of the legend of Lancelot and his adulterous affair with King Arthur's wife Guinevere became a particular favorite. Called "the perfect romance," his *Chevalier de la Charette* expresses the doctrines of courtly love in their most refined form. Identifying Lancelot with Jesus, Chrétien goes so far as to equate Lancelot's noble suffering with Jesus's passion.

MUSIC

Hildegard of Bingen. Only relatively few women, those of the nobility, could enjoy the pleasures of the court of love. Most women worked the fields alongside their husbands. Women who did not marry and thus could not hope to inherit property from their husbands often became nuns and lived in convents.

The head of one such convent was Hildegard of Bingen (1098–1179). Born to noble parents, Hildegard had a mystical vision at the age of five, and when she was eight was put into the care of a small community of nuns attached to the Benedictine monastery outside Bingen, near Frankfurt, Germany. She became a playwright and poet, and composed a cycle of seventy-seven songs in plainchant. She also wrote a book on medicine, and a book of visionary writings.

Hildegard of Bingen's music was written for performance by the nuns of her convent. Her major work, *The Symphony of the Harmony of Celestial Revelations*, which occupied her for much of her creative life, contains some of her finest work. One of her most popular compositions, O Viridissima (O Greenest Twig) features a soaring vocal live that creates a feeling of joy and serenity.

Cultural Impact

The cross page from the *Lindisfarne Gaspels*, ca. 700, in which an underlying geometric plan organizes the composition, exemplifies the emphasis on abstraction and ornamentation in the painting of the early Middle Ages. In the centuries to come, artists emphasized observation and greater realism; but in the twentieth century the pendulum of artistic taste swung back in the direction of abstraction. Thus Piet Mondrian's *Composition in Red, Yellow, and Blue* of 1920 (fig. 22.14) stresses the two dimensionality of the picture plane; the pattern created of horizontal and vertical lines is as flat as the surface on which it is painted.

The same history is found in sculpture. During the early Middle Ages and the Romanesque era, the human body is represented symbolically, as in the overtly distorted figure of Jesus at Vézelay (fig. 11.13). Artists of the Renaissance and for several centuries thereafter preferred a high degree of anatomical accuracy. The twentieth century saw the return to abstraction and distortion in sculptures such as Henry Moore's *Recumbent Figure* of 1938 (fig. 22.17).

Romanesque church architecture emphasizes massive dimensions, thick walls, semicircular arches, and barrel vaults; the barrel vault at Saint-Sernin in Toulouse, begun in the later twelfth century (fig. 11.9), represents the form of nave vaulting most frequently used during the Romanesque era. The same form reappears in the nineteenth-century Crystal Palace (fig. 17.12), designed by Joseph Paxton to display the new architectural materials (cast iron and glass) of the time—the effect very different! The massive stone forms of the Romanesque were used especially by the American architect Henry Hobson Richardson (1838–1886), himself a man of comparably generous proportions. Richardson is perhaps best known for Trinity Church in Boston, built 1873–1877, which revives the solid dimensions, semicircular arches, and barrel vaults of Romanesque architecture.

KEY TERMS

animal style
illuminated manuscript
parchment
vellum
folio
feudalism
chanson de geste
assonance
cloister
garth
refectory
guild
mystery play
plainchant
monophony
Gregorian chant
tropes
polyphony
neumes
tapestry
crusade
pilgrimage
relic
Romanesque
basilica
facade
bay
barrel vault (tunnel vault)
voussoirs
cross vault (groin vault)
campanile
blind arcade
tympanum
trumeau
mandorla
archivolt
reliquaries
troubadours
lais
romance

www. Websites for Further Study

http://www.fordham.edu/halsall/sbook.html
(The Internet Medieval Sourcebook is an excellent site with many links regarding all aspects of medieval society.)

http://www.mayo-ireland.ie/Mayo/Towns/MayAbbey/HistMAbb/Alcuin.htm
(A site focusing on Alcuin of York, the chief architect of educational reform on the continent under Charlemagne.)

http://users.aol.com/butrousch/augustine/gregory.htm
(Visit this site for a biography of Pope Gregory the Great, with relevant websites and his writings.)

http://www.medieval.org/
(The Medieval Music and Arts Foundation has many pertinent links and a wealth of information regarding medieval music.)

http://www.historymedren.about.com
(Comprehensive directory of Medieval and Renaissance art, literature, music, philosophy, religion, science, and militaria, with an emphasis on key individuals.)

http://www.history-world.org/dynamic_culture_of_medieval_euro.htm
(History and culture of early Middle Ages.)

http://www.stanford.edu/~jrdx/medieval.html
(The birth of polyphony.)

http://www.medieval.org/emfaq
(A selection of early medieval music.)

Chapter 12

History

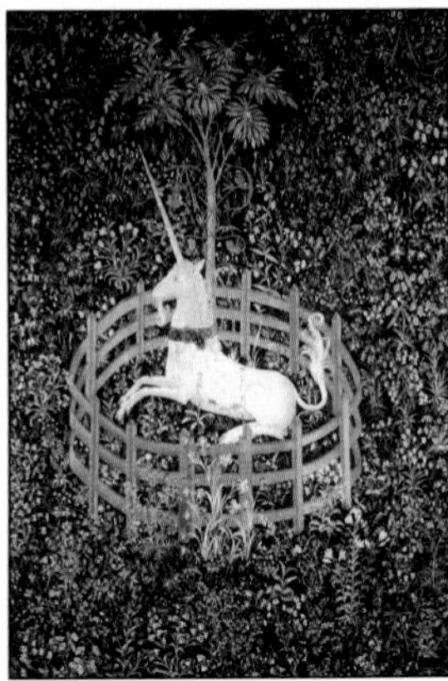

1152	Louis VII marries Eleanor of Aquitaine
1180–1223	Philip Augustus reigns
1189–99	Richard the Lionhearted reigns
1215	Magna Carta
1226–70	Louis IX reigns
1285–1314	Philip the Fair reigns
1327–77	Edward III reigns
1337–1453	Hundred Years' War
1348	Worst outbreak of bubonic plague in western Europe
1358	Étienne Marcel revolts against crown
1364–80	Charles V reigns
ca. 1550	Gothic era ends in France, aspects continue in Germany and England

Arts and Architecture

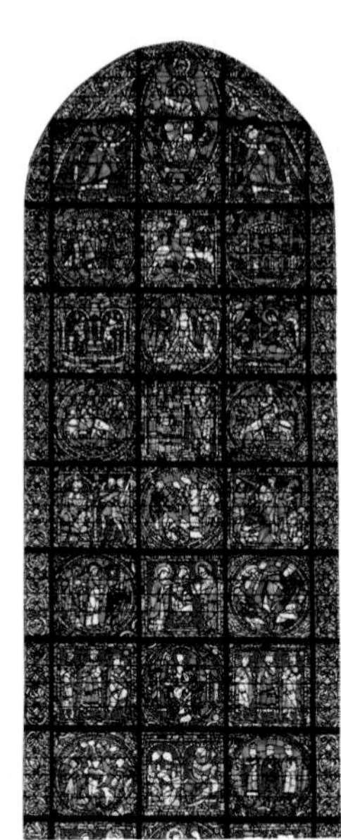

1140–45	Saint-Denis, choir and ambulatory
1145–55	Column figures of Royal Portals, cathedral, Chartres
1145–1220	Notre-Dame Cathedral, Chartres
begun 1163	Notre-Dame Cathedral, Paris
ca. 1175	Leonin, chant composer active
ca. 1200	Perotin, chant composer active
1220–66/70	Nicholas of Ely et al., Salisbury Cathedral
1243–48	Sainte-Chapelle, Paris
1259–60; 1302–10	Nicholas and Giovanni Pisano depictions of the *Nativity*
ca. 1260	*Psalter of St. Louis,* illuminated manuscript
begun 1296	Florence Cathedral
1300–77	Machaut, *ars nova* composer
1305–06	Giotto, Arena Chapel
1308–11	Duccio, *Madonna and Child Enthroned*
1346	Machaut, *Mass of Notre Dame*
late fourteenth century	Milan Cathedral
1413–16	Limbourg brothers, *Les Très Riches Heures*
ca. 1500	*Unicorn tapestries*
1503–19	Robert and William Vertue, Chapel of Henry VII, Westminster Abbey, London

Literature and Philosophy

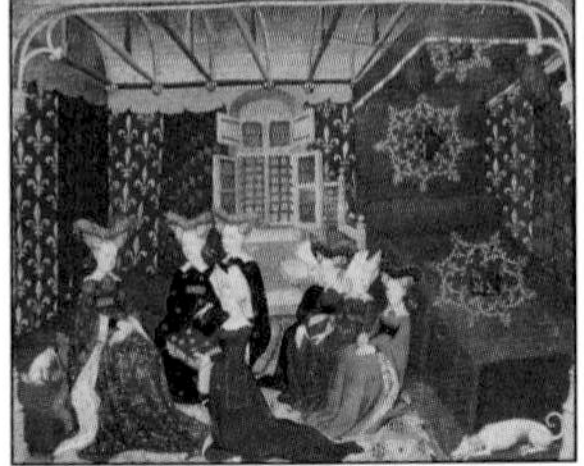

1181–1226	Francis of Assisi
1265–74	St. Thomas Aquinas, *Summa Theologica*
1320	Dante, *Divine Comedy*
1349–51	Boccaccio, *Decameron*
1386–1400	Chaucer, *The Canterbury Tales*
1405	Christine de Pizan, *Book of the City of Ladies*

Gothic and Late Middle Ages

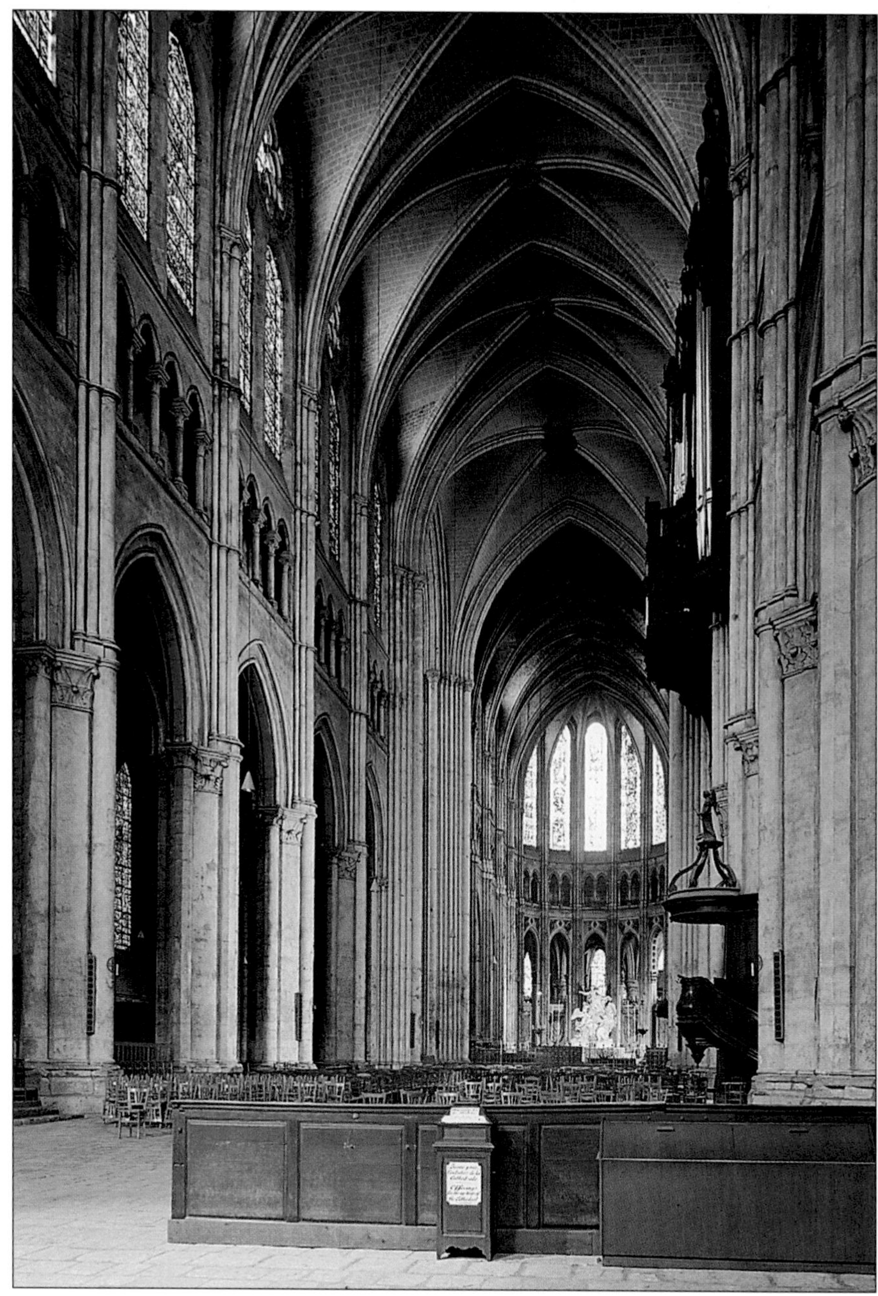

Cathedral of Notre-Dame, Chartres, nave looking toward altar, rebuilding begun 1145, vault finished by 1220.

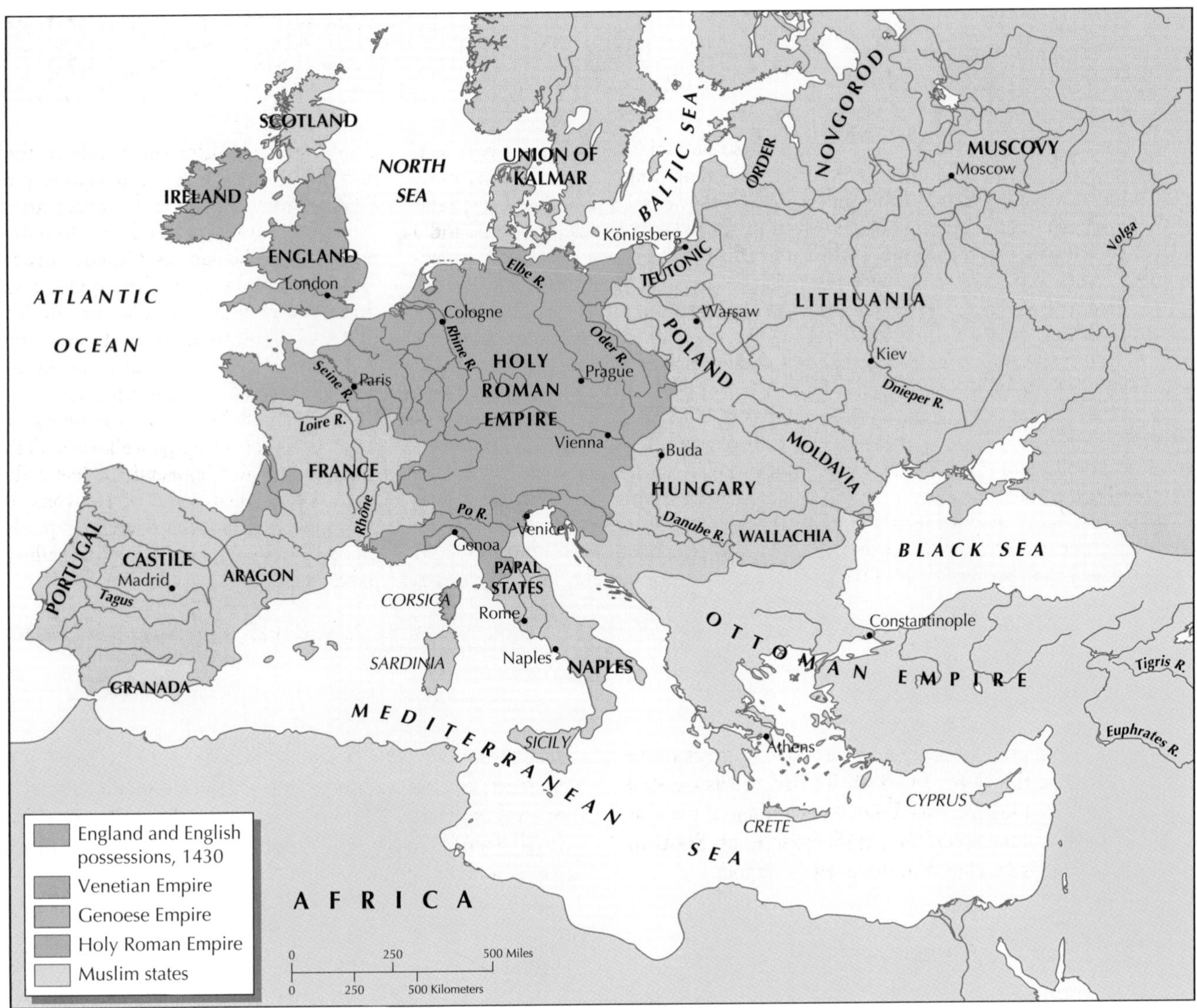

MAP 12.1 Europe during the Hundred Years' War, 1337–1453.

CHAPTER OVERVIEW

GOTHIC ERA

Age of the great cathedrals of western Europe, richly embellished

TOWARD THE RENAISSANCE

Trends toward naturalism and realism in painting and sculpture

GOTHIC ERA

PARIS IN THE LATER MIDDLE AGES

NO CITY DOMINATED THE LATER MIDDLE AGES more than Paris. Home to a revival in learning at the newly founded university, Paris was also the seat of the French government, overseen by King Louis IX (later St. Louis) (r. 1226–70). The monarchy had not enjoyed such power and respect since the time of Charlemagne. Louis made a determined effort to be a king to all his people, sending royal commissioners into the countryside to monitor the administration of local government and to ensure justice for all. He outlawed private warfare and granted his subjects the right to appeal to higher courts. Furthermore, he became something of a peacekeeper among the

Then & Now

THE LOUVRE

The Louvre today is one of the most famous museums in the world. It is also the largest royal palace in the world, a building that has undergone more redevelopment through the ages than any other building in Europe. The first building on the site was a fortress, erected in 1200 by Philip Augustus, with a keep, the symbol of royal power, surrounded by a moat. Today, remnants of the moat and keep can be viewed on the bottom floor of the museum.

Charles V used the building as a royal residence, but over the years its galleries and arcades have also served as a prison, an arsenal, a mint, a granary, a county seat, a publishing house, a ministry, the Institute for Advanced Studies, a telegraph station, a shopping arcade, a tavern, and a hotel for visiting heads of state. The expansive and open plan of the Louvre today, with its two great arms extending from the original building west to the Tuileries Gardens, is the result of later additions. In the latter part of the sixteenth century, Henry IV added the Grand Galleries, initially conceived as a covered walkway connecting the palace to the garden. In the seventeenth century, Louis XIV closed off the east end, forming the Cour Carrée.

The result of these additions and alterations is a building that represents almost every architectural style in the history of the West. A Romanesque fortress forms its basis, and outward from it spread two Gothic and two Renaissance wings. Baroque and Rococo ornamentation can be found throughout, and the closed-off end is Neoclassical. In this spirit of heterogeneity and plurality, architect I. M. Pei designed a glass pyramid to serve as the museum's new entrance in 1988. Set above a network of underground rooms and walkways, Pei's pyramid is 61 feet high and 108 feet wide at the base, constructed of 105 tons of glass. Beside it are flat triangular pools that reflect the walls of the surrounding palace.

other European powers, and he was in most matters more influential than the pope. In short, he became associated with fairness and justice, and France consolidated itself as a nation around him, with Paris as its focal point. Soon all roads led to Paris, as they had once led to Rome.

GOTHIC ARCHITECTURE

The term **Gothic** refers to the style of visual arts and culture that first developed, beginning about 1140, in the Ile-de-France, and reached its zenith in the thirteenth century. From the mid-thirteenth through the mid-fourteenth century, Paris was an important source of artistic inspiration for the rest of France, Germany, and England; Italy remained quite separate aesthetically. By the middle of the sixteenth century, the Gothic style was at an end in France, although aspects of it continued to influence artists in Germany and England until the seventeenth century.

What is now called "Gothic art" was originally called the "French style," and referred to architecture. Architecture, in fact, dominates the era, for this is the age of the great **cathedrals** of northern Europe. However, it was the Italians who gave the style its name; preferring the classical style, the Italians thought the Gothic barbaric and identified it with the most notorious of the barbarian tribes, the Goths. Thus the style was labeled "Gothic," with a decidedly derogatory intent.

The Gothic style developed out of the Romanesque. Romanesque buildings are broad and massive, characterized by semicircular arches, thick walls, and closely spaced supports that create a feeling of security. Solid and heavy, Romanesque buildings seem to be bound to the earth. In contrast, Gothic buildings have a soaring quality, for the vertical is constantly emphasized and the walls are thin. Small Romanesque windows give way in Gothic architecture to vast windows of stained glass.

Gothic architecture was confident and daring. The tremendous height of the buildings was a reflection of religious ideals and enthusiasm, of inspiration and aspiration. The vast naves of the Gothic cathedrals create an extraordinary atmosphere of spirituality. The chants sung here reverberated from the high vaults.

The structural innovations (fig. 12.1) that characterized this new style include the following:

1. **Pointed arches and vaults** that exert less lateral thrust than the semicircular Romanesque arches and vaults. The pointed ribbed vault can be constructed in a variety of floor plans and, in theory, built to any height.
2. **Ribs** that serve to concentrate the weight of the vault at certain points, making it possible to eliminate the wall between these points.
3. **Flying buttresses** that were introduced in response to the problem created by the lateral thrust exerted by a true vault. The idea of a buttress, a solid mass of masonry used to reinforce a wall, was an old one. But the "flying" part, the exterior arch, was an invention of the Gothic era. Flying buttresses project outward on the exterior of the building and cannot be seen from the inside through the stained glass windows.

Royal Abbey, Saint-Denis. The Gothic style began at the Royal Abbey of Saint-Denis, located just north of Paris.

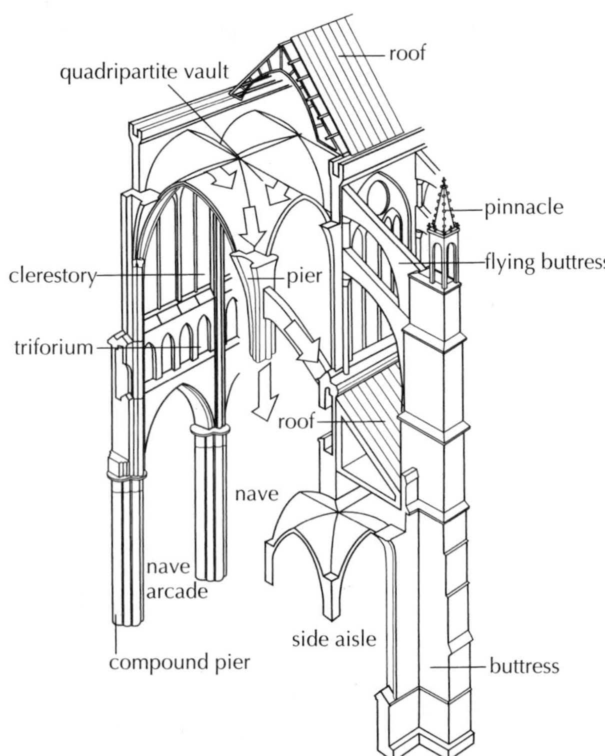

FIGURE 12.1 The principal features of a Gothic church include the nave and aisles; triforium/gallery; clerestory, pointed arches; ribbed vaults; and flying buttresses.

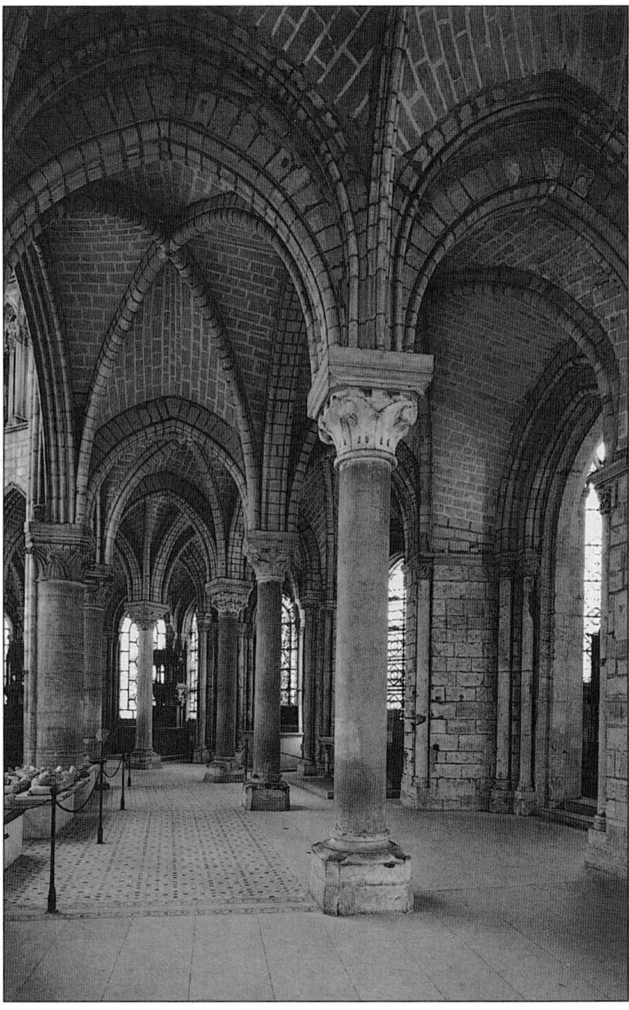

FIGURE 12.2 Royal Abbey, Saint-Denis. Ambulatory, 1140–44. The eccentric and egocentric Abbot Suger initiated the Gothic style of architecture, characterized by a new lightness of proportion and sense of flowing space. The pointed Gothic arches exert less lateral thrust than the Romanesque semicircular arches, and the ribs reinforce the vaults.

The first church on the site was erected in 475 in honor of St. Denis, who went to Paris around 250 C.E. to convert the Gauls and was rewarded for his efforts by being tortured on a hot grill and then decapitated. St. Denis is said to have picked up his head and walked north to the site where the abbey was subsequently built.

The parts of the abbey of Saint-Denis that herald the beginning of the Gothic were built under Abbot SUGER [SOO-zjay] (1081–1151) around 1140. A Benedictine monk, Suger advised successive kings of France and was even regent of the country during the Second Crusade. He regarded the church as symbolic of the kingdom of God on earth and was intent on making Saint-Denis as magnificent as possible. Suger rebuilt the facade, the narthex, and the east end of Saint-Denis. He commissioned a golden altar, jeweled crosses, chalices, vases, and ewers made of precious materials. This richness was in honor of God, France, and possibly also Suger. At a time when humble anonymity was the norm, Suger had himself depicted in stained glass and sculpture and his name included in inscriptions.

The first large and truly Gothic building, Saint-Denis served as the prototype for other Gothic structures. The facade of Saint-Denis was the first to synthesize monumental sculpture and architecture. Its two towers, **rose window** (a circular window with tracery radiating from its center to form a roselike symmetrical pattern), rows of figures representing Jesus' biblical ancestors, and column figures on the jambs all became standard features of later Gothic cathedrals. Today, the ambulatory and the seven chapels of the ambulatory remain as they were in Suger's day (fig. 12.2).

In Suger's plan, the divisions between the chapels are almost eliminated. Each chapel has two large windows. This introduction of light was a new concept. The space is not divided into distinct units, as in Romanesque architecture. Instead, without the solid walls and massive supports of the Romanesque, Gothic space flows freely and areas merge with each other.

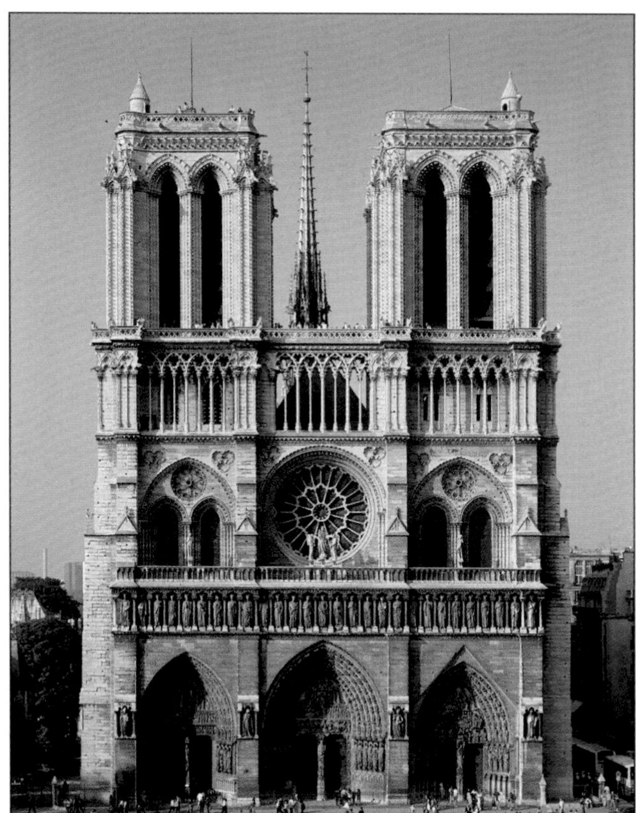

FIGURE 12.3 Cathedral of Notre-Dame, Paris, west facade, 1163–ca. 1250, mostly first half of thirteenth century. This celebrated cathedral is an example of the first phase of the Gothic, referred to as Early Gothic. In Romanesque architecture horizontals dominated; here horizontals and verticals balance; soon the verticals will dominate.

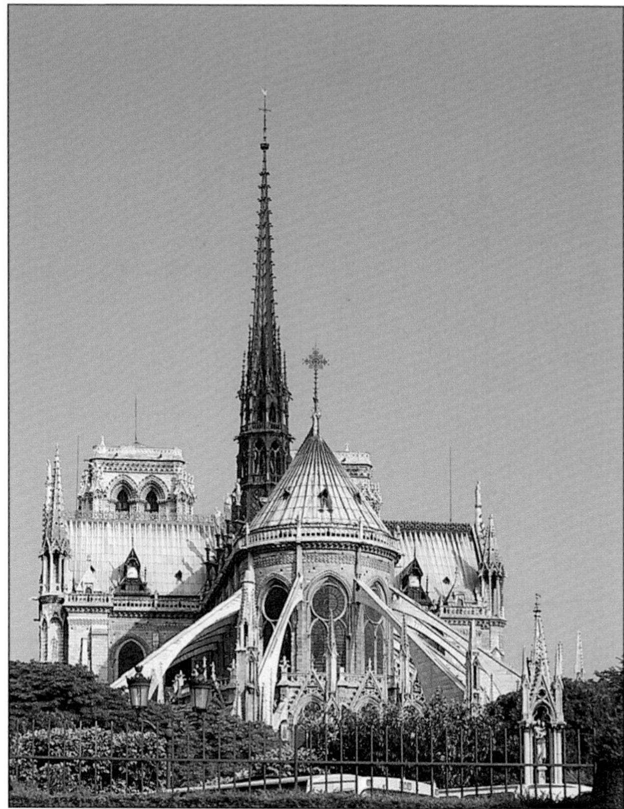

FIGURE 12.4 Cathedral of Notre-Dame, Paris, 1163–ca. 1250, apse, flying buttresses added in the 1180s. Exterior wall buttresses have a long history; innovative are the arch-shaped flying buttresses, used especially on large multistoried buildings to absorb the lateral thrust exerted by the vaulting. The solid walls of Romanesque architecture were replaced by the characteristically Gothic flying buttresses.

Notre-Dame, Paris. The Cathedral of Notre-Dame-de-Paris (Our Lady of Paris) (fig. 12.3), is located in the heart of Paris on the Ile-de-la-Cité, an island in the Seine River. The historical center of the city, Gallo-Roman ramparts once fortified the site, and earlier churches had been built there as well. Bishop Maurice of Sully, founder of the cathedral, had these removed, however.

Construction of Notre-Dame started in 1163. Work began with the choir—the construction of a church or cathedral usually commences at the choir end. With few exceptions the Christian altar is oriented to the east, the church entrance toward the west. Notre-Dame was first finished in 1235. Reconstruction began almost immediately. The vaulting of the choir was redone; almost all the clerestory windows were enlarged; the flying buttresses were doubled; the transepts were rebuilt; and work was carried out on over forty chapels. All this remodeling took several decades.

The facade (fig. 12.3) dates, for the most part, from the first half of the thirteenth century. Large amounts of wall are still evident, a holdover from the Romanesque period. The facade's equilibrium of horizontals and verticals creates a masterpiece of balance. Based on a sequence of squares, one inside another, the entire facade is one large square, 142 feet on each side. The towers are one-half the height of the whole solid area—a simple, satisfying geometry.

In the 1180s, the first flying buttresses (fig. 12.4) were added at Notre-Dame to stabilize its great height. The buttresses are in two parts: The outer buttress is exposed; the inner buttress is hidden under the roof of the inner aisle. From this time forward, flying buttresses would play an important structural and visual role in Gothic architecture.

Notre-Dame, Chartres. The Cathedral of Notre-Dame in Chartres (fig. 12.5), a spectacular structure with splendid sculpture and sparkling stained glass, begins the **High Gothic.**

Chartres Cathedral was intended to be a "terrestrial palace" for Jesus' mother Mary, built on the highest part of the city in order to bring it closer to heaven. This cathedral possesses an important relic of Mary. Known as the

Connections

NUMEROLOGY AT CHARTRES

At the cathedral school at Chartres, Plato's theory of the correspondence between visual and musical proportions and the beauty of the cosmos was carefully studied. The number three, also important in Christian theology, assumed special importance for the builders at Chartres. It symbolized the Holy Trinity and Plato's secular trinity of truth, beauty, and goodness.

The architecture of Chartres is replete with threes—on the exterior a three-story facade is matched by three corresponding interior levels, culminating in the colored light of the clerestory. There are three semicircular chapels off the apse, and each clerestory window consists of one rose and two lancet windows. The six-petaled rose in the mosaic in the center of the nave represents the sum of one, two, and three.

The number nine, associated with Jesus' mother Mary, is also of special importance. The cathedral, which houses fabric said to be part of her veil from the Nativity, celebrates her number. Mary is, as Dante said, "the square of the Trinity." Chartres has nine entrance portals—three times three—and in its original plan it was to have nine towers, two on the facade, two on each of the transepts, two flanking the apse, and one rising over the crossing.

FIGURE 12.5 Cathedral of Notre-Dame, Chartres, rebuilding 1145–1220; north spire 1507–13. This cathedral dominates the surrounding landscape and is visible for miles around; Gothic cathedrals were routinely built on the highest site available. The typical French Gothic facade has one rose (wheel) window, two towers, and three entry portals.

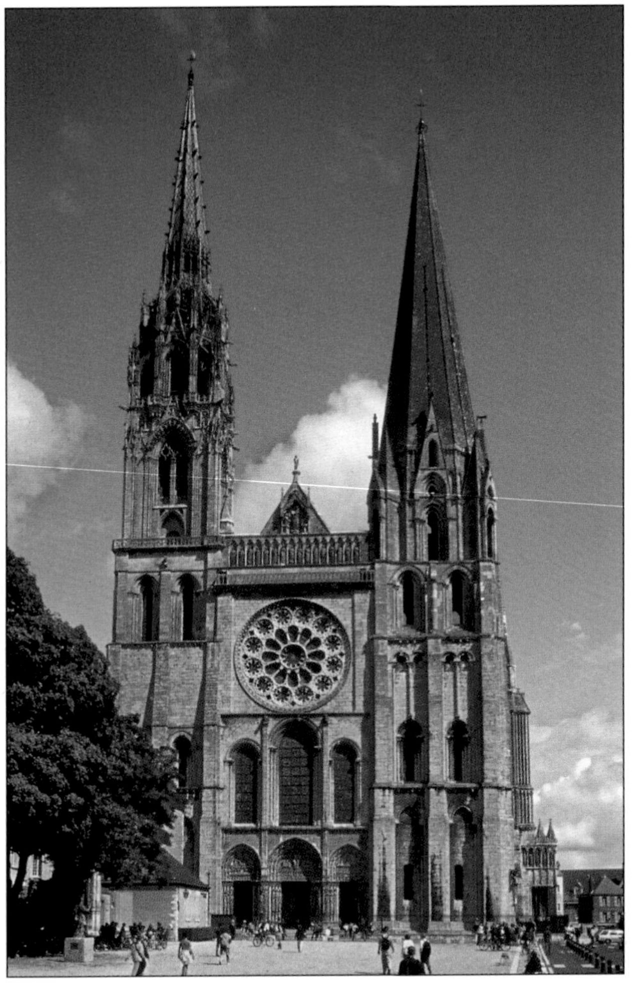

sancta camisia, it is a piece of cloth, said to have been worn by Mary when Jesus was born. Chartres was believed to be protected by Mary and became an extremely popular pilgrimage site. Although it was believed to have produced many miracles, the relic could not fend off fire, constant enemy of churches during the Middle Ages and the cause of the cathedral's destruction in 1020. Rebuilding began immediately and, by 1024, a new crypt was finished. Known as "Fulbert's Crypt," it is still the largest crypt in France. A Romanesque cathedral was then constructed on the site, but in 1134 fire destroyed the town, and the building was damaged. The Royal Portals and the stained glass windows on the west facade were made 1145–55. In 1194, there was yet another fire in which the cathedral suffered great damage. Little more than Fulbert's Crypt and the Royal Portals and windows survived.

Mary's cloth, safe in the crypt, did survive the fire of 1194. Taken as a sign to build a yet more magnificent monument, the people of Chartres gave money, labor, and time, all social classes participating, from the high nobility to the humble peasantry. Rough limestone was brought from five miles away in carts, an activity referred to as the "cult of the carts." By 1220, the main structure and the vaults were finished, built with great speed and in a consistent style. In 1260, the cathedral was dedicated. Like the facade of Notre-Dame in Paris, Chartres has four buttresses, three portals, two towers, and one rose window. Yet, at Chartres, the two facade towers are strikingly dissimilar. The south spire is 344 feet high, built at the same time as the rest of the upper facade. But the north steeple of the early sixteenth century, built in a much more **Flamboyant Gothic** style, rises 377 feet. Each tower was constructed in the style popular at the time of its construction.

Chartres is the first masterpiece of the High Gothic, the first cathedral to be planned with flying buttresses (at Notre-Dame in Paris they are later additions), and to use them for the entire cathedral, as made clear by the plan (fig. 12.6). The buttresses at Chartres are designed as an integral part of the structure. They join the wall at the critical point of thrust, between the clerestory windows, where there is a minimum of stone and a maximum of glass.

The nave (fig. 12.7) is soaring, open, and airy. Whereas the nave at Notre-Dame in Paris is just over 108 feet high, Chartres' is 121 feet high and 422 feet long. The three-story elevation consists of the arcade, the triforium, and the clerestory. The clerestory windows are tall and narrow, emphasizing the vertical rather than the horizontal. A vast amount of window area is permitted by the exterior buttressing, yet this does not produce a brightly lit interior. Instead, stained glass provides colored and changing light in the windows themselves and flickering light over the stone interior.

Sainte-Chapelle, Paris. By the middle of the thirteenth century, a new **Rayonnant** style of Gothic architecture had begun to emerge. The name "Rayonnant" comes from the French *rayonner*, which means "to shine" or "to radiate." The move to this new phase was the result of a changing sense of harmony and the gradual substitution of window for wall. In this Rayonnant style, stone tracery divisions between the areas of glass in rose windows were made thinner and ever more intricate.

Paris under King Louis IX was the center for the Rayonnant style. Louis acquired a portion of Jesus' crown of thorns and many other relics, including a piece of Jesus' cross, iron fragments of the holy spear that pierced his side, the holy sponge, the robe, the shroud of Jesus, a nail from the crucifixion, and part of the skull of St. John the Baptist. Louis had these relics placed in an ornate shrine in the Sainte-Chapelle.

Rich and refined, the Sainte-Chapelle looks like an enormous reliquary. Its architectural importance is not due to great scale; when compared to other Gothic buildings, the Sainte-Chapelle is extremely small—the interior is a mere 108 feet long, and 35 feet wide. Divided into a lower and an upper chapel, the lower is only a little under 22 feet high, and the upper only just over 67 feet. The upper chapel (fig. 12.8) was dedicated to the Holy Crown of

FIGURE 12.6 Cathedral of Notre-Dame, Chartres, plan. When building with pointed arches, ribbed vaulting, and flying buttresses (shown projecting from the aisles, transepts, and apse), in theory, there is no limit to the height attainable. Soaring heavenward, the nave of Notre-Dame in Paris rises over 108 feet and that of Notre-Dame in Chartres 121 feet. Beauvais Cathedral, at 158 feet, collapsed, demonstrating the practical limits of the structural system.

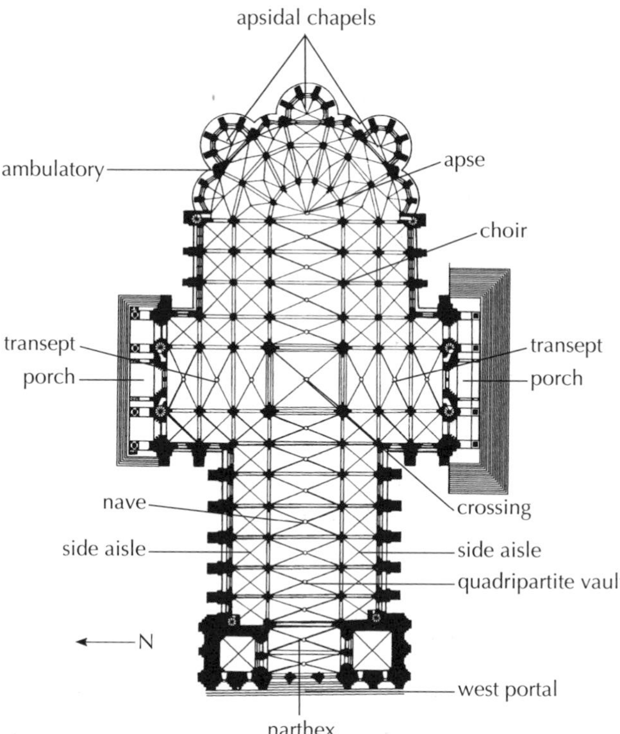

FIGURE 12.7 Cathedral of Notre-Dame, Chartres, nave looking toward altar, rebuilding begun 1145, vault finished by 1220. The first architectural masterpiece of the second phase of the Gothic, known as the High Gothic, Chartres Cathedral was designed from the start to have flying buttresses. In this three-story nave elevation, large clerestory windows allow light to enter directly into the nave, the deep colors of stained glass creating an atmosphere of multicolored light.

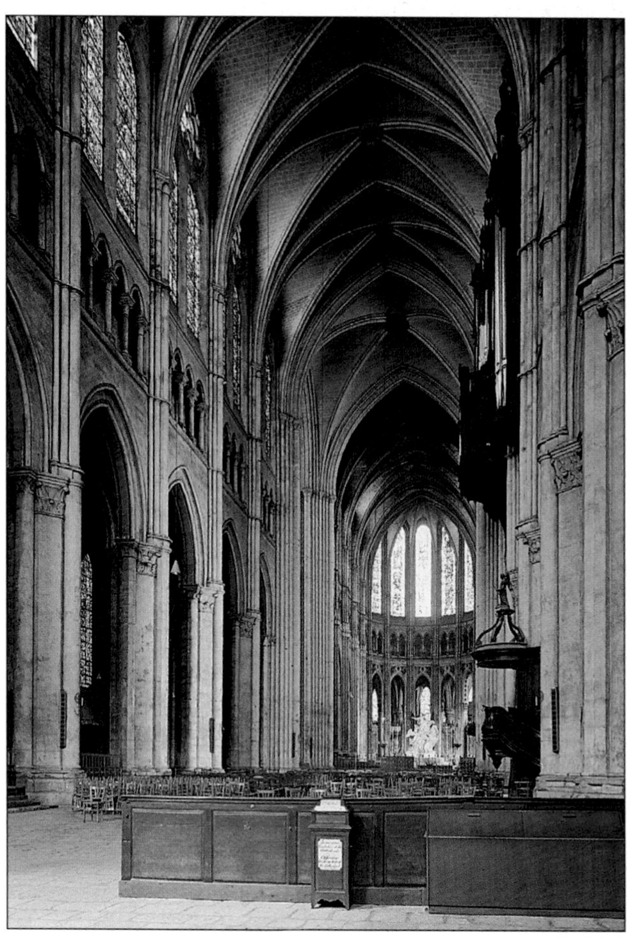

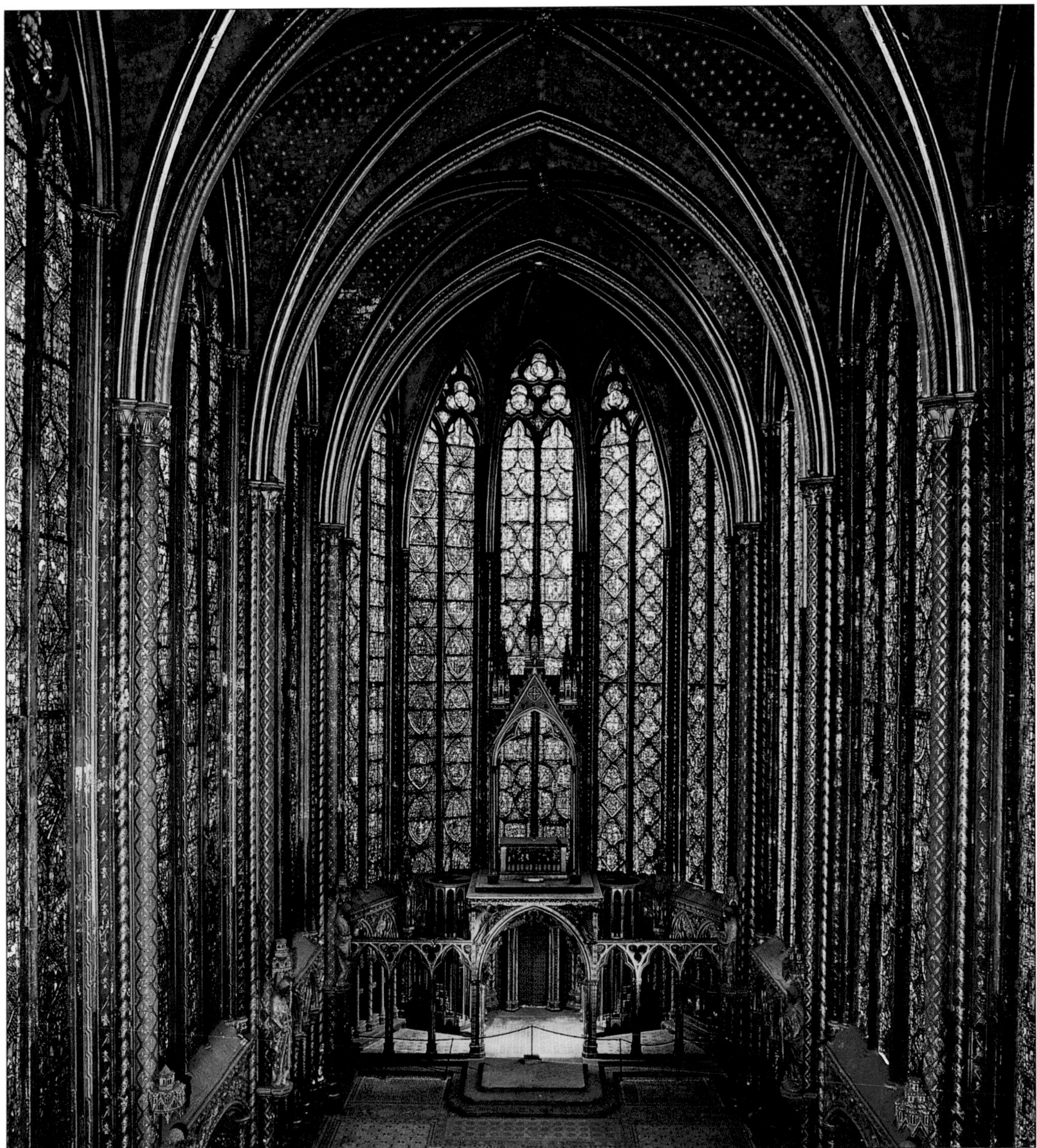

FIGURE 12.8 Pierre de Montreuil (?), Sainte-Chapelle, Paris, upper chapel, looking toward apse, 1243–48. In this example of the third phase, the Rayonnant Gothic, the amount of masonry is reduced and the building becomes a cage of glass. Standing inside the upper chapel, when sunlight streams through the stained-glass windows, it is as if one is standing inside a sparkling, multicolored, multifaceted jewel.

Thorns and the Holy Cross. The plan is simple, consisting of only the nave of four rectangular bays and a seven-sided apse. The walls disappear. The lines soar. The windows are shafts of light. A cage of glass and stone, the Sainte-Chapelle appears to defy the laws of gravity. All the space between the piers is given over to huge windows, with more than three-quarters of the walls actually stained glass. The piers project inward over three feet, but their bulk is masked by groups of nine colonettes. All other supports are placed outside, leaving the interior a continuous uninterrupted space. In 1323, Master Jean de Jandun described his experience of the chapel in the following way: "On entering, one would think oneself transported to heaven and one might with reason imagine oneself taken into one of the most beautiful mansions of paradise."

The program of the upper chapel glass relates to the relics kept there. The central apse window shows Jesus' passion, introduced by the Old Testament stories in the nave. The cycle begins on the north side with the Book of Genesis and concludes on the south side with the story of the relics of the passion, especially the crown of thorns, and their arrival in Paris. The French king is depicted alongside kings David and Solomon. The windows of the Sainte-Chapelle include a great number of coronation scenes—twenty plus that of Jesus, seemingly linking French royalty and biblical royalty.

Saint-Maclou, Rouen. Saint-Maclou in Rouen (fig. 12.9), a small parish church, is the paradigm of the Flamboyant Gothic style, the final phase in the development of Gothic architecture. The church was designed in 1434 by Pierre Robin, although the facade was probably designed by Ambroise Havel. Its most striking feature is the porch, which is faceted into three planes and thus bows outward.

Called Flamboyant because of the flamelike curving stone tracery (*flamboyant* is the French for "flaming"), this style is characterized more by ornament than by structure. Delighting in delicacy and complexity, the masons covered the church in lace-like fantasy. Indeed, the ornament obscures the structure beneath it. Exuberant and interlacing, the steeply pitched openwork gables form a surface tangle that is animated by light and shadow as the sun moves.

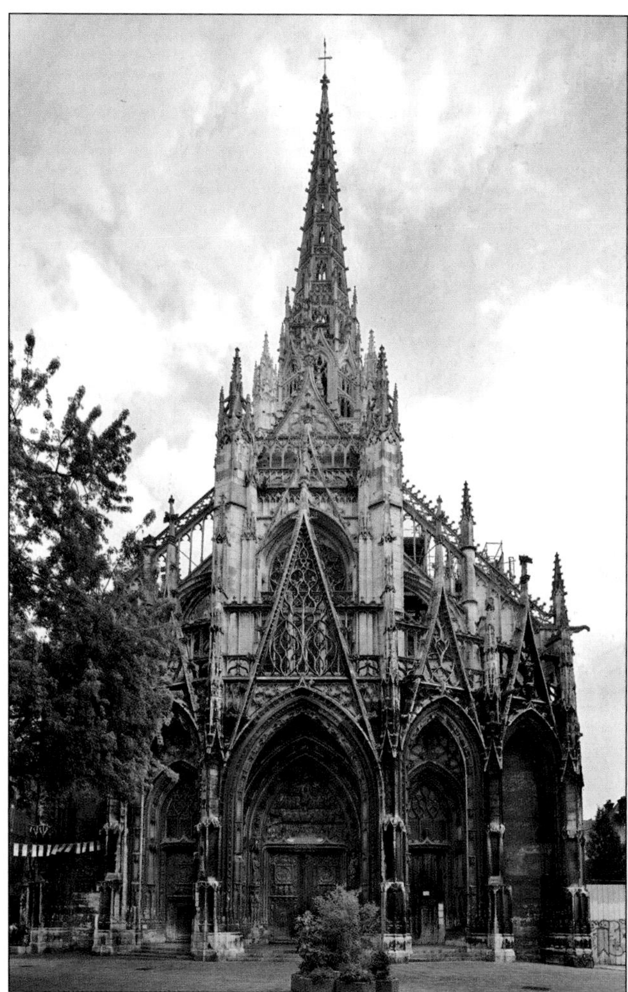

FIGURE 12.9 Pierre Robin, Saint-Maclou, Rouen, designed 1434, west facade designed by Ambroise Havel (?) 1500–21. The finest example of the fourth and final phase of the Gothic, the Flamboyant or Late Gothic, this small building has enough decoration to equal that of a huge cathedral. The lacy stone tracery is "flamboyant"—flamelike—with its undulating curves.

GOTHIC ARCHITECTURE OUTSIDE FRANCE

Salisbury Cathedral. The French Gothic spread outside France, each country modifying it to its own tastes. In England, the Early Gothic was relatively understated, but the Late Gothic reached extremes of eccentricity beyond anything found in France.

Early English Gothic is represented by Salisbury Cathedral (fig. 12.10). The choir, Lady Chapel, transepts, and nave were built between 1220 and 1258 by Nicholas of Ely and work was finally completed by 1270. The expansive structure, which measures 473 by 230 feet, lacks a rounded apse, ambulatory, and radiating chapels found in France, having instead, as is typical of English Gothic, a square east end. The nave has ten bays instead of the seven usually found in France.

The facade of Salisbury Cathedral, although begun in the same year as Amiens Cathedral, has very different proportions. Salisbury is low and wide, as if stretched horizontally, with no particular emphasis on height. The facade is wider, in fact, than the church and is treated as a screen, divided into horizontal bands with emphasis placed on the sculpture, not on the portals. English cathedrals are usually entered by a porch on the side of the nave or on the transept. Flying buttresses, so characteristic of French Gothic, were used only sparingly in England.

Westminster Abbey, London. After English Gothic architects had thoroughly mastered initial structural problems, they refined and enriched their forms. Vaulting

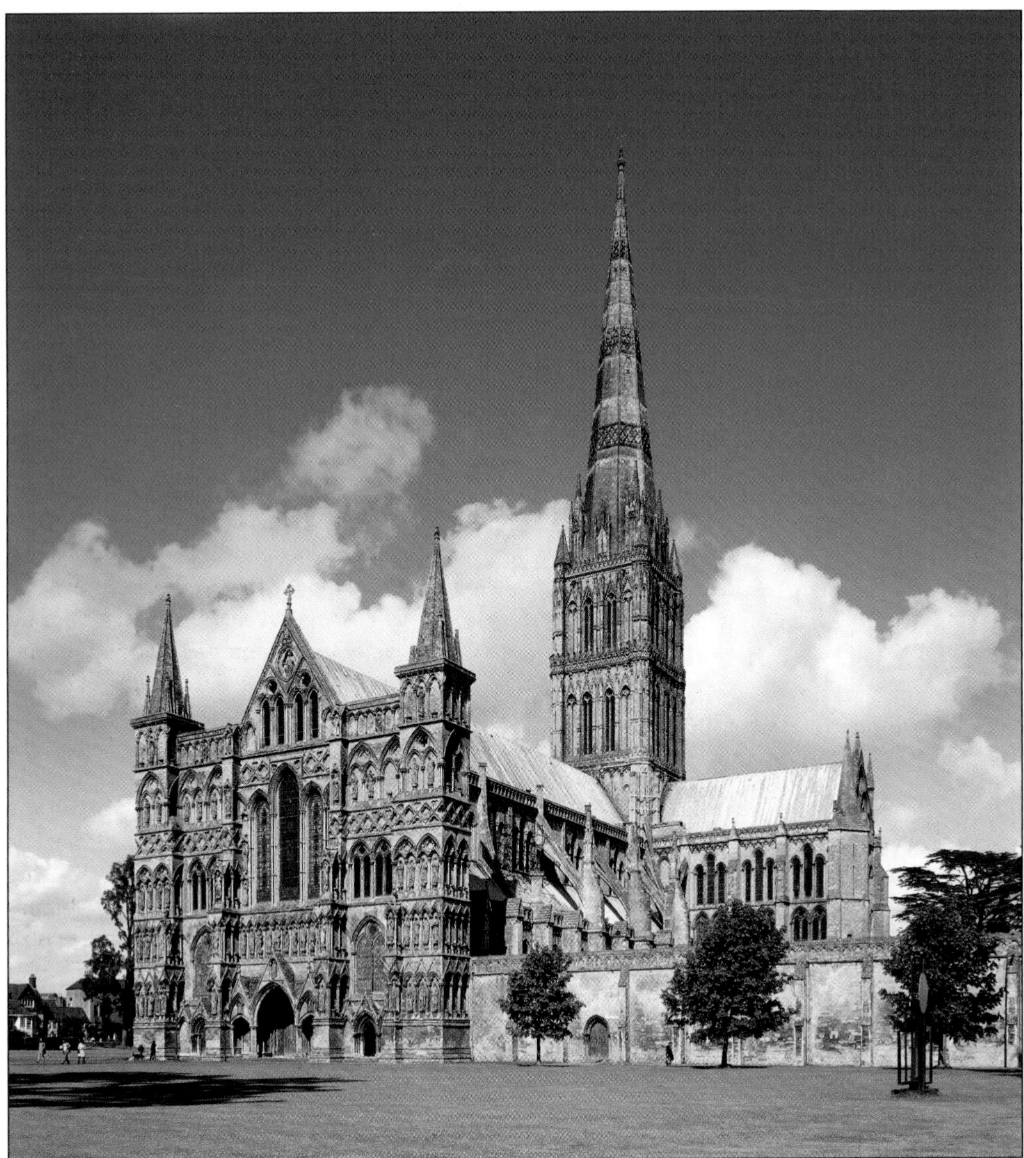

FIGURE 12.10 Nicholas of Ely, Cathedral, Salisbury, west facade, 1220–70. Typical of early English Gothic, Salisbury is sprawling in plan, surrounded by a green lawn, and makes little use of flying buttresses—as opposed to French Gothic cathedrals, which are typically compact in plan, located in the city center, and rely on flying buttresses for structural support.

became progressively more adventurous. The ultimate example of English vaulting is in Westminster Abbey, London, culminating in the fantastic chapel of Henry VII (fig. 12.11), by the architects Robert and William Vertue. The tomb of Henry VII is behind a grill at the back of the altar. William Vertue replaced the axial chapel, originally built in 1220, with this one, built 1503–19. The most remarkable feature is the ceiling, an example of **fan vaulting,** thus called because the ribs radiate in a manner similar to those on a fan. But here the idea is carried to an extreme, to become pendant vaults hanging down in knobs, apparently denying both logic and gravity. Describing the chapel, one historian noted, "Its extraordinary, petrified foliage gives the impression of some fantastic, luminous grotto encrusted with stalactites." Elaborate designs cover the entire surface, an indication of the English inclination toward the architectural extreme, the eccentric, the intricate, and the opulent.

Florence Cathedral. Italy was little affected by the Gothic style. Instead of the elaborate buttress systems and large windows popular in the north, Italian architects favored large wall surfaces with emphasis on the horizontal, as is evident in the landmarks of the city of Florence—its cathedral (*duomo*), bell tower (*campanile*), and baptistery (fig. 12.12).

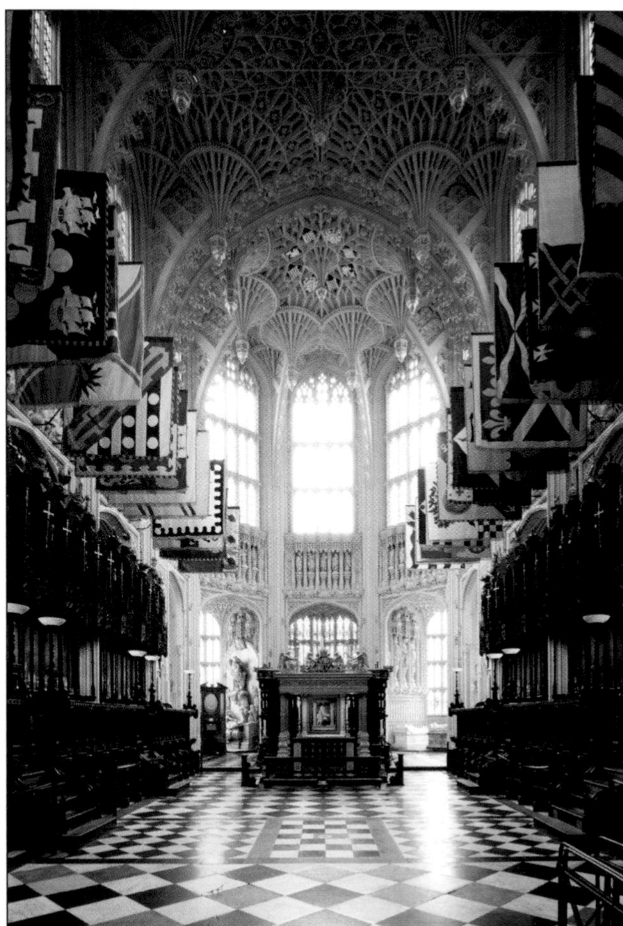

FIGURE 12.11 Robert and William Vertue, Chapel of Henry VII, Westminster Abbey, London, 1503–19, interior. The radiating ribs of fan vaulting are taken to an extreme here, becoming pendant vaults that actually hang down into the space of the chapel. The surface dissolves in this late and extreme example of English architectural eccentricity.

The single most important construction work carried out during the Gothic era in Florence was that done on the cathedral. There had been an older church on the site, but in 1296, Arnolfo di Cambio began to build a new cathedral. Work started atypically at the west (entrance) end and proceeded quickly, until Arnolfo's death in 1302. Work gradually continued over a long period of time, with various architects involved. The cathedral is distinctive for its flat, colorful marble incrustation.

In 1334, Giotto was appointed architect-in-chief of the building of Florence Cathedral. Giotto, however, was a painter who knew little about architectural structure and was to design only the campanile. His original drawing of it survives, from which it is known that he intended the tower to be topped by a spire. When Giotto died in 1337, only the first floor of the tower was finished. Work was continued by Andrea Pisano among others, and finished by Francesco Talenti in a somewhat different design around 1350–60. The interior of the tower consists of a series of rooms connected by staircases.

The campanile is referred to as "Giotto's Tower." Although the freestanding campanile is typically Italian, it is not an invention of the Italian Gothic; the campanile of Pisa, the famous "leaning tower," was built in the Romanesque era (see fig. 11.11). The richly ornamented Gothic campanile of Florence, with its multicolored marble incrustation and sculpture, served not only as the bell tower but also as a symbol of the sovereignty of the Florence commune.

SCULPTURE

Notre-Dame, Chartres. The logical place to find the earliest Gothic sculpture would be Saint-Denis, but the work there has been badly damaged. Fortunately, the sculpture at Chartres Cathedral has fared better. The cathedral has three triple portals, on the west facade and the north and south transepts, all richly adorned with sculpture. On the west are the Royal Portals (fig. 12.13), from the early Gothic era, dated ca. 1145–55. All the sculpture was once painted and gilded, but now only beige stone remains.

Each of the three entrances of the Royal Portal is flanked by statues. Symmetrical, ordered, and clear, Gothic compositions can typically be grasped at a glance, whereas the Romanesque preferred greater complexity. These **jamb** figures form what is known as a "precursor portal," of a type first seen at Saint-Denis and perhaps started by Abbot Suger. The visitor passes by Old Testament figures to enter the church. Those without crowns are the prophets, priests, and patriarchs of the Old Testament, Jesus' spiritual precursors. Those with crowns are the kings and queens of Judah—Jesus and Mary's physical ancestors. Medieval iconography is complex, with layered meanings, permitting multiple interpretations. Thus, in addition to being the royal ancestors of Mary and Jesus, the kings and queens of Judah are also associated with the kings and queens of France, joining together religious and secular authority. Further, the church was an earthly version of the heavenly Jerusalem, and these portals were regarded as the "gates of heaven," through which Christians could enter a symbolic journey through biblical history to arrive at Jesus in the present.

Such jamb figures are also called "column figures," as the shape of the figure follows that of the column. Sculpture here is very closely tied to architecture. Unlike their energetic Romanesque forerunners, these figures are calm and serene, with a noble dignity. There is no twisting, turning, or bending; they do not interact with one another or with the viewer. The drapery, of many linear folds that fall to perfect zigzag hems, looks much like the fluting of a column, stressing the architectural role of these figures.

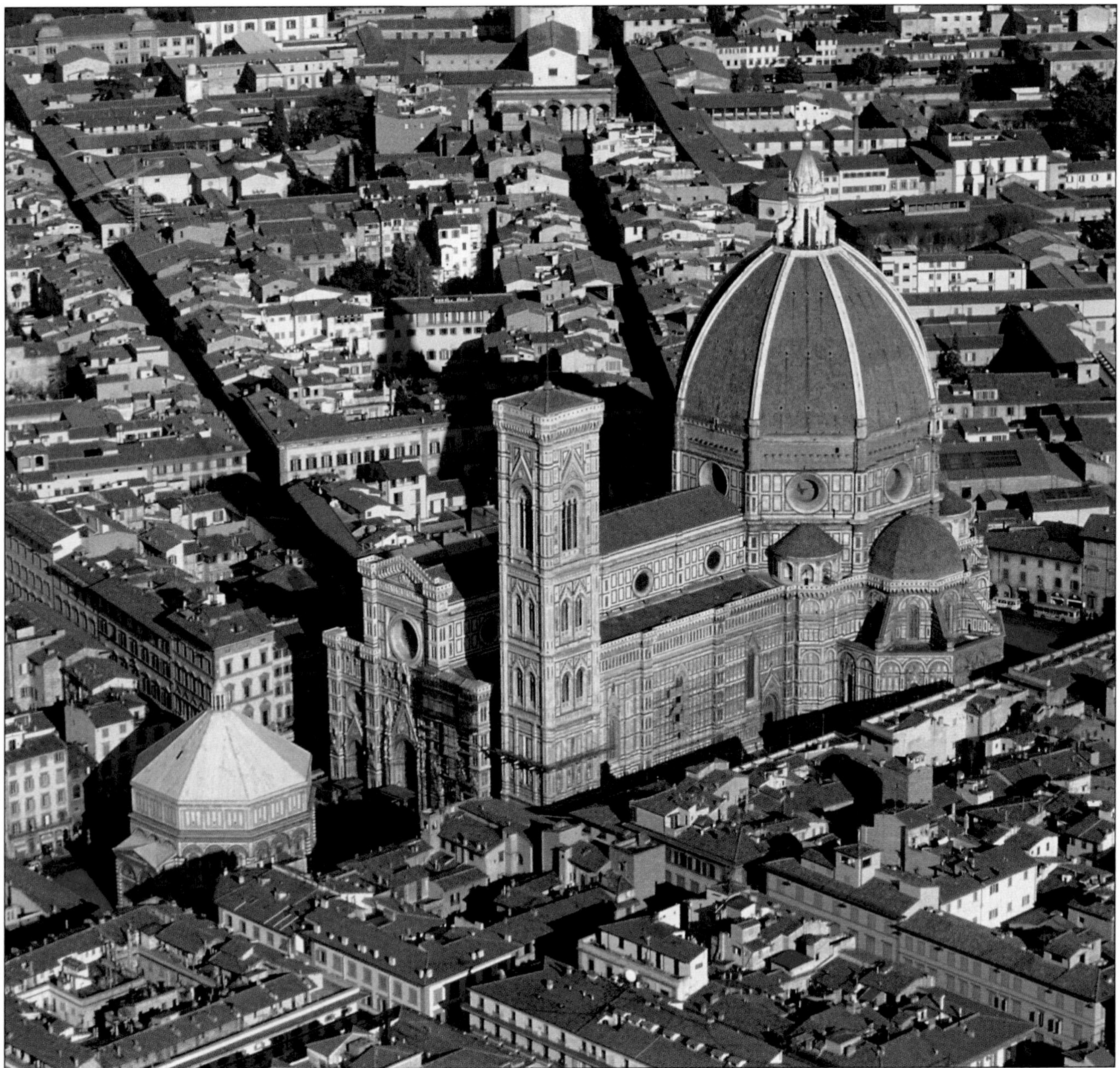

FIGURE 12.12 Arnolfo di Cambio, Francesco Talenti, Andrea Pisano, and others, Cathedral, Florence, begun 1296; redesigned 1357 and 1366, drum and dome 1420–36; campanile designed by Giotto, built ca. 1334–50. The dome of the cathedral could not be built as originally designed. It was only in the early part of the Renaissance that Filippo Brunelleschi would solve the engineering problems that had prevented its earlier construction (see Chapter 13).

Only slightly wider than their columns, the figures are not bodies with weight, but immaterial beings, seemingly hovering as their feet dangle.

Notre-Dame, Reims. The High Gothic figures who act out the *Annunciation and Visitation* (fig. 12.14) on the west facade of Reims Cathedral, dated to the 1230s or early 1240s, are descendants of the column figures at Chartres. Yet at Reims, rather than standing unaware of the next figure's presence, they interact. Moreover, the columns from which they extend are less noticeable.

The *Annunciation* depicts the moment when the angel Gabriel tells Mary that she will give birth to Jesus. In view of the extraordinary news she has just received, Mary shows little response. She is severe, standing erect, her heavy drapery falling in broad sharp folds to completely obscure her legs. But Gabriel is different. He holds his

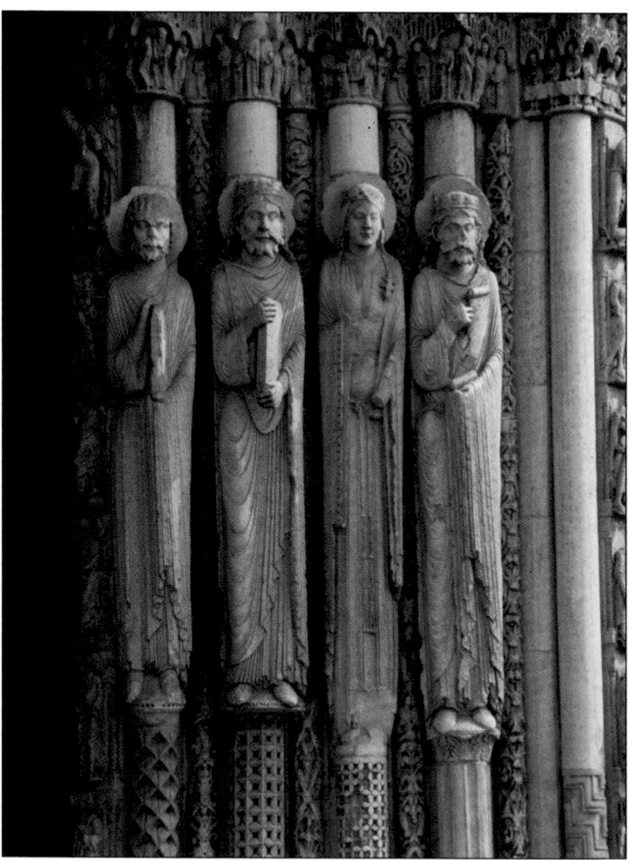

FIGURE 12.13 Column figures, flanking the Royal Portals, west facade, Cathedral of Notre-Dame, Chartres, ca. 1145–55, stone. Early Gothic figures perpetuate the distortion seen in Romanesque figures, but no longer have their agitated animation. Instead, these stiff, elongated figures maintain the shape of the column to which they are attached, emphasizing their architectural function.

drapery so it falls diagonally, his slender body forms an S curve and he moves gracefully, with a relaxed elegance. And he gives a Gothic grin! The new interest in emotion is a characteristic of the Gothic era.

The *Visitation* shows the meeting of Mary, now pregnant with Jesus, and her cousin Elizabeth, pregnant with John the Baptist, as they exchange their happy news. According to the story, Elizabeth is older, and this is shown by the sculptor. Both figures form an S curve—a revival of the *contrapposto* pose of antiquity—so that they seem to move in space. Many small drapery folds run on diagonals and horizontals, the creases following the outlines of the body.

Notre-Dame-de-Paris. Medieval art includes many images of Mary and the infant Jesus. From the late eleventh century on, popular devotion to the Virgin Mary was great; many churches, cathedrals, religious orders, and brotherhoods were dedicated to Mary. She was portrayed as the ideal woman, the second Eve. As religion became more humanized, the Church intentionally appealed to the tenderer emotions. Additionally, Mary was seen as able to intercede on behalf of sinners on Judgment Day. People appealed to Mary for help as the Madonna of Mercy. Members of all levels of society participated in the Cult of the Virgin. Images of Mary were commissioned by those who could barely afford a humble work, and by those who could have a work made in gold by the finest metalworkers and set with glittering gems. By the fourteenth century, Mary was often shown being crowned by Jesus and was given comparable status.

A devotional image of Mary known as *Notre-Dame-de-Paris* (Our Lady of Paris) (fig. 12.15), a marble statue

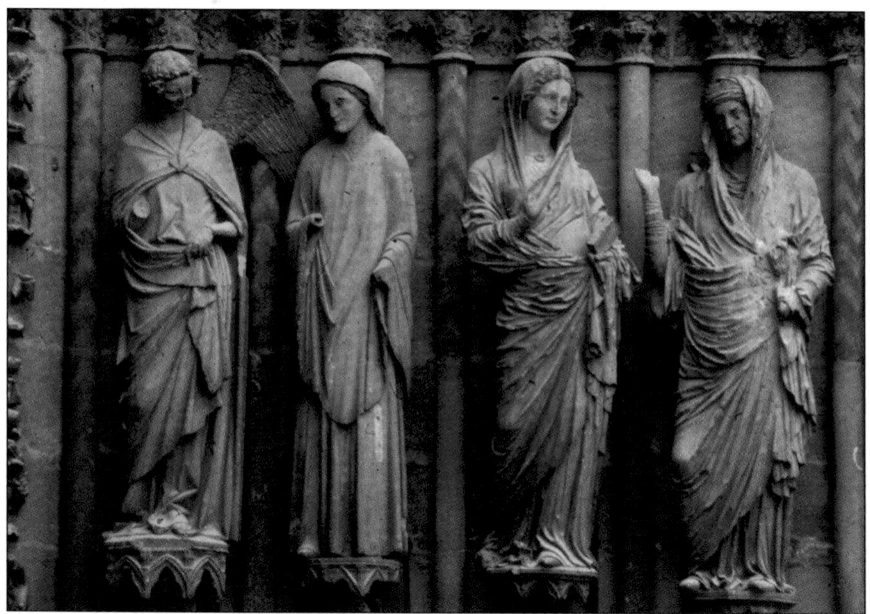

FIGURE 12.14 *Annunciation* and *Visitation*, west facade, Cathedral of Notre-Dame, Reims, ca. 1230–45, stone. Descendants of column figures, these High Gothic sculptures dominate their architectural setting and have little to do with the columns behind. Characteristic of the increased realism and idealism of the Gothic era, the proportions and movements of these figures are now normal, and they even turn toward one another as if conversing.

that dates from the early fourteenth century, stands in the crossing of the Cathedral of Notre-Dame in Paris. Graceful and elegant, Mary pulls a garment across her body, indicating the form beneath. Rather than a pattern of parallel pleats, the drapery now has broader sweeping folds. The silhouette is broken and animated. The infant Jesus plays with his mother's clothing and is portrayed with the bodily proportions of a baby, looking quite different from his portrayal as a little man in the Romanesque era.

FIGURE 12.15 *Notre-Dame-de-Paris,* French, in the crossing of the Cathedral of Notre-Dame, Paris, early fourteenth century, marble. Gracefully swaying in space, with Jesus on her hip, this image of Mary is very different from the stiff images of her created during the Romanesque era. Mary is now shown as an elegant French princess.

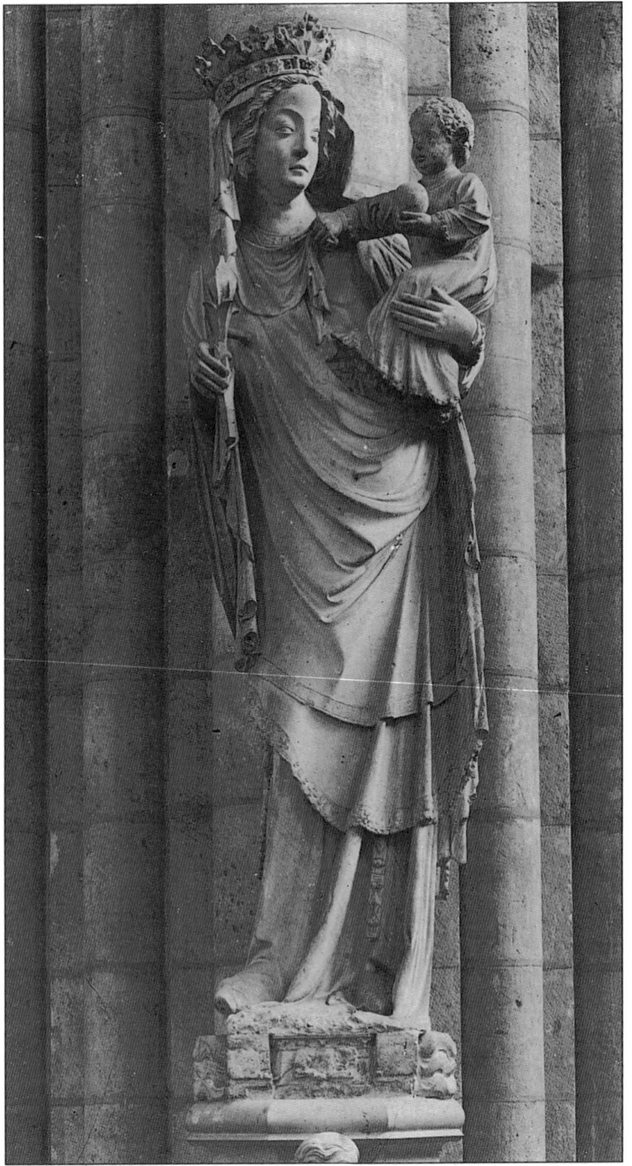

PAINTING AND DECORATIVE ARTS

Manuscript Illumination. Manuscript illumination reached a peak in the Gothic period. Books were written in finer lettering than ever before, and the size of the books was reduced. Stained glass affected painting after the mid-thirteenth century, for reds and blues dominate, the figures are outlined in black, and the effect is ornamental and flat. A good example is *Joshua Bidding the Sun to Stand Still* (fig. 12.16), a folio in the *Psalter of St. Louis,* made ca. 1260 for King Louis IX of France. Gothic architecture, including rose windows and pinnacles, forms the background in this miniature. The two-dimensional buildings contrast with the long, thin, three-dimensional, modeled figures.

In the years just before and following 1400, a single style of painting was popular throughout Europe. Typical of this **International Style** are bright contrasting colors, decorative flowing lines, elongated figures, surface patterns, a crowded quality, and opulent elegance. A prime example is the manuscript known as *Les Très Riches Heures* (*The Very Rich Hours*) of the duke of Berry, which dates from 1413–16.

FIGURE 12.16 *Joshua Bidding the Sun to Stand Still,* from the *Psalter of St. Louis,* French, ca. 1260, manuscript illumination, $5 \times 3\frac{1}{2}''$ (13.6 × 8.7 cm), Bibliothèque Nationale, Paris. Manuscript illumination reached a high point during the Gothic era, with the finest manuscripts produced in Paris. The elegant, animated, modeled figures are not in scale with the building they enter, and contrast with the flat patterned background, which is based on contemporary architecture.

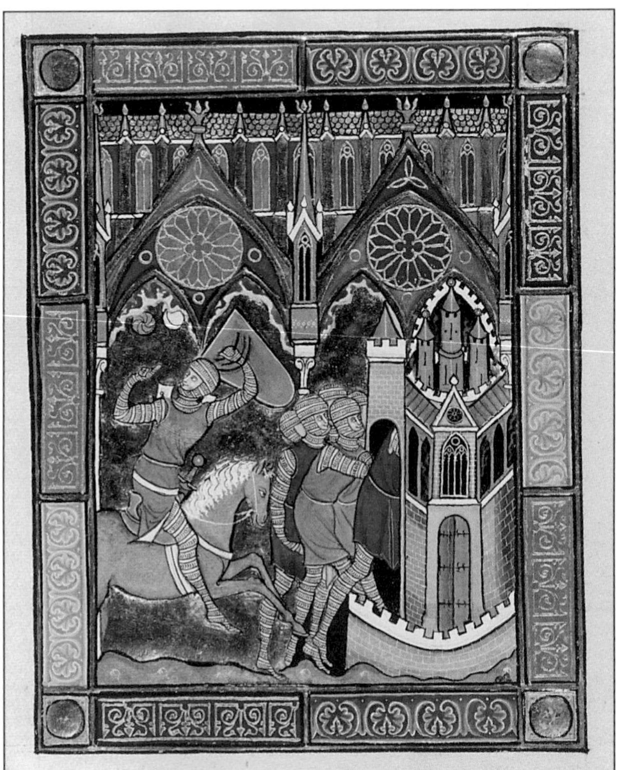

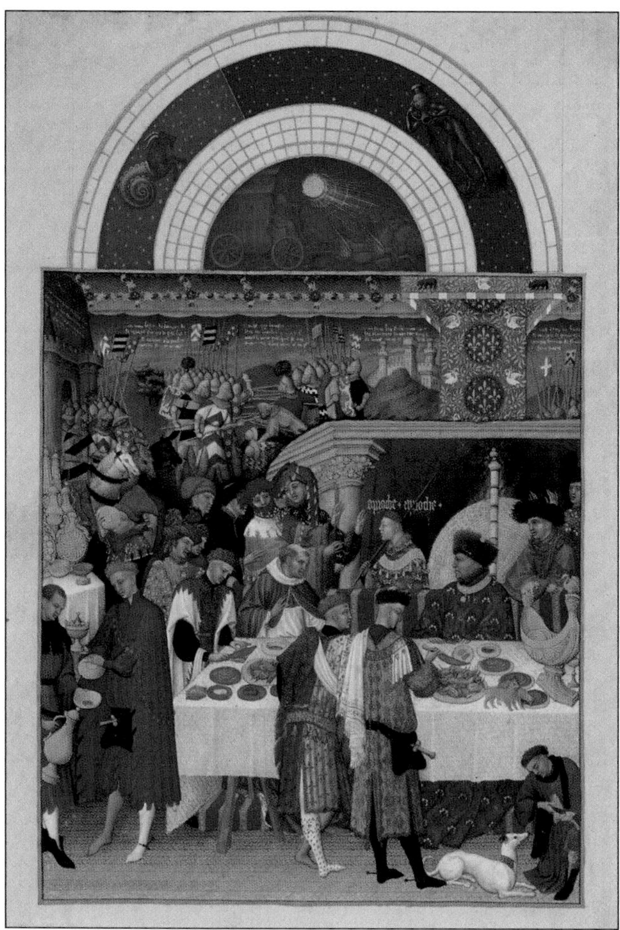

FIGURE 12.17 Limbourg brothers, *January*, from *Les Très Riches Heures* of the duke of Berry, French, 1413–16, manuscript illumination, $11\frac{1}{2} \times 8\frac{1}{4}''$ (29.2 × 21 cm), Musée Condé, Château of Chantilly. This manuscript includes twelve folios, one for each month of the year, that record how the upper and the lower classes lived, including pleasures and hardships.

It is the work of the Limbourg brothers, Pol, Herman, and Jean, who were probably German or Flemish but worked in France for the duke of Berry, brother of the French king Charles V, and a patron of the arts. *Les Très Riches Heures* is a book of hours or private prayer book. It contains a series of illuminations, one for each calendar month. *June* includes a depiction of the Sainte-Chapelle in Paris, and *October* shows the Louvre. In both, women and men are shown working in the fields. A different level of society is portrayed in *January* (fig. 12.17), one of several scenes of aristocratic life. The duke of Berry is hosting a banquet, perhaps in celebration of the Twelfth Night, the day the magi, following the star of Bethlehem, arrived to present gifts to the infant Jesus. The duke sits in front of a large fireplace that creates a halo around him. Above the head of the man behind him—some think this is a portrait of Pol de Limbourg—are the words *aproche, aproche*, "come in, come in," signifying the duke's hospitality. The manuscript is an extraordinary record detailing the customs, costumes, and consumption that characterized medieval life.

Stained Glass. Gothic architecture offered new possibilities for glass. The solid walls of the Romanesque period were covered with murals simultaneously decorative and instructive. In the Gothic period the dual functions passed to stained-glass windows. To create colored glass, various metallic oxides are added while the glass is still in a molten state. A stained-glass window is made of many small pieces of colored glass held together by lead strips. From the exterior of the building there is little to see in a stained-glass window, for stained glass is interior decoration, intended to be seen illuminated from behind by sunlight.

The colored light that floods the interior of Gothic buildings through their stained-glass windows had special importance in the Middle Ages. Light was believed to have mystical qualities as an attribute of divinity. John the Evangelist saw Jesus as "the true light" and as "the light of the world who came into the darkness." St. Augustine called God "light" and distinguished between types of physical and spiritual light.

In addition to the twelfth-century rose window and three lancets on the west facade (fig. 12.18), Chartres Cathedral has over 150 early thirteenth-century stained-glass windows. Local merchants donated forty-two windows, which include over a hundred depictions of their occupations. These windows document medieval tools, materials, and working methods. The masons, for instance, are depicted carving royal figures and show us just how Chartres' sculptures themselves were created.

Tapestry. Also characteristic of the Gothic era, tapestries were a form of insulation as well as decoration, for these woven wall hangings helped keep the cold air from seeping through the stone walls to the interior living space. Tapestries were luxury items, to be coveted and collected.

To produce a tapestry, the artist first makes a small-scale color drawing. This is then copied and enlarged on paper to the dimensions intended for the tapestry. This enlarged design is called the **cartoon.** Next, the weavers translate the cartoon into tapestry. A tapestry is woven on a loom, which is worked by several people sitting side by side. If a set of tapestries was to be produced, as was often the case, several looms were employed. The loom is strung with warp threads of tightly twisted wool. The number of warp threads per inch determines how fine the tapestry will be. The warp threads will be hidden by the weft threads of wool, silk, and even silver and gold. Tapestries are woven from the back; the finished image is an inversion of the artist's original design. When the design is woven, every change of color requires a change of thread; the weaving of a tapestry is a slow tedious process.

The *Unicorn Tapestries*, made in Brussels around 1500, tell the story of the hunt, capture, and murder of the unicorn. The first and the last tapestry (fig. 12.19) are in the *millefleurs* ("thousands of flowers") style, which is characterized by dense backgrounds of plants. These plants are meticulously observed and many can be identified, yet they represent an unreal realm, in which plants from different

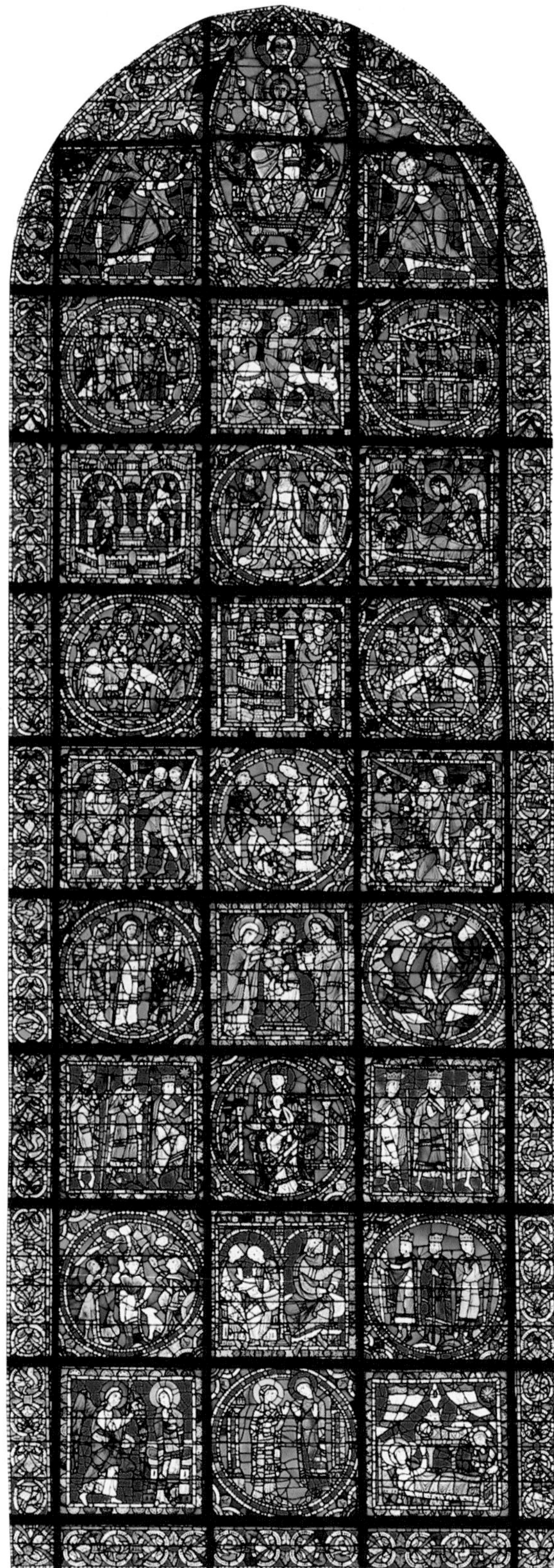

FIGURE 12.18 *Life of Jesus*, west facade, Cathedral of Notre-Dame, Chartres, ca. 1150, stained glass, central lancet window. Stained glass reached its peak during the Gothic era, filling the huge windows permitted by the skeletal architectural system, creating constantly changing patterns of colored light flickering over the interiors. Narratives that had been told in paintings on walls and vaults were now told in stained-glass windows.

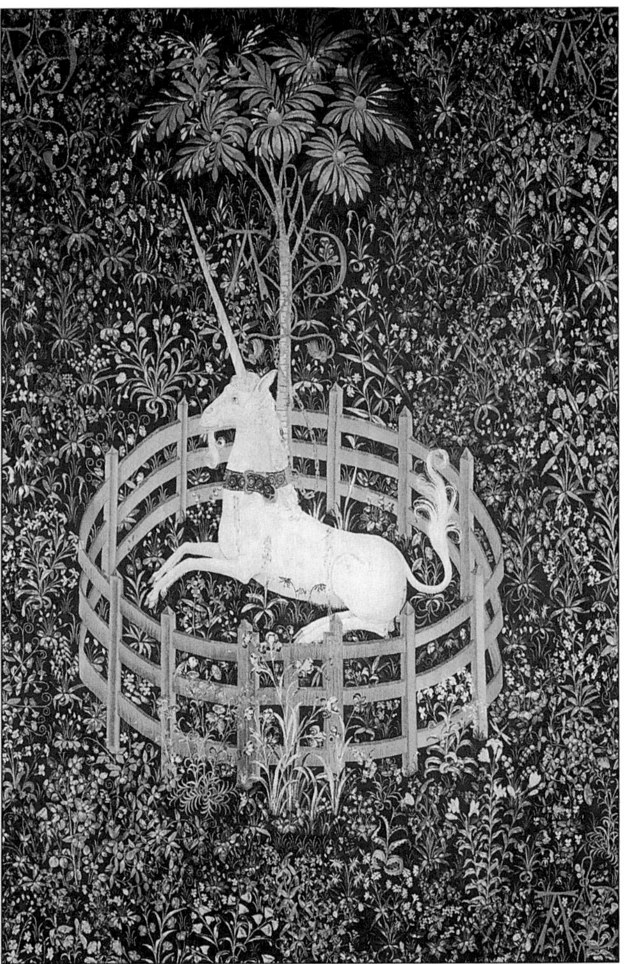

FIGURE 12.19 *The Unicorn in Captivity*, from the *Unicorn Tapestries*, Franco-Flemish, made in Brussels, ca. 1500, wool and silk tapestry, 12′ 1″ × 8′ 3″ (3.68 × 2.51 m). Gift of John D. Rockefeller Jr, 1937. Cloisters Collection, Metropolitan Museum of Art, New York. Art Resource, NY. During the Middle Ages, people believed in the existence of the unicorn, a fabulous animal said to have a single horn in the center of its forehead. When a tapestry is made, the picture is formed as the fabric is woven from colored threads. This type of tapestry is known as *millefleurs*—"thousands of flowers," shown scattered over the background.

geographic areas and climates all bloom simultaneously, the weavers accomplishing what nature could not.

These tapestries may have been made as a wedding gift. According to religious interpretation, the unicorn represents Jesus at the Resurrection, in a heavenly garden. According to secular interpretation, the unicorn represents the lover, now wearing the *chaîne d'amour* (chain of love) around his neck and surrounded by a fence, perhaps tamed and domesticated by obtaining his lady's affection. Red juice falls on the unicorn's white fur from the pomegranates above. Like the unicorn, the pomegranate can be read in both religious and secular terms. Taken from a religious point of view, the many seeds of the pomegranate represent the unity of the church and hope for the resurrection. In a secular light, the crownlike finial represents royalty, and

Cross Currents

MUSLIM SPAIN

The Gothic cathedrals of northern Europe are contemporaneous with one of Spain's most beautiful Islamic buildings, the Alhambra in Granada (see fig. 6.7). Spain was the most multicultural country in Europe, a legacy of the arrival of the first Muslim conquerors in Spain in 711. Spain had been controlled since 589 by Visigoth kings, but by the turn of the eighth century most Spaniards were unwilling to serve in the Visigoth army, a duty required of all free men. Furthermore, until 650, Jews had controlled most of the commerce in Spain, but in 694, the Visigoth kings, who had become Christian, enslaved Jews who would not accept Christian baptism. Thus Spaniards greeted the Muslim army in 711 as liberators.

And liberators they were. Both the Jews and the Christians were tolerated as "protected" groups. They paid taxes to the Muslim lords, but they were free to practice their own religion and to engage in business as they pleased. Thus Spain became a multicultural country like no other, with Jews, Islamic Moors, and Christians working together in a spirit of *convivencia*, "coexistence." The population consisted of six groups: (1) *Mozárabes*, Christians who had adopted Muslim culture; (2) *Mudéjares*, Moors who were vassals of Christians; (3) *Muladíes*, Christians who had adopted the Islamic faith; (4) *Tornadizos*, Moors who had turned Christian; (5) *Enaciados*, those who sat on the fence between both Islam and Christianity, and who pretended to be one or the other as the occasion warranted; and (6) the large Jewish community.

The cultures invigorated each other. An older Christian man, writing in 854, lamented the acceptance of Muslim ways by the Christian youth, but his protest reveals much of the culture's vitality:

> Our Christian young men, with their elegant airs and fluent speech, are showy in their dress and carriage, and are famed for the learning of the Gentiles; intoxicated with Arab eloquence, they greedily handle, eagerly devour and zealously discuss the books of the Mohammadans. . . . They can even make poems, every line ending with the same letter, which display high flights of beauty and more skill in handling meter than the Gentiles themselves possess.

The odes of the Islamic poets that the Christian youth were imitating began with an erotic prelude, then moved through a series of conventional themes such as descriptions of camels and horses, hunting scenes, and battles, and then culminated in the praise of a valiant chieftain. The odes soon developed into independent love songs and drinking songs, and it was out of this tradition that the troubadour poets sprang.

Moorish influence on medieval and Renaissance Europe extended beyond this. For instance, Arab scholars passed back much classical learning into Europe (see Chapter 6). Nonetheless, by 1492, the last traces of this happy cohabitation were erased when Ferdinand and Isabella of Aragon reclaimed Granada for Christianity and expelled the Moors and Jews.

Table 12–1 SYMBOLS USED IN MEDIEVAL CHRISTIAN ART: COLORS AND OBJECTS

Colors	
Black	symbol of mourning, death
Blue	symbol of heaven, truth, fidelity—"true blue"
Green	symbol of fertility, springtime growth
Red	symbol of passion, of both love and hate—to "see red"
White	symbol of purity, innocence
Yellow/gold	symbol of God, of the sun, of truth, yet also of deceit and cowardice
Objects	
Globe/orb	symbol of the world
Grapes	used to make wine, a symbol of Jesus' blood
Hourglass	symbol of the shortness of life
Keys	identifying attribute of St. Peter because Jesus is said to have given him the keys to heaven
Lamp	symbol of intelligence
Pomegranate	due to the fruit's many seeds, a symbol of the unity of the church; hope for resurrection
Scallop shell	worn by pilgrims to Santiago de Compostela, Spain
Ship	symbol of the Christian church

Connections

Scholasticism and Gothic Architecture

During the Middle Ages, from about 1130 to 1270 the philosophy of Scholasticism reached its culmination in the grand *Summa Theologica* of St. Thomas Aquinas, and Gothic architecture reached its zenith in the cathedrals in and around Paris.

Scholastic philosophy and Gothic architecture both embody the aspiration toward a unity of truth. The grandness of both enterprises, their vastness and inclusivity manifest an all-encompassing belief centered on the divine creation of the world, the Incarnation and divinity of Jesus, the mystery of the trinity, and the role of faith in achieving salvation.

In Aquinas and in the cathedrals, the sacred doctrine was clarified through the use of human reason. Aquinas' *Summa* manifested reason in the careful ordering of its parts in their comprehensiveness and distinctness. Analogously, in their overall structure and design, the cathedrals revealed a rational order. The Gothic cathedral—in every element of its construction, from its portals to its apse, its sculpture to its architectural design, its stained glass windows to its gargoyles—collectively embodied the whole of Christian knowledge. The cathedral exemplified a visual structure analogous to the logical organization of Scholastic thought.

the many seeds, fertility. The iconography of medieval art is often multilayered in meaning.

SCHOLASTICISM

As the Middle Ages progressed, the attitude of the Roman Catholic Church toward secular learning and the wisdom of ancient writers began to change. More often than not, the church incorporated into its own teaching the learning it acquired from other cultures, including the literature and philosophy of ancient Greece and Rome, along with the Byzantine and Islamic religious and philosophical traditions. In this intellectual climate, forms of learning that derived from observation of the natural world rather than the written word of scripture were no longer at odds with a Christian perspective. Such natural knowledge was seen as a foundation for the more advanced states of religious contemplation.

Growth of Universities. The shift in the church's intellectual perspective was stimulated by the preservation and translation by Muslim scholars of Aristotle's writings, which passed back into Christian Europe in the twelfth and thirteenth centuries. This new perspective was complemented by the rise of the universities, which were evolving into major centers of learning. The University of Paris was the result of the expansion of the cathedral school at Notre-Dame. In turn, the University of Paris gave rise to institutions like Oxford and Cambridge in England, the former founded by teachers and students who had left Paris, the latter created by a group disenchanted with the Oxford curriculum. Debate about what should be studied led to the foundation of more and more universities. Soon universities in Spain, Portugal, and Germany joined the approximately eighty institutions of higher learning that existed by the end of the Middle Ages.

The university curriculum consisted of seven "liberal arts": the *trivium* (grammar, logic, and rhetoric) and the *quadrivium* (arithmetic, astronomy, geometry, and music). Soon degrees were awarded in both civil and canonical law, in medicine, and in theology.

Prior to the thirteenth century, medieval philosophy had centered on demonstrating the truths of religious faith through reason. But now a focus on the empirical observation of the natural world began to emerge, divorced from the service of Christian belief. Tensions between faith and reason resulted.

Peter Abelard. Peter Abelard (1079–1144) was one of the first to wield the twin powers of logic and language in a philosophical approach called *dialectic*, a razor-sharp form of logic. The most able student of the renowned William of Champeaux (Sham-POE) of the Cathedral school of Paris, Abelard renounced Champeaux's philosophical approach as he challenged church authorities in his *Sic et Non (Yes and No)* by calling attention to apparently contradictory statements they made. Abelard suggested that such conflicting statements could be resolved by analyzing their language to see if the same words were being used in differing ways. Believing that most theological and philosophical confusion resulted from confusion about language, Abelard argued that words signify or refer only to individual things rather than to general concepts.

At stake for Abelard and for many medieval philosophers was a debate about "universals" that had its origin in the Greek philosophy of Aristotle and Plato. The issue debated was whether general concepts, or universals, actually exist. The realists believed that they do—and that, for example, goodness actually exists irrespective of its manifestation in particular good individuals. The nominalists, led by Abelard, denied the existence of such concepts as real entities, arguing that no such thing as goodness, redness, or catness actually exists, but only particular examples of good men, red objects, or of actual cats. Abelard did not deny that the concepts existed; he argued that they exist only as mental words signifying an abstract concept, which itself has none other than mental existence.

Although Abelard is known in philosophical circles as a gifted logician who exerted an influence on subsequent philosophical thought, including that of Thomas Aquinas, he is better known as the teacher and then lover of his brilliant student Heloise. Abelard was hired by Heloise's uncle as a guardian and tutor. He fell in love with Heloise and secretly married her. Her uncle hired a group of thugs to attach and punish Abelard by castrating him. He became a monk, and Heloise entered a convent. The letters they wrote during their years of solitude are among the richest reflections on love ever written.

The Synthesis of St. Thomas Aquinas. Using Aristotle's focus on the natural world to explain how God's wisdom is revealed, the Dominican friar ST. THOMAS AQUINAS [a-KWHY-ness] (1225–1274) effected a synthesis of Aristotelian philosophy and Catholic religious thought. Aquinas, like Aristotle, began with empirical knowledge. Unlike Aristotle, however, Aquinas then moved from the physical, rational, and intelligible to the divine. Aquinas claimed that the order of nature, a beautiful harmonious structure in its own right, reflected the mind of God.

Aquinas saw no conflict between the demands of reason and the claims of faith. Nor did he see a conflict between the requirements of belief and the inducements of independent thought. For Aquinas, the exercise of intellectual freedom was granted by God according to the divine plan. This freedom not only makes a person human, but also presents the opportunity for every individual to choose or deny God by using the tools of reason.

Unlike his forebears Plato and Augustine, for whom physical reality and material circumstance were not as real or important as spiritual essences or qualities, Aquinas argued, much like Aristotle, that the soul and body are inextricable. The body needs the soul to live; the soul needs the body's experience. Each completes the other in a unity. According to Aquinas, spiritual knowledge and theological understanding require a grounding in the body's experience and observation of the world.

In this integration, Aquinas showed that philosophy and theology need not conflict, that they could coexist. Nevertheless, with the introduction of rational analysis into theological speculation, and the acceptance of empirical evidence as elements of philosophical truth, critics of Aquinas began to question the validity of his unification of faith and reason.

The most important of Aquinas' writings was his *Summa Theologica*, or summary of theology, a monumental work consisting of 518 questions and 3,652 responses, over which Aquinas labored for seven years. The work is written in the style of disputation and challenge, in which auditors of an idea were expected to either assent, dissent, or doubt it—challenge—it in some way. The first and second disputes in the *Summa Theologica* involved the nature of theology and God's existence.

The story of Thomas Aquinas' early life is as interesting as his theological work is significant for Catholic belief. A member of a well-off Italian family, Thomas, like his many brothers, was expected to become an important religious leader—the Head of a Benedictine Abbey. Thomas, however, had other ideas, as he wanted to be a humble Dominican friar—a begging monk, who would forsake his wealth and status. Two of his brothers interfered with this plan by kidnapping Thomas and imprisoning him. When Thomas used his quiet time to think, pray, and write, his brothers sent a courtesan to his room to tempt him. Thomas drove her out with a flaming brand that he plunged into the fire, scaring the woman into a hasty retreat. When his family realized that Thomas was adamant about how he wanted to spend his life, they relented, after which he traveled to Cologne to study under the then well-known theologian Albertus Magnus, who is generally recognized as the Father of Scholasticism; Thomas Aquinas is its most famous proponent.

Duns Scotus and William of Ockham. Two who refused to accept Aquinas' grand synthesis were Duns Scotus (1265–1308) and William of Ockham (1285–1349), both of whom were Franciscan friars. Scotus was a Scotsman who had studied at Oxford and Paris; Ockham was an Englishman, who had also studied at Oxford, and who wound up vilified and excommunicated for what were perceived as heretical views. Duns Scotus, known as "the subtle doctor," reacted against the theological views of both Aquinas and Augustine. In place of Augustine's divine illumination and Aquinas' integration of faith and reason, Scotus posited the central importance of will, emphasizing the freedom of individuals in their actions. Scotus believed that a person's will is guided on the one hand by what is good for the individual, and on the other by what is good for all, the two being modulated according to a sense of justice.

Scotus also rejected Aquinas' notion that the identity of an individual thing depends on its matter, while sharing its form with all other things of the same kind. For Scotus, the individual identity of a thing is part of its form, as distinguished between a thing's "common nature" (its *quiddity* or whatness) and its individualizing difference, a notion that inspired the Jesuit priest-poet Gerard Manley Hopkins, who celebrated Scotus in his poem *Duns Scotus at Oxford.* Such philosophical hairsplitting among scholastic philosophers gave rise to the criticism that such subtleties had little, if anything, to do with faith and everyday living. Ironically, though, Scotus came to emphasize faith as superior to reason and to argue that philosophy and religion should be separated because they have different tasks.

William of Ockham went beyond Scotus by denying the existence of any correspondence between concrete individual beings or things. Like Peter Abelard, he eschewed the notion of universals except as mental concepts. Similarities among individual human beings, or, say, particular dogs or trees, exist strictly in the mind as mental abstractions, as ideas rather than as real things. For Ockham, the issue of the universal existing beyond the physical was a matter for theology or for logic rather than a concern of philosophy. Thus he rejected Aquinas' notion that the human mind possessed a divine light that guided the intellect toward a proper understanding of reality, and he severed the link between faith and reason that Aquinas had so carefully established. With "Ockham's razor," his principle that the best explanation is the simplest and most direct, Ockham also broke away from the elaborate and subtle explanations of the scholastic philosophers or "schoolmen," whose ideas had dominated medieval philosophical thinking. In doing so, Ockham helped prepare the ground for the developments of Cartesian rationalism and Baconian empiricism.

Francis of Assisi. The intellectualism of scholars was challenged by the life and teachings of Giovanni Bernadone (1181–1226), nicknamed "Francesco" by his father, who was born in the Italian town of Assisi. Captured as a youth in a battle against the neighboring town of Perugia and held in solitary confinement, Francis of Assisi (fig. 12.20), decided in prison that real freedom demanded complete poverty. On his release, he gave up all worldly goods and, identifying closely with Jesus, began to lead the life of a wandering preacher. St. Francis' identification with the passion was so strong that his body was said to bear the crucifixion marks, or *stigmata*, of Jesus. Best known for his love of birds and animals, Francis' lifestyle made him wholly dependent on the generosity of others. His many followers, who came to be known as Franciscans, were already a powerful monastic order of the church by the time of his death in 1226.

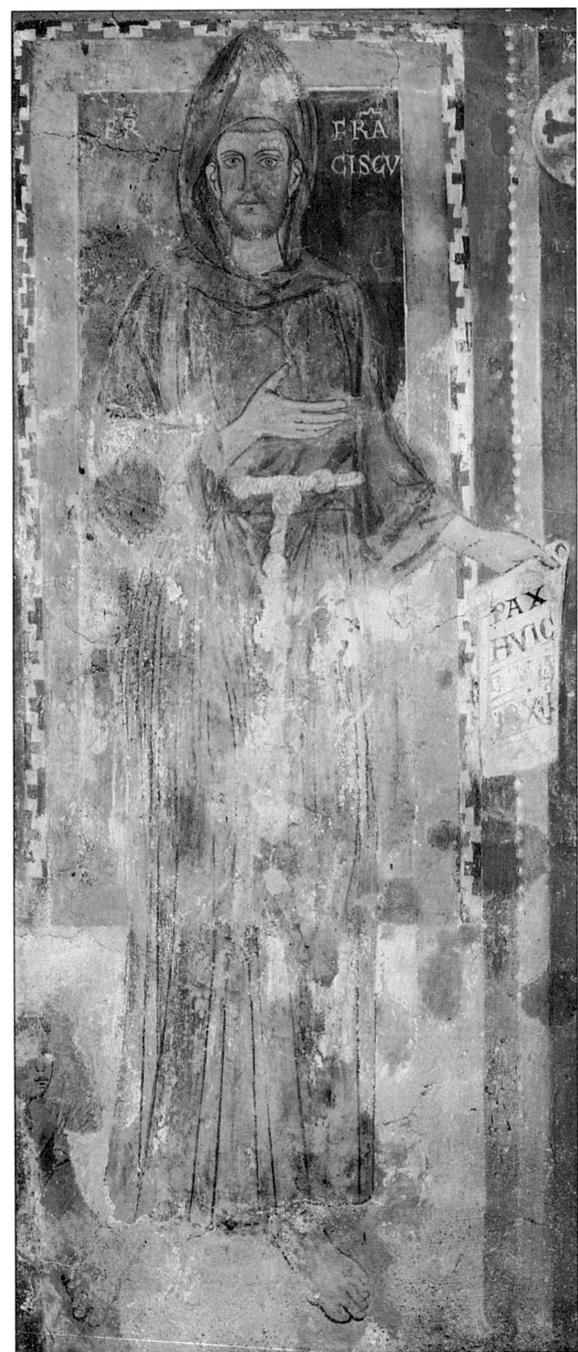

FIGURE 12.20 *St. Francis of Assisi*, thirteenth century, fresco, Sacro Speco, Subiaco, Italy. The earliest known portrait of St. Francis, this fresco may have been executed during his lifetime. St. Francis founded his own monastic order, the Franciscan order, in 1209, and it had already grown to be a powerful movement within the medieval church by the time of his death in 1226. One of the most important features of the order was its acceptance of poverty by its members.

LITERATURE

Dante's Divine Comedy. The most celebrated literary work of the Middle Ages is the epic poem *The Divine Comedy* by the Italian poet DANTE ALIGHIERI [DAHN-tay] (1265–1321) (fig. 12.21). Born in Florence in 1265, Dante was involved in politics as well as literature. When a rival party seized power in 1302, Dante was exiled from his home city, never to return. *The Divine Comedy* was completed in Ravenna shortly before Dante's death. In the poem, Dante makes numerous references to the politics of his day, especially to the rivalry between the Guelphs and the Ghibellines, two opposing Florentine political parties.

The Divine Comedy is divided into three parts: *Inferno* (*Hell*), *Purgatorio* (*Purgatory*), and *Paradiso* (*Heaven*). These are the three different places in medieval theology to which the soul can be sent after death. In the poem Dante ascends through Hell and Purgatory to Heaven, guided in the first stages by the pagan poet Virgil, who represents human reason, and at the end by his beloved, Beatrice, who represents divine revelation. Though indebted to the classical poetic tradition, *The Divine Comedy* is an explicitly Christian poem.

The poem contains one hundred cantos equally divided among the three sections, with the opening canto of the prologue prefacing the *Inferno*. Dante's attention to organization, especially structural symmetry, is apparent in

Critical Thinking

SIN AND ERROR

In his *Inferno*, Dante punishes sinners according to the type of sin they committed during life and according to the degree of their guilt, making the punishment fit the crime. Although this idea reflects medieval religious thought, especially that of Thomas Aquinas, in some attenuated sense, perhaps, it remains alive today in the criminal justice system, in which "crimes" rather than "sins" are prosecuted and punished. To what extent do you think that punishment—of whatever type—is the appropriate response to "sin" and to "crime"? To what extent are contemporary attitudes toward punishment for crimes similar to medieval ideas regarding punishment for "sin"? How do they differ?

every aspect, particularly in the use of *terza rima*, a succession of three-line stanzas that rhyme ABA, BCB, CDC, and so on, in which the unrhymed line ending in each stanza is picked up in the following stanza, where it becomes the principal rhyme. Dante employs this pattern of interlocked rhyme through the entire work.

One of the most notable features of Dante's *Inferno* is the law of symbolic retribution, which suggests how a punishment should fit a sin. In depicting opportunists, for example, Dante positions them outside of Hell proper, in a kind of vestibule. Because they were unwilling to take firm positions in life, they are not completely in or out of Hell after death. And as they were swayed by winds of change and fashion, their eternal punishment is to follow a waving banner that continually changes direction.

Other punishments that seem particularly well suited to their corresponding sins include those who have committed carnal offenses, who in life were swayed by sexual passion and in death are swept up in a fiercely swirling

FIGURE 12.21 Domenico di Michelino, *Dante and His Poem*, 1465, fresco, Cathedral, Florence. Dante stands holding his poem. To his right is the Inferno, behind him Mount Purgatory, and to his left, representing Paradise, is Florence Cathedral itself, with its newly finished dome by Brunelleschi.

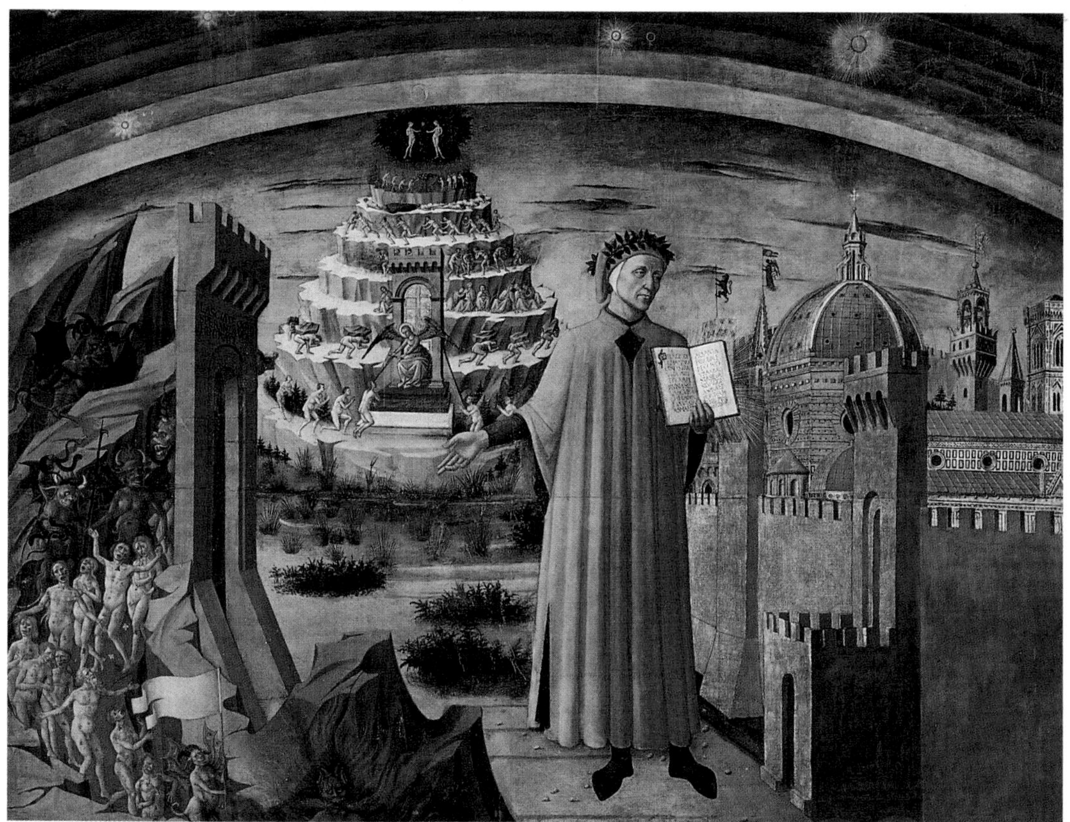

wind. Murderers are punished by being immersed in a river of boiling blood, the degree of their immersion determined by the degree of their bloodlust in life. Gluttons are punished by being made to lie in the filthy slush of a garbage dump while the giant three-headed dog, Cerberus, tears at their flesh with claws and teeth. The souls of those who committed suicide are imprisoned in trees, whose limbs are torn and eaten by giant ugly birds, the fearful Harpies.

This law of symbolic retribution is complemented by another—that the most grievous and heinous of sinners are punished more severely than those who committed less odious crimes in life. Dante's poem is a synthesis of all the learning of his day—astronomy, history, natural science, philosophy—and this differentiation among sinners is indebted to the theology of Thomas Aquinas. Dante follows Aquinas, for example, in suggesting that sins of the flesh, such as lust, are not as serious as those of malice or fraud. Thus lust, gluttony, and anger are punished in the upper portion of Hell, where the punishments are less painful; sins of violence and fraud are punished in the deeper recesses of the Inferno.

Because deceit and treachery are, for Dante, the most pernicious of sins, these are punished at the very bottom of hell. Dante's scheme is so carefully worked out that he even divides the betrayers into categories—betrayers of their kin, of their country, of their guests and hosts, and, finally, those who betrayed their masters. This last and worst kind of sin Dante represents by the crimes of Brutus and Cassius, who betrayed Julius Caesar; by Judas Iscariot, the betrayer of Jesus; and, worst of all, by Satan, who betrayed God. These sinners are the furthest from God, deep in the cold, dark center of Hell. Satan, a three-headed monster, lies encased in ice; in his three mouths he chews incessantly on the bodies of Brutus, Cassius, and Judas. Many of Dante's political enemies in Florence are discovered by the poet suffering the torments of Hell.

Just as Dante's *Inferno* reflects the type and degree of sinners' guilt, so his *Purgatorio* reflects a concern for justice. Dante's Purgatory is a mountain that is also an island. The mountain is arranged in tiers, with the worst sins punished at the bottom, since the sinners punished there are furthest from the Garden of Eden and from the heavens. In ascending order, the sins punished on the mountain of Purgatory are pride, envy, anger, sloth, avarice, gluttony, and lust—roughly the reverse of their positions in the *Inferno*.

Dante's *Paradiso* is based on the seven planets of medieval astronomy—the Moon, Mercury, Venus, the Sun, Mars, Jupiter, and Saturn. Just as the *Inferno* and the *Purgatorio* describe the subject's movement through hell and the purgatorial mountain, Dante's *Paradiso* also describes a journey, this one celestial, from planet to planet and beyond, to the Empyrean, the heavenly abode of God and his saints.

Table 12–2 THE STRUCTURE OF DANTE'S COMEDY

Hell

The Anteroom of the Neutrals

Circle 1: The Virtuous Pagans (Limbo)

Circle 2: The Lascivious

Circle 3: The Gluttonous

Circle 4: The Greedy and the Wasteful

Circle 5: The Wrathful

Circle 6: The Heretics

Circle 7: The Violent Against Others, Self, God/Nature/ and Art

Circle 8: The Fraudulent (subdivided into ten classes, each of which dwells in a separate ditch)

Circle 9: The Lake of the Treacherous against kindred, country, guests, lords, and benefactors. Satan is imprisoned at the center of this frozen lake.

Purgatory

Ante-Purgatory: The Excommunicated/The Lazy/ The Unabsolved/Negligent Rulers

The Terraces of the Mount of Purgatory

1. *The Proud*
2. *The Envious*
3. *The Wrathful*
4. *The Slothful*
5. *The Avaricious*
6. *The Gluttonous*
7. *The Lascivious*

The Earthly Paradise

Paradise

1. *The Moon: The Faithful who were inconstant*
2. *Mercury: Service marred by ambition*
3. *Venus: Love marred by lust*
4. *The Sun: Wisdom; the theologians*
5. *Mars: Courage; the just warriors*
6. *Jupiter: Justice; the great rulers*
7. *Saturn: Temperance; the contemplatives and mystics*
8. *The Fixed Stars: The Church Triumphant*
9. *The Primum Mobile: The Order of Angels*
10. *The Empyrean Heavens: Angels, Saints, the Virgin, and the Holy Trinity*

MUSIC

The Notre-Dame School. One of the more elegant features of Gregorian plainchant is the way its single melodic line molds itself to the words of the Latin text. The rounded shape of its vocal melody and the concentrated focus of its single melodic line suit the devotional quality of the liturgy.

Then & Now

Dante's *Inferno* has remained popular for many centuries. Now, in the twenty-first century, a new version has been created—a video game with a brawny, armor-clad Dante as its protagonist. The video game creators have made Dante a much less passive figure and a more robust action hero; much less poetic and philosophical and much more aggressive. In this new game version of the *Inferno*, Dante is a knight who returns home from the Crusades to find that his beloved Beatrice has been murdered and that her soul has been taken captive by Lucifer. Dante goes down into hell to find her, fighting off legions of demons and monsters along the way. And although Dante's original story line has been altered in the video game, the creators have retained many features of the original work, such as the basic physical organization of hell and the mythological figures Minos and Cerberus, whose functions remain the same as in Dante's original. The question remains as to whether Dante's vision of hell, even altered in this manner, will appeal to a new generation, and whether, if it does, the game will draw players to read the *Inferno* in one of the many fine translations currently available.

In the ninth and tenth centuries, however, chants began to be composed with multiple voice lines. Those with two voice lines an interval of a fourth, fifth, or octave apart were known as a parallel **organum,** the simplest kind of polyphonic, or multivoiced, musical practice. In parallel organum, the two melodic lines move together, note for note, parallel, and with identical rhythmic patterns. The lower, or bottom, line is the main melody, or ***cantus firmus,*** above which the second line is composed. By the eleventh century, the organum developed from the entrance of a second voice into music moving in parallel, oblique, and contrary motion. The harmonies were random and, although the two singers were on the same note when starting, intervals between the notes would sound to our modern ears dissonant and hollow. The original chant, which was sung as the bottom line of the organum, could not be varied and provided the polyphonic basis to the upper voice, which began to expand movement and range.

As polyphonic music became standard in church ritual, the organum grew to three, four, or as many as five separate voice parts. Moreover, the melodies above the cantus firmus began to change with each of the voice lines, thus imparting an independent quality absent in simpler forms of parallel-voiced polyphony.

The two most prominent chant composers of the twelfth century, LEONIN [LAY-oh-nan] (ca. 1135–ca. 1200) and PEROTIN [PEAR-oh-tan] (ca. 1170–ca. 1236), were associated with the Cathedral of Notre-Dame in Paris. Though the church was not completed until the 1220s, during the 1180s an altar was consecrated and services were held. Léonin, who was active around 1175, favored a chant for two voices called *organum duplum,* in which the lower cantus firmus spread slowly over long held notes while a second voice, scored higher, moved more quickly and with many more notes through the text. This top line was called the *duplum* and the bottom cantus firmus line the **tenor,** from the Latin *tenere,* which means "to hold." (This "tenor" has nothing to do with the later development of "tenor," referring to one of the voice ranges, as in soprano, alto, tenor, and bass.)

Working a generation later, at the turn of the thirteenth century, Pérotin was Léonin's most notable successor in composing polyphonic chants. Pérotin wrote mostly three- or four-voiced chants called respectively *organum triplum* and *organum quadruplum.* Pérotin's more complex polyphony still used the cantus firmus tenor voice, but over it were placed two or three lively voice parts, which the tenor imitated from time to time. An additional distinguishing feature of the polyphonic chants of Léonin and Pérotin was their use of measured rhythm. Unlike the free unmeasured rhythms of plainchant, the polyphonic chants of Léonin and Pérotin had a clearly defined meter with precise time values for each note. Initially, the rhythmic notations for the music were restricted to only certain patterns of notes, with the beat subdivided into threes to acknowledge the Trinity. Later, however, these rules were loosened, and polyphonic chant became even freer in structure and more richly textured.

Probably the most viable result from the addition of rhythm by the Notre Dame school was that music fit melody to the rhythm of words. The result was more form in music, liturgy became easier to memorize and the rhythmic flow lent a steady pulse to the movement of clerics in procession. The extemporaneous lines of the upper voice, which was sometimes left to the improvisation of the performer, provided the basis for new musical forms—both sacred and secular.

It has been suggested that the metrical regularity of Léonin's and Pérotin's chants are especially suited to the Gothic cathedral. The repeating and answering patterns of polyphonic chant music have their architectural counterpart in the Gothic cathedral's repetitive patterns of arches, windows, columns, and buttresses, and its visual rhythms.

MEDIEVAL CALAMITIES

BLACK DEATH

Among the most devastating calamities to befall Europe during the Middle Ages was the plague, which caused the deaths of more than a third of Europe's seventy million people. There were many outbreaks of the plague, which was carried over sea and land trade routes to most parts of Europe. The carriers of the plague bacillus were fleas that had bitten infected rats, and which then bit other rats and humans. Three forms of the plague existed: bubonic, or infected lymph nodes; pneumonic, or infected lungs; and septicemic, or infected blood. These forms of the plague were so virulent that death would result within a few days and sometimes within hours. The symptoms of those afflicted were painful and horrifying. Abscesses, or *buboes*, appeared in the armpits or groin lymph nodes, filling them with pus and turning the body black—hence the term by which the disease is best known, the "Black Death."

References to the Black Death appear in the *Decameron*, a collection of linked short stories, by Giovanni Boccaccio, who lived through the plague. Boccaccio set his collection of stories in the hills around Florence, to which the stories' narrators flee to escape the ravages of the disease. In the introduction to the *Decameron*, Boccaccio noted both the physical and psychological consequences of the pestilence, as he describes the despair of the citizens of Florence.

The plague disrupted societies and economies throughout Europe and into Asia and North Africa, where the plague had spread by travelers and merchants plying land and sea trade routes. The disease caused massive labor shortages, which fed social unrest exacerbated by the conflicting interests of landlords and workers. In addition to the social and economic consequences there were religious effects. Boccaccio describes how many Florentines abandoned funeral rites and burial rituals, as they feared contagion from infected victims. People also wondered about a world that could include such a horrifying form of death for so many people and a God who allowed such a calamity to occur. Lack of understanding of the causes of the Black Death and absence of information about its transmission created fear and confusion. This, in turn, gave rise to a greater preoccupation with death, which resulted in various artistic renderings, such as the *danse macabre*, or the Dance of Death, portrayed by skeletons and by cadavers leading the living to their graves.

HUNDRED YEARS' WAR

To the horrors of the Black Death, which raged throughout the second half of the fourteenth century, were added the blood and gore of more than a hundred years of war between France and England. The Hundred Years' War, which lasted from 1337 to 1453, was fought completely on French soil. Although the proximate cause of the war was the English claim to the French throne upon the death of Charles IV in 1328, the major and longer contributing cause was the English claim to French lands, a claim dating from the time of the Norman Conquest, when English kings held land in France.

Although French soldiers greatly outnumbered the English invaders, the English won most of the battles, including those of Poitiers and Agincourt, which Shakespeare immortalized in his play *Henry V*. Although the battles themselves were deadly, with foot soldiers and archers slaughtering one another with improved weapons such as the English longbow, the time between battles also brought destruction, as mercenaries roamed the countryside pillaging and killing. And even though the English were consistently victorious in the battles of the Hundred Years' War, they suffered serious financial losses due to the cost of waging war abroad and maintaining garrisons there. The war depleted the French aristocracy and rendered obsolete the institution of knighthood and feudal vassalage.

TOWARD THE RENAISSANCE

We begin to detect the seeds of scientific inquiry, an increasing urge to know the world in its every detail. Life, more and more people believed, should be a quest for "truth." And the realization of visual and literary truth—the depiction of things in a manner "true to nature"—began to seem more urgent. Scholars increasingly found what seemed to be the "truth" in the writings of antiquity and artifacts of the classical past.

NATURALISM IN ART

The Pisanos. Sculpture in Italy differs from that of the rest of Gothic Europe. NICOLA PISANO [pea-SAH-noh] (ca. 1220/25 or before–1284) reintroduced a classical style, as demonstrated by the marble pulpit he made for the baptistery in Pisa, 1259–60. He may have studied the ancient Roman sarcophagi preserved in Pisa, for in the panel that portrays the *Nativity* (fig. 12.22) he has carved classical figures and faces. Included are three separate events: the Annunciation on the left; the Nativity itself in the middle; and the Adoration at the top right. Mary appears twice in the center of the composition, once with the angel Gabriel at the Annunciation, and directly below, lying prostrate at the Nativity. She is recognizably the same individual in each instance, although her expression changes. Deeply undercut, solid and massive, the forms bulge outward from the background. The crowding is typically Gothic, but the **naturalism** and classicism of the figures looks forward to the Renaissance.

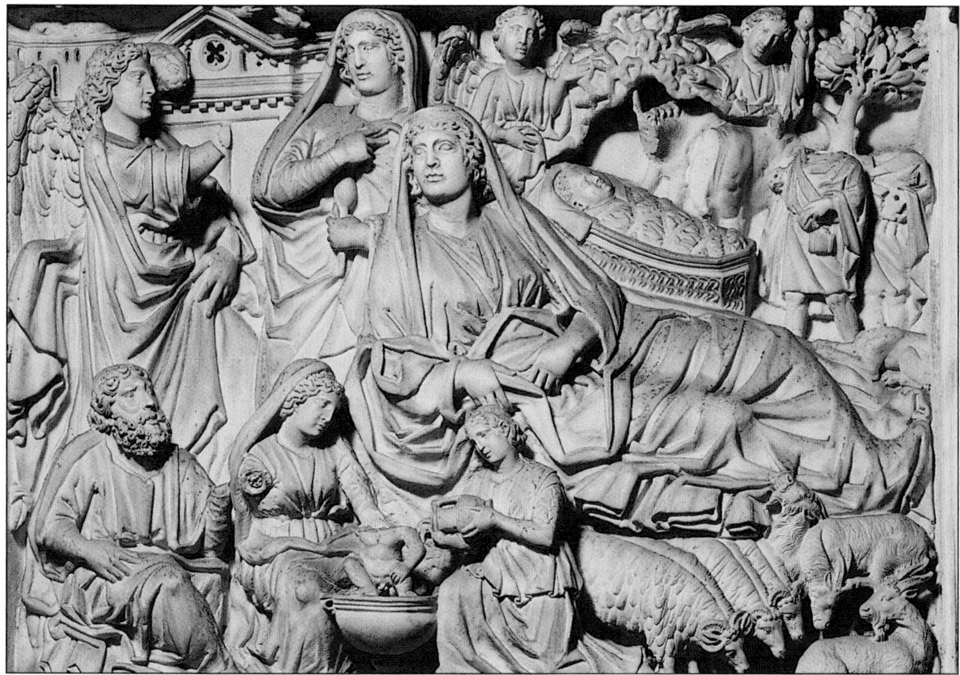

Figure 12.22 Nicola Pisano, *Nativity*, panel on pulpit, Baptistery, Pisa, Italy, 1259–60, marble, $33\frac{1}{2} \times 44\frac{1}{2}''$ (85.1 × 113 cm). Important interests in antiquity and in reviving Italy's cultural past, which were to lead to the Renaissance, are already evident in the sculpture of Nicola Pisano. Ancient Roman sarcophagi reliefs provided inspiration for the classical type of figures.

Nicola's son Giovanni Pisano (ca. 1240/45–after 1314) also carved a *Nativity* for Pisa, this time for the cathedral (fig. 12.23). Executed between 1302 and 1310, the figures are slimmer than his father's, and the Mary seems more a young woman than the matronly figure in the earlier work. Her drapery is more flowing, her body almost substantial beneath its folds. The composition is not as crowded as Nicola's, the effect more energetic than serene. Each figure now has a logical amount of space, and the viewer seems to look down from above, thereby making the composition clearer. Giovanni includes more landscape and setting in his depiction than his father, creating a greater sense of depth, and in his sculpting uses even deeper undercutting for a greater play of light and shade.

Duccio and Giotto. At the end of the thirteenth and beginning of the fourteenth century, two trends emerged in Italian painting, associated with the rival cities of Siena and Florence. Conservative Siena, represented by the artist Duccio, clung to the medieval and Byzantine traditions, favoring abstract patterns, gold backgrounds, and emphasis on line. Progressive Florence, however, represented by the artist Giotto, displayed a greater concern for depiction of the physical world and three-dimensional space and mass. This is the more naturalistic style that Europe would follow for the next several centuries.

DUCCIO [DOOCH-chee-OH] (ca. 1255–before 1319) is frequently mentioned in the Sienese archives, not only for his art but also for disturbing the peace, for his

Figure 12.23 Giovanni Pisano, *Nativity*, panel on pulpit, Cathedral, Pisa, Italy, 1302–10, marble, $34\frac{3}{8} \times 43''$ (87.2 × 109.2 cm). The greater naturalism of Nicola Pisano's son, Giovanni, when carving the same subject half a century later, is evidenced in his work by less crowding, a greater sense of space, and increased attention to the setting.

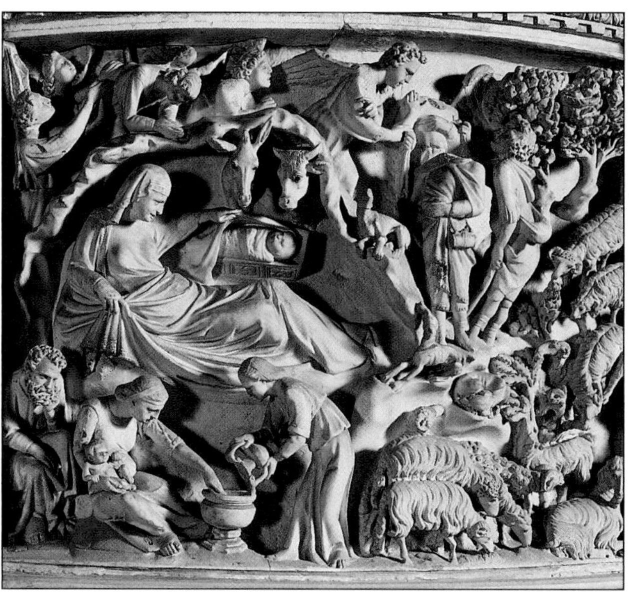

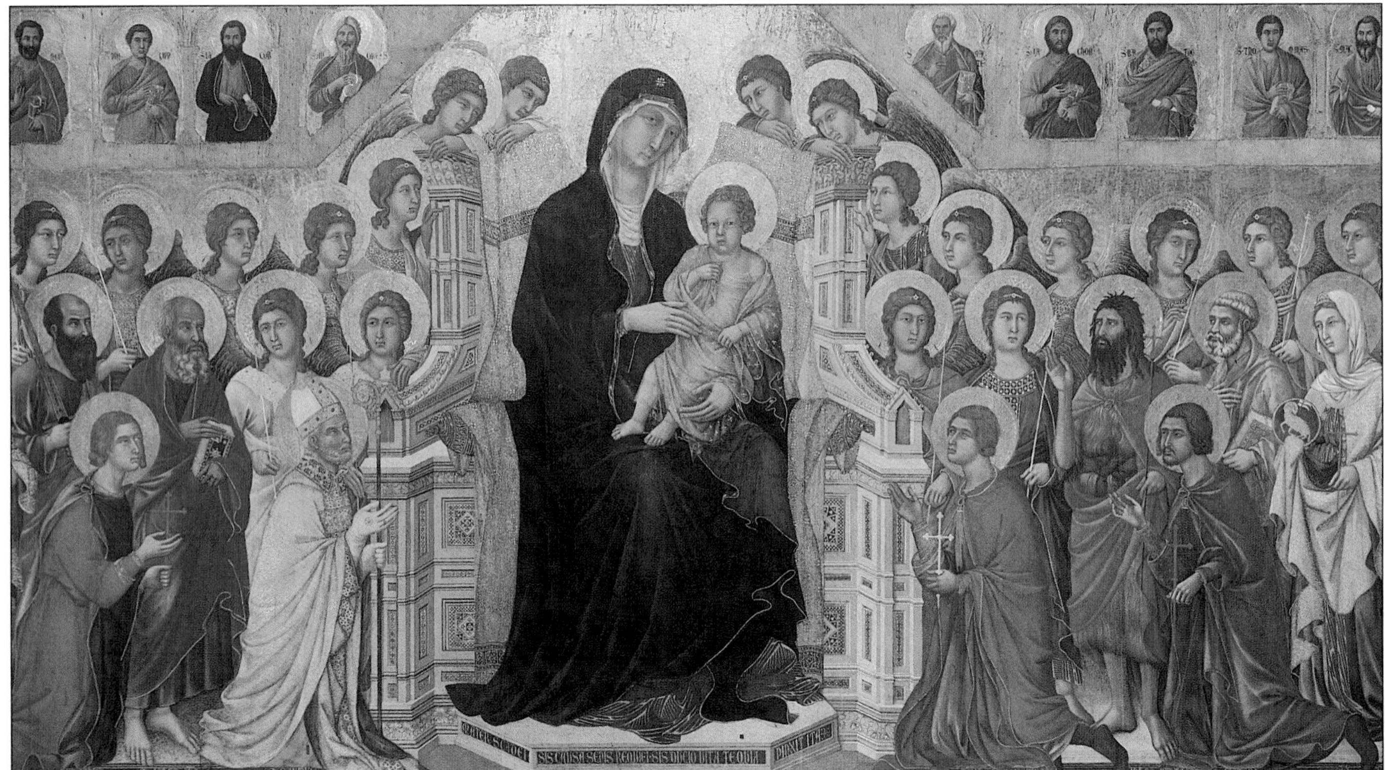

FIGURE 12.24 Duccio, *Madonna and Child Enthroned*, main panel of the *Maestà Altarpiece*, 1308–11, egg tempera and gold on wooden panel, 7′ × 13′6¼″ (2.13 × 4.12 m), Museo dell'-Opera del Duomo, Siena. The paintings by Duccio were the final flowering of the medieval Byzantine tradition in Italy. The *Maestà*, which means "majesty" of the Madonna, portrays Mary as extremely elongated, enormous in size, flanked by angels and saints, as if she were a feudal queen holding court. Bright color and flowing outline are stressed rather than three-dimensionality of solid forms in space.

many wine bills, and for having debts. His most famous work, the *Maestà Altarpiece*, 1308–11, on the front of which is the *Madonna and Child Enthroned* (fig. 12.24) (the Italian word *maestà* refers to the "majesty" of the Madonna), was made for the high altar of the cathedral of Siena. It was painted entirely by Duccio (the contract has survived), although the usual practice at this time was for the artist to employ assistants. When the painting was finished a feast day was proclaimed in Siena.

In this rigidly symmetrical composition, Mary and the infant Jesus are enthroned, surrounded by tiers of saints and angels. Still in the medieval manner, much larger than any of the other figures, Mary is elongated, ethereal, and immaterial. Her drapery has a linear quality emphasized by the gold edging. Outline and silhouette play a major role; the effect of shading is minor. The faces are wistful and melancholic, and the angels look tenderly at Mary. The throne appears to splay outwards, is not rendered with scientific perspective, and does not suggest depth. Duccio represents the culmination of the old Byzantine style rather than the start of a new one.

GIOTTO [JOT-toh] (1267?–1336/7) was Duccio's contemporary. Giotto's naturalism is apparent if we compare his *Madonna and Child Enthroned* (fig. 12.25) to Duccio's. Although Duccio's Madonna seems like an icon, insubstantial and elongated, Giotto's Mary appears more realistic. Not only does she appear to sit in actual physical space, but it is as if real bones lie beneath her skin.

Giotto's most famous work is the extensive fresco cycle portraying the lives of Mary and Jesus in the Arena Chapel (Scrovegni Chapel) in Padua, painted 1305–06. In the scene of the *Lamentation over the Body of Jesus* (fig. 12.26), the composition is used to emphasize the sadness of the subject. Here, the focus of attention is low and off center. Figures bend down to the dead Jesus. The diagonal of the hill leads down to the heads of Mary and Jesus. The figures form a circle around Jesus, leaving a space for one more person—the viewer, who thereby joins in their grieving. Emphasis is on mass rather than line, figures are three-dimensional, solid, and bulky, and seen to occupy the actual space of the landscape. Most important of all, the mourners convey emotion, a tangible sense of grief and loss.

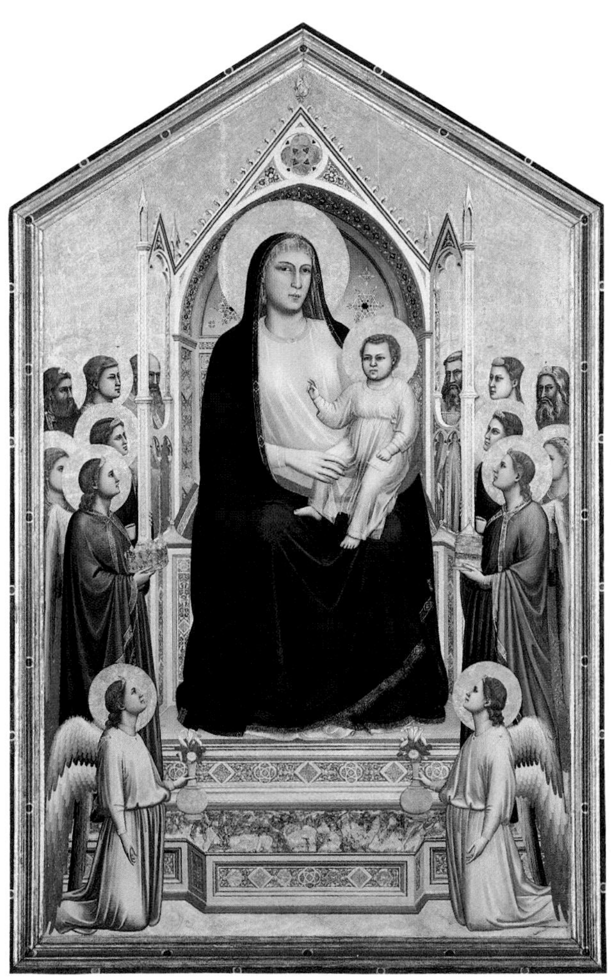

FIGURE 12.25 Giotto, *Madonna and Child Enthroned*, 1310, egg tempera and gold on wooden panel, $10'8'' \times 6'8\frac{1}{4}''$ (3.53×2.05 m), Galleria degli Uffizi, Florence. In contrast to Duccio's slender Mary, Giotto's is solid and appears to sit within the space implied by her throne.

REALISM IN LITERATURE

Boccaccio's Decameron. If the visual arts were becoming more and more naturalistic by the end of the fourteenth century, literature achieved something of the same effect by forsaking Latin for the spoken language, the **vernacular,** of the day. This is especially true of the work of GIOVANNI BOCCACCIO [bo-CAH-choh] (1313–1375). His most famous prose work, the *Decameron*, has similarities with Dante's *Divine Comedy*, on which Boccaccio wrote a commentary. Furthermore, his interest in classical antiquity, his translations of ancient Greek texts, his Latin writings, and his search for lost Roman works make him an early Italian Renaissance figure.

Boccaccio spent much of his youth in Naples, where his father was a merchant and attorney. Trained in banking himself, Boccaccio nonetheless preferred literature, and spent most of his adult life in Florence pursuing a literary career. *The Decameron* is a collection of a hundred ***novelle,*** or short stories, told by ten Florentines, seven women and three men, who leave plague-infested Florence for the neighboring hill town of Fiesole. Written in the vernacular Tuscan, their tales center on the lives and fortunes of ordinary people, who are given a voice for the first time in Western literature. An eye for detail, convincing characters, wit, frankness, and worldly cynicism make Boccacio a lively read.

Chaucer's Canterbury Tales. As a well-educated medieval intellectual, the English poet GEOFFREY CHAUCER [CHAW-ser] (ca. 1342–1400) was, like Boccaccio, familiar with Latin literature, history, and philosophy. He read Ovid and Virgil in their original language, and was familiar with Greek myth, literature, and history through his knowledge of the Latin writers.

The most important influence on Chaucer's work, however, was not Latin but Italian. Chaucer's trip to Italy in 1372 immersed him in Italian literature, especially the works of Dante and Boccaccio. A number of Chaucer's *Canterbury Tales*, as well as the basic narrative structure, derive from Boccaccio's *Decameron.*

Unfinished at the time of his death in 1400, Chaucer had been working on *The Canterbury Tales*, a collection of stories told by a group of pilgrims traveling from London to Canterbury, for nearly fifteen years. The tales depict medieval figures from the highest to the lowest social classes.

Chaucer had originally planned to write 120 tales (or so the Host of the tavern where the pilgrims all first gather tells us in the General Prologue), two for each of his thirty pilgrims to tell on the pilgrimage to Canterbury, and two on the return trip. However, Chaucer only completed twenty-two tales and composed fragments of two others. He also composed a General Prologue, which provides a pretext for the tales—the pilgrimage to the shrine of St. Thomas à Becket at Canterbury introduces the characters, who later narrate their own tales. Chaucer further reveals the characterizations of these narrators through the tales they tell and the manner in which they tell them.

Chaucer's attitude toward the characters in the General Prologue varies. Some, such as the Clerk and the Knight, he depicts as models, whose behavior is to be emulated; others, such as the Monk and the Pardoner, he portrays negatively, with their warts (both literal and figurative) showing. The ironic and satiric portraits of the other pilgrims are constructed through the voice of Chaucer's narrator. Yet this narrator himself is slightly naïve. The "naïve" narrator sometimes fails to discriminate between good and evil manifestations of human behavior or to distinguish between the supposed ideals of certain characters and the less admirable qualities they embody.

Chaucer employs irony as an instrument of satire. His wit and observation—evident throughout the work, though perhaps most clearly in the General Prologue—reveal a

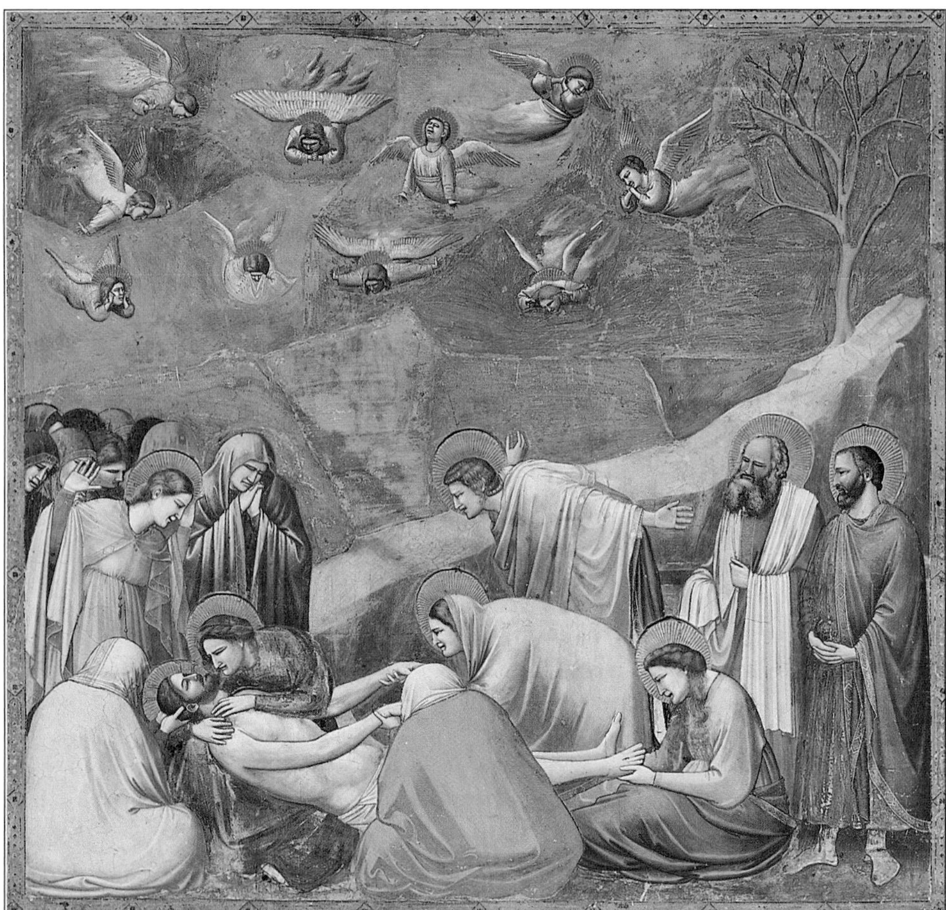

FIGURE 12.26 Giotto, *Lamentation over the Body of Jesus*, Arena (Scrovegni) Chapel, Padua, 1305–06, fresco, $6'6\frac{3}{4}'' \times 6'\frac{7}{8}''$ (2.00 × 1.85 m). The profound grief of this subject is magnified by the way in which it is depicted by Giotto. The center of attention, usually in the physical center of the composition, is instead low on the left, emotionally "down," and the barren background leads the viewer's eyes down to the heads of Jesus and his mother Mary.

zest for life from its lowest and bawdiest to its most elegant and spiritual manifestations.

Christine de Pizan. One of the outstanding writers of the later Middle Ages, CHRISTINE DE PIZAN [PEA-zan] (1364–ca. 1431) was a scholar and court adviser, as well as a poet and writer of prose pieces (fig. 12.27). Born in Venice, Christine de Pizan moved with her father to France, where he served as court astrologer to the French monarch Charles V. There she learned to write French and Italian as well as to read Latin, an unusual accomplishment for a woman at the time.

At the age of fifteen, she married a court notary, Eugène of Castal, who died four years later in an epidemic. As a widow with three young children, she began writing to support her family. Before long she was a recognized literary luminary, an accomplished poet and the officially sanctioned biographer of Charles V. In her works, she consistently argued for the recognition of women's status and abilities.

Among her many works are a poem about Joan of Arc; a set of letters challenging the depiction of women in the influential medieval poem *The Romance of the Rose;* a book of moral proverbs; a dream vision; a collection of a hundred brief narratives accompanied by their own commentary; a manual of instruction for knights; an admonitory essay on the art of prudence, *The Book of Feats of Arms and Chivalry;* and her best known work, *The Book of the City of Ladies.* A universal history of women, *The Book of the City of Ladies* includes discussion of pagan as well as Christian women, of those long deceased as well as those of her own time, and of fictional characters as well as actual people. Throughout the book, she attempts to alter the reader's perceptions of women. It is this desire to represent women from a woman's point of view that makes the writing of Christine de Pizan unique. Her book is a refutation of misogynistic images of women constructed by male writers of the past. In particular, she rebuts the images of women portrayed in Giovanni Boccaccio's *De mulieribus claris (Concerning Famous*

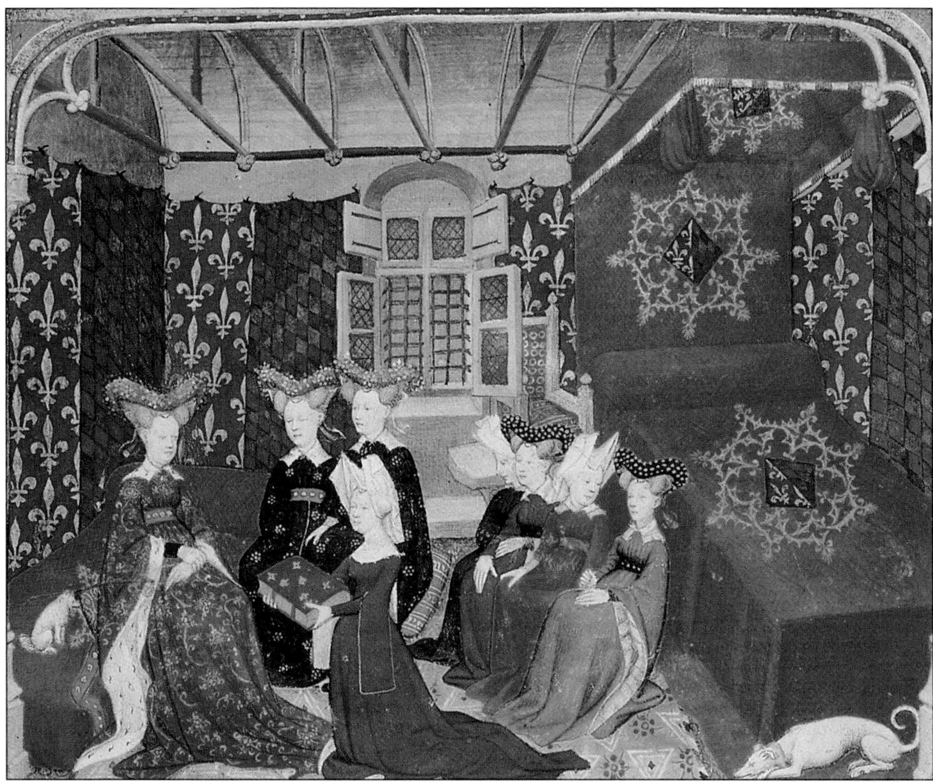

FIGURE 12.27 *Christine de Pizan Presenting Her Poems to Isabel of Bavaria*, manuscript illumination, British Library, London. The illumination shows the world of women that Christine de Pizan celebrates in her writing.

Women). For example, in response to the charge that women are greedy, she states that what appears as greed in women is a prudent and sensible response to male profligacy. Because men squander, women have to protect themselves against such destructive behavior. She counterattacks by arguing that women are fundamentally generous.

Even as she argued for opportunities for women, Christine de Pizan echoed the ideals of Christian life as espoused in church teaching. She supported the goals of Christian marriage, in which a commitment between spouses enables them to advance in grace and spirituality while fulfilling their roles as husband and wife. To a large extent, she appears to have been an idealist, one who aspired to achieve the highest values articulated in her religious tradition while ridding it of its entrenched bias against women.

While urging women to accept their place in the hierarchy of the time, she also encouraged them to fulfill their potential—intellectually, socially, and spiritually—by developing nobility of soul, whatever their particular social status or individual circumstances. Nobility, for Christine de Pizan, was a matter of mind, heart, and spirit, rather than of birthright. She believed that through patient and persistent striving, women of her time could become embodiments of the highest ideals of heart and mind.

SECULAR SONG

Guillaume de Machaut. In the fourteenth century, medieval music underwent significant changes, including the rise of secular music along with church music. Drinking songs and music that drew on the everyday began to be composed and performed as often as devotional music inspired by religious faith. In addition, a new system of musical notation had developed by the fourteenth century so composers were now able to spell out the rhythmic values as well as the melodic pitches of notes. Other changes in musical style, such as the use of syncopation (which emphasizes notes off the regular beat), became so significant that theorists referred to the new music as ***ars nova*** (new art) to distinguish it from the *ars antiqua* (ancient or old art) of previous centuries.

One composer who wrote both sacred and secular music in the *ars nova* style was GUILLAUME DE MACHAUT [ghee-OHM duh mash-OH] (1300–1377), the foremost French composer of the time and one of France's leading poets. Like Giotto in painting, Machaut helped usher in the Renaissance by breaking away from the older medieval style. Machaut wrote the first complete polyphonic setting of a mass, called *La Messe de Nostre Dame* (Our Lady's Mass). Until this time, the mass was a collection of Gregorian chants by anonymous composers; Machaut's was the first by

Cultural Impact

Fundamental structural and aesthetic changes occurred in architecture during the Gothic period. The supporting role of the thick walls and the small windows of Romanesque architecture were superceded by exterior flying buttresses and vast stained-glass windows in Gothic architecture (Chartres Cathedral, figs. 12.5, 12.6, 12.18).

In modern times, rather than flying buttresses of hand-hewn stone, architecture employs modern materials and techniques, such as skeletal steel supports, reinforced concrete, and cantilevered construction. Rather than windows of meticulously assembled stained glass, modern windows are mass produced in great volume in factories. Slender skeletal constructions with glass walls are a characteristic of modern urban life, as seen in Mies van der Rohe's Lake Shore Drive Apartment Houses, Chicago, 1950–52 (fig. 23.8), and the sweeping space and colored glass of Gothic churches reappear occasionally in modern variation, such as Corbusier's Notre-Dame-du-Haut, Ronchamp, France, 1950–55 (fig. 23.9).

The interest in human emotions and everyday life increased in the art of the Gothic period, as evidenced in numerous images of Mary and the infant Jesus. *Notre-Dame-de-Paris*, sculpted in the early fourteenth century (fig. 12.15), portrays a fashionable young French mother and her endearing child. In the same years, the painter Giotto portrayed Mary as a real Italian mother holding her son. (fig. 12.25).

In more recent years, images of maternal love and devotion may be created for reasons connected with political/social problems rather than with religion. Thus Käthe Kollwitz's *The Mothers*, a lithograph of 1919, (fig. 22.9), refers to the plight of widowed German mothers in the aftermath of World War I, and Dorothea Lange's photograph of 1936 of a widowed *Migrant Mother* (fig. 22.26) with several of her children comments on the Great Depression in the United States.

an identified composer. As the liturgy's most important musical form, the mass, which reenacts the last supper of Christ, became a foundation for many other multimovement musical forms that followed.

Machaut spent most of his life at court. Born in the French province of Champagne, he traveled throughout Europe and spent his later years in Reims. During his many travels, he presented carefully written and decorated copies of his music and poems to court patrons and foreign nobility. The great care he took in making these copies has ensured their survival.

English Song. The English song "Sumer Is Icumen In" is unlike anything else that has survived from the thirteenth century in providing a foretaste of musical tendencies and techniques that were to emerge over a century and a half later, in the works of Renaissance madrigalists such as Thomas Weelkes and Thomas Morley (see Chapter 14). The words of the text were composed in English, not Latin, and they celebrate nature rather than religion, the physical life of earth rather than the spiritual joys of heaven. The composer set the words to a lively tune, which is sung by all four voice parts in a canon, or round. Each voice enters before the others have finished so all four sing simultaneously, although they are at different places in the music at any given time.

KEY TERMS

Gothic
cathedral
flying buttress
rose window
High Gothic
Flamboyant Gothic
Rayonnant Gothic
fan vaulting
jamb
International Style
cartoon
organum
cantus firmus
tenor
naturalism
vernacular
novelle
ars nova

www. Websites for Further Study

http://www.elore.com/Gothic/Glossary/components.htm
(A good site on Gothic architecture, with a glossary and links.)

http://web.kyoto-inet.or.jp/org/orion/eng/hst/gothic.html
(Visit many of the greatest Gothic cathedrals on this site.)

http://www.metmuseum.org/works_of_art/collection.asp
(This site discusses the seven individual tapestries known as the "Unicorn Tapestries," some of the most beautiful and complex works of the late Middle Ages.)

http://w3.rz-berlin.mpg.de/cmp/machaut.html
(This site has a brief but thorough discussion on Machaut, one of the most important Gothic composers.)

http://worldart.sjsu.edu/prt31*1$596
(This site covers select sculptural works of the Gothic era found on and in French cathedrals.)

http://wsu.edu/~dee/MA/INTRO.HTM
(Overview of later medieval culture and history.)

http://www.press.uchicago.edu/Complete/Series/LMERMF.html
(Late medieval and Renaissance music in facsimile.)

Chapter 13

History

1494	First French invasion of Italy
ca. 1495	Savonarola takes control of Florence
1494–1512	Medici exiled from Florence
1516–23	Leo X controls Florence
1519	Charles V becomes Holy Roman Emperor
1523–27	Clement VII controls Florence
1527	Sack of Rome
1553–63	Council of Trent

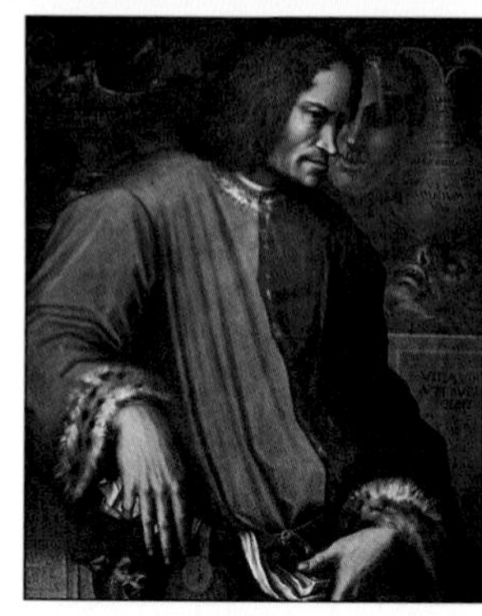

Arts and Architecture

ca. 1425–30s	Donatello, *David*
1427–28	Masaccio, *Trinity*
1425–52	Ghiberti, *Gates of Paradise*
1430	Dufay Alma Redemptoris Mater
1436	Brunelleschi finishes dome for Florence Cathedral; Dufay, "Il Duomo"
1453–55	Donatello, *Mary Magdalene*
1438–45	Fra Angelico, *Annunciation*
1445–ca. 1452	Michelozzo, Palazzo Medici-Riccardi
ca. 1484–86	Botticelli, *Birth of Venus*
ca. 1499	Michelangelo, *Pietà*
1502	Josquin des Près, "Ave Maria . . . virgo serena"
ca. 1503	Leonardo da Vinci, *Mona Lisa*
1508–12	Michelangelo, ceiling of Sistine Chapel
1510–11	Raphael, *School of Athens*
ca. 1520	Properzia de Rossi, *Joseph and Potiphar's Wife*
1524–59	Laurentian Library
1534–40	Parmigianino, *Madonna with the Long Neck*
1543–54	Cellini, *Perseus*
ca. 1559	Sofonisba Anguissola, *Portrait of the Artist's Sister Minerva*
1565	Palestrina, *Pope Marcellus Mass*

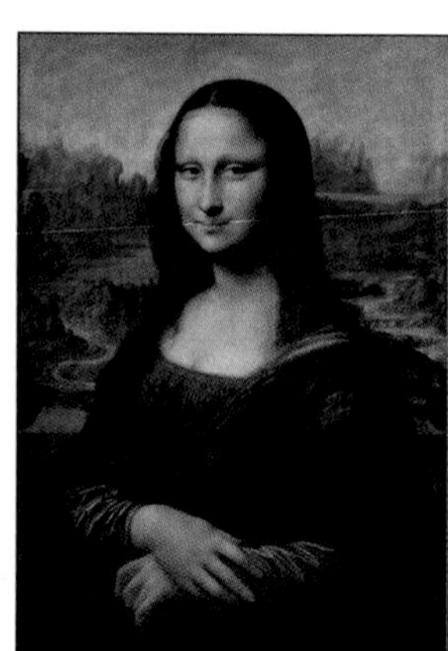

Literature and Philosophy

1327–72	Petrarch, *Canzonieri*
1429	Bruni finishes *History of Florence*
1435–50	Alberti, *De pictura/De re aedificatoria*
ca. 1455	Gutenberg and the printing press
1462	Platonic Academy of Philosophy
ca. 1484–86	Ficino, *Theologia Platonica*
1486	Pico, *Oration on the Dignity of Man*
1524–59	Castiglione, *Book of the Courtier*
1534–40	Machiavelli, *The Prince*
1550	Vasari, *Lives*
1553–63	Cellini, *Autobiography*

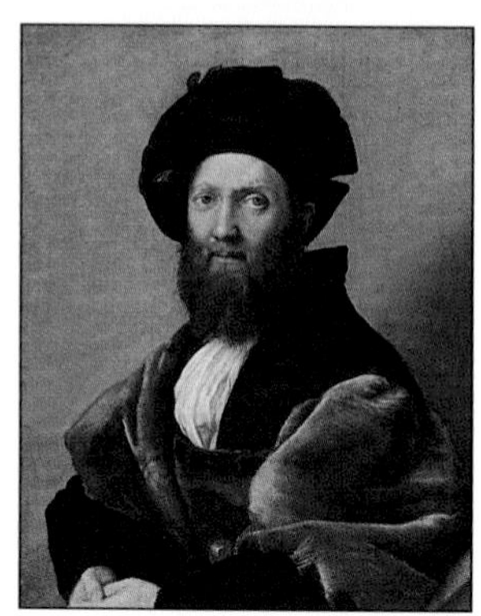

Renaissance and Mannerism in Italy

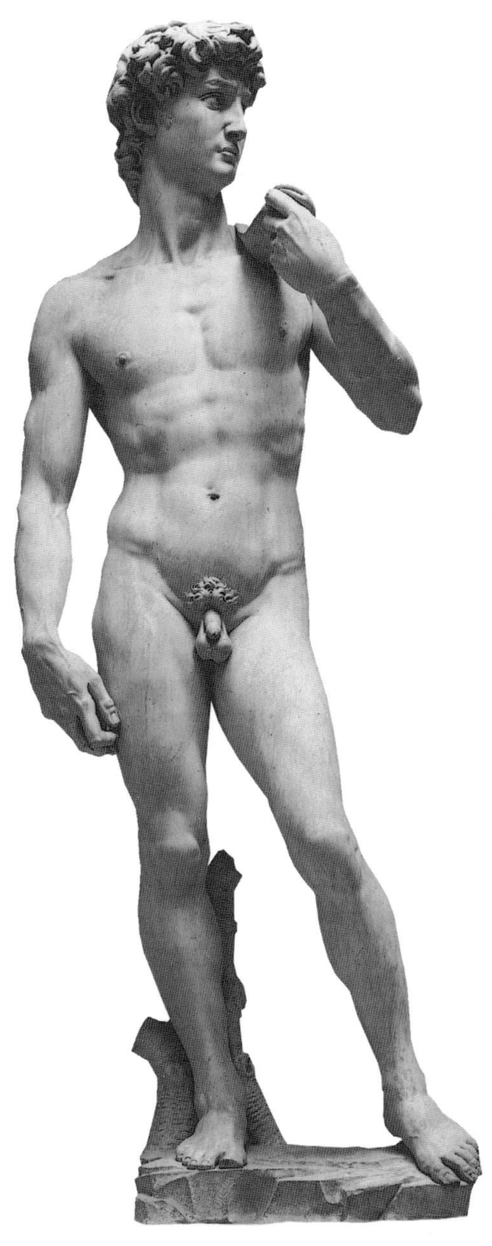

Michelangelo, *David*, 1501–04, marble, height 13′5″ (4.09 m), Galleria dell'Accademia, Florence.

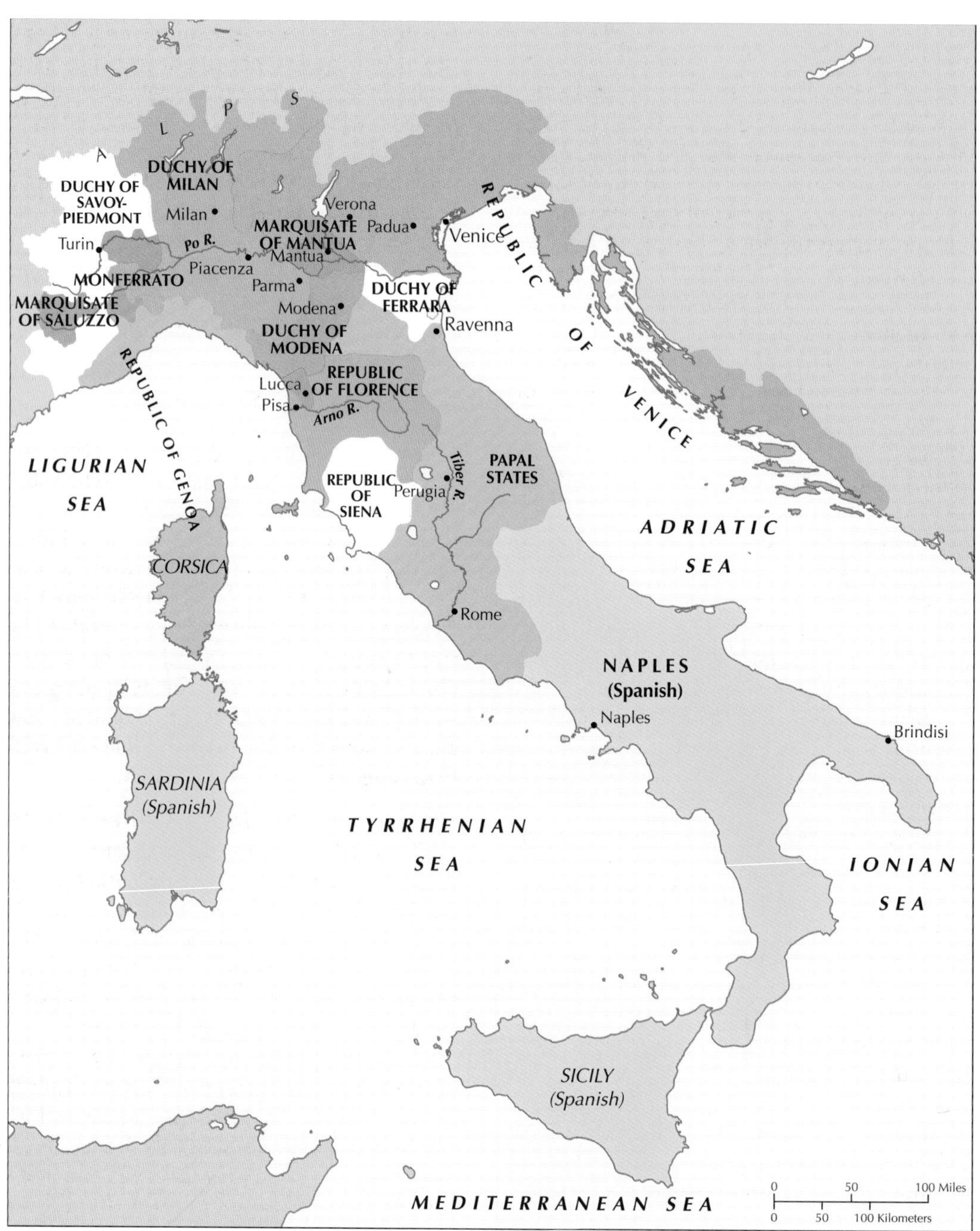

MAP 13.1 The division of Italy into city-states at the end of the fifteenth century.

CHAPTER OVERVIEW

EARLY RENAISSANCE

Rebirth of interest in antiquity, the individual, and nature

HIGH RENAISSANCE

Maturation of the arts

MANNERISM

Moving away from the classical ideal

EARLY RENAISSANCE

THE TRANSITION FROM THE MIDDLE AGES to the Renaissance was gradual. The intense religiosity of the Middle Ages persisted into the Renaissance, though it came to coexist with a more worldly philosophy and a more secular outlook. A number of important broad changes developed during the Renaissance, such as the development of nation states, the advent of commercial capitalism, the emergence of the middle class, and the rise of rationalist thought. European exploration of the Americas was abetted by scientific and technological developments, especially in navigation. And the invention of movable type, which allowed for printing, expanded the world of learning.

Of particular importance in Europe, originally in Italy, was a reinvigoration of classical learning based on the literary and philosophical writings of the Greeks and Romans. This development, called "classical humanism," was a defining Renaissance intellectual preoccupation. The influence of Greco-Roman antiquity on Renaissance Europe was pervasive, and included an impact on social, political, and diplomatic life, as well as upon education and the arts. Of great importance is the part played by Arab scholars in preserving ancient Greek scholarship, which enabled European scholars like Petrarch and Boccaccio to benefit from their labors.

In Italy, changes were developing across the social, political, and economic spectrums. Italy underwent significant urbanization, increased political stability, and economic expansion, along with increasing contact with other societies. Venice, for example, was a crossroads for East–West commercial exchanges, and also for exchange of customs and ideas.

The French word **Renaissance,** meaning "rebirth," was first employed in the nineteenth century to describe the period from the early fifteenth century to the middle of the next. The Italians of the time believed this period marked a radical break from the past and a reinvention of the civilization and ideals of classical Greece and Rome.

The Renaissance was characterized by—in addition to this interest in classical art, literature, law, and ideals—an interest in the individual person, now emerging from the anonymity of the Middle Ages, as well as a new fascination with nature and the physical world. A number of Italian city-states had grown powerful in Italy—the kingdom of Naples in the south, the church states around Rome, and in the north, the duchy of Milan and the republics of Venice and Florence. Located on the main road connecting Rome with the north, Florence had become the center of trade, and European banking had been established with credit operations available to support and spur on an increase in trade.

Florence itself was ruled by its guilds, or *arti.* The seven major guilds, which were controlled by bankers, lawyers, and exporters, originally ran the civic government, but by the middle of the fourteenth century all the guilds, even the lesser guilds of middle-ranking tradesmen, had achieved some measure of political voice, and the city prided itself on its "representative" government and its status as a republic. Still, the long-standing division between those who favored the Holy Roman Emperor and those who favored the popes continued unabated. Such civil strife, sometimes marked by street battles, had one inevitable result. By the fifteenth century, what Florence needed most was a leader with enough political skill, power, and wealth to stop the feuding.

THE MEDICIS' FLORENCE

A single family, the Medici, led Florence to its unrivaled position as the cultural center of Renaissance Europe in the fifteenth century. The family had begun to accumulate its fortune by lending money to other Florentines out of income derived from its two wool workshops. GIOVANNI DI BICCI DE' MEDICI [geo-VAHN-nee dee BEE-chee deh MED-uh-chee] (1360–1429) multiplied this fortune by setting up branch banks in major Italian cities and creating close financial allegiances with the papacy in Rome, allegiances that tended to switch the balance of power, making secular concerns more important than religious ones to the Vatican.

Cosimo de' Medici. COSIMO [CAH-zee-moh] (1389–1464), the son of Giovanni Di Bicci, led the family to a position of unquestioned preeminence, not only in Florence but, as branches of the Medici banks opened elsewhere, throughout Europe. Although never the official leader of the city, Cosimo ruled from behind the scenes. By 1458, Pope Pius II said of Cosimo that "He is King in everything but name."

Cosimo's power was based on calculated acts of discretion and benevolence. Cosimo built the first public library since ancient times and stocked it with ancient manuscripts and books, chiefly Greek and Roman, with a special eye toward the works of Plato and Aristotle. At some point, Cosimo employed virtually every major Italian artist, architect, writer, philosopher, or scholar of the day.

In many ways, Cosimo's largesse simply solidified what was already fact—Florence had been a cultural center since the middle of the fourteenth century (see Chapter 12). The growing wealth of the city itself, together with the peace brought by Cosimo's leadership, created an atmosphere in which the arts could prosper, and this in turn contributed to the increasing sophistication of its citizenry.

Lorenzo the Magnificent. The city's dream of achieving the status of the Golden Age of Athens was fully realized by LORENZO [LOR-enn-zoh] (1449–1492), Cosimo's grandson, who assumed his place as head of the Medici family at the age of twenty in 1469, inaugurating twenty-three years of influence. Lorenzo's father, PIERO [pea-AIR-oh] (1416–1469), cursed with ill health, had ruled for only five years after Cosimo before his own death, but he had raised Lorenzo in Cosimo's image, and Lorenzo quickly established himself as a force to be reckoned with. "Lorenzo the Magnificent" he was called (fig. 13.1), and he lived with a sense of grandeur. He was one of the leading poets of his day, as well as an accomplished musician, playing the lute and composing dances. He surrounded himself with scholars, built palaces and parks, sponsored festivals and pageants, all the while dipping deeply into the city's coffers, which he controlled, as well as his own. He commissioned little in the way of painting, preferring instead to spend money on gemstones and ancient vases, which he believed to be better investments. Many of the precious stones in his collection, for example, were valued at over a thousand florins (the coin of the day), whereas a painting by Botticelli might be bought for as little as a hundred florins. Spend Lorenzo did, and by the time of his death in 1492, the Medici bank was in financial trouble and Florence itself was verging on bankruptcy.

Although the Medici ruled Florence with minor interruptions until 1737, they never again held the same power and authority as Cosimo and Lorenzo. Outside Florence, the most important patron of the Renaissance in Rome would be Lorenzo's son, Pope Leo X. In generations to come, several female Medici descendants would marry the most powerful figures in Europe—Catherine de' Medici (1519–1589) was queen to Henry II of France, and Marie de' Medici (1573–1542) was queen consort to Henry IV of France.

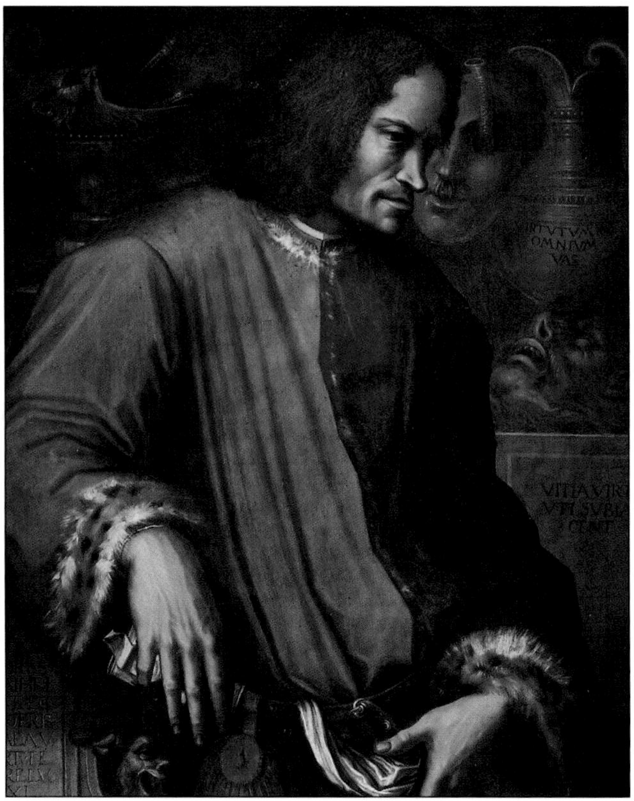

FIGURE 13.1 Giorgio Vasari, *Posthumous Portrait of Lorenzo the Magnificent*, oil on canvas, Galleria degli Uffizi, Florence. SCALA/Art Resource, NY. The impressive presence of Lorenzo, as well as his broken nose, are recorded in this painting by Vasari, author of the *Lives of the Most Excellent Painters, Sculptors, and Architects*.

THE HUMANIST SPIRIT

Cosimo, Piero, and Lorenzo de' Medici were all **humanists**—they believed in the worth and dignity of the individual. Celebrating human reason, spirit, and physical beauty, the humanists echoed the Greek philosopher Protagorus in seeing human beings as the measure of all things. Seeking to discover what was best about humanity, they turned to the culture of classical antiquity. In the literature, history, rhetoric, and philosophy of ancient Greece and Rome, they discovered what the Latin scholar and poet PETRARCH [PEH-trark] (1304–1372) a century before had called a "golden wisdom." Cosimo and Lorenzo worked to make Florence the humanist capital of the world, a place where the golden wisdom of the ancients might flourish.

Table 13–1 POPES DURING THE RENAISSANCE AND MANNERIST PERIODS

The Catholic popes of the fifteenth and sixteenth centuries and the dates they reigned:

Boniface IX	1389–1404	Innocent VIII	1484–1492	Paul IV	1555–1559
Innocent VII	1404–1406	Alexander VI	1492–1503	Pius IV	1559–1565
Gregory XII	1406–1415	Pius III	1503	St. Pius V	1566–1572
Martin V	1417–1431	Julius II	1503–1513	Gregory XIII	1572–1585
Eugene IV	1431–1447	Leo X	1513–1521	Sixtus V	1585–1590
Nicholas V	1447–1455	Adrian VI	1522–1523	Urban VII	1590
Callistus III	1455–1458	Clement VII	1523–1534	Gregory XIV	1590–1591
Pius II	1458–1464	Paul III	1534–1549	Innocent IX	1591
Paul II	1464–1471	Julius III	1550–1555	Clement VIII	1592–1605
Sixtus IV	1471–1484	Marcellus II	1555		

Cross Currents

MONTEZUMA'S TENOCHTITLAN

While Florence stood as the center of the Early Renaissance world, in the other hemisphere stood a city of equal grandeur, one that the Europeans did not know existed until Hernán Cortés invaded Mexico in 1519. It was called Tenochtitlan, and it was the capital of Montezuma's Aztec empire.

The Aztecs, who founded the city, believed they had been ordered by their god Huitzilopochtli to wander until they saw an eagle perched upon a prickly pear, or *tenochtli*. They finally encountered such a vision in 1325 on an island in the marshes of Lake Texcoco in the Valley of Mexico. There they built their city, connecting it to the mainland by four causeways. By the end of the fifteenth century, it was a metropolis inhabited by 150,000 to 200,000 people and ruled by a priest and emperor, Montezuma.

The *Codex Mendoza* (fig. 13.2) is the fullest account that we have of early sixteenth-century Aztec life. It consists of seventy-two annotated pictorial pages together with sixty-three more pages of related Spanish commentary. It was compiled under the supervision of Spanish friars and at the request of the Spanish crown in about 1541 to aid in their colonial expansion.

As depicted by Aztec scribes, the city is represented by the eagle on the cactus, the shield and arrows symbolizing war, and the waterways dividing the city into equal quadrants. At the heart of the city was the Great Pyramid, imaged by the scribes in the temple at the top. Here, the Aztecs worshiped both Huitzilopochtli, god of the sun and of warfare, and Tlaloc, god of rain and fertility, and here they engaged in ritual human sacrifice to both gods by cutting out the still-beating hearts of their victims, then decapitating them.

As the cultural center of the Aztec civilization, Tenochtitlan was magnificent, grander in fact than anything in Europe at the time. In the words of one of Cortés's soldiers: "When we saw . . . that straight and level causeway going towards Tenochtitlan, we were amazed. . . . Some of our soldiers even asked whether the things that we saw were not a dream."

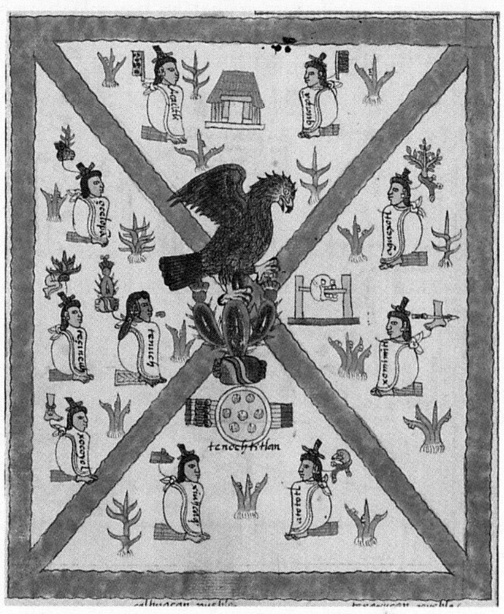

FIGURE 13.2 *The Founding of Tenochtitlan*, page from the *Codex Mendoza*, Aztec, sixteenth century, ink and color on paper, $81\frac{7}{10} \times 12\frac{3}{8}''$ (21.5 × 31.5 cm), The Bodleian Library, Oxford. The skull rack just to the right of center is one of the very few images in the Codex that openly acknowledges the practice of human sacrifice in Aztec life.

Petrarch is often called the father of humanism, and in many ways he determined its high moral tone. He believed that learning was the key to living a virtuous life, and that life should be an eternal quest for truth. Every individual leading a virtuous life in the pursuit of knowledge and truth would provide a basis for improving humanity's lot. He encouraged an appreciation of beauty, in nature and in human endeavor, which he thought to be a manifestation of the divine. For Petrarch, reading the ancients was like having conversations with them, and he took to writing letters to the ancients as if they were personal friends, even family. He called the poet Virgil his brother and Cicero his father. In the writings of the ancients, Petrarch sensed their uniquely human (noble and ignoble) qualities.

In the middle of the fourteenth century, Petrarch's friend, the writer Boccaccio, was one of the first men to study Greek since the classical age itself. During the next fifty years, humanist scholars combed monastery libraries for long-ignored ancient Greek texts and translated them into Latin and Italian. By 1400, the works of Homer, Aeschylus, Sophocles, Euripides, Aristophanes, Herodotus, Thucydides, and all of Plato's dialogues were available. In addition, after the fall of Constantinople to the Muslim forces of the Ottoman Turks in 1453, ending the already weakening Byzantine Empire, Greek scholars flooded into Italy. Greek learning spread with the rapid rise of printing in Italy following Johann Gutenberg's invention of printing with movable type in 1455. Between 1456 and 1500, more books were published than had been copied by manuscript scribes in the previous thousand years. Many of these were in vernacular (or native) Italian, which contributed to the growing literacy of the middle class. By the sixteenth century, many educated persons owned the complete works of Plato.

THE PLATONIC ACADEMY OF PHILOSOPHY

The center of humanist study was the Platonic Academy of Philosophy in Florence, founded by Cosimo de' Medici in 1462 and supported with special enthusiasm by Lorenzo the Magnificent. The academy sponsored **Neoplatonism,** or a "new Platonism," which sought to revive Platonic ideals in contemporary culture, especially as espoused by the Roman philosopher PLOTINUS [Ploh-TINE-us] (205–270 C.E.). The Platonic Academy was an important example of the shift of interest from Aristotle during the Middle Ages to Plato during the Renaissance.

Marsilio Ficino. At the head of the academy was MARSILIO FICINO [fi-CHEE-noh] (1433–1499), who translated both Plato and Plotinus into Latin and wrote the *Theologia Platonica* (1482). Ficino's Neoplatonism was a conscious rereading of Plato (see Chapter 3), particularly his dualistic vision of the psyche (roughly equivalent to the soul or spirit) trapped in the body, but Ficino thought we could glimpse the higher world of forms or ideas through study and learning, and so he looked to Plotinus. Plotinus argued that the material and spiritual worlds could be united through ecstatic, or mystical, vision. Following Plotinus, Ficino conceived of beauty in the things of this world as God's means of making himself manifest to humankind. The contemplation and study of beauty in nature—and in all things—was a form of worship, a manifestation of divine or spiritual love, and Plato's ideas about love were central to Ficino's philosophy. Like erotic love, spiritual love is inspired by physical beauty, but spiritual love moves beyond the physical to an intellectual plane and, eventually, to such an elevated spiritual level that it results in the soul's union with God. Thus, in Neoplatonic terms, Lorenzo's fondness for gems was a type of spiritual love, as was Petrarch's love for Laura, celebrated in his sonnets, and so was the painter Botticelli's love of the human form (both discussed later in this chapter). If in real things one could discover the divine, realism became, in Neoplatonic terms, a form of idealism. In fact, Ficino saw "Platonic love," the love of beauty, as a kind of spiritual bond on which the strongest kind of community could be constructed. In this way, Neoplatonism even had political implications. The Neoplatonists envisioned Florence as a city whose citizenry was spiritually bound together in a common love of the beautiful.

Pico della Mirandola. Another great Neoplatonic philosopher at the academy was PICO DELLA MIRANDOLA [PEA-coh DELL-ah mee-RAN-doh-lah] (1463–1494), whose religious devotion, intense scholarship, and boundless optimism attracted many followers. His *Oration on the Dignity of Man* (1486) encapsulates one of the central impulses of the Renaissance: humankind serving as a link between the lower orders of nature, including animals, and the higher spiritual orders, of which angels are a part. For Pico, human beings possess free will; they can make of themselves what they wish. Though linked with the lower order of matter, they are capable of rising to the higher realm of spirit and ultimately being united with God. Each person's destiny is thus a matter of individual choice.

In the *Oration*, Pico presents God speaking to Adam, telling him that "in conformity with thy free judgment in whose hands I have placed thee, thou art confined by no bonds, and constrained by no limits." God also tells Adam directly that he is "the molder and maker" of himself, who "canst grow downward into the lower natures which are brutes" or "upward from the mind's reason into the higher natures which are divine." This central tenet of humanist philosophy is often misunderstood to mean that an emphasis on the individual results in or implies a rejection of God. Although Pico, and humanists in general, place the responsibility for human action squarely on humans and not on the Almighty, Pico also believed the human mind—with its ability to reason and imagine—could conceive of and move toward the divine. It follows that individual genius, which was allowed to flower in Renaissance Italy as never before in Western culture, is the worldly manifestation of divine truth.

ARCHITECTURE

Renaissance architecture reflects a renewed interest in ancient Roman models for mathematically derived proportions as well as logic of construction.

Filippo Brunelleschi. The greatest architect of the Early Renaissance was FILIPPO BRUNELLESCHI [brew-nuh-LESS-key] (1377–1446), whose triumph is the dome of Florence Cathedral (fig. 13.3). Measuring $138\frac{1}{2}$ feet wide and 367 feet high, it was the largest dome since the Pantheon built in 125 C.E. (see Chapter 4). Although influenced by antique architecture, the octagonal dome of Florence Cathedral does not look like the hemispherical dome of the ancient Roman Pantheon. Using the basic structural principles perfected in the pointed arches of Gothic cathedrals, Brunelleschi produced a dome with less outward thrust than a hemispherical one. Because his predecessor, Arnolfo di Cambio, had designed the base of the dome to be extraordinarily wide, Brunelleschi flanked his octagonal dome with three half domes to buttress it.

Brunelleschi used stone at the bottom of the dome; for the upper portion, he used brick. The heavier material at the bottom produced a self-buttressing system, an idea seen in the Pantheon. Brunelleschi's innovation was to build a double dome with an inner and an outer shell—a dome within a dome that was much lighter than the solid concrete dome of the Pantheon. The octagonal dome is reinforced by eight major ribs, visible on the exterior, plus three minor ribs between every two major ribs. Finally, Michelozzo added an open structure to crown the roof, a **lantern.** The metal lantern's weight stabilized the whole, its downward pressure keeping the ribs from spreading apart at the top.

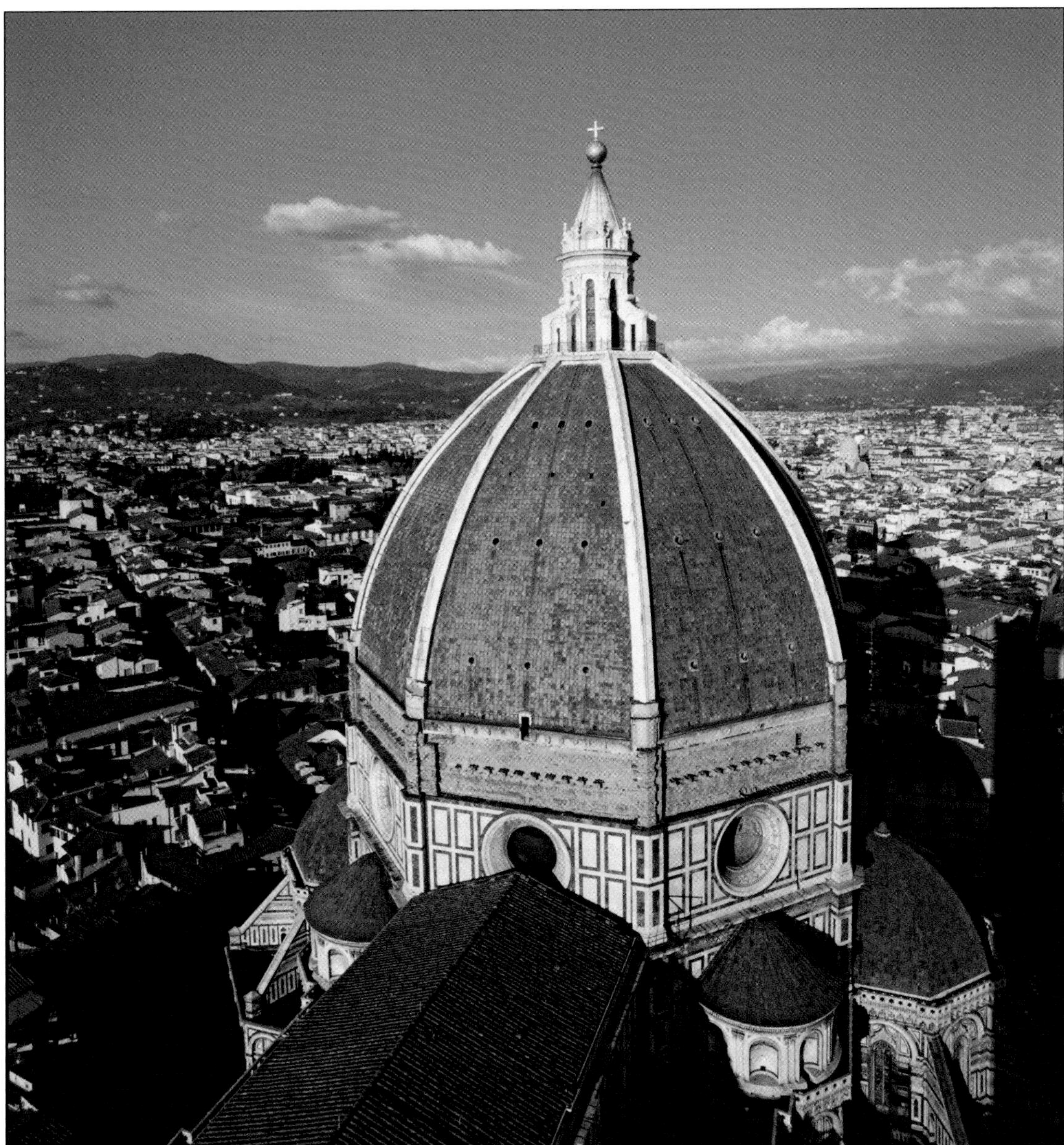

FIGURE 13.3 Filippo Brunelleschi, Florence Cathedral, dome, 1420–36; lantern completed 1471. Brunelleschi managed to erect this enormous double-shell pointed dome without the use of temporary scaffolding. It is the major landmark of Florence.

Leon Battista Alberti. The other great architect of the day, LEON BATTISTA ALBERTI [al-BEAR-tee] (1404–1472), was celebrated both as an architect and as an author. He was the first to detail the principles of linear perspective in his treatise *De pictura* (*On Painting*), written in 1434–35. His ten books on architecture, *De re aedificatoria*, completed about 1450, were inspired by the late-first-century B.C.E. Roman writer Vitruvius, who had himself written an encyclopedic ten-volume survey of classical architecture.

Alberti worked to create beauty in architecture that derived from harmony among all parts, using mathematics to determine the proportions of his buildings. A prime example is the church of Sant' Andrea in Mantua (fig. 13.4), designed in 1470 and completed after his death. Hampered by an older building on the site, Alberti had to adapt his ideal design for the church to the preexisting surroundings. His solution exemplifies Renaissance theory. For the facade he combined the triangular pediment of a classical temple with the arches characteristic of ancient Roman triumphal arches—one large central arch flanked by two smaller arches. The facade balances horizontals and verticals, with the height of the facade equaling the width. Four colossal Corinthian pilasters paired with small pilasters visually unite the stories of the facade. Large and small pilasters of the same dimensions

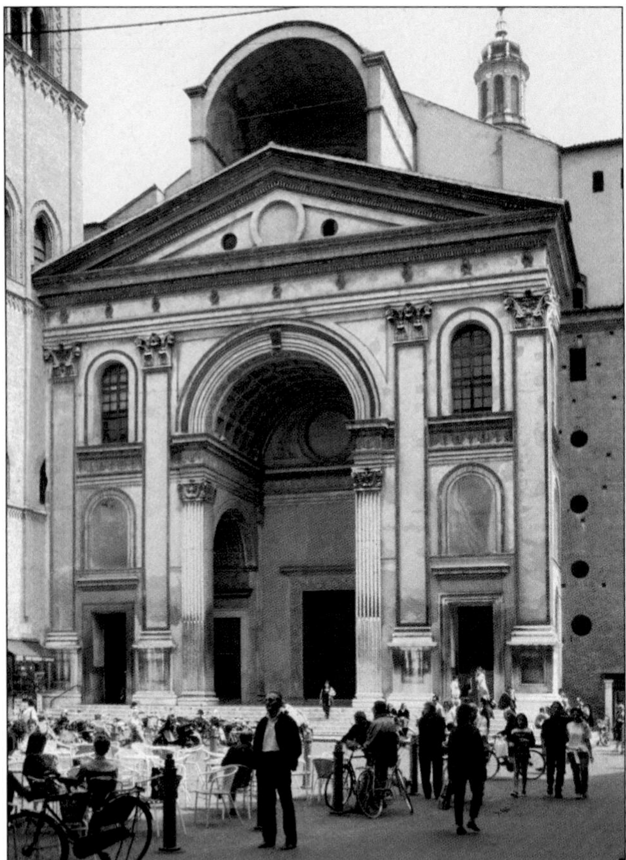

FIGURE 13.4 Leon Battista Alberti, Sant' Andrea, Mantua, facade, designed 1470. An ideal demonstration of the Early Renaissance devotion to the antique, the design of this facade combines the form of an ancient temple with that of an ancient triumphal arch.

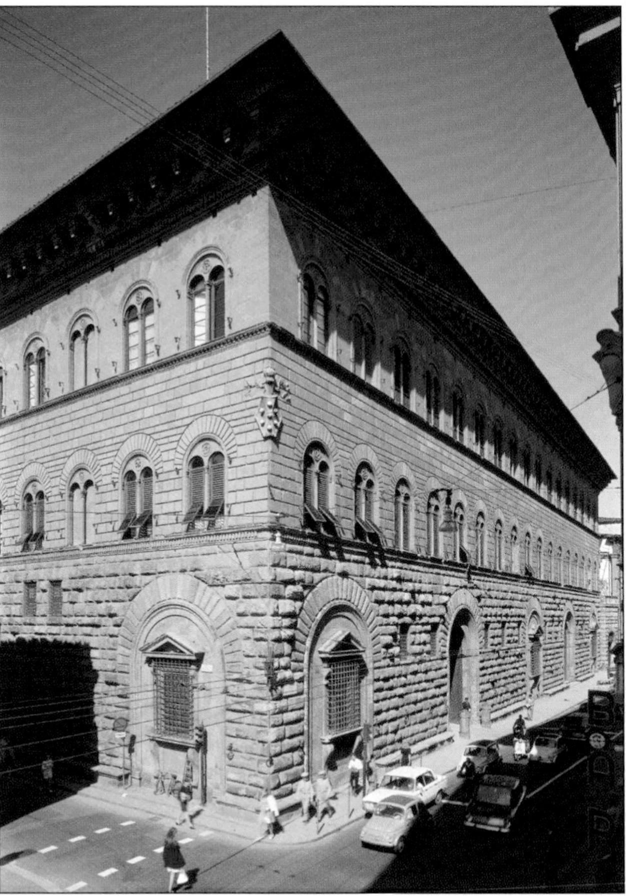

FIGURE 13.5 Michelozzo di Bartolommeo, Palazzo Medici-Riccardi, Florence, exterior, begun 1445, probably completed by 1452; ground-floor windows by Michelangelo, ca. 1517. Typical of Early Renaissance palazzi, the facades of this massive city residence, built for Cosimo de' Medici the Elder, are neatly divided into three stories with evenly spaced windows.

appear in the nave, linking the exterior and interior in a harmonious whole.

Michelozzo di Bartolommeo. In fifteenth-century Florence, wealthy families customarily hired architects to build fortresslike palaces, emblematic of their power. The Palazzo Medici-Riccardi (fig. 13.5), designed by MICHELOZZO DI BARTOLOMMEO [MEE-kel-LOTZ-oh] (1396–1472), was begun in 1445 and probably completed by 1452. Although built for Cosimo de' Medici, the Riccardi family acquired the palazzo in the seventeenth century. Located on a corner of the Via Larga, the widest street in Florence, it is an imposing residence, dignified yet grand, that heralded its resident—the city's most powerful person—literally and metaphorically at the center of the city's cultural and political life.

Michelozzo created an austere three-story stone building. The stonework, beginning with a ground level of rusticated stone (the same rough-hewn masonry used in fortifications), becomes increasingly smoother from bottom story to top. Michelozzo further differentiated the levels visually by successively diminishing the height of each, although they all remain over twenty feet high. Typical of the Renaissance, the division of the stories is neat and clear, and the divisions are formed by classical moldings.

The Renaissance interest in orderliness is seen also in the even spacing of the windows. The form of window used—two arched openings within an overriding arch—was already popular in the Middle Ages. At the top of the palazzo, a heavy projecting cornice fulfills both aesthetic and architectural roles. The cornice serves visually to frame and conclude the architectural composition; it also sent the rainwater wide of the wall. The Medici coat of arms with its seven balls appears on the corners of the second story. What are now its ground-level windows were originally arches that opened onto the street creating a *loggia*, or covered gallery. (The arches were filled and the windows added in the sixteenth century by Michelangelo.) The first story provided offices and storage rooms for the

Medici business; the family's living quarters were on the second level.

The rooms of the Palazzo Medici-Riccardi are arranged around a central colonnaded courtyard, a typical Florentine system in which the palace is turned in on itself, ostensibly for protection but also for privacy and quiet. Whereas the plain exterior reflected the original owner's public posture as a careful, even conservative man, the inside, especially the second floor, or *piano nobile* (the grand and "noble" family rooms of the palace), displayed ostentatious grandeur.

SCULPTURE

Renaissance culture promoted the notion of individual genius by encouraging competitions among artists for prestigious public and religious commissions. In 1401, the Florentine humanist historian Leonardo Bruni sponsored a competition to determine who would make the doors of Florence Cathedral's octagonal **baptistery,** the small structure seen in the left foreground in fig. 12.12, separate from the main church, where baptisms are performed. Seven sculptors were asked to submit depictions of the sacrifice of Isaac.

Lorenzo Ghiberti. The winner of the competition was the young sculptor LORENZO GHIBERTI [ghee-BAIR-tee] (1378–1455), and his reaction typifies the heightened sense of self-worth that Renaissance artists felt about their artistic abilities and accomplishments: "To me was conceded the palm of victory by all the experts. . . . To me the honor was conceded universally and with no exception. To all it seemed that I had at that time surpassed the others."

So well were these doors received that as soon as they were completed Ghiberti was commissioned to make a second set for the east side of the baptistery. These, depicting ten stories from the Old Testament, were completed in 1452. Impressed by their beauty, Michelangelo called them the "gates of paradise," and the name stuck. *The Gates of Paradise* face the cathedral facade, occupying the most prominent position on the baptistery.

The panels are fewer in number and larger in size; scenes are set in simple square formats, and this time the whole square is gilded rather than just the raised areas. Each panel includes several scenes. The first, *The Creation* (fig. 13.6), portrays five scenes from Genesis. At the top, God creates the heavens and earth. At the bottom left, Adam is created from the earth. The central scene depicts Eve being created from Adam's rib. To the left and behind, Adam and Eve are tempted by Satan in the guise of a serpent. And to the right, Adam and Eve are expelled from the Garden of Eden. This is simultaneous presentation of events that took place sequentially, a technique called continuous narration.

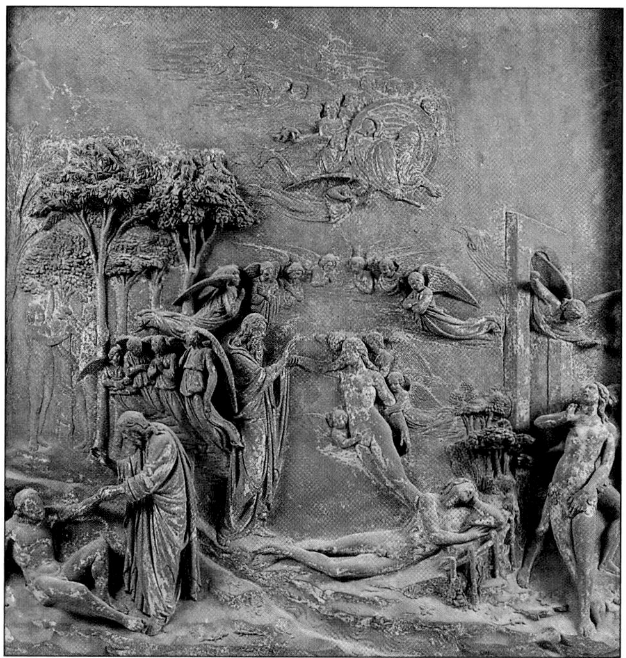

FIGURE 13.6 Lorenzo Ghiberti, *The Creation of Adam and Eve*, relief panel from the *Gates of Paradise*, east doors, Baptistery, Florence, 1425–52, gilt bronze, $31\frac{1}{4}'' \times 31\frac{1}{4}''$ (79.4 × 79.4 cm), now in the Museo dell'Opera del Duomo, Florence. Because of their beauty, Michelangelo referred to these doors as the "Gates of Paradise."

Donatello. DONATELLO [don-ah-TELL-oh] (1386–1466) depicted a subject popular in the Early Renaissance, the shepherd boy David (fig. 13.7) who slew the giant, Goliath, with a stone from his slingshot. In Donatello's *David* (ca. 1425–30s), the stone is still in David's sling, although Goliath's head lies beneath David's foot. By depicting David both before and after the conflict, Donatello provides a condensed version of the story. With the first large-scale nude created since Roman antiquity, Donatello portrays his hero as an adolescent male wearing only a hat and boots. According to the Bible, David casts off only his armor as too cumbersome for battle. To depict David in the nude is to link him to heroic nudes of antiquity. In addition, David adopts the antique *contrapposto* posture, in which the weight of the body rests on one leg, elevating the hip and the opposite shoulder, putting the spine into an S curve.

Between 1453 and 1455, Donatello carved and painted a wooden figure of *Mary Magdalene* (fig. 13.8), which stands over six feet high. After a sermon by Pope Gregory the Great in 594, in which he made a suggestive comparison to Mary Magdalene's sinfulness, she came to be identified as a prostitute. She remained among the followers of Jesus, is said to have annointed him with oil after his crucifixion, to have attended to his burial, and discovered his resurrection. Donatello depicts her after years of living in the desert, rejecting the life of the body in anticipation of the immortal life of the soul after a spiritual resurrection.

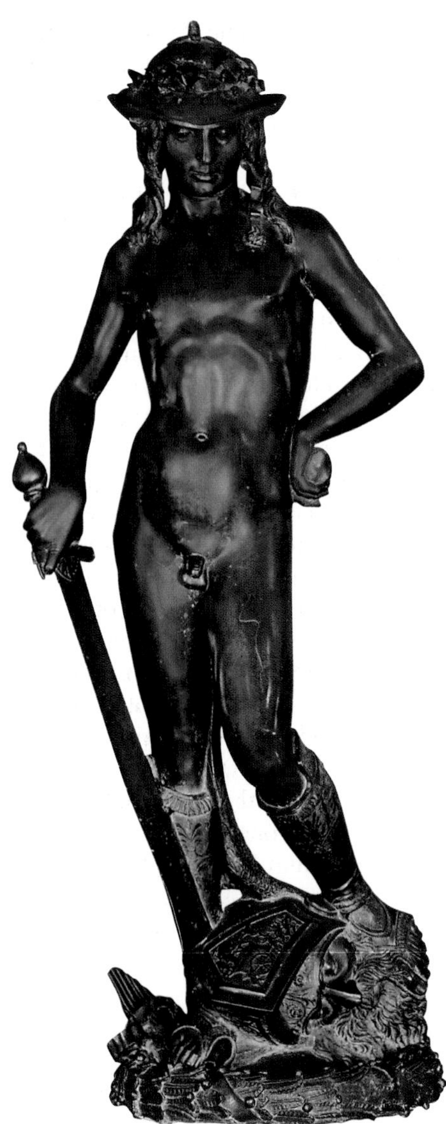

FIGURE 13.7 Donatello, *David*, ca. 1425–30, bronze, height 5′2$\frac{1}{4}$″ (1.58 m), Museo Nazionale del Bargello, Florence. SCALA/Art Resource, NY. The Early Renaissance interest in antiquity and the accurate portrayal of the nude are evidenced in Donatello's work.

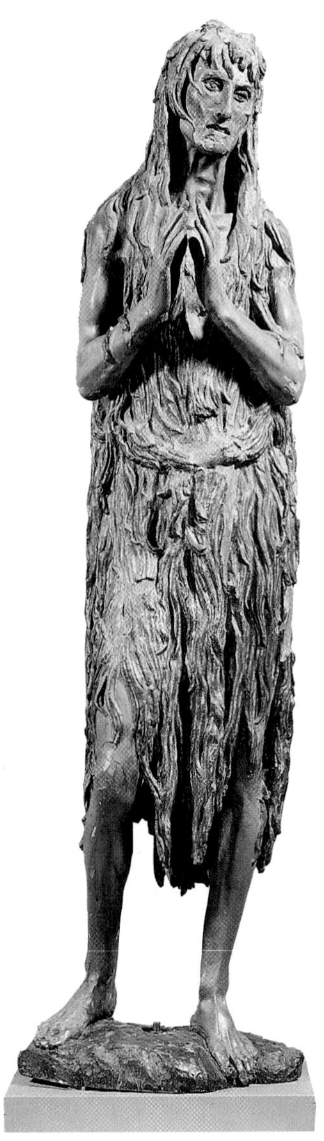

FIGURE 13.8 Donatello, *Mary Magdalene*, 1453–55, wood, painted and gilded, height 6′2″ (1.88 m), Museo dell' Opera del Duomo, Florence. SCALA/Art Resource, NY. Not only beauty, but also its absence can be used to create emotionally moving art, as in this portrayal of the repentant sinner.

Her body now gaunt, her arms and legs withered, she prays. Donatello's figure is intentionally unnerving, even repulsive. It is the striking absence of beauty that makes her both powerful and memorable.

PAINTING

Masaccio. Of all the Early Renaissance painters, it was MASACCIO [mah-SAH-chee-oh] (1401–1429), in his short life, who carried the naturalistic impulse in painting furthest. In the 1436 Italian edition of *On Painting*, Alberti named Masaccio, along with Brunelleschi, Donatello, and Ghiberti, as a leading artist of the day.

Masaccio's fresco of the *Trinity with the Virgin, St. John the Evangelist, and Donors* (fig. 13.9), in Santa Maria Novella in Florence, of ca. 1427–28, summarizes several characteristics of the Renaissance. The Renaissance interest in lifelike portraiture can be seen in the life-size depictions of two members of the Lenzi family who commissioned the work. Unlike the anonymous marginal figures of donors seen in medieval paintings, these donors have a real presence in the scene. So successful was Masaccio in his use of linear perspective that the chapel appears to recede into the wall; the vanishing point is just below the bottom of the cross, five feet from the floor, approximately eye level for the adult viewer. Situated deeper in the space and therefore drawn smaller than the Lenzis, Mary and John the Evangelist plead with Jesus on behalf of humankind. The only figure to defy natural logic is God, for his feet are on the back wall, yet he holds the

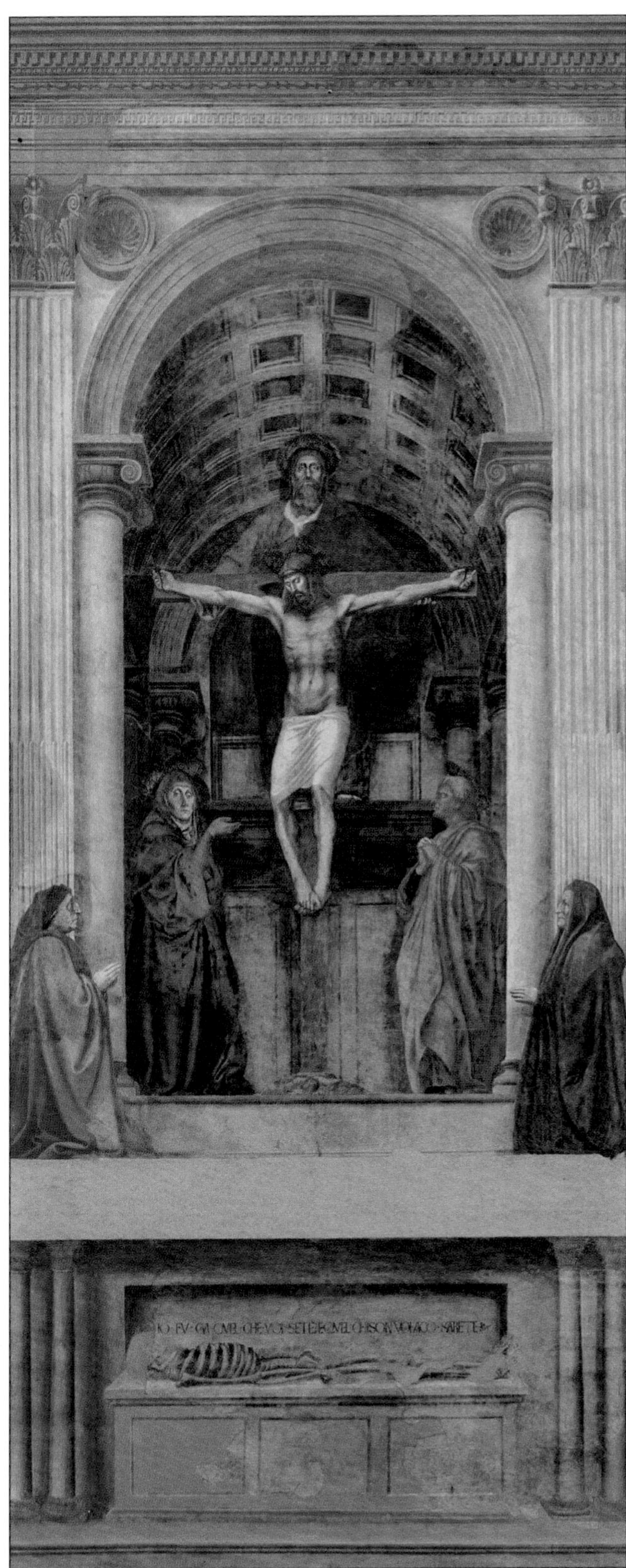

FIGURE 13.9 Masaccio, *Trinity with the Virgin, St. John the Evangelist, and Donors,* Santa Maria Novella, Florence, probably 1427 or 1428, fresco, 21′ × 10′5″ (6.5 × 3.2 m). The architectural setting demonstrates the Early Renaissance interest in the antique and in spatial illusion; the naturalistic portrayal of the life-size donors indicates the new concern for the individual.

cross in the foreground. The Renaissance interest in the antique is seen in the coffered barrel vault, Ionic and Corinthian capitals, and the moldings—all based upon ancient Roman models.

Piero della Francesca. PIERO DELLA FRANCESCA [pea-AIR-oh del-uh fran-CHES-kah] (ca. 1406/12–1492) was also deeply interested in portraiture, a reflection of the Renaissance concern for the individual. His double depiction of Battista Sforza and Federico da Montefeltro (figs. 13.10 and 13.11) shows wife and husband holding their heads motionless, high above the landscape behind them. They are noble, elevated, grand. The profile presentation was especially popular in the Early Renaissance, revealing the sitter's most distinctive features.

Piero began the portraits in 1472, the year the countess died, suggesting her portrait was made from her death mask. She is shown in the fashion of the times, with her plucked and shaved forehead, her elaborate hairstyle, and sparkling jewels. The count was ruler of Urbino, which had begun to compete with Florence as an intellectual center. He was a gentleman, scholar, bibliophile, and warrior, whose court included humanists, philosophers, poets, and artists. A left profile view was chosen because the count had lost his right eye and the bridge of his nose to a sword in a tournament. It is nonetheless with unsparing realism that Piero presents him "warts and all." We can assume the countess and count looked exactly like this, and that Piero faithfully recorded all the crannies and crevices of their facial terrain.

Fra Angelico. FRA ANGELICO [FRAH an-JELL-ee-coh] (ca. 1400–1455), nicknamed "Angelic Brother" by his brother Dominican monks, was the most popular painter in Florence in the first half of the fifteenth century. His *Annunciation* (fig. 13.12), painted between 1438 and 1445 in the monastery of San Marco in Florence, was part of a vast project in which Fra Angelico painted on the walls in one of the cloisters, the chapter house, upstairs in the corridors, and especially in the monks' dormitory cells with the help of assistants. It would be difficult to create gentler, more graceful gestures than those of Mary and Gabriel in this scene. Their crossed arms are a sign of respect as well as a reference to Jesus's cross and prefiguration of his crucifixion. In the garden to the left are accurate depictions of real plants, but Fra Angelico, in medieval fashion, has spaced them evenly across the ground so each maintains its separate identity. The architecture of the space is rendered with typical Early Renaissance respect for the laws of perspective, but Fra Angelico has placed his figures in the architectural setting without regard to proper relative scale. The scene is accurately set within the architecture of San Marco, newly finished by the architect Michelozzo; thus the Annunciation is shown to take place in a specific and contemporary building. The immediacy and conviction of the event were enhanced for the monks

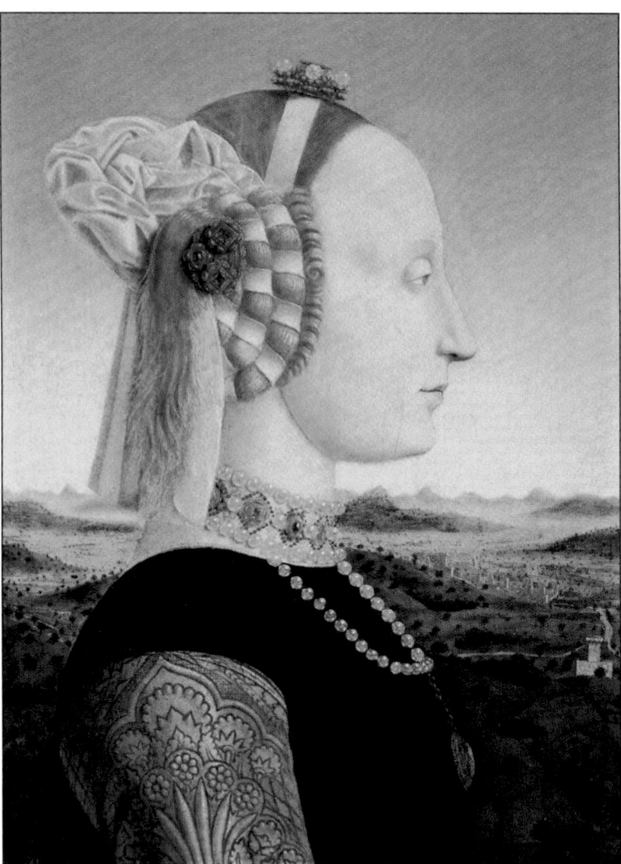

FIGURE 13.10 Piero della Francesca, *Battista Sforza*, 1472–73, oil on panel, $18\frac{1}{2}'' \times 13''$ (47 × 33 cm), Galleria degli Uffizi, Florence. SCALA/Art Resource, NY. The profile portrait was favored in the Early Renaissance; later the three-quarter view became popular.

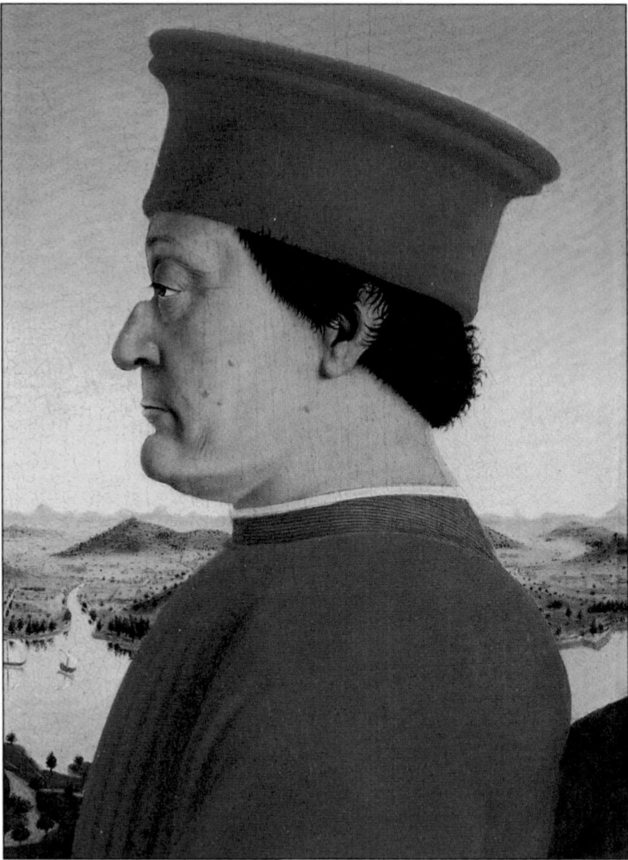

FIGURE 13.11 Piero della Francesca, *Federico da Montefeltro*, 1472–73, oil on panel, $18\frac{1}{2}'' \times 13''$ (47 × 33 cm), Galleria degli Uffizi, Florence. SCALA/Art Resource, NY. In this pair of portraits, wife and husband are recorded with unsparing realism. An accident in combat accounts for the count's curious profile.

who saw the angel Gabriel addressing Mary in their own monastery.

Sandro Botticelli. SANDRO BOTTICELLI [bott-tee-CHEL-lee] (1445–1510) received his artistic training as an assistant to Fra Filippo Lippi, a painter who had worked with Fra Angelico.

Botticelli's *Birth of Venus* (fig. 13.13), of ca. 1484–86, depicts the goddess born from the sea, a subject from antique pagan mythology, made acceptable to the Christian Church by equating Venus with Jesus's mother Mary on the grounds that both were sources of love. According to Neoplatonic interpretation, the birth of Venus is equivalent to the birth of the human soul, as yet uncorrupted by the matter of the world. In Neoplatonic terms, the soul is free to choose for itself whether to follow a path toward sin and degradation or to attempt to regain, through the use of reason, a spiritual perfection manifested in the beauty of creation and felt in the love of God. To love beauty is to love not the material world of sensual things, but rather the world's abstract and spiritual essence.

Botticelli is a master of line—which is simultaneously descriptive and decorative. So lovely are his flowing lines that the viewer will forgive Venus her anatomical inaccuracies and the wind gods their confusion of legs.

In 1494, a Dominican friar, Girolamo Savonarola, who had lived in the same monastery of San Marco in Florence that Fra Angelico had painted, took control of the city. Savonarola proclaimed that Florence had condemned itself to perdition, saying that its painters—artists such as Botticelli—"make the Virgin look like a harlot." A bonfire was built in the Piazza della Signoria, the main square of the city, and on it signs of vanity—clothing, wigs, false beards, make-up, and mirrors—as well as books, board games, and paintings were burned.

EARLY RENAISSANCE MUSIC

March 15, 1436, was a day of dedication for the completed Florence Cathedral, now crowned by Brunelleschi's extraordinary dome. A procession wound its way through the city's streets and entered the cathedral, led by Pope Eugene IV and seven cardinals, thirty-six bishops, and

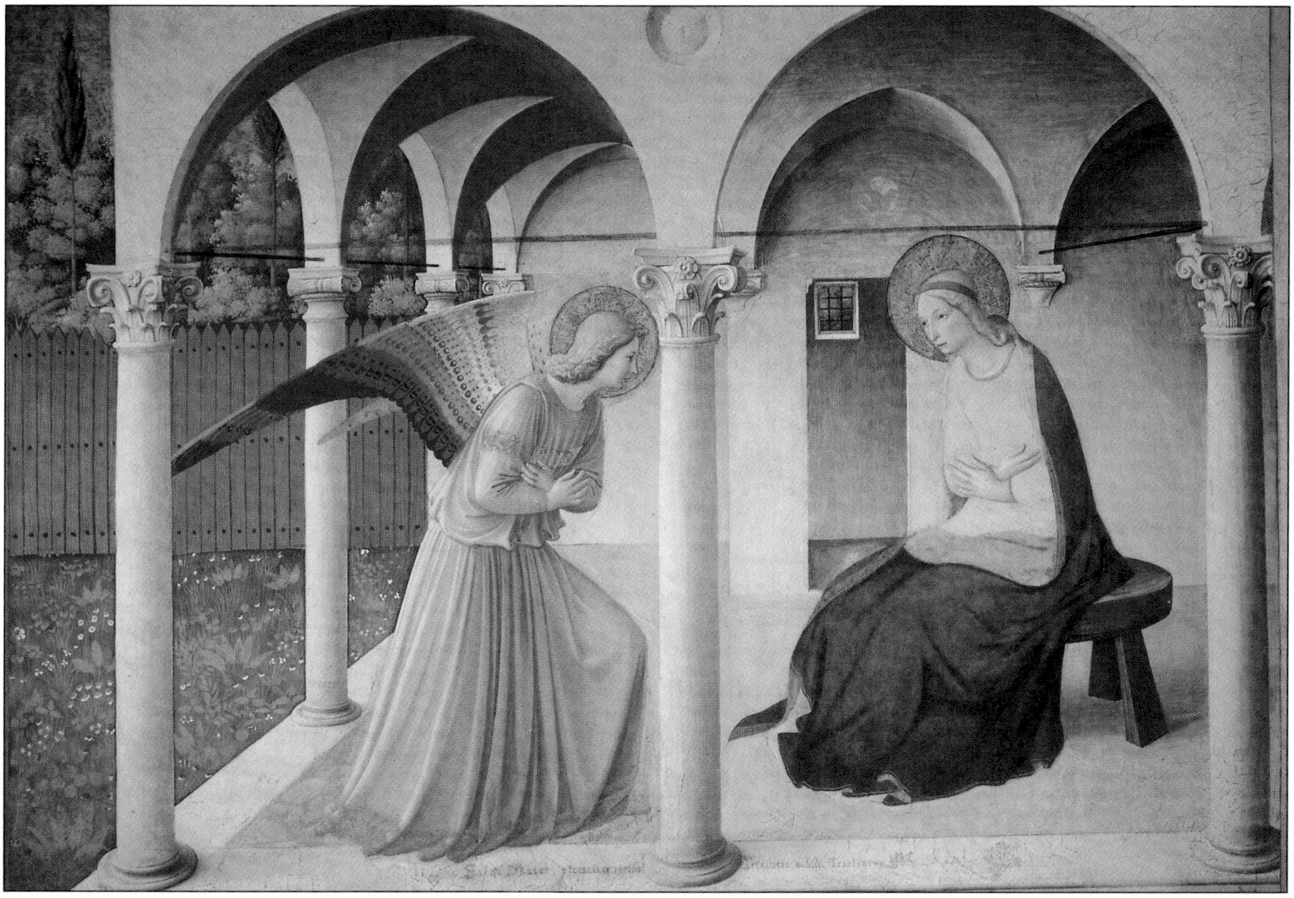

FIGURE 13.12 Fra Angelico, *Annunciation*, monastery of San Marco, Florence, 1438–45, fresco, 7′6″ × 10′5″ (2.29 × 3.18 m). Fra Angelico cleverly painted the Annunciation as if it were taking place within the actual architecture of the monastery of San Marco.

untold numbers of church officials, civic leaders, artists, scholars, and musicians. The papal choir included one of the greatest figures in Renaissance music, the composer Guillaume Dufay. The choir performed a motet called informally "Il Duomo" composed by Dufay especially for the occasion. As one eyewitness recalled, "The whole space of the temple was filled with such choruses of harmony, and such a concert of diverse instruments, that it seemed (not without reason) as though the symphonies and songs of the angels and of divine paradise had been sent forth from Heaven to whisper in our ears an unbelievable celestial sweetness."

Guillaume Dufay. More than any other composer, GUILLAUME DUFAY [dew-FAY] (1400–1474) shaped the musical language of the Early Renaissance. Born in northern France, Dufay served first as a music teacher for the French court of Burgundy, then as a court composer in Italy, working at various times in Bologna, Florence, and Rome. A musical celebrity, he was often solicited to compose music for solemn occasions, such as the dedication of "Il Duomo."

The English had developed pleasing harmonies using a three-note interval (rather than the four-, five-, or eight-note intervals of the Middle Ages), but it was Dufay who used this triadic harmony in polyphonic and imitative style. Dufay was a composer of the increasingly popular "parody mass," where a popular song of the day was inserted into a liturgical mass. Congregations loved the familiar secular tune used in their daily worship. However, composers of parody masses were careful to hide the pop tune in a slow-moving tenor line to escape criticism from the clergy.

Dufay wrote music in all the popular genres of his time: masses for liturgies, Latin motets, or compositions for multiple voices; music for ceremonies; and French and Italian *chansons*, or songs, for the pleasure of his patrons and friends. In each genre, Dufay's melodies and rhythms were more easily identifiable than those of earlier composers.

Motets. Dufay wrote many **motets:** one-movement compositions that set a sacred text to polyphonic choral music, usually with no instrumental accompaniment. Dufay's motet *Alma Redemptoris Mater*, composed in about 1430, fuses medieval *polyphony*—that is, the simultaneous singing of several voices each independent of the others—with a newer Early Renaissance form. The result

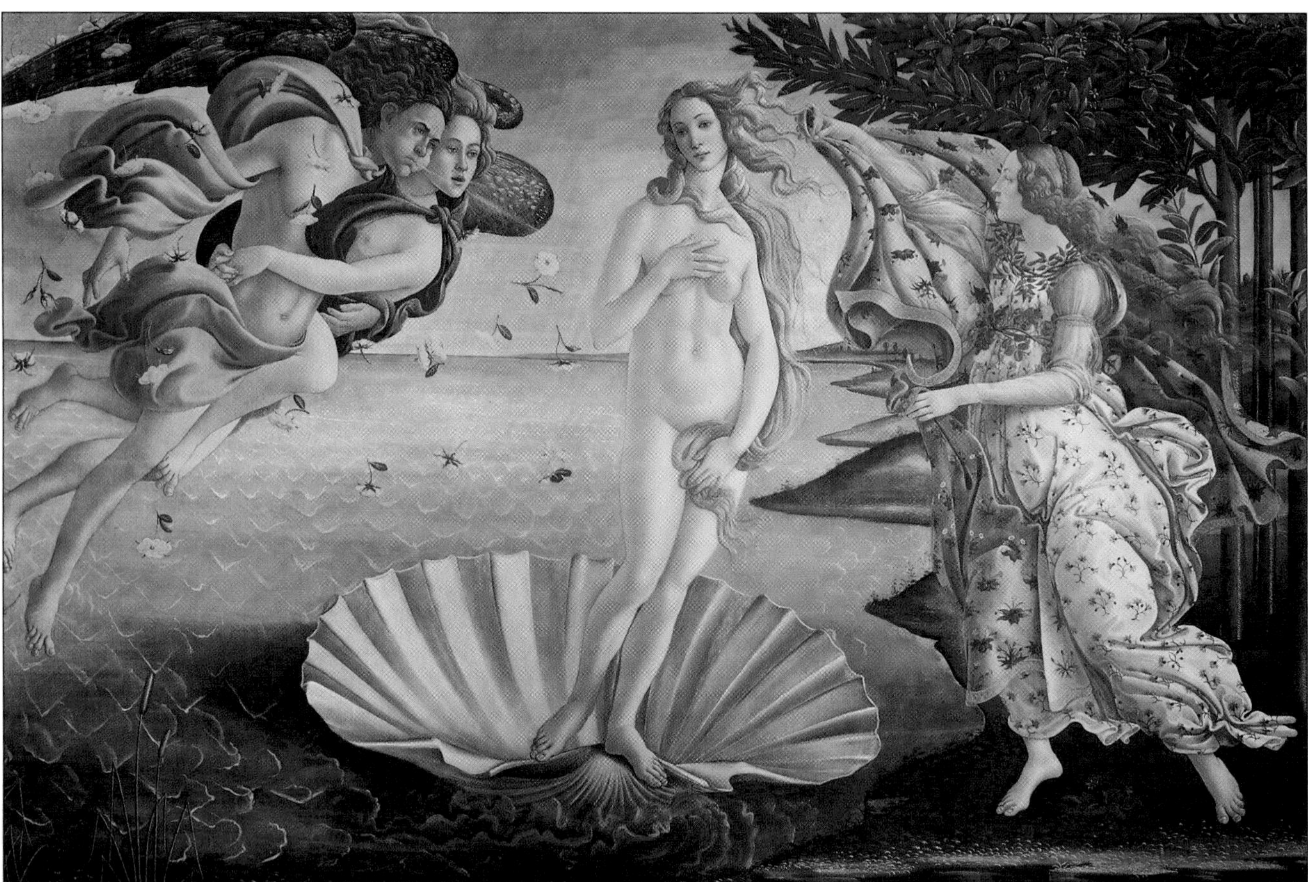

FIGURE 13.13 Sandro Botticelli, *Birth of Venus*, ca. 1484–86, tempera on canvas, 6′7″ × 9′2″ (2.01 × 2.79 m), Galleria degli Uffizi, Florence. SCALA/Art Resource, NY. Botticelli painted this important revival of the nude based upon antique prototypes.

was a multimelodic, rather than merely a multivoiced, musical style, with more lyrical, less chantlike melodies and a more sensuous sound. Earlier composers typically put the *plainchant* melody, or main melody, in the lowest voice, but Dufay puts the main melody in the highest or uppermost voice, where it can be better heard. He also avoids the rhythmic distortion of medieval composition. The three voices of Dufay's *Alma Redemptoris Mater*—bass, tenor, and soprano—maintain rhythmic independence (also a late medieval characteristic) until the third and last section of the motet. Then Dufay blocks them together in chords to emphasize the text's closing words, which ask Mary to be merciful to sinners; the chords, arranged in graceful harmonies, soothe the listener's ears more than those of the traditional medieval motet. In this last part Dufay adds an additional voice by giving the sopranos two different parts to sing. In doing so, he moves toward the four-part texture of soprano, alto, tenor, and bass that was to become the norm for later Renaissance vocal music.

Word Painting. Dufay's emphasis on lyrics is an early example of **word painting,** in which the meaning of words is underscored and emphasized through the music that accompanies them. One sixteenth-century musical theorist offered composers this suggestion: "When one of the words expresses weeping, pain, heartbreak, sighs, tears, and other similar things, let the harmony be full of sadness." A composer might also employ a descending melodic line (going from high to low), or a bass line, to express anguish; conversely, an ascending line (going from low to high), utilizing soprano voices, might express joy and hope. This increasing sense of the drama of language, comparable to the Renaissance artists' attention to the drama of the stories they chose to depict—Donatello's *Mary Magdalene* (see fig. 13.8), for example—led Renaissance composers to use music to enrich the feelings their music expressed, and to support the meaning of a song's text, whether sacred or secular. Though little music had survived from ancient Greece, humanist philosophers like Ficino understood that Aristotle had considered music the highest form of art and the rhythms of Greek music imitated the rhythms of Greek poetry, for which it served as a setting. Thus word painting as the intimate relation of sound and sense has classical roots.

As in the Middle Ages, musicians like Dufay were employed by the churches, towns, and courts. However, unlike music in the Middle Ages, which served mostly

Connections

MATHEMATICAL PROPORTIONS: BRUNELLESCHI AND DUFAY

Mathematics played an important part in all the arts of the Renaissance. Architects designed buildings guided by mathematical ratios and proportions. Painters and sculptors employed mathematics to determine ideal human proportions, as well as to depict buildings in scientific linear perspective. Composers wrote music that reflected mathematical ratios between the notes of a melody and in the intervals between notes sounded together in harmony. Poets structured their poems according to mathematical proportions.

One especially striking set of relationships exists between the proportions of the dome built by Filippo Brunelleschi for Florence Cathedral and "Il Duomo," the motet for four voices that Guillaume Dufay wrote for its dedication in 1436. Its formal title is *Nuper Rosarum Flores (Flowers of Roses)*, the word *flores* referring to Florence itself. The mathematical ratios in Dufay's motet are evident in its rhythm rather than its melody. The slower-moving lower voices of the two tenors proceed in strict rhythmic progressions that reflect the ratio of 6:4:2:3. The initial ratio of 6:4 is reducible to 3:2; thus it is a mirror reverse ratio of 3:2:2:3, which appears in the number of beats in each of the work's four sections: 6, 4, 4, and 6. In addition, Dufay's motet contains a total of 168 measures, proportionally divided into four harmonious parts of 56, 56, 28, and 28 measures each. The last two parts contain exactly half the number of measures of the first two, creating a mathematically harmonious and intellectually pleasing structure.

Brunelleschi's dome's proportions exhibit mathematical ratios that are 6:4:2:3, just as in Dufay's motet. This is the ratio of the internal dimensions to the external ones. And motet and dome both have a doubling. Dufay's motet employs a doubling of the tenor voices, which sing the lower melody five notes apart. Brunelleschi's dome is a double shell, having an internal and an external structure.

The structure of a Petrarchan sonnet also employs a harmonious mathematical ratio for its basic structure. The Petrarchan sonnet is composed of fourteen lines, which typically break into two parts: an octave of eight lines and a sestet of six that yield a ratio of 8:6, which reduces to 4:3. Moreover, both the octave and the sestet usually split evenly into two equal parts: 4 + 4 and 3 + 3, yielding a further neatly symmetrical balanced pair of proportions in both octave and sestet of 1:1.

In these and numerous other instances of Renaissance architecture and music, as well as perspectivist painting, sculptural proportions, and poetry, mathematics lies at the heart of the harmonious nature of the works. This concern with geometric symmetry and mathematical proportions illustrates one more way in which the arts of the Renaissance were a legacy of the golden age of Greece.

religious ends, music in the Renaissance became increasingly secularized. Musicians still depended on such patronage, but commissions came from wealthy burghers and aristocrats such as the Medici family, as well as from the church, which remained the staunchest of musical patrons. The nobility commissioned secular works to accompany formal occasions such as coronations, weddings, processions, and even political events. However, before long secular music also found its way into sacred settings. Dufay, for instance, introduced the popular French folksong "*L'Homme arme*" ("The Man in Armor") into a mass, and other composers soon followed suit, creating an entire musical genre known as *chanson masses*, or "song masses."

Musical accomplishment was one of the marks of an educated person in the Renaissance, and most people among the nobility both played an instrument and sang. Moreover, many uneducated people were accomplished musicians; in fact, the music of the uneducated masses—their songs and dances—was most influenced by the secular music of the age. Music was an integral part of an evening's entertainment. Although it was common for professionals to provide this entertainment, increasingly individuals at a party might entertain the group. Dance, too, became the focus of social gatherings, and much of the instrumental music of the day was composed to accompany dances. By the Early Renaissance, instruments had evolved to look much as they do today. The lute was used both as a solo instrument and to accompany singers. Bowed instruments came in all sizes; wind instruments with brass mouthpieces and single and double reeds were used in festivals and in church. Instruments were classified as either loud (*haut*) or soft (*bas*), which also designated the activity for which the instrument was intended. Before this time, instruments had always performed vocal parts. During the Renaissance, music was written specifically for particular instruments without regard for the capability of the human voice.

Movable type contributed to the growth and popularity of music during the Renaissance. The first collection of music printed in movable type, *One Hundred Songs*, was published in 1501 in Venice by Ottaviano de' Petrucci. Half a century later, printed music was widely available to scholars and amateurs alike. With the greater availability of printed scores, Renaissance composers became more familiar with each other's works and began to influence one another. Amateurs were able to buy and study the same music, and soon songs and dances in particular achieved the kind of widespread popularity that today might put a song into the "Top Ten."

LITERATURE

Petrarch. The first great figure of Italian Renaissance letters, and the first important representative of Italian Renaissance humanism, was Petrarch, a scholar and prolific writer, whose work simultaneously reflects the philosophy of Greek antiquity and the new ideas of the Renaissance. Born Francesco Petrarca in Arezzo and taken, at the age of eight, to Avignon, where the papal courts had moved in 1309, Petrarch studied law in Bologna and Montpellier, then returned in 1326 to Avignon. Petrarch once said of himself, "I am a pilgrim everywhere," for he also traveled widely in France and Italy, hunting down classical manuscripts.

Unlike his Florentine predecessor, Dante Alighieri, whose *Divine Comedy* (see Chapter 12) summed up the sensibility of late medieval culture, Petrarch positioned himself at the beginning of a new literary and artistic era, one that placed greater emphasis on human achievement. Without rejecting the importance of spirituality and religious faith, Petrarch celebrated human accomplishment as the crowning glory of God's creation but praised human beings for their achievements as well.

Petrarch's work is poised between two powerful, intertwined impulses: the religious and moral impulse of the early medieval thinkers, such as St. Augustine, and the humanist dedication to the disciplined study of ancient writers, coupled with a desire for artistic excellence.

Petrarch was especially affected by the elegance and beauty of early Latin literature. However, he disliked the Latin of the Middle Ages, seeing in it a barbarous falling off from the heights of eloquence exemplified by ancient Roman writers such as Virgil, Horace, Ovid, Seneca, and Cicero. Petrarch strove to revive classical literature rather than absorb its elements into contemporary Italian civilization. He considered classical culture a model to be emulated and an ideal against which to measure the achievements of other civilizations. For Petrarch, ancient culture was not merely a source of scientific information, philosophical knowledge, or rhetorical rules; it was also a spiritual and intellectual resource for enriching the human experience. Petrarch would help first Italy, and then Europe, recollect its noble classical past. And although Petrarch did not invent humanism, he breathed life into it and was its tireless advocate.

Soon after his return to Avignon in 1326, Petrarch fell in love with a woman whose identity is unknown, but whom he called Laura in his *Canzoniere (Songbook)*. This collection of 366 poems—**sonnets, ballads, sestinas,** madrigals, and **canzoni** (songs)—was written and reworked over more than forty years. Many of the poems are about love, and they are notable for their stylistic elegance and formal perfection. The poems about Laura are the most famous and the most beautiful.

The Petrarchan Sonnet. Thematically, Petrarch's sonnets introduced what was to become a predominant subject of Renaissance lyric poetry: the expression of a speaker's love for a woman and his experience of the joy and pain of love's complex and shifting emotions. Laura's beauty and behavior cause the poet/speaker to sway between hope and despair, pleasure and pain, joy and anguish. Throughout the sequence of poems, Laura remains unattainable. Like so many figures in Renaissance painting, she is at once a real person and an ideal form, a contradiction expressed in the ambivalent feelings the poet/speaker has about her. Petrarch's popularity spawned a profusion of imitators, who borrowed from his situations, psychological descriptions, figurative language, and particularly his sonnet form. Petrarch's sonnets also inspired poets throughout Europe to write their own sonnet sequences. The most famous examples in English are Philip Sidney's *Astrophel and Stella* (1591), Edmund Spenser's *Amoretti* (1595), and William Shakespeare's 154 sonnets. Petrarch's sonnet structure established itself as one of the two dominant sonnet patterns used by poets.

The Petrarchan (sometimes called the Italian) sonnet is organized in two parts: an octave of eight lines and a sestet of six. The octave typically identifies a problem or situation, and the sestet proposes a solution; or the octave introduces a scene, and the sestet comments on or complicates it. The rhyme scheme of the Petrarchan sonnet reinforces its logical structure, with different rhymes occurring in octave and sestet. The octave rhymes *abba abba* (or *abab abab*), and the sestet rhymes *cde cde* (or *cde ced; cde dce;* or *cd, cd, cd*).

The following sonnet was the most popular poem in the European Renaissance; it depicts the lover's ambivalence in a series of paradoxes.

I find no peace and all my war is done,
I fear and hope, I burn and freeze like ice;
I fly above the wind yet can I not arise,
And nought I have and all the world I sesan.
That loseth nor locketh holdeth me in prison
And holdeth me not, yet can I escape nowise;
Nor letteth me live nor die at my devise,
And yet of death it giveth me occasion.
Without eyes, I see, and without tongue I plain,
I desire to perish, and yet I ask health,
I love an other, and thus I hate my self,
I feed me in sorrow and laugh in all my pain,
Likewise displeaseth me both death and life,
And my delight is cause of this strife.

HIGH RENAISSANCE

In the High Renaissance, focus shifted from Florence to Rome due to the wealth and power of the popes. Lavish artistic patronage was provided especially by Pope Julius II (r. 1503–13), patron of Bramante, Raphael, and Michelangelo, and Pope Leo X (r. 1513–21), who also patronized Michelangelo (and excommunicated Martin Luther). Rome had now become a city in which the two major national traditions of Italy converged—Classicism and Christianity.

The High Renaissance begins around 1485 or 1490 in Italy. Only one generation long, the High Renaissance was a short yet extremely important period that was to prove enormously influential on future art. Although there is no precise conclusion to the High Renaissance, the period may be said to come to a close at the death of Raphael in 1520, because this artist's paintings are widely held to epitomize the Renaissance style. Alternatively, the Renaissance may be said to have ended when Rome was sacked and burned by troops serving the Holy Roman Emperor Charles V (in Germany) in 1527. Many artists fled the city, thereby further spreading the ideas of Italy over western Europe.

The High Renaissance continued Early Renaissance interests in humanism, classicism, and individualism, artists and authors perfecting some of the ideas of their Early Renaissance predecessors and developing ideas of their own.

PAINTING

Leonardo da Vinci. Born in Vinci, about twenty miles west of Florence, LEONARDO DA VINCI [lay-o-NAR-doh dah VIN-chee] (1452–1519) was the illegitimate son of a peasant named Caterina and Ser Piero, a Florentine lawyer, or notary. Leonardo later joined his father in Florence, and in 1469 he entered the workshop of Andrea del Verrocchio. Giorgio Vasari wrote of Leonardo's "beauty as a person," describing him as "divinely endowed" and "so pleasing in conversation that he won all hearts." But he was, Vasari noted, unstable in temperament, often abandoning projects, constantly searching and restless.

Leonardo painted *The Last Supper* (fig. 13.14) between 1495 and 1499. The orderly composition clarifies the painting's meaning. The largest of the three windows on the back wall is directly behind Jesus, thereby emphasizing him. The curved pediment, which arches above his head, serves as a halo. He is perfectly centered in the mural, and all perspective lines converge toward a vanishing point directly behind his head, leading the viewer's eyes to him. The twelve apostles are arranged six on each side, divided into four equal groups of three figures. The result is a composition that is symmetrically balanced on either side around the central figure of Jesus, whose arms are extended diagonally so that he forms an equilateral triangle in the center. The arrangement of the five segments is somewhat theatrical—action building from the wings, leading to the central calm figure of Jesus.

FIGURE 13.14 Leonardo da Vinci, *The Last Supper*, refectory, Santa Maria delle Grazie, Milan, 1495–98, tempera and oil on plaster, 15′2″ × 28′10″ (4.60 × 8.80 m). Scala/Art Resource, NY. The mural's poor condition is due to the experimental media in which Leonardo painted. Nevertheless, his ability to merge form and content, using perspective to create simultaneously an illusion of a cubic space and focus the viewer's attention on Jesus, can still be appreciated.

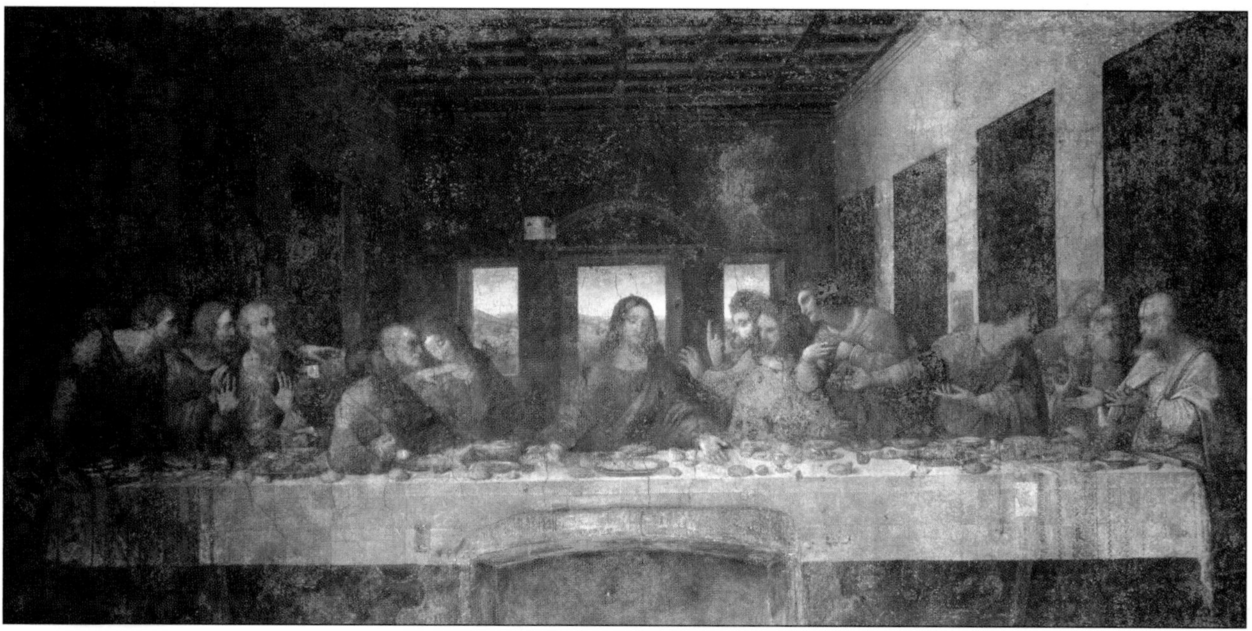

Leonardo chose the most psychologically powerful moment in the story: Jesus has just announced that one of his apostles will betray him, and they respond with dismay. Judas, his betrayer, sits with John and Peter directly to the left of Jesus, his face lost in shadow as he leans away, clutching a money bag in his right hand. We know from preparatory sketches that Leonardo wanted to depict a different emotion on each of the apostles' faces. The most difficult thing to paint, Leonardo said, was "the intention of Man's soul." It could only be shown by pose, facial expression, and surrounding events and figures. Painting Judas and Jesus, apparently, gave Leonardo the most difficulty. Vasari tells the story:

> The prior [of Santa Maria delle Grazie] was in a great hurry to see the picture done. He could not understand why Leonardo would sometimes remain before his work half a day together, absorbed in thought. . . . [Leonardo] made it clear that men of genius are sometimes producing most when they seem least to labor, for their minds are then occupied in the shaping of those conceptions to which they afterward give form. He told the duke [Sforza, under whose protection the monastery was] that two heads were yet to be done: that of the Savior, the likeness of which he could not hope to find on earth and . . . the other, of Judas. . . . As a last resort he could always use the head of that troublesome and impertinent prior.

Leonardo solved his problem with Judas by grouping him with Peter and John. "I say," Leonardo explained in his *Notebooks*, "that in narratives it is necessary to mix closely together direct contraries, because they provide a great contrast with each other, and so much more if they are adjacent, that is to say the ugly to the beautiful."

He returned to Florence and painted the *Mona Lisa* (fig. 13.15), ca. 1503, a portrait of Lisa di Antonio Maria Gherardini, the twenty-four-year-old wife of a Florentine official, Francesco del Gioconda—hence the painting is sometimes called *La Gioconda*. Mona Lisa appears relaxed and natural. Leonardo presents his sitter in a half-length, three-quarter view, the hands showing. With this pose, set against a landscape background, Leonardo established a type. In accordance with the fashion of the time, her high forehead indicates Mona Lisa's nobility—the effect achieved by her shaved hairline and absence of eyebrows. The sitter's lofty mind is indicated by the stormy weather shown in the background. The fame of this painting rests on the sitter's facial expression. Leonardo was concerned with not only the exterior, but also with the interior, with the psychological subtleties of individual personality.

Leonardo developed a technique for modeling forms in light and dark called **chiaroscuro** (in Italian, chairo means "clear" or "light," and oscuro means "obscure" or "dark"). He also developed a painting technique known as **sfumato** (in Italian, "smoky") in which the outlines of objects are hazy, as if in a smoky atmosphere.

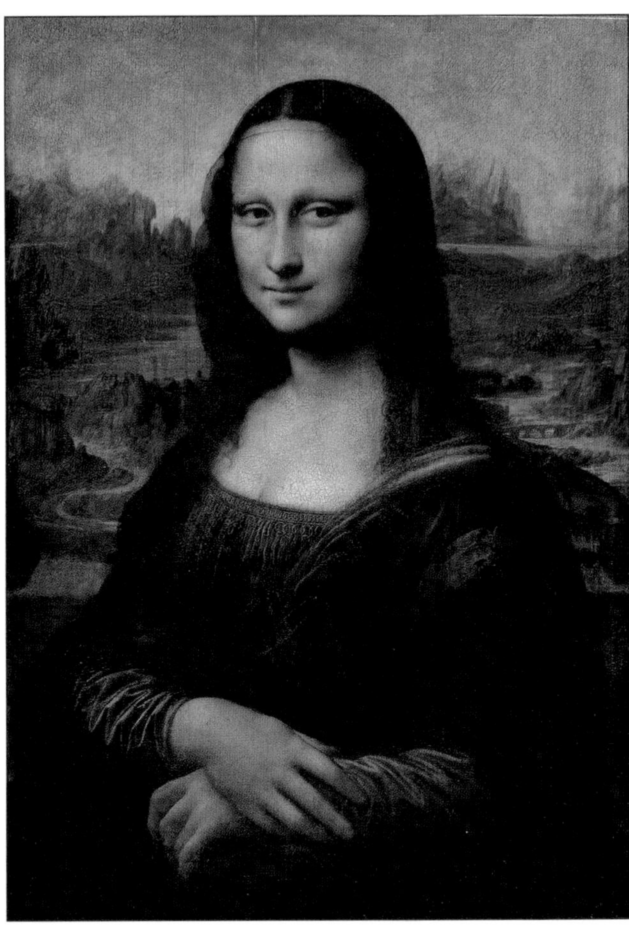

FIGURE 13.15 Leonardo da Vinci, *Mona Lisa*, ca. 1503, oil on panel, $2'6\frac{1}{4}'' \times 1'9''$ (76.8 × 53.3 cm). Photo: Lewandowski/LeMage/Gattelet. © Musée du Louvre, Paris/Reunion des Musées National/Art Resource, NY. Probably the most famous painting in the world, Mona Lisa's mysterious smile continues to intrigue viewers today.

THE REINVENTION OF ROME

In the middle of the fifteenth century, Pope Nicholas V had close ties to the Florentine humanists, especially to Leon Battista Alberti, who made a massive survey of classical architecture, *De re aedificatoria*. With Alberti as his chief consultant, Nicholas V began to rebuild Rome's ancient churches and initiated plans to remake the Vatican as a new sacred city. Nicholas V also began to assemble a massive classical library, paying humanist scholars to translate ancient Greek texts into Latin and Italian. The Vatican library became one of the chief preoccupations of Pope Sixtus IV (r. 1471–84). With Platina as its head, the library became a true "Vatican," or "public," library, with rules for usage, a permanent location, and an effective, permanent administration. By 1508, the Vatican Library was said to be the "image" of Plato's Academy. Athens had been reborn in Rome.

Archaeological discoveries led to Rome's reinvention as the classical center of learning and art. Sixtus established a museum in 1474 to house the recently uncovered

Etruscan bronze statue of the she-wolf that had nourished Romulus and Remus, the mythical twin founders of the city (see Chapter 4). Other discoveries followed: *Spinario*, a Hellenistic bronze of a youth pulling a thorn from his foot; *Hercules*, the life-size bronze discovered in the ruined temple of Hercules in the Forum Boarium; and two antique marble river gods that came from the ruins of the Constantinian baths.

To execute Pope Nicholas's plans for a new Vatican palace, Sixtus IV commissioned the Sistine Chapel, which he named after himself, and inaugurated plans for its decoration. Perugino and Botticelli, among others, painted frescoes for the chapel's walls, which were completed in 1482. Sixtus's nephew, Pope Julius II (r. 1503–13), continued Sixtus's plans. Classical sculpture was placed in the Vatican's sloping gardens: the *Apollo Belvedere*, which had been discovered during excavations, and the *Laocoön* (see Chapter 3), found buried in the ruins of some Roman baths. Composers were hired to write new hymns. Josquin des Près served in the sixteen- to twenty-four-member *Sistina Cappella*, or Sistine Choir, from 1476 to 1484. Soon the rough rhythms of medieval poetry were supplanted by the softer, finer meter of the Horatian odes. To add to the pomp of the liturgical processions, Julius established a large chorus to perform exclusively in St. Peter's, the *Cappella Giulia*, or Julian Choir, which remains active to this day. And, most important, Julius invited Raphael and Michelangelo to work in Rome.

PAINTING AND SCULPTURE

Raphael. When RAPHAEL [RAFF-ay-el], born Raffaello Santi of Urbino (1483–1520), was invited to Rome in 1508, he was not yet twenty-five years old, but his renown as a painter was well established. He had grown up surrounded by culture and beauty. He studied painting under his father, Giovanni Santi, a painter for the dukes of Urbino. In Perugia he studied with Perugino.

Raphael became famous for his paintings of the Madonna and Child. His *Madonna of the Meadows* (fig. 13.16), painted in 1505, is typical of his style: pale, sweet, and serious. She is maternal and meditative, thinking ahead to Jesus's passion, prefigured by the cross offered by the infant St. John, who in turn is identified by the camel-hair garment he would wear as an adult. In most Early Renaissance depictions of this subject, the Madonna is elevated on a throne. Raphael's Madonna has descended to our earthly level; she even sits upon the ground—in this pose she is referred to as the "Madonna of Humility." The differences between the sacred and the secular are minimized—even the figures' halos have become thin gold bands. A master of composition, with ease and grace, Raphael contrasts the curved and rounded shapes of his substantial figures with their triangular and pyramidal positions in space.

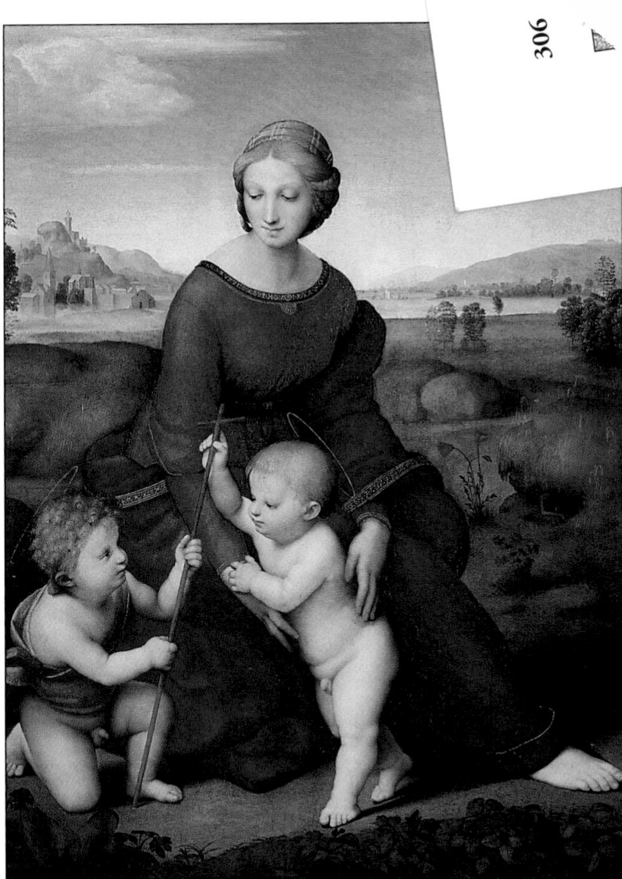

FIGURE 13.16 Raphael, *Madonna of the Meadows*, 1505, oil on panel, $44\frac{1}{2}'' \times 34\frac{1}{4}''$ (113 × 87 cm), Kunsthistorisches Museum, Vienna. Erich Lessing/Art Resource, NY. Often considered the epitome of High Renaissance painters, Raphael was celebrated for his ability to arrange several figures into compact units. Mary, Jesus, and John the Baptist form a pyramid, a favorite Renaissance compositional device.

Beginning in 1508, Julius II commissioned Raphael to paint frescoes in several rooms in the Vatican Palace, including the Stanza della Segnatura, the room where papal documents were signed. The *School of Athens* (fig. 13.17) embodies the Renaissance humanist's quest for classical learning and truth. In the center of this bilaterally symmetrical composition are the ancient Greek philosophers, Plato and Aristotle. The figure of the older Plato, which might be a portrait of Leonardo da Vinci, holds Plato's *Timaeus* and points upward, indicating the realm of his ideal Forms. The younger Aristotle holds his *Ethics* and points toward earth, indicating the philosopher's emphasis on material reality. The scene includes representations of Diogenes or Socrates, sprawling on the steps in front of the philosophers; Pythagoras, calculating on a slate at the lower left; Ptolemy, holding a globe at the right; and Euclid in front of him, inscribing a slate with a compass. Michelangelo is shown as the philosopher Heraclitus in the foreground leaning on a block of marble while sketching. Raphael painted his own portrait, the second figure from the right, looking at us. Pope

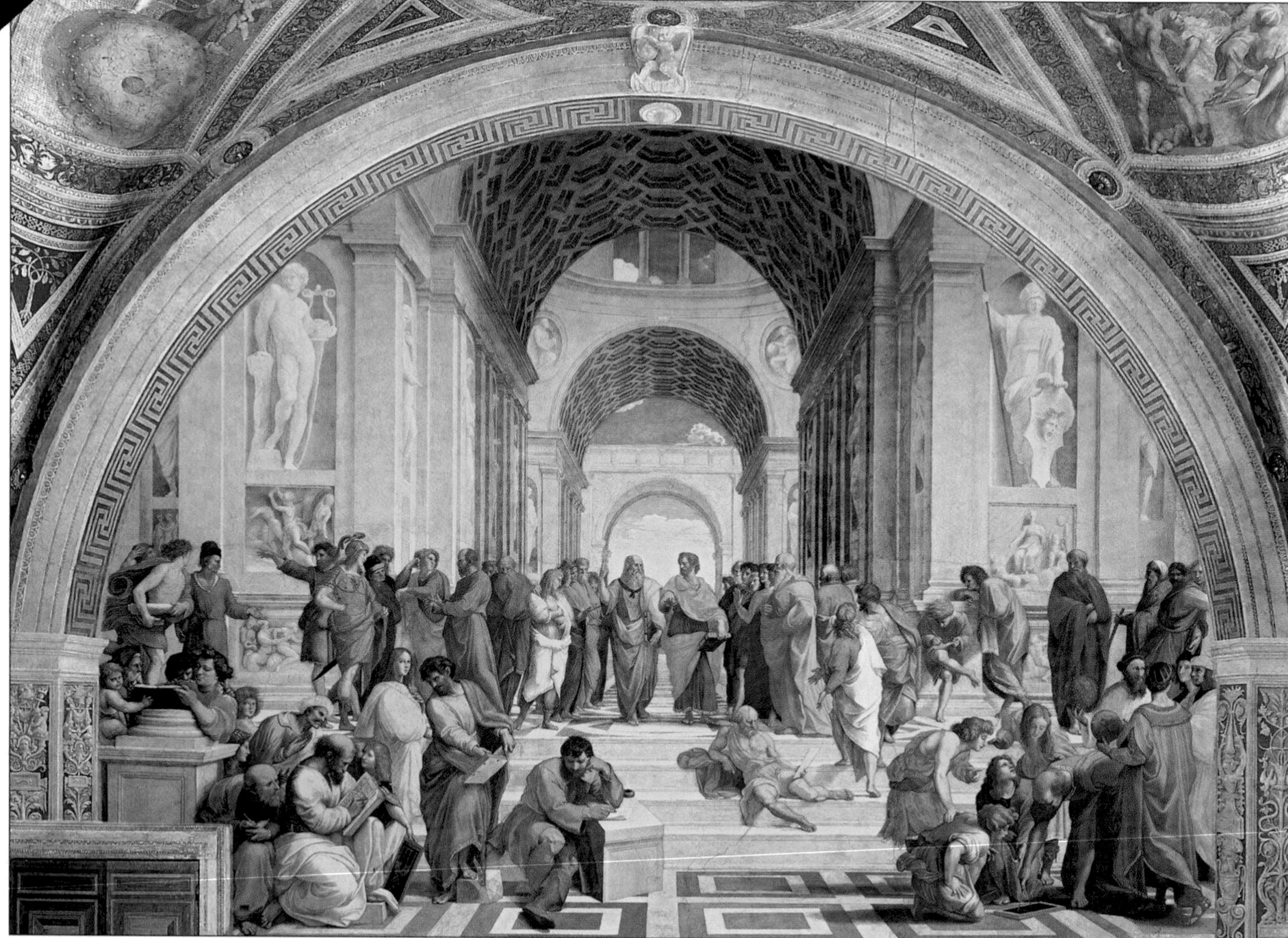

FIGURE 13.17 Raphael, *School of Athens*, 1510–11, fresco, 19′ × 27′ (5.79 × 8.24 m), Stanza della Segnatura, Vatican Museums, Rome, Italy. Raphael painted several rooms in the Vatican for Pope Julius II, a great patron of the arts. Statues of Apollo and Minerva flank Plato and Aristotle, shown surrounded by scientists and philosophers of antiquity, some of whom have been given the facial features of Raphael's contemporaries.

Julius had made Raphael "prefect of antiquities," in charge of the papal excavation and preservation of antiques. Perhaps because of this, the setting is based on the ancient Roman baths and has the classical statues of Apollo (god of sunlight, rationality, and poetry) and Minerva (goddess of wisdom).

Michelangelo. MICHELANGELO BUONARROTI [my-kuhl-AN-gel-oh] (1475–1564), born near Florence, lived as a child in the Palazzo Medici there (fig. 13.5), which served not only as Lorenzo the Magnificent's home but also as an art school, and there he studied sculpture under Giovanni Bertoldo, once a student of Donatello. In Lorenzo's palace, bursting with Neoplatonic and humanist ideas, Michelangelo was nurtured on the virtues of antique classical sculpture. As a boy, in Florence, he studied fresco painting under Domenico del Ghirlandaio and copied the frescoes by Giotto in Santa Croce and those by Masaccio in Santa Maria del Carmine. He was, like so many Renaissance artists, skilled in many areas—painting, architecture, poetry—but in his own mind he was a sculptor.

Michelangelo believed the figure is imprisoned within the block of marble in the same way the soul is trapped within the body. In fact, to release the figure from the marble was a matter of subtraction, as the sculptor chiseled away the shell of stone that hid the figure within. Unlike Leonardo, who believed beauty was found in nature, Michelangelo believed beauty was found in the imagination.

Michelangelo carved the enormous *David* (fig. 13.18) between 1501 and 1504. The statue, which is over 13 feet tall, was intended to stand 40 feet above the ground on a buttress on Florence Cathedral. However, when it was

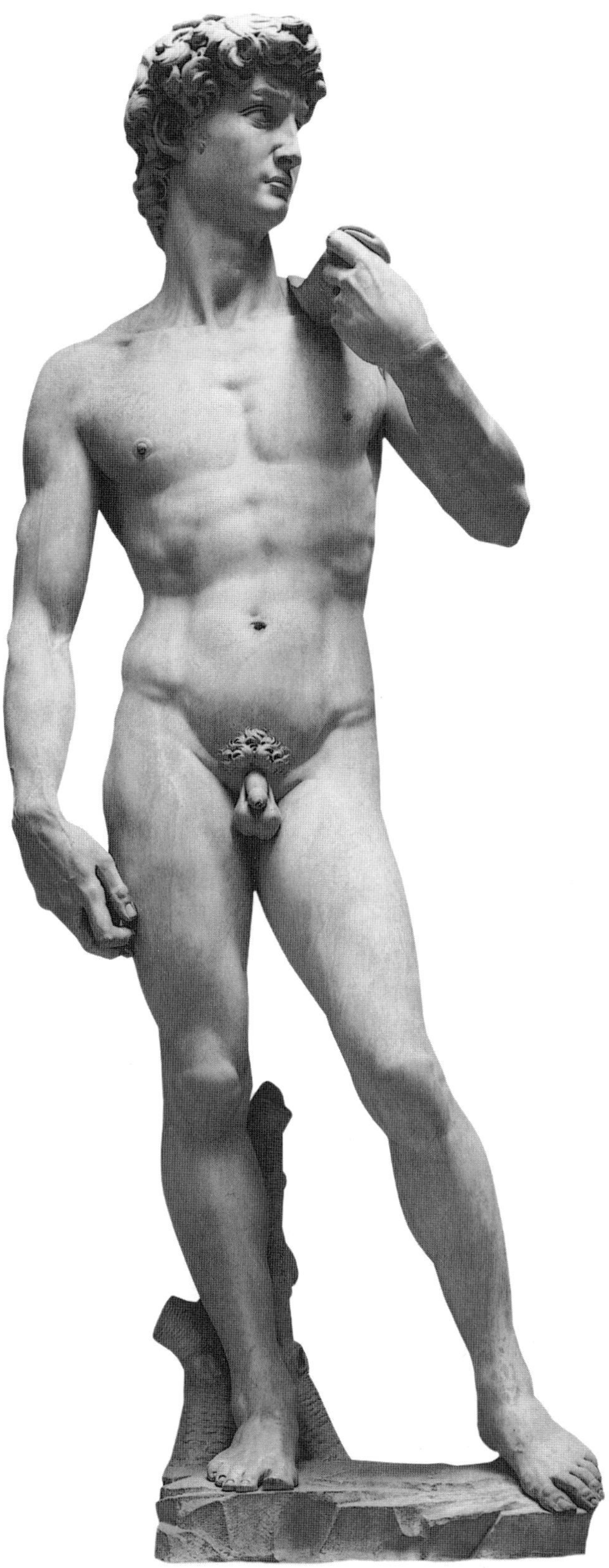

FIGURE 13.18 Michelangelo, *David*, 1501–04, marble, height 13′5″ (4.09 m), Galleria dell'Accademia, Florence. A magnificent marble man, akin to the heroic nudes of antiquity and undated by costume, David becomes a universal symbol of the individual facing unseen conflict.

finished, the city officials designated it a "masterpiece," too good to be placed so high on the cathedral; instead it was placed in front of the Palazzo Vecchio in the Piazza della Signoria. There, in the square where political meetings took place, it would symbolize not only freedom of speech, but the Republic of Florence itself, free from foreigners, papal domination, and Medici rule. (The Medici had been exiled in 1494.)

The *David*'s pose is taken from antiquity, with the weight on one leg in the *contrapposto* position. The sculptor's virtuosity is most evidenced in David's tightly muscled form, his tendons and veins recorded. A sense of enormous pent-up energy emerges, of latent power about to explode, and the question seems to be less *if* he will move than *when*. The absence of attire recalls the heroic nudes of antiquity and avoids linking the *David* to a specific time period; instead *David* has universal meaning. He represents the battle between good and evil, as well as every person who must face their foe.

Michelangelo was called to Rome in 1505 to create the monumental tomb of Pope Julius II. The project was halted by Julius II himself soon after Michelangelo's arrival when the pope decided that finishing the painting of the Sistine Chapel, a project initiated by his predecessor Sixtus IV, should take priority. Michelangelo is reputed to have said, "Painting is for women, sculpture for men." Reluctantly, he began to paint. The ceiling, which covers more than 5,800 square feet, is nearly seventy feet high. Michelangelo would have to work long hours on scaffolding, paint dripping on him. The center of the ceiling features the story of Creation—nine scenes from Genesis. Four further scenes from the Old Testament appear in the corners. Old Testament prophets and ancient pagan sibyls (female prophets) are included, along with Jesus's ancestors, and assorted medallions, *putti* (cherubs), and male nudes. There are over three hundred figures in all, many of which have no known meaning. Michelangelo claimed that Julius II let him paint what he pleased, but the complexity of the program suggests he had advisers. Neoplatonist numerology, symbolism, and philosophy inform many of the subjects and pagan stories and motifs are also evident. Old Testament stories are used to prefigure those in the New Testament.

In the scene of the *Creation of Adam* (fig. 13.19), God, noble and powerful, flies in swiftly, bringing Eve with him under his arm. Compare this scene with Ghiberti's depiction in the *Gates of Paradise* (see fig. 13.6). Michelangelo's dynamic God contrasts with a listless Adam, whose figure Michelangelo derived from an ancient Roman coin. Momentarily, God will give Adam his soul and bring him fully to life, for their fingers are about to touch. Note the masculine musculature of the figures; even the female figures on the Sistine ceiling are based on male models. Michelangelo's figures are heroic and powerful, yet they have a grace and beauty.

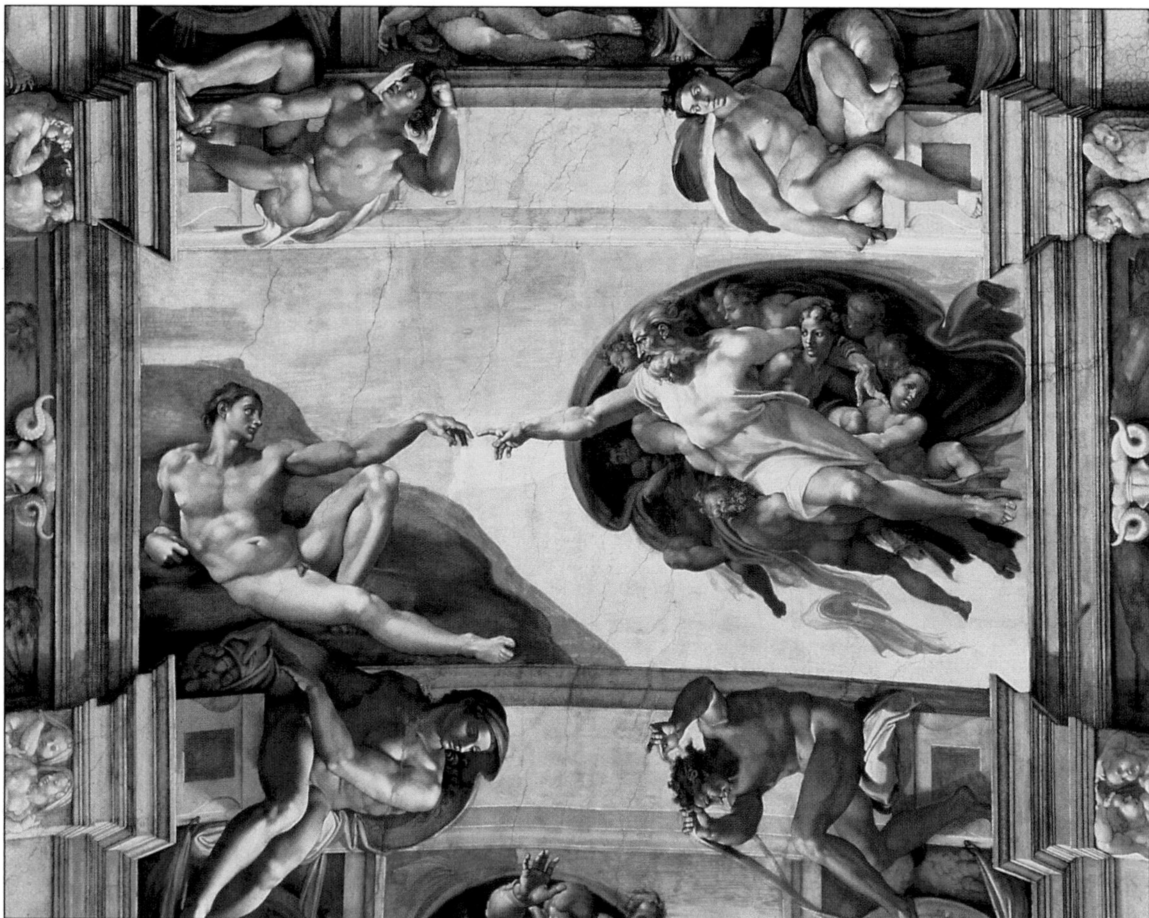

FIGURE 13.19 Michelangelo, *Creation of Adam*, detail of Sistine Chapel ceiling, 1511–12, fresco, 9′2″ × 18′8″ (2.79 × 5.69 m), Vatican, Rome. Adam's enormous latent power will be released in the next instant when swift-moving God, with Eve already under his arm, brings him to life.

In both the tenseness of its mood and its distortion of human anatomy, Michelangelo's fresco of *The Last Judgment* (fig. 13.20) reflects the Mannerist style. Although his plan for St. Peter's, built in 1546, embodies the ideals of the High Renaissance, much of Michelangelo's late work leaves those ideals far behind. A new spirit entered his art in *The Last Judgment*, commissioned for the altar wall of the Sistine Chapel in 1534 by a dying Pope Clement VII. Painted between 1536 and 1541, it lacks the optimism and sense of beauty that define Michelangelo's work on the ceiling. His figures, no longer beautifully proportioned, now look twisted and grotesque, with heads too small for their giant, inflated bodies. The space is filled with bodies that are larger at the top of the picture than the bottom; no illusion of realistic depth is even intended here.

However, this style befits Michelangelo's subject. The dead are dragged from their graves and pulled upward to be judged by Jesus. Mary, at his side, cringes at the vision. At his feet, to his right, is St. Bartholomew. Legend states that Bartholomew was martyred by being skinned alive, and he holds his skin in his hand. But the face is a self-portrait of Michelangelo, and such grimness extends to the whole painting. The hands of Bartholomew's flayed skin seem to reach downward, to the chasm of hell that opens at the bottom of the painting, where a monstrous Charon (the ferryman of the dead) guides his boat across the River Styx, driving the damned before him into perpetual torment.

Properzia de' Rossi. PROPERZIA DE' ROSSI [Pro-PEHR-tzee-ah deh RAW-see] (ca. 1490–1530), from Bologna, is known for her work in miniature, carving entire scenes on the pit of an apricot or a peach! Yet she also sculpted on a huge scale, for de' Rossi won a competition to create sculpture for the facade of the church of San Petronio in Bologna, from which the scene of *Joseph and Potiphar's Wife* (fig. 13.21) is believed to come. The semiclad wife of the Egyptian officer Potiphar has failed to seduce Joseph; she reaches quickly to grab for his cloak as he flees her bed. The sense of animation achieved is notable, the draperies and hair of Joseph and of Potiphar's wife shown to respond to the speed of their movements. Properzia de' Rossi died at the age of 39—one can only wonder what she would have achieved had her productive years been extended.

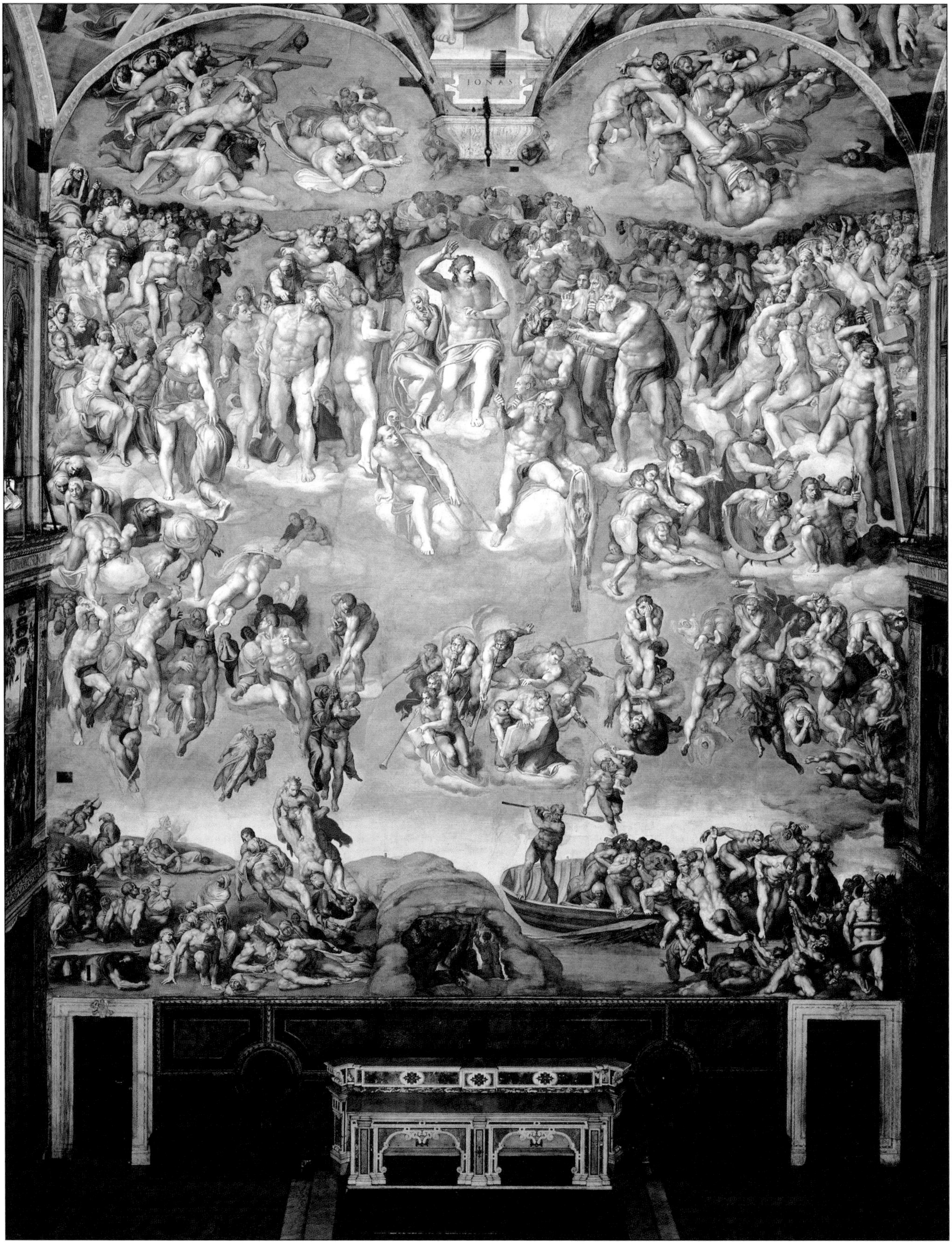

FIGURE 13.20 Michelangelo, *The Last Judgment*, Sistine Chapel, 1536–41, fresco, 48′ × 44′ (14.63 × 13.41 m), Vatican Museums, Rome, Italy. Michelangelo's optimism and the idealized beauty of the ceiling of this chapel are now replaced with a pessimistic view and anatomical anomalies.

Critical Thinking

The Question of Art Restoration

Among questions debated strongly in recent years is the extent to which works of art that have deteriorated over the centuries should be restored, or even cleaned. Cleaning refers to removing grime and soot, or layers of varnish from works. Restoration involves repairing elements that have become damaged and replacing missing elements. One major example that occasioned strenuous debate was the cleaning of the Sistine Chapel frescoes painted by Michelangelo, and which had, over the centuries, become darkened with dirt. Another example is the restoration of Leonardo da Vinci's *Last Supper*, which took twenty years, and involved not only cleaning, but also filling in some missing sections of the image with new paint.

Among the arguments against cleaning Michelangelo's work was that the cleaning agents might also remove some of the original pigment, and could damage the painting irretrievably by removing the darkened colors that over many generations people had become accustomed to seeing and revealing a brighter set of hues that some considered garish. Against adding newly painted sections to Leonardo's work were those who said the great painting would effectively no longer be Leonardo's. Countering these arguments were those who claimed that cleaning the Sistine frescoes would restore them to how Michelangelo originally painted them. Similarly, those who favored restoring Leonardo's *Last Supper* believe that the painting has now been restored to its former glory.

Which point of view do you find more convincing, and why? What other issues do you think should be evaluated when a major art masterpiece is being considered for cleaning and/or restoration? What do you think should be done with Leonardo's *Mona Lisa*, which is the most famous prime candidate for cleaning today?

FIGURE 13.21 Properzia de' Rossi, *Joseph and Potiphar's Wife*, ca. 1520, marble bas-relief, $19'\frac{1}{4}'' \times 18'\frac{1}{8}''$ (49 × 46 cm), Museo di San Petronio, Bologna. Powerful full figures, so admired during the High Renaissance, move rapidly through space in this compact composition, the garments revealing the bodies beneath as well as enhancing the action.

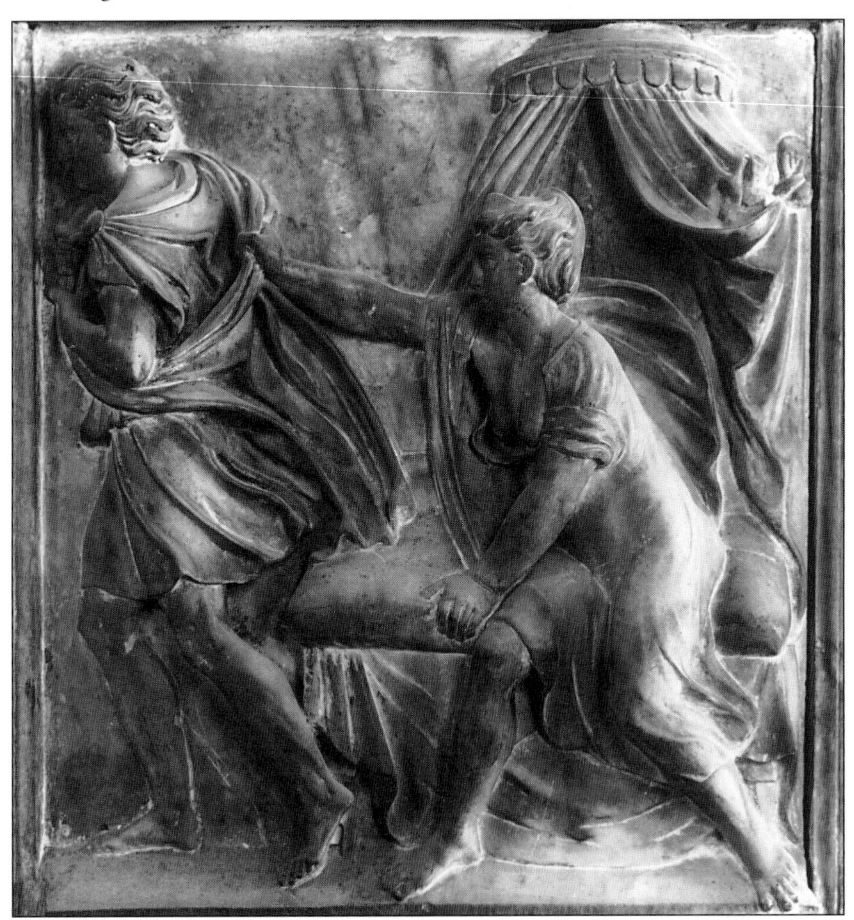

ARCHITECTURE

Donato Bramante. DONATO BRAMANTE's [bra-MAHN-tay] (1444–1514) reputation was based largely on a building called the Tempietto, or "little temple" (fig. 13.22) constructed from 1502 on the site where St. Peter was believed to have been crucified. Commissioned by Ferdinand and Isabella of Spain (patrons of the explorer Christopher Columbus), the Tempietto is an adaptation of a classical temple of the Doric order (see Chapter 2), including a complete entablature.

The building itself is set on a stepped base and surrounded by a **peristyle,** or continuous row of columns. The first story is topped by a balustrade, or carved railing, inside of which is a **drum,** or circular wall, on which Bramante set a classically hemispheric dome. The plan, with its deeply recessed spaces, creates a dramatic play of light and dark, despite the relatively small scale of the building itself.

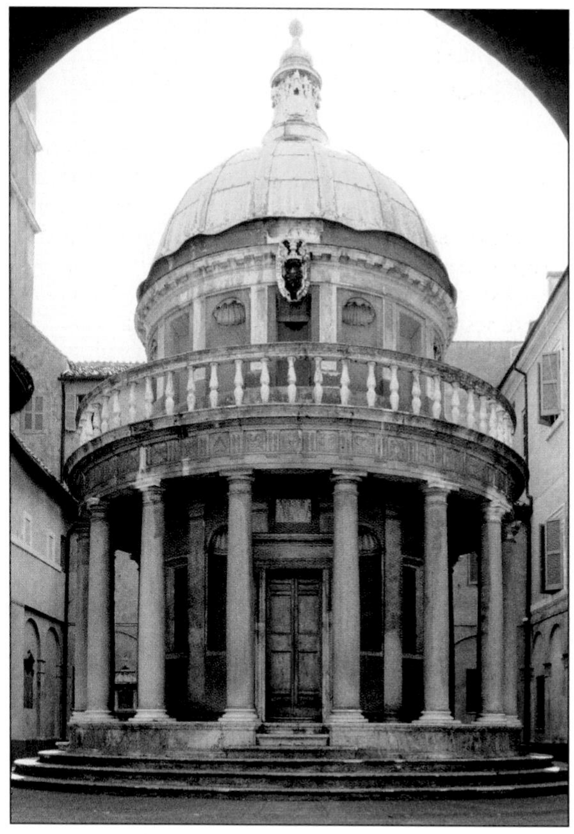

FIGURE 13.22 Donato Bramante, Tempietto, San Pietro in Montorio, Rome, 1502–after 1511. Small in size but of great importance, the Tempietto demonstrates the reuse of ancient pagan architecture for Renaissance Christian purposes.

VENICE

Throughout the fifteenth century and into the sixteenth, Venice was one of the most powerful city-states in all of Europe, exercising control over the entire Adriatic and much of the eastern Mediterranean. It was celebrated in Vittore Carpaccio's *Lion of St. Mark* (fig. 13.23), painted in 1516 for a government office in the city's Ducal Palace. The lion is the symbol of the city's patron saint, Mark the Evangelist, whom God was said to have visited on the

FIGURE 13.23 Vittore Carpaccio, *Lion of St. Mark*, 1516, oil on canvas, $4'6\frac{3}{4}'' \times 12'1''$ (1.40 × 3.70 m), Ducal Palace, Venice. The winged lion was a symbol of the Evangelist Mark and of Venice. This painting documents the early sixteenth-century appearance of the city, with its campanile, Ducal Palace, and the domes of St. Mark's Cathedral.

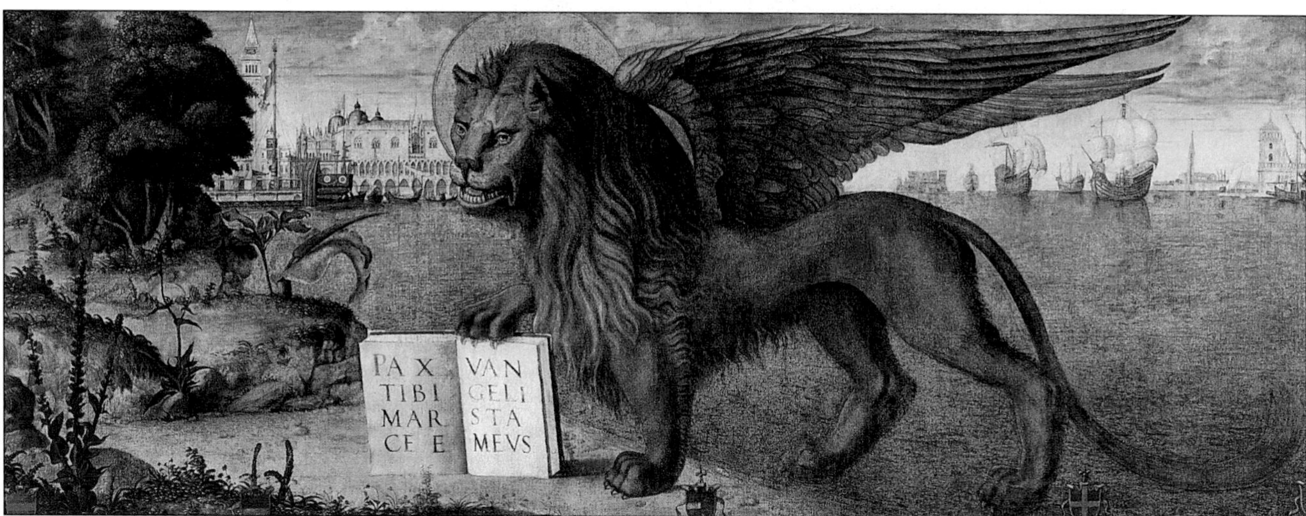

Evangelist's arrival at the Venice lagoon, thereby designating Venice as the saint's final resting place. Greeting St. Mark, God's angel is said to have announced, "Peace unto you, Mark, my evangelist," the Latin words inscribed on the tablet held in the lion's paws. The lion stands with its front paws on land and its hind paws in the water, signifying Venice's dominion over land and sea. Behind the lion, to the left, is the Ducal Palace, the seat of government and law and the source of the city's order and harmony. The Byzantine domes of St. Mark's Cathedral rise behind it, the basis of the city's moral fabric, and the giant campanile (bell tower) that dominates St. Mark's Square stands on the far left housing the five bells of St. Mark's, one of which chimed to announce the beginning and end of each working day. Behind the lion to the right is a fleet of Venetian merchant ships, the source of the city's wealth and prosperity.

Venetian Oil Painting. Surrounded by water and built over a lagoon, humidity made fresco painting, so popular elsewhere in Europe, virtually impossible in Venice. From 1475, after **oil painting** (pigments mixed with linseed oil) was developed in The Netherlands, fresco painting in Venice gradually ceased. The use of oil on canvas led in turn to a new kind of painting. Applying colors in glazes—that is, in layers of transparent color—created by mixing a little pigment with a lot of linseed oil, painters were able to create a light that seemed to emanate from the depths of the painting itself. Furthermore, the texture of the canvas itself was exploited. Stroked over a woven surface, the brush deposits more paint on the top of the weave and less in the crevices. This textured surface in turn "catches" actual light, lending an almost shimmering vibrancy.

Titian. Tiziano Vecelli of Venice, known as TITIAN [TISH-un] (ca. 1488/90–1576) favored paintings with complex iconography—in fact, Titian classified his paintings as poetry. Characteristic of the Renaissance interest in antiquity, the subject of Titian's festive *Bacchanal* (fig. 13.24), painted ca. 1518, derives from Classical mythology; Bacchus is the ancient Roman god of wine. Titian popularized the type of strawberry blond female seen here, portrayed with his characteristically sensuous

FIGURE 13.24 Titian, *Bacchanal*, ca. 1518, oil on canvas, 5′8$\frac{7}{8}$″ × 6′4″ (1.75 × 1.93 m), Museo del Prado Madrid. Botticelli's slender Early Renaissance figure type (fig. 13.13) matured in the work of High Renaissance painters such as Titian to a full-bodied ideal of beauty.

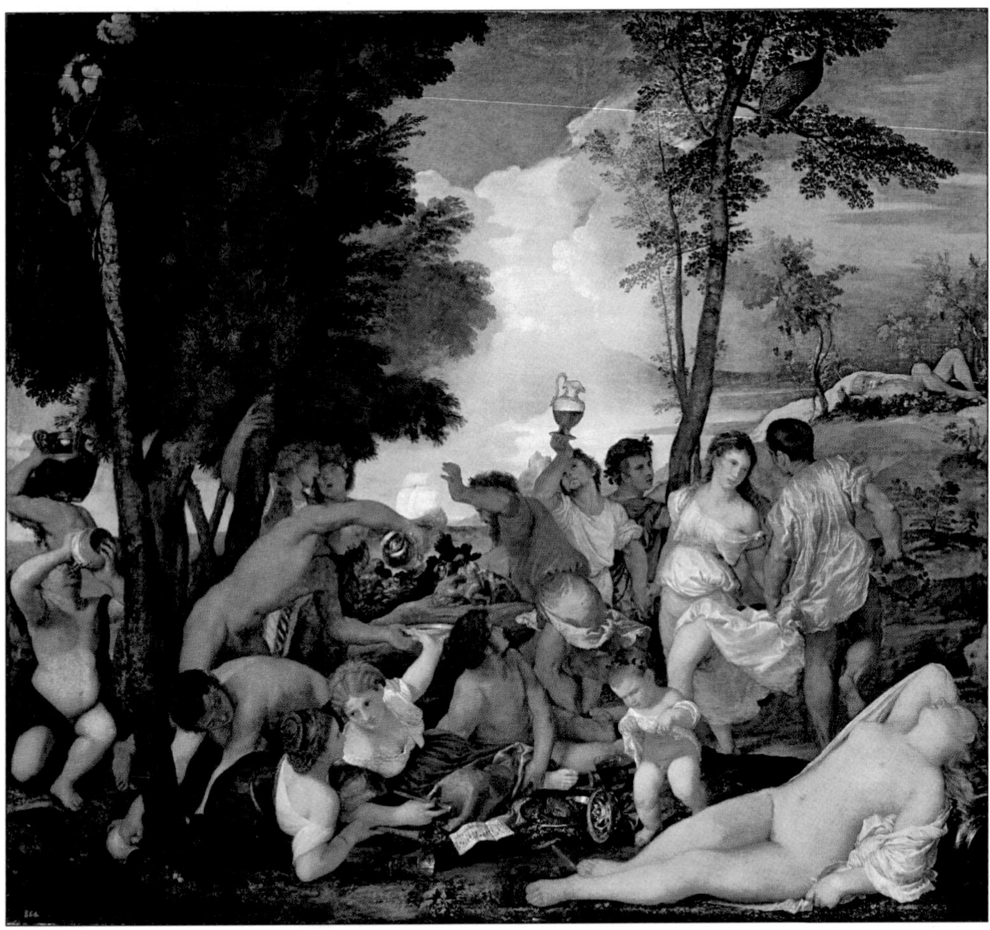

handling of flesh. The richness of Titian's paintings is due in part to his use of an underpainting of red bolus (an earth pigment) in many of his works, rather than the usual green-black underpainting. He also used **impasto**—thick paint made by mixing the pigment with beeswax. Titian is associated with the so-called "golden glow" of Venetian painting, achieved, in part, by adding a bit of yellow pigment to the final protective glaze applied to the painting.

MUSIC

The reinvention of Rome required the reinvention of music—a new St. Peter's needed a new mass to fill its vast space with sound.

Josquin des Près. The most important composer of the new Rome took on the job: JOSQUIN DES PRÈS [JOZ-skanh de-PRAY] (1440–1521), from Flanders. It was Josquin who led the Sistine Choir as Michelangelo painted the ceiling and Raphael worked in the papal suites. Like Dufay, Josquin spent many years in Italy, serving the Sforza family in Milan, the Estes at their court in Ferrara, and finally several Roman popes, including Sixtus IV (for whom he directed the Sistine Choir), Julius II, and Leo X. So highly regarded was Josquin that the French king Louis XII and the Austrian queen Margaret both bid for his services. His contemporaries extolled him as "the Father of Musicians" and "the best of composers." An enchanted Martin Luther remarked that Josquin was "the master of the notes; they must do as he wills."

Josquin composed approximately two hundred works—motets, **masses,** and **chansons** (songs). His many motets and chansons attest to his interest in exploring new trends in setting words to music. His motet "Ave Maria . . . virgo serena" ("Hail, Mary . . . Serene Virgin") (1502) exemplifies his style. The opening employs imitative counterpoint with the melody for the words "Ave Maria" first heard in the soprano, then repeated in succession by the alto, the tenor, and the bass while the original parts continue, as in a round. On the words *gratia plena* ("full of grace") Josquin introduces a new, second melody, again in the soprano, which is again passed from one voice to the next. Josquin overlaps the voices in both melodies, allowing the altos to enter, for example, before the sopranos have sung the complete melody. This overlapping of voices enriches the music's texture, giving it body and providing it with a continuous and fluid motion. Josquin also allows two voices, and sometimes three or four, to sing the same melody simultaneously—a duet between the two lower voice parts (tenor and bass), for instance, will imitate a duet between alto and soprano. The motet concludes serenely with emphatic slow chords on the words *O mater Dei, memento mei* ("O mother of God, remember me"). Just before this ending, Josquin introduces a significant silence that sounds at first like an ending. He uses this silence to focus the listener's attention on the true ending, which comes immediately after. The dignified serenity and graceful restraint of Josquin's "Ave Maria . . . virgo serena" can be compared with the quiet beauty and restrained elegance of Raphael's madonnas.

Palestrina. The music of the Italian GIOVANNI PIERLUIGI DA PALESTRINA [pal-uh-STREE-nah] (1525–1594) came to dominate the church throughout most of the sixteenth century. As the church came under attack from the north for its excessive spending and ornate lavishness, it responded by simplifying the mass and the music designed to accompany it. Although it considered banning polyphony altogether, thinking it too elaborate to be easily understood by laypeople, in the end the church endorsed the controlled and precise style of Palestrina.

Palestrina held a number of important church positions. He was organist and choirmaster of the large chorus that performed exclusively in St. Peter's, the *Cappella Giulia* (Julian Choir), and he was music director for the Vatican. His music evokes the Gregorian roots of traditional church music and relies directly on the emotional appeal of the listener's potential union with God. He wrote nearly a thousand compositions, including over a hundred masses. Among the most beautiful of all Palestrina's works is his *Pope Marcellus Mass,* written in honor of the pope and set for an **a cappella**—or unaccompanied—choir in six voice parts: soprano, alto, two tenors, and two basses. It contains music for the Kyrie, Gloria, Credo, Sanctus, Benedictus, and Agnus Dei, as did the Gregorian Mass before it, and Palestrina utilizes the traditional Gregorian melodies connected with each of these parts of the mass. Still, it is clearly Renaissance in its style, utilizing an orderly and clear imitative polyphony that allows the listener to follow each of the voices in the mass as they weave together with precision.

LITERATURE

Baldassare Castiglione. BALDASSARE CASTIGLIONE [KAS-till-YOH-nay] (1478–1529) was a courtier to the Italian ducal courts, first at the court of Francesco Gonzaga, the ruler of Mantua in the early sixteenth century, and then at the court of Urbino, established by Federico da Montefeltro, the father of Guidobaldo da Montefeltro, in whose service Castiglione prospered. Later unrest caused him to return to service in Duke Francesco's court. After serving as ambassador to Rome, Castiglione was appointed by Pope Clement VII as papal ambassador to Spain, where he lived out the remaining years of his life.

While at Urbino, Castiglione wrote the *Book of the Courtier,* which memorializes, celebrates, and idealizes life at court, especially Urbino. It is cast in the form of a series of dialogues spread out over four evenings at the court of Urbino. The central topic is the manners, education, and behavior of the ideal courtier, whose virtues Castiglione extols. The courtier must be a man of courage with experience in war; he must be learned in the classics and in classical languages; he must be able to serve his prince with generosity.

Castiglione's ideal courtier had to be physically and emotionally strong, able to perform feats requiring agility, skill, courage, and daring. His physical prowess was measured by his grace as a dancer and elegance as a singer and musician. He was also expected to be an engaging and witty conversationalist, a good companion, an elegant writer, even a bit of a poet. In short, Castiglione's courtier was the ideal Renaissance gentleman—of sound mind, body, and character, and learned in the ideas of Renaissance humanism.

Castiglione's blending of the soldier and the scholar, his merging of the ideals of medieval chivalry with those of Renaissance humanism, made his *Book of the Courtier* popular both in its own time and afterward. Castiglione himself was no exception and embodied the ideals his book celebrated. Raphael's portrait of Castiglione (fig. 13.25) displays many of the qualities Castiglione extols, from the nobility of the graceful head to the intelligence of the shining eyes, complemented by the elegant refinement of the attire.

Niccolò Machiavelli. A contemporary of Castiglione, NICCOLO MACHIAVELLI [mak-ee-ah-VEL-ee] (1469–1527), also wrote a guidebook on behavior—*The Prince*, a manual for princes and rulers.

FIGURE 13.25 Raphael, *Baldassare Castiglione*, ca. 1515, oil on panel, transferred to canvas, $32\frac{1}{4}'' \times 26\frac{1}{2}''$ (81.9 × 67.3 cm). Photo: Arnaudet. Musée du Louvre, Paris. Reunion des Musées National, France/Art Resource, NY. Castiglione wrote about the qualities of the ideal courtier; it is not surprising that Raphael, a refined gentleman, was a personal friend of his. Perhaps some of the calm restraint recommended by Castiglione is seen in Raphael's portrait with its restricted range of color.

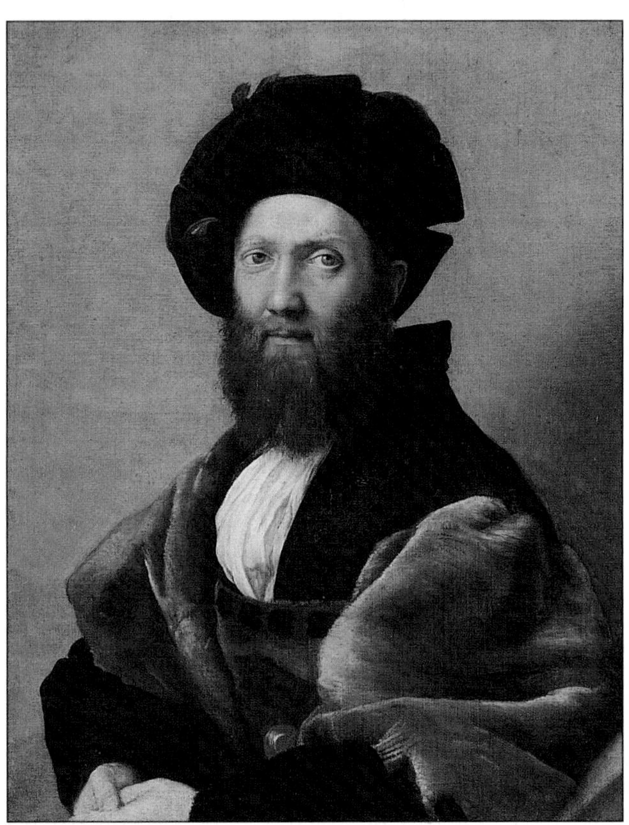

Like Castiglione, Machiavelli was well educated in the Renaissance humanist tradition. Like Castiglione's courtier, Machiavelli's prince is a model of an ideal. The difference between the two writers' "ideals," however, is dramatic: Castiglione supported the tenets of Renaissance humanism, but Machiavelli challenged them by introducing a radically different set of standards, standards that inform, among other things, Mannerist art.

Young Machiavelli was employed as a clerk and secretary to the Florentine magistrates responsible for war and internal affairs. From 1498 to 1512, he also served as an ambassador to, among others, the Holy Roman Emperor Maximilian, the king of France, and Pope Julius II. During his lifetime, the Italian city-states were almost continually at war either with one another or with other countries, such as France and Spain. Machiavelli himself suffered from the changing fortunes of the ruling families: When the Medici came to power in Florence, for instance, he was accused of conspiracy, tortured, and imprisoned. Later, when the Medici government collapsed, he was accused of being a Medici sympathizer.

The Prince was written in 1513 and published in 1532 after Machiavelli's death. It quickly acquired fame or, as some would have it, notoriety. Based on a series of premises about human nature—none favorable—*The Prince* asserts that people are basically selfish, deceitful, greedy, and gullible. Accordingly, Machiavelli advises princes to rule in ways that play on these fundamental human characteristics. A prince can be—indeed, should be—hypocritical, cruel, and deceitful when necessary. He should keep faith with no one but himself and employ ruthlessness and cunning to maintain his power over the people. As Machiavelli writes, "it is far better to be feared than loved," although he notes, "the prince must nonetheless make himself feared in such a way that, if he is not loved, he will at least avoid being hated."

The view of human beings that forms the foundation of Machiavelli's arguments in *The Prince* reflects political expediency, based on Machiavelli's observation of Florentine politics and the politics of other city-states and countries he visited as a Florentine ambassador. Having witnessed the instability of power in Italy, particularly the surrender of parts of Italy to France and Spain, Machiavelli wrote that a ruler must be strong enough to keep himself in power, for only with the strength of absolute power could he rule effectively.

Machiavelli's *The Prince* was the most widely read book of its time, after the Bible. The questions it raises about the relationship between politics and morality, the starkly realistic depiction of power it presents, and the authority, immediacy, and directness with which it is written, ensured its success. Whatever we may think of its vision of human nature or of the advice it offers rulers, it is hard to deny the power of its language, the strength of its convictions, and the force of its arguments.

MANNERISM

Mannerism was defined as a style in 1914 by Walter Friedländer; the term **Mannerism** derived from the Italian *manièra* (manner of style, suggesting affectation). The style is also referred to as the Manièra as well as the anti-Classical style, although the artists today labeled as Mannerists considered themselves classical. Mannerism originally referred only to painting, and meant that one painted "in the manner of . . ." Later, it came to have a negative connotation, one associated with affectation, academicism, and decadence: Mannerism became a derogatory term connoting artificiality and artistic decline on the grounds that artists did not assimilate the style of a master, but only affected it. Today, Mannerism is no longer considered a decline, for it is felt the distorted elements that characterize the style give spiritual feeling and convey emotion. The Mannerist period dates from approximately 1520 to 1600, the style seen especially in Italy, centering in Rome and Florence, although it was also fashionable in France and elsewhere.

Mannerism coincides with a period of political and religious unrest. The sack of Rome in 1527 by the troops of Charles V, six months of murder and destruction, undermined the confidence of the Renaissance humanists. Religious feelings were strong in the time of the Reformation and Counter-Reformation. In an age of anxiety, an era of crisis, the clarity and confidence of the High Renaissance was lost, replaced by ambiguity and despair. The emotional impact of Mannerist art is likely to be tense and disturbing.

Never intended to have broad public appeal, Mannerism was a court style oriented to the tastes of the upper class. It was formulated to appeal to the sophisticated, elegant, aristocratic sensibilities of the sixteenth century. Thus, although the style was in vogue for a long period of time, its audience was restricted and it was not to have significant impact on future artistic trends. Mannerism, therefore, is not considered as important in the history of culture as the preceding Renaissance style or the succeeding Baroque style.

PAINTING

Mannerism was a departure from Renaissance ideals. Whereas Renaissance painting was characterized by clear presentations of subject matter, balanced compositions, normal body proportions, scientific spatial constructions, and preference for primary colors, Mannerist painting, in contrast, was characterized by intentionally obscure subject matter, unbalanced compositions, bodies with distorted proportions and contorted poses, confusing spatial constructions, and a preference for secondary and acidic colors. Facial expressions may be strained or inappropriate for the subject. Aesthetic forms became of greater concern than content.

Parmigianino. Among the most characteristic examples of the Mannerist departure from the Renaissance norm is the *Madonna with the Long Neck* (fig. 13.26), painted 1534–40 by PARMIGIANINO [par-mee-jah-NEE-noh] (1503–1540) of Parma. The figures are perfect, but, in contrast to the classical canon of proportions admired in the Renaissance, they have become unreal, other worldly, elongated and ethereal, artificial and affected, graceful and refined beyond nature's capabilities. Mary is especially large, with an almost balloonlike inflation through the hips and thighs. Only a complete absence of bones and joints would explain the curving contours of Mary's right hand.

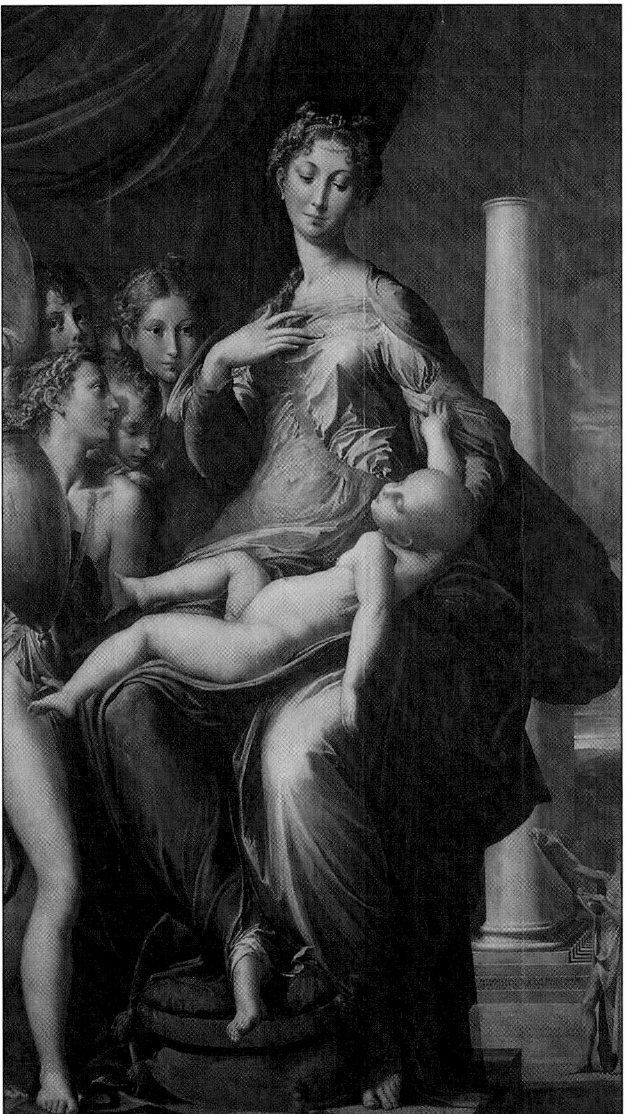

FIGURE 13.26 Parmigianino, *Madonna with the Long Neck*, 1534–40, oil on panel, 7′1″ × 4′4″ (2.16 × 1.32 m), Uffizi Gallery, Alinari, Florence, SCALA/Art Resource, NY. Comparison with Raphael's High Renaissance *Madonna of the Meadows* (see fig. 13.16) makes obvious the Mannerist preference for distorted figures and spatial ambiguity.

The composition is unbalanced and spatially ambiguous. The figures are crowded on the left side, yet the open area on the right side is almost empty. The column in the background is a symbol of the torture of Jesus, because he was bound to a column and flagellated. The tiny prophet emphasizes the odd and unclear spatial arrangement—the viewer looks up to the foreground figures but down to the prophet.

Bronzino. Another representative of the Mannerist or anti-Classical style is Bronzino (1503–1572), court painter to Cosimo de' Medici. Mannerism was noted to be the style of the courts and was not intended to appeal to the general public. Bronzino's painting of the *Allegory of Venus* (fig. 13.27), ca. 1546, demonstrates the intentional ambiguity of Mannerist iconography. The two main figures are Venus and Cupid, their relationship shown to be uncomfortably erotic. On the right, Folly throws roses. In the upper right, Father Time uncovers the follies of love—or perhaps he tries to hide them! The figure in the right background, with the body of a snake and the left and right hands reversed, is Deceit—the masks suggest falseness. The figures in the left background are probably Hatred and Inconstancy. Typically Mannerist is the complexity and obscurity of the **allegory,** which has been interpreted in various ways by historians.

Like the subject, the composition is also unclear. Characteristic of Mannerism is the absence of a single center of focus—the figures seem to compete with each other for the viewer's attention. The figures completely fill the composition, choking the space. Still and tense, their poses are elegant but affected, agitated, and exaggerated—and certainly difficult for a person to actually assume. Relative scale of the figures is inconsistent. Their uneasy expressions cause them to appear disturbed, and they are intended to disturb the viewer in this style that is distorted psychologically and physically. The colors are acid and metallic, the style of painting linear and hard with harsh lighting. Figures weave in and out in a paper-thin space, crowded, limited, and confined, set against a heavy and impenetrable background. Spatial contradictions abound—a floor plan of this space and its inhabitants cannot be drawn, for neither linear nor aerial perspective is used.

FIGURE 13.27 Agnolo Bronzino, *Allegory with Venus and Cupid,* ca. 1546, oil on panel, $4'9\frac{1}{2}'' \times 3'9\frac{1}{4}''$ (1.46 × 1.16 m), National Gallery, London. Typically Mannerist are the intentionally complex iconography (including an oddly erotic encounter between Venus and Cupid) and the pictorial space choked with figures.

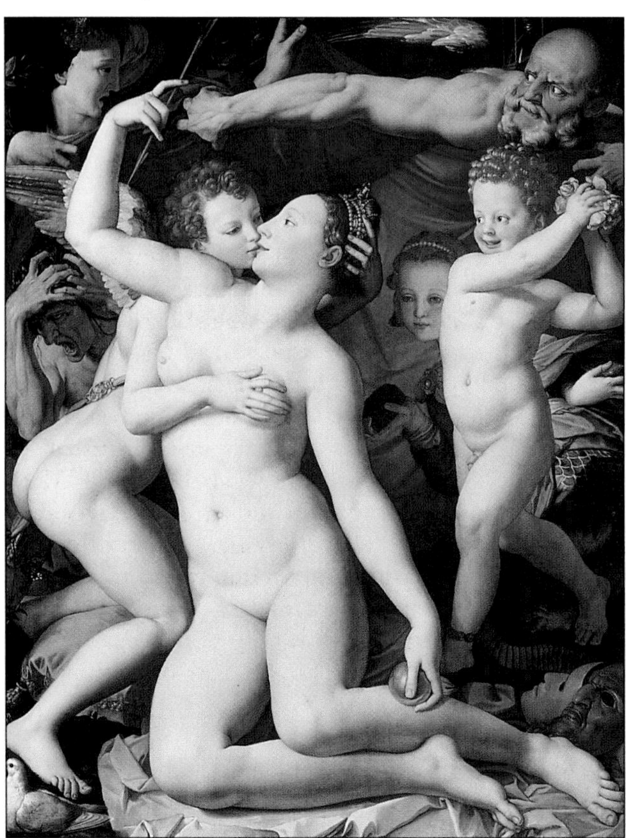

Tintoretto. The leader of the Mannerists in Venice was Tintoretto (1518–1594), whose real name was Jacopo Robusti, painter of the *Last Supper* (fig. 13.28) of 1592–94. The coveted Renaissance iconographic clarity, seen in Leonardo da Vinci's depiction of this subject (fig. 13.14), is gone. In fact, the viewer may need some time to find Jesus in this scene, for the perspective leads the viewer's eyes away from Jesus and out of the composition, many figures compete with Jesus for the viewer's attention, and Jesus is pushed back into the space. He is singled out only by his central position and aureole of light. The lighting is unnatural, radiating from Jesus and the hanging lamp, from which the smoke turns into floating transparent angels. Judas is singled out from the apostles as the only figure on the opposite side of the table. The table is not parallel to the picture plane, as in Renaissance portrayals of the Last Supper, but placed on a strong diagonal into depth—the rapid recession is characteristic of Tintoretto. This Mannerist portrayal of the Last Supper is set in a tavern, an unusually commonplace location for a religious event.

Yet there is no possibility of mistaking this for a genre scene. Religious drama and emotion derive from Tintoretto's striking composition and lighting. Far from a calm, stable, static depiction, Tintoretto's verve changed Leonardo da Vinci's format for the Last Supper and broke Leonardo's hold on this subject. But Tintoretto's presentation has been criticized for losing sight of the spirituality of the subject, with too much stress placed on the incidental activity in the foreground. Instead, Tintoretto's greatest concern was the aesthetic problem and the potential of light, movement, and drama.

El Greco. One of the most interesting artists whose work displays Mannerist qualities is known as EL GRECO [el GRECK-oh] (1541–1614), or "the Greek." Domenikos Theotokopoulos was born on the island of Crete. He studied in Venice from about 1566, where he was deeply influenced by Titian, and then for seven years in Rome. In 1577, he emigrated to Spain, going first to Madrid and then to Toledo.

The most important of his major commissions is *The Burial of Count Orgaz* (fig. 13.29) of 1586. Legend held that

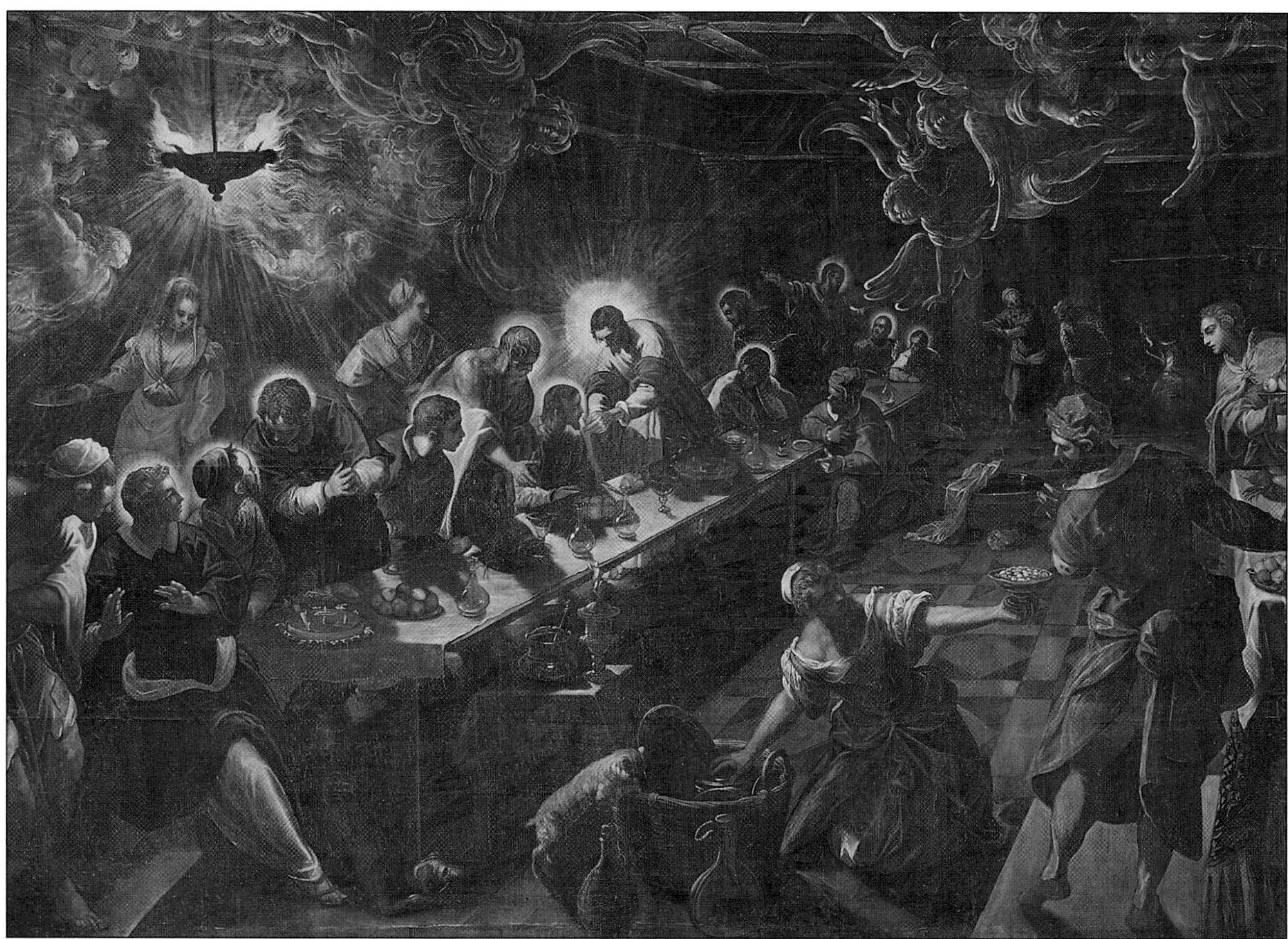

FIGURE 13.28 Tintoretto, *The Last Supper*, 1592–94, oil on canvas, 12′ × 18′8″ (3.66 × 5.69 m), San Giorgio Maggiore, Venice. SCALA/Art Resouce, NY. In striking contrast to the compositional clarity of Leonardo da Vinci's High Renaissance depiction (see fig. 13.14), the viewer may have some difficulty in locating Jesus in Tintoretto's Mannerist version of this subject, for the perspective leads away from, rather than toward, Jesus.

at the count's burial in 1323, Saints Augustine and Stephen appeared and lowered him into his grave even as his soul was seen ascending to heaven. In the painting, the burial and the ascension occur in two separate realms, neither of which fits spatially with the other, and both of which are packed with figures. On the lower portion, El Greco has painted the local contemporary aristocracy—people he knew—in attendance at the funeral, not the aristocracy of the count's day. In fact, El Greco's eight-year-old son stands at the lower left next to St. Stephen, and above him, looking out at the viewer from the back row, is quite possibly El Greco himself.

The top half of the scene is as spatially ambiguous as any example of Mannerist painting. A crowd of saints enters from a deep space at the top right. A chorus of angels playing instruments occupies a sort of middle space on the left. In the foreground, St. John and the Virgin Mary greet the angel who arrives with the soul of the count, shown about the size of a baby, as if to emphasize its innocence. John and Mary plead the count's case with Jesus, who is peculiarly small and seated far enough in the distance almost to occupy the vanishing point to the heavens. The most notable aspect of El Greco's style is exemplified by Jesus' right arm, which stretches far forward into the space above Mary's head. The elongated hands and arms are the most "mannered" feature of El Greco's art, and yet it is difficult to label his work "Mannerist." His aim is to move his audience by conveying a sense of the spiritual, almost mystical power of deeply religious faith and conviction. In this, his painting anticipates that of the Baroque age, and captures something of the power of the great Spanish mystics of his own day, Teresa of Avila and Ignatius Loyola, both of whom would be made saints in Rome in 1622.

Sofonisba Anguissola. Castiglione's *Book of the Courtier* advocated that aristocrats, be they male or female, be educated in social arts, and that women, specifically, should

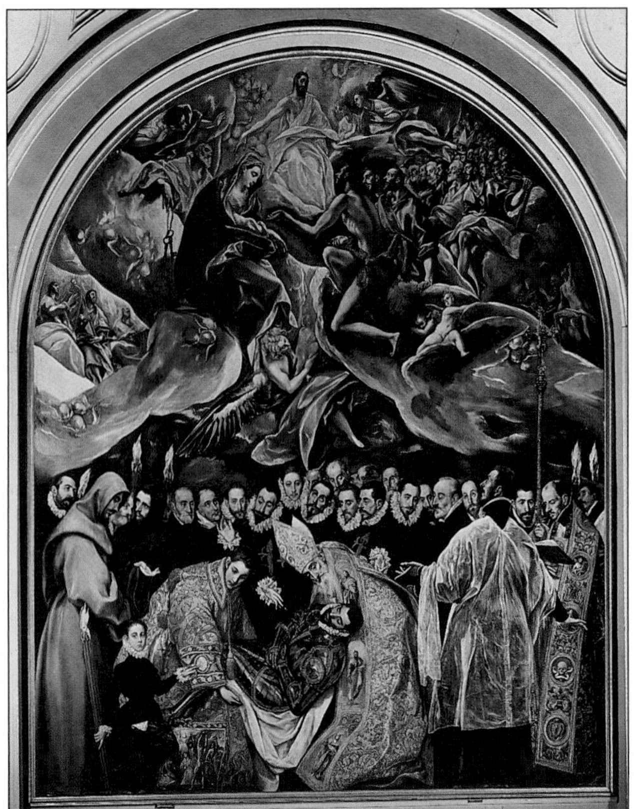

FIGURE 13.29 El Greco, *The Burial of Count Orgaz*, 1586, oil on canvas, 16′ × 11′10″ (4.88 × 3.61 m), Church of San Tomé, Toledo. Although El Greco's distorted figures were once attributed to astigmatism, they are now recognized as part of the Mannerist preference for elongated bodily proportions.

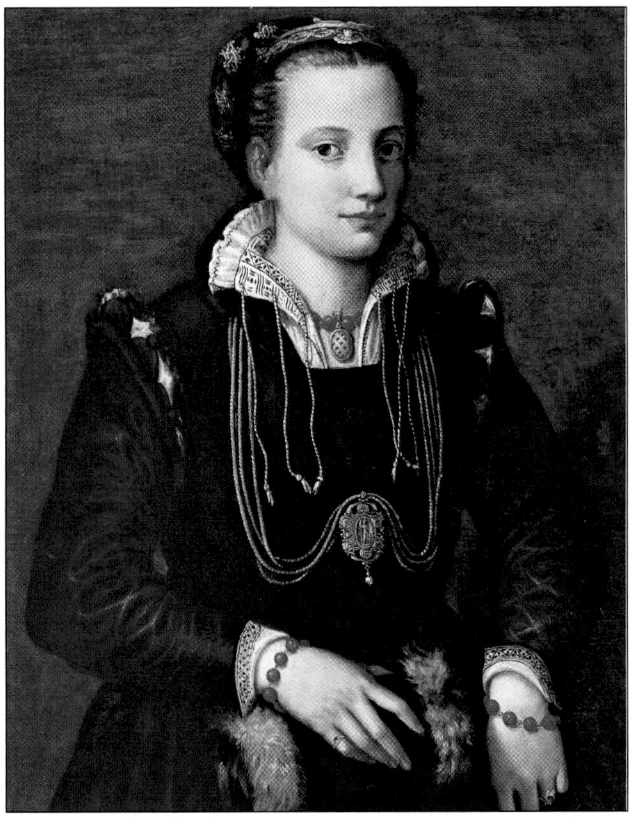

FIGURE 13.30 Sofonisba Anguissola, *Portrait of the Artist's Sister Minerva*, ca. 1564, oil on canvas, $33\frac{1}{2} \times 26''$, Milwaukee Art Museum. Gift of the family of Mrs. Fred Vogel, Jr, L1952.1. As was customary for women artists of this era, Anguissola specialized in portraits. Such realistic records are one of the manifestations of the interest accorded the individual that began during the Renaissance.

learn to paint, not as a career, but as part of training for aristocratic life. SOFONISBA ANGUISSOLA [So-fo-NEES-bah Ahn-gwee-SO-lah] (1528/35– 1625), from Cremona, and her five younger sisters studied painting and all became painters; only the youngest sibling, a boy, did not. In 1560, Anguissola became a painter at the court of Philip II in Madrid, indicating her international fame. The high regard in which she was held is made clear by the generous dowry the Spanish monarchy provided for her first marriage in 1570.

Sofonisba Anguissola frequently painted self-portraits, which were much in demand due to her fame, as well as portraits of her family, such as fig. 13.30 of one of her sisters, Minerva. Her sitters appear relaxed, almost alive; Giorgio Vasari noted that she created "breathing likenesses." Minerva wears a large gold medallion of the ancient Minerva, goddess of wisdom and the arts.

Lavinia Fontana. LAVINIA FONTANA [La-VEEN-nee-eh Fohn-THAN-nah] (1552–1614) grew up in Bologna, where she was instructed by her father, the artist Prospero Fontana. She is believed to be the first woman in western Europe to establish herself as a professional artist equal to her male contemporaries in fame. Her *Portrait of a Noblewoman* (fig. 13.31) is representative of her work; although women artists were likely to specialize in portraiture, Fontana's repertoire included religious and mythological subjects as well. Her husband and fellow painter Gian Paolo Zappi worked as her assistant. She was the mother of eleven children, although was survived by only three of them. In 1604 she moved to Rome to work as a portrait painter for Pope Paul V. The appeal of Fontana's style lies in the meticulously painted details of the costume, her superb technical skill in depicting various textures, and the absence of a distracting background, thereby placing all attention on the subject.

SCULPTURE

By the mid-sixteenth century, Mannerism was the dominant style in France, largely as a result of the influence of Italian artists who moved there after the sack of Rome in 1527. Benvenuto Cellini's sculpture and writings reflected the full flowering of the style.

Cultural Impact

The Renaissance changed the way human beings thought of themselves. People were no longer content to see themselves simply as a part of a larger social or religious group. With the Italian Renaissance emerged the notion of the individual self, an idea that would be celebrated two centuries later in the age of Romanticism.

One legacy of the Italian Renaissance was a restless intellectual energy. The independent thought and critical scrutiny encouraged during the Renaissance would result in the scientific revolution of the seventeenth century, as thinkers like Copernicus and Galileo built on the advances of that earlier time.

The power of individual artistic genius is most evident perhaps, among Italy's painters and sculptors. Who better than Raphael, Leonardo, and Michelangelo epitomize the genius of the Renaissance and its cultural influence? The very concept of the "Renaissance man," a multitalented individual who operates at the peak of perfection in many areas, is synonymous with these splendid artists, whose achievements have never been surpassed.

Outside the arts proper, the political ideas of Macchiavelli have been profoundly influential. Machiavelli's realistic approach to governing established principles by which rulers not only of his own day, but also of future eras, would rule. More quiet but no less influential were the social ideals of Renaissance court etiquette, especially those set down by Castiglione. His ideals of behavior established a standard for educated people of his own and future centuries to emulate.

Figure 13.31 Lavinia Fontana, *Portrait of a Noblewoman*, ca. 1580, oil on canvas, $45\frac{1}{4}'' \times 35\frac{1}{4}''$ (114.9 × 89.5 cm), National Museum of Women in the Arts, Washington, DC. Gift of Wallace and Wilhelmina Holladay. This portrait of an unknown Bolognese lady is believed to be a marriage portrait because red was the customary color of a wedding gown in Bologna; she is shown wearing one of the garments, and some of the gems, in her trousseau. The dog is a standard symbol of marital fidelity.

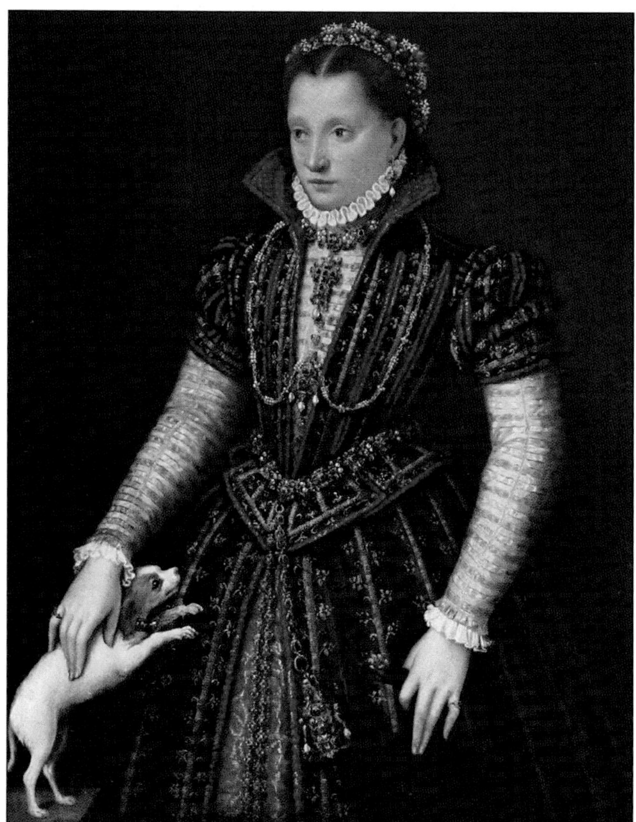

Benvenuto Cellini. BENVENUTO CELLINI [che-LEE-nee] (1500–1571) was a Florentine who worked in France for King Francis I (r. 1515–47). Cellini made an extraordinary gold and enamel *Saltcellar of Francis I* (fig. 13.32), between 1539 and 1543. It is functional, yet elegant and fantastic. Salt is represented by the male figure Neptune, because salt comes from the sea (the salt is actually in a little boat), and pepper is represented by the female figure Earth, because pepper comes from the earth (the pepper is actually in a little triumphal

Figure 13.32 Benvenuto Cellini, *Saltcellar of Francis I*, 1539–43, gold with enamel, $10\frac{1}{4}'' \times 13\frac{1}{8}''$ (26 × 33.3 cm), Kunsthistorisches Museum, Vienna, Austria. An example of extreme elegance and opulence, this table ornament contained salt and pepper.

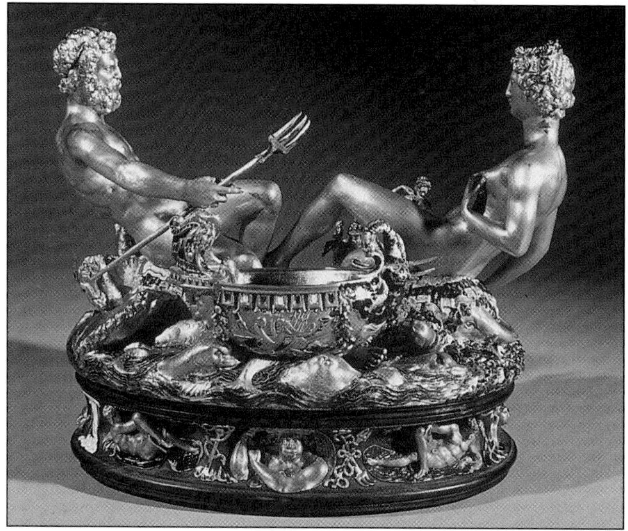

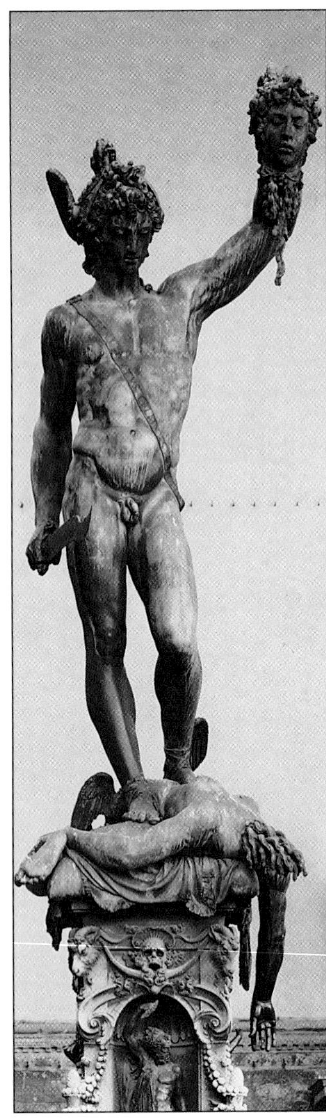

FIGURE 13.33 Benvenuto Cellini, *Perseus*, 1545–54, bronze, height 18′ (5.4 m), Loggia dei Lanzi, Florence. Even the depiction of the decapitation of the ancient mythological gorgon Medusa, blood gushing, attains elegance in the Mannerist style.

arch). On the base are complex allegorical figures of the four seasons and four parts of the day, meant to evoke both festive seasonal celebrations and the daily meal schedule. Cellini wrote that figures should be elongated; these with small heads and boneless limbs are graceful and charming.

The Autobiography of Benvenuto Cellini. Among the most widely read of Renaissance works, Cellini's *Autobiography* is notable for the way in which it portrays the Italian Mannerist sculptor and goldsmith. His response to his patron, the duke of Florence, Cosimo de' Medici, who had just commissioned a new sculpture, *Perseus* (fig. 13.33), shows his Mannerist extravagance. When the duke questioned Cellini's ability to complete a sculpture in bronze, the artist responded with supreme confidence. In Cellini's account of the incident, the artist is portrayed as heroic, brave, violent, passionate, promiscuous, and entirely committed to his art.

Like the elongated figures in Parmigianino's paintings, Cellini's exaggerated portrayal of himself and others, in his *Autobiography*, typifies the Mannerist tendency. Unlike Parmigianino's delicacy and grace, however, Cellini is all drama and vigor. Cellini's *Autobiography*, in the end, is akin to his *Saltcellar of Francis I.* His sculpture extends the Mannerist style to its limits—the decorous Classical ideal of his Renaissance predecessors is gone.

ARCHITECTURE

Mannerist architects responded to the revival of the antique in unorthodox ways. The vestibule of the Laurentian Library in Florence (fig. 13.34) was built as the Medici family library above the monastery of the church of San Lorenzo. Begun by Michelangelo in 1524, the staircase was designed between 1558 and 1559, and the room was completed by BARTOLOMEO AMMANATI [ah-mahn-AH-tee] (1511–1592). One of the most peculiar rooms ever built, the foyer has among its oddities that it is two stories high and thus higher than it is long or wide. The niches (wall recesses) are smaller at the bottom than at the top, and the same inversion of the norm is true of the pilasters that flank the niches. The columns are set into the wall, not in front of it, reversing the usual column and wall relationship. Scroll brackets, usually supporting elements, are rendered nonfunctional by their placement. The impression is one of walls pushing in, crushing the visitor. Finally, the staircase has three separate flights at the bottom but only one into the doorway at the top—a guaranteed traffic problem. This intriguing and uncomfortable room, in which everything is contrary to the classical rules of architecture, may be regarded as an ingenious Mannerist interpretation of the antique vocabulary.

The architect ANDREA PALLADIO (1508–1580), from Vicenza in northern Italy, created a building in the Mannerist style that was to be highly influential—the Villa Rotunda (fig. 13.35), ca. 1567–70, one of many villas he built in and around Vicenza. The Villa Rotunda demonstrates the extreme to which Palladio carried his passion for symmetry and ancient architecture, since all four sides are identical, each mimicking an ancient temple facade with a triangular pediment supported on columns. The central dome recalls that of the ancient Roman Pantheon (Chapter 4, fig. 4.11). Certainly the result is harmonious, dignified, majestic, with an impressive

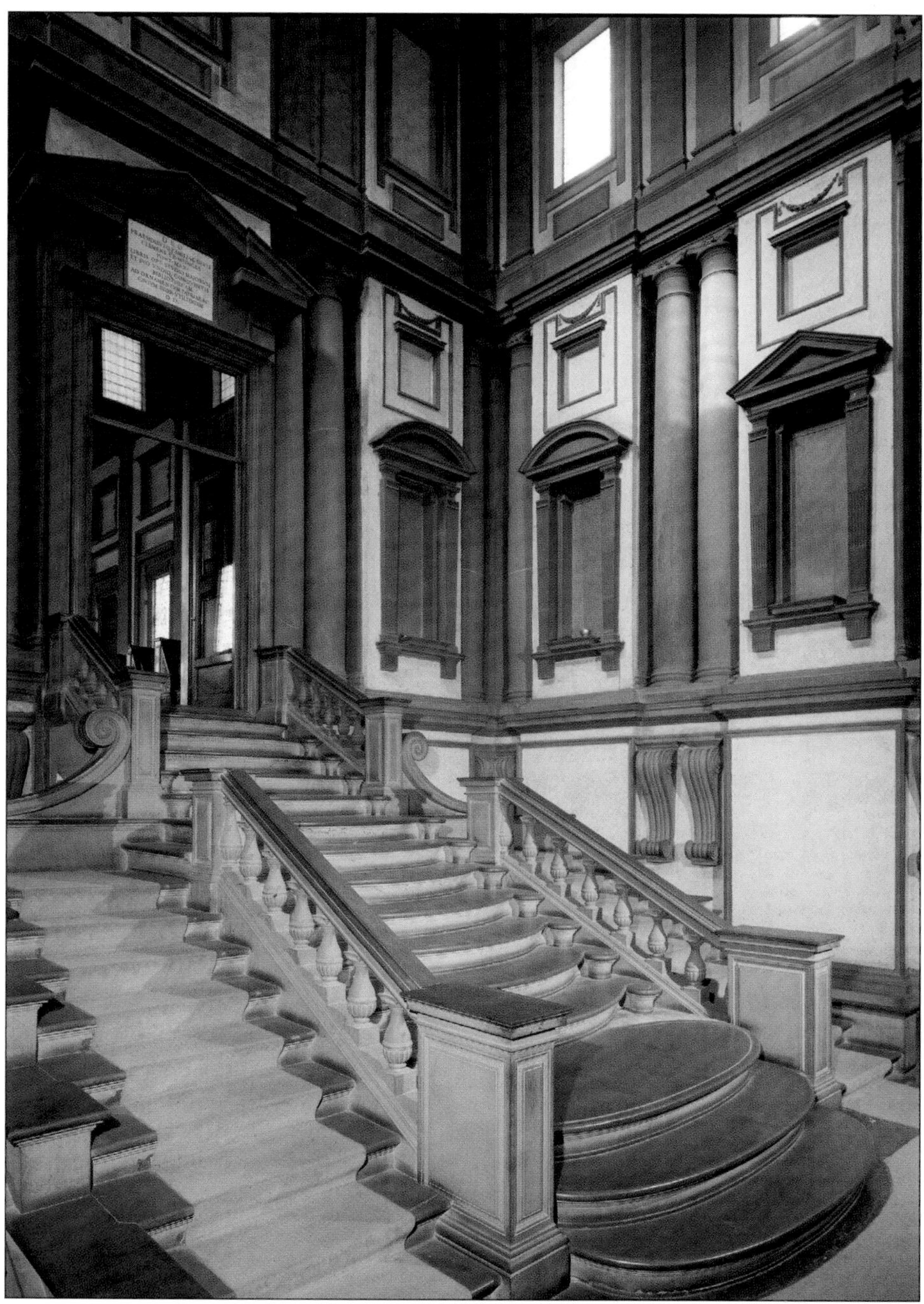

FIGURE 13.34 Designed by Michelangelo, vestibule of Laurentian Library, begun 1524, staircase completed 1559 by Bartolomeo Ammanati monastery of San Lorenzo, Florence. The antique architectural vocabulary has been used to create a space in which the visitor is unlikely to feel comfortable. The stairs, which seem to flow downward, fill most of the floor space and, because three flights lead to a single doorway at the top, a traffic jam is likely.

grandeur. Yet the idea of a home as inviting and welcoming has been transformed into something intimidating: The visitor is humbled by the ascent of many steps required to gain entry, and, although the spacious main floor was used for entertaining, the bedrooms upstairs have low ceilings.

Palladio was not only an architect but also an author: His *Four Books on Architecture*, published in 1570, became the handbook of architects. An admirer of classical architecture, as the Villa Rotunda demonstrates, the ancient architect's logic is replaced by impracticality in the Mannerist's reinterpretation.

Then & Now

The Venice Ghetto

One of the most horrifying events in twentieth-century history is the Holocaust, the anti-Semitism movement in Hitler's Germany that led to the murder of more than six million Jews. One of the reasons Hitler could so easily control the Jewish population in Europe was that he created ghettos for the vast majority of Jews in the major European capitals. The earliest known segregation of Jews into their own distinct neighborhoods occurred in Spain and Portugal in the fourteenth century, but a large ghetto was established in Frankfurt in 1460. Ghettos in Venice appeared early in the sixteenth century.

A Jewish presence in Venice dates to the early fourteenth century, and by 1381 the city had authorized Jews to live in the city, practice usury—the lending of money with interest—and sell secondhand clothes and objects, which led to the profession of pawnbroking. In 1397, all Jews were expelled, ostensibly because of irregularities that had been discovered in the monetary practices of Jewish bankers and merchants. They were permitted to visit the city for no more than fifteen consecutive days and forced to wear an emblem identifying their religion. But this order became more and more laxly enforced, and the Venetian Jewish community flourished until 1496, when they were once again banished, and this time only permitted to stay in Venice for two weeks a year.

In 1508, Julius II formed an alliance with the rest of Italy and Europe against Venice, and when his army approached the city in the spring of 1509, the large Jewish community that lived on the mainland at the lagoon's edge fled to Venice proper. Many Jewish leaders offered much-needed financial support, and the city found itself in a quandary about where they should be allowed to live. The issue was hotly debated for seven years. Franciscan sermons routinely warned that God would punish the city if Jews were admitted. Finally, on March 29, 1516, a substantial majority of the Senate approved a proposal to move the Jews en masse to an islet linked to the rest of the city by two points of access that could be closed at night. In this way, Venice could make use of the skills—and money—of the Jewish community and still segregate them.

The island to which they were banished was the site of a new foundry. The Venetian word for the smelting process is *gettare*, and the new foundry built on the island was named *getto nuovo*. Soon the island itself was called Ghetto Nuovo, and the word "ghetto" entered the language, and came to be used throughout Europe to describe the areas in cities where Jewish communities were to be found.

Figure 13.35 Andrea Palladio, Villa Rotunda, Vicenza, ca. 1567–70. This home takes the idea of symmetry and repetition beyond the limits of practicality, for all four sides look exactly the same. Palladio's passion for his antique prototype—the Roman Pantheon (see Chapter 4)—led him to create this Mannerist example.

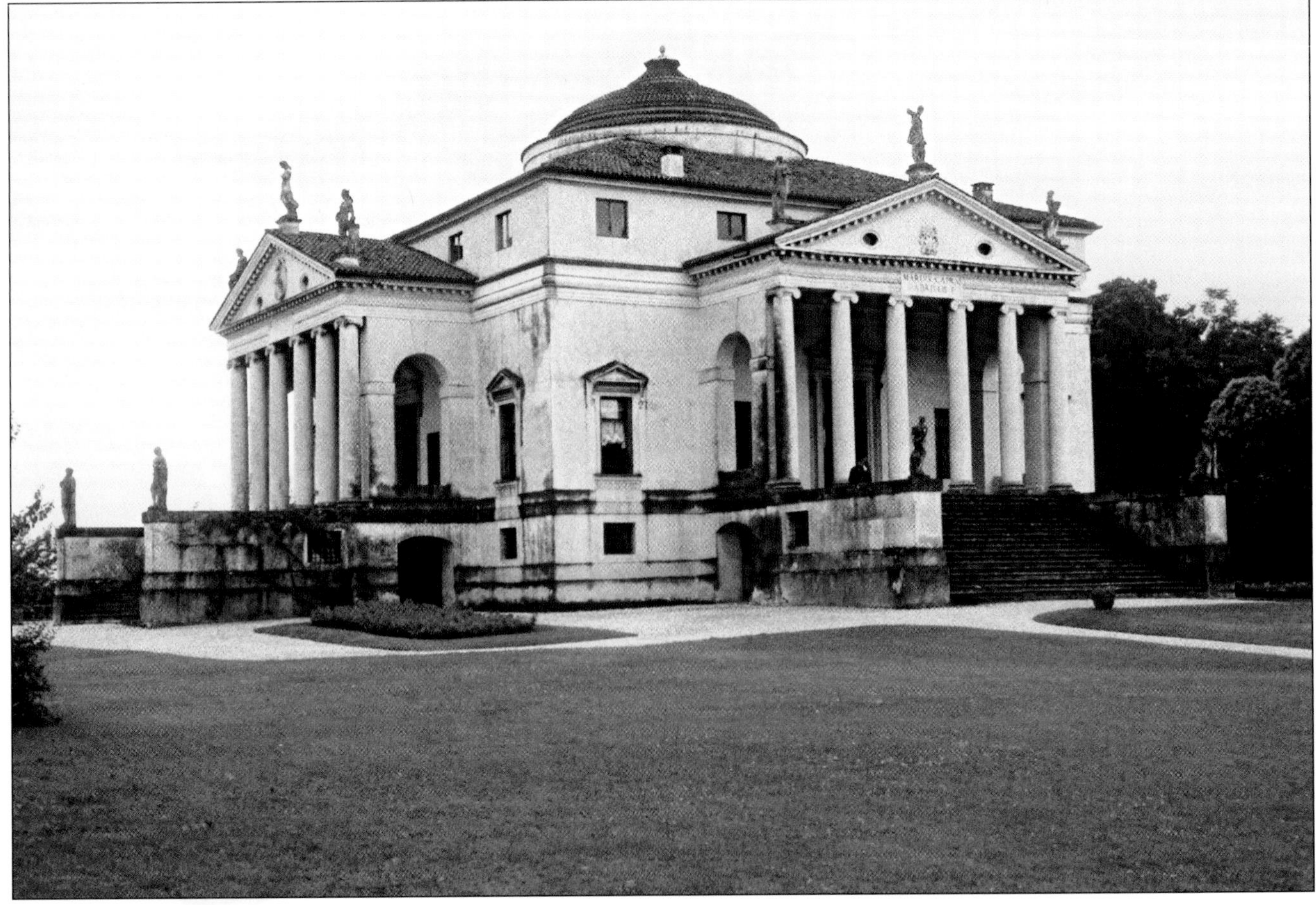

KEY TERMS

Renaissance
humanist
Neoplatonism
lantern
baptistery
motet
word painting
sonnet
ballad
sestina
canzoni
chiaroscuro
sfumato
peristyle
drum
oil painting
impasto
mass
chanson
a cappella
Mannerism
allegory

www. WEBSITES FOR FURTHER STUDY

http://www.nga.gov/collection/gallery/gg4
(A virtual tour of the early Renaissance in Florence, with many excellent images from the period.)

http://www.artchive.com/artchive/D/donatello.html
(This is the Artchive, a website with virtually every major artist in every style from every era in art history. It is an excellent resource.)

http://www.michelangelo.com/buon/bio-index2.html
(This site is a comprehensive resource for the life and career of Michelangelo.)

http://www.GreatBuildings.com/buildings/St Peters of Rome.html
(The Great Buildings site is an excellent tool for architecture of all eras.)

http://www.naxos.com/person/Giovanni_Pierluigi_da_Palestrina/25625.htm
(Biography, pictures, albums, notes on his music.)

http://www.wsu.edu:8080/~dee/REN/LIT.HTM
(Useful overview of Renaissance literature organized by genre and with references to Petrarch, Castiglione, and Macchiavello, among others.)

http://www.historyguide.org/intellect/humanism.html
(Overview of Renaissance philosophy in historical context.)

Chapter 14

History

1520	Pope Leo X excommunicates Luther
1521	Diet of Worms condemns Luther
1529–35	Reformation Parliament in England
1534	Henry VIII declared head of Church of England
1535	Shrine to St. Thomas à Becket in Canterbury Cathedral destroyed; Henry VIII orders monasteries destroyed
1542	Frisius invents triangulation
1550	Images and altars ordered removed from English churches
1553–58	Mary restores Catholicism in England
1555	Peace of Augsburg ends German religious wars
1559	Elizabeth reestablished as head of Church of England
1566	Van Eyck's *Ghent Altarpiece* hidden by church supporters
1598	Edict of Nantes ends French religious wars
1609	Galileo adapts telescope to astronomy

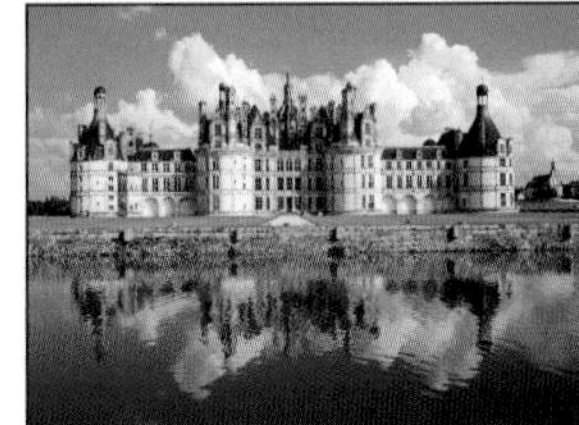

Arts and Architecture

ca. 1426	Campin, *Mérode Altarpiece*
1425–32	Van Eyck, *Ghent Altarpiece*
1500	Dürer, *Self-Portrait*
1505–10	Bosch, *Garden of Earthly Delights*
c. 1514 f.	Hampton Court Palace
1519 f.	Da Cortona (?), Château of Chambord
1529–35	Luther, lyrics to "A Mighty Fortress Is Our God"
1540	Holbein the Younger, *Henry VIII*
1551	Van Hemessen, *Portrait of a Lady*
1566–67	Bruegel the Elder, *Peasant Wedding*
1595	Morley, madrigal composer, "Now Is the Month of Maying"
1598	Weelkes, madrigal composer, "As Vesta Was Descending"

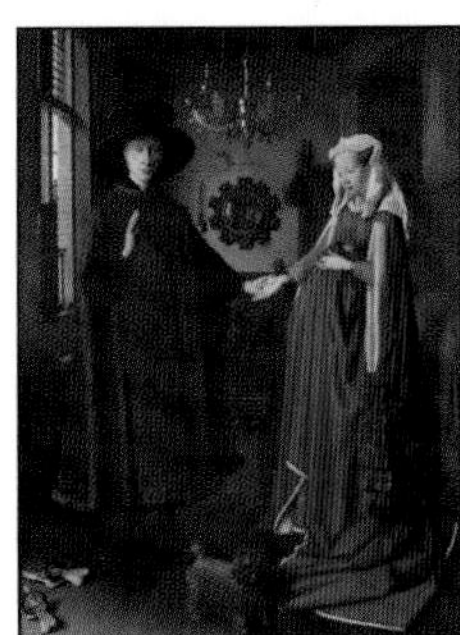

Literature and Philosophy

1509	Erasmus, *The Praise of Folly*
1517	Sir Thomas More, *Utopia*
1519	Luther, "Ninety-Five Theses"
1520	Erasmus, *Familiar Conversations*
1536	Calvin, *Institutes of the Christian Religion*
1542	Jesuit order founded
1543	Vesalius, *Seven Books on the Structure of the Human Body*
1549	Copernicus, *On the Revolutions of Celestial Bodies*
1550	Cranmer's *Book of Common Prayer* required in all English churches
1559	First Index of Prohibited Books
1593	Montaigne, *Essays*
1595	Marlowe, *Dr. Faustus*
1601	Shakespeare, *Hamlet*
1603	Gilbert, *Concerning the Magnet*
1620	Kepler, *On the Motion of Mars*
1628	Bacon, *Novum Organum*
1628	Harvey, *On the Circulation of Blood*

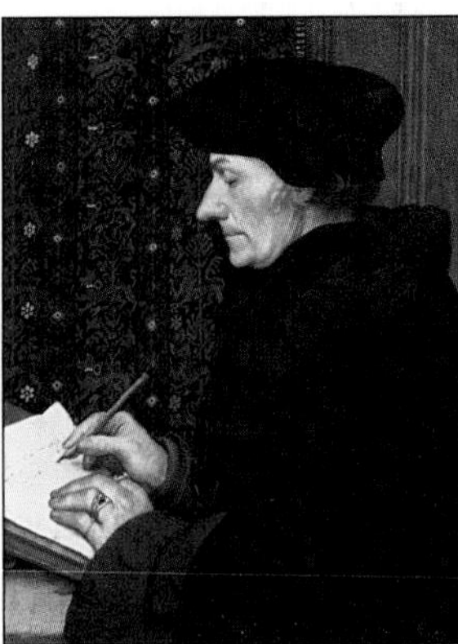

Renaissance in Northern Europe

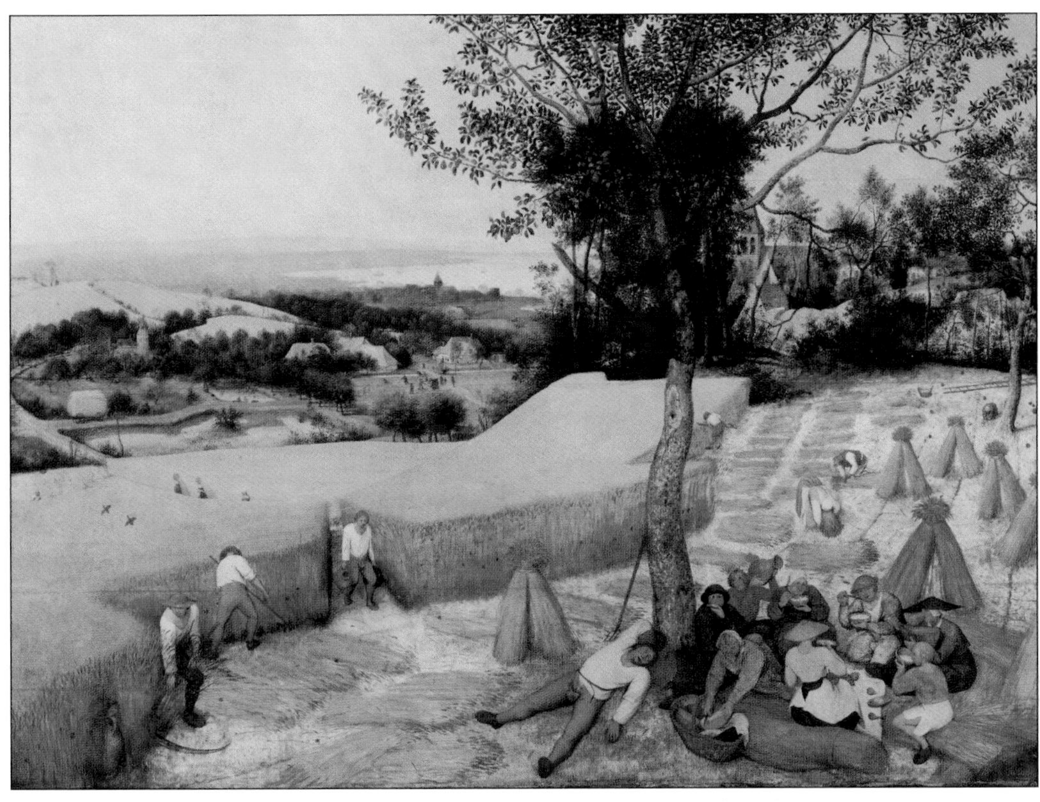

Pieter Bruegel the Elder, *Harvesters*, 1565, oil on panel, 3′10 $\frac{1}{2}$″ × 5′3 $\frac{1}{4}$″ (1.18 × 1.61 m), Rogers Fund, 1919. Metropolitan Museum of Art, New York.

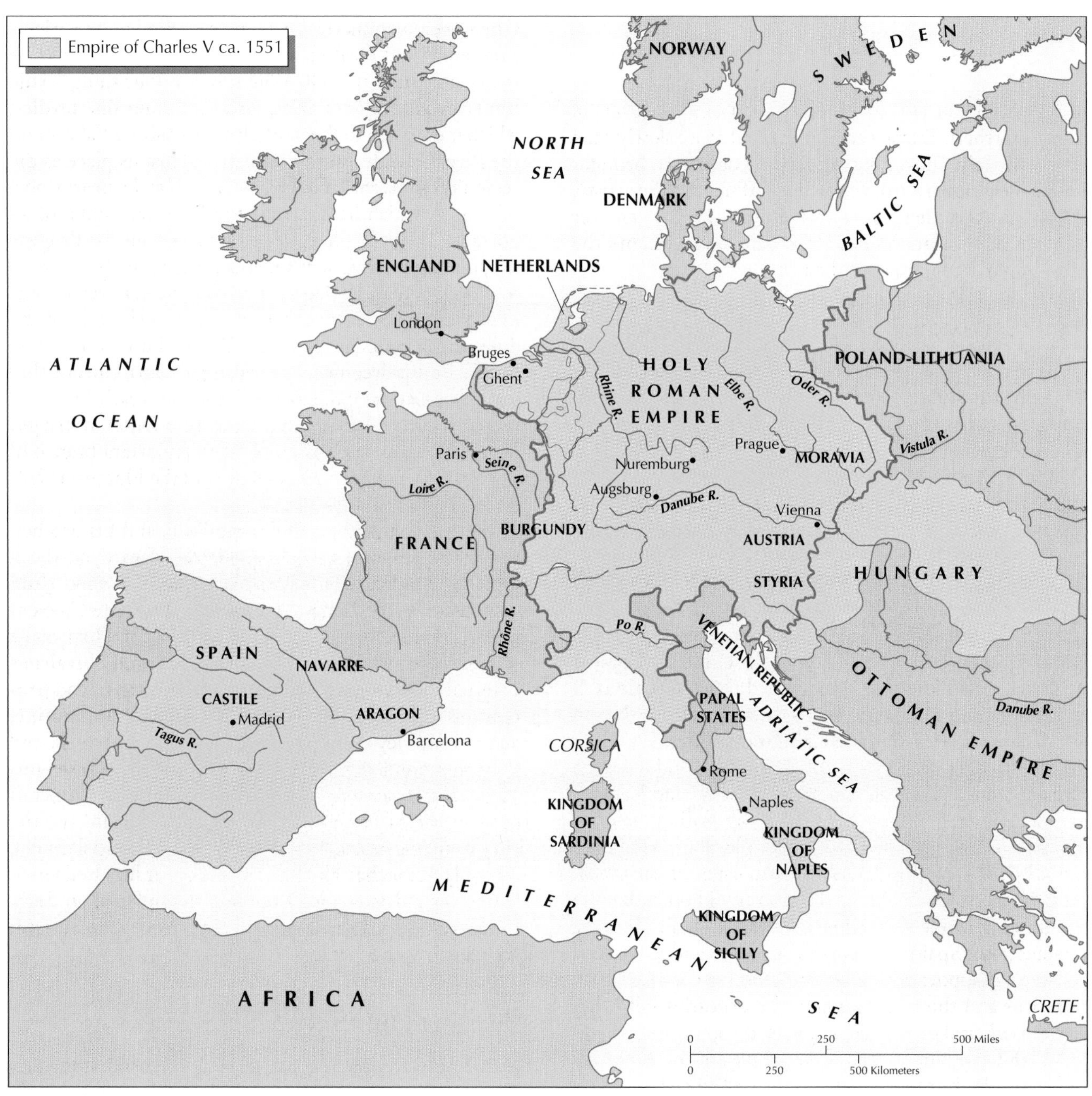

Map 14.1 The empire of Charles V, ca. 1551.

Chapter Overview

EARLY RENAISSANCE IN NORTHERN EUROPE

The Low Countries establish high standards in the visual arts

HIGH RENAISSANCE IN NORTHERN EUROPE

The age of discovery, political and religious conflict, Shakespeare, and the portrait

EARLY RENAISSANCE IN NORTHERN EUROPE

THE "REBIRTH" OF CLASSICAL VALUES EMERGED in northern Europe and in England more slowly than in Italy. Inevitably, trade and commerce brought Italian ideas northward, where they influenced the artistic traditions. As trade grew, it brought prosperity to an ever more influential merchant class, who soon became the most important patrons of their day.

THE COLUMBIAN EXCHANGE

With the voyages of the Italian navigator Christopher Columbus and the Portuguese navigator Vasco de Gama, European penetration of the Americas became well established, following previous voyages of Portuguese mariners, especially those of Henry the Navigator in the early fifteenth century. Successive Portuguese voyages resulted in their colonizing the Madeira and Azores islands in the Atlantic, as well as the Cape Verde islands off the west coast of Africa. By the mid-fifteenth century, Portuguese traders had expanded their trade in guns and textiles for African gold to include trade in slaves. Although Africa had long engaged in its own slave trade, the Portuguese vastly increased its volume and varied the destinations of slaves to offshore African islands, Atlantic islands, North and South America, and the Caribbean region.

The voyages of Christopher Columbus, underwritten by the Spanish King and Queen, Ferdinand and Isabella, did not reach the "Indies" in Asia by sailing west, as Columbus had calculated. Nor did Columbus bring back the silks and spices he had envisioned when he set sail on these voyages. These voyages, however, did open the way for other European mariners from England, France, Holland, and Spain to follow in his wake and to explore and exploit opportunities for trade and for colonizing the Americas and the Caribbean. In the centuries following Columbus's and de Gama's voyages, the conquest, settlement, and exploitation of native peoples of the Americas and Africa by Europeans was firmly established.

The natural resources of the new world were brought to Europe, such that to a large degree, the wealth of the Americas fueled the amassing of fortunes in art by European courts. Moreover, new world products, such as cocoa, cotton, and tobacco, became staples of European consumers. One of the great ironies of the period from the fourteenth through sixteenth centuries is that an age grounded in humanistic ideals and anchored in religious morality could result in the exploitation of African slaves and the destruction of native Indian civilizations in Mexico and Peru.

GHENT AND BRUGES

In the Low Countries, the areas known today as Belgium and The Netherlands, there was a number of substantial cities by the dawn of the fifteenth century. Cities such as Ghent were commercial centers, surrounded by agricultural lands and located, for trading purposes, along the rivers and coast. In 1340, Ghent was a flourishing textile center producing tapestries, lace, and other fine textiles, which it exported to the world from its substantial port on the River Scheldt. But by 1400, it had lost its place as the region's commercial center, supplanted by the nearby port of Bruges, which had become the financial capital of all northern Europe. There were many reasons for Bruges's rise, among them Ghent's devastating population loss to the Black Plague. Perhaps the most important reason was that Bruges, not Ghent, became the favorite city of the dukes of Burgundy, especially Philip the Good (1396–1467). Philip dreamed of creating a court culture that might compete with that of the French, and early in the fifteenth century he moved his court from Dijon to Bruges. Meanwhile, the Medicis founded an important branch of their bank in Bruges and fresh news of the Florentine cultural scene was always at hand.

Philip's grandfather, Philip the Bold, and his brother, Jean, duke of Berry, were great patrons of art in northern Europe, just as the Medici were in southern Europe. (Jean commissioned the Limbourg brothers' illuminated book of hours, completed in 1416; see Chapter 12.) Their court was obsessed with chivalry and encouraged chivalrous entertainments—jousts, tournaments, pageants, and processions. They dressed in gold-threaded cloth, ermine, and jewels; they commissioned the finest tapestries; and they surrounded themselves with poets, musicians, scholars, and painters. Unfortunately, by the late fifteenth century, the harbor at Bruges was filled with silt, and the city, dwindling in size, lost importance as a financial capital. Virtually untouched and forgotten for four hundred years, it remains today as one of the best examples of an Early Renaissance city in Europe, its streets and buildings still very much as they were.

FLEMISH OIL PAINTING

Oil paint had been used for centuries to paint stone and metal, but it was not used on wood panels until the early fifteenth century. In the past, painters had used egg tempera. In **egg tempera** (pigments mixed with egg yolk), an artist must work quickly because the mixture dries rapidly. Subtle modeling is difficult to achieve in egg tempera, since the paint does not blend readily and is fairly opaque. Oil paint (pigments mixed with linseed oil) stays wet a long time, so color can be blended and reworked right on the painting surface. Depicting subtle texture—soft skin, fluffy hair, velvet, wood, metal, or plaster—is possible in oil paint.

Robert Campin. One of the first important examples of the oil painting technique is the *Mérode Altarpiece* (fig. 14.1), attributed to the Master of Flémalle, ROBERT CAMPIN [cam-PEN] (ca. 1375–1444), a member of both the Tournai painters' guild and the city council.

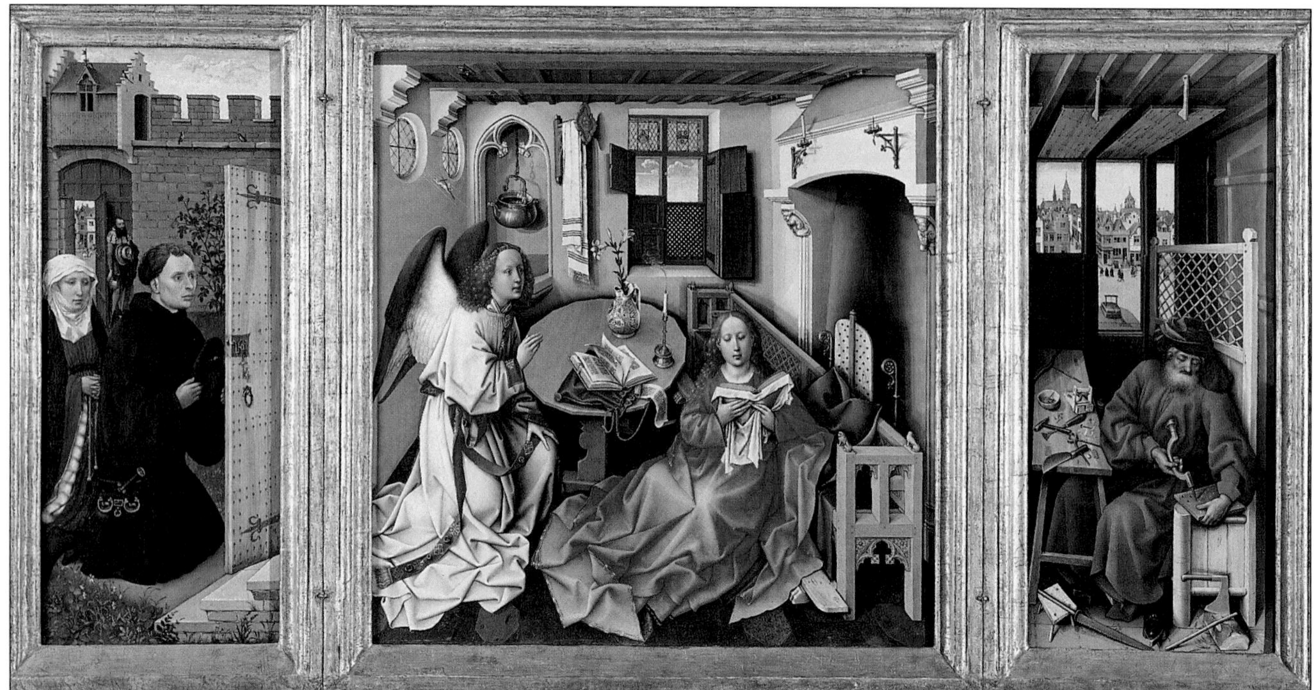

FIGURE 14.1 Robert Campin (Master of Flémalle), *Mérode Altarpiece*, ca. 1426, egg tempera and oil on panel, center $25\frac{3}{16}'' \times 24\frac{7}{8}''$ (64.1 × 63.2 cm), each wing $25\frac{3}{8}'' \times 10\frac{7}{8}''$ (64.5 × 27.6 cm), The Cloisters Collection, 1956 (56. 70), Metropolitan Museum of Art, New York. Illusions of texture and atmosphere are made possible by painting in oil rather than egg tempera, the medium favored during the Middle Ages. Equally innovative is the depiction of the Annunciation in a middle-class fifteenth-century Flemish home.

The altarpiece still echoes medieval conventions: For instance, the large size of Mary and Gabriel indicates their importance, not realistic relative scale. Yet it also introduces a new matter-of-fact attention to the details of reality, facilitated by the use of oil paint. Painting around 1426, Campin employed a mixed technique in the altarpiece, using egg tempera for the underpainting, then proceeding immediately to paint over it in oil.

The altarpiece is a **triptych**—a three-paneled painting. The triptych wings are hinged and can be closed to protect the painting inside, and when they are opened out at an angle, the altarpiece can stand up unaided. This is the earliest known depiction of the Annunciation as taking place not in a church or holy realm but in a home. Here the traditional religious subject has been combined with an accurate observation of daily life.

The central panel depicts the Annunciation. In the left panel, a prosperous merchant, the patron, Ingelbrecht of Mechlin, and his wife look in through an open doorway, witnessing the miraculous event. This clever device establishes an ingenious spatial relationship uniting the two panels.

The artist documents each object in tiny detail. Every part of the painting catches and holds the viewer's eyes. This interest in detail is suffused with religious symbolism. For example, the lion finials on the bench are symbols of watchfulness as well as of Jesus and his resurrection; the dog finials are symbols of fidelity and domesticity. The candle refers to the light brought into the world by Jesus. The lily, a symbol of purity, is the flower of Jesus's mother Mary (Madonna lily). Perhaps the most interesting symbolic detail is the tiny figure coming in the window on rays of light, heading for Mary's abdomen. This miniature man, carrying a tiny cross, is a prefiguration of Jesus—in the next instant the Incarnation will take place. Every object, even an ordinary household item, could carry **iconographic** (or symbolic) implications. An unusual example of symbolism is seen on the right panel, where Mary's husband Joseph makes mousetraps in his carpentry shop, a fifteenth-century Flemish carpenter's shop complete with tools. Presumably this iconography derives from St. Augustine's description of the Lord's cross as a mousetrap for the devil, and his death as the bait by which the devil would be caught.

Jan van Eyck. In the 1420s, the painter JAN VAN EYCK [van IKE] (ca. 1390–1441) served Philip the Good, not only as a painter but also as a diplomat to Spain and Portugal. In Portugal, he painted portraits of Philip's future bride, Princess Isabella, so that Philip, back in Flanders, could assess her appearance. Giorgio Vasari was to refer to him in his *Lives* as the "inventor of oil painting."

Like Robert Campin, van Eyck recorded the world in minute detail. Jan van Eyck completed his *Ghent Altarpiece*, in 1432. Located in St. Bavon Cathedral in Ghent, this enormous **polyptych**—a painting consisting of multiple panels—has twenty-six panels.

An inscription on the outer frame reads: "Hubert van Eyck, the most famous painter ever known, started this work of art at the request of Joos Vijd; his brother Jan, who was the second in art, finished the monumental commission. . . ." Little is known about Hubert van Eyck. Still, mention of the artists on the work itself indicates a shift from the anonymity of the medieval guild system toward the recognition of individual artists.

When opened, the altarpiece focuses on the salvation and redemption of humankind (fig. 14.2). The central panel on the lower level depicts the *Adoration of the Lamb:* The sacrifice of the Mystic lamb symbolizes Jesus's sacrifice. In the foreground is the Fountain of Life. The crowds of people paying homage to the lamb include Old Testament prophets and patriarchs, classical poets and philosophers, New Testament apostles, and people of all classes, times, and places. Various body types and facial expressions individualize the figures with their blemishes and deformities included. Realism is heightened by the use of atmospheric perspective (see Chapter 13). The colors and the edges of objects in the background are not as intense or as sharp as those in the foreground; distant hills merge with the sky. This differs from the *Mérode Altarpiece* in which the artist gave each object equal focus, whether in the foreground or background.

Unlike the lower panels, the upper panels do not form a unified composition. In the center is either God or Jesus, adorned in a scarlet mantle and gemstones that appear to catch the light. The outermost figures are Adam and Eve, the earliest large-scale nudes in northern European panel painting. Highly naturalistic, they were presumably painted from models. Eve's protruding abdomen is the fashionable physique of the day rather than an indication of pregnancy. Adam is shown with his mouth slightly open, as if speaking. Seen slightly from below, the bottom of Adam's foot is visible as he steps on the frame, because the viewer must look up at these figures.

Van Eyck painted a double portrait of *Giovanni Arnolfini and His Wife Giovanna Cenami*, often called

FIGURE 14.2 Jan and Hubert van Eyck, *Ghent Altarpiece* (open), ca. 1425–32, oil on panel, $11'5\frac{3}{4}'' \times 15'1\frac{1}{2}''$ (3.4 × 4.6 m), St. Bavon, Ghent. Because of the lower center scene in which the multitudes are shown venerating the Lamb of God (Agnus Dei), this monumental polyptych is sometimes referred to as the *Mystic Lamb.*

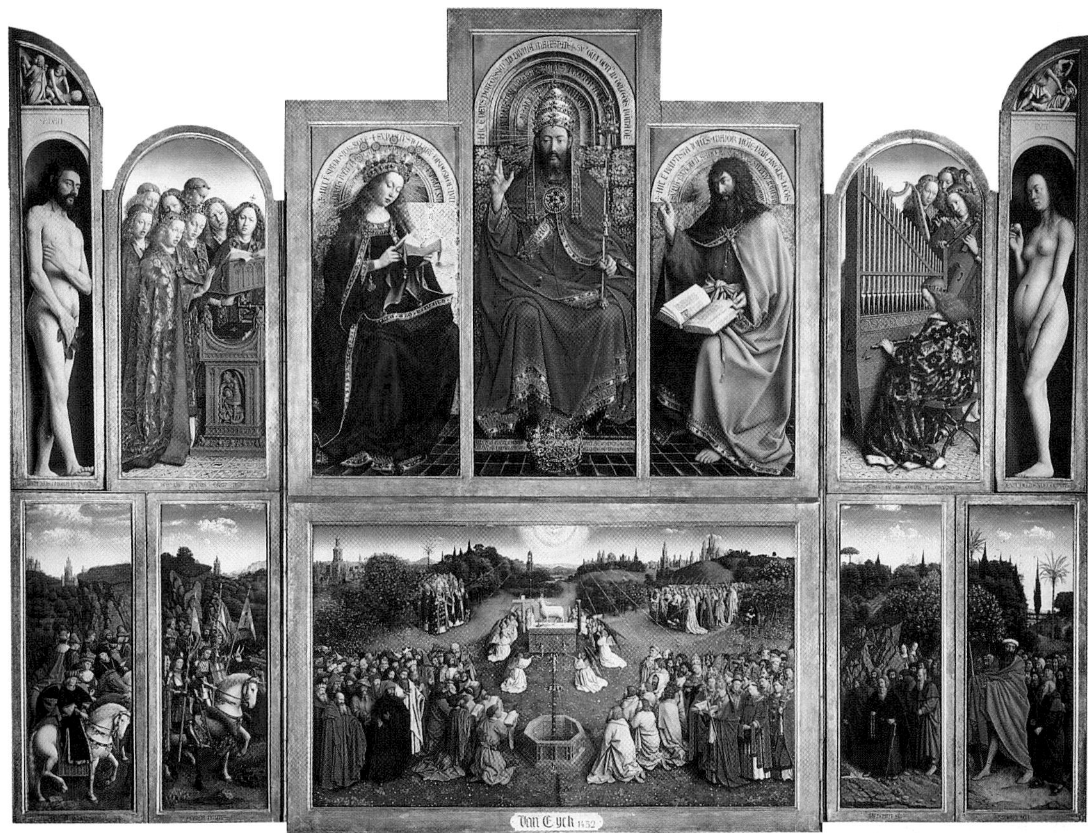

The Arnolfini Wedding (fig. 14.3). On the back wall, above the mirror, are the words "*Johannes de Eyck fuit hic. 1434*" ("Jan van Eyck was here. 1434"). We see reflections in the mirror: the backs of Arnolfini and Cenami and, beyond them, two other figures, standing in the same place as the viewer. The man in the red turban is perhaps the artist himself, suggesting he was, in fact, present as witness.

Giovanni Arnolfini was an Italian merchant working in Bruges as an agent for the Medicis. The painting expresses the prosperity of the merchant class in fifteenth-century Bruges with their lavish textiles and dazzling finery. His wife's protruding abdomen again does not suggest pregnancy but a fashionable physique, probably achieved by a small padded sack over the abdomen and emphasized by the cut of the garment and posture of its wearer.

FIGURE 14.3 Jan van Eyck, *Giovanni Arnolfini and his Wife Giovanna Cenami*, signed and dated 1434, oil on panel, $32\frac{1}{4}'' \times 23\frac{1}{2}''$ (83.8 × 57.2 cm), National Gallery, London. The growing interest in portraiture is evidenced here. Cenami's protruding abdomen was a fashion of the times, achieved by padding and posture (note Eve's comparable contour in the *Ghent Altarpiece*) rather than an impetus for the exchanging of wedding vows.

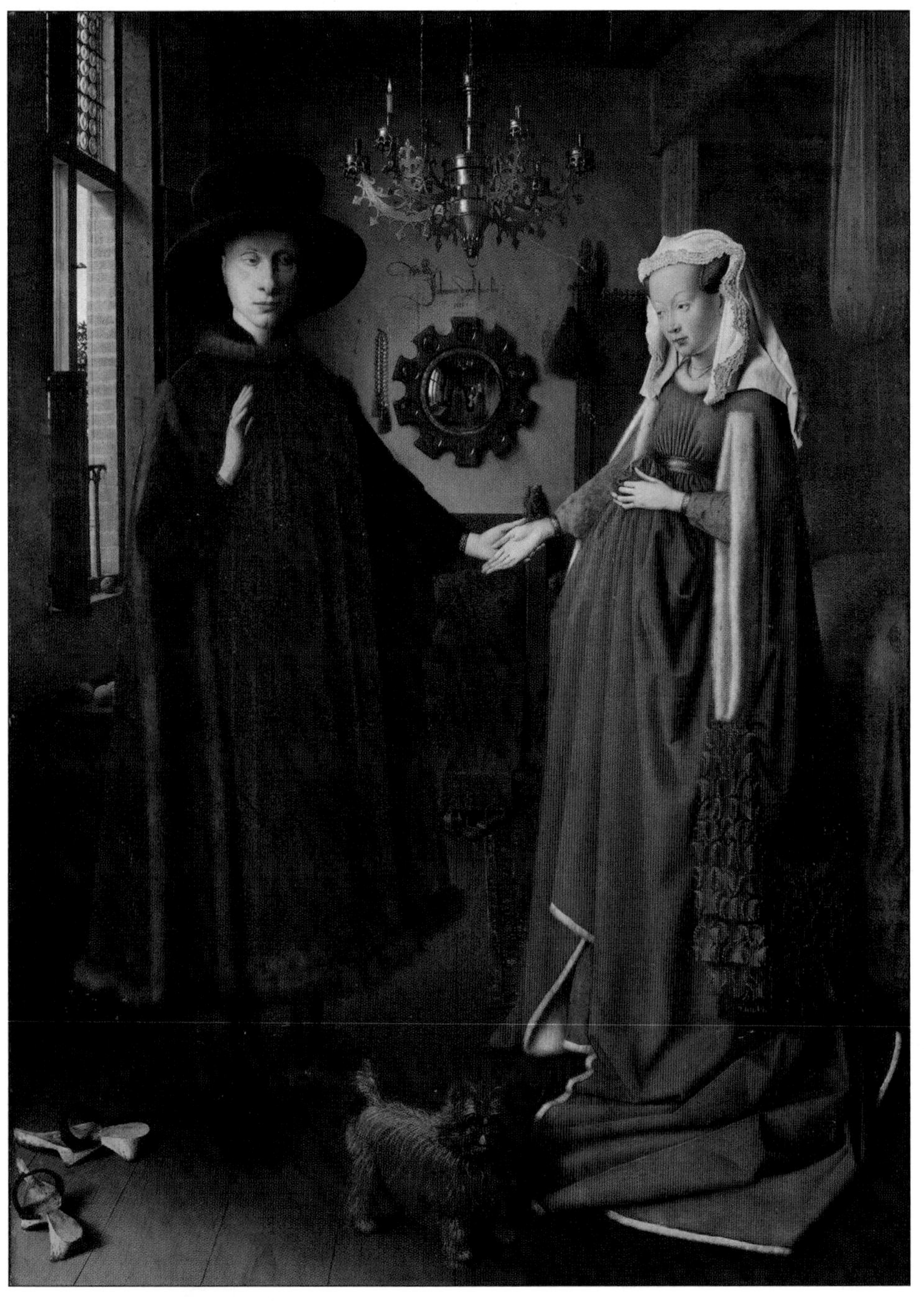

Although it has long been assumed the couple are shown in a bridal chamber, exchanging marriage vows, recent arguments suggest instead we are witness here not to a marriage but to an engagement, and the room is not a bedroom but the main room of Arnolfini's house. The moment is not unlike that described by Shakespeare in *Henry V*, when the English king proposes to Katherine, the French princess: "Give me your answer; i' faith, do; and so clap hands and a bargain: how say you lady?" Such a touching of the hands was the common sign of a mutual agreement to wed. As for the room itself, it has been pointed out that canopy beds were "furniture of estate," commonly displayed in the principal room of the house as a sign of the owner's prestige.

The painting is replete with objects that hold iconographic significance, in **disguised symbolism.** Thus St. Margaret, patron saint of childbirth, adorns the bedpost. The couple's shoes are off to signify they stand on holy ground. Ten scenes in the mirror frame represent the passion of Jesus, and the single candle in the chandelier represents the all-seeing God. The dog, as noted, is a symbol of fidelity and domesticity. God's presence on earth was believed to be found in ordinary everyday objects.

Hieronymus Bosch. Very different from Jan van Eyck's efforts to portray the real world are those of HIERONYMUS BOSCH [BOSH] (1450 or 1453–1516). He takes his name from s-Hertogenbosch [s-HER-toe-gen-bos] in southern Holland (now called Den Bosch) where he grew up and worked. Off the main roads, isolated from progressive ideas, this was a middle class, commercial town situated within an area of religious, political, social, and economic unrest. In Bosch's world, people believed in witches, astrology was taught at the universities, and visions were accepted as fact. Although a member of a Catholic fraternity until his death in 1516, Bosch was openly critical of certain religious practices.

Bosch's work displays an extraordinary imagination and a highly personal style, his painting teeming with bizarre and menacing creatures, part human, part animal. Painting ***alla prima*** [AH-la PREE-ma]—without any preliminary drawing. Where other Flemish painters stressed solid dimensionality, Bosch's draftsmanship looks fragile and delicate. While his contemporaries painted illusions of nature, Bosch painted a phantasmagorical world. Bosch was less interested in the painterly problems of light and shadow, and more concerned with the moralistic import of his subjects.

Bosch's *Hay Wain* (fig. 14.4), a triptych painted ca. 1495–1500, illustrates the Flemish proverb, "The world is a hay wagon and each seeks to grab what he can." The hay

FIGURE 14.4 Hieronymus Bosch, *Hay Wain*, ca. 1495–1500 (?), oil on panel, center 4′7$\frac{1}{8}$″ × 3′3$\frac{3}{8}$″ (1.40 × 1.00 m), each wing 4′9$\frac{1}{8}$″ × 2′2″(147 × 66 cm), Museo del Prado, Madrid. Another version of this painting is in the Escorial, near Madrid—scholars debate which is the original. People of all types try to grab the hay, which, according to a proverb, represents material possessions.

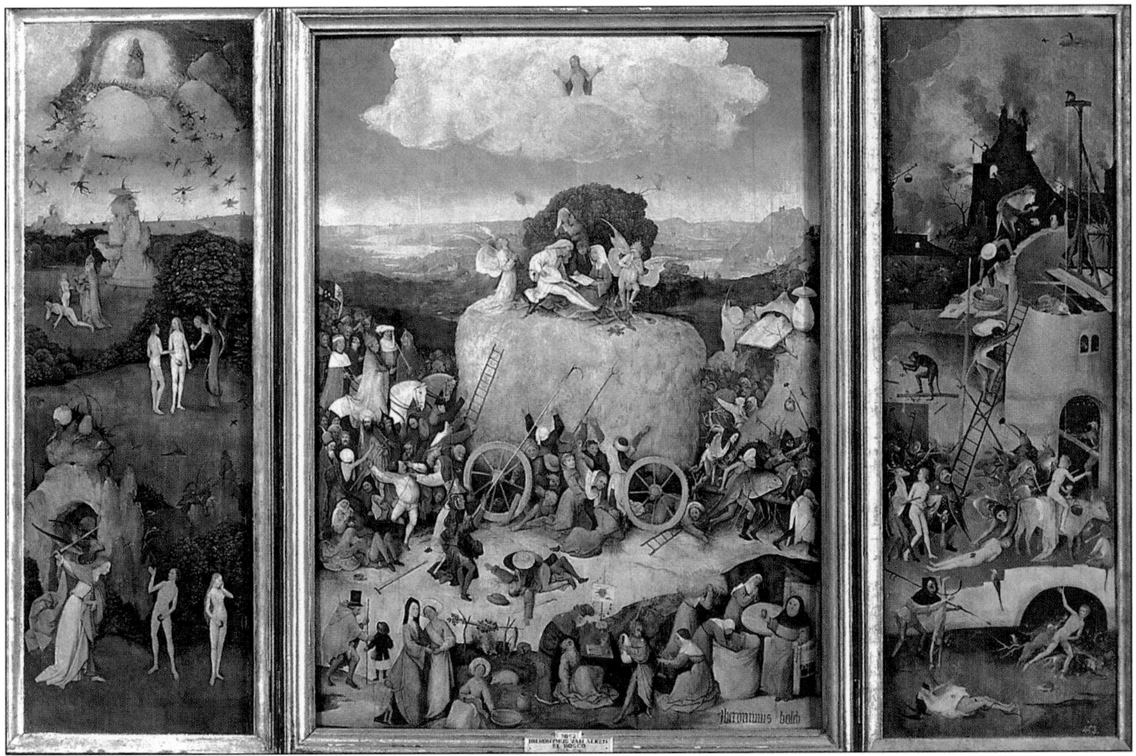

wagon is a symbol of worldly goods and pleasures, and the painting is a satire on the evils of greed. Characteristically, Bosch fills this painting with a multitude of vignettes. In the center panel all classes of people fight each other for the hay. Some are crushed under the wheels. A quack physician fills his purse. Nuns, supervised by a gluttonous monk, stuff hay into a bag. On top of the hay a man plays a lute while the dancing demon on the right plays his nose like a flute, and a couple kiss in the bushes. Only the angel on the left notices Jesus above. The left panel is a scene of Original Sin. Rebel angels are thrown out of heaven and the sky is full of monsters. On the right panel is hell—to which the wagon, pulled by devils, is rolling.

HIGH RENAISSANCE IN NORTHERN EUROPE

The Habsburg Patronage

Bosch became the favorite northern painter of Philip II of Spain, the richest and greatest collector of art in the last half of the sixteenth century. Not only did Philip own the *Garden of Earthly Delights*, but he owned over thirty other paintings attributed to Bosch. The painter's work evidently struck a chord with the elegant, highly educated, and refined prince.

Philip II was the nephew of Charles V, emperor of the Holy Roman Empire, and of Mary of Hungary, the emperor's sister. The HABSBURG [HAPS-burg] Charles V controlled Spain, the Low Countries, the German empire, Hungary, Spanish America, and parts of Italy. Although not a strong supporter of the arts, Charles discovered the paintings of Titian in 1532 and became, together with Mary, the artist's chief patron. Mary of Hungary also served as governor of the Netherlands from 1531 to 1556, and in that time developed a passion for fifteenth-century Flemish painting, acquiring, among others, van Eyck's portrait of *Giovanni Arnolfini and His Wife Giovanna Cenami* (see fig. 14.3).

Financed by gold and silver from the Americas, Philip added to the great collections of his uncle and aunt. Like Charles V and Mary before him, he favored Titian, granting him an annual stipend and allowing him to paint whatever he chose. When Titian died in 1576, Philip had amassed dozens of his paintings. From Flanders, Philip collected works by Campin and Bosch. By the time Philip was done, he had brought more than 1,500 paintings to Spain.

Erasmus and Northern Humanism

Like Bosch, the northern humanist scholar DESIDERIUS ERASMUS [ee-RAZ-mus] (1466–1536), born in Rotterdam, The Netherlands, saw the religious world of late-fifteenth- and early-sixteenth-century Europe through a critical lens, but he was no iconoclast. In *A Pilgrimage for Religion's Sake*, he marveled at the shrine to Thomas à Beckett in Canterbury Cathedral: "Ye Gods! What a show was there of silken vestments, what a power of golden candlesticks. . . . Treasures beyond all calculation [were] displayed. The most worthless thing there was gold, every part glowed, sparkled and flashed with rare and large gems, some of which were bigger than a goose egg."

Erasmus blended the study of classical civilization with Christian faith. Combining critical intelligence with spiritual conviction, Erasmus brought together the thought of Plato with that of St. Paul, and the philosophy of Aristotle with that of St. Augustine. Educated by the Brethren of the Common Life, an order of laymen who modeled their lives on that of Jesus Christ, he joined an Augustinian monastery in 1487 and was ordained a priest in 1492. Erasmus traveled widely, studying and teaching in most of the cultural centers of Europe, including England. At Oxford, he became friends with Sir Thomas More; at Cambridge, he was Professor of Divinity and of Greek.

Erasmus wrote his *Familiar Conversations* (1519) to attack abuses within the Catholic Church. Erasmus's readers found the satire scathingly accurate. His *Conversations* was so antagonistic to the clergy that Charles V, the Holy Roman Emperor, issued an edict that any teacher using the work in the classroom would be liable to immediate execution. Forty editions of the book were published in Erasmus's lifetime, and John Milton, more than a hundred years later, remarked that everyone was still reading it at Cambridge. His most famous work, however, is *The Praise of Folly*, a satire of hypocrisy and pretension in his time.

Erasmus did not set himself up as a counterauthority to the Catholic Church. His goal was to purify the church from within by ridiculing its abuses and thereby stimulating internal reform.

Thomas More

Sir Thomas More (1478–1535), to whom Erasmus dedicated his *Praise of Folly*, was, like Erasmus, a scholar and a Christian humanist. More rose to power during the reign of King Henry VIII, the English king who broke away from the Roman Catholic Church to establish the Church of England. A man of conscience, More lost his life for refusing to support Henry in his split with the Roman Church, and especially in his effort to annul his marriage. Henry had More executed for treason.

More is also known for his *Utopia*, which depicts an ideal state in which economic and social equality prevail and in which citizens are free to pursue religion and learning as they wish. In More's utopian society, citizens worked, studied, and took recreation in a balanced life guided by moral values and ethical principles, although not dominated by any particular religion.

Then & Now

Iconoclasm and the Attack on the Arts

The iconoclastic practices of sixteenth-century European Protestants were focused on the destruction of "idolatrous" images of God. From the Protestant point of view, such images diminished God by making him appear like humankind. This logic quickly extended to all images within churches, which could distract the worshiper from the true contemplation of salvation. It was not a question of artistic merit; the statues were viewed solely for their sacrilegious content.

Since 1985, artists in the United States have also been attacked for creating art considered obscene or blasphemous, specifically those works that, to some people, challenge the very idea of Christianity and the values they associate with a Christian lifestyle. Recent attacks have had a political flavor because the art and artists in question—Robert Mapplethorpe and Andreas Serrano, for example—were funded in part by the National Endowment for the Arts. The attackers argue that the government, supported by taxpayers' money, should not fund work that offends or upsets those who pay for it.

Senator Alphonse D'Amato, a Republican from New York, tore a photograph of one of Serrano's works into pieces on the floor of the U.S. Senate on May 18, 1989. "This so-called piece of art is a deplorable, despicable display of vulgarity," he exclaimed. On July 26, 1989, Senator Jesse Helms, a Republican from North Carolina, introduced an amendment to legislation funding the National Endowment that would prohibit the use of appropriated funds to, among other things, "promote, disseminate, or produce . . . obscene or indecent materials, including but not limited to depictions of sadomasochism, homoeroticism, the exploitation of children, or individuals engaged in sex acts; or . . . material which denigrates the objects or beliefs of the adherents of a particular religion or non-religion."

Supporters of artists' rights of self-expression found the last word of that statement particularly alarming, because, if the amendment were to be passed, the government could prohibit funding of any material that denigrated *anyone's* belief about *anything*. It seemed to many like government-supported censorship.

The amendment failed, and thus began a legislative battle that continues to this day. Should the government take on the role of artistic patron? If not, who will? Many of the country's great dance companies, symphony orchestras, theater companies, artists, and writers depend on government funds to complete their projects.

Thus the link between Renaissance iconoclasm and today's debates over funding of the arts is clear. How our current society settles the debate remains in question.

Martin Luther and the Reformation

If one individual could be said to dominate the history of sixteenth-century Europe, that person would be MARTIN LUTHER [LOO-ther] (1483–1546), the key figure in the Protestant **Reformation.** Like Erasmus, Luther (fig. 14.5) was an Augustinian monk and a humanist scholar, and, again like Erasmus, he was no iconoclast, although he was well aware that his teachings sparked iconoclastic frenzy. He was an avid lover of the arts, especially music. He wrote hymns for his new Protestant church services. Many are still sung, especially "A Mighty Fortress Is Our God." Two centuries later, Johann Sebastian Bach used Luther's chorales, embellishing them in his cantatas.

Luther was a professor of philosophy and biblical studies at Wittenberg [VIT-en-burg] University. At Wittenberg Latin was the language of instruction, and the method of teaching was a detailed study of the classics with particular attention to Aristotle's logic. The learning process depended on **disputations,** or debates. Faculty and students attended weekly disputations, which were judged on success according to the rules of logic.

The faculty of Wittenberg University came largely from an Augustinian monastery in the city, where Luther was a monk. Luther specialized in the language and grammar of the Bible. After 1516, he studied in particular the Greek New Testament in the edition of Erasmus. The task of making his own translation into German led him to rethink the question of salvation. Salvation, he now believed, was not delivered through achievement but through faith. According to Luther, the gospel repudiates "the wicked idea of the entire kingdom of the pope . . . [with its idea that] a Christian man must be uncertain about the grace of God toward him. If this opinion stands, then Christ is completely useless. . . . Therefore the papacy is a veritable torture chamber of consciousness and the very kingdom of the devil."

Such language would obviously offend Rome, but the incident that drew Luther to the attention of Pope Leo X was the publication, on October 31, 1517, of his "Ninety-Five Theses." The clergy had long accepted payment for indulgences, which supposedly remitted penalties to be suffered in the afterlife (including release from purgatory) and paved the purchaser's way to heaven. Luther was particularly incensed by the conduct of the Dominican monk TETZEL [TET-sel]. "As soon as the coin into the box rings," Tetzel would remind his audience, "a soul from purgatory to heaven

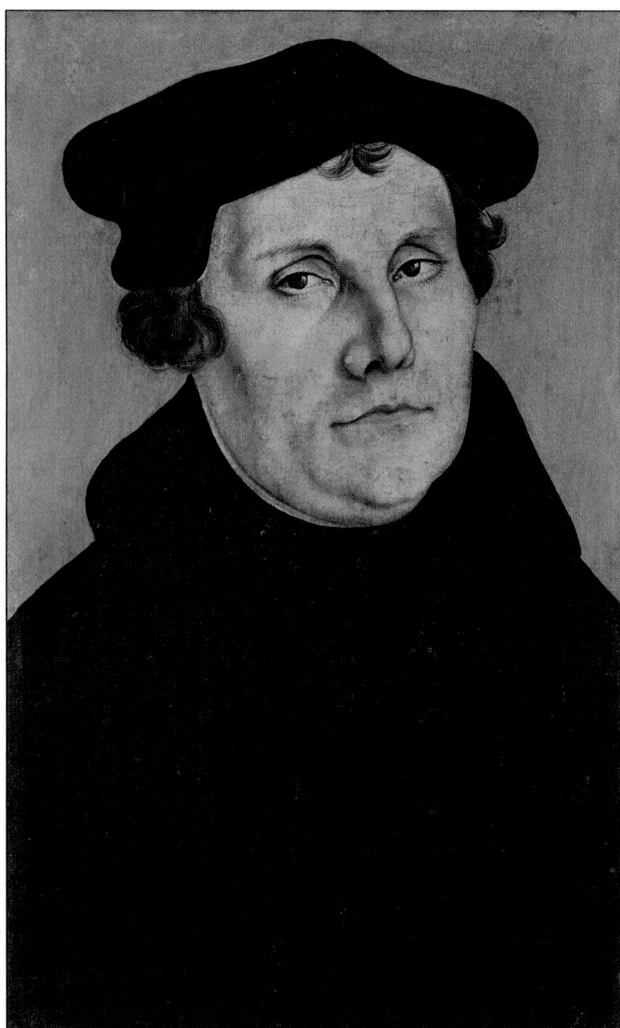

FIGURE 14.5 Lucas Cranach, *Portrait of Martin Luther*, ca. 1526, oil on panel, 15″ × 9″ (38.1 × 22.9 cm), Uffizi Gallery, Florence. Cranach. SCALA/Art Resource, NY. Cranach was a staunch supporter of Luther, whose criticism of church practices, such as indulgences, began the Protestant Reformation.

springs." Frederick the Wise had banned Tetzel from Wittenberg, but the city's populace simply went out to meet him in the countryside. When the people informed Luther, who also served as their pastor, that they no longer needed to confess or attend mass because they had purchased lifetime indulgences from the Dominican monk, Luther was outraged, and the "Ninety-Five Theses" soon followed.

Luther's ideas were given greater impact by the advent of printing—Luther considered the printing press a gift from God. In 1500, there were over two hundred printing presses in Europe; soon there were seven in Wittenberg alone, pumping out the writings of the so-called heretic Martin Luther as fast as they could. Over 750,000 copies of Luther's German translation of the Bible were in circulation by the time of his death in 1546.

Luther concluded that every nonessential religious practice needed to be stripped away. For Luther, nonessentials included scholastic philosophy and church ritual, along with its hierarchy, sacraments, organizational structure, and even its prayers and services. Believers could be "justified by faith alone."

Luther crystallized reformist ideas that were simmering in other countries besides Germany, most importantly Switzerland and England. Aside from the sale of indulgences, at issue were three fundamental concerns: (1) the opulence and worldliness of the Roman Church; (2) the idea that faith, not good works, led to a person's salvation; and (3) the tension between religious tradition as embodied in the papacy and Scripture, including both Old and New Testaments, as the supreme authority in matters of faith and morals. Luther and other Protestant reformers sought to simplify the elaborate rituals of the Roman Church by returning to spiritual essentials. In addition, Protestant reformers, especially Luther, believed that in order to achieve salvation one had to believe in God, and that God's mercy alone, not an individual's good acts, determined one's spiritual salvation. Moreover, central to the reformers' ideas was an emphasis on the importance of the individual conscience—one's unmediated, personal relationship with God, rather than a relationship mediated by priests, doctrines, and religious tradition.

Luther was also community minded. No one, he believed, should have to beg in Wittenberg. Every city should take care of its poor. Disappointed by the unwillingness of the populace of Wittenberg to contribute to the community chest (established by him in late 1520 to provide social welfare), Luther scolded his congregation for being "unthankful beasts," and, declaring his unwillingness to be "the shepherd of such pigs," actually quit preaching until the situation was remedied. He argued, "Christ and all saints are one spiritual body, just as the inhabitants of a city are one community and a body, each citizen being a member of the other and of the entire city." Thus Luther laid religious grounds for social democracy and equality, ideas that would, in the next century, lead to social revolution throughout Europe and the Americas.

JOHN CALVIN AND THE *INSTITUTES OF THE CHRISTIAN RELIGION*

While Luther was reforming in Germany, another more radical Protestant leader was active in Geneva in Switzerland, JOHN CALVIN [KAL-vin] (1509–1564), a French humanist who underwent a religious conversion of great intensity. Calvin's reformist views were not well received in France, and he fled to Switzerland, where he published his *Institutes of the Christian Religion* in Basel and later set up a theocratic state—that is, a state ruled by a religious figure or group—in Geneva.

Calvin's reforms, like Luther's, involved stripping away what he considered external and distracting to true Christian piety. He rejected images of saints and limited the use of music

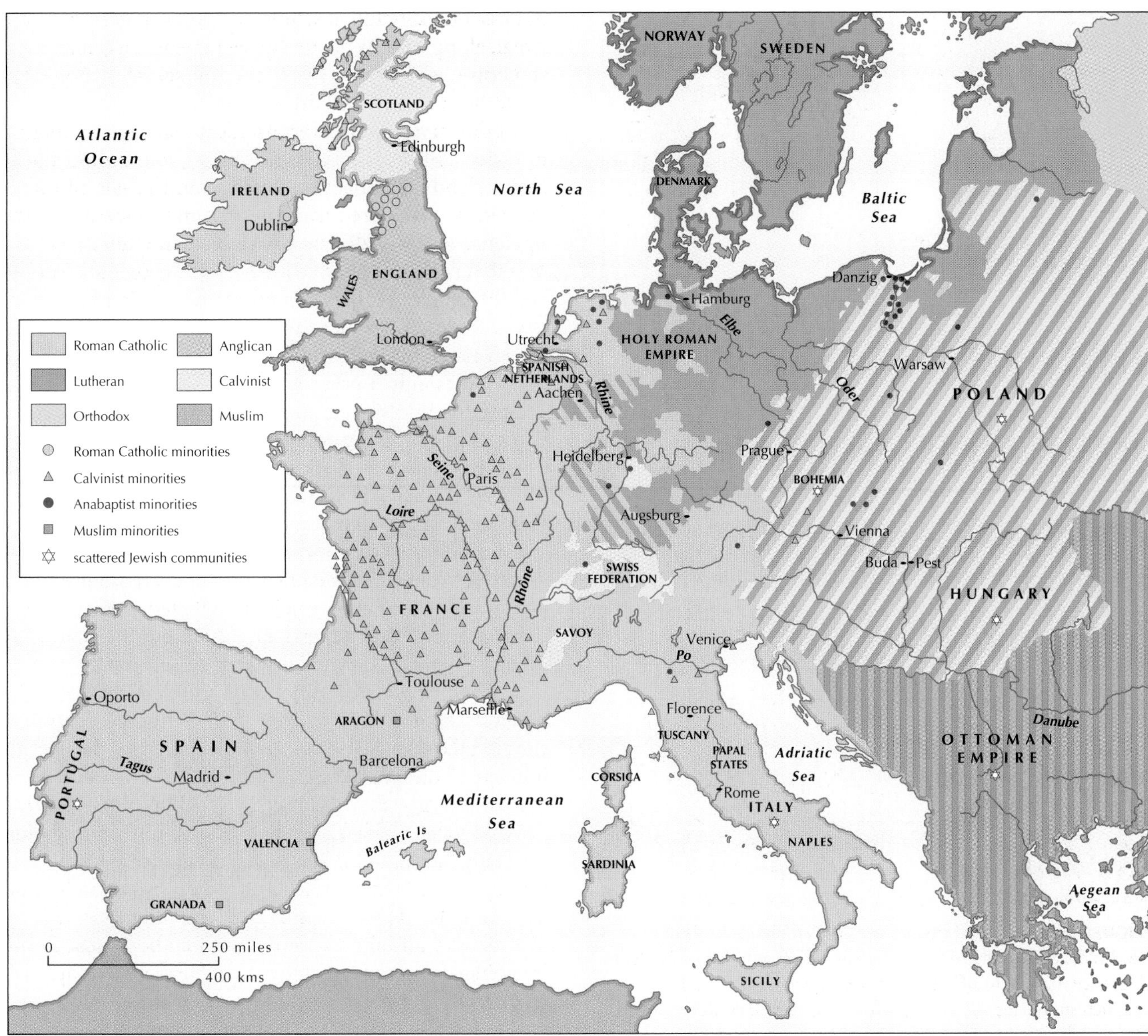

MAP 14.2 The Reformation in Europe, ca. 1560.

to psalms. Many other activities were prohibited in Calvin's Geneva, including feasting and dancing; wearing rouge, jewelry, and lace, and dressing immodestly; swearing, gambling, and playing cards; reading immoral books and engaging in sexual activity outside of marriage. People caught breaking the rules were warned the first time, fined the second, and severely punished after that. Some were banished, others executed.

Like Luther, Calvin recognized the Bible as the supreme source of knowledge and the only recourse for religious living. His *Institutes* drew out the principles embedded in biblical teaching. They include the following:

1. Human beings are born in total depravity as a result of Adam's fall, whereby they inherit original sin.
2. The will of God is absolute and all-powerful.
3. Faith is superior to good works, since humans lack the capacity to choose to do works that are truly good in God's eyes.
4. Salvation comes through God's freely given grace rather than through any acts of the people.
5. God divinely predestines some to eternal salvation—the Elect—and others to eternal perdition—the Damned; and since no one knows with absolute certainty whether he or she is one of the Elect, all must live as if they were, obeying God's commands.

Calvin identified the Elect by their unambiguous profession of faith, their upright life, and their pious participation in the sacraments, whose number, like Luther, Calvin reduced.

Cross Currents

Dürer Describes Mexican Treasures

When Hernán Cortés landed in Mexico in 1519, he did so as the representative of King Charles V of Spain, the Habsburg ruler who actually lived in Vienna. Cortés sent Charles a series of letters recounting his conquests there, and with them a collection of treasures. When these treasures arrived in Brussels, Albrecht Dürer was among the many who came to see them.

Among the collection was the famous Dresden Codex, a folding-screen manuscript made of bark paper dating to as early as the thirteenth century. It recounts agricultural rituals, establishes the Mayan calendar, and, in its drawings of costumes and gods, is by far the most detailed description of Mayan life we have today. Only its having been sent back to Europe saved it from the total destruction of all "pagan" and "idolatrous" manuscripts ordered by Diego de Landa, Charles V's first appointee as bishop of Yucatán.

But Dürer was most impressed by the extraordinary gold- and metalwork sent from the "New World": "I saw the things brought to the King from the New Golden Land," Dürer wrote, "a sun entirely of gold, a whole fathom wide; likewise, a moon, made entirely of silver, and just as big; also, a variety of other curiosities from weapons, to armor, and missiles. . . . These things were all so precious that they were valued at a hundred thousand gilders. But I have never seen in all my days anything that caused my heart to rejoice so as these things have. For I saw among them amazing art objects, and I marveled over the subtle ingenuity of the men in distant lands who made them." This Aztec goldwork was, however, soon melted down by Charles for currency, the fate of almost all such metalwork sent to Europe from Mexico.

From Geneva Calvinism spread into France, the Netherlands, England, Scotland, and North America, impacting the social, political, and intellectual life of all these countries. The Calvinist attitude can be traced in the rise of the Puritans, in Milton's *Paradise Lost* and the works of seventeenth-century American Puritan writers Edward Taylor and Cotton Mather, and in nineteenth-century works such as Nathaniel Hawthorne's *The Scarlet Letter* and Herman Melville's *Moby-Dick*.

Iconoclasm

Iconoclasm [eye-KON-o-KLAZ-em] is the systematic destruction of religious icons because of their religious connotations. As anti-Catholic reform movements spread throughout northern Europe in the sixteenth century, an iconoclastic fever spread with them. The widespread destruction of religious images resulted from popular resentment against a church grown worldly and corrupt. The Old Testament prohibition against images that led to idolatry was cited as the justification for this destruction. The art that had flourished under the patronage of Julius II and Leo X became the very symbol of the papacy's corruption. In Zurich, the religious leader ULRICH ZWINGLI [ZWING-glee] even prohibited the use of music in worship. John Calvin wrote, "Therefore it remains that only those things are to be sculpted or painted which the eyes are capable of seeing: let not God's majesty, which is far above the perception of the eyes, be debased through unseemly representations." Such sentiments led church supporters to dismantle the *Ghent Altarpiece* in 1566 and safeguard it in the tower of St. Bavon.

The most virulent iconoclasm occurred in England, beginning when King Henry VIII (fig. 14.6) ordered the destruction of the monasteries in 1535. Henry's motives were as much political as they were religious. When he wanted to divorce Catherine of Aragon and marry Anne Boleyn, from whom he hoped for a male heir, as a Catholic he could not do so. Frustrated after six years of negotiations with Pope Clement VII in Rome, Henry eliminated papal authority in England. Thus the Church of England was born—the Anglican Church—and it granted his divorce. (An heir was born, although Henry was disappointed, since the child was a girl—the future Queen Elizabeth I.)

Henry first attacked the monasteries, the ruins of many of which still stand: Glastonbury, the mythological burial place of King Arthur, and Tintern Abbey, which later inspired a poem by William Wordsworth. When Shakespeare wrote of "these bare ruin'd choirs where late the sweet birds sang," he was referring to such ruins. Thomas Cromwell, Henry's minister, ordered the destruction of the objects of idolatry, particularly "feigned images . . . abused with pilgrimages or offerings." Soon the shrine to St. Thomas à Beckett in Canterbury Cathedral was torn down and his sainthood recanted.

Age of Discovery

Ever since Marco Polo had returned from China in the thirteenth century, the European view of the globe had undergone continual revision. In the two centuries after 1450,

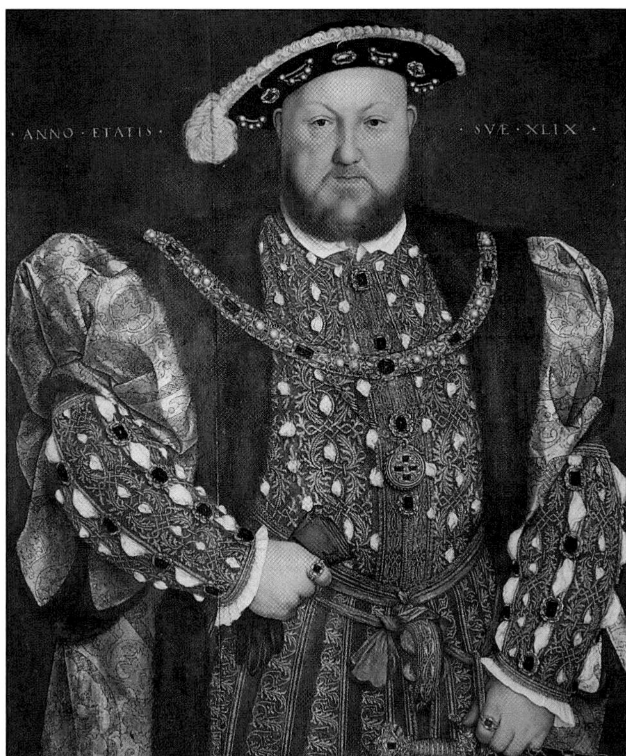

FIGURE 14.6 Hans Holbein the Younger, *Henry VIII*, ca. 1540, oil on panel, $2'9\frac{1}{2}'' \times 2'5\frac{1}{2}''$ (82.6 × 75 cm), Galleria Nazionale d'Arte Antica, Rome. SCALA/Art Resource, NY. The English monarch is shown in wedding dress—attire he donned six times. As Holbein records, at the age of forty-nine he was already, as he was described in his later years, a "man-mountain."

European explorations mapped the details of the world. Fueled by both missionary and economic zeal, European exploration also spawned an encounter with peoples and cultures hitherto unknown.

Renaissance Explorers. In 1488, the Portuguese explorer BARTOLOMEU DIAS [DEE-es] was blown far south off the West African coast by an enormous storm. Heading northeast afterwards, he had rounded what came to be called the Cape of Good Hope, thus suggesting that Africa was surrounded by water. In 1497, the Portuguese explorer VASCO DA GAMA [VAS-koe de GAM-uh] followed Dias's route and reached India ten months and fourteen days after setting out from Lisbon. Meanwhile, Christopher Columbus had made landfall in the Bahamas in 1492, and in 1500 the Portuguese PEDRO CABRAL [ka-BRAHL] pushed west from the bulge of Africa and landed in what is now Brazil. Magellan sailed around the tip of South America, across the Pacific to the Philippines, across the Indian Ocean and around Africa, thus circumnavigating the globe. On September 8, 1522, the eighteen survivors of Ferdinand Magellan's crew arrived back in Cadiz, Spain, three years after setting out.

European exploration was stimulated by a variety of motives. Foremost were economic motives, such as the search for lands with resources sutiable for cultivating crops that could be sold for cash. Equally important was the goal of establishing trade routes to Asian markets, along with the desire to spread the influence of Christianity. Portuguses mariners were successful in finding such land resources in the Azores and Madeira Islands, as well as some Atlantic islands, with sugar an important commodity, along with gold, ivory, and slaves from Africa.

Accompanying these economic and material incentives were others, such as the European desire to expand the boundaries of Christianity, which, like Islam and Buddhism, is a missionary religion. Franciscan and Dominican missionaries had travelled to India, central Asia, and China, with the Jesuits soon to follow. Although they began peacefully, missionary efforts developed later into a series of crusades and holy wars against Muslims in Palestine, Iberia, and the Mediterranean islands.

These various impulses for exploration combined and overlapped, such that in 1498 the Portuguese mariner Vasco de Gama told authorities in Calicut, India, that he had come there for "Christians and spices." In fact, European countries, via their seafares, had sought to control the spice trade in the Indian Ocean, though with only partial success. Nonetheless, Portuguese merchants built more than fifty trading posts between West Africa and East Asia. Portuguese mariners controlled access to the Persian Gulf; they organized trade in African gold, Indian pepper, and in cloves and nutmeg in the Spice Islands. Following the Portuguese were English and Dutch merchants, who formed respectively the English East India Company, founded in 1600, and the Dutch United East India Company, in 1602. These companies were highly profitable, multiplying many times over the financial values of the investments made in in them.

The age of discovery was an age of doubt. Thus not only geography underwent revision in the sixteenth century. Likewise, the Reformation placed in doubt the authority of institutional orthodoxy. In asserting that authority resided in the individual, Luther echoed a humanist trend. Luther's emphasis on individual conscience, on private judgment, and the individual act of faith was part of the cultural transformation that led to the secularization of society and the rise of scientific investigation.

Nicolas Copernicus. In the spirit of geographical "discovery" the Polish astronomer NICOLAS COPERNICUS [koh-PUR-ni-kus] (1473–1543) published *On the Revolutions of Celestial Bodies* in the year of his death. Building on the work of the ancient Greek geographer and astronomer Ptolemy, whose writings had been rediscovered and translated in 1410, Copernicus argued that Earth and the other planets orbit the sun, rather than the sun and planets revolving around Earth. But theologians refused to believe the Earth was not at the center of the universe, and Copernicus's book was placed on the Index of Prohibited Books in 1616. Even so, Copernicus's work could not be suppressed.

Table 14-1 RELIGIOUS REFORMERS IN WESTERN EUROPE

Reformer	Country	Significance
Desiderius Erasmus (1466–1533)	The Netherlands	*The Praise of Folly*
Martin Luther (1483–1546)	Germany	The 95 Theses
Ulrich Zwingli (1484–1531)	Switzerland (Zurich)	Iconoclasm
John Calvin (1509–64)	Switzerland (Geneva)	Predestination
King Henry VIII (1491–1547)	England	Destruction of monasteries

New Scientists. In England, Francis Bacon (1562–1626) advocated a "scientific method" in which actual observations needed to be made in planned experiments. Hypotheses could be tested and proved; there was no room in science for blind "faith."

In the same year that Copernicus published *On the Revolutions of Celestial Bodies*, ANDREAS VESALIUS [vi-SAY-lee-es] (1514–64) published his *Seven Books on the Structure of the Human Body*, which illustrated the anatomy of the human body based on actual observations. In England, Sir William Harvey discovered capillaries in the human circulation system, solving the mystery of how blood returned to the heart from the arteries. The English mathematician JOHN NAPIER [NAY-pee-er] discovered the logarithm, freeing mathematicians from arduous calculation. In 1542, GEMMA FRISIUS [FREE-zi-yus] discovered new principles for increasing accuracy in surveying and mapmaking, using the technique of triangulation.

PAINTING AND PRINTMAKING

Albrecht Dürer. If any artist in the north can be said to embody the ideals of the Renaissance and the spirit of discovery that defines it, it is ALBRECHT DÜRER [DYOU-ruhr] (1471–1528), painter, printer, draftsman, theoretician, writer, humanist, and publisher. His output was enormous, consisting of more than a hundred paintings and over a thousand drawings and prints.

Dürer was born in Nuremberg; his mother was a German, his father a Hungarian goldsmith. Like his Italian counterpart Leonardo da Vinci, Dürer was fascinated with nature and studied it intensely. Throughout his career, Dürer made various studies of animals, birds, and plants, all sketched or painted from life. "Art," he wrote, "derives from God; it is God who has created all art; it is not easy to paint artistically. Therefore, those without aptitude should not attempt it, for it is an inspiration from above." Dürer believed he was endowed with a God-given gift, a humanistic and individualistic view that he shared with Michelangelo and other Renaissance artists.

Dürer's fame derives especially from his prints. In **woodcuts** and **engravings,** through the precision and detail of his work as well as the richness and variety of his effects, Dürer was able to achieve monumentality on the scale of a sheet of paper. Among the many series of prints that Dürer produced is the *Apocalypse*, published in 1498, consisting of fifteen woodcuts with the text printed on the reverse. Reissued several times, this series did much to spread his fame. From the *Apocalypse* series comes the gruesome *Four Horsemen of the Apocalypse* (fig. 14.7). Death, War, Pestilence, and Famine are riding rampant over the burghers, artisans, merchants, and other citizens of Nuremberg. In a woodcut, the negative, or white, areas of

FIGURE 14.7 Albrecht Dürer, *Four Horsemen of the Apocalypse*, 1497–98, woodcut, $15\frac{1}{2}'' \times 11\frac{1}{8}''$ (39.4 × 28.3 cm), gift of Junius S. Morgan, 1919 (19.73.209). Location: Metropolitan Museum of Art, New York, NY, U.S.A. Photo Credit: Image copyright © The Metropolitan Museum of Art/Art Resource, NY. Dürer's genius elevated graphic art (printmaking) to a fine art. When making a woodcut, the artist draws a reverse image on a block of wood, then cuts away the wood from the drawing. The remaining raised areas of the wooden block are inked, the paper is pressed onto the block, and an image of the raised area is made.

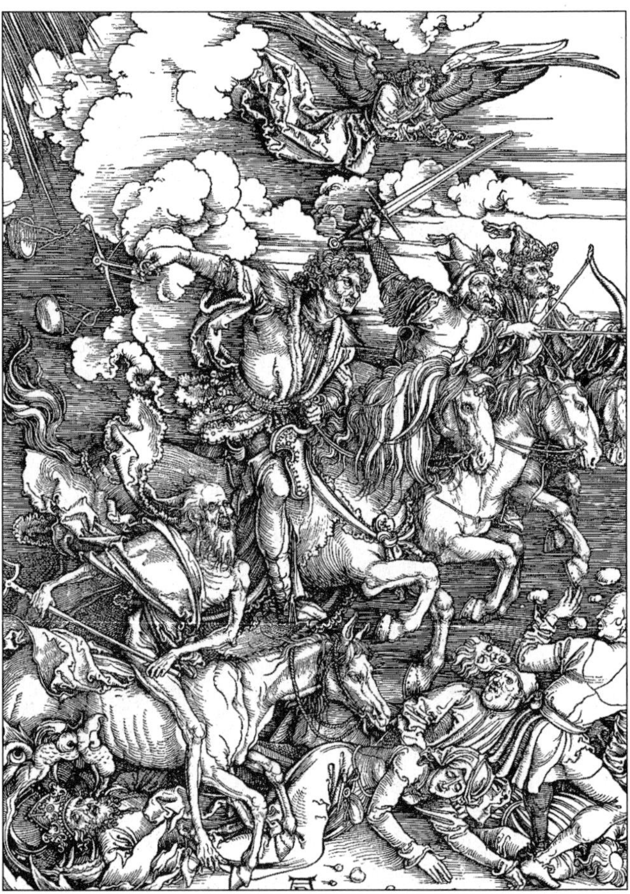

the final print are cut into the block while the black areas are uncut, and remain raised in relief. Ink is rolled over the surface, paper is placed on the inked surface, and the image transferred to the paper by applying pressure to the back of the paper.

Adam and Eve (fig. 14.8) is an engraving, signed and dated on the plaque on the tree branch, "Albrecht Dürer of Nuremberg made this in 1504." An engraving is printed from a design inscribed in the surface of a metal plate. Using a sharp **burin,** or steel gouging tool, the design is cut into the surface of a metal plate. In an ***etching,*** as in engraving, the design comes from incisions made in the surface. When an etching is made, first, a metal plate is coated with a waxy film. Next, the design is scraped or scratched through the wax to expose the plate, a process far less arduous than engraving the plate itself. The plate is then placed in a mild acid bath that eats into the exposed areas of metal. Ink is rubbed into these recesses and the surface of the plate is wiped clean. Damp paper is then placed on the inked plate. The pressure of a printing press is required to force the paper into the recesses to pick up the ink. The image that is printed is a mirror reversal of the original.

FIGURE 14.8 Albrecht Dürer, *Adam and Eve*, 1504, engraving, $9\frac{1}{8} \times 7\frac{5}{8}''$ (25.1 × 19.4 cm), Philadelphia Museum of Art, Philadelphia. In an engraving, the recessed areas are printed. The artist cuts the lines into a metal plate, the recessed lines take the ink, paper is applied to the inked plate, and the ink is transferred to the paper by the pressure of a printing press.

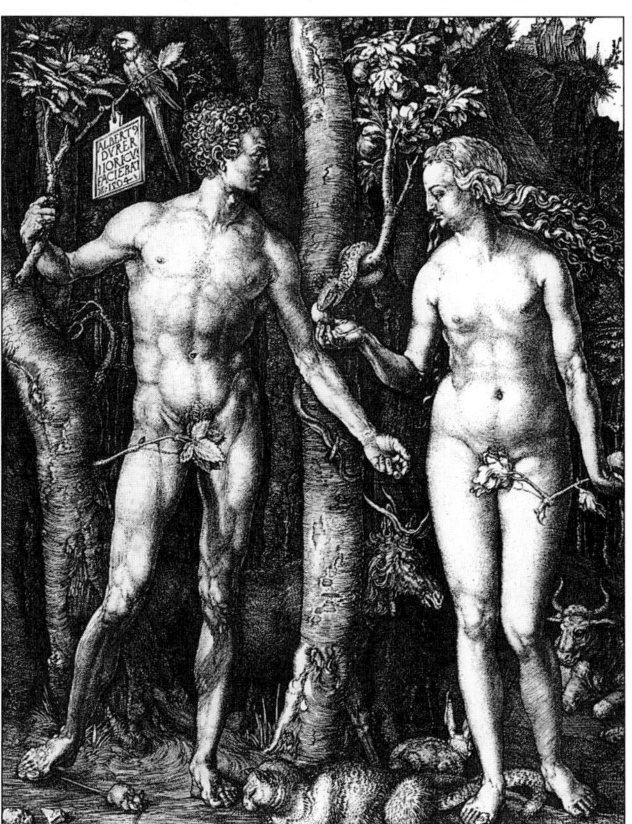

After visiting Italy, Dürer became increasingly interested in the human figure, and his depictions of Adam and Eve essentially an excuse to study the male and female nude. Dürer used mathematical proportions and drew from Italian works and interpretations of antiquity. His Adam resembles the Hellenistic Greek *Apollo Belvedere,* which had been recently discovered, and his Eve recalls the classical *Venus de Milo.*

Dürer included symbols of the four humors, a notion derived from classical philosophy, in the background of *Adam and Eve:* The cat is choleric (angry); the rabbit sanguine (confident); the elk melancholic (depressed); and the ox phlegmatic (impassive).

In 1515, Dürer was made court painter to Emperor Maximilian I. Now among the rich and famous, Dürer had a shop of people working for him. In later years he worked more and more on theories of measurement and proportion. Like Leonardo da Vinci, Dürer relied on Vitruvius's scheme of human proportions, and in 1525 he published *The Teaching of Measurements with Rule and Compass (Manual of Measurements)* and later *Four Books on Human Proportions.* Concerned with practical application, Dürer designed devices to aid the artist in doing perspective drawings. In all, his interests in antiquity, the natural world, anatomy, and perspective were analogous to those of his Italian contemporaries.

Although Dürer did paint and print religious subjects, most were executed early in his career. In 1519, Dürer became a follower of Martin Luther. As the Reformation gained momentum, painters in the north turned more and more to secular subjects.

Hans Holbein the Younger. The art of HANS HOLBEIN THE YOUNGER [HOLE-bine] (1497/98–1543) reflects this increasing secularity. Holbein's fame grew from his portraiture, and he painted many important people. Born in Augsburg into a family of artists, he worked in the shop of his father, Hans Holbein the Elder, and he studied in Basel, Switzerland, where in 1519 he set up shop. Around 1523, Holbein painted *Erasmus of Rotterdam* (fig. 14.9), a portrait of the famous Dutch humanist who had settled in Basel in 1521. Holbein revered Erasmus, became his close friend, and portrayed him several times.

Erasmus provided Holbein with letters of introduction to the English court, where he was to become famous. In 1536, Holbein became court painter to Henry VIII, producing portraits of the king and his family (see fig. 14.6). As Henry's court painter, Holbein painted portraits of his prospective brides. Holbein's working method was to begin with a chalk sketch, the face drawn in careful detail, the body and costume loosely indicated. Later, the portrait was painted in his studio. The sitter could send to Holbein's studio any garment she or he wished to be shown wearing; no one was expected to pose while waiting for Holbein to craft every puff and pleat. These portraits display exquisite line and sensitive modeling. Holbein varied the format of his portraits, but he always made the sitter look dignified.

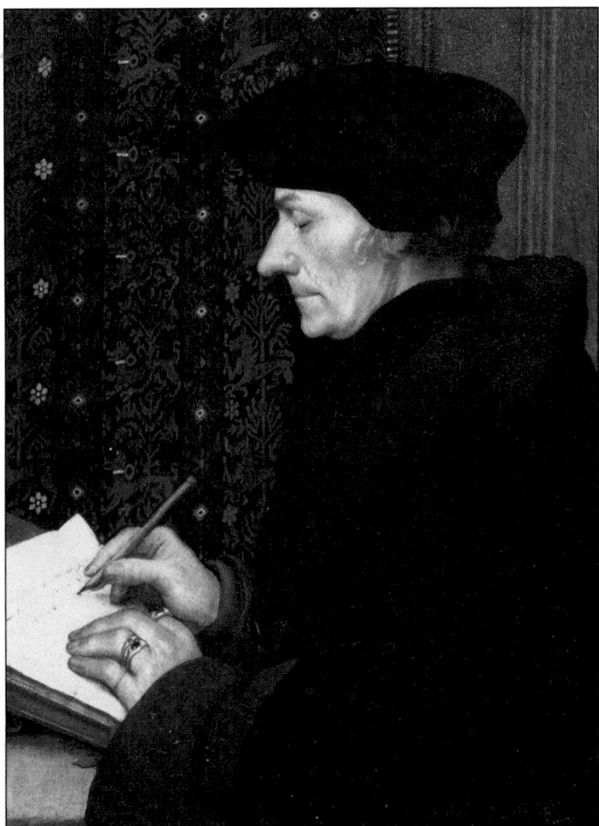

FIGURE 14.9 Hans Holbein the Younger, *Erasmus of Rotterdam*, ca. 1523, oil on panel, $16\frac{1}{2}'' \times 12\frac{1}{2}''$ (42 × 31.4 cm), Musée du Louvre, Paris. Reunion des Musées Nat'l/Art Resource, NY. Holbein's portrait of the Dutch humanist Erasmus, shown as he records his ideas, conveys his intellectual authority.

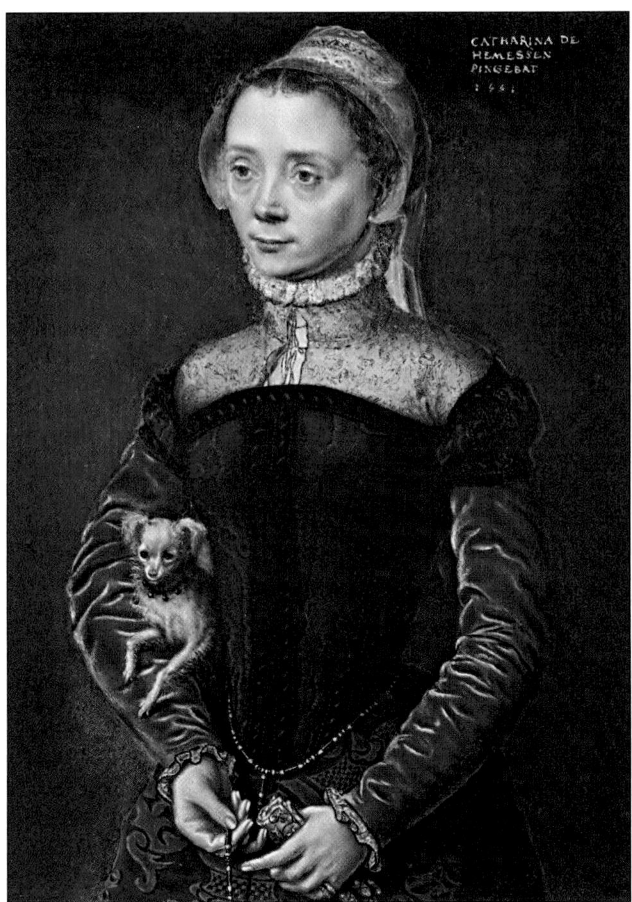

FIGURE 14.10 Caterina van Hemessen, *Portrait of a Lady*, 1551, oil on oak, 9″ × 7″ (23 × 18 cm), National Gallery, London. Tiny in size, this portrait is an example of the sixteenth-century vogue for miniature portraits. Van Hemessen's sitters, seemingly avoiding eye contact with the viewer, maintain their quiet composure.

Caterina van Hemessen. Caterina Van Hemessen (1527/8–ca. 1566), one of the most important women painters of the Renaissance in northern Europe, also specialized in portraiture, as many women artists did. Her father was the Flemish Mannerist painter Jan Sanders van Hemessen of Antwerp. The example seen in fig. 14.10 is typical of her work in its small-scale depiction of a single figure standing against a dark monochromatic background. This reserved simplicity accorded with the taste of the time and brought her great success, for she was patronized by Queen Mary of Hungary, then ruling the Low Countries for her brother, Charles I of Spain. In 1556, when Mary returned to Spain, her invitation to van Hemessen and her husband to join her there was accepted. When Mary died, she left van Hemessen and her husband ample funds to allow them to return to Antwerp and live comfortably.

Pieter Bruegel the Elder. In contrast to Holbein's and van Hemessen's work at court, PIETER BRUEGEL THE ELDER [BROY-gul] (ca. 1525–1569) portrayed the peasantry and the countryside. Little is known about his life. When he was born remains uncertain; where, perhaps in Flanders. He visited Rome to study humanism, classicism, and the new trends, but the trip seems to have had little impact on his art. In 1563, he married his teacher's daughter and moved from Antwerp to Brussels, where he was to remain. His two sons became painters.

Bruegel earned considerable income by imitating the paintings of Hieronymus Bosch, which were extremely popular by the middle of the sixteenth century. But his best paintings depict the daily life of ordinary people, known as **genre painting.** Typical of his paintings is the *Harvesters* (fig. 14.11) of 1565. Bruegel was commissioned to paint a series of scenes of the months of the year with, presumably, one painting representing every two months; the *Harvesters* represents August and September. Bruegel gave the landscape prominence; nature no longer served merely as a setting for a portrait or religious event. The Limbourg brothers (see Chapter 12) had completed a series on the months of the year in their book of hours in 1416; what is new in Bruegel's paintings is the way in which the landscape is shown. The figures, rather than being placed in front of a landscape background, are now

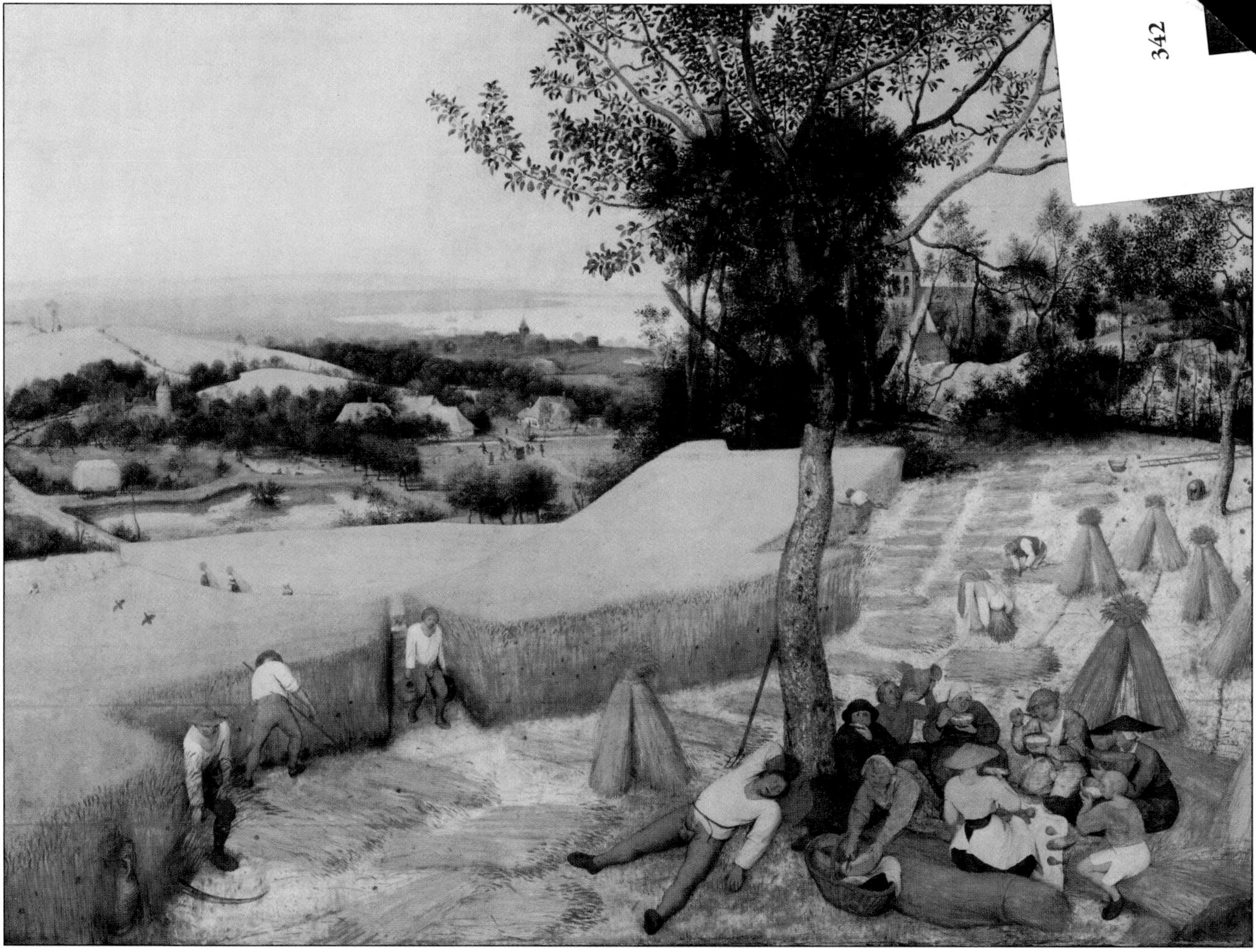

FIGURE 14.11 Pieter Bruegel the Elder, *Harvesters*, 1565, oil on panel, 3′10½″ × 5′3¼″ (1.18 × 1.61 m), Rogers Fund, 1919. Metropolitan Museum of Art, New York. A genuine interest in landscape as a subject, rather than as mere background, first appears in Bruegel's series of paintings depicting the months and their corresponding labors.

integrated into the setting. The colors convey the feeling of a warm summer afternoon—rich yellows and tans in the foreground, cool greens in the background.

Bruegel's *Peasant Wedding* (fig. 14.12), of ca. 1566–67, records the commotion of a rustic wedding. The smiling bride sits before a dark hanging cloth, hands clasped. Two men carrying bowls of rice pudding on wooden planks create the foreground. The bagpiper looks at this dessert, which, because rice was not a local product, was considered a delicacy. The composition of the *Peasant Wedding* is carefully constructed to appear informal and draw the viewer into the event. The foreground is brought close to the viewer by the figures in the lower left, including a child licking his fingers. The arrangement in space is diagonal; the diagonal line of the planks on which the dessert is served continues to recede down the table all the way to the back of the hall. Bruegel uses areas of flat color and simplified forms to create a decorative, patterned quality. His strong, stocky figures convey the robustness and earthy liveliness of this celebration.

ARCHITECTURE

As the merchant class rose in importance, secular patronage of the arts grew, along with interest in personal luxury and the display of wealth as a means of expressing power and prestige. Castles were obvious examples of the owner's importance. The most splendid of these were the **châteaux** (castles) of France. A concentration of Renaissance castles is found in the Loire [LWAR] valley, which was an especially agreeable area because of its fine climate and abundant game.

Château of Chambord. Perhaps the most extraordinary of the French Renaissance châteaux is that of Chambord [sham-BORE] (fig. 14.13), begun in 1519 for the king, Francis I. The original architect is believed to have been an Italian, DOMENICO DA CORTONA [dah kor-TOE-nuh] (d. 1549). The largest of all Renaissance châteaux, Chambord has 440 rooms, 365 chimneys (one for every day of the year), fourteen big staircases, and seventy smaller staircases. The plan of

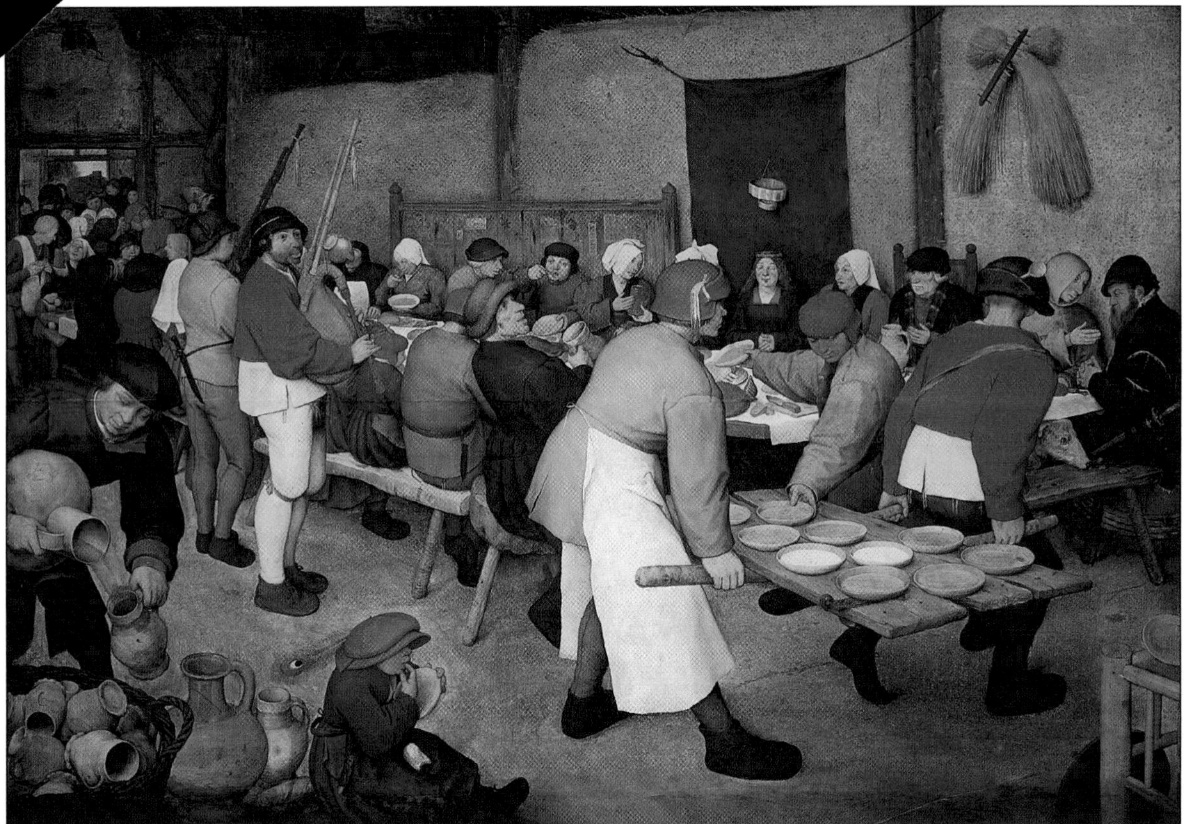

FIGURE 14.12 Pieter Bruegel the Elder, *Peasant Wedding*, ca. 1566–67, oil on panel, $3'8\frac{1}{8}'' \times 5'4'$ (1.10 × 1.60 m), Kunsthistorisches Museum, Vienna. Unlike his contemporaries, Bruegel was concerned not so much with the individual as with the type and, in particular, with the peasant class.

FIGURE 14.13 Domenico da Cortona (?), Château of Chambord, Loire Valley, begun in 1519, north facade. It is possible to ascend the monumental double-spiral staircase to the roof—where a little town has been constructed atop this extraordinary French castle.

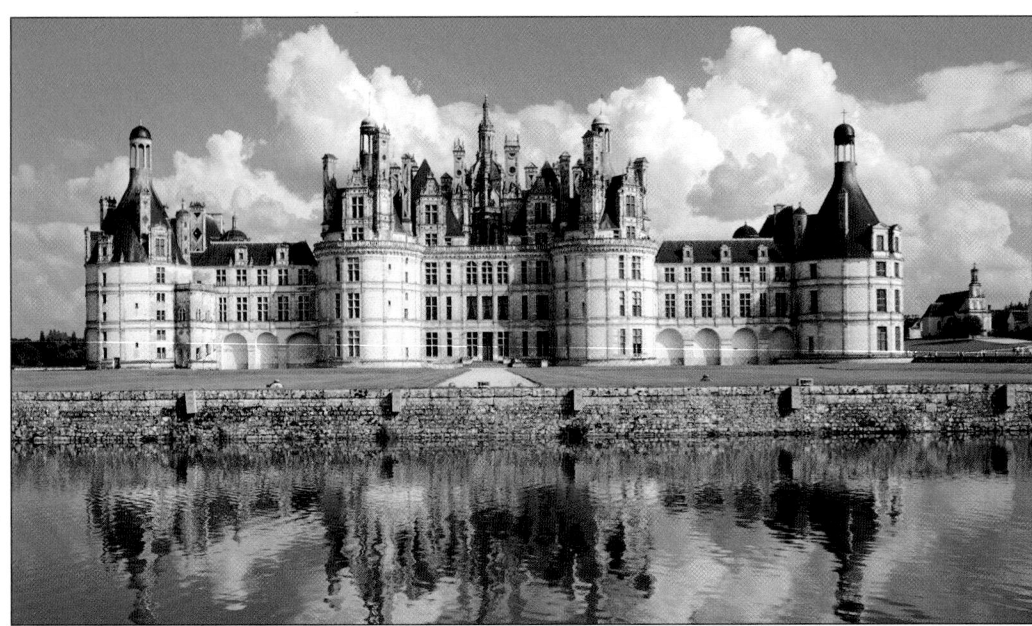

Chambord is that of a medieval castle with a central keep, four corner towers, a surrounding wall, and, originally, a moat. Yet Chambord was built not for defense but for display.

The château at Chambord has two extraordinary features, one outside, the other inside. Outside, on the flat roof, is a tiny town with winding streets, squares, and turrets. To walk on the roof is to wander in an intricate fairyland in the sky. Inside, the main attraction is the central double-spiral staircase. Built within a circle 30 feet in diameter and 80 feet to the roof, the two spiral staircases intertwine, but do not meet—two people on opposite staircases can see each other across the central well, but they cannot touch.

Hampton Court Palace. The English contemporary of France's King Francis I was Henry VIII (r. 1509–47), who lived with five of his six wives at Hampton Court Palace on the southwest outskirts of London, beside the Thames River (fig. 14.14). In England, medieval fortified castles with massive stone walls and small windows gradually gave way to more luxurious dwellings with large windows. Hampton Court Palace is constructed of brick, which is not as strong as stone. The dry moat, towers, battlements, and crenelations are only minimally militaristic, and Hampton Court decidedly domestic rather than defensive. This early Tudor mansion, originally built for Cardinal Wolsey around 1514, came to be owned by, and enlarged by, Henry VIII. (Later it was futher enlarged by William III in a different style.) Sprawling Hampton Court Palace, organized around several courtyards and somewhat symmetrical in plan, was claimed to have one thousand rooms. It is surrounded by 60 acres of gardens.

Although Henry VIII lived during the Renaissance era, he perpetuated the late medieval Gothic style at Hampton Court Palace. Thus, the Great Hall, although built in the 1530s, is still Gothic in style and is covered by a characteristically English wooden hammerbeam roof, impressive as it spans a width of 40 feet in a hall over 100 feet long. Similarly, the Royal Chapel has a Gothic style fan-vaulted ceiling (thus-called because the many small ribs radiate out like the vanes of a fan) and pendant bosses, yet it was built for Henry VIII, 1535–36. The chapel's ceiling looks like stone, as would have been used during the Gothic era, yet this Renaissance version is actually made of wood.

SECULAR MUSIC

During the Renaissance, **secular music** (music not associated with religious meanings or ceremonies) became increasingly popular. Giorgione and Titian's *Fête champêtre* documents this popularity in its depiction of people playing instruments. Unlike sacred vocal music, which typically set Latin or Greek texts to music, secular vocal

FIGURE 14.14 Hampton Court Palace, London, seen from the Great Gatehouse, c. 1514 and later. This main entrance, built with walls of pink brick pierced with large windows, rather than with solid walls of stone, indicates that the fortified castles of the Middle Ages were no longer required in sixteenth-century England. Yet defensive elements such as crenelations and moats were retained for their picturesque appeal.

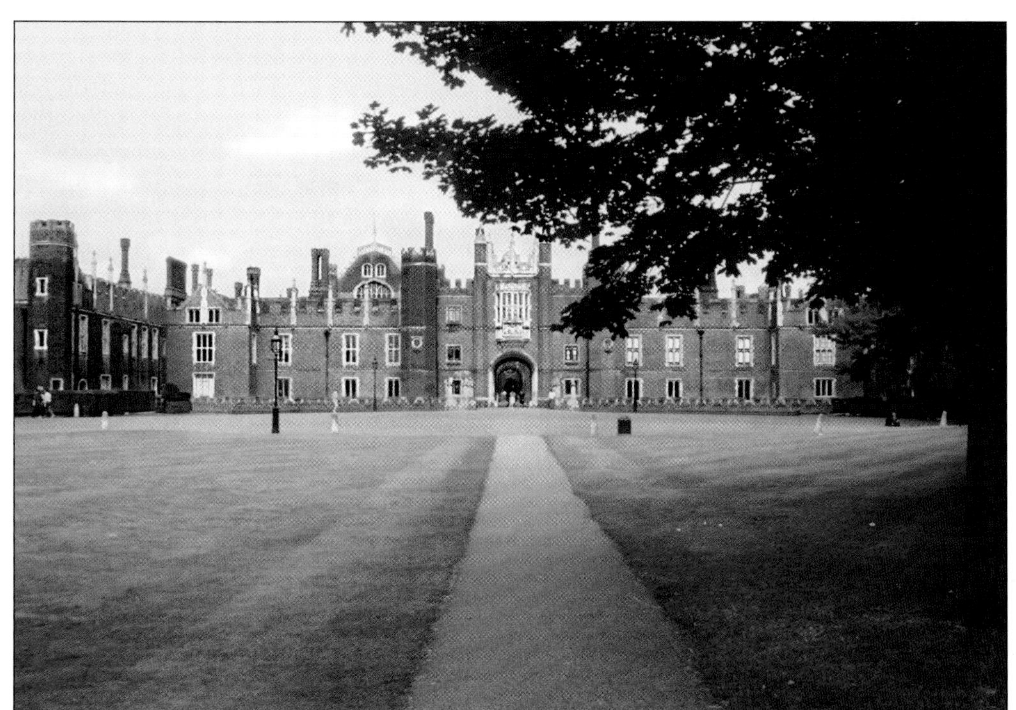

music was composed for lyrics in the vernacular, the spoken language. Although secular vocal compositions were written in Italian, French, Spanish, German, Dutch, and English, there were two main schools of madrigal writing—English in the north and Italian in the south.

The **madrigal** is a vocal composition for a small group of singers, usually with no accompaniment. Like sacred motets (religious texts set to a polyphonic composition), madrigals were composed in polyphonic style, with multiple voice parts. (For an explanation of polyphony, see Chapter 13.) Unlike motets, however, which were performed by a small choir singing the same text in polyphony, madrigals were performed by a few singers, each of whom sang a different vocal part. The madrigal particularly appealed to an educated audience and was a popular court entertainment.

Typically settings of short lyric poems, madrigals were often about love and frivolity. The madrigalist's challenge was to set the poem to music perfectly. Madrigalists often tried to outdo each other, and their language and musical settings were often witty. They were especially inventive in setting words associated with weeping, sighing, trembling, and dying.

Thomas Weelkes. A composer best known for his madrigals, THOMAS WEELKES [WILKS] (1575–1623) was the organist at Chichester Cathedral. His madrigal "As Vesta Was Descending" was included in an early-seventeenth-century collection of madrigals, *The Triumph of Oriana*, to honor Queen Elizabeth I (fig. 14.15). Written for six voices—two sopranos, alto, two tenors, and bass—Weelkes's madrigal was a setting of the following poem:

As Vesta was from Latmos hill descending,
She spied a maiden Queen the same ascending,
Attended only by all the shepherds swain,
To whom Diana's darlings came running down amain:
First two by two, then three by three together,
Leaving their goddess all alone, hasted thither,
And mingling with the shepherds of her train,
With mirthful tunes her presence entertain.
Then sang the shepherds and nymphs of Diana,
Long live fair Oriana.

Weelkes takes advantage of the poem's opportunities for word painting. On the words "descending" and "ascending," for example, he uses descending and ascending musical lines, respectively. He also expresses the description of the attendants running "two by two, then three by three together, / Leaving their goddess all alone," by having first two singers then three, and finally all six join in before dropping back to a solo singer. Weelkes also uses fast notes for the words "running down amain," and he writes lively and upbeat music for the line "With mirthful tunes her presence entertain." Finally, for the word "long" in the last line, Weelkes provides singers with their longest held note. (For a further explanation of word painting, see Chapter 13.)

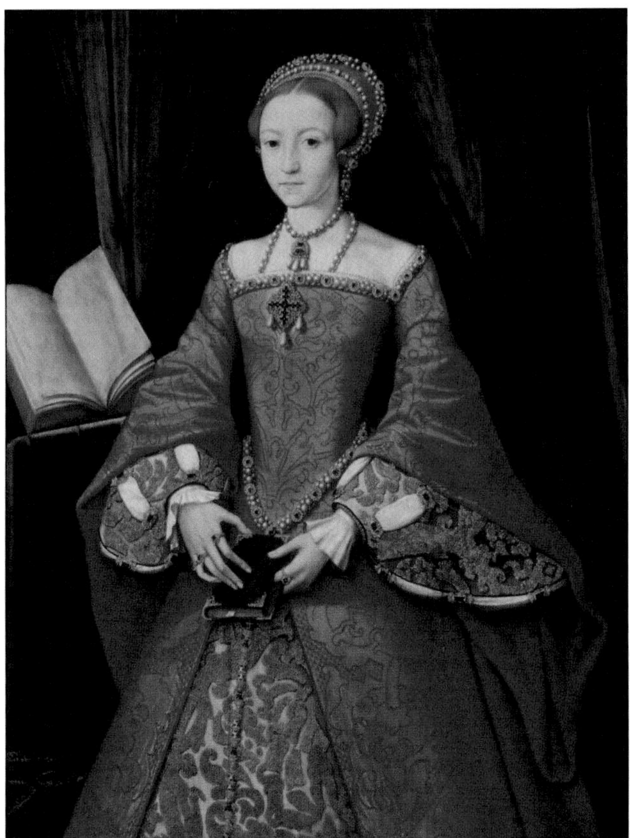

FIGURE 14.15 Levina Bening Teerling, *Elizabeth I as a Princess*, ca. 1559, oil on oak panel, $42\frac{3}{4}'' \times 32\frac{1}{4}''$ (108.5 × 81.8 cm), The Royal Collection © 2004 Her Majesty Queen Elizabeth II, Windsor Castle, Windsor. Royal Collection Enterprises Ltd. The books are indicative of Elizabeth's love of learning and support of the arts.

Thomas Morley. Another well-known composer of madrigals was Thomas Morley (1557–1603). Morley favored **homophonic texture,** in which a single melody, not several, is employed with harmonic support. He also uses the same music for each stanza of the poem below, with the nonsense syllables *fa-la* sung as a refrain. The playfulness of the music complements the playfulness of the words, which, as with much Elizabethan poetry, reveal a true love of the language.

Morley's madrigal, "Now Is the Month of Maying," scored for five voices, describes the flirting and courtship games common in the countryside. Morley's melody has the rhythm and tunefulness of a folk dance. It is structured in two parts, each of which is repeated and each of which concludes with the *fa-la* refrain. Here is the text:

Now is the month of maying,
When merry lads are playing, fa la,
Each with his bonny lass
Upon the greeny grass. Fa la.
The spring, clad all in gladness,
Doth laugh at winter's sadness, fa la,
And to the bagpipe's sound

The nymphs tread out their ground. Fa la.
Fie then! why sit we musing,
Youth's sweet delight refusing? Fa la,
Say, dainty nymphs, and speak,
Shall we play barley break? Fa la.

The lyrics to both Weelkes's and Morley's madrigals depict delicate nymphs and good-natured shepherds, lighthearted diversions that appealed to the privileged classes.

LITERATURE

Michel de Montaigne. The fame of MICHEL DE MONTAIGNE [mahn-TAYN] (1533–1592) rests on his *Essays*, which exemplify Renaissance individualism grounded in a humanism derived from Greco Roman antiquity. Montaigne's *Essays*, however, are distinguished less by depth of knowledge of the past than by a profound knowledge of the self.

Montaigne was born in Bordeaux, southern France. Montaigne studied law, spent time at court, and became a member of the Bordeaux parliament, serving as an arbitrator between the warring Protestant and Catholic royal factions. At thirty-eight, Montaigne retired to his castle, where he had a library, and devoted himself to reflection and writing. (At forty-eight, he came out of retirement to serve two terms as mayor of Bordeaux in 1581–85.)

Montaigne's early essays (in French, *essais*) contain numerous quotations from antiquity. In his second book of essays, however, he relied less on the authority of the past and more on expressing views in his own voice. In his third and last book of essays, Montaigne used quotations sparingly, presenting an original self-portrait.

Montaigne said that he wrote about himself because he knew himself better than he knew anything else. In "Of Experience," he wrote that "no man ever treated of a subject that he knew and understood better than I do this . . . and in this I am the most learned man alive." Montaigne notes, however, that he exists in a state of flux. "I must adapt my history to the moment," he wrote, for "I may presently change, not only by chance, but also by intention." And thus his essays are "a record of diverse and changeable events, of undecided, and . . . contradictory ideas."

Montaigne asks questions in his essays, without providing answers. "Perhaps" and "I think" are among his most frequently used expressions, and "*Que sais-je?*" ("What do I know?") is his most recurring question. The very name for the genre he created, *essai*, means trial or attempt, suggesting a process rather than a product, openness rather than conclusiveness, a journey and not a destination. As much as his essays reveal him, they also reveal readers to themselves. Montaigne's search for questions rather than answers, coupled with his affirmation of the individual, makes his work a landmark of Renaissance humanism. The modern novelist Virginia Woolf put it this way: "This talking of oneself, following one's own vagaries, giving the whole map, weight, colour, and circumference of the soul in its confusion, its variety, its imperfection—this art belonged to one man only: to Montaigne."

William Shakespeare. WILLIAM SHAKESPEARE [SHAYK-speer] (1564–1616) is the greatest writer in the English language, a reputation that rests on thirty-seven plays and 154 sonnets exploring complex states of mind and feeling in exuberant language rich with metaphor. His command is particularly evident in his **soliloquies,** meditative reflections spoken aloud. From *Hamlet* (fig. 14.16) alone, we glean the following sayings:

In my mind's eye;
I must be cruel only to be kind;
Brevity is the soul of wit;
To be or not to be, that is the question;
Neither a borrower nor a lender be;
Something's rotten in the state of Denmark;
What a piece of work is a man.

Shakespeare was born in Stratford-upon-Avon in April 1564. He attended the local school, but did not go on to Oxford or Cambridge. Instead, in 1582, at the age of

FIGURE 14.16 Title page, *Hamlet* (1603), The Huntington Library, California. This is the title page of the first quarto edition of the play that was printed.

THE

Tragicall Hiſtorie of

HAMLET

Prince of Denmarke

By William Shake-ſpeare.

As it hath beene diuerſe times acted by his Highneſſe ſeruants in the Cittie of London : as alſo in the two Vniuerſities of Cambridge and Oxford, and elſe-where

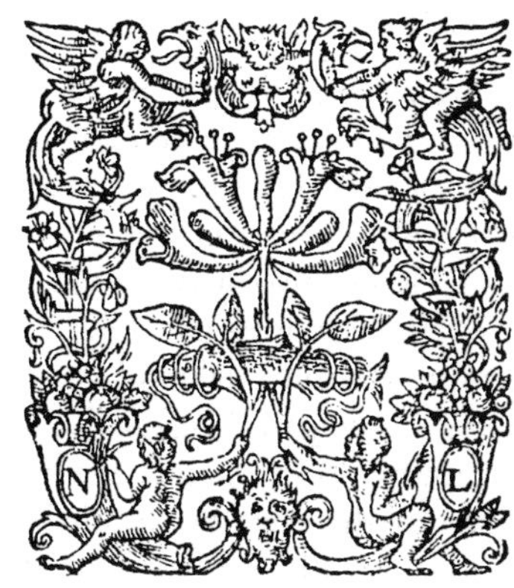

At London printed for N.L. and Iohn Trundell.
1603.

Connections

SHAKESPEARE AND MUSIC

Shakespeare employs music in his plays for various purposes. He uses music to suggest a change in locale and time, indicating that the action of a play has shifted scene. Music signals the entrance or exit of an important character; trumpet flourishes announce the arrival or departure of royalty. Trumpets also sound a battle charge.

Music and Character Revelation

Perhaps the most important function of music in Shakespeare's plays is to reveal character. Shakespeare's characters disclose their states of mind through the songs they sing. In *Hamlet*, the young Ophelia reveals her unstable mental state through singing about love, loss, and death. In *Othello*, Desdemona, Othello's wife, conveys an ominous foreboding about her imminent death in the "Willow Song."

Musical Imagery

Shakespeare's plays are also rife with musical images. Some of these are simple passing references, such as those in *Romeo and Juliet*. When Romeo and Juliet part, Juliet cries out in disappointment, "the lark sings so out of tune, / Straining harsh discords and unpleasing sharps." Often, however, Shakespeare developed elaborate patterns of musical imagery. A striking example occurs when Hamlet speaks to his boyhood friends Rosencrantz and Guildenstern, who are about to betray him. In complaining about their deceit, Hamlet likens himself to a recorder, or flute, playing in the background, and also to a plucked and fretted instrument:

> HAMLET Why, look you now, how unworthy a thing you make of me! You would play upon me, you would seem to know my stops, you would pluck out the heart of my mystery, you would sound me from my lowest note to the top of my compass; and there is much music, excellent voice, in this little organ, yet cannot you make it speak. 'Sblood, do you think I am easier to be played on than a pipe? Call me what instrument you will, though you can fret me, you cannot play upon me.
>
> *Act III, Scene ii, ll. 349–57*

In this elaborated metaphor, everything Hamlet says proves to be literally true.

Composers and Instruments

Instruments used for Shakespearean music include brass, woodwind, strings, and percussion (fig. 14.17). Trumpets were the most frequently used brass instrument; wooden flutes and recorders of various sizes were the most common woodwind instruments. Stringed instruments included the violin, harp, lyre, and lute, among others. Percussion was almost always supplied by a tabor or drum, which often was accompanied by a fife, the smallest of the flutes.

Shakespeare did not compose the music that accompanied his plays. In Shakespeare's lifetime, his contemporaries, such as Thomas Morley, set his words to music, including "O Mistress Mine" from *Twelfth Night*, which Morley may have written at Shakespeare's request. Other music used to accompany songs included traditional arrangements that antedated the plays, as with the "Willow Song," sung by Desdemona in *Othello*, and the gravedigger's song "In Youth When I Did Love" from *Hamlet*.

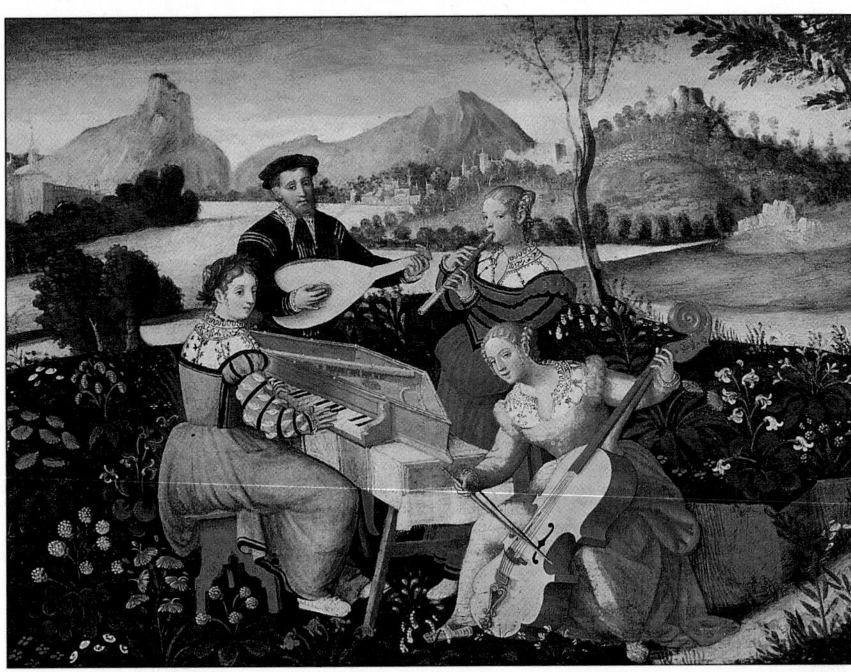

FIGURE 14.17 Anonymous, *The Country Concert*, Italian School, sixteenth century. Musée de l'Hotel l'Allemant, Bourges. Giraudon/Art Resource, New York. Here is a depiction of a typical chamber music ensemble, consisting of a harpsichord, lute, recorder, and bass viol.

Critical Thinking

WHO WROTE "SHAKESPEARE'S PLAYS"?

Among issues in literary studies that have reappeared over the centuries is that of whether William Shakespeare is the actual author of plays such as *Hamlet*, *Julius Caesar*, and *Romeo and Juliet*. Those arguing against Shakespeare's authorship claim that he was not sufficiently well educated to have written such masterpieces, with their wide range of knowledge and their brilliant language. These critics of Shakespearean authorship offer alternative authors, including, among others, Sir Francis Bacon and Edward De Vere, the Seventh Earl of Oxford, and the Renaissance playwright Christopher Marlowe, all of whom were extremely well educated and themselves very good writers.

Defenders of Shakespeare claim that the preponderance of evidence is in favor of his authorship of the plays. These defenders offer as evidence that Shakespeare's name is on the first printed editions and that he was an actor and part owner of an acting company that needed new material, which he wrote as a normal part of his theatrical work. They refer to contemporary paintings of Shakespeare and to his extensive knowledge of Italy, classics, and the law, which runs throughout his plays.

How would you go about deciding whether Shakespeare wrote the plays attributed to him? What questions would you have in pursuing your investigation of the matter? What kinds of evidence would you look for? What types of sources would you consult, and what kinds of credentials for the writers of those sources would you find credible?

eighteen, he married Anne Hathaway, who bore him three children in as many years. At that time Shakespeare began writing and acting in plays. Although many tributes have been paid to Shakespeare, one stands above the rest: his contemporary Ben Jonson's judgment that "he is not for an age, but for all time."

Shakespeare's sonnets have drama as well as melodic lyricism. Their range is wide, including melancholy, despair, hope, shame, guilt, fear, jealousy, and exhilaration. Written during the 1590s, they were not published until 1609—(though two were printed in a 1599 collection, *The Passionate Pilgrim*, without Shakespeare's authorization). Like John Donne's poems, Shakespeare's sonnets circulated in manuscript before publication and were much admired.

Shakespeare's soliloquies further reveal the human spirit. In a soliloquy, Macbeth uses obsessive, bitter language to lament his ruined scheme. The following from Act V, Scene i occurs when Macbeth discovers that though he is now king, his wife is dead:

> Tomorrow, and tomorrow, and tomorrow
> Creeps in this petty pace from day to day,
> To the last syllable of recorded time;
> And all our yesterdays have lighted fools
> The way to dusty death. Out, Out, brief candle!
> Life's but a walking shadow, a poor player
> That struts and frets his hour upon the stage
> And then is heard no more. It is a tale
> Told by an idiot, full of sound and fury
> Signifying nothing.

Written in **blank verse**—verse in unrhymed **iambic pentameter** (each line has ten syllables with alternating stresses)—the soliloquy portrays Macbeth's despair over the apparent meaninglessness of life.

Shakespeare's plays capture the imagination. The political astuteness in *Julius Caesar* and *Antony and Cleopatra* is complemented by the playful comedy in *As You Like It* and *Much Ado About Nothing*, and the tempered romance of Shakespeare's final plays, of which *The Tempest* is a glorious example.

The drama of the Elizabethan Age (1558–1603) shares features with Greek drama. The Elizabethan dramatists wrote domestic tragedies, tragedies of character, and revenge tragedies, of which *Hamlet* is the great example. The Elizabethan dramatists also wrote comedies of manners and comedies of humors, which extended the range of earlier romantic and satiric comedies. In both Greek and Elizabethan theater, props were few, scenery was simple, and the dialogue alone indicated changes of locale and time.

An Elizabethan playhouse such as the Globe (fig. 14.18), where Shakespeare's plays were staged, had a much smaller seating capacity than the large Greek amphitheaters, which could seat thousands. The Globe could accommodate about 2,300 people, including roughly eight hundred groundlings who, exposed to the weather, stood around the stage. The stage itself projected from an inside wall into their midst. More prosperous spectators sat in one of the three stories that encircled the stage. The reduced size of the Elizabethan theater and the projection of its stage made for a greater intimacy between actors and audience. Although actors still had to project their voices and exaggerate their gestures, they could be heard and seen without the aid of the megaphonic masks and elevated shoes of the ancient Greek theater. Elizabethan actors could modulate their voices to vary pitch, stress, and intonation in ways unsuited to the Greek stage. They could also make wider and more subtle use of facial expression and gesture.

Cultural Impact

The Reformation of the Roman Church, which emerged from the Renaissance emphasis on individualism, had profound effects on western European society. With the decline of the authority of the Catholic Church, Europeans began to follow alternative religious beliefs and practices. Soon after Luther, Calvin, Zwingli, and Henry VIII had splintered the Catholic Church, their own churches fragmented and factionalized. In the ensuing centuries, numerous religious denominations were established, and hundreds of Protestant churches emerged.

A more general consequence of the Protestant Reformation was an emphasis on wealth. Personal wealth commanded respect as a mark of social status and a sign of divine favor. The virtues of discipline and effort necessary to achieving worldly success were Protestant values and fed directly into the emergence of capitalism.

The invention of movable type led to mass printing of reformist theological tracts. Gutenberg's press changed the way information was packaged, processed, and disseminated. Among the world's major revolutions, mechanized printing had an effect that lasted to the end of the millennium; only now in the twenty-first century, is the new age of electronic technology vying to displace print as the prime medium of communication.

The power of the individual genius creating works of enduring influence also finds expression in the north, more powerfully perhaps, in the work of its writers than in that of its painters, sculptors, and architects, who led the Renaissance in Italy. Who better than Montaigne and Shakespeare to epitomize the heights of achievement during the Elizabethan age, as they invented genres such as the personal essay and perfected those of the sonnet and the revenge tragedy? Moreover, Shakespeare set the standard for poetic excellence and dramatic accomplishment, his 37 plays having been translated into many of the world's languages and continue to be studied and dramatized today.

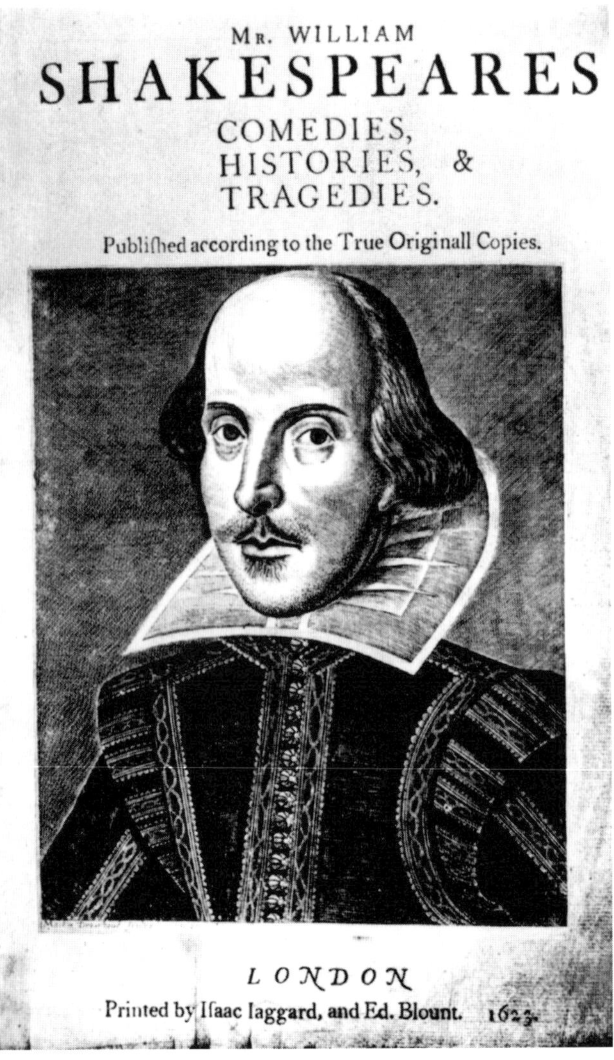

FIGURE 14.18 Cover of Shakespeare's First Folio, published in 1623, seven years after his death. This image of Shakespeare has become iconic.

In addition to greater intimacy, the Elizabethan stage also offered more versatility than its Greek counterpart. Although the Greek *skene* building could be used for scenes occurring above the ground, such as a god descending from above by means of a crane (***deus ex machina***), the Greek stage was really a single-level acting area. Not so the Elizabethan stage, which contained a second-level balcony, utilized in *Othello* and in *Romeo and Juliet*, for instance. Shakespeare's stage also had doors at the back for entrances and exits, a curtained alcove useful for scenes of intrigue, and a stage-floor trapdoor, used for the ghost's entrance in *Hamlet*.

These and other of Shakespeare's plays were given varied readings. *Julius Caesar* and other Roman plays, such as *Coriolanus*, were given classical settings to highlight Renaissance interest in the classical world. *Romeo and Juliet*, in contrast, was set in the Italian Renaissance, and *Hamlet* was set in the north, in Denmark.

KEY TERMS

egg tempera
triptych
iconographic
polyptych
disguised symbolism
alla prima
Reformation
disputation
iconoclasm
woodcut
engraving
burin
etching
genre painting
châteaux
secular music
madrigal
homophonic texture
soliloquy
blank verse
iambic pentameter
deus ex machina

www. WEBSITES FOR FURTHER STUDY

http://www.metmuseum.org/works_of_art/collection.asp
(Campin's The Annunciation Triptych exhibits the stylistic tendencies of the early Netherlands style.)

http://artchive.com/artchive/V/van_eyck.html
(This is the Artchive, a Website with virtually every major artist in every style from every era in art history. It is an excellent resource.)

http://mexplaza.udg.mx/wm/paint/auth/bosch/delight/
(The Webmuseum of Paris displays and discusses Bosch's most famous and unconventional picture, The Garden of Earthly Delights.*)*

http://www.iep.utm.edu/h/humanism.htm#Erasmus
(The Internet Encyclopedia of Philosophy is an excellent source for all the major philosophers.)

http://www.txdirect.net/users/rrichard/science.htm
(This is the Internet Chronology of Scientific Developments, listing all the important scientists from the sixteenth through the twentieth century.)

http://www.oldmusicproject.com/madrigals
(English madrigal site that includes information on numerous composers, as well as texts and music of their madrigals. Morley and Weelkes are both included.)

http://www.folger.com.edu
(The website of the Folger Library in Washington, D.C. Excellent site devoted to all aspects of Shakespeare's life and works.)

http://www2.lib.virginia.edu/rmds/portfolio/gordon/literary/montaigne
(Site devoted to works and life of Montaigne. Useful links to travel narratives about cannibals; helpful links to images.)

Chapter 15

History

1575	Order of Oratorians founded by St. Philip Neri
1598	Edict of Nantes ends French religious wars
1609	Galileo, telescope
1610	Henry IV assassinated
1622	Philip Neri, Teresa of Avila, Ignatius of Loyola canonized
1648	Peace of Westphalia ends Thirty Years' War
1649–52	Fronde rebellions against absolute monarch
1661	Louis XIV begins personal reign
1682	Louis XIV moves court to Versailles
1683	Leeuwenhoek sees microorganisms
1685	Louis XIV revokes Edict of Nantes

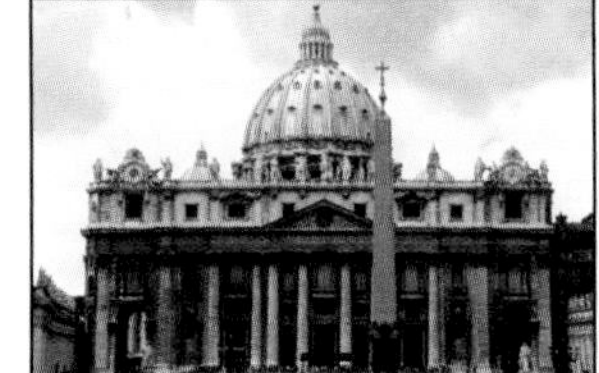

Arts and Architecture

ca. 1599–1602	Caravaggio, *Calling of St. Matthew*
1611	Peeters, *Table with a Tart and a White Pitcher*
1607	Pope Paul V commissions Maderno for St. Peter's Basilica; nave and facade completed; 1607–15 Monteverdi, *Orfeo*
ca. 1620	Gentileschi, *Judith Slaying Holofernes*
1622–25	Rubens, *Marie de' Medici, Queen of France, Landing in Marseilles*
1629	Pope Urban VIII commissions Bernini to finish St. Peter's Basilica; colonnade designed, 1657
1630	Hals, *Jolly Toper;* Moillon, *Still Life with Cherries, Strawberries, and Gooseberries*
1635	Leyster, *Boy Playing a Flute;* Van Dyck, *Portrait of Charles I*
1637	Poussin, *Rape of the Sabine Women*
1642	Rembrandt, *The Night Watch*
1645–52	Bernini, *Ecstasy of St. Teresa*
1648	Royal Academy of Painting and Sculpture established
1656	Velázquez, *Maids of Honor*
1663	Sirani, *Virgin and Child*
1665	Vermeer, *Young Woman with a Water Pitcher*
1638–67	Borromini, *San Carlo*
1667–70	Le Vau, Le Brun, Perrault, east facade of the Louvre
ca. 1670	Beale, John Wilkins DD
1669–85	Le Vau, Hardouin-Mansart, Le Brun, and Coysevox, Palace of Versailles
1694	Pozzo, *Triumph of St. Ignatius Loyola*
1710	Wren, St Paul's Cathedral
1721	J. S. Bach, *Brandenburg Concertos*
ca. 1725	Vivaldi, *The Four Seasons*
1742	Handel, *Messiah*

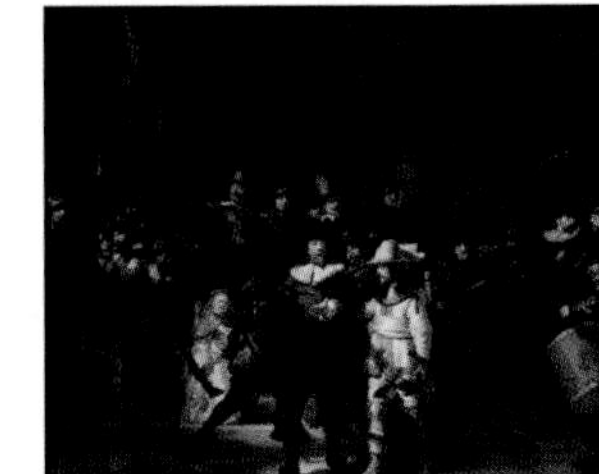

Literature and Philosophy

1548	St. Ignatius of Loyola, *Spiritual Exercises*
1565	St. Teresa of Avila, *Life*
1582–84	St. John of the Cross, *The Dark Night of the Soul*
1601	Donne, *Songs and Sonnets*
1605	Cervantes, *Don Quixote*
1641	Descartes, *Meditations*
1651	Hobbes, *Leviathan*
1658	Louis XIV becomes patron of Molière, Molière, *Tartuffe,* 1664
1667–70	Milton, *Paradise Lost*
1690	Locke, *Essay on Human Understanding*

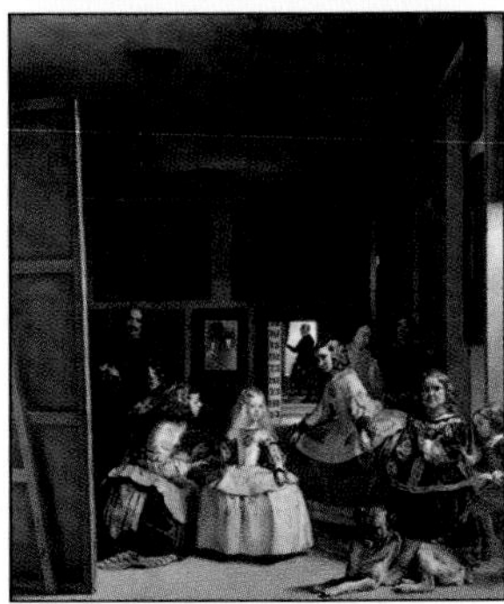

Baroque Age

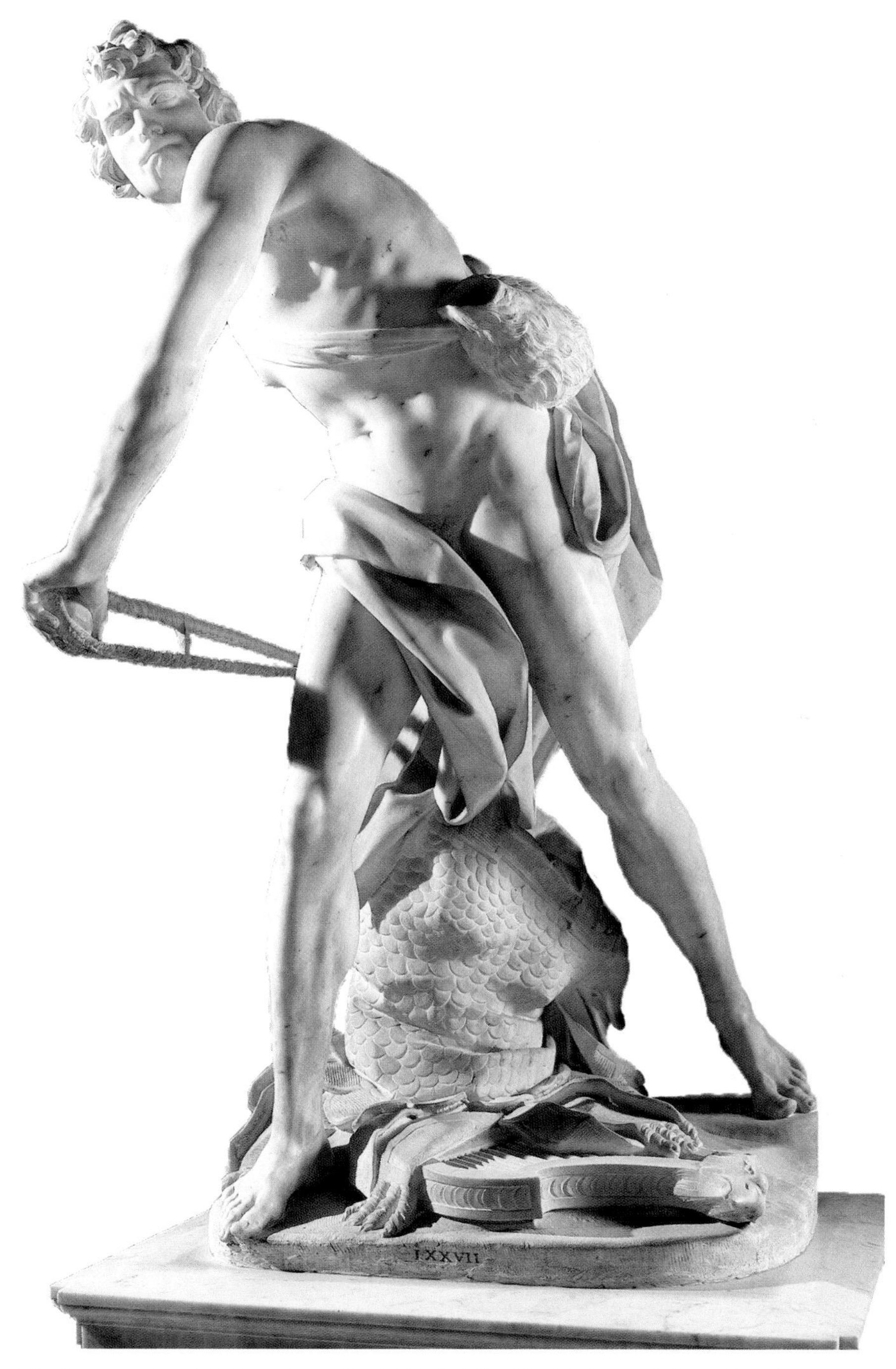

Gianlorenzo Bernini, *David*, marble, 1623, height 5′70″ (1.7 m), Galleria Borghese, Rome.

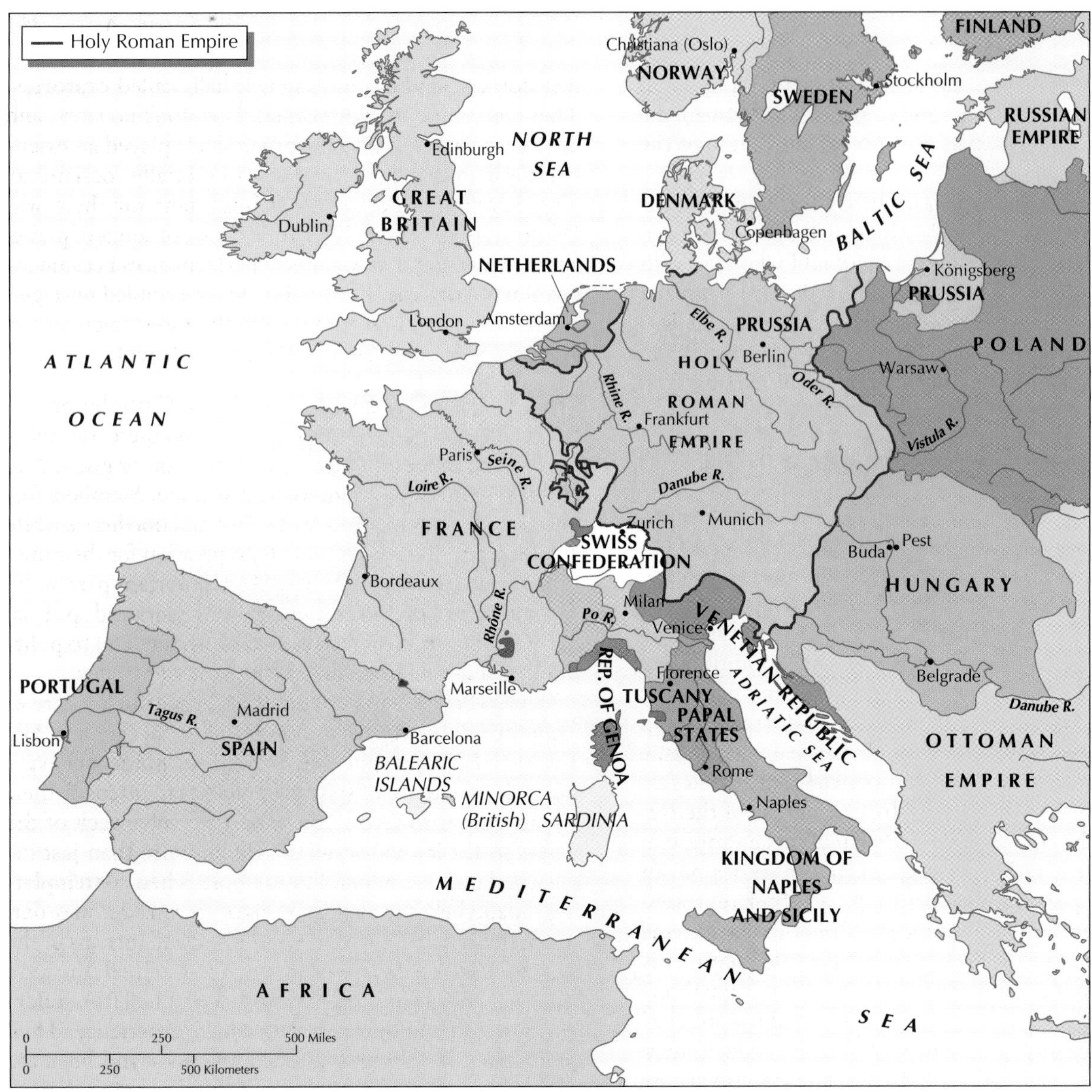

Map 15.1 Europe in the early 1700s.

CHAPTER OVERVIEW

BAROQUE IN ITALY

Drama and illusion dominate the arts

BAROQUE OUTSIDE ITALY

Diversity rules the arts and sciences

BAROQUE IN ITALY

THE TERM **BAROQUE,** FROM THE PORTUGUESE word *barrocco,* meaning a large, irregularly shaped pearl, was initially used as a pejorative, or negative, term. Gradually it came to describe the complex, multifaceted, international phenomenon of the Baroque. Baroque artists intended to involve their audiences emotionally. Formally, the style is characterized by drama and theatricality seen in a heightened realism and illusions of motion. Classical elements are used without classical restraint. Emotionalism is enhanced by striking contrasts of light and shadow.

At least as important in defining the Baroque style is understanding the patronage that supported it. Church-sponsored art in Rome thrived during the Counter-Reformation. Although secular patrons were important in the development of Baroque art (particularly Philip IV in Spain and Marie de' Medici and Louis XIV in France), the Church in Rome assumed the role of the center of the Baroque art world.

As pope succeeded pope, each brought with him an entourage of family and friends who expected and received lucrative positions in the government and who vied with each other to give expression to their newfound wealth and position. The popes commissioned palaces and chapels—along with paintings and sculptures to decorate them. Artists flocked to Rome to take advantage of the situation.

THE COUNTER-REFORMATION IN ROME

In response to Martin Luther's "Ninety-Five Theses" and the Protestant Reformation that followed, the Catholic Church sought to remake Rome as the cultural center of the Western world. Thus once again Roman popes became great patrons of art and architecture. The strategy to defend Rome's prestige and dominion was continued for over a hundred years, culminating in the twenty-one-year pontificate of Urban VIII (r. 1623–44).

The theological justification for this patronage came at the Council of Trent, which convened in three sessions from 1545 to 1563 to address the crisis of the Reformation. The council decided to counter the Protestant threat "by means of the stories of the mysteries of our Redemption portrayed by paintings or other representations, [whereby] the people [shall] be instructed and confirmed in the habit of remembering, and continually revolving in mind the articles of faith." The council further suggested that religious art be directed toward clarity (to increase understanding), realism (to make it more meaningful in everyday fashion), and emotion (to arouse piety and religious fervor). Taken together, these goals epitomized the Catholic **Counter-Reformation.**

According to the council's recommendations, art ought to be easily understood. Music had to be accessible and lyrics intelligible. Literature should celebrate religious values and ideals. These recommendations were intended to counter the Mannerist style. Mannerist painting tended to be refined, stylized, virtuosic, decorative, and complex in color, structure, and allegorical content. Baroque art was to make direct statements on religious subjects familiar to the common people. Still, from the Mannerists, Baroque artists inherited a reliance on emotionally charged and dramatic action. The Council of Trent began a renewal of faith, stirring religious fervor through church art and architecture, and through liturgies, rituals, and dogmas.

Two new religious orders emerged from the Council of Trent, the Oratorians and the Jesuits. Both were of central importance to the religious mission.

Oratorians. Founded by St. Philip Neri, the Oratorians were groups of Catholics, laymen and clergy, who met informally for spiritual conversation, study, and prayer. They met not in churches but in prayer halls called **oratories.** They were not a religious order: They took no vows, and members could leave at any time. Music played an essential role in their religious devotions, especially vocal music. The composer who was most important for them was Palestrina (see Chapter 13), whose *Laude*, or songs of praise, were easy to sing. Later, musical performances became increasingly dramatic. Eventually, they resembled unstaged miniature music dramas and were the forerunners of the oratorios written by George Frederick Handel.

Jesuits. In 1534, the Jesuit order of Catholic priests was established by St. Ignatius Loyola, and there was nothing informal about the Jesuits' organization or goals. The order was to follow a militaristic discipline. Members followed strict vows of poverty, chastity, and obedience while pursuing a rigorous education in preparation for their missionary role. Jesuit priests played an important part in the religious life of the age, serving as confessors and spiritual advisers to prominent artists such as Bernini and to political leaders, including Queen Christina of Sweden.

The most influential aspect of Jesuit spirituality derives from the writings of the order's founder, St. Ignatius. His *Spiritual Exercises*, published in 1548, guide believers through a sequence of spiritual practices to intensify their relationship with God. The *Exercises* involve each of the senses so the individual might obtain more than just intellectual understanding. For example, when contemplating sin and hell, the soul is exhorted to consider in order: the sights of hell (flames); the sounds of hell (groans of the damned and shrieks of devils); the smells of hell (the fetid stench of corrupting bodies); the tastes of hell (the suffering of hunger and thirst); and the tactile experience of hell (the intense heat, which scorches the body and boils the blood). Such exercises involved the emotions in religious experience, the hallmark of Baroque sensibility.

Complementing the work of the Oratorians and the Jesuits were the writings of sixteenth- and seventeenth-century Spanish mystics such as St. John of the Cross, who wrote *The Dark Night of the Soul*, and St. Teresa of Avila, who wrote an autobiography. Both blended the contemplative life with a commitment to a life of action. Teresa of Avila was canonized by Pope Gregory XV in 1622, along with Philip Neri and Ignatius of Loyola.

THIRTY YEARS' WAR

During the thirty-year period from 1618 to 1648, a series of wars raged throughout central Europe. On one side was a coalition consisting of the Austrian Hapsburg Holy Roman Emperors, Ferdinand I and II, with their Spanish cousin King Philip IV. Opposing them were Denmark, France, Holland, and Sweden. In addition, various German principalities fought on both sides. There was also a religious dimension to the war, with Lutherans, Catholics, and Calvinists fighting one another at various times.

The war occurred when the Peace of Augsburg (1555), which had ended violence between Lutherans and Catholics in Germany, became frayed. Tensions were exacerbated by rising political tensions throughout Europe, as Denmark, France, Spain, and Sweden all had designs, for different reasons, on German lands. Fought primarily on German lands, the war resulted in the deaths of about one-third of the German population.

The consequences of the war were significant. Spain declined both politically and militarily, with Portugal declaring its independence from Spain in 1640. With Germany fractured into many competing territories, France grew in power. Other effects included an end to the age of mercenaries, or hired soldiers. The Peace of Westphalia (1648), which concluded the Thirty Years' War, ended the era of the Holy Roman Empire and religious unity, inaugurating a new era in which sovereign nation states controlled politics and diplomacy in Europe.

ARCHITECTURE AND SCULPTURE IN ROME

St. Peter's Basilica. The Church's most visible effort to arouse the faithful was the continued work on St. Peter's Basilica (fig. 15.1), work initiated by Pope Julius II in 1502. In 1607, Pope Paul V commissioned CARLO MADERNO [mah-DEHR-no] (1556–1629) as Vatican architect to convert Michelangelo's unfinished Greek-cross plan into a Latin cross plan complete with a new facade. There was a practical reason for this: The long nave of the Latin cross plan provided space for more people to attend services. The interior space Maderno created was the largest of any church in Europe, meant to evoke the vastness of God himself.

Maderno's facade (fig. 15.2) followed Michelangelo's conception of using the colossal order to unite the stories and of topping the entrance with a triangular pediment. In fact, Maderno's composition is even more theatrical than Michelangelo intended. Pope Paul V conceived of the

FIGURE 15.1 Bramantés' view of St. Peter's, Rome. St. Peter's underwent so many changes that only a hint of the simplicity of Bramantés and Michelangelo's original Greek cross plans remains.

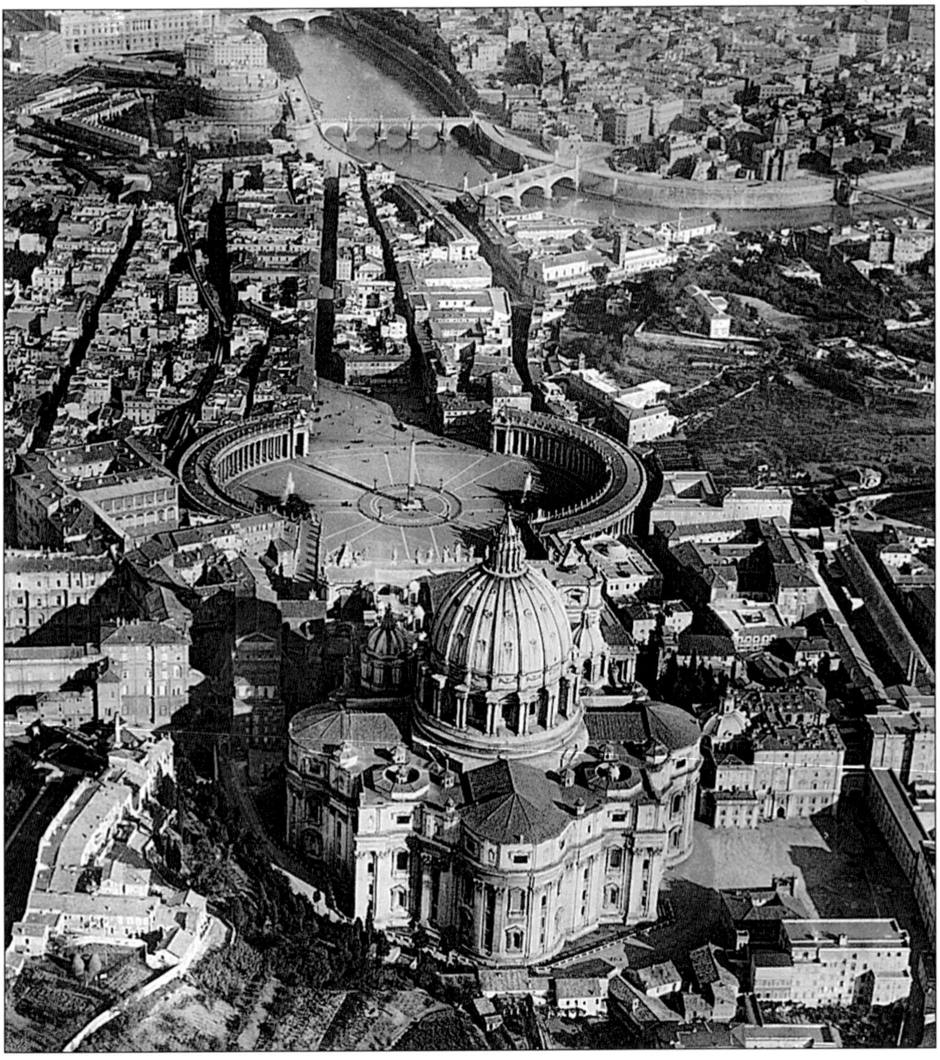

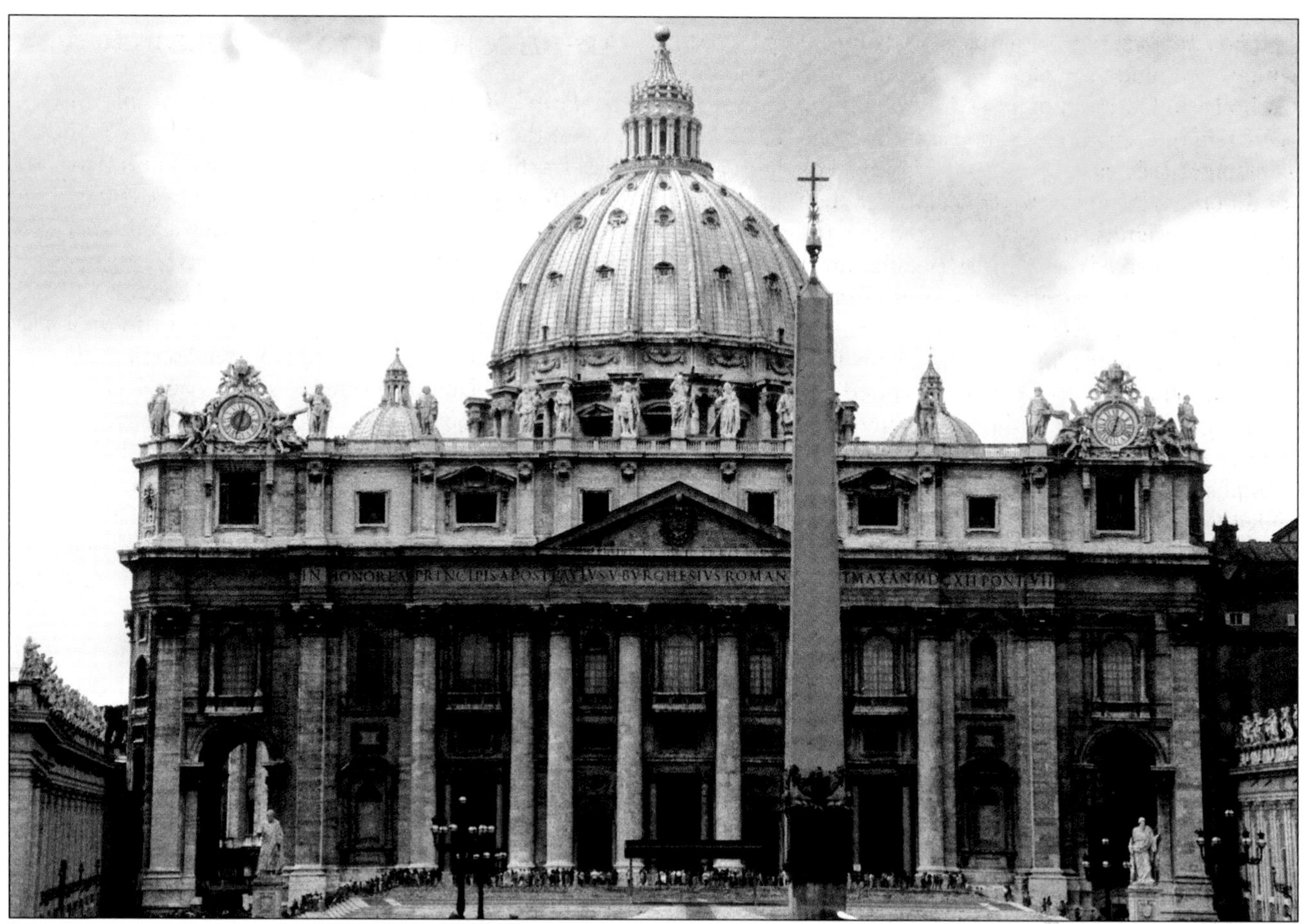

FIGURE 15.2 Carlo Maderno, facade of St. Peter's, Rome, 1607–15, height 147′ (44.81 m), width 374′ (114 m). The facade is treated like a theatrical performance that builds from the wings: Starting from the corners, the pilasters double, then become columns, which then also double, and, finally, the center section seems to push out to meet the visitor.

church facade as a backdrop to his own public appearances and required a balcony from which he could bless the people below. An architectural crescendo rises from the sides of the facade toward the central portal, generating a dramatic, which is to say Baroque, effect.

Gianlorenzo Bernini. The theatricality of Maderno's facade was only a beginning. When Maderno died in 1629, Pope Urban VIII replaced him with GIANLORENZO BERNINI [ber-NEE-nee] (1598–1680), who had collaborated with Maderno for five years. Although Bernini considered himself a classicist, he fused his classicism with extraordinary drama and emotion. His sculpture and architecture are the essence of Baroque art.

In 1657, Bernini, now working for another pope, designed and supervised the building of a ***colonnade,*** or row of columns, in front of St. Peter's. Beginning in two straight covered walkways, or **porticoes,** the Doric columns extend down a slight incline from the church facade, then swerve into two enormous curved porticoes, surrounding and embracing the open space of the piazza, like "the motherly arms of the church," as Bernini himself put it (fig. 15.3). Forgoing the square and circular forms of the Renaissance, Bernini's colonnade uses the more dynamic ellipse and trapezoid. In the center of the oval plaza stands an **obelisk,** or four-sided shaft topped by a pyramid. From there, lines on the pavement radiate out to the colonnade. Finally, surmounting each inner column is a different statue, creating an irregular silhouette along the top of the colonnade.

Bernini's sculpture of *David* (fig. 15.4), carved in 1623 and characteristic of his style, deserves comparison to Michelangelo's High Renaissance *David* (see Chapter 13). In its depiction of drama, Bernini's work is close to Hellenistic sculpture as embodied in the *Laocoön* (Chapter 3), which Bernini had studied. Michelangelo's *David*, by contrast, seems restrained. Bernini captures the split second before David flings the stone that kills Goliath, implying a second figure to "complete" the action. *David's* pose and facial expression charge the space surrounding the sculpture with tension, so effectively that people viewing the statue avoid standing between *David* and his implied target.

Bernini's *Ecstasy of St. Teresa* (fig. 15.5) is the most impressive sculpture created to celebrate the life of a Counter-Reformation saint. Bernini designed it for the Cornaro Chapel of Santa Maria della Vittoria in Rome and positioned it in an oval niche above the altar, framed by green

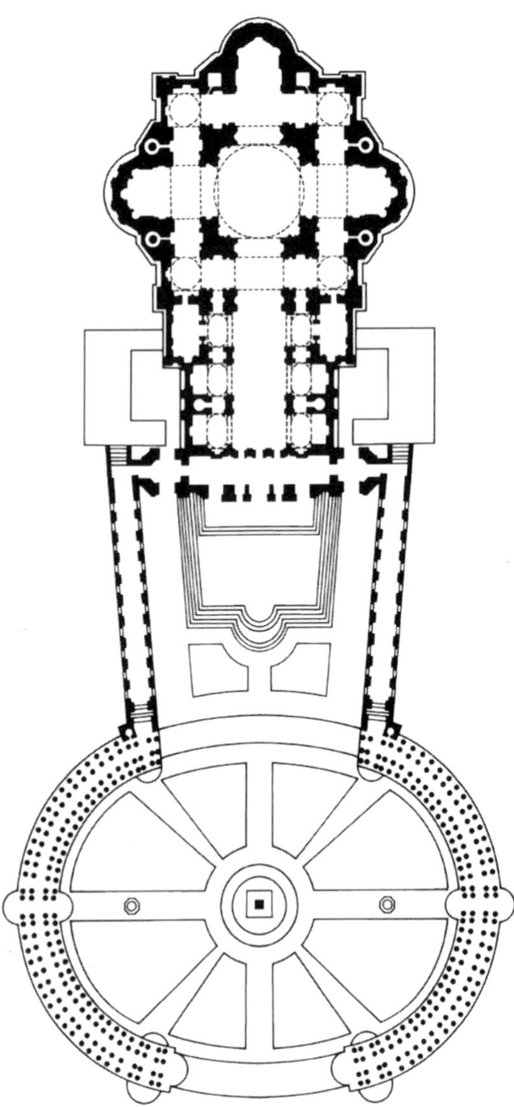

FIGURE 15.3 St. Peter's Rome, plan. Maderno's Latin cross plan of St. Peter's is preceded by Bernini's colonnades that create a dynamic architectural environment of elliptical and trapezoidal shapes.

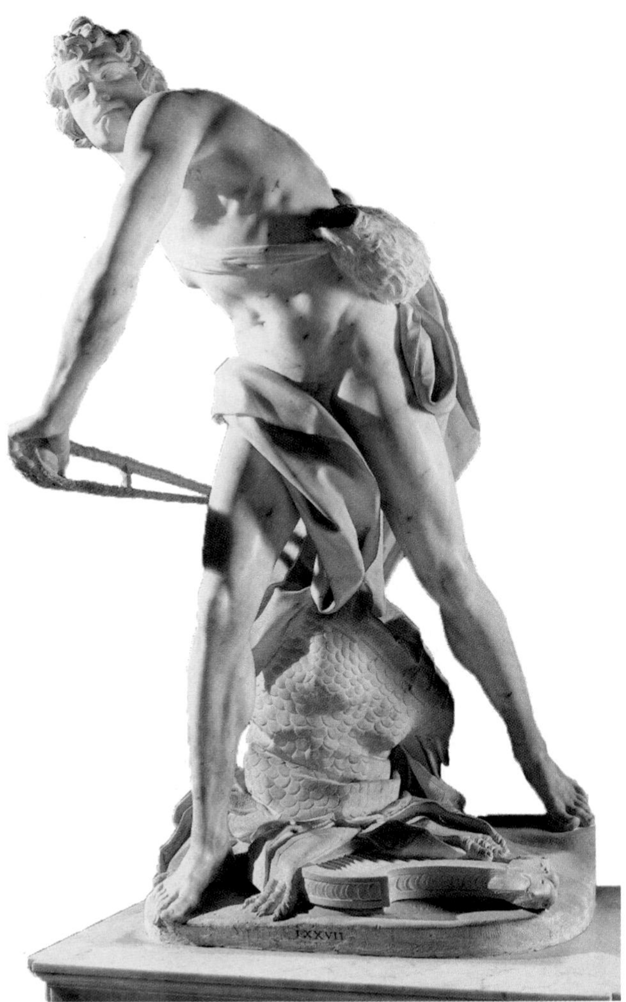

FIGURE 15.4 Gianlorenzo Bernini, *David*, marble, 1623, height 5′7″ (1.7 m), Galleria Borghese, Rome. Unlike Michelangelo's static *David*, Bernini's is caught at the split second when the direction of the action is about to reverse—much like the ancient Greek *Discus Thrower* (fig 3.13). Bernini effectively indicates the position of the giant Goliath, something that is sensed by viewers, who quickly move out of the implied line of fire.

marble pilasters. Created between 1645 and 1652, the multimedia sculpture depicts the moment in St. Teresa's autobiography when she says an angel pierced her heart with a flaming golden arrow, causing her to swoon in pleasure and agony. "The pain was so great that I screamed aloud," she wrote, "but at the same time I felt such infinite sweetness that I wished the pain to last forever. . . . It was the sweetest caressing of the soul by God." Abandoning Renaissance restraint, Bernini captures the sensuality of her ecstasy.

Francesco Borromini. FRANCESCO BORROMINI [Bor-ro-MEE-nee] (1599–1667) joined his uncle, Carlo Maderno, in Rome in 1619 and was soon working for Bernini in St. Peter's. But Borromini quickly became Bernini's chief rival, and unlike the worldly Bernini, Borromini was a secretive and unstable man whose life ended in suicide.

Borromini is best known for San Carlo alle Quattro Fontane (fig. 15.6), or St. Charles of the Four Fountains, named for the fountains at the junction where it is located in Rome. The interior of the church was designed between 1638 and 1641, and the facade between 1665 and 1667. On a tiny and irregular plot, Borromini built a tiny and irregular church: San Carlo could fit easily within Saint Peter's. Deviating from the classical tradition, the columns are of no known order—instead, Borromini designed a new order of his own. Rather than building with the traditional flat surfaces of ancient architecture, Borromini made the stone facade seem elastic, curving in and out, the stone appearing to undulate in a serpentine concave-convex motion. So three dimensional is this facade that it almost becomes sculpture, rippling with light and shade in Rome's sunlight.

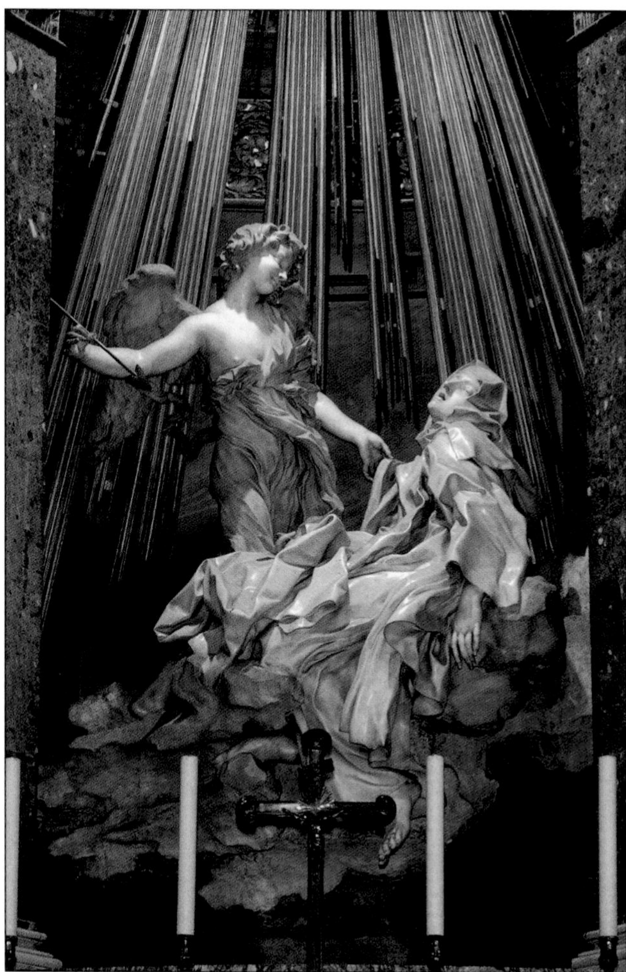

FIGURE 15.5 Gianlorenzo Bernini, *Ecstasy of St. Teresa*, overview of Cornaro Chapel, 1645–52, height of figure group 11′6″ (3.51 m), Santa Maria della Vittoria, Rome. This dramatic depiction of Teresa's written description is literally theatrical, for the chapel is arranged like a theater, complete with box seats occupied by marble figures of members of the Cornaro family.

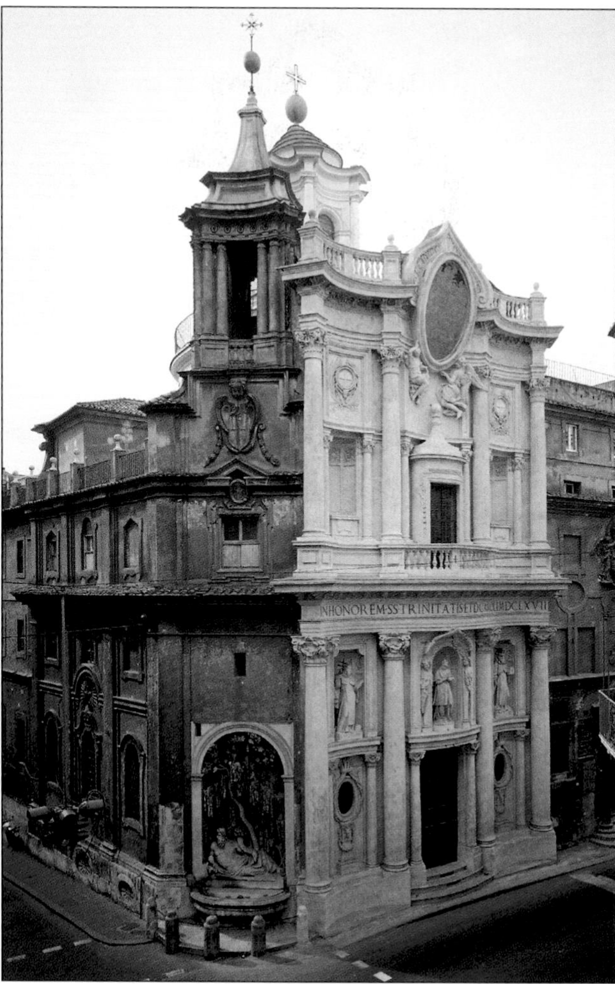

FIGURE 15.6 Francesco Borromini, San Carlo alle Quattro Fontane, Rome 1638–67, width of facade 34′ (10.36 m). Because this church is located at an intersection of narrow streets, the viewer cannot easily see the entire facade. Borromini therefore created two separate compositions, undulating and sculptural, linked by the entablature of the lower story that forms a balcony for the upper story.

Borromini designed San Carlo alle Quattro Fontane with a double facade, a clever solution to a practical problem. The church faces so small an intersection that it is not possible to stand back far enough to view the facade in its entirety. Borromini's double facade divides the surface into two smaller compositions, yet the entablature of the lower story forms the balcony of the upper story, typical of the Baroque concern for unity of design.

Borromini's extravagant style was popular. The head of the religious order for whom San Carlo alle Quattro Fontane was built wrote with great pride, "Nothing similar can be found anywhere else in the world. This is attested by the foreigners who . . . try to procure copies of the plan. We have been asked for them by Germans, Flemings, Frenchmen, Italians, Spaniards, and even Indians."

PAINTING IN ITALY

As with sculptors and architects, the demand for painters during the Counter-Reformation was enormous. Although some were hired to work permanently for a given patron, by far the majority worked in studios in Rome, displaying their works in progress and seeking commissions. Competition for the best artists was fierce, and as a result their social standings (and fees) rose ever higher.

Caravaggio. One of the most important art patrons was Cardinal Scipione Borghese, nephew of Pope Paul. Borghese's villa contained a vast quantity of paintings and frescoes and was set in a large park full of niches and statuary. One of Borghese's favorite painters was CARAVAGGIO [ka-ra-VAH-joh] (1573–1610), whose real name was Michelangelo Merisi but who took his name from his birthplace, the village

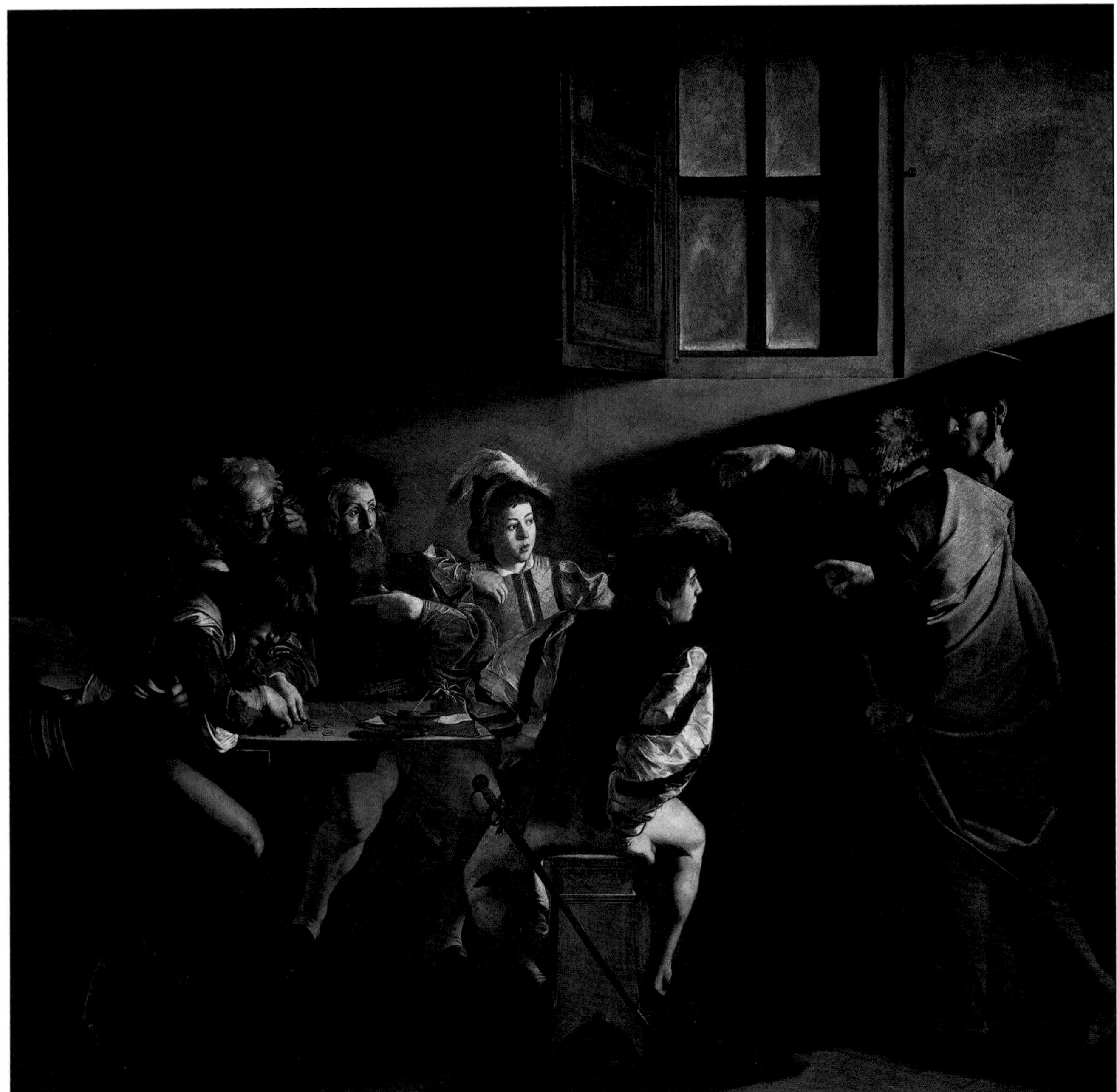

FIGURE 15.7 Caravaggio, *Calling of St. Matthew*, ca. 1599–1602, oil on canvas, 11′1″ × 11′5″ (3.38 × 3.48 m). Contarelli Chapel, San Luigi dei Francesi, Rome. Although Matthew is seated in a tavern when he receives Jesus's call, Caravaggio uses tenebristic lighting to reveal the religious nature of this event.

of Caravaggio near Milan. Caravaggio was a Bohemian artist with a terrible temper who led a short and turbulent life (with a long police record bordering on the criminal). Despite his lifestyle, Caravaggio was a great religious painter whose work established the major direction of painting in the Baroque age.

Caravaggio painted the *Calling of St. Matthew* (fig. 15.7) in about 1599–1602 for the private chapel of the Contarelli family in the Church of San Luigi dei Francesi in Rome. A large painting, it depicts the climactic moment of Matthew's calling. As told in the Bible, Matthew 9:9. Jesus points to the tax collector Matthew, who gestures with disbelief, as if to say, "Who? Me?"

This biblical tale, shown in the everyday environment of a Roman tavern, is enacted by people who could have been Caravaggio's contemporaries (who were probably the models for the work). Although Matthew and his associates are richly attired, the two figures on the right are in rags. Jesus's halo is barely visible. Yet a religious atmosphere is created by Caravaggio's dramatic use of light, known as **tenebrism**—a "dark manner," in which light and dark contrast strongly, the highlights picking out only what the artist wants the viewer to see. The light comes from above, like a spotlight centering on an actor on stage, but no obvious light source is shown.

Artemisia Gentileschi. The emotional and dramatic side of the Baroque is demonstrated also by ARTEMISIA GENTILESCHI [jen-tee-LESS-kee] (1593–ca. 1653). Born in Rome, her style seems to have been influenced by that of her father, Orazio Gentileschi, a painter in Caravaggio's style. She was herself known as one of several "Caravaggisti," or "night painters," whose work was identifiable by the use of tenebrism.

Gentileschi's paintings often depicted the popular biblical subjects of Bathsheba and David and of Judith and Holofernes. Her *Judith Slaying Holofernes* (fig. 15.8), painted ca. 1620, conveys intrigue and violence. The beautiful Jewish widow Judith saved her people from Nebuchadnezzar's Assyrian army by enticing their leader, Holofernes, into a tent where he drank himself to sleep. She then cut off his head with his own sword. The unnerving drama is enhanced by the dark tenebristic lighting that spotlights the actors as if on stage. The large figures fill the picture and seem to crowd forward as if about to burst through the picture plane.

Gentileschi's paintings have been linked to a sexual assault at the age of fifteen by one of her teachers. Later she was tortured in court with a thumbscrew (a device designed to compress the thumb to the point of smashing it) to verify the validity of her accusation.

Elisabetta Sirani. During her brief life of only twenty-seven years, the extremely prolific painter ELISABETTA SIRANI [Elis-ah-BEHT-tah see-RAH-nee] (1638–1665) of Bologna was in charge of the family shop and supported her parents and three siblings through the sale of her art. Known for the speed with which she produced finished paintings, she achieved international fame and her paintings were sought by the most important patrons. Her early death followed immediately after severe abdominal pains. When an autopsy discovered perforated ulcers, the maid accused of poisoning her was acquitted.

Her painting of the *Virgin and Child* (fig. 15.9), dated to 1663, shows the sentimentality that charmed her patrons. Mary's gesture could be no gentler without losing

FIGURE 15.8 Artemisia Gentileschi, *Judith Slaying Holofernes*, ca. 1620, oil on canvas, 6′6$\frac{1}{3}$″ × 5′4″ (1.99 × 1.63 m). Galleria degli Uffizi, Florence. SCALA/Art Resource, NY. Drama and horror are magnified by the proximity of the figures and by the powerful spotlight focusing attention on the beheading, leaving all else in shadow.

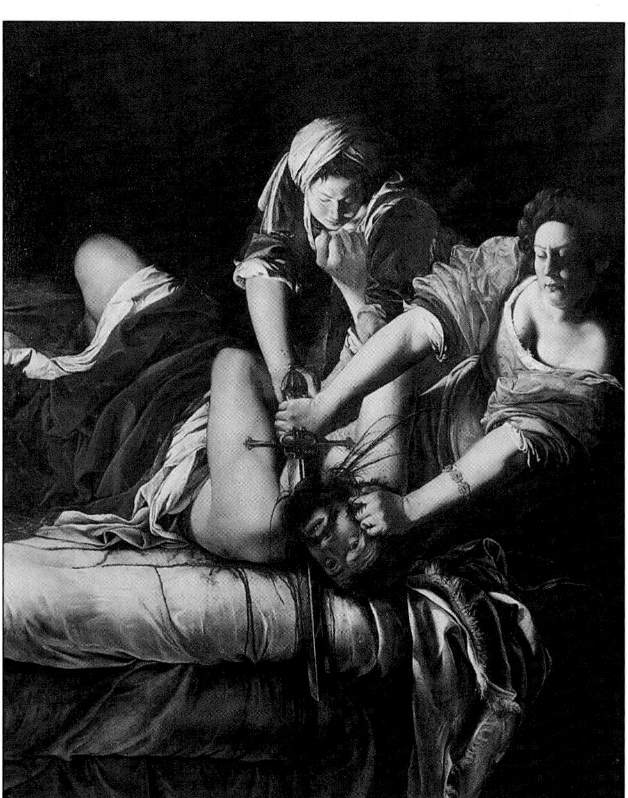

FIGURE 15.9 Elisabetta Sirani, *Virgin and Child*, 1663, oil on canvas, 34″ × 27$\frac{1}{2}$″ (86.4 × 69.9 cm), National Museum of Women in the Arts, Washington, DC. Gift of Wallace and Wilhelmina Holladay. Conservation funds generously provided by the Southern California State Committee of the National Museum of Women in the Arts. The Baroque interest in emotion, in this case sweet, sentimental, and touching, is seen in Sirani's painting. Also characteristic of the Baroque are the lush full-bodied figures and the facility with which they are painted.

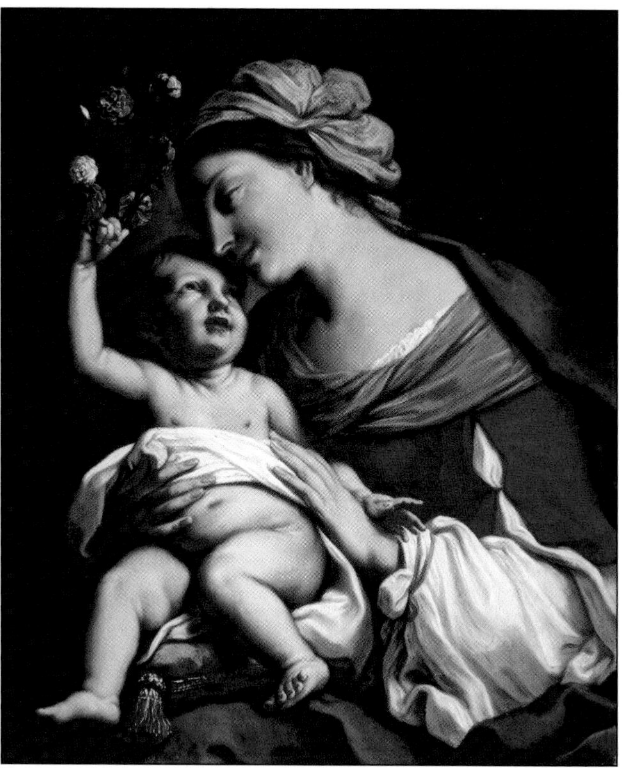

hold of her twisting infant, whose animation contrasts to Mary's slow movement. The exchange of gazes endears, as Mary leans forward so that Jesus may crown her with a flower garland. Sirani signed her work in the embroidered band on the pillow on which Jesus sits.

Giovanna Garzoni. In contrast to the Baroque emotional drama and obscuring shadows is the work of GIOVANNA GARZONI [Gee-oh-VAHN-nah Gar-ZONE-ee] (1600–1670), for although she painted various subjects, she is remembered for her depictions of still life, a subject already popular in Northern Europe from the late sixteenth century onward. In the *Plate of White Peas* (fig. 15.10) the composition is simple and the subject is ordinary, down to the degree of decay beginning to appear on the leaves and pods. The appeal of Garzoni's paintings is based largely upon her impressive technical skill and ability to simulate in paint what the eye sees, down to the tiniest and most meticulously rendered detail.

Like some successful male artists of her day, Garzoni did not marry and instead traveled from one city to the next. Thus, she accommodated her patrons in Venice, Florence, Naples, and Rome, arriving there by 1654 and remaining in this city thereafter.

Fra Andrea Pozzo. The epitome of the illusionistic Baroque ceiling fresco was achieved by FRA ANDREA POZZO [POT-zoh] (1642–1709), in his depiction of the *Triumph of St. Ignatius of Loyola* (fig. 15.11), of 1691–94, on the nave ceiling of Sant'Ignazio, Rome. The effect is astonishing; the solid vault of the ceiling has been painted away. It is an extreme example of what the Italians called *quadratura*, used to trick the eye into believing that the architecture of the church, its columns and arches, extends past the actual ceiling. The perspective is calculated to be seen from a specific point marked on the floor. When standing there, it is difficult to determine where the real architecture ends and the painted architecture begins. The center of the ceiling appears to be open sky from which saints and angels descend. Some sit on painted architecture or clouds; others fly through space in a dazzling display of Baroque artistic dexterity.

FIGURE 15.10 Giovanna Garzoni, *Plate of White Peas*, undated, tempera on parchment, $9\frac{3}{4}'' \times 13\frac{1}{2}''$ (25 × 33 cm). Palazzo Pitti, Florence. Technically, working in a water-based medium on animal skin and painting the tiniest details, this recalls medieval manuscript illuminations. But the extreme degree of fidelity to the visible world and direct study from a model in Garzoni's work contrasts with the medieval preference for distortion and avoidance of firsthand study of nature.

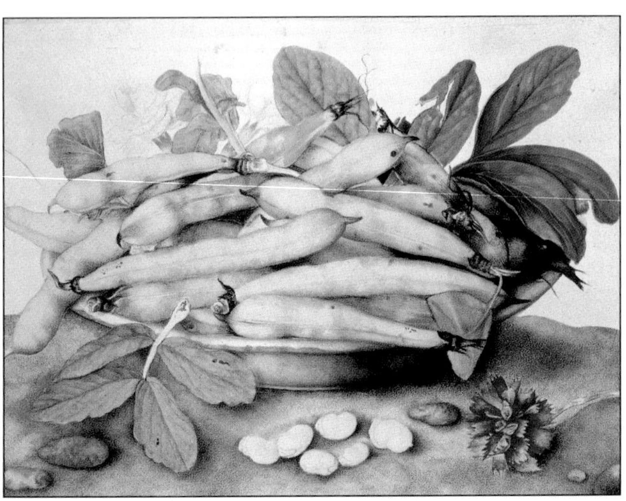

MUSIC IN ITALY

Claudio Monteverdi and Early Opera. It is hardly surprising, given the dramatic theatricality of Baroque painting, that the Baroque era produced the musical form known as **opera,** the Italian word for "a work." *Opera drammatica in musica*, "a dramatic work in music," has been abbreviated to "opera." Combining vocal music, instrumental music, and theater, an opera is a staged drama sung to the accompaniment of an orchestra. Opera developed among a group of humanists in Florence, who were interested in reviving the arts of ancient Greece. The creation of accompanied melodies with dramatic presentation was thought to be similar to the original Greek performances that had occurred between acts of plays. The emotional content of the voice, accompanied by instruments and combined with drama, was one of the most powerful forms to develop during the Baroque era. Opera epitomized the spirit of the Baroque in its flamboyant and theatrical style.

The first operas were written and performed before 1600, but the first notable work in the genre, *Orfeo* (*Orpheus*) by CLAUDIO MONTEVERDI [mon-teh-VAIR-dee] (1567–1643), was composed for his patron, the duke of Mantua, in 1607. It retells the Greek myth of Orpheus, the poet and musician who goes down to Hades, the underworld, to bring back his dead wife, Eurydice.

The opera includes **recitative,** a form of musically heightened speech midway between spoken dialogue and melodic aria. Orpheus's recitative is a monologue in the "agitated style," which expresses musically the feelings described by the text. For example, the melody descends on the words *più profondi abissi* ("deepest abysses") and ascends to accompany the words *a riverder le stelle* ("to see again the stars").

Singing the women's parts in opera throughout the Baroque were "castrati," men who had been castrated before puberty to maintain their "boy soprano" vocal qualities. The high register of the boy, coupled with the strength and power of an adult voice, was popular with audiences during the seventeenth and eighteenth centuries. The demand for vocal virtuosity in lead singers in opera and later in solo performances meant castrati often had much wealth and prestige.

The orchestra accompanying Baroque operas consisted of groups of small ensembles and was used to affect the "feelings" produced by the libretto, or text. Pastoral scenes

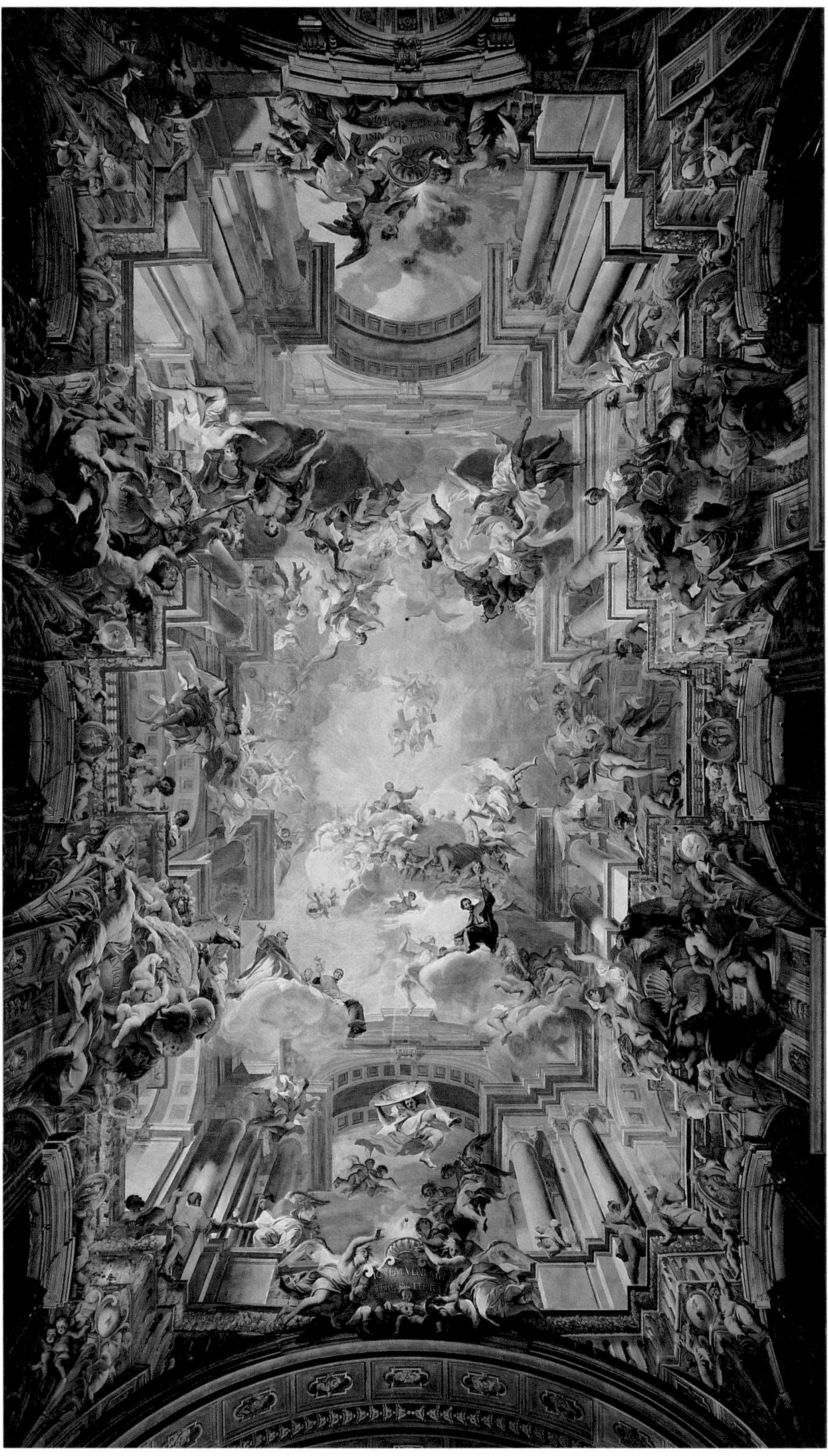

FIGURE 15.11 Fra Andrea Pozzo, *Triumph of St. Ignatius of Loyola*, 1691–94, ceiling fresco, Sant Ignazio, Rome. If the viewer stands directly below the center of this quintessentially Baroque illusionistic ceiling painting, it is not possible to see where the actual architecture ends and the painted architecture begins.

might be accompanied by recorders or scenes of heaven by a harp. This process paved the way for program music in the centuries to follow.

Antonio Vivaldi and the Concerto Grosso. Invented by ARCANGELO CORELLI [ko-REL-lee] (1653–1713), the ***concerto grosso*** is an instrumental musical form consisting of three parts, or movements, for soloists and orchestra pitted against one another in dramatic contrast. Typically, the first movement of a Baroque concerto is energetic and spirited, the second is slow but with increasing tension, and the third and final movement more vigorous than the first, releasing the tensions built up earlier.

One of the most prolific Baroque composers of the concerto was ANTONIO VIVALDI [vee-VAHL-dee] (1678–1741), who wrote 450 concertos, forty operas, and numerous vocal and chamber works. Born in Venice in 1678, Vivaldi, an ordained priest, spent most of his life as music master at a Venetian school for orphaned girls here, the Ospedele della pietà, which had an excellent choir and orchestra, and which was one of Venice's main attractions. Many of Vivaldi works were composed for student recitals.

Vivaldi's most popular work is *The Four Seasons*, a set of four concertos for solo violin and orchestra. Each of Vivaldi's four concertos—Winter, Spring, Summer, and Fall—is accompanied by a sonnet describing the appropriate season. In the original edition, the words were printed above musical passages that depicted the words in sound. The Spring Concerto, for instance, includes descriptions of chirping birds returning to the meadows, and has accompanying sections called "bird calls" in which one violin "calls" and another answers it.

The first eight lines of the sonnet are distributed throughout the first movement of the Spring Concerto, an Allegro in E major. The movement opens with a phrase played twice in succession, once loud and once softly as an echo. This is followed by a ***ritornello*** passage that will return repeatedly throughout the movement. The ritornello section is played by the entire instrumental group in alternation with sections for the solo violin. The ritornello form pervades not only Vivaldi's music but the Baroque concerto generally. Different textures in solo and ensemble sections are supplemented by abrupt contrasts in dynamics from loud to soft (terraced dynamics) and by contrasting imitations of bird-song and storm.

But interesting as such musical scene painting may be, the primary interest of Vivaldi's music is its use of themes, textures, and tone colors in structured repetitions and contrasts that identify him as a master of the concerto style. Inventive within a formal structure, Vivaldi's music was soon admired throughout Europe, and closely studied by Johann Sebastian Bach, the great composer of the age. The play between control and freedom appealed to an age at once attracted to the classicism of a Bernini colonnade and the fantasy of a Borromini facade.

BAROQUE OUTSIDE ITALY

Baroque art, especially painting, originated in Italy. Many of the Baroque artists whom we identify with other countries either lived, worked, or studied in Rome, including the French painter Nicolas Poussin, the Spanish painter Diego Velázquez, and the Flemish painter Peter Paul Rubens. If they did not go to Rome, they were usually influenced by Roman Baroque painting, particularly Caravaggio, who enjoyed a considerable reputation outside Italy. Nonetheless, the Baroque thrived outside Italy: in the low countries, Flanders and Holland, where a flourishing mercantile class became deeply interested in the arts; in Spain, where Philip IV amassed a collection; in England, where Charles I did the same; in France, where Marie de' Medici, regent for the young King Louis XIV, exerted influence over the French court; and in Germany, where Baroque music was particularly well received.

PAINTING IN HOLLAND

During the reign of Philip II of Spain, the northern provinces of The Netherlands rebelled against his repression of Protestants and formed a new Dutch republic; the southern provinces remained Catholic and loyal to Spain, thus creating the separate countries of Holland and Flanders.

A distinct brand of Baroque painting emerged in Holland, which in the seventeenth century was a country of merchants and tradespeople who found themselves, freed of Spanish rule, the sudden beneficiaries of having Amsterdam, the maritime center and commercial capital of Europe, as their capital city.

In Holland not just religious and political leaders but also merchants and tradespeople collected art. The English traveler Peter Mundy in 1640 claimed that "none go beyond" the Dutch "in the affection of the people to pictures. . . . All in general strive to adorn their houses, especially the outer or street room, with costly pieces. Butchers and bakers not much inferior in their shops, which are fairly set forth, yea many times blacksmiths, cobblers, etc., will have some picture or other by their forge and their stall."

Frans Hals. FRANS HALS [hals] (ca. 1580–1666) was born in Antwerp and worked in Haarlem as a portraitist. An extrovert, the painter's jovial personality comes across in a number of his paintings. Hals's sitters usually appear to be in a good mood, more at home in a tavern than in a church. Differing from the stiff formality of earlier portraiture, the *Jolly Toper* (fig. 15.12) of ca. 1628–30 is balancing a wine glass and gesturing broadly, perhaps caught in conversation. Hals broke with the fashion of the time, which was to paint with careful contours, delicate modeling,

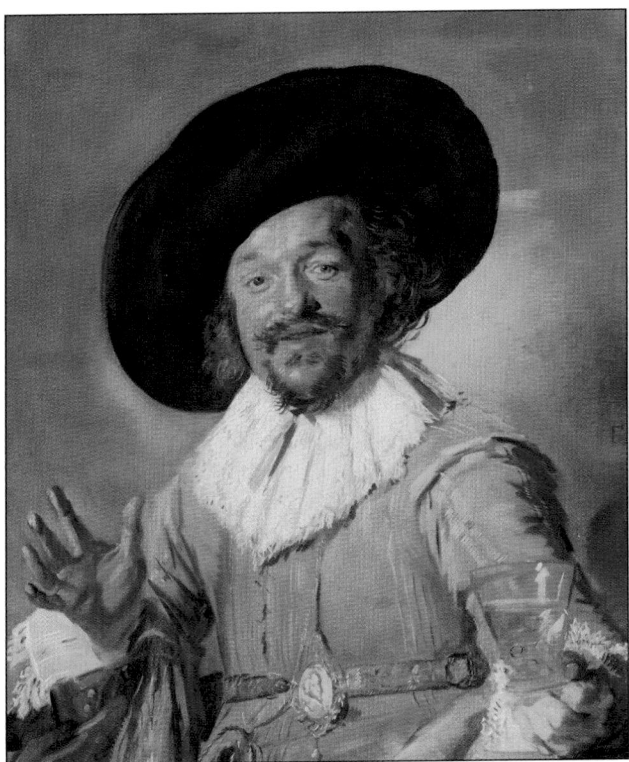

FIGURE 15.12 Frans Hals, *Jolly Toper*, ca. 1628–30, oil on canvas, $31\frac{7}{8}'' \times 26\frac{1}{4}''$ (81.0 × 66.7 cm), Rijksmuseum, Amsterdam. Breaking from the stiffness of earlier portraits, this man appears to have been caught in mid-sentence—perhaps offering that glass of wine. Hals's dashing brushstrokes accord with and enhance the quality of spontaneity.

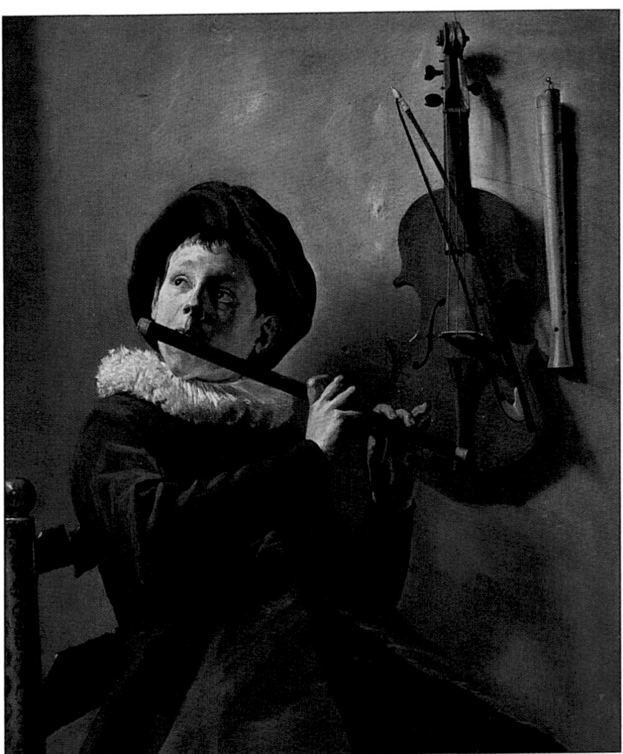

FIGURE 15.13 Judith Leyster, *Boy Playing a Flute*, 1630–35, oil on canvas, $28\frac{1}{2}'' \times 24\frac{1}{8}''$ (72.4 × 61.3 cm), National museum, Stockholm. Leyster's ability to convey a sense of life, of animation, is comparable to Hals's. The seemingly casual quality of both subject and painting technique is actually achieved with great care.

and attention to detail. Instead, his paint ranged from thick impasto to thin fluid glazes and he left the separate brushstrokes clearly visible. This spontaneity of technique matched the liveliness of his subject.

Judith Leyster. The most important follower of Frans Hals was JUDITH LEYSTER [LIE-ster] (1609–1660), a Dutch painter whose name came from her family's brewery in Haarlem, the Leysterre (Pole Star). So close are their painting styles that several works long thought to be by Hals have been found to be by Leyster. Like Hals, Leyster depicted animated scenes from daily life, as in the *Boy Playing a Flute* (fig. 15.13), painted 1630–35. Like Caravaggio, Leyster used limited colors and tenebristic lighting. And, as in Caravaggio's paintings, the figure occupies a shallow space, close to the picture plane. The boy's glance to the left would endanger the balance of this composition, were it not for the musical instruments hanging on the wall to the right. As with Hals, the seemingly casual brushwork and composition skillfully create an impression of relaxed ease.

Rembrandt van Rijn. In Amsterdam, the most important painter was REMBRANDT VAN RIJN [REM-brant] (1606–69), who took Caravaggio's Baroque lighting to new heights. Born in Leyden, the son of a miller, Rembrandt abandoned his studies of classical literature at the University of Leyden to study painting. In 1634, he married Saskia van Ulenborch, who came from a wealthy family. Between 1634 and 1642, now extremely successful, Rembrandt had many commissions and owned a large house and art collection in Amsterdam. Saskia was his great joy and often his model, but her early death in 1642 marked a turning point in Rembrandt's life—it was in this year that he painted *The Night Watch*.

The Night Watch (fig. 15.14) was one of Rembrandt's most important public commissions, paid for by the Amsterdam civic guard. All the men portrayed in this huge informal group portrait had contributed equally to the cost (their names appear on the shield hanging on the far wall). Its original title was *Captain Frans Banning Cocq Mustering His Company*, but it was dubbed *The Night Watch* in the eighteenth century because it had darkened with age. In actuality, the painting shows Cocq's company in the morning, welcoming Marie de' Medici, Queen of France, at Amsterdam's city gate.

The composition moves along diagonals. Originally, Captain Cocq and his lieutenant were not in the center but walking toward it (the painting has been cut on all four sides, but especially on the left). Originally their next steps would have placed them in the center; because the viewer

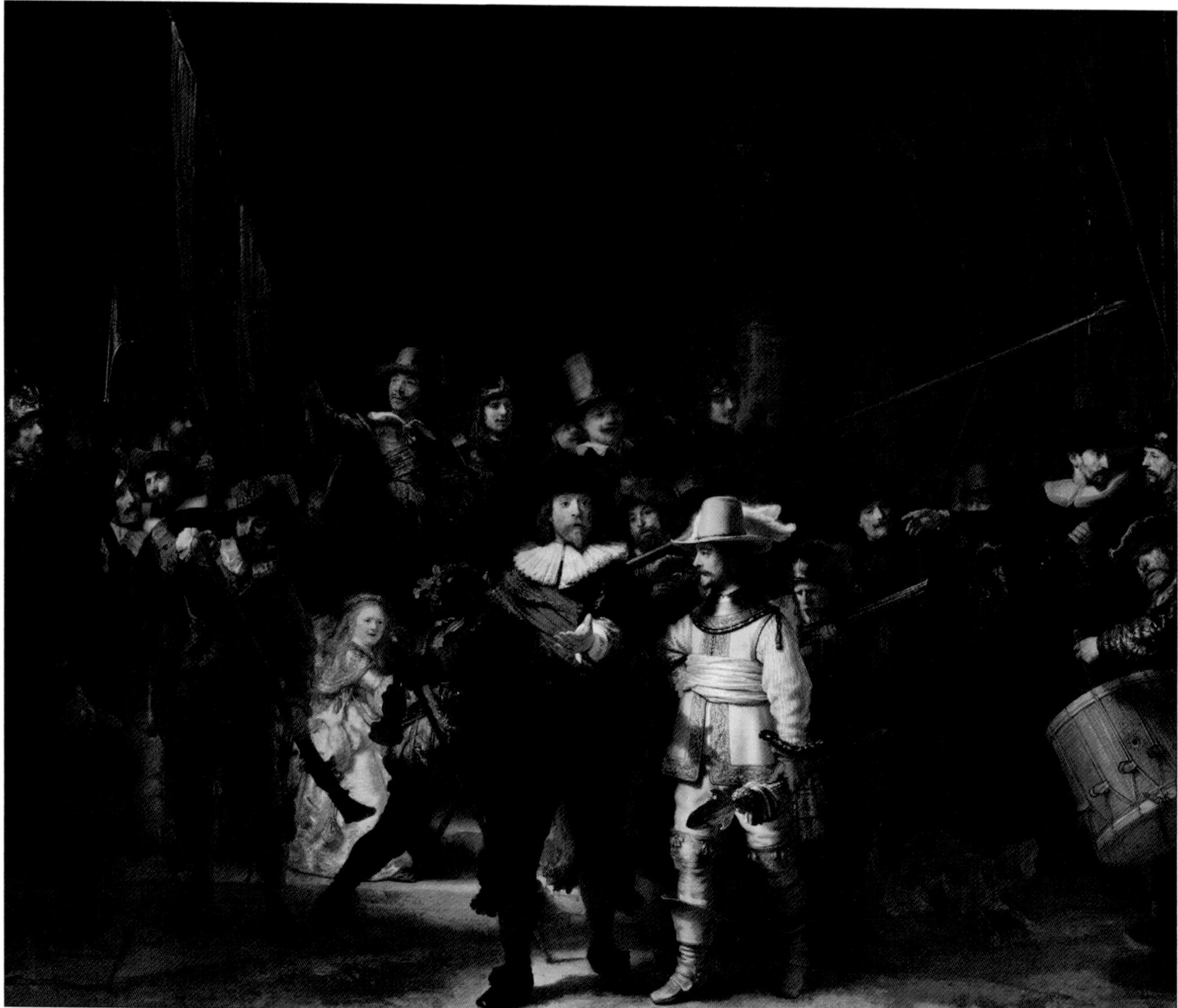

FIGURE 15.14 Rembrandt van Rijn, *Captain Frans Banning Cocq Mustering His Company (The Night Watch)*, 1642, oil on canvas, 11′11″ × 14′4″ (3.63 × 4.37 m), Rijksmuseum, Amsterdam. This enormous group portrait is often interpreted as marking the turning point in Rembrandt's life. His wife Saskia died in 1642, his popularity as an artist declined, and his financial problems began. The event depicted took place in the morning, but, because of gradual darkening, the painting has come to be known as *The Night Watch*.

intuitively expects the focal point to be in the center, Rembrandt cleverly implies their movement.

The most remarkable aspect of the painting is the light, which creates atmosphere, unifies the composition, links the figures, highlights expressive features, and subordinates unimportant details. The figures of Captain Cocq and his lieutenant received the greatest emphasis; the others felt cheated, but the picture was considered good enough to hang in the company's clubhouse.

Rembrandt recorded his own life in many self-portraits—sixty in oil alone. His last *Self-Portrait* (fig. 15.15) was painted in 1669, the year of his death. The textured handling of paint is masterful, the colors luminous and glowing, but the contours are looser, the brushstrokes broader, the surface not as smooth as in his earlier paintings. Rembrandt is weary and disillusioned. Yet he remains dignified; in none of his self-portraits does he appear bitter, resentful, or self-pitying. Introspective and honest, he presented himself as he was.

Jan Vermeer. Born in Delft, JAN VERMEER [vur-MEER] (1632–1675) painted only for local patrons. He specialized in domestic scenes that document everyday life. Like Rembrandt Vermeer was fascinated by light, but of a very different kind. Where Rembrandt's light is theatrical, Vermeer's is scientific. Vermeer's use of light reveals every textural nuance.

In *Young Woman with a Water Pitcher* (fig. 15.16) of ca. 1664–65, characteristic of Vermeer, a single female figure

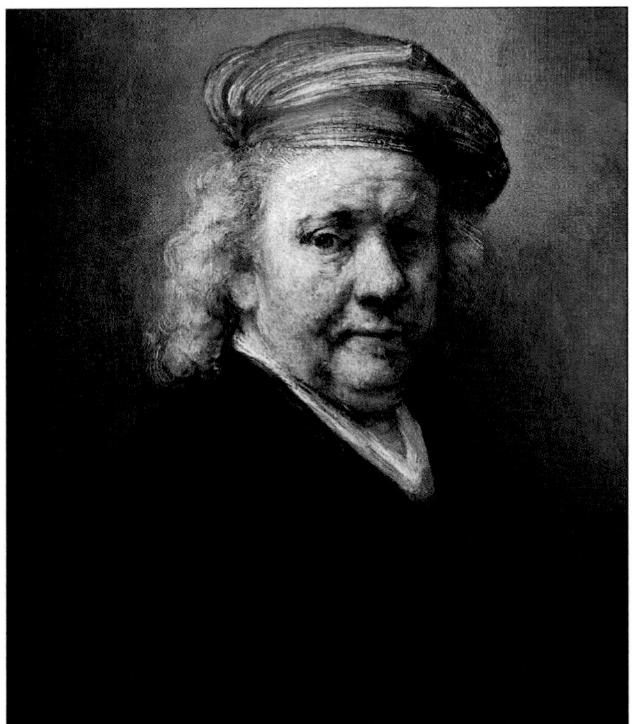

FIGURE 15.15 Rembrandt van Rijn, *Self-Portrait as an Old Man*, 1669, oil on canvas, $23\frac{1}{4}'' \times 20''$(59.0 × 51.0 cm), Royal Picture Gallery Mauritshuis, The Hague. Rembrandt painted himself throughout his life, not in a laudatory manner like Albrecht Dürer, but as a means of self-analysis and personal reflection more akin to the later self-portraits of Vincent van Gogh.

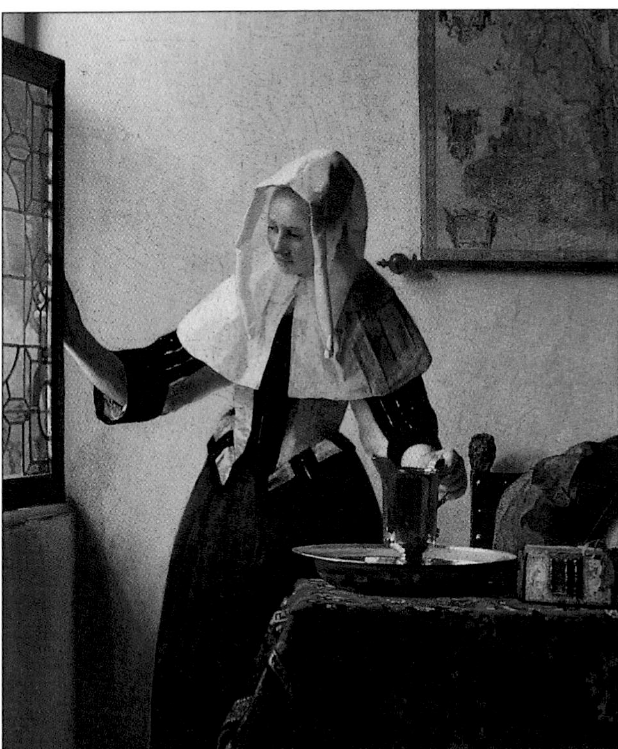

FIGURE 15.16 Jan Vermeer, *Young Woman with a Water Pitcher*, ca. 1664–65, oil on canvas, 18″ × 16″ (45.7 × 40.6 cm). Gift of Henry G. Marquand, 1889. Metropolitan Museum of Art, New York. Great importance is given by Vermeer to light—not for Baroque bravura, but to scientifically observe and record every detail, and to note every subtle gradation and reflection.

is depicted performing an ordinary action, indoors, at a table with objects on it, light coming from a window on the left, the figure silhouetted against a pale-colored wall. Vermeer's clear and luminous light pervades the space, unlike Rembrandt's light, which falls in shafts. Neither the subtle gradations across the back wall nor the reflections of the table rug in the metal basin are overlooked. The viewer can almost feel the starched linen headdress, its two sides subtly differentiated by the fall of light, the polished metal pitcher, and the basin. The woman is posed within a composition of rectangles drawn in perspective. Vermeer's intimate scene of a woman absorbed in household tasks conveys a mood of serenity and peace.

Rachel Ruysch. This interest in careful observation and detailed recording done with an almost scientific attention to detail is seen in the work of the Dutch artist RACHEL RUYSCH (1664–1750), whose fame derives from the many still lifes of flowers she executed during a long and productive life. In 1679 she began an apprenticeship with a flower painter. Her *Roses, Convolvulus, Poppies, and Other Flowers in an Urn on a Stone Ledge* (fig. 15.17), an early work from the 1680s, shows her to have been an especially adept student. This scientifically accurate record of a variety of flowering plants includes both familiar and exotic species. Some are still buds, others are in full bloom, and still others are now decaying. Ruysch's interest in variety includes the decorative shapes, colors, and textures. She had learned the importance of careful observation of Nature from her father, the scientist Frederik Ruysch; later she returned the favor by teaching her father to paint.

Ruysch joined the painters' guild in The Hague in 1701. Commissions for her large flower still lifes came from various parts of the globe. In 1708, she accepted an invitation to be court painter to Johann Wilhelm, the Elector Palatine of Bavaria, in Düsseldorf.

PAINTING IN FLANDERS

Peter Paul Rubens. Although born in Germany, PETER PAUL RUBENS [REW-bens] (1577–1640) established himself as an artist in Antwerp, the capital of Catholic Flanders. Between 1600 and 1608, at the very height of Caravaggio's career, he was in Italy, where he studied the Baroque masters, the antique, and the High Renaissance. He copied the "old masters" and enjoyed a good reputation in Italy, painting in a style that combined influences from the north and the south.

Intelligent, talented, sociable, energetic, and equipped with a good business sense, Rubens became extremely successful. He set up shop in Antwerp, and by 1611, with two hundred painters and students working in his studio, was the most financially successful artist of the age. He built a large home

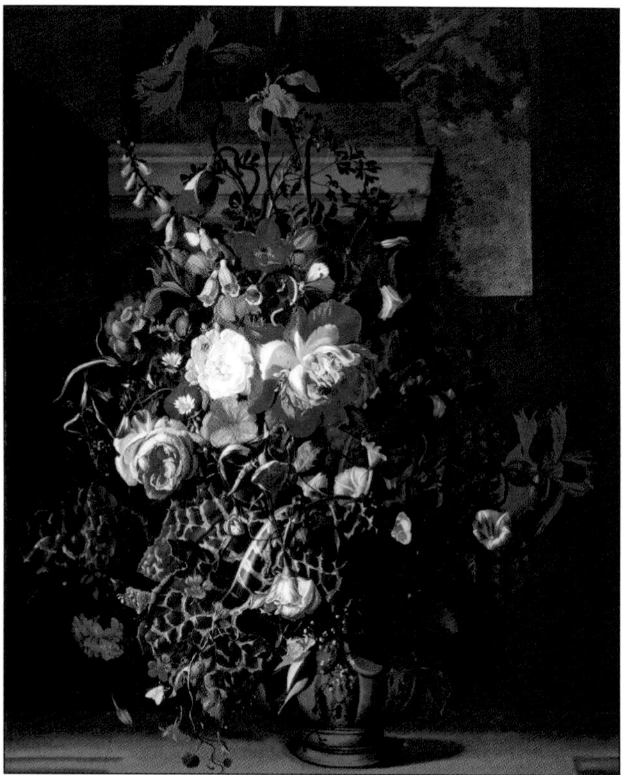

FIGURE 15.17 Rachel Ruysch. *Roses, Convolvulus, Poppies, and Other Flowers in an Urn on a Stone Ledge*, ca. 1745, oil on canvas, $42\frac{1}{2}'' \times 33''$ (108 × 84 cm), National Museum of Women in the Arts, Washington, DC. Gift of Wallace and Wilhelmina Holladay. A much-appreciated painter of flower still lifes, a subject favored by the Dutch, Ruysch's popularity was based on her perfect assymetric flower arrangements, the most colorful flowers emerging from the characteristically dark gloom. Taking a scientific approach to Nature, she included a variety of types of plants and recorded the tiniest details of each.

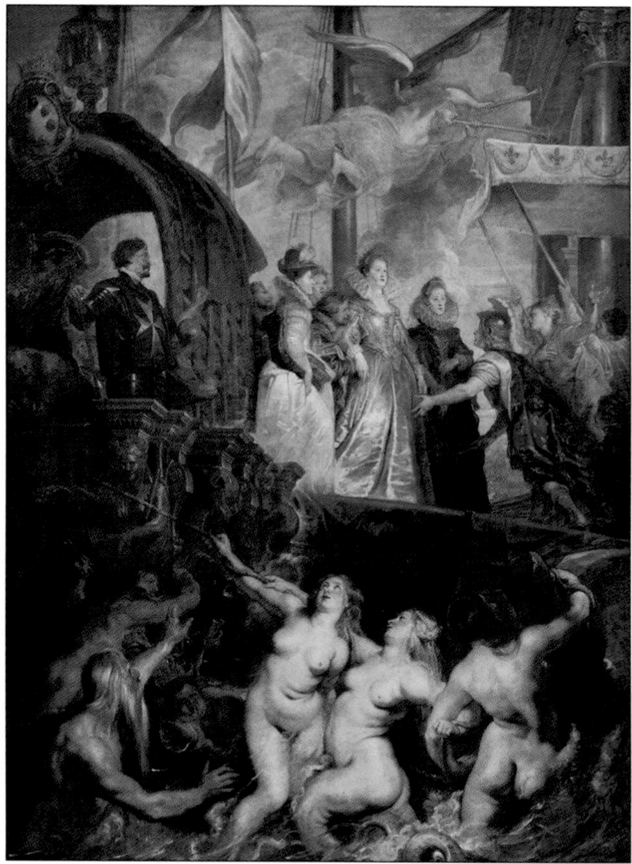

FIGURE 15.18 Peter Paul Rubens, *Marie de' Medici, Queen of France, Landing in Marseilles*, 1622–25, oil on canvas, $5'1'' \times 3'11\frac{2}{3}''$ (1.55 × 1.21 m). Photo: Jean/Lewandowski. Musée du Louvre, Paris, Reunion des Musées Nationaux/Art Resource, NY. With the diagonal movements typical of the Baroque, brilliant color, sensuous textures, and dashing brushwork, Rubens raised his depiction of an unglamorous queen at an ordinary event to the level of high drama.

containing his studio and an art collection including works by Raphael, Titian, Tintoretto, van Eyck, and Bruegel. He received commissions from the Church, the city of Antwerp, and private individuals, but it was the royal courts of Europe that garnered him the most fame and fortune. He was court painter to the Duke of Mantua, and to the Spanish regents of The Netherlands, Albert and Isabella. Commissions came also from Charles I of England and Philip IV of Spain, both of whom presented him with a knighthood. In 1621, Marie de' Medici of France gave him the commission that would establish his international reputation.

After the death of her husband, Henry IV, Marie de' Medici served as regent for her young son, Louis XIII. She asked Rubens to create a cycle of twenty-one large oil paintings portraying her life. His aim was to glorify the queen. A master of narrative, Rubens's solution was to dramatize even the ordinary. In the scene of *Marie de' Medici, Queen of France, Landing in Marseilles* (fig. 15.18), the queen is merely disembarking in the southern French city of Marseilles, yet Fame flies above, blowing a trumpet, and Neptune, god of the sea, accompanied by mermaids, rises from the waves to welcome her.

The drama of the composition is characteristic of the Baroque style, as is the love of movement in an open space. Everything becomes active to the point of agitation, even when not required by the subject. Rubens painted in terms of rich, luminous, glowing color and light rather than in terms of line. Every stroke, every form, is united by the sweeping movements of Rubens's design and the sheer exuberance of his lush forms, which appeal more to the eye than to the mind.

Aided by his early experience as a court page as well as his fluency in five languages (Greek, Italian, French, Spanish, and Flemish), Rubens served as an adviser and emissary for the Flemish court. When he visited the court of Philip IV in Spain from September 1628 until late April 1629, he stayed in the royal palace in Madrid and was visited almost daily by the young king.

After his first wife died in 1626, Rubens married Hélène Fourment, a distant relative, and began a second family. He was fifty years old, his bride sixteen, and they had four children in five years. *The Garden of Love* (fig. 15.19),

Connections

VERMEER AND THE ORIGINS OF PHOTOGRAPHY

It appears that Vermeer used a device known as the ***camera obscura*** to execute his paintings. First used in the Renaissance for verifying perspective, the camera obscura was used by Dutch painters as a tool for observation comparable to the microscope and the telescope. At its simplest, the device is an enclosed box with a tiny hole in one side through which shines a beam of external light, projecting the scene outside as an inverted image on the opposite, interior wall of the box. Thus the *camera obscura* is like the modern-day camera, but it lacks light-sensitive paper or film on which to record the image. In Vermeer's time, it could be the size of a room in which the artist could stand fully upright and trace the image, Or, as is probable in the case of Vermeer, the pinhole was lensed in such a way that he could focus the image on a translucent intermediary screen that he could closely copy.

Not only did the camera obscura transform a three-dimensional view to a two-dimensional image; it revealed intriguing details about the play of light. Often in Vermeer's paintings the light seems to force the image out of focus. Photographers call such spots in a photograph "discs of confusion." Although fleeting to the naked eye, Vermeer could study this optical effect through the lens of his camera obscura and capture it on canvas.

While it would be another 150 years until photographic chemistry was perfected, the physics upon which photography is based was already at work in Vermeer's images.

FIGURE 15.19 Peter Paul Rubens, *The Garden of Love*, ca. 1638, oil on canvas, $6'6'' \times 9'3\frac{1}{2}''$ (1.98 × 2.83 m), Museo Nacional del Prado, Madrid. Rubens is known for his rich, lush style—applied to the setting and, especially, to the figures. The term *Rubenesque* has been coined to describe voluptuous, fleshy females.

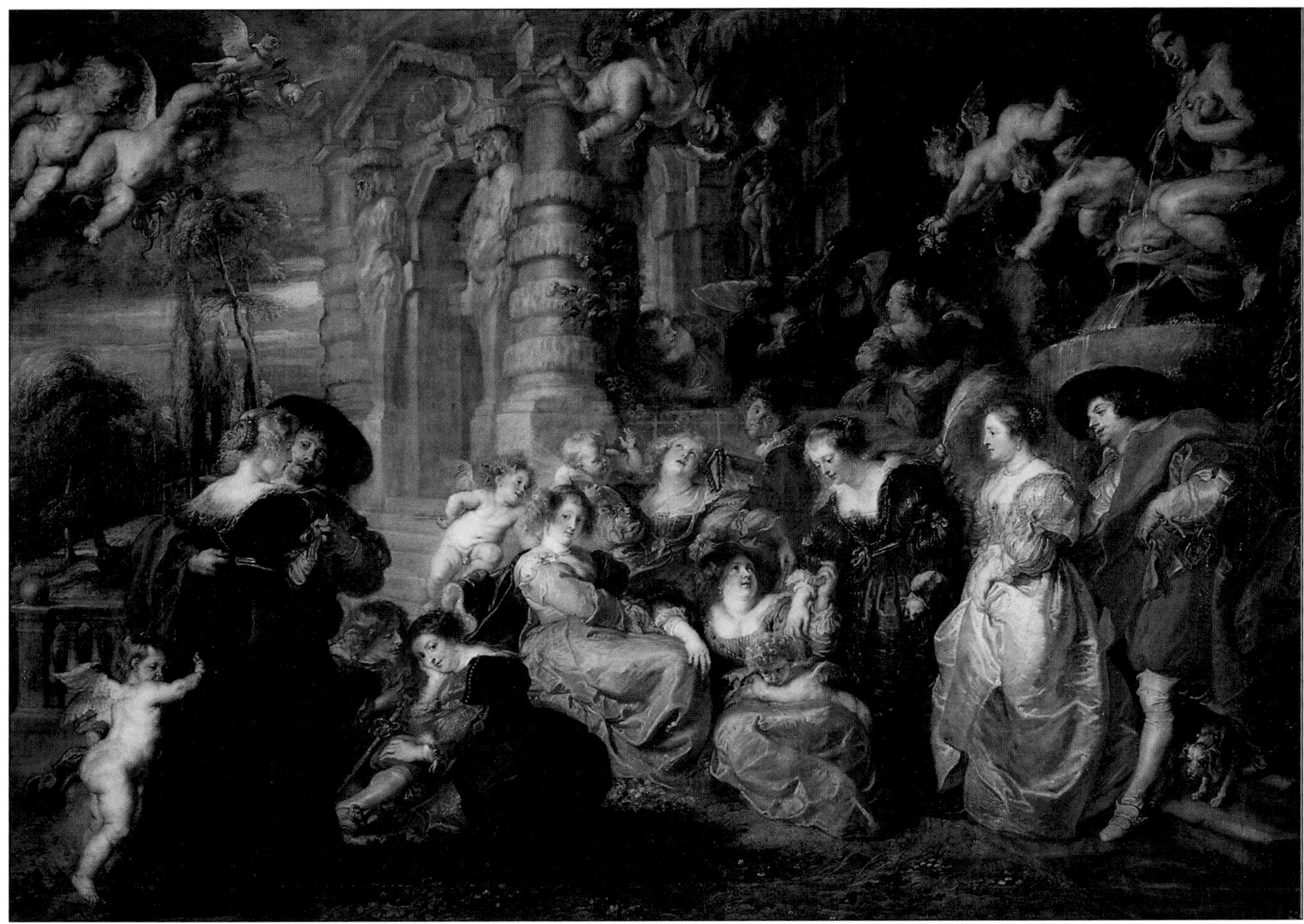

ca. 1638, expresses the pleasures of life, with a robust grandeur approaching animal exuberance. Certainly Rubens's main interest in this work is in the voluptuous female figure. Only with difficulty could this scene be made any more sumptuous—or sensuous.

Anthony van Dyck. Rubens's assistant from 1618 to 1620, Anthony van Dyck (1599–1641), became painter to the court of Charles I in England and perhaps the greatest portrait painter of the age. His *Portrait of Charles I at the Hunt* (fig. 15.20), of 1635, captures the king's self-assurance. Van Dyck contrasts the king with the anxious groom and the pawing, nervous horse behind him, underscoring Charles's command of all situations.

Clara Peeters. Another aspect of Flemish painting is represented by Clara Peeters (1594–after 1657) from Antwerp, who signed her first painting at the age of fourteen. A still life painter, her specialty was the depiction of breakfasts or elaborate banquet tables. Of the latter type is her *Table with a Tart and a White Pitcher* (fig. 15.21) of 1611, painted when she was only seventeen years old.

FIGURE 15.20 Anthony van Dyck, *Portrait of Charles I at the Hunt*, 1635, oil on canvas, approx. 9′ × 7′ (2.74 × 2.13 m), Musée du Louvre, Paris. Reunion des Musées Nationaux. Art Resource, NY. Working in Rubens's rich, painterly style with loose brushwork and a range of textural effects, van Dyck captures the haughtiness of the posturing king.

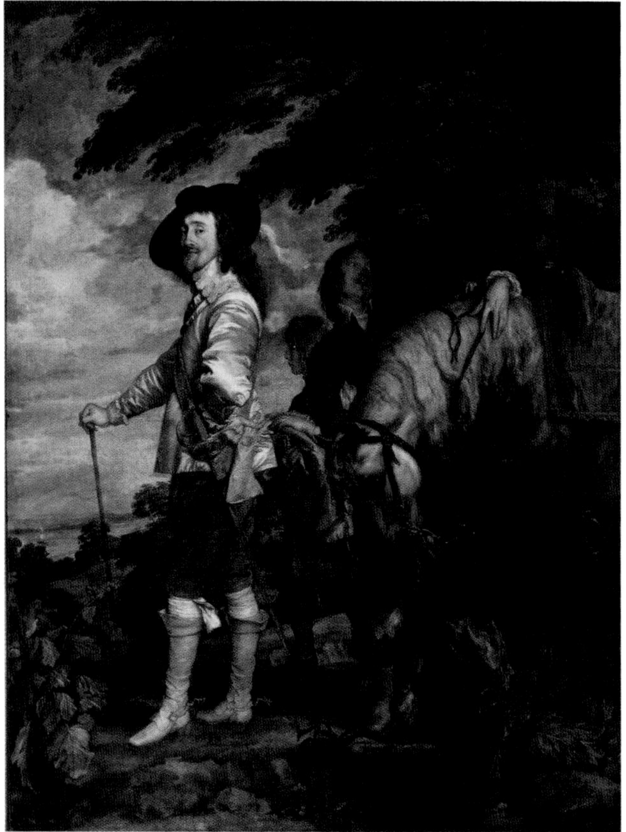

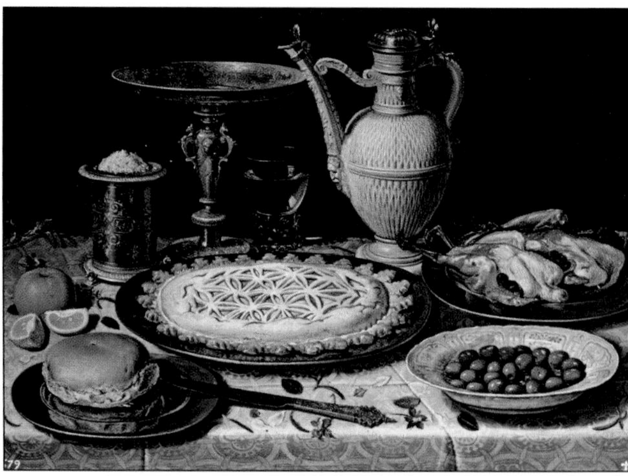

FIGURE 15.21 Clara Peeters, *Table with a Tart and a White Pitcher*, 1611, $29\frac{1}{2}'' \times 28\frac{3}{4}''$ (75 × 73 cm), Museo del Prado, Madrid, Spain. Erich Lessing/Art Resource, NY. Such still life paintings appeal to our senses—of visual beauty and, as encouraged by the level of realism, also to our senses of taste and of smell. A luxurious way of life is implied, perhaps the viewer's for the taking: Objects extend over the edge of the table, suggesting that we might reach across the picture plane and help ourselves to these delicious foods.

This complex table setting records a complete gourmet meal. Her technical ability in depicting different textures and surfaces reached a peak in the skillful handling of reflections, as here on the polished metal plate or glass goblet, which sometimes included miniature self-portraits.

Beneath the surface beauty of such still life paintings lies deeper symbolic meaning, often alluding to the brevity of life. In moralizing *vanitas* pictures, obvious symbols are a snuffed-out candle, hour glass, or skull, while more subtle are flowers that are dying or eaten by insects and fruits that are decaying or peeled, as seen here. The meaning of such symbols was well known to Peeters's intended audience.

PAINTING IN ENGLAND

Mary Beale. The interest in portraiture in seventeenth-century Europe also appears in the work of Mary Beale (1632–1697), who specialized in portraiture, a genre particularly appreciated by the British. The artist Sir Peter Lely invited Beale to copy paintings in his extensive personal art collection in London. After Lely's death, Beale satisfied the demand for copies of his paintings: So adept was she at this, and so similar were their styles, that it is possible some portraits by Beale have been incorrectly attributed to Lely. After marrying Charles Beale, she began a professional apprenticeship and by 1670 was working independently as an artist. An example of her skill at this time in portraiture is seen in the likeness she created of *John Wilkins DD* (fig. 15.22) of ca. 1670. Painted in subdued colors, the Bishop of Chester is shown seated, the depiction straight forward, as he looks directly at the viewer.

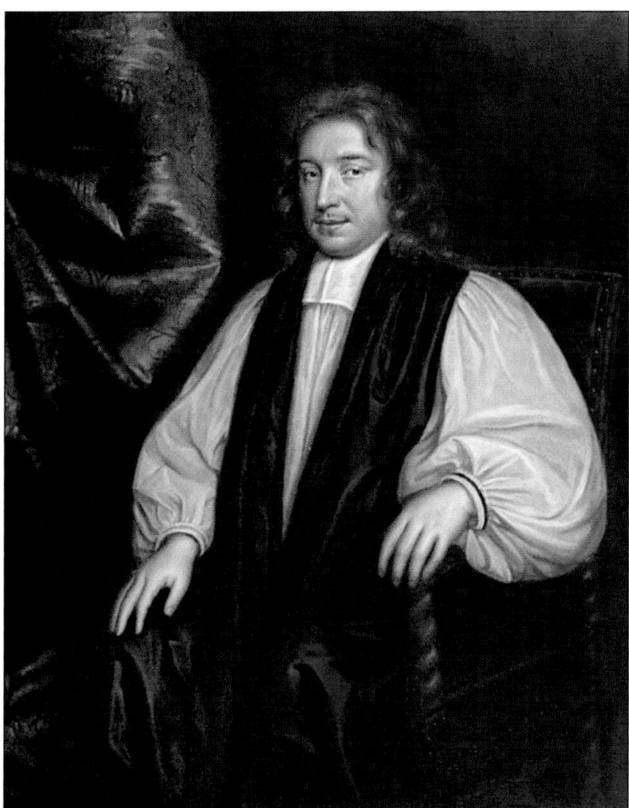

FIGURE 15.22 Mary Beale, *John Wilkins DD*, ca. 1670, oil on canvas, 49″ × 39½″ (124.5 × 100.5 cm). Bodleian Library, Oxford. The British interest in portraiture is evidenced here. The abundant and richly textured textiles of the costume, furniture, and curtain add to the sought-after impression of elevated social standing.

Beale's husband aided her by preparing her canvases and colors, and even becoming an art dealer. Notebooks survive in which he kept track of her work and the large number of commissions she completed each year. One of her two sons became a portraitist.

PAINTING IN SPAIN

Diego Velázquez. Philip IV had become king of Spain in 1621 at the age of sixteen, and from the outset he relied heavily on the advice of Gaspar de Guzmán, the count of Olivares. Olivares wanted Philip's court to be recognized as the most prominent in Europe; he appointed DIEGO VELAZQUEZ [ve-LAHS-kez] (1599–1660) to the position of royal painter. Velázquez was highly honored by the king, who ultimately knighted and conferred on him the Order of Santiago, usually reserved for noblemen. Velázquez painted many portraits of the royal family, and he seems to have made his sitters no prettier or more handsome than they actually were. Velázquez lived most of his life in Madrid, although shortly after Rubens's visit and at Rubens's suggestion, Philip granted Velázquez permission to visit Italy in order to study art in 1629. There he absorbed the lessons of the Italian Baroque and brought them back to Spain. Throughout his career, his style became progressively richer, the color lusher, the figures more animated.

Velázquez's most celebrated painting is the *Maids of Honor*, or *Las Meninas* (fig. 15.23), painted in 1656. Originally called *Family of Philip IV*, the painting raises the question: Is this a formal portrait? Or is it a genre scene? In fact, it is both. A glass of water has just been brought to Princess Margarita, the five-year-old daughter of Philip IV and his second wife, Queen Mariana. Margarita's maids, friends, a nun, a dwarf, a dog, and others gather round. Yet this scene from everyday life is portrayed on a huge scale. Velázquez includes himself painting a large canvas in the foreground.

On the back wall of the room are the reflections of the queen and king, apparently in a mirror. They stand where the viewer stands in relation to the pictorial space. Is the viewer looking at a portrait of the Infanta Margarita, or are the king and queen having their portraits painted by Velázquez and their child has come to watch? Velázquez unites the world of the sitter and the world of the viewer. Velázquez implies yet a third space to be reached by ascending the stairs on the back wall.

When Velázquez's masterpiece took its place in Philip IV's collection, it joined over 1,500 paintings in the king's collection at the Buen Retiro, the new residence that Olivares and Philip built on the outskirts of Madrid in the early 1630s. Together with Philip II's massive collection, Spain, by 1650, owned much of the Western world's great art.

PAINTING IN FRANCE

Nicolas Poussin. NICOLAS POUSSIN [poo-SAN] (1594–1665) represents the classicizing and restrained tendency within the usually dramatic Baroque.

Favoring academic history painting, his *Rape of the Sabine Women* (fig. 15.24), of ca. 1636–37, shows Romulus, on the left, raising his cloak to signal his men to abduct the Sabine women to be their wives. The figures make wild gestures and expressions, yet the action is frozen and the effect unmoving. This style is intended to appeal more to the mind than to the eye; appreciation of the painting depends largely upon knowing the story depicted. Poussin said the goal of painting was to represent noble subjects to morally improve the viewer. His approach to painting was disciplined, organized, and theoretical. Poussin worked in terms of line rather than color—in this he was the opposite of Rubens.

Louise Moillon. Among all seventeenth-century French painters of still life, LOUISE MOILLON [Loo-EEZ Mwa-YON] (1610–1696) of Paris is regarded as the finest. Both her father, Nicolas Moillon, who died when she was

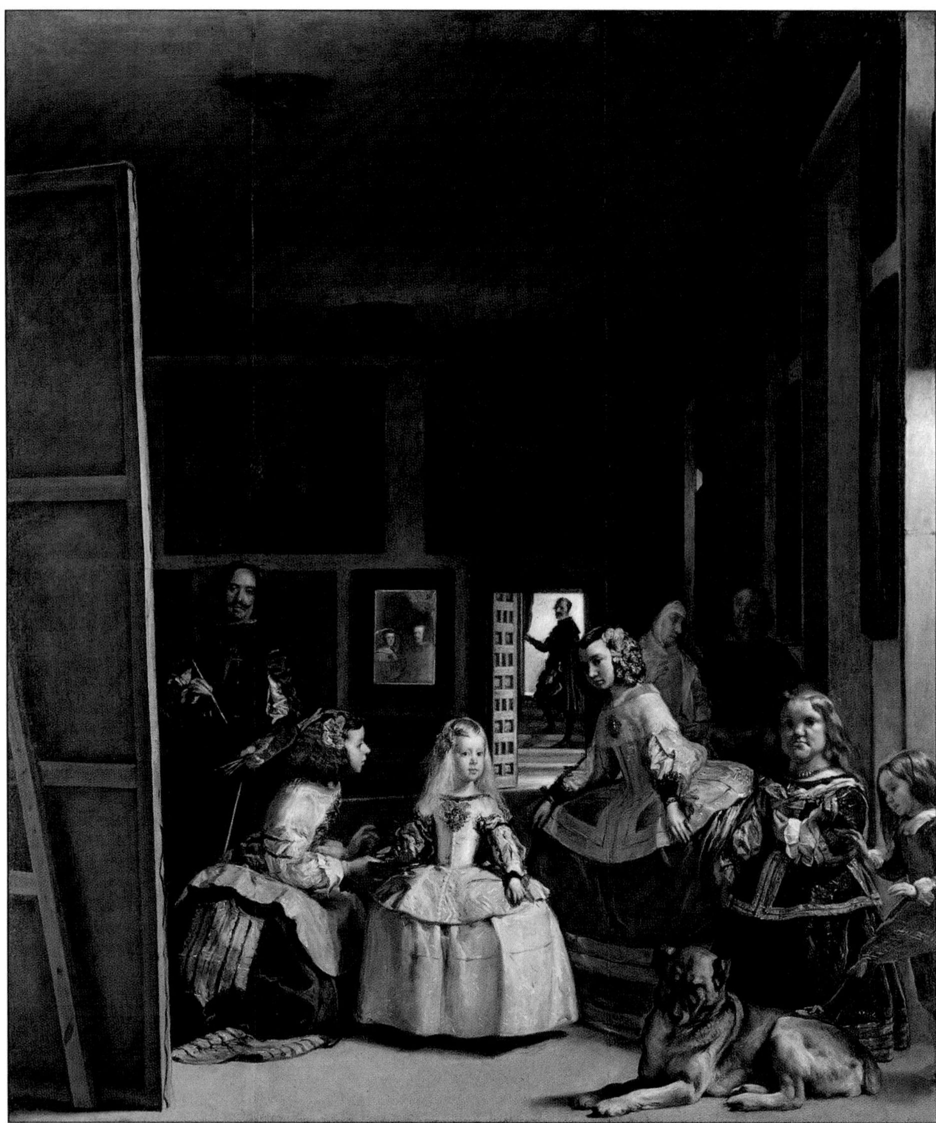

FIGURE 15.23 Diego Velázquez, *Maids of Honor* (*Las Meninas*), 1656, oil on canvas, 10′5″× 9′ (3.17 × 2.74 m), Museo del Prado, Madrid. Velázquez depicts himself in this group portrait in the process of painting just such a large canvas. Much as in Jan van Eyck's Arnolfini wedding portrait (fig. 14.3), the presence of people (here the king and queen) in the viewer's space is indicated by their reflection in the mirror on the back wall.

nine, and her stepfather, François Garnier, were painters and art dealers. A child prodigy, she was selling paintings by the time she was ten. Although the Royal Academy of Painting and Sculpture regarded still life as of less merit than religious or historical subjects or portraiture, the artists elected to membership during the seventeenth century included still life painters. In fig. 15.25, *Still Life with Cherries, Strawberries, and Gooseberries*, painted when she was only twenty and already an artist of note, Moillon created a simple composition, perfectly balanced, the blank background focusing all attention on the objects. The textures, sizes, and shapes of the fruits as well as of their containers form intentional contrasts.

The French Academy. Beginning with the reign of KING LOUIS XIV [LOO-ee] (1638–1715), who came to the throne as a child in 1643 and ruled outright from 1661 until 1715, Paris became increasingly the center of the Western art world, even if many of its most important painters, such as Poussin, preferred to live and work in Rome. Louis XIV's reign was the longest in European history, and assisted by his chief adviser, Jean-Baptiste Colbert, he soon established control over art and architecture. He did this through the Royal Academy of Painting and Sculpture, established in Paris in 1648 and known more simply as the French Academy. Its purpose was to define absolute standards by which to judge the art of the period.

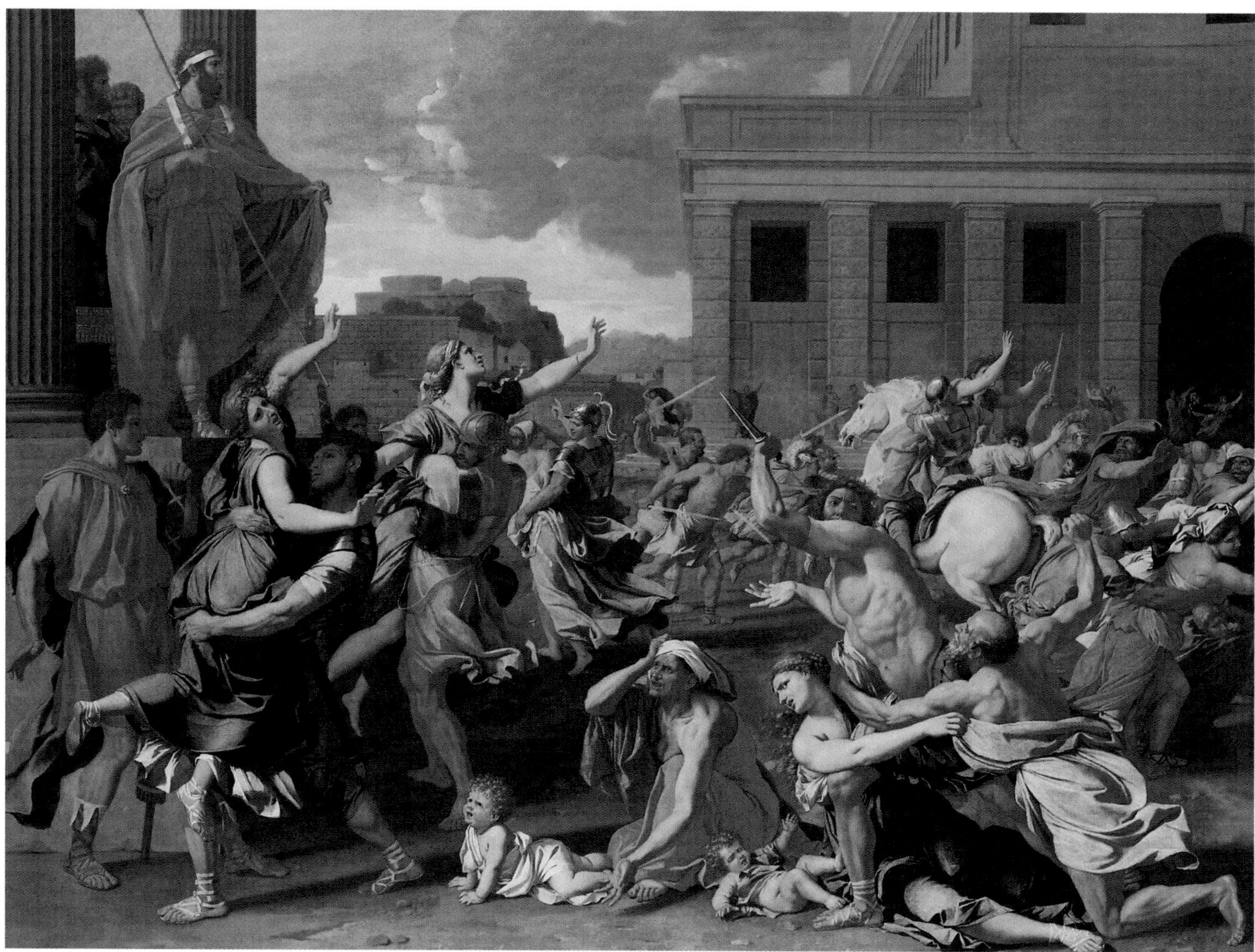

FIGURE 15.24 Nicolas Poussin, *Rape of the Sabine Women*, ca. 1636–37, oil on canvas, $5'\frac{7}{8}'' \times 6'10\frac{5}{8}''$ (1.55 × 2.10 m). Metropolitan Museum of Art, New York. In spite of the dramatic subject and technical perfection of drawing, Poussin's academic style renders his characters as frozen actors on a stage, unlikely to elicit an emotional response in the viewer.

Favored above all other painters was Poussin, but the Academy's insistence on Poussin's supremacy alienated many younger members of the Academy inclined not toward Poussin's cool classicism, but toward Rubens's dashing bravura. By the end of the seventeenth century, the Academy had split into two opposing groups—those who favored line and those who favored color. The former, adherents to the style of Poussin and referred to as ***poussinistes,*** argued that line was superior because it appealed to the mind, whereas color appealed only to the senses. The latter, preferring the style of Rubens, were called ***rubénistes*** and maintained that color was truer to nature; line appealed only to an educated mind, but color appealed to all. Both sides agreed on this point. Thus, to ask whether line or color is superior is to question whether the educated person or the lay person is the ultimate audience for art, a debate that continues to this day.

ARCHITECTURE

Louvre. As head of the French Academy, Colbert invited Bernini to Paris in 1664 to present plans for the facade for the new east wing of the royal palace of the Louvre [LOOV]. But Bernini's approach was deemed too radical, and furthermore, French architects did not think the design of a French palace should fall to an Italian. Therefore, to conceive a new plan, Colbert appointed a French council: architect LOUIS LE VAU [luh VO] (1612–1670), painter CHARLES LE BRUN [luh BRUN] (1619–1690), a previous director of the French Academy, and architect CLAUDE PERRAULT [peh-ROH] (1613–1688), who later published a French edition of the ancient architect Vitruvius. A strict, linear classicism was the result (fig. 15.26). The center of the facade looks like a Roman temple with Corinthian columns; wings of paired columns extend on each side, and the building ends in forms reminiscent of a Roman triumphal arch.

Critical Thinking

Art Forgeries

Among the problems confronting art dealers and purchasers today is that of forgery—works of art which have been created to look like important paintings, sculptures, or artifacts from the past, usually from ancient times, but are copies meant to deceive. Forgery exists because artworks are valuable, and forgers aim to cash in on that fact.

Among recent forgeries is that of an ancient Greek sculpture of a kouros, or young male nude standing figure, purchased by the J. Paul Getty Museum in California. Although the work appeared to be from the sixth-century B.C.E. historians were divided as to its authenticity. After listening to arguments on both sides, the museum purchased the statue, in large part because geological analysis indicated that its marble had come from an ancient quarry site and because it had appropriate papers to designate its provenance—its history of former ownership.

In a recent book, *Blink*, Malcolm Gladwell explains how the forged sculpture was created, why some people were fooled by it, and how some experts knew, seemingly instinctively, that the Getty kouros was a fake, even though many details suggested its authenticity.

What do you think is necessary for an expert to detect a forgery? What kinds of tests might be done as part of the investigation into a work's authenticity? To what extent do you think tests, such as those done on the dating of a work's materials, are enough to decide such issues? To what extent is an art historian's experience of value in deciding such matters?

FIGURE 15.25 Louise Moillon, *Still Life with Cherries, Strawberries, and Gooseberries*, 1630, oil on panel, $12\frac{5}{8}'' \times 19\frac{1}{8}''$ (32 × 48.5 cm). The Norton Simon Foundation. Moillon's speciality was fruit still lifes. This display of her extraordinary technical skill includes the drops of water on the table which are given a prominent location in the center foreground, ensuring that they do not go unnoticed by the viewer. More realistic records of the visible world would have to wait until the invention of photography.

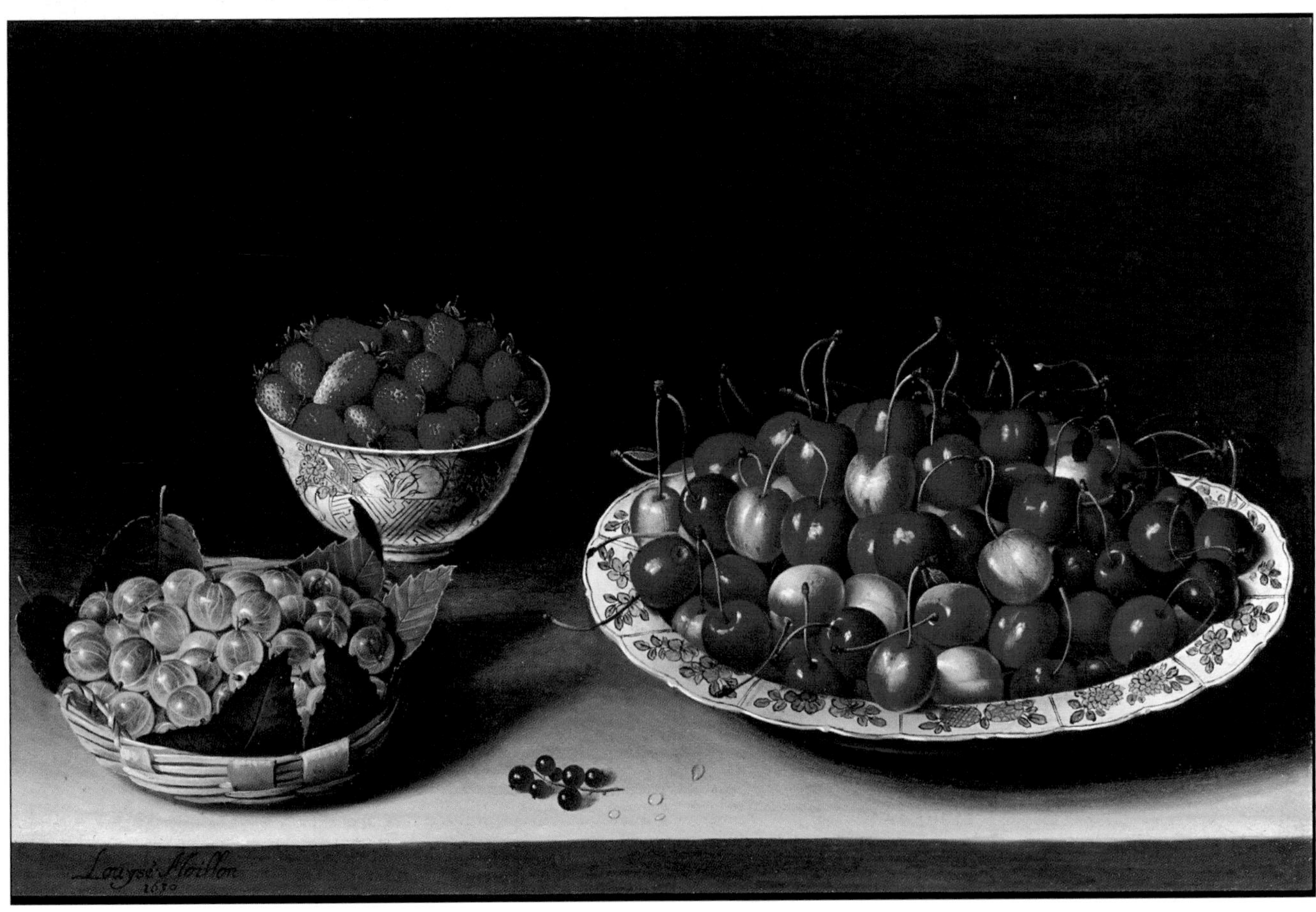

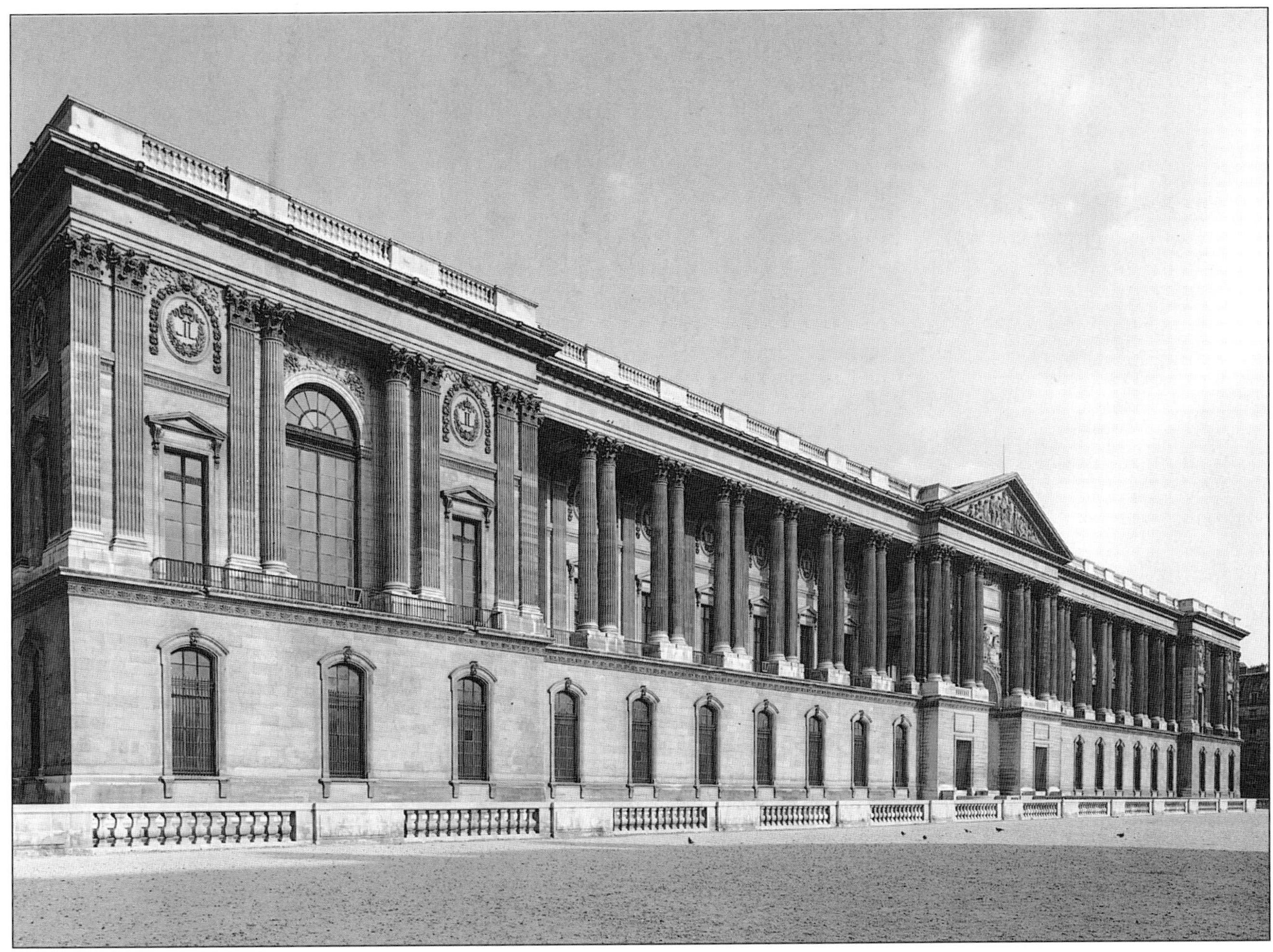

FIGURE 15.26 Louis Le Vau, Charles Le Brun, Claude Perrault, east facade, Palais du Louvre, Paris, 1667–70. All vestiges of Baroque sensuality have been banished in favor of a revival of elements found in ancient Roman architecture, used here to create a classical elegance.

The king was so pleased that he insisted the new facade be duplicated on the palace's other faces.

The Palace of Versailles. Louis XIV then turned his attention to the building of a new royal palace at Versailles [vair-SIGH], eleven miles southwest of Paris. It was begun in 1669 by Le Vau, who managed to design the garden facade but died within the year. JULES HARDOUIN-MANSART [man-SAR] (1646–1708) took over and enlarged the palace to the extraordinary length of 1,903 feet.

The visitor arriving at Versailles from Paris is greeted by the principal facade, designed to focus on the three windows of Louis XIV's bedroom in the center. The entire palace and gardens are arranged symmetrically on this axis.

Versailles was the seat of the government of France and once housed ten thousand people. Even the humblest attic room at Versailles was preferred to living on one's own estate, because only through contact with the king was there the possibility of obtaining royal favor. The most spectacular of the many splendid rooms of the palace of Versailles is the Hall of Mirrors (fig. 15.27), designed about 1680, the work of Hardouin-Mansart, Le Brun, and Antoine Coysevox. Tunnel-like in its dimensions (240 feet long, but only 34 feet wide, and 43 feet high), the Hall of Mirrors overlooks the gardens through seventeen arched windows reflected in seventeen arched mirrors. Furnished with silver furniture and orange trees, and hung white brocade curtains, lit by innumerable flickering candles, mirrored to reflect marble, gilding, stucco, wood, and paint, it is one of the ultimate examples of French Baroque elegance.

St. Paul's Cathedral. Although England had lagged behind the continent artistically, Sir Christopher Wren (1632–1723) quickly brought it to the fore. In addition to being an architect, Wren was professor of astronomy at Oxford University and was also knowledgeable in anatomy, physics, mathematics, sailing, street paving, and embroidery. He even invented a device for copying documents by having a second pen attached to the first and writing double.

During the Great Fire of 1666, much of London was destroyed, including the original Gothic church of St. Paul's. Wren joined the royal commission for rebuilding the city,

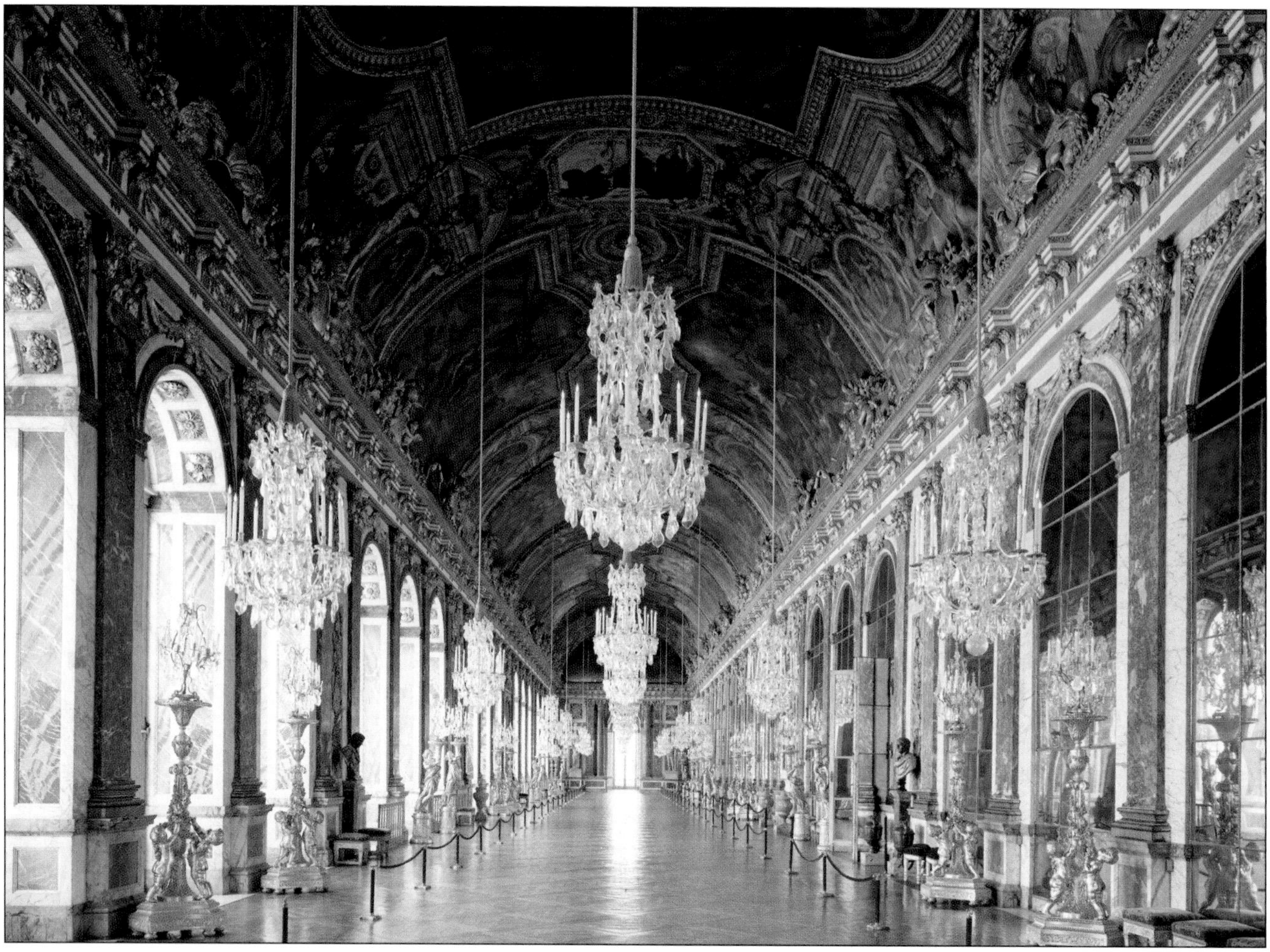

FIGURE 15.27 Jules Hardouin-Mansart and Charles Le Brun, Hall of Mirrors, Palace of Versailles, ca. 1680. Typically Baroque is the combination of a variety of materials to enhance the opulence of the overall impact. Imagine the effect with the flickering light of hundreds of candles reflected in the arched mirrors.

and although his master plan for its reconstruction was rejected, he did design many local churches. His masterpiece was the new St. Paul's cathedral (fig. 15.28), built 1675–1710.

St. Paul's cathedral may be regarded as a Baroque reinterpretation of the ancient Roman Pantheon (see Chapter 4). Wren designed a dome like that of the Pantheon, but raised it high on double drums and topped it with a lantern, and he modeled his triangular pediment on the Pantheon's but supported it on two stories of columns, which, characteristic of the Baroque, are grouped in pairs. The lower story of columns is as wide as the nave and aisles, the upper as wide as the nave. Particularly Baroque are the broken silhouettes of the towers at each corner.

It is possible that Wren intended St. Paul's to be the St. Peter's of the north. Like the dome of St. Peter's in Rome, the dome of St. Paul's is as wide as the nave and aisles. Although smaller than St. Peter's, St. Paul's is considered artistically superior for its stylistic consistency; St. Paul's is also the only major cathedral in Western Europe to be completed by the person who designed it. St. Peter's lacks small-scale features with which to interpret its vastness; St. Paul's includes such details on both the exterior and interior.

BAROQUE MUSIC OUTSIDE ITALY

Handel and the Oratorio. Late in the Baroque age, Italian opera such as Monteverdi's began to go out of style, particularly in the north where Protestants thought the form frivolous. One of the most successful composers of Italian opera of the day was GEORGE FREDERICK HANDEL [HAN-del] (1685–1759), a German composer who emigrated to England in the early 1700s. Handel was renowned as an organist and a prodigious composer in many musical genres, including operas, keyboard works, orchestral suites, and concertoes for various instruments. Lauded and commissioned by the Hanoverian kings, he profoundly influenced English music for a century after his death.

By the mid-1720s Handel had composed nearly forty operas, but recognizing the growing English distaste for the form, he turned to composing **oratorios.** An oratorio is a sacred opera sung without costume and without acting

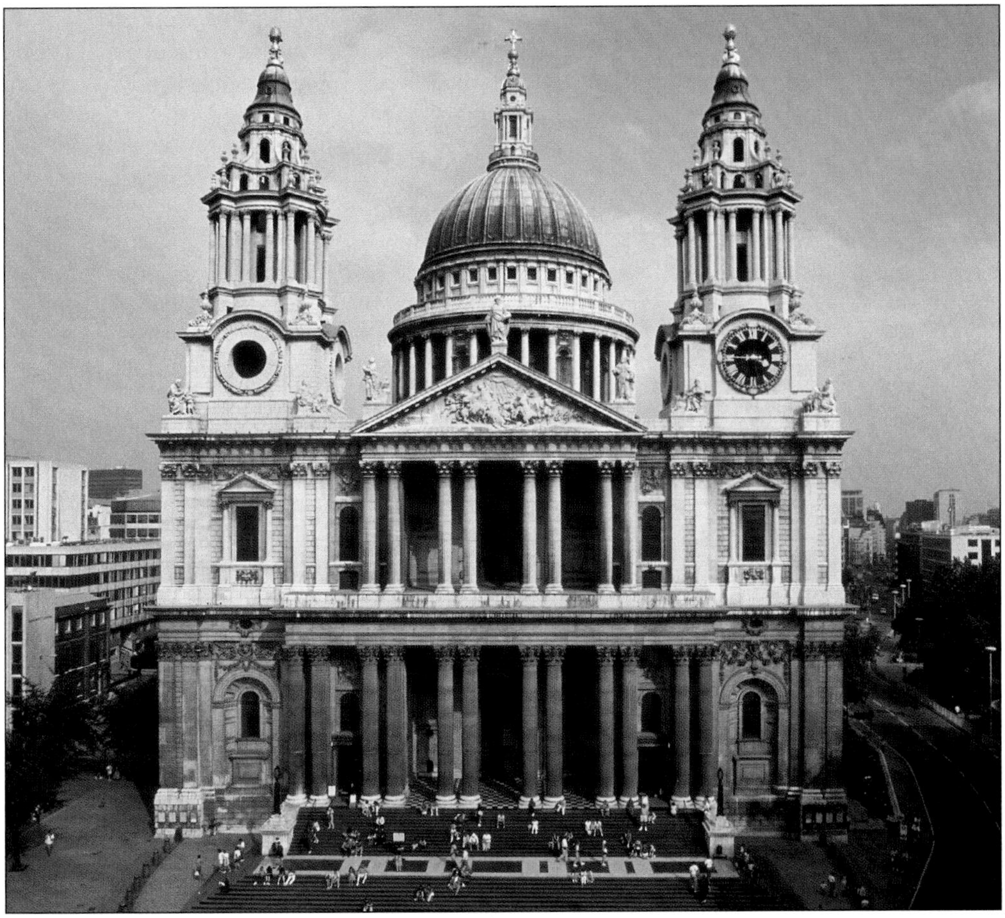

FIGURE 15.28 Sir Christopher Wren, facade, St. Paul's Cathedral, London, 1675–1710, length 514′ (156.67 m), width 250′ (76.20 m), height of dome 366′ (111.56 m). The facade of St. Paul's in London deserves comparison with that of St. Peter's in Rome (fig. 15.2). Although the basic dome, pediment, and columns derive from antiquity, the Baroque influence is evident in the paired columns and double facade.

because it was forbidden to present biblical characters in a public theater. Handel relied on a heightened musical drama to make up for the lack of theater. Written in English, Handel's oratorios employ the many musical forms of opera, such as **arias** (solo songs), recitatives, duets, ensemble singing, and choruses, and all were set to orchestral accompaniment.

Handel's most famous oratorio is his *Messiah*, a composition of enormous scope that rivals the most ambitious projects of Baroque art and architecture—Bernini's colonnade for the Vatican square, Rubens's cycle of paintings celebrating the life of Marie de' Medici and Milton's epic *Paradise Lost*. *Messiah* includes approximately fifty individual pieces, lasting, collectively, about three hours. Its three parts are based on the biblical texts of Isaiah, the Psalms, the Gospels, Revelations, and the Pauline Epistles. The first part concerns the prophecy of the birth of Christ; the second focuses on his suffering, especially the crucifixion; the third encompasses his resurrection and the redemption of the world.

The tone of *Messiah* is jubilant and celebratory. One particularly inspirational section is the second part of the oratorio, concluding with the famous "Hallelujah Chorus," which is based on Revelations 11:15. The text is as follows:

a. Hallelujah! Hallelujah!
b. For the Lord God omnipotent reigneth
c. The Kingdom of this world is become the Kingdom of Our Lord and of His Christ.
d. And He shall reign for ever and ever
King of Kings and Lord of Lords
And He shall reign for ever and ever
Hallelujah! Hallelujah!

The opening of this exultant chorus is noteworthy for its repeated and emphatic Hallelujahs (a), followed by a sudden contrasting quieter section (b). An even softer section begins with (c) "The Kingdom of this world," which is quickly followed by the majestic fugue of (d) "And he shall reign for ever and ever." As the chorus moves exuberantly toward its dramatic conclusion, Handel splits the voices. The top voice is split into two voices, soprano and alto, and they rise higher and higher on the phrase "King of Kings and Lord of Lords." The bottom voice is also divided into two voices, tenor and bass, which sing "for ever and ever,

Hallelujah!" The four voices are bolstered by the jubilance of beating drums and trumpeting brass. The entire effect is one of Baroque drama, a play between the "light" of the soprano voices and brass contrasted with the "darkness" of the drums and bass line, capturing the essence of the crucifixion's simultaneous sorrow and joy.

Composed in an astonishing twenty-three days, *Messiah* was first performed not in London but in Dublin, in 1742, for the relief of prisoners and wards of the state. It was not until 1750 that the London public fully responded to the work. Upon completing *Messiah* Handel's eyes are said to have filled with tears, and he is reputed to have said, "I did think I did see all Heaven before me, and the Great God Himself!"

Another story regarding *Messiah* concerns its premiere, in Dublin, when Handel had to rely on a number of nonprofessional singers. One bass was recommended as a good singer who could sight-read unfamiliar music. At the rehearsal, however, he had trouble reading his part, prompting Handel to shout, "You scoundrel! Did you not say you could sing at sight?" "Yes sir," the bass replied, "but not at first sight."

Last, we might wonder whether, since Handel was an almost exact contemporary of Johan Sebastian Bach and since they both lived and worked in Germany, they might have known each other or have been friends. But they actually never met, although Bach tried to arrange a meeting on more than one occasion. Bach, however, was far less famous and important a figure than Handel then, and Handel was less interested in such a meeting.

Henry Purcell and English Opera. Before Handel began his career as a composer of operas and oratorios, Henry Purcell (1659–1695) had established himself as one of the premier Baroque composers. Purcell wrote instrumental works in a variety of genres, but he is best known for his opera *Dido and Aeneas*, based on Virgil's *Aeneid*. Among the most popular musical moments in this opera is "Dido's Lament," a mournful melody whose shape declines in tones to reflect Dido's thoughts about the suicide she is contemplating when she learns that her lover Aeneas has abandoned her.

Johann Sebastian Bach. The other great Baroque composer (many would claim the greatest) is JOHANN SEBASTIAN BACH [BAHK] (1685–1750), the grand master of the Baroque style and musical art forms of his age, and as thorough and thoughtful a musician as ever lived. Bach's output includes music for voices and instruments in every major form of the era except opera. His works for keyboard include hundreds of pieces that are used today as teaching pieces. He played and composed solo works for a number of instruments, including violin and harpsichord (fig. 15.29), and was master of the organ, on which he could improvise at will the most complicated fugues.

A **fugue** is composed of three or four independent parts of which one part, or voice, states a theme, which is then imitated in succession by each of the other voices. As the second voice takes over the theme from the first, the first continues playing in **counterpoint,** music that differs from the main theme. The third voice takes over from the second, the second continues on in counterpoint, and so on. The driving rhythm of Bach's fugues create drama and tension, as the musical voices seem to chase one another, only to be resolved when they come together peacefully at the end.

Bach developed to perfection the art of such *polyphonic* music, or music for multiple voices. As a young church organist, Bach demonstrated a talent for improvising on hymn tunes, so much so that complaints were lodged against him "for having made many curious variations in the chorale and mingled many strange tones in it." He was at work on his *Art of the Fugue*, an encyclopedic compendium of fugues for study and performance, when he died.

Bach's professional career began with a position as organist at a church in Arnstadt. Then he served for nine years as court organist and chamber musician at the court of the duke of Weimar, composing many works for the organ. Next Bach served as director of music for the prince of Cöthen, where he composed a set of six concertos dedicated to the Margrave of Brandenburg, subsequently known as *The Brandenburg Concertos*. Bach's longest musical post was as music director of the Church of St. Thomas in Leipzig, where for twenty-seven years he served as organist, choirmaster, composer, and music director. At Leipzig, Bach produced his religious vocal music, including the *B Minor Mass*, the *St. John* and *St. Matthew Passions*, and numerous church cantatas, of which he wrote nearly three hundred, more than two hundred of which survive. A **cantata** is a work for a single singer or group of singers accompanied by instruments.

FIGURE 15.29 Jerome de Zentis, harpsichord, 1658. Maker: Girolamo Zenti. Robet Harding/Metropolitan Museum of Art, New York. Art Resource, NY. A keyboard instrument that was often intricately decorated, the Baroque harpsichord had strings that were plucked by mechanical plectra inside the body of the instrument.

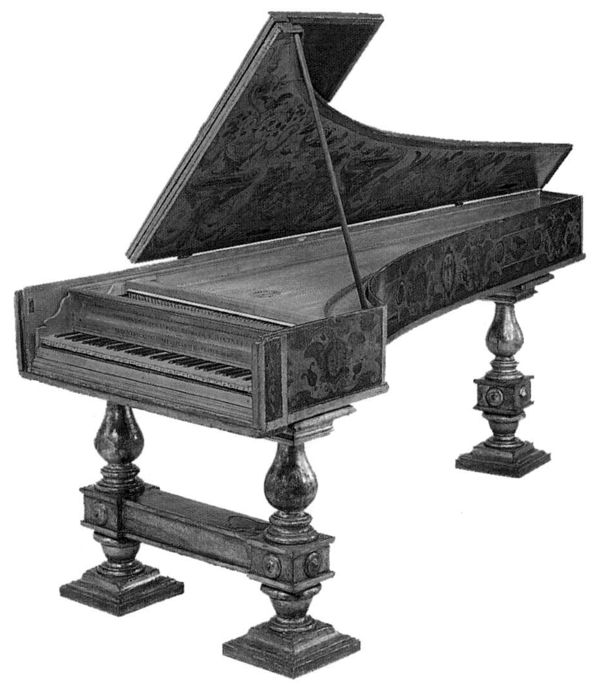

Cross Currents

THE BAROQUE IN MEXICO

When the Spanish explorers led by Hernán Cortés came to America in 1519, they spread Catholicism with zeal. With the support of Jesuits, missionaries, and the political and financial backing of European governments, seventeenth-century South America boasted a strong European cultural connection, including no fewer than five universities, the largest and most important of which was in Mexico City.

Mexican-born writers and artists worked hand in hand with their European-born counterparts to create a native architecture and literature that spoke to the European cultural heritage. Great Baroque structures were built, the leading example of which is the Chapel of the Rosary in the Church of Santo Domingo in Puebla (fig. 15.30), completed about 1690. Like much Mexican art, it melds local traditions and Catholic icons. Here local artisans crafted images in polychrome stucco that, although they represent Christian figures, possess the faces and dresses of native Mexicans. Meandering vines weave across the ceilings, and gold leaf covers the altar. So elaborate is the whole that the style is called the "exuberant Baroque."

Among the most noteworthy and influential of Mexican Baroque writers was SOR JUANA INÉS DE LA CRUZ [soar HWA-nah] (1648–1695), who was born near Mexico City. Hailed as the "Phoenix of Mexico" and "America's Tenth Muse" during her lifetime, Sor Juana is considered one of the finest Spanish American writers of her time. Although a nun, she also became the confidante of prominent leaders and intellectuals throughout Spanish America.

Her poetry speaks to women across cultures and centuries in a language that is by turns playful and ironically critical of men's failures, as shown in the first and last stanzas from her aptly titled poem, "She Demonstrates the Inconsistency of Men's Wishes in Blaming Women for What They Themselves Have Caused":

> Silly, you men—so very adept
> at wrongly faulting womankind,
> not seeing you're alone to blame
> for faults you plant in woman's mind . . .
> I well know what powerful arms
> you wield in pressing for evil:
> your arrogance is allied
> with the world, the flesh, and the devil.

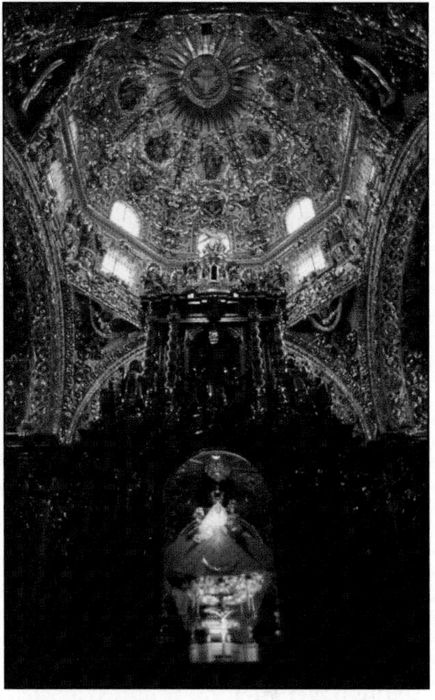

FIGURE 15.30 Chapel of the Rosary, Church of Santo Domingo, Puebla, Mexico, ca. 1690. Free of any preconceptions that would limit their decorative impulses, the artists who fashioned this interior were able to press the Baroque sensibility to its very limits.

Among these is the famous *Cantata No. 80: Ein feste Burg ist unser Gott* (*A Mighty Fortress Is Our God*), composed in 1715, revised in 1724, and based on the hymn, or chorale, by Martin Luther. Like many of Bach's sacred, or church, cantatas, this one was written for Lutheran services. The cantatas were performed by eight to twelve singers and an orchestral ensemble of eighteen to twenty-four musicians (although Bach often complained he had to make do with wretched musicians and underprepared vocalists). Luther's original chorale, which is in itself a centerpiece of Protestant hymnology, appears in eloquent and simple majesty in a four-part harmonization as the final movement of Bach's cantata.

Bach's music gained worldwide popularity when a composer of the Romantic era, Felix Mendelssohn (1809–1847), arranged for a performance of Bach's *Passion According to St. Matthew* some eighty years after Bach's death. Since that time, Bach has been considered the consummate composer of Baroque music. His musical style has been adapted to a variety of genres. Jazz performers study Bach's improvisational style and his theoretical techniques. Groups such as the Swingle Singers and the Thomas Gabriel Trio have adapted Bach's works in a fusion of jazz and Baroque styles. His polyphonic compositions are well suited to computer-generated music such as the series of Wendy Carlos's *Switched On Bach*.

Among the numerous children of J. S. Bach were four sons who were composers, some more famous in their time than their illustrious father—Wilhelm Friedemann, Carl Philipp Emanuel, Johann Christoph Friedrich, and Johann Christian. An additional claimant to the Bach pedigree is P.D.Q. Bach, the invented humorous alter ego of the contemporary composer and musicologist Peter Schickele (b. 1935). Professor Schickele perennially "discovers" musical compositions of P.D.Q. Bach. He then arranges performances with friends and colleagues of works with titles such as "Oedipus Tex," "1712 Overture,"and "Grand Serenade for an Awful Lot of Percussion." Although musicians derive the deepest pleasure from Schickele's musical shenanigans, his antics provide amusement for a wide audience who like their music seasoned with comedy.

THE SCIENCE OF OBSERVATION

The precision of Bach's fugues and Vermeer's paintings echo the scientific spirit of the Baroque age. Francis Bacon's development of the principles of the scientific method (see Chapter 14), with its emphasis on the careful observation of physical phenomena, resounded throughout the Baroque age in a vast array of scientific discoveries and inventions. Precise observation required new tools for seeing, and these new observations in turn created new knowledge.

Anton van Leeuwenhoek. In Holland, for instance, a lens maker named ANTON VAN LEEUWENHOEK [LAY-ven-huck] (1632–1723) transformed the magnifying glasses used by lace makers and embroiderers into powerful microscopes capable of seeing small organisms. He investigated everything under his microscope (including all of his bodily fluids). Leeuwenhoek quickly realized that the world was teeming with microorganisms he called "little animals." He was the first person to see protozoa and bacteria and the first to describe the red blood cell. Leeuwenhoek was also fascinated with the mechanisms of sight, particularly with the fact that the eye is itself a lens. He dissected insect and animal eyes, and actually looked through them himself. He describes looking at the tower of the New Church through the eye of a dragonfly: "A great many Towers were presented, also upside down, and they appeared no bigger than does the point of a small pin to our Eye."

Johannes Kepler. JOHANNES KEPLER [KEP-ler] (1571–1630) had been equally interested in the eye, and in 1604 he was the first to describe it as an optical instrument with a lens used for focusing (fig. 15.31). "Vision," he wrote, "is brought about by a picture of the thing seen being formed on the concave surface of the retina."

"I leave to natural philosophers to discuss the way in which this picture is put together by the spiritual principles of vision residing in the retina and the nerves," he wrote, "and whether it is made to appear before the soul or tribunal of the faculty of vision by a spirit within the cerebral cavities, or the faculty of vision, like a magistrate sent by the soul, goes out from the council chamber of the brain to meet this image in the optic nerves and retina, as it were descending to a lower court." Kepler is interested in the *fact* of vision, not its metaphysical meaning.

Galileo Galilei. Kepler's friend GALILEO GALILEI [gali-LAY-o] (1564–1642) was the first to develop the telescope and use it to observe the heavens. Through it he saw and described craters on the moon, the phases of Venus, and sunspots, and he theorized, in one of the important advances of physics, that light takes time to get from one place to another—that, either as a particle or wave, it travels at a uniform speed that is measurable. Galileo's astronomical findings confirmed Copernicus's theory that the earth circled the sun, a position the Church still did not accept. In 1615, Galileo was forced to defend his ideas before Pope Paul V in Rome, but his efforts failed, and he was prohibited from either publishing or teaching his findings. When Pope Urban VIII, an old friend, was elected pope, Galileo appealed to the papacy again, but again he was condemned, this time much more severely. He was made to admit the error of his ways in public and sentenced to prison for the rest of his life. Friends intervened, and in the end he was merely banished to a comfortable villa outside Florence.

PHILOSOPHY

René Descartes. Kepler's effort to distinguish the science of observation from the contemplation of the subjective or spiritual matters of the mind was well known to RENÉ DESCARTES [day-CART] (1595–1650). Descartes actually

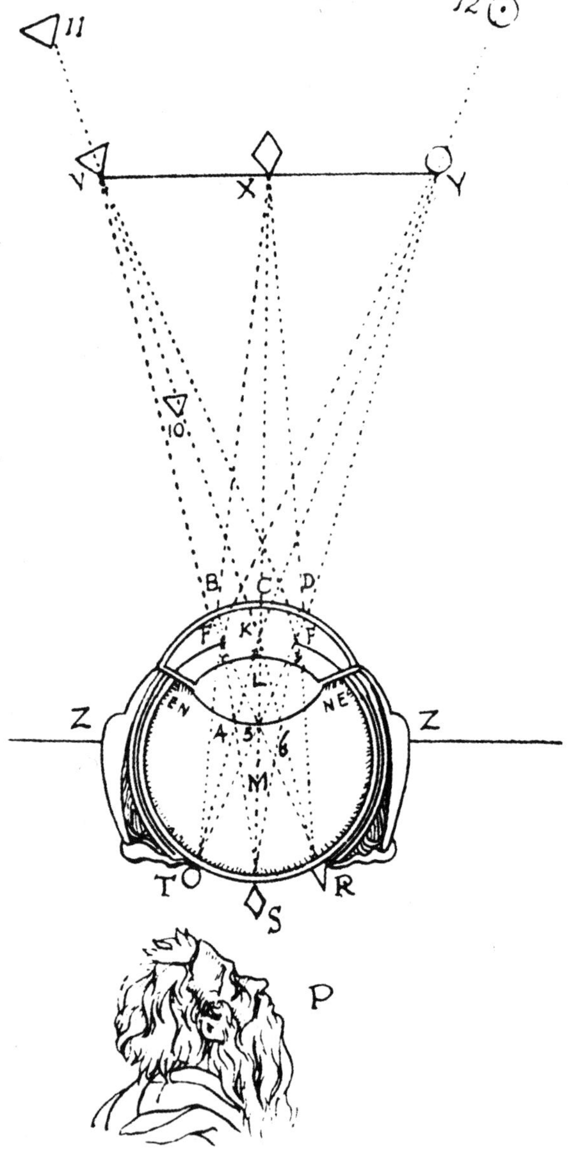

FIGURE 15.31 Illustration of the theory of the retinal image, from René Descartes, *La Dioptrique* (Leiden, 1637), Bancroft Library, Berkeley, California. No image better illustrates the importance of scientific observation to the Baroque sensibility. Even the eye itself is defined here as a scientific instrument.

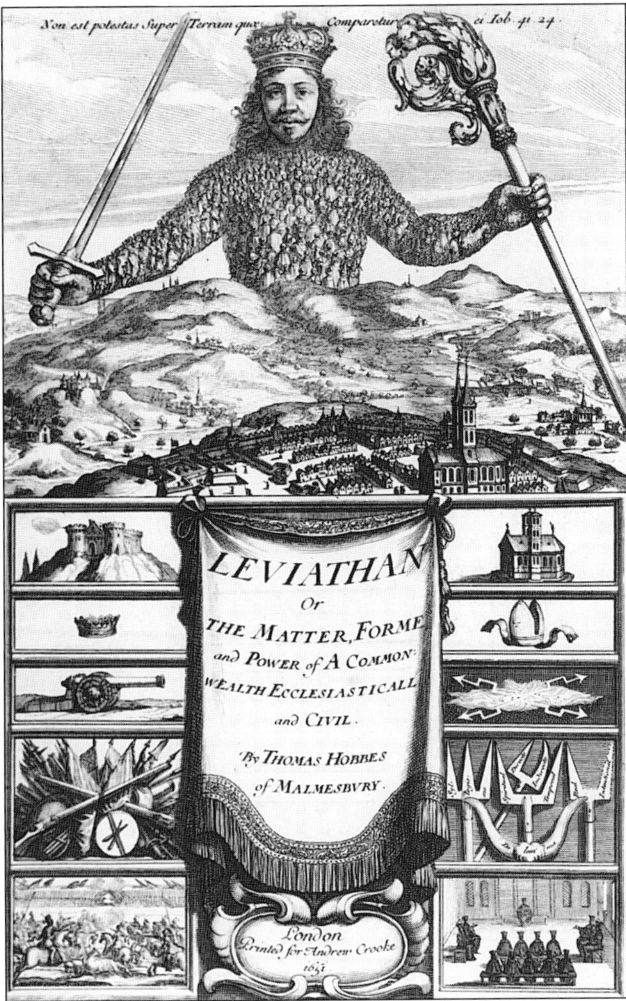

FIGURE 15.32 Frontispiece of *Leviathan*, 1651, Bancroft Library, Berkeley, California. An image of the social contract, the body of the king is made up of hundreds of his subjects. He rules over a world at peace, its cities well-fortified and its countryside well-groomed.

published the illustrated model of the retinal image (fig. 15.32) in his own work. But Descartes was interested in what Kepler was not. He was, in fact, the very "natural philosopher" to whom Kepler left the problem of what happened to the image once it registered itself on the retina. Descartes did for modern philosophy what Bacon had done for science, and so he is often called the "Father of Modern Philosophy."

Descartes used doubt as a point of departure and philosophical debate. He began with a series of systematic questions that led him to doubt the existence of everything. At that point, he asked himself if there was anything at all he could know with certainty. His answer was that the only thing he could conceive of "clearly" and "distinctly" (his two essential criteria) was that he existed as a doubting entity. Descartes formulated this fundamental concept in Latin: *Cogito, ergo sum*, which means "I think, therefore I am." According to Descartes, this *cogito* provided the foundation, principle, and model for all subsequent knowledge, which he held to the same standards of evidence and rationality.

Descartes began by doubting the existence of the external world. He surmised that he might, perhaps, be dreaming or hallucinating the world outside himself. Eventually, he tried to doubt his own existence. With this, he realized that he was the doubter, that it was his mind that did the doubting. And, therefore, Descartes reasoned, "I think (or perhaps "I doubt"), therefore, I exist."

Turning his attention from himself to the world, Descartes allowed that the only thing he could *know* for certain about the material world is that it too exists. He believed there was an absolute division between mind and matter. Matter could be studied mathematically and scientifically, its behavior predicted by the new science of physics. How the mind knows something is altogether different. When we observe an object in the distance—the sun, for instance—it appears to be small, but we know through scientific observation that it is much larger than it appears. Knowledge, Descartes recognized, cannot rest on perception alone. This had been demonstrated by Copernicus's theory of the universe: We may perceive ourselves to be standing still, but we are on a planet spinning quickly through space.

This recognition led Descartes to ask how we can know that which we cannot perceive. Most important, how can we know that God exists, if we cannot perceive him? Descartes decided, finally, that if we are too imperfect to trust even our own perceptions, and yet we are still able to *imagine* a perfect God, then God must exist. If he did not, then he would be unimaginable. In other words, what is "clearly" and "distinctly" perceived by the mind—*Cogito, ergo sum*—must be true. Descartes's answer was somewhat paradoxical and would lead to much philosophical debate in the centuries to come.

Thomas Hobbes. During the Baroque age, the question of how to govern increasingly occupied philosophical thinkers. In England, the situation reached a crisis point when Charles I challenged Parliament's identity as the king's partner in rule. Civil war erupted, and in 1649, a Commonwealth was established, led by the Puritan Oliver Cromwell as, essentially, a military dictatorship. The monarchy was restored in 1660 after the republic failed, but the relationship between parliament and monarch remained murky. Finally, in 1688, James II was expelled in the bloodless "Glorious Revolution," and Mary and William of Orange, James's daughter and son-in-law, ascended the throne. They immediately accepted the rights of all citizens under the law, recognizing in particular Parliament's right to exercise authority over financial matters, and England became a limited monarchy.

In this atmosphere, the debate about who should govern and how was addressed by two political philosophers with very different points of view. Mirroring Descartes's emphasis on the primacy of perception was the philosopher Thomas Hobbes (1588–1679). Educated as a classicist, Hobbes was particularly impressed by the geometry of Euclid, and he came to believe the reasoning on which geometry is based could be extended to social and political life.

After visiting with Galileo in Italy, Hobbes became even more convinced this was true. The power of Galileo's science of observation and its ability to describe the movement of the solar system could be extended to the observation of human beings in their relations to one another.

Hobbes's philosophy, published in 1651 in a book entitled *Leviathan* (see fig. 15.32), would be read by many as an apology for, or defense of, monarchical rule. Hobbes believed that humans are driven by two primal forces, the fear of death and the desire for power. If government does nothing to check these impulses, humankind simply self-destructs. He put it famously that, without governments, man's natural state wars "solitary, poor, nasty, brutish, and short." But Hobbes also believed that humans recognize their essential depravity and therefore choose to be governed. They enter into what he called the **social contract,** by which the people choose to give up sovereignty over themselves and bestow it on a ruler. They agree to carry out all the ruler's commands, and in return the ruler agrees to keep the peace.

Despite his belief in the need for a "visible Power" to keep people in "awe and tie them to their Covenants," Hobbes attacked the idea of the divine right of kings. In this he was branded a heretic, if not an atheist, and he was called such names as "Apostle of Infidelity" and "Bugbear of the Nation." Even so, Hobbes's *Leviathan* had a profound influence on political theory, social ethics, and international law.

John Locke. JOHN LOCKE [lock] (1632–1704), repudiating Hobbes, believed people are perfectly capable of governing themselves. Locke's *Essay on Human Understanding*, published in 1690, argues that the human mind is at birth a *tabula rasa*, or "blank slate." Then two great "fountains of knowledge," our environment as opposed to our heredity, and our reason as opposed to our faith, fill this blank slate with learning as the person develops. Locke argued, furthermore, in his *Second Treatise on Government*, also published in 1690, that humans are "by nature free, equal, and independent." They accept the rule of government, he argues, because they find it convenient to do so, not because they are innately inclined to submit to authority. Such ideas set the stage for the political revolutions of the eighteenth century.

Locke's *Two Treatises of Government* have been acknowledged as inspiring both the American and French revolutions, with their emphasis on freedoms and fundamental rights. Locke's influence is felt in the Declaration of Independence and in the Bill of Rights. His impact is felt further in the French doctrine of natural rights and in the French Declaration of the Rights of Man. The philosopher and writer Voltaire considered Locke a man of great wisdom. Benjamin Franklin was inspired by him, and Thomas Jefferson valued Locke as a great philosopher of liberty.

LITERATURE

Unlike Renaissance writers, who were often content to catalog the beauties of the beloved, Baroque writers explore the mysteries of love, both erotic and divine. Baroque writers, overall, also spend considerably more time exploring their relationship to God, often in passionate and dramatic terms. Religious and secular Baroque writing, poetry in particular, often dramatizes emotional and personal encounters between speaker and listener (whether God or lover).

Molière and the Baroque Stage. During the Baroque era, stage plans differed from those of Shakespeare and classical Greece. Seventeenth-century plays took place indoors on a stage, with a **proscenium arch,** an arch that stands in front of the scene and divides the stage from the auditorium. A supporting curtain separates the audience from the actors. The plays were enacted on a box stage, which represented a room with a missing fourth wall, allowing the audience to look in on the action. This is still the most popular stage in use.

Unelaborate painted scenery served as a backdrop for the action. Candles and lanterns illuminated actors and audience. Costume tended toward the ornate, as in Elizabethan drama. On both Elizabethan and Baroque stages, actors were costumed in the contemporary dress appropriate to the social status of the characters they portrayed. An innovation in seventeenth-century drama was that female actresses assumed women's roles for the first time, enabling more extensive, more frequent, and more realistic love scenes. As in the earlier eras of drama, however, language still did much of the work.

The conventions of the French theater of the time were inspired by the classical drama of Greece and Rome. Like its ancient antecedents, the seventeenth-century French theater observed what are known as the three **unities:** the unity of time, the unity of place, and the unity of action. A play's action had to be confined to a twenty-four-hour period. The place should be a single setting. The action must be unified in a single plot. Plays that violated these

Table 15–1 SEVENTEENTH-CENTURY SCIENTISTS AND PHILOSOPHERS

Scientists	Anton van Leeuwenhoek (1632–1723): The microscope
	Johannes Kepler (1571–1639): The science of vision
	Galileo Galilei (1564–1642): The telescope
Philosophers	Thomas Hobbes (1588–1679): *Leviathan* social contract
	René Descartes (1595–1650): *Cogito, ergo sum* (I think, therefore I am)
	John Locke (1632–1704): *Essay on Human Understanding;* tabula rasa (blank slate)

Then & Now

THE TELESCOPE

Galileo's telescope (fig. 15.33) changed the way people thought of their solar system. It demonstrated conclusively that the earth and other planets orbited around the sun. The modern-day Hubble Space Telescope is rapidly enhancing our understanding of the solar system's place in the universe. Deployed into Earth's orbit on April 24, 1990, from the space shuttle *Discovery*, the 12.5-ton satellite is able to look directly at the cosmos unhindered by Earth's atmosphere. It has revealed galaxy forms as far as twelve billion light-years away, which may be the furthest reaches of our universe.

Galileo was able to see other galaxies, which he called *nebulae* (clouds). Hubble's photographs suggest that these *nebulae* are really clumps of gas that generate new stars. Enormous jets of gas erupt out of these gas clumps at speeds up to 300 miles per second and are shot trillions of miles out into space. This is the stuff, scientists believe, of which solar systems are made. Hubble has shown these whirling jets all at once form a star and shoot out jets of matter that will form something like our own solar system. The implication is that some stars, even in our own galaxy, may possess solar systems similar to our own, and hence the possibility of life.

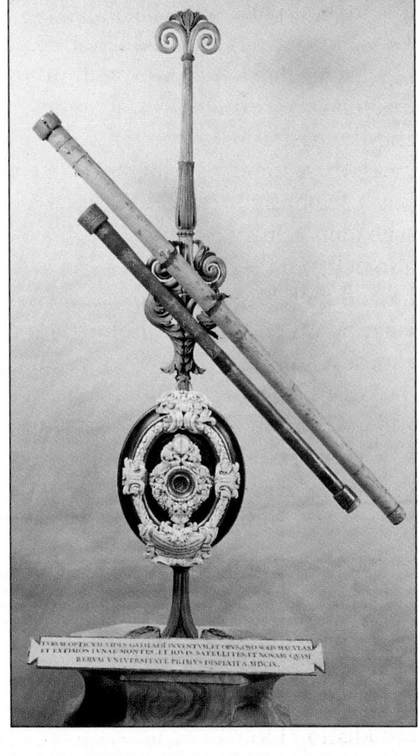

FIGURE 15.33 Galileo Galilei, Telescope, 1609, Museo di Scienza Florence. With a telescope such as this, Galileo was able to contradict the Ptolemaic view of the universe.

unities were thought crude and inelegant by their audience, which consisted largely of courtiers and aristocrats. The three great practitioners of the French Baroque theater all observed the unities—its two great tragedians, PIERRE CORNEILLE [kor-NAY] (1606–1684) and JEAN RACINE [ra-SEEN] (1639–1699), and its great comic genius Jean-Baptiste Poquelin, known by his stage name MOLIÈRE [mol-YAIR] (1622–1673).

Corneille's themes are patriotism and honor. Racine's plays concentrate on the moral dilemmas of the Greek tragedies. But of the three, Molière's satiric comedy is the most accessible, resorting, as it often does, to slapstick, pratfalls, and the sorts of comic predicaments modern audiences still enjoy. Among his masterpieces is *Tartuffe*, which satirizes fraud and religious hypocrisy. The play also pokes fun at the gullibility of those who allow themselves to be taken in by greedy, self-serving sanctimony.

When *Tartuffe* was first staged in 1664, it antagonized some who considered it an attack on religion. Even though Molière retitled it *The Impostor* to indicate Tartuffe's fraudulence, the play was censored and banned. To defend himself and his play against such charges, Molière wrote three prefaces and later changed his original ending. The publicity enhanced the play's popularity, and the work was returned to the stage under the protection of the king. Its unending popularity, however, is due neither to royal protection nor to notoriety, but rather to the ingenuity of its plot, the vitality of its characters, and the brilliance of its language.

John Donne. JOHN DONNE [dun] (1572–1631) is considered among the finest poets of his, or indeed of any, age. He wrote prose as well as verse, and his poetry includes amorous lyrics, philosophical poems, devotional sonnets and hymns, elegies, epistles, and satires.

Born into a Roman Catholic family in anti-Catholic England, Donne attended Oxford and Cambridge Universities, though he neither took an academic degree nor practiced law. He later converted to Anglicanism and was appointed private secretary to Sir Thomas Egerton, a high court official. When Donne secretly married his employer's niece, Anne More, he was dismissed and prohibited from obtaining court appointment, first by Egerton and later by King James I, who wanted Donne to become an Anglican preacher. This Donne eventually did, being ordained to the ministry in 1615 and made dean of St. Paul's Cathedral in London in 1621, where he served until his death ten years later.

Donne's "A Valediction: Forbidding Mourning," a philosophical love poem, is noted for its extended analogy or conceit comparing lovers to the two feet of a geometrician's compasses.

As virtuous men pass mildly away,
  And whisper to their souls to go,
While some of their sad friends do say,
  The breath goes now, and some say, no:
So let us melt, and make no noise,
  No tear-floods, nor sigh-tempests move;
'Twere profanation of our joys
  To tell the laity our love.
Moving of th' earth brings harms and fears,
  Men reckon what it did and meant,
But trepidation of the spheres,
  Though greater far, is innocent.
Dull sublunary lovers' love
  (Whose soul is sense) cannot admit
Absence, because it doth remove
  Those things which elemented it.
But we by a love so much refined,
  That ourselves know not what it is,
Inter-assured of the mind,
  Care less, eyes, lips, and hands to miss.
Our two souls therefore, which are one,
  Though I must go, endure not yet
A breach, but an expansion,
  Like gold to airy thinness beat.
If they be two, they are two so
  As stiff twin compasses are two;
Thy soul the fixed foot, makes no show
  To move, but doth, if th' other do.
And though it in the center sit,
  Yet when the other far doth roam,
It leans, and hearkens after it,
  And grows erect, as that comes home.
Such wilt thou be to me, who must
  Like th' other foot, obliquely run:
Thy firmness makes my circle just,
  And makes me end, where I begun.

Contemporary sources note that Donne addressed this poem to his wife as he was preparing in 1611 for a continental journey. He had premonitions of disaster, which turned out to be well founded because his wife gave birth to a stillborn child while he was abroad. In the first two stanzas the speaker urges his wife not to make a public spectacle of their grief on parting. The poet/speaker compares their leave-taking with the death of virtuous men, who depart life quietly and peacefully. He urges her to emulate their behavior, arguing that theatrical displays of unhappiness profane their deeply private relationship.

Throughout the next four stanzas the speaker contrasts the couple's higher, more spiritual love with the love of the sensual. Their love, intellectual and spiritual, transcends the senses. In these stanzas, Donne introduces the first of his two important conceits: that the lovers' souls are not really separated but are almost infinitely expanded to fill the intervening space between them, as gold expands when beaten into paper-thin sheets. The comparison with gold suggests the value of love and its prominent position in their lives. This use of concrete reality to illuminate a spiritual condition typifies Donne's amalgamation of disparate realms of experience.

The last part of Donne's "A Valediction: Forbidding Mourning," however, extends his conceit over three stanzas. The compass is a symbol of constancy and change, since it both moves and remains stationary. The compass also inscribes a circle, symbol of perfection. These ideas of constancy and perfection are worked through in detail as the speaker/poet explains how one foot of the compass moves only in relation to the other, returning "home" when the two feet of the compass are brought together.

Anne Bradstreet. Among Donne's near contemporaries is Anne Bradstreet (1612–1672), the first major poet in American literature. Born Anne Dudley to a Puritan family in Northampton, England, she sailed with her parents and her new husband, Simon Bradstreet, to Massachusetts in 1630. As secretary to the Massachusetts Bay Company, Simon often traveled on company business, leaving Anne alone. On several occasions she wrote poems about their separation. "A Letter to Her Husband, Absent upon Public Employment" is an example.

Though best known today for her domestic lyrics, in her own day Bradstreet was known for a cycle of historical poems based on the four ages of humanity. Donne's philosophical poems, and Bradstreet's domestic ones, can be compared with the art of Vermeer, whose paintings, although few in number, embody near perfection of form and idea. The following poem to her husband is an example.

TO MY DEAR AND LOVING HUSBAND

If ever two were one, then surely we.
If ever man were lov'd by wife, then thee.
If ever wife was happy in a man,
Compare with me, ye women, if you can.
I prize thy love more than whole Mines of gold
Or all the riches that the East doth hold.
My love is such that Rivers cannot quench,
Nor ought but love from thee give recompetence.
Thy love is such I can no way repay.
The heavens reward thee manifold, I pray.
Then while we live, in love let's so persever
That when we live no more, we may live ever.

John Milton. John Milton (1608–1674) represents a facet of Baroque sensibility that John Donne lacked. Unlike Donne, whose poems are mostly brief lyrics, Milton had a monumental conception of poetry attuned to the epic. Like the architect Bernini, the painter Rubens, and the composers Bach and Handel, Milton worked on a grand scale.

No poet more than Milton embodies a grand ideal of the poetic vocation. He believed a poet had to prepare the mind and soul through study and prayer before attempting to produce great art.

One kind of preparation was his study of the classical writers of ancient Greece and Rome—Homer, Virgil, Ovid, and Theocritus. Another was his study of the complete Bible, which he is said to have memorized. Following these studies Milton wrote poetry at once serious in outlook and grand in manner, befitting one who wanted to "leave something so written to aftertimes as they should not willingly let it die."

Combining the ideals of classical humanism and biblical morality more thoroughly and more profoundly than any other writer in English, Milton presents a summation of High Renaissance art and Christian humanism. From the Greeks and Romans Milton derived a sense of civic responsibility. Milton valued statesmen, who by virtue of their nobility, intellectuality, and vision might ensure the survival of humane values. In later life, Milton found his ideal in the Puritan leader Oliver Cromwell, for whom he wrote a series of prose works.

Milton's life can be divided into three parts. First, he prepared for his vocation. This period culminated in the publication of "Lycidas," his elegy on the death of a drowned friend, followed by a two-year tour of Europe. Second, from about 1640 to 1660 was a twenty-year span of political involvement, during which he wrote prose rather than poetry. In the service of the Puritan cause, Milton produced pamphlets and tracts on various theological and ecclesiastical issues, such as Christian doctrine and divorce. When the English monarchy was restored to the Stuart line, Milton was imprisoned and his property confiscated. Set free a short time later, he lived out the third part of his life in relative isolation working on his great epic poems. Milton lived the last two decades of his life in blindness caused, in part, by his exhausting work on behalf of the Puritans.

Milton spent the last fifteen years of his life writing and publishing his most ambitious works: *Paradise Lost* (1667), *Paradise Regained* (1671), and *Samson Agonistes* (1671). In these poems, especially in *Paradise Lost*, Milton attempted, in his words, "to justify the ways of God to man." This idea of justification reflected Milton's blend of Puritan theology and classical humanism. Milton reinterpreted the events of Genesis—humankind's fall from grace, and its banishment from the Garden of Eden. Milton emphasized the central belief of Christianity: the incarnation of God-as-man in Jesus Christ, who came to atone for the sin of humanity's first parents. Christ's sacrifice thus gained for human beings the chance for eternal life—providing they live in accordance with biblical teachings.

We should note, however, that although Milton's major life work was his epic, *Paradise Lost*, he also wrote a few exquisite sonnets. The two reprinted here, one on his blindness, the other on his deceased wife, are perhaps his finest efforts in the genre.

When I Consider How My Light Is Spent

When I consider how my light is spent
Ere half my days in this dark world and wide,
And that one talent which is death to hide
Lodg'd with me useless, though my soul more bent
To serve therewith my Maker, and present
My true account, lest he returning chide,
"Doth God exact day-labour, light denied?"
I fondly ask. But Patience, to prevent
That murmur, soon replies: "God doth not need
Either man's work or his own gifts: who best
Bear his mild yoke, they serve him best. His state
Is kingly; thousands at his bidding speed
And post o'er land and ocean without rest:
They also serve who only stand and wait."

On His Deceased Wife

Methought I saw my late espoused saint
Brought to me like Alcestis from the grave,
Whom Jove's great son to her glad husband gave,
Rescued form death by force, though pale and faint.
Mine, as whom wash'd from spot of child-bed taint
Purification in the old Law did save,
And such, as yet once more I trust to have
Full sight of her in Heaven without restraint,
Came vested all in white, pure as her mind:
Her face was veil'd yet to my fancied sight
Love, sweetness, goodness, in her person shin'd
So clear, as in no face with more delight.
But O, as to embrace me she inclin'd,
I wak'd; she fled; and day brought back my night.

Miguel de Cervantes. During the sixteenth century in Spain, a narrative form known as the **picaresque** began to develop. The picaresque novel details the life of a *pícaro*, a rogue or knave who wanders from adventure to adventure, and marks the birth of the novel as a literary art form. Like Chaucer's *Canterbury Tales*, the picaresque novel probably developed out of the pilgrimage tradition, in particular the pilgrimage across northern Spain to Santiago de Compostela, the burial place of St. James, which in the eleventh and twelfth centuries had been the object of European pilgrimages. Whereas the *Canterbury Tales* is a compendium of stories about different pilgrims, the picaresque novel focuses on a single hero.

One characteristic feature of the picaresque novel is its pseudo-autobiographical nature. Narrated always by the hero, the point of view is clearly his, prejudiced and partial. He is an observer of society, and, perhaps as a result, he is expert at recognizing fraud and deception.

The greatest of all picaresque novels is *Don Quixote*, by MIGUEL DE CERVANTES [ser-VAHN-tez] (1548–1616). It is in fact more than a picaresque novel, satirizing the form even as it goes beyond it in complexity and ambition. Composed between 1603 and 1615, *Don Quixote*

Cultural Impact

The Baroque era celebrated individual genius while endorsing new forms of social cooperation and artistic patronage. Begun in Italy, the Baroque style spread throughout Europe. In Italy the Counter-Reformation fueled an emotional embrace of the spiritual world, seen especially in the sculpture and architecture of Bernini.

The Baroque style influenced the creation of public buildings and monuments, as well as domestic architecture. The monuments of southern Baroque architecture were funded not by private donors but by public commission of court or church. Piazzas and fountains abounded in Italy, with forms alluding to religious history and Greco-Roman mythology.

The Roman Church and Counter-Reformation spirituality retained influence on the music of the southern Baroque. However, Baroque music became as much a secular as a religious art. Opera, invented in Italy during the early Baroque, initially took its subjects from myth, history, and legend. This trend continued in later centuries, as the influence of opera became more prominent.

The impact of the Baroque in northern Europe was quieter and less flamboyant, with the north revealing a more subdued but no less sustained shift of cultural expression. In England and in Holland, for example, artistic patronage shifted from court and church to wealthy patrons, who commissioned works honoring themselves and their world. This celebration of social ideals and middle-class prosperity are hallmarks of the northern Baroque. Portraits by Rembrandt of prominent individuals and of members of civic organizations exemplify this desire for recognition and honor.

Northern Baroque painters such as Rembrandt and Rubens amassed huge fortunes. Rembrandt was to lose his and died nearly destitute. Rubens, however, oversaw a large studio and inaugurated a major industry—the production of masterpieces with the aid of teams of assistants.

The situation was otherwise for literature, which was only occasionally commissioned and almost exclusively composed by an individual. John Donne's poems circulated in manuscript only to be published after his death. While employing Renaissance poetic conventions and playfully undermining them, Donne and his followers seasoned poetry with wit and ingenuity. Donne's influence appears in such later poets as Emily Dickinson in the nineteenth century and T. S. Eliot in the twentieth.

Unlike their counterparts in the south, composers of the northern Baroque were not exclusively in the employ of the Roman Church. Thus, although J. S. Bach and G. F. Handel both wrote reams of music for religious occasions, both composed much music for court and private entertainment as well. Their music, and the music of Baroque masters in the south such as Antonio Vivaldi, was designed to challenge the virtuosity of the performer, an emphasis that would be taken much further later, especially during the Romantic era.

Perhaps the greatest legacy of the northern Baroque was the emergence of objectivity with the inductive method of Baconian science and the rational analytical method of Cartesian philosophical thought. Casting everything into doubt until proof could be established, Bacon and Descartes changed science and philosophy forever.

Finally, the expansion of colonial empires spread European values and ideals around the globe, particularly to the shores on the Americas, where they took root and sprouted during the eras of the Enlightenment and Romanticism.

was translated in the seventeenth century into English, French, Italian, and German. The central character, Don Quixote, the hero, wants, most of all, to become a "knight errant," the kind of hero he has read about in books, who saves ladies from evil and defeats dragons in combat. In fact, he is at once noble and a buffoon. What he sees and what is the truth are two entirely different things. His horse is "all skin and bones," but in his eyes, it is a noble "steed." His companion is a peasant boy, redubbed his "squire," Sancho Panza. His lady, the lovely Dulcinea, is actually one Aldonza Lorenzo, who "never knew or was aware of" his love for her. And the giants he fights are not giants at all, but windmills. The novel represents, for the first time in Western literature, the conflict between reality and the imagination, and although Don Quixote's imagination brings him to the edge of total madness, it ennobles him as well.

KEY TERMS

Baroque
Counter-Reformation
oratories
colonnade
portico
obelisk
tenebrism
opera
recitative
concerto grosso
ritornello
camera obscura
poussinistes/rubénistes
oratorio
aria
fugue
counterpoint
cantata
social contract
proscenium arch
unities
picaresque

www. WEBSITES FOR FURTHER STUDY

http://galileo.rice.edu/gal/urban.html
(A site on the Maffeo Barberini, also known as Pope Urban VIII, one of the most powerful and influential popes.)

http://www.fordham.edu/halsall/source/loyola-spirex.html
(An excerpt from The Spiritual Exercises of Ignatius Loyola, founder of the Jesuit order.)

http://www.artchive.com/artchive/C/caravaggio/calling of st matthew.jpg.html
(This is the Artchive, a website with virtually every major artist in every style from every era in art history. It is an excellent resource.)

http://w3.rz-berlin.mpg.de/cmp/monteverdi.html
(A good site on Monteverdi and the beginning of opera.)

http://www.ucmp.berkeley.edu/history/leeuwenhoek.html
(The biography of Antony Leeuwenhoek, discoverer of bacteria and inventor of the microscope.)

http://www.jsbach.org
(A wide-ranging array of linked sites on every aspect of the life, career, and music of Johann Sebastian Bach.)

http://www.gfhandel.org
(Handel site that includes information ranging from biographical, critical, historical to discographies, conferences and workshops, concerts and festivals, and more.)

http://www.classical-composers.org/comp/vivaldi
(A website devoted to the life and works of a wide range of classical composers; Baroque favorites like Vivaldi among them.)

http://www.cambridge.org/catalogue
(The Cambridge history of seventeenth-century philosophy—which discusses Thomas Hobbes, among others of the era.)

http://www.wwnorton.com/college/english/nael/17century/welcome.htm
(Site of the Norton Anthology of English Literature with special features and links for John Milton's Paradise Lost*, including contexts, related texts, illustrations, and other web resources.)*

http://www.luminarium.org/sevenlit/donne/
(Donnes' life, quotes, works, books about, and more. Links to other seventeenth-century writers. The site ranges across literature of earlier and later periods, as well.)

CHAPTER 16

HISTORY

1710	Leibniz invents new notations of calculus
1715	Louis XV ascends to French throne
1733	James Key invents flying shuttle
1735	Linnaeus establishes biological classification system
1740–48	War of the Austrian Succession
1756–63	Seven Years' War
1759	Wedgwood opens English pottery factory
1769	Watt patents steam engine
1775–83	American Revolution
1776	American Declaration of Independence
1787	Edmund Cartwright invents power loom
1789–99	French Revolution
1789	Declaration of the Rights of Man and Citizen
	Gathering of Estates General and Declaration of National Assembly; fall of Bastille
1792	French monarchy abolished
1793	Louis XVI and Marie Antoinette executed
1799	Napoleon overthrows Directory
1804	Napoleonic Code established

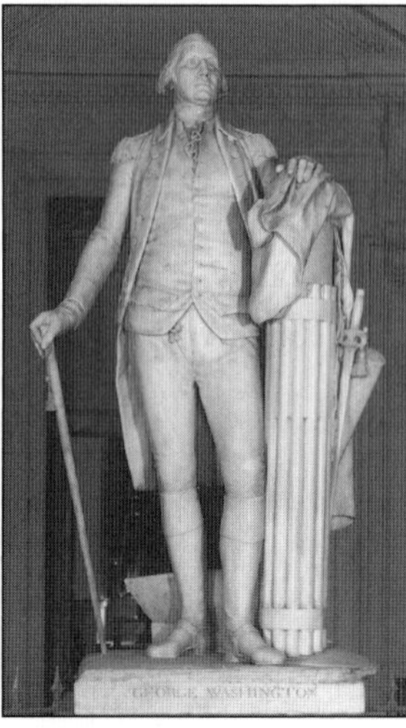

ART, ARCHITECTURE, AND MUSIC

1717	Watteau, *Pilgrimage to Cythera*
1725	Burlington/Kent, Chiswick House
1744	Hogarth, *Marriage à la Mode*
1763	Chardin, *The Brioche*
1769	Jefferson designs Monticello
1770	West, *Death of General Wolfe*
1772	Haydn, *Farewell Symphony*
1777–80	Reynolds, *Lady Elizabeth Delmé and Her Children*
1785	David, *Oath of the Horatii*
1785	Kaufmann, *Cornelia Pointing to Her Children as Her Treasures*
1786	Mozart, *The Marriage of Figaro*
1787	Vigée-Lebrun, *Portrait of Marie Antoinette with Her Children*
1787	Mozart, *Don Giovanni*
1788	Labille-Guiard, *Louise-Elisabeth of France*
1788–92	Houdon, *George Washington*
1796–98	Beethoven, early piano sonatas, op. 1–14
1807–8	Beethoven, Symphony No. 5 in C Minor

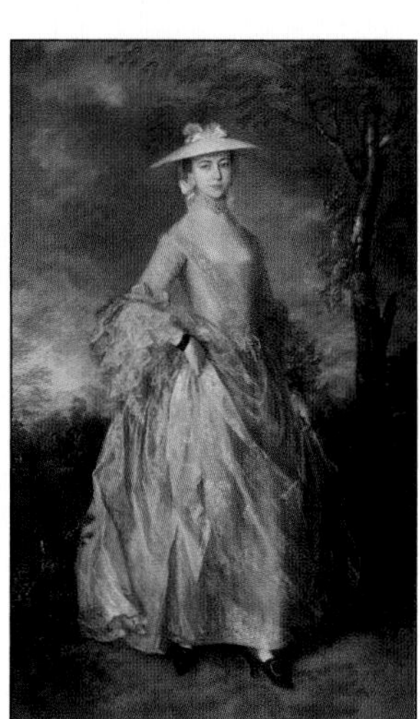

LITERATURE AND PHILOSOPHY

1712	Pope, *The Rape of the Lock*
1726	Swift, *Gulliver's Travels*
1751–72	Diderot, *Encyclopédie*
1755	Voltaire, *Candide*
1762	Rousseau, *Social Contract*
1776	Smith, *Wealth of Nations*

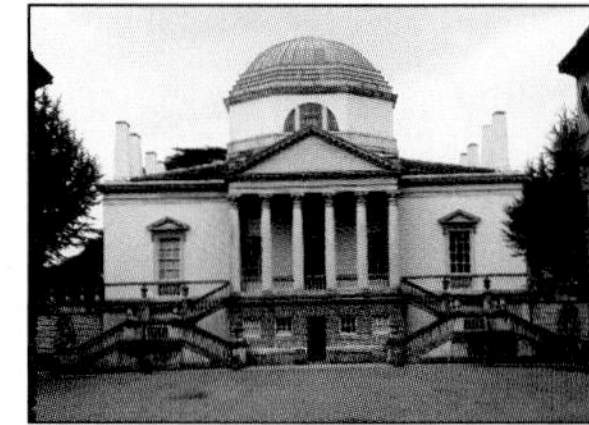

Eighteenth Century

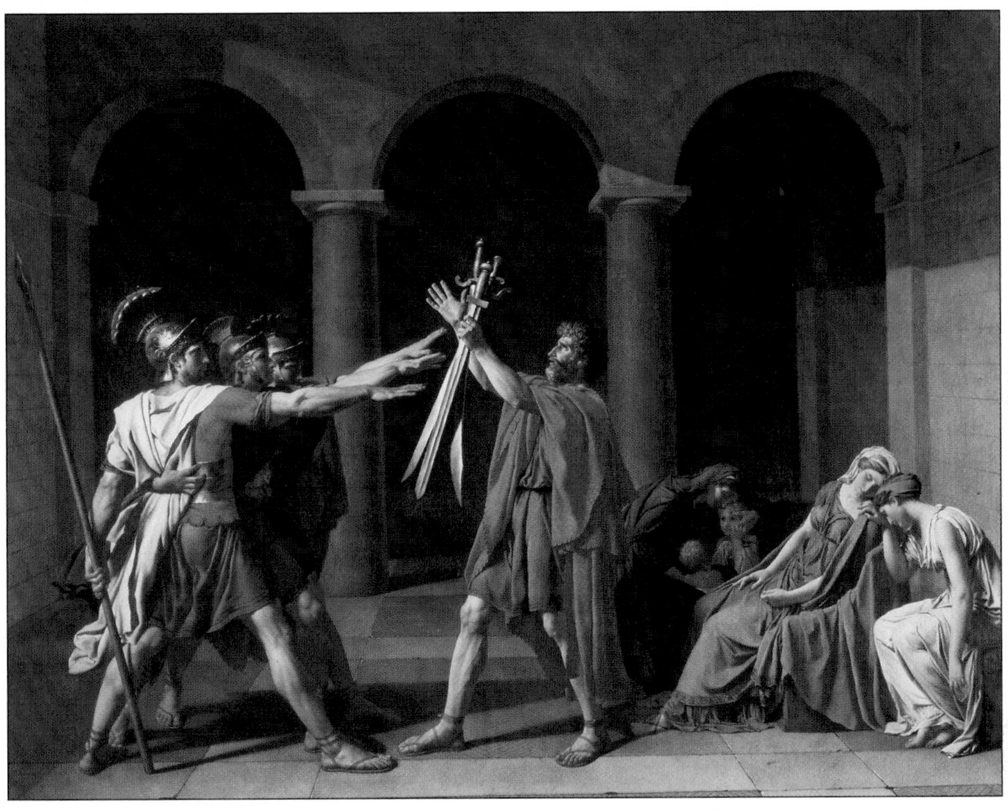

Jacques-Louis David, *Oath of the Horatii*, 1785, oil on canvas, 4′3″ × 6′5$\frac{1}{4}$″ (1.30 × 1.96 cm), G. Blot/C. Jean. © Musee du Louvre/RMN Reunion des Musées Nationaux/Art Resource, NY.

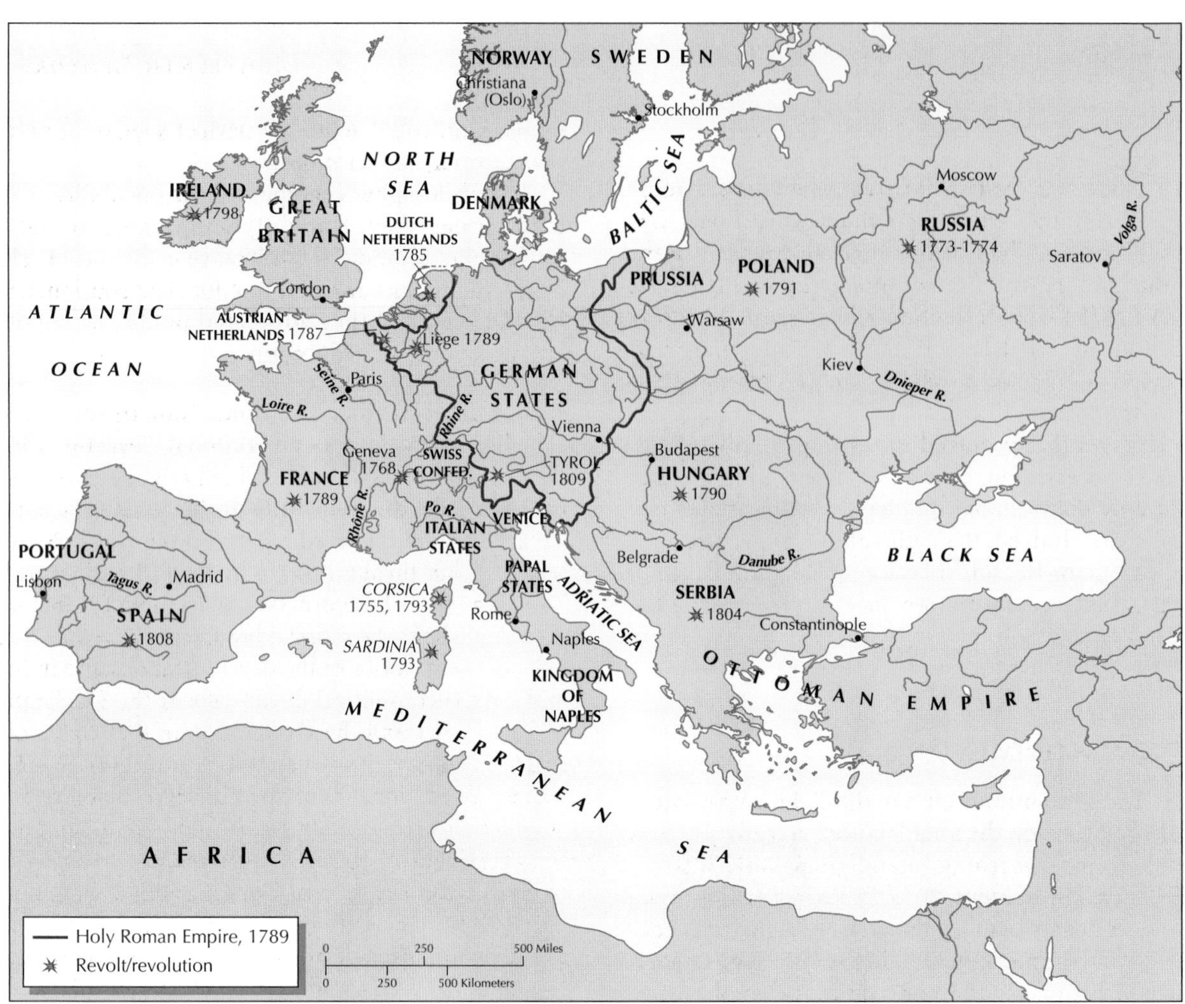

MAP 16.1 Revolts and revolutions in Europe, 1705–1809.

CHAPTER OVERVIEW

ENLIGHTENMENT

The philosophers enlighten the world

REVOLUTIONS

Politics, philosophy, industry, and science change the world

ROCOCO

Romance and luxury permeate the arts

LITERATURE OF RATIONALISM

VOLTAIRE'S PHILOSOPHY OF CYNICISM

NEOCLASSICISM

Clarity, balance, and antiquity dictate the arts

TOWARD ROMANTICISM

Restraint of expression begins to crumble

ENLIGHTENMENT

BETWEEN 1700 AND 1800, THE WORLD WAS transformed. At the beginning of the century, Louis XIV, the Sun King, had firm control of France. By the end of the century, the French monarchy had fallen, as Louis XVI (1754–1793), the Sun King's great-grandson, and his Queen, MARIE ANTOINETTE [anntweh-NET] (1755–1793), were executed by the National Assembly of the French Revolution.

The changes that occurred in the eighteenth century were swift and extreme, encompassing revolutions that were not only political, but intellectual, scientific, industrial, and social. Indeed, the eighteenth century has been called the "Age of Reason" because of the dominance of the intellectual revolution we have come to call the Enlightenment.

THE ENLIGHTENMENT

The term **Enlightenment** refers to the eighteenth-century European emphasis on the mind's power to reason, in contrast to the mind's yearning for religious faith, which a number of Enlightenment thinkers saw as superstition. The late seventeenth century through the eighteenth century saw two great movements: that of the "Age of Reason," which hallmarks the contemporary emphasis on rationality, and the Neoclassical, which testifies to the influence of classical antiquity.

The Enlightenment continued an emphasis on secular concerns that began during the Renaissance and continued with the rise of scientific and philosophical thought during the seventeenth century. Eighteenth-century political and philosophical ideals included freedom from tyranny and superstition, and a belief in the essential goodness of human nature and the equality of men (although not all men, and not women).

Enlightenment thinkers emphasized the common nature of human experience, ignoring differences in social, cultural, and religious values. Enlightenment composers sought universal musical forms. Enlightenment writers celebrated constancy and continuity, encouraging a respect for tradition and convention, especially in literature and the arts. Enlightenment artists and thinkers were not, however, simply supporters of the status quo. They used their analytical powers to attack the hypocrisies of the age. As much as they celebrated the powers of reason, they did not fail to notice when human behavior was guided by passion, selfishness, and irrationality. Voltaire, Swift, and Pope all composed scathing attacks on political and social misconduct.

The Philosophes. The Enlightenment was embodied in a group of intellectuals called by the French name **philosophes.** These thinkers believed that through reason, humankind could achieve a perfect society of perpetual peace, order, and harmony.

The philosophes championed the possibility of democratic rule; they feared tyranny most of all. The philosophes denounced intolerance in matters of religious belief which, since the Reformation, had continued to disrupt society, and they advocated public, as opposed to church-controlled, education.

Rational Humanism. **Rational humanism** is based on the belief that through rational, careful thought, progress—which is good and benefits everyone—is inevitable. Like the humanists of the Renaissance, the rational humanists believed progress is possible only through learning and through the individual's freedom to learn. Humans must, therefore, be free to think for themselves. This logic links the rational humanists with the two great political revolutions of the day, in America and in France, and with such political documents as the Declaration of Independence and the Declaration of the Rights of Man and Citizen, as well as with the Constitution of the United States. The rational humanists believed that any political system that strives to suppress freedom of thought must be overthrown as an obstacle to progress.

In France, the Age of Enlightenment was called Le Siècle des Lumières (The Century of Illumination). During this time French luminaries such as Diderot, Montesquieu, Rousseau, and Voltaire shed their philosophical light of reason on all things. Rationalism spawned such broad concepts as individual rights, religious freedom, equality, humanism, tolerance, and the sanctity of nature.

The Age of Enlightenment waas a time of new ideas that presented challenges to established orthodoxies, political, religious, social, and economic. The *French Encyclopedia*, published between 1751 and 1776 by Dennis Diderot and Jean d'Celembert, collected and celebrated this new knowledge.

Philosophically, the age was split between two competing perspectives. On one side were the empiricists, such as David Hume, who studied what had happened, analyzed what could be tested and verified by the senses, and then predicted what could follow. On the other side were the idealists or visionaries, such as Jean Jacques Rousseau, who postulated theories about society, basing their ideas on what could be dreamed, hoped, or imagined.

REVOLUTIONS

THE AMERICAN REVOLUTION

Enlightenment ideals had a profound effect on eighteenth-century America. The first and most important was as a source of inspiration that spurred the colonists philosophically and politically to revolt against England. A later but no less significant Enlightenment influence was to keep religion separate from politics, leaving church and state to operate in distinct and separate realms.

But why did the American Revolution occur? What precipitated it? One major cause was the imposition of new taxes by the British in an attempt to exert more control over the colonies. Colonists were deeply angered over taxes on molasses, on publications and legal documents, and most famously, on tea. They also resented Britain's enforcement of laws requiring cargo to travel at sea in British vessels, and they objected to being required to house and accommodate British troops.

The colonists responded to Britain's authoritative stance by boycotting British products, attacking British officials, generating anti-British slogans like "no taxation without representation," and staging protests. The most famous of these was the "Boston Tea Party," in which colonists dumped a cargo of tea into Boston Harbor rather than pay the tax for it. Shortly afterward, colonists exchanged gunfire with British troops in Lexington, a suburb of Boston.

On July 4, 1776, the Continental Congress, which had been established two years earlier to coordinate resistance to British policies, adopted the Declaration of Independence. According to this important document inspired by Enlightenment ideas of liberty and sovereignty, "all men are created equal," and all are endowed by God with the "unalienable rights" of "Life, Liberty, and the Pursuit of Happiness." The Declaration also asserted that the colonists had the right to establish a government to secure these rights, and that the government derived its authority from the people.

The Declaration led to the colonists' armed resistance of Britain, and even though Britain was the preeminent economic and military power of the western world, the colonists prevailed, and the balance of world power was dramatically altered. The war lasted five years, with the surrender of British troops to General George Washington in 1781. Two years later, the Peace of Paris was signed, in which the British recognized American independence.

The Americans could not have won the war without the help of European nations, including France, Holland, and Spain, which all wanted to see Britain weakened. Another factor in the colonists' favor was that they were defending their own land and fighting for a set of principles, not the least of which was freedom.

Paine, Washington, Jefferson, and Franklin. Among the men who had a decisive impact leading up to the war with Britain, and who continued to exert a significant influence in America and beyond afterwards were Thomas Paine, George Washington, Thomas Jefferson, and Benjamin Franklin. Thomas Paine (1737–1809) was a journalist and pamphleteer whose writings roused readers' passions against the British and inspired them to believe that military resistance was both necessary and justified. The first of his famous pamphlets, *Common Sense*, begins with these rousing words: "These are the times that try men's souls; the summer soldier and sunshine patriot will, in this crisis, shrink from the service of their country, but he that stands by it now deserves the loving thanks of man and woman."

George Washington (1732–1799) took charge of the army during the war. As a military leader, General Washington consistently outsmarted and outmaneuvered his British antagonists, culminating in their surrender to him. After the war, Washington served two terms, from 1789 to 1797, as the country's first President.

Thomas Jefferson (1743–1826) is credited as the primary author of the Declaration of Independence. Jefferson served as governor of Virginia, as U.S. minister to France, as Secretary of State under Washington, and as Vice President under John Adams, before becoming himself the third President of the United States. Jefferson was also a writer who argued that liberty was a God-given right. In addition, Jefferson founded the University of Virginia, which he planned, designed, and supervised.

The most versatile of the American Founding Fathers was Benjamin Franklin (1706–1790), one of five men who helped draft the Declaration of Independence. Franklin was a statesman and diplomat, printer and writer, merchant and newspaper editor, and an inventor who experimented with electricity, and who invented both the lightning rod and bifocals. During a long and illustrious career, Franklin founded the first lending library in America, established the first fire company, and created a college that merged later with the University of Pennsylvania. Among his greatest accomplishments, however, was his service as Minister to France prior to and during the Revolution. Franklin deserves much of the credit for securing a treaty with France, including financial support to secure American independence.

Enlightenment Thought and Women. During the eighteenth century, advocates for the rights of women were active in a number of countries, including Britain, Canada, France, and the United States. The British writer Mary Wollstonecraft was one of the best known, with her influential essay "A Vindication of the Rights of Women," published in 1792. Following John Locke's arguments for human freedom, Wollstonecraft argued that women would make better and more successful wives and mothers if they were educated, and that they would be fuller and abler participants in the political process.

In the United States, Elizabeth Cady Stanton would take up the cause for the full slate of women's rights, including the right to vote. The word *suffrage* means the right to vote, a right denied women in the United States and the United Kingdom until the suffragist movement in both countries reversed that denial. The movement for women's suffrage in the United States lasted more than seventy years, from the time of the first women's convention in Seneca Falls, NY, in 1848, until the passage of the nineteenth amendment to the U.S. Constitution in 1920. In the U.K., women were given restricted voting rights in 1918, and then full voting rights equal to those granted

U.S. women, in 1928. (U.S. blacks had gained the right to vote with the ratification of the fifteenth amendment in 1870, although it took the Voting Rights Act of 1965 to make it a reality.)

Propelling the movement for women's suffrage in the United States was the general movement for women's rights, including property rights and educational opportunities. These were announced at the Seneca Falls Convention in the Declaration of Sentiments. Fueling the movement for women's suffrage in the United Kingdom was the shortage of able-bodied men during World War I, requiring women to take on many traditional male roles and responsibilities, which led before long to a fuller understanding of the capabilities of women, and then to their being granted property, educational, and voting rights.

In other countries, too, women's rights were being contested. New Zealand gave women full voting rights in 1893, the first country to do so. In 1902 Australia gave women the right to vote in national elections. Other countries granting voting rights to women in the early 1900s included Canada, Finland, Germany, and Sweden.

THE FRENCH REVOLUTION

The executions of Louis XVI and Marie Antoinette in 1793 represented not only the death of the monarchy, but also an end to the privilege and extravagance that the monarchy had come to represent in the minds of the people. In death, all are equal. The century's growing belief in the equality of all, in the right of the individual to live free of tyranny, and in the right of humankind to self-governance, culminated in political **revolution,** the overthrow of the existing order for a new one. In fact, revolution itself seemed to many an "enlightened" course of action.

The American Revolution began to stir in 1774, when the colonists convened for the new Continental Congress. An American Declaration of Independence, authored by Thomas Jefferson (1743–1826), unified the colonies in their successful war against the British, and in the following years, a constitutional convention met in Philadelphia to draft a new charter for the American republic. At the convention, mechanisms were devised to assess and collect taxes, regulate commerce, and make enforceable laws, all within a government framework of "checks and balances." The legislative, judicial, and executive branches of government all had their own powers, but powers that were overseen by the other branches.

The French bourgeoisie watched with interest. They wanted a "National Assembly" like the Continental Congress; a document drafted along the same principles as the American Declaration; and a republican constitution that would give them life, liberty, and the right to own property. But the French situation was different from the American one. Where the American Revolution pitted against one another two groups with similar cultural values, one simply seeking economic autonomy from the other, the French Revolution was essentially an internal class struggle and, as such, expressed a clash in values.

Each of the French kings of the eighteenth century—Louis XIV (r. 1643–1715), Louis XV (r. 1715–74), and Louis XVI (r. 1774–93), guillotined on January 21, 1793—had successively led the country further into debt. In May 1789, Louis XVI succumbing to mounting pressures to deal with the ever-increasing national debt, called for an assembly of the Estates General. This assembly of the clergy (the First Estate), the aristocrats (the Second Estate), and the bourgeois middle class (the Third Estate) resulted in the "The Declaration of the Rights of Man and Citizen," a document modeled on the American "Declaration of Independence."

THE NATIONAL ASSEMBLY

In the Estates General, each of the three estates had one vote. The Third Estate quickly realized it would be outvoted 2–1 on every question. Thus, on June 20, 1789, the deputies of the Third Estate along with their aristocratic sympathizers declared a "National Assembly" in a building called the Jeu de Paume, the king's tennis court. Together they swore they would not separate until France had a new constitution.

Rumors that the king was planning to overthrow the National Assembly led to the formation of a volunteer bourgeois militia, which, on July 14, 1789, went to the Bastille prison in Paris in search of arms and gunpowder. The prison governor panicked and ordered his guard to fire on the militia, killing ninety-eight and wounding seventy-three. An angry mob quickly formed and stormed the Bastille, decapitating its governor and slaughtering six of the guards. The next day, Louis XVI asked if the incident had been a riot. "No, your majesty," was the reply, "it was a revolution."

The National Assembly continued to meet while rioting spread throughout the French countryside, and finally, on August 4, 1789, in a night session, the viscount of Nouilles and then the duke of Aiguillon renounced their feudal privileges and revenues. Other nobles did the same, and the clergy in attendance relinquished their tithes. By the end of the evening, all French people suddenly found themselves subject to the same laws and taxes. On August 27, 1789, the Assembly ratified its Declaration of the Rights of Man and Citizen, and a constitutional monarchy was established.

DEMISE OF THE MONARCHY

Despite the events of August 27, as early as October 5, 1789, Parisian women were back in the streets demonstrating for bread. It was on this day that Marie Antoinette is supposed to have declared, notoriously, "Let them eat cake!"—an exclamation some historians doubt was ever made. The women marched on the palace at Versailles and invaded the inner rooms, causing the queen to flee for her life, but Louis and Marie Antoinette were escorted back to Paris later that day.

The king ostensibly cooperated for a while with the National Assembly, but in June 1791 he attempted to flee with his family to Luxembourg. The royal retinue was captured and returned to Paris. Then, in April 1792, Austria and Prussia took the opportunity to declare war on the weakened nation, and the Prussian duke of Brunswick declared he would restore Louis XVI to full sovereignty, revealing an already widespread suspicion that the king was collaborating with the enemy. And so the bourgeois leaders, aided by the working class, invaded the Louvre on August 10, 1792, butchering the king's guard and the royal servants, and over the next forty days arrested and executed more than a thousand priests, aristocrats, and royalist sympathizers. On September 21, 1792, a newly assembled National Convention abolished the monarchy in France, and on January 21, 1793, Louis XVI was executed by guillotine in the Place de la Révolution, known today as the Place de la Concorde.

The situation continued to deteriorate. In the summer of 1793, a Committee of Public Safety was formed, headed by MAXIMILIEN DE ROBESPIERRE [ROBES-pea-air] (1758–1794). For fifteen months, France endured the committee's Reign of Terror. The Terror had three goals: to win the war with Austria and Prussia; to establish a "Republic of Virtue"; and to suppress all its enemies. To achieve the latter, the Revolutionary Tribunal of Paris alone handed out 2,639 death sentences, including that of Marie Antoinette, who by this time was referred to simply as "the widow Capet." Throughout France, an estimated twenty thousand people were executed.

NAPOLEON BONAPARTE

In 1795, when the term of the National Convention expired, a political body known as the Directory succeeded to power. It managed to establish peace, but otherwise France was effectively rudderless. Finally, in November 1799, General NAPOLEON BONAPARTE [BONE-ah-part] (1769–1821) staged a coup d'état, abolishing the Directory and installing himself, on the Roman model, as First Consul.

Napoleon was a common man who rose to power through talent and civic sacrifice. Yet he was also a man of uncommon presence. He had no shortage of ego, either, for in 1802 he inquired of the people, "Is Napoleon Bonaparte to be made Consul for Life?" The people answered in the affirmative by 3.5 million votes to 8,000. After another election in 1804, he declared himself Emperor for Life, and was crowned Emperor Napoleon I in December 1804. France had, effectively, restored the monarchy.

Napoleon's power and appeal tell us much about the Enlightenment itself. He was the very model of enlightened leadership that the philosophes longed for, although his decision to crown himself emperor disillusioned many of his republican supporters. Under Napoleon's regime, the economy boomed again, and he vigorously supported industrial expansion. Cotton production, for instance, quadrupled between 1806 and 1810. In 1800, Napoleon created the Bank of France, which made government borrowing a far easier and more stable matter. But his greatest achievement was the **Napoleonic Code,** which provided a uniform system of law for the entire country. This code was brief and clear, with the aim that every citizen should be capable of understanding it. Together with the Declaration of Independence, the U.S. Constitution, and the Declaration of the Rights of Man, the Napoleonic Code is one of the great monuments of Enlightenment thought.

The causes of the revolution were complex, ranging from a resentment of royal absolutism, a desire for liberty in tune with enlightenment ideals, to gross economic class inequities, a scarcity of food, and the king's failure to deal with precipitating crises. The consequences of the French Revolution were momentous; the revolution was, in fact, a turning point in French history, with significant consequences for Europe. It marked a pronounced shift from monarchy and absolutism to republicanism and democracy. Furthermore, enlightenment ideals embodied in both the French and American revolutions, especially freedom, equality, and sovereignty, spurred revolutionary movements in the Caribbean and in Central and South America, especially in Bolivia, Haiti, and Mexico.

INDUSTRIAL REVOLUTION

The Birth of the Factory. On May 1, 1759, in Staffordshire, England, a twenty-eight-year-old man named Josiah Wedgwood (1730–1795) opened his own pottery manufacturing plant. Wedgwood initially specialized in unique pottery made by hand, but began to produce ceramic tableware on which designs were printed by mechanical means. In the same year, Wedgwood's friend Matthew Boulton (1728–1809) inherited his father's toy factory (small metal objects such as belt buckles, buttons, and clasps were known as "toys"). Soon he had built a factory in London, employing six hundred people in mechanized large-scale production. The steam engine, patented by James Watt in 1769, transformed the way in which these new factories could be powered. Mechanical looms were soon introduced into the cotton cloth industry, powered by Watt's steam engines. Where once workers had woven fabric at home as piecework, they now watched over giant looms that did the work for them, in a fraction of the time. Mass manufacturing, and with it what we have come to call the **Industrial Revolution,** had begun.

Adam Smith. In 1776, the Scotsman Adam Smith (1727–1790) provided the rationale for the entire enterprise. His *Inquiry into the Nature and Cause of the Wealth of Nations* barely mentioned manufacturing, concentrating instead on

Then & Now

RIGHTS OF WOMEN

When the French National Assembly ratified the Declaration of the Rights of Man and Citizen on August 27, 1789, its members did not include women among the "citizens." In 1791, Olympe de Gouges (1748–1793) wrote a "Declaration of the Rights of Women" and demanded that the National Assembly act on it. This stated that "Woman is born free and remains equal to man in rights," arguing that "the only limit on the exercise of woman's natural rights is the perpetual tyranny wielded by men; these limits must be reformed by the law of nature and the law of reason." The declaration continued with the then radical claim that women were "equally entitled to all honors, places, and public employments according to their abilities, without any other distinction than that of their virtues and their talents."

The Englishwoman Mary Wollstonecraft (1759–1797) wrote another important revolutionary manifesto supporting women's rights. *A Vindication of the Rights of Woman*, published in 1792, is a treatise embodying Enlightenment faith in reason and in the revolutionary concepts of change and progress. Wollstonecraft held that women, having an equal capacity for reason, should have an equal standing in society. She offered a scathing critique of the social forces that kept women in a position of inferiority. Wollstonecraft developed her revolutionary ideas in the company of a radical group of English artists and writers, including Tom Paine and William Godwin, who sympathized with the aims of the French Revolution.

To the contemporary American, these demands may seem reasonable enough, but it is worth remembering that women did not gain the right to vote in the United States until 1920. And women continue to fight for equality in the workplace, both in competing for jobs on an equal footing and receiving comparable pay for comparable work. Such demands were certainly not considered reasonable at the time of the French Revolution. De Gouges was charged with treason by the National Assembly and sentenced to the guillotine in 1793.

agriculture and trade, but the businesspeople who ran the new factories saw in his writings the justification for their practices. In a free-market system based on private property, Smith argued that prices and profits would automatically be regulated to the benefit, theoretically, of everyone, not just the factory owners. He contended that the economy would operate as if with an "invisible hand" beneficently guiding it. The new "working class" that arose out of the Industrial Revolution, however, would find that the free-market system benefited the factory owners a great deal more than themselves, and by the dawn of the nineteenth century, the factory owners had become the new "kings" of industrial culture—as spendthrift and tyrannical as the monarchs of the previous age.

SCIENTIFIC REVOLUTION

Isaac Newton. The positivism of the age was driven by advances in scientific learning. The philosophes seized on the discovery by Isaac Newton (1642–1727) of the principle of gravitation, the first physical description of the forces holding the known universe together. The Earth and its moon, Jupiter and its four moons, the sun and its planets all formed a harmonious system, with each celestial body relying on the others to maintain its place and position. Transferring this vision to human society, the philosophes suggested that with a comparable system of mutual reliance humans could live in harmony. Throughout the eighteenth century, scientists explored the natural world to such a degree that new sciences had to be defined: geology (1795), mineralogy (1796), zoology (1818), and biology (1819).

Denis Diderot and Carolus Linnaeus. The French essayist DENIS DIDEROT [DEED-eh-roe] (1713–1784) conceived of an idea for an ***Encyclopédie,*** twenty-eight volumes designed to encompass the whole of human knowledge, from science and technology to philosophical thought. The volumes contain thousands of illustrations showing the mechanical principles of production and commerce.

In the middle of the century, CAROLUS LINNAEUS [leh-NAY-us] (1707–1778) established the biological classification system that is still used to identify species. Both Linnaeus's classification system and the *Encyclopédie* are undertakings that reveal the optimism of the age, the result of two hundred years of scientific advances that had convinced many people that humankind could in fact eventually know everything—and catalog it.

Table 16–1 EIGHTEENTH-CENTURY TECHNOLOGICAL ADVANCES
The steam engine: United States, 1769
The flush toilet: England, 1775
The bicycle: France, 1779
The hot air balloon: France, 1783
The flintlock musket: United States, 1793

ROCOCO

The Rococo style of art was, in the eyes of many, entirely decadent and self-serving. It was commissioned by the same powerful aristocratic French families who were seen as suppressors of the people's freedom. Its abundant extravagance was interpreted as a reflection of its patrons' self-aggrandizement. The Rococo art of this aristocracy, the poetry, architecture, painting, and sculpture of the court of Louis XV (r. 1715–74), is precisely what the Enlightenment came to define itself against.

The name **Rococo** is thought to come from the French word *rocaille*, a type of decorative work or grotto work made from pebbles and shells. It is also very likely a pun on the Italian word for the Baroque, *barocco;* the style's connection to certain elements of the Baroque is strong. Associated especially with the reign of Louis XV of France, Rococo artists reshaped and refined the more elaborate aspects of the Baroque style.

FRENCH MUSIC

Couperin and Rameau. Next to the drama and grandeur of Baroque music, Rococo music is playful and light. The gallantry and polish of Rococo painting are echoed in Rococo music, especially music written for harpsichord by Francis Couperin (1668–1733) and Jean-Philippe Rameau (1683–1764).

During the mid- to late-eighteenth century, when the Rococo style was in full bloom, France successfully resisted the influence of foreign musical styles. King Louis XIV, in his effort to establish things French as the epitome of taste and culture, subjected the arts to a consistent national policy and set up an operatic monopoly that excluded foreign composers. A tight musicians' guild effectively limited outsiders from participating through strict apprenticeship and accreditation requirements. In addition, creative efforts in music, as in the other arts, were concentrated in areas approved and supported by the court. Thus music during the reign of Louis XIV was largely designed to accompany court functions, ceremonies, and entertainments. Couperin and Rameau supplied much of this music.

FRENCH PAINTING

Jean-Antoine Watteau. JEAN-ANTOINE WATTEAU [WAH-toe] (1684–1721) was most noted for his ***fêtes galantes***, depictions of elegant out-of-doors parties known for their amorous conversations, graceful fashion, and social gallantry.

Watteau's *Pilgrimage to Cythera* (fig. 16.1), of 1717, is a mythologized vision of just such an event. The party takes place on Cythera, the birthplace of Venus and the island of love. Lovers go there to honor Venus, portrayed by a statue on the far right. Cupids fly above the crowd, the sun is low, and the lovers are boarding the boat that will return them to the real world. The departure is sad; some people glance back, reluctant to leave the idyllic setting.

Watteau's painting gained entry into the Royal Academy of Painting and Sculpture even though it did not

FIGURE 16.1 Jean-Antoine Watteau, *Pilgrimage to Cythera*, 1717, oil on canvas, 4′3″ × 6′4$\frac{1}{2}$″ (1.30 × 1.90 m). Photo: Gerard Blott. Musée du Louvre, Paris. Reunion des Musées Nationaux/Art Resource, NY. The Rococo style is characterized by lightness both of content and of color; romantic pastimes are portrayed in an atmosphere of lighthearted aristocratic hedonism.

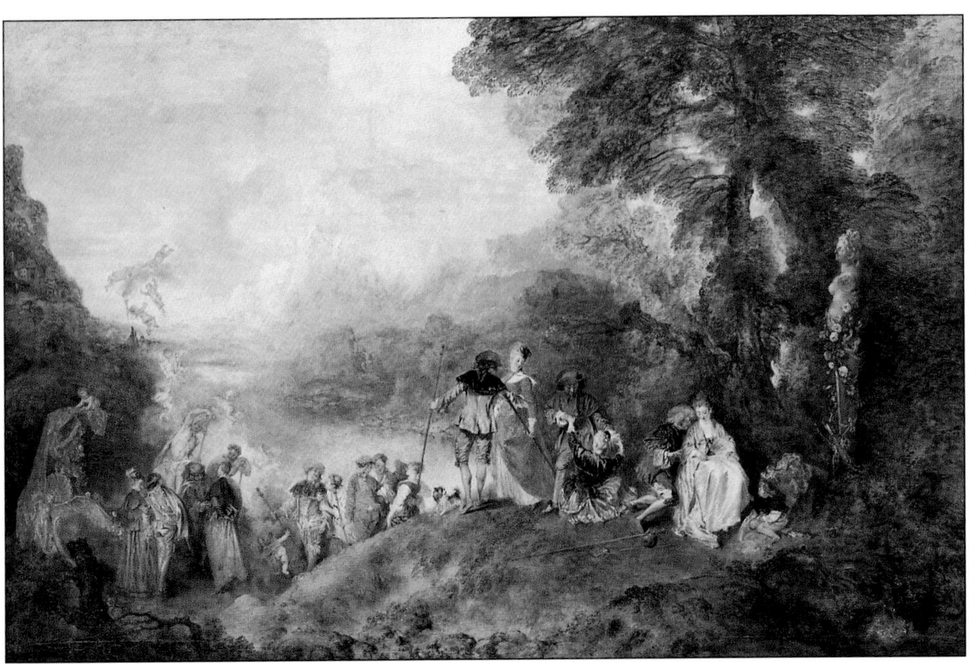

adhere to Academy rules of size or subject. It is relatively small, and the subject was neither history nor religion nor portraiture, the subjects the Academy favored. Watteau did not glorify the state or flatter the king. Nonetheless, the Academy recognized Watteau's achievement, and in a moment of triumph for the *rubéniste* sensibility, it created a new official category expressly for *fêtes galantes.*

By the time Louis XV assumed personal rule of the country in 1743, the court had enjoyed a free rein for many years. The king essentially adapted himself to its carefree ways, dismissing state officials at whim. In thirty years of personal rule, he had fourteen chief fiscal officers and eighteen different foreign secretaries, creating ceaseless instability in government. Part of the problem can be attributed to France's growing fiscal crisis and the high costs of government and court life. Nonetheless, life, for Louis XV, was something of an endless *fête galante.* He surrounded himself with mistresses, at least one of whom, Madame de Pompadour, wielded as much, or more, power than the king himself.

François Boucher. Madame de Pompadour's favorite painter was FRANÇOIS BOUCHER [boo-SHAY] (1703–1770), who began his career, in 1725, by copying the Watteau paintings owned by Jean de Jullienne, the principal collector of the artist's work. Jullienne had conceived of the notion of having all of Watteau's works engraved so they could be enjoyed by a wider public. Boucher was the best of the printmakers hired by Jullienne to undertake the task. With his earnings, he set off for Rome in 1727 to study the masters. But he found Raphael "trite" and Michelangelo "hunchbacked," so he returned to Paris. By 1734, he was an established member of the Academy, specializing in *fêtes galantes* and other similar subjects. Soon he was appointed director of the Royal Academy and first painter to Louis XV, and patrons of society clamored after his work.

Boucher's painting of the *Bath of Diana* (fig. 16.2), of 1742, displays the delicate French grace and charming Rococo sentiment that made him so successful. Boucher painted many female nudes, then a popular subject; but on this occasion, to make it socially acceptable, he presented the figure as the mythological Diana. His goddess of the hunt, however, is hardly strong or powerful. She is aristocratic, delicate, and soft, seemingly straight from the hairdresser. The curving shapes are characteristic of the Rococo style, as are the lush colors that he favors—tender pinks, blues, and soft whites. The artist's friends likened his colors to "rose petals floating in milk." The overall effect is one of quiet sensuality, conveying an air of relaxed indiscretion.

Jean-Honoré Fragonard. The other great painter of the Parisian Rococo was JEAN-HONORE FRAGONARD [frah-goh-NAR] (1732–1806), Boucher's student,

FIGURE 16.2 François Boucher, *Bath of Diana*, 1742, oil on canvas, $22\frac{1}{2}'' \times 28\frac{3}{4}''$ (57.2 × 73 cm). Photo: Herve Lewandowski. Musée du Louvre, Paris. Reunion de Musées National/Art Resource, NY. The portrayal of female nudity was made acceptable by the antique context in which it was presented. The female type admired was not athletic or rugged but pale and pampered.

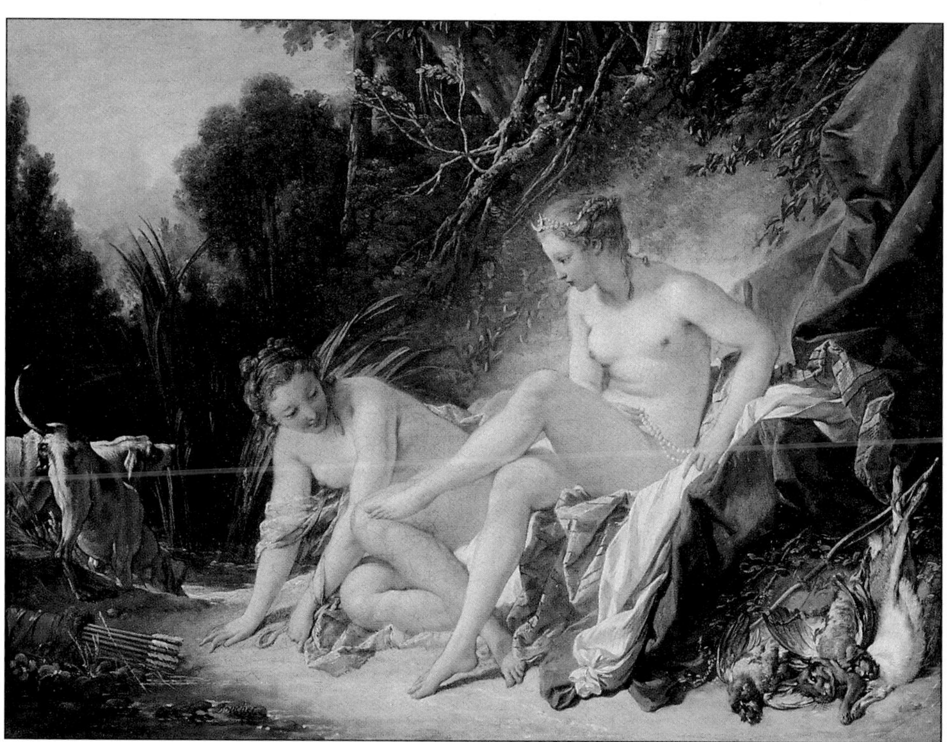

whose work is even more overtly erotic than his teacher's. Sensuous nudes inhabit his paintings, and they are depicted in an equally sensual style, much like that of Rubens in its use of strong fluid color and areas of light and shade. Fragonard is noted for his rapid brushwork—sometimes he could paint an entire work inside an hour. His figures float softly, ever graceful, always courtly. Fragonard's most famous work, however, was a series of fourteen canvases commissioned around 1771 by Madame du Barry, Louis XV's last mistress. Designed to decorate her château, they depict a series of encounters between lovers in garden settings, like the gardens of the château itself. *The Meeting* (fig. 16.3) has elements characteristic of the whole series. Below a statue of Venus, a young woman waits to meet her lover, who is climbing over the garden wall. Depictions of flirtation and romance, enjoyed by elegantly attired aristocrats in imaginary garden settings, are typically Rococo.

Fragonard endured constant interruption by Madame du Barry, and in the end the paintings were rejected, perhaps because the Rococo was becoming increasingly unpopular. Seen by many as the embodiment of the decadence of the aristocracy, the style was on the wane.

FIGURE 16.3 Jean-Honoré Fragonard, *The Meeting*, 1771–73, oil on canvas, 10′5$\frac{1}{4}$″ × 7′$\frac{5}{8}$″ (3.18 × 2.15 m), copyright the Frick Collection, New York. The pastel colors, delicate graceful gestures, and curving forms—including the twisting pose of the statue of Venus—are Rococo characteristics.

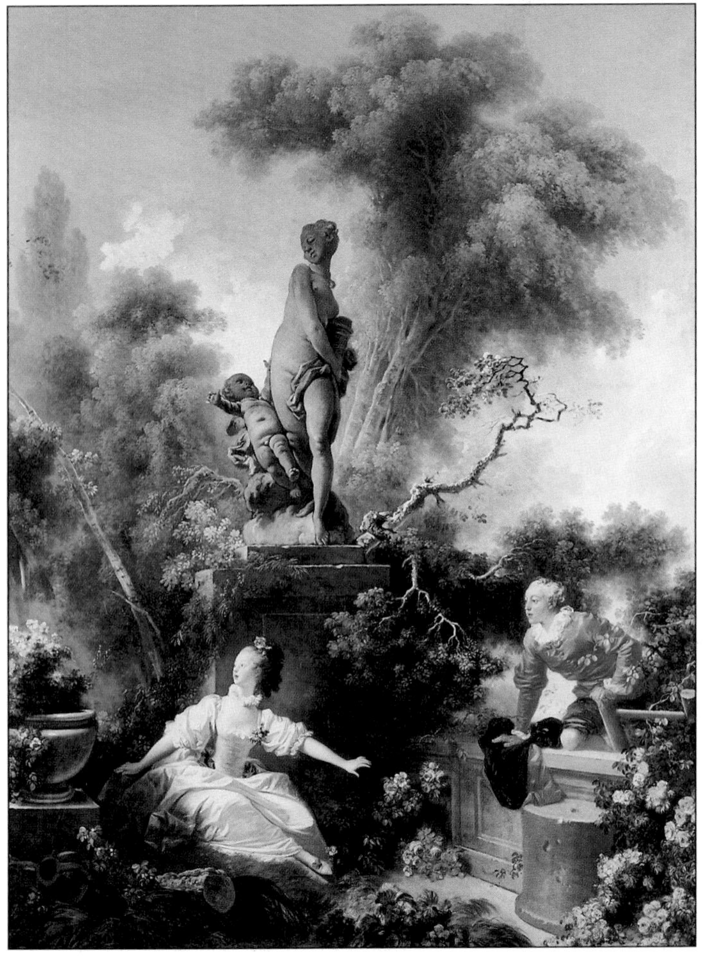

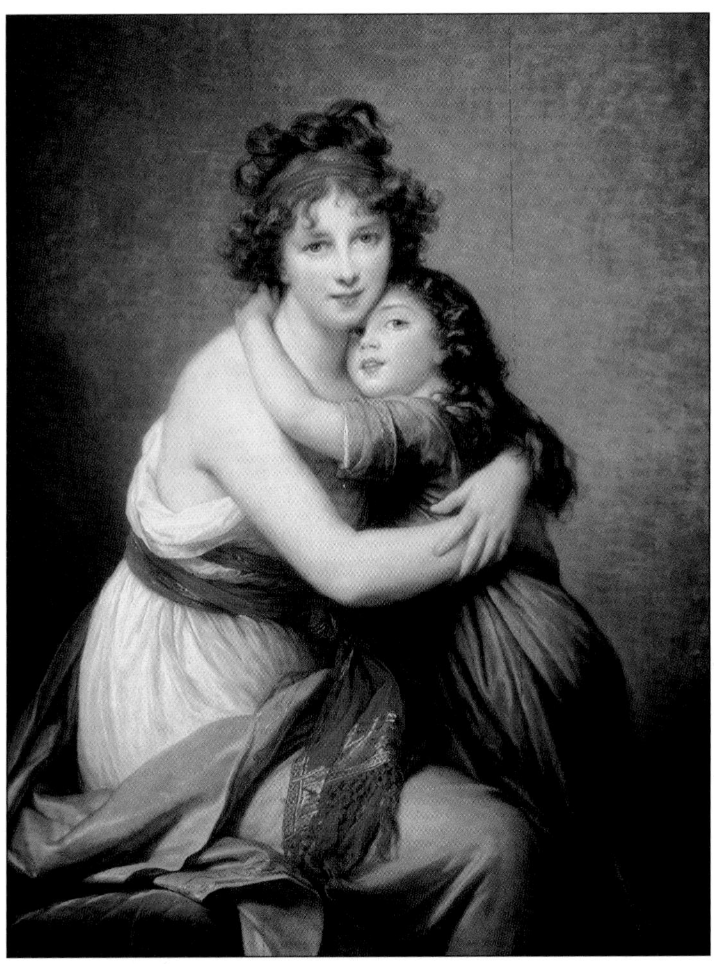

FIGURE 16.4 Marie-Louise-Elisabeth Vigée-Lebrun, *The Artist and Her Daughter*, ca. 1785, oil on canvas, 4′3″ × 3′1″ (139.7 × 94 cm). Musée du Louvre, Paris. Photo: G. Blot/ C. Jean./Photo credit: Reunion des Musées Nationaux/Art Resource, NY. Vigée-Lebrun's style coincided perfectly with upper-class tastes, making her the highest-paid portrait painter in France (by the age of twenty!) and court painter to Queen Marie Antoinette.

Marie-Louise-Elisabeth Vigée-Lebrun. Paintings like *The Artist and Her Daughter* (fig. 16.4) by MARIE-LOUISE-ELISABETH VIGEE-LEBRUN [vee-JHAY le-BRUN] (1755–1842) signaled the arrival of a more restrained and naturalistic classical style. Her father died when she was young, and Vigée-Lebrun supported her mother and brother by her painting. She was a child prodigy; by the time she was twenty, her portraits were commanding the highest prices in France. Highly sought after, Vigée-Lebrun painted portraits of all the important members of the aristocracy, including Louis XVI's queen, Marie Antoinette. Vigée-Lebrun was able to convey a sense of power combined with grace and intimacy. Her subjects often seem to be turning to glance at the viewer, as if the viewer just happened into their presence a moment ago. Closely linked to royalty, Vigée-Lebrun fled France during the revolution, spent many years traveling and painting in Europe, and published three volumes of memoirs, which give an insight into her art and era.

Adélaïde Labille-Guiard. Like her contemporary Vigée-Lebrun. ADÉLAÏDE LABILLE-GUIARD [ahd-LAID la-BEE ghee-YAR] (1749–1803) was a French portraitist who received commissions from some of the same patrons. Both were admitted to the French Academy on the same day in 1783. Whether their rivalry was real or invented by the hostility of other artists is unknown. Several of Labille-Guiard's pupils went on to notable artistic careers. She was active in promoting the rights of women artists.

In her capacity as the Peintre des Mesdames (Painter of the Ladies) to Louis XVI, she was commissioned to portray *Louise-Elisabeth of France* (fig. 16.5) in 1788. This is a commemorative portrait, as Louise-Elisabeth had died almost thirty years earlier of smallpox when only thirty-two years old. In this poignant memorial, her expression is almost wistful as she looks out at the viewer, while her son reaches up to take her hand. Although shown on a balcony, the sweep of red drapery was customary in portraiture.

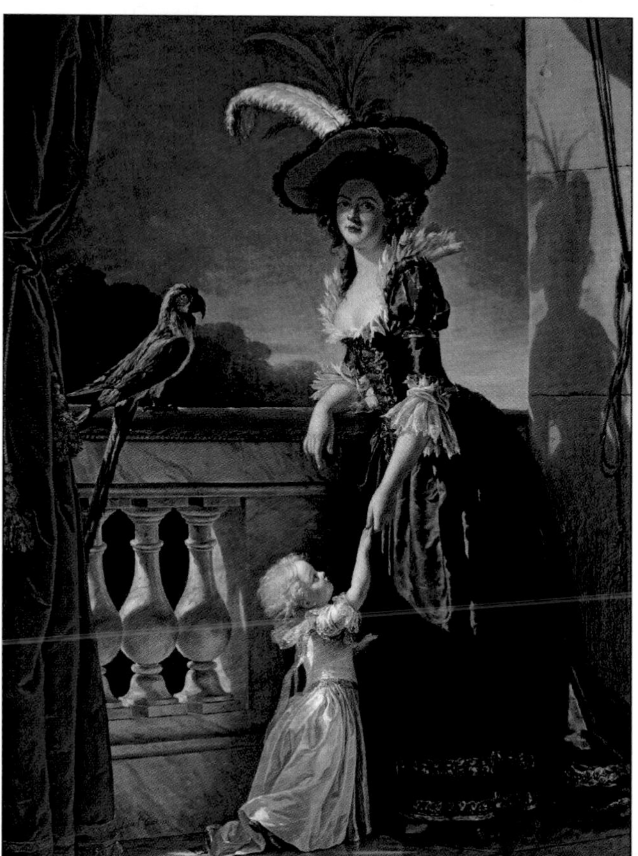

FIGURE 16.5 Adélaïde Labille-Guiard *Posthumous portrait of Louise-Elisabeth of France, Duchess of Parma.* 1788, oil on canvas, 8′9″ × 5′3′ (2.72 × 1.6 m). Chateaux de Versailles et de Trianon, Versailles, France. RMN Reunion des Musees Nationaux/Art Resource, NY. This is a memorial portrait to a member of the family of Louis XVI, the former Duchess of Parma, who died of smallpox leaving the young son seen here, Don Ferdinand, the future Duke of Parma. Labille-Guiard evokes the viewer's sympathy by the child's gaze and gesture and especially by the use of shadows, as that across her face, for the sun is symbolically low and soon to set.

The New Hôtels. In almost all things, the French court indulged its newfound sense of freedom. When Louis XIV died, and the Duc d'Orléans assumed the role of regent for the child-king, Louis XV, Versailles was immediately abandoned. The court was reestablished in Paris, although not so much at the Palace of the Louvre, as in ***hôtels***, or townhouses, where clever hostesses oversaw weekly **salons**, fashionable social gatherings of notable people. These salons were the scene of conversations that turned, very often, into battles of wit and intelligence, or dwelt on matters of love and courtship. Musicians, frequently the finest of the day, entertained the guests.

The hostesses were free to pursue their own tastes in Paris, unhampered by any official court style such as they had experienced at Versailles, and they decorated their *hôtels* elaborately. One salon was created for the Princess de Soubise (fig. 16.6). Designed by France's royal architect,

FIGURE 16.6 Salon de la Princesse, Hôtel de Soubise, Paris, ca. 1737–38, decorated by Gabriel-Germain Boffrand. Turning away from the vast spaces of Baroque architecture, Rococo architects preferred small rooms, as demonstrated by those in this elegant townhouse. This room measures ca. 33 × 26′ (ca. 10.06 × 7.92 m), an ideal space in which to cultivate the art of conversation.

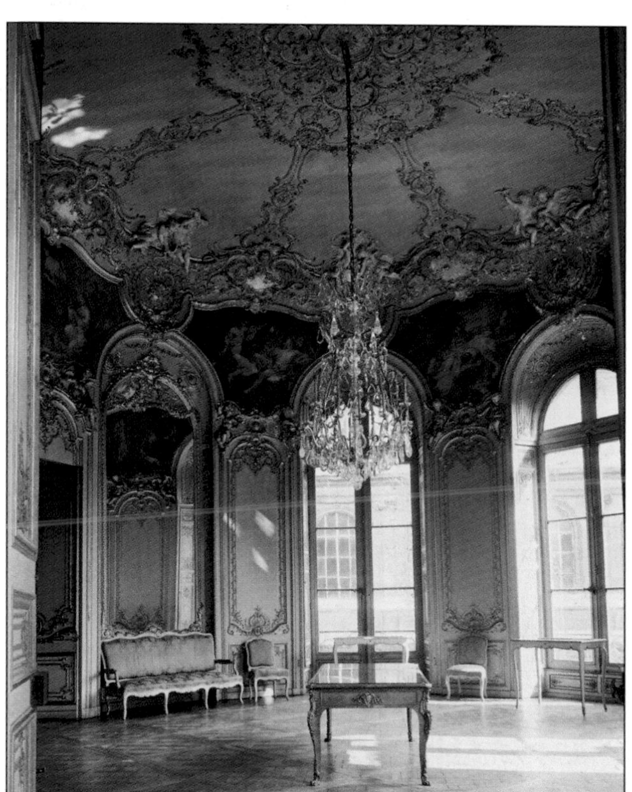

GABRIEL-GERMAIN BOFFRAND [boo-FRAHN] (1667–1754), it displays the typical Rococo pale pastel colors, small details, and concern for melding ceiling and walls into one curvilinear flow of delicate ornament and grace.

ENGLISH PAINTING

William Hogarth. William Hogarth (1697–1764) painted series of pictures that were equivalent to scenes in a play or chapters in a novel. He used similar details to help viewers interpret the different scenes of his works, which were much like morality plays. He sought to teach by example, referring to his narratives as "modern moral subjects." A social critic, he satirized the decadent customs of his day by exposing the "character" of society. Thus, unlike his French counterparts, who painted the life of the aristocracy in an unabashedly erotic and glowing light, Hogarth's view of England's aristocracy is overtly critical and moralistic. The engravings he made of these paintings were sold to the public and became wildly popular. Hogarth's financial success was based on the fact that lurid stories sell well.

Hogarth's *Marriage à la Mode* is a series of paintings made in 1744. The first scene, called *The Marriage Contract* (fig. 16.7), introduces the cast of characters. On the right sits the father of the groom, a nobleman who points to his family tree. Through this arranged marriage, he is trading his social position for money that will ensure the mortgage on his estate is paid off. The bride's father, a wealthy tradesman, inspects the contract. On the left, the engaged couple have their backs to each other. The groom preens himself in the mirror. The bride talks to the lawyer, counselor Silvertongue.

FIGURE 16.7 William Hogarth, *Marriage à la Mode: The Marriage Contract*, 1744, oil on canvas, 35 × 27″ (89 × 69 cm), © National Gallery, London/Art Resource, NY. Through a series of paintings, comparable to scenes in a play, Hogarth told moralizing tales focusing on the hypocritical or dishonest practices of his day. *Marriage à la Mode* shows the disastrous outcome of a marriage arranged for the benefit of the parents of the bride and groom.

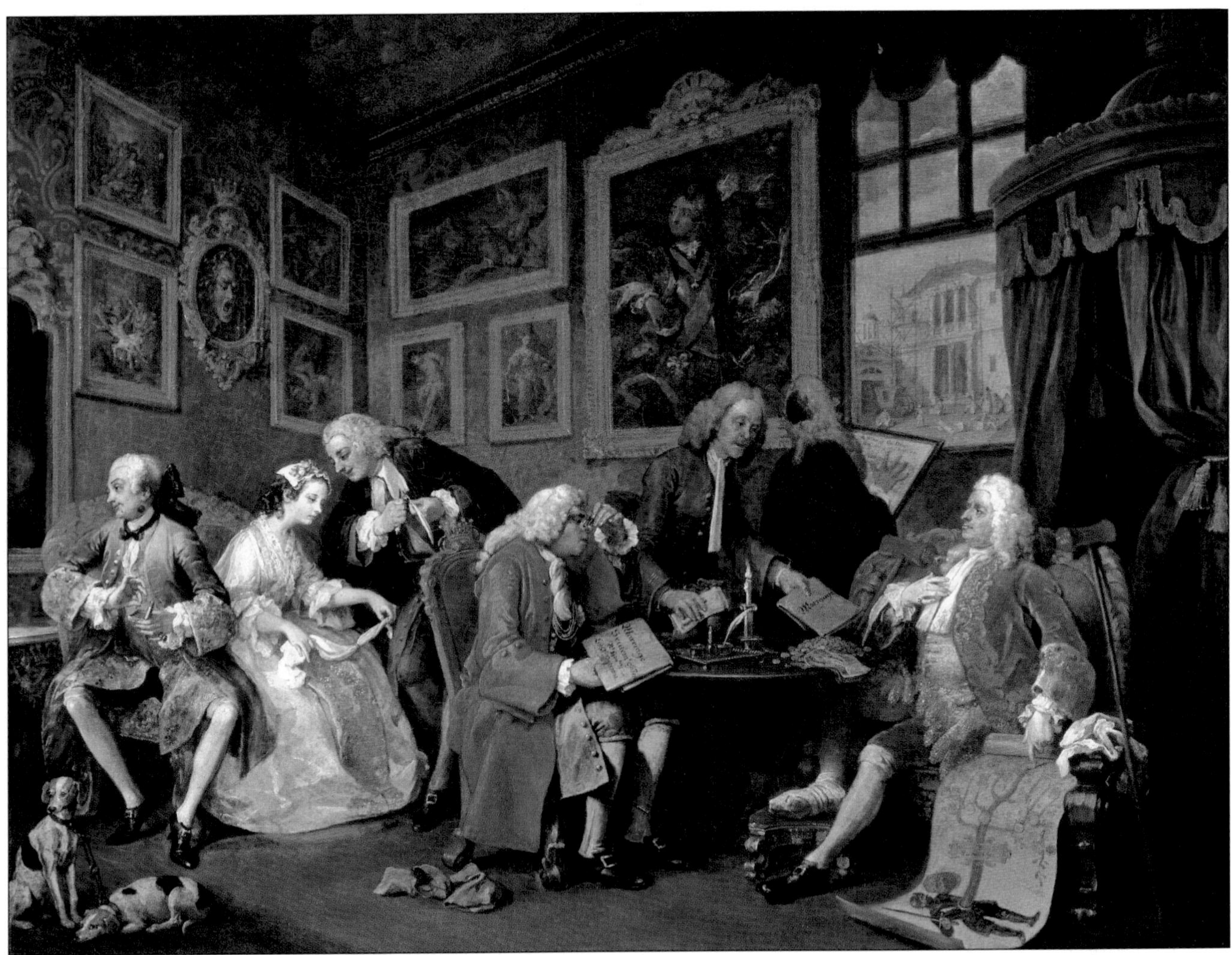

Connections

DIDEROT AS ART CRITIC

One of the very first art critics—certainly the first art critic of any substance—was Denis Diderot (1713–1784), the philosophe. He enjoyed art, and his enjoyment is evident in every page of his essays, called the *Salons.* He reviewed all the exhibitions sponsored by the French Academy from 1759 on for a private newspaper, *La Correspondance littéraire.* Subscribers to this newspaper were the elite of Europe—princesses and princes—and it was intended to keep potential patrons abreast of the latest news from Paris.

Although he considered Boucher the most talented painter of his generation, Diderot generally disapproved of his subjects, and went so far as to condemn him and his contemporaries in the *Salon of 1767* for the essentially erotic content of most of what was on display. Four years earlier he had asked, "Haven't painters used their brushes in the service of vice and debauchery long enough, too long indeed?" He preferred what he called "moral" painting that sought "to move, to educate, to improve us, and to induce us to virtue." Diderot could also be cruel. Addressing a now-forgotten painter by the name of Challe, he asked, "Tell me, Monsieur Challe, why are you a painter? There are so many other professions in which mediocrity is actually an advantage."

Anticipating the Impressionists a century later, he celebrated a **still life** painting entitled *The Brioche* (fig. 16.8) by JEAN-BAPTISTE-SIMEON CHARDIN [shar-DAN] (1699–1779), "Such magic leaves one amazed. There are thick layers of superimposed color, and their effect rises from below to the surface. . . . Come closer, and everything becomes flat, confused, and indistinct; stand back again, and everything springs back into life and shape."

Diderot's writing style is anything but as direct as his criticisms. Some of his *Salons* are so long that they cannot be read at a single sitting. They exercise every excuse for a digression. Still, their acuteness of vision and moral purpose continue to influence art criticism.

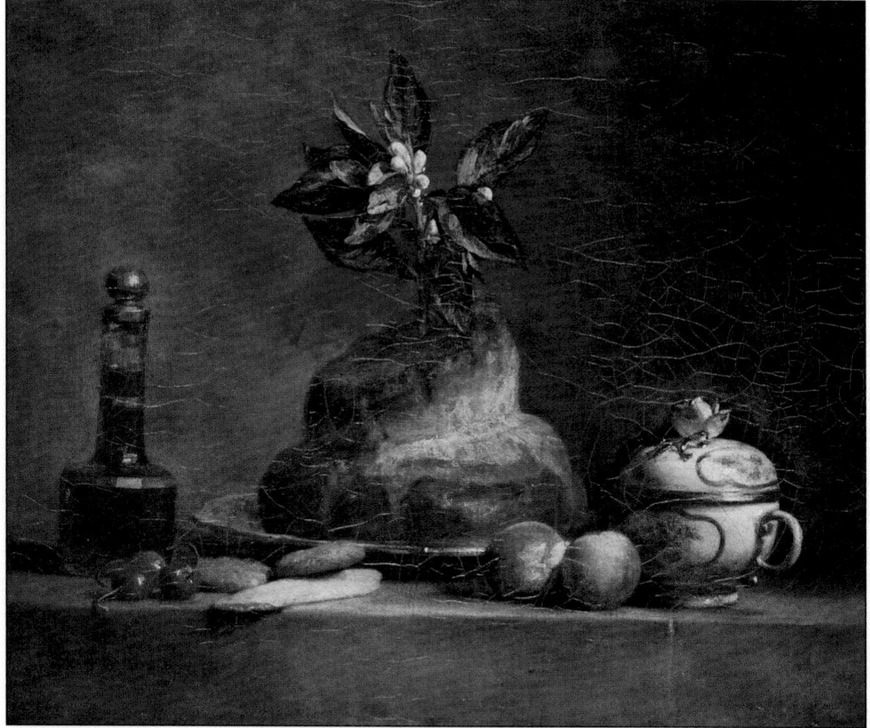

FIGURE 16.8 Jean-Baptiste-Siméon Chardin, *The Brioche*, 1763, oil on canvas, $18\frac{1}{2}'' \times 22''$(47 × 55.9 cm), photo: Herve Lewandowski. Musée du Louvre, Paris. RMN Reunion des Musees National/Art Resource, NY. A master of still life, which in his day was considered the lowest form of painting, Chardin was nevertheless recognized by his contemporaries as applying paint and color as no one before him had ever done. But his technique was not, he thought, what mattered most. "Who told you that one paints with colors?" he once asked a fellow artist. "One uses colors, but one paints with feelings."

In the five scenes that follow, the marriage, as expected, sours. Husband and wife are both unfaithful. When the husband finds his wife with Silvertongue, the lover stabs him. The wife is disgraced and takes poison. As she is dying, her father, mercenary to the end, removes her valuable rings. In *Marriage à la Mode* the guilty go unpunished.

Sir Joshua Reynolds. One of the leading painters of London society was Sir Joshua Reynolds (1723–1792). Thoughtful, intelligent, and hard working, Reynolds was named the first president of the Royal Academy of London in 1768 and was knighted the following year. Favoring an academic art similar to that championed by Lebrun in France a century earlier, Reynolds developed a set of theories and rules in his fifteen *Discourses*, positioning history painting as the highest form of art.

The majority of Reynolds's works, however, are portraits, presumably because portrait painting was lucrative. His style is seen in his portrait *Lady Elizabeth Delmé and Her Children* (fig. 16.9), executed 1777–80 at the peak of his career. Reynolds often portrayed aristocratic ladies as elegant and gracious, refined and dignified. Lady Delmé sits on a rock and embraces her oldest children. All are fashionably dressed. The colors and textures are lush in Reynolds's "Grand Manner"—indeed, the canvas itself is enormous and the figures almost life size.

Reynolds painted rapidly with full, free brushstrokes, without first making sketches. In his fourth *Discourse*, he says a portrait painter should give a general idea of his subject and "leave out all the minute breaks and peculiarities in the face . . . rather than observing the exact similitude of every feature." Thus Reynolds painted people the way he thought they should look, rather than how they actually did look.

Thomas Gainsborough. Reynolds's chief rival was Thomas Gainsborough (1727–1788). Although Gainsborough began as a landscape painter, a subject he always preferred, he painted portraits to make a living and became the most fashionable portraitist in British society. Gainsborough's *Mary, Countess Howe* (fig. 16.10), of 1765, like most eighteenth-century portraiture, flatters the

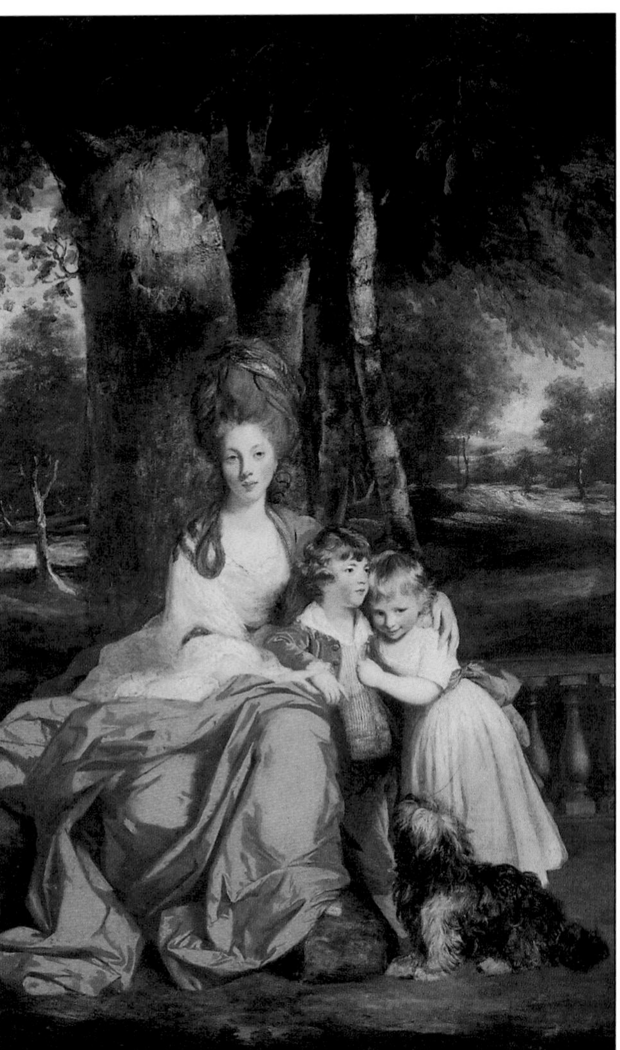

FIGURE 16.9 Sir Joshua Reynolds, *Lady Elizabeth Delmé and Her Children*, 1777–80, oil on canvas, 7′10″ × 4′12$\frac{1}{8}$″ (2.39 × 1.48 m), Andrew W. Mellon Collection. 1937.1.95. Photograph © Board of Trustees, National Gallery of Art, Washington, D.C. Reynolds, Gainsborough's rival, places his aristocratic subjects in a landscape setting indicative of the eighteenth-century appreciation of nature.

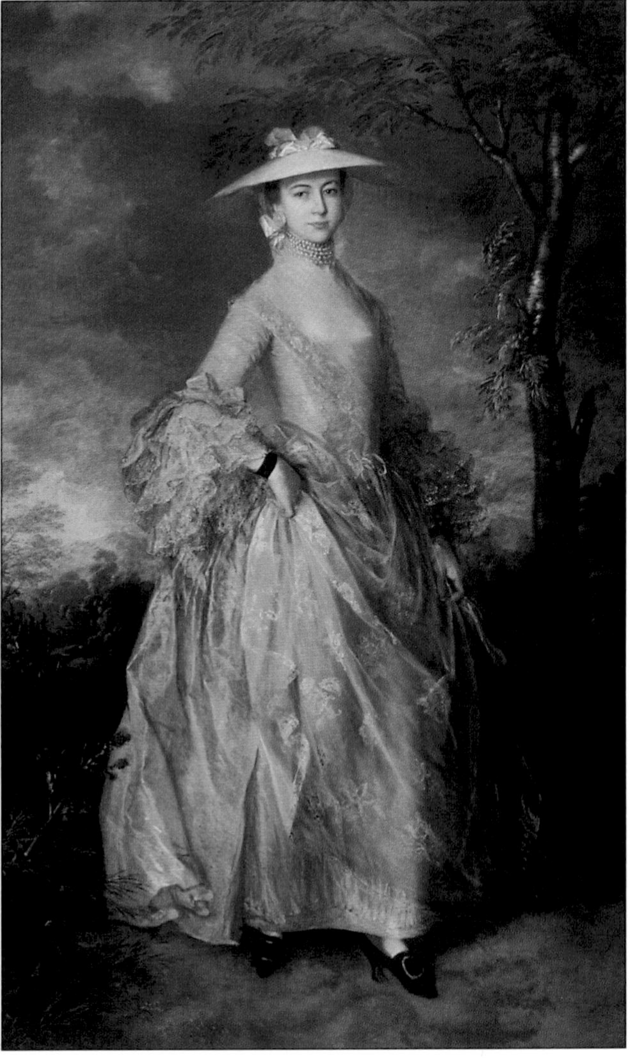

FIGURE 16.10 Thomas Gainsborough, *Mary, Countess Howe*, 1765, oil on canvas, 8′ × 5′ (2.59 × 1.52 m), London County Council, Kenwood House (Iveagh Bequest). English Heritage, London. Although he thought of himself first and foremost as a landscape painter, Gainsborough is best known for large-scale portraits that present his subjects as aristocratic and refined.

subject. Set in a landscape worthy of Watteau, Gainsborough depicts the countess of Howe as if she were strolling in a *fete galante.* She is impeccably dressed, elegant, possessing social poise and a self-confident air of distinction. Painting with dash and freedom, using a fresh and fluid technique emphasizing lush textures in decorative colors, Gainsborough displays a technical virtuosity typical of the Rococo.

LITERATURE OF RATIONALISM

During the eighteenth century, literary works throughout Europe reflected the rationalism of the Enlightenment. The emphasis on reason occurred across genres, from essays and fiction to poetry and drama. Benjamin Franklin and Thomas Paine wrote essays that relied on careful reasoning and incisive logic to support their claims about human political and social behavior, as well as humanity's irrational beliefs, especially those concerning religious faith. Novelists and satirists, including Daniel Defoe and Jonathan Swift, often used irony to satirize humans' claim to reason. Swift suggested, in fact, that although human beings are theoretically capable of being rational, few actually behave rationally. English poets in particular employed irony and sarcasm as weapons in their fiercely satirical verses on all manner of subjects, especially the behavior of courtiers.

Samuel Johnson's "Club." The London of Hogarth's day was, above all, a city of contrasts. On the one hand, there was Fleet Street, largely rebuilt after the Great Fire of 1666 and dominated at one end by Wren's St. Paul's Cathedral. Fleet Street was the gathering place of the Club, a group of London intellectuals, writers, editors, and publishers. One of its founders was Samuel Johnson (1709–1784), author of the 1755 *Dictionary of the English Language* and editor of Shakespeare's complete plays. The Club was also home to members of refined society. Artists, too, among them Sir Joshua Reynolds, sought each other's company at the Cock Tavern or at Ye Olde Cheshire Cheese. "When a man is tired of London, a man is tired of life," Johnson boasted of the city's intellectual and cultural stimulation.

On the other hand, there was Grub Street, a lane just outside the London Wall. As Johnson put it in his *Dictionary*, Grub Street was "inhabited by writers of small histories, dictionaries, and temporary poems"—the hacks of the burgeoning publishing trade. A world of difference lay between it and Fleet Street; Newgate Prison was between them, and Bethlehem Royal Hospital, known as Bedlam, the lunatic asylum, was nearby. This was the monstrous side of London, a side that members of Johnson's Club witnessed every day as they strolled from Fleet Street to the tavern where they met. On the way, they passed through Covent Garden, where the city's street-walkers plied their trade.

Alexander Pope. Alexander Pope (1688–1744) set the standard for satiric poetry in eighteenth-century England. No work captures the spirit of Grub Street better than Pope's *Dunciad*, written in 1743. Pope equates the Grub Street writers with the lunacy of the city itself, and the poem ends with a "dunces" parade through the city.

In the face of the monstrosities of Grub Street, Pope writes, "Morality expires." Satire was Pope's chief tool, and the lowly hacks of Grub Street were by no means his only target. Like Hogarth, he attacked the morality of the aristocracy. Perhaps his most famous poem is *The Rape of the Lock.* This is a **mock epic**—it treats a trivial incident in a heroic manner and style more suited to the traditional epic subjects of war and nation building. *The Rape of the Lock* is based on an actual incident in which a young man from a prominent family clipped a lock of hair from one Miss Arabella Fermor, an event that caused her family considerable consternation. Pope describes the gentlemen and ladies of polite society in the same terms as the heroes and heroines of Homer's epic *Iliad* and *Odyssey*, his translations of which first established his reputation. Pope's "war" is chiefly one of the words and deeds exchanged between the sexes, all described in heroic style. Applied to the frivolous world of snuffboxes, porcelain, and cosmetics, the effect is undeniably comical, as if Sir Joshua Reynolds's Grand Manner had been brought low.

Jonathan Swift. A far crueler satirist was Jonathan Swift (1667–1745). Born in Ireland, Swift traveled to London, where he became a renowned poet and political writer, as well as an Anglican clergyman. After his appointment as dean of St. Patrick's Cathedral in Dublin in 1713, he spent the rest of his life in Ireland. Best known for his satirical prose work *Gulliver's Travels*, Swift for many years was considered a cynical misanthrope—a person who hates the human race. Much has been made of a comment from *Gulliver's Travels*, spoken by the King of Brobdingnag (the land of the giants). Addressing Lemuel Gulliver, Swift's representative of humanity, the Brobdingnagian king describes human beings as "the most pernicious race of little odious vermin that Nature ever suffered to crawl upon the face of the earth."

This bitter satirical strain, however, is only one side of Swift's literary persona; his satirical imagination also had a lighter, more playful dimension. *Gulliver's Travels* is full of fantastic and marvelous events, delightful even to children. The book recounts the adventures of a ship's physician, Lemuel Gulliver, over four voyages. His first voyage takes him to Lilliput, where the people are only six inches tall; the second to Brobdingnag, the land of giants; the third to Laputa, a region where thought and intellect are privileged; and the fourth and final voyage to the land inhabited by the Yahoos and their masters the Houyhnhnms, horselike creatures whose lives are governed by reason, intelligence, and common sense. Nonetheless, throughout *Gulliver's Travels*, Swift uses his hero's adventures to satirize the political, social, and academic institutions of his own time and country, with their abundant display of human folly, stupidity, baseness, and greed. Thus he contrasts the sensible and wise

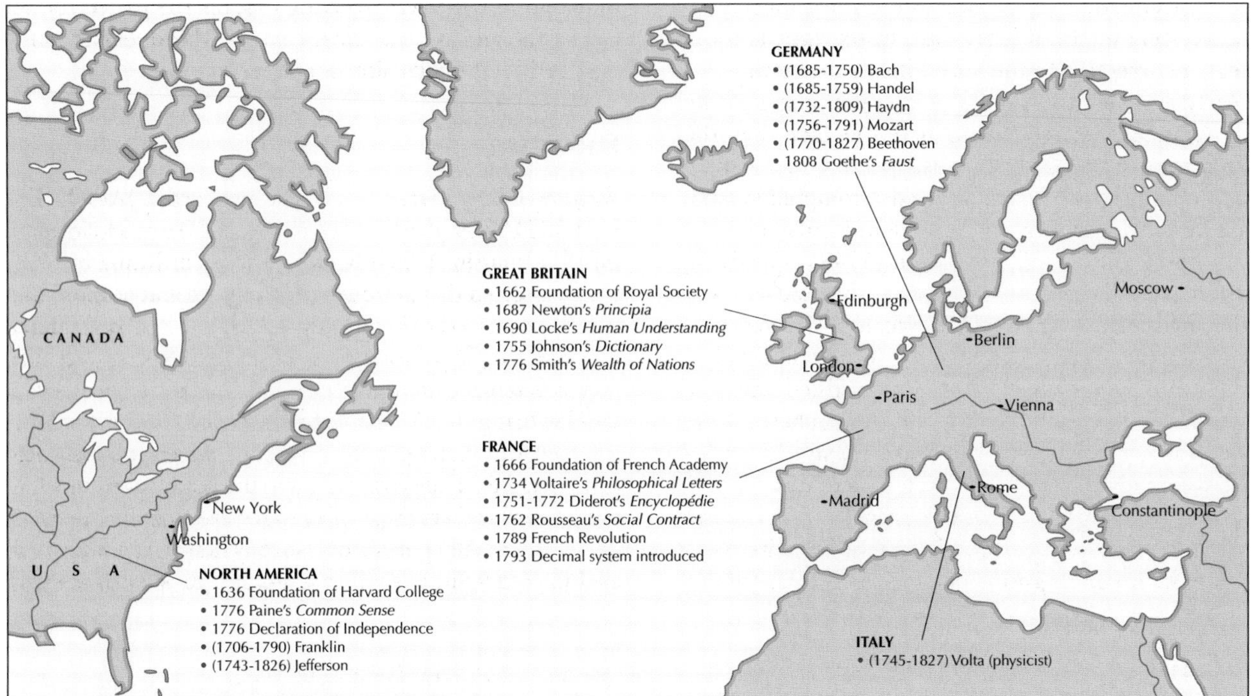

MAP 16.2 The Enlightenment in America and Europe.

Houyhnhnms with both the ignorant and filthy Yahoos and with the impractical and eccentric Laputians, who are so far from living effectively in the real world that they carry a large sack filled with a multitude of objects, which they need to communicate with one another.

VOLTAIRE'S PHILOSOPHY OF CYNICISM

One of the most important thinkers of the eighteenth century, François Marie Arouet, known by his pen name VOLTAIRE [Vole-TAIR] (1694–1778), shared Swift's general sense of human folly, as well as Hogarth and Pope's recognition of the moral bankruptcy of the aristocracy. Voltaire was deeply influenced by English political thought, especially by the freedom of ideas that, among other things, allowed writers such as Pope and Swift to publish without fear. Voltaire himself was jailed for a year, then exiled to England in 1726, for criticizing the morality of the French aristocracy. When he returned to France, in 1729, he promptly published his *Philosophical Letters Concerning the English*, in which, once more, he criticized French political and religious life. This time, his publisher was jailed, and Voltaire himself retreated to Lorraine, in eastern France, where he lived for the next fifteen years.

Voltaire's best known work, *Candide*, is a scathing indictment of those who agreed with the philosopher Leibniz that this is the best of all possible worlds, regardless of occasional misfortunes, and that everything that happens is part of the providential plan of a benevolent God. *Candide* was written just after the 1755 Lisbon earthquake, in which thousands were killed. Voltaire argued that those who explained the catastrophe away, minimizing its destructive consequences, were deceiving themselves. Voltaire reasoned that either God refused to prevent the existence of evil, in which case he was not benevolent, or he lacked the power to avert evil, in which case he was not omnipotent. Voltaire also rejected the Christian notion of a personal God. Voltaire was a Deist, one who subscribed to a belief system that envisioned a divine being as the maker of the universe, but a creator who lacked interest in the world once it had been created. According to Deism, the creator was like a clockmaker and the world like a complex machine, which was set in motion by the creator but into which he did not intervene. For Voltaire, religious traditions such as biblical Christianity that promise eternal joy, happiness, and salvation were responsible for creating unrealistic expectations and vain hopes. In fact, one of the strongest impetuses for rationalism was a disillusionment with religious belief—faith and revelation—because differences among religious factions had accounted for more than 150 years of bloody war throughout Europe.

NEOCLASSICISM

Many people in France were suspicious of the behavior and tastes of their own aristocracy. To painters, it seemed as if the sensuous color and brushwork of the *rubénistes* had led not merely to the excesses of the Rococo but had themselves become the visual sign of a general moral decline. Thus *poussinistes* once again began to take hold.

Poussin's intellectual classicism offered not merely an alternative style to the Rococo but, in its rigor and orderliness, a corrective to the social ills of the state.

As early as 1746, in reviews of the exhibition of the French Academy, critics bemoaned the fact that the grandiose history paintings had disappeared, replaced by the Rococo fantasies Diderot abhorred. Prompted in large measure by the rediscovery of the ancient Roman cities of Herculaneum and Pompeii, in 1738 and 1748 respectively, which were partially excavated from the ashes and volcanic mud that had buried them when volcanic Mt. Vesuvius erupted in 79 C.E., many people began to reestablish classical values in art and state. People indentified with the public-minded values of the Greek and Roman heroes who placed moral virtue, patriotic self-sacrifice, and "right action" above all else, and they wanted to see these virtues displayed in painting. By 1775, the French Academy was routinely turning down Rococo submissions to its biennial Salon in favor of more classical subjects, just as Madame du Barry was rejecting Fragonard's panels for her new château. A *new* classicism—a **Neoclassicism**—replaced the Rococo almost overnight.

PAINTING

Jacques-Louis David. The French artist JACQUES-LOUIS DAVID [dah-VEED] (1748–1825) was a follower of Nicolas Poussin. When he left to study in Rome in 1775, David asserted that antique art lacked fire and passion; but, in fact, he was to be thoroughly seduced by it. David offered his stark, simple painting as an antidote to Rococo frivolity.

His first major commission was for Louis XVI, the *Oath of the Horatii* (fig. 16.11). Three brothers from Rome, the Horatii, pledge an oath upon their weapons, which are being held by their father. They vow to fight to the death against the Curatii, three brothers from Alba, to resolve a conflict between the two cities. All figures are accurately drawn, carefully modeled in cold light, as solid as sculpture. In accordance with

FIGURE 16.11 Jacques-Louis David, *Oath of the Horatii*, 1785, oil on canvas, 4′3″ × 6′5$\frac{1}{4}$″ (1.30 × 1.96 cm). Photo: G. Blot/C. Jean. © Musee du Louvre/RMN Reunion des Musees Nationeux/Art Resource, NY. Neoclassical artists favored subjects taken from ancient literature and history that illustrated high principles or ideals. Excavation of the ancient Roman cities of Herculaneum and Pompeii generated a renewed and widespread interest in the antique.

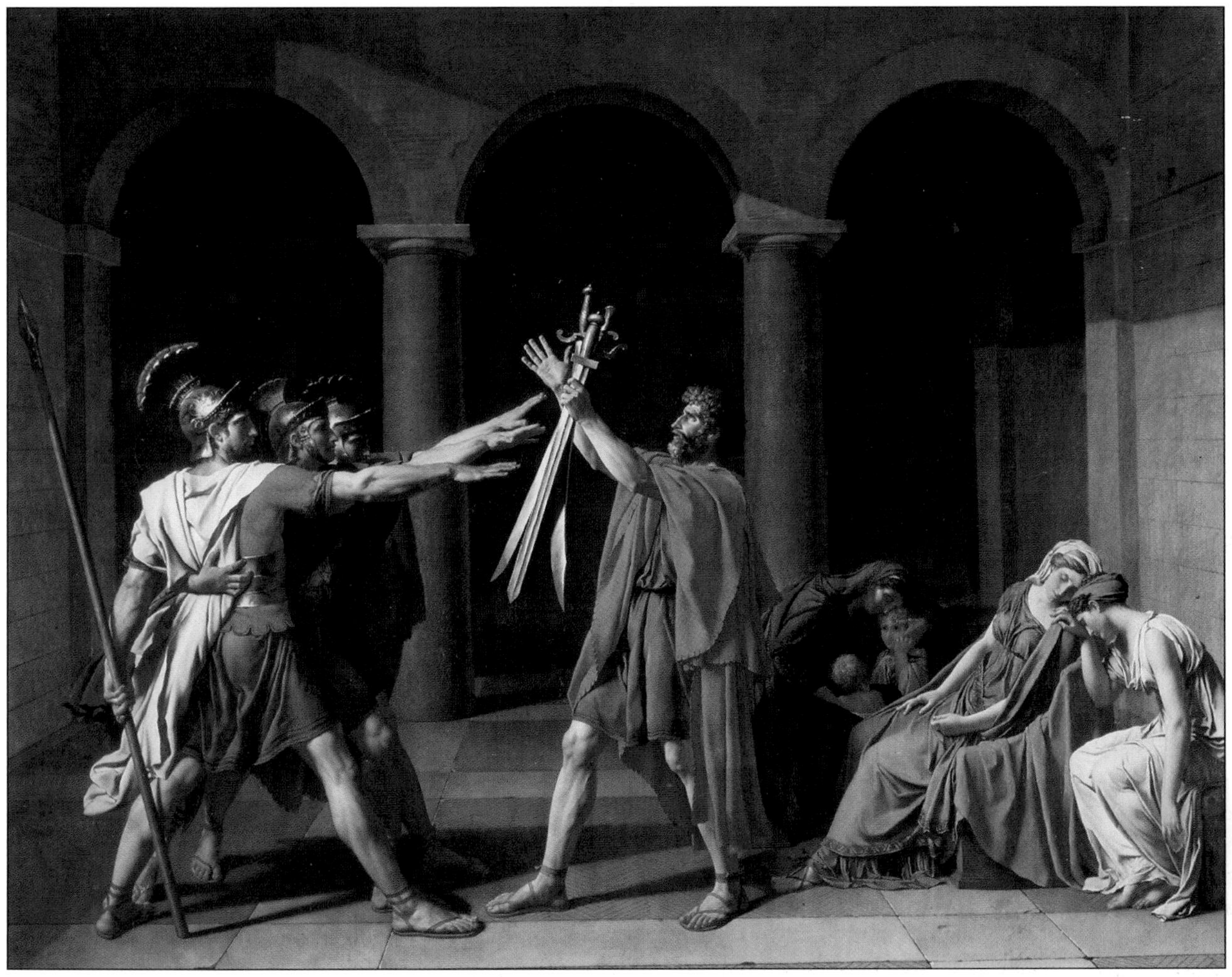

Neoclassical ideals, the scene is set against the severe architecture of the Roman revival. David, like Poussin, constructed his composition in a series of horizontal planes arranged parallel to the picture plane. Also like Poussin, David subordinated color to line, because he believed clarity of statement was most important and was best achieved by drawing. As a result, his paintings appear to be drawings that have been colored. David's subject is a display of Roman heroic stoicism and high principles. The Horatii place patriotic duty above concern for themselves and their family.

When the painting was exhibited at the Salon of 1785, it caused an immediate sensation, not so much because of its Neoclassical style, but because it promoted values that many people recognized were lacking in the king and his court. By the time of the French Revolution in 1789, the painting was read almost universally as an overtly antimonarchist statement, although David probably did not originally intend it as such. Interpreted as a call for a new moral commitment on the part of the French state, David's art quickly became that most closely associated with the revolution. David himself was soon planning parades gala festivals, and public demonstrations, all designed to rally the people behind the revolution's cause. He persuaded the revolutionary government to abolish the French Academy, and in its stead to create a panel of experts charged with reforming the public taste.

Angelica Kauffmann. The work of ANGELICA KAUFFMANN [KOFF-mahn] (1741–1807) provides an even clearer example of painterly representation of virtuous behavior and high moral conduct. The Swiss-born Kauffmann was trained in Italy, where she modeled her figures after the wall paintings at Pompeii and Herculaneum. In 1766, she moved to England, and, with her friend Sir Joshua Reynolds, helped found the new British Royal Academy.

Kauffmann's *Cornelia Pointing to Her Children as Her Treasures* (fig. 16.12), of 1785, champions family values,

FIGURE 16.12 Angelica Kauffmann, *Cornelia Pointing to Her Children as Her Treasures*, 1785, oil on canvas, 3′4″ × 4′2″ (1.02 × 1.27 m), Virginia Museum of Fine Arts, Richmond. The Adolph D. and Wilkins C. Williams Fund. Photo: Katherine Wetzel. © Virginia Museum of Fine Arts. In contrast to Rococo frivolity, Neoclassical art was intended to serve a public role in encouraging virtue. In this story from ancient republican Rome, when asked about her treasures, Cornelia points to her children, who went on to do good deeds on behalf of the poor.

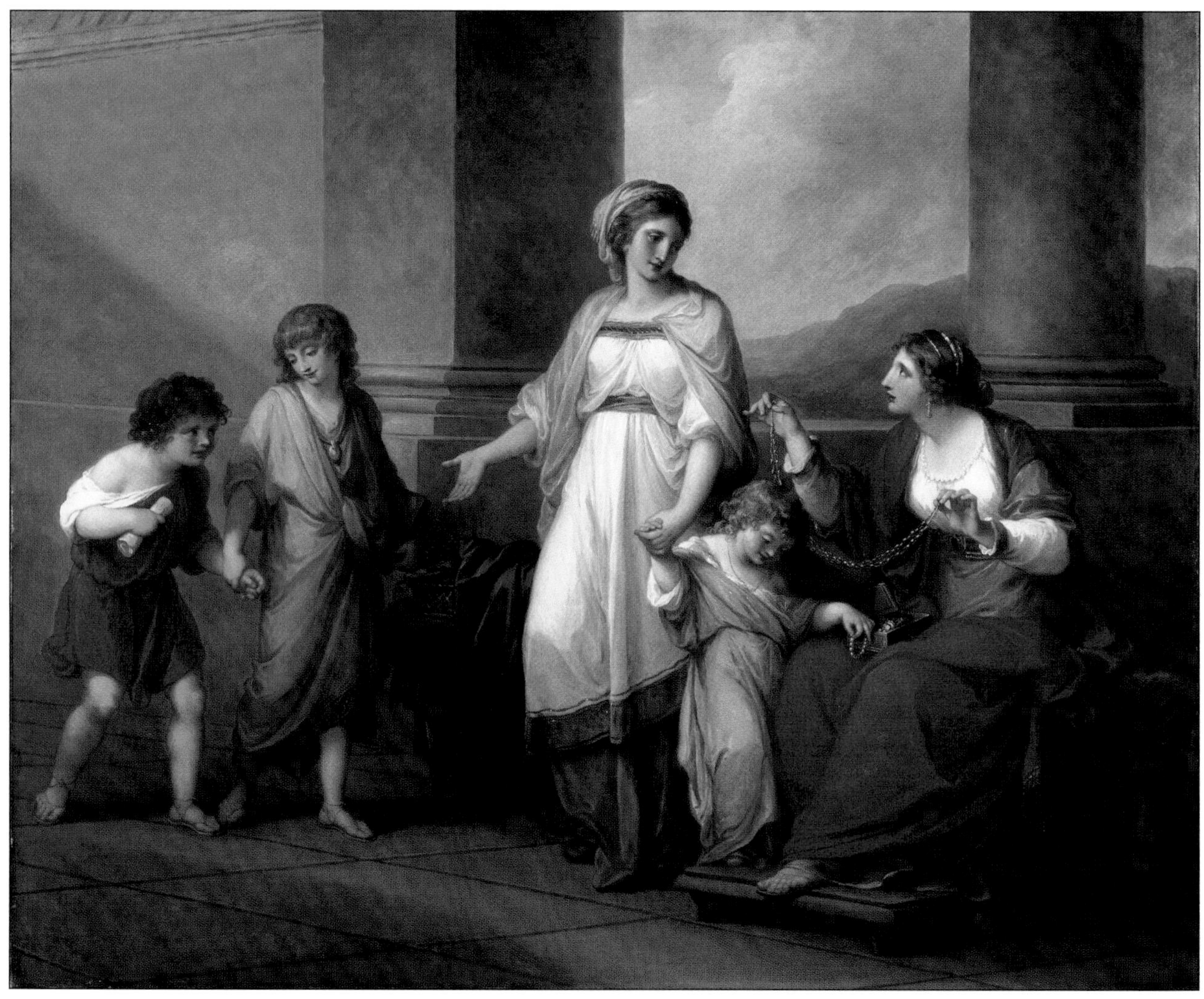

simple dress, and austere interiors. Gone are Rococo depictions of women wearing the elegant and refined dress of the Rococo salon. Instead, when a visitor asks to see her family treasures, Cornelia points with pride to her two sons (the Gracchi), both of whom were to grow up to become leaders of the Roman Republic, repossessing public land from the decadent Roman aristocracy and redistributing it to the poor—precisely the spirit that drove the leaders of the French Revolution.

John Singleton Copley. An American expatriate working in London, JOHN SINGLETON COPLEY [COP-lee] (1738–1815) of Boston was New England's leading portraitist. Copley went to England in 1774, studied in London, gained admission to the Royal Academy, and remained there the rest of his life. Copley's *Watson and the Shark* (fig. 16.13), of 1778, depicts a contemporary event with a kind of immediacy and realism that anticipates the painting of the next century. The event depicted was real: A man named Brook Watson had indeed encountered a shark while swimming in the harbor of Havana, Cuba. The painting shows the shark lunging for Watson while two men reach out for him, straining, their faces showing their anguish, and another man grasps the shirt of one to prevent him from falling overboard. The drama is increased by the dramatic lighting and the dynamic diagonal movements. Copley paints a cliff-hanger—the viewer is left wondering whether Watson will survive. In fact, Watson had long escaped the shark when he commissioned the painting years later as a publicity ploy while running for political office.

SCULPTURE

Jean-Antoine Houdon. One of France's greatest sculptors was JEAN-ANTOINE HOUDON [ooh-DON] (1741–1828), born at the Palace of Versailles where his father was a servant. Later his father became the caretaker for the school for advanced students in the French Academy of Painting and Sculpture, enabling Houdon to associate with artists from the time he was eight years old. It is said that as a child he would sneak into class, steal some

FIGURE 16.13 John Singleton Copley, *Watson and the Shark*, 1778, oil on canvas, $6'\frac{1}{2}'' \times 7'6\frac{1}{4}''$ (1.84 × 2.29 m). Gift of Mrs. George von Lengerke Meyer. Courtesy Museum of Fine Arts, Boston. Reproduced with permission. © 2005 Museum of Fine Arts, Boston. All Rights Reserved. Copley's painting has all the drama of a modern adventure film—a struggle for survival against nature depicted at the climactic moment and with the outcome left uncertain—combined with heroic nudity.

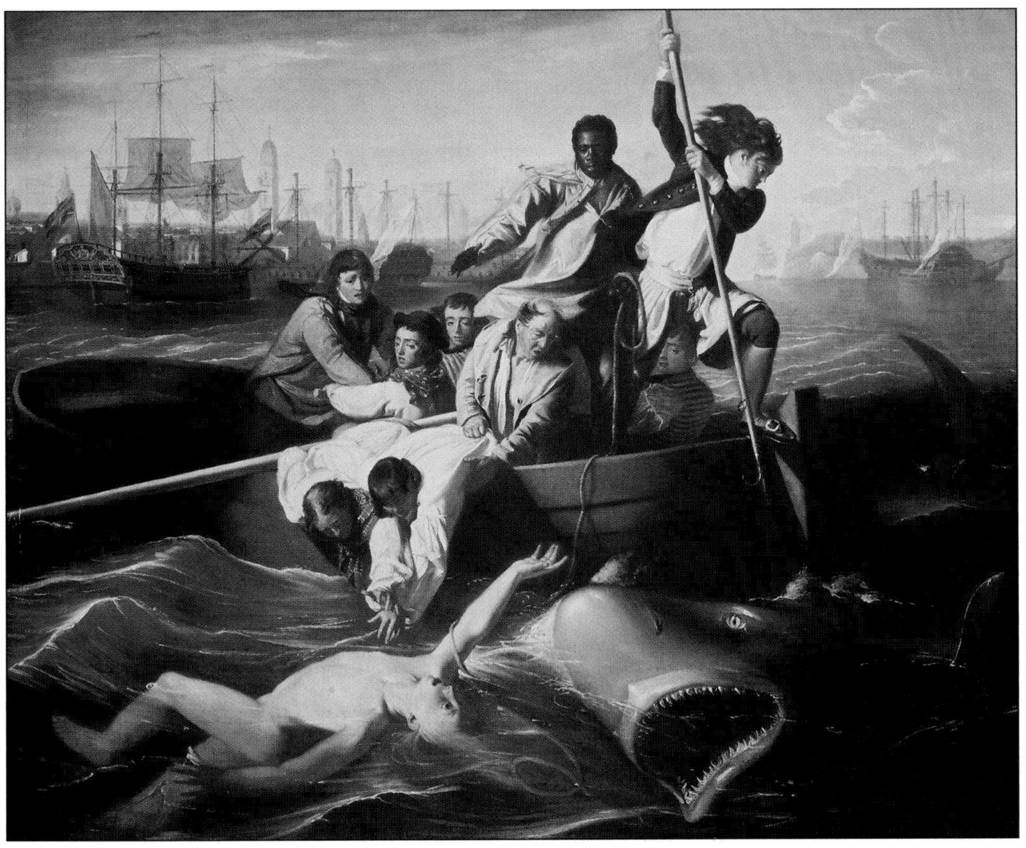

clay, and imitate what he saw. He learned well, for he won the Prix de Rome, which enabled him to study in Italy from 1764 to 1769.

Houdon was unrivaled in his day as a portrait sculptor. Even Americans ventured forth to commission him while they were in Paris: Benjamin Franklin (1778), John Paul Jones (1780), and Thomas Jefferson (1789). To create life-like images, Houdon took precise measurements of his sitters and usually made a terra cotta model while working with the sitter. This model was given to his assistants, who blocked out the form in marble; then Houdon did the fine carving and polishing.

In order to portray George Washington (fig. 16.14), Houdon went to America and stayed for two weeks in October 1785 as a guest in Washington's home at Mount Vernon, Virginia. Houdon made a cast of Washington's face and a plaster bust, but returned to Paris to carve the life-size figure in stone, working on the project from 1788 to 1792.

During that time Houdon also made a statue of Washington in classical garb. Although the version finally selected shows Washington wearing contemporary attire, it, too, has links to the classical past. Washington stands in the antique *contrapposto* pose. His left hand rests on thirteen bound rods, or ancient *fasces*, symbolizing both the original states of the Union and the power and authority of ancient Rome. Behind the *fasces* are sword and plow, representing war and peace.

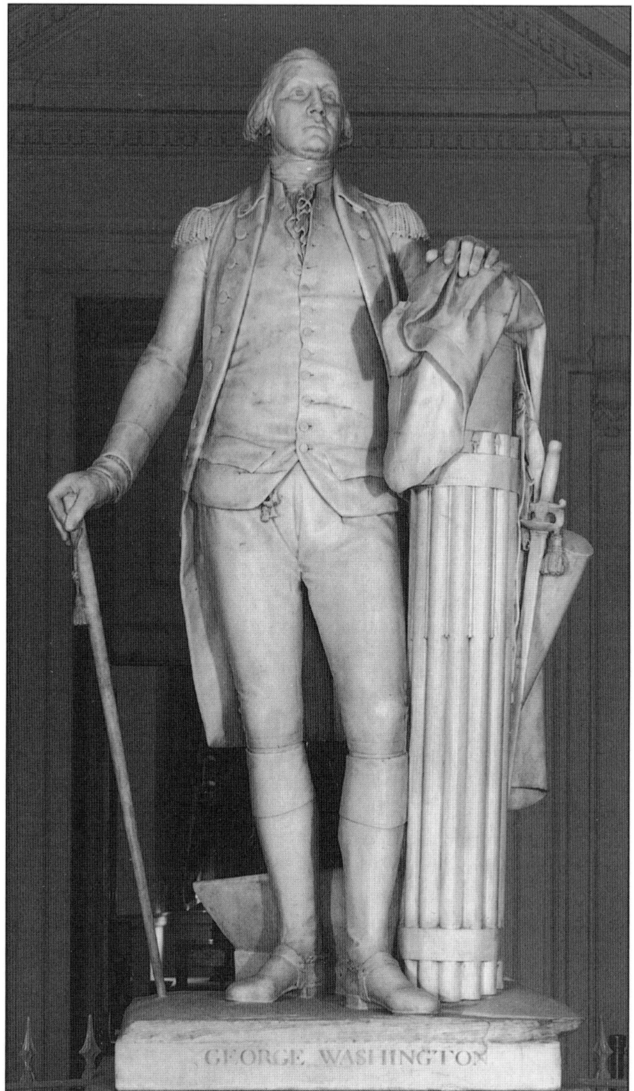

FIGURE 16.14 Jean-Antoine Houdon, *George Washington*, 1788–92, marble, height 6′2″ (1.88 m). State Capitol, Richmond, Virginia. Collection of the Commonwealth of Virginia. Photo Courtesy of the Library of Virginia. Calm, composed, and commanding, this version of Washington in his general's attire was favored over another version in classical garb. Still, antique echoes are seen in the *contrapposto* pose and the thirteen *fasces* (rods) bound together, representing the states of the Union.

ARCHITECTURE

Chiswick House. Chiswick House (fig. 16.15) is an excellent example of Neoclassical architecture in England. It was begun in 1725, built by Lord Burlington (1694–1753) and William Kent (1685–1748). Burlington was himself an amateur architect, but his team included trained architects.

Like its prototypes, including the Roman Pantheon (see fig. 4.11) and Palladio's Villa Rotunda in Vicenza, Italy (see fig. 13.35), Chiswick House is geometrically simple yet stately. The classical vocabulary and proportions are most important. Symmetry is maintained at all costs, even when it makes things inconvenient within the home. In the academic Neoclassical style, regularity, reason, and logic dominate imaginative variation. This is in marked contrast to the emotion and drama of the Baroque and Rococo styles. In Neoclassical buildings, the walls are flat and the decoration relatively austere compared to that of Rococo interiors, with their abundantly ornamented, animated, even undulating architectural elements.

La Madeleine. In France, the Neoclassical style was promulgated in particular by Napoleon, who longed to rebuild Paris as the new Rome. The church of La Madeleine in Paris (fig. 16.16) had been started by Louis XVI, but Napoleon rededicated it in 1806 as a Temple of Glory to be designed by PIERRE-ALEXANDRE VIGNON [VEE-nyonh] (1762–1829).

Napoleon conceived of La Madeleine as a monument to his military victories and as a repository for his trophies. Reflecting the great interest in archaeology at this time, the exterior is an accurate reconstruction of an ancient Roman temple. It has a raised base, steps across the front only, a colonnade of the Corinthian order, entablature, pediments,

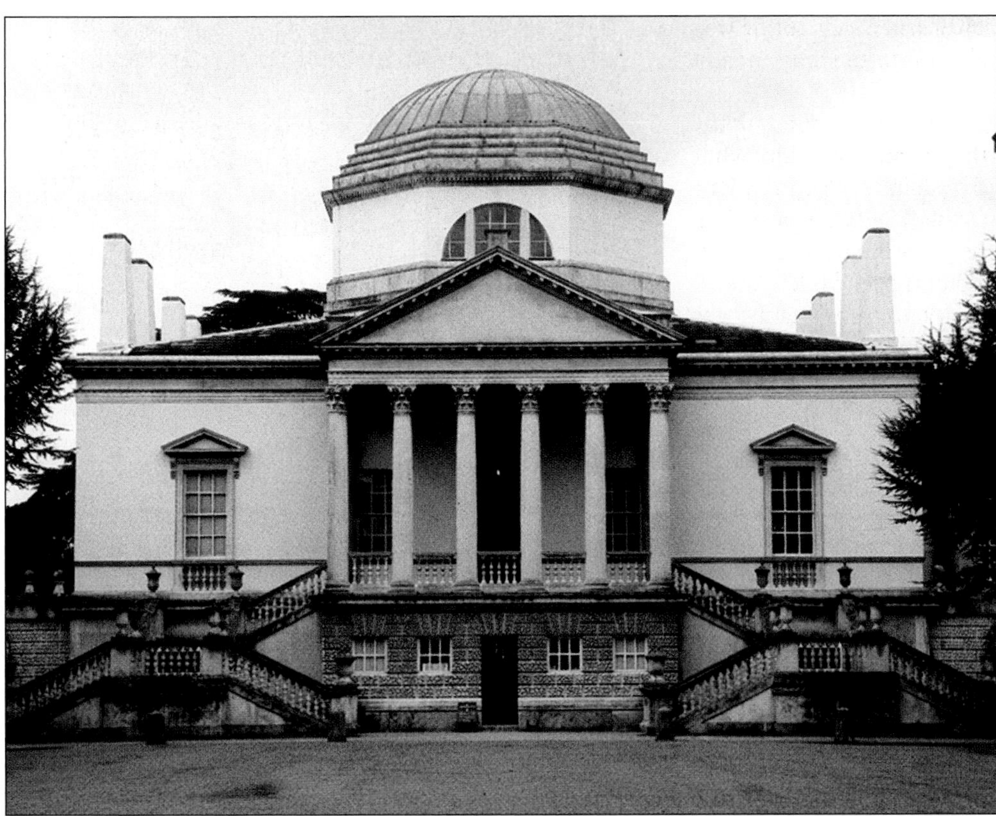

FIGURE 16.15 Lord Burlington and William Kent, Chiswick House, west London, begun 1725. The architectural lineage of this house, with its central dome, triangular pediment, and columnar portico, can be traced back to the ancient Roman Pantheon (see fig. 4.11).

and a peaked roof. Although highly dignified, there is something stark about La Madeleine's archaeological accuracy. Individual imagination seems absent. The interior belies the exterior, for its ceiling consists of three consecutive domes; thus, unlike its ancient Greek and Roman prototypes, the exterior and interior are not coordinated. After Napoleon's death the building was once again used as a church.

Monticello. The Neoclassical style of architecture was prominent in the United States, where the new American presidents, believing it to embody enlightened democratic leadership, championed its use in public architecture. One of the most notable Neoclassical designs in the United States is the private home of President Thomas Jefferson (1743–1826), known as Monticello [MON-tih-CHELL-o], in Charlottesville, Virginia (fig. 16.17). Jefferson drew up the designs for it himself in 1769. An adaptation of Burlington and Kent's Chiswick House, it was built between 1770 and 1806. Monticello is constructed of brick and wood and capped with a polygonal dome. The deep portico, or porch, here supported on Doric columns, was to become very popular in the southern United States, as seen in some of the great antebellum homes in Mississippi. In southern climates the portico provided protection from the sun and added dignity and splendor to the building; the northern equivalent was much shallower. The plan of Monticello is almost perfectly symmetrical, with entrances on each of the four sides, and the rooms laid out on either side of a central hall and drawing room.

A leading architect of his time, Jefferson fostered classical ideas in America. He studied the ancient Roman temple known as the Maison Carrée in Nîmes, France, and used it as the model for the Virginia state capitol (1785–98). An example of austere Neoclassicism, it represents a deliberate rejection of the Baroque and the Rococo.

LITERATURE

The Rise of the Novel. Although the novel can be said to have originated in the ancient world with stories told by Greek and Roman writers, it did not rise to significance as a literary genre until the eighteenth century in Europe. Preceding the rise of the novel as a major literary genre

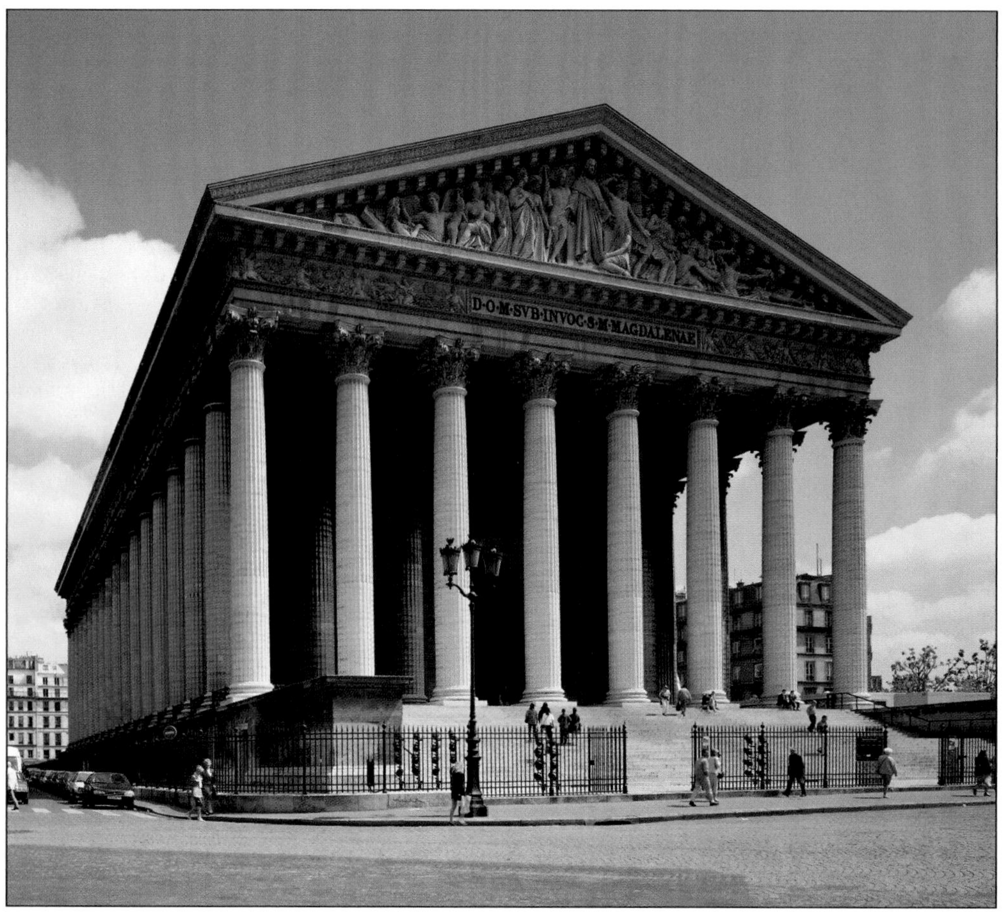

FIGURE 16.16 Pierre-Alexandre Vignon, La Madeleine, Paris, 1806–42, main facade, length 350′ (106.68 m), width 147′ (44.81 m), height of podium 23′ (7.01 m), height of columns 63′ (19.20 m). La Madeleine is based on the ancient rectangular temple type, such as the Greek Parthenon (see fig. 3.3).

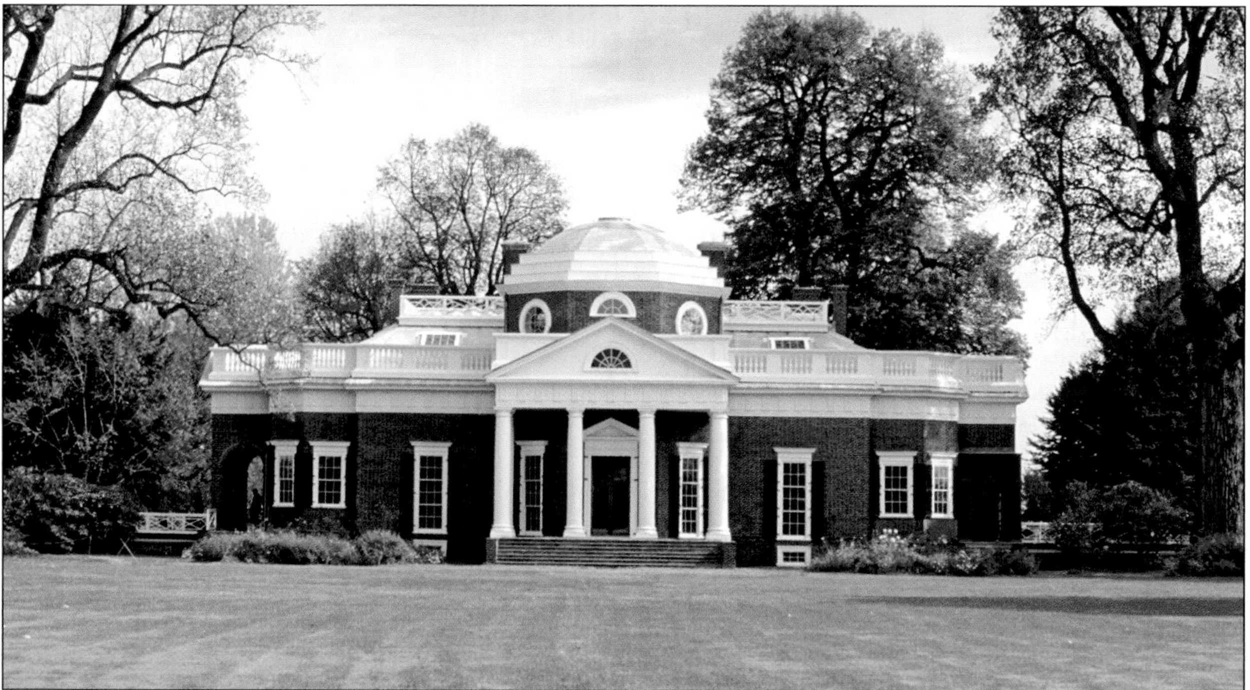

FIGURE 16.17 Thomas Jefferson, Monticello, Charlottesville, Virginia, main facade, 1770–1806. Neoclassical architecture was favored in America for its formal symmetry and antique associations. At Monticello a temple of stone and concrete, the ancient Roman Pantheon (see fig. 4.11), via Chiswick House (fig. 16.15), has been translated into a home of brick and wood.

Critical Thinking

The Popularity of the Novel

The novel became a popular literary genre in the eighteenth century with the serial publication of books such as *Tom Jones* in England and *Les Liaisons Dangereux* in France. These novels told the stories of fictional characters whose adventures their authors chronicled as if the characters were real and their stories biography rather than fiction. In the case of Defoe's *Robinson Crusoe* and *A Journal of the Plague Year*, as well as with the case of his novel, *Moll Flanders*, the characters and events seem as real as any actual person's life story or any actual historical chronicle of events.

To what extent do you think that the novel's popularity in the eighteenth century can be attributed to authors' attempts to make their books appear factual—either as biography or as history? What other factors contributed to the appeal of novels for readers then? To what extent do you think those appealing aspects of novels continue to make the novel popular in the twenty-first century? And, finally, as with the eighteenth century, so today, the majority of novel readers are women. Why do you think this genre has always been more popular with women than with men?

were occasional earlier prose fiction masterpieces, most notably Miguel Cervantes' *Don Quixote*, the picaresque tales of the famous knight of the woeful countenance and his comic sidekick the paunchy Sancho Panza.

But Cervantes' book and occasional other works of prose fiction did not manage to create an audience with an appetite for longer works of fiction. That did not happen until a leisured class of educated readers emerged in eighteenth century Europe, particularly in England and France. These readers had the time and the interest to read longer prose fictional works created by writers such as Henry Fielding and Samuel Richardson in England and Chaderlos la Clos in France. Fielding's *Tom Jones*, Richardson's *Pamela*, and La Clos' *The Dangerous Liaisons (Les Liaisons Dangereux)* were immensely popular works. They were published in stages, one part at a time, and offered to readers in periodicals, or magazines that come out monthly or quarterly, thus keeping readers' interest keen as to what was to happen in forthcoming episodes.

All of these novelists and many that followed in both France and England wrote about a handful of basic subjects—mostly about love and marriage, money, and class status. Novelists offered a panorama of society by depicting the various social classes interacting with each other. Novelists recreated in fictional form their social worlds, capturing the aura and ethos of city life and country life, of the rich and the poor, of social changes that occurred during their lifetimes, as for example the shift from an agricultural to an industrial economy. What these eighteenth century novelists began in earnest continued through the nineteenth century, in England with Jane Austen and Charles Dickens among many other notable English novelists, and with Honoré de Balzac and Gustave Flaubert, among noteworthy French novelists of the next century.

One of the great paradoxes of the rise of the novel in Europe was the extent to which novelists made an effort, largely successful, to invest their characters with life-likeness, to the extent of giving them historical and biographical ballast. Daniel Defoe, the author of *Robinson Crusoe*, another famous eighteenth-century novel, based his fiction on a factual account of a man, Alexander Selkirk, who experienced some of what Defoe describes as happening to Crusoe. In another novel, *A Journal of the Plague Year*, Defoe pretends to be chronicling actual history—what happened in London during the Great Plague in the 1660s, in which a large percentage of the city's population succumbed to the ravages of the disease. In one case Defoe writes fiction as a kind of biography and in another as a kind of history. And yet both works are fiction.

Jane Austen. One of the most important novelists of her day, Jane Austen (1775–1817) was the daughter of a clergyman and spent the first twenty-five years of her life at her parents' home in Hampshire, where she wrote her first novels, *Northanger Abbey*, *Sense and Sensibility*, and *Pride and Prejudice*. None of these works was actually published until the second decade of the nineteenth century, when Austen was almost forty. She came from a large and affectionate family, and her novels reflect a delight in family life; they are essentially social comedies. Above all else, they are about manners, good and bad. They advocate the behavioral norms by which society deemed decent must and should operate. They are also deeply romantic books that have marriage as their goal and end. Austen was not so naive as to believe good marriages could come from alliances built solely on social advantage; it is her scenes showing romantic love, not expedient matrimony, that draw the reader's sympathy.

Austen called herself a "miniaturist," by which she meant her ambition was to capture realistic and intimate portraits of her characters and the time in which they lived. Many readers have found that her presentation of human beings, with all their foibles, attempting to enjoy and prosper in life with one another, is utterly convincing.

Classical Music

The Classical period of music is distinguished by the growth of a popular audience for serious music, highlighted by the rise of the public concert. A middle class began to demand from composers a more accessible and recognizable musical language than that provided by the complex patterns of, say, a Baroque fugue. The classical composers Haydn and Mozart developed this new musical language by reshaping old forms like the concerto and establishing new forms, such as the symphony.

The Symphony. The **symphony** is known as a large form: It consists of several distinct parts, called movements, that proceed in a predictable pattern. The challenge the composer faces is to create fresh and inventive compositions without diverging from the predictable format. A symphony typically consists of four movements:

First movement: The pace of the movement is fast, usually *allegro*, and its mood usually dramatic.
Second movement: This movement is slow (*adagio* or *andante*, for instance), and its mood reflective.
Third movement: The pace picks up moderately, and the period's most popular dance, the stately and elegant aristocratic minuet, often serves as the basis for the movement.
Fourth movement: Once again, the fourth movement is fast (*allegro*), spirited (*vivace*), or light and happy.

Over the course of the eighteenth century, audiences became educated in these conventions; in part the excitement of hearing a new composition centered on the anticipation the listeners felt as the composer moved inventively through this predictable pattern.

Each symphonic movement also possessed its own largely internal form. The first and fourth movements usually employed a **sonata** (or sonata-allegro) form, the second was sometimes in this form but just as often a **theme and variations** or a **rondo,** and the third was generally a **minuet and trio.**

The word sonata derives from the Italian *sonare*, "to sound," as distinguished from cantata, which derives from the Italian *cantare*, meaning "to sing." Sonata form itself consists of three sections: exposition, development, and recapitulation, the last of which is sometimes followed by a coda. The overall structure suggests a pattern of departure and return. The exposition introduces the movement's themes, the development section modifies and advances them, and the recapitulation returns home to the main themes.

Each of the other movements of the symphony employs this pattern of departure and return, but in slightly different terms. In the theme and variations (a second movement form), the main theme is introduced and then recurs again and again in varied form. In a rondo, used in the second and fourth movements, a single theme repeats itself with new material added between each repetition. The minuet and trio (a third movement form) possesses an ABA structure. That is, a minuet ("A") is presented, followed by a contrasting trio section ("B"), before the return of the minuet ("A"). The trio section contrasts with the minuet in that it is written for fewer instruments, although not necessarily for three instruments, as the name suggests.

Franz Joseph Haydn. Raised as a choirboy at St. Stephen's Cathedral in Vienna, FRANZ JOSEPH HAYDN [HIGH-din] (1732–1809) served as a court musician for Prince Esterházy for nearly thirty years, beginning in 1761. Haydn composed so many symphonies—more than a hundred—in so many variations that he is known as the "father" of the form. It is Haydn to whom we are indebted for the classical characteristics of musical clarity, balance, and restraint. As his nickname implies, Papa Haydn developed the basic classic form of the sonata, the symphony, and the string quartet. He set the guidelines for the classical style while adapting his music to his patrons' needs and desires. His career not only defines this transition from court to public music, but it also marks the moment when musicians and composers finally attained the social status that painters, sculptors, and architects had enjoyed since as early as the Renaissance.

Haydn's "Farewell" Symphony no. 45 of 1772 was conceived as an explicit protest at the living conditions at Eisenstadt palace, about thirty miles south of Vienna, where the court musicians lived in isolation. Esterházy did not allow his musicians to bring their families to the palace. Thus, living in crowded servant quarters, they were forced to be away from their loved ones for long periods at a time. Performing one evening at court, the musicians played the symphony's three uneventful movements, but in the middle of the fourth movement, the second horn player and the first oboist suddenly stopped playing, packed up their instruments, blew out the candles that illuminated their scores, and left the hall. Slowly, the rest of the orchestra followed suit until no one was left except two violinists, who finished the symphony. The prince immediately understood the implications of the performance and granted his musicians an extended leave to visit their families.

When Esterházy died in 1790, his son, who did not much care for music, disbanded the orchestra, and Haydn returned to Vienna. By now he was internationally renowned. A concert promoter from London, Johann Peter Salomon, offered him a commission, and in 1791, he left Vienna for England. There, he was received by the royal court, awarded an honorary doctorate at Oxford, and began to reap the financial benefits by conducting public subscription concerts of new work, particularly the famous "London" symphonies, which were acclaimed by the public as no other symphonic music had been before. Among Haydn's best-loved symphonies is Symphony 94, is nicknamed. "The Surprise Symphony," due to the unexpected outbursts of loudness in its second movement.

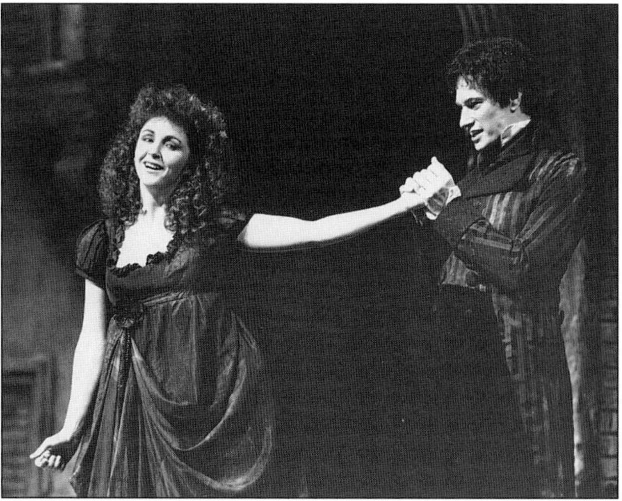

FIGURE 16.18 A scene from *Don Giovanni* by Wolfgang Amadeus Mozart. The opera premiered in 1787. Here, in Act I, Don Giovanni (played by Sherrill Milnes) seduces the innocent Zerlina (Teresa Stratas) in the duet "Là ci darem la mano."

Wolfgang Amadeus Mozart. Perhaps the greatest of the Classical composers was WOLFGANG AMADEUS MOZART [MOAT-zart] (1756–1791), born and raised in Salzburg, Austria. His first music teacher was his father, Leopold, himself an accomplished musician and composer. Young Mozart's musical genius was immediately evident in his early piano and violin playing and in his composing, which he began at the age of five. Although he had enormous musical gifts, Mozart suffered from depression and illness, and as an adult, had a difficult time securing a regular income. He achieved stunning successes in Vienna, especially with his operas, but when he died at the age of thirty-five he was heavily in debt.

During his brief life, Mozart composed more than six hundred works. He wrote forty-one symphonies along with twenty-seven piano concertos and nine concertos for other instruments. He composed large numbers of chamber works and a significant volume of choral music, including his great ***Requiem,*** or mass for the dead, which remained unfinished at his death. Mozart also composed some of the most popular operas ever written, including *The Marriage of Figaro* (1786), *Don Giovanni* (1787), and *The Magic Flute* (1791). Reviving the drama of the Baroque, he created operas in both *opera seria* (usually with historical or mythological stories) or *opera buffa* (comic operas). His singspiels, which combined spoken dialogues and arias, duets and ensembles, were his main contribution to German opera.

Don Giovanni is based on the story of the legendary Spanish nobleman, Don Juan, who was notorious for his seduction of women. Mozart, well aware of the amorous goings-on in all the great courts of Europe, subtly mocks them in this work. His opera begins with Don Giovanni killing the outraged father of a young noblewoman he has just seduced. At the end of the opera, the dead man returns in the form of a statue that comes sufficiently alive to drag Don Giovanni down to hell. Between these two dramatic episodes, Mozart portrays Don Giovanni's seduction of three women, blending seriousness with humor.

An early scene from Act I reveals Don Giovanni at work in music that captures the Don's persuasive appeal for the peasant girl Zerlina (fig. 16.18), whom he has promised to marry if she comes to his palace. Mozart has the would-be lovers sing a duet entitled "Là ci darem la mano" ("There, you will give me your hand"). Don Giovanni begins with an attractive image of their intertwined future. Zerlina's ambivalent response indicates her desire for the Don and her fear that he may be tricking her. Following this initial exchange, Mozart speeds up their interaction to show Zerlina's increasing acquiescence and then blends their voices to suggest their final mutual accord. The scene is doubly pleasing. It portrays an actual seduction, one that any audience can enjoy, and it exposes Don Giovanni for the rake that he is, thus allowing the audience both to warm to and detest Mozart's antihero. The wide range of feelings typifies Mozart's music and in part accounts for his enduring popularity.

One of Mozart's best-loved comic operas, *The Marriage of Figaro*, is based on the play of the same title by the French dramatist Beaumarchais, One of the play's—and the opera's—major motifs is the way social-class relationships are wittily and skillfully undermined by the servent hero Figaro and his fianceé Susanna. Early in the opera's first scene, Mozart writes a charming duet for them, "Cinque . . . Diecie (Five. . . . Ten), in which Figaro counts out and paces the size of their bed and where it will be positioned, while Susanna stands before a mirror adjusting her bridal bonnet. Mozart begins and ends the duet with orchestral music, the duet proper starting with Figaro's counting cinque to dieci before Susanna enters singing her thoughts. Mozart quickly has their two voices harmoniously intertwined, then responding back and forth to one another, and finally synchronized to conclude the duet.

In addition to his operatic and other vocal masterpieces, Mozart's symphonies remain a staple of today's worldwide concert repertoire. Among his symphonic masterpieces is the Symphony #40 in g minor, the first movement of which can be heard on the accompanying disc.

Mozart's life, with its dramatic swings of fortune and his tragic early death, has inspired, among other works, the 1979 play and 1984 film *Amadeus*, Mozart's middle name. (Amadeus was actually not Mozart's given name, but rather a Latin transalation of the German Gottlieb,) Both the Broadway play and the movie *Amadeus* won numerous awards. Though based on fact, a number of aspects of *Amadeus* are fictional, including the intense rivalry and deep animosity between Mozart and the Italian composer Antonio Salieri. Other liberties taken with the facts include the mystery surrounding the commission and composition of Mozart's final work, the *Requiem*, which became, in a manner, music for his own death.

TOWARD ROMANTICISM

BEETHOVEN: FROM CLASSICAL TO ROMANTIC

LUDWIG VAN BEETHOVEN [BAY-tove-in] (1770–1827) was born during the age of the Enlightenment, came to maturity during a period of political and social revolution, and died as the **Romantic** era was in full flower. His work and his life reveal a tension between the Classical style of the past and the newly emerging Romantic tendencies in art. In his middle period, Beethoven enlarged the scope of the Classical style; in his later works, he transcended it, moving in new musical directions.

Beethoven was born and raised in Bonn, in the German Rhineland. At the age of twenty-one he went to Vienna, where he remained for the rest of his life. He became known for his prodigious ability on the piano, especially for his improvisational skill. By the time he was thirty, Beethoven was recognized as an innovative and creative composer. Unlike other musicians and composers of his time, he was determined to remain a free artist, and, with the help of a number of sympathetic patrons, he supported himself solely through composing and performing his music. Beethoven was aided by the growth of music publishing and an increase in concert life fueled by the rise of a middle-class public with an appetite for serious music.

Among the most significant experiences of Beethoven's life was the onset of deafness, which began to afflict him around 1800, just as his music was attracting serious acclaim. He nearly committed suicide. In 1802, he wrote his famous Heiligenstadt testament, an agonized letter to his brother describing his suicidal thoughts and his eventual victory over them: "I would have ended my life—it was only my art that held me back. Ah, it seemed to me impossible to leave the world until I had brought forth all that I felt was within me."

Living through this traumatic experience strengthened Beethoven, and the music he wrote afterward exhibited a new depth of feeling and imaginative power. By 1815, Beethoven was almost entirely deaf, but this did not stop him from composing and conducting his music. In the end, Beethoven's deafness was more of a social affliction than a musical one. He increasingly separated himself from society, for which his rebellious and fiery temperament ill suited him.

Beethoven produced an abundance of music, including thirty-two piano sonatas and nine symphonies, which set the standard against which the sonata and symphonic efforts of all subsequent composers have been measured.

Three Periods of Beethoven's Music. Beethoven's music can be divided into three periods, each reflecting differences in stylistic development. During the first period, which lasted until about 1802, Beethoven wrote works mainly in the Classical style, adhering to the formal elements established by Haydn and perfected by Mozart before him. In the middle period (1803–14), referred to as the "heroic" phase, his works become more dramatic; they are also noticeably longer than those of his Classical predecessors, as they begin to stretch the requirements of Classical form. The first movement of the Third Symphony is, for instance, as long as many full symphonies of Haydn and Mozart. And his compositions in this period modulate between the most gentle and appealing melodies and the most dynamic and forceful writing—not only between works, but within each work, as well.

Beethoven's final period of composition spans the years 1815–27, during which he was almost completely deaf. In this period, Beethoven not only departed from the constraints of Classical compositional practice, but also entered new musical territory and reached new levels of spiritual profundity. Works from the late period include, among many others, his Ninth Symphony, considered by many the greatest symphony ever written; the last piano sonatas; and the deeply spiritual *Missa Solemnis*.

Symphony no. 5 in C Minor; op. 67. Beethoven's most famous work remains his middle period Symphony

Cross Currents

TURKISH MILITARY MUSIC AND VIENNESE COMPOSERS

Western Europeans had long been fascinated with the so-called exotic. During the eighteenth century there was increased cultural interaction with Turkey, then part of the Ottoman empire. Although at the time it represented a threat to Austria, the Austrian Hapsburg empire enjoyed a taste for things Turkish and Ottoman. Viennese cuisine reflected the influence of Turkish spices. Viennese fashion exhibited Turkish influence in flowing garments and brightly decorative ribbons and braiding in women's attire. Viennese music incorporated elements of the music of Turkish military bands, composed of musicians mounted on horseback playing drums and shawms, long-tubed horns used in medieval Western as well as medieval Turkish music. In the seventeenth century, trumpets, cymbals, bells, and additional types of drums were added to Turkish military bands. Later, during the nineteenth century, some pianos were equipped with a special pedal for creating unusual percussive effects reminiscent of these instruments.

All three of the great Viennese composers of the time reveal the influence of the Turkish military band. Haydn wrote three military symphonies, whose titles reflect the martial nature of their music, including the "Drum Roll" and the "Military." Mozart included Turkish percussive musical elements in his opera *The Abduction from the Seraglio.* He also entitled the rondo movement from his piano sonata K. 331 "Rondo alla Turca," a spirited piece with a section reflective of Turkish military music. Beethoven was also inspired by Turkish music, as is evidenced by his "Turkish March" and in themes from the fourth movement of his Ninth Symphony. Moreover, inspired by the whirling dance of Islamic Turks, Beethoven wrote his "Chorus for Whirling Dervishes," a work whose theme is repeated in increasing intensity and in quicker tempos, imitating the trance induced by the whirling dance of the Sufi dervishes (see Chapter 6).

no. 5 in C Minor, op. 67, a work that defines the idea of the symphony in the popular imagination. He completed it in 1808. One of the most tightly unified compositions Beethoven ever wrote, its opening four-note motif is perhaps the best known of all symphonic themes. Out of that brief fragment of musical material, Beethoven constructs a dramatic and intense opening movement. He uses its rhythmic pattern of three short notes followed by a longer one in each remaining movement and further unifies the work by returning to the theme of the third movement during a dramatic passage in the fourth movement. Overall, the symphony moves from struggle and dramatic conflict to triumphant and majestic exultation.

The first movement, marked Allegro con brio, "fast with spirit," opens abruptly with the famous "Fate knocking on the door" theme—short-short-short-long:

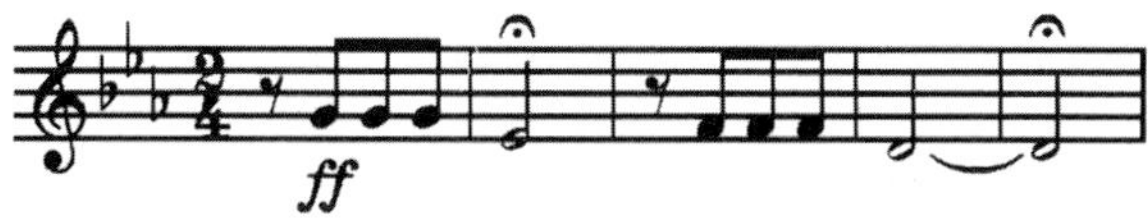

Beethoven repeats this musical motif relentlessly throughout the exposition before a bridge passage leads to a second, contrasting, and more lyrical theme, which is accompanied in the cellos and basses by the first fournote theme. Additional musical ideas fill out the movement, including a development section that breaks the main theme into smaller and smaller units and a recapitulation that features a surprising lyrical oboe solo.

The second movement, in theme and variations form, provides relief from the unabating tension created in the first. Two themes dominate the movement, the first sung by cellos and violas, the second by clarinets. Both receive extensive variation throughout the movement. The overall effect combines noble grandeur with sheer lyrical beauty.

The third movement, a scherzo, begins with a mysterious theme introduced quietly by cellos and basses, followed by a loud theme blared out by the horns on a single repeated note. Instead of a break between movements, Beethoven creates a sense of tension with a long sustained tone that forms a bridge to the fourth and final movement.

The fourth movement, a scherzo, in C major, is cast in sonata form, with an extensive coda, one of the most dramatic Beethoven wrote. For this, he enlarged the orchestra: A high-pitched piccolo extends the orchestral range upward, a low-pitched contrabassoon extends it downward, and three extra trombones add power. Beethoven presents four themes first, then a stunning coda that appears to end a number of times before he finally brings the movement and the symphony to a triumphant conclusion.

Cultural Impact

Politically and socially, the eighteenth century was a period of dramatic change. Government by aristocracy gave way to more democratic political structures. Although absolutist forms of government persisted in Europe, they were challenged by republican advocates of divided, complementary forms of political organization and by supporters of democratic rule. The seeds of democratic government were sown not only in America, but also in Europe, where democracy would eventually emerge as the prevalent form of government in the modern Western world.

The Enlightenment had a profound impact on the development of Western civilization. It was during this period that the ideals of "liberty, equality, and fraternity" animated the French Revolution. Similar ideals of "life, liberty, and the pursuit of happiness" provided the new American nation with its foundational principles.

The arts saw a return to the aesthetic ideals of classical antiquity, especially order, balance, symmetry, and proportion. Aspects of eighteenth-century architecture, for example, are modeled after that of ancient Greece and Rome. Enormously influential, the Neoclassical style is seen in government and public buildings constructed in the nineteenth and twentieth centuries in the United States and around the world.

Classical ideals of balance, symmetry, and proportion were also important in music and literature. So were qualities of wit and elegance: The spirit of the music and literature of the age is reflected in a propensity for irony, in sparkling dialogue between characters in novels, plays, and operas, and in a strong tendency toward satire. Concern for elegance in the formal structure of musical and literary works remains an important legacy of the Enlightenment.

It is perhaps because Beethoven became isolated from the natural world by his deafness that he was able to redefine the creative act of composition. It was no longer, as it had been for centuries, considered a function of objective laws and rules of harmony, but the expression of deeply personal and often introspective feelings. It is to this interior world that artists of the nineteenth century, the so-called Romantics, turned their attention.

KEY TERMS

Enlightenment
philosophes
rational humanism
revolution
Napoleonic Code
Industrial Revolution
Encyclopédie
Rococo
fêtes galantes
hôtels
salons
still life
mock epic
Neoclassicism
symphony
sonata
theme and variations
rondo
minuet and trio
Requiem
Romantic

www. Websites for Further Study

http://www.infidels.org/library/historical/john_remsburg/six_historic_americans/chapter_2.html
(This is a site entitled Six Historic Americans, which includes Thomas Jefferson, as written by John E. Remsburg.)

http://csep10.phys.utk.edu/astr161/lect/history/newtongrav.html
(A good physics site on Sir Issac Newton and studies on gravity.)

http://artchive.com/artchive/W/watteau.html
(This is the Artchive, a website with virtually every major artist in every style from every era in art history. It is an excellent resource.)

http://w3.rz-berlin.mpg.de/cmp/mozart.html
(A good site on Wolfgang Amadeus Mozart's biography.)

http://www.historyworld.net
(Site devoted to the history of literature with a focus on European literature. The eighteenth-century section features Austen, Johnson, Swift, and Voltaire, among others.)

http://www.history-world.org/age or enlightenment
(Site about the Age of Enlightenment, including arts and music contextualized with history and philosophy. Includes Diderot, Rousseau, Voltaire, and others.)

http://www.w3.rz-berlinmpg.de/cmp/haydnj.html
(Broad site on Franz Joseph Haydn, with articles, images, biography, links, and more.)

http://www.lvbeethoven.com
(Comprehensive site for Beethoven, including the text of the Heilingenstadt Testament*, as well as links to books by friends of Beethoven and much more, including images and texts form Beethoven's funeral.)*

Chapter 17

History

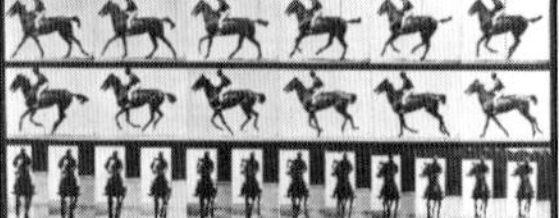

1789–99	French Revolution
1804	Napoleon declared emperor
1848	Revolutions spread through Europe
1854	Pasteur develops pasteurization
1860s	American Civil War
1868	German empire proclaimed

Art, Architecture, and Music

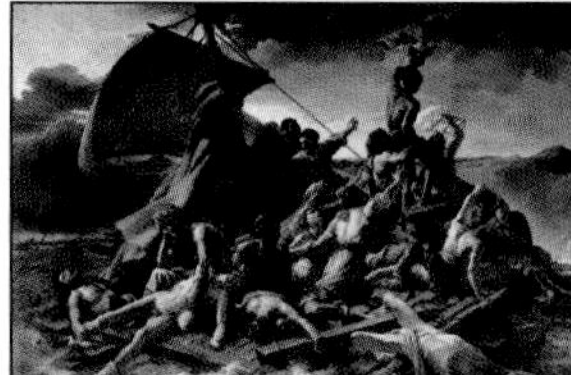

1814	Ingres, *La Grande Odalisque*
1814–15	Goya, *The Third of May*
1819	Gericault, *Raft of the Medusa*
1821	Constable, *The Haywain*
1824	Delacroix, *Scenes from the Massacres at Chios*
1830	Berlioz, *Symphonie Fantastique*
1830	New York Philharmonic founded
1833–36	Rude, *La Marseillaise*
1836	Barry and Pugin, Houses of Parliament
1840	Turner, *The Slave Ship*
1842	Chopin, Polonaise in A—flat, Op. 53
1849	Mozart's *Requiem* played at Chopin's funeral
1849	Bonheur, *Plowing in the Nievernais*
1851	Paxton, Crystal Palace
1863	Manet, *Luncheon on the Grass*
1868	Brahms' "Lullaby"
ca. 1872	Lewis, *The Old Indian Arrow Maker*
1875	Whitney, Charles Sumner
1887	Verdi, *Otello*
1887	Brownscombe, *Love's Young Dream*

Literature and Philosophy

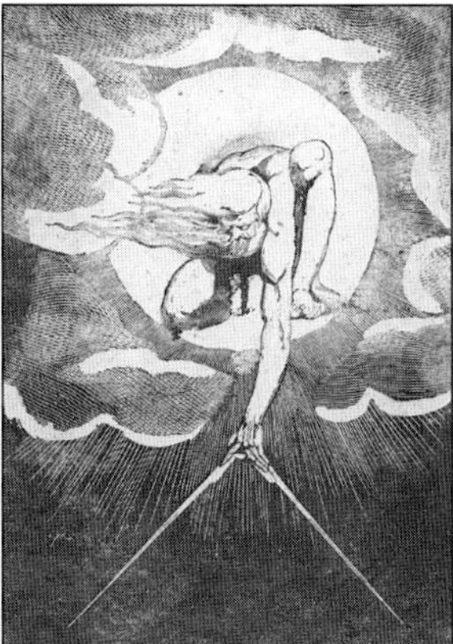

1798	Wordsworth and Coleridge, *Lyrical Ballads*
1808	Goethe, *Faust*
1819–24	Lord Byron, *Don Juan*
1836	Emerson, *Nature*
1838	Dickens, *Oliver Twist*
1851	Melville, *Moby Dick*
1854	Thoreau, *Walden*
1855	Whitman, *Leaves of Grass*
1856	Flaubert, *Madame Bovary*
1859	Darwin, *On the Origin of the Species*
1860s	Dickinson, *Poems*
1872	Rousseau, *Confessions*
1877	Tolstoy, *Anna Karenina*
1881	Dostoyevsky, *The Brothers Karamazov*

Romanticism and Realism

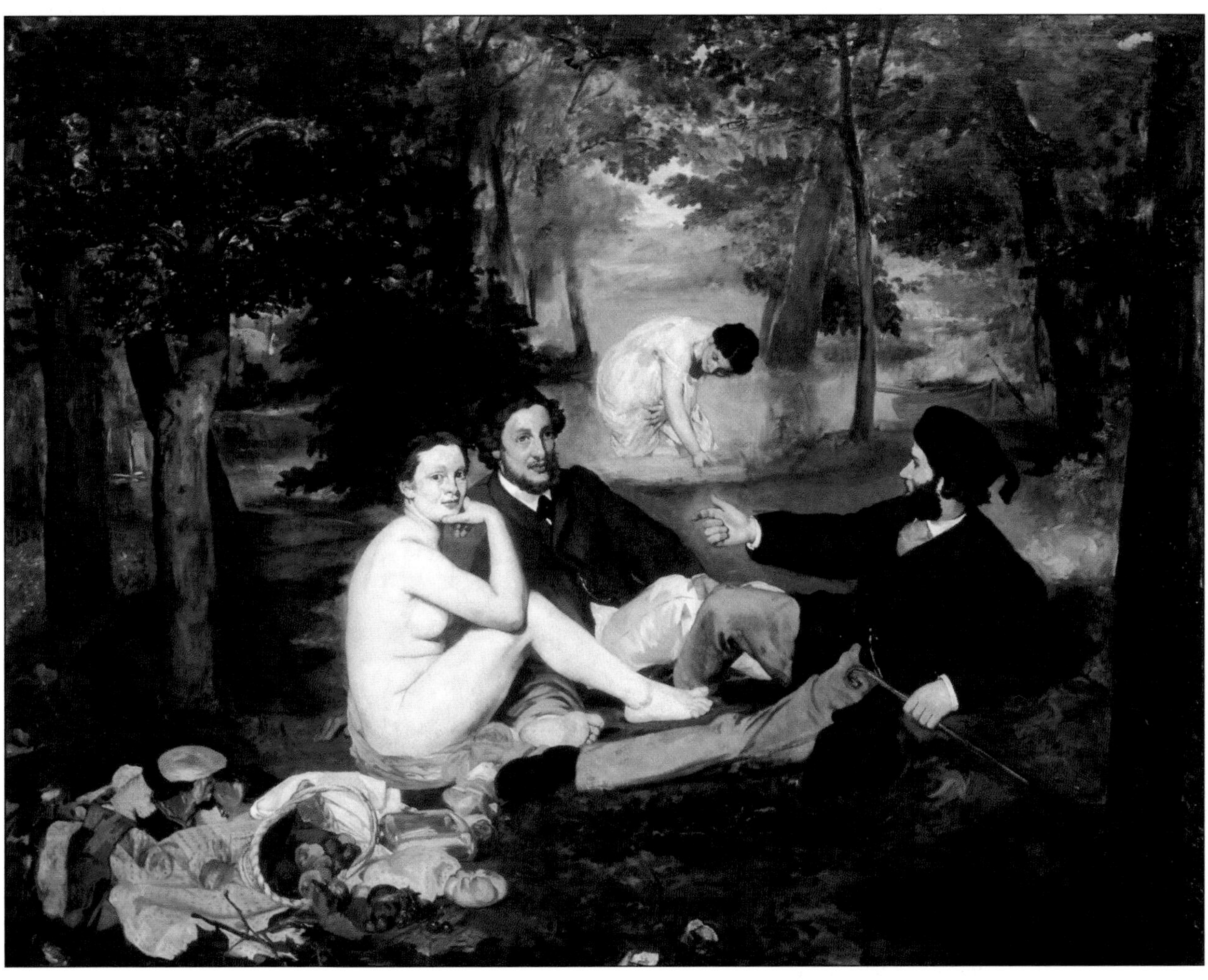

Edouard Manet, *Luncheon on the Grass (Le Déjeuner sur l'herbe)*, 1863, oil on canvas, 7′ × 8′10″ (2.67 × 4.06 m), Musée d'Orsay, Paris.

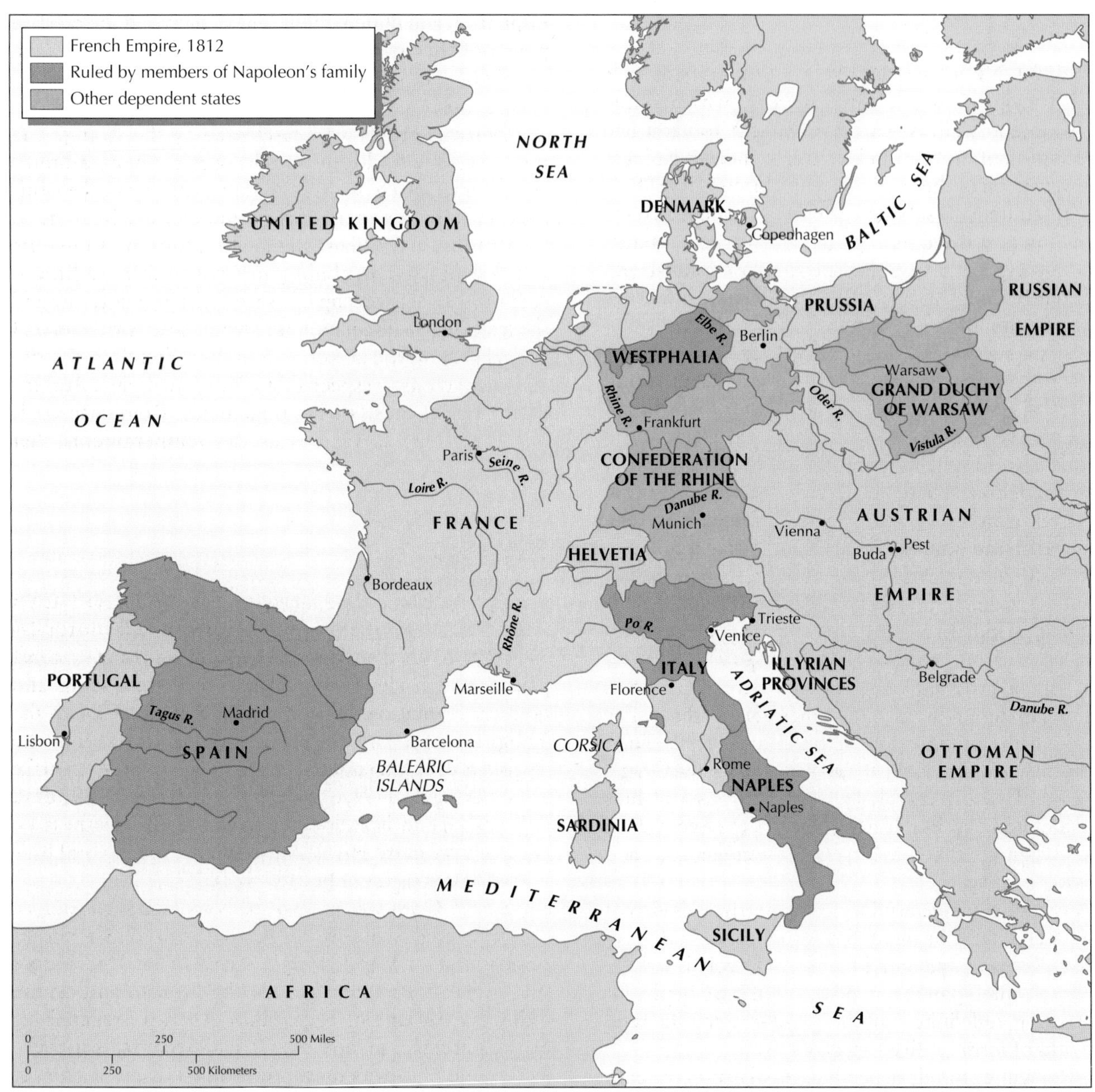

MAP 17.1 Napoleon's Empire 1812.

CHAPTER OVERVIEW

ROMANTICISM

The imagination runs wild

REALISM

The European sociopolitical scene turns the arts to everyday life

ROMANTICISM

By 1800, Neoclassicism was the dominant style in European art and architecture, which suited Napoleon well. As early as 1805, Napoleon had begun to speak of his "Grand Empire," conceiving of it as a modern version of the Holy Roman Empire. In 1808, as part of his strategy to subdue the entire European continent, his troops crossed the Pyrenees into Spain, ostensibly on their way to Portugal, which was closely allied with the British. But once in Spain, Napoleon took advantage of the abdication of the unpopular Charles IV, refused to recognize his successor, Ferdinand VII, and took control of the country. At first, there was little resistance, but Napoleon discovered that just because the Spanish did not care for their king did not mean they were prepared to be ruled by a French emperor. Skirmishes broke out across the country. These "little wars," or *guerrillas* (the origin of our word for guerrilla warfare), forced Napoleon to withdraw large numbers of troops from Germany to fight in Spain, and soon full-scale war broke out.

In the meantime, an emerging new movement, **Romanticism,** provided a countertendency to the Neoclassical style. Romanticism is an attitude more than a style, but it depends on a growing trust in subjective experience, particularly in the emotions and feelings of individuals. The Romantics had a love for anything that elicits such feelings: the fantastic world of dreams, the exotic world of the Orient, the beauty of nature revealed in a sudden vista of hills exposed around a turn in an English garden, the forces of nature in a magnificent or unpredictable moment, such as a sunset after a storm.

Inexactitude and indeterminacy characterize this view of the world, and it can be discovered everywhere in this period. The Romantic painter Eugène Delacroix loved the **études** by a contemporary composer, Frédéric Chopin, for "their floating, indefinite contour . . . destroying the rigid frameworks of form . . . like sheets of mist."

The Romantic attitude depends particularly on the concept of **originality.** Just as no aspect of an English garden should be like any other, no painter or author should imitate any other. The new Romantic genius stands alone, different from the rest, and unsurpassed—a true original.

In addition, the Romantic attitude is a mixture of belief in the natural goodness of man as expressed by Rousseau and in the autonomy of rational beings. Emanating from these central Romantic conceptions was empathy for the disadvantaged and the downtrodden apparent in the writings of William Blake and the paintings of Géricault, Turner, and Goya. The ethical law of Immanuel Kant (1724–1804), never to treat another human being as an object, bolsters these conceptions, as does Kant's advice to behave as if the maxim that guides your action were to become a universal law.

The Romantic glorification of the self found expression in many ways. Artists, composers, and writers were seen as divinely inspired visionaries with Promethean powers of inspiration and illumination. Many compared the creative power of the artist to the power of the biblical creator. They saw God's power as residing within their own creative genius.

Romantic artists were fascinated by the strange and the marvelous, by dreams and the occult. They celebrated the commonplace, seeing the extraordinary in the ordinary, infinity in a grain of sand and eternity in an hour, to paraphrase William Blake. In addition, Romantic artists expressed an abiding interest in folk traditions. And they were preoccupied as well with the uncanny and the irrational, a fascination that would lead, by the end of the century, in the person of Sigmund Freud, to the rise of psychiatry as a respected branch of medicine. Accommodating all these varied tendencies, Romantic art is multiplicitous, as various as the temperaments that created it.

PAINTING

Francisco Goya. The Spaniard FRANCISCO GOYA [GOY-uh] (1746–1828) began his career as a favorite portraitist of Madrid society and in 1789 was made a court painter to Charles IV of Spain. Goya was a social and political revolutionary, whose sympathies were with the Enlightenment and the failed French Revolution; he worked for the king not out of loyalty but in order to make a good living. In 1794, a serious illness left him totally deaf, and within the isolation produced by his deafness he became ever more introspective. Slowly, gaiety and exuberance were replaced by bitterness.

At first, Goya was in favor of Napoleon's invasion of Spain, hoping Spain would be modernized as a consequence. But on May 2, 1808, the civilians of Madrid rose up in a guerrilla action against the French, and on the following day one of Napoleon's generals executed his Spanish hostages in retaliation. That execution is the subject of one of Goya's most powerful works, *The Third of May, 1808* (fig. 17.1). Painted several years after the event, the painting marks Goya's change of heart. The French presence had brought Spain only savage atrocity, death, famine, and violence.

The soldiers on the right, faceless, inhuman, and machine-like, turn their backs to the viewer in anonymity and raise their weapons to destroy. The lighting of this night scene is theatrical; the square light in front of the soldiers illuminates their next victim. Christlike, with arms extended, his portrayal here evokes the image of the Savior, but he is simply one man among many. Several lie dead in their own pools of blood to his right, and those about to die await their turn. *The Third of May, 1808* is a painting that gives visual form to a sense of hopelessness. Although it possesses all the emotional intensity of religious art, here people die for liberty rather than for God; and they are killed by political tyranny, not Satan.

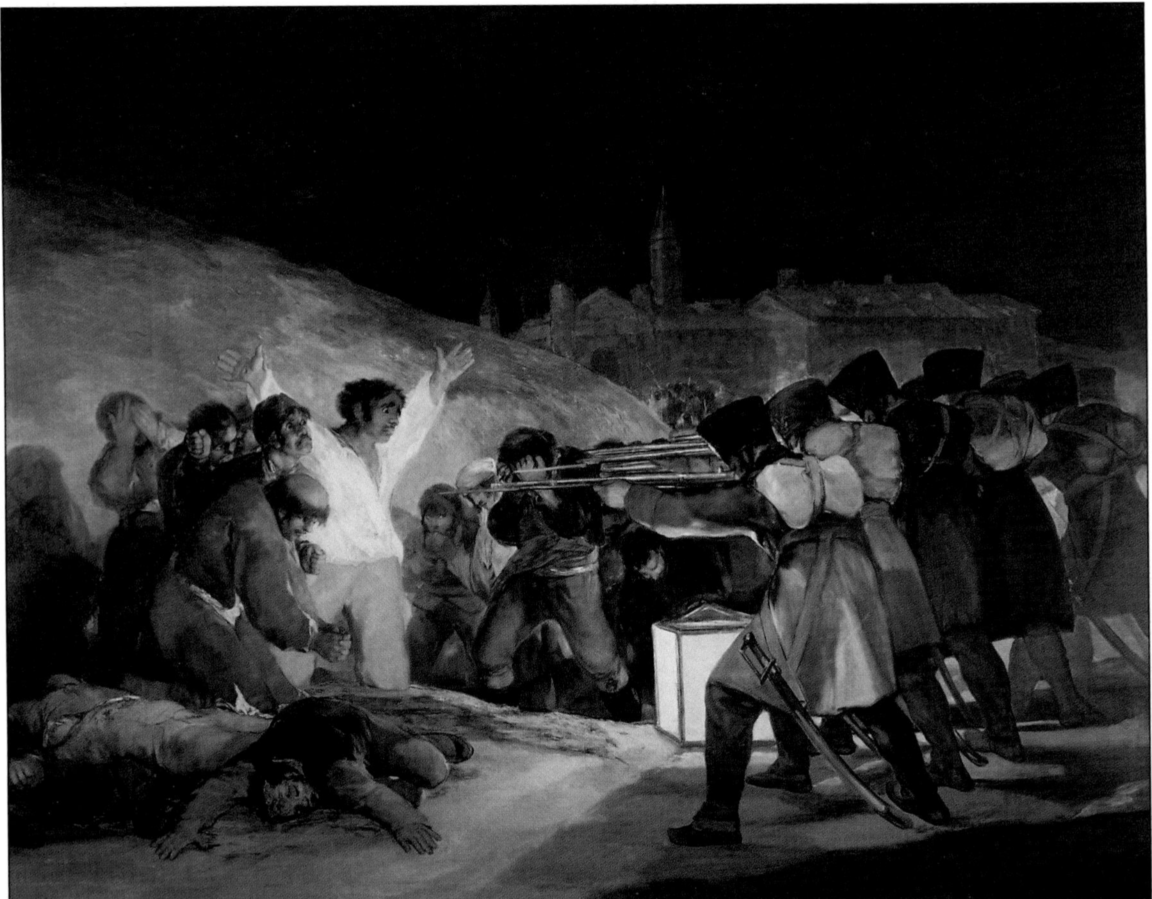

FIGURE 17.1 Francisco Goya, *The Third of May, 1808*, 1814–15, oil on canvas, 8′9″ × 13′4″ (2.67 × 4.06 m), Museo del Prado, Madrid. One of the most powerful antiwar statements ever made, Goya's painting documents the execution of Madrid citizens for resisting the French occupation of their city. The killers are faceless, dehumanized, mechanized; the victim, Christlike in pose, dies for liberty rather than religion.

Théodore Géricault. Goya's equal among the French painters of the Romantic movement is THÉODORE GÉRICAULT [jay-ree-COH] (1791–1824). Like Goya, Géricault painted subjects that affected him emotionally. His most famous painting, the *Raft of the Medusa* (fig. 17.2), painted 1818–19, was inspired by an infamous incident in 1816. The government ship *Medusa* set sail overloaded with settlers and soldiers bound for Senegal. When it sank on a reef off the coast of North Africa, the ship's captain and officers saved themselves in the six available lifeboats and left the 150 passengers and crew members to fend for themselves on a makeshift raft. These people spent twelve days at sea before being rescued; only fifteen survived, the others having died from exposure and starvation. Some went insane and there were even reports of cannibalism. The actions of the captain and officers were judged criminally negligent and intentionally cruel, and the entire incident reflected poorly on the French monarchy, newly restored to the throne after Napoleon's defeat. The captain had been commissioned on the basis not of his ability but of his noble birth. His decision to save himself was considered an act inspired by his belief in aristocratic privilege.

Géricault completed the enormous painting (16′1″ × 23′6″) in nine months. In an attempt to portray accurately the raft and the people on it, Géricault interviewed survivors, studied corpses in the morgue, and even had the ship's carpenter build a model raft, which he then floated. His search for the uncompromising truth led him to produce a vividly realistic painting of powerfully heroic drama. Géricault elected to portray the moment of greatest emotional intensity—when the survivors first sight the ship that will eventually rescue them, just visible on the horizon. It is a scene of extraordinary tension, a thrilling combination of hope and horror. Those who have died or given up are shown at the bottom of the composition, close to the viewer, large, and extremely realistic. The strongest struggle hysterically upward, led by a black man in a diagonal surge of bodies that rises toward the upper right.

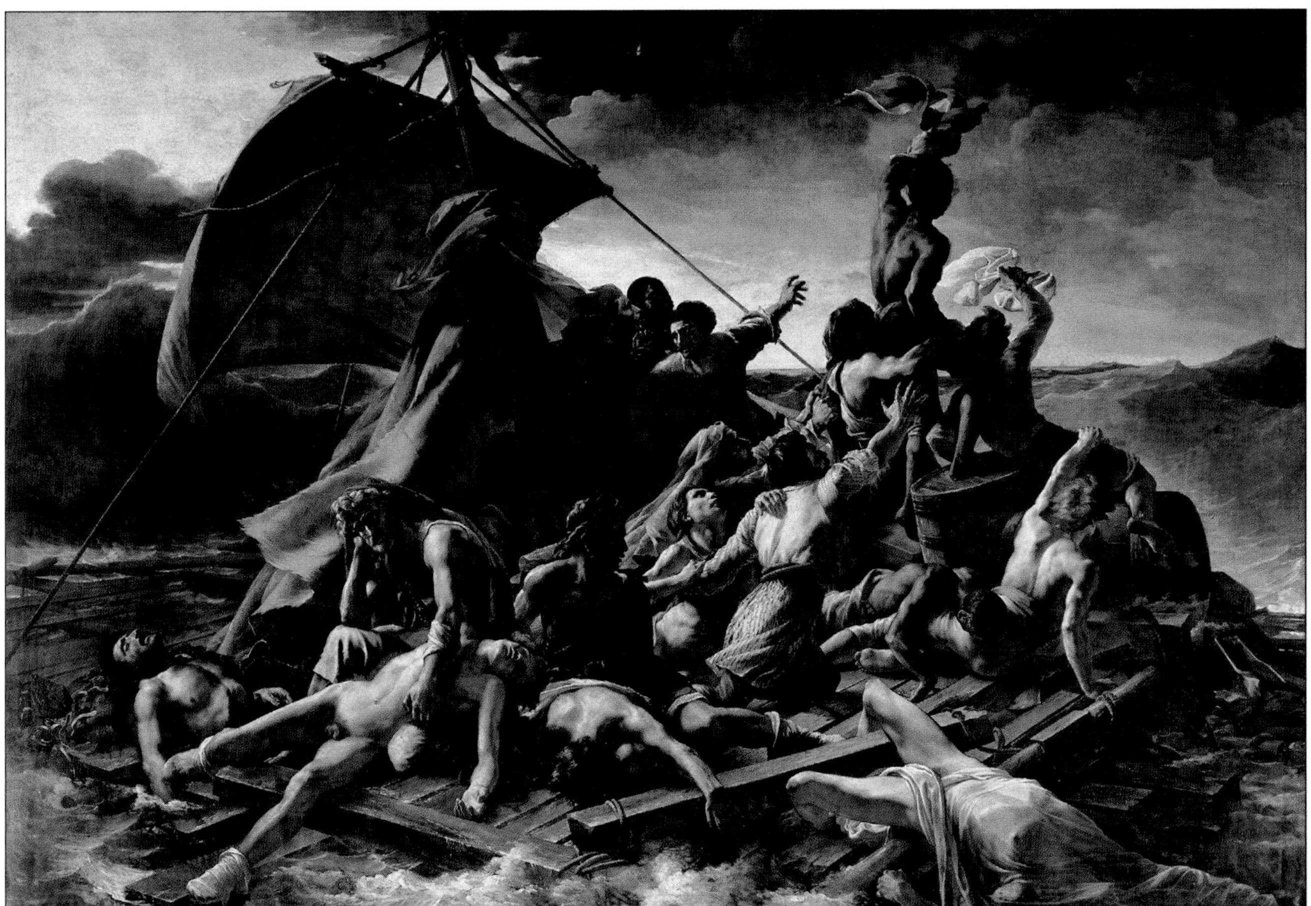

FIGURE 17.2 Théodore Géricault, *Raft of the Medusa*, 1818–19, oil on canvas, 16′1″ × 23′6″ (4.9 × 7.16 m). Musée du Louvre/RMN Reunion des Musées Nationaux, France. Bridgeman/Giraudon/Art Resource, NY. In this moving depiction of a tragedy in which many lives were lost after days at sea, the impact is enhanced by the raft jutting obliquely into the viewer's space, by the proximity of extremely realistic dead bodies, and by the dramatic contrasts of light and shadow.

THE JULY MONARCHY

For Romantic painters such as Géricault and his friend EUGENE DELACROIX [duh-lah-KWA] (1798–1863), who served as the model for the central corpse lying face down below the mast in the *Raft of the "Medusa,"* art could serve as an effective social and political tool.

In France particularly, the plight of the working people was at issue throughout the reign of Louis-Philippe, who became king shortly after July 28, 1830, when violent fighting broke out in the streets of Paris, supported by almost every segment of society, and the rule of Charles X quickly came to an end. Within days, Louis-Philippe, who was the former king's cousin, was named the head of what would come to be called the July Monarchy. Eugène Delacroix quickly went to work on a large painting to celebrate this new revolution, so reminiscent of the glorious days of 1789.

Delacroix named his painting *The Twenty-Eighth of July: Liberty Leading the People* (fig. 17.3). It was finished in time for the Salon of 1831, but instead of the accolades he thought he would receive, Delacroix was roundly attacked for the painting. It was purchased by the new government of Louis-Philippe and quickly removed to storage. The scene is set in barricades of the kind traditionally built by Parisians by piling cobblestones up in the street, thus creating lines of defense against the advance of government troops. Behind it, to the right, are the towers of Notre-Dame Cathedral, seen through the smoke of battle across the Seine River. The composition rises in a pyramid of human forms, the dead sprawled along the base of the painting, and Liberty herself, waving the French tricolor, crowns the composition. Beside Liberty is a youth of the streets. To Liberty's right, a working-class rebel in white and a bourgeois gentleman, distinguished by his tie, coat, and top hat, advance with her. Delacroix depicts the cross-section of society that actually took part in the uprising.

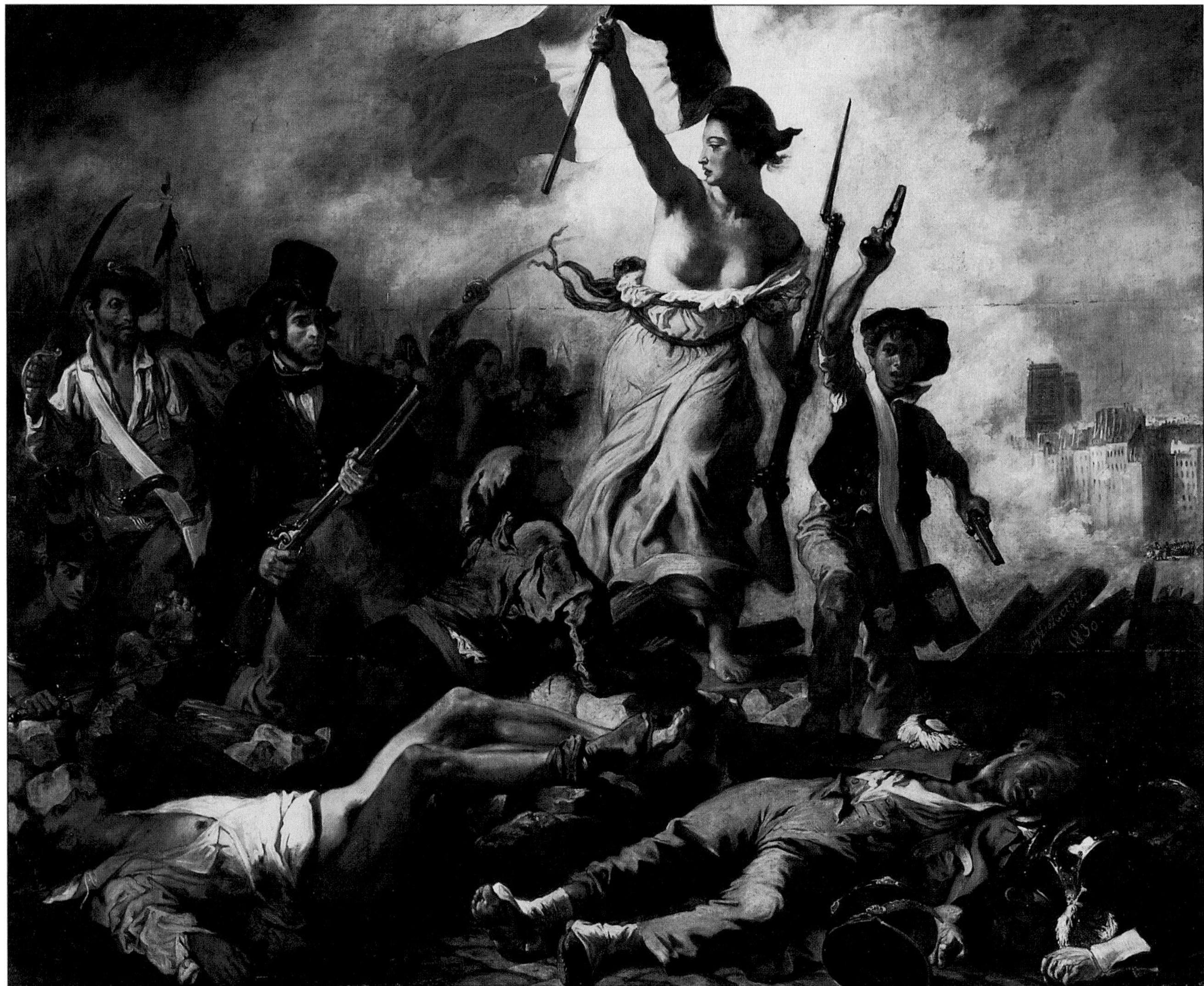

FIGURE 17.3 Eugène Delacroix, *The Twenty-Eighth of July: Liberty Leading the People*, 1830, oil on canvas, $8'6\frac{3}{8}'' \times 10'8''$ (2.59×3.25 m), Photo: Hervé Lewandowski. Musee du Louvre, Paris. Reunion des Musees National/Art Resource, NY. In this romanticized representation of the Revolution of 1830, Liberty is personified by a seminaked woman leading her followers through Paris. The revolution resulted in the abdication of Charles X and the formation of a new government under Louis-Philippe.

Jean-Auguste-Dominque Ingres. A pupil of David, JEAN-AUGUSTE-DOMINIQUE INGRES [AN-gruh] (1780–1867) is perhaps the last Neoclassical painter, for he opposed all Romantics of his day, particularly Delacroix. Stubborn and plodding, he was described as a "pedantic tyrant." Through his position as head of the French Academy, he restricted official art for generations.

In Ingres's approach, precision of line is all important. His *La Grande Odalisque* (fig. 17.4), the word **odalisque** meaning "harem woman" in Turkish, painted in 1814, is the kind of exotic subject also favored by the Romantics. The odalisque is not an individual, and her anatomy is neither academic nor accurate. The elongated, large-hipped proportions recall the Mannerist style (see Chapter 13) rather than the classical ideal. Ingres perhaps had more in common with the Romantics than he would have liked to admit, since it is hard to remove *all* sensuality from such a subject. He was shocked when the Neoclassical painters found his work unclassical.

Still, compared to a Delacroix *Odalisque* (fig. 17.5) of 1845–50, Ingres's painting seems positively tame. Delacroix's nude is unabashedly sensual. His painting style is loose, physical, not at all intellectual. Where Ingres explores the external human form, Delacroix explores the internal emotions the body can generate.

John Constable. In England, painters were attracted to the physical aspects of nature. John Constable (1776–1837) immersed himself in the scenery of his native land and painted places he knew and loved such as Suffolk and Essex. The valley of the River Stour, which divides Suffolk from Essex, was his special haunt.

In the 1820s, Constable began painting a series of "six-footers," which were large ambitious landscapes

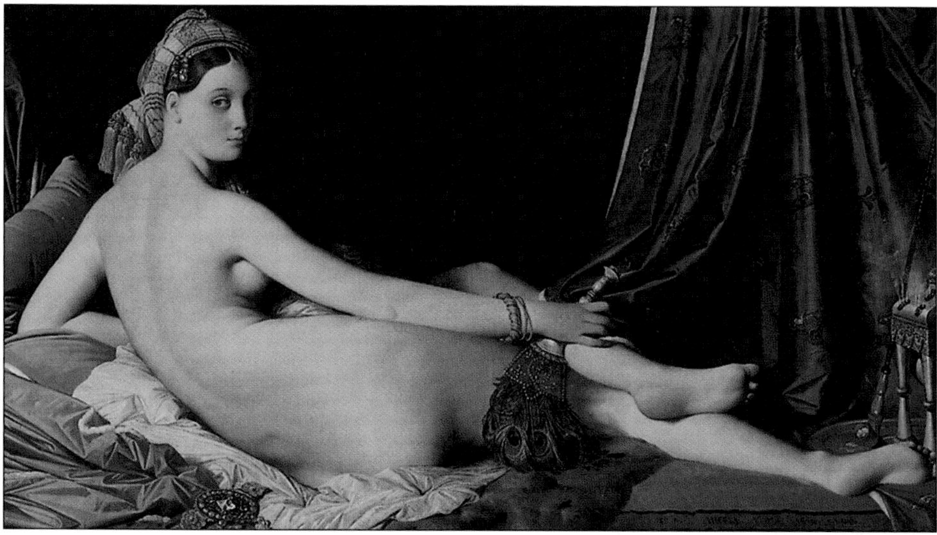

FIGURE 17.4 Jean-Auguste-Dominique Ingres, *La Grande Odalisque*, 1814, oil on canvas, $2'11\frac{1}{4}'' \times 5'3\frac{3}{4}''$ (89.7 × 162 cm), Musée du Louvre, Paris. Reunion des Musées National. Erich Lessing/Art Resource, NY. The treatment of the anatomy of this odalisque (harem woman), an exotic and erotic subject, is less academic than Ingres might have liked to believe. In fact, she has much in common with the smooth elongated bodies created by Mannerist artists, such as Parmigianino's *Madonna with the Long Neck* (fig. 13.26).

celebrating rural life. *The Haywain* (fig. 17.6), of 1821, depicts a wagon mired beside Willy Lott's cottage in the millstream at Flatford that ran beside the Stour proper, adjacent to Constable's own property. Willy Lott lived in this cottage for eighty years and spent only four nights away from it during his entire life. He embodied, for Constable, the enduring attachment to place so fundamental to rural life. Constable was interested in the transience of nature, the momentary effects of atmosphere and light, of storm and sunlight, and the contrast of dense foliage and open field.

FIGURE 17.5 Eugène Delacroix, *Odalisque*, 1845–50, oil on canvas, $14\frac{7}{8}'' \times 18\frac{1}{4}''$ (37.6 × 46.4 cm). Fitzwilliam Museum, Cambridge, England. It is hard to say which is more sensual in Delacroix's painting, the subject or the brushwork. There is an obvious contrast with Ingres's treatment of an odalisque subject thirty-odd years earlier (see fig. 17.4). Whereas in Ingres's version the emphasis is very much on line, Delacroix is a *rubéniste* and delights in an ecstatic use of color.

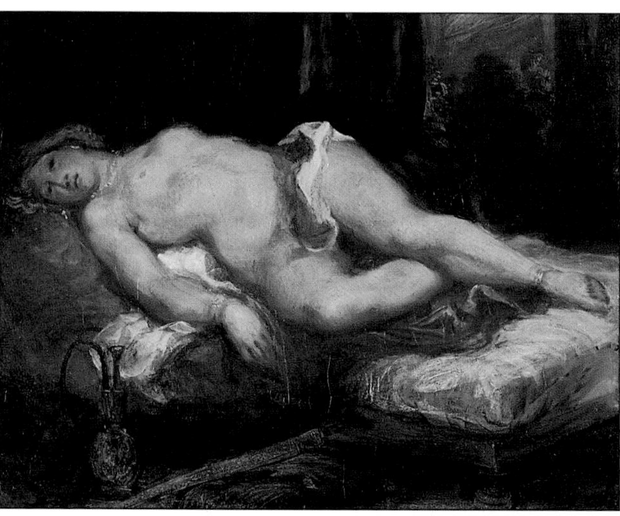

J. M. W. Turner. Constable's love of nature was shared by his fellow Englishman Joseph Mallord William Turner (1775–1851). The son of a barber, Turner had no formal education but was interested in art from childhood. His talent was quickly recognized for he was already a full member of the Royal Academy in 1802, when he was only twenty-seven. Opposing the Academy's classicism, he was to become England's leading Romantic painter.

Although Turner worked from nature, he took even greater liberties with the facts than Constable did. Consequently, it is not always possible to recognize his sites or fully to comprehend his subject. For example, Turner's painting *The Slave Ship* (fig. 17.7), of 1840, originally titled *Slavers Throwing Overboard the Dead and Dying—Typhoon Coming On*, illustrates a specific contemporary event with all the outrage of Géricault and Delacroix. A ship's captain had thrown overboard slaves who were sick or dying from an epidemic that had broken out on board. The captain was insured against loss of slaves at sea, but not against their loss owing to disease.

Turner's figures are lost in the wash of colors of sea and sky, and the political subject threatens to become, in Turner's hands, an excuse for a study of atmosphere. The forms dissolve into a haze of mist. The swirl of storm and colored light is the result of layers of oil glazes. So radical was Turner's style that he was dubbed "the over-Turner."

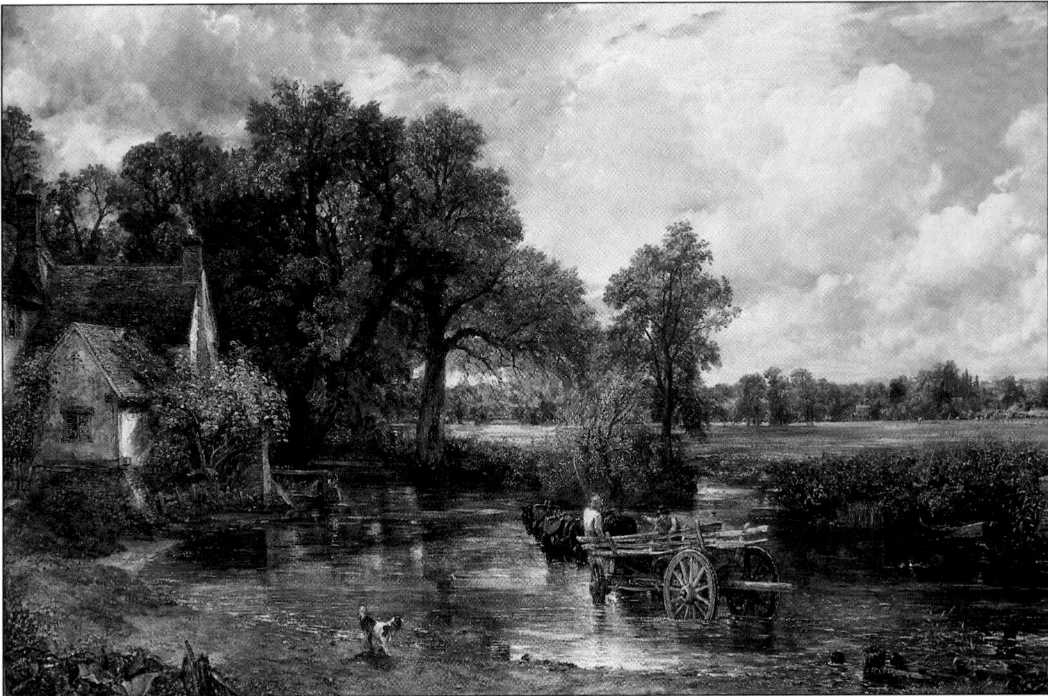

FIGURE 17.6 John Constable, *The Haywain*, 1821, oil on canvas, 4′3$\frac{1}{4}$″ × 6′1″ (1.30 × 1.90 m), National Gallery, London. The English penchant for landscape painting indicates a growing interest in nature and weather conditions that prefigures late-nineteenth-century Impressionism. Although Constable sketched from nature, he did the final painting in his studio.

FIGURE 17.7 Joseph Mallord William Turner, *The Slave Ship*, 1840, oil on canvas, 2′11$\frac{3}{4}$″ × 4′ (90.5 × 122 cm), Henry Lillie Pierce Fund. Courtesy, Museum of Fine Arts, Boston. Reproduced with permission. ©2005 Museum of Fine Arts, Boston. All Rights Reserved. Constable called Turner's paintings "tinted steam." The original title, *Slavers Throwing Overboard the Dead and Dying—Typhoon Coming On*, in spite of its unusual length, hardly clarifies the subject, which is, above all, Turner's Romantic response to nature.

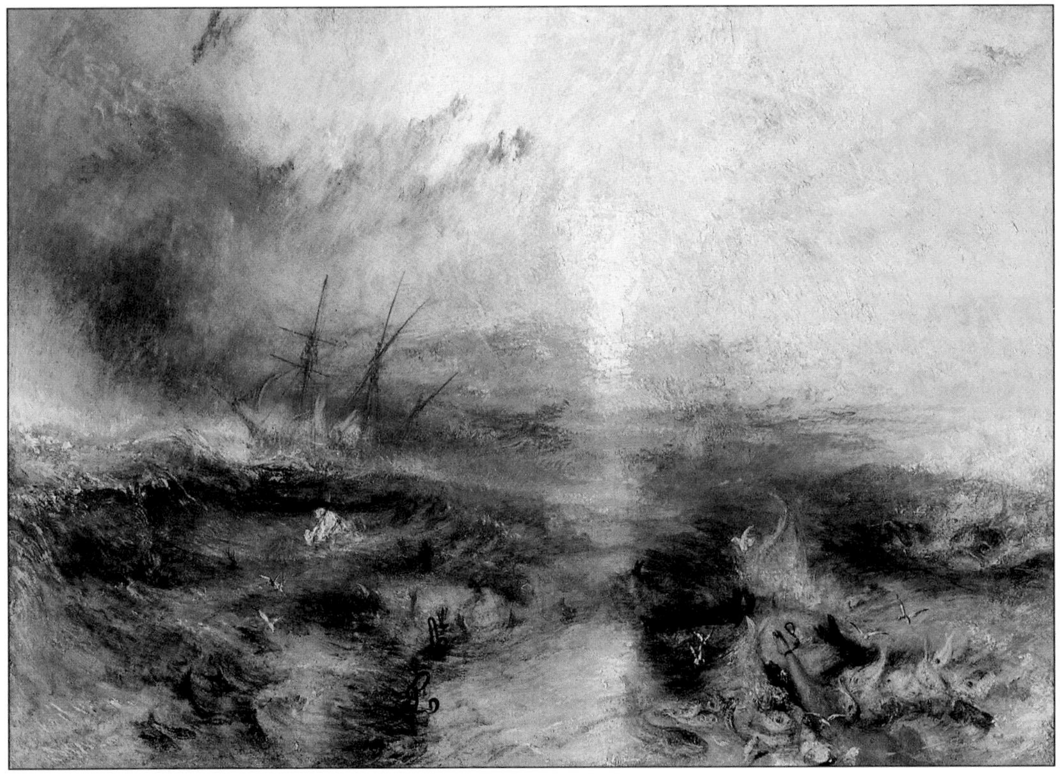

Then & Now

AMERICA'S NATIONAL PARKS

In the early eighteenth century, the new American nation prided itself on its political system, but it lagged far behind Europe in cultural achievement. Rather than in authors and artists, the country took pride in the one thing it had in abundance—land. After Thomas Jefferson purchased the Louisiana territory from Napoleon in 1803, the American landscape became, in effect, the nation's cultural inheritance. And as the country was subsequently explored, the treasures it held, in beauty as well as gold, excited the American populace.

It was the artists and photographers who accompanied the expeditions to the West who publicized the beauty of the landscape. The painter ALBERT BIERSTADT [BEER-shtaht] (1830–1902) accompanied Colonel Frederick Lander to the Rockies in 1859. The photographer C. E. Watkins (1829–1916) traveled to Yosemite in 1861. The painter Thomas Moran (1837–1926) went with Colonel Ferdinand V. Hayden of the National Geographic Survey through the Rockies to Yellowstone in 1871.

Bierstadt's paintings and Watkins's photographs were the primary reason that Lincoln signed into law a bill establishing Yosemite as a national preserve in 1864. In 1872, Congress purchased Moran's *Grand Canyon of the Yellowstone* (fig. 17.8) for $10,000 and later hung the massive painting in the lobby of the Senate. On March 1, 1872, President Ulysses S. Grant signed the Yellowstone Park Act into law, establishing the national park system.

Today the national park system is increasingly threatened. Automobiles have been banned from Yosemite, parts of Mesa Verde, and other parks as well. In the early 1980s, developers proposed building a geothermal power plant fifteen miles west of Upper Geyser Basin and "Old Faithful" Geyser in Yellowstone. The project was halted only because no one could demonstrate the exact boundaries of the Yellowstone geothermal reservoirs. In 1980, the National Park Service explained the situation this way: "Yellowstone, Great Smoky Mountains, Everglades, and Glacier—most of these great parks were at one time pristine areas surrounded and protected by vast wilderness regions. Today, with their surrounding buffer zones gradually disappearing, many of these parks are experiencing significant and widespread adverse effects associated with external encroachment."

The nation is losing one of its myths—the myth that people can live harmoniously with nature, which was illustrated in the landscapes of American Romantic painters.

FIGURE 17.8 Thomas Moran, *Grand Canyon of the Yellowstone*, 1872, oil on canvas, 7′ × 12′ (2.13 × 3.66 m), Lent by the Department of the Interior Museum. Smithsonian American Art Museum, Smithsonian Institution, Washington, DC. Art Resource, NY. On a visit to England in 1862, Moran studied and copied the paintings of J. M. W. Turner, whose use of light and color he particularly admired.

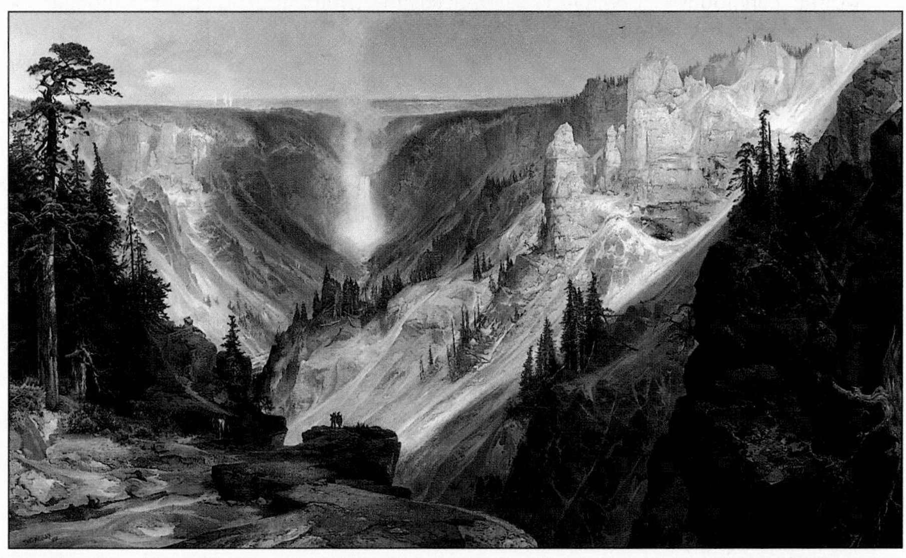

His distortion of the subject and interest in nature and light would pave the way to Impressionism.

SCULPTURE

Perhaps surprisingly, during the Romantic era, sculpture fell out of favor. In fact, in 1846, the poet Charles Baudelaire argued that the idea of Romantic sculpture was impossible. Sculpture, he suggested, can neither arouse subjective feelings in the viewer nor express the personal sensibility of the artist because, as a three-dimensional object, it asserts its objective reality too thoroughly. Baudelaire summed up Romantic sculpture in the title of his essay, "Why Sculpture Is Boring."

Baudelaire did argue, however, that sculpture could escape this fate in the service of architecture; attached to a larger whole, it could evoke profound feelings. One example is *The Departure of the Volunteers of 1792*, popularly known as *La Marseillaise* (fig. 17.9), by François Rude (1784–1855), a huge stone sculpture made for the Arc de Triomphe in Paris. Although sculpted between 1833 and 1836, the subject refers to an event that occurred in

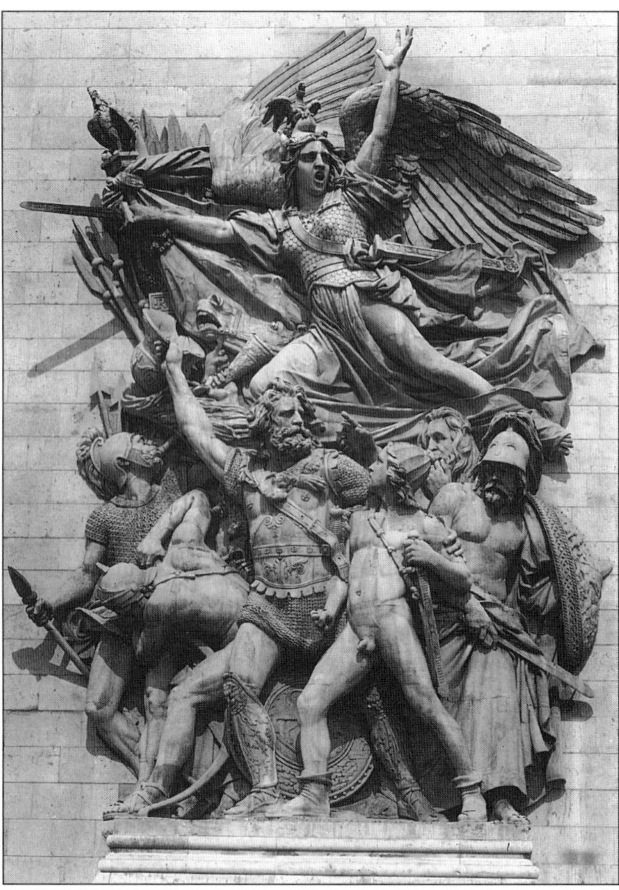

FIGURE 17.9 François Rude, *La Marseillaise (The Departure of the Volunteers of 1792)*, Arc de Triomphe, Place de l'Etoile, Paris, 1833–36, limestone, ca. 42′ × 26′ (12.80 × 7.90 m). The use of a triumphal arch to commemorate a military victory, as well as the use of a winged female figure to represent victory, derives from Greek and Roman antiquity.

1792—the defense of the French Republic by volunteers rallying to repel invaders from abroad. For Rude, the subject was deeply emotional because his own father had been among the volunteers.

The figures are costumed in both ancient and medieval armor, and the nude youth in front is Neoclassical in pose and physique. A winged female figure representing Victory (as in antiquity) leads the soldiers forward, and the group below appears to surge upward with a diagonal force that points in the direction of the tip of her sword. Thus, in a rectangular format necessitated by the architecture of the arch itself, Rude created a dynamic triangular thrust to the left that creates an emotional thrust as well, one that many French people associate with their national anthem to this day.

ARCHITECTURE

Like painting and sculpture, architecture of the Romantic era also borrowed freely from the past, creating revivals of earlier architectural styles. The Gothic and the Baroque, in particular, were revived, and often several styles were combined.

Houses of Parliament. The Gothic Revival is seen in the Houses of Parliament in London (fig. 17.10), begun 1836, by Sir Charles Barry (1795–1860) and Augustus W. N. Pugin (1812–1852). The Gothic revival was strongest in England, where it was mistakenly believed to have originated. In fact, as discussed in Chapter 12, the Gothic style originated in France and was associated primarily with ecclesiastical architecture. Somewhat incongruously, this style was applied to the buildings of the British government. Gothic features on the Houses of Parliament are the irregular silhouette, broken surface, incessant accenting of the vertical, and multiplicity of small delicate surface forms. The whole was designed to evoke the spiritual and ethical values of the Middle Ages.

Opéra. In contrast, it was the Baroque that provided the inspiration for Charles Garnier (1825–1898) when he designed the Opéra in Paris (fig. 17.11) between 1861 and 1874. Made to accommodate large audiences, the Opéra was built on a grand scale. The quantity of sculptured ornament is neo-Baroque, and the overall effect is of extreme sumptuousness. The three-story facade consists of a series of arches, surmounted by a story with two sizes of orders, topped by an ornamental attic. The forward-jutting corner pavilions are typically French.

By the second half of the nineteenth century, new technological achievements, particularly the development of cast iron as a construction material, offered architects and sculptors new possibilities. In fact, two of

FIGURE 17.10 Sir Charles Barry and Augustus Welby Northmore Pugin, Houses of Parliament, London, 1836–60, length 940′ (286.5 m). The delicacy of Gothic religious architecture is applied to government office buildings. Among the plethora of pointy pinnacles, turrets, and towers rises the famous clock tower, the largest of its bells known as Big Ben.

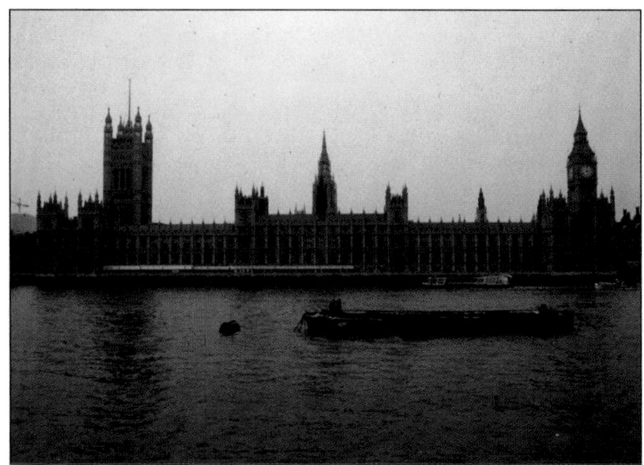

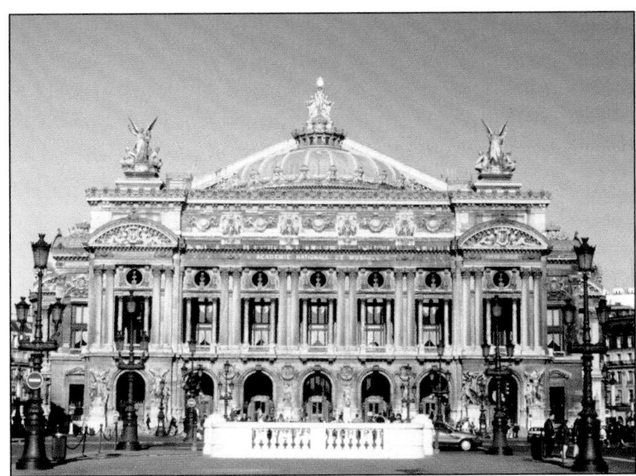

FIGURE 17.11 Charles Garnier, Opéra, facade, Paris, 1861–74, width ca. 200′ (62.96 m), height 95′ (28.96 m). The Opera, with its Neo-Baroque combination of arcades, colonnades, and luxuriously opulent ornament, is well suited to performance of opera, a Baroque form of music.

the most innovative works of the day, Crystal Palace in London and the Statue of Liberty in New York harbor, were considered by some to be more feats of engineering than works of art.

Crystal Palace. Built for the Great Exhibition of 1851, Crystal Palace (fig. 17.12) was designed by Joseph Paxton (1803–65), who was once gardener to the duke of Devonshire and was trained neither as an architect nor as an engineer. When Prince Albert called for a competition to design the exhibition site, the judges, among them Charles Barry, who had designed the Gothic Revival Houses of Parliament, deemed none of the large number of entries suitable. The judges themselves prepared a design, but it, too, was rejected. Finally Paxton offered his proposal. Instead of a giant brick edifice, as everyone else had proposed, Paxton extended the concept of the glassframe greenhouse. Employing a cast-iron prefabricated modular framework—the first such building of its kind—Paxton used glass for his walls. Over 900,000 square feet of glass—nearly a third of Britain's total annual production—were fitted into a building 1,851 feet long and 408 feet wide. The result was not only in harmony with the building's site in Hyde Park, but offered the simplest solution to the problem of lighting the interior of a vast exhibition space. Soon Paxton's model was adapted to other similar spaces, particularly to railway stations.

FIGURE 17.12 Joseph Paxton, Crystal Palace, London, 1851, cast iron and glass, length 1851′ (564.18 m), width 408′ (124.36 m), height 108′ (32.92 m). Designed by a gardener, Crystal Palace was, in its time, the largest enclosed space ever created. Built as an exhibition hall to display industrial and technological accomplishments, it was in itself an impressive demonstration of new technology.

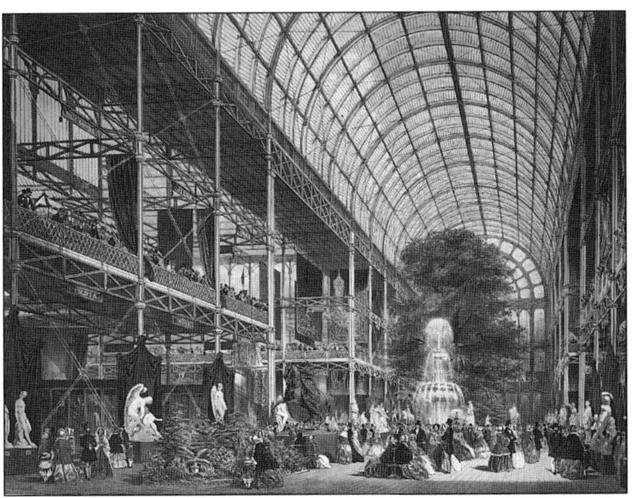

PHILOSOPHY

Hegel and Historical Change. Another key thinker of the Romantic era, German philosopher George Friedrich Wilhelm Hegel (1770–1831) saw reality and history as a dynamic process rather than a series of static ideals. For Hegel, historical change reflects a dialectical process in which opposing ideas collide to produce a new result, or synthesis, that combines elements of the original two contradictory forces. Every thesis has its antithesis, with the conflict between them resulting in a synthesis, which becomes the basis for a further synthesis. Hegel used this approach to analyze the history of philosophy and to understand the history of the world. He argued that history is a series of moments, each of which evolves out of a previous conflict.

Hegal's dialectical approach was grounded in the idea that history is the unfolding in time of something he called "Absolute Spirit." For example, the spirit of one era, such as the conformist 1950s, gave rise to its opposite: the rebellious 1960s in a pattern of "thesis and antithesis." Out of their collision emerges, according to Hegel, a new "synthesis" in which 1950s conservatism and 1960s liberalism yield "Wall Street bankers with Beatles haircuts," as one writer has comically described the synthesis. Moreover, according to Hegel, the Absolute Spirit of an age was something of a transcendent point of view, looking down from on high, above the inevitable swings of the pendulum and the continual shifting of historical forces.

Originally designed to explain the conflicting ideas and ideals of great men, Hegel's dialectic was later adapted to explain opposing economic forces and class conflicts between owner/managers and labor. Karl Marx and Friedrich Engels, in *The Communist Manifesto* (1844), argued for the influence of economic factors on all aspects of human experience, including social, political, and intellectual matters.

Jean-Jacques Rousseau and the Concept of Self. The autobiographical *Confessions* of the French philosophical writer JEAN-JACQUES ROUSSEAU [roo-SEW] (1712–1778) was the first and most influential exploration of the self in the West outside the tradition of religious autobiography.

Rousseau's *Confessions* serves as a powerful example of reflective self-analysis, a model for future philosophical self-explorations. This celebration of the self became so prevalent during the Romantic era that even in the face of crisis, as with the dashed hopes of many in Britain and France at the outcome of the French Revolution, there was a belief that those aspirations could be profitably redefined.

Rousseau's early works concern social themes. In his *Discourse on Inequality* (1754), he provides a critique of the philosophy of Thomas Hobbes, who argued that human beings are spurred by self-interest and that to exist in a state of nature is to exist in a state of war (see Chapter 15). Rousseau argued that although humans are motivated by self-interest, they also possess a natural instinct of compassion.

As a Romantic rather than an Enlightenment figure, Rousseau stood in stark contrast to many of his contemporaries, particularly Swift and Voltaire. Rousseau believed in the basic goodness of humanity, in naturally positive instincts rather than naturally negative ones. Society, he felt, corrupted a person's basic instincts, making people competitive, greedy, and uncaring. Like the Romantic poets and painters who were to follow, he celebrated the claims of the imagination above all else.

Thus, Rousseau marks a radical shift from a philosophy that emphasizes authority and power to one that celebrates freedom and individualism. In doing so, Rousseau offered a complete reversal of the values of his time. With Voltaire an age ended; with Rousseau a new age began.

Ralph Waldo Emerson and Transcendentalism. The sentiments about nature expressed by the Romantic painters were quickly adopted in the United States, where in the nineteenth century more people lived in close communion with nature than in Europe. The union of humanity with nature was a special theme of Ralph Waldo Emerson (1803–1882), author of the widely influential essay "Nature," first published in 1836. Emerson was one of a number of American thinkers who called themselves Transcendentalists. The Transcendentalists built a philosophical perspective from the poetry of William Wordsworth, on the one hand, and the philosophy of the German Immanuel Kant (1724–1804), on the other. Kant had argued there are two basic elements, "those that we receive through impressions, and those that our faculty of knowledge supplies from itself." The first he called **phenomena,** the second **noumena.** We can never truly know the essence of the things that the mind creates for itself. "In the world of sense, however far we may carry our investigation, we can never have anything before us but mere phenomena . . . The transcendental object remains unknown to us." The "transcendental object" is known only through intuition. Emerson was able to intuit the transcendental in nature. As he puts it in the most famous passage in "Nature": "Standing on the bare ground,—my head bathed by the blithe air, and uplifted into infinite space,—all mean egotism vanishes. I become a transparent eyeball; I am nothing; I see all; the currents of the Universal Being circulate through me; I am part or particle of God. . . . In the wilderness, I find something more dear and connate than in streets or villages. In the tranquil landscape, and especially in the distant line of the horizon, one beholds somewhat as beautiful as one's own nature."

Henry David Thoreau. The American wilderness was raw and vast, and even along the eastern seaboard, where civilization had taken firm hold, it was still easy to leave the city behind, as Henry David Thoreau (1817–1862) did at Walden Pond. "I went to the woods," Thoreau wrote in *Walden* (1854), "because I wished to live deliberately, to front only the essential facts of life, and see if I could not learn what it had to teach, and not, when I came to die, discover that I had not lived." Living close to nature was, for Thoreau, the very source of humankind's strength. In an essay entitled "Walking" he echoed the sentiments Emerson had expressed in "Nature":

> What I have been preparing to say is, that in Wildness is the preservation of the world. Every tree sends its fibres forth in search of the Wild. . . . From the forest and wilderness come the tonics and barks which brace mankind. Our ancestors were savages. The story of Romulus and Remus being suckled by a wolf is not a meaningless fable. The founders of every State which has risen to eminence have drawn their nourishment and vigor from a similar wild source. It was because the children of the Empire were not suckled by the wolf that they were conquered and displaced by the children of the Northern forests who were. I believe in the forest, and in the meadow, and in the night in which the corn grows.

THE ANTISLAVERY MOVEMENT

The growth of humanitarian feeling during the eighteenth century Age of Enlightenment and the spreading of democratic ideals through revolutions in France and the Americas led to increased criticism of the slave trade. In the United States, the prohibition of the foreign slave trade was not realized until 1805. In Britain, slavery was abolished with the Abolition Act of 1833, which was followed by its gradual abolition in all lands under British control.

In the northern United States a group opposed to slavery emerged, with members calling themselves "abolitionists." Believing that slavery was evil, the abolitionists fought for its eradication on idealistic moral grounds, arguing against its spread to the western U.S. territories and in favor of its elimination in all states where it existed. Among the most famous of the abolitionists were William Lloyd Garrison, who published an abolitionist newspaper, *The Liberator*, for thirty-five years, and Frederick Douglass, a former slave, whose *Narrative of the Life* revealed the shocking brutality and degradation slavery encouraged. Douglass's autobiographical work was complemented by Harriet Beecher Stowe's immensely successful novel *Uncle Tom's Cabin* (1852), the best-selling novel of the nineteenth century. Upon meeting the author, President Abraham Lincoln is said to have remarked: "So this is the little lady who wrote the big book that started this great war."

In other countries the emancipation of slaves was also at issue. As South American countries acquired their independence, they abolished slavery. Some countries, such as Chile (1823), Mexico (1829), and Bolivia (1831) made the prohibition against slavery absolute. In other countries, however, including Argentina (1810), Colombia (1814), and Venezuela (1821), the abolition of slavery was more gradual. In Brazil, the issue was explosive, and although slavery was abolished in 1888, fierce opposition fueled revolution there in 1889.

THE CIVIL WAR

Civil War erupted in the United States over slavery and a suite of other factors, social, political, and economic. With the election of Abraham Lincoln as president in 1860, a number of tensions came to a head. Prominent among them was the issue of slavery, with Lincoln a firm believer that slavery was immoral and in need of abolishment. Equally important political issues, such as states rights versus the authority of the federal government, and the competing claims of the agrarian south versus the industrial northern states, drove a wedge between the two parts of the country.

A firm believer in the sacredness of the Union, Lincoln refused to allow the southern states to secede, which they considered their right. Believing that they could sustain a separate southern union of states on the backs of their slaves, eleven southern states withdrew from the Union in 1860 and 1861. The war followed swiftly and became the bloodiest ever fought on American soil, lasting four agonized years, until 1865.

Midway through the war, President Lincoln announced his *Emancipation Proclamation*, which promised freedom to slaves and the abolition of the institution of slavery in all the United States. When the northern states finally prevailed, slavery was ended as an institution in the country, and the central government was strengthened. The issues that divided the country, however, would do so in attenuated form for more than another century, as the problem of freed slaves during the Reconstruction era and the rights of blacks would become and long remain major social and political issues.

THE CRIMEAN WAR

During the nineteenth century, European imperialist tendencies increased. The first major Ottoman war, the Crimean War occurred from 1854 to 1856, with Russia, which had been annexing Muslim lands in Central Asia. Eager to absorb Muslim provinces in Eastern Europe, Russia attacked the Ottomans, ostensibly over the right to defend Christian sites in the Holy Land. Alarmed at further Russian expansionist tendencies, Britain and France sided with the Ottomans and declared war on Russia. Although the Turks and their allies were victorious, both sides suffered heavy casualties.

The Crimean War initiated a decline in Ottoman power and influence. It was the first Ottoman war in which the Ottomans did not control the outcome. After the Crimean War, the European powers no longer considered the Ottomans a serious global political and military force. For Russia, the effects of the war were equally disastrous. In addition to losing more than 100,000 men and suffering humiliating military defeat on its own soil, Russia could no longer sustain its expansionist ambitions. The war clearly showed that Russia's agrarian economy based on the labor of serfs was no match for the European industrial powers.

LITERATURE

The theme of much nineteenth-century literature is our ignorance of things. In Herman Melville's (1819–1891) novel *Moby-Dick* (1851), Captain Ahab is bent on capturing the great white whale, which comes to stand, in his imagination, for something close to a final truth or a first cause. But the whale eludes him, and even when Ahab does indeed "capture" it, the whale drags him to his death. He seeks a knowledge he cannot possess.

Robert Louis Stevenson (1850–1894), another important author of the era, wrote a short novel, *Dr. Jekyll and Mr. Hyde* (1886), which embodies the conflict between the classical mind, with its urge for order, and the new Romantic mind, and in which the rational, scientific Dr. Jekyll has to battle with his alter ego, the violent, irrational Mr. Hyde. In other popular literature, the mystery tale rises into fashion in France in the 1830s and is seen in America a decade later, but culminates, at the end of the century, in the English writer Sir Arthur Conan Doyle's great detective, Sherlock Holmes. In the typical mystery, everyone is, metaphorically, thrown into a fog by murder. No one knows "who done it," a situation that has excited the passions of readers ever since. As a sort of Enlightenment hero, the detective penetrates the fog, clarifies the situation, resolves the conflict, and explains it logically. If our Romantic spirit is excited by inexactitude and indeterminacy, we nonetheless long to be rescued from them.

William Blake. A product of the industrial slums, the poet and artist William Blake (1757–1827) was born in poverty and, unable to attend school, taught himself to read and studied engravings of paintings by such Renaissance masters as Raphael, Dürer, and Michelangelo. At the age of twenty-two, Blake entered the Royal Academy as an engraving student, but unsettling clashes over artistic differences returned him to a life of nonconformist study.

Blake insisted that his "great task" as a poet was "To open the Eternal Worlds, to open the immortal Eyes of Man inwards into the Worlds of Thought." His was a poetry of revelation, not technique. As a boy Blake saw "a tree filled with angels, bright angelic wings bespangling every bough with stars." This ability to see beyond the physical, what he called his "double vision," fueled Blake's imaginative and poetic flights (fig. 17.13).

FIGURE 17.13 William Blake, frontispiece to *Europe: A Prophecy*, 1794, $12\frac{1}{4}'' \times 9\frac{1}{2}''$ (31.1 × 24.1 cm), © The Trustees of the British Museum/Art Resource, NY. Blake's idea of God, Urizen, is depicted here on the second day of Creation. He holds a pair of compasses as he measures out and delineates the firmament.

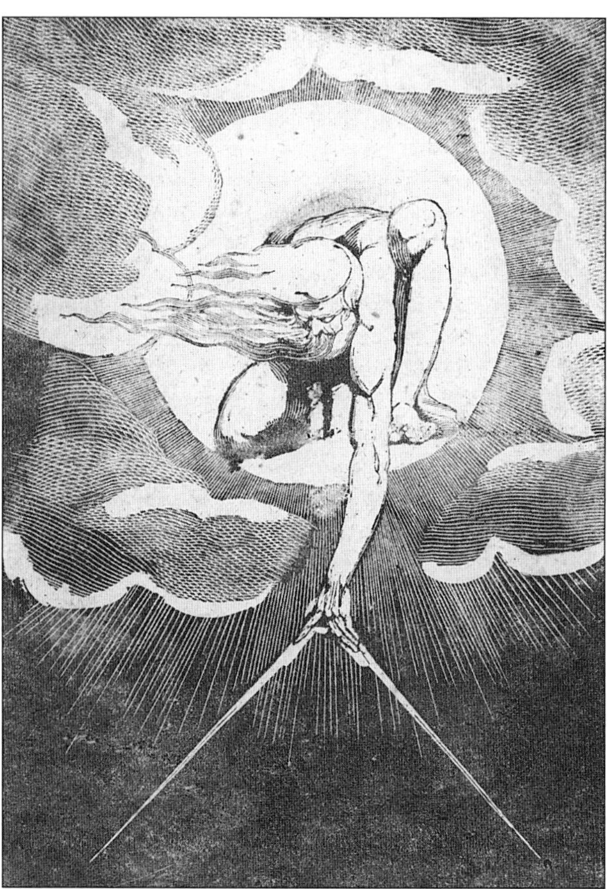

Blake saw himself as a prophet, and he drew heavily on both the Hebrew and the Christian sacred texts. At the core of Blake's work are two contrary archetypal states of the human soul: innocence and experience. Humanity's oscillation between these states forms the focus of much of his poetry.

For Blake, innocence and experience are psychological states that carry political implications. "The Chimney Sweeper" in *Songs of Innocence* is a young boy who rationalizes his misery and naively declares, "Those that do their duty need not fear harm." Historically, nothing could have been further from the truth. Young sweeps who endured this forced labor rarely lived to reach adulthood. The irony of his final pronouncement escapes the innocent boy, unaware of the horrors of the Industrial Revolution. Readers would have understood the implications nonetheless.

William Wordsworth and Samuel Taylor Coleridge. The year 1798 saw the publication of the *Lyrical Ballads*, co-authored by William Wordsworth (1770–1850) and Samuel Taylor Coleridge (1772–1834). Turning their backs on the sophisticated syntax and vocabulary of Neoclassical writing, they insisted that the language of poetry should be natural; as natural, in fact, as its subject, nature—both human nature and the natural world. Coleridge was particularly interested in folk idioms and songs. Wordsworth's ear was tuned to the everyday language of common folk, "a language really used by men," as he put it. He wrote about everyday subjects, a poetry of the individual, of the inner life and "the essential passions of the heart."

Exactly how the human imagination delineates a sense of place in nature, and by extension in daily reality, also underlies Wordsworth's lyric "I Wandered Lonely as a Cloud." According to his sister Dorothy's journal of April 15, 1802, they had gone for a walk "in the woods beyond Gowbarrow Park." Together they stumbled upon a stretch of daffodils that "grew among the mossy stones . . . some rested their heads upon these stones as on a pillow for weariness; and the rest tossed and reeled and danced, and seemed as if they verily laughed with the wind, that flew upon them over the Lake; they looked so gay, ever glancing, ever changing." The daffodils of Wordsworth's poem are the personified flowers of Dorothy's journal entry, but in the end brother and sister witness different events. Whereas Dorothy draws simple pleasure from her walk among the flowers, the poet's attention becomes fixed on how the imagination interacts with nature. For although Wordsworth takes pleasure in his walk, the "wealth" the poem refers to comes into focus only with the "inward eye" of the imagination. The poem reflects many of Wordsworth's Romantic preoccupations, particularly the power of nature and of remembered experience to restore the human spirit.

John Keats. Probably no poet of the period was more aware of his inability to know the world fully, yet at the same time more compelled to explore it, than John Keats (1795–1821). Like Wordsworth, Keats believed in the vitality of sensation, but did not limit himself to sight and sound. Keats often uses imagery designating one sense in place of imagery suggesting another. For example, he writes of "fragrant and enwreathed light," "pale and silver silence," "scarlet pain," and "the touch of scent." Keats's images register on palate and fingertip as well as within the ear and eye, making the world, the poet, and the poem one complete sensation. This blurring of borders reflects the empathic power Keats termed "negative capability," the poet's ability to empathize with other characters, or entities, living or imagined, animate or inanimate.

Perhaps the most affecting of Keats's efforts at negative capability is "This Living Hand," written shortly before he died of tuberculosis at the age of twenty-five:

This living hand, now warm and capable
Of earnest grasping, would, if it were cold
And in the icy silence of the tomb,
So haunt thy days and chill thy dreaming nights
That thou wouldst wish thine own heart dry of blood
So in my veins red life might stream again,
And thou be conscience-calmed—see here it is—hold it
towards you.

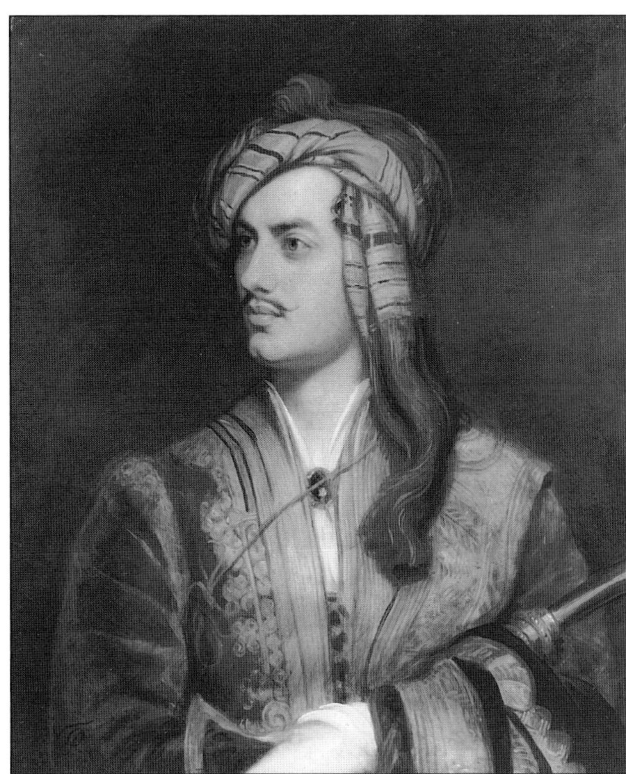

FIGURE 17.14 Thomas Philips, *Lord Byron in Albanian Costume*, 1814, oil on canvas, $29\frac{1}{2}'' \times 24\frac{1}{2}''$ (75 × 62 cm), National Portrait Gallery, London. Byron looks particularly dashing in this costume, which signifies the love of the exotic and interest in the cultures of the Balkans reflected in his writing.

Lord Byron. Another great English Romantic poet, George Gordon, Lord Byron (1788–1824), embodies the Romantic self. A free spirit, he was notorious for his unconventional behavior. One of his first books of poems, *Hours of Idleness* (1807), was subjected to severe criticism in the *Edinburgh Review*, to which Byron retorted, in 1809, with a biting satire in the style of Swift and Pope, entitled *English Bards and Scotch Reviewers*. It won him instant fame. That same year, he left England to travel extensively in Spain, Portugal, Italy, and the Balkans (fig. 17.14). Good-looking and flamboyant, Byron socialized with a variety of upper-class and aristocratic women. His most famous poem, *Don Juan* (1819–24), portrayed the seducer already well known to most audiences. Most of his followers assumed the poem to be semiautobiographical, since it was begun soon after he formed a relationship with Contessa Teresa Guicioli in Italy, who remained his mistress for the rest of his life. As one female friend said of him, not without some real admiration, "He is mad, bad, and dangerous to know." Byron died in the Balkans fighting for the Greeks in the war against Turkey in 1824, the same year that Delacroix painted his *Massacres at Chios*.

Emily Brontë. *Wuthering Heights* (1847), the masterpiece of EMILY BRONTË [BRON-tay] (1818–1848), is organized with the same structural care in the Classical manner of Jane Austen, but it is a fully Romantic work that breaks new ground in the violence of its scenes and the extravagance of its style.

Gone is the decorum that marked Austen's world (the "artificial rudeness" of the English garden) and in its place is a world of storm and turmoil. The novel's central characters display passionate and socially disruptive tendencies entirely at odds with the rational and serene world of the Enlightenment, and it is as if the landscape around them responds. Reason and social decorum are replaced by intense feeling and individual expression. The demands and needs of the self are paramount. Nature is untamed, unruly, and grand, exhibiting patterns of storm followed by calm, similar to the contrasting emotions displayed by Brontë's characters, and analogous to the alternation of quiet lyricism and passionate drama heard in Romantic music such as Schubert's. Moreover, in the work of both artists, drama explodes in the midst of serenity and calm, suggesting thereby the potential for abrupt change in both inner and outer weather.

Johann Wolfgang von Goethe. Perhaps the most influential writer of the Romantic era was JOHANN WOLFGANG VON GOETHE [GUR-tuh] (1749–1832), who lived half his adult life during the Enlightenment and half during the Romantic era. He witnessed the shift in consciousness from the Enlightenment emphasis on reason, objectivity, and scientific fact to the Romantic concern for emotion, subjectivity, and imaginative truth.

Born and raised in Frankfurt, Goethe studied law at the University of Strasbourg, where he met the German critic and thinker J. G. Herder. With Herder and Friedrich Schiller, Goethe contributed to the beginnings of German Romanticism in the 1770s, leading what was called the **Sturm und Drang** (storm and stress) movement. Goethe's contribution to this movement was his novel *The Sorrows of Young Werther* (1774). Enormously influential throughout Europe, the work expressed discontent with Enlightenment ideals of objectivity, rationality, and restraint. In it, an educated young man, Werther, gives up a government position to search for greater meaning in his life. He becomes alienated and unhappy until he meets and falls in love with a young woman, who is unfortunately engaged to a businessman, whom she marries. Werther becomes obsessed with her and finally commits suicide.

The work for which Goethe is best known, *Faust* (1808), is based on the life of the medieval German scholar Johann Faust, who is reputed to have sold his soul to the devil in exchange for knowledge. *Faust* has been described as a defining work of European Romanticism, one that epitomizes the temper and spirit of the Romantic era and serves to represent the anxiety-ridden Romantic imagination in all its teeming aspiration.

Throughout his life and literary career, Goethe was torn between the intellectual ideals of the Enlightenment and the emotional passions of the Romantic period. In *Faust*, readers confront alternative perspectives on life, represented by the characters Faust and the devil, Mephistopheles. Faust is a man of the mind, a knowledgeable scholar, who abandons himself to the exploration of physical experience, represented by Mephistopheles, who offers Faust the chance to live a more active life of sensation. Faust remains a divided figure, one who cannot integrate harmoniously the two different aspects of his consciousness—his scientific rationalism and his poetic intuition.

Walt Whitman. Of the American poets writing during the nineteenth century, two stand out above all others: Walt Whitman (1819–1892) and Emily Dickinson. Unlike Dickinson, whose idiosyncratic and elliptical style has found few imitators, Whitman greatly influenced later American poets. William Carlos Williams emulated Whitman's attention to the commonplace and his experiments with the poetic line. Wallace Stevens displayed the meditative, philosophical cast of mind found in poems such as Whitman's "Crossing Brooklyn Ferry." Later, Allen Ginsberg exhibited something of Whitman's early extravagance and outrageousness.

Instead of using the poetic structures of his day, Whitman developed more open, fluid forms. And rather than using old-fashioned poetic diction, he wrote in familiar and informal language, following Wordsworth's "language really used by men." Whitman also mixed exalted language with common speech, resulting in, as he remarked, a "new style . . . necessitated by new theories, new themes," far removed from European models. Whitman's stylistic innovations in *Leaves of Grass*, which he wrote and revised over nearly fifty years and once described as "a language experiment," were intended to "give something to our literature which will be our own . . . strengthening and intensifying the national." In this he was like many nineteenth-century artists who expressed their nationalistic tendencies in music, painting, and literature.

Emily Dickinson. In his exalted ambition, Whitman differed markedly from Emily Dickinson (1830–1886), whose poetic inclination gravitated inward. Although Whitman and Dickinson each brought something strikingly original to American poetry, their poems could not be more different. A glance at a page of their poetry reveals a significant visual difference. Whitman's poems are expansive, with long lines and ample stanzas. Dickinson's poems, by contrast, are very tight, with four-line stanzas that distill feeling and thought.

The openness of Whitman's form is paralleled by the openness of his stance, his outgoing public manner. Dickinson's poetry, in contrast, is much more private. Her meditative poems are rooted partly in the metaphysical poetry of seventeenth-century writers such as John Donne and partly in the tradition of Protestant hymnology. Dickinson made frequent and ingenious use of Protestant hymn meters and followed their usual stanzaic pattern. Her adaptation of hymn meter accords with her adaptation of the traditional religious doctrines of orthodox Christianity. For although many of her poems reflect her Calvinist heritage—particularly in the ways their religious disposition intersects with intensely felt psychological experience—Dickinson was not an orthodox Christian. "Some keep the Sabbath going to Church," she wrote. "I keep it, staying at Home." Her love of nature separates her from her Puritan precursors, allying her instead with such Transcendentalist contemporaries as Emerson, Thoreau, and Whitman, although her vision of life was starker than theirs.

Dickinson spent nearly all of her life in one town, Amherst, Massachusetts, living as a near recluse and dying in the house where she was born. Dickinson's poems probe deeply into a few experiences—love, death, doubt, and faith. In examining her experience, Dickinson makes a scrupulous effort to tell the truth, but she tells it "slant," as one of her poems puts it: "Tell all the Truth but tell it slant." Part of her artistry includes the way she invites readers to share her search for truth. Her poems' qualified assertions, along with their riddles and questioning stance, cumulatively suggest that life is mysterious and complex, as it was for so many Romantic artists.

MUSIC

Because it seems capable of unleashing emotions beyond mere words or images, music is perhaps the most "romantic" of Romantic art forms. Romantic music was not a break with the classical ideas of Haydn and Mozart but an expansion of techniques to express emotion in symphonies and other absolute musical forms. Both in length and substance, Romantic music served as an aural palette of new colors and expression. Romantic composers wrote music that expressed individuality and innovation, exalted nature, and broke new ground formally, harmonically, and stylistically. They also developed a musical language that reflected changing political and social attitudes. Their concern was with freedom and self-expression, with the grandeur of nature, with folk traditions, and with the vicissitudes of romantic love. And above all, their music expressed intense feeling.

Some features of Romantic music resulted from technological advances, such as the invention of valves for brass instruments and key systems for woodwinds, which increased their orchestral prominence, and the development of thicker strings for the piano, which deepened and enhanced the instrument's tonal properties. Other features of the Romantic style reflected social changes, such as the movement of musical performance from church and palace to the public concert hall, which occasioned opportunities for musical compositions of larger scope performed by bigger orchestras and choruses. This type of change enriched the orchestral sound, along with new timbres.

Although some Romantic works tended to be, on the whole, larger and longer than their counterparts from earlier centuries, there developed alongside the monumental impulse one toward the miniature. Chopin and Schubert, for example, wrote numerous short piano pieces of only a few minutes' duration. Schubert and Schumann, among others, developed the **Lied** (or art song), also a small form, designed for performance by a singer and accompanist in a room in someone's house. The monumentality of Romantic music is evident in the size of the orchestra needed to perform symphonic and choral works and the sheer magnitude of some of the works themselves. Some symphonies of Gustave Mahler (1860–1911), for example, last two hours, and require more than a hundred orchestral players as well as a hundred choral singers. And four operas of Richard Wagner (1813–1883) create a linked cycle, the *Ring of the Niebelung*, which takes thirteen hours to perform.

Program Music. Program music is a characteristic form of Romantic composition. As opposed to **absolute music**, which does not refer to anything outside of musical sound, form, and tone color, **program music** describes, in musical tones, a scene, story, event, or other nonmusical situation. Exploiting the mind's capacity to suggest and evoke, program music attempts to imitate something beyond the music itself by emphasizing an instrument's special properties or tone.

Earlier composers had used the flute to imitate birdsong, as did the Baroque composer Antonio Vivaldi in *The Four Seasons*. Renaissance composers such as Thomas Weelkes had imitated human sighing with a downward melodic motion. But composers of the Romantic era developed the idea of musical description into something far more ambitious, creating a musical program that governed an entire symphonic movement or work. In his Symphony no. 6, nicknamed "the Pastoral Symphony," for example, Beethoven provides all five movements with descriptive titles, including "Awakening of joyful feelings upon arriving in the country" and "The thunderstorm."

Hector Berlioz. One of the most innovative of Romantic composers was HECTOR BERLIOZ [BEAR-lee-ohz] (1803–1869). After pursuing a medical degree, he turned instead to music, analyzing scores, attending operas, giving lessons, singing in a theater chorus, and composing. Not long out of the Paris Conservatory of Music, Berlioz wrote his *Symphonie Fantastique*, a work that shocked Parisian audiences with its innovative orchestration, its musical recreation of a bizarre witches' sabbath, and its autobiographical theme about Berlioz's own "endless and unquenchable passion" for the English actress Harriet Smithson, whom he pursued and married against the wishes of both their families.

The *Symphonie Fantastique* contains five movements: (1) Reveries, Passions; (2) A Ball; (3) Scene in the Country; (4) March to the Scaffold; and (5) Dream of a Witches' Sabbath. Each movement uses distinctive musical material. The first movement, for example, combines a mood of reverie with an agitated and impassioned section that employs dramatic crescendos and obsessive repetitions of a musical theme Berlioz used throughout this movement and the entire symphony. This "fixed idea," or **idée fixe,** as he called it, exemplifies musically the image of "the beloved one herself [who] becomes for him a melody, a recurrent theme that haunts him everywhere." Berlioz transforms the beloved's theme of the *idée fixe* in each movement according to the needs of the program. The *idée fixe* unifies the symphony and carries it forward to a tragic conclusion. Throughout, Berlioz continually expands the orchestral palette, introducing a wide range of instruments including bells, cymbals, sponge-tipped drumsticks, a snare drum, and four harps.

Berlioz was a big fan of Beethoven. On one occasion when Berlioz was attending a Beethoven performance, he was seen sobbing—a common emotional experience for Berlioz when he listened to the music of Beethoven. Today, Berlioz's reputation remains in dispute. Some see him as a musical innovator and genius; others criticize his flash and fire, arguing that his music lacks substance. A fine music critic himself, amply demonstrated in his *Memoirs*, Berlioz would likely be amused at the debate occasioned by his intensely Romantic music.

Franz Schubert and Johannes Brahms. Inspired by the outburst of lyric poetry of the age, many composers turned to writing songs. FRANZ SCHUBERT [SHU-bert] (1797–1828) lived in Vienna and was a contemporary of Beethoven's. Over the course of his career, he wrote more than six hundred songs, many of which were settings of Goethe's verse. He also wrote three **song cycles,** or groups of linked songs, including *Die Schöne Müllerin* (*The Pretty Miller-Maid*) of 1824, which tells the story of a love affair that starts joyously only to end in tragedy.

Song was also one of the favorite forms of Johannes Brahms (1833–1897), who composed later in the century. As a boy he played piano in the bars and coffeehouses of his native Hamburg, and during the Hungarian uprising of 1848, when the city was inundated with refugees, he became particularly intrigued by gypsy songs and melodies. His most famous song, known today as "Brahms's Lullaby," was written in 1868 for the baby son of a woman who sang in the Hamburg choir. Only just over two minutes long, the song is one of the most peaceful and serene ever written.

In addition to his songs, Brahms wrote three significant concertos, two for piano and one for violin and orchestra. He composed four important symphonies, along with a multitude of chamber works and pieces for solo piano. His orchestral music especially reflects the formalist Romantic style, hewing more closely to classical musical structures inherited from Beethoven.

Clara Schumann and Fanny Mendelssohn. Two composers of the nineteenth century, whose works have been overshadowed in one case by a husband and in another by a brother, are Clara Wieck Schumann, wife of Robert Schumann, and Fanny Mendelssohn Hensel, sister of Felix Mendelssohn. Fanny Mendelssohn (1805–1847) was a German pianist and a composer of Lieder and chamber music. Her works were long neglected, but in recent years have begun to be published and performed. Her songs are particularly accomplished, with the well-crafted piano accompaniments playing an important role as settings for the poetic texts set to music. Their lyricism appears as well in her "songs without words," short piano pieces in the style of the Lied, a genre in which her brother Felix was also accomplished and which he is often credited with having invented (though Fanny may have an equal claim to that honor).

Clara Schumann (1819–1896), like her husband Robert and also like Fanny Mendelssohn, was a pianist and composer. Clara Schumann's first public appearance as a pianist was at age nine, followed by a complete recital at age eleven, and a concert tour a year later. Over the objections of her father, Clara Wieck married Robert Schumann when she was twenty-one, and became a close musical collaborator, studying symphonic and chamber music scores with him, and composing some pieces together, including a series of songs with their Lied settings intertwined. Johannes Brahms was a friend of both Robert and Clara Schumann, and was acknowledged to have been in love with her. After Robert Schumann's death, Clara continued to champion his music, as well as that of Brahms, and is believed to have been a direct influence on the music of both composers.

Chopin and the Piano. If Berlioz represents one pole of the Romantic composer's spectrum, FREDERIC CHOPIN [SHOW-Pan] (1810–1849) represents the other. Where Berlioz wrote mostly in large forms, Chopin wrote in small ones. Where Berlioz composed for orchestra, Chopin wrote almost exclusively for the piano, which he played brilliantly. The few who heard him play were swept away by his delicate, evocative style of playing. His music serves as a counterforce to the big and the bold. His intimate pieces show that genius can exist in miniature as well as in majestic forms.

During the eighteenth and the early nineteenth centuries, the **piano** (then called the pianoforte) was a smaller instrument than the concert version of today. Throughout the Romantic period, it was used as a solo instrument for short lyric pieces, as an accompaniment to songs, and for orchestral use. Unlike the harpsichord, which plucks its strings, the piano strikes them with small felt-tipped hammers, giving the musician the ability to modulate between soft and loud simply by exerting more or less pressure on the keys—hence the name, *piano* (soft) *forte* (loud), later shortened simply to *piano*.

Chopin composed two piano concertos, two large-scale piano sonatas, and a series of semilong works for solo piano, as well as two sets of études (or studies), a group of **preludes** in different keys, a set of **nocturnes** (or night pieces) mostly melancholy in tone, along with **waltzes,** polonaises, and mazurkas, which capture the spirit and flavor of the Parisian salon and of the Polish peasant world. The **polonaises** and the **mazurkas** reflect Chopin's nationalistic spirit during a time when Poland was partly under Russian domination. The majestic Polonaise in A Flat, op. 53, one of Chopin's best known pieces, expresses both joy and pride in a spirit of noble grandeur. The spirit of the polonaise ennobles it, its melody makes it memorable, and its technical demands make it a bravura piece for the piano virtuoso.

Another bravura solo piano piece is his Etude op. 10, #12, "The Revolutionary Etude," so-called because it appeared when the Poles staged an uprising against Russia, their master. Chopin poured his revolutionary fervor into the piece as his contribution to the Polish protest.

Giuseppe Verdi and Grand Opera. Opera first appeared as a distinct form early in the seventeenth century in Italy. Its popularity was increased by Claudio Monteverdi, who further contributed to its development. During the eighteenth century, it became popular in England and Austria, with Mozart composing his consummate operatic masterpieces, including *Don Giovanni* and *The Marriage of Figaro.* It was during the nineteenth century, however, that opera became internationally popular, with Romantic composers of many countries participating in the grand flowering of the genre.

The rise of the middle class after 1820 helped usher in a new kind of opera, grand opera, which appealed to the masses because of its spectacle as much as its music. Alongside the drama and passion of grand opera there remained comic opera, which continued to flourish as it had in the previous century.

Italy's greatest and most important Romantic composer of any kind was GIUSEPPE VERDI [VAIR-dee] (1813–1901), whose music epitomizes dramatic energy, power, and passion. Born in northern Italy near Parma, Verdi had little formal musical training. Verdi's career began with a series of early operas in the 1850s—*Rigoletto*, *Il Trovatore*, and *La Traviata;* continued with a series of popular operas in the 1860s—*Un Ballo in Maschera*, *La Forza del Destino*, and *Don Carlos;* and concluded triumphantly with a series of grand operas in the 1870s and 1880s—*Aida*, *Otello* (based on Shakespeare's *Othello*), and *Falstaff* (based on Shakespeare's *Merry Wives of Windsor*).

Rigoletto, composed in 1851, is one of Verdi's most dramatic works. Based on a play by the French Romantic writer Victor Hugo, *Rigoletto* depicts intense passion and violence in a tale of seduction, revenge, and murder. Rigoletto is a court jester, a hunchback who serves the duke of Mantua. When the Duke seduces his daughter Gilda, Rigoletto plans to kill him in revenge and lures the Duke to a quiet inn with Maddalena, the sister of his hired assassin, Sparafucile. He hopes that Gilda will renounce her love for the Duke when she sees him attempt to seduce Maddalena. His hopes, however, are dashed when Gilda sacrifices her own life to save the Duke.

The melodies Verdi provides for his characters perfectly express their feelings. The Duke sings one of the most famous of all operatic arias, "La donna è mobile" ("Woman is fickle"), which perfectly captures his frivolous and pleasure-loving nature. Following this song, Verdi provides a quartet for the Duke, Maddalena, Gilda, and Rigoletto, giving voice to their individual concerns. In response to the Duke's elegantly seductive melodic line, Maddalena voices a series of sharp broken laughs. Gilda's melody is fraught with pain and sorrow; Rigoletto's reveals his heated anger as he curses the Duke. Verdi deftly balances the individual singers so their ensemble singing is blended into a unified and dramatic expression of feeling.

A distinctive feature of Verdi's operas is the catchy tunes they contain. After the premiere of a Verdi opera, local singers and musicians would be singing and playing his melodies, which remain among the most popluar and hummable pieces of all time. One example is "La donna e mobile," which Verdi kept secret until the opening night of his opera *Rigoletto*. Verdi extracted a promise of secrecy from the tenor who would sing it, from the orchestra, and from other singers and stage hands not even to whistle the tune anywhere until the first performance. "La donna e mobile" was thus a complete surprise and an immediate success. It remains one of Verdi's (and of opera's) most popular tunes to this day.

Richard Wagner. As Beethoven had dominated the musical world of the first half of the nineteenth century, RICHARD WAGNER [VAHG-ner] (1813–1883) dominated the musical world of the second half. It was, in fact, through intense study of Beethoven's works that Wagner became a composer. Late in life, Wagner explained that he had wanted to do for opera what Beethoven had done for symphonic music—to make it express a wide range of experience and to have it achieve overwhelming emotional effects. Wagner called the new kind of opera he would create "music drama." Unlike Beethoven, whose works express a profound hope in human possibility, Wagner displays a more pessimistic attitude toward life, emphasizing the blind forces of irrationality and passion that drive human behavior. Wagner's works include the comic *Die Meistersinger von Nürenberg*, the mystical *Lohengrin*, and the sensuous *Tristan and Isolde*, which influenced subsequent European musical style perhaps more than any work of the late nineteenth century. His operas portray characters whose lives are made unhappy by circumstances they cannot control, as in *Tristan and Isolde*, in which the two lovers are kept apart only to be finally united in death.

Wagnerian music drama brings together song and instrumental music, dance and drama and poetry in a single unbroken stream of art. Wagner's ambitious goals were to restore the importance of music in opera, to establish a better balance between orchestra and singers, and to raise the quality of the librettos, or texts of operas. This last Wagner accomplished by finding his subjects in medieval legend and Nordic mythology and by writing his own librettos, or little books, for his operatic music.

Designed to do more than simply provide beautiful accompaniments for arias, Wagner's operatic orchestral writing was meant to arouse intense emotion, to comment on stage action, to be associated with incidents in the plot, and to reflect characters' behavior. Wagner accomplished these goals in part by using what were called **leitmotifs.** These were usually brief fragments of melody or rhythm that, when played, would remind the listeners of particular characters and actions, somewhat in the way a movie or television theme triggers associations in the mind of the audience.

Connections

GOETHE AND SCHUBERT: POETRY AND SONG

During the nineteenth century there occurred an explosion of lyric poetry fueled by the Romantic movement. In England, France, and Germany especially, poetry poured from the pens of writers such as William Wordsworth, Samuel Taylor Coleridge, John Keats, Lord Byron, Alfred de Musset, Victor Hugo, and Heinrich Heine, among many others. Of the German poets, the poetry of Johann Wolfgang von Goethe was especially inspiring to the young Viennese composer Franz Schubert.

Schubert set many poems to music, perfecting a form of musical art called the *Lied* (plural *Lieder*). The Lied was a type of art song set to an accompaniment, usually for piano, that suited the tone, mood, and details of a poem. Schubert composed more than six hundred Lieder, more than fifty of them to poems by Goethe. Among the most accomplished of Schubert's settings of Goethe texts is a song he wrote as a teenager: *Erlkönig (The Erlking)*.

Based on a Danish legend, Goethe's narrative poem has the Romantic qualities of strangeness and awe. The poem tells the story of a boy who is pursued, charmed, then violently abducted by the king of the elves, as the child rides on horseback through the forest with his father.

FATHER My son, why hide your face so anxiously?
SON Father, don't you see the Erlking?
The Erlking with his crown and his train?
FATHER My son, it is a streak of mist.
ERLKING Dear child, come, go with me!
I'll play the prettiest games with you.
Many colored flowers grow along the shore,
My mother has many golden garments.
SON My father, my father, and don't you hear
The Erlking whispering promises to me?
FATHER Be quiet, stay quiet, my child;
The wind is rustling in the dead leaves.
. . .
ERLKING I love you, your beautiful figure delights me!
And if you're not willing, then I shall use force!
SON My father, my father, now he is taking hold of me!
The Erlking has hurt me!
NARRATOR The father shudders, he rides swiftly on;
He holds in his arms the groaning child,
He reaches the courtyard weary and anxious:
In his arms the child—was dead.

In setting Goethe's poem, Schubert was faced with the challenge of delineating in music the lines and voices of four characters—father, son, narrator, and Erlking. His response to the challenge exhibits his early musical genius. Schubert differentiates the poem's characters by giving them very different melodies and by putting their music in different vocal registers. The child's vocal line is high pitched and fearful. The father's is in a lower register and conveys confidence. The Erlking's melody is lilting and seductive. Schubert also characterizes the horse by using galloping triplets in the piano accompaniment. Throughout the alternation of the characters' lines, Schubert builds tension by raising the child's vocal line in pitch and increasing its intensity. By altering the character of the Erlking's music toward the end, he suggests the Erlking's shift from charm and seduction to threatening menace.

Throughout his setting of Goethe's poem, Schubert finds musical analogues for the poet's language, imagery, and story. One of his more dramatic strategies is to slow down the music at the end, and he actually stops singer and accompanist in a dramatic pause in the middle of the final line: "In his arms the child—was dead."

Among the best-known and most frequently heard of Wagner, *Melodies* is the famous Bridal Chorus from Lohengrin.

MUSIC IN RUSSIA

Before Peter the Great's Europeanization drive in the eighteenth century, Russian music consisted primarily of religious and folk music. After the czar's return from the West, however, European music, particularly that composed during the eighteenth and nineteenth centuries, greatly influenced what was being produced in Russia. Among the composers who were able to synthesize the two musical styles were Modest Mussorgsky, whose operas commemorate great Russian leaders, and Peter Ilyich Tchaikovsky, whose ballets, operas, symphonies, and chamber works made him an internationally acclaimed figure.

Table 17–1 ROMANTIC COMPOSERS AND REPRESENTATIVE WORKS
Ludwig von Beethoven (1770–1827): Symphony no. 5
Franz Schubert (1797–1828): *The Erlking* (Lied or art song)
Hector Berlioz (1803–69): *Symphonie Fantastique*
Frederic Chopin (1810–49): Revolutionary Etude (piano piece)
Richard Wagner (1813–83): *Tristan and Isolde* (music drama)
Giuseppe Verdi (1813–1901): *Rigoletto* (opera)
Johannes Brahms (1833–97): Piano Concerto #2
Peter Ilyich Tchaikovsky (1840–93): *The Nutcracker* (ballet)

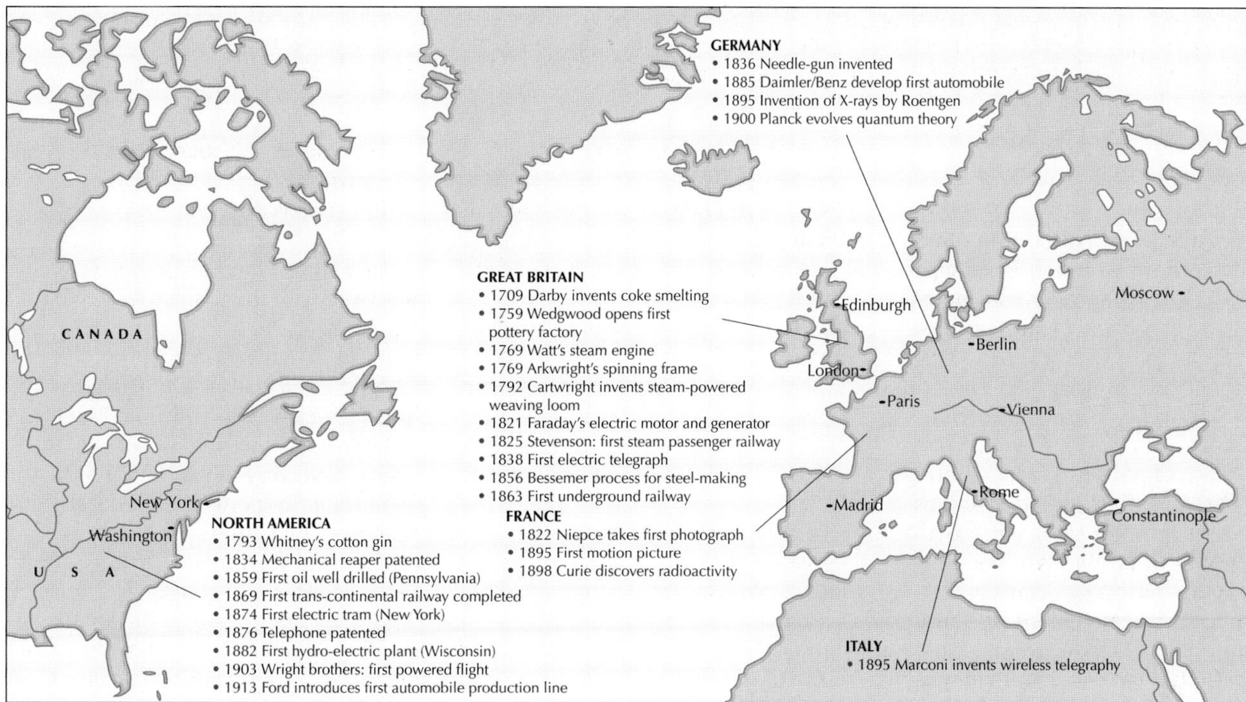

MAP 17.2 The Industrial Revolution in Europe and America.

Modest Mussorgsky. Supporting himself by working as a government clerk, MODEST MUSSORGSKY (moo-ZORG-skee] (1839–1881) composed relatively few works; although each reflected important qualities of the Russian national character. Mussorgsky led the school of Russian nationalist music in the 1860s that incorporated elements of Russian folk music into its compositions and used ancient Russian church modes in addition to the Western major and minor scales.

Most prominent among Mussorgsky's works is *Boris Godunov*, an opera based on a poem by the Russian Alexander Pushkin (1799–1837). It is in four acts and opens with a prologue that contains two important choral scenes, set in front of the Kremlin churches, which convey the national and religious spirit of old Russia. Mussorgsky includes the sound of the church bells, almost as important an emblem of Russian religious fervor as religious icons.

Peter Tchaikovsky. If Mussorgsky is to be considered one of the most nationalistic of Russian composers, PETER ILYICH TCHAIKOVSKY [cheye-KOV-skee] (1840–1893) can be said to be one of the most European. At the age of thirty, Tchaikovsky was introduced to a wealthy patron, Nadezhda von Meck. His patron agreed to attend to his material needs on condition that they never meet but only correspond. The more than three thousand letters they exchanged have given us an intimate picture of Tchaikovsky, the artist and the man. Although he was often reproached for his excessive sentimentality, his six symphonies are some of the most beautiful examples of Western influence on a Russian composer. Tchaikovsky was one of the first Russian composers to visit America, and his music remains popular in the United States as well as in his homeland today. A favorite among Americans, his *1812 Overture* was commissioned to celebrate the seventieth anniversary of Russia's victory over Napoleon. With booming cannons, familiar tunes, ringing bells, and fireworks, this piece is frequently performed at Fourth of July celebrations.

Tchaikovsky is best known for his ballet music, such as *Swan Lake*, *Sleeping Beauty*, and *The Nutcracker.*

Composed in 1892, *The Nutcracker* was, for years, rarely performed. In the 1930s, a number of ballet companies outside Russia discovered it, and it premiered in the United States in 1940 in a production of the Ballets Russes de Monte Carlo. But the ballet really took flight with the choreography of George Balanchine for the New York City Ballet in 1954. Today, *The Nutcracker* is a Christmas-time ritual in many major cities worldwide, New York included, making it ballet's greatest hit of all time.

Tchaikovsky's music exhibits a gift for melodic invention and demonstrates his skill as an orchestrator, highlighting the tonal color and varied expressive qualities of the full range of orchestral instruments. In its sense of drama and intense emotion, Tchaikovsky's music shares important affinities with other nineteenth-century Romantic composers from France, Italy, Germany, and Austria.

REALISM

Realism is the term used to describe a development in the arts in which many artists tried to convey in a nonidealized way the realities of modern life. The artist's role was no longer simply to reveal the beautiful and the sublime, but to open the public's eyes to the world around them, not just its grandeur but its brute reality as well. In Realist art and literature, the aim is to tell the truth, not to be true to some higher, perfect ideal. Ordinary events and objects were, to the Realist, as interesting as heroes or the grand events of history. Increasingly, after the revolution of 1789, it was no longer the aristocracy who made history, but the ordinary working class people. And so it was to the lives of the working class that Realist art turns for its inspiration.

In Lyons in 1831, silk workers had gone on strike for better wages. The situation fomented for three years until, in 1834, strikers fought police and national troops in a six-day battle that resulted in hundreds of deaths. A few days later, Louis-Philippe suspended publication of a radical newspaper and arrested the leaders of the working-class Society of the Rights of Man. In protest, workers again took to the streets, battling with government troops. In one working-class neighborhood, troops invaded an apartment building from which, they claimed, shots had been fired.

Honoré Daumier. The cartoonist HONORÉ DAUMIER [DOME-yay] (1801–1879) depicted the aftermath in a lithograph exhibited in a storefront window a few days later, *Rue Transonain, April 15, 1834* (fig. 17.15). A father, in a nightshirt, lies dead by his bed. Beneath him, face down, lies his child. His wife is sprawled in the shadows, and another, older man, perhaps the child's grandfather, lies to the right. Such a slaughter of the innocent outraged not only the Parisian working class but the intelligentsia as well.

FIGURE 17.15 Honoré Daumier, *Rue Transonain, April 15, 1834*, 1834, lithograph, $11\frac{1}{2}'' \times 17\frac{5}{8}''$ (29.2 × 44.8 cm). Charles Derring Fund, 1953. 530. Photograph © 2005, The Art Institute of Chicago. All Rights Reserved. Daumier wrote that "One must be part of one's times." This stark and moving image records the repression of the people by the troops of Louis-Philippe.

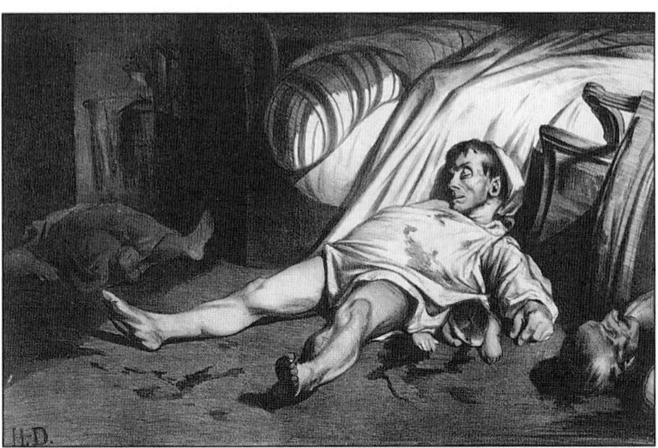

KARL MARX AND FRIEDRICH ENGELS

It was precisely such conditions, common across Europe, that influenced the thinking of Karl Marx (1818–1883) and his colleague Friedrich Engels (1820–1895). Workers, they realized, had no effective political voice other than revolution and, alienated from their labor by an increasingly mechanized industrial system from which they also received no real economic benefit, they were bound to rebel. "The bourgeoisie . . . has converted the physician, the lawyer, the priest, the poet, the people of science into its paid wage-laborers," they wrote in *The Communist Manifesto* (1848). "Constant revolutionizing of production, uninterrupted disturbance of all social conditions, everlasting uncertainty and agitation distinguish the bourgeois epoch. . . . All that is solid melts into air, all that is holy is profaned, and one is at last compelled to face, with sober senses, the real conditions of life."

Even as Marx was writing these words, Europe was undergoing an unprecedented economic decline. Revolution quickly followed, first in France in February 1848, then in Germany, Austria, Hungary, Poland, and Italy. In France, the government formed National Workshops, known as **ateliers,** in order to put the people back to work. But enrollment quickly swelled to a size that the government could not handle—120,000 by June—and, fearing they had inadvertently created an army of the dissatisfied and unemployed, the government disbanded the workshops. The reaction was swift and, on June 23, the working class rebelled. Three days later, after some of the bloodiest street fighting in European history, the rebels found themselves surrounded in their neighborhoods, with an estimated ten thousand dead. More died in the struggles that followed, and eleven thousand others were imprisoned and deported to the French colonies, particularly to North Africa. It was, Marx wrote, "the first great battle . . . between the two classes that split modern society." For a few brief weeks, Delacroix's *Liberty Leading the People* was removed from storage and put on public view, and on December 10, 1848, Louis Napoleon Bonaparte, nephew of the first emperor, was elected president of France in a landslide election.

FRENCH PAINTING

Rosa Bonheur. One of the first truly successful painters of working class subjects was ROSA BONHEUR [BON-ur] (1822–1899). She disliked life in Paris, where she had grown up, preferring the rural life. A student of zoology, Bonheur made detailed studies out of doors and even painted there, directly from nature, which was not yet common practice. When studying the anatomy of animals at the Paris slaughterhouses or when observing horses at the Paris horse fairs, Bonheur dressed in men's suits because, she explained, women's clothing interfered with her work. By dressing as a man she was able to move in a world from which she would have otherwise been excluded. She described herself as of a "brusque and almost savage nature," as well as "perfectly feminine" and proud of being a woman.

After winning a first-class medal at the 1848 French Salon, Bonheur was commissioned in 1849 by the French government to paint *Plowing in the Nievernais: The Dressing of the Vines* (fig. 17.16), which established her as a leading painter in France. The painting portrays peasant life in harmony with nature, especially with the animal kingdom. Depicted with almost photographic realism is a scene of the good agrarian life in which the soil is fertile, the oxen are strong, and the weather is favorable. It seems to illustrate lines written by Bonheur's contemporary George Sand (another woman who dressed in men's clothing) in her 1846 novel *The Devil's Pond*, which describes "a truly beautiful sight, a noble subject for a painter. At the far end of the flat ploughland, a handsome young man was driving a magnificent team [of] oxen."

Gustave Courbet. While Sand and Bonheur admired the French peasantry, GUSTAVE COURBET [koor-BAY] (1819–1877) refused to idealize working life. A Realist, Courbet preferred simply to tell things as they were. A group of large paintings he exhibited in the Paris Salon of 1850–51 outraged conservative critics, and Courbet found himself defending not only his works but the "honest truth" of the people who were their subjects. He had, in fact, returned to his native village, Ornans, in 1849, after the revolution and painted the realities of life experienced by the peasant farmers.

A Burial at Ornans (fig. 17.17) angered the public in part because it seemed, at the very least, pretentious. At 10′3″ 20′10″, it is of a size generally reserved for only the most serious allegories and histories. A distant relative of Courbet's, one C. E. Teste, is being buried, and the mayor of Ornans, the justice of the peace, Courbet's father, and his three sisters are among the mourners who line up across the painting, echoing the horizon line's contour. Even the grave seems an extension of the Loue valley that cuts through the plateau behind them. Nevertheless, the painting is emotionally unfocused. No one's eyes are fixed on the same place, not even on the grave or the coffin. The dog stares away uninterestedly. The religious import of the scene is undermined by the way the cross seems to sit askew on the far horizon. The emotional impact of death is entirely deromanticized as well. We are witness here to a simple matter of fact.

The work's lack of idealism is especially evident if we compare it to Bonheur's *Plowing in the Nivernais.* Where

FIGURE 17.16 Rosa Bonheur, *Plowing in the Nivernais: The Dressing of the Vines*, 1849, oil on canvas, 5′9″ × 8′8″ (1.75 × 2.64 m), F. R. 64. Musée d'Orsay, Paris, France. Erich Lessing/Art Resource, NY. Bonheur studied directly from her subject to create this factual record of nature's grandeur. Previously, such subject matter was not considered worthy of an artist's attention and certainly would not have been depicted on such a large scale.

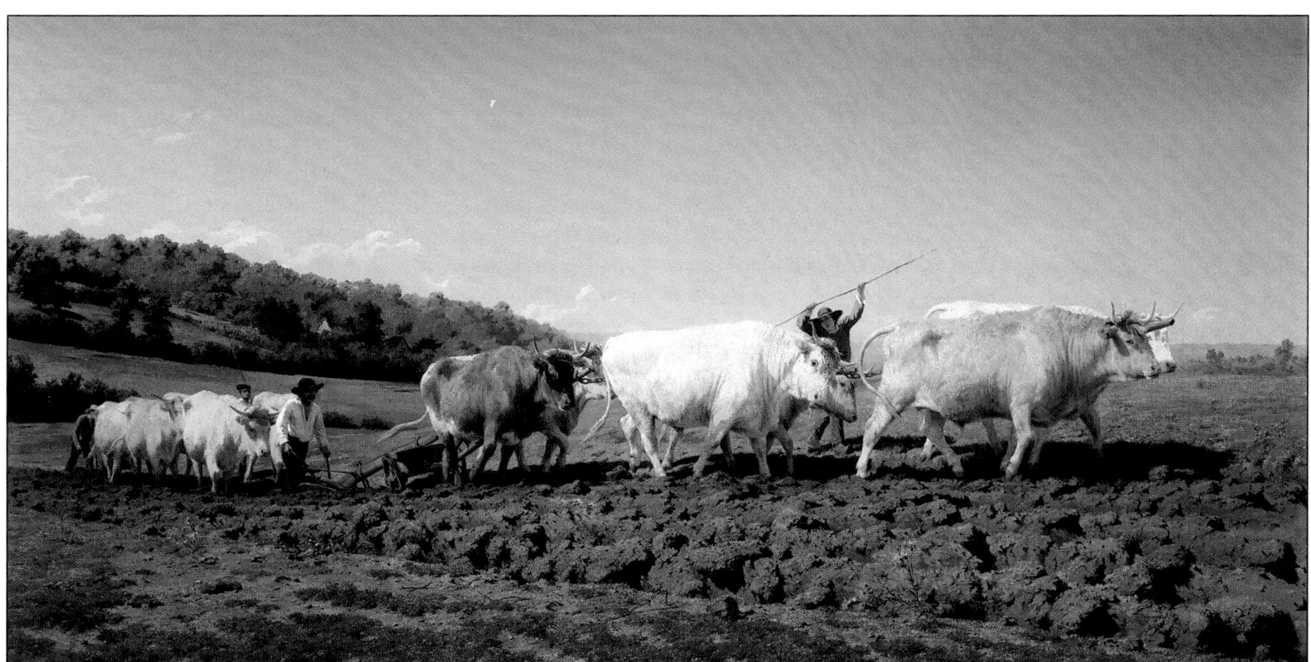

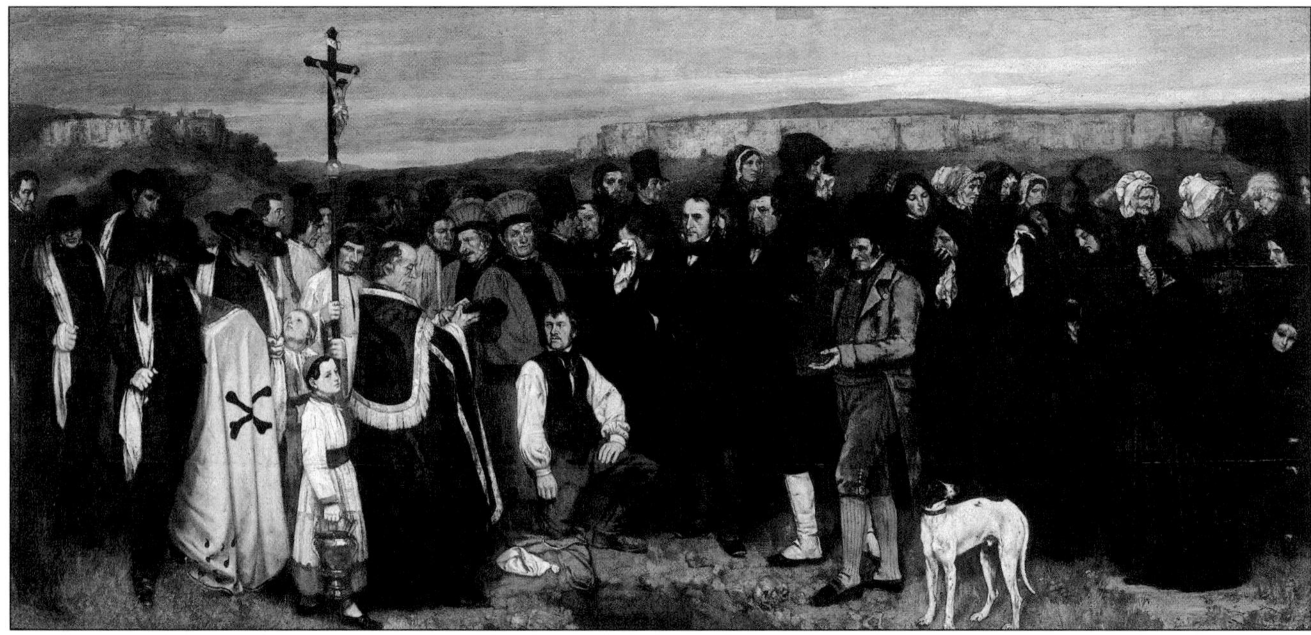

FIGURE 17.17 Gustave Courbet, *A Burial at Ornans*, 1849, oil on canvas, ca. 10′3″ × 20′10″ (3.10 × 6.40 m). Musee d'Orsay, Paris, France. Photo: Herve Lewandowski. © Reunion des Musees Nationaux/Art Resource, NY. The extremely hostile reaction of the public to this painting was due to the fact that the subject was not elevated, glorified, or romanticized—Courbet referred to this as the burial of Romanticism. He said, "Show me an angel and I'll paint one."

the figures in Courbet's painting seem static, forming an almost flat wall of humanity in front of the viewer, Bonheur's similarly horizontal format is dynamic. On the left, the hills lead downward and away from the viewer; on the right, the oxen move upward and toward the viewer.

Edouard Manet. The most characteristic Realist painter was EDOUARD MANET [man-AY] (1832–1883). Born into a well-to-do family, Manet was a sensitive and cultured man who studied literature and music (he married his piano teacher). After Manet twice failed the entrance exam to the Naval Training School, his family permitted him to study art. Manet had an academic training, which included copying paintings at the Louvre. He particularly admired the artists Hals, Velázquez, and Goya, all of whom worked in a painterly style, letting the brushstrokes show.

His *Luncheon on the Grass* (fig. 17.18), often referred to by its French title *Le Déjeuner sur l'herbe*, was painted in 1863. That year, the official Salon jury rejected over four thousand paintings, producing such an uproar from disappointed painters and their supporters that Napoleon III set up a separate salon to exhibit the rejected paintings, the Salon des Refusés (Salon of the Rejected). Thus, there were two salons, and the monopoly of academicism had been broken. But even at the Salon des Refusés, *Luncheon on the Grass* was regarded as shocking and scandalous by many. In fact, Manet had not painted an actual event, as the public thought; instead, his sources were highly respectable. The poses of the three central figures were derived from an engraving made about 1520 by the Italian artist Marcantonio Raimondi after a painting of the *Judgment of Paris* by Raphael.

It was his painting style, above all, that offended many. He painted directly on the canvas with thinned oil paint, which permitted him to wipe off any mistakes, the traces of which may sometimes still be seen. When the composition was determined, he executed the final painting directly with large brushstrokes. Instead of the smooth surfaces admired by the public, Manet's brushstrokes were strong, quick, and remain fully visible.

Manet's way of painting was fresh and direct. Rather than using carefully wrought highlights and shadows to make forms appear three dimensional, Manet intentionally flattened forms and used rapid, loose brushwork. This was criticized as carelessness or incompetence by many critics.

AMERICAN PAINTING

Winslow Homer. During the time that France and the rest of Europe were enduring class struggle and adjusting to the new industrial world, Americans had one thing on their minds—the Civil War, which gave impetus to American Realism. Recording events in the Civil War for *Harper's Weekly* was a young illustrator named Winslow Homer (1836–1910). He specialized in camp

Critical Thinking

REALISM AND FEMINISM

In the last quarter century, feminist scholars of literature, music, and art began an intensive study of works created by women. Bringing sociological, economic, and historical approaches to the study of works by women, feminist scholars raised questions about the ways in which women have been portrayed in art created by men. One example of this concern is the extent to which paintings that include both men and women may show the men clothed and the women nude, as Edouard Manet's *Le Déjeuner sur l'herbe* (fig. 17.18). In this painting, two fully clothed men sit in a park-like setting with a nude woman. Why, we might ask, are the men clothed, yet the woman unclothed? Why is the nude woman looking directly out at the viewer? Why is there a second woman, clothed, in the background? What is suggested about the relations of the men and women in the painting? What roles are assumed by each?

To what extent do feminist considerations enhance your understanding and appreciation of a painting like *Le Déjeuner sur l'herbe?* To what extent does the painting reflect a particularly male or masculine sensibility? To what extent does the representation of women (and men) in the painting reflect the time and place in which it was created?

FIGURE 17.18 Edouard Manet, *Luncheon on the Grass (Le Déjeuner sur l'herbe)*, 1863, oil on canvas, 7′ × 8′10″ (2.10 × 2.60 m), Musée d'Orsay, Paris. An outraged public deemed this painting indecent for depicting a naked woman out of doors with two clothed men. Actually painted in Manet's studio from models, it was based on a print by Marcantonio Raimondi after a painting by Raphael, ca. 1520, of the *Judgment of Paris*.

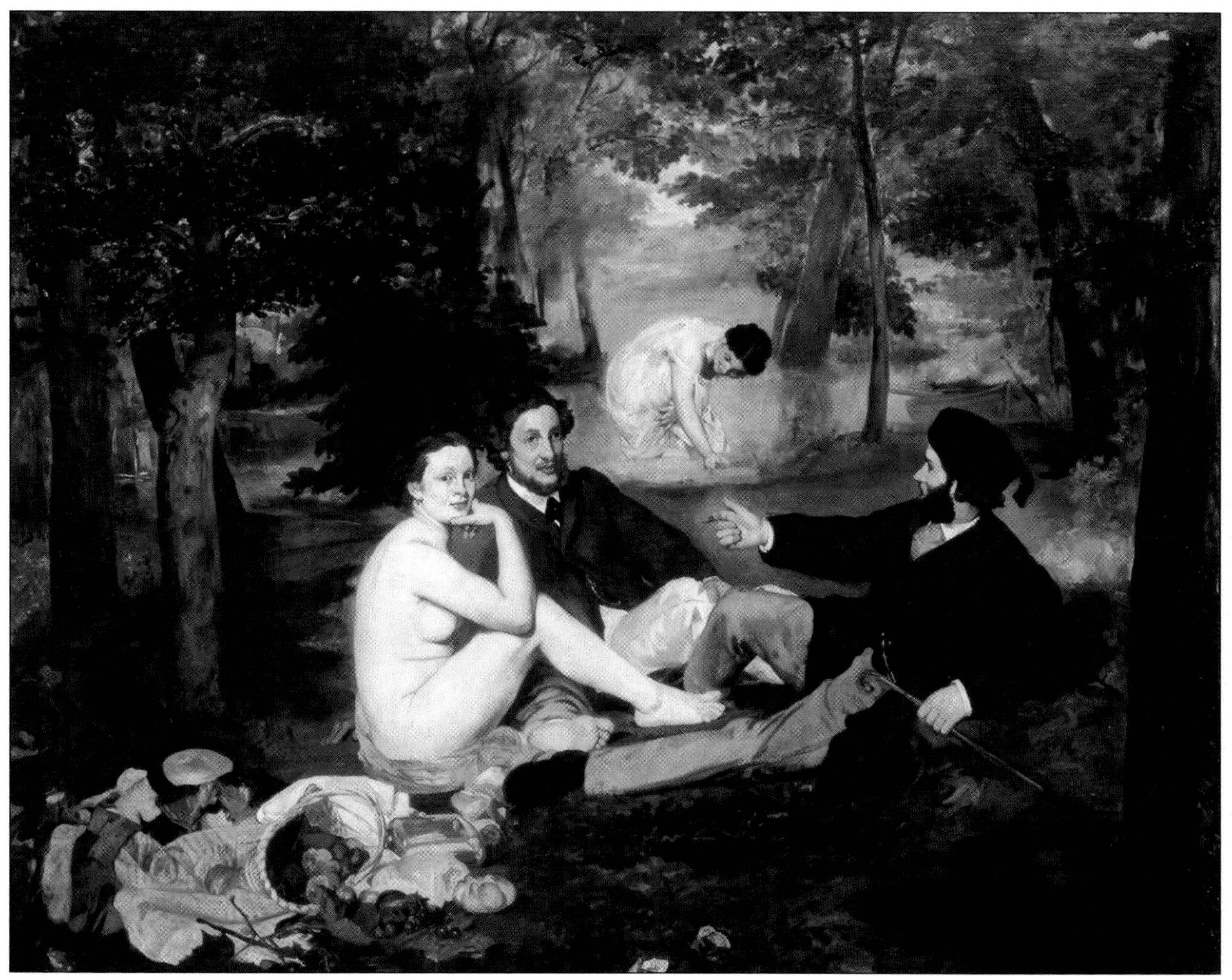

life and avoided the brutal scenes of battle captured by the new medium of photography. Homer's painting career began soon after the war with *Prisoners from the Front* (fig. 17.19), of 1866. This work depicts the surrender of three Confederate soldiers to a Union officer, a recognizable portrait of General Francis Channing Barlow, a distant cousin of Homer's. The painting was considered remarkable, even at the time, for the unrepentant, even arrogant attitude of the central figure, who, hand on hip, stares defiantly at General Barlow. Here, some felt, was an image of a nation at odds with itself.

After the painting's exhibition at the National Academy of Design in 1866, it was displayed in Paris at the World Exposition of 1867. Homer accompanied it and, once there, became acquainted with the work of Gustave Courbet and Edouard Manet. Manet's willingness to paint everyday life in a direct and informal way especially appealed to Homer. His later paintings continued to evoke the aesthetics of photography, but they also showed brilliant color and brushwork, borrowed from Manet, which insisted on their status as paintings by emphasizing the quality of pigment on canvas.

Thomas Eakins. Another American Realist was THOMAS EAKINS [AY-kins] (1844–1916). Eakins, from Philadelphia, referred to himself as a scientific realist. He was interested in human anatomy, in the construction of the human body, its muscles and bones, saying that he learned more from watching his fellow students wrestling in the studio than he did from drawing a posed model. He even took medical courses in anatomy at Jefferson Medical College in Philadelphia for two years. He saw no reason for artists to study the antique, as was customary in his time, favoring instead the study of nature, saying that nature is "just as varied and just as beautiful in our day as she was in the time of Phidias," noting that "the Greeks did not study the antique."

In *The Swimming Hole* (fig. 17.20), painted 1883–85, Eakins creates a composition around a series of studies of nude boys seen from different angles and in different poses, some still and other more active—especially the boy caught in mid-air as he dives off the rocks. Eakins was fascinated by the human body and dedicated to depicting it accurately in motion. He used photographs in his figure studies. Eakins taught at the Pennsylvania Academy of Fine Arts in Philadelphia from 1870 to 1886,

FIGURE 17.19 Winslow Homer, *Prisoners from the Front*, 1866, oil on canvas, 24″ × 38″ (60.9 × 96.5 cm), signed and dated (lower right): HOMER 1866. The Metropolitan Museum of Art. Gift of Mrs. Frank B. Porter, 1922. (22.207). Photograph © 1985 The Metropolitan Museum of Art, NY. For such factual narrative depictions of aspects of life in America, Homer was known during his lifetime as "the greatest American artist."

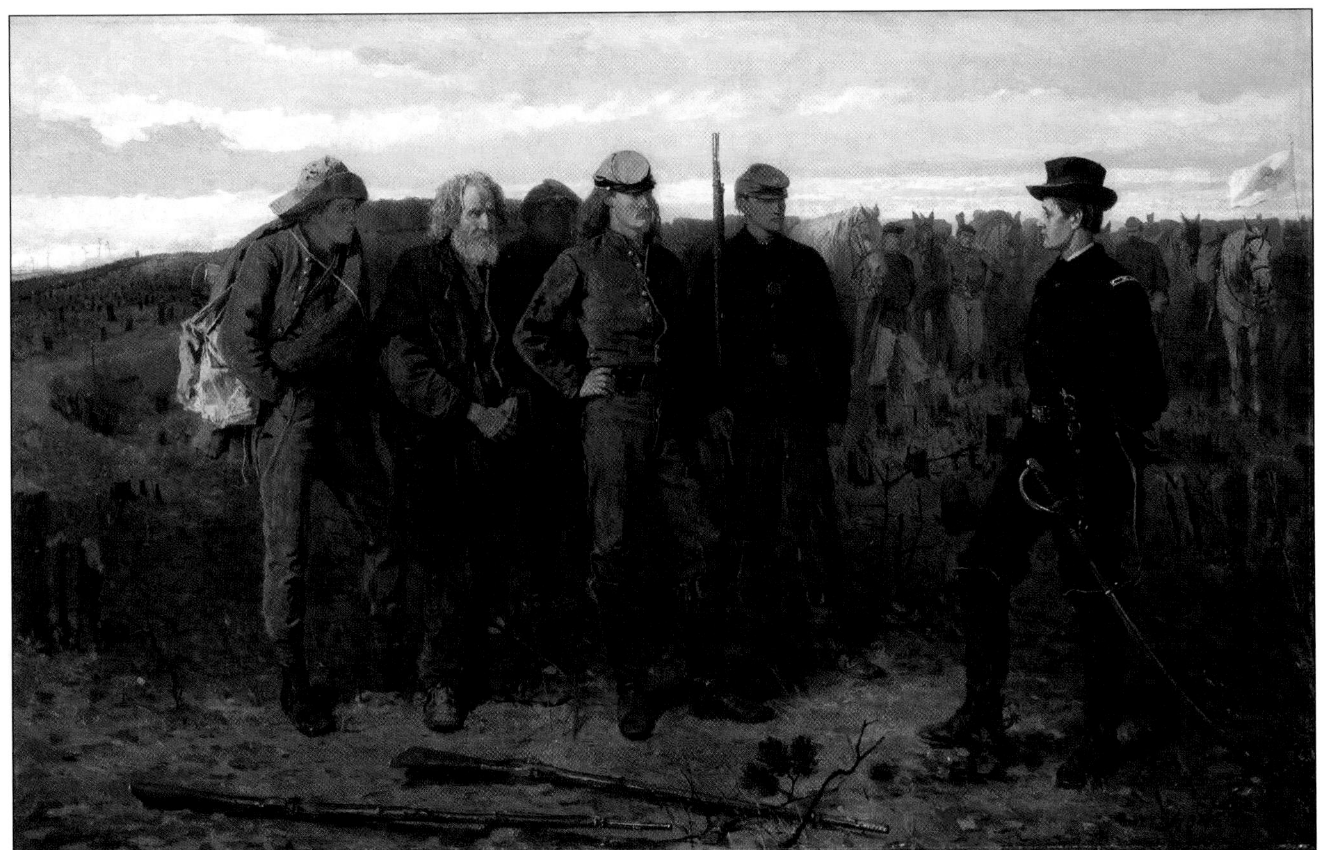

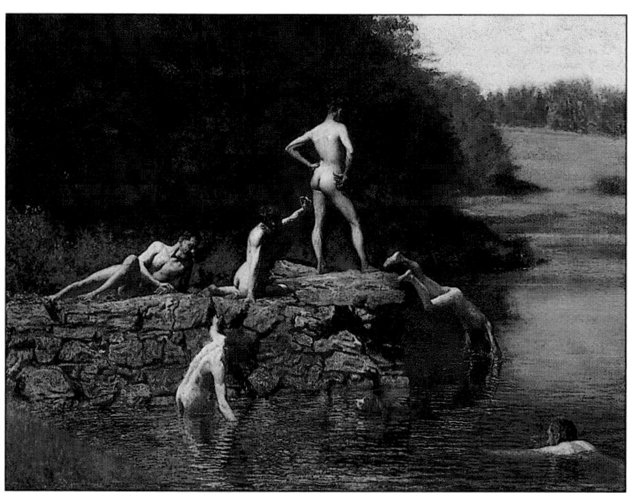

FIGURE 17.20 Thomas Eakins, *The Swimming Hole*, ca. 1883–85, oil on canvas, 27″ × 36″ (68.5 × 91.4 cm), Amon Carter Museum. Purchased by the Friends of Art, Fort Worth Art Association, 1925; acquired by Amon Carter Museum, 1990 from the Modern Art Museum of Fort Worth through grants and donations from the Amon G. Carter Foundation, the Sid W. Richardson Foundation, the Anne Burnett and Charles Tandy Foundation, Capital Cities/ABC Foundation, Fort Worth Star-Telegram, The R.D. and Joan Dale Hubbard Foundation and the people of Fort Worth. As part of his quest for realistic factuality, in the foreground, Eakins painted himself as part of the group.

until forced to resign because of a scandal he created by introducing a nude male model to a women's drawing class. Eakins had a serious personality and his approach was intellectual and methodical. But his realism was too harsh for most people and he sold few paintings during his lifetime.

Jennie Augusta Brownscombe. Another American. Jennie Augusta Brownscombe (1850–1936), after the death of her father when she was eighteen, earned a living by selling her paintings to be reproduced on Christmas cards and calendars. Consequently, her art became widely known. She moved to Manhattan, studied art, and was one of the founders of the Art Students League, where she later taught.

The setting in her *Love's Young Dream* (fig. 17.21), painted in 1887, must have been familiar to her, for she was born in rural Pennsylvania in a log cabin. She often depicts country life, family, and tradition in sentimental ways. Her narrative paintings are realistic, the details enhancing the appeal of a charming story—as the cat playing with the ball of yarn that has fallen from the lap of the older woman, presumably the mother in this family—which also recalls the artist's own, as Brownscombe was an only child.

THE RISE OF PHOTOGRAPHY

Photography was invented simultaneously in England and France: in 1839 by William Henry Fox Talbot (1800–1877) and LOUIS-JACQUES-MANDE DAGUERRE

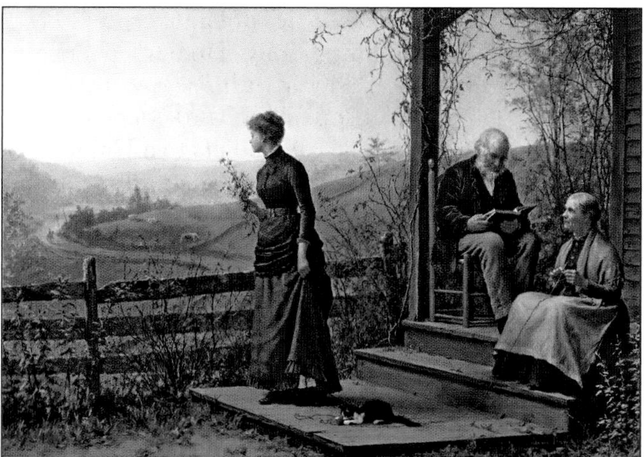

FIGURE 17.21 Jennie Augusta Brownscombe, *Love's Young Dream*, 1887, oil on canvas, $21\frac{1}{4}''$ × $32\frac{1}{2}''$ (54 × 81.6 cm), National Museum of Women in the Arts, Washington, DC. Gift of Wallace and Wilhelmina Holladay. Brownscombe suggests complex stories and relationships through simple compositions painted in a realistic detailed style.

[duh-GARE] (1787–1851). Before photography, an image could *look* spontaneous and immediate; now it could *be* spontaneous and immediate. Moreover, because the photographic image was the product of a machine, it had the aura, at least, of being purely objective, lacking the subjective intervention of the artist. Talbot's images made on sensitized paper between 1833 and 1839 were precursors of modern photographic prints.

Daguerreotypes. Through competition from photography, painted portraits underwent a rapid decline and photographs largely replaced them for a while. The **daguerreotype,** named for Daguerre's process, was the earliest photograph, produced on silver or silver-covered copper plate. In Paris in 1849 alone, over a hundred thousand photographic daguerreotypes, mostly portraits, were sold to people of every rank and class. In England, photography studios sprang up everywhere to satisfy the craze for photographic portraits (fig. 17.22). The photograph had the advantage of capturing reality accurately and immediately, and as its technology rapidly developed, making it easier and easier to use, it captured the Realist imagination.

Eadweard Muybridge. As camera technology quickly improved, it revealed more and more about the nature of reality. When, in 1872, the former governor of California, Leland Stanford, bet a friend $25,000 that a running horse had all four feet off the ground when either trotting or galloping, he hired EADWEARD MUYBRIDGE [MWE-bridge] (1830–1904) to photograph one of his horses in motion. Along a racetrack at Stanford's ranch in Palo Alto, California, Muybridge lined up a series of cameras with trip wires that would snap the shutter as the horse ran by. For the first time, the muscular and physical movements of an animal in motion were recorded. Muybridge's studies of animal

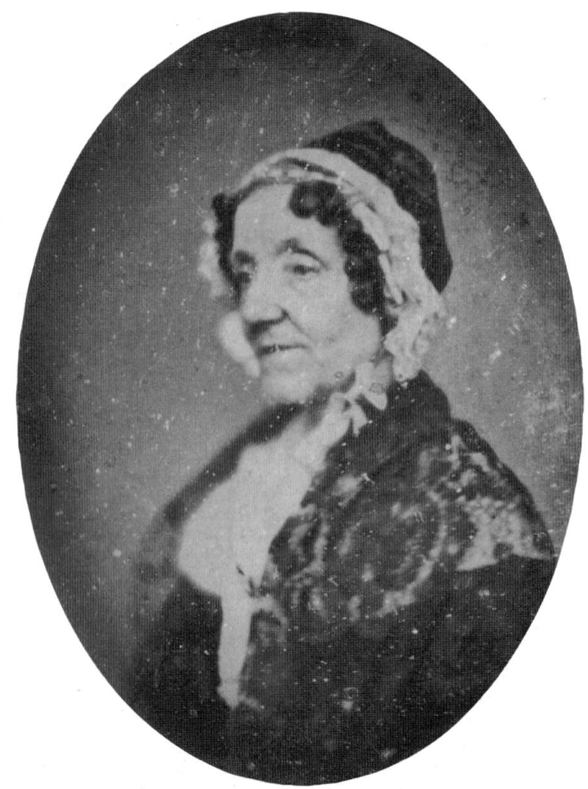

FIGURE 17.22 Richard Beard, *Maria Edgeworth*, 1841, daguerreotype, $2\frac{1}{8}'' \times 1\frac{3}{4}''$ (5.4 × 4.4 cm), National Portrait Gallery, London. Beard's was the first British portrait studio, and the author Edgeworth one of his earliest customers. "It is a wonderful mysterious operation," she wrote. Daguerre's process was used until the end of the nineteenth century.

(fig. 17.23) and human locomotion at the University of Pennsylvania in 1883 would have a major impact on later painters.

Alfred Stieglitz. Photographer Alfred Stieglitz (1864–1946) had been interested in European modernist work since the turn of the century. Stieglitz was the first American to buy a Picasso. His own photographic talents captured the early modern era, its hustle, streets, and skylines. One classic photograph, *Winter, Fifth Avenue* (fig. 17.24), records Manhattan's main thoroughfare. Even progress and the growth of industry cannot protect those unlucky enough to be caught in this fierce snowstorm.

Gertrude Stanton Käsebier. The American Gertrude Stanton Käsebier (1852–1934) is considered among the finest photographers. She opened a portrait studio on Fifth Avenue, the most fashionable street in Manhattan. The studio was an immediate success with clients, and her own work exhibited there received favorable reviews.

Using photography as an aesthetic rather than a documentary medium, her subjects were frequently landscapes and figure compositions. This approach, known as **pictorialism,** is seen in *The Manger* (fig. 17.25), a print made around 1899. The lines are softened, the image intentionally slightly out of focus, the details obscured. This differs from the more frequent use of photography to capture a detailed record of a temporary scene. In fact, it has been questioned if there was even a baby in this posed photo. The reference to the birth of Jesus in a stable (the setting was a stable in Newport, RI) is evident.

Working with the photographer Alfred Stieglitz (fig. 17.24). Käsebier founded the Photo-Secession in

FIGURE 17.23 Eadweard Muybridge, *Annie G. Cantering, Saddled*, 1887, collotype print, sheet: 19″ × 24″; image: $7\frac{1}{2}'' \times 16\frac{1}{4}''$ (19 × 41.3 cm), Philadelphia Museum of Art, City of Philadelphia Trade and Convention Center, Dept. of Commerce (Commercial Museum). Muybridge's sequence studies would lead to the invention of the motion picture by the century's end.

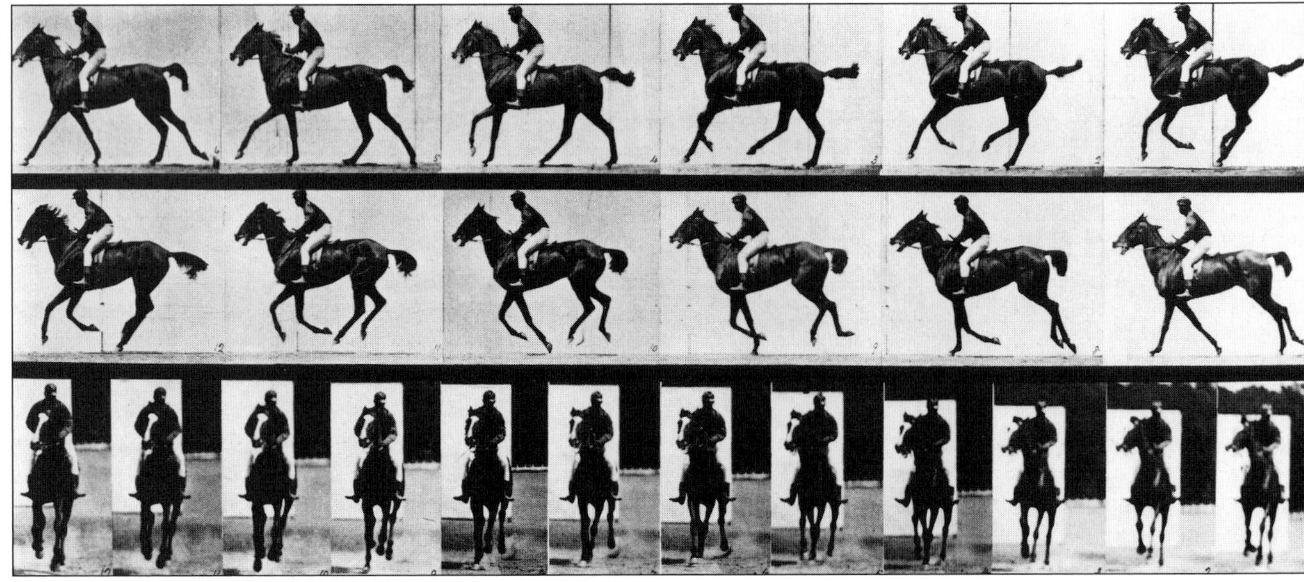

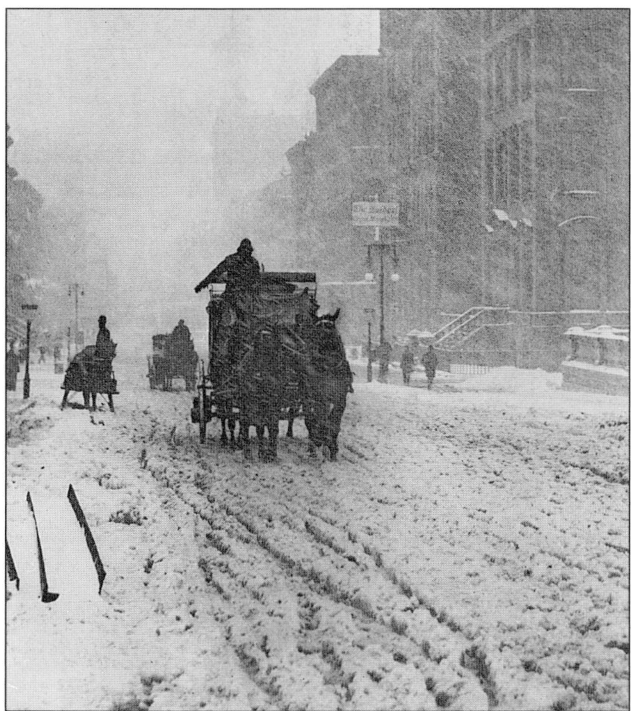

FIGURE 17.24 Alfred Stieglitz, *Winter, Fifth Avenue*, 1893, photogravure, $8\frac{5}{8}'' \times 6\frac{1}{16}''$ (21.9 × 15.4 cm), Museum of Modern Art, New York/Licensed by SCALA, Art Resource, NY. Stieglitz was not only the leading photographer of his day but, through his Gallery 291 in New York, the person most responsible for introducing European *avant-garde* art to the United States.

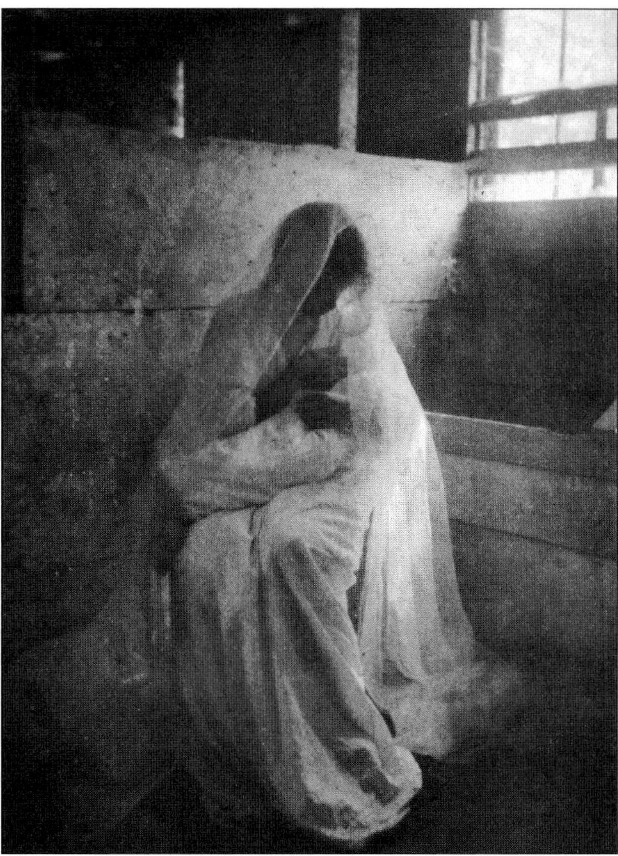

FIGURE 17.25 Gertrude Stanton Käsebier (1852–1934), American, *The Manger (Ideal Motherhood)*, ca. 1899, platinum print, $7\frac{5}{8}'' \times 5\frac{1}{2}''$ (19.4 × 14 cm), National Museum of Women in the Arts, Washington, D.C. Gift of the Holladay Foundation. One of the most popular photographs taken by Käsebier, this is an example of pictorialism in which photography is used, like other artistic media, to create an aesthetically satisfying image, rather than a documentary record.

1902, which encouraged the pictorial, rather than the documentary, use of photography.

SCULPTURE

The Statue of Liberty. In 1875, a year before the centennial celebration of the American Revolution, organizers in France conceived the idea of commemorating the event with a colossal statue. A Franco-American Union was founded to raise funds, and the architect Frédéric-Auguste Bartholdi (1834–1904) was hired to design the work. *Liberty Enlightening the World*, commonly known as the *Statue of Liberty* (fig. 17.26), was the result. Bartholdi first made a nine-foot model of the sculpture, and then GUSTAVE EIFFEL [EE-FELL] (1832–1923)—the French engineer who created the Eiffel Tower—designed a huge iron framework to support the giant sheets of copper, molded in the shape of Bartholdi's model. All the components were transported across the ocean, and in 1884, construction began on Liberty Island in New York Harbor. The sculpture, dedicated in 1886, is itself over 151 feet high and rests on a 150-feet-high concrete pedestal faced with granite. Sculpture and pedestal in turn sit on an eleven-point star, the walls of which are part of old Fort Wood. The Statue of Liberty remains a symbol of welcome and freedom to generations of people immigrating to the United States.

Edmonia Lewis. Among the more interesting sculptors of the era was Edmonia Lewis (1845–after 1911), an American, born outside Albany, to an American Indian mother and an African-American father. After both parents died while she was still a child, she was raised by aunts on her mother's side. Her brother financed her education, and, in 1859, she entered Oberlin College in Ohio. There, however, she was accused of poisoning two classmates, beaten, tried, and acquitted. She moved to Boston and then on to Rome in 1865, were she was highly successful as a sculptor.

Lewis carved a variety of subjects, including portraits and religious themes, but perhaps most notable are those that relate to her biracial family background, such as *The Old Arrow Maker and his Daughter* (fig. 17.27), ca. 1872. Lewis created, a series of contrasts with exquisite carving, between flesh and muscle structure of old and young, male and female. The natural poses of the figures, their attention seemingly caught by the viewer's presence, convey a sense of latent energy.

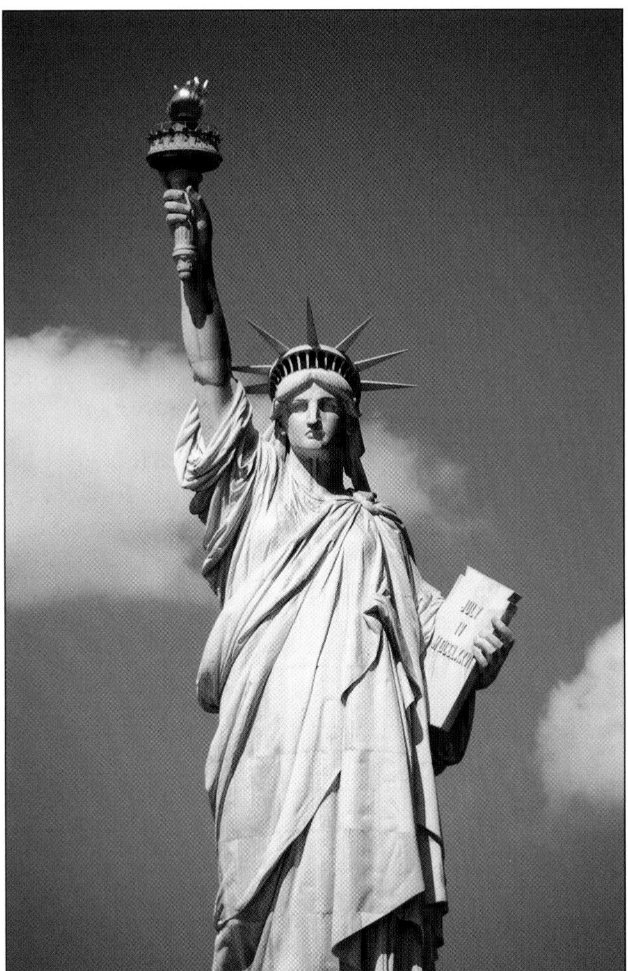

FIGURE 17.26 Frédéric-Auguste Bartholdi, *Statue of Liberty (Liberty Enlightening the World)*, Liberty Island, New York Harbor, 1875–84, copper sheeting over iron armature, height of figure 151′6″ (46.18 m). A gift of the French people, the *Statue of Liberty* has become the symbol of the United States. The monument portrays a crowned woman in classical garb, holding the torch high, while breaking underfoot the shackles of tyranny.

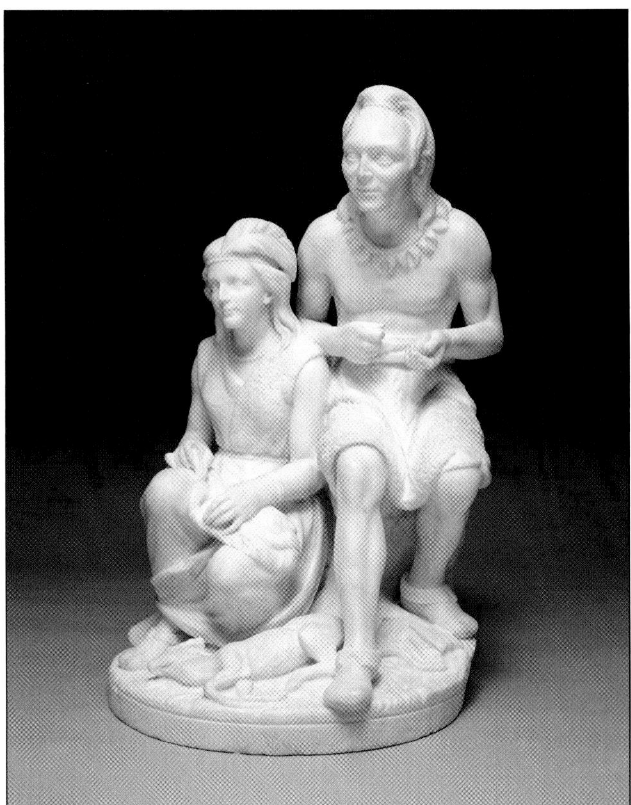

FIGURE 17.27 Edmonia Lewis, *The Old Arrow Maker and His Daughter*, ca. 1872, carved marble, $21\frac{1}{2}'' \times 12\frac{5}{8}'' \times 13\frac{3}{8}''$ ($54.75 \times 34.5 \times 34$ cm) Smithsonian American Art Museum, Washington, DC. Art Resource, NY. Lewis's mixed racial heritage is referenced in several of her sculptures. This work relates to her mother, a Chippewa Indian, while Lewis's *Forever Free*, the title referring to the end of slavery, relates to her father, an African American.

Anne Whitney. From a very different background was another American who moved to Rome to sculpt. ANNE WHITNEY (1821–1915), from Massachusetts, turned from writing poetry to creating sculpture when she was in her thirties. Independently wealthy and politically liberal, she was a member of a group of expatriate American women sculptors working in Rome. She returned to the United States in 1871, and made the model for the figure of the abolitionist senator *Charles Sumner* (fig. 17.28) in 1875, although it was not cast in bronze until 1902. She won the competition held by the Boston Art Committee for this commission, but it was rescinded when the Committee learned that Whitney was a woman. She completed the piece independently, many years later; it was her final work. In the Neoclassical style, the monument is grand in scale, and Sumner impressively powerful in Whitney's straightforward depiction.

LITERATURE

Honoré de Balzac. Like the painters of modern life, Realist writers aimed, above all, to represent contemporary life and manners with precision. In the case of HONORE DE BALZAC [BALL-zak] (1779–1850), the project was extensive: Balzac sought to represent contemporary life with encyclopedic completeness. In the nearly one hundred novels and stories that make up his series *La Comédie humaine*, Balzac touched on virtually every aspect of French society, from the urban working class and the country peasant, to the middle-class merchant, the new industrialists, and the bankrupt aristocracy. By 1816, while working as a law clerk in Paris, he would spend his evenings wandering through the streets, gathering details for his novels. "In listening to these people," he later recalled, "I felt I could champion their lives. I felt their rags upon my back. I walked with my feet in their tattered shoes; their desires, their wants—everything passed into my soul." His characters—there are over two thousand—often appear in more than one novel, establishing a sense of the interconnectedness of French life. Chief

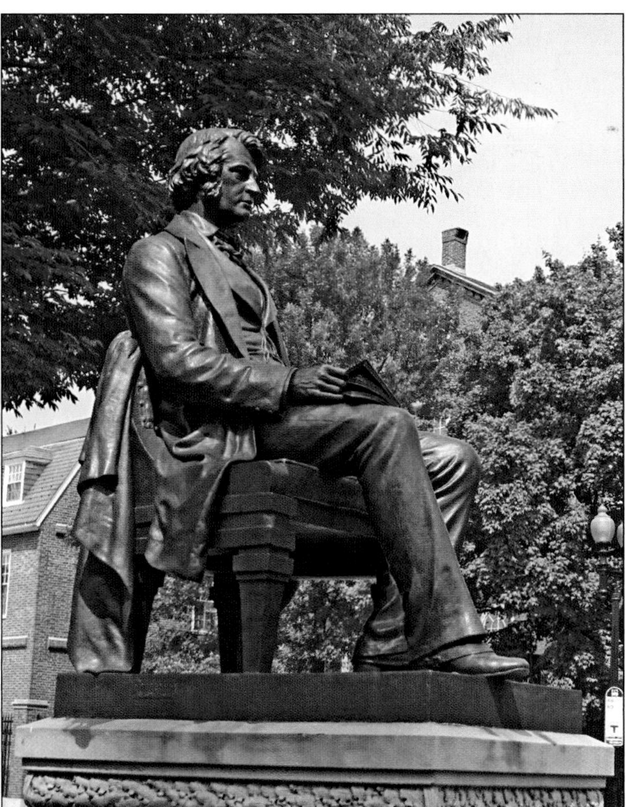

FIGURE 17.28 Anne Whitney, *Charles Sumner*, Harvard Square, Cambridge, MA, modeled 1875, cast 1902, bronze, ca. 7′1″ × 3′2″ × 4′8″ (2.16 × .97 × 1.4 m) (without base). This realistic portrayal of the abolitionist senator is in the Neoclassical style, which returned to the ideals of harmony and balance of the ancient Greeks and Romans, here used to create a sense of stately, noble grandeur.

among them is Eugéne Rastignac, the son of a poor provincial family who comes to Paris, mixes with nobility, builds a career as a politician, and generally leads a life of gambling and debauchery. At the climax of *Le Père Goriot*, Rastignac climbs to the top of the hill at Père Lachaise cemetery and, in one of the most famous moments in French literature, faces the city that threatens to consume him: "There lay the glittering world that he had hoped to conquer. He stared at the humming hive as if sucking out its honey in advance and pronounced these impressive words, 'It's you or me now!'" Rastignac's moment on the top of the hill is entirely Romantic. Pitting himself against the world, he is caught in the web of his own Romanticism: from a Realist's point of view, a self-indulgent fate.

Gustave Flaubert. The Realist novel that represents the most thorough attack on the Romantic sensibility is *Madame Bovary*, published in 1857 after five years in the writing, by GUSTAVE FLAUBERT [floh-BEAR] (1821–1880). Flaubert's heroine—if, indeed, *heroine* is a word that can be used to describe her, she is such a banal figure—is Emma Bovary, the wife of a country doctor who seeks to reinvent her life in the manner of the romantic novels she reads so voraciously.

Emma desperately takes lovers to overcome the incessant boredom of everyday life, spends money as if she were nobility, falls into the deepest debt, and finally, in the most romantic gesture of all, commits suicide by swallowing arsenic.

The novel took five years to write because Flaubert sought, in every sentence, to find what he called "*le mot juste*," exactly the right word needed to describe each situation. In this, Flaubert felt, he was proceeding like the modern scientist, investigating the lives of his characters in precisely the same way that the scientist pursues research through careful and systematic observation.

Emile Zola. Flaubert's scientific approach to writing became the standard for all subsequent French Realist writing, particularly the work of the so called French naturalists, who emphasized the influence of heredity and environment in determining the fate of the literary characters they created. A prominent naturalist, EMILE ZOLA [ZOH-la] (1840–1902) saw society as a kind of grand laboratory and the people in it as data for his study of the ways in which humans were determined. In books such as *Germinal*, which chronicled the life of French miners, and *Nana*, which detailed the life of a prostitute, Zola used naturalistic techniques to reflect his fatalistic vision of the world.

Realist Writing. Important English Realist novelists of the time include Charles Dickens (1812–1870), Anthony Trollope (1815–82), and George Eliot (1819–1880), the pen name of Mary Ann Evans. Eliot's *Middlemarch* (1872) is a portrayal of nineteenth-century life in an English country village. Trollope, an inspector of rural mail deliveries, created an imaginary English country called Barsetshire, the cathedral town of which he named Barchester, and he set a long series of novels in and around this fictional locale. The Barchester novels capture the spirit of nineteenth-century rural life in a series of similarly interconnected tales. Where Trollope and Eliot chronicled country life, Dickens wrote mostly about the increasingly dark urban environment epitomized by London, attacking conditions in the English workhouses in *Oliver Twist*, published serially in 1837–38, and the evils brought on by industrialization in *Hard Times* (1854). Like their continental counterparts, the English novelists wrote about the world in which they lived and that they knew most thoroughly.

In America, nineteenth-century fiction writers tended toward Romantic themes and styles until very late in the century. While Realism was spreading through Europe, American writers, such as Edgar Allan Poe (1809–1849), Nathaniel Hawthorne (1804–1864), and Herman Melville (1819–1891), wrote fiction characterized, in Hawthorne's terms, as "romances" rather than as "novels." In the fiction of these romance writers, characters and settings were not depicted with the social realism of their European counterparts. In Hawthorne, dialogue borders on the archaic and in Melville on the theatrical. Description in the

Then & Now

EMERSON, THOREAU, AND THE AMERICAN ENVIRONMENT

During the nineteenth century, the American landscape was considered a source of consolation as well as of sustenance. Nature was celebrated in poems and letters, essays, lectures, and books, most notably by the New England Transcendentalist writers Ralph Waldo Emerson and Henry David Thoreau. For Emerson, nature was a moral teacher, a guide that contained lessons in how to live life properly. Nature was intimately connected with the life of humanity, and thus was not something to be conquered or contested, but rather a dimension of reality to bond with. For Emerson, nature was less to be used as a resource than to be treasured as a gift from God.

Emerson's embrace of the spirit of nature reflects the reverence felt toward the natural world by those who have long made their living from its bountiful resources. And his perspective is shared by a number of contemporary groups concerned with finding the physical, spiritual, and intellectual common ground necessary for sustaining the earth's life.

Emerson's spiritual counterpart in appreciating nature, Henry David Thoreau, was less mystical in his attachment to the natural world but no less devoted to it. Thoreau loved to ramble in the woods, to scrutinize their every nook and cranny to see what he could find there. At the same time, Thoreau found in nature time to deliberate about those few essentials things in life that really matter. "Let us spend one day as deliberately as Nature," he admonishes his readers in *Walden*. For Thoreau, perhaps even more than for Emerson, nature provided an escape from the corruptions of civilization, a place to retreat for spiritual recreation.

In the thought and work of Emerson and Thoreau lie the seeds of the modern environmental movement. Today's Sierra Club and other ecologically minded groups are working to preserve the American land, to conserve the country's resources. They continue the tradition of valuing the natural world not for the profits that can be made from it or even for the solace it can provide, but simply for itself, for its beauty. Environmentalists lament the heedless destruction of natural resources, recognizing they are limited. Environmentalists also view nature as a treasure to be preserved, enjoyed by all and owned by none, most truly possessed by those who have learned to understand the glory and the grandeur Emerson and Thoreau discovered in nature.

works of both is highly symbolic and often poetic, rather than serving as a vehicle for a sharp-edged realism.

RUSSIAN LITERATURE

One of the glories of Russian literature is the development of the Russian novel in the middle to late nineteenth century. Of the many novels written during this half-century period, those of Fyodor Dostoyevsky and Leo Tolstoy tower above the rest. Among the most accomplished of Realist writers, they wrote novels on a grand scale, covering all aspects of Russian culture and society.

Fyodor Dostoyevsky. FYODOR DOSTOYEVSKY [doss-toh-YEF-skee] (1821–1881) was the son of a Moscow doctor and landowner who was murdered by his serfs when Fyodor was eighteen. After studying military engineering, Dostoyevsky spent a year in the army before taking up a literary career, the most dramatic event of which was his arrest and imprisonment for conspiring to set up a secret printing press and discussing political and social ideas banned by the czarist regime. After eight months, Dostoyevsky was sentenced to death, only to receive a last-minute reprieve; his sentence was commuted to four years of hard labor and an additional four years of military service. His prison reading was restricted to the New Testament, which he read avidly, and which informs the novels he wrote upon his release, especially *Crime and Punishment* (1866) and *The Brothers Karamazov* (1881).

Dostoyevsky's realism (which he described as a "higher realism") is underpinned by the psychological rather than the social. His interest lies not so much in presenting a panorama of Russian urban life, but in probing the tensions and anxieties that animate and motivate behavior.

His narrative impulse is richly dramatic, realizing itself forcefully in scenes of conflict. The interview scenes with the ax-murderer Raskolnikov and the detective Porfiry Petrovich in *Crime and Punishment* exemplify the drama inherent in his dialogue. Raskolnikov's behavior throughout the novel reflects Dostoyevsky's acute understanding of human psychology, and reveals the author's belief that any transgression of the moral law—in Raskolnikov's case, murder—no matter how reasonable it may appear, results in the guilt of a tormented conscience. The punishment is internal, undeniable, and torturous.

Leo Tolstoy. LEO TOLSTOY [TOHL-stoy] (1828–1910) was born into an aristocratic world, one replete with the trappings of high society, including servants, fine cuisine, extravagant clothing, and the manifold opportunities that come with great wealth. As a young man, Tolstoy studied oriental languages at the University of Kazan, but left without taking a degree, returning to run the family estate in Yosnaya Polyana, south of Moscow.

War and Peace was published in 1869. Set in the Napoleonic age, the novel explores the nature of history and the role that great men play in influencing the development of historical events. The book combines speculation

Critical Thinking

MEMOIR, FACT, AND TRUTH

Autobiography and memoir have long been important as an overlapping literary genre. Among the earliest autobiographies, St. Augustine's *Confessions* set the standard for self-analysis and self-reflection. Autobiography continued to be of interest to readers, particularly autobiographies of great men, such as those of the religious writer John Bunyan, the historian Edward Gibbon, the scientist Charles Darwin, and the social philosopher, such as Jean-Jacques Rousseau. Autobiography and memoir continue to draw readers into the twenty-first century. Some recent critics believe that these nonfiction prose genres have now outstripped the novel in popularity and importance as a literary genre—though other critics contest that claim.

But there is no question as to the popular appeal of memoir, so much so that the television host Oprah Winfrey chose a memoir, James Frey's *A Million Little Pieces* for her enormously popular and influential Oprah's Book Club. When reports surfaced that the author had fabricated significant portions of his memoir, wildly exaggerating some of his experiences and brazenly inventing others, Oprah withdrew her endorsement of the book. A national debate ensued about the extent to which an autobiographer or memoirist was obliged to tell the truth by sticking to facts and events, and leave invention and fiction to novelists—or to reclassify the work as a novel.

What is your view? To what extent do you think writers of autobiography and memoir should include in their books only actual facts and real events? Or should they, perhaps, identify them as fiction, instead? Is it possible for there to exist autobiographical works, such as memoirs, that contain some invented parts or that exaggerate some details to get at what their authors have called a "larger truth"?

on philosophical questions, such as necessity and free will, causation, and human destiny, with social concerns, such as agrarian reform. It also dramatizes ideas about the nature of the Russian state, as well as being a chronicle of the lives of several Russian families, with an emphasis on the philosophy of marriage. The novel contrasts the glories of nature and the simple life with the superficiality and artifice of civilization, celebrating the natural, privileging intuition over analysis, and emphasizing hope in the basic goodness of life rather than more studied forms of civilized learning and behavior.

During the writing of his second masterpiece, *Anna Karenina* (1873–77), Tolstoy experienced a moral and religious crisis that set him on a course that would change his life. *Anna Karenina* possesses all the realism of Tolstoy's earlier novel, but during its writing, the author began to have doubts about the book's secular emphasis, and so introduced a tone of moral criticism into the work, not only of Anna's adultery, but also of other characters' violations of society's moral norms. Even so, Tolstoy keeps the didactic impulse from overwhelming his literary artistry. Although he disapproves of Anna's adulterous behavior, he portrays her as a powerfully attractive woman, the site of struggle between his artistic sympathy and his moral judgment.

Anton Chekhov. The finest examples of Russian drama are the plays of its foremost dramatist, ANTON CHEKHOV [CHECK-off] (1860–1904). A short-story writer as well as a playwright, Chekhov began publishing fiction and sketches in newspapers and journals while studying medicine, in order to help support his large family. His fiction was well received, far better, initially, than the plays he would begin writing in the 1880s. Although Chekhov is celebrated as a major influence for later writers such as James Joyce and Ernest Hemingway, his plays are heralded in their own right as Modernist masterpieces and as precursors of important trends in modern theater.

Chekhov's plays, such as *The Three Sisters* and *The Cherry Orchard*, lack the intense melodramatic character of those by other realist dramatists, such as Henrik Ibsen. They don't tell stories, nor do they build toward tragic climaxes. Instead, Chekhov creates characters that are very lifelike in their inability to find happiness, their uncertainty about the future, and their indecisiveness in achieving their desires.

Because Chekhov was writing at a time when the old social order in Russia was dying, his plays have often been seen as dramatizations of the disappearance of the land-owning gentry as a source of authority and cultural value. Yet the playwright's interest lies in human nature, in individuals caught in a world undergoing great transformation. The characters in plays like *The Three Sisters* and *The Cherry Orchard* are neither heroes nor villains. They do not operate as mouthpieces for the dramatist's views. Indeed, their very inability to articulate their feelings, or even to act on them, adds poignancy to their suffering. Chekhov's insight into the truths of human experience is unmatched in modern drama.

NEW SCIENCES: PASTEUR AND DARWIN

The interest in the precise, objective description of things evidenced in Realist painting and literature was shared as well by the philosophers and scientists of the age. In France, the scientist LOUIS PASTEUR [pass-TER] (1822–1895) began to look at organisms smaller than the eye can see—micro-organisms that he claimed

Cultural Impact

The Romantic era saw radical changes in the political makeup of Europe and America. Greece achieved independence; Germany and Italy became unified nations. America, which had gained its independence in the last quarter of the eighteenth century, became a political world power and established itself as a distinctive artistic presence, especially in painting, fiction, and poetry. France, which shared with America the revolutionary ideals of freedom and equality, established the Napoleonic Code, which continues to govern the legal system of the French-speaking world today.

Deep social changes took root during the Romantic age and throughout the nineteenth century. The primary cause of social change was the Industrial Revolution, which altered the way in which many people made their living; with the rise of industry, the demise of agrarian life began. Instead of living on farms and in small country villages, people began migrating to large urban centers, where they found work in manufacturing.

Romanticism profoundly influenced not only nineteenth-century political, social, and artistic concerns, but also twentieth-century attitudes toward these aspects of life. During the Romantic era, writers and artists continued to reflect the respect for human freedom that Enlightenment thinkers had celebrated, retaining the Enlightenment's belief in human possibility. With rare exception, Romantic artists and writers avoided the satiric thrust of Enlightenment art and literature; nor did they emphasize the importance of reason celebrated by the Enlightenment predecessors. Instead, Romantic-era artists and writers emphasized the primacy of feeling, making the heart as important as the head, emotion as significant a human experience as thought.

In music, the artistic forms and structures popular during the eighteenth century significantly changed. Beethoven's symphonies broke the mold of the classical symphonic form established by Haydn and perfected by Mozart, clearing the ground for more radical changes not only in musical forms, but also in harmony, rhythm, and musical texture. Wagnerian music drama took opera in new directions and was paralleled by the explosion of Romantic Italian opera, which extended the scope and range of opera far beyond what Handel and Mozart had envisioned.

The literature of the Romantic era also reflected a significant break with the past. Wordsworth and Coleridge changed the direction of English poetry by describing familiar scenes from everyday life in common, everyday language. The Romantic literary and artistic revolution had as significant an impact on literature and art as the political and industrial revolutions had on society. The legacy of all four types of revolutions continues to affect the way life is lived and art is produced and enjoyed throughout the world today.

were responsible for the spread of disease. Sterile practices could radically reduce the chance of infection in medical procedures, and by heating food, spoilage could be eliminated, a process that led to the **pasteurization** of milk.

But by far the most influential scientist of the age was Charles Darwin (1809–1882). Darwin's *On the Origin of Species,* drafted in 1844 but not published until 1859, laid out his theory of **evolution** by **natural selection.** A landmark work, it had an immediate and profound impact on late-nineteenth-century thought.

Darwin noted that, in the struggle for existence, since nature cannot provide sufficiently for all the animals that come into being, only the fittest will survive, suggesting that more than simple luck accounted for the survival of individual members of a species. Darwin proposed that, in any given environment, those individuals best able to adapt to that environment, have the greatest chance of surviving. He suggested it was the strongest members of the species that survive long enough to breed and pass on to future generations genes enabling them to survive as well. He also suggested that as an environment changes, those individual members of a species that adapt to the changes will survive to pass on their genetic inheritance.

Darwin's emphasis on the mechanism of natural selection undermined conventional theological and philosophical assumptions about the special place of human beings in the divine order of creation. Instead of a world providentially designed by God with humankind as its guardian and guide, Darwin postulated a world that followed the blind laws of chance and saw human beings simply as a species of animal that has successfully adapted to its world, ensuring its capacity for survival. Moreover, there was no indication that humans were the highest point of creation, nor was their survival assured in future centuries.

Darwin did not deny that humankind represented the high point of creation so far, only that its origins were other than had been believed for centuries. His *The Descent of Man* (1871) suggested that humans were derived from lower life-forms that evolved. The distinguishing feature of humans, their spiritual nature and their consciousness, was diminished to emphasize their biological origins and their relationship to their simian ancestors. At stake in this revolutionary shift was humanity's ultimate place in the cosmos. At stake, too, were theological beliefs that had withstood the scientific revolution of the seventeenth century, but which seemed incompatible with Darwinian scientific explanation and the profusion of evidence he brought to support it.

KEY TERMS

Romanticism
études
originality
odalisque
phenomena
noumena
Sturm und Drang
Lied
absolute music
program music
idée fixe
song cycles
piano
prelude
nocturnes
waltz
polonaise
mazurka
leitmotif
Realism
atelier
daguerreotype
pictorialism
pasteurization
evolution
natural selection

www. WEBSITES FOR FURTHER STUDY

http://artchive.com/artchive/I/ingres.html
(This is the Artchive, a website with virtually every major artist in every style from every era in art history. It is an excellent resource.)

http://www.beautiful-london.co.uk/big-ben.htm
(An excellent site on the Houses of Parliament and many other London landmarks.)

http://www.wabash.edu/Rousseau/home.htm
(The Rousseau Association, where one can find a biography, his written works, and many associated links.)

http://www.r-cube.co.uk/fox-talbot/history.html
(William Henry Fox Talbot, philosopher, classicist, Egyptologist, mathematician, philologist, transcriber and translator of Syrian and Chaldean cuneiform text, physicist, and photographer.)

http://www.wagnersocietyny.org/
(The Wagner Society of New York, with many links and information about one of the greatest opera composers of all time.)

http://www.photo.net
(History of photography timeline, includes links to Muybridge, Beard, Brady, and others.)

http://www.infoplease.com
(Broad survey of Russian writers, with links to Tolstoy, Dostoyevsky, Chekhov, and others. And other links to French writers, including Flaubert and Balzac.)

http://www.historyworld.net
(The history of opera from early times to the present. Included are links for Wagner, Verdi, Puccini, and other great opera composers before and after them.)

http://saintpaulsunday.publicradio.org/
(What makes Russian music Russian? Focuses on nineteenth-century Russian composers to answer that question.)

http://www.philosophypages.com
(Overviews of the life and works of eighteenth- and nineteenth-century philosophers including Hegel, Marx, and Kant, as well as others before and after.)

http://www.answers.com/topic/romanticism
(Brief descriptions of romanticism from various perspectives—literary, political, artistic, and architectural—across Europe.)

Chapter 18

History

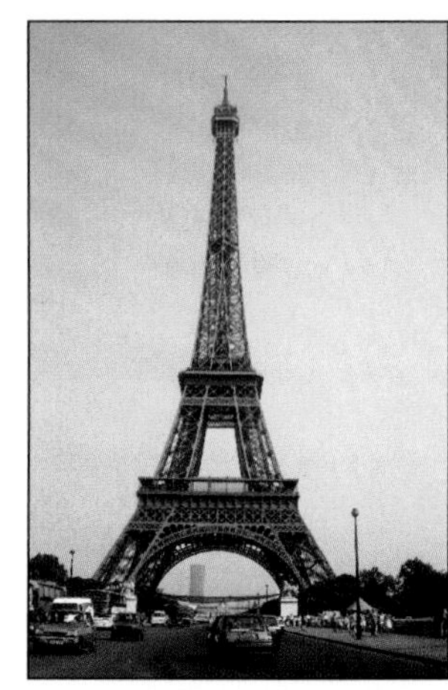

1845–48	Mexican American War
1870	Haussmann rebuilds Paris
1877	Edison invents the phonograph
1880s	Economic depression in England
1889	Paris International Exposition
1895	X-ray invented
1897–99	Thomson detects electrons in the atom
1898	Hawaiian Islands annexed
1898–99	Spanish American War

Arts and Architecture

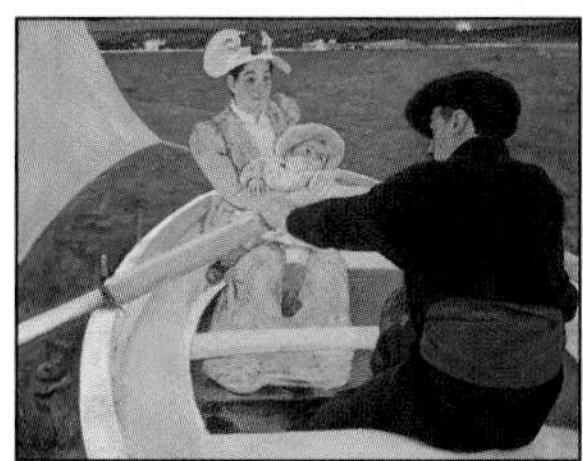

1872	Monet, *Impression, Sunrise*
1876	Renoir, *Dance at the Moulin de la Galette*
1879	Morisot, *Summer's Day*
1884–86	Seurat, *Sunday Afternoon on La Grande Jatte*
1889	Eiffel Tower
1889	Rodin, *The Thinker,*
1889	van Gogh, *Starry Night*
1891	Sullivan, Wainwright Building
1892	Claudel, *The Waltz*
1893–94	Cassatt, *The Boating Party*
1894	Cézanne, *Still Life with Peppermint Bottle*
1894	Debussy, *Prelude to the Afternoon of a Faun*

Literature and Philosophy

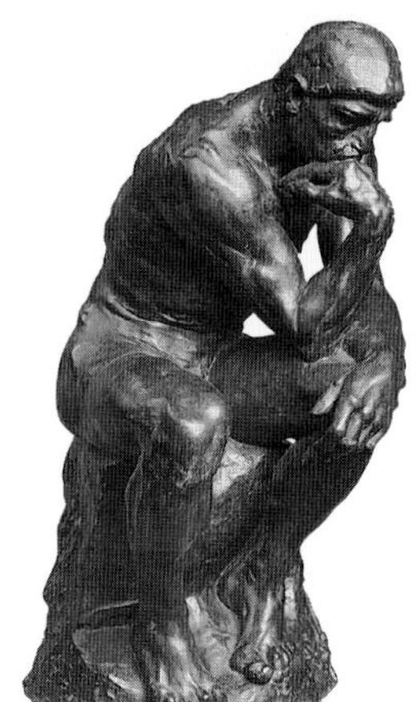

1857	Baudelaire, *The Flowers of Evil*
1876	Mallarmé, "The Afternoon of a Faun"
1879	Ibsen, *A Doll House*
1883	Nietzsche, *Thus Spoke Zarathustra*
1887	Strindberg, *The Father*
1899	Chopin, *The Awakening*
1899	Freud, *The Interpretation of Dreams*

Impressionism and Post-Impressionism

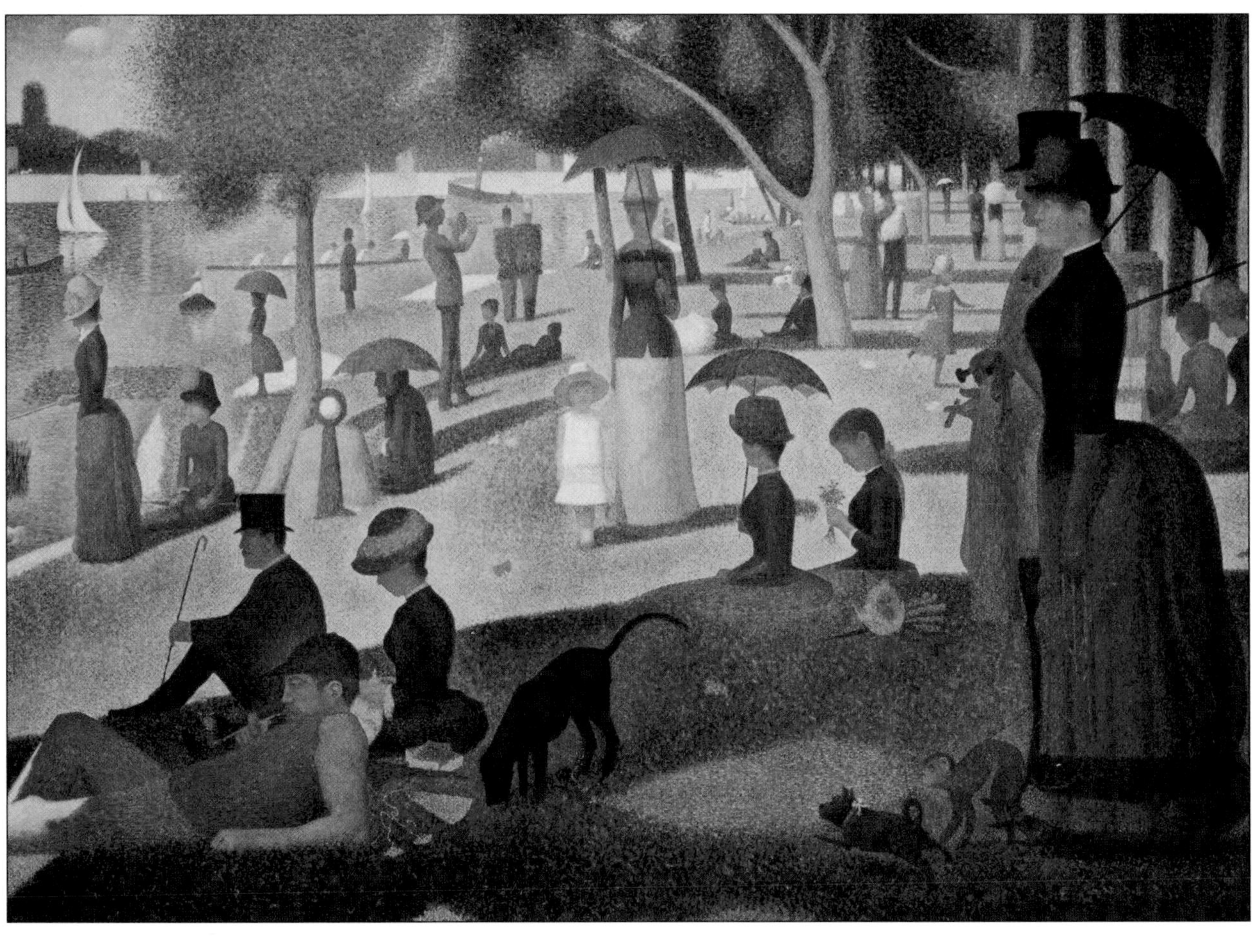

Georges Seurat, *A Sunday Afternoon on La Grande Jatte*, 1884–86, oil on canvas, $6'9\frac{3}{4}'' \times 10'1\frac{1}{4}''$ (2 × 3 m). Helen Birch Bartlett Memorial Collection. Photograph © 2005, The Art Institute of Chicago. All Rights Reserved.

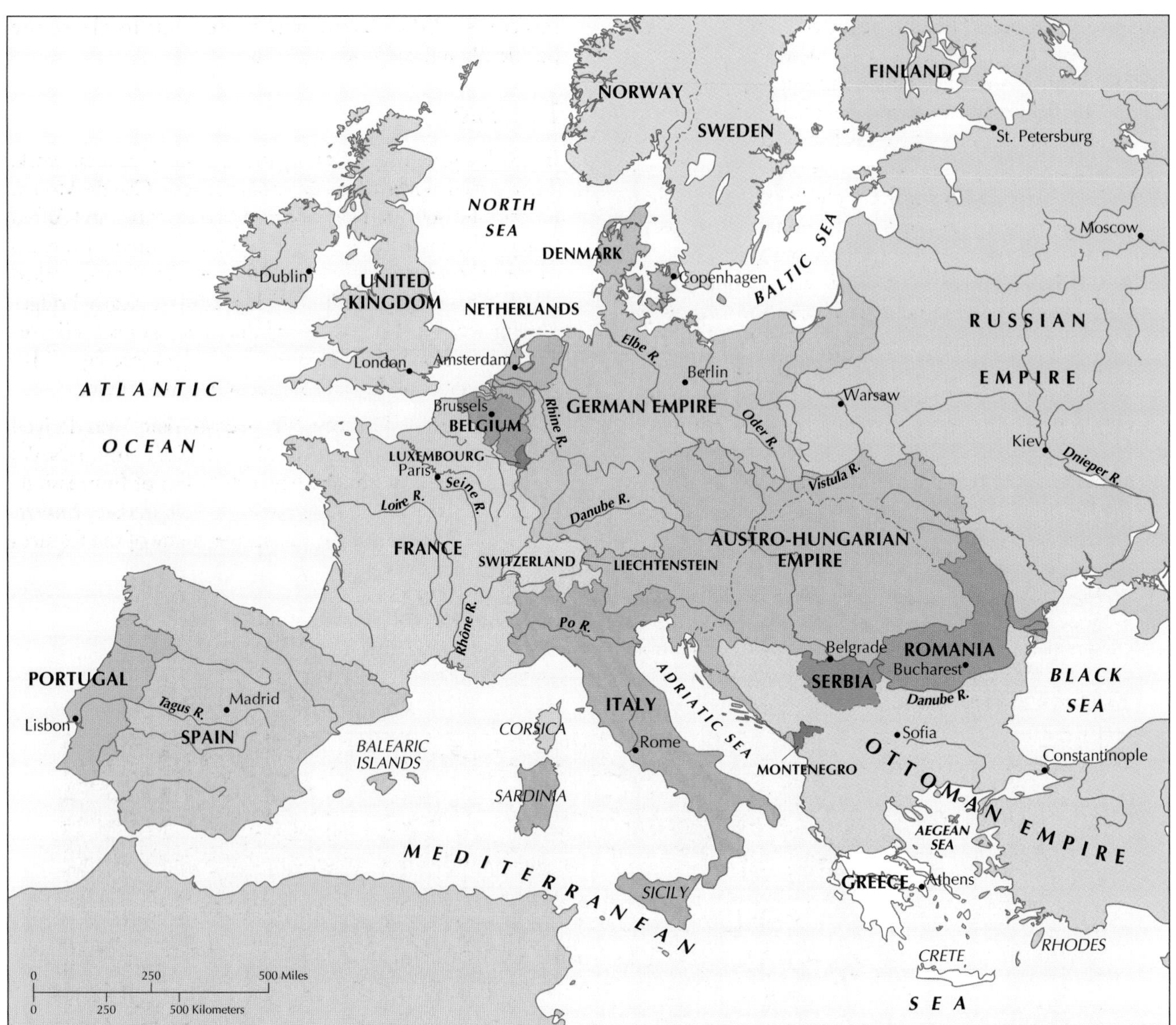

Map 18.1 Europe in 1871.

Chapter Overview

IMPRESSIONISM

Art and science converge

POST-IMPRESSIONISM

Technology and nature influence the arts

IMPRESSIONISM

BEFORE 1848, PARIS WAS CHARACTERIZED BY narrow streets and dark alleys, a maze that had been fortified with rebel barricades nine times since 1830. GEORGES EUGENE HAUSSMANN [OUSE-mun] (1809–1891) was commissioned to rebuild the city. He had three principal aims, the first being "to disencumber the large buildings, palaces, and barracks in such a way as to make them more pleasing to the eye, afford easier access on days of celebration, and a simplified defense on days of riot." Second, he recognized that slum conditions had a detrimental effect on public health, a situation he sought to rectify by the "systematic destruction of infected alleyways and centers of epidemics." Finally, he stated his plans "to assure public peace by the creation of large boulevards which will permit the circulation not only of air and light but also of troops." By the time Haussmann had completed his work in 1870, hundreds of miles of streets had been widened, new water and sewage systems were in place, the boulevards of modern Paris had been built, the banks of the Seine cleared of hovels, new bridges built, and tens of thousands of working-class poor evicted to the suburbs.

Due to Baron Haussmann, Paris was suddenly nearly as much a park as it was a city. It was, moreover, purged of its politically dangerous working class. In 1850, there were forty-seven acres of parkland in the city; by 1870, there were over 4,500, an increase of almost 100-fold. Haussmann doubled the number of trees lining the streets to over 100,000. The Bois de Boulogne, a neglected royal hunting ground to the west of the city, was redesigned between 1852 and 1858 as a giant English garden, with twisting, meandering paths, and a racecourse, Longchamp, which was built to please the politically powerful Jockey Club.

PAINTING

In 1874, a group of artists organized a show of their work. They included Mary Cassatt, Edgar Degas, Claude Monet, Berthe Morisot, Camille Pissarro, Pierre Renoir, and Alfred Sisley. Although he did not exhibit with them, Edouard Manet, who was particularly good friends with Monet, worked closely with the Impressionists. Manet most clearly bridges the gap between the Realists and the Impressionists. His Realist painting of 1863, *Luncheon on the Grass* (see fig. 17.18) was a precursor of the new Impressionist movement.

Claude Monet. The term **"Impressionism"** was derived from a painting by CLAUDE MONET [moh-NAY] (1840–1926) shown at the first exhibition of Impressionist art. Painted in 1872, it was called *Impression, Sunrise* (fig. 18.1). The painting encapsulates many of the features

FIGURE 18.1 Claude Monet, *Impression, Sunrise*, 1872, oil on canvas, $17\frac{3}{4}'' \times 21\frac{3}{4}''$ (48 × 63 cm). Painted in Le Havre, France. © Estate of Claude Monet/ARS Artists Rights Society, NY. The term "Impressionism," originally meant as an insult, derives from the title of this painting. Critics objected to the style, saying artists created *merely* an impression of a scene, without detail or compositional structure.

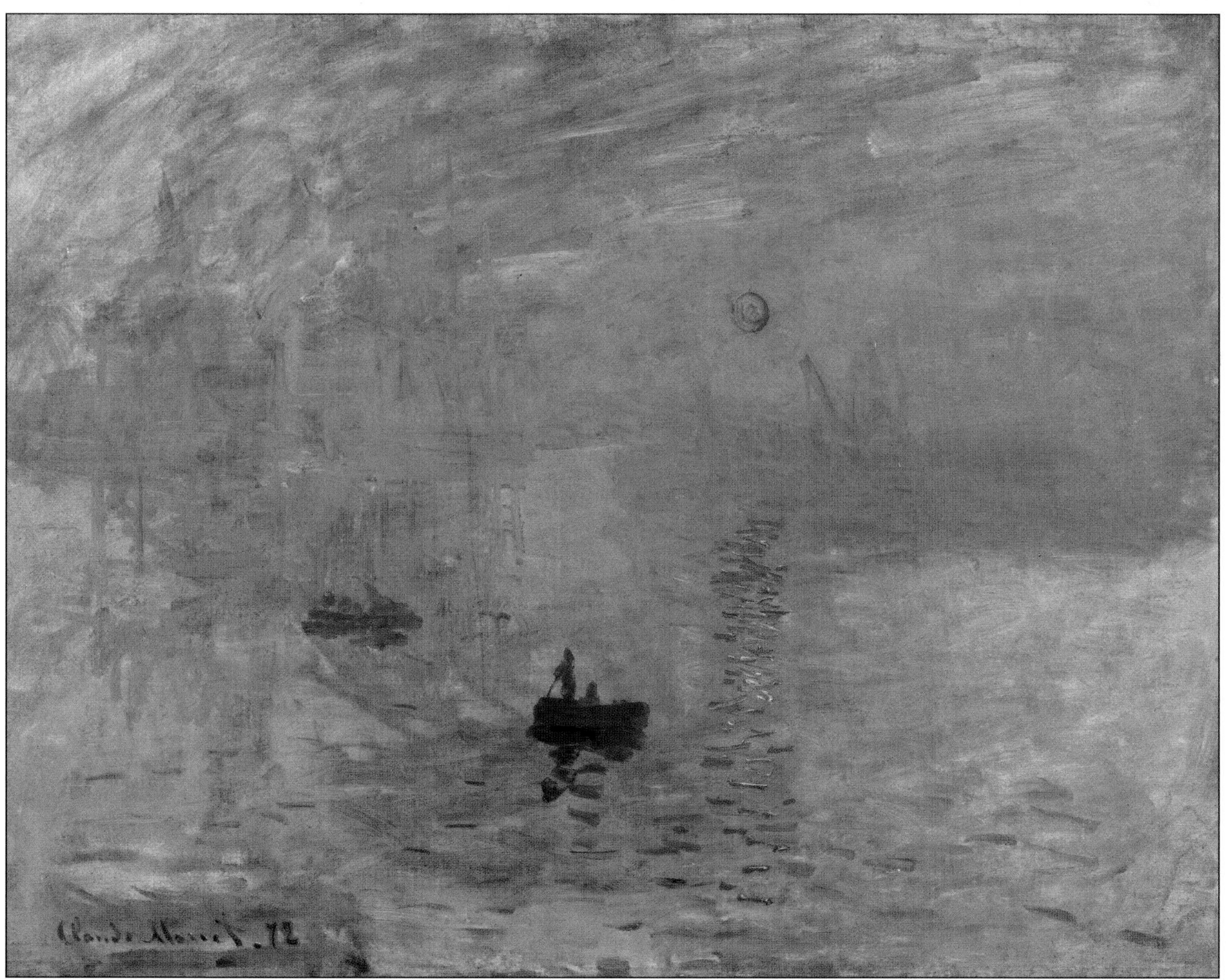

characteristic of Impressionist art. The *way* the Impressionist painters worked was as important to them as the subjects they painted. The traditional method of oil painting was to begin with a dark background color and work up to the lighter colors. The Impressionists reversed this, beginning with a white canvas and building up to dark colors. To convey a sense of natural light, they painted in the open air, rather than in the studio. They also tried to depict a momentary impression of nature's transitory light, atmosphere, and weather conditions; in Monet's painting the sun rises on a misty day over the harbor at Le Havre on the northern French coast. Behind this painting, and Impressionism as a whole, there also lies a major technological advance—the availability of oil paint in small, portable tins and tubes, which allowed painters to transport their paints out of doors.

Monet's brushwork is deliberately sketchy, consisting of broad dashes and dabs of paint. He suggests waves in the water with strokes of black. He shows the reflection of the sunrise in a series of orange and white strokes mixed together while still wet, right on the canvas. Although Monet's brushwork is loose, his composition is tightly controlled. Everything is carefully placed within a grid, defined horizontally by the horizon and vertically by the masts and the pattern of light and shadow that forms vertical bands across the composition.

Monet embarked on a number of projects designed to investigate the way in which changes in light and weather alter what we see by repeatedly painting the same subject at different times of the day and in different seasons: Rouen Cathedral, poplars, water lillies, and haystacks. Among the most famous of these projects, begun in 1888, is the series of paintings of haystacks. In *Haystacks at Giverny* (fig. 18.2), the color actually creates a feeling of heat. Monet realized that natural light changes color constantly and that many different colors make up what is perceived to be a single one. The myriad dabs of "broken" color are intended to blend in the viewer's eyes, creating sparkle and vibration. When a group of fifteen of these paintings was exhibited in Paris in 1891, they caused an immediate sensation. As the critic Gustave Geffroy wrote in the introduction to the show's catalog, "[Monet] knows that the artist can spend his life in the same place and look around himself without exhausting the constantly renewed spectacle. . . . These stacks, in this deserted field, are transient objects whose surfaces, like mirrors, catch the mood of the environment, the states of the atmosphere with the errant breeze, the sudden glow."

Pierre-Auguste Renoir. PIERRE-AUGUSTE RENOIR [ren-WAH] (1841–1919) was a good friend of Monet when both were poor and struggling, and the two often painted together in Paris and at Argenteuil where Renoir was a frequent visitor. His joyous personality and his zest for living, which reflect the age itself, inform his paintings.

Impressionists changed the focus of artistic subject matter. In turning away from traditional religious, mythological, historical, and literary subjects, they were similar to the Realists in temperament, but instead of looking objectively at the ordinary life of the working class, they looked to the good life and the entertainments

FIGURE 18.2 Claude Monet, *Haystacks at Giverny (end of summer, morning)*, 1891, oil on canvas, $23\frac{3}{4}'' \times 39\frac{1}{2}''$ (60.5 × 100 cm). Photo R. G. Ojeda. Musée d'Orsay, Paris. Reunion des Musées Nationaux/Art Resource, NY. B. Hatala/Art Resource, NY. Rather than painting in the studio as did earlier artists, Monet painted out of doors. Instead of mixing colors on a palette beforehand, he applied paint in dabs of pure color, referred to as "broken color."

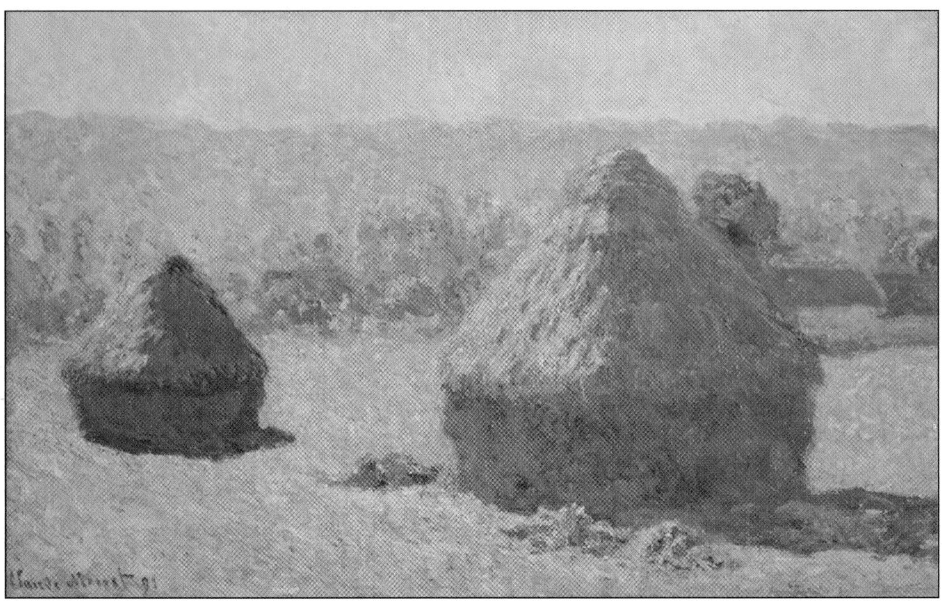

of the middle class in a new "beautiful age"—the ***belle époque.*** It was an age of pleasure-seeking in which life focused on Paris's *grands boulevards*, weekend outings in its suburbs and gardens, a day at the races, boating on the Seine, the theatre, or dancing.

Dance at the Moulin de la Galette (fig. 18.3), of 1876, is a good example. The painting, of a restaurant and open-air dance hall in Montmartre, a northern section of Paris, captures the sense of gaiety that marks the belle époque. Renoir painted outdoors, working rapidly with his colors to capture the atmosphere of the moment. Light comes through the trees, falling in patches, dappling the surface—note the pattern of round splotches of light on the back of the man in the foreground. Renoir's figures appear relaxed, rather than stiffly posed. Interestingly, the couple dancing on the left gaze at the viewer. They seem aware they are being watched, a photographic effect that lends the painting an aura of spontaneity. They are, in fact, friends of the artist: Margot, one of his models, and Solares, a Cuban painter. As in all of his paintings, the men are handsome, the women are pretty, the activity in which they engage is pleasant, and the sun is shining. According to Renoir, "A picture ought to be a lovable thing, joyous and pretty, yes, pretty. There are enough boring things in this world without our making more."

Berthe Morisot. The only woman to exhibit at the first Impressionist exhibition was BERTHE MORISOT [more-ee-SOH] (1841–1895). Married to Manet's younger brother Eugène, her work was almost immediately given the negative label "feminine" by the critics, perhaps because her subject matter was, almost exclusively, women and children. Whatever she depicted, it is clear she was

FIGURE 18.3 Pierre-Auguste Renoir, *Dance at the Moulin de la Galette*, 1876, oil on canvas, $4'3\frac{1}{2}'' \times 5'9''$ (1.30 × 1.80 m), ©2004 Artists Rights Society (ARS), New York. Louvre Museum/Art Resource, NY. Instead of choosing traditional subjects, the Impressionists depicted pleasant places where people congregated. In Renoir's paintings the people are always attractive and the weather is usually good—here the sun falls in patches through the leaves.

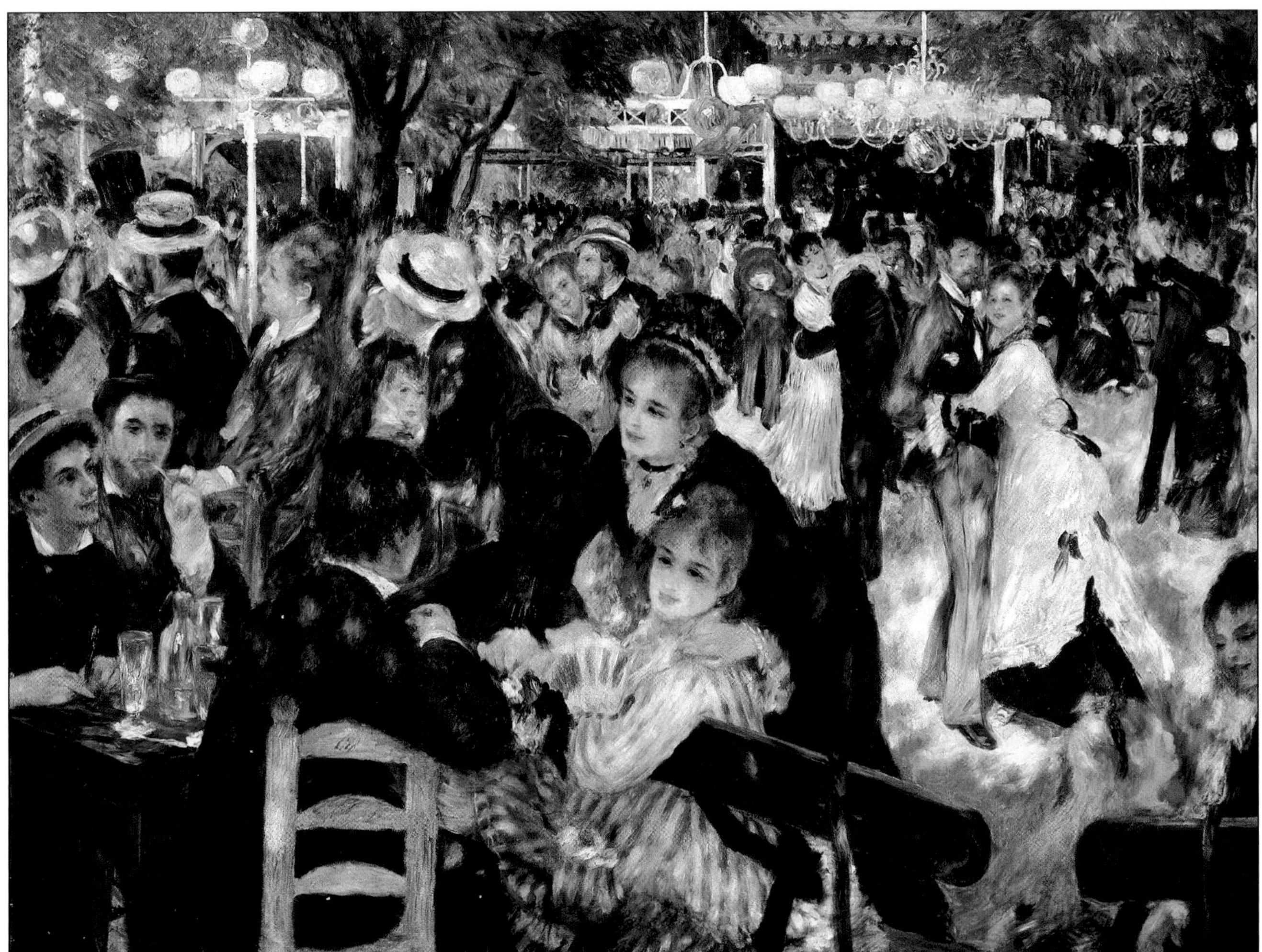

the most daring of all the Impressionist painters. *Summer's Day* (fig. 18.4), exhibited at the fifth show in 1880, is remarkable for the looseness of its brushwork, which is hardly contained within the contours of the forms it depicts. It zigs and zags across the surface in a seemingly arbitrary manner. Yet in the small rapid movements of her strokes, we can almost feel the breeze on the water, see the lapping and splashing of the water on the oars, and hear the wisps of conversation between the two women as they enjoy their outing.

Edgar Degas. A very different type of French Impressionism was created by EDGAR DEGAS [DAY-GAH] (1834–1917). An aristocrat from a banking family, Degas was independently wealthy and therefore able to paint to suit himself. Many other painters disliked him, and with reason, for he was snobbish and unfriendly, with a nasty wit. Politically and socially conservative, Degas did not think art should be available to the lower class.

Degas' strict academic training resulted in a style based on draftsmanship. In 1865, he met Ingres, then eighty-five years old. Ingres told him to "do lines and more lines, from nature or from memory, and you will become a good artist." Because of this approach, Degas has been called a "linear Impressionist," which may seem at first to be a contradiction. Degas, however, hated the word "Impressionist" because of the negative connotations of "accidental" or "incomplete." He worked methodically, sometimes determining the proportions of the work by ruling off squares and often making many sketches before painting. He once remarked, "No art was ever less spontaneous than mine. What I do is the result of reflection and study of the great masters; of inspiration, spontaneity, temperament, I know nothing."

What makes Degas an Impressionist, nonetheless, is the *sense* of spontaneity visible in his work, not only in the looseness of his brushwork, but also in the choice and treatment of his subject matter. However calculatingly hard he worked, he aimed to *appear* unstudied. His effect is one of instantaneous and immediate vision. Degas seems to have been influenced by photography, and by the snapshot in particular. His paintings often appear severely cropped, cutting figures in half, as if they are just entering or leaving the viewfinder of a camera.

In Degas' depictions of ballet dancers, for which he is perhaps best known, he takes us behind the scenes. In *The Dancing Class* (fig. 18.5), of about 1874, he seems to have tried deliberately to capture the dancers at their least graceful—straining, stretching, scratching, and yawning. Known for his unusual compositions, Degas constructs a boxlike space in which the walls are not parallel to the picture plane but instead on oblique angles. The point of view from which the scene is recorded is striking—from above and to the side. It anticipates, in effect, the freedom of perspective that photographers would discover with the handheld camera, an invention that the Kodak Corporation had introduced by the end of the century.

Mary Cassatt. In addition to French Impressionist painters, there were a number of American Impressionists.

FIGURE 18.4 Berthe Morisot, *Summer's Day*, 1879, oil on canvas, 18″ × 29¾″ (45.7 × 75.2 cm), National Gallery, London. Note in particular Morisot's handling of the three ducks swimming on the right. They are so loosely painted that they have become almost unrecognizable.

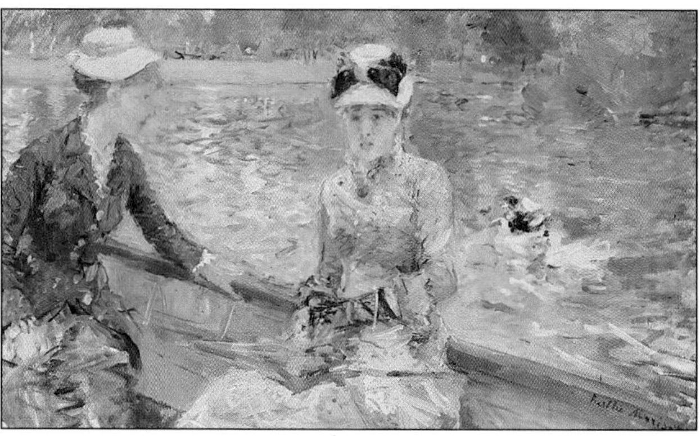

FIGURE 18.5 Edgar Degas, *The Dancing Class*, ca. 1874, oil on canvas, 33½″ × 29½″ (85 × 75 cm), Musée d'Orsay, Paris. Degas was called a "linear Impressionist"—seemingly an oxymoron. Interested in figures in motion, he made many pictures of ballerinas. He seems to have preferred them at their least graceful, as when leaning tired against the barre, stooping over their aching feet, or adjusting their costumes.

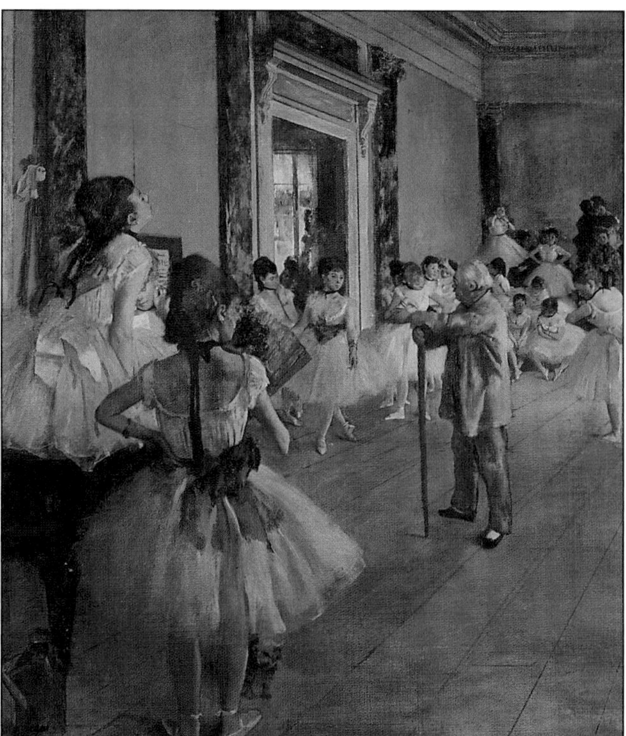

One of the foremost was MARY CASSATT [kah-SAHT] (1844–1925), who left her wealthy Pittsburgh family and moved to Europe where she became absorbed in the art world. Her parents opposed her study of art so strongly that her father is reported to have said, "I would almost rather see you dead." She soon gained recognition, however—she was called a madwoman because of her style. Cassatt was a close friend of Degas, who claimed he never would have believed a woman could draw so well. As early as 1879, Cassatt was exhibiting with the Impressionists.

Cassatt's *The Boating Party* (fig. 18.6), painted 1893–94, was criticized when first shown, for the foreground figure has rudely turned his back on the viewer. Rather than being the center of attention, however, he acts as a compositional device directing the viewer's gaze into the composition. His arm and oar point inward, and he looks toward the mother and child, just as the viewer does. The contours of the boat and sail also lead to the mother and child. A sense of realism is achieved in the squirming movement of the child.

The influence of Japanese prints is apparent in the asymmetrical composition, the emphasis on sharp silhouettes and linear rhythms, the broad flat areas of color, the snapshot quality of the scene, the high positioning of the horizon, and, moreover, the unusual perspective—we look down into the boat, which is abruptly cut off. The brilliant light effects so typical of Impressionism are not achieved through the use of broken color. Instead, Cassatt juxtaposes large areas of bright color. The light appears intense, but is not realistic: the interior of the boat should, in fact, be dark. Facts are manipulated for art, and in this respect Cassatt's painting, and that of other Impressionists, can be seen as anticipating the art of the next century.

FIGURE 18.6 Mary Cassatt, *The Boating Party*, 1893–94, oil on canvas, $35\frac{1}{2}'' \times 46\frac{1}{8}''$ (90 × 117 cm), Chester Dale Collection. Photograph © Board of Trustees, National Gallery of Art, Washington, D.C. 1963.10.94 (1758)/PA. An American working in France, Cassatt paints a typical Impressionist subject—pleasant and out of doors. The composition directs the viewer's eyes to the squirming child.

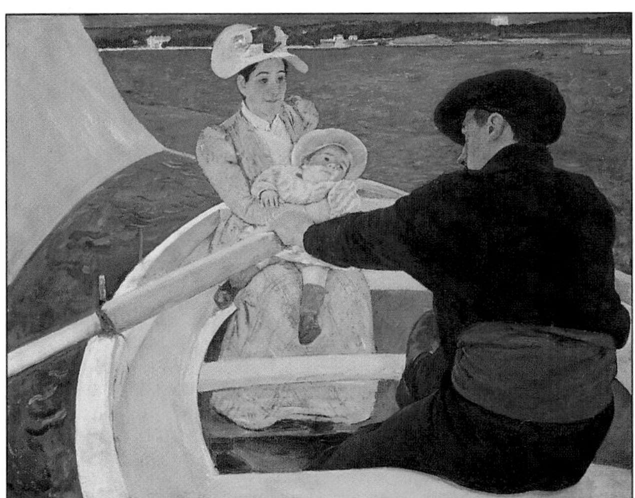

James Abbott McNeill Whistler. The work of another expatriate American, James Abbott McNeill Whistler (1834–1903), also foreshadows twentieth-century art. After a disappointing stint at West Point, and being fired from a government job in Washington, DC, Whistler went to Paris in 1855, where he lived as a Bohemian art student. Then in 1859, he moved to London, and was to remain there for the rest of his life. He visited Paris several times and learned about Impressionism, but he never used Impressionistic broken color or light effects.

In 1863, his mother came to keep house for him (she supported him financially), and in 1871 he immortalized her in a work entitled *Arrangement in Black and Gray: The Artist's Mother* (fig. 18.7), known popularly as *Whistler's Mother.* Whistler referred to his paintings by musical terms such as nocturnes, symphonies, and harmonies. This painting is first and foremost an "arrangement," and only secondarily a portrait. Abstract and formal, the pictorial space is flattened, depth receives little emphasis, and light, shadow, and modeling are minimal. Whistler maintained that art should not be concerned with morality, education, or storytelling, but should appeal to the aesthetic sense. He believed in art for art's sake.

FIGURE 18.7 James Abbott McNeill Whistler, *Arrangement in Black and Gray: The Artist's Mother*, 1871, oil on canvas, $4'9'' \times 5'4\frac{1}{4}''$ (1.50 × 1.60 m), Photo: Jean Schormans. Musee d'Orsay, Paris. Reunion des Musees Nationaux/Art Resource, NY. Whistler's mother, as subject, is treated much the same as the other elements in this intellectual arrangement in restricted colors.

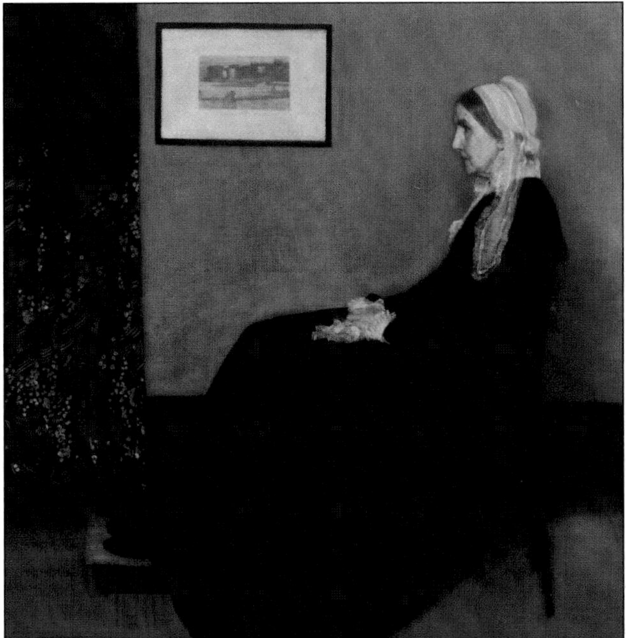

Connections

DEBUSSY AND MALLARMÉ: IMPRESSIONIST AND SYMBOLIST

Claude Debussy's chamber orchestral composition *Prelude to the Afternoon of a Faun* was inspired by Stéphane Mallarmé's poem "The Afternoon of a Faun." Both composer and poet convey the faun's experience through suggestive uses of sound and language. Mallarmé's poem describes the reveries of a creature from classical mythology, with the body of a man and the horns, ears, legs, and tail of a goat. The poem's dreamlike tone raises the question as to whether the faun has actually been chasing nymphs or whether he has only been dreaming about doing so. Equally ambiguous is the poem's sense of time and place. Debussy's composition does not attempt to portray the content of the poem so much as to evoke its atmosphere of languor and fantasy.

Debussy wrote the music to suggest "the successive scenes through which pass the desires and dreams of the faun in the heat of [an] afternoon." He accomplishes this with a musical language that includes the sounds of woodwind and harp while excluding those of trumpets and trombones. Rather than the clearly articulated, symmetrical themes of the Classical and Romantic styles that were developed and recapitulated, Debussy creates a more dreamlike and evocative music. His themes appear and disappear, often in misty fragments and brief orchestral swells. The music ebbs and flows continuously in a series of subtly shifting rhythms, the flute suggesting the musical pipes associated with the mythological faun. The overall musical effect is one of reverie, which suits the mood of Mallarmé's poem.

LITERATURE

Symbolists. Like the Impressionists, the **Symbolist** poets also attempted to convey reality by impression and sensation. They felt liberated by their medium, words, and from the necessity of rendering the "facts" of vision. Words, they believed, could do more than simply portray these "facts" of external experience; indeed, they could capture a sense of the shifting and fluid nature of our entire mental experience. Language could encompass not only our perceptions of the outside world, but our internal lives as well. The Symbolists sought to evoke states of mind and feeling beyond the surface of everyday reality. And because they did not believe they could successfully render the external world objectively, they were free to present it from their own unique and idiosyncratic perspectives. Reality was at best, they argued, an irretrievably personal affair.

Poetry, they felt, had long been mired in the ordinary, caught up in conventions of meaning and usage that blinded the reader to language's potential to reveal the extraordinary and the unknown. For the Symbolists, an image or symbol did not so much stand for something as suggest a cluster of ideas and feelings. They preferred the vagueness of symbolic suggestion to a more precise rendering of experience. As Stéphane Mallarmé wrote, "To name an object is to do away with three-quarters of the enjoyment of the poem, which is derived from the satisfaction of guessing little by little; to suggest it, to evoke it, this is what charms the imagination."

Among the poets associated with the Symbolist movement, CHARLES BAUDELAIRE [bow-duh-LAIR] (1821–1867) is an important precursor, but STÉPHANE MALLARMÉ [mal-are-MAY] (1842–1898) was the group's leading theoretician and its most influential practitioner. Both Baudelaire and Mallarmé attempted to create poems using images that fuse the senses and attain the expressiveness of music. In Baudelaire's "Hair," for example, the speaker pays homage to a lover's hair by describing it as "A port resounding where, in draughts untold, / My soul may drink in colour, scent, and sound." A similar combination of the senses occurs in Mallarmé's "Windows," in lines such as "His eye on the horizon gorged with light, / Sees golden ships, fine as swans, / On a scented river of purple." In addition to this attempt to convey the rich sensuousness of imagined experience, Symbolist poets tried to make their verse musical, so the sounds of the words themselves would be suggestive in a musical sense rather than purely representational, a characteristic difficult to demonstrate in translation.

Naturalism. The impulse toward Romanticism in the nineteenth century was countered by the writing of a number of American women. Writers such as Sarah Orne Jewett (1849–1909), Charlotte Perkins Gilman (1851–1904), and KATE CHOPIN [SHOW-panh] (1851–1904) all deal with the concerns of middle-class women in naturalistic detail, with a psychological realism often reminiscent of Freud. Jewett's stories center on the everyday lives of New England characters; Gilman focuses on the ways in which nineteenth-century attitudes toward women kept them physically and psychologically imprisoned; and Chopin's fiction depicts strong women who insist upon their independence and their right to determine their own destinies.

Kate Chopin was especially adept at depicting the lives of the Creole, Cajun, African-American, and Native American communities of Louisiana, and her popularity soared as readers consumed her stories filled with local customs and dialects. Chopin's best known work is the short novel *The Awakening*, published in 1899. It is intensely psychological in its portrayal of its heroine Edna Pontellier's passionate emotional life, her boredom with her constricting marriage, and her flirtatious adventures with another man. But the novel was considered virtually obscene in its day, banned from most libraries, and Chopin's reputation suffered until the 1950s, when the work was rediscovered.

Drama, too, began to develop along naturalistic lines, especially in Europe. Among the great nineteenth-century realist dramatists was the Norwegian playwright Henrik Ibsen (1828–1906), whose plays touched on such themes as the roles and rights of women (*A Doll House*), the scourge of venereal disease (*Ghosts*), and the death of a child (*Little Eyolf*). Ibsen's dramatic intensity and electrifying revelations were matched by the Swedish playwright August Strindberg (1849–1912), whose plays *The Father, Creditors*, and *Comrades* were all written in a strongly realistic style. The plays of Russian writer ANTON CHEKHOV [CHECK-off] (1860–1904), such as *The Three Sisters* and *The Cherry Orchard*, lack the intense melodramatic character of those by Ibsen and Strindberg. They don't have a clear cause and effect plot structure, and they do not build toward tragic climaxes. Instead, Chekhov's characters are lifelike in their inability to find happiness, their uncertainty about the future, and their indecisiveness in achieving their desires.

The plays of Ibsen, Strindberg, Chekhov, and the numerous other naturalist dramatists of the time were staged to emphasize the authenticity of the characters, settings, and situations. Chekhov's plays were produced at the Moscow Art Theater, which was run by Konstantin Stanislavsky, whose theory of acting asked actors to "live" their roles based on their own psychological reactions to the characters. Chekhov's plays, with their complex portraits of character relationships, were particularly suited to the Stanislavsky system. Together, Chekhov and Stanislavsky profoundly influenced subsequent modern realistic theater in the West.

Music

Debussy's Musical Impressionism. The composer CLAUDE DEBUSSY [day-byou-SEE] (1862–1918) revolutionized his artistic medium. Just as Claude Monet altered the way external reality was rendered in pigment, so Debussy altered the way music suggested extramusical sensations and impressions. Working with a palette of sound instead of color, he mixed musical tones, combining them in ways never heard before, thus influencing the music that would be written after him.

Debussy insisted that "French music is clearness, elegance, simple and natural declamation. French music aims first of all to give pleasure." This he did in a wide range of compositions—some for orchestra, such as *Fêtes* (*Festivals*) and *La Mer* (*The Sea*), and others for piano, including the popular *Clair de Lune* (Moonlight), inspired by the Symbolist poet Paul Verlaine. Rather than duplicating the poem's images or details, Debussy created a parallel or analogous musical image of moonlight through beautiful sounds and suggestive harmonies, without a long lyrical melodic line. Based on a poem by Stéphane Mallarmé, his innovative *Prélude à l'après-midi d'un faune* (Prelude to The Afternoon of a Faun) feels improvisational and somewhat free of form. Debussy masks its structural complexity beneath a long, languorous melodic line and a shimmering surface of complex harmonies.

Debussy rejected the dramatic dynamics of theme employed by Classical and Romantic composers in favor of greater tonal variety. He accomplished this effect partly by encouraging the use of the piano's damper pedal, which allows the strings for different notes to resonate simultaneously, creating a hazy but rich blend of sounds. He complemented this with a fluctuating sense of rhythm. In masking the basic musical pulse, Debussy created music that avoided the familiar melodic, harmonic, and rhythmic patterns of the past. At the Paris International Exposition in 1889, Debussy heard Javanese and Southeast Asian music that he could not duplicate on Western instruments. In response, he explored a scale of six whole tones, entirely of whole-step intervals. The effect of using such a scale was to make all the scale tones equal in weight, without the strong pull of any one home key. The unfocused quality of music that resulted from a whole-tone scale is comparable to the effects Impressionist painters used in creating a shimmering atmosphere across a canvas, and to the lack of representation achieved by Symbolist poets in their deliberate avoidance of strict linguistic referentiality.

Opera at the Turn of the Century

If Giuseppe Verdi was Italy's most revered composer of the Romantic era, Giacomo Puccini (1858–1924) became an equally popular successor in the following era. Nearly a century after his death, Puccini's popularity remains as great as ever, with productions of his operas performed around the world as frequently as Verdi's and almost as often as Mozart's. Among Puccini's most acclaimed operas are *Madama Butterfly, Tosca*, and *La Bohème*, each of which centers on a young woman. Cio-Cio-San of *Butterfly* loves unselfishly, the flamboyant Tosca is a mix of temperament and passion, and Mimi of *La Bohème* becomes entangled in a love affair with an unhappy ending.

By the time of *La Bohème's* inaugural performance in 1896, Claude Debussy had already composed a number of remarkable orchestral pieces, including *La Mer* and *L'apres-midi d'une faune*, and the Symbolist poets had written the bulk of their poems. It is to the poets, composers, and artists of the late nineteenth century that *La Bohème* plays tribute. In fact, the story of the opera comes in part from a mid-century novel, *Scenes from La Vie de Bohème*, and partly from Puccini's own Bohemian life experiences. For example, Puccini once pawned his only coat during winter in order to take a ballet dancer out for a night on the town.

Part of what accounts for the popularity of *La Bohème* is that in this work, as in his other operas, Puccini describes believable characters in real-life situations, often involving love. He creates for his characters simple plots, which he accompanies with richly melodic music. And though Puccini's operas lack the deeper intellectual bite and the structural complexity of Verdi's, they have remained a staple of the repertory due to the appeal of their characters and the accessibility of their music.

POST-IMPRESSIONISM

As the nineteenth century came to a close, the Western world was overtaken by a sense that an era was ending. It was a time of extraordinary material innovation: In the 1880s and 1890s, the telegraph, telephone, bicycle, automobile, typewriter, phonograph, elevator, and electric lamp all came into being.

The end of the century was also a time of profound and disturbing social unrest and, to many, one of moral decay. Starting in the 1880s, severe economic depression in England marked the beginning of the end of the country's supremacy as a world power. The Dockers' Strike of 1889 led to the unionization of unskilled workers, and by 1900, the Labour Party had been founded. In France, meanwhile, the working classes, it seemed, turned more and more to alcohol for pleasure. Beginning in 1891 and continuing for twenty more years, three thousand new bistros opened in Paris every year, and by 1910, there was one for every eighty-two Parisians. By 1906, most French workmen drank over three liters of wine a day. Drug use was on the rise, with opium, and its derivative morphine, finding special favor. With addiction and poverty came crime, so much so that electric light was championed more for its ability to deter criminal behavior than for anything else.

The period also witnessed a challenge on the part of European intellectuals to the accepted code of moral behavior of the day. Some writers styled themselves "decadents." Oscar Wilde (1854–1900) flaunted his homosexuality. This identifiable "type" suddenly became visible to such a point that in Vienna, in 1905, Sigmund Freud would include homosexuality in his *Three Essays on the Theory of Sexuality.* George Sand and Rosa Bonheur had worn men's clothing in mid-century, but now, in the 1890s, many women, particularly intellectuals, wore trousers, and they were consequently decried for betraying their sex. Moreover, they asked with increasing intensity for the right to vote. In the late nineteenth century, many conventional standards of behavior were being questioned and reevaluated.

AMERICAN EXPANSION

Throughout the nineteenth century, the United States engaged in territorial expansion. Territories had been added through purchase, most famously with Thomas Jefferson's negotiated purchase of the Louisiana Territory from the French in 1803, and later the purchase of Alaska from Russia in 1867. In addition to these land purchases, under the banner of "manifest destiny," Native American Indians were routinely displaced from their lands and relegated to reservations. Many lost their lives in the Indian Wars.

Other kinds of expansion proved equally troublesome. When the United States accepted Texas, which had seceded from Mexico in 1836, into the union, Mexico protested and the resulting tensions led to the Mexican American War of 1845–48. The main result of this war was Mexico's sale of its territories in California and New Mexico and its recognition of the U.S. annexation of Texas.

One place where the United States did not succeed in expanding was north into Canada. During the War of 1812 between the United States and Britain, Canadians consistently repelled U.S. incursions, serving to unite the previously splintered French and British Canadians, and propelling Canada toward political sovereignty.

The United States also had mixed experiences in expanding its territory into other areas. The Hawaiian islands were annexed in 1898, after the last Hawaiian monarch was ousted in 1893. The United States took possession of Cuba and Puerto Rico after a brief military encounter with Spain in the Spanish-American War of 1898–99. Each of these has had a different fate, with Hawaii becoming the fiftieth U.S. state in 1959, Puerto Rico rejecting U.S. statehood and remaining a U.S. associated commonwealth, and Cuba becoming independent.

Spain also lost its colonial possessions in the Pacific to the United States, with Guam and the Philippine islands coming under U.S. control in 1898. As a result of the Spanish-American War, Spain lost control of the last remnants of its overseas colonial empire, with a new imperialist force, the United States, recognized as a major world power.

BOER WAR

Seeking gold in South African mines, thousands of prospectors from Britain and other countries came to South Africa. British imperialism also found expression in the Boer Wars, especially the Second Boer War, also known as the South African War (1899–1902). The war was fought between the British Empire and the two independent Boer Republics in South Africa. Victorious, Britain absorbed into the British Empire the Orange Free State and the Transvaal Republic, as the Union of South Africa.

Although the war was fought among whites, many black Africans who served on both sides were killed. British concentration camps held as many as 100,000 black Africans, 10,000 of whom died. Other groups who suffered from severe treatment were Chinese laborers, or "coolies," who, employed by the British colonial governor after the war, were poorly paid, segregated from the local population, and left to live in appalling conditions.

NEW SCIENCE AND NEW TECHNOLOGIES

Even as prosperity seemed to promise a limitless future, the technology it spawned contributed to the breakdown of established patterns of social organization. New means of communication, such as the telephone, and new forms of transportation, such as the automobile, complicated life rather than simplifying it. The rules of the road remained largely uncodified, and the continuing process of industrialization spurred the growth of urban centers at the expense of agrarian life. Modern intellectual developments greatly accelerated the transformation of traditional ways of thinking. In particular, discoveries in quantum physics and depth psychology transformed twentieth-century thought. The most important of these developments were Freud's invention of psychoanalysis and Einstein's promulgation of his theory of relativity.

The Theory of Relativity. In 1905, Albert Einstein (1879–1955) proposed that space and time are not absolute, as they appear to be, but are instead relative to each other in a "space-time continuum." Not until 1919 could the mathematical equations central to Einstein's special theory of relativity be confirmed through scientific experiment. Subsequent experiments further established the legitimacy of his ideas. All modern developments in space technology were influenced by his discoveries, those developments proving the accuracy of his theory right into the 1980s. Einstein's notion of relativity was widely circulated even though it undermined traditional ways of thinking about the universe, similar to the way in which Copernicus's theory had overturned the Ptolemaic concept of the universe.

The Atom. Equally important in its implications was the work of J. J. Thomson (1856–1940) in Cambridge, England, who between 1897 and 1899 managed to detect the existence of separate components, which he called electrons, in the structure of the **atom,** which had previously been thought indivisible. By 1911, his colleague Ernest Rutherford (1871–1937) had introduced his revolutionary new model of the atom. It consisted of a small positively charged nucleus, which contained most of the atom's mass, around which its electrons orbited. To many, the world no longer seemed a solid whole.

PHILOSOPHY AT THE TURN OF THE CENTURY

Friedrich Nietzsche. The philosopher FRIEDRICH NIETZSCHE [NEE-chuh] (1844–1900) emphasized the rebellious nature of the **superman,** a superhuman being who refused to be confined within the traditional structures of nationalist ideology, Christian belief, scientific knowledge, and bourgeois values. According to Nietzsche, the exceptional individual is above ordinary people and has the right to exert his superior strength over others. Proclaiming "God is dead," Nietzsche asserted the complete freedom of the individual, who could now begin to channel **Dionysian** (instinctual) and **Apollonian** (intellectual) tendencies in ways that were unrestricted by social conventions. Early modernist art, in part, owes its rebellious antiauthoritarianism to Nietzsche's example. So too, in part, do developments in literary theory and in philosophy, especially existentialism.

Sigmund Freud. The psychology of SIGMUND FREUD [FROYD] (1856–1939) further influenced modernist trends in culture and the arts. Freud's analysis of unconscious motives and his description of instinctual drives reflected an antirationalist perspective that undermined faith in the apparent order and control in human individual and social life. Although he was a psychoanalyst and not a philosopher, Sigmund Freud had an influence on philosophy with his claim that biological drives determine human behavior. According to Freud, humans are at the mercy of their unconscious rather than under the control of their conscious, rational thought. His emphasis on the irrational provided a quasi-scientific explanation of impulses and behaviors that had formerly been displayed in works of literature, which could now be analyzed with the language and concepts of **psychoanalysis** he developed. Freud's splitting of the human psyche into the **ego,** the **id,** and the **superego** provided a psychoanalytical analogue for the growing concern with social fragmentation and cultural disharmony, the distressing feeling that all was not well, even if the period was known as the belle époque.

POST-IMPRESSIONIST PAINTING

By the early 1890s, the Impressionist style of painting was widely accepted. However, since the time of Courbet, painters had defined themselves against the mainstream of approved art. The next wave of artists to challenge the public's expectations were called the Post-Impressionists.

The term **Post-Impressionism** is, in fact, an extremely broad one, for the Post-Impressionists did not band together but worked in isolation. Rather than a rejection of Impressionism, Post-Impressionism, which began in France in the 1880s, was an attempt to improve on it and to extend it. The Post-Impressionists considered Impressionism too objective, too impersonal, and lacking control. They did not think that recording a fleeting moment or portraying atmospheric conditions was sufficient. Placing greater emphasis on composition and form, the Post-Impressionists worked to control reality, to organize, arrange, and formalize. The Post-Impressionist painters wanted more personal interpretation and expression, as well as greater psychological depth.

Paul Cézanne. PAUL CÉZANNE [say-ZAHN] (1839–1906) was in Paris at the beginning of the Impressionist phenomenon. Introverted to the point of being reclusive, he led an almost completely isolated existence in the south of France from 1877 to 1895. People there considered him a madman and jeered at him. He became ever more irritable as a consequence and turned increasingly inward.

Reacting against the loose and unstructured quality of Impressionist art, Cézanne's greatest interest was in order, stability, and permanence. He said he wanted "to make of Impressionism something solid and durable, like the art of the museums." All of Cézanne's paintings are carefully constructed. His usual technique was to sketch with thin blue paint and then apply the colors directly. He washed his brush between strokes so that each color would be distinct, sometimes taking as long as twenty minutes between brushstrokes. In fact, he referred to his brushstrokes as "little planes." An apple, for example, is viewed as a spherical form consisting of a series of small planes—each plane is a specific color according to the apple's form. This revolutionary style of painting would lead to the innovative ideas of the early twentieth century. Indeed, some historians feel Cézanne was the first artist to profoundly redirect painting since Giotto (see Chapter 12) in the early fourteenth century.

Cézanne's favorite subjects were still life and landscape, and indeed, landscape may be regarded as enlarged still life. Inanimate objects permitted Cézanne's intensive and lengthy study. In his painting of *Mount Sainte-Victoire from the Large Pine Tree* (fig. 18.8), of 1885–87, one of several paintings he made of this mountain, Cézanne used his "little planes" to analyze and carefully construct the view. Tree trunks mark the foreground plane, yet the curves of their branches echo the silhouette of the most distant hills, linking foreground and background, compressing pictorial space.

In his *Still Life with Peppermint Bottle* (fig. 18.9), of ca. 1894, Cézanne makes apparent that the subject was not as important to him as *how* he painted it, and he often combined unrelated objects in his still lifes. No attempt at photographic reproduction was made, for he consciously distorted edges and shapes, emphasizing the contours and the space between objects. Disregarding the conventions of perspective, he created a tension between the three-dimensional subject and the two-dimensional surface.

FIGURE 18.8 Paul Cézanne, *Mount Sainte-Victoire from the Large Pine Tree*, 1887, oil on canvas, $23\frac{1}{2}'' \times 28\frac{1}{2}''$ (60 × 73 cm), The Phillips Collection, Washington, DC, acquired 1925. Cézanne's innovative approach to depicting objects in space, without using traditional methods of perspective, would prove to be influential for twentieth-century painting.

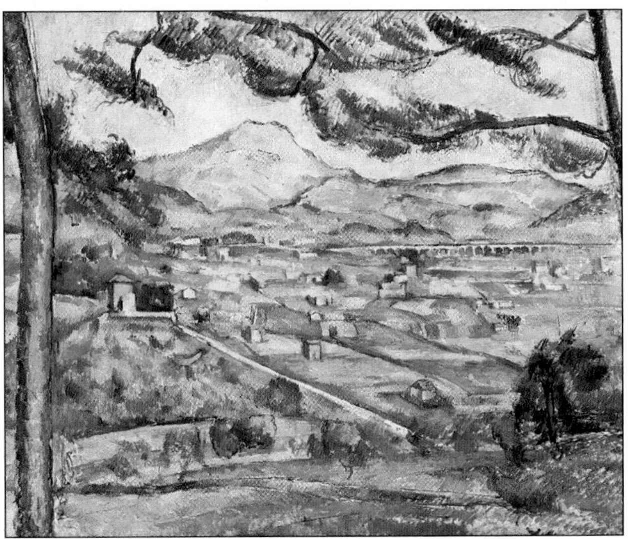

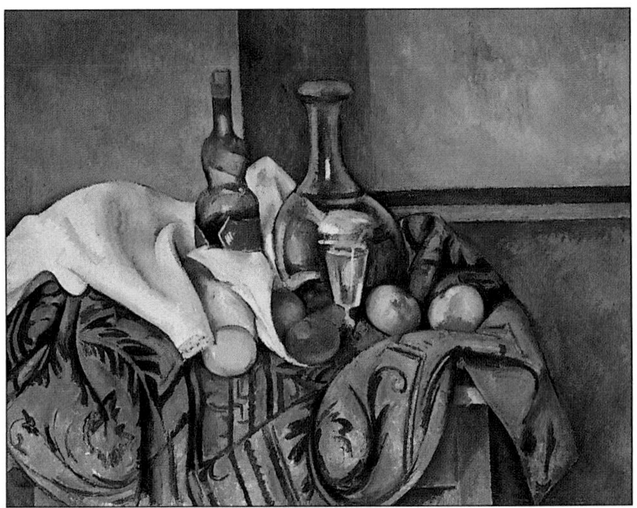

FIGURE 18.9 Paul Cézanne, *Still Life with Peppermint Bottle*, ca. 1894, oil on canvas, $26'' \times 32\frac{3}{8}''$ (66 × 82.3 cm), Chester Dale Collection. Photograph © Board of Trustees, National Gallery of Art, Washington, D.C. Post-Impressionists perpetuated the bright colors of Impressionism, but for different purposes. Using broken color in a more scientific and studied way, Cézanne referred to each brushstroke as a "little plane," which he used to establish the contours of an object in space.

Always striving, yet chronically dissatisfied with his work, Cézanne felt he did not reach his goal. "I am the primitive of the way I have discovered," he claimed. Yet much of early twentieth-century painting is indebted to Cézanne, who has been called the "Father of Abstract Art." His phrase, "You must see in nature the cylinder, the sphere, and the cone," became the basis of the Cubist painting of Pablo Picasso and Georges Braque.

Georges Seurat. Another important French Post-Impressionist artist, GEORGES SEURAT [sir-AH] (1859–1891), had an approach to painting that was still more intellectual and scientific, for he believed that art could be created by a system of rules. Like Cézanne, he made many sketches and studies before painting and worked very slowly.

Sunday Afternoon on La Grande Jatte (fig. 18.10), painted between 1884 and 1886, is a monumental work. The subject is the type favored by the Impressionists—a sunny afternoon in a public park with a gathering of French society. Yet, in an effort to give structure to the disintegrating forms of Impressionism, Seurat solidified and simplified them and defined their boundaries. Edges reappear and silhouettes are sharp. All is tidy, balanced, and arranged with precision.

Then & Now

POINTILLISM AND TELEVISION

Seurat's Pointillist technique involved putting small dabs of different colored paint next to one another and allowing the eye to blend them into a single tone. Television works in much the same way. A standard set contains one picture tube and three electron guns. Each gun makes a complete picture on the screen in one of the primary light colors—red, blue, and green (not yellow as in surface primary colors). The screen itself is made of small dots, each dot capable of being hit by only one of the guns. When the three primary colors are projected simultaneously through the dots on the screen, they blend, projecting a full range of colors to the viewer's eye. If you look at the screen of a color television with a magnifying glass before turning it on, you can see the pattern of dots. Then look at the screen after turning it on, and you can see how the manufacturer has arranged the different primary colors (every manufacturer employs a different pattern) in an array intended to create vivid color images.

Seurat's working method was first to create silhouettes of simple lines and precise contours. He then organized the composition's surface and depth. Spaces between figures and shadows were considered part of the composition, and shapes were repeated for unity. Finally, he painted in his *petits points*, a technique called "Pointillism," although Seurat called it "divisionism." **Pointillism** is the almost mathematical application of paint to the canvas in small dots or points of uniform size, each dot precisely placed. This technique is underpinned by color theory—Seurat believed the human eye could optically mix the different colors he applied as dots. Thus, where a blue dot was placed next to a red dot, theoretically the eye would see purple. It is difficult to imagine the patience required to paint in this technique, which Seurat even used to sign his name and to paint the frames. Each shape, its color, size, and location, is calculated—very different from Impressionism's informal, seemingly accidental quality.

FIGURE 18.10 Georges Seurat, *A Sunday Afternoon on La Grande Jatte*, 1884–86, oil on canvas, 6′9$\frac{3}{4}$″ × 10′1$\frac{1}{4}$″ (2 × 3m), Helen Birch Bartlett Memorial Collection. Photograph © 2005, The Art Institute of Chicago. All Rights Reserved. Seurat systematically applied bright color in tiny dots intended to blend in the viewer's eyes when the painting is seen from a distance. The technique is scientific, and the composition is carefully unified by the repetition of curving shapes.

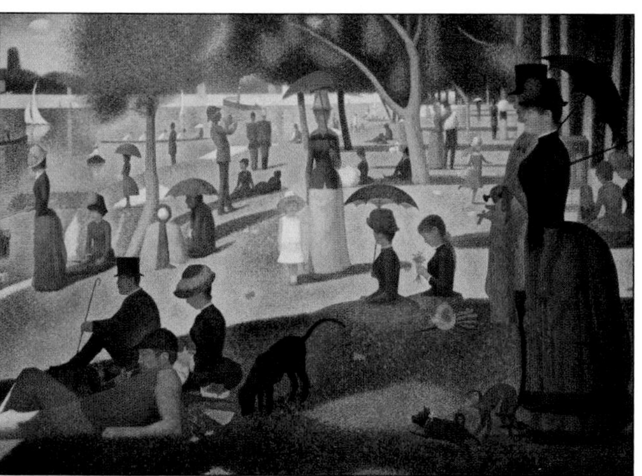

Vincent van Gogh. In contrast to Seurat, VINCENT VAN GOGH [van GOH] (1853–1890) is famed for his rapidly executed paintings, which use expressive and emotional color. Dutch by birth, van Gogh lived and worked in France for most of his life. His brother Theo, director of a small art gallery, supported him. Van Gogh met the Impressionists and used their bright colors and vivid contrasts, not to capture light effects but to convey emotion.

Van Gogh's *Starry Night* (fig. 18.11), of 1889, was painted on a hillside overlooking St.-Rémy, a small town

FIGURE 18.11 Vincent van Gogh, *Starry Night*, 1889, oil on canvas, 28$\frac{1}{4}$″ × 36$\frac{1}{2}$″ (73 × 92 cm). Acquired through the Lillie P. Bliss Bequest. The Museum of Modern Art/Licensed by Scala-Art Resource, NY. Although seemingly conceived and executed without restraint, as if painted in a fevered rush, this painting was actually preceded by a complete preliminary drawing.

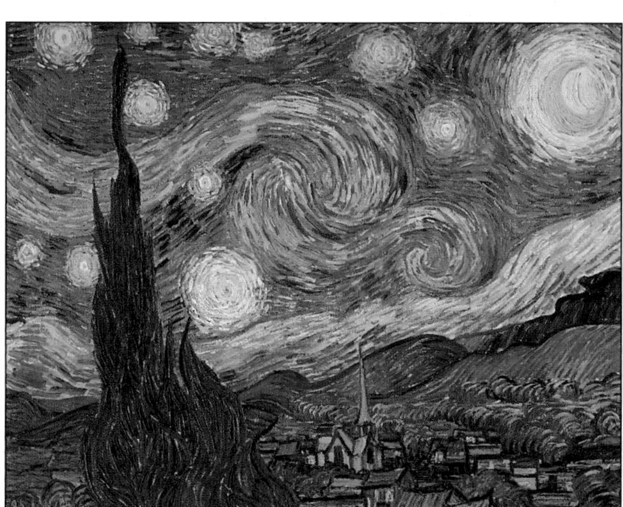

Cross Currents

JAPANESE PRINTS AND WESTERN PAINTERS

The influence of the Japanese prints on Western painters of the nineteenth century, especially on the Impressionists, is the direct result of the opening of Japan to trade with the West after Commodore Matthew Perry sailed into Tokyo Bay in 1853, demanding that Japanese ports be opened to foreigners. Perry's arrival ended over two hundred years of Japanese isolationism, which had started as a result of the negative reception of Christian ideas introduced into the country by foreign missionaries.

After trade began, Japanese prints flooded Europe to such an extent that they became commonplace. Western artists were attracted especially to the flatness of Japanese forms, the compressed pictorial space, and the oblique perspective that characterizes Japanese prints. The cropped but close-up renderings of occurrences in everyday life that so enthralled the Japanese artists influenced, in particular, the work of Edgar Degas and Mary Cassatt.

Claude Monet discovered the first of the many Japanese prints that would decorate his house at Giverny wrapped around a cheese purchased at the market. What especially attracted him to Japanese landscapes were the ways in which they organized the natural elements, such as rocks and trees. Perhaps the clearest example of Monet's enthusiasm for Japanese art and culture is the garden he created at Giverny and the paintings it inspired. The Far Eastern influence is evident in the small pond he created, which was spanned by a little arched bridge, with blue wisteria flowers arranged so as to hang down on either side. There were irises, bamboo, and willows, all common plants in Japanese paintings.

Perhaps the artist most thoroughly influenced by the Japanese print was Vincent van Gogh. He owned hundreds of prints, and one of the reasons he went to Arles in 1888 was that he believed he would find a landscape there similar to that of Japan. His letters to his brother Theo repeatedly refer to his idealized image of Japanese life, in which painters and printmakers lived in close contact with ordinary people and in harmony with the rhythms and cycles of nature. While still in Paris, in 1887, van Gogh copied a print by Ando Hiroshige, *Plum Estate*, of 1857. Van Gogh's painting, entitled *Japonaiserie: The Tree* (fig. 18.12), is an almost exact copy. What particularly impressed van Gogh was the relation between the tree in the foreground, and the space behind it, the gulf between the nearby detail and the landscape beyond. This is an effect that would dominate his paintings in the future.

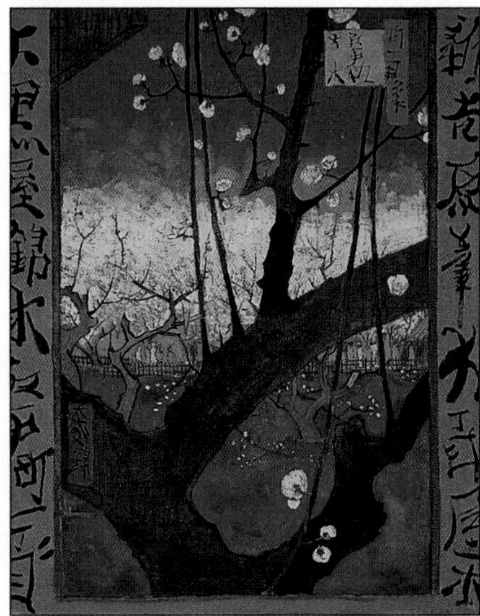

FIGURE 18.12 Vincent van Gogh, *Japonaiserie: The Flowering Plum Tree (after Hiroshige). Paris Summer/Autumn*, 1887, oil on canvas, $21\frac{3}{8}'' \times 18\frac{1}{8}''$ (55 × 46 cm), National Museum Vincent van Gogh, Amsterdam. Van Gogh was influenced in this painting and in others by the unusual vantage point, flat pattern, and dark outlines characteristic of Japanese prints.

just south of Arles. *Starry Night* is anything but calm. In this unusually turbulent landscape, his highly expressive brushwork implies the precarious balance of his emotions. Pigment appears slapped on, sometimes applied with a brush, sometimes a palette knife, sometimes squeezed directly from the tube—as if van Gogh were desperate to get his ideas on canvas as quickly as possible. This appears spontaneous, almost as if he started painting and could not stop himself. The result is an emotional landscape, frenzied, passionate, flamelike, undulating, the sky swirling and writhing. Yet, in fact, the composition was planned in advance and is organized and balanced by traditional methods. The composition flows from left to right, the trees and church steeple slowing the movement down, with the hills rising on the right-hand side of the picture for balance. Vincent wrote to Theo explaining his working method, saying he would think everything out "down to the last detail" and then quickly paint a number of canvases.

Van Gogh suffered from extreme emotional swings. During one of his periods of depression, he shot himself in a field in Auvers. He died two days later, on July 21, 1890, in Theo's arms. He was thirty-seven years old. He never knew fame, but today he is one of the most celebrated of all painters.

Paul Gauguin. Fellow Post-Impressionist PAUL GAUGUIN [go-GAN] (1848–1903) was born to a Peruvian mother and a French father. A successful

Critical Thinking

ARTISTS' LIVES

One question that has interested readers of literature and viewers of art for centuries is the relationship between a writer's or artist's work and his or her life. Some scholars believe that a thorough knowledge of an artist's or writer's life is essential to understanding a particular book or painting. Others contend, on the contrary, that such biographical knowledge is not vital for such understanding, and that it may actually distract readers and viewers from the literary and artistic achievement of the work alone. Still others argue that a work can be appreciated and understood without knowing the details of an author's or artist's actual life, but that such biographical knowledge enriches that appreciation and understanding without either distracting us from or displacing the work aesthetically.

We might consider, for example, the weight we might give the knowledge that William Wordsworth wrote his poem "I Wandered Lonely as a Cloud" after having read in his sister Dorothy's journal an account of a walk he had taken with her some years earlier. Or, to take another example, we might consider the relevance of Vincent van Gogh's suicide for an analysis of his paintings, particularly those he painted near the end of his life. How important is what van Gogh wrote in a letter to his brother Theo in connection with his painting *Starry Night*? "I go out at night to paint the stars, and I dream always of a picture like of the house with a group of figures. . . . I have a terrible lucidity at moments when nature is so beautiful; I am not conscious of myself any more, and the pictures come to me as in a dream."

banker and stockbroker in Paris, Gauguin had a personal crisis at the age of thirty-five. He decided to become a full-time artist, leave his wife and five children, and embark on an exotic life, which he recorded in his autobiography, *Noa Noa* (*Fragrance*). Gauguin shared with the Symbolist poets a desire to escape the everyday world and retreat into what Mallarmé called metaphorically "the afternoon of a faun." To that end, he auctioned off about thirty of his paintings and sailed to Tahiti in 1891. There he lived in a wooden hut, painted all day, naked, and referred to himself as Monsieur Sauvage (Mr. Savage). He learned the native language and myths, took a Tahitian wife, and had a son.

Gauguin wrote about his painting *Manao Tupapau* (*Spirit of the Dead Watching*) (fig. 18.13), of 1892, in *Noa Noa.* One night, he returned to his hut, only to find it in complete darkness. Lighting a match, he found Tehura lying as shown, terror-stricken by the dark. The woman in the background is the "Spirit of the Dead." The white areas in the background are phosphorescent fungi which, according to Maori legend, symbolize the spirits of ancestors. Gauguin wrote that he tried to convey fear through "somber, sad, frightening" colors. The painting is treated as a pattern of rhythmically arranged colored shapes. Rather than emphasizing the three-dimensionality of solid forms, the picture plane is emphasized by the areas of flat color and by the stress on outline.

Gauguin called this style of painting *Synthetism*, characterized by heightened color, flattened forms, and heavy outlines. The style is also called **Symbolism,** the intent being to give concrete form to abstract ideas—Gauguin is considered the leader of the French Symbolist movement. Gauguin's willingness to distort shapes and colors for symbolic purposes was important for the future of painting. By turning away from realistic academic painting, Gauguin led others to use arbitrary shape and color, and to free art from the restraints of nature.

FIGURE 18.13 Paul Gauguin, *Manao Tupapau (Spirit of the Dead Watching)*, 1892, oil on burlap mounted on canvas, $28\frac{1}{2}'' \times 36\frac{3}{8}''$ (72.4 × 92.5 cm). A. Conger Goodyear Collection, 1965. Albright-Knox Art Gallery, Buffalo. The phosphorescent spots were believed by the Maoris to signify the spirits of the dead. In spite of his claims, Gauguin remained a sophisticated artist, drawing more on the art of the museums than from his surroundings.

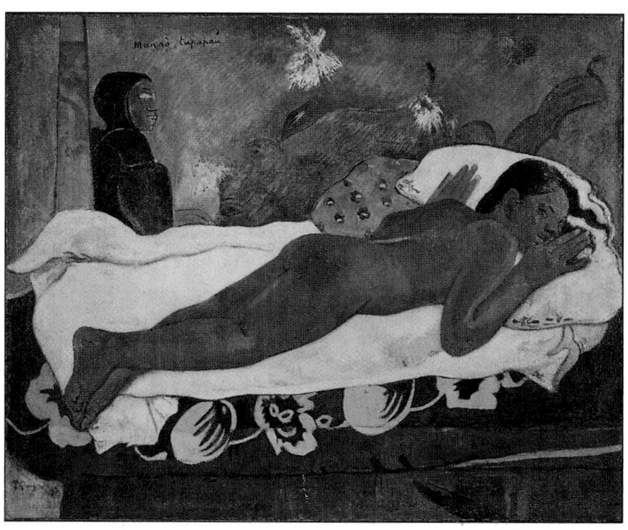

Table 18–1 IMPORTANT PAINTINGS OF IMPRESSIONISM AND POST-IMPRESSIONISM

	Artist	Painting and Date
Impressionism	Whistler	*Arrangement in Black and Gray,* 1871
	Degas	*The Dancing Class,* ca. 1874
	Renoir	*Dance at the Moulin de la Galette,* 1876
	Morisot	*Summer's Day,* 1879
	Monet	*Haystacks at Giverny,* 1891
	Cassatt	*The Boating Party,* 1893–94
Post-Impressionism	Seurat	*Sunday Afternoon on La Grande Jatte,*1884–86
	van Gogh	*Starry Night,* 1889
	Gauguin	*Spirit of the Dead Watching,* 1892
	Cézanne	*Still Life with Peppermint Bottle,* ca. 1894

NEW DIRECTIONS IN SCULPTURE AND ARCHITECTURE

Auguste Rodin. For the better part of the nineteenth century, many sculptural concepts had amounted to little more than variations on classicism, but toward the end of the century a major sculptor appeared. The Frenchman AUGUSTE RODIN [roh-DAN] (1840–1917) became the most influential sculptor in Europe. He studied the human form from nude models in his studio, but rather than having them remain immobile as was the tradition, Rodin's models walked around so he could study the human body in motion.

Rodin's bronze sculpture *The Thinker* (fig. 18.14), made between 1879 and 1889, was intended to form part of a larger work for the entrance to the Museum of Decorative Arts in Paris, *The Gates of Hell,* based on Dante's *Inferno* (see Chapter 12), with *The Thinker* looking down on hell, brooding over the gates. Rodin's superb understanding of "body language" can be seen in the details, for example, in the tension in the toes of the figure that seem to grip the base.

Also created for this entrance was an over-lifesize marble sculpture called *The Kiss* (fig. 18.15), made between 1886 and 1898. In this work Rodin displays a sensuous love of the body as well as virtuosity in carving two intertwined figures. The completed sculpture has portions of stone that have been intentionally left rough, thereby emphasizing a contrast of textures between the illusion of soft skin and the hard marble from which it came. Some of Michelangelo's work also has this contrast, but this is because he lacked time to finish his work. Rodin, in contrast, did this as a conscious aesthetic.

Camille Claudel. Rodin's art was closely linked with that of the French sculptor CAMILLE CLAUDEL [ka-ME claw-DEL] (1864–1943). She was a prodigy; when only

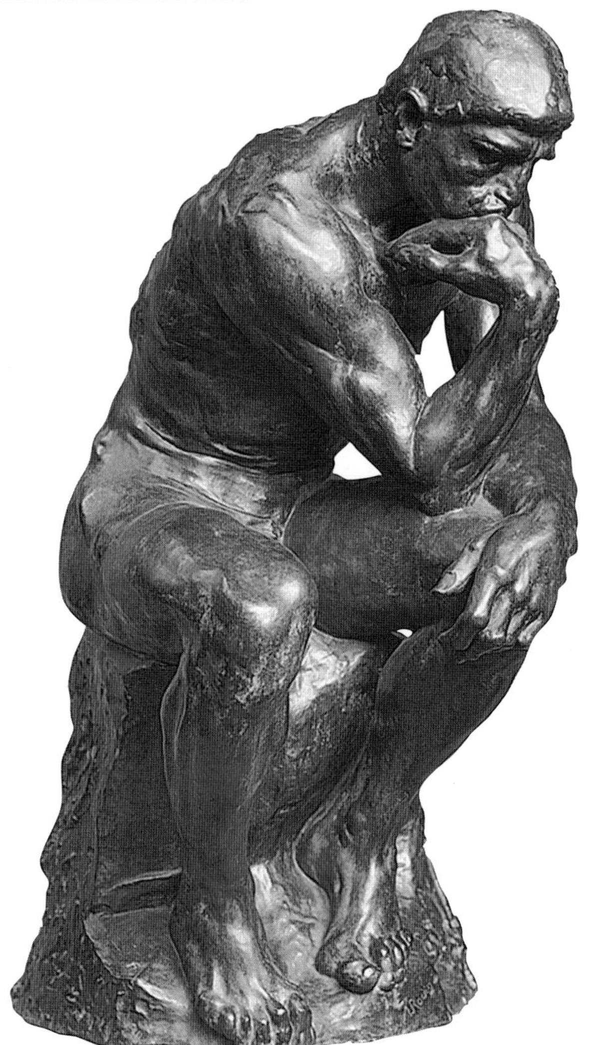

FIGURE 18.14 Auguste Rodin, *The Thinker,* 1879–89, bronze, height $27\frac{1}{2}''$ (69.8 cm), Metropolitan Museum of Art, NY. Gift of Thomas F. Ryan, 1910 (11.173.9). Art Resource, NY. Like the Impressionist painters' concern with light flickering over forms, Rodin's broken surface creates a similarly dappled and unfinished effect.

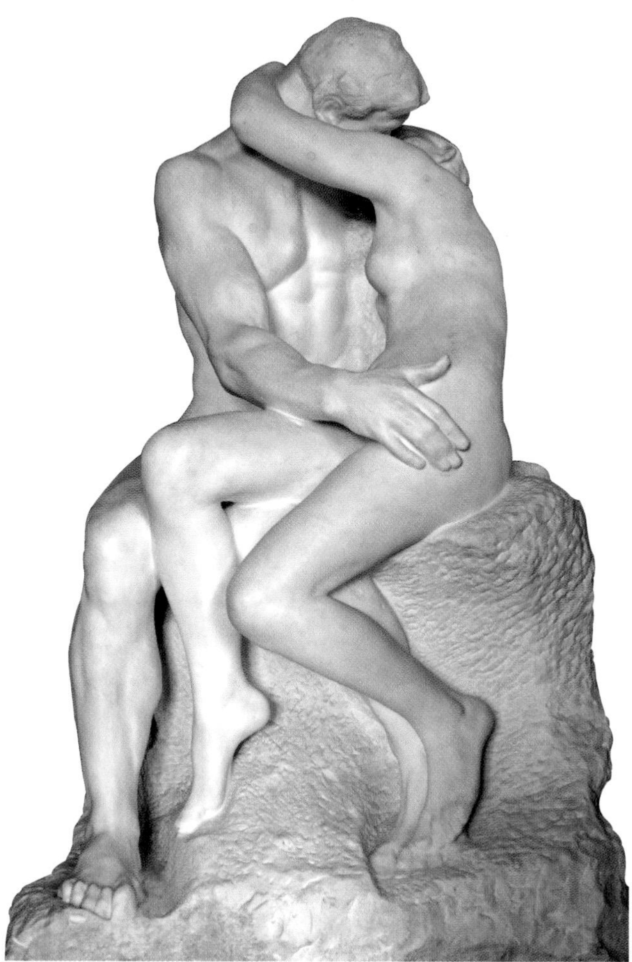

FIGURE 18.15 Auguste Rodin, *The Kiss*, 1886–98, marble, over-lifesize, height 6′2″ (1.90 m), Musée Rodin, Paris. The seemingly warm soft flesh is emphasized in contrast to the hard cold stone from which it was carved.

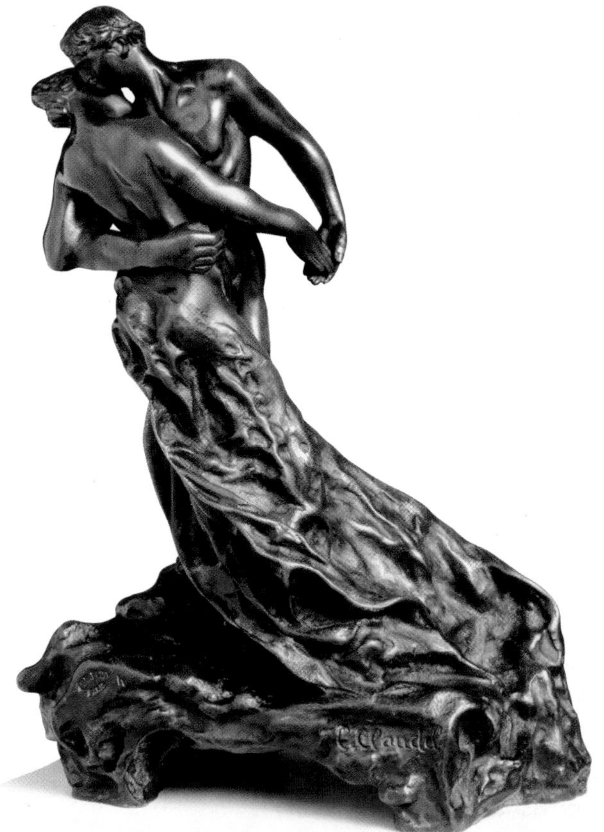

FIGURE 18.16 Camille Claudel, French, *The Waltz*, 1892, bronze, height $9\frac{7}{8}$″ (25 cm), Bayerische Staatsgemaldesammlungen, Neue Pinakothek, Munich. Claudel, long in the shadow of Rodin—her teacher, collaborator, and lover—was certainly his artistic equal. Her work is unmatched for the exquisite refinement of the forms and the graceful fluidity of the movements.

thirteen years old she was presented to the Director of the École Nationale des Beaux-Arts. Claudel and Rodin both focused on the human body as a vehicle for emotional expression. Their styles were so similar that there were instances in which he signed her work—and she was furious. Twenty-four years younger than Rodin, Claudel was first his student, then his collaborator, and soon his lover.

Claudel created a sculpture of a couple dancing, but, because the nudity of the figures shocked the public, she added the costumes, creating the version of *The Waltz* seen in fig. 18.16 in 1892. The work was very well received when it was exhibited in 1893 and various versions were created in later years.

After Claudel's definitive split with Rodin in 1898, she freed herself from his influence and was at her most creative. Although she thrived artistically, she suffered emotionally, and concerns about her mental health began with initial signs of paranoia. In her "madness," as it was called, she destroyed what she had created. At her family's request, she was institutionalized for the last thirty years of her life.

Architecture. At the 1889 World Fair in Paris, which marked the one-hundredth anniversary of the revolution, the engineer Gustave Eiffel (1832–1923) constructed the tallest structure in the world, a tower that stood 984 feet high (fig. 18.17). At first, many Parisians hated it. The author Guy de Maupaussant, for instance, preferred to lunch at the restaurant in the Eiffel Tower because, he said, "It's the only place in Paris where I don't have to see it." Despite the negative reception, its skeletal iron frame prepared the way for the most prevalent of twentieth-century buildings—the skyscraper.

Toward the end of the nineteenth century, a new style developed in architecture, seen in public and commercial buildings—stores, offices, and apartments. The use of iron, steel, concrete, and large sheets of glass radically changed

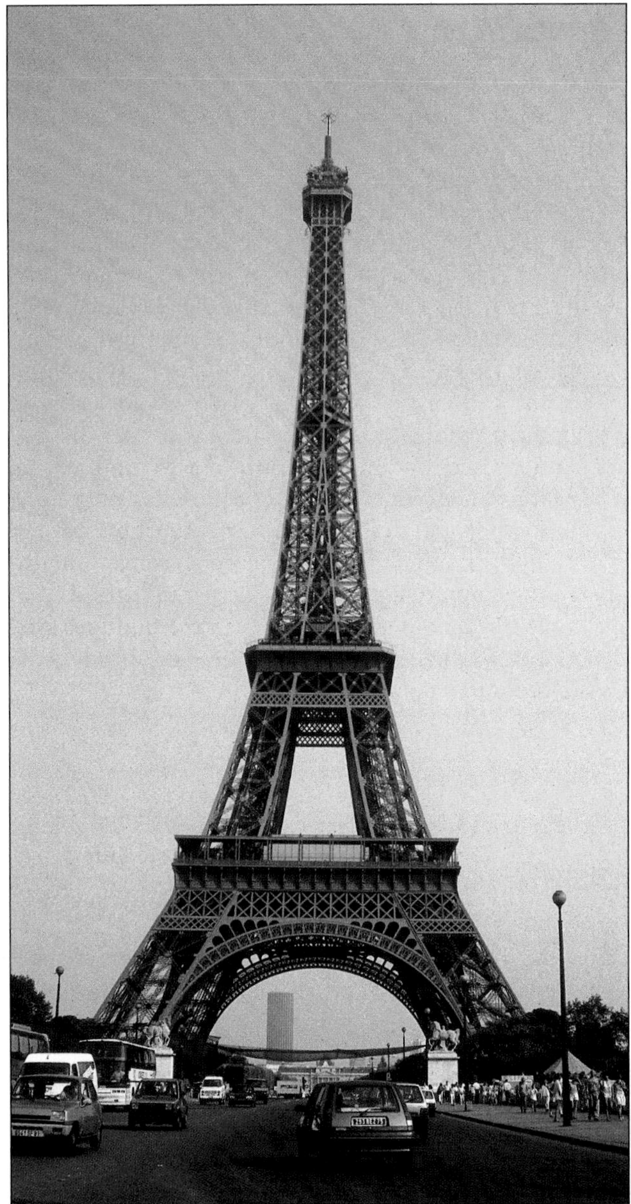

FIGURE 18.17 Gustave Eiffel, Eiffel Tower, Paris, 1889. This demonstration of engineering technology, which was extremely controversial when erected and has remained unique, is now considered the symbol of France. An elevator takes tourists up to enjoy a spectacular view of Paris.

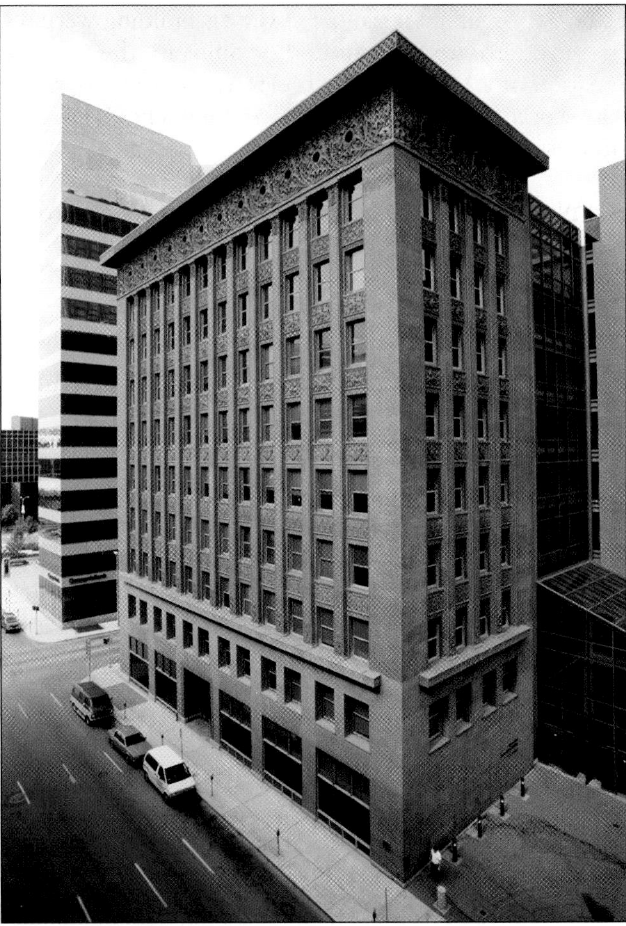

FIGURE 18.18 Louis Sullivan, Wainwright Building, St. Louis, Missouri, 1890–91. Moving in the direction of the skyscraper, the Wainwright Building has an underlying steel skeleton and brick skin. The architect Louis Sullivan's now famous phrase, "form follows function" sums up his beliefs.

architectural language. As steel construction and concrete forms were developed, thick masonry walls were no longer required to support the whole structure of a building. Expression was given freely to the new underlying skeletal frames. The idea of the building as a solid closed space was replaced by that of the building as an open airy environment. As height could be more easily increased, tall buildings began to define the city skyline.

The American architect Louis Sullivan (1856–1924) designed such a structure with the Wainwright Building in St. Louis, Missouri (fig. 18.18). Built between 1890 and 1891, it uses a supporting steel structure and has a brick exterior. Sullivan's design stresses the continuous verticals that reflect the internal steel supports, thus emphasizing the building's height. Sullivan doubled the number of piers necessary, creating a dense effect. The corners are stressed and thereby visually strengthened. Horizontals at the top and bottom provide a visual frame—in a sense, a start and a conclusion to the compostion.

Sullivan saw a building as being like the human body: The steel is the bone; the brick is the flesh and skin. It was Sullivan who coined the phrase "form follows function." Yet this does not mean the decorative elements of the design are integral to the architectural design. For Sullivan, "the function of all functions is the Infinite Creative Spirit," and this spirit could be revealed in the rhythm of growth and decay we find in nature. Thus the elaborate organic forms that cover his building were intended to evoke the infinite. For Sullivan, the primary function of a building was to elevate the spirit of those who worked in it. His ideas led to a new school of Functionalist architecture.

Art Nouveau. Sullivan's belief in nature was mirrored in **Art Nouveau** (literally, New Art), a short-lived style that began in Europe and was popular from the 1890s to the early 1900s. It is characterized by decoration, especially curvilinear patterns, based on the forms of nature. The influence of Art Nouveau extended beyond architecture to include home furnishings, clothing, and typography.

The home of Dr. Tassel in Brussels, designed by the architect VICTOR HORTA [OAR-ta] (1861–1947) and built 1893, is an ideal example of the Art Nouveau style. Horta liked to be able to design "each piece of furniture, each hinge and door-latch, the rugs and the wall decoration." Consequently, in the Tassel house every part is in harmony, characterized by curve and counter-curve, by its small scale, grace, and charm. The staircase (fig. 18.19) is illuminated by a skylight and made with large amounts of glass and metal, used both for ornamentation and for structure. It is especially characteristic of the Art Nouveau style with its swirling and sensuous forms.

In Spain, another exponent of Art Nouveau was ANTONÍ GAUDÍ [GOW-dee] (1852–1926), the architect of the Casa Milá in Barcelona (fig. 18.20), built 1905–07. This apartment building bears no relation to anything that had gone before. Gaudí's Art Nouveau style has few flat areas or straight lines, favoring instead constantly curving lines and asymmetry over symmetry. Although made of cut stone, the Casa Milá looks like it was molded from soft clay. Gaudí created an organic style influenced by the forms of the natural world. The building appears eroded, as if nature has worn away all the sharp angles. The facade seems to ripple around the corner of the building, and the roof seems to undulate. The chimneys look like abstract sculptures. Gaudí did much of his designing on the actual building site, which was unusual then (as it is now), and produced a highly personal and eccentric style.

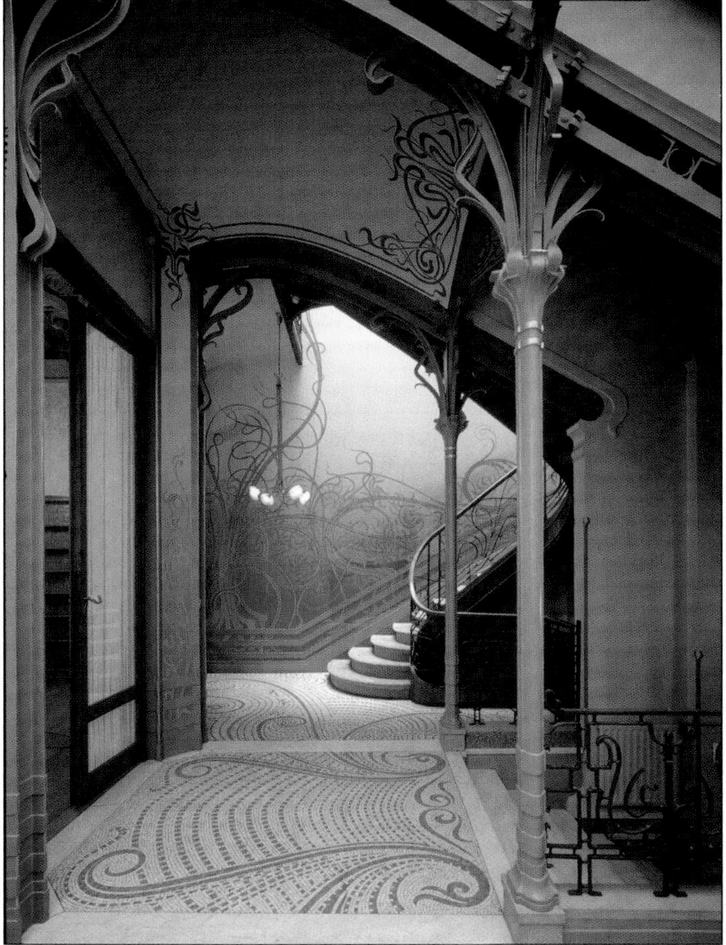

FIGURE 18.19 Victor Horta, staircase, Dr. Tassel's house, Brussels, 1893. Art Nouveau favored forms derived from nature such as foliage and curling tendrils. To achieve a certain harmony, Horta designed everything in the house, from the furniture and rugs down to the small details such as the hinges.

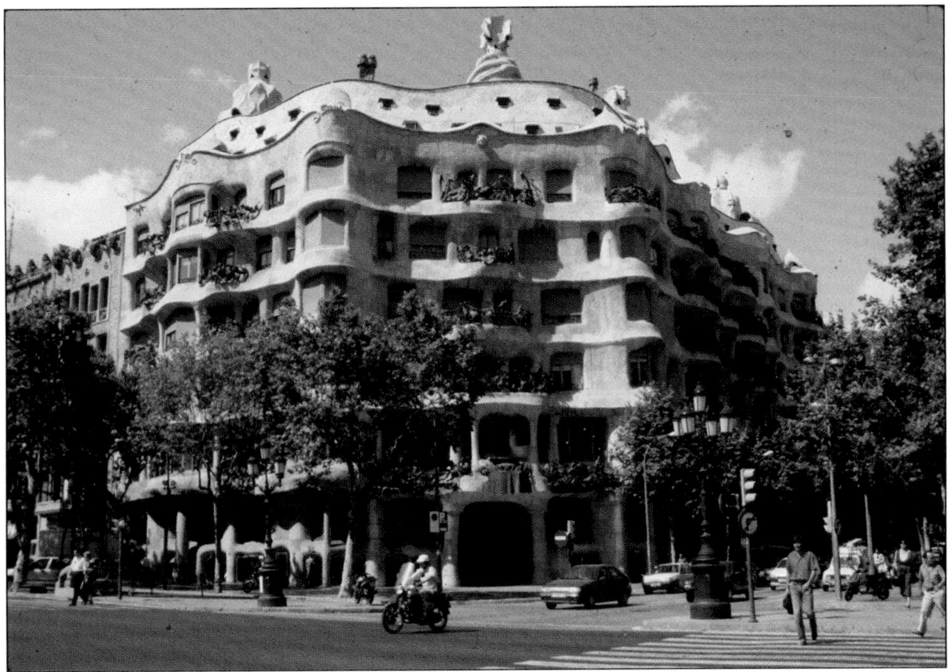

FIGURE 18.20 Antoní Gaudí, Casa Milá Apartment Building, Barcelona, 1905–07. Although made of traditional cut stone, the forms appear eroded by nature, weathered into curves, and the metal balcony railings look like seaweed.

Cultural Impact

During the second half of the nineteenth century, Romanticism gave way to Realism and then to Impressionism and Post-Impressionism. These artistic changes occurred in a climate of political and social unrest. In America, the Civil War raged from 1861 to 1865, with a death toll of more than 658,000. The war was a watershed in American history, and its legacy continues in issues of race and regionalism in contemporary America. In Europe, German unification resulted in increased military and economic power, a precursor to the German might of the Hitler era and to the consolidation of German political and economic enterprises following the collapse of communism and the fall of the Berlin Wall in 1989.

Of intellectual currents important during the later nineteenth century, none has been more significant than Darwin's theory of evolution through the process of natural selection. Darwin's ideas profoundly affected how human beings thought about themselves, unsettling their religious beliefs and challenging their understanding of science and history. Karl Marx's adaptation of Hegel's theory of historical change through conflict and resolution provided the foundation for the Russian Revolution of 1917. Finally, the emergence of liberalism as an applied political philosophy encouraged the spread of middle-class values, including thrift, ambition, and work, as well as an emphasis on the value of the individual.

The rise of the middle class created an audience for fiction and propelled it to primacy among the literary genres. In the later nineteenth century, drama too became increasingly popular as Ibsen and Strindberg, among others, wrote plays that reflected the issues of the time, including individual rights, inherited diseases, and the struggle for power between men and women. Realism continues to be enormously influential. In some senses, Realism has never gone out of style, although other styles have emerged to compete with it.

The Impressionist painters Claude Monet and Auguste Renoir enabled people to look at the everyday world in new ways, and their experiments with light, color, and atmosphere redirected the history of painting. In music, too, Impressionism was a significat stylistic development: The French composers Claude Debussy and Maurice Ravel achieved the sonorous equivalent of the color and light of Impressionist painting. Debussy created new harmonies and introduced new melodic possibilities, partly influenced by the music of other cultures, especially those of Asia. Ravel exploited instrumental sonorities of individual instruments and combined them in ways that expanded the orchestral sound palette.

The literary analogue of Impressionism was Symbolism, which sought to achieve with words effects similar to those of Impressionist painting and music. French Symbolist poetry attempted to create musicality with verbal sounds, inspiring Impressionist composers such as Debussy, in turn, to create musical equivalents of Symbolist poems. The work of Impressionist and Symbolist artists continue to influence contemporary painters, composers, and poets.

KEY TERMS

Impressionism
belle époque
Symbolists
atom
superman
Dionysian
Apollonian
psychoanalysis
ego
id
superego
Post-Impressionism
Pointillism
Symbolism
Art Nouveau

www. WEBSITES FOR FURTHER STUDY

http://www.artchive.com/artchive/M/manet.html
(This is the Artchive, a website with virtually every major artist in every style from every era in art history. It is an excellent resource.)

http://www.hf.uio.no/ibsensenteret/index_eng.html
(A comprehensive site on Henrik Ibsen, dramatist and author, with many links.)

http://www.westegg.com/einstein/
(An excellent, comprehensive site on all the work of Albert Einstein.)

http://www.freudfile.org
(An excellent comprehensive site on the life and work of Sigmund Freud.)

http://www.answers.com/topic/impressionist-music
(Overview of impressionist music with links to impressionism in other arts.)

http://en.thinkexist.com/quotes/friedrich_nietzsche/
(Site of quotes from Nietzsche's works, including links to quotes from others on Nietzsche's themes and ideas.)

Chapter 19

History

1260–94	Kublai Khan reigns
1275–92	Marco Polo in China
1368–1644	Ming dynasty
1402–24	Forbidden City rebuilt under Emperor Yongle's rule
1405–33	Cheng Ho travels to India and Africa
1514	Portuguese appear off coast of Canton
1644–1911	Qing dynasty
1689	British East India Company arrives in China
1784	American traders arrive in China
1840–42	Opium War with Great Britain
1898–1900	Boxer Rebellion
1911	Republic Revolution begins, dynastic rule overthrown
1911–49	Period of political instability
1965–76	Cultural Revolution
1989	Tiananmen Square protests
1997	Control of Hong Kong reverts to China

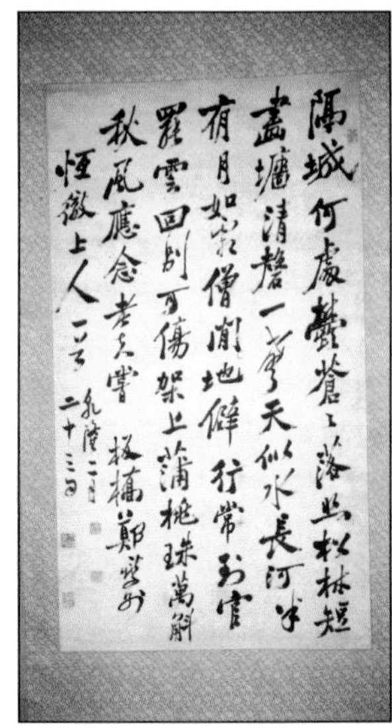

Arts and Architecture

1350	Wu Zhen, *Bamboo*
Early fifteenth century and later	Forbidden City
ca. 1500	Shen Zhou, *Poet on a Mountaintop*
ca. 1740	Zheng Xie, *A Country Temple*

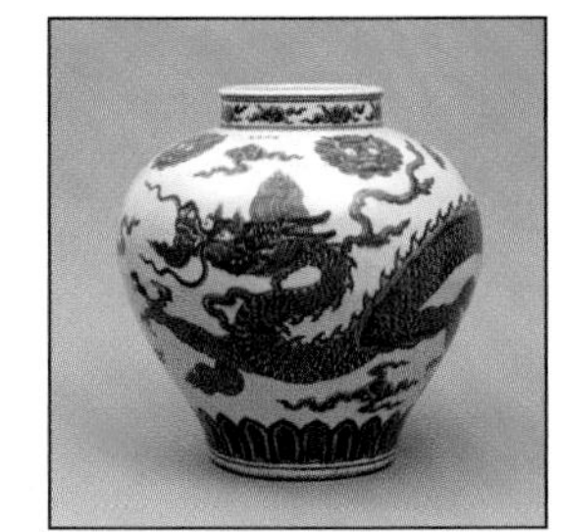

Literature and Philosophy

ca. 1750	Cao Xueqin, *The Dream of the Red Chamber*
1991–96	Bei Dao, Poems

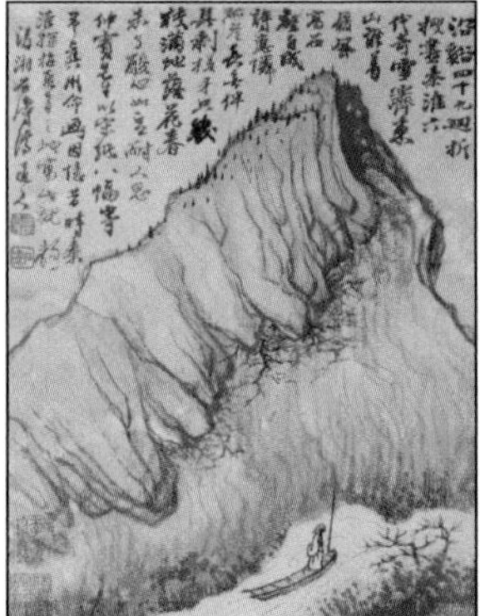

Later Chinese Civilization

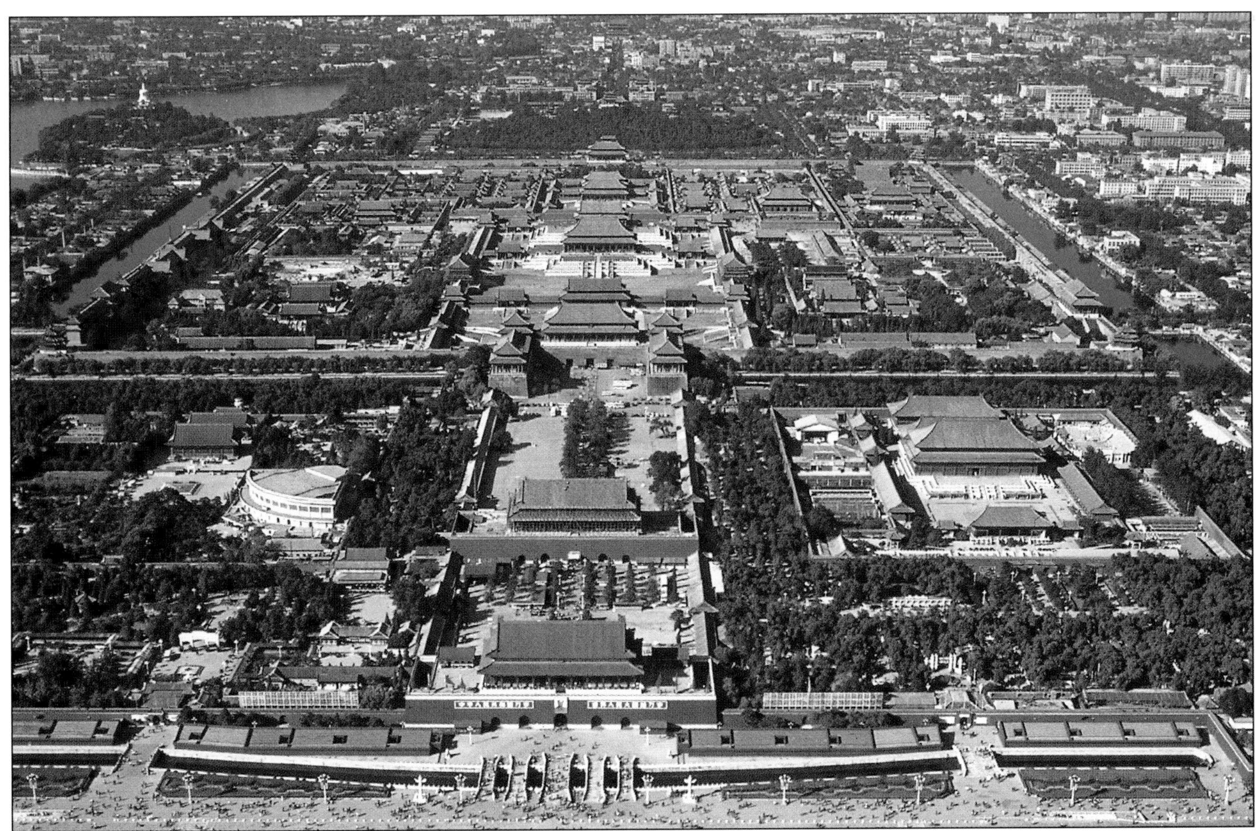

The Forbidden City, Beijing, seen from the north.

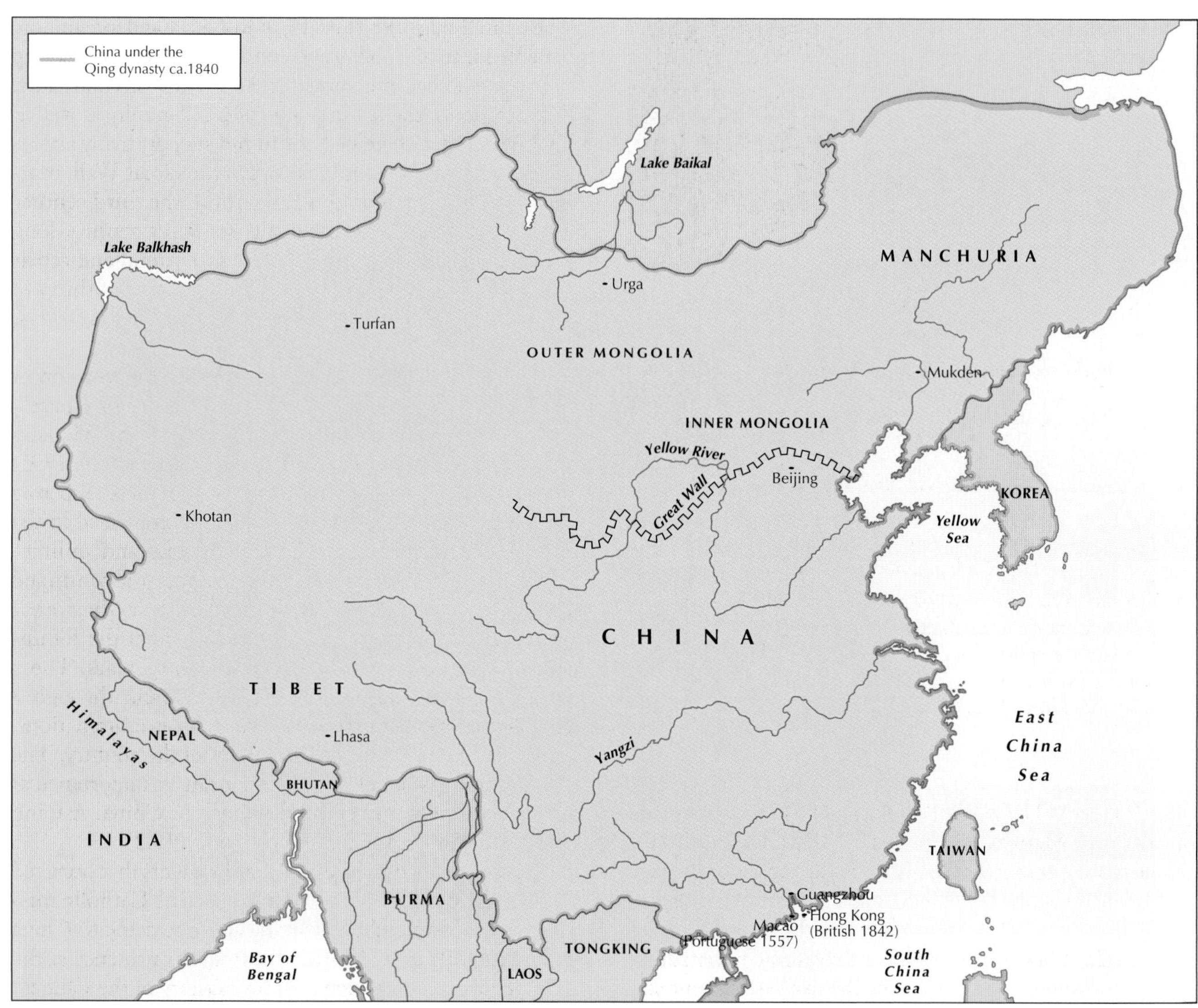

Map 19.1 China under the Qing Dynasty, ca. 1840.

Chapter Overview

LATER CHINESE CULTURE

An isolated China gradually absorbs Western ideas

LATER CHINESE CULTURE

The last of the great medieval dynasties of China was the Yuan (1271–1368), a Mongol dynasty. In 1271, the Mongolian leader KUBLAI KHAN [koob-lie KON] (1214–1294), a grandson of Genghis Khan, adopted the Chinese dynastic name Yuan. By 1279, Kublai Khan had conquered the Southern Song and ruled from Beijing [bay-JHING] as emperor of China. He turned Beijing into a walled city and extended the Grand Canal to provision it. The Mongol ruling class kept the principal offices of governmental administration to themselves, but appointed Chinese to the lowest posts. Although the Mongols wanted to maintain their ethnic separateness during their rule, they nonetheless needed Chinese officials to maintain order, collect taxes, and settle disputes.

The period of Yuan rule was the shortest of China's major dynasties, but it was culturally significant. A subtle and quiet resistance to the uneasy foreign occupation pervaded almost every aspect of Chinese life, including its painting. *Bamboo*

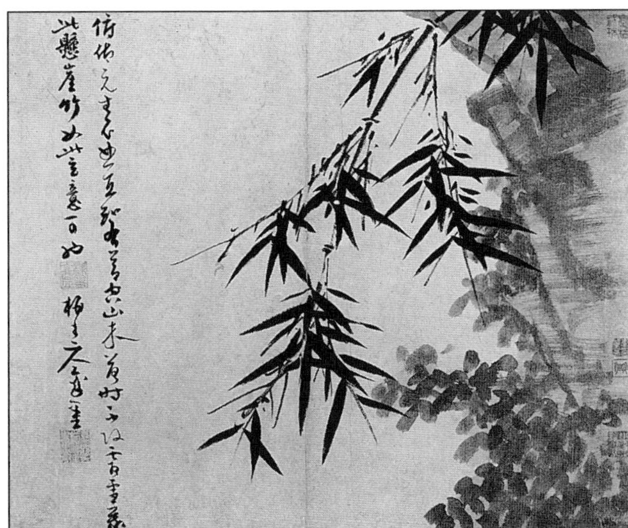

FIGURE 19.1 Wu Zhen, *Bamboo*, Yuan dynasty, 1350, album leaf, ink on paper, 16″ × 21″ (40.5 × 53.3 cm), National Palace Museum, Taipei, Taiwan, Republic of China. Despite Mongol rule, Wu Zhen worked in an intensely intellectual Chinese environment, dominated on the one hand by gatherings organized for the appreciation and criticism of poetry, calligraphy, painting, and wine, and, on the other, by deep interest in Buddhist and Taoist thought.

(fig. 19.1) by WU ZHEN [WOO JUN] (1280–1354), one of the "Four Masters" of the Yuan dynasty, is ostensibly a simple representation of the plant, but its social significance was widely recognized. Bamboo, one of the strongest of materials and a symbol of survival, is like the Chinese under foreign rule: They might bend, but they would never break. Similarly, orchids, which nurture themselves without soil surrounding their roots, are a common symbol of Chinese culture in this period. Like the nation, the orchid could survive, even though the native Chinese soil had been stolen by the Mongol invaders. In 1368, Zhu Yuanzhang drove the last Yuan emperor north into the deserts and declared himself the first emperor of the new Ming dynasty. China was once again ruled by the Chinese.

MING AND QING DYNASTIES

The Ming (1368–1644) and Qing [CHING] (1644–1911), China's last dynasties, maintained the centralized bureaucratic political organization developed by the earlier Tang and Song dynasties. Although the Qing was ruled by Manchus, rather than ethnic Chinese, the Ming and Qing were remarkably alike in their reliance on Confucian ideals and in their high level of cultural achievement. The patriarchal nature of Confucian society (see Chapter 8) was evident at every level: The family, headed by the father, was the model unit. Politically, the emperor, as the Son of Heaven, was the father of the country. The magistrates, who carried out the rule of the emperor, also served as authority figures. The entire Ming–Qing system, one of unity and integration, benefited from the ability and commitment of its governing officials, who became known as *mandarins*, or counselors. These officials, trained in poetry and calligraphy as well as Confucianism, also helped create and support many arts.

Later Ming emperors reinforced the Great Wall, originally built by the first Qin Emperor in the third century B.C.E. The Ming emperors made the wall a century-long project, using thousands of workers to extend and repair the 1,500-mile-long wall that reached heights of thirty to fifty feet, and which included watchtowers, signal towers, and accommodations for troops.

The Ming dynasty ended in 1644 with the invasion of the Manchu from the north, who created the Qing ("pure") dynasty, which ruled until 1911. Two of the Manchu emperors, Kanxi (1661–1772) and Qianlong (1736–1795) solidified Manchu control of China. Both of these emperors were sophisticated and learned men, accomplished in the arts, while also being brilliant diplomats and military tacticians. These and other Qing emperors continued the governmental structure developed by their Ming predecessors, with a highly centralized state under the administrative control of Confucian mandarin scholars. These scholar-bureaucrats, who earned their rank through a complex series of competitive civil services examinations, controlled the political and social life of the country. The examination system ensured the continued importance of Confucianism to the cultural history of China. A Qing period scholar's study can be seen in fig. 19.2.

Among the many and varied developments that occurred during Qing rule was the arrival of Jesuit Catholic missionaries. Most notable of the Jesuits who came to China was Matteo Ricci (1552–1610), a frequent presence at the Ming courts, a consequence of his mastery of the Chinese language and the Confucian classics. Among the many ways that Ricci and his Jesuit colleagues and successors charmed their Chinese hosts was with their mathematical, scientific, and technical knowledge. Through these and other forms of Western knowledge brought by the Jesuits to China, the Jesuits gained access. Although this did not yield many converts, it did serve to build a metaphorical bridge of knowledge and understanding between China and Europe, the first since the time of Marco Polo.

Although China was generally self-sufficient during these centuries, it gradually became apparent that technical and scientific advances in the West had left China behind. By the end of the nineteenth century, China was politically weak, and European countries had established trading relations that were decidedly unfavorable to China. Something had to be done, and in the early-twentieth century, China abandoned the tradition of imperial rule that had provided social stability for many centuries. First, Confucian ideals of governance began to be discarded. Then, with the overthrow of the Qing dynasty in 1911, came a period of political instability that lasted until the establishment of the communist state in 1949.

Cross Currents

THE JESUITS IN ASIA

In the latter half of the sixteenth century, inspired by Francis Xavier, the Jesuits explored India, China, and Japan, establishing mission stations throughout Asia. Although the architecture of their buildings reflected a distinctive missionary style, the Jesuits were prone to acculturation. They learned the local languages; acquired, studied, and preserved sacred texts; and adapted their preaching and teaching to local customs. They even wore local attire.

Among the most prominent of the Jesuit missionaries was Matteo Ricci (REE-chee, 1552–1610), whose goal was to convert China to Christianity. Brilliant, learned, and highly skilled in diplomacy, Ricci became a prominent figure at the Ming court. Having thoroughly grounded himself in Chinese literature, philosophy, history, and culture, Ricci had a flair for languages. His exceptional memory enabled him to become highly literate and fluent in classical Chinese. Ricci's mastery of Chinese language and culture enabled the Jesuits to gain the trust of Chinese scholars, diplomats, and administrators, such that Ricci and his compatriots could share European science, technology, and medicine with the Chinese. The Jesuits prepared maps of the world for the Chinese and they supervised the casting of high-quality bronze cannons for Ming and Qing dynasty armies.

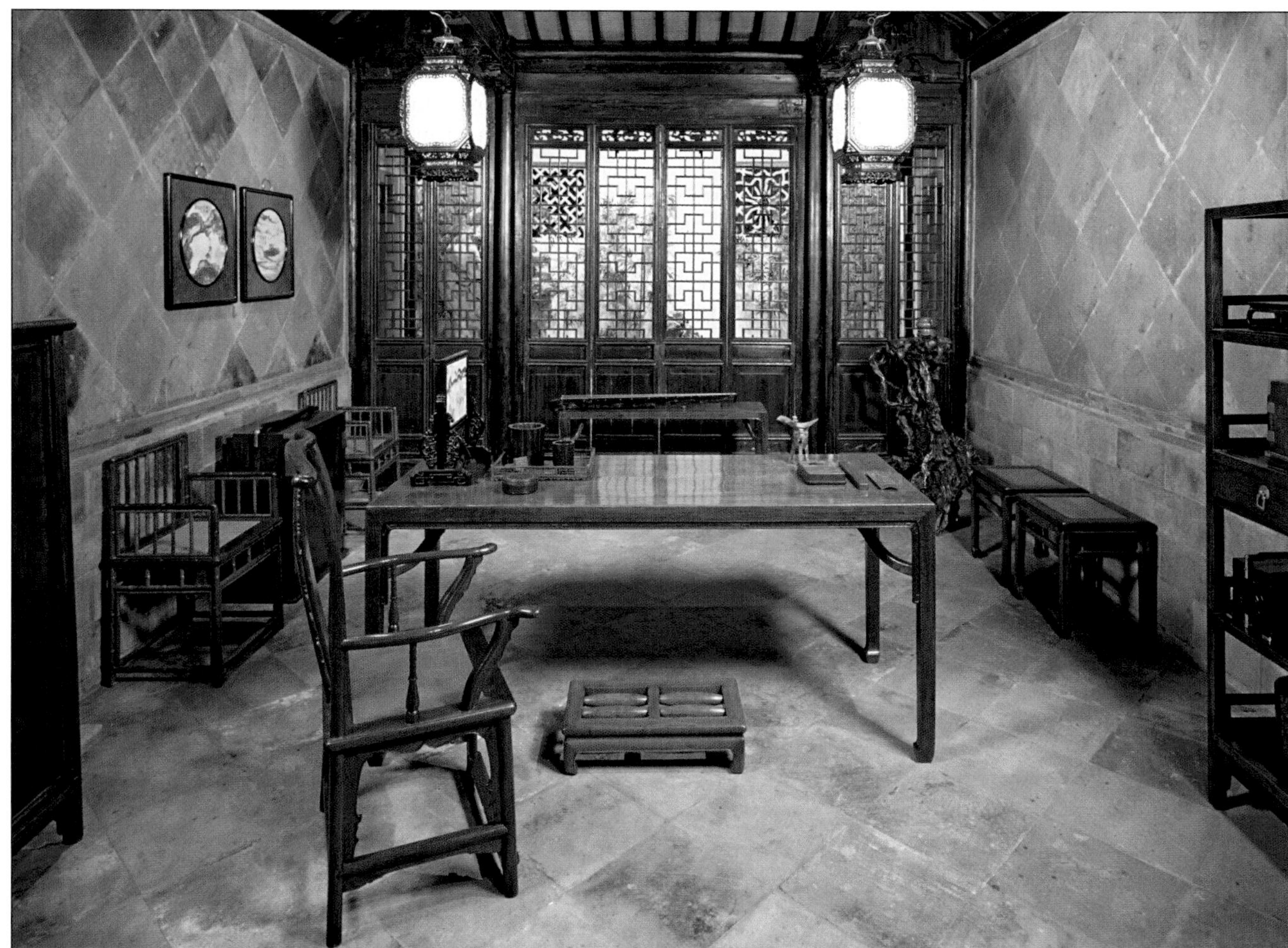

FIGURE 19.2 *The Studio of Gratifying Discourse*, Qing dynasty, 1797, wood, ceramic tile, stone, lacquer. Gift of Ruth and Bruce Dayton. The Minneapolis Institute of Arts. This scholar's study with a desk and footrest in the center and the delicate window grate offering a view of the garden, provides a serene space for contemplation, meditation, and inspiration.

Communism remains the dominant political system in contemporary China. Despite the tumultuous Cultural Revolution in the late 1960s—a period of upheaval in all aspects of Chinese culture and society—and despite the Tiananmen Square protests in 1989, which sought greater democratic liberties for the Chinese people, the Communist Party has maintained its political control. Nevertheless, a more liberal attitude toward capitalistic economic growth has led in the last decades to many changes in China, including modernization and emergence into the network of world trade.

Until a hundred years ago, however, the system that kept China organized was based on the national examination system. The examination system allowed the brightest and most capable men to join and advance in government, and these scholar-officials were most influential in the arts.

PAINTING

Formats. The four traditional formats of Chinese painting are: horizontal hand scrolls, vertical hanging scrolls, album leaves, and fans.

The hand scroll, which is characteristically Chinese, was used at least as early as the second century B.C.E. Initially, most Chinese paintings were horizontal in format. The earliest hand scrolls are on silk woven in very long panels. Paper was made in smaller sheets and, therefore, several sheets of thick paper were glued together to make a hand scroll. A wooden rod was attached to each end of the silk or paper so that it could be rolled and unrolled. The height of hand scrolls remained quite standard, ranging from approximately 9 1/2 to 14 inches high, while the length varied greatly. A hand scroll is meant to be seen lying flat, a section at a time, by an individual or a limited number of people. The scale of painting is small, suitable for close scrutiny. The unrolling and rolling of the hand scroll is controlled by one person, encouraging an intimate experience with the art. The entire scroll is never seen at one time—instead, it is unrolled, from the right to the left. As one end is rolled up, the other is unrolled; as one scene disappears, another appears, making the hand scroll ideal for narratives.

The increase in the number of *hanging scrolls* coincided with the rise in popularity of landscape painting, which gradually became the subject most frequently depicted, reaching its peak during the Northern Song dynasty (960–1127). A vertical scroll is meant to be seen in its entirety, hanging on a wall, and may be viewed by a number of people simultaneously. The scale of the painting is likely to be larger than on hand scrolls.

Chinese *albums* contain collections of small paintings. Because Chinese paintings are usually executed on paper or silk, both relatively fragile, they may be mounted on a sturdier support. Within the album, they are protected and preserved. Album leaves are intended to be seen close up. Subject matter, style of painting, number of paintings, and even the size and shape of the leaves may vary within an album.

Fans have long been used for comfort in warm weather. Early Chinese fans were flat; the folding fan was introduced to China from Korea in the eleventh century. The originally humble functional fan became an important personal accessory, elaborately decorated, that comprised a category of decorative art. Eventually, the fan's wedge shape, without the fan's function, was used as a format for painting. Although the artist's composition might simply defy or ignore the fan's wedge shape, more pleasing is an arrangement of elements curved to conform to the shape of the fan. As works of art, fans are meant to be contemplated carefully and close up. They are often given as gifts of friendship—a dedication inscription may refer to this or to an event, such as a meeting or a journey, even indicating the season and year.

Subjects. Landscape was the most important subject in Chinese painting until the late-nineteenth century, when influences entered China from the West. Some landscapes are based on the work of older masters, others are imaginary fantasies, and still others record with varying degrees of fidelity a place the artist visited. Chinese landscapes often incorporate an interest in weather conditions, recording an aspect of Nature's infinite variety, amalgamating the artist's imagination and experience. Small figures may be included, but they are likely to be dwarfed by the depictions of the vastness of Nature. In other paintings a closer scrutiny of Nature is evident in carefully rendered depictions of flowers, fruits, vegetables, and even insects. An encyclopedic variety may be shown, combining a genuine affection for Nature with scientific renderings. The human figure was depicted in scenes ranging from aristocratic life at court to the everyday life of ordinary people such as craftspeople and street vendors. Hunting scenes document customs and weaponry.

Composition. Chinese landscape painters preferred panoramic vistas with multiple focal points. To compose a landscape painting was regarded as a mental exercise. Often dominated by diagonals, the compositions used in Chinese paintings are of several types, each having a descriptive name. These include: "vertical-axis" composition, "banks on two sides of the river" composition, "S-shape" composition, and "diagonal" or "one-corner" composition.

A characteristic of Chinese painting is that a significant portion may be left empty, the void or negative spaces contrasting with the solid or positive areas that are densely filled with trees, stones, and other elements of Nature. These empty areas serve as foils to the representational areas and may enhance their clarity while also encouraging the viewer to contemplate what exists in the infinite space beyond the picture. That is, the unpainted areas are not meant to suggest nothingness. Rather, the empty areas are intended to suggest something tangible; to encourage the viewer to have thoughts that go far beyond the painted image; to entice the viewer to imagine more than what is depicted there by the artist.

Materials and Techniques. Chinese paintings are executed in ink and color. Chinese painters and calligraphers work with what are called the "Four Treasures of Study": paper, brush, ink-stick, and ink-stone, on which the ink is mixed with water. Usually only black ink is used but, depending on the amount of water added, the tone may be infinitely varied from the darkest shade of black to the palest pastel tint of grey. It is said that "black ink has many colors." The different shades of ink as well as the different types of brush strokes became increasingly more important in Chinese painting. The techniques with which the ink is applied to the paper or silk vary, and are known by descriptive terms such as "broken-ink," "splashed-ink," and "layered-ink."

Literati Painting. Many of the most important paintings created in China after the thirteenth century were by the scholar-official amateurs called **literati,** such as Wu Zhen (see fig. 19.1). During the Yuan, Ming, and Qing periods, these poet artists utilized brushwork to express their understanding of humankind and nature, usually communicating their poetic vision in landscapes.

Shen Zhou. The literati movement in the Ming dynasty was exemplified by SHEN ZHOU [SHUN JOH] (1427–1509), who was less a professional artist than a gentleman scholar. Unlike a typical member of his social class, he never held an official government position. Described as a "poet of the brush," Shen Zhou was the founder of the Wu school, a group of amateur scholar-painters for whom painting was an intimate expression of personal feeling. (The name "Wu" derives from Wuhsien, the Yangtze River Delta where Shen Zhou and other painters lived and worked.)

Among Shen Zhou's most striking compositions is *Poet on a Mountaintop* (fig. 19.3), one of five album paintings mounted as a hand scroll. Using black ink with a few touches of color, the artist balances white spaces (unpainted paper) with bold strokes and spots of black, to define the forms of rocks, trees, and other vegetation. He sets off the poet and the mountain in the center against lighter surroundings—washes of soft ink and white space. The poet, tiny and simply sketched, stands poised at the edge of a cliff on an inclined plane, propped up by his walking staff. Tucked away on the right is a mountain pavilion, a part of the natural scene, which is used as a place for people to put themselves in tune with the natural surroundings. Unlike many of his predecessors, Shen Zhou does not attempt to portray nature in an especially beautiful fashion, nor render the natural scene in carefully drawn, realistic detail. Instead, his painting conveys a sense of nature's serene grandeur.

FIGURE 19.3 Shen Zhou, *Poet on a Mountaintop*, Ming dynasty, ca. 1500, album painting mounted as a hand scroll, ink and color on paper, $15\frac{1}{4}'' \times 23\frac{3}{4}''$ (38.1 × 60.2 cm), Nelson-Atkins Museum of Art, Kansas City, Missouri. Like much Chinese nature painting, this work portrays human beings as a small element within a large natural scene.

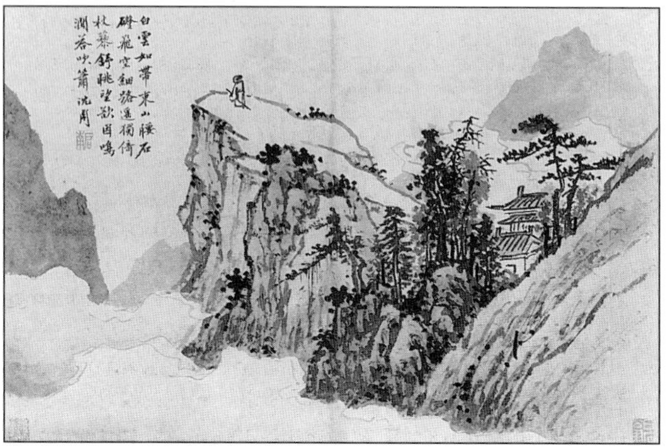

Dong Qichang. On a vertical hanging scroll, the Chinese artist Dong Qichang (1555–1636) painted *Shaded Dwellings among Streams and Mountains* (fig. 19.4) in the early seventeenth century, during the later Ming dynasty. Dong Qichang founded a school of painting that advocated reverence for the past by reviving or imitating earlier artists. Inspiration was taken from painters of the Tang, Song, and Yuan dynasties. Dong Qichang's own landscapes were inspired by masters from the tenth through thirteenth centuries; the painting illustrated here (fig. 19.4) is based on that of the tenth-century artist Dong Yuan. Literati painters, including Dong Qichang, promoted the idea of *shigu*, which means "the ancients as teachers," *fanggu*, which means "imitating the ancient," as well as *fugu*, which means "reviving the ancient." Admiration for one's own master was also encouraged. The beliefs of Dong Qichang remained unchallenged until the late-nineteenth century.

Shi Tao. The paintings of SHI TAO (Shee DOW) (1642–1707) are more overtly expressive than those of Shen Zhou, reflecting an adventurous life in which he traveled extensively through China, became a Ch'an (Zen) monk, and finally returned to secular life. He became known for his eccentricities, such as naming one of his paintings, "*Ten Thousand Ugly Ink Dots.*" He excelled in **wet-brush technique** in which the ink and colors merge and fuzz out on the paper or silk as in his work *Reminiscences of the Qin-Huai River* (fig. 19.5). His dramatic compositions often seem to put the viewer directly into the scene.

Like many literati, Shi Tao wrote about painting, emphasizing that one could not rely on following the past styles of painting, but must find one's own way based on timeless truths. His ideas rely on Taoist and Zen ideals (see Chapter 8) but apply them in a new way to art. He wrote, "In ancient times there were no methods, since the state of natural simplicity had not been shattered. But when this state was dispersed, methods arose. What was their basis? The true single stroke of the brush! This is the origin of all methods for depicting anything in existence and it is the root of all images. Revealed through the spirit, it is innate in all people but they do not realize this. I have established for myself, this method of no-method, from which all methods emerge." More specifically, he wrote, "When the wrist does not move freely, the painting will not be alive, but if each single stroke is created without hesitation, all methods are mastered."

Zhu Da. Another eccentric Qinu dynasty artist was ZHU DA (Joo DAH) (1626–1705). Related to the Ming imperial family, he was raised in wealth and privilege. At the age of eighteen, however, he saw the downfall of the

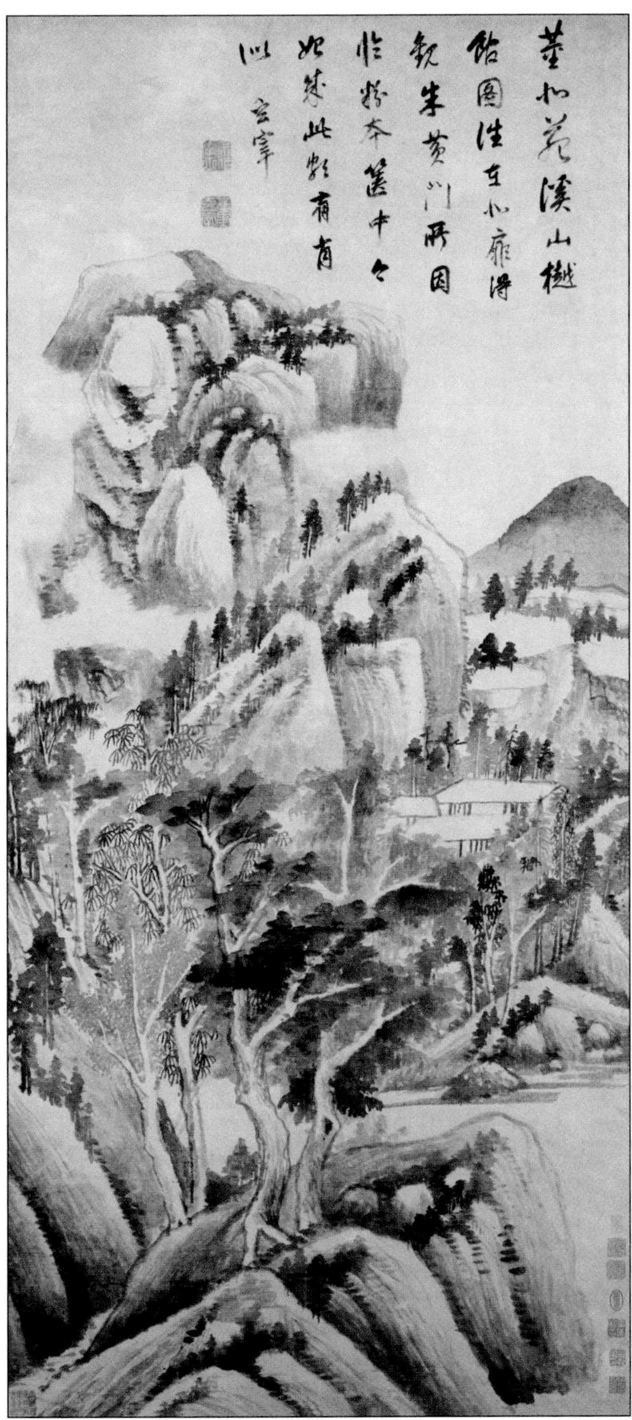

FIGURE 19.4 Dong Qichang (1555–1636), *Shaded Dwellings among Streams and Mountains*, later Ming dynasty, ink on paper, $62\frac{3}{8}'' \times 28\frac{3}{8}''$ (158.4 × 72.1 cm), Metropolitan Museum of Art, New York (1979.75.2). In this monumental style of landscape painting, the compact composition is compiled of a multitude of fragments. The expressive dynamic distortions and contortions of the erratically shaped hills are not dependent on duplicating observed Nature.

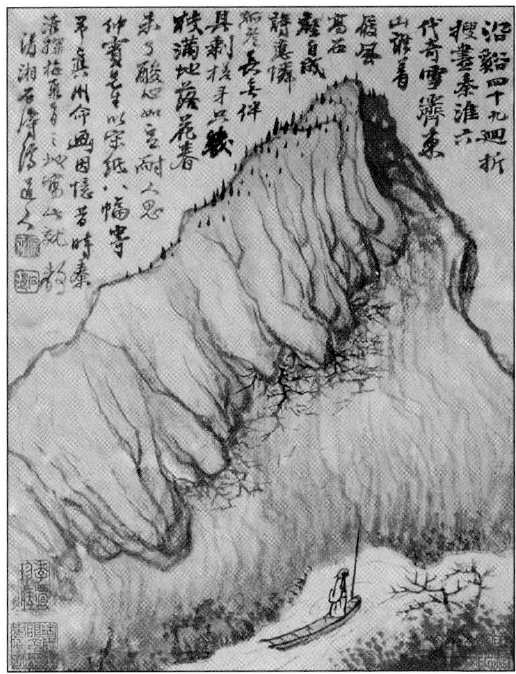

FIGURE 19.5 Shi Tao (1642–1707), *Reminiscences of the Qin-Huai River*. Qing dynasty, 1704. From album of eight leaves. Ink and light color on paper, $10\frac{1}{3}'' \times 8''$ (25.5 × 20.2 cm). © The Cleveland Museum of Art, John L. Severence Fund, 1966. 31.8. The scholar-sage is sailing along the river and, according to his poem, he is searching for the remains of past dynasties while composing poems.

Ming dynasty to the Manchus and he became, or pretended to be, dumb for some years. He served as a Buddhist monk but began to act as though he were insane; scholars still debate whether he was truly mad or was pretending in order to live his life without constraints. In his final years he turned more and more to painting, sometimes depicting landscapes but more often birds, animals, and plants in a distinctive ink style all his own. His painting *Fish and Rocks* (fig. 19.6) illustrates his unique style.

CALLIGRAPHY

The Chinese have long believed that the flexible brush is the perfect means to express one's inner spirit. Thus calligraphy with ink on paper or silk, whether by scholars, poets, monks, or government leaders, is often considered the highest form of art. Great masterworks from earlier periods such as the Tang dynasty were used as models for the proper style and proportion of the more than fifty thousand Chinese characters. There were also a number of different scripts to choose from. Ancient seal script, used even today for carving seals (or "chops"), conveys an archaic flavor, as does clerical script, developed in the Han Dynasty by clerks to record government documents. Calligraphy, however, could also be written in regular (printed), running (more rapid), or cursive (with strokes joined together) script, not unlike our own choices in English—for example, most of us do not write the small letter *a* in this printed form, but in more rapid pencil or pen movement. Similarly, Chinese calligraphers usually preferred less formal and more dramatic styles of brushwork to regular script. Some masters, however, combined scripts, such as the painter-poet-calligrapher

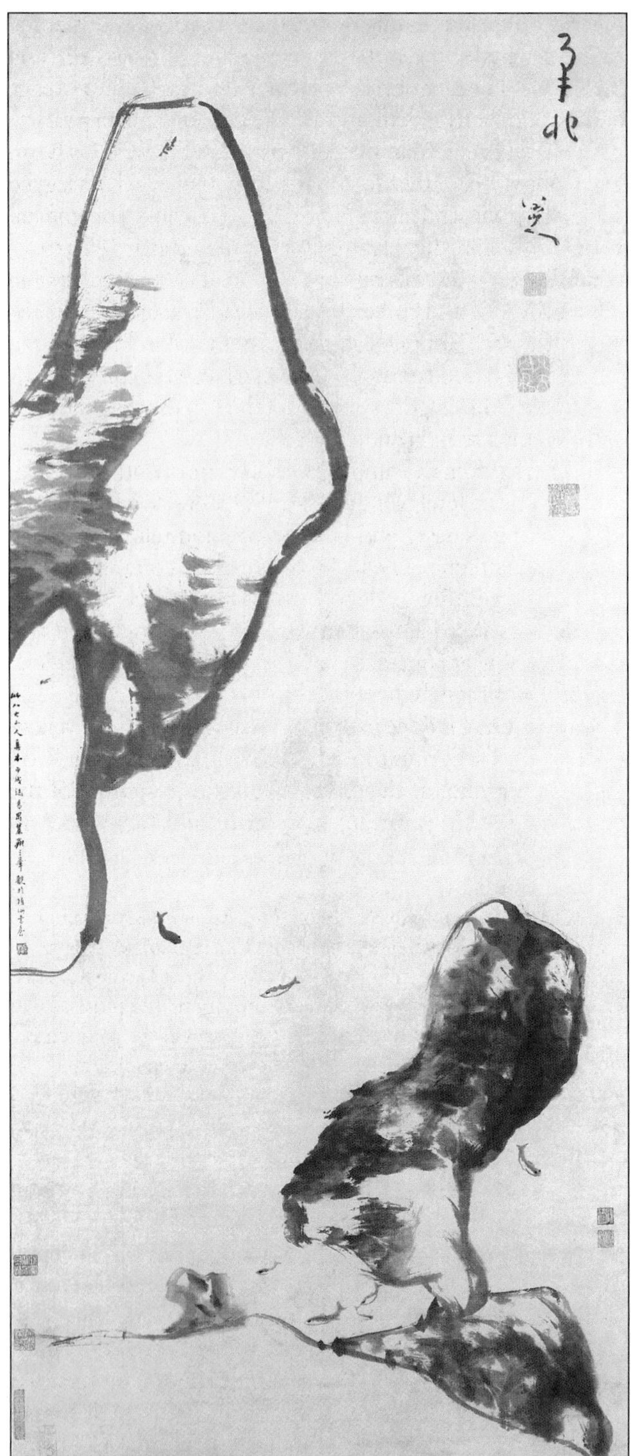

FIGURE 19.6 Zhu Da (1626–1705), *Fish and Rocks*, Qing dynasty, 1699, hanging scroll, ink on paper, $53'' \times 23\frac{7}{8}''$ (134.6 × 60.6 cm). Bequest of John M. Crawford, Jr., 1988 (1988. 363.137). The Metropolitan Museum of Art, New York, NY, U.S.A. Photo credit: Image copyright © The Metropolitan Museum of Art/Art Resource, NY. The fish swim around unnatural rock formations that seem to float in space, resembling the heads of rabbits. The result of Zhu Da's intentional avoidance of convention is hauntingly powerful as well as whimsical.

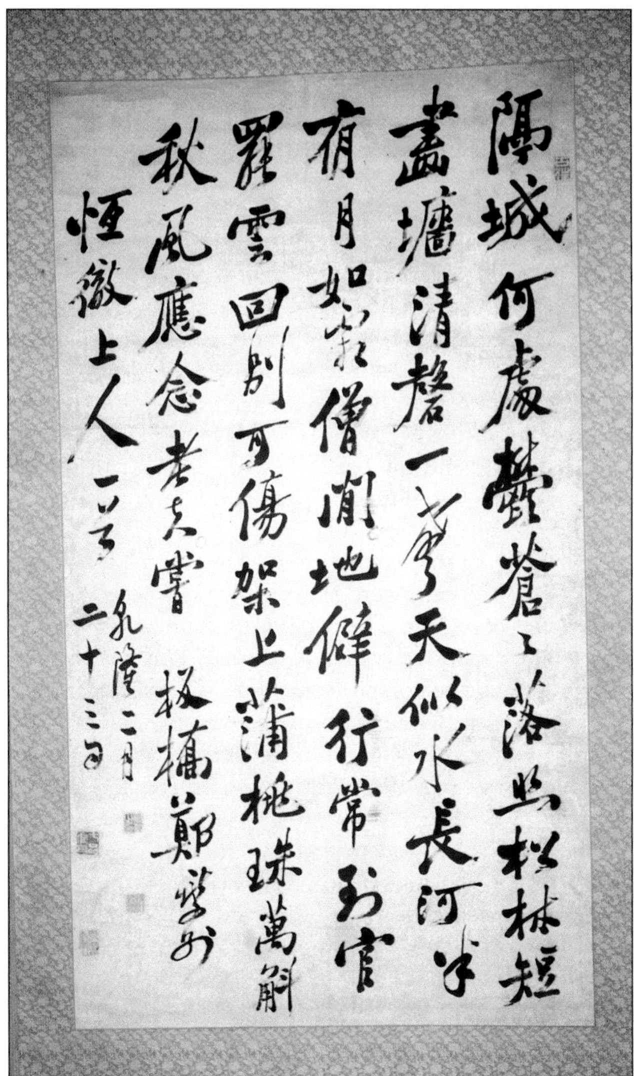

FIGURE 19.7 Zheng Xie, *A Country Temple*, Qing Dynasty, ca. 1740, hanging scroll, ink on paper, $62'' \times 34\frac{3}{4}''$ (162.3 × 88.2 cm), Hsaio Hua Collection. Chinese is written in columns from top to bottom and then right to left, so this poem begins in the upper right and ends with the seals on the lower left.

ZHENG XIE [CHENG SHEE-EH] (1693–1765), who enjoyed mixing clerical, regular, running, and cursive scripts. Zheng's eight-line verse (fig. 19.7) reflects the nostalgia for country life felt by the official who must live and work in the city.

A Country Temple

Outside the city, where is the foliage most lush?
By the decorated walls where the setting sunlight filters through the pine forest.
A single note comes from the pure sounding-stone, the sky seems like water;
On the evening river, the reflection of the moon is like frost.
The monks are calm at this remote place, and I often visit,
Floating like a cloud from my government office; I am pained when I must depart.

On the trellis are grapes like ten thousand pearls:
The autumn wind must have remembered that this old man loves to eat them.

CERAMICS

Porcelain was first produced in China and is manufactured from volcanic porcelain stone clay that contains quartz, kaolin, and feldspar. These clays, when fired in kilns at very high temperatures (1100–1400 degrees centigrade), form glass crystals. Porcelain is noted for its strength, translucence, and whiteness. During the Ming and Qing dynasties, imperial kilns were well-established in areas where porcelain clays and the pine forests needed for firing the kilns was available. Porcelain production in imperial kilns was distinguished by specialization, a different person performing each of the required steps. One source says that a minimum of 72 steps were required to create a single piece of imperial porcelain. The result of this specialization was a far higher quality of ceramics than was produced at private kilns where one person performed many of the steps.

A specialty of Chinese porcelains in which cobalt blue painting is done on a white ground is referred to as blue-and-white porcelains (fig. 19.8). The technique was at its peak in the early-fifteenth century during the Ming dynasty. Preferred subjects include flowers, birds, people, and animals—real and imaginary. The dragon, seen here, is a favorite Chinese image and his popularity is demonstrated by his depiction in a variety of media. Extremely animated, if not agitated, with his beard and mane flowing, this dragon is fully equipped with a jagged spine, scaly skin, and talons. The number of claws a dragon has reveals his stature; five claws per paw indicates that he is an imperial dragon—and this jar a luxury item. The Chinese dragon is typically long and limber, his body readily adapted to fit any space available. Although associated with evil in Western art, the dragon is a good creature conveying favorable connotations in the East. The dragon, symbolic of the emperor, is associated with power, strength, and good luck.

Differing from the simplicity of blue-and-white porcelain, polychrome enamel painting (fig. 19.9) developed at the end of the Ming dynasty and became the dominant porcelain painting technique. The technique is more complicated because, first, painting is done with an underglaze blue, then other colors are added as overglaze. With its bright and varied colors, this jar is an example of *wucai*, meaning "five color," decoration, although there may be more than five colors. The delicate painting is done in orange, green, blue, red, and yellow, on a white background. Fish are frequently depicted on Chinese ceramics of this time. The fish is a symbol of the desire for wealth: *yu* means both "fish" and "abundant" in

FIGURE 19.8 Jar with *Dragon*, Ming dynasty, Xuande period (1426–35), porcelain, height 19″ (48.3 cm). The Metropolitan Museum of Art, New York, NY, U.S.A. Image copyright © The Metropolitan Museum of Art/Art Resource, NY. Ming dynasty porcelains are world famous for their masterful technical quality and sophisticated decoration. The blue-and-white porcelains painted in underglaze blue produced in the early-fifteenth century are considered the finest of this type.

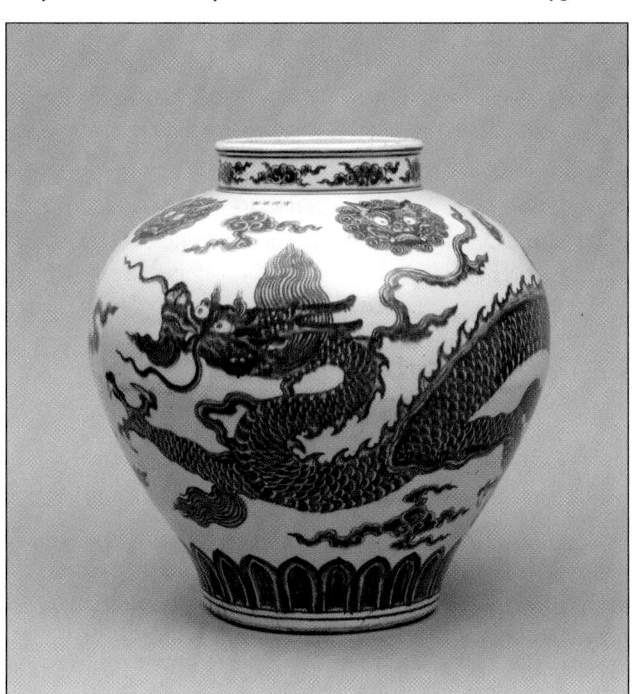

FIGURE 19.9 Jar with *Swimming Fish*, Ming dynasty, Jiajing period (1522–66), porcelain, height $9\frac{1}{8}$″ (23.2 cm). Metropolitan museum of Art, NY (17.127.2). This wide-mouthed jar appears to contain fish that twist and turn as they swim among the plants. In this colorful and complicated porcelain technique, the painting is first done with an underglaze blue and then other colors are added as overglaze enamels.

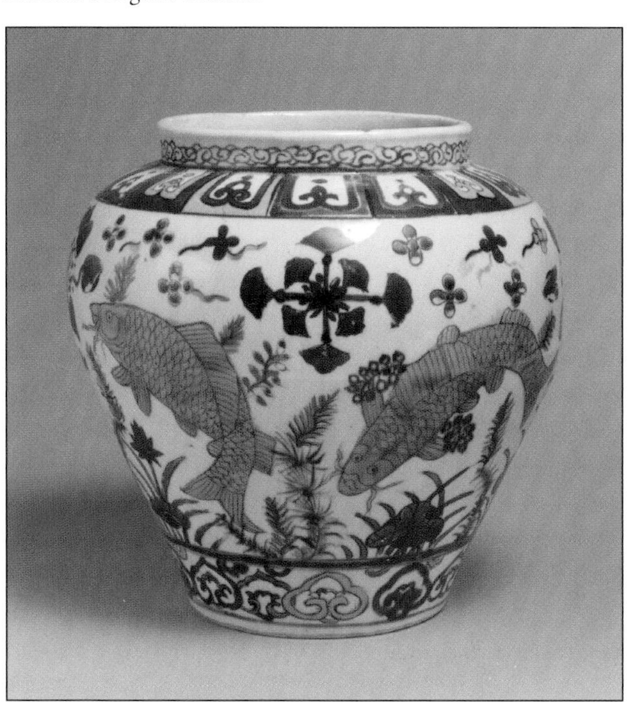

Then & Now

Hong Kong

The history of Hong Kong, the island city just off the coast of the Chinese mainland, has long been important to China's relations with the West. In the nineteenth century, the West began to pursue colonial ambitions in Asia, and the emperors of the declining Qing dynasty were forced to make trade and territorial concessions to encroaching Western powers. Defeated by Great Britain in the Opium War (1840–42), China ceded Hong Kong to Britain by the Treaty of Nanking (Nanjing) in 1842. In a renegotiated settlement in 1898, Hong Kong, along with two other local Chinese territories, was "leased" to Britain until 1997, when control of the city reverted to China.

With one of the greatest deep-water harbors in the world, Hong Kong has always been a trading center, in part because the land is unsuitable for agriculture and lacks minerals and other natural resources. Since the 1960s, Hong Kong has developed one of the most successful economies in Asia, outperforming those of some Western countries, including Great Britain. As Hong Kong's economic value has increased, the city became a symbolic bone of contention between China and Britain. Although the countries share an interest in Hong Kong's stability and prosperity, they had contrasting visions of Hong Kong's purpose and management. For Britain, Hong Kong represented the crowning achievement of its global economic expansion. For China, Hong Kong stands as an economic catalyst for the rest of the country.

In 1984, an agreement between China and Britain called for the termination of British rule in Hong Kong while maintaining its capitalist economy and democratic governmental structure until 2047. Since 1997, with Hong Kong officially incorporated into the People's Republic of China, it ostensibly retains a social structure and democratic government elected by the people of Hong Kong. However, Beijing's control over the transitional governing council, and its increasing disregard for Hong Kong's democratic political culture, raise questions about the city's future as an engine of free economic enterprise. It remains to be seen whether, with its new political status, Hong Kong will sustain its economic vitality and global influence.

FIGURE 19.10 The Forbidden City, Beijing, seen from the north.

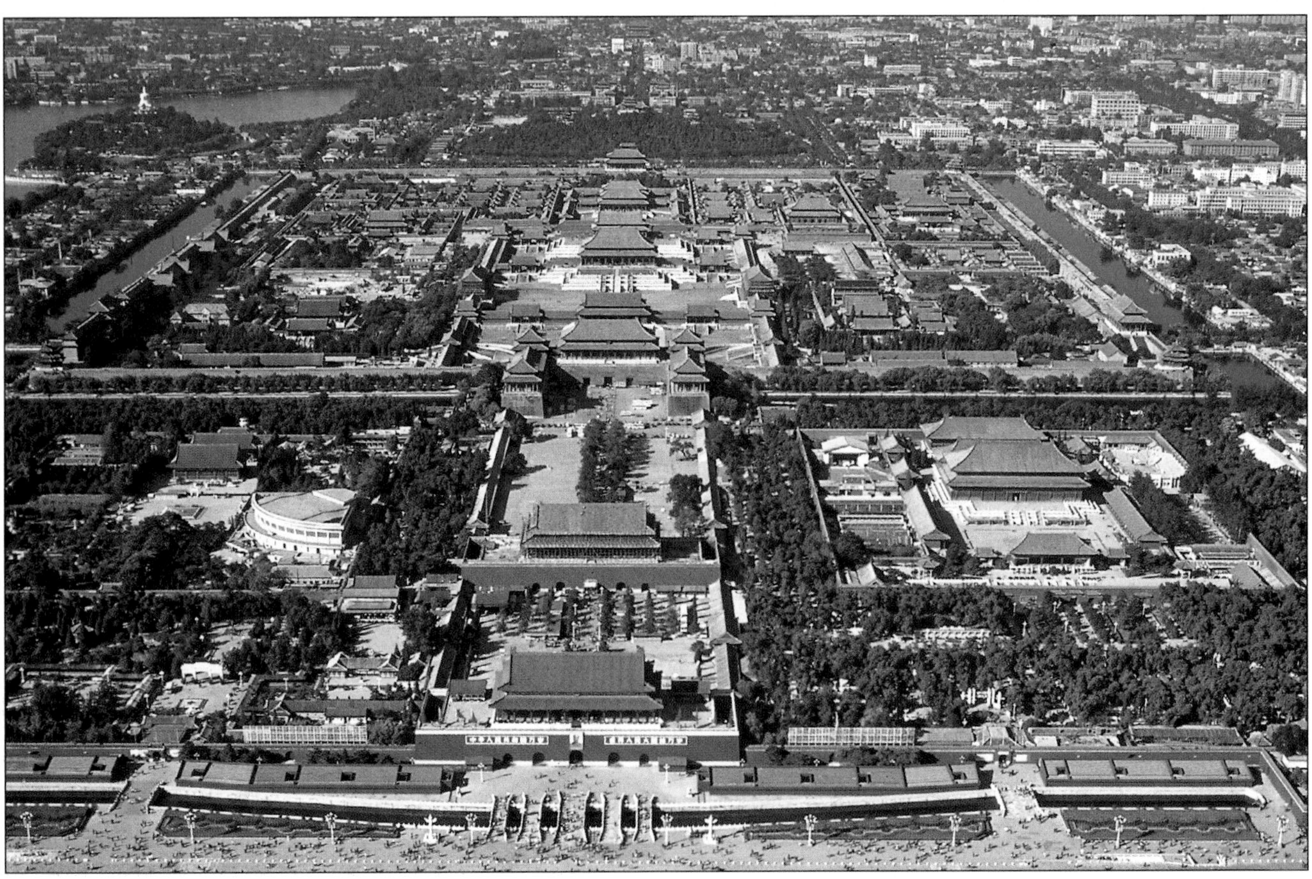

Chinese. Here, as elsewhere, Chinese art has both beauty and meaning, often including many auspicious symbols.

ARCHITECTURE: CITY PLANNING

Architecture in traditional China signified the connection between the rule of the emperor and the order of the universe. Cities were constructed on a grid system, surrounded by walls, which represented stability. The ruler's palace was generally situated at the north end, looking south, so the emperor's back was turned against the north from which evil (including the Mongol invaders) was always believed to come, and so his gaze overlooked and protected the people, who lived in the city's southern half. The emperor looked down on the city just as the Pole Star, from its permanent position in the north, looks down on the cosmos. So long as the emperor fulfilled his function as the Son of Heaven, peace and harmony, it was believed, would be enjoyed by all.

Under the rule of the Yongle Emperor (r. 1402–24), present-day Beijing was reconstructed as the imperial capital (fig. 19.10). Following traditional architectural plans, the principal buildings and gates of the government district, called the Imperial City, faced south, and almost all structures were arranged in a gridded square (fig. 19.11). The palace enclosure where the emperor and his court lived, called the Forbidden City, was approached through a series of gates: The Gate of Heavenly Peace (called Tiananmen) is first, then the Noon Gate, which opens into a giant courtyard. Next, the Meridian Gate leads into the city's walled enclosure and opens out onto the first spacious courtyard, which has a waterway with five arched marble bridges. These bridges represent the five Confucian relationships as well as the five virtues (see Chapter 8). Past the bridges, high on a marble platform, stands the Gate of Supreme Harmony. Beyond the gate is the largest courtyard with three ceremonial halls. The most important is the Hall of Supreme Harmony, used for the emperor's audiences and special ceremonies. Large-scale sculptures of a lion and a lioness appear together as a pair more than once in the Imperial Palace flanking entrances to buildings (fig. 9.12).

FIGURE 19.11 Plan of the Forbidden City (Imperial Palace), Beijing. Outside the palace enclosure is Tiananmen Square. 1 Gate of Divine Pride; 2 Pavilion of Earthly Peace; 3 Imperial Garden; 4 Palace of Earthly Tranquillity; 5 Hall of Union; 6 Palace of Heavenly Purity; 7 Gate of Heavenly Purity; 8 Hall of the Preservation of Harmony; 9 Hall of Perfect Harmony; 10 Hall of Supreme Harmony; 11 Gate of Supreme Harmony; 12 Meridian Gate; 13 Kitchens; 14 Gardens; 15 Former Imperial Printing House; 16 Flower Gate; 17 Palace of the Culture of the Mind; 18 Hall of the Worship of the Ancestors; 19 Pavilion of Arrows; 20 Imperial Library; 21 Palace of Culture; 22 Palace of Peace and Longevity; 23 Nine Dragon Screen.

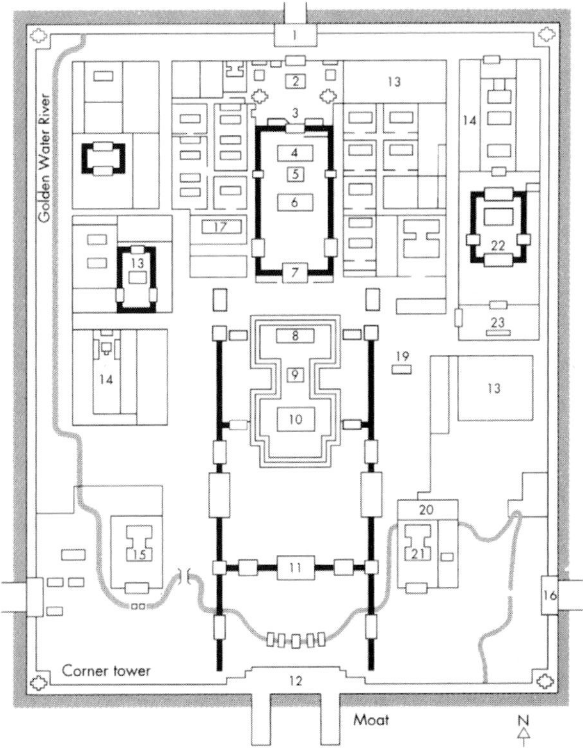

FIGURE 19.12 *Lioness Suckling Club*, bronze, Forbidden City, Beijing. Typically, the lion and lioness both have manes and are general symbols of power and majesty in China. More specifically, the lioness with a cub under her paw, which she suckles in this implausible manner, as seen here, symbolizes the fertility of the royal family. The lion with a ball under his paw symbolizes imperial power.

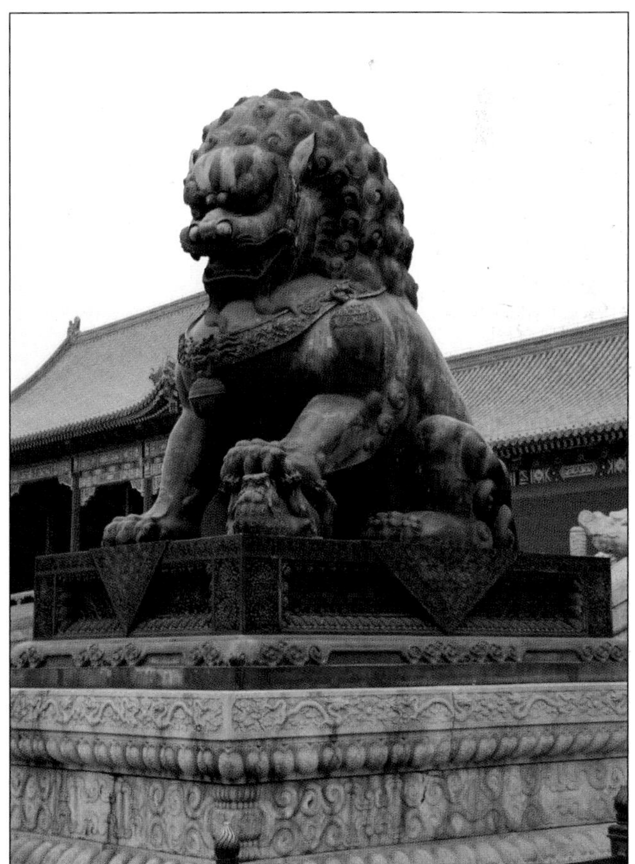

Critical Thinking

FENG SHUI

When the British handed Hong Kong over to the Chinese in 1997, the new Chinese governor of the province, Tung Chee-hwa, had to select a site for his offices. In order to do so, he brought with him a Feng Shui (Fung-SHWAY) master, who advised him regarding the appropriateness of various prospective office locations. **Feng Shui,** which combines the Chinese words for "wind" and "water," is the Chinese art of harmonizing people and their environment. With its origins in Daoism and a three-thousand-year-old heritage, Feng Shui addresses the design and layout of cities and villages as well as houses and public buildings to achieve harmony with the environment.

Feng Shui is grounded in the idea that influences in the natural environment affect people's fortunes. In deciding where to build a temple or a home, or where to situate a grave, the topography of terrain, its hills and fields and bodies of water, and their relationships to each other are analyzed. Such considerations and calculations can be quite complex; hence the need for an expert geomancer with the requisite esoteric knowledge.

Feng Shui, though not so popular among young Chinese in the People's Republic, is still used in rural China, Hong Kong, Taiwan, Singapore, and Malaysia, and it has practitioners in Japan and Korea as well. One example of a building purportedly built with Feng Shui in mind is the Citigroup building in Hong Kong, which was designed with a curved façade to shield it from and deflect negative elements emanating from a neighboring Bank of China building. Another is the Cheonk Kung Tower, which is a "green" building inside and built with its major entrance facing east because the Feng Shui master, who advised the Li Ka Shing family who own it, believed it would have a favorable effect on their wealth and fortune.

What do you think of the idea of Feng Shui and the beliefs associated with it? To what extent do you agree that it is important to consider the placement of a home, tomb, or building with respect to its natural environment? And how does this concept of Feng Shui compare with the principles guiding the work of an architect such as Frank Lloyd Wright, especially in the location of homes that he designed?

In recent years, the practice of Feng Shui has become quite popular in the West. Decisions in the West, however, about where to build offices and houses, may need to take into account historical factors or practical environmental considerations. How important do you think these other factors are, and why?

With its series of interlocking gates and courtyards, its walled-in sections within larger walled-in areas, Beijing gives the visitor a different experience from Western cityscapes, which have open vistas with numerous opportunities to see up and down thoroughfares. An analogy can be made by comparing a Western landscape painting, which is seen in totality from a fixed perspective, to a Chinese landscape hand scroll, which must be viewed section by section as it is unrolled. In Chinese architecture and in such scrolls, the viewer experiences a series of discrete visual incidents, which only cumulatively provide an impression of totality.

LITERATURE

Traditional Poetry. Much of the poetry written during the Ming dynasty was used in other art forms such as drama, fiction, music, and painting. The calligraphy at the upper left of Shen Zhou's *Poet on a Mountaintop* (fig. 19.3) is, in fact, a poem. Shen Zhou was not only an accomplished painter but a fine poet and, like many of his fellow artists of the Yuan and Ming dynasties, he was skilled at many of the literati arts, which include music, seal carving, and prose essays. Shen Zhou's poem reads:

> White clouds like a belt encircle the mountain's waist
> A stone ledge flying in space and the far thin road.
> I lean alone on my bramble staff and gazing contented into space
> Wish the sounding torrent would answer your flute.

Not only does the poem express an affinity for nature, it contrasts the speaker's isolation with the need for companionship, the sound of the flute announcing the arrival of a companion along the "far thin road" shrouded in mist. The comparison of the fog to a belt, furthermore, transforms the landscape into human terms. Removing the belt of clouds would cause the landscape's robe to fall open and reveal its natural beauty to the poet's eye, offering the promise of human intimacy—which the image on its own does not even begin to suggest.

Yuan Hong-dao. Shen Zhou's poem continues a long tradition of Chinese poetry and fits comfortably within it. But by the late Ming dynasty, poetry began to change. The finest poet of the era was Yuan Hong-dao (1568–1610), who wrote, "The good painter learns from things, not from other painters. The good philosopher learns from his mind, not from some doctrine. The good poet learns from the panoply of images, not from writers of the past." Yuan served, as did so many literati, as an official, but he semihumorously complained that "Superiors visit you like gathering clouds, travelers stop by like drops of rain, papers pile up like mountains, and oceans of taxes in cash or grain must be collected; if you work and write morning and night, you still can't keep up with all of it! Misery, misery!" Nevertheless Yuan was able to write a number of poems as well as prose on subjects as unusual as spider fights, before his death at the age of forty-two. His brother Yuan Zhong-dao was also an excellent poet, and he too sometimes chose unusual subjects for his verse: One poem, for example, is about keeping a pet rooster.

The Chinese poetry tradition continued into the Qing dynasty (fig. 9.12), including among the Manchus who now ruled the country. Almost all of the emperors themselves were poets, and some wrote vast quantities. For example, over 42,000 poems have been attributed to the emperor Qianlong (1736–1796). However, prose fiction, focusing on the lives of merchants, servants, and petty officials, was the most innovative literary development of the Qing dynasty.

Cao Xueqin's Dream of the Red Chamber. The most important work of Chinese literature written in the eighteenth century, considered by some the greatest Chinese novel, is *The Dream of the Red Chamber* by CAO XUE-QIN [TSAO SOOEH-CHIN] (1715–1763). The novel is enormous, with 120 chapters. The "red chamber" is where the female characters live; the "dream" refers to the foretelling of the fates of these characters.

The Dream of the Red Chamber has been read as a story about the decline of a family, an allegory of Buddhist attitudes toward the world, and an autobiographical fiction adhering closely to the life of its author. It has also been considered a love story, a search for identity, and a quest for understanding the purpose of human existence. The book can be seen as a reflection of the many elements of mid-Qing elite life, including politics and religion, economics and aesthetics, love and family. Blending realism with dream and fantasy, *The Dream of the Red Chamber* has been hailed as one of the most revealing works ever written about Chinese civilization.

Modern Chinese Poetry. Although fiction and drama have long been a part of Chinese literary tradition, pride of place has always been accorded to poetry. Even when poets swerved away from refined classical Chinese and began to write in the modern vernacular, poetry continued to command more respect than other literary genres. While frequently working within ancient Chinese traditions, modern Chinese poets have also experimented with free verse and other styles and forms that emerged in Europe during the nineteenth and twentieth centuries. Without directly imitating the literature of the Western world, modern Chinese writers absorbed Western influences to express contemporary Chinese cultural experiences, including the political circumstances of the age. Chairman MAO ZEDONG [ZAY-DUNG] (1893–1976), the father of Chinese communism, wrote a number of poems celebrating the revolutionary ideal. Also political, but in direct opposition to the established order of contemporary China, the poems of BEI DAO [BAY DOW] (b. 1949) repudiate the oppressiveness of a society that, if it does not execute its dissenters, jails them. The Tiananmen Square massacre of 1989 gives urgent meaning to the sentiments expressed in the poems by Bei and other contemporary Chinese poets, who sometimes feel lost between old traditions and new realities.

I'M FOREVER A STRANGER

I'm forever a stranger
to this world.
I don't understand its language.
It doesn't understand my silence.
As if we'd met in a mirror,
a shadow of contempt
is all we exchange.
I'm forever a stranger
to myself.
Afraid of the dark,
I block with my body
the only light.
My only lover is my shadow,
my only enemy my heart.

MUSIC

Chinese Theater Music. From the fourteenth through the seventeenth centuries, Chinese music was largely associated with drama, especially with a form of musical drama known as ***Hsi-wen***, which included musical arias or lyrical songs, spoken dialogue, dance, and mime—all with instrumental accompaniment. Two different styles developed. There was a northern style, ***'ei-chu***, in which a pear-shaped lute (***pipa***) was the primary instrument for accompaniment, and singing was performed by one individual. In the southern style, ***ti***, the transverse flute (*dizi*) was the primary instrument for accompaniment and nearly all the characters sang.

During the 1500s, these two styles of musical drama merged in the Kun opera, which incorporated elaborate poetic texts and intricate plots with numerous scenes. Although Kun opera became a more or less elitist form of musical drama owing to its intricacy and complexity, it did have an influence on more popular forms of musical drama that emerged in later centuries, including the Beijing opera, a nineteenth-century development.

Beijing Opera. Beijing opera has become one of the most popular musical forms of the twentieth century. Incorporating traditional styles of acting absorbed from the history of Chinese drama, Beijing opera

Connections

KANGXI AND QIANLONG: CHINESE RULERS, WRITERS, AND SCHOLARS

Two of the most important Chinese emperors, KANGXI [KANNG-shi] (1661–1722) and QIANLONG [SHIEN- lahng] (1736–1795), reigned during the Qing dynasty (1644–1911). Both were members of the Manchu, a people from Manchuria, who had been given important court responsibilities under the Ming emperors (1368–1644), especially toward the end of Ming rule, when Manchu rulers supplanted them. Manchu rulers preserved their own cultural identity by outlawing intermarriage with Chinese and by forbidding the Chinese to travel to Manchuria or to learn the Manchus' language.

The emperor Kangxi was a strong ruler, who helped the Manchus consolidate their power early in the Qing dynasty. He expanded the Qing empire, absorbing the island of Taiwan, conquering nomadic peoples of Mongolia and central China, and establishing a protectorate in Tibet. A voracious reader, Kangxi was also a poet, and an advocate of the Confucian classics, whose teachings he incorporated into his political policies. His agricultural program of flood control, for example, was based on Confucian precepts. In addition, he was an avid supporter of Confucian schools.

Kangxi's grandson, Qianlong, continued his grandfather's expansion of the empire into Turkestan and made Vietnam, Burma, and Nepal vassal states. Like Kangzi, Qianlong was well versed in scholarship. In addition to being a more prolific poet than his grandfather (he is reputed to have composed 100,000 poems), Qianlong was a connoisseur of painting and calligraphy. Under his reign, China prospered, remaining a well-organized, efficient, and extremely wealthy country.

possesses a distinctive liveliness, with colorful, fast-paced scenes based on ancient Chinese myths, legends, and fables.

The dramatic action of Beijing opera is highly stylized. There are, for example, twenty-six distinct ways to laugh and thirty-nine specific ways to manipulate the twenty different types of beards. The performers' roles are divided into four major categories: male (**sheng**), female (**dan**), painted male face (**jing**), and clown (**chou**). The male and female roles, all performed by men, are subdivided into roles for old men and roles without beards for young men, including the flirtatious female and the lady of propriety (fig. 19.13).

The music for Beijing opera is performed by an orchestra arranged in two parts: a percussion section composed of gongs and drums, and a melodic section of strings and wind instruments. The percussion instruments play introductory music prior to the characters' entrances; they also play between the singing and acting. The melodic instruments accompany the singing. Although the melodies for the Beijing opera arias derive

Table 19-1 CHINESE ARTS
Landscape painting: Shen Zhou
Calligraphy: Zheng Xie
City planning: The Forbidden City
Theater music: Beijing Opera
Fiction: *The Dream of the Red Chamber*
Poetry: Bei Dao

FIGURE 19.13 An actor from the Beijing opera performing as the heroine Mu Guiying, a popular character who comes from the Yang family of the eleventh century. She is the most important of the women generals of the family—women who fought their enemies from the north.

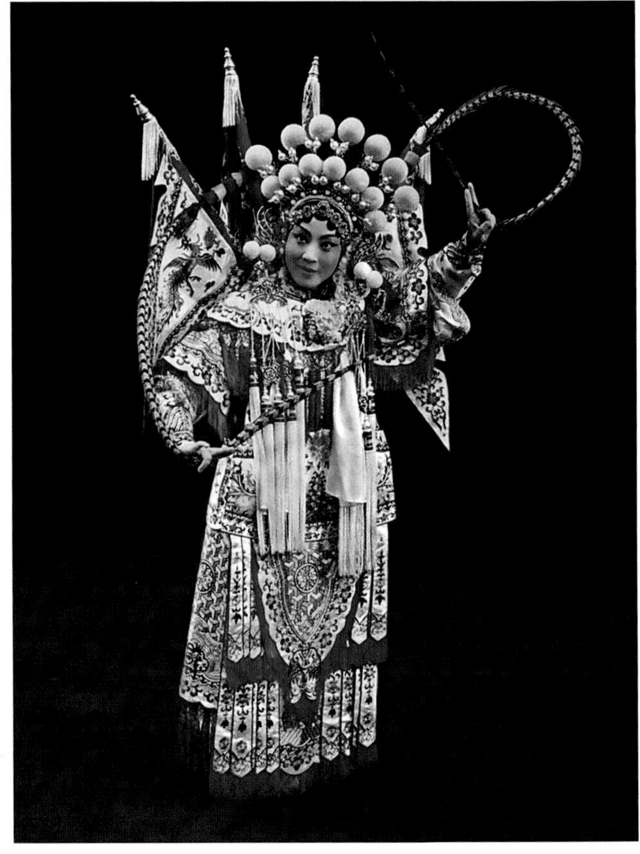

Cross Currents

THE PIPA AND THE GUITAR

The pipa (fig. 19.14) is a four-stringed lute of middle-eastern origin with a pear-shaped body of different sizes and which included differing numbers of frets, as few as 10 and as many as 30. The pipa's frets are made of wood, ivory, or jade and its strings are made of silk. The pipa's history is a long one, being mentioned in texts dating from the Han dynasty (206 B.C.E.–220 C.E.). Since the Tang dynasty, the pipa has been among the most popular of Chinese musical instruments, maintaining its appeal as both a chamber instrument and as a solo instrument.

The popularity of the pipa can be compared to that of the Spanish or classical guitar. Both instruments are plucked with the fingernails, with the pipa producing a sound resembling that of a harpsichord. They have three open-string tunings in common: A, D, and E. And performers on the two instruments share some plucking techniques, including rapidly wheeling the fingers of the right hand over a string to create a sustained tremolo effect.

Contemporary professional players of the pipa perform both traditional music and modern compositions written for the instrument. They also play music of other cultures, including western music, both popular and classical. The contemporary performers Wu Man and Liu Fang play pieces that embrace a variety of world music, including the Indian music of Ravi Shankar, as well as music from Korea, Japan, Ethiopia, Europe, and the United States. Both of these artists also play traditional Chinese music, such as "Dance of the Yi People," a popular favorite often required by conservatory juries of prospective students.

Another Chinese professional musician, Xuefei Yang, a classical guitarist, plays traditional Western classical guitar repertoire and also makes her own arrangements for guitar of traditional Chinese music as well as contemporary music of Chinese composers. A recent album, Si Ji, which translates as "Four Seasons," is an example of this kind of musical cross current. Sharon Isbin, still another contemporary classical guitarist, has played in concert and has recorded a guitar concerto by the contemporary Chinese composer Tan Dun. In her live and recorded performances of this music, she has, in certain moments, attempted to imitate the sound of the pipa with her guitar, yet another example of how these two stringed instruments, one of ancient Chinese lineage, and the other developing its repertory in nineteenth-century Spain, continue to influence each other.

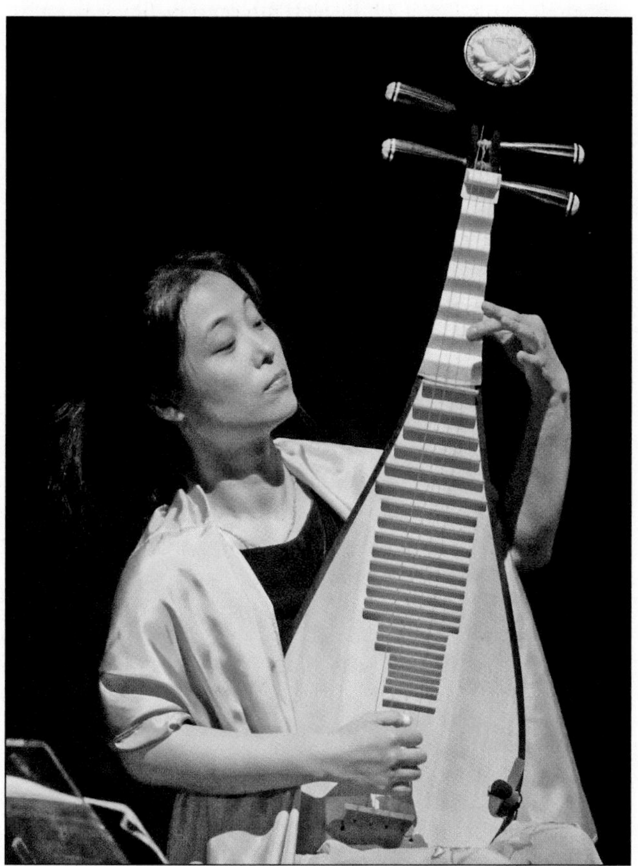

FIGURE 19.14 Wu Man playing the Chinese pipa during a performance of "Night Banquet," directed by Cher Shi-Zheng, Lincoln Center Festival, LaGuardia Concert Hall, NY. Photograph © 2002 Linda Vartoogian/FrontRowPhotos. All Rights Reserved. The pipa is typically played in a vertical position, unlike the lute, which is held across the body horizontally.

Cultural Impact

China's impact on the rest of the world continues to be felt in many ways. Politically, China has developed its own version of Marxist-Leninist communism. Economically, it has become a major player on the international scene, having joined the World Trade Organization and established trade relationships with a number of important African, Asian, and European countries.

Chinese cultural influence has extended into Asian countries, including Korea and Vietnam. Korean ceramics owe a debt to China's long tradition of ceramic ware, having been influenced especially by the ceramic artisans of the Tang, Song, and Ming dynasties. The impact of China on Vietnam has been both cultural and political. Well into the eighteenth century, the most important Vietnamese poetry, including the country's epic, *The Tale of Kieu*, existed primarily in Chinese. Politically, modern Vietnam inherited Chinese communism. In addition, both Vietnam and Korea exhibit the influence of Confucianism and Taoism, although Buddhism is a stronger religious presence in Vietman.

The impact of the Chinese aesthetic ideal has been felt in the West as well, particularly in interior design and decor, with modern and contemporary architects and interior designers following Chinese aesthetic principles of simplicity, balance, elegance, and harmony. Chinese furniture of the Ming dynasty continues to be popular in Western countries, as do various period styles of ceramic ware. In the earlier twentieth century, Chinese poetry, with its emphasis on images rather than discursiveness, influenced American poets such as Ezra Pound, T. S. Eliot, and William Carlos Williams.

from traditional music, there is often originality in their embellishment.

With the founding of the Communist People's Republic of China in 1949, Chinese music was directed toward social revolutionary purposes. Mao Zedong conscripted all the arts, remarking that they "operate as powerful weapons in unifying and educating the people and for attacking and destroying the enemy." Mao introduced two influential artistic directives: (1) a return to folk tradition and (2) an emphasis on political ideals and content in music. From 1966 to 1969, at the height of the Cultural Revolution, the only opera performances permitted in China were eight revolutionary works deemed pure of the taint of so-called bourgeois ideas and influences.

Music played an important role throughout the Cultural Revolution in extolling the glories of China and providing ceremonial background to public events. One early revolutionary song has been adapted for several purposes. "East Is Red" was written by a peasant in 1946 and performed by three thousand workers, students, and soldiers in 1964 to celebrate the fifteenth anniversary of the Proletarian Republic of China. This same song played as background music in radio broadcasts of the time and as a wake-up call—from loudspeakers in the streets—every morning. China's best known composer, XIAN XINGHAI (SHEE-EN SHINH-he) (1905–1940), wrote *Yellow River Cantata*, which continued the persistent theme of revolutionary music by combining folk songs that extolled the beauty of China and memorialized the hardships of the people. This cantata spawned the Yellow River Concerto, for piano and orchestra, which had its premiere during the Culture Revolution in 1969 and remains popular both in China and the West.

In the late twentieth and early twenty-first centuries, the necessity for such strict adherence to political ideology for musical composition and performance has diminished. Although revolutionary themes dominate many modern Chinese musical works, Western influences, instruments, and performance practices are now apparent.

KEY TERMS

literati
wet-brush technique
Feng Shui
Hsi-wen
'ei-chu
pipa
ti
sheng
dan
jing
chou

WWW. WEBSITES FOR FURTHER STUDY

http://www-chaos.umd.edu/history/imperial3.html
(An article that summarizes the Mongol and Ming dynasties ruling in China.)

http://www.chinats.com/beijing/index.html
(The Forbidden City, Beijing, China.)

http://www.sinologic.com/literature.html
(A page devoted to the poetry of Bei Dao and a brief biography.)

http://www.kirjasto.sci.fi/luxun.htm
(Lu Xun bio and overview of key works.)

http://www.philmultic.com
(Site devoted to stringed Chinese musical instruments and pictures. Link to detailed discussion of the pipa, with multiple images and excellent history of the instrument.)

CHAPTER 20

HISTORY

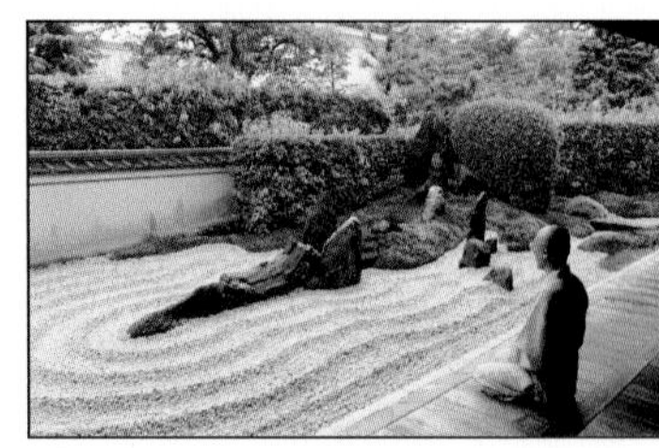

1542	Portuguese merchants first reach Japan
1868	Meiji Restoration establishes imperial government
1894–95	First Sino-Japanese War
1904–05	Russo-Japanese War
1937–45	Second Sino-Japanese War
1941–45	Japan at war with Western Allies

ARTS AND ARCHITECTURE

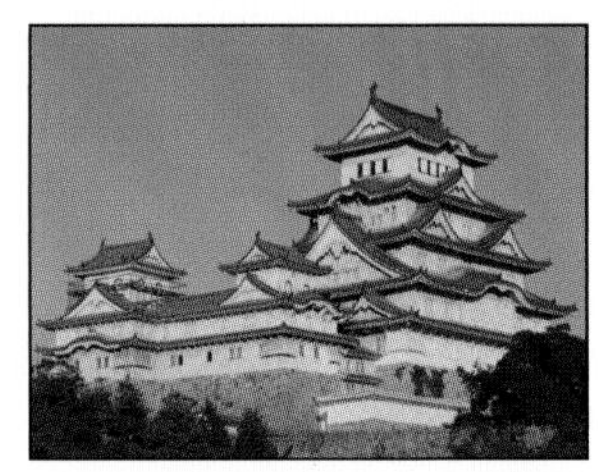

1581–1609	Himeji Castle
ca. 1794–95	Utamaro Kitagawa, *Painting the Lips*
ca. 1831	Hokusai Katsushika, *Thirty-Six Views of Mount Fuji*
1857	Ando Hiroshige, *One Hundred Views of Edo*

LITERATURE AND PHILOSOPHY

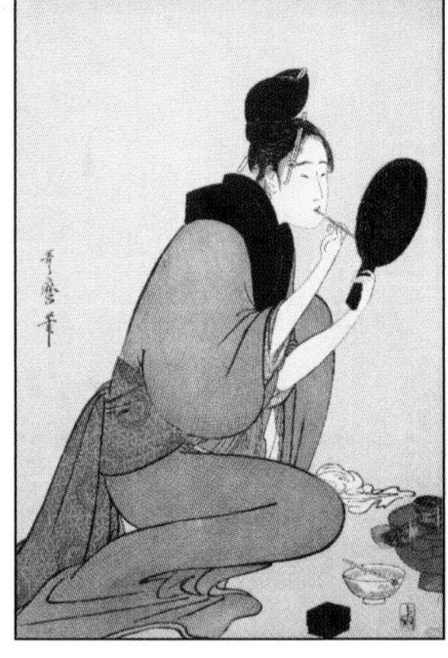

1689	Basho Matsuo, *The Narrow Road of Oku*
1967	Takemitsu Toru, *November Steps*
1994	Oe Kenzaburo wins Nobel Prize for Literature

Later Japanese Civilization

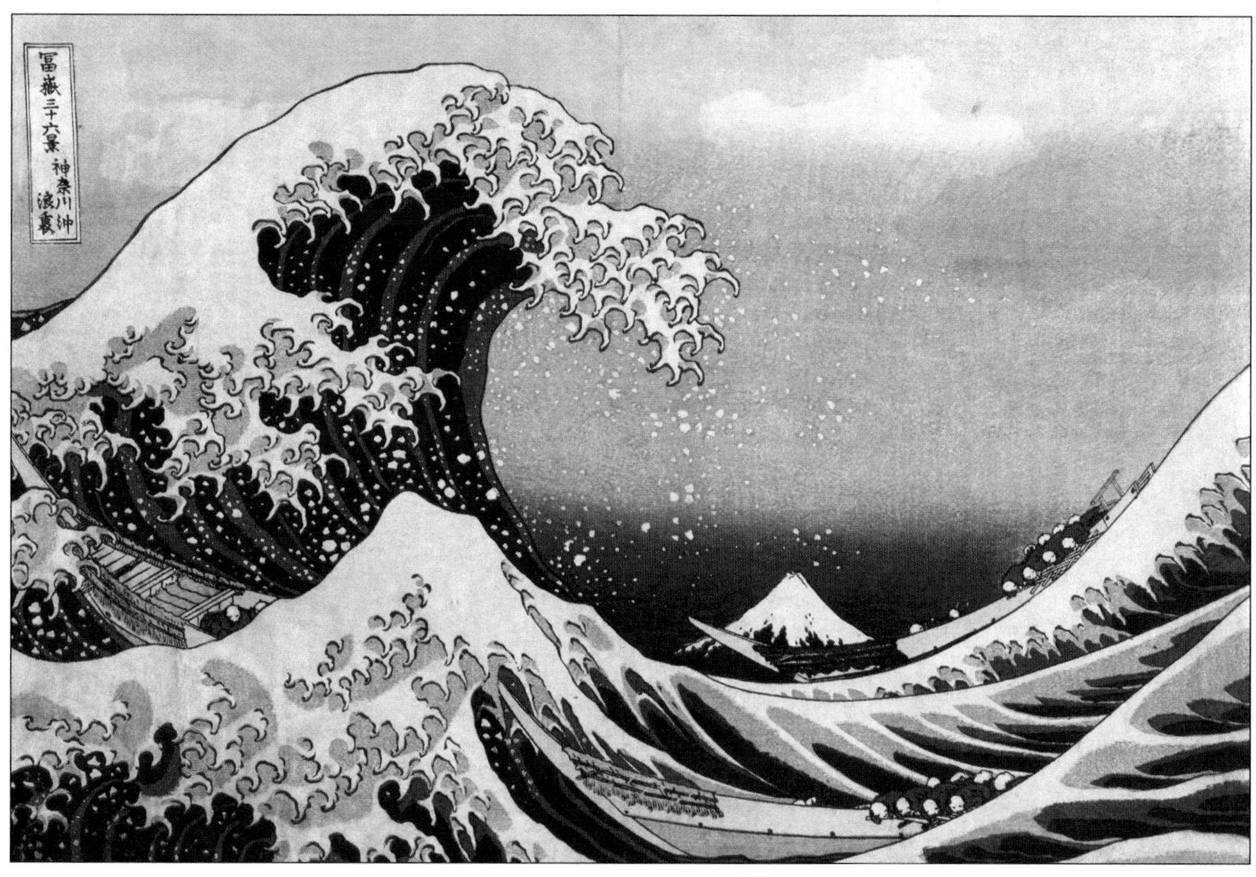

Katsushika Hokusai, *The Great Wave of Kanagawa*, from the series *Thirty-Six Views of Mount Fuji*, Tokugawa period, ca. 1831, color woodblock print, $9\frac{7}{8}'' \times 14\frac{5}{8}''$ (25.5 × 37.1 cm). Private Collection, Art Resource, NY.

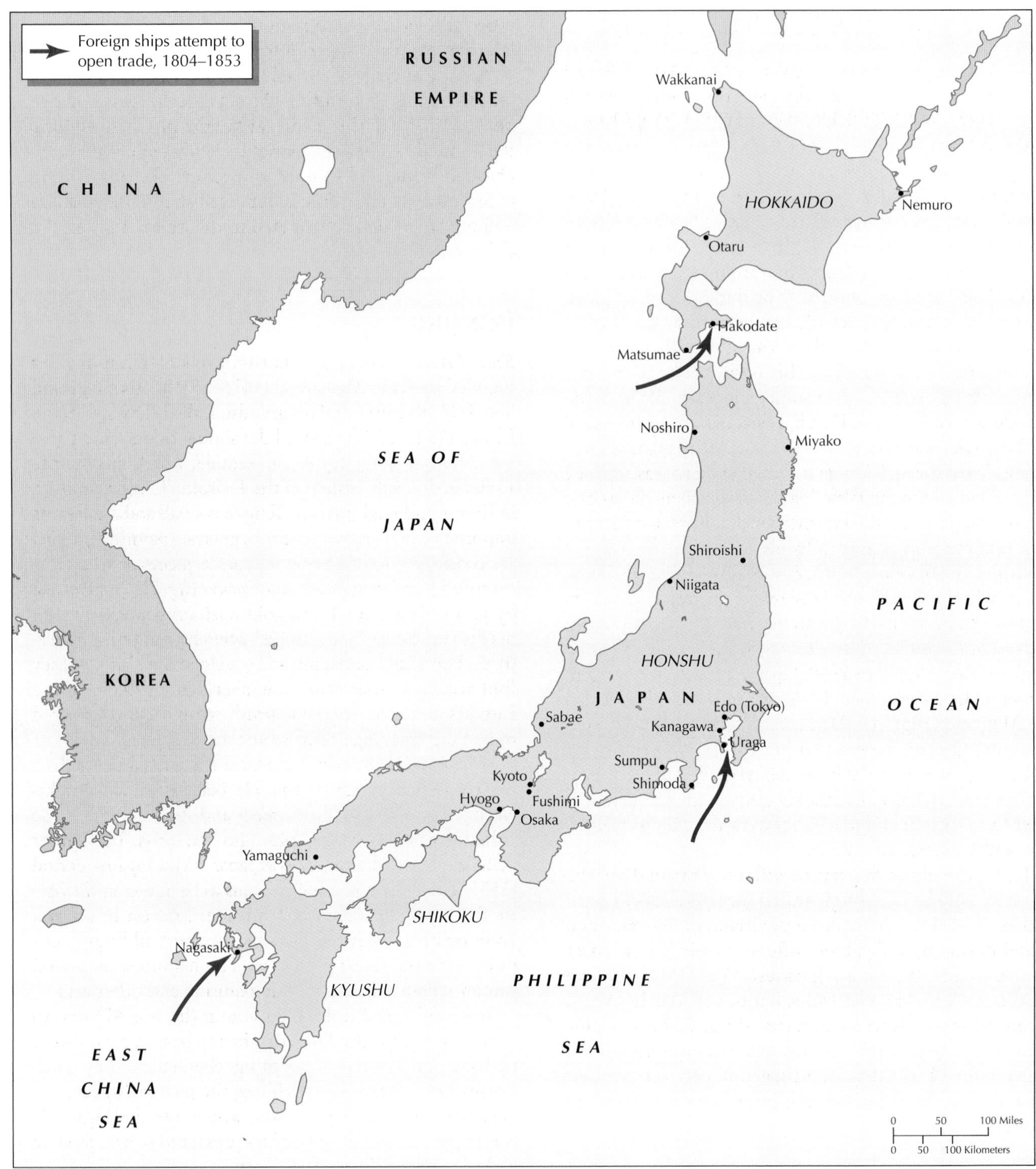

Map 20.1 Japan in 1853, when Commodore Perry reopened trade with the West.

Chapter Overview

LATER JAPANESE CIVILIZATION

Japan carefully gleans from the West what will make it an international power, while maintaining its own cultural identity

LATER JAPANESE CIVILIZATION

Toward the end of over a century of feudal warfare, known as the Warring States period (1477–1600), TOKUGAWA IEYASU [TOH-KOO-GAH-WA HYEH-YAH-SOO] (1542–1616) became the **shogun,** or military ruler, of a newly unified Japan. The Tokugawa family ruled the country from 1600 until 1868, retaining emperors as cultural and symbolic figures in Kyoto, while making Edo (present-day Tokyo) the effective capital of the country. Under Confucian influence, society was ordered into classes of **samurai** (who during an age of peace became government officials), farmers, artisans, and merchants, who theoretically had the lowest status but who rose in power and importance in this period. The Tokugawa **shogunate** both unified the country and isolated it from the outside world. Only the Dutch, relegated to a small island off Nagasaki, were permitted to trade with Japanese merchants. It was through Dutch traders that Japan was apprised of developments in the West, but the government did its best to preserve Japan's distinctive national culture and identity almost immune to outside influence.

After the American military expedition led by Commodore Perry forced the Tokugawa regime to open its trade doors in the 1850s, Japan began to look to the West, instead of to China, in its effort to transform itself into a modern nation-state. In 1868, Japan returned to rule by an emperor and a parliament, inaugurating a period known as the Meiji era (1868–1912), during which it enjoyed rapid economic development and a growth in national power. Japan adopted a constitution modeled on that of Germany; it eliminated the power of the shogunate, the samurai, and their local vassals; and it began programs of industrialization and universal education.

Japan also began to exert its influence throughout the western Pacific. Through its victory in the war with China of 1894–95, it acquired the island of Taiwan (then called Formosa) and gained influence over Korea. After its triumph in the Russo-Japanese War (1904–05) and its alliance with the victorious nations in World War I, Japan colonized Korea and parts of the Chinese mainland. When Japan had to face the consequences of its defeat after World War II, it turned to economic rather than military means to achieve international power and influence.

The Shinto Revival

With the rise of the Tokugawa dynasty, Shinto was resurrected as a state religion. **Shinto,** which literally means "the way of the gods," is a belief system indigenous to Japan; it involves rituals and veneration of local deities, known as ***kami.*** In its most general sense, Shinto is a "religion" of Japanese patriotism. Less a system of doctrines than a reverential attitude toward things Japanese, Shinto emphasizes the beauty of the Japanese landscape, especially its mountain regions, and views the Japanese land and people as superior to all others.

Accompanying the revival of Shinto was the rise of the feudal knight, or samurai, who was idealized as a native hero. Much like the medieval knight of Christendom, the samurai was held to a strict code of conduct that emphasized loyalty, self-sacrifice, and honor. The rejuvenation of Shinto and of the samurai reflected an intense Japanese ethnocentrism and contributed to the isolationism of the Tokugawa dynasty.

Painting

Kano Eitoku. An important family school of painting was founded by Kano Motonobu (1476–1559). His son, Kano Shoei (1519–1592), and his grandson, the celebrated Kano Eitoku (1543–1590), painted the sliding doors (*fusuma*) in the abbot's lodging of Juko-in Temple, which was built in 1566 and is a sub-temple of the Daitoku Temple complex in Kyoto. Although Juko-in Temple is small and modest, its importance derives from these large-scale paintings, which are considered to be among the masterpieces of sixteenth-century art in Japan. *Birds and Flowers* (fig. 20.1), executed by Kano Eitoku in ink and gold wash on paper, is among his first works, and was finished when he was only twenty-three. Panoramas surround and envelope the visitor as they fold around corners and flow over sliding doors. Kano Eitoku's dynamic, energetic brush strokes are considered to be the beginning of the Momoyama style.

These paintings secured Kano Eitoku's fame and he received many commissions. He became known for his large paintings on folding screens and sliding doors in the palaces and castles of nobles and warlords. His career benefitted from the warlords of Japan's Momoyama Period (1573–1615) because a warlord was to be adept on the battle field, yet also cultivated, with an interest in art and architecture, evidenced by constructing buildings decorated with the finest paintings. The Momoyama period was an artistic renaissance—in painting and other arts.

It is said that Eitoku died young (he was 47) due to overwork and the deadlines that had to be met for insistent patrons. Eitoku's style of painting, characterized by quick brushwork and large forms filling the pictorial space, was described by his own grandson, who wrote that this style was in part the result of Eitoku's pressured work schedule and the warlords' need for display.

Hakuin Ekaku and Zen. Hakuin Ekaku (1685–1769) is considered the most important Zen master of the past five hundred years. Hakuin reached a wide audience, from farmers to samurai, with his paintings and writings.

Hakuin was only seven or eight years old when his mother, a devout Buddhist, took him to a fire-and-brimstone sermon by a famous traveling preacher. Deeply affected by the sermon, Hakuin determined that in order to save his soul he would become a monk. He began his formal Buddhist

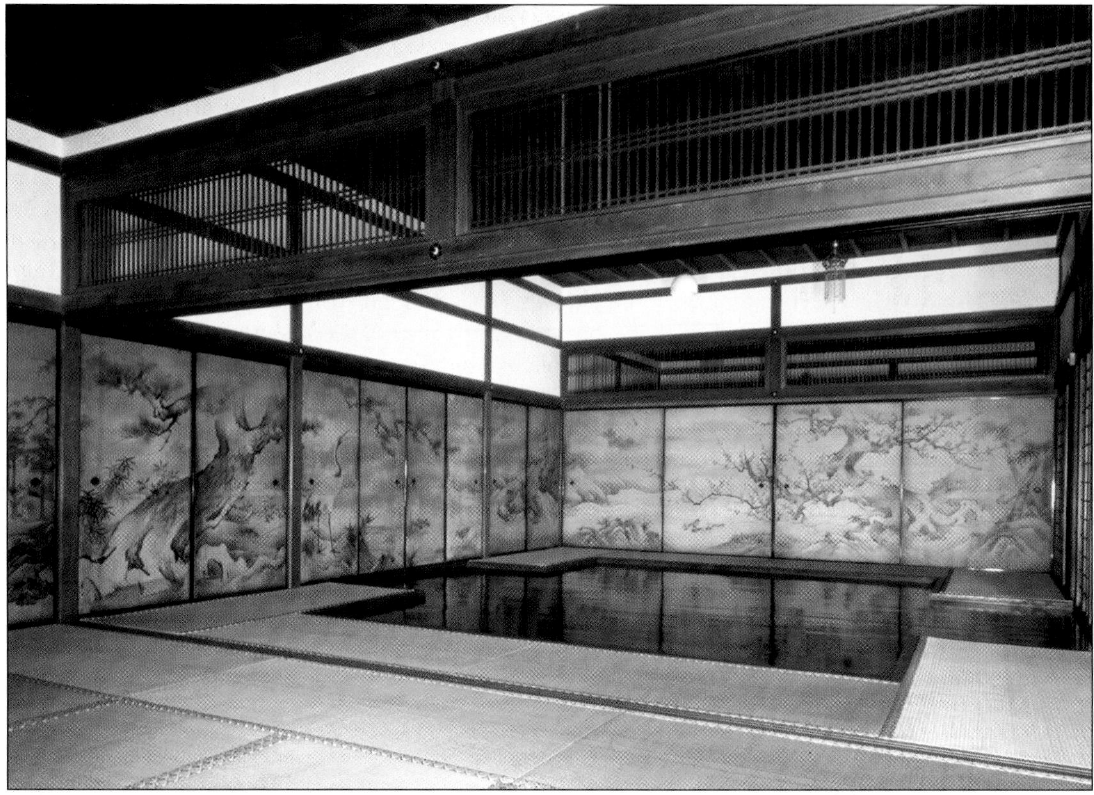

FIGURE 20.1 Kano Eitoku (1543–1590), *Birds and Flowers*, finished 1566, ink and gold wash on paper, on the sliding doors (*fusuma*) in the abbot's lodging of Juko-in, a sub-temple of the Daitoku Temple complex in Kyoto. Large paintings turn the walls and doors into, in effect, windows with views of lovely landscapes. The images are strong, bold, powerful, and dramatic—in accord with the temper of the times.

training at the age of fourteen, learning classical Chinese texts and Zen practice. He continued his training for many years, practicing ***zazen*** (seated Zen meditation) and meditating on the ***koan*** (Zen riddle) in which the Zen master Joshu is asked, "Does a dog have the Buddha-nature?" Although all living beings possess this Buddha-nature, Joshu replies, "*Mu*" (literally, "no" or "nothing").

This koan is traditionally the first that Zen monks begin meditating on trying to break through to their own Buddha-nature. Such koans, seemingly nonsensical questions and statements, are used by Zen masters to help their students achieve enlightenment by breaking through the barriers of rational dualistic thought. Students do not solve koans logically, but rather dissolve them by transcending their illogicality without providing a logical explanation. In understanding a koan, students bypass logic to arrive at an intuitive understanding.

Hakuin began having enlightenment experiences at the age of twenty-four and eventually established himself as a Zen master and teacher. He strove to convert complex Zen ideas into everyday form by writing folk songs and poems that could be easily understood, such as his *Song of Meditation*. Just as significantly, he painted images that conveyed Zen teachings clearly, simply, directly, and often humorously. Hakuin produced thousands of paintings and calligraphies and gave them to his monk and lay followers to help guide them on their own Zen journeys. In his painting of *Meditating Daruma* (fig. 20.2), Hakuin reveals the intense concentration of the first Zen patriarch with bold brushstrokes. The striking eyes are typical of portraits of Daruma; it is said that, because he was angry at himself for falling asleep while meditating, he cut off his own eyelids.

Hakuin also created his own Zen koan, "What is the sound of one hand clapping?" which has gained notoriety in contemporary Western society. Although Hakuin stressed the importance of traditional *zazen* and *koan* study, he also strongly believed Zen should not be an isolated, solitary experience, but should take place within every aspect of one's existence. He taught that meditation within the activities of daily life was just as important as seated silent meditation, and his influence continues to the present day.

WOODBLOCK PRINTS

During the seventeenth and eighteenth centuries, a style of art called ***ukiyo-e*** became especially associated with woodblock prints. *Ukiyo* means "floating world" in the Buddhist sense of "transient" or "evanescent," and

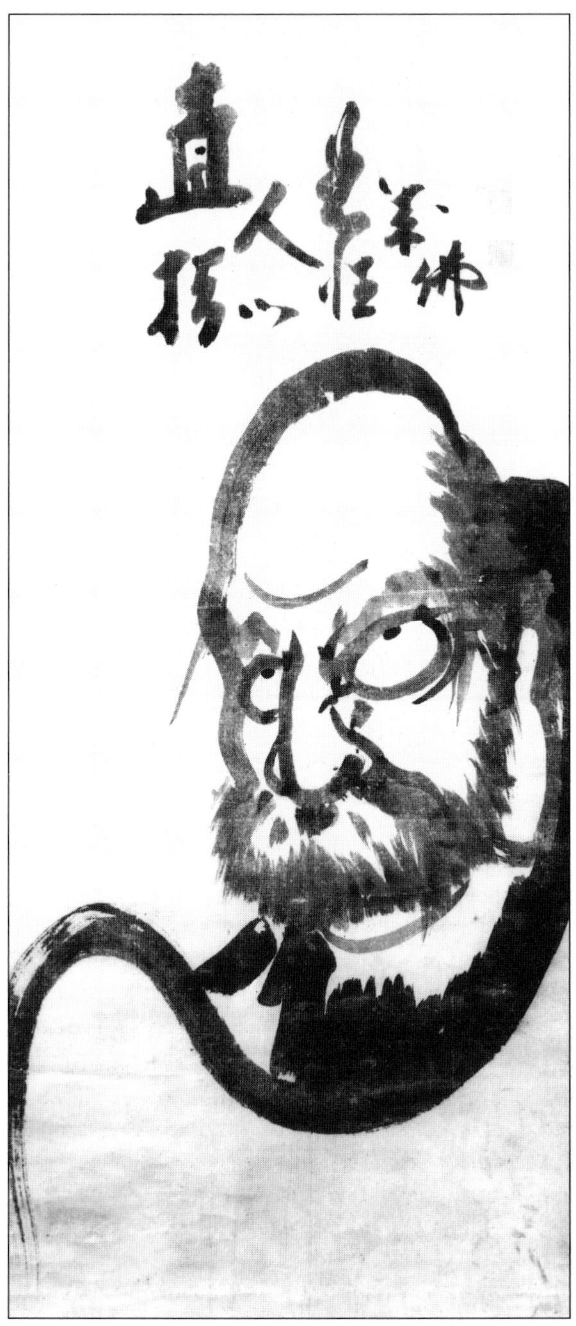

FIGURE 20.2 Hakuin Ekaku (1685–1768), *Meditating Daruma*, 49″ × 21″ (126 × 55 cm), ink on paper, Chikusei Collection. The inscription comes from words attributed to Bodhidharma (Daruma), the first Zen Patriarch: "Pointing directly to the human heart/See your own nature and become Buddha."

ukiyo-e means "pictures of the floating world." The Impressionist painters of nineteenth-century Europe admired *ukiyo-e* prints enormously because, like them, Japanese artists were concerned with the world of everyday life, particularly of cultural enjoyments, such as dance, theater, music, games, and travel.

Prior to the seventeenth century, woodblock prints were used almost exclusively to make inexpensive Buddhist images for the public. With the increased interest in everyday life of the Tokugawa period, the subject matter of prints expanded, and the spread of literacy meant a wider public for woodblock-printed books, often with illustrations. Gradually, single-sheet prints of the "floating world" became popular, and new techniques for color reproduction were developed.

For the expanding public in big cities such as Edo (Tokyo) with an appetite for entertainment, color woodblock prints represented the world of human pleasures. Many eighteenth-century prints celebrated the beautiful courtesans of the Yoshiwara, the pleasure district of Tokyo; a significant percentage of prints were erotic. In the nineteenth century, artists also turned their attention to the Japanese landscape, providing fresh interpretations of nature.

Woodblock prints were closely linked with the world of the Kabuki theater, which had a large and enthusiastic audience. Prints of Kabuki actors were popular, as were posters and programs featuring the actors in Kabuki roles. In fact, print publishers frequently asked artists to create up-to-date images of the actors to sell during the run of a play. These prints usually showed the most dramatic moments, such as when an actor paused in a crucial action to cross his eyes and hold a dramatic pose.

Utamaro Kitagawa. Of the artists producing woodblock prints for popular consumption, UTAMARO KITAGAWA [OO-TAH-MAH-ROH] (1753–1806) is among the best known. Utamaro's elegant, willowy, and languorous women are typically rendered in full-length portraits characterized by delicacy and refinement, but he also helped to develop the close-up print showing little more than the face of some beautiful courtesan, often with a mica background to enhance the decorative quality of the portraits. One of the full-color woodblock prints, *Painting the Lips* (fig. 20.3), shows a woman who has just blackened her teeth now applying color to her lips before a mirror. She has not shaved her eyebrows, however, which women did when they married, so she can be identified as a courtesan. The slightly turned position of her head and torso adds visual drama without disrupting the elegance of her posture.

Katsushika Hokusai. KATSUSHIKA HOKUSAI [HOK- KOO-SAI] (1760–1849), created a multitude of designs and prints, which were produced in large editions. Hokusai created some of his finest works after age seventy, including his popular series *Thirty-Six Views of Mount Fuji.* His *The Great Wave of Kanagawa* (fig. 20.4) is remarkable for its depiction of the power of nature, with Mount Fuji, a symbol of Japan's enduring beauty and stability, small in the distance. Although almost centered in the print, Fuji is dwarfed by a giant wave, which threatens to crash on the boat beneath it. In this image, which is now known worldwide, Hokusai contrasts the transience of everyday existence, the fragility of life, to the more enduring majesty of Fuji.

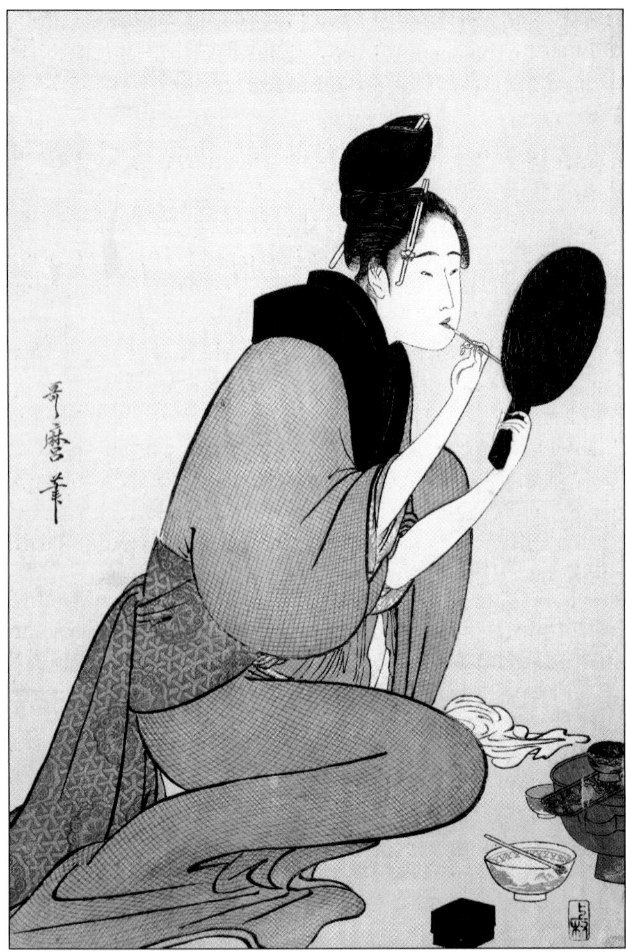

FIGURE 20.3 Utamaro Kitagawa, *Kuchi-bini* (Painting the Lips), Tokugawa period, color woodcut with printed glue, ca. 1794–95. $14\frac{1}{3}'' \times 9\frac{3}{4}''$ (36.5 × 24.8 cm). New York Public Library. Art Resource, NY. The strong composition contrasts with the delicate face of this woman as she applies her makeup.

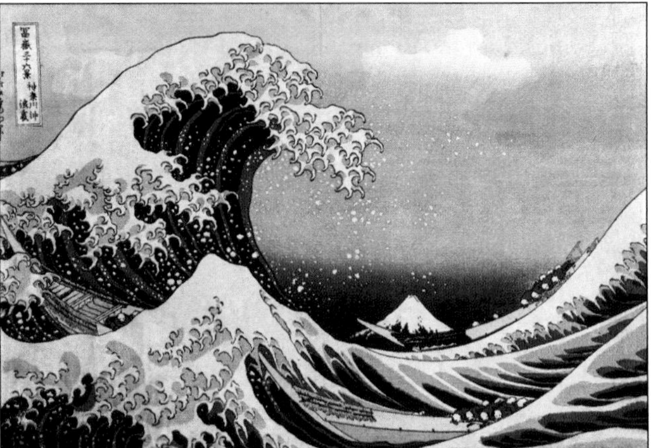

FIGURE 20.4 Katsushika Hokusai, *The Great Wave of Kanagawa*, Japan, from the series *Thirty-Six Views of Mount Fuji*, Tokugawa period, ca. 1831, color woodblock print, $9\frac{7}{8}'' \times 14\frac{5}{8}''$ (25.5 × 37.2 cm), Private Collection, Art Resource, NY. Among the best known of all Japanese woodblock prints, this image, an icon representing Japan, contrasts the powerful energy of the ocean's waves with the stable serenity of the distant snow-capped mountain in the background.

FIGURE 20.5 Ando Hiroshige, *Sudden Shower Over Atake*, *Number 58* of *One Hundred Views of Edo*, 1857. Woodblock print, color, $10\frac{1}{2}'' \times 15''$ (26.7 × 38 cm). British Museum, London. As with many of Hiroshige's masterpieces, this print represents not just the view, but also mood and atmosphere.

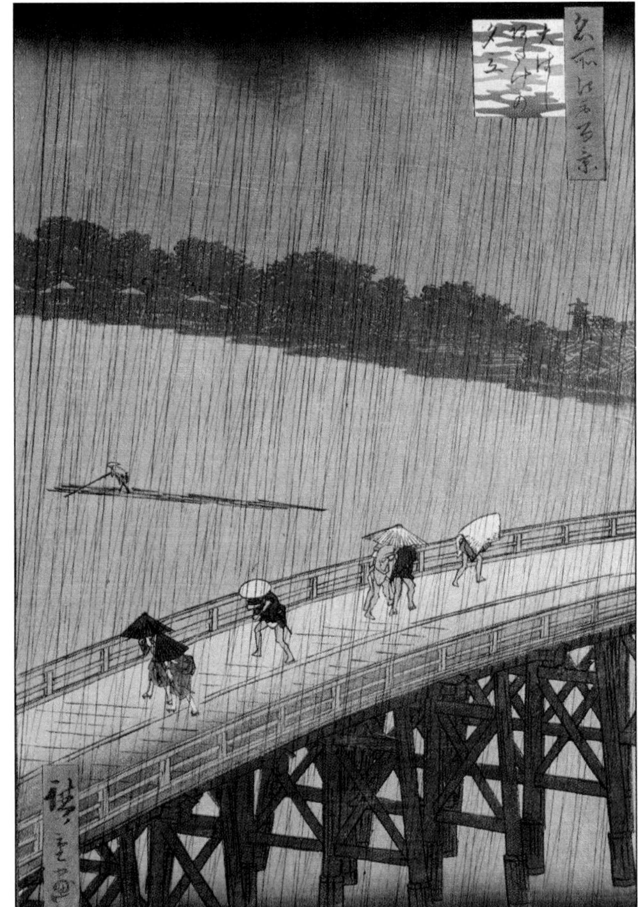

Ando Hiroshige. HIROSHIGE [HE-ROH SHEE-GUH] (1797–1858), like Hokusai preferred landscapes to portraits. Also like Hokusai, Hiroshige produced many prints as parts of various series of woodblock prints of landscapes. Among his most famous and important works are the series of prints *One Hundred Views of Edo.* Number 58 of that series (fig. 20.5) shows a characteristic scene of high summer when the humid heat dissolves into streaking slanting rain. Hiroshige captures the suddenness of the downpour, showing elegant ladies and bare-legged men caught unawares on a bridge, while other figures are depicted crouching under umbrellas, huddling under straw capes, or rushing for the nearest protection.

LACQUERWARE AND CERAMICS

Lacquerware. Use of lacquer as an artistic medium began during the Neolithic period and became important especially in China, Japan, and Korea. To an underlying object made of wood, the artist applies lacquer, which is a varnish that comes from the lacuer tree (Rhus verniciflua) and dries as a clear, hard, durable surface. A number of layers of varnish are applied to build up a smooth coating. Lacquered surfaces may be inlaid with mother-of-pearl and precious metals. Gold may be sprinkled on the surfaces before the lacquer is completely dry, causing the powder to adhere. Rather than painted or inlaid, lacquer may also be carved. To do this, layer upon layer of lacquer is applied until thick enough that the design may be carved out. Characteristically, the scale of the carving is nearly microscopic and the display of manual dexterity extraordinary. Beautifully crafted lacquered objects were manufactured in workshops. Because of the relative fragility of the medium, few early examples of lacquerware survive today.

Wealthy people of the Momoyama period (1573–1615) enjoyed the use of luxury utensils in their homes, such as the sake pitcher seen in fig. 20.6 made c. 1596–1600, of lacquered wood. In this example, the simple shape of the perfectly symmetrical vessel contrasts to the extreme asymmetry of its decoration. The decoration itself consists of contrasts: shapes large, simple, and abruptly angular to small, curved, complex floral forms of two kinds, set against different backgrounds—one black and the other sprinkled gold, separated by angular zig-zag lines. The aesthetic, based on intentionally striking contrasts, is characteristic of Japanese works of art created in various materials at this time; the technical perfection is a general characteristic of Japanese art.

FIGURE 20.6 Wine container, Momoyama period (1573–1615), c. 1596–1600, lacquered wood, height 9 $\frac{7}{8}$″ (25 cm). The Metropolitan Museum of Art, New York, NY, U.S.A. Image copyright © The Metropolitan Museum of Art / Art Resource, NY. Lacquer on wood was a favored medium in the East and was used to create luxury items. Characteristically Japanese are both the technical perfection and the striking asymmetry of the decoration.

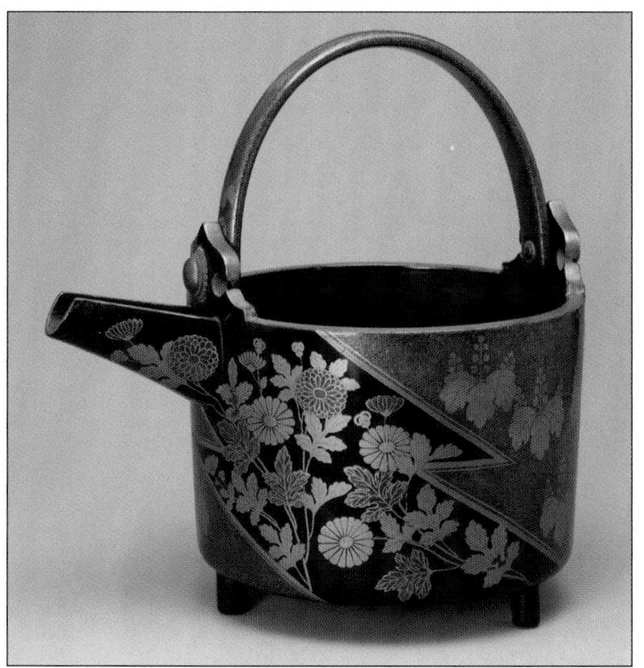

Ceramics. The same aesthetic of extreme asymmetry of design applied to symmetrical objects is seen in Japanese ceramics. The porcelain plate shown in fig. 20.7, made in the nineteenth century during the Edo period (1615–1868), is a perfect circle; here, too, it is not the shape of the object, but the way in which it is painted that favors asymmetry. Beginning in the early nineteenth century, there was a revival in Japan of Ko-Kutani (meaning "old Kutani") porcelain, which had been made in the early Edo era, c.1655, in Kutani. The kilns here continued to produce until around 1730. The highly praised Ko-Kutani ware is typically seen in large dishes with strikingly simple designs painted in a restricted range of thickly applied colors. This example is painted with overglaze green, yellow, black, and brown enamels.

Architecture

Architectural styles in early modern Japan differ from those of previous eras and from one another. During the Muromachi period, the Ashikaga shoguns attempted to fuse styles inherited from their predecessors. During the next era, the Momoyama era, secular architecture became increasingly grandiose and elaborate. This architectural exuberance was tempered during the Tokugawa, with a more restrained aesthetic.

FIGURE 20.7 Plate, Arita ware, Ko-Kutani style, Edo period (1615–1868), nineteenth century, overglaze enamel on porcelain, diameter 8 $\frac{5}{8}$″ (21.9 cm). The Metropolitan Museum of Art, New York, NY, U.S.A. Image copyright © The Metropolitan Museum of Art / Art Resource, NY. Depictions of fans, so abstracted as to be barely recognizable, form a vigorous, energetic pattern. The boldness and simplicity are characteristics of the Ko-Kutani style.

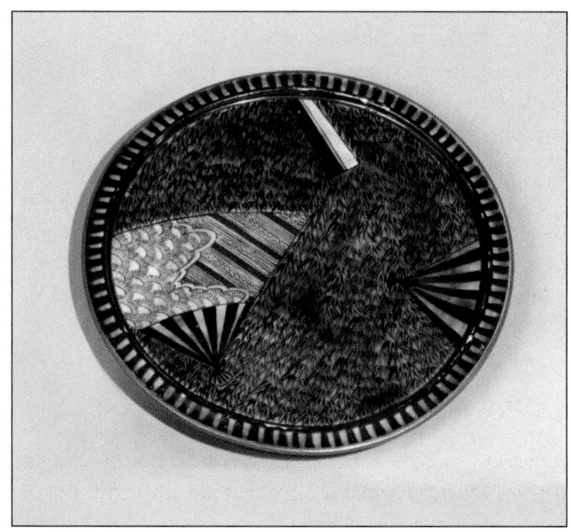

Himeji Castle. In contrast to the elegant simplicity of Muromachi religious and domestic architecture, military architecture developed in the Momoyama period. In earlier military fortresses, the living quarters of the ***daimyo***, or lord, were separated from the defensive fortifications. During the Momoyama, home and fortifications were combined into a single massive edifice designed to discourage attack. The interior, however, was richly decorated to impress visitors with its owner's wealth.

Himeji (fig. 20.8), begun by the shogun Hideyoshi in 1581 and enlarged and completed in 1609, is an outstanding example of castle architecture. The exterior of the castle's main building is constructed of massive masonry, made necessary by the introduction of Western firearms and cannons. The castle rises from a moat, with towers soaring fifty to sixty feet above the water. Atop this impregnable masonry foundation sits a four-story wooden structure reminiscent of temple architecture.

Great Buddha Hall, Todai-ji Temple. The first construction of a temple on the site of today's vast Todai-ji Temple in Nara dates back to 728. In 741, the emperor began to establish Buddhist temples throughout Japan. Other buildings that now constitute the Todai-ji Temple complex were begun in 751 or 752 and built at different times. This temple is mentioned in *The Tale of Genji* (see Chapter 9).

The Great Buddha Hall (Daibutsu-den) (fig. 20.9), started in 745, is the Main Hall of Todai-ji Temple. This building has suffered repeated damage, especially by fire in the twelfth and sixteenth centuries, and has been rebuilt several times. The current building, finished in 1709, measures 187′ long by 164′ wide (57 × 50 m) and is 157′ (48 m) high. Although this Great Buddha Hall is a reconstruction and is approximately 30 percent smaller than the original, it is the largest wooden building in the world. The Great Buddha Hall is thus named because it houses an enormous cast bronze statue of the seated Buddha. Started in 743 at the request of the emperor, it was finished in 752 and dedicated in the same year. The Great Buddha (Daibutsu) is 49′1″ (15 m) high and the largest gilded bronze statue of Buddha in the world.

FIGURE 20.8 Himeji Castle, Hyogo (near Osaka), Japan, Momoyama period (1581–1609). Popularly known as White Heron Castle, Himeji was built as a fortress by powerful Japanese warlords.

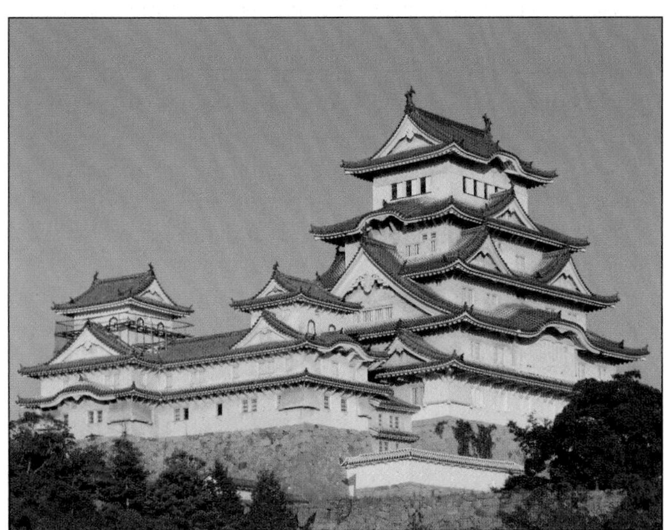

JAPANESE GARDENS

Japanese gardens are essentially landscape architecture. Aesthetically, they are tied to Japanese painting. Many gardens were designed by prominent artists, who shaped the raw materials of nature to appear like carefully inked scrolls. Some gardens were designed for contemplation, others for meandering. In either case, with their neatly raked patterns of sand and carefully positioned shrubs and stones, Japanese gardens are conducive to meditation.

The characteristically Japanese Zen "dry" gardens, which represent nature in microcosm, might be designed with carefully raked pebbles or sand, which was used to suggest water, punctuated by "islands" of rocks.

One of the most famous of these gardens is at the Daisen-in monastery garden (fig. 20.10) in Kyoto, designed by the painter Soami (d. 1525). This 1,100-square-foot garden lies alongside the priest's house. Its vertical rocks represent cliffs, while horizontal stones represent embankments and bridges. The trees in the background symbolize distant mountains.

Larger, more elaborate Japanese gardens include bridges and pagodas as well as plants. These designs are meant to evoke the essence of the Japanese landscape as well as to follow representations of nature in Japanese art. As a result, gardens reflect Japanese cultural aesthetics, including asymmetrical balance, subtle proportion, overall unity, and visual harmony, as seen at the Katsura Palace gardens near Kyoto (fig. 20.11).

LITERATURE

Prior to 1600, literature in Japan had been aristocratic or religious in focus, written by court figures or monks for an educated audience. After 1600, however, literature developed more popular subject matter and was produced by writers from a wider social spectrum.

Saikaku Ihara. While Murasaki's twelfth-century *The Tale of Genji* (see Chapter 9) is generally considered the first great Japanese novel, the novels of SAIKAKU IHARA [SIGH-KAY-KOO] (1642–1693), especially his *The Life of an Amorous Man*, *The Life of an Amorous Woman*, and *Five Women Who Loved Love*, achieved great popularity in their

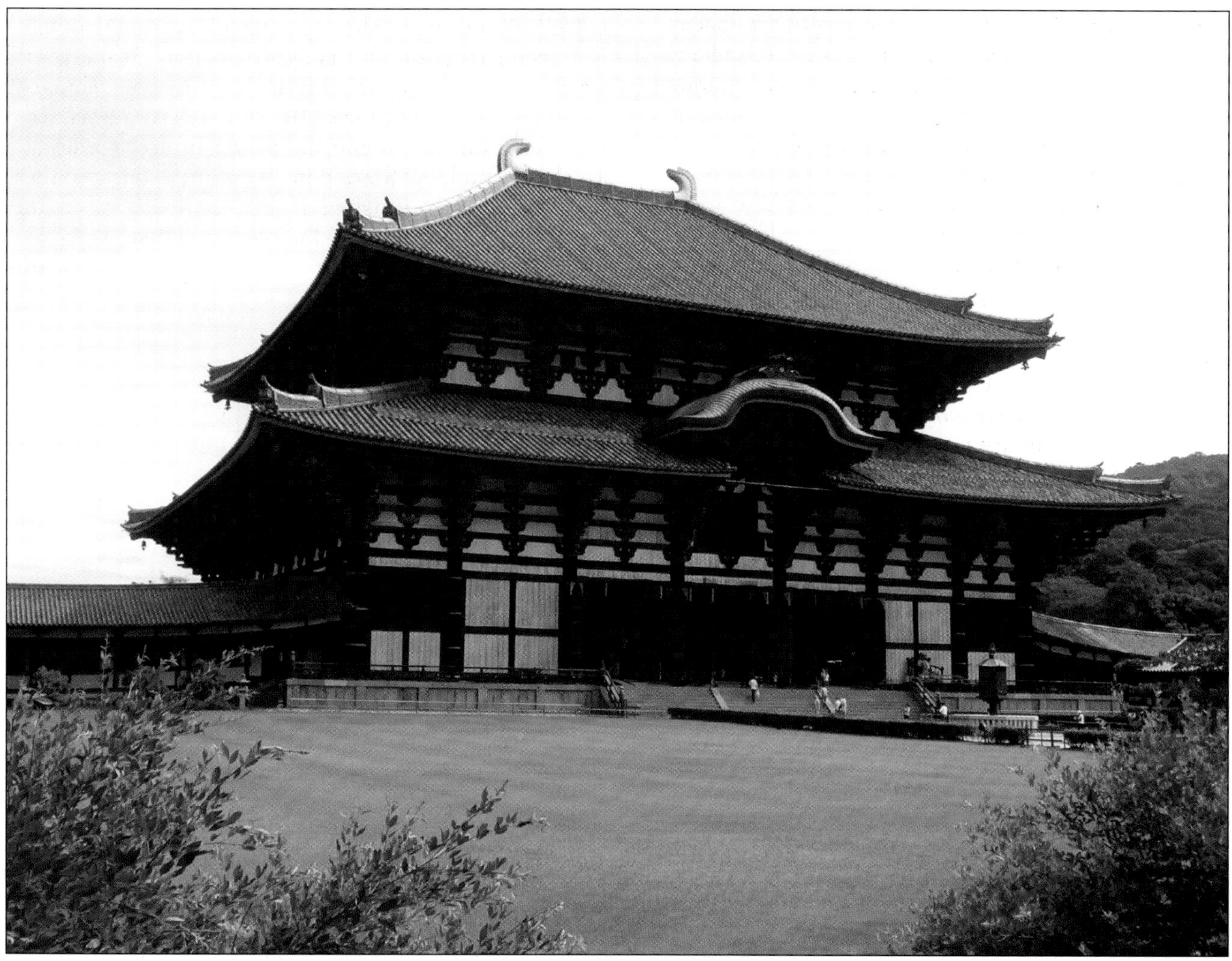

FIGURE 20.9 Great Buddha Hall (Daibutsu-den), Todai-ji Temple, Nara. Buddhism was introduced to Japan from Korea, and encouraged by the Japanese emperors who built temples throughout their country. Some, as Todai-ji Temple, were very large complexes comprised of various gates, halls, and sub-temples.

day. Earlier adventure novels had explored sexuality, but Saikaku's inventive technical experiments with style and point of view were largely responsible for the legitimization of the subject matter.

Five Women Who Loved Love remains Saikaku's most highly regarded book. By exploring the desires of his five female protagonists, Saikaku suggests their kinship with the court ladies of earlier Japanese literature. His merchant wives experience the same passions as courtesans, but they are more willing to sacrifice everything, even their lives, for love. Although modeled on actual people, Saikaku's five heroines are not as highly individualized as characters from nineteenth-century European novels such as Flaubert's Emma Bovary or Tolstoy's Anna Karenina. Saikaku's characters, however, are engaging figures, whose actions anticipate the behavior of more modern Japanese fictional heroines.

Haiku. **Haiku** are three-line poems consisting of a total of 17 syllables in a pattern of 5, 7, and 5 syllables per line. In the past four hundred years, haiku has been the most popular form of poetry in Japan, and in the past century it has also been extremely influential in the West. The essence of a good haiku is a momentary, implicitly spiritual, insight presented without explicit comment. According to conventions established in the seventeenth century, the haiku must have imagery from nature, and usually includes reference to a season, while avoiding rhyme. The haiku poet attempts to create an emotional response in the reader by penetrating to the heart of the poem's subject, thus evoking a sudden moment of awareness.

Basho Matsuo. Haiku reached its greatest artistic heights with the poems of BASHO MATSUO [BAH-SHOH] (1644–1694). Basho began his life as a member of the

Cross Currents

EAST MEETS WEST: TAKEMITSU TORU

Of contemporary Japanese composers, among the best known in the West is TAKEMITSU TORU [TAH-KEY-MEET-SOO] (1930–1996). Takemitsu wrote for film and television as well as for the concert hall. His concert works include symphonic orchestral pieces, compositions for chamber orchestras, and works for voices. Takemitsu scored his orchestral works for both Western and traditional Japanese instruments such as the ***biwa*** (lute) and the ***shakuhachi*** (bamboo flute originally played by Zen monks).

Takemitsu became known in the West through Igor Stravinsky (see Chapter 18), who championed his work, and Aaron Copland (see Chapter 21), who considered him "one of the outstanding composers of our time." Serving as a bridge between East and West, Takemitsu brought works by Japanese composers to the attention of Western performers and introduced Western musical innovations to Japan. He was also instrumental in organizing cultural exchanges between Japan and the United States. Takemitsu enriched his harmonic palette through the influence of French Impressionist composers such as Debussy. He also found inspiration for his music in nature, at one time describing himself as "a gardener of music," a title that reflects his interest in the combination of natural beauty and cultured formality typical of Japanese landscape gardens. Titles of his works often reflect connotations of nature, as in "Riverrun," "Eclipse," and "Toward the Sea."

FIGURE 20.10 Attributed to Kagaku Soku, Garden of the Daisen-in monastery, Daitokuji temple, Kyoto, Japan, sixteenth century. Although used primarily for meditation, this garden served also as a place of assembly for Zen priests and samurai to compose *renga*, linked verses of poetry composed communally.

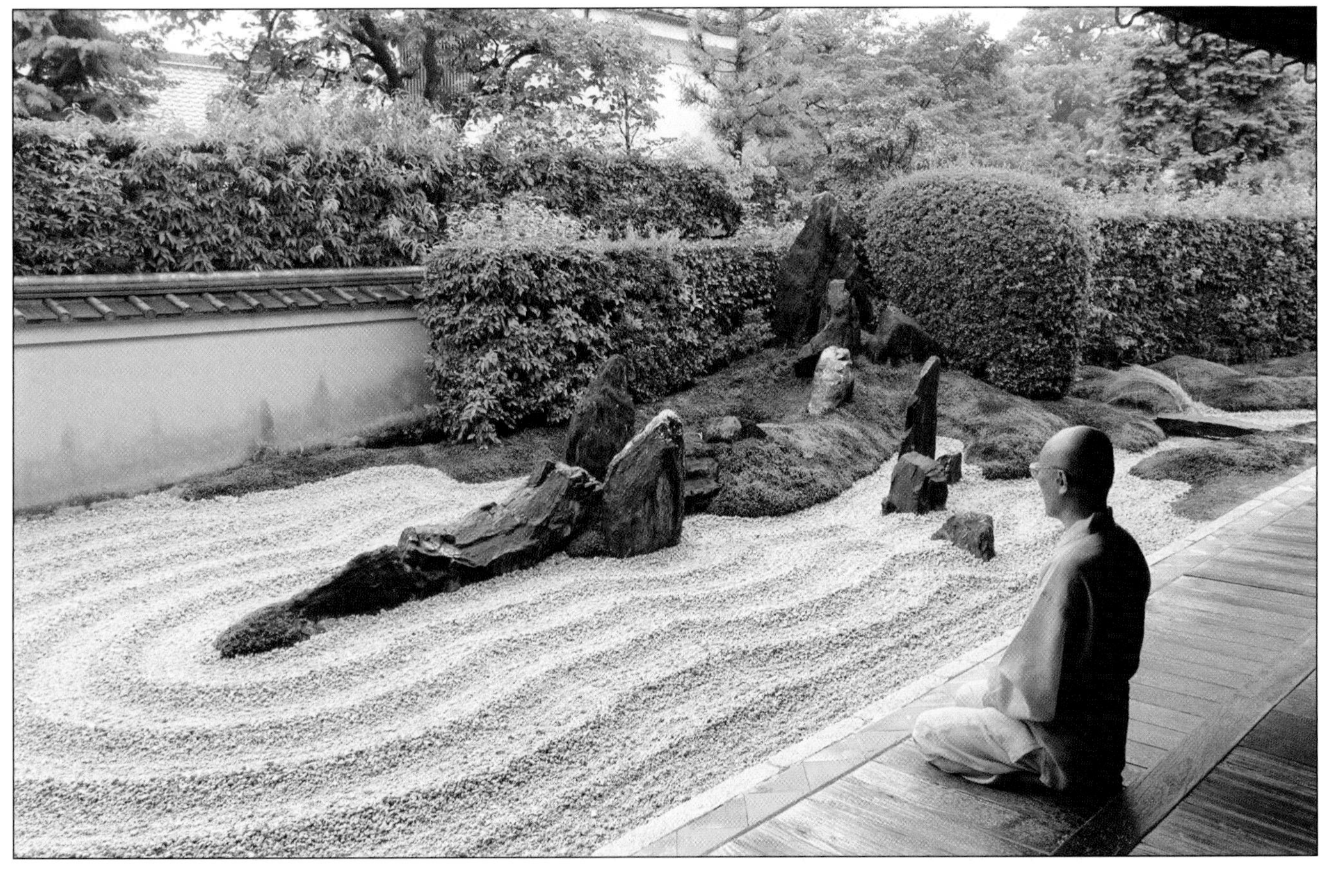

Then & Now

The Samurai Code

The code of the samurai consisted of five aspects: loyalty, hierarchy, bravery, self-control, and shame. Samurai were loyal to their aristocratic lords, who rewarded them with land in return for military service. The samurai themselves were warrior aristocrats with a keen sense of rank and hierarchy. And although the age of the samurai ended in the late twelfth century during the Kamakura shogunate, the samurai ideal has had a strong influence on Japanese culture, both in peacetime and during wartime. Many samurai values, in fact, remain embedded in the fabric of contemporary Japanese society.

The importance of loyalty, for example, can be seen in the way Japanese workers and businesspeople bind themselves to a single company for their working lives. Japanese baseball players, too, play for a single team in Japan rather than looking for better and better deals with different teams, as players do in the United States. To some extent, this kind of total loyalty is beginning to break down, as global markets undermine Japanese businesses and some Japanese ball players come to America to play in the major leagues. Nonetheless the cultural ideal of loyalty to a single entity remains pervasive in Japan.

Hierarchy, too, remains pervasive in Japanese culture. It can be found in relationships in every sector and level of society, from business and government to university life, from religion to the military, and among spouses and relatives of those holding positions of rank and authority. The flip side of the emphasis on rank carries with it a set of responsibilities such that honor is always at stake. In situations where an individual has failed or disappointed his superiors, there is a sense of shame and dishonor. In medieval times, the failed samurai warrior would commit ritual suicide with his own sword. During the financial setbacks of the 1990s, a number of Japanese businessmen committed suicide for failing their companies, families, and coworkers.

The Japanese warrior code, *bushido*, was apparent during World War II as Japanese kamikaze pilots defended the honor of country and emperor by flying their airplanes on suicide missions into enemy ships. And although contemporary Japanese are questioning their allegiance to the ancient samurai code of *bushido*, its cultural values continue to exert a strong pull, even in the midst of cultural change.

Figure 20.11 Shokintei (Pavilion of the Pine Lute), Katsura Palace gardens, near Kyoto, early 1660s. Named after the sound of wind in the pines that surround it, the pavilion is larger than many tea huts, but its setting conveys the harmony with nature that is such an important feature of Japanese aesthetics.

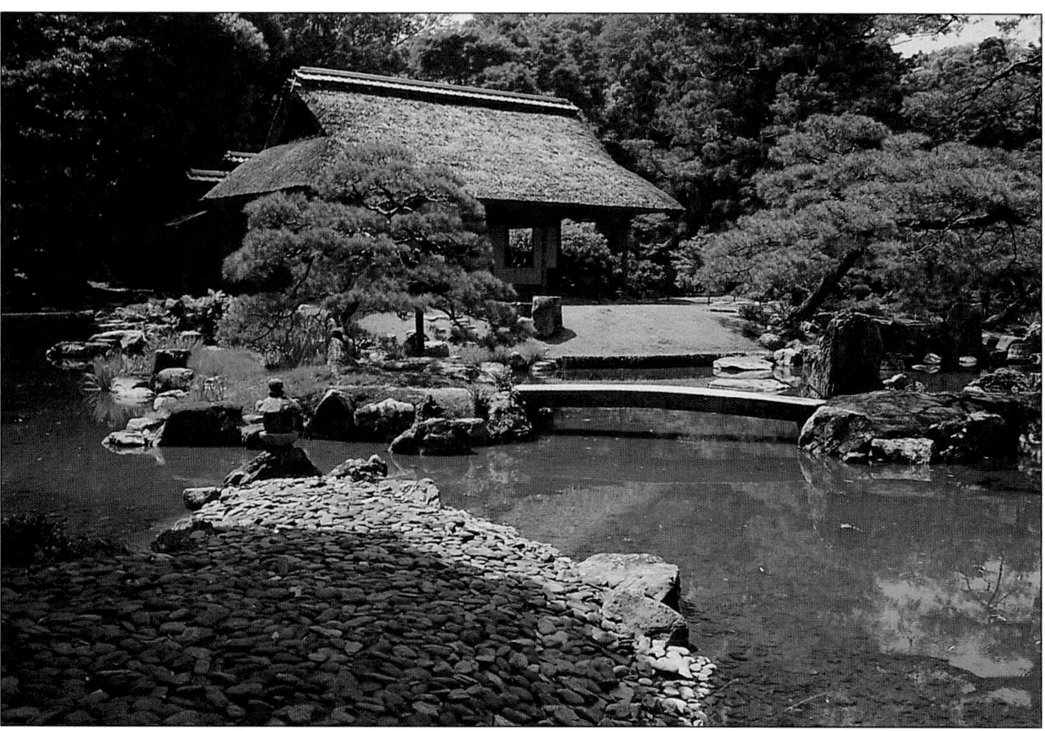

samurai class, but he gave up this life to become a wandering poet. Strongly influenced by the Tang masters Du Fu and Li Bai (see Chapter 8), Basho took from his Chinese predecessors their austerity and loneliness while absorbing their sense of humor. His poems, like theirs, convey an enjoyment of life and express regret at life's impermanence, in Basho's case with a minimum of words and images.

In his desire to distance himself from the clever haiku popular in his day, Basho developed a distinctive style that reflected the realities of everyday living while suggesting spiritual depths and intellectual insights. Humor is readily apparent in this haiku, written on a journey Basho made in 1689. On the road he saw a monkey caught in a sudden rain shower, and moved by its evident distress, he composed the following:

hatsushigure	First rain of winter—
saru mo komino wo	the monkey too seems to want
hoshige nari	a little straw raincoat.

Even in this humorous vision, we can detect Basho's profound sense of what the Latin poet Virgil called "the tears of things." When Basho was ill and approaching death, he composed the following haiku, which evokes his sense of solitude.

tabi ni yande	Sick on a journey,
yume wa kareno wo	my dreams wander over
kakemeguru	withered fields.

This haiku, the last Basho ever wrote, was titled "Composed in Illness" by the poet. Providing a title was highly unusual; Basho knew the severity of his illness. He used the image of the journey both literally, for he became ill while traveling, and metaphorically, for the journey of life. The final word *kakemeguru*, translated here as "withered fields," brings home with precision and elegance the inevitable fact of his dying.

Yosa Buson and Kobayashi Issa. Haiku master Yosa Buson (1716–1784) was equally well known as a literati painter. Many of his haiku have a strong visual element. Buson taught that the poet should use ordinary language to express what is beyond the ordinary.

Shojo to shite	Bleak and lonely
Ishi ni hi no ireru	the sun penetrates the rocks
kareno kana	in the withered field

Poet Kobayashi Issa (1763–1827) lived a tragic life; his wife and several children died before he did. Issa, who invested his poetry with great compassion for all living creatures, may be the best loved of all Japanese poets.

Yare utsu na	"Don't hit me!"
hae ga te wo suru	the fly wrings his hands
ashi wo suru	and wrings his feet

In more modern times, the poet and critic Masaoka Shiki (1867–1902) admired Buson for his ability to express emotion through imagery; his own haiku often convey a tinge of melancholy. One of Shiki's finest haiku has been misattributed to Buson:

Yuku ware ni	For me leaving
todomaru nare ni	and you staying—
aki futatsu	two autumns

Haiku in modern Japan has gone in two directions. A great number of poets strive to follow the traditional rules of seventeen syllables and a seasonal reference; others advocate an approach that breaks the formal rules in order to follow the spirit of haiku: a subtle expression of meaning through natural images through which the reader becomes an equal partner with the poet.

The monk Taneda Santoka (1882–1940) was a leading exponent of free haiku. He wrote of himself, "A foolish traveler, I have only a life of wandering, like grasses floating from one bank to the other, the shadows of my heart changing as life provides for me." One of his rule-breaking poems has a combination of eight and seven syllables in its two lines:

Yama no shizukasa e	To the mountain silence—
shikuzanaru ae	silent rain

Haiku has become the most international of all forms of poetry. Most writers in other countries do not follow the 5-7-5 rule, since languages such as English compress more meaning in fewer syllables, but the ideal of brief poems expressing meaning indirectly through images from nature, including human nature, continues to inspire people all over the world.

Modern Fiction. Modern Japanese literature is traditionally dated from the beginning of the reign of the Meiji emperor in 1868. During the Meiji era (1868–1912) a number of Westernizing reforms were introduced into Japanese economic, social, educational, and cultural life. Literacy was increasing dramatically, and writers began to use colloquial Japanese rather than the language of classical Japan. These changes, which parallel those in China at the turn of the twentieth century, inaugurated a period of modern fiction that is recognized for its elegance, subtlety, and grace. Japanese authors, such as Nobel Prize winner Oe Kenzaburo, have frequently written what are called "confessional novels" centering on the experience of the protagonist told from his or her own point of view. In most cases, however, modern Japanese novels reflect a larger-scale struggle between traditional Japanese values and new influences from the Western world.

The fiction of modern Japan therefore reflects a strong concern with identity, both cultural and individual. Prizing communal values, Japanese have wondered at the Western emphasis on the autonomy of the individual self. TANIZAKI JUN'ICHIRO [TAH-NEE-ZAH-KEE] (1886–1965) explored these themes. Depicting Japan's changing cultural terrain, his works examine the consequences individuals face when set free from cultural

Connections

BUNRAKU: JAPANESE PUPPET THEATER

Although puppets were used in Japanese ceremonies and festivals at least as early as the eleventh century, it was during the Tokugawa period that the puppet theater, or **Bunraku,** developed and flourished. The texts of Bunraku plays were more distinguished than those of Kabuki, with the best of them composed by CHIKAMATSU MONZAEMON [CHICK-A-MAHT-SU] (1653–1724), who is considered by many the greatest Japanese dramatist. Written in poetic language, Chikamatsu's Bunraku plays had a narrator and were accompanied by a ***samisen*** (three-string banjo) player, both of whom typically sit on a dais set off to the side of the stage. Unlike Kabuki actors, who are the main attraction for a Kabuki audience, the puppeteers, the *samisen* accompanist, and the narrator are all self-effacing. Their job is not to impress the audience and win applause, but rather to bring the play to the audience in such a way that they are all but forgotten while the audience concentrates on the action of the puppets and the language of the play.

In its reliance on the rhythmic pacing of the stringed *samisen* and the narrator's chanting, Bunraku can be compared with the earliest Greek dramas, in which a single actor-speaker recounts tales from the ancient myths and legends. In Bunraku the narrator is the voice of all the puppets, whose movements are controlled by puppet masters dressed in black. Like their ancient Greek counterparts, the early Bunraku plays celebrate ancient tales of Japanese culture, such as stories from *The Tale of Genji* (see Chapter 9). Chikamatsu, however, shifted the grounds of Bunraku from an emphasis on heroic stories of the past to situations involving ordinary people in his own time. Foreigners who view Bunraku are usually amazed how much depth of feeling can be evoked in a form of theater that in the West is usually performed as entertainment for children.

constraints to pursue personal ambitions and desires. Many of Tanizaki's characters live as modern Japanese, and the results of their self-assertion and self-aggrandizement produce guilt and alienation: guilt for abandoning long-valued cultural norms, and alienation as a result of being cut off from the solidarity of the group.

THEATER

There are two primary types of Japanese music for theater: Noh and Kabuki. Each is a distinctive form, with different musical conventions. Noh drama was developed in the fifteenth century, during the age of warrior control; Kabuki theater emerged in the seventeenth century under the influence of merchant culture.

Noh. Literally meaning "an accomplishment," **Noh** consists of dances, dialogue, and songs by the main actors, and music from a ***ji,*** or chorus. The instruments used to accompany the singing are collectively referred to as the ***hayashi.*** The *hayashi* ensemble consists of a ***nokan,*** or flute; an ***o-tsuzumi,*** a type of hourglass drum held on the hip; a ***ko-tsuzumi,*** a shoulder drum; and a ***taiko,*** or stick drum on a stand. During the entire time actors perform a Noh drama, the musicians of the *hayashi* remain on stage, their musical actions choreographed as part of the drama alongside the words and gestures of the actors.

Noh is distinguished from other forms of drama by its solemnity. Even the happier moments are performed with a seriousness and gravity that make them sound ritualistic. Originally, Noh plays were performed by Shinto priests to placate the gods. Later, from the fourteenth through the seventeenth centuries, the plays were performed by professional actors wearing masks, one of the genre's distinguishing features. The limited plot action, the highly poetic texts, and the understated stylized gestures differentiate Noh plays from the realistic plays of Western theater.

Kabuki. During the first years of the Tokugawa period, a type of theater that includes more lively song and dance was performed in Kyoto. The first **Kabuki** were short dramatic dances, performed by women, accompanied by song and percussion, that celebrated the exploits of heroes, especially the samurai. However, scandals concerning relations between noblemen and the actresses led to this form of theater, like Noh, being performed only by men. During the eighteenth century, with the works of Chikamatsu, Kabuki developed a repertoire of plays based on the daily lives of peasants and merchants. Unlike Noh drama, which looked back to the glories of the Middle Ages, Kabuki focused on the present. In contrast to the solemnity and decorum of Noh drama, Kabuki performances were melodramatic and suggestive of the actors' seductive charms. Developed in response to the needs of an urban audience, Kabuki includes popular drama along with various types of dance and music, some of which are performed onstage and some offstage.

Cinema/Anime. Japan has long had a vibrant film industry and a proud cinematic tradition. In the early twentieth century, most Japanese films were simply cinematic renditions of staged plays and other theatrical performances. During the 1920s, however, Japanese films began to deal with both period and modern themes and to exist independently of theater productions.

Cross Currents

EAST MEETS WEST: FILMS OF AKIRA KUROSAWA

One of the greatest Japanese film directors, producers, and screenwriters, Akira Kurosawa (1910–98), is also one of the most popular in the West. His *Rashomon* (1950) was remade by Hollywood as *The Outrage* (1964) and his *Seven Samurai* (1954) as the *Magnificent Seven* (1960). Both Hollywood versions of Kurosawa's films were Westerns, a cinematic form that Kurosawa himself knew well and to which he was deeply indebted. *Seven Samurai,* notable for its dramatic and violent action, closeups, moving cameras, and contrasting scenes of lyricism, presents a Japanese variation on the opposition between Western ranchers and farmers familiar from American Westerns. The film depicts the breakdown of social barriers, as aristocratic samurai fight victoriously alongside peasants against an alien enemy.

Rashomon, based on a story by Ryunosuke Akutagawa, is a very different kind of film. Set in the Heian period (794–1184), the film depicts an encounter between a husband, wife, and bandit, during which the wife is raped and the husband killed. The film's narrative action is described four times from four points of view, that of each of its three protagonists and a fourth narrated by a woodcutter who witnessed the event. Kurosawa's film calls truth and objectivity into question, as each of the four tells a different version of the story. Replete with ambiguity, uncertainty, and contradiction, the four versions undercut the attempt to fix the truth with any certainty.

A number of Kurosawa's films were inspired by, or adapted from, Western literary works. His *Throne of Blood* was inspired by Shakespeare's *Macbeth; Ran* by *King Lear;* and *The Bad Sleep Well* by *Hamlet.* Tolstoy's *The Death of Ivan Ilych* inspired Kurosawa's *Ikiru,* and another of his films adapted Dostoyevsky's *The Idiot.* In addition, Kurosawa was influenced by the American film maker John Ford, who made many Westerns, and Kurosawa was himself a significant influence on a number of American filmmakers, including George Lucas, maker of the *Star Wars* films.

Table 20–1 JAPANESE ARTS
Landscape painting: Sesshu
Woodblock prints: Hokusai
Architecture: Himeji Castle
Landscape gardens: Garden of the Daisen-in Monastery
Haiku poetry: Basho
Theater: Noh and Kabuki

Samurai films became a staple, and they remain an important film genre to this day.

The golden era of Japanese filmmaking began in 1950 with the production of *Rashomon* by the acclaimed director Akira Kurosawa, which won a number of international prizes. Kurosawa also based a number of films on the plays of Shakespeare, most notably, perhaps, *Throne of Blood,* a modernized samurai adaptation of *Macbeth.* Other Japanese directors of the 1950s include Mizoguchi Kenji, whose *Tales of Ugetsu* and *The Life of Oharu* joined Kurosawa's *Seven Samurai* as popular films in both Japan and abroad.

A contemporary cinematic development in Japan is **anime,** a word derived from French and English and denoting highly sophisticated animated films. In Japan animated films occupy a place of pride in the film genre hierarchy, and they are taken as seriously as any other kind of film. Anime films in Japan are not just cartoons for children, but rather extend to many genres, including science fiction, action and adventure films, as well as romantic films and historical dramas. Targeting all age groups, anime films explore philosophical questions and social issues, develop complex plots, and provide stunningly realistic animated visuals.

World of the Geisha. Historically, **geisha,** or women who served as "professional entertainers," or "artist entertainers," were skilled at art, music, dance, storytelling, and even a simple kind of juggling. They are typically hired to attend parties, sometimes at tea houses, sometimes at traditional Japanese restaurants. Arrangements are made through a geisha union office. Geisha originated as skilled professional entertainers, with most of them being male. Over time, the number of male geisha dwindled, and by the early nineteenth century, female geisha vastly outnumbered them.

Popular Western misconceptions of geisha confuse them with prostitutes. However, this has not, historically, been the case, but rather the exception. This confusion has been exacerbated by Japanese prostitutes, who have traded on the image of the geisha by presenting themselves to tourists as "geisha." Additional confusion has resulted from the portrayal of geishas in popular novels and films like the recent *Memoirs of a Geisha.*

Like other kinds of work involving the development of skills, such as the skilled trades in western countries, the path for the **maika,** or geisha in training, to full geisha status was long and arduous. It required dedication and commitment over a span of many years. Traditionally, geisha began their training while very young, with some girls sold to geisha houses as children. Today, however,

Critical Thinking

The Economic Future of Japan

After the Second World War, Japan embarked on a program of education and business innovation that led the country to develop one of the world's most successful economies. Japanese auto manufacturers modeled their products on luxury cars made in Germany, and before long were taking a large percentage of the high-end auto market from the Germans, after having successfully taken much of the lower and middle range auto market from American auto manufacturers.

Japan had a similar success with consumer electronics goods, especially with televisions, radios, and the "Sony Walkman," at least until the Apple Computer Corporation displaced the Walkman with its ubiquitous and wildly successful Ipod. Japan is facing fierce competition in consumer electronics both from American companies like Apple and from South Korean companies like Samsung, which has surpassed Japan as the leading electronics company. And it is also facing competition in the auto market both from a resurgence of makers of luxury cars, including Mercedes, Audi, and BMW, as well as from South Korean manufacturers of mid and lower priced cars, such as Hyundai.

What does Japan need to regain its position as a market leader in these industries? To what extent is it possible for Japan to become a world leader again? To what extent does the rise of China as an economic power complicate Japan's economic future? How much time, effort, initiative, and investment will be needed for Japan to achieve economic success?

many women begin their careers as geisha in adulthood, while others begin their training after high school. Geisha, today, still study traditional Japanese musical instruments, such as the shamisen and the shakuhachi, and they still learn classical Japanese dance, the tea ceremony, flower arranging (ikebana), along with literature, especially poetry, which has long been popular in Japan.

Contemporary Music

Oe Hikari. The story of the contemporary composer OE HIKARI [OH-AY HEE-KAH-REE] (b. 1963), son of the Nobel Laureate for Literature in 1994, Oe Kenzaburo, is one of the more unusual accounts of the making of an artist. Oe Hikari was born with a life-threatening growth on his brain. Against the advice of doctors, his parents decided to have the growth removed, even though part of Hikari's brain had to be sacrificed. The surgery saved his life but left him severely brain damaged, so that it was difficult for him to communicate using language. He did not make a sound until the age of six, when he responded to bird calls in the wild by imitating them perfectly, an early indication that he possessed an unusual aural ability. His parents soon realized he had memorized more than seventy distinctive bird calls at the age of four from a recording given to him.

Although Oe's verbal language remains limited, his imagination has allowed him to compose music, beginning after piano lessons at the age of eleven. His work shows an instinctive appreciation of melody and an inclination toward the harmonic traditions of Western music from the seventeenth through the nineteenth centuries. Oe's music is deeply indebted to the musical styles of Bach, Mozart, and Chopin. Most of his compositions are brief and lyrical, conveying sorrow and joy, serenity and exuberance.

Koto Music. Like much else in Japanese culture, a predecessor of the koto came to Japan from China during the late seventh and early eighth centuries. Chinese and Korean musicians came with this zither-like instrument to play it in the Japanese court orchestra. About two hundred years later, the koto was being used as a solo instrument of the aristocracy. The earliest extant koto music dates from the sixteenth century and was used in Buddhist temple ceremonies. Performance of koto music at that time was restricted to priests, scholars, and aristocrats.

The best known and most important traditional koto music dates from the Edo period (1615–1868) when Japan's capital moved to Edo, currently Tokyo. Although Japanese society was isolated during most of this period, Japanese merchants served as catalysts for artistic developments in music, kabuki, and woodblock prints. Music for the koto during the early Edo was intended for entertainment rather than to accompany religious ceremonies. It was composed not by priests or scholars but by professional musicians, most of whom were blind, and who belonged to a special guild. As with other crafts, the koto repertoire was passed down through apprenticeship and was played from memory. The most famous of the koto masters was a blind musician named Yatsuhashi Kengyo, considered the father of modern koto music; like other koto masters, he was also a teacher of young women from wealthy Japanese families.

The koto (fig. 20.12) is used for solos, for duets, often with the shakuhachi, a five-holed end-blown bamboo flute, and for vocal accompaniments. It is also sometimes coupled with the shamisen, a plucked lute-like instrument with three strings. Most koto music is based on pentatonic (five-tone) scales that correspond to CDEGA or CDE♭GA♭ on the piano. In fact, the koto is to Japanese music what the piano is to western music—an extremely important instrument.

Cultural Impact

Japan's impact on the rest of the world continues to be felt in various ways. Since the 1950s, Japan has been an important world economic power and a significant trading partner of the United States and Europe as well as of Asian countries. Its dominance of electronics, particularly CD players, radios, speakers, and stereo equipment, is paralleled by the popularity of its automobiles across a range of price categories, from the Lexus and Infiniti at higher prices to its Hondas and Toyotas at midrange.

In the previous century, European painters, in particular Claude Monet and Vincent van Gogh, were inspired by Japanese woodblock prints, especially those of Hokusai, to produce paintings that imitated particular Hokusai prints or incorporated details from them. Monet produced a number of paintings on Japanese themes, emphasizing the elegance and graceful lines of Japanese art. Van Gogh collected Hokusai's woodblock prints, many of which can be seen today, hanging alongside van Gogh's own paintings in the van Gogh museum in Amsterdam. Other Western painters, including the American James McNeill Whistler, introduced Japanese elements into their works.

Japanese music influenced Western composers of both the nineteenth and twentieth centuries. The Impressionist composers Claude Debussy and Maurice Ravel experimented with Japanese melodic and harmonic elements. Contemporary composers such as Steve Reich incorporate Japanese musical motifs into their compositions. Japanese music for flute, especially, remains popular, as CDs by flutists Jean Pierre Rampal and James Galway attest.

In filmmaking, director Akiru Kurosawa's samurai films have influenced American Westerns, especially the films of John Ford and Sam Peckinpah, and can be seen in the recent *The Last Samurai*, although Kurosawa's influence extends beyond this genre. His *Rashomon*, which presents a single story told from the perspectives of a narrator and each of its three characters, remains influential as an example of multiple perspectivism and the relativity of truth.

Finally, the influence of Zen continues to reverberate in both Europe and America. Zen meditation practices have been adapted by contemporary spiritual and psychological movements such as EST. Zen aesthetics, especially floral arranging and the tea ceremony, continue to have their adherents in the West, as does Zen-inspired calligraphy, painting, and poetry, particularly haiku.

FIGURE 20.12 Yuki Yamada playing the Japanese koto with the Kifu Mitsuhashi Ensemble at the Japan Society, NY. Photograph © 2003 Jack Vartoogian/FrontRowPhotos. All Rights Reserved. In the *Tale of Genji*, Japan's earliest novel, Prince Genji falls in love with a woman after hearing her play the koto.

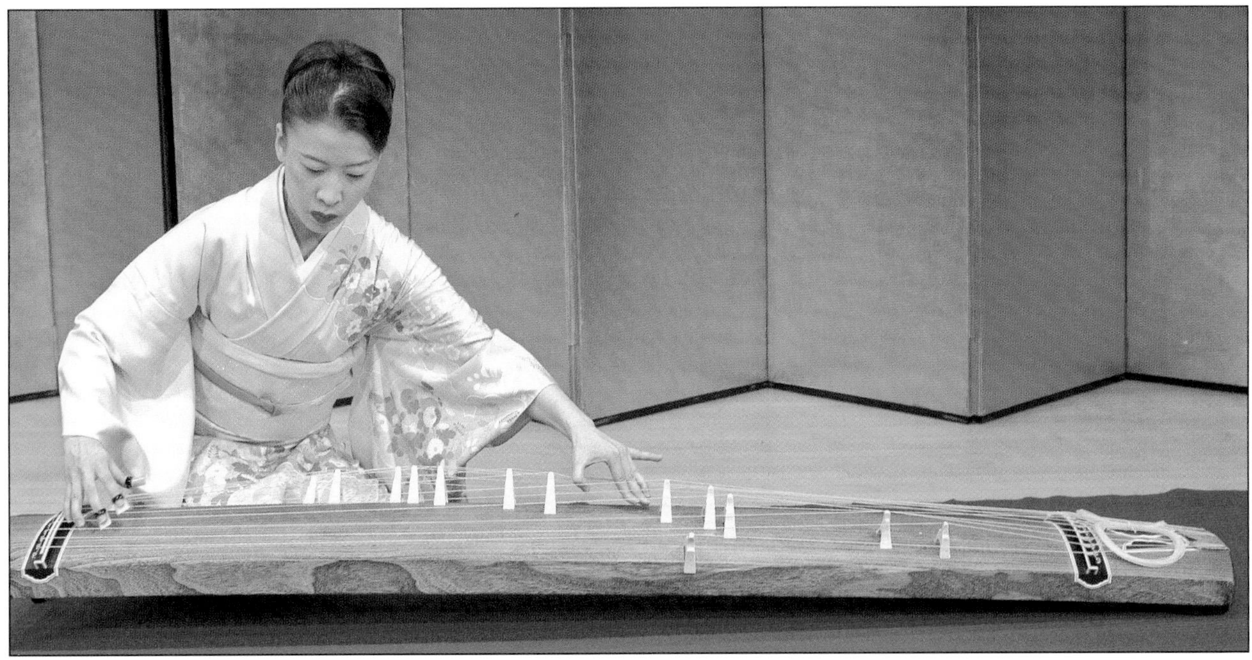

KEY TERMS

shogun
samurai
shogunate
Shinto
kami
zazen
koan
ukiyo-e
daimyo
haiku
biwa
shakuhachi
Bunraku
samisen
Noh
ji
hayashi
nokan
o-tsuzumi
ko-tsuzumi
taiko
Kabuki
anime
geisha
maika

WWW. WEBSITES FOR FURTHER STUDY

http://www.japan-zone.com/omnibus/shinto.shtml
(A history of Shinto: from its early history through the revival and to modern Shinto.)

http://web-japan.org/atlas/architecture/arc16.html
(Himeji Castle, Hyogo [near Osaka], Japan, Momoyama period, 1581–1609.)

http://web.kyoto-inet.or.jp/org/orion/eng/hstj/histj.html
(History of architecture in Kyoto, including the Daisen-in Gardens.)

http://jtrad.columbia.jp/eng/inst.html
(Overview with images of traditional Japanese instruments, including the koto and shakuhachi, among others.)

http://www.pbs.org/wnet/gperf/shows/kurosawa/kurosawa.html
(Multimedia site about Kurosawa's life and films, with interviews, essays, dialogue, filmography, and more.)

http://www.jlit.net
(Site devoted to Japanese authors and their works, including Akutagawa and Saikaku.)

Chapter 21

History

1801	L'Ouverture conquers present-day Hispaniola and abolishes slavery
1807	Great Britain and United States outlaw transatlantic slave trade
1830–47	French invasion of Algeria
1846–48	Mexican War
ca. 1875	Slave trade to Americas ends
1884–85	Conference of Berlin sets rules for European colonization of Africa
1898	Spanish-American War
1899–1902	Boer War in South Africa
1914	Panama Canal completed
1943–56	Perón rules in Argentina
1948	Apartheid formalized in South Africa
1960	Congo gains full independence from Belgium
1961	U.S. Bay of Pigs invasion of Cuba fails
1970	Allende elected president of Chile
1990	Nelson Mandela released from prison
1991	Apartheid abolished in South Africa

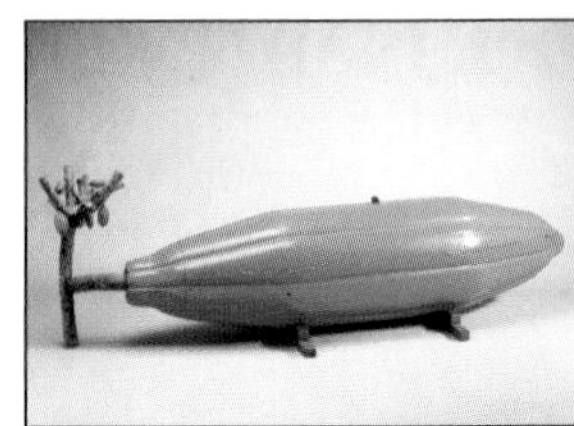

Arts and Architecture

ca. 1660	Followers of Quispe Tito, *Corpus Christi Procession with the Parishioners of Santa Ana*
1909	Yoruba *gelede mask*
1919	Villa-Lobos, *Cancões Típicas Brasileirias*
1929	Kahlo, *Diego and I*
1932–44	Villa-Lobos, *Bachianas Brasileiras*
1943	Lam, *The Jungle*
1944	Siqueiros, *Cuauhtémoc against the Myth*
1959	Botero, *Mona Lisa at the Age of Twelve*
1970s	Kane Kwei, Cocoa-Pod-Shaped Coffin
1978	Sonny Okosun, *Fire in Soweto*

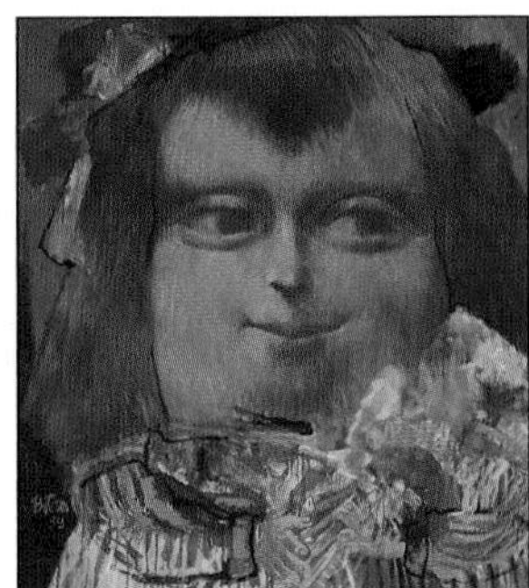

Literature and Philosophy

1958	Chinua Achebe, *Things Fall Apart*
1967	García Márquez, *One Hundred Years of Solitude*
1980	Coetzee, *Waiting for the Barbarians*
1984	Wole Soyinka, *A Play for Giants*

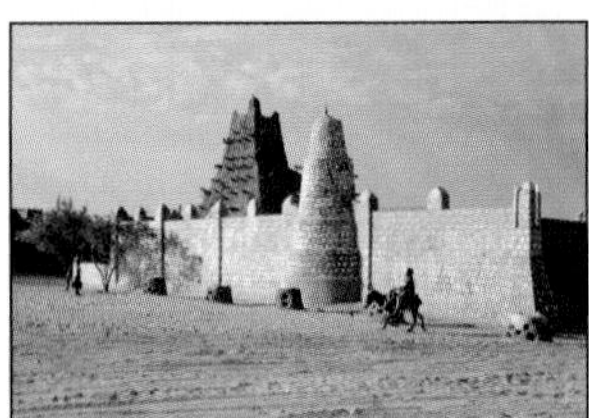

Later Africa and Latin America

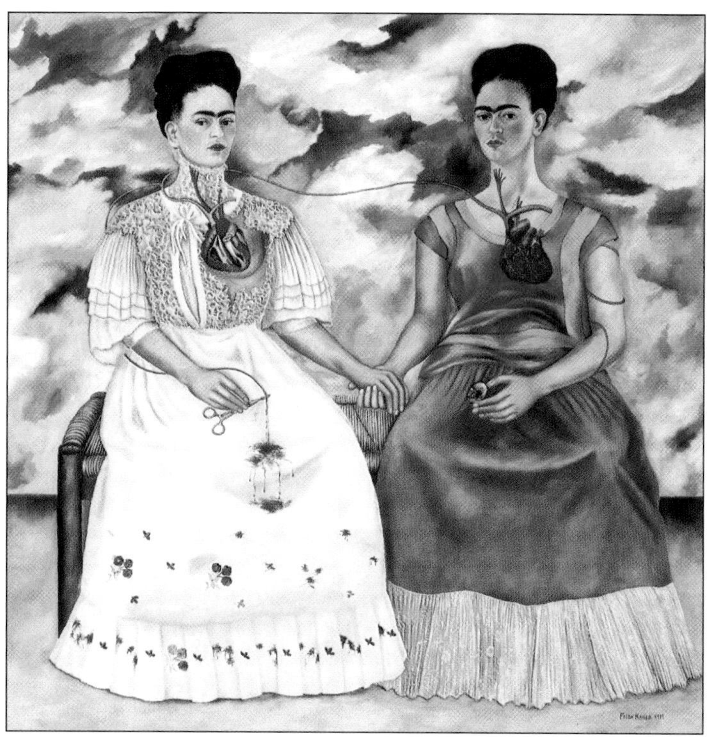

Frida Kahlo, *The Two Fridas*, 1939, oil on canvas, 5′9″ square (1.73 m square), Museo Nacional de Arte Moderno, © 2001 Banco de Mexico, Diego Rivera & Frida Kahlo Museums Trust/Artist Rights Society (ARS), NY. AV Cinco de Mayo No. 2, Col. Centro, Del. Cuanhtemoc 06059, Mexico, D.F. Reproduction authorized by the Instituto Nacional de Bellas Artes y Literatura. Bob Schalkwijk/Art Resource, NY.

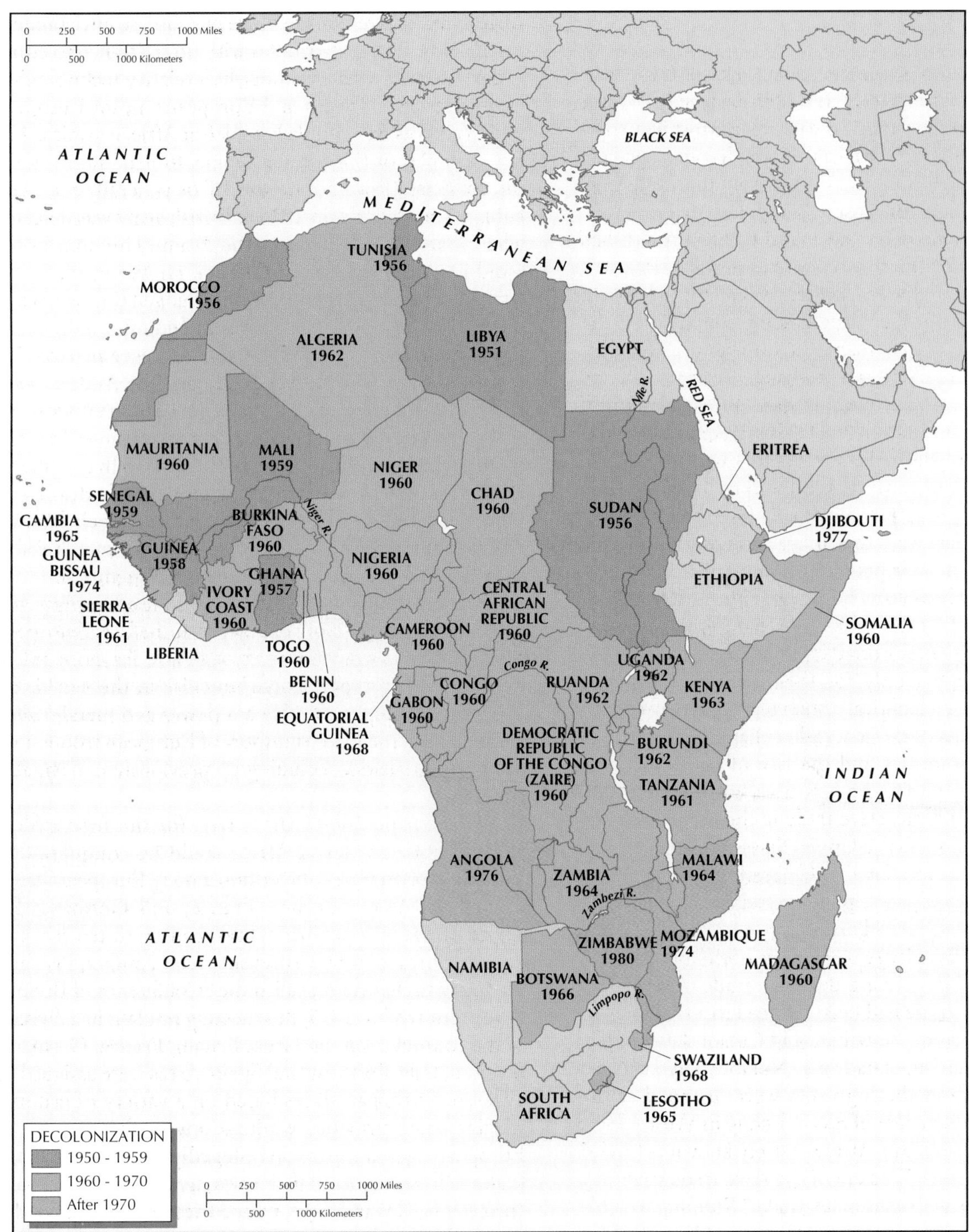

MAP 21.1 The decolonization of Africa in the twentieth century.

CHAPTER OVERVIEW

MODERN AFRICA

The "Dark Continent" moves into the light of modern culture despite European attempts at colonialism

MODERN LATIN AMERICA

Central American culture is enriched through a multiracial society composed of indigenous and colonial peoples

MODERN AFRICA

IN 1800, THE TRANSATLANTIC SLAVE TRADE was reaching its peak, with nearly 100,000 enslaved Africans transported to the Americas each year. Most were destined for Brazil and the Carribean, although some 5 percent were taken to North America. Profits from this trade were high for slave traders; the cost was high for Africa. Where once the inhabitants of Western and Central Africa had provided largely for their own needs in terms of industry, the economy of the regions had increasingly turned toward slave trading. Now, rather than making iron, textiles, and household implements, many African states chose to capture slaves and sell them in exchange for materials and finished goods from European traders. Firearms, in particular, were an important part of this system of exchange. Ironically, even those African states that determined the trade in human beings to be immoral, such as Benin in south-central Nigeria, were eventually forced to take part, since one of the few ways to acquire enough firearms and powder to protect their people from enslavement was to sell slaves. Many historians believe the increased sense of insecurity created by the slave trade undermined existing systems of political legitimacy because new rulers were increasingly selected only for their ability to organize military force. Such a political system tended to concentrate power in the hands of the few, rather than the many.

Changing economics and the rise of an abolitionist movement in Europe and the Americas, however, began to turn the tide against the slave trade in the early 1800s. In 1807, Great Britain and the United States unilaterally outlawed the transatlantic slave trade, treating any slave ship found on the high seas as a pirate vessel (neither country outlawed slavery within its borders for some decades, however). By the 1820s, a large percentage of the British navy was involved in interdicting the slave trade. After 1850, the Atlantic slave trade had been reduced to a trickle, with only a few Portuguese, Brazilian, and Cuban slave traders risking the antislaving squadrons. Notably, any enslaved Africans rescued on the high seas were dropped at the small British protectorate of Sierra Leone in West Africa, creating a remarkable pan-African society known as "Krio" [KREE-oh] **(creole).** The era of the slave trade gave way to a period known as "Legitimate Trade." Running roughly from 1850 to 1880, the regions of West and Central Africa saw substantial economic growth as European demand shifted from human labor to commodities such as palm oil (used to lubricate machinery), latex (natural rubber), and gum arabic (a dye fixer).

THE SCRAMBLE FOR AFRICA AND COLONIAL RULE

By the latter 1800s, the relationship between Africa and Europe was changing once again. For centuries, European traders had been largely relegated to the coastlines of Africa's tropical regions because of a disease environment particularly hostile to peoples with no resistance to either malaria or yellow fever. Similarly, a relative technological parity between Africans and Europeans meant European military forces were unlikely to defeat African armies. The few examples of European attempts to penetrate beyond the coasts of Africa before the 1870s generally met with failure. For example, in 1824, a British army was defeated when it attempted to attack the Asante kingdom in the Gold Coast (now modern Ghana). However, three important technological innovations changed this balance of power. The first was the discovery of quinine, a drug that allowed Europeans to both prevent and cure malaria. Interestingly, quinine was originally used by Andean societies in South America, and it was not so much discovered as it was refined by Europeans after they witnessed its use. Nonetheless, now Europeans could hope to live in malarial regions without it being the equivalent of a death sentence. Second was the development of breech-loading cartridge-firing rifles. These weapons were far more reliable than flintlocks, especially in wet environments, and they also allowed individual soldiers to fire more rapidly and with greater range and accuracy than before. European soldiers, even in small numbers, were now far more deadly than their counterparts anywhere else in the world. Finally, the development of steam power and metal-hulled boats allowed the rapid transport of European troops anywhere in the world, including up previously unnavigable rivers.

Thus, by the 1880s, there was, for the first time, a possibility that tropical Africa could be conquered by Europeans. Growing competition among European states, particularly Great Britain, France, and Germany, for African trade and territories was leading to tension and even the threat of war. To prevent such a conflict, Bismark, the German chancellor, called the "Conference of Berlin." Held from 1884 to 1885, this meeting resulted in a division of the continent among Great Britain, France, Germany, Belgium, Italy, Portugal, and Spain. Areas were assigned to different European states based on a variety of criteria, ranging from previous explorations of the regions by European agents to treaties allegedly signed by African leaders who surrendered their sovereignty over to European "protectors." By and large, most African rulers had no idea they had been labeled as subjects of the various European powers. Ironically, the European powers involved declared they were partitioning the continent for the Africans' own good, specifically stating they were doing so to help bring an end to slavery and to bring the benefits of civilization to Africa.

Of course, declaring the partition of Africa on paper was different from actually colonizing the continent, and the final declaration of the Conference of Berlin demanded that the various European states establish "effective occupation" of the regions assigned to them if the other states were to respect the assigned boundaries. The outcome was, in effect, a declaration of war on Africans by Europeans. From the mid-1880s to the early 1900s, European armies (sometimes largely consisting of African troops under European command) sought to establish European control over the areas allotted by the Conference of Berlin. These campaigns were often bloody and hard fought. Even with their newfound technology, European armies were not guaranteed an easy victory. For example, a West African leader named Samori Ture led his people against the French from 1882 to 1898, winning numerous battles before eventually being overcome by his enemies. In 1896, the Ethiopians successfully defeated the Italians at the Battle of Adowa, guaranteeing their independence from colonial occupation. They were the only African country to do so. However, even stateless societies, such as the Igbo of Nigeria or the Herero of Namibia, often proved particularly difficult for European forces to defeat, in part because the absence of a single leader or even a capital made it hard to overthrow these societies' flexible systems of political authority. As a result the British spent more than a decade before defeating the Igbo.

The horrors of colonialism did not come to a close with the successful military occupation of the continent. Under even the most benevolent colonial regimes, African subjects were faced with a denial of the most basic rights enjoyed by the citizens of the states that had colonized them. Colonial governments used forced labor, a sort of temporary slavery, to build roads, railways, and harbors that helped facilitate the export of African commodities and the import of finished goods from Europe. Similarly, African farmers were often required to grow fixed quantities of crops (such as cotton, cocoa, peanuts, or palm oil) in demand in Europe and sell them to the new colonial government at non-negotiable prices. All colonial powers sought to make colonialism profitable by supporting industries in Europe with cheap materials from Africa and control over African markets.

Perhaps the greatest abuse of colonial political and economic power came in the Congo Free State, a Central African region roughly the size of Western Europe that the Conference of Berlin made the personal property of King Leopold of Belgium. The potential wealth of the Congo Free State was largely in the form of latex (natural rubber). Following the imposition of colonial rule, the traders and agents of the Congo Free State ordered adult males in the colony to produce a weekly quota of latex. If a town or village failed to meet its collective quota, women and children might be taken hostage and homes might be burned down. If production still failed to meet demand, the hostages could be shot—with their hands cut off and returned to company officials along with the spent bullet casing—just to prove no ammunition had been wasted. As demand for latex in Europe and the United States skyrocketed in the 1890s and early 1900s (thanks to the growing demand for bicycle tires), the Congo Free State's administrators simply increased the quotas demanded of the region's inhabitants. So great was the demand that hundreds of thousands died each year from overwork, starvation, or in rebellion against the colony's brutal policies. Not until missionaries helped expose the brutality of the system did other colonial powers raise protests. Dubbed the "red rubber scandal," this situation resulted in the dissolution of the Congo Free State and the creation of a Belgian government-run colony in the region. King Leopold and his agents had already left their mark, however. At least a million people had died (some estimate the total as high as ten million) as a result of policies that had greatly enriched the Belgian king and his government.

VARIETIES OF COLONIAL RULE

The various colonial powers shared similar economic goals, but they often had very different ideas about the sort of political and administrative systems to use to attain these financial ends. In general, these policies can be distinguished as direct rule, as practiced by the French, Germans, Belgians, and Portuguese, and indirect rule, as practiced by the British. Under direct rule, the colonial power established a top-to-bottom bureaucracy staffed with nationals of the ruling country and organized along European lines. Thus, for a French West African colony such as Senegal, a post office would be run by a French postal officer, a police detachment by a French lieutenant, and a court presided over by a French judge. Each of these officials probably oversaw numerous African clerks and functionaries, but the immediate source of authority was still a French official. Similarly, all laws, rules, and practices were as French as possible. More so, the language of government was French as well. Thus, in order to have any interaction with the new colonial state, Africans under French colonial authority had to learn to speak French.

The principle behind this system was known as *assimilation*, the idea that the more French (or Belgian or Portuguese) the Africans learned to act, the more civilized they were considered. Such standards included not just language, but what and how people ate, how they dressed, the music they listened to, and so on. The colonial powers practicing direct rule argued that once Africans assimilated, they would be granted full rights of citizenship, and the colonies would eventually become, for example, part of an expanded "Greater France." In reality, very few Africans were ever deemed adequately assimilated to receive full rights. By 1922, only about a hundred Africans had been granted French citizenship, for example. Nonetheless, with all government jobs and even schools biased toward the exclusion of those who did not accept and embrace the culture of the ruling country, there was considerable pressure to adopt some degree of European culture. Not surprisingly, in former French, Belgian, and Portuguese colonies (the Germans lost their colonies after World War I), a wide variety of European cultural practices are to be found. Anywhere in former French Africa, for example, it is easy to buy French bread and even croissants for breakfast. Similarly, French is the near universal language in former French colonies. In Belgian colonies, in particular, the Catholic Church was used as a major tool to help people assimilate, and it continues to be very influential in those regions today.

Quite different from direct rule was the British policy of indirect rule, based on the assumption it was better to rule through existing African systems of political authority than to replace them with European-style bureaucracies. Thus, wherever possible, the British incorporated local rulers into the British colonial governments. For example, after defeating the Sokoto Caliphate (a precolonial state located largely in the region of contemporary northern Nigeria) and killing the sultan of Sokoto in 1903, the British then built the administration of the region around the structures of the Caliphate, keeping the local **emirs** (kings) as the heads of local government and tasking them with such duties as maintaining police forces and courts and collecting taxes. Thus, rather than overthrowing local political systems, the British often reinforced them. Notably, however, in regions previously inhabited by stateless societies, the British created "chiefs" where none had existed before, simply as a means to facilitate colonial administration. In general, British rule rested more lightly on the shoulders of colonized Africans, in part because it was more familiar and not so culturally disruptive. Rather than demanding that Africans learn to speak English, for example, British colonial officers were required to learn local languages themselves.

COLONIALISM AND CULTURE

Religion. Many of the outcomes of colonialism, however, were different from what the colonial powers expected. Although the British, French, and Belgians ultimately held political and economic power, they were often at a loss to control the cultural path of their colonies. For example, although European missionaries sought to bring established European churches to the continent, Africans soon created their own independent forms of Christianity. Indeed, the most successful forms of Christianity in Africa came to be known as "independent churches," which had no institutional ties to European denominations of Christianity. Today, for example, the Aladura churches are prevalent in coastal West Africa and the Zion churches are found throughout southern Africa. Both denominations emphasize ecstatic possession by the Holy Spirit, the power of God to heal the sick, and the ability of belief to protect church members from witchcraft. Colonialism certainly introduced Christianity to many Africans, but it could not define the final form Christianity would take.

Another outcome of colonialism, interestingly, was the rapid expansion of Islam in Africa. Islam had long been established in North Africa, the West African savannahs, and the East African coast, but its expansion elsewhere in the continent had been slow. Colonialism, however, changed this situation. In only a few decades, colonial rule facilitated the spread of Islam deep into the East African interior and also into the forest and coastal regions of West Africa. This growth occurred for two main reasons. First, colonial economic systems, no matter how abusive, served to help connect regions of Africa previously separated by distance and natural barriers. As such, rail lines extending from the coastal ports to the interior were not only conduits for goods, but also culture. Muslim traders not only exported products from the West African savannahs, but they also brought Islam to the people of the coastline. Conversely, Swahili Muslims used similar railway links in East Africa to carry Islam into the interior. Similarly, since assimilationist colonial powers saw Islam as a potential barrier to making Africans "more European," they often sought to repress or restrict the religion, which often had the effect of making conversion to Islam a means of resisting colonial cultural imperialism.

Nationalism. One of the most important cultural developments that came out of Africa's colonization was African identity and nationalism. Faced with the common experience of colonization, and also taking advantage of the expanded opportunities for travel and communication afforded by colonial infrastructures, an increasingly large number of Africans, particularly those who were able to acquire European-style educations, began to think of themselves as a single people.

For example, the Senegalese scholar (and later president) Leopold Senghor was one of the few Africans granted full French citizenship. Nonetheless, he became a leading founder of the movement called **negritude,** which, beginning in the 1930s, stressed the cultural unity and achievements of all people of African descent. Elsewhere, many Western-educated Africans began to use the very rhetoric of colonialism as a tool to destroy it. It did not take long for Africans who read about democracy, human rights, or free-market capitalism to understand that they were receiving little of these so-called benefits of modernization under colonial rule. Thus African nationalists such as Kwame Nkruma (who would become president of Ghana) and Jomo Kenyatta (first president of Kenya) were able to use the very underpinnings of Western philosophy to demand an end to colonialism. It was an argument that European democracies could not deny.

Beginning in the 1940s and becoming increasingly vocal in the 1950s, these nationalists built upon Europe's weakened position following World War II to demand greater self-determination and even an end to colonialism. In this they shared in the mid-twentieth-century phenomenon of liberation movements that included the end of colonialism in Asia and the Middle East and the civil rights and women's rights movements in the United States.

By 1960, it was clear the winds of change were blowing in Africa, and most colonial powers took steps to end their formal administrations in Africa. Portugal, itself ruled by a fascist dictatorship, refused to relinquish its African colonies despite years of war. Only with the overthrow of the Salazar government in 1974 did Portugal withdraw from Africa. The white minority government of Southern Rhodesia was replaced with a new nonracial government following years of bloody conflict in 1980. In South Africa, decades of internal and international protest against the system of racial oppression and segregation known as **apartheid** came to a head when Nelson Mandela was released from prison in 1990 after twenty-seven years of incarceration. Mandela was soon elected president of a new South Africa.

INDEPENDENT AFRICA

Euphoria greeted African independence in the 1960s. Decades of colonial occupation and exploitation were finally at an end, and the expectations for economic growth and improved quality of life were great. For most Africans, however, these hopes have not yet come to pass. The reasons for this failure lie both outside of Africa and within. Externally, the Cold War made it difficult for new countries to find their footing, particularly in Africa. During this period the United States and the Soviet Union both interfered in African political affairs, often arming and shoring up brutal dictators and fostering civil wars to pursue their own international political and economic agendas. Internally, many of Africa's new rulers focused on enriching themselves rather than helping the people they were elected to serve. One-party states and military regimes increasingly became the norm in Africa over the course of the latter twentieth century. Many, such as Idi Amin in Uganda and Robert Mugabe in Zimbabwe, oversaw brutal abuses of human rights. Some countries, such as Somalia and the Democratic Republic of the Congo, effectively collapsed from the combined pressures of international meddling and internal corruption, leaving large areas under the control of local warlords. In recent years, the pandemic of HIV has added greatly to Africa's suffering, especially in the southern regions of the continent, where infection rates sometimes exceed 25 percent of the population.

There have been notable success stories, however. Despite an economic collapse in the 1970s, Ghana's economy has rebounded in recent years. The country also returned to democracy in 1992, after over a decade of military rule. Current annual "happiness surveys" now list Ghanaians as among the most cheerful people on the face of the earth. Similarly, in countries such as Uganda, aggressive public-education campaigns have helped reverse the spread of HIV. Elsewhere the end of apartheid in South Africa and a resurgence of democratically elected governments around the continent have been seen as signs that Africa's post-independence fortunes may be changing.

Africa's economic and political upheaval, however, has not meant Africa has failed to make a substantial cultural contribution to the modern world. Indeed, the artistic expression of African artists, authors, and musicians continues to change and develop in response to new influences and contemporary needs.

SCULPTURE

As we saw in Chapter 10, Africans have long produced significant works of sculpture in wood, metal, and clay. Modern African sculpture reflects both the preservation of local sculptural traditions and the introduction of styles and techniques from outside the continent. For example, the ***gelede*** masking tradition (fig. 21.1) shows the continuity of older artistic forms even in the present. Indeed, the *gelede* performances of the Yoruba are still popular, and the masks continue to be made. Other forms of physical art are quite innovative. African art enjoys huge markets in the West, and African artists have responded by creating *tourist art*, which combines African styles with the expectations of international customers. Still, some art historians argue that even as the form of the artwork changes, the purpose of the art remains consistent. Susan Vogel, a prominent African art historian, suggests that content is of primary significance for African artists, as well as for audiences and critics of African art. Each of these constituencies assumes that works of art convey meaning,

FIGURE 21.1 Mask, Yoruba, Republic of Benin, polychrome, wood, height $14\frac{1}{2}$"(37 cm), Musée du Quai Branley. Reserved rights. The reference to the moon in the crescent-shaped horns of this mask echoes a *gelede* song that begins, "All-powerful mother, mother of the night bird."

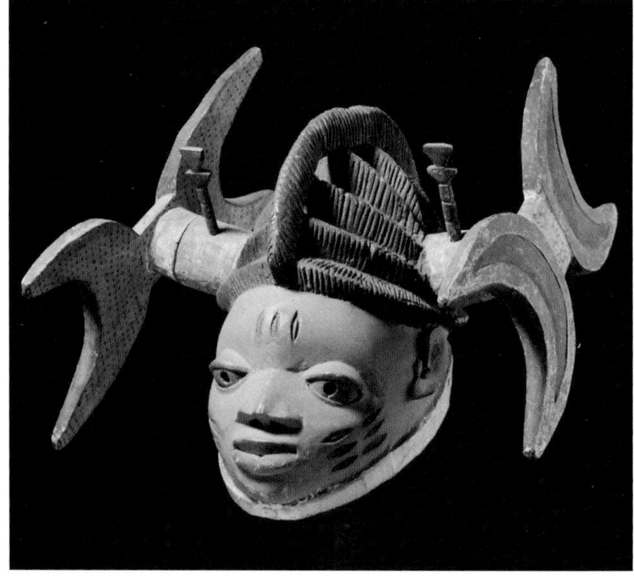

often through stories that recount important social, cultural, and religious values and beliefs. In addition, African art is traditionally viewed as functional, even purposeful. African art, thus, is considered to be a serious endeavor and one that is never merely ornamental. There is common agreement among interested parties that African art should always be directed toward a meaningful end and that it should serve an important purpose.

The coffins of KANE KWEI [KWHY] (b. 1924) of Ghana are a good example. Kwei never received any formal training as a carpenter. In the mid-1970s, a dying uncle, who had worked as a fisherman, asked him to produce a coffin in the shape of a boat. Kwei's work delighted the entire community, and he was soon creating many types of coffins—fish and whales (for fishermen), hens with chicks (for women with large families), Mercedes-Benz coffins (for the wealthy), and cash crops (for farmers), among them the cocoa bean (fig. 21.2). These coffins disappeared underground soon after they were made. Coffins in Ghana are seen as serving the community and also have a spiritual purpose: They celebrate the successful life of the person and form part of the traditional Ghanaian funeral celebrations that often last for days. In 1974, an American art dealer exhibited Kwei's coffins in San Francisco, and now Kwei's large workshop turns out coffins for both funerals and the art market.

MUSIC

Africa is home to a great variety of musical traditions, encompassing a diversity of rhythmic and melodic styles. As discussed in Chapter 10, some West and Central African musical styles were carried by enslaved Africans to the Americas, where they interacted with European and Native American musical traditions to form such musical styles as rumba, blues, and jazz. Of particular influence was the West African minor pentatonic scale. This scale differs from the eight-note European chromatic scale (do-re-mi) in that it has five key notes, the third and fifth of which are flat, known to blues and jazz players as the "blue notes." Critical to the development of not only blues and jazz, this five-note scale often plays a significant role in gospel, country, folk, and rock and roll. Further, rather than stressing only the pure notes, African music often explores the tonal spaces in between. Thus many African instruments or musical styles encourage the musician to bend notes. For example, the **talking drum**, an instrument that also blurs the line between melody and rhythm, constantly slides between notes, as do the slide guitars so popular in blues, country, and rock music. Similarly, many African musical forms include a **call-and-response format** in which lines are called out by a leader and sung back by the band, chorus, or audience. As previously noted, African musical styles also emphasize participation by a community rather than performance to an audience, and call and response is a critical way that nonmusicians are made a part of the music.

African music is also rhythmically complex. Rather than just making sure the instruments play in unison, as is the function of the beat in classical Western music, African beats serve to both propel the music and serve as instruments in their own right. Critical to this is the interplay between multiple rhythms, a form known as **polyrhythms.** Here, multiple rhythms, such as a 4/4 and a 3/4 beat, are intertwined—intersecting at certain times and diverging at others in a complex musical interplay. But this complexity

FIGURE 21.2 Kane Kwei (Teshi tribe, Ghana, Africa), *Coffin, Orange, in the Shape of a Cocoa Pod*, ca. 1970, polychrome, wood, 34″ × 105$\frac{1}{2}$″ × 29″ (86.4 × 268 × 61 cm). Fine Arts Museums of San Francisco, gift of Vivian Burns, Inc. 74.8. When reproduced in a photograph, as it is here, Kwei's coffin seems smaller than it actually is. It is, literally, a coffin, over 8$\frac{1}{2}$ feet long.

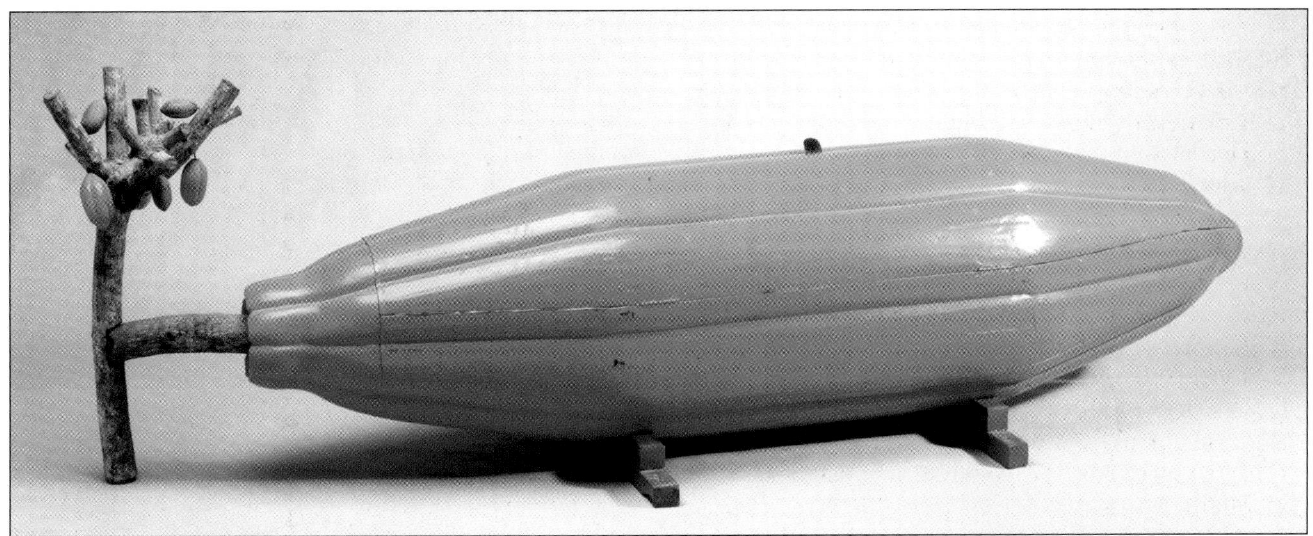

Connections

THE MASK AS DANCE

For the Baule [BOW-LAY] carvers of the Ivory Coast, the helmet mask illustrated here (fig. 21.3) is a pleasing and beautiful object but has another significance as well. It is the Dye sacred mask. As the carver explained to Susan Vogel, "The god is a dance of rejoicing for me. So when I see the mask, my heart is filled with joy. I like it because of the horns and the eyes. The horns curve nicely, and I like the placement of the eyes and ears. In addition, it executes very interesting and graceful dance steps. . . . This is a sacred mask danced in our village."

The Baule carver pays attention to the physical features of the mask, and he also sees the mask *as* dance. In its features, he sees its performance. A mask is thus more than an ornament disguising or hiding the face. These Africans have no separate word for mask; rather the word *mask* includes the whole person performing the dance. In this sense, masks can be said to dance, and the mask or the dancer is a vehicle through which the spirit of the place passes.

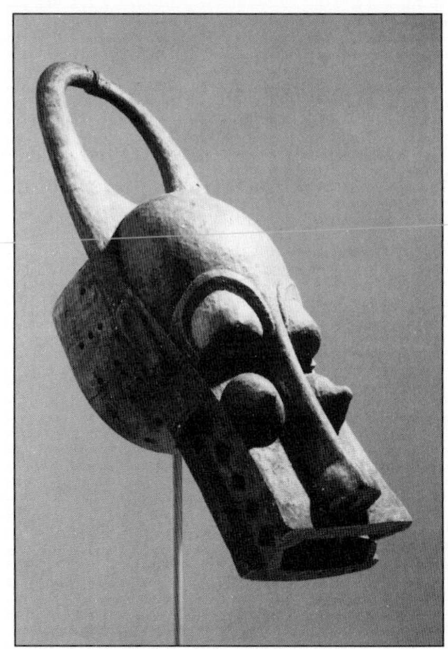

FIGURE 21.3 Helmet mask. Baule style, Ivory Coast, nineteenth–twentieth century, polychrome, wood, length 38″ (95.8 cm). Style: Baule. The Metropolitan Museum of Art, The Michael C. Rockefeller Memorial Collection, gift of Adrian Pascal LaGamma, 1993. (1978.412.664). Art Resource, NY. This African mask "makes us happy when we see it," explains a Baule carver.

is not random, and the musicians use the synergy and tension inherent in the cross rhythms to guide the songs. Like the minor pentatonic scale, the powerful nature of African rhythms has had a powerful influence on contemporary music. Although few modern musicians invest the time necessary to master the complexity of polyrhythms, the prevalence of a strong **backbeat** and the omnipresence of the drum set in popular music are testimonies to the influence of African music on the global stage.

Inside Africa, musical forms have continued to develop as African musicians have embraced instruments and styles from elsewhere in the world. Electric guitars, drum machines, and electronic keyboards are now ubiquitous in African popular music. Contemporary musicians like SONNY OKOSUN [OAK-ka-sun] (b. 1947) blend African and Western sounds. Okosun's work is based on a brand of Ghanaian music known as *highlife*, itself a blend of local rhythms and melodies with Western musical forms. Indeed, African-influenced musical forms such as jazz and country music have been of great influence in Africa. **Soukous** styles in Central Africa themselves reflect the popularity of Afro-Cuban music reintroduced to Africa in the 1950s and 1960s. African bands also often perform versions of Johnny Cash songs. In the 1970s, funk music from the United States greatly influenced the development of **Afrobeat** music in Nigeria and Ghana. In recent years, hip-hop has become a significant musical influence in Africa. For example, young Ghanaian musicians have combined hip-hop with local highlife styles to create a new musical form called **hip life.**

Like most African artwork, African music often makes overt political commentary. Chimurenga songs, for example, were a key form of protest against white minority rule in Southern Rhodesia. Anti-apartheid music was produced throughout the continent. Sonny Okosun produced *Fire in Soweto* in 1978, despite the fact that he is from Ghana. The song and album became a popular statement against apartheid throughout Africa. Perhaps no musician better represents the political side of African music, however, than Nigeria's FELA KUTI [KOO-ti]. Born into a wealthy Western-educated family, Kuti studied jazz and classical music in London. Returning to Nigeria in the late 1960s, he not only helped create the musical style of Afrobeat, but also repeatedly attacked the Nigerian government for corruption. Albums such as *Coffin for Head of State*, *VIP (Vagabonds in Power)*, and *Africa Stealing* landed him in jail repeatedly, and made him a popular hero in Nigeria.

The Lion King: The Saga of a Song. One of the most popular songs of the twentieth century, "The Lion Sleeps Tonight," originated in Africa. A centerpiece of the 1994 Disney movie *The Lion King*, as well as the Broadway show later developed from the hit film, the original song upon which it was based was written decades earlier by a Zulu

Then & Now

TIMBUKTU

Timbuktu (also spelled Timbuctu or Timbuctoo) is a city in the West African country of Mali, about eighty miles from the Niger River. Its location made it a logical meeting point for local African populations and nomadic Arab peoples to the north. Timbuktu was for many years a trading post linking Africa with Jewish and Islamic traders throughout North Africa, and through them, with European traders. Its most enduring contribution to world civilization is scholarship, with important books and manuscripts written, copied, and preserved in its well-endowed library. It is also known for the Great Mosque of Timbuktu (fig. 21.4), which is actually located in the nearby village of Djénné. In modern times, especially in the West, Timbuktu has become a metaphor for the exotic and far away, as in the expression "from here to Timbuktu."

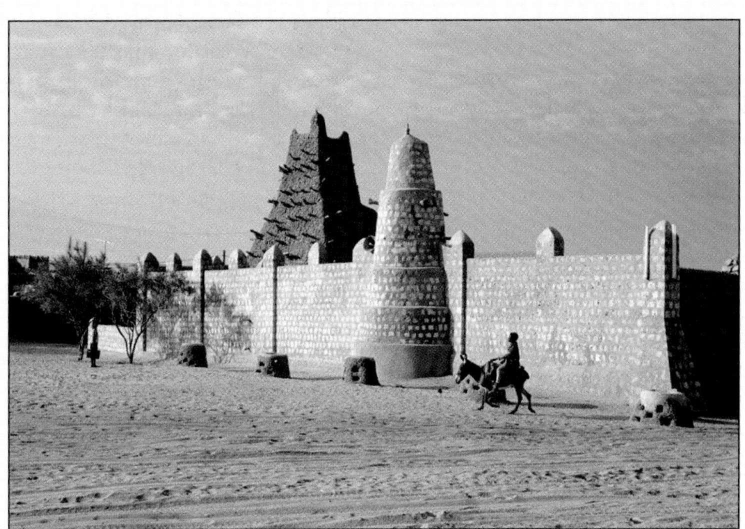

FIGURE 21.4 Great Mosque of Timbuktu, also known as the Great Mosque of Djénné. The color, design, and rough surfaces of the mosque and surrounding walls harmonize with the landscape.

musician, Solomon Linda. Linda's original song, "Mbube," which is Zulu for lion, and which was recorded in 1939, includes simple lyrics, background chanting, and harmonies that made it an immediate popular success initially in Africa and then around the world.

When the American folk singer Pete Seeger recorded it, "Mbube" became "wimoweh," a mispronunciation that became standard in subsequent renderings of the song by American and European artists. An American songwriter adapted the song, adding lyrics that began his version with the words, "In the jungle, the mighty jungle, the lion sleeps tonight." This version was recorded by the Tokens and became a worldwide phenomenon. Since then, more than 150 artists have recorded it, and it lives on in its stage and screen versions.

One unfortunate fact of the song's saga is that its originator, Solomon Linda, earned less than one dollar when he sold the rights to "Mbube" in 1952. Millions of dollars have been made by singers, songwriters, record producers, and studios since. Recently, though, Mr. Linda's family was awarded royalties reverting to 1987 and onward.

LITERATURE

In the modern era, many African authors have continued a tradition of protest begun by early African nationalists. Jomo Kenyatta's famous ethnography/autobiography *Facing Mount Kenya* is a prime example of how early authors used literature to challenge colonialism. In more recent years, African authors have turned their pens on their own rulers when they deemed them corrupt. An example of this theme is Ayi Kwei Armah's *The Beautiful Ones Are Not Yet Born,* which indicts the corruption of early independence in Ghana in the 1960s.

Chinua Achebe. Nigerian CHINUA ACHEBE (ah-CHAY-bay) (b. 1930) has set his most famous works in the fictional town of Umofia. They deal with the coming of colonial rule or trace the lives of a series of characters from Umofia as they cope with the changing economic, political, and cultural situation in their country. These novels include *Things Fall Apart, Arrow of God, A Man of the People, No Longer at Ease*, and *Anthills of the Savannah* and roughly chronicle the fate of Nigeria from the advent of colonialism in the latter 1800s to independence and the struggle for stability in the 1990s. By tracing the development of Nigeria over such a long span of time, Achebe is able to critically examine the complex interactions of African and European cultures. A profound realist, Achebe is perfectly willing to attack what he sees as the shortcomings of Igbo or Nigerian culture, just as he assaults the inequities of colonialism and international economics.

Wole Soyinka. WOLE SOYINKA [shoy-INK-ah] (b. 1934) from Nigeria became the first African writer to win the Nobel Prize for Literature in 1986. Although best

Then & Now

TWINS

The Yoruba have one of the highest rates of twin births in the world. Yet, for the Yoruba, twins remain "gifts of the gods" who possess, or rather are possessed by, the deities of creativity. They are empowered by their inborn ability to perceive a dimension beyond the everyday, communicating with a universe beyond our own.

The Yoruba believe a mother is blessed with twins as a reward for her patience and virtue, and hence, after their birth, she is treated as if she were a member of the highest royalty. Indeed, any woman who gives birth to twins three times is considered the most powerful person of all, higher than kings. This is a particularly remarkable honor given that the Yoruba have a patriarchal culture, in which the oldest male member leads his entire clan.

For some time, it has been Yoruba tradition to have images carved of the twins, or *ere ibeji*, which are kept in case one of the twins should die, which sometimes happens, since twins are often smaller and more fragile than single babies. Until the twentieth century, these figures were carved out of wood, but they have been increasingly replaced by mass-produced Western dolls (fig. 21.5). The mother cares for the "twin" doll of the dead child as if it were still alive, placing it in a shrine in her bedroom. Its spirit, the Yoruba believe, will bring good fortune to the family.

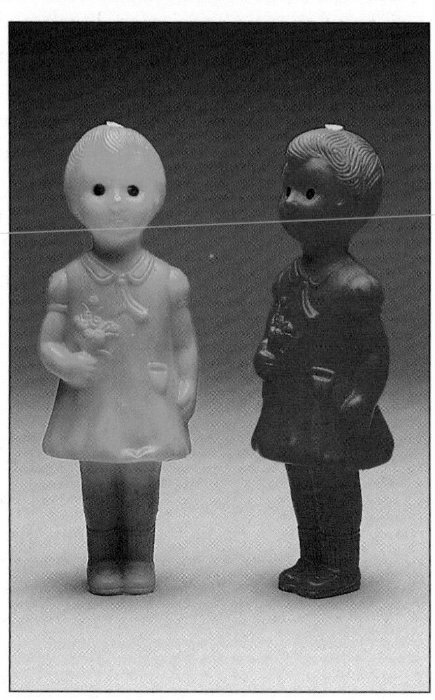

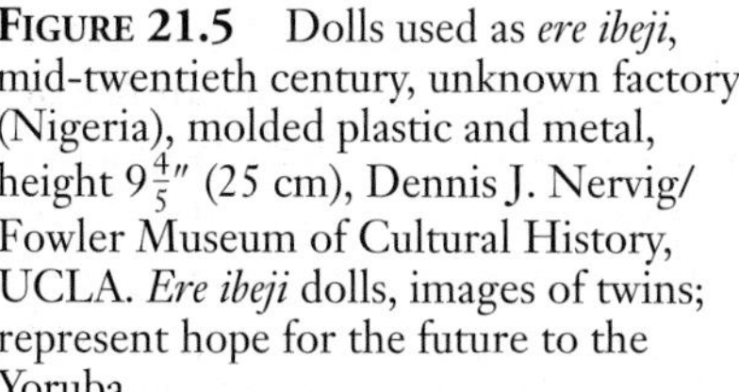

FIGURE 21.5 Dolls used as *ere ibeji*, mid-twentieth century, unknown factory (Nigeria), molded plastic and metal, height $9\frac{4}{5}$" (25 cm), Dennis J. Nervig/ Fowler Museum of Cultural History, UCLA. *Ere ibeji* dolls, images of twins; represent hope for the future to the Yoruba.

known as a playwright, Soyinka is also a poet, essayist, political activist, social critic, and literary scholar. His poetry and plays are deeply political: as he noted in a *New York Times* interview, "I cannot conceive of my existence without political involvement."

During the Nigerian Civil War, Soyinka was imprisoned and kept in solitary confinement for his antigovernment activism. There he composed *Poems from Prison* (1969) and *The Man Died: Prison Notes of Wole Soyinka* (1988), both written in secret on toilet paper and later smuggled out. During the 1960s he worked tirelessly to develop a Nigerian national drama. Two of his best-known plays depict political intrigue in an imaginary kingdom, *Death and the King's Horseman* (1976) and *A Play for Giants* (1984), a satire on African dictators.

John Maxwell Coetzee. The South African author J. M. Coetzee (b. 1940) first came to international prominence with his novel *Waiting for the Barbarians* in 1980 and for *Life and Times of Michael K.* in 1983. A South African of Afrikaaner (Dutch) and English descent, Coetzee nonetheless uses his novels as a platform for a thinly veiled criticism of apartheid, the white South African government's policy of racial segregation and oppression, although he generally sets his novels in fictional surroundings that could be anywhere in the world. Coetzee's books are bleak and unremittingly realistic, sometimes brutally so. They chronicle the inhuman cruelties that powerful human beliefs inflict on the weak, the marginalized, and the disenfranchised. And yet for all their unflinching honesty, Coetzee's novels offer testimony to human beings' power to survive, to endure in the face of even the most oppressive hardships. He twice won the prestigious British Booker Prize (the first author to do so), and in 2003 was awarded the Nobel Prize for Literature.

MODERN LATIN AMERICA

Like Africa, Latin America had long been under the rule of colonial Europeans—chiefly the Spanish and Portuguese. Then, in the early nineteenth century, grassroots movements fueled wars of independence throughout the region and inspired the Latin American social elite to break the economic trade monopolies of the colonial rulers while preserving the existing social structure.

Latin America is marked by the collision and intermingling of two separate cultural and economic traditions.

The colonists and their heirs are largely well-to-do Roman Catholics, whereas the diverse indigenous peoples maintain their own traditional cultural practices and make up an underprivileged, subsistence-based social class. A variety of types of societies developed among different Latin American countries. In Argentina and Uruguay, the few natives were essentially wiped out by European diseases in the early years of colonization. A **Eurocentric** culture developed when over one million Europeans, mostly Spanish and Italian, emigrated to these countries between 1905 and 1910. In Central America and Peru, in contrast, strong native communities, of Mayan and Incan ancestry, survive to this day, with their own thriving indigenous cultures.

FIGURE 21.6 *Virgin of the Rosary of Guápulo*, ca. 1680, Peruvian (Cuzco), oil on canvas, 67 $\frac{1}{4}$″ × 43 $\frac{1}{2}$″ (170.8 × 110.5 cm). The Metropolitan Museum of Art, New York, NY, U.S.A. Image copyright © The Metropolitan Museum of Art/Art Resource, NY. Depictions of actual dressed statues of religious figures, as this, believed to work miracles, were revered. Mother and son wear matching luxurious, voluminous gowns.

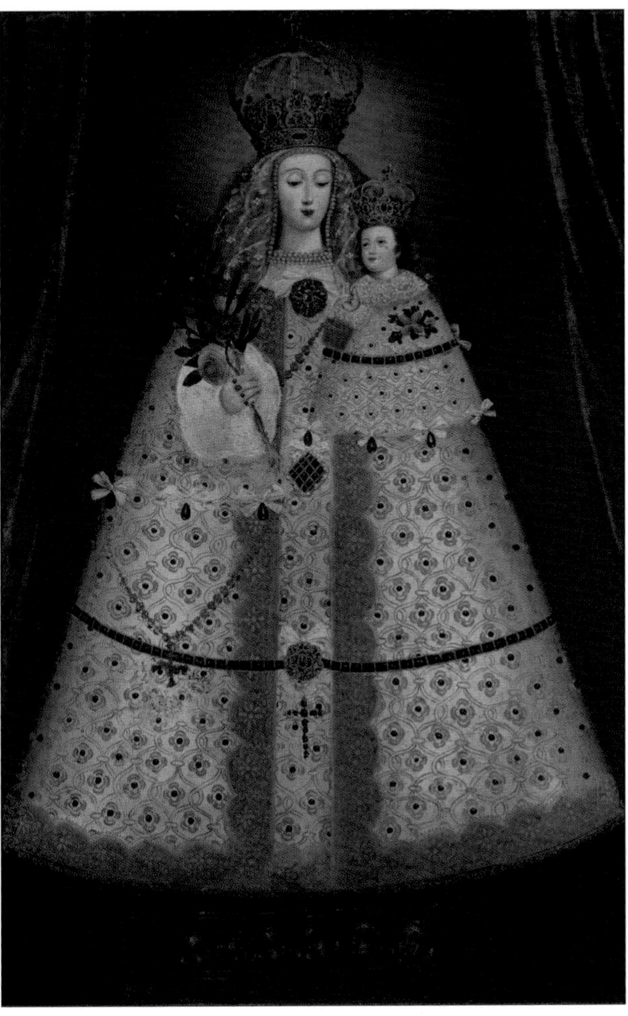

PAINTING

For a large and striking Peruvian painting made in Cuzco, in oil on canvas, around 1680, consider the *Virgin of the Rosary of Guápulo* (fig. 21.6). This is a painting of an actual statue that is located in a parish church in Guápulo, Ecuador, and is claimed to produce miracles. Maternal Mary glances down, and Jesus up to her lovingly. Mary and Jesus are dressed in identical garments. In Ecuador, the Spanish custom of garbing statues in costumes was copied. This practice already existed in Andean cultures where ritual items and images were adorned and dressed with textiles and other gifts. The transition to Christianity in this area of South America was facilitated by linking the native earth-mother goddess Pachamama to Jesus' mother Mary.

Mexican Mural Movement. Despite the merging of traditions evident in colonial art, the Church and the European cultural elite wanted to suppress native customs. In Mexico particularly, where strong native populations had begun to rebel against the European elite by the early twentieth century, these customs were a source of identity and pride. Beginning in 1910 with a violent revolt against the regime of Porfirio Diáz, Mexico was rocked by social and political unrest. Civil war lasted until the inauguration of the revolutionary leader, Alvaro Obregón, as president in 1920. Obregón believed the aesthetic faculty, and the appreciation of painting in particular, could lead the way to revolutionary change. He also believed in restoring Mexico's indigenous cultural identity. He thus began a vast mural project designed to cover the walls of public spaces across the country with images celebrating Mexico's past and future. By the mid-1920s, the mural movement was in the hands of three painters, *Los Tres Grandes*, as they were called, "The Three Giants"—DIEGO RIVERA [rih-VAY-rah] (1886–1957), JOSE CLEMENTE OROZCO [oh-ROZ-coe] (1883–1949), and DAVID ALFARO SIQUEIROS [see-KAYR-ohs] (1896–1974).

All three artists began their careers painting **al fresco,** but the sun, rain, and humidity of the Mexican climate damaged their efforts. In 1937, Siqueiros organized a workshop in New York City, close to the chemical industry, to develop and experiment with new synthetic paints. One of the first media used in the workshop was **pyroxylin,** commonly known as Duco, a lacquer developed as an automobile paint. It is used in the large-scale mural by Siqueiros, *Cuauhtémoc Against the Myth* (fig. 21.7), which was painted in 1944 on panel so it could withstand earthquakes and is housed today in the Union Housing Project at Tlatelco, Mexico. It depicts the story of the Aztec hero who shattered the myth that the Spanish army could not be conquered. This message had great significance for the people: The indigenous people could regain power. Siqueiros also meant it as a

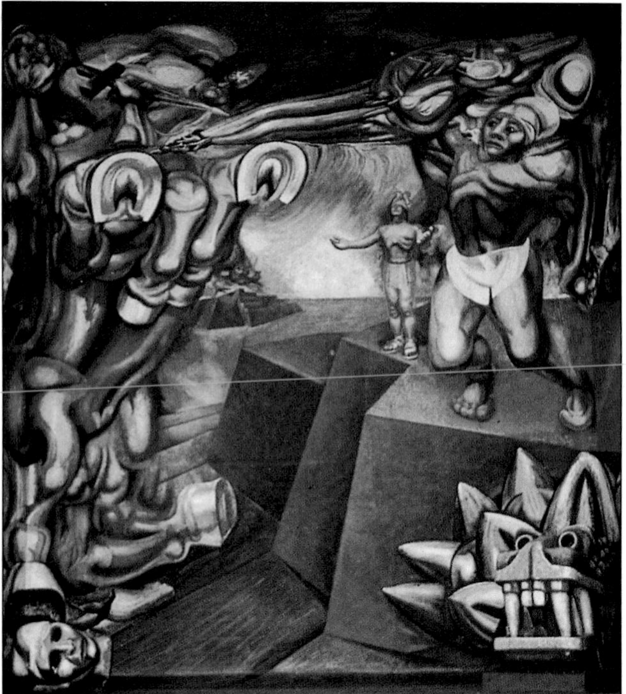

FIGURE 21.7 David Alfaro Siqueiros, *Cuauhtémoc Against the Myth*, 1944, mural, pyroxylin on celtex and plywood, 1,000 sq. ft. (92.9 sq. m). Teepan Union Housing Project, Tlatelco, Mexico. Photo by Dr. Desmond Rochfort. Reproduction authorized by the Insitituto Nacional de Bellas Artes y Literatura. Siqueiros's experimentation with synthetic paints would lead to the invention of acrylics, widely used today.

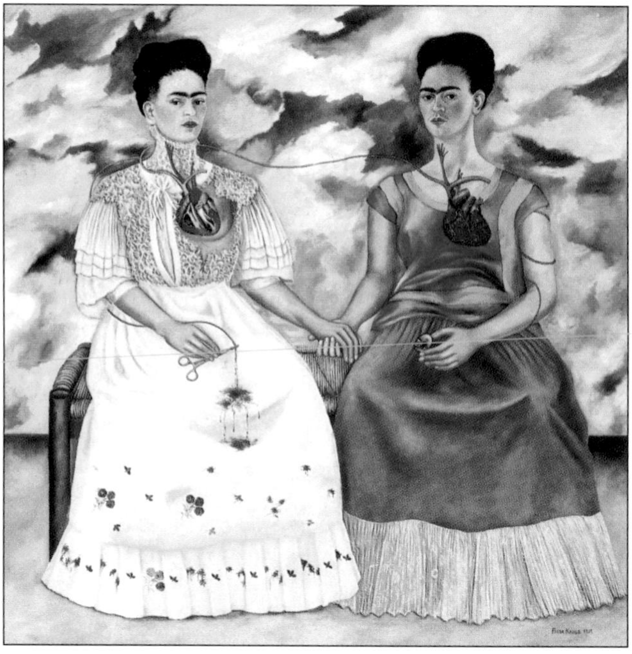

FIGURE 21.8 Frida Kahlo, *The Two Fridas*, 1939, oil on canvas, 5′9″ square (1.73 m square), Museo Nacional de Arte Moderno, © 2001 Banco de Mexico, Diego Rivera & Frida Kahlo Museums Trust/Artists Rights Society (ARS), NY. Av. Cinco de Mayo No. 2, Col. Centro, Del. Cuanhtemoc 06059, Mexico, D.F. Reproduction authorized by the Instituto Nacional de Bellas Artes y Literatura. Bob Schalkwijk/Art Resource, NY. The marriage between the artists Rivera and Kahlo was described by her parents as "like the marriage between an elephant and a dove." Kahlo described marriage to Rivera as her "second accident"—a nearly fatal traffic collision at the age of eighteen was her first.

commentary on the susceptibility to defeat of the Nazis in Europe.

Frida Kahlo. Rivera was married to another prominent Mexican painter, FRIDA KAHLO [KAH-loh] (1910–1954), whose work was initially overshadowed by that of her husband, but whose reputation has increased to such a degree that she is now considered the greater artist and is surely the more famous. Kahlo is best known for her highly distinctive self-portraits in a wide range of circumstances and settings. "I paint self-portraits because I am so often alone," she once said, "because I am the person I know best." Her self-portraits, it has been argued, created a series of alternative selves that helped exorcise life's pains. She suffered almost her entire life: first from polio, which she contracted at age six and left her with a withered right leg; then from a bus and trolley collision at age eighteen, in which her pelvis and spinal column were broken, her foot was crushed, and her abdomen and uterus were pierced by a steel handrail, resulting in a life-long series of operations; and finally from her volatile relationship with Rivera, whose many adulterous affairs, including one with her own sister, hurt her deeply.

The Two Fridas (fig. 21.8), 1939, alludes to Kahlo's mixed ancestry, physical suffering, and troubled marriage to Rivera. On the left is the European Frida, a reference to her German-Jewish father; on the right is the Mexican Frida, a reference to her Mexican mother. The two Fridas are linked by their clasped hands and the shared artery between their hearts. The Mexican Frida holds a tiny image of Rivera, while the European Frida tries to stop herself from bleeding, without success.

Wilfredo Lam. The work of Cuban painter Wilfredo Lam (1902–1982), of Chinese and mulatto ancestry, demonstrates the close connection between European and Latin American cultures. Lam left for Europe in 1923 at the age of twenty-one and did not return to the Caribbean for eighteen years, until 1941, when he was sent by the Nazis to a prison camp in Martinique. Within forty days, he was released and sent back to Havana, where he discovered that

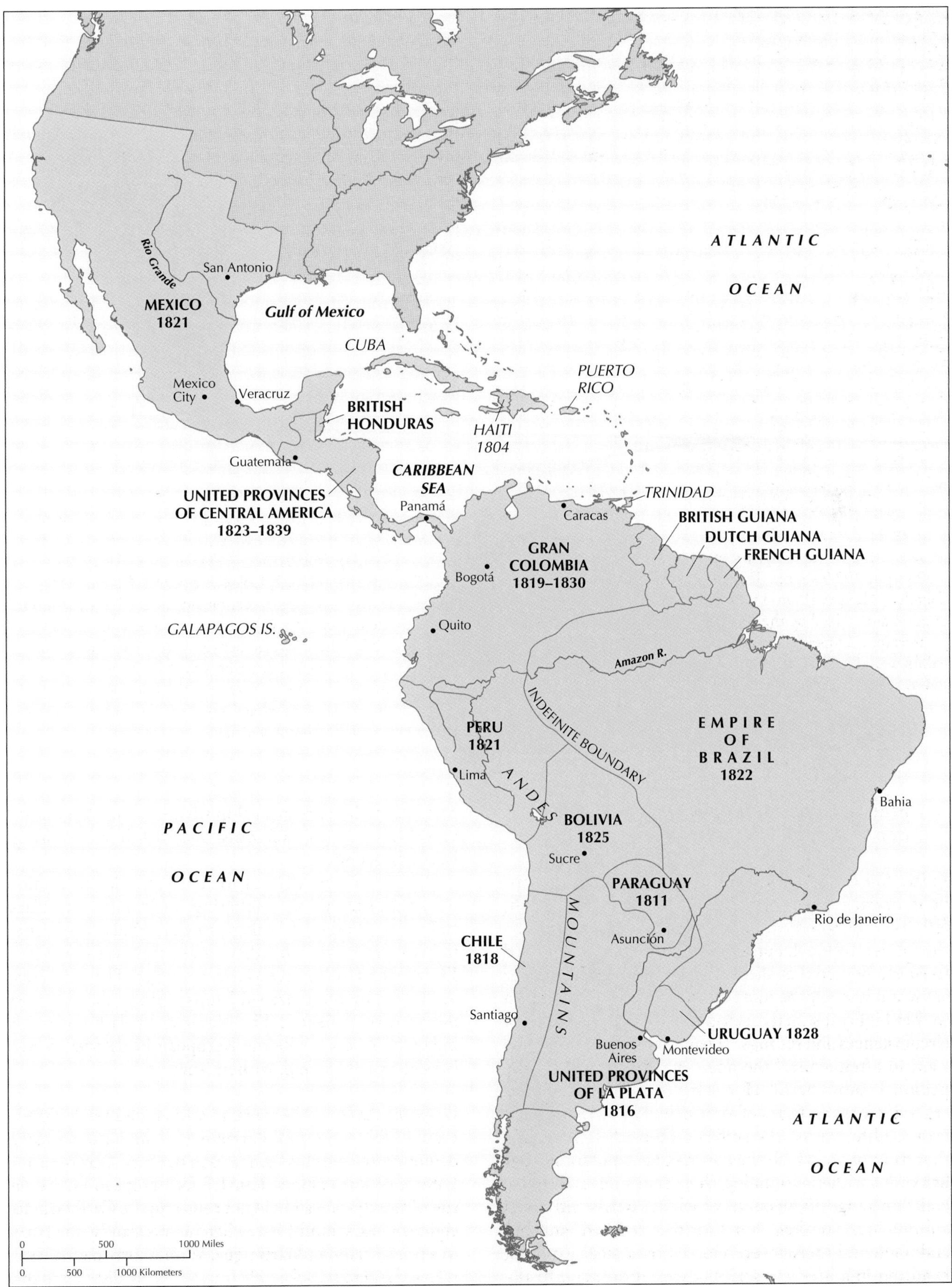

MAP 21.2 The decolonization of Latin America 1800–36.

the idyllic Cuba of his childhood had been destroyed by the collapse of sugar prices.

Lam's masterpiece, *The Jungle* (fig. 21.9), painted in 1943, is a record of his reaction. It is almost exactly the same size as *Les Demoiselles d'Avignon* (see fig. 22.2) by Picasso, who had befriended Lam in Paris in 1939. The faces of Lam's totemic figures are based, like Picasso's, on African masks. But crucially different from Picasso's painting is the density of Lam's image. Every space is occupied, not only by shoots of sugarcane and jungle foliage, but by the figures themselves, whose arms and hands seem to reach to the ground. This natural world is inhabited by a mysterious, mythical virgin-beast, both productive and destructive, whose origins are to be found in Lam's fascination with the world of ***santería*** or voodoo.

Fernando Botero. Columbian artist FERNANDO BOTERO [bo-TAIR-oh] (b. 1932) is known for his "swollen" or "inflated" figures that fill the canvas like balloons and satirize the Latin American ruling elite. "When I inflate things," he has explained, "I enter a subconscious world rich in folk images." *Mona Lisa at the Age of Twelve* (fig. 21.10), painted in 1959, condenses three images: Leonardo da Vinci's original painting (see fig. 13.15), the Infanta Margarita in Diego Velázquez's *Maids of Honor* (see fig. 15.23), and *Alice in Wonderland.* Mona Lisa's oft-noted "inscrutable" smile here becomes grotesquely piglike, Botero revealing in it the gluttony of the Latin American aristocracy and their ability to "consume" the land and its people.

MUSIC

Latin America has a rich musical heritage, both popular and traditional. The most prevalent forms of popular music are those associated with dance. The tango came from Argentina, the **samba** from Brazil, and the pasillo from Colombia. Latin-inspired dances include the Caribbean **calypso,** the Cuban rumba, the Brazilian lambada, and even the macarena.

One of the most popular instruments used in Latin American music is the guitar, which has a long history in Spain and Spanish American cultures. The guitar has been used both in folk and classical music, by many composers,

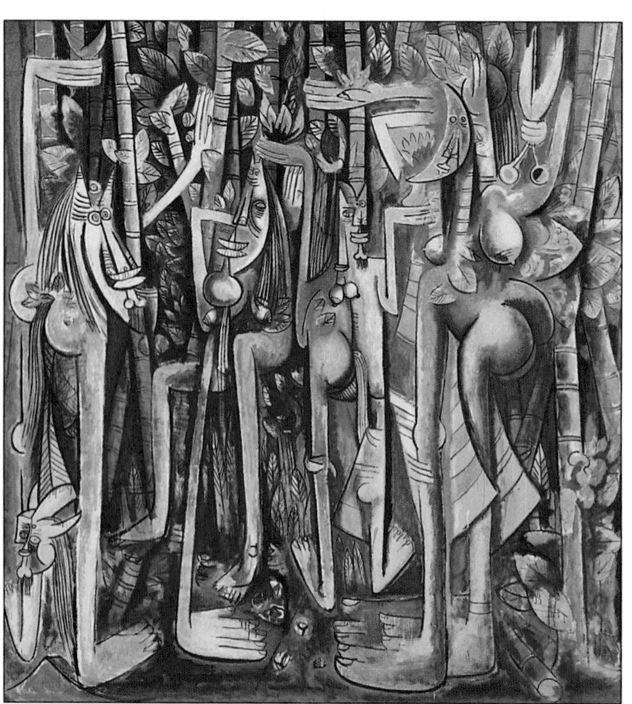

FIGURE 21.9 Wilfredo Lam, *The Jungle*, 1943, gouache on paper, mounted on canvas, 7′10″ × 7′6½″ (2.39 × 2.30 m). Inter-American Fund, Museum of Modern Art, NY/Licensed by Scala-Art Resource, NY. © 2005 Artists Rights Society, (ARS) NY. The son of a Chinese immigrant and an Afro-Cuban mother, Lam studied African art in Paris and adopted Picasso's style in an attempt to explore his own origins.

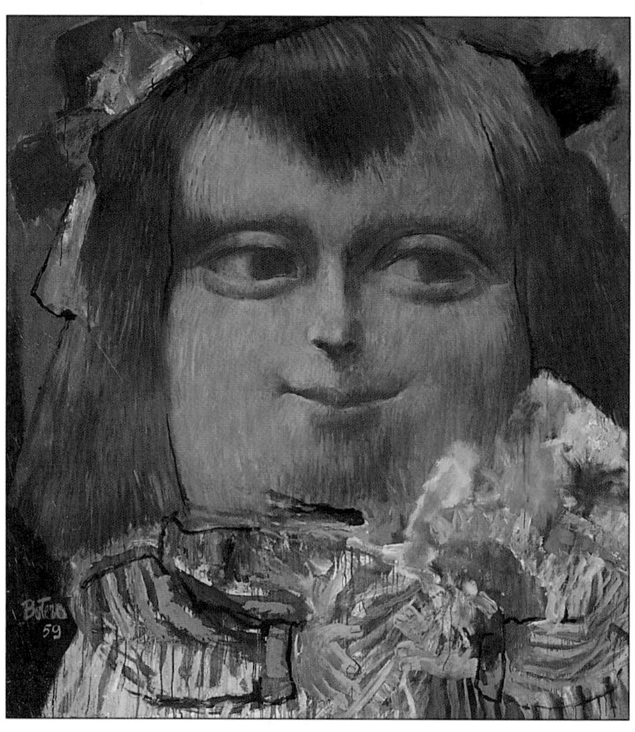

FIGURE 21.10 Fernando Botero, *Mona Lisa at the Age of Twelve*, 1959, oil and tempera on canvas, 6′ 11″ × 6′ 5″ (2.11 × 1.96 m). Inter-American Fund. Museum of Modern Art, NY/Licensed by Scala/Art Resource, NY. In the 1970s, Botero moved to Paris, where he began to make large bronze sculptures of his swollen figures.

Cross Currents

BACH IN BRAZIL

One interesting musical cross current between Latin America and Europe is Villa-Lobos's *Bachianas Brasileiras*, a piece inspired by the German Baroque composer Johann Sebastian Bach and written as a tribute to his memory and legacy. In this work, Villa-Lobos couples Brazilian rhythms with Bachian counterpoint to create a fusion of Latin and Germanic musical styles that spans cultures, oceans, and centuries.

Bach was the archetypal composer for Villa-Lobos, since Bach also drew inspiration from simple folk melodies, which he then developed into complex polyphonic compositions. *Bachianas Brasileiras* consists of nine parts, each scored for different instrumental combinations. No. 1, for example, is scored for eight cellos, No. 3 for piano and orchestra, No. 6 for flute and bassoon.

One of the most notable parts of *Bachianas Brasileiras* is No. 5, which includes a beautiful aria based on a Brazilian folk song. Villa-Lobos sets this piece for soprano and eight cellos, with a solo cello line. Its elegant beauty in the alternative arrangements is but one example of the way cultures interact to produce new and exciting artistic forms and styles.

including the Brazilian HEITOR VILLA-LOBOS [VEE-yah-LOW-bows] (1887–1959).

Latin America's best known classical composer, Villa-Lobos was born in Rio de Janeiro. After studying music with his father, he earned a living by playing the cello in cafés. He researched and collected authentic folk and Indian songs, both of which he later used as melodies in his classical compositions. Villa-Lobos believed that folk music reveals the special vitality and spirit of a people, their unique essence, and he conveys this in his large works for chorus and orchestra.

LITERATURE

The literature of Latin America is written primarily in two languages, Spanish and Portuguese. Yet the plurality of voices and visions that emerge in modern and contemporary Latin American fiction is staggering. A concern many writers share is an exploration of the imagination. Three writers in particular can be singled out for special attention: the Argentinean novelist, essayist, and short-story writer Jorge Luis Borges; the contemporary Colombian novelist and short-story writer Gabriel García Márquez; and the Chilean novelist Isabel Allende.

Jorge Luis Borges. JORGE LUIS BORGES [BOR-haze] (1899–1986) is best known for what he calls his *ficciones*—short, enigmatic fictional works that invite philosophical reflection, especially speculation about the mysterious universe that human beings inhabit. Borges's fiction is situated at the interface between the genres of essay and autobiography; he mixes facts and names from his family chronicles with reflections on philosophical matters. His stories frequently involve a central character confronted with a puzzle or problem, which has to be unraveled much in the manner of detective stories.

One of Borges's most powerful metaphors is that of the labyrinth, a maze into which the central character (and the reader) is placed, and from which extrication comes as the character gains realization about the imaginative world. Borges often merges the "real" with the imaginary, what is historical with what is invented, so his readers become disoriented and are forced to reconsider the relationship between fiction and reality.

Gabriel García Márquez. If Borges is the master of the short story, GABRIEL GARCÍA MÁRQUEZ [gar-SEE-ah MAR-kez] (b. 1928) is the master of the novel. His *One Hundred Years of Solitude* (1967) blends the "real" with the imaginary in unpredictable yet convincing ways, in a style that has come to be known as **magic realism.** Magic realism weaves realistic events together with incredible and fantastic ones, in an attempt to convey the truths of life. In magic realism, key events do not necessarily have a logical explanation; mystery is an integral part of experience. Remarking that "There's not a single line in all my work that does not have a basis in reality," García Márquez, like other magic realists, sees his work as conveying simultaneously the truths of the imagination and those of "reality."

Isabel Allende. In the same year that García Márquez won the Nobel Prize for Literature, ISABEL ALLENDE

Critical Thinking

MAGIC REALISM

Magic realism is a term that was coined to attempt to describe the literary movement that began in South America and had its greatest and most sustained success there. It refers to a style of writing (and also films and paintings) that mixes sharply etched realistic descriptive details with fantastic and dreamlike elements, that include motifs from myths and fairy tales. Related to surrealism, a movement in art primarily and secondarily in literature that combines elements of dreams and myth with everyday experience, magic realism hews more closely to everyday experiential reality, without pretending to supersede, surpass, or transcend it. Magic realism includes the following aspects:

- elements of the fantastic or marvelous
- a lack of discursive explanation
- an acceptance of the irrational and nonlogical
- an abundance of sensory images and details
- temporal distortions and causal inversions
- elements of folklore and legend
- multiple perspectives and points of view
- ambiguity and uncertainty

Why do you think writers and other artists in the twentieth century developed such an approach to their art? How might elements of magic realism, such as those identified in the list above, contribute to meaningful literary and artistic productions and performances? What is your own personal response to works that employ elements of magic realism?

[ay-END-eh] (b. 1942) published her noteworthy novel *The House of Spirits* (1982). Like García Márquez's *One Hundred Years of Solitude*, Allende's novel creates a fictional world that reconstructs the history of a country—in her case, modern Chile, her homeland, from which she was exiled when her uncle, President Salvador Allende of Chile, was assassinated in 1975. Like García Márquez, Allende uses techniques of magic realism to weave realistic events with incredible and fantastic ones to convey the truths of life.

Allende explains that she uses these techniques because, as she says, "in Latin America, we value dreams, passions, obsessions, emotions." It is also partly attributable to, as she says, "our sense of family, our sense of religion, of superstition, too." But mostly it is because "Fantastic things happen every day in Latin America—it's not that we make them up."

Table 21–1 MODERN AFRICAN AND LATIN AMERICAN WRITERS
African Writers
Chinua Achebe (b. 1930), Nigeria, *Things Fall Apart; Arrow of God* (novels)
Wole Soyinka (b. 1938), Nigeria, *Poems from Prison; Death and the King's Horseman* (play)
J. M. Coetzee (b. 1940), South Africa, *Waiting for the Barbarians; Disgrace* (novels)
Latin American Writers
Jorge Luis Borges (1899–1966), Argentina, *Ficciones* (stories)
Gabriel García Márquez (b. 1928), Colombia, *One Hundred Years of Solitude* (novel)
Isabel Allende (b. 1942), Chile, *The House of Spirits* (novel)

Cultural Impact

Twentieth-century Africa has been a continent in flux. Its political makeup has shifted from a continent of European colonial empires to one of modern nation-states. It has been a battleground for competing ideologies, both native and foreign, including Marxist-inspired revolutions, Christian proselytizing, and Islamic cultural incursions.

Parts of contemporary Africa continue to suffer from a high incidence of contagious diseases, including malaria and AIDS. Some African countries are becoming increasingly modernized, and some increasingly democratic. Recent developments in South Africa testify to the vitality and influence of the continent's impact politically, socially, and economically. Artistically, African music continues to influence Western composers and performers, and African music and dance groups perform to acclaim around the world, especially in the United States.

Modern Latin America has undergone significant social and political change. Revolutions in a number of countries, including Argentina, Brazil, and Mexico, occurred early in the century. Among later centers of unrest, the Mexican revolution of 1910 was the most successful in reorganizing social structures and fostering economic and political renewal.

The legacy of Latin American arts continues to influence painters, writers, and musicians around the globe. The social scope and political focus of the Mexican mural tradition has had a major impact on twentieth-century artists in the Americas and in Europe. The psychological complexity of Mexican portrait painting, especially in the paintings of Frida Kahlo, has had a lasting influence on the art world. In addition, the magic realism of South American novelists, especially in the work of Gabriel García Márquez, has been imitated and adapted by writers worldwide. Finally, the music of Latin America continues to be among the most internationally influential of any in the world.

KEY TERMS

creole
emirs
negritude
apartheid
gelede
talking drum
call-and-response format
polyrhythms
backbeat
Soukous
Afrobeat
hip life
Eurocentric
al fresco
pyroxylin
santería
samba
calypso
magic realism

www. WEBSITES FOR FURTHER STUDY

http://cti.itc.virginia.edu/%7Ebcr/Bayly/Bayly.html
(African art from the Bayly Museum.)

http://globetrotter.berkeley.edu/Elberg/Soyinka/soyinka-con0.html
(Harry Kreisler interviews Nobel Laureate Wole Soyinka about writing, theater arts, and political activism.)

http://www.rdpl.red-deer.ab.ca/villa/heller.html
(An excellent website featuring the life and works of composer Heitor Villa-Lobos.)

http://www.themodernword.com/gabo/
(An extensive site on one of the world's greatest writers, Gabriel García Márquez.)

http://www.isabelallende.com
(Site focused on life and works of Isabel Allende, her books, roots, curiosities, and her foundation.)

http://www.mnsu.edu/emuseum/cultural/music/african_music.shtml
(Site devoted to traditional African music.)

http://www.mnsu.edu/emuseum/cultural/music/south_america.shtml
(Site featuring South American music, especially the music of the Andes.)

Chapter 22

History

1900	Labour Party founded in England
1905	Einstein formulates theory of relativity
1908	Ford introduces Model T
1913	Assembly line introduced at Ford plant
1914	World War I begins
1917	Russian Revolution
1920	Nineteenth Amendment grants women the right to vote
1920s	Harlem Renaissance flourishes
1920s	"Roaring Twenties" and prohibition
1927	Lindbergh's solo flight across Atlantic Ocean
1929	Stock Market crashes; Depression begins
1933	FDR introduces New Deal
	Nazis gain control of Germany
1935	WPA begun: FSA begins photography program
1936–39	Spanish Civil War
1939	World War II begins
1941	United States enters World War II

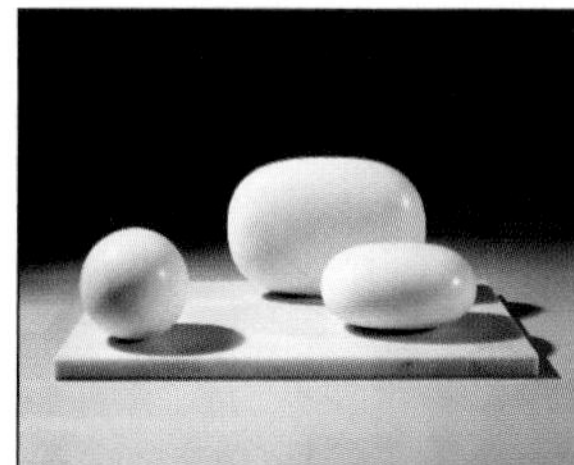

Arts and Architecture

1905	Matisse, *Woman with a Hat*
1907	Picasso, *Les Demoiselles d'Avignon*
1913	Stravinsky, *The Rite of Spring*
1915	Severini, *Suburban Train Arriving at Paris*
1917	Duchamp, *Fountain*
1920	Mondrian, *Composition in Red, Yellow, and Blue*
1924	Gershwin, *Rhapsody in Blue*
1926	O'Keeffe, *Yellow Calla*
1928	Armstrong, *West End Blues*
1928	Brancusi, *Bird in Space*
1931	Dali, *The Persistence of Memory*
1931	Schoenberg, *Variations for Orchestra*
1933	Rivera, *Detroit Industry*
1936	Oppenheim, *Breakfast in Fur*
1937	Picasso, *Guernica*
1938	Moore, *Recumbent Figure*
1939–41	Lawrence, *The Migration of the Negro*
1940	Ellington, *Concerto for Cootie*
1942	Hopper, *Nighthawks*
1944	Copland, *Appalachian Spring*

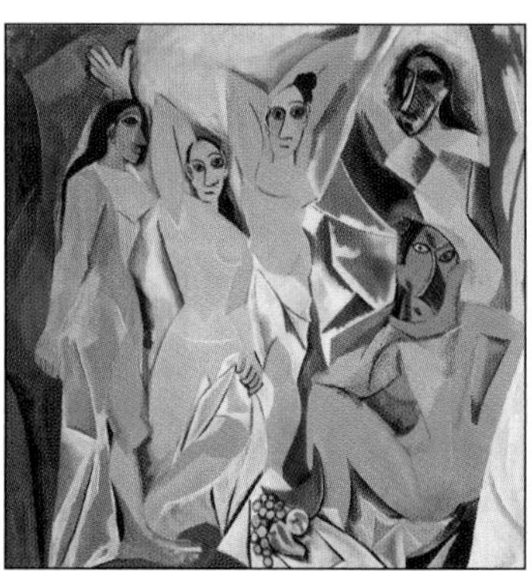

Literature and Philosophy

1905	Freud, *Three Essays on the Theory of Sexuality*
1922	Eliot, *The Waste Land*
1922	Joyce, *Ulysses*
1926	Hemingway, *The Sun Also Rises*
1927	Woolf, *To the Lighthouse*
1929	Cocteau, *Les Enfants Terribles*
1929	Faulkner, *The Sound and the Fury*
1939	Steinbeck, *The Grapes of Wrath*

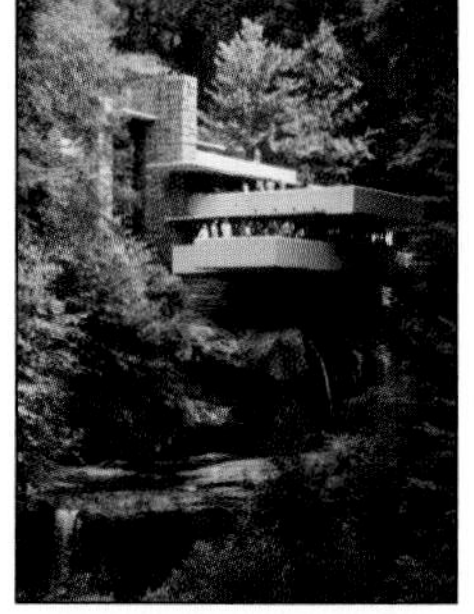

Early Twentieth Century

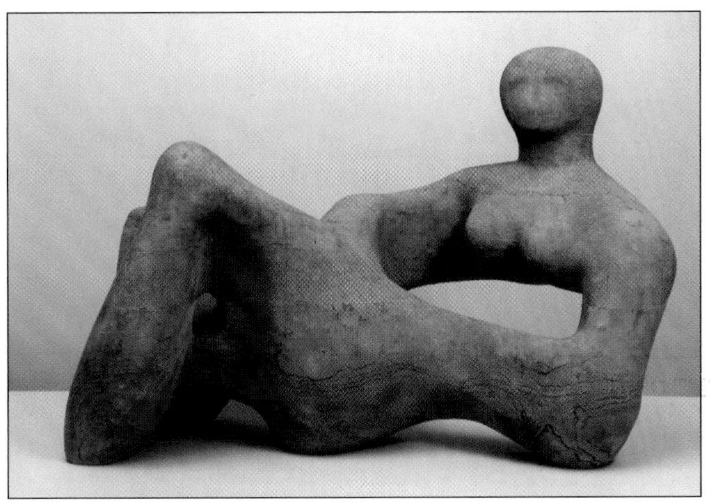

Henry Moore, *Recumbent Figure*, 1938, green hornton stone, length 55″ (141 cm), Henry Moore Foundation/Tate Picture Gallery, London, UK.

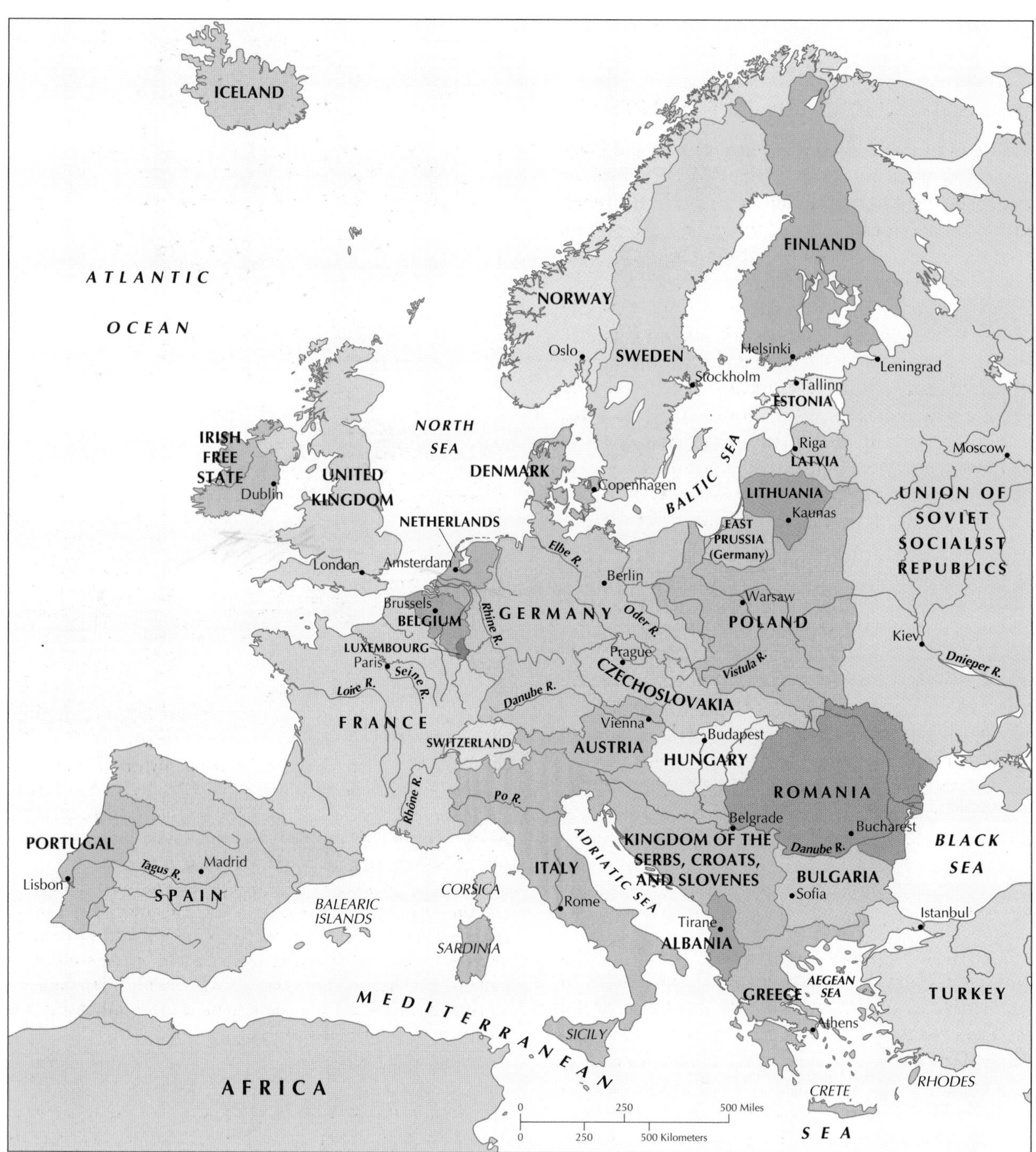

MAP 22.1 Europe after World War I, ca. 1920.

CHAPTER OVERVIEW

NEW DIRECTIONS IN THE ARTS

Picasso and Cubism impact the arts

THE GREAT WAR AND AFTER

Changes in a civilization altered by war

REPRESSION AND DEPRESSION: THE THIRTIES

Global instability infuses the arts

NEW DIRECTIONS IN THE ARTS

Picasso and Cubism Impact the Arts

By the early twentieth century, the Impressionist and Post-Impressionists were no longer regarded as radical or shocking; they were now accepted by the official French Salon that had previously scorned them. In 1901, a huge retrospective exhibition of van Gogh's work was held in Paris. The 1907 Salon featured Cézanne's paintings. The Impressionists and Post-Impressionists were now the leaders of art that went against tradition and expectation, preferring to seek what was unique and innovative, even startling or shocking, the ***avant garde.*** In the never-ending quest for the new, movement after movement, "ism" after "ism," came and went. Thus, Romanticism, Realism, Impressionism, and Post-Impressionism were followed in the early twentieth century by Fauvism, Cubism, Futurism, and German Expressionism. In general, the later nineteenth-century trend toward abstraction of the visual world, the willingness to distort its form and color, was still more extreme in early twentieth-century art.

The interest in **abstraction** takes three forms: (1) an *expressive* art that is emotional, gestural, and free in its use of color; (2) a *formalist* art that is concerned with structure and order; and (3) an art of *fantasy* that is concerned with the individual imagination and the realm of dreams. In all three, the world of surface appearances is gradually left behind. Abstract art is based less and less on the artist's *perception* and increasingly on the artist's *conception* of things.

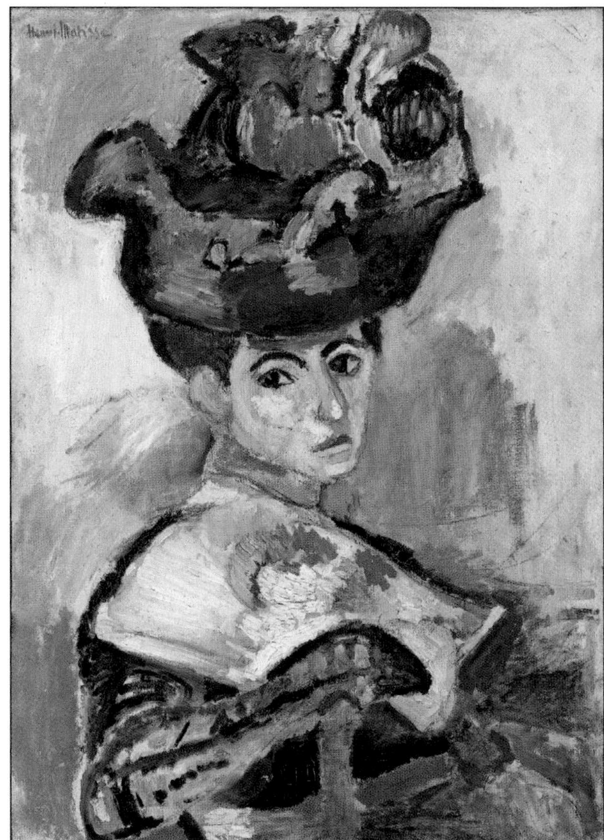

Figure 22.1 Henri Matisse, *Femme ou chapeau* (*Woman with the Hat*), 1905, oil on canvas. $31\frac{3}{4}''\times 23\frac{1}{2}''$ (80.65 × 59.69 cm). Bequest of Elise S. Haas. Photo: San Francisco Museum of Modern Art. © Succession H. Matisse/Artists Rights Society (ARS), NY. Photography: Ben Blackwell. The American author Getrude Stein and her brother Leo purchased this painting at the Autumn Salon in 1905, inaugurating one of the greatest collections of modern art in Paris in the twentieth century. Americans, in particular, flocked to Stein's evening gatherings in her apartment on the Rue des Fleurs to see the work of Matisse and Picasso and to meet the artists themselves, who were in regular attendance.

Fauvism

The 1905 Salon d'Automne (Autumn Salon) in Paris was liberal in its acceptance policy and included a room of paintings by Henri Matisse, Maurice de Vlaminck, André Derain, Georges Rouault, and others who were exhibiting together for the first time. The art critic Louis Vauxcelles reviewed the show and was quick to label these artists *Les Fauves* (The Wild Beasts) because of their paintings' violent and arbitrary colors. The artists who launched **Fauvism,** like van Gogh and Gauguin, believed color could be an expressive force in its own right and it could correspond, not to reality, but to what van Gogh had called "the artist's temperament." Furthermore, they rejected the small "dots and dashes" of color that characterized Impressionist painting and, particularly, the Post-Impressionist paintings of Seurat. Their work was intended to shock the viewer, visually and psychologically, with its intensely surprising color. It was, above all, new.

Henri Matisse. The leader of the Fauves was HENRI MATISSE [mah-TEES] (1869–1954). At the age of twenty-two, Matisse had abandoned a career in law for one in art. At the 1905 Autumn Salon, he exhibited *Woman with the Hat* (fig. 22.1), a portrait of Madame Matisse. It appeared to many viewers to be little more than a smearing of brilliant, arbitrary, and unnatural colors across the subject's face and background. In its subject matter, this could be an Impressionist painting depicting Madame Matisse dressed for an outing in gloves and an enormous hat, yet it bears almost no resemblance to any earlier work. Rather than employing dabs of color, Matisse broke the color into broad zones. Not only are the colors seemingly arbitrary, the artist makes no attempt to harmonize them. Red, green, and purple are used at maximum intensity.

Cubism

The Fauvist emphasis on the reality of the picture plane is also apparent in the work of the Cubist painters. Derived from Cézanne's famous dictum, "You must see in nature the cylinder, the sphere, and the cone," **Cubism** differs from earlier styles of painting in its depiction of objects in their most reduced geometric form, particularly, as its name implies, in cubes. It also differs in the way in which objects are represented simultaneously from several different points of view; rather than presenting an object from a single vantage point, the intent was to present all aspects of the object simultaneously. Reality, they argued, is not just what we see, but what we know about what we see, in the same way that when we see a person's back, we can infer that person's face.

Cubism was the invention of two relatively unknown painters at the time, Pablo Picasso and Georges Braque, both of whom arrived separately at the same conclusions about the nature of our experience of the world. They soon discovered one another's shared convictions and proceeded to work together for seven years until the outbreak of World War I.

Pablo Picasso. Often considered the single most important painter of the twentieth century, PABLO PICASSO [pi-KAH-soh] (1881–1973) never ceased searching for the new. He went through many styles in his long life and worked in a wide variety of media including painting, graphics, sculpture, and ceramics. He might draw and paint with extraordinary realism one day and with a high degree of abstraction the next—although he never abandoned a subject entirely.

Picasso's famous *Les Demoiselles d'Avignon* (*The Ladies of Avignon*) (fig. 22.2), of 1907, was a turning point in the history of painting. Although the word *demoiselles* means "gentlewomen," here it refers to prostitutes, and

FIGURE 22.2 Pablo Picasso, *Les Demoiselles d'Avignon*, 1907, oil on canvas, 8′ × 7′ 8″ (2.40 × 2.30 m), Museum of Modern Art, New York. With motifs that echo African art, the angular lines and overlapping planes of this painting initiated a new way of analyzing three-dimensional forms in space. The work's primitive energy sent shock waves through the art world when it was first shown in Paris, allying it with Stravinsky's *Rite of Spring*, which had a similar effect on the world of music six years later.

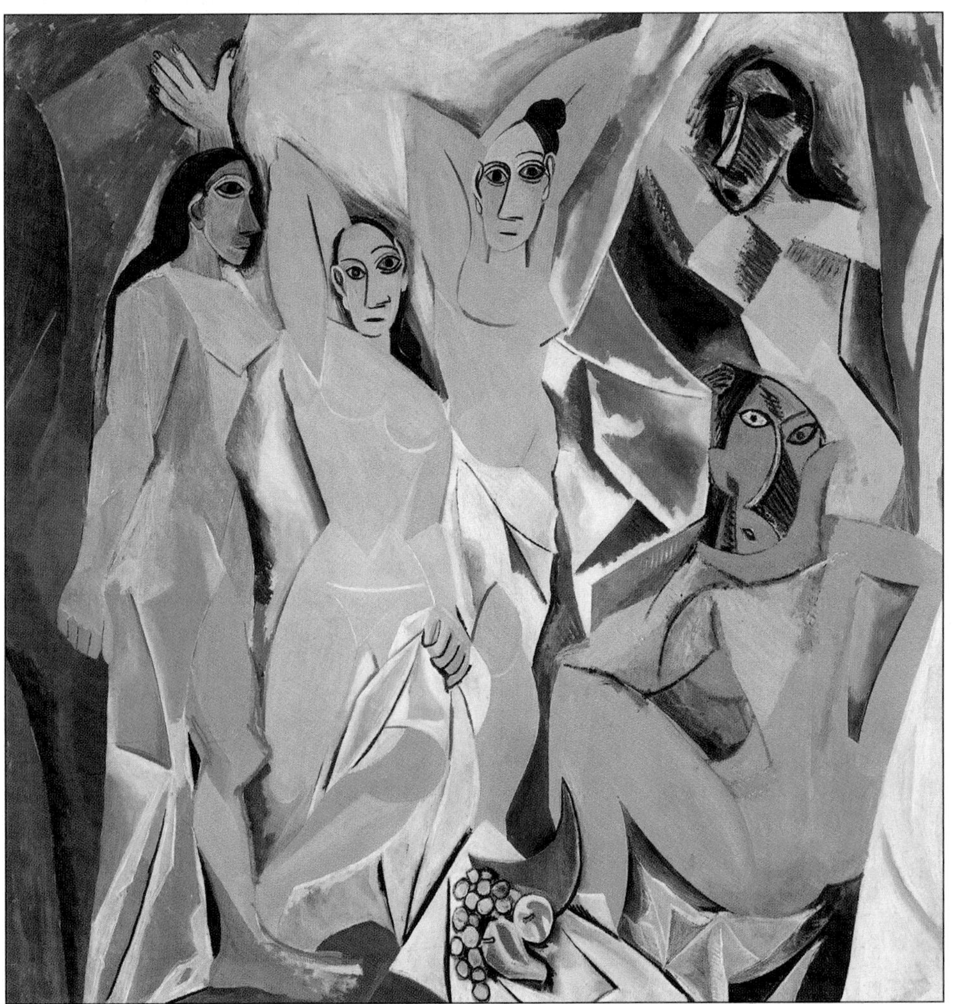

Avignon refers to Avignon Street in Barcelona rather than the city of the popes in southern France. The anatomy of the figures shows distorted proportions, their bodies turned into rhythmic shapes and broken angular pieces. Space is treated in the same way. Solid and void are depicted in terms of structural units, similar to Cézanne's "little planes." The style is also deliberately "primitive." African sculpture, particularly masks, inundated Paris in the first decade of the century, and Picasso took full advantage of their expressive force.

Georges Braque. One of the first people to see *Les Demoiselles*, and to approve of it, was GEORGES BRAQUE [BRAHK] (1882–1963). Braque had worked with Matisse as a member of the Fauves, and it was probably Matisse, who was himself horrified by *Les Demoiselles*, who introduced him to Picasso. But Braque saw in it a flattening and simplification of form that he believed Cézanne had championed.

FIGURE 22.3 Georges Braque, *The Portuguese*, 1911, oil on canvas, $45\frac{1}{8}'' \times 32\frac{1}{8}''$ (114.5 × 81.5 cm), Kunstmuseum, Basel, Switzerland. © 2005 Artists Rights Society (ARS), NY. © ADAGP, Paris and DACS, London 1998. In cubism the forms are broken and faceted as if portions of cubes, and the forms are portrayed from multiple viewpoints. The range of color is restricted so it will not distract from this new way of analyzing form in space.

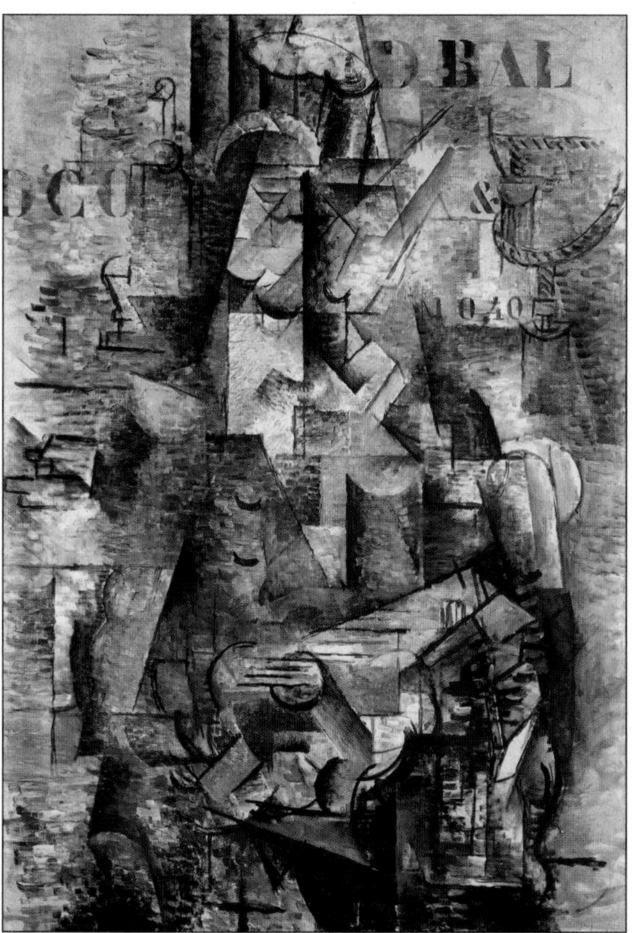

Braque's *The Portuguese* (fig. 22.3), of 1911, depicts a guitarist playing at a café, but there is no fully realized figure. We can see the guitar's soundhole and strings in the lower-middle part of the painting. There are fragments of lettering—OCO and BAL—and something is offered at a price of 10.40 francs. A rope is wrapped around a post, and perhaps that is the guitarist's broad smile in the upper-middle part of the piece. All is a fleeting glance as if seen through a window in which the reflections of activity and movement outside distort everything seen inside.

Both Braque and Picasso began to introduce recognizable pieces of material reality into their compositions, asking the questions: What is real and what is art? If something is real, can it be art? And vice versa, if something is art, is it real? By pasting real materials on the canvas they engaged in a technique called **collage** (from the French word *coller*, "to glue" or "to paste"). Picasso's *Still Life with Chair Caning* (fig. 22.4), of 1912, contains rope and a piece of oilcloth with imitation chair caning printed on it, a cigarette, and a fragment of a newspaper (*Le Journal*). All we see are the first three letters, a fragment of the whole, but this fragment tells us much about Braque and Picasso's intentions. The letters "jou" also form the beginning of the verb *jouer*, the French for "to play." Collage became the new playground of the artist.

FIGURE 22.4 Pablo Picasso, *Still Life with Chair Caning*, 1912, oil, oilcloth, and pasted paper simulating chair caning on canvas, rope frame, $10\frac{1}{2}'' \times 13\frac{3}{4}''$ (26.7 × 35 cm). Photo: R.G. Ojeda. Musée Picasso, Paris. Reunion des Musées Nationaux. Art Resource, NY. © 2008 Estate of Pablo Picasso/Artists Rights Society (ARS), NY. This collage (from the French for "to paste" or "to glue") is created from scraps of ordinary materials that became art when arranged into a composition.

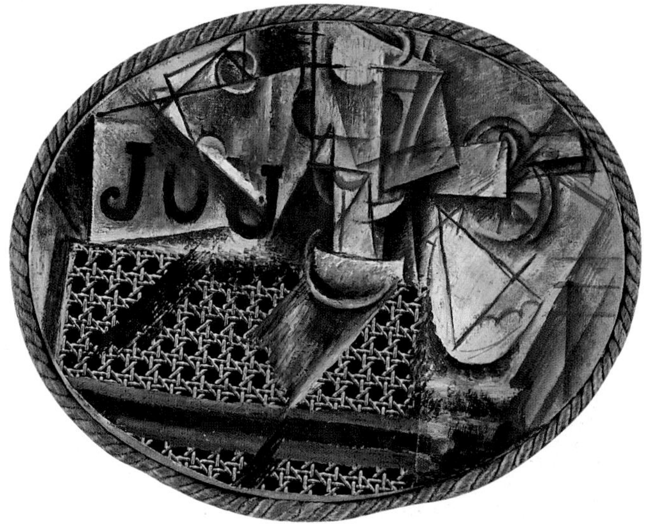

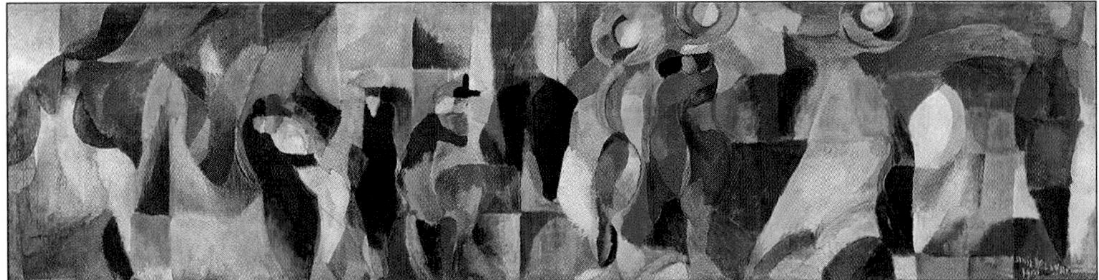

FIGURE 22.5 Sonia Delaunany-Terk, *Tango au Bal Bullier*, 1913, oil on canvas 3′ 2″ × 12′ 8″ (97 × 390 cm), Musée National d'Art Moderne, Centre National d'Art et de Culture, Georges Pompidou. Philippe Migeat/Reunion des Musées Nationaux/Art Resource, NY. The title of this painting is the name of a dance hall in Paris where the artist danced the tango wearing her *simultanéiste* costumes, which her husband Robert Delaunay described as "living paintings."

Sonia Delaunay-Terk. Sonia Delaunay-Terk (1885–1979) was born Sarah Stern in the Ukraine, but grew up in St. Petersburg under the care of a relative, the art collector Heinrich Terk. In 1909, she married an art dealer, Wilhelm Uhde, who exhibited her work in his Paris gallery. In 1910, she married again, now to the artist Robert Delaunay, with whom she formed a long creative partnership.

The couple developed a style of abstract painting called **Simultanéisme** based on color theory, using vivid colors and geometric shapes, intended to be experienced simultaneously. Sonia Delaunay's *Tango au Bal Bullier* (fig. 22.5), 1913, conveys the rapid graceful movement of dancers, including a sense of their animation and energy. She applied this style to clothing created from various materials, thereby combining art and attire, blurring the traditional distinction between Fine Art and Applied Art. She designed costumes for Diaghilev's Russian Ballet and for Tristna Tzara's play *Le Coeur à Gaz*. With the fashion designer Jacques Heim, she opened the Boutique Simultané in Paris in 1925, featuring garments and accessories in this style.

FUTURISM

The **Futurism** movement, based in Italy before World War I, used Cubist forms in a dynamic way. It was the first art movement to have been founded almost exclusively in the popular press, conceived by its creator, the poet FILIPPO MARINETTI [mah-ri-NET-ee] (1876–1944), in his "Manifesto of Futurism," published on February 20, 1909, in the French newspaper *Le Figaro*.

The "Manifesto" outlines an eleven-point pledge, including the Futurists' intention to "sing the love of danger," to "affirm that the world's magnificence has been enriched by a new beauty, the beauty of speed," to "glorify war—the world's only hygiene," to "destroy the museums, libraries, and academies of every kind," and, finally, to "sing of great crowds excited by work, by pleasure, and by riot."

Gino Severini. In February 1910, seven painters, including GINO SEVERINI [sev-err-EE-nee] (1883–1966), signed a "Manifesto of Futurist Painters" that pledged, among other things, "to rebel against the tyranny of terms like 'harmony' and 'good taste,'" "to demolish the works of Rembrandt, of Goya, and of Rodin," and, most importantly, "to express our whirling life of steel, of pride, of fever, and of speed." The Furturists wanted, they claimed, to render "universal dynamism" in painting.

The Futurists' interest in expressing speed was aided by the forms of Cubism. Severini's *Suburban Train Arriving at Paris* (fig. 22.6), of 1915, depicts speed as a sequence of positions of multifaceted forms. Similar to a series of movie stills, or to a multiple exposure photograph, the artist expresses the direction of the force by the abstract fragmentation of the speeding forms. The Futurists valued simultaneous perspective, as did the Cubists, but the Futurists recorded the various aspects of a moving object, whereas the analytical Cubists recorded those of a static one.

GERMAN EXPRESSIONISM

The last of the great prewar avant-garde movements was **German Expressionism** which consisted of two separate branches, *Die Brücke* (The Bridge), established in Dresden in 1905, and *Der Blaue Reiter* (The Blue Rider) formed in Munich in 1911. Both were directly indebted to the example of the Fauves in Paris, especially in terms of the liberation of color and the celebration of sexuality.

Emil Nolde. One of the most daring members of *Die Brücke* was EMIL NOLDE [NOHL-(duh)] (1867–1956). What distinguishes his *Dancing Around the Golden Calf* (fig. 22.7) from the work of Matisse and the

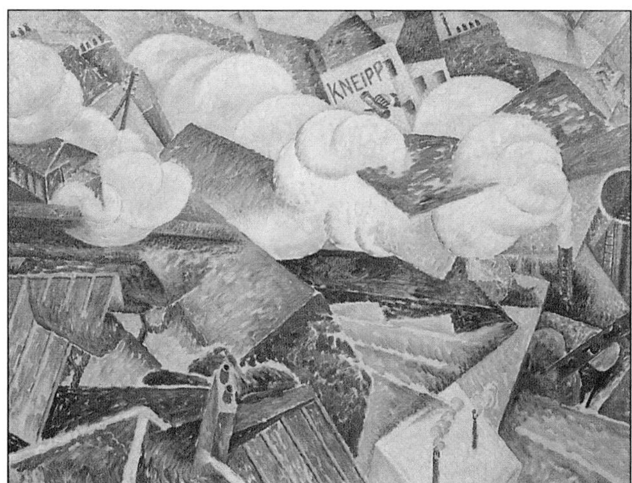

FIGURE 22.6 Gino Severini, *Suburban Train Arriving at Paris*, 1915, oil on canvas, $35'' \times 45\frac{1}{2}''$ (88.6 × 115.6 cm), Tate Gallery, London. © 2005 Artists Rights Society (ARS), NY. The Italian Futurists sought to destroy museums and anything old, praised what they called the "beauty of speed," glorified war and machinery, and favored the "masculine" over the "feminine."

Fauves is the painting's lack of contour and outline. Instead, emphasis is on the use of color, which fully exploits the dissonances between its bright reds, orange-yellows, and red-violets. The energy of this style—almost slapdash in comparison to Matisse—helps create a sense of violence, fury, and wanton sexuality that is alien to Matisse's vision. This rough-hewn, purposefully inelegant approach is typical of *Die Brücke* work, and it owes much to the example of Picasso's *Les Demoiselles* and its so-called primitivism.

FIGURE 22.7 Emil Nolde, *Dancing Around the Golden Calf*, 1910, oil on canvas, $34\frac{3}{4}'' \times 39\frac{1}{2}''$ (88 × 100 cm), Staatsgalerie Moderner Kunst, Munich. Much of the shock of this painting derives from its depiction of a biblical subject in such openly sexual terms.

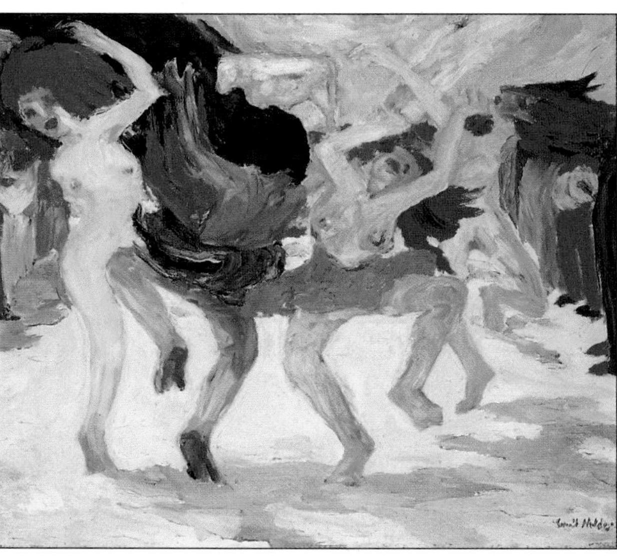

Vassily Kandinsky. The leader of *Der Blaue Reiter* was VASSILY KANDINSKY [kan-DIN-skee] (1866–1944), who was born in Moscow. A practicing lawyer with a professorship in Moscow, Kandinsky saw one of Monet's *Haystacks* paintings in 1895 and was so moved by the experience that he traveled to Munich to study art. He became friendly with the Fauves and the Cubists, bringing their work to Germany in 1911 for a major exhibition.

The name *Der Blaue Reiter* refers to St. George slaying the dragon, the image that appeared on the city emblem of Moscow. Tradition held that Moscow would be the capital of the world during the millennium, the thousand-year reign of Jesus on earth after the Apocalypse. *Improvisation No. 30 (Warlike Theme)* (fig. 22.8) includes, at the bottom of the composition, two firing cannons, which announce the second coming of Jesus. Crowds of people march toward the millennium across the canvas. Above them are the churches of the Kremlin and, circling around the horizon, the streets of Moscow itself. Kandinsky did not so much want to convey the meaning of his work through its imagery as through its color. Color, he

FIGURE 22.8 Vassily Kandinsky, *Improvisation No. 30 (Warlike Theme)*, 1913, oil on canvas, $43\frac{1}{4}'' \times 43\frac{1}{4}''$ (110 × 110 cm), Photograph © 2005, The Art Institute of Chicago. All Rights Reserved. © 2005 Artists Rights Society (ARS), NY. Although Kandinsky did produce completely nonrepresentational paintings, beginning in 1910, that were intended to stir the viewer's emotions, this painting includes recognizable subjects having political and religious implications.

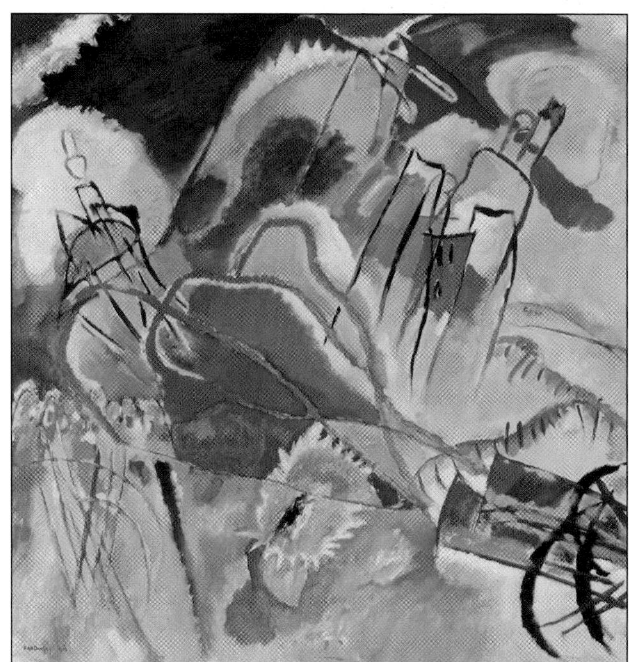

believed, caused "vibrations (in German, *Klangen*) in the soul," and his painting was designed, he wrote in 1912 in his *Concerning the Spiritual in Art*, to "urge" the viewer to a spiritual awakening in preparation for the second coming.

MUSIC

Igor Stravinsky. IGOR STRAVINSKY [strah-VIN-skee] (1882–1971) is considered the most influential composer of the modern era. His works revolutionized twentieth-century musical styles and affected artists such as Picasso, writers such as T. S. Eliot, and ballet choreographers such as George Balanchine. Stravinsky was born in Russia, near St. Petersburg. Although groomed for a law career, Stravinsky studied music and achieved early success composing for the Ballets Russes, a Russian ballet troupe performing in Paris under the artistic direction of Serge Diaghilev. His early scores, *The Firebird* (1910) and *Petrushka* (1911), were both ballets based on Russian themes and musically influenced by Debussy.

The Rite of Spring. The most spectacular of Stravinsky's early ballet scores was *Le Sacre du Printemps (The Rite of Spring)* of 1913. *The Rite of Spring* broke new ground. The music was filled with harmonic shifts, rhythmic surprises, and melodic irregularities. The public was shocked by the near violence of the sound and by its disruption of their emotional expectations. During the performance, the audience hissed and booed, shouted and screamed, and even began fighting amongst themselves. The police had to be called in to quell the riot.

The origin of *The Rite of Spring* came to Stravinsky in a vision: "a solemn pagan rite: wise elders, seated in a circle, watch a young girl dance herself to death. They are sacrificing her to propitiate the god of spring." Stravinsky linked this vision to his childhood memories of the "violent Russian spring that seemed to begin in an hour and was like the whole earth cracking." The work depicts the fertility rites of a primitive tribe in pagan Russia. The first part, "The Fertility of the Earth," opens with a suggestion of the rebirth of spring. A bassoon solo begins the introductory section and is soon followed by other woodwinds, and then the brasses that play the melody, all without a home key, that is, without a harmonic center. The music builds to a climax and then abruptly stops, leaving the solo bassoon to echo the introductory notes.

Without pause, a brief four-note theme repeated softly by the violins opens the second part, "The Sacrifice." Immediately comes the "Dance of the Youths and Maidens," in which Stravinsky builds intensity through the heavy use of percussion, sharply irregular rhythmic accents, and the shrill syncopation of the horns. All this is emphasized further by both polytonal harmonies and strong dissonance. Stravinsky's "Introduction" to *The Rite of Spring* reflects the modern composer's new directions in melody and harmony; "The Dance of the Youths and Maidens" displays a corresponding rhythmic freedom.

One of Stravinsky's most unusual musical commissions came when he was asked to compose a ballet for elephants. Barnum and Bailey Circus had approached George Balanchine, the ballet master and choreographer, who came up with the idea. Stravinsky delivered a work that was performed in New York City's Madison Square Garden. The work was described in the program as "Fifty Elephants and Fifty Beautiful Girls in an Original Choreography Tour de Force."

THE GREAT WAR AND AFTER

"ON OR ABOUT DECEMBER 1910 HUMAN character changed," wrote English novelist Virginia Woolf. "All human relations shifted, those between masters and servants, husbands and wives, parents and children. And when human relations shift there is at the same time a change in religion, conduct, politics and literature." These changes were dramatized by the Great War (as World War I was then called), which began in August 1914. As another English novelist, D. H. Lawrence, wrote, "in 1915 the old world ended." The war gave frightening meaning to the radical changes of the early twentieth century. It was a time of "disorder and early sorrow," as German writer Thomas Mann wrote in one of his stories; where "things fall apart; the centre cannot hold," as the Irish poet William Butler Yeats noted. Change, disorder, sorrow, and disintegration: These forebodings ushered in an age of anxiety.

WORLD WAR I

On June 28, 1914, a Serbian nationalist named Gavrilo Princip assassinated the Habsburg archduke, Francis Ferdinand, heir to the throne of Austria and Hungary, and his wife, Sophie Chotek, on the street in Sarajevo, Bosnia. Within weeks, Europe was at war, the Central Powers (Austria, Hungary, Germany, Turkey, and later, Bulgaria) against the Allies (Serbia, Russia, France, and Britain, and later, the United States).

It is hard to overstate the impact of the Great War on the public in the West. It took the lives of over eight million soldiers in action, and many millions more through malnutrition and disease. Along the Western Front, which extended from the English Channel to the Swiss border with Alsace, near Basel, hundreds of thousands of soldiers faced each other in parallel trenches across a stationary line. British historian Charles Carrington (1897–1981) remembers life in the trenches on the Somme, as a young man barely twenty years of age:

> The killed and wounded were all lost by harassing fire, mostly on their way up or down the line. Once in position . . . you could not show a finger by daylight, and by night every path by which you might be supposed to move was raked by machine-guns which had been trained on it by day. . . . If you could reach your funk-hole and crouch in it, there was a fair chance of your coming out of it alive next day to run the gauntlet . . . again. In your funk-hole, with no room to move, no hot food, and no chance of getting any, there was nothing worse to suffer than a steady drizzle of wintry rain and temperature just above the freezing point. A little colder and the mud would have been more manageable. Life was entirely numbed; you could do nothing. There could be no fighting since the combatants could not get at one another, no improvement of the trenches since any new work would instantly be demolished by a storm of shell-fire.

Another chronicler of the war, the German Erich Maria Remarque, described in his novel *All Quiet on the Western Front* (1929) the sense of doom that dominated the German lines: "Monotonously the lorries sway, monotonously come the calls, monotonously falls the rain. It falls on our heads and on the heads of the dead up the line, on the body of the little recruit with the wound that is so much too big for his hip; it falls on Kemerich's grave; it falls in our hearts." After the Great War, it seemed as if the whole world mourned, a mood evoked in this lithograph by the German artist KATHE KOLLWITZ [KOL-vits] (1867–1945) (fig. 22.9).

FIGURE 22.9 Kathe Kollwitz, *The Mothers*, 1919, lithograph, $17\frac{3}{4}'' \times 23''$ (45×58.4 cm), Philadelphia Museum of Art. © DACS 1998. © 2005 Artists Rights Society (ARS), NY. Kollwitz captures the tragedy of World War I in this image of lower-class German mothers left to fend for themselves and their children after the war. The black-and-white medium emphasizes the harshness of their reality.

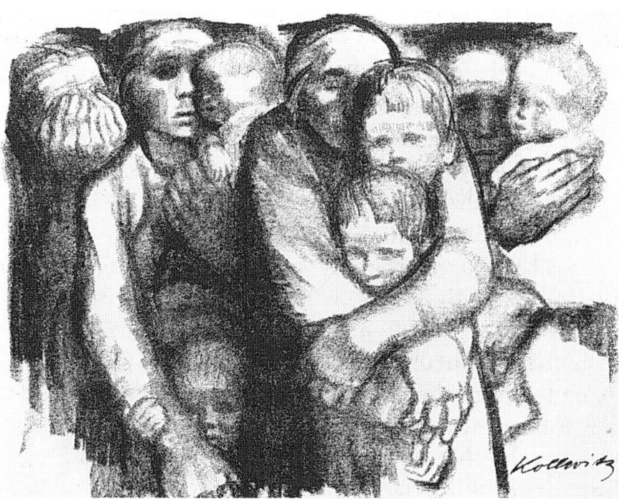

RUSSIAN REVOLUTION AND AFTER

The influence of the West on Russia, so evident in St. Petersburg, was counterbalanced by later political developments that undermined the autocratic monarchy of the Tsars. The Russian Revolution officially began when the last Russian Tsar, Nicholas II, abdicated in 1917. However, it had in fact started earlier, on Bloody Sunday, January 9, 1905, when government troops fired on a peaceful demonstration by workers outside the Winter Palace in St. Petersburg. The workers quickly organized themselves into "soviets," or councils of workers elected in the factories, while the police responded swiftly by arresting dissenters. Most leaders were either sent to Siberia or chose self-imposed exile, as did Lenin, removing himself with many others to Switzerland.

Yet it was World War I that precipitated the real crisis. The Russian army was crushed in the fight with Germany, resulting in over five million casualties between 1914 and 1917. Germany penetrated deep into western Russia. The flow of refugees into Moscow could almost not be supported.

In February 1917, popular demonstrations forced Nicholas from power. (He and his family were later executed on the night of July 16, 1918.) A democracy was promised, the nature of which was to be determined by a constituent assembly, elected by the people at the earliest opportunity. From February to October 1917, Russia was ruled by a provisional government, but in October, to cries of "all power to the soviets," the Bolshevik party seized power, led by Vladimir Ilyich Lenin (1870–1924). The Bolsheviks were Marxists—that is, those who believed in the writings of Karl Marx and called for a new society ruled by the proletariat, the working class. In Marx and Engels's words, from *The Communist Manifesto:* "In place of the old bourgeois society, with its classes and class antagonisms, we shall have an association, in which the free development of each is the condition for the free development of all."

Within a few months, Russia was embroiled in a bitter civil war, which would last for three years. The war pitted the Red Army of the working proletariat against the White Army of the anti-Bolshevik bourgeoisie. The Reds won, but since Britain and France had openly supported the Whites, and Japan and the United States had sent troops to Siberia, the new Bolshevik government was almost totally isolated from the West. It nationalized almost all industry, organizing the workers, and created what it called a "dictatorship of the proletariat." Yet a deep economic crisis soon followed, and Lenin, recognizing that he had moved too quickly, inaugurated a New Economic Policy (NEP) in 1921, legalizing private trade, abandoning the nationalization of industry, and allowing the private sector of the economy to reestablish itself. It was a full retreat from Communist principles, but one necessitated, Lenin believed, by reality.

Meanwhile, the new Soviet bureaucracy began to establish itself. Rising to the position of General Secretary of the Bolshevik party was Joseph Stalin (1879–1953). When Lenin died in 1924, Stalin overcame his rival Leon Trotsky (1879–1940) and took over, making it clear that the primary goal of the Soviet Union was industrialization. His Five-Year Plan, implemented in 1929, modernized the country and built the basic structure of Soviet society, which remained intact until December 1991.

The Russian Revolution created a new order that affected not only Russians, but other peoples around the globe. Its complex web of causes included popular grievances, radical ideas espoused by intellectuals, idealism coupled with a lust for power, and a breakdown of public order. Its consequences included helping to prevent the restoration of peace after World War I—which contributed to the rise of Nazi Germany and the outbreak of World War II—and increasing world tension throughout the twentieth century, resulting in a "cold war."

DADA

The war had an immense impact on art. Profoundly affected by the destruction, a group of artists, writers, and musicians founded a new art movement—**Dada,** from a nonsense word indicating a child's first utterance of 'Da, da' or 'yes, yes' to life. Beginning in Zurich and New York during the war, it flourished in Paris and Germany after it.

As early as 1916, artists and intellectuals who had escaped the war gathered regularly at the Café Voltaire in Zurich. Swiss sculptor Hans Arp (1886–1966) defined Dada in the following way: "Repelled by the slaughterhouses of the world war, we turned to art. We searched for an elementary art that would, we thought, save mankind from the furious madness of these times." This it attempted to do in an irreverent manner. Arp himself made relief sculptures by dropping liquid into a series of small puddles, outlining each, and then cutting out wooden replicas and finally putting them together. His friend, TRISTAN TZARA [ZAHR-ah] (1896–1963), a Dada poet, wrote poems using these same "laws of chance." Tzara would cut up a newspaper article word by word, then draw the words out of a hat, and write a poem. Tzara also performed a kind of poetry at the Café Voltaire—*bruitisme*, he called it, after the French word for "noise"—consisting of vowels, consonants, and guttural sounds, strung together in a nonsense parody of German *Lieder* (songs). The Dadaists thought that if tradition was responsible for the madness of the Great War, then tradition deserved no respect. The childlike, absurd behavior of the Dadaists was a conscious attempt to start again from square one.

Marcel Duchamp. One of the most important Dadaists, MARCEL DUCHAMP [doo-SHAHM] (1883–1968), worked as a painter before the war. When Duchamp arrived in New York in 1915, he said that Dada meant "hobby horse" in French (yet another meaning), and claimed he had picked the word at random from a French dictionary (yet another conflicting story of its origins). Duchamp saw Dada as a kind of **anti-art** one that embodied imagination, chance, and irrationality, and opposed all recognized values in art and literature.

In 1917, Duchamp submitted a "sculpture" to the Independents exhibition in New York. Entitled *Fountain* (fig. 22.10), it was a porcelain urinal signed with a pseudonym, "R. Mutt." It caused an uproar. Duchamp let it be known that he was "Mutt" himself, suggesting that what mattered most about a "work of art" was not aesthetic concerns, but who made it. Furthermore, the significance of the urinal changed in different contexts. It was one thing in a plumbing shop or bathroom, quite another on a plinth in an art exhibition, demonstrating that where things were seen changed how they were understood. Duchamp had taken something mundane and, by reframing it, had revealed its aesthetic dimension.

Duchamp engaged in many other demonstrations and attacks on traditional aesthetics. He retouched a poster of Leonardo da Vinci's *Mona Lisa* (see fig. 13.15), adding a mustache and goatee, and a series of letters which, when pronounced phonetically result in an off-color pun. Duchamp used puns in many of his works because he thought that wordplay undermined the stability of meaning, and in so doing encouraged new ways of seeing.

SURREALISM

The spirit of the *avant-garde* continued to thrive after the war. Paris was its center, "the laboratory of ideas in the arts," as the American poet Ezra Pound put it. Tristan Tzara organized a massive Dada festival in Paris in 1920. In May 1917, Diaghilev's Ballets Russes performed *Parade*, a dance with music by French composer Eric Satie and complete with the sounds of dynamos, sirens, express trains, airplanes, and typewriters. The stage set was designed by Picasso.The whole creation seemed to the poet Guillaume Apollinaire like the space of a *sur-réalisme*, or "super-realism."

In 1924, the poet André Breton appropriated the word *sur-réalisme* to name his own new movement in the arts. Delighting in the irrational, and its lack of "aesthetic or moral concern," **Surrealism** was indebted to Dada. Where it differed was in its fascination with the realm of dreams, supported by a willful misunderstanding of Freud. Where Freud considered neurosis as an illness demanding psychoanalysis and cure, Breton found it liberating. The neurotic person, for Breton, was free to behave in any manner, and the dreams opened up whole new vistas of subject matter, many of them previously taboo.

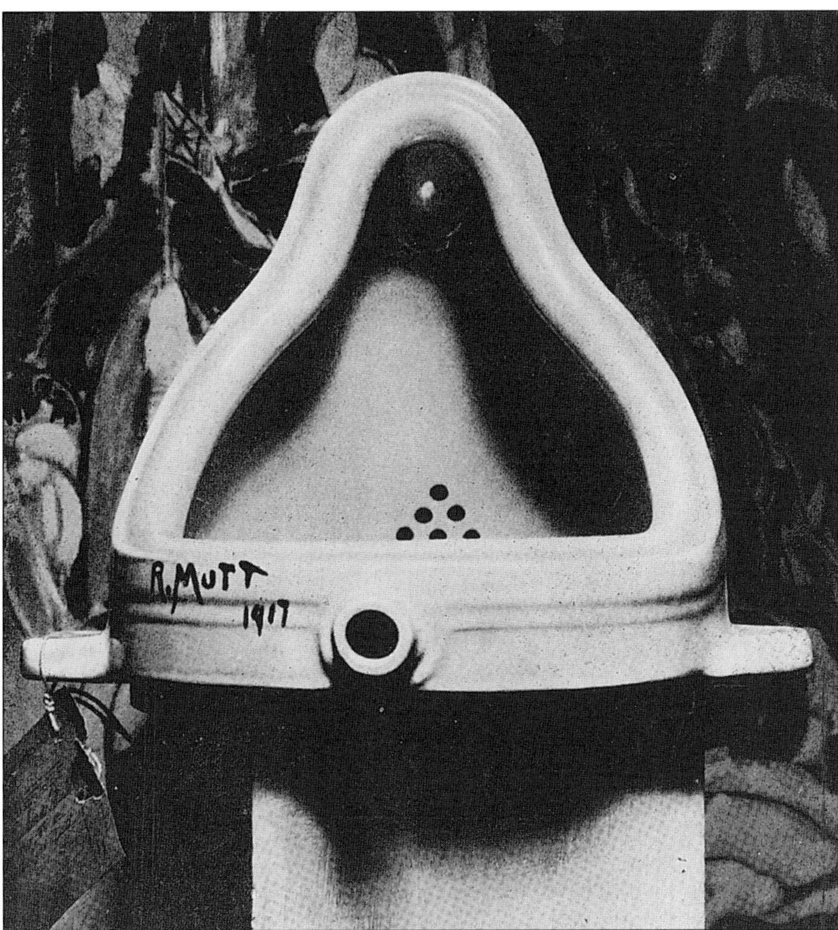

FIGURE 22.10 Marcel Duchamp, *The Fountain*, 1917, height $24\frac{5}{8}''$ (62.2 cm), Fountain by R. Mutt. Glazed sanitary china with black paint. Photograph by Alfred Stieglitz in *The Blind Man, no. 2*, May 1917; original lost. © Philadelphia Museum of Art: The Louise and Walter Arensberg Collection. 1998-74-1 © 2003 Artists Rights Society (ARS), New York/ADAGP, Paris/Estate of Marcel Duchamp. Duchamp argued that he "created a new thought for that object" by forcing the viewer to see it in a new context. He labeled such works "ready-mades."

There were two approaches to this new subject matter: one abstract, the other representational. The abstract vein was based on Breton's notion of psychic **automatism**—that is, drawing liberated from the necessity of plan. Surrealists, according to this idea, should accept any apparent accident as psychologically predetermined and therefore revelatory. The second approach was focused on representing the world of dreams accurately, deliberately, and particularly without self-censorship.

Joan Miró. One of the practitioners of automatism is JOAN MIRO [mee-ROH] (1893–1983). Although Miró never called himself a Surrealist, he acknowledged the Surrealist influence on his art. Soon after arriving in Paris from his native Spain in 1922, he was, he said, "carried away" by their example, and by 1925 "was drawing almost entirely from hallucinations. At the time I was living on a few dried figs a day."

His *Painting* (fig. 22.11) of 1933 is a rendering of machine forms he saw in a catalog, transformed into abstract shapes, more organic than mechanical. The two bands of color in the background create a landscape, which the forms inhabit, existing at the very edge of rational thought.

FIGURE 22.11 Joan Miró, *Painting*, 1933, oil on canvas, $4'3\frac{1}{4}'' \times 5'3\frac{1}{2}''$ (1.30 × 1.61 m), Courtesy Wadsworth Atheneum, Hartford, Connecticut. © 2005 Artists Rights Society (ARS) NY. ADAGP, Paris/DACS, London 1998. One of the reasons this painting, when it is seen in real life, seems so alive, as if inhabited by abstract creatures, is that it is very large, so the forms depicted in it are on a human scale.

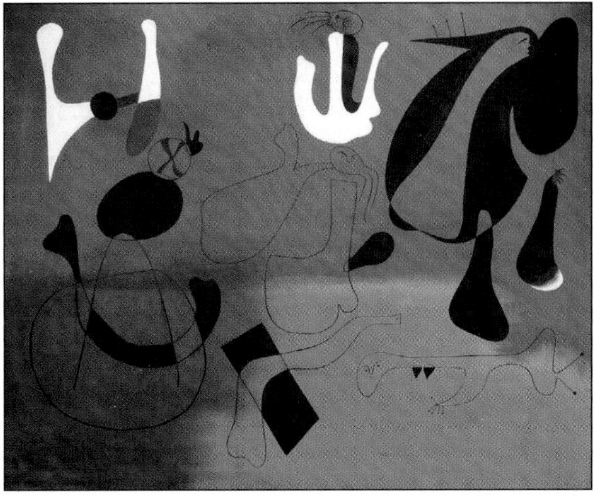

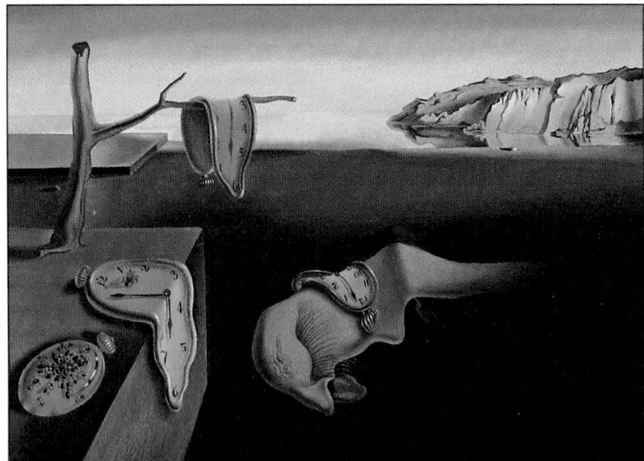

FIGURE 22.12 Salvador Dali, *The Persistence of Memory*, 1931, oil on canvas, $9\frac{1}{2}'' \times 13''$ (24.1 × 33 cm). Digital Image © Museum of Modern Art/Licensed by Scala/Art Resource, NY. (162. 1934). Given anonymously. © 2002 Kingdom of Spain. © 2005 Salvador Dail, Gala-Salvador Dali Foundation/ Artists Rights Society (ARS), NY. Combining psychology and art, Surrealist artists sought to express the unconscious. Intentionally enigmatic and mysterious, Dali's painting depicts the impossible and irrational with absolute conviction.

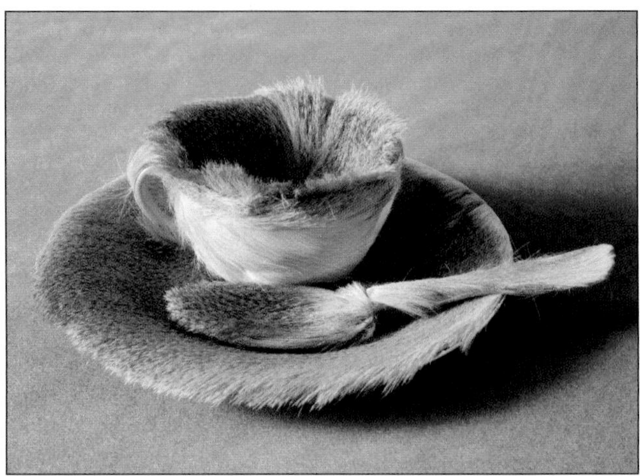

FIGURE 22.13 Méret Oppenheim, *Object (Le Déjeuner en Fourrure) (Luncheon in Fur)*, 1936, fur-covered cup, saucer, and spoon, diameter of saucer $9\frac{3}{8}''$ (23.7 cm), overall height $2\frac{7}{8}''$ (7.3 cm), Purchase. The Museum of Modern Art/Licenced by Scala-Art Resource, NY. © 2007 Artists Rights Society, NY. In this paradigm of the peculiar, this icon of incongruous materials, Oppenheim combined tableware and fur, making this one of the most memorable examples of Surrealist sculpture.

Salvador Dali. The most famous Surrealist is SALVADOR DALI [DAH-lee] (1904–1989), also from Spain, who arrived in Paris in 1929 and consciously invented himself as a Surrealist cult figure. He manipulated his foot-long mustache into various shapes. He claimed he could remember life in his mother's womb. He had himself buried and resurrected. Dali's life of irrational behavior garnered fame and fortune—highly rational results.

Dali's painting *The Persistence of Memory* (fig. 22.12), of 1931, depicts four watches that are limp, corroded by rust, and attacked by ants. What can this puzzling vision mean? Is time itself wilting, even as it causes decay and destruction? Has time become flexible, or is it distorted? Can the artist "bend time"? Is creativity a means to immortality? Can art defeat time? Such are the questions the painting seems to pose.

The slug-like object on the ground appears to be a distorted self-portrait. "I want to paint like a madman," Dali said. As he pointed out, if Surrealism were to investigate the unconscious, then it had to explore whatever the unconscious had to offer. In this painting and others, Dali depicted illogically juxtaposed objects, impossibly distorted forms, and undefined spatial settings. Yet when rendered with his meticulous technique, the inconceivable becomes real.

Méret Oppenheim. Surrealist artists did not limit themselves to painting. One of the best-known Surrealist works is the *Object (Le Déjeuner en Fourrure) (Luncheon in Fur)* (fig. 22.13), 1936, created by MÉRET OPPENHEIM [OP-pen-hime] (1913–1985). Born in Berlin, she moved to her mother's native Switzerland, and continued on to Rome when eighteen or nineteen years old, to study art. As Surrealist painters combined ordinary objects in extraordinary ways, Oppenheim combined the refined teacup, saucer, and spoon with the wildness of animal fur. This evokes the intentionally disturbing thought of drinking from a fur-lined cup: imagine the sensation of sipping tea through the fur of a Chinese gazelle. Or might the fur keep the tea warm? The title of the work, *Le Déjeuner en Fourrure*, was given by Andre Breton, one of the leaders of the Surrealists, as a reference to *Le Déjeuner sur l'herbe* painted by Manet in 1863 (fig. 17.18), which certainly disturbed the public when first exhibited. Oppenheim also created Surrealist drawings, paintings, sculptures, appliances, furniture, and clothing as well as poems and descriptions of dreams.

DE STIJL

If Dada represents a nihilistic reaction to World War I, **De Stijl** ("The Style" in Dutch), sometimes called **Neo-Plasticism,** represents an affirmative, hopeful response. Founded in 1917 in Holland, the movement sought to integrate painting, sculpture, architecture, and industrial design, and championed a "pure" abstraction. In the movement's first manifesto, the De Stijl artists wrote, "The war is destroying the old world with its contents. . . . The new art has brought forward what the new consciousness of the time contains: balance between the universal and the individual."

Piet Mondrian. The leading painter of the Neo-Plastic school was PIET MONDRIAN [MON-dree-on] (1872–1944). Dutch by birth, he moved to Paris in 1911 attracted by and turned his attention to Cubism, which he quickly took to its logical conclusion. When he returned to the Netherlands in 1914, where he stayed until the end of

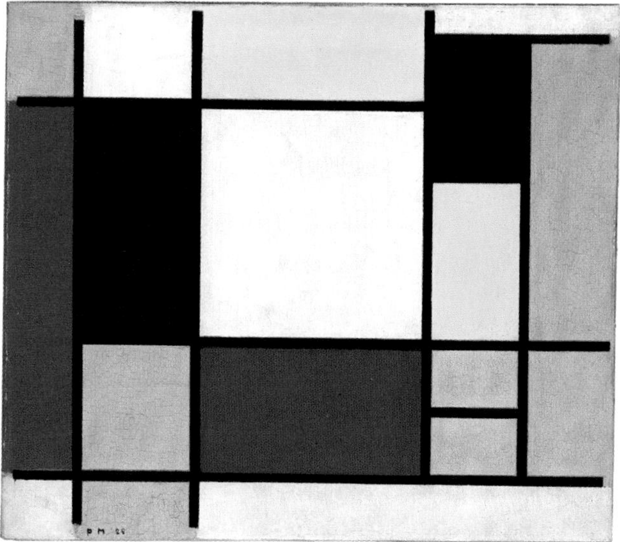

FIGURE 22.14 Piet Mondrian (1872–1944), *Composition with Yellow, Red, Black, Blue, and Grey*, 1920. Oil on canvas, $20\frac{1}{4}'' \times 24''$. Stedelijk Museum, Amsterdam. © 2011 Mondrian/Holtzman Trust c/o HCR International, Virgina. In 1917 Mondrian co-founded the journal *De Stijl* in which he published his book on Neoplasticism in the first 12 issues. The ideas expressed in the Journal attracted a group of artists who actively explored new ideas of artistic expression until the early 30's.

World War I, his work referred less and less to nature, until it finally became completely nonobjective and abstract.

By 1920, Mondrian had defined a mature style, as seen in *Composition with Yellow, Red, Black, Blue, and Grey* (fig. 22.14). Believing the flat plane was integral to painting and that it must be respected rather than falsified by perspective, and seeking perfection within strictly imposed limitations, Mondrian created a surface grid of horizontal and vertical lines; the rectangle and square are its basic shapes. The colors are restricted to the primary colors—red, yellow, and blue—plus black, white, and, in a few places, gray. Using these simple elements, Mondrian established a sense of balance. As he would assert, while writing about a drawing of this time, "If one does not represent things, a place remains for the Divine."

ABSTRACTION IN SCULPTURE

A number of sculptors sought to explore the possibilities of abstraction in three dimensions. They created shapes that were organic and fluid, suggesting natural forms. Thus their work appears mysterious and elemental, universal in its simplicity.

Constantin Brancusi. A Romanian who moved to Paris in 1904, CONSTANTIN BRANCUSI [Bran-KOO-zee] (1876–1957) "rediscovered" primitive sculpture while working with the Expressionist painters. Brancusi favored simple geometric forms—rectangles, ovals, and verticals. His *Bird in Space* (fig. 22.15), in polished bronze, for example, is an elongated vertical shape. Its purity of form does not depict a bird, but rather evokes the flight of the bird. The work is completely abstract; its expressive quality is completed by our knowing the title. "Don't look for obscure formulas or mystery," Brancusi said of his work. "It is pure joy that I am giving you."

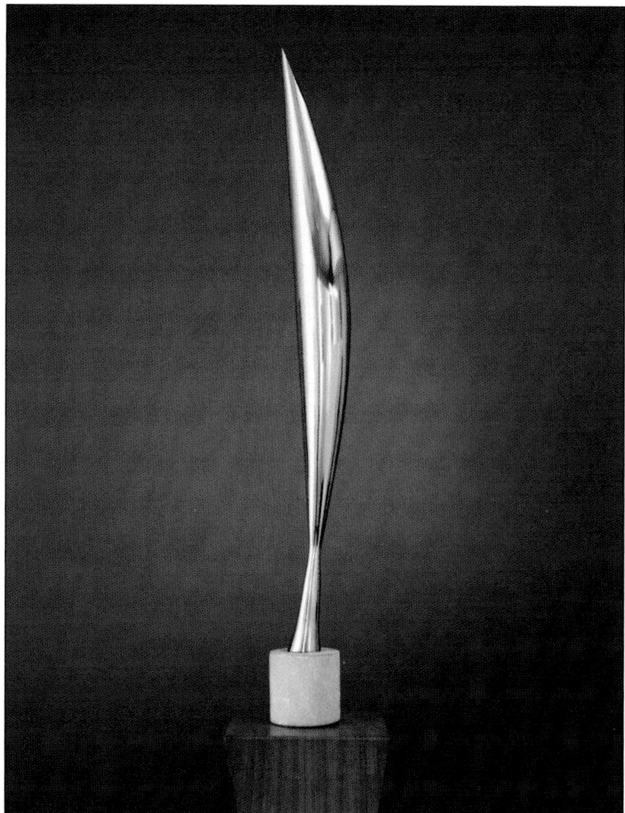

FIGURE 22.15 Constantin Brancusi, *Bird in Space*, 1920, bronze (unique cast), $54'' \times 8\frac{1}{2}'' \times 6\frac{1}{2}''$ (137.2 × 21.6 × 16.5 cm). Museum of Modern Art/Licensed by Scala-Art Resource, NY. Given anonymously. Photograph © 2000 The Museum of Modern Art, NY. © 2000 Artists Rights Society (ARS), New York ADAGP, Paris. One of Brancusi's *Bird in Space* sculptures was the center of a battle between Brancusi and the U.S. Customs Office in 1927. Customs officials called it "bric-à-brac" and said it should therefore be taxed, whereas Brancusi said it was a work of art and was thus duty free. Brancusi won—a victory for modern art, now officially recognized as abstract art.

Barbara Hepworth. The British sculptor Barbara Hepworth (1903–1975) perfected abstraction. Her *Three Forms* (fig. 22.16) was carved in 1935 of white serravezza marble. Hepworth's sculptures have a biological quality, as if nature created this organic abstraction of three egg-like ovoids, molding and shaping not only the masses but also the spaces between them. Hepworth said she was "absorbed . . . in tensions between forms." Although these forms are simplified to the point of severity, they are gently rounded, the surfaces perfectly finished.

Henry Moore. The human figure was the point of departure for British sculptor Henry Moore (1898–1986). Yet

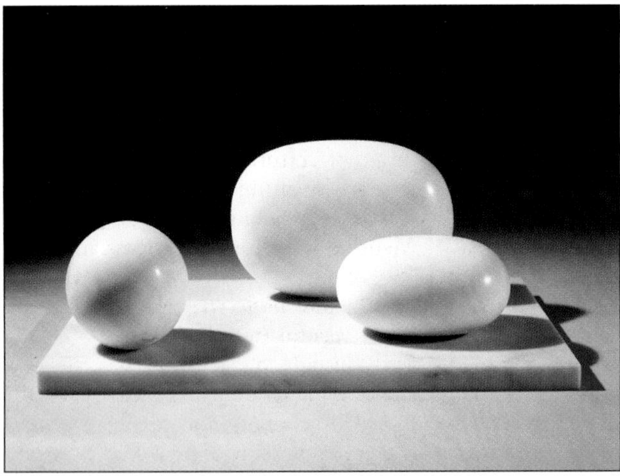

FIGURE 22.16 Barbara Hepworth, *Three Forms*, 1935, marble, Tate Gallery, London. Art Resource, NY. © Copyright Henry Moore Foundation. Hepworth created this soon after the birth of her triplets in 1934. Her work achieves a timelessness—primitive in its elemental simplicity, classical in its subtle refinement while simultaneously modern in its organic quality and tense spatial relationships.

Moore's figures are so simplified and abstract that they are barely identifiable, often appearing to be forms of nature, capable of growth but beaten by the elements. He admired prehistoric Stonehenge and similar forms eroded by nature and time. His *Recumbent Figure* (fig. 22.17), of 1938, looks weathered and suggests the power of natural forces at work. Moore's sculptures are often more effective when seen in a park than in a museum.

Moore's smooth flowing forms include large openings and hollows. He shapes the solids but gives equal importance to the voids. The masses can be viewed as "positive volumes" and the depressions and holes may be seen as "negative spaces."

FIGURE 22.17 Henry Moore, *Recumbent Figure*, 1938, green hornton stone, length 55″ (141 cm), Henry Moore Foundation/Tate Picture Gallery, London, UK. Moore's monumental figure, although in a classical reclining pose, appears to have been weathered into this organic shape.

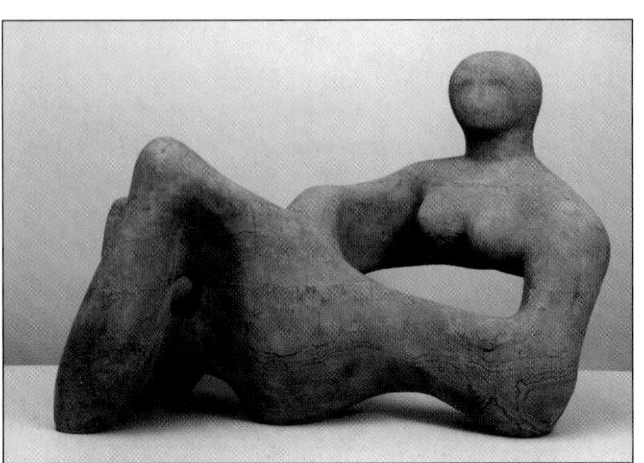

ARCHITECTURE

Unlike the other modern arts, in architecture a single **international style** developed over the first half of the twentieth century that almost all architects acknowledged, if not wholly accepted. The Museum of Modern Art in New York held an exhibition of modern architecture in 1932 that identified a new "International Style . . . based primarily on the nature of modern materials and structure . . . slender steel posts and beams, and concrete reinforced by steel." Many leading architects fled the worsening situation in Europe in the 1930s and came to the United States. The booming economic climate after the war called for many new buildings.

Walter Gropius. A leading architect in Germany before World War II, Walter Gropius (1883–1969) directed the **Bauhaus** art school in Dessau, Germany, and designed its chief buildings (fig. 22.18), built 1925–26. When Adolf Hitler closed the Bauhaus, Gropius moved to America and became the chair of the Architecture Department at Harvard University.

The main principle of the Bauhaus was to interrelate art, science, and technology so there was no dividing line between the fine arts, architecture, and industrially produced functional objects. The artist, the architect, the craftsperson, and the engineer were brought together.

The Bauhaus building is essentially a cage of glass. Its steel frame makes possible walls entirely of glass because the walls do not support the structure. The cornice at the top is not functionally necessary to protect a building of glass, steel, and concrete from the elements, but it is aesthetically necessary as a visual conclusion to the architectural composition, to frame the building.

FIGURE 22.18 Walter Gropius, Bauhaus, Dessau, Germany, 1925–26. Museum of Modern Art/Licensed by SCALA/Art Resource, NY. The Bauhaus (House of Building), closed by the Nazis in 1933, was a school that sought to adapt to the modern world by combining the methods and disciplines of fine art, craft, graphic design, architecture, and industry. Built of reinforced concrete, steel, and glass, the Bauhaus building itself looked like a painting by Mondrian made three dimensional.

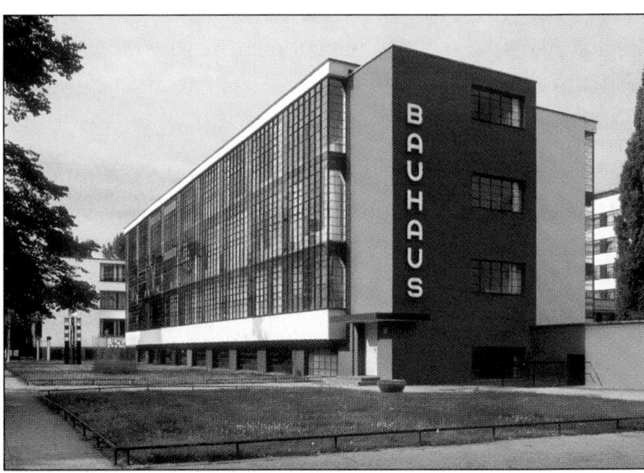

Cross Currents

RUSSIA AND THE WEST: THE BALLETS RUSSES

Ballet as a dance form did not originate in Russia, but it certainly flourished there. The most influential nineteenth-century choreographer in Russia was the French-born MARIUS PETIPA [PET-ee-pah] (1819–1910), who worked for the czar in St. Petersburg. Petipa collaborated with Tchaikovsky on both *Sleeping Beauty* and *The Nutcracker* to create two of the most popular ballets ever. After Petipa, Michel Fokine rose to prominence and became the principal choreographer of the Ballets Russes, a Russian dance company set up in Paris under the direction of the impresario SERGEI DIAGHILEV [dee-AHG-uh-LEF] (1872–1929), who was responsible for popularizing ballet throughout Europe.

Diaghilev set himself the goal of bringing Russian culture to the attention of the West, moving to Paris to do so. In 1906, he held a large-scale exhibition of Russian art, and in 1907, he began a series of concerts of Russian music. It was his presentation of Mussorgsky's *Boris Godunov* in 1908 that dazzled Western audiences with its originality and splendor. In 1909, he ventured a second season, which featured some ballets that included scenes from Borodin's opera *Prince Igor*, arranged for dancers rather than singers. The Russian ballerina Tamara Karsavina and her male counterpart, Vaslav Nijinsky, so stunned and enthralled Parisian audiences that they streamed onto the stage during the intermission of the first performance.

With dancers like Nijinsky and choreographers that included George Balanchine, and with set designs commissioned by painters such as Pablo Picasso and Henri Matisse, the Ballets Russes brought together a wealth of talent from a wide range of cultures and art forms. Composers who produced music for the Russian ballet included Claude Debussy, Maurice Ravel, and the Russian Serge Prokofiev.

The international acclaim of Russian ballet was furthered when George Balanchine defected from Russia in 1924 and eventually came to the United States in 1933 to choreograph. He founded and directed his own company, The New York City Ballet, and his own school. Here, Balanchine created a style of ballet that suited the American ethos—fast, sleek, conceptual, and thoroughly modern. During the communist era, many dancers, including Rudolf Nureyev and Mikhail Barishnikov, defected from the Soviet Union to enjoy the artistic freedom of the West, much to the delight of Western audiences.

Le Corbusier. Another influential architect of the international style was Charles Edouard Jeanneret, known as LE CORBUSIER [cor-BOO-see-ay] (1886–1965). The Savoye House in Poissy-sur-Seine in France (fig. 22.19), built 1929–30, is a private home that caused a revolution in domestic architecture. Corbusier called such houses he designed *machines à habiter* ("machines for living"), reflecting Corbusier's admiration for the neatness and precision of machines.

The Savoye House is elevated on stilts of **reinforced concrete.** Smooth walls in pure geometric shapes enclose space in an abstract composition of simple planes and clean lines, like a large sculpture that can be inhabited. Because the house is elevated, outsiders cannot see in, although the inhabitants can see out. The materials used are ornamental, without extraneous decoration.

Frank Lloyd Wright. The American Frank Lloyd Wright (1867–1959) believed that a building must be related to its site and blend with the terrain. Contrary to critics who call modern architecture "impersonal," Wright used the term "organic" to describe his buildings. Wright's best known home is Fallingwater, in Bear Run, Pennsylvania (fig. 22.20), built in 1936 for the Kaufmann family. The house projects out over a waterfall and blends into the rising cliffs of the landscape. Inside, Fallingwater is open and is oriented to the outdoors with windows that extend floor to ceiling. Walls are made of screens. The furniture, as in other Wright homes, is largely built-in.

FIGURE 22.19 Le Corbusier (Charles Edouard Jeanneret) Exterior. Villa Savoye, Poissy, France. Anthony Scibilia/Art Resource, NY. © 2001 Artists Rights Society (ARS), New York/ADAGP, Paris/FLC. Le Corbusier called the functional homes he designed *machines à habiter*—"machines for living." Made of reinforced concrete and glass in simple geometric shapes, this home is an example of the International Style of the 1920s.

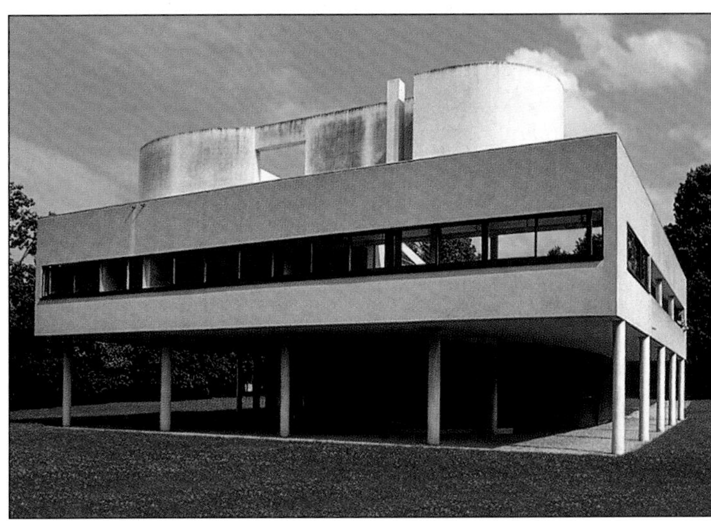

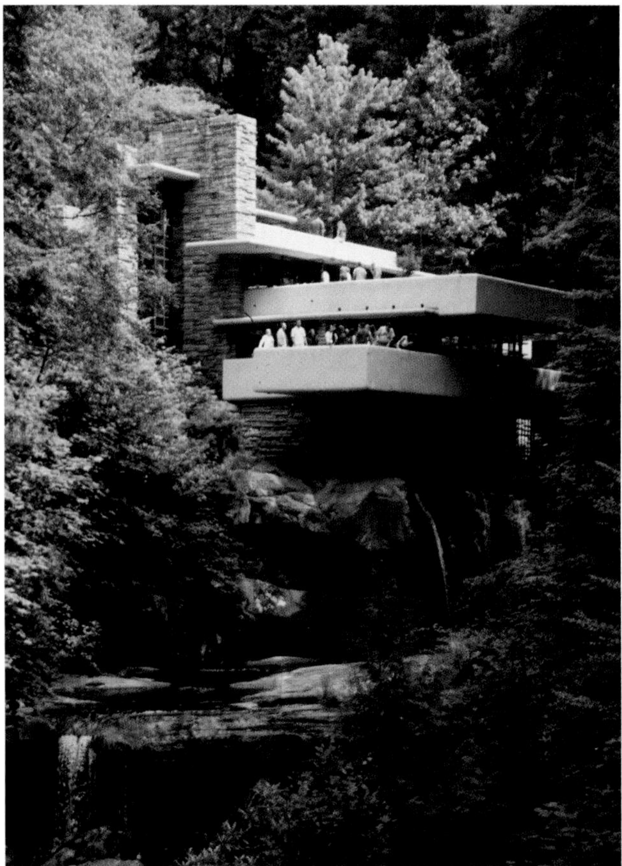

FIGURE 22.20 Frank Lloyd Wright, Fallingwater, Bear Run, Pennsylvania, 1936. Seeking to unite structure and site, Wright used cantilevered construction to build this home over a waterfall. As in contemporary painting and structure, solid and void are given equal consideration in this composition.

AMERICAN MODERNISM

In 1913, just before World War I, a number of American artists worked together to plan an International Exhibition of Modern Art at the 69th Street Regiment Armory, in New York City. Thousands of people jammed into what was soon known as "the Armory Show" to see the Post-Impressionist, Fauve, and Cubist works. Most visitors gawked at the show and ridiculed it, but some American artists were inspired, especially those who frequented the New York City gallery known simply as 291, run by Alfred Stieglitz.

Georgia O'Keeffe. Among the painters most influenced by Stieglitz's style was Georgia O'Keeffe (1887–1986). Born in Wisconsin, O'Keeffe was a student at the Art Institute of Chicago and the Art Students League in New York. When, in 1915, she sent Stieglitz a bundle of drawings and watercolors, he immediately exhibited them. They later married.

Favoring flowers and animal bones as her subjects, O'Keeffe is best known for the type of painting represented by *Yellow Calla* (fig. 22.21), of 1926, a large-scale abstraction of a natural form. *Yellow Calla* is a flower seen close up and painted large scale, emphasizing its abstract form and pattern. Simple yet carefully designed, O'Keeffe's painting makes use of shading to create filmy, translucent, fluttering forms that are rich and sensuous. Intrigued by light and color, she said, "Color is one of the great things in the world that makes life worth living to me." Although many saw sexual symbols in her work, O'Keeffe repeatedly made clear that this was not true. She was, she explained a painter of nature and of nature's forms and colors.

The same year she painted *Yellow Calla*, O'Keeffe began spending her summers near Taos, New Mexico. After Stieglitz's death in 1946, she moved there permanently. The forms of the desert Southwest became her primary subject matter and its colors her palette.

Charles Demuth. Among the other American artists championed by Stieglitz was Charles Demuth (1883–1935). Unlike O'Keeffe, whose primary interest was in natural forms and colors, Demuth was concerned with the architectural forms of the American scene. He reduced them to flat compositions in a manner reminiscent of the Cubist landscape paintings of Picasso and Braque. In *Aucassin and Nicolette* (fig. 22.22), of 1921, for instance, the geometric shapes of the industrial landscape near Demuth's home in Lancaster, Pennsylvania, are rendered in flat, hard-edged forms, the lines of which extend into the sky like facets on a polished gem.

MODERNIST LITERATURE

American expatriates flocked to Paris and Europe to escape Prohibition and other social restrictions at home. There, they discovered liberation from what they considered the stultifying Puritanism of America.

During and after the war, the most adventurous new writing in English was published in Paris: James Joyce's *Ulysses*, in 1922, banned for obscenity in America and Britain until 1933; T. S. Eliot's *The Waste Land*, in 1922; William Carlos Williams's prose and poetry *Spring and All*, in 1923; F. Scott Fitzgerald's *The Great Gatsby*, in 1925; Ezra Pound's first sixteen *Cantos*, in 1926; and Ernest Hemingway's *The Sun Also Rises*, also in 1926. It was Hemingway who defined the mood of what he called the "lost generation."

Ezra Pound and T. S. Eliot. Ezra Pound (1885–1972) and T. S. Eliot (1888–1965), two influential American Modernist poets, wrote complex, multifaceted poems that were technically innovative and densely allusive. Pound and Eliot relied heavily on rapidly shifting images, typically presented without explanation. Readers are left to make connections among the poems' images and allusions and to arrive at understanding for themselves.

Pound and Eliot are sometimes considered difficult for all but the most learned and experienced readers. Both poets believed poetry *should* be difficult, in part to reflect the difficulty of experience, especially that of World War I,

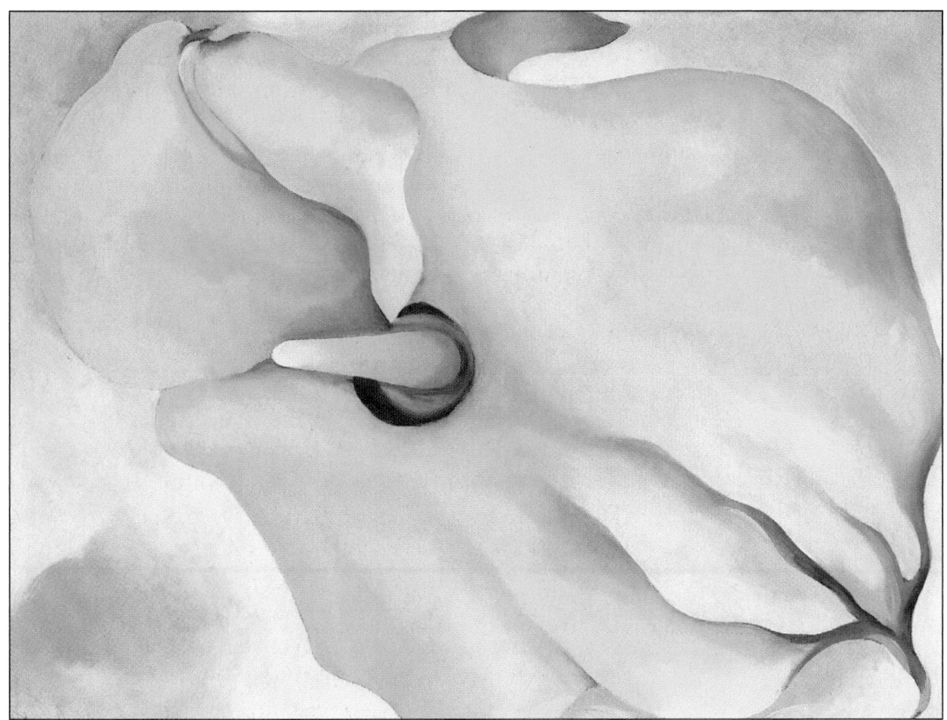

FIGURE 22.21 Georgia O'Keeffe, *Yellow Calla,* 1926, oil on fiberboard, 9″ × 12$\frac{3}{4}$″ (22.9 × 32.4 cm), Smithsonian American Art Museum, Washington, DC. Art Resource, NY. © 2005 Artists Rights Society (ARS), NY. Concerned with expressive organic abstractions of nature throughout her long career, O'Keeffe made it clear she was an artist—not a "woman artist."

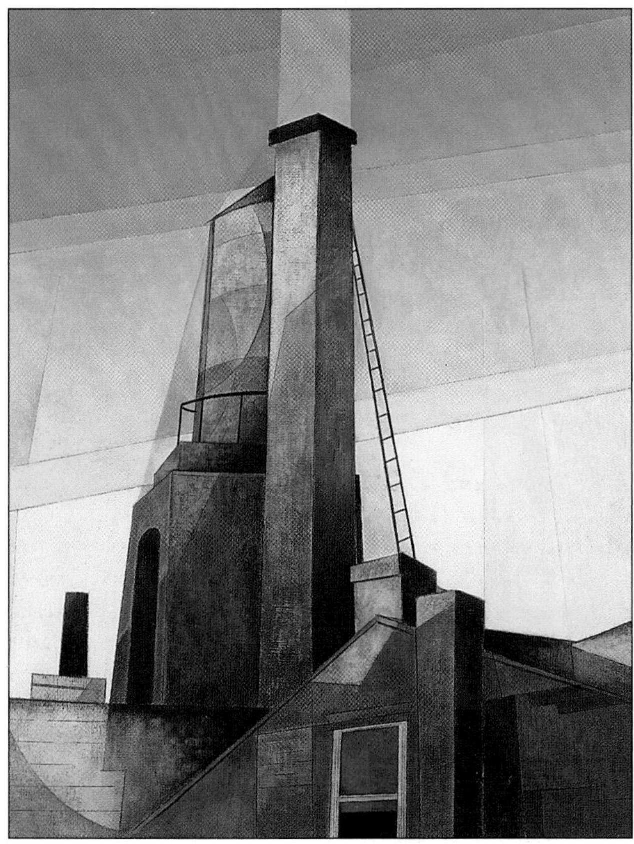

FIGURE 22.22 Charles Demuth, *Aucassin and Nicolette,* 1921, oil on canvas, 23$\frac{9}{16}$″ × 19$\frac{1}{9}$″ (59.8 × 49.5 cm), Gift of Ferdinand Howland. Columbus Museum of Art, Columbus, Ohio. The painting's ironic title, referring to the famous lovers of medieval romance, is attributed to another member of the Stieglitz circle during World War I, Marcel Duchamp. In fact, Demuth records the industrialization of rural Pennsylvania.

Connections

Graham and Noguchi: The Sculpture Of Dance

For the pioneer of modern dance Martha Graham (1894–1991), modern sculpture proved to be a useful way of thinking about the movement of the body in space. Dance was, for Graham, a trajectory into space, a composition of mass moving through void. She also perceived that set design could move from its position as backdrop to occupy the territory of the dance itself. Dancers could move in it, around it, over it, under it, through it, and beside it. They could lean on it, jump over it, hide behind it. Her dances showed humans interacting with art.

In 1935, for the dance *Frontier* (fig. 22.23), Graham initiated what was to be a long-lasting relationship with the Japanese sculptor Isamu Noguchi (1904–1988). (See Chapter 23, fig. 23.12.) Noguchi devised a simple fence, set at center stage, with two ropes attached to it, extending from each end of the fence forward and upward to the portals of the theater. This giant V shape created the illusion of space when viewed from a traditional, single-point perspective, receding in a steep plane toward a vanishing point below and behind the fence rail. "It's not the rope that is the sculpture," Noguchi later explained, "but the space that it creates that is the sculpture. It is an illusion of space. . . . It is in that spatial concept that Martha moves and creates her dances. In that sense, Martha is a sculptor herself." Graham herself forms the apex of the V as the dance opens, and as she moves forward and backward in front of the fence, it is as if she is in a vast landscape, the prairies and basins of the American frontier.

"Isamu Noguchi's vision of space," Graham later said, "and the integral meaning of his sculpture set me on a direction which sustained me throughout my career."

FIGURE 22.23 Martha Graham in *Frontier*, set by Isamu Noguchi, 1935. © ADAGP Paris and DACS, London 1998. Noguchi designed over thirty-five sets for Graham, this being his first. To create sculptural forms with her body, Graham had her costume designed with a full circle skirt to swoop and arc through the air, creating linear curves as she moved.

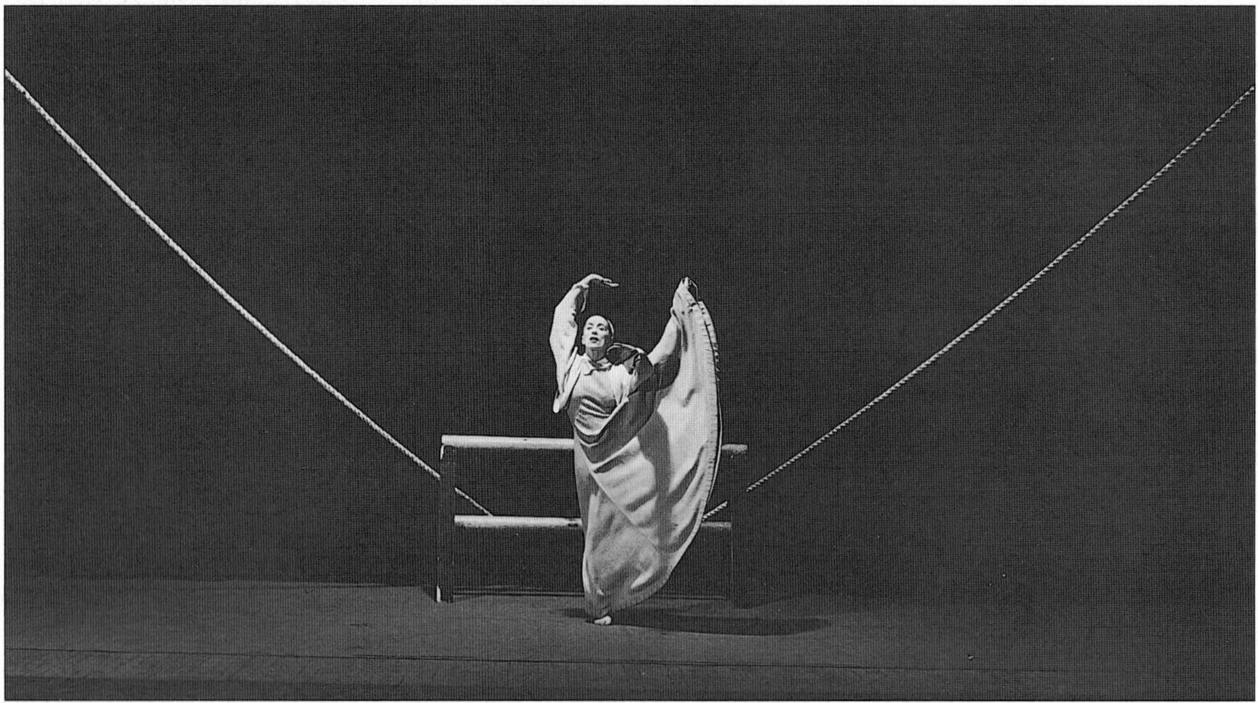

which Eliot once described as an "immense panorama of futility and anarchy." Eliot's most influential poem, *The Waste Land*, burst onto the literary scene in 1922. Eliot was aided in his work by his friend Ezra Pound, who cut more than a hundred lines from an early draft and suggested alterations to help unify the poem. In appreciation Eliot dedicated the poem to Pound and honored him further as *il miglior fabbro* ("the better maker").

"I had not thought death," Eliot writes in the poem, "had undone so many," speaking of the benumbed people inhabiting the "unreal city" of postwar London. To Eliot, London seemed as if it had been stricken by the gas warfare on the Western Front. His poem is but a holding action, to stop the bleeding, so to speak—"fragments I have shored against my ruin," as he describes it at poem's end.

Pound's early poetry is a concerted attack on World War I. The five-part "Hugh Selwyn Mauberley," published in 1920, ends with this indictment of the cause the soldiers had been fighting for:

There died a myriad,
And of the best, among them,
For an old bitch gone in the teeth,
For a botched civilization . . .

So disillusioned was Pound with the political and economic policies of England, France, and the other Allies that, when Mussolini took power in Italy in the early 1930s, he became one of his champions. Fascism, and the anti-Semitism that went with it, appealed to Pound, and he supported Mussolini throughout World War II. After the war he was imprisoned, tried for treason, and certified insane. For thirteen years, he was kept at St. Elizabeth's mental hospital in Washington, D.C. Finally, at the request of writers including Hemingway, Williams, and Eliot, he was released, and returned to Italy, where he died in 1972.

James Joyce. James Joyce (1882–1941) accomplished for modern fiction what T. S. Eliot did for modern poetry: He changed its direction by introducing startling innovations. Like Eliot, who employed abundant and wide-ranging literary and historical allusions in *The Waste Land*, Joyce, in his monumental *Ulysses*, published in the same year, complicated the texture and structure of his narrative with intricate mythic and literary references.

Joyce used a **stream of consciousness** narrative technique to take readers into the minds of his characters. His innovations include shifting abruptly from one character's mind to another; moving from description of an action to a character's response to it; mixing different styles and voices in a single paragraph or sentence; combining events from the past and the present in one passage. These and similar devices convey a sense of a mind alive, a consciousness that is absorbing and connecting the experiences it perceives—what one critic has described as "the shifting, kaleidoscopic nature of human awareness." In his *Portrait of the Artist as a Young Man*, for example, Joyce uses stream of consciousness to recreate the early memories of his protagonist partly by imitating the toddler's baby talk and partly by emphasizing the sights, smells, and tastes of a young child's consciousness. Despite the modernist style, Joyce still casts his novel in the tradition of the *bildungsroman*, or the novel of education, the preferred genre of eighteenth- and nineteenth-century novelists.

Ulysses grows out of the tradition of the nineteenth-century realist novel. Combining a microscopic factual accuracy in depicting Dublin with a rich language, it is an intricate recreation of the events of one day (June 16, 1904) in the life of Leopold Bloom. Organized into eighteen increasingly complex chapters, it echoes major events in Homer's *Odyssey*.

Virginia Woolf. As James Joyce was experimenting with techniques in fiction, Virginia Woolf (1882–1941), one of the founders of the Bloomsbury group in London, was developing ways of rendering a literary character's inner thoughts. Both writers explored techniques for conveying stream of consciousness, the representation of the flow of mental impressions and perceptions through an individual's consciousness, conveying a sense of his or her subjective psychic reality. Woolf, in particular, was interested in revealing a character's inner being through what that character thinks and feels, rather than what that character says or does.

Mrs. Dalloway (1925) and *To the Lighthouse* (1927) are two of Woolf's novels that illustrate her use of the stream of consciousness technique. Like Joyce, Woolf in *Mrs. Dalloway* focuses on a single day in the life of a person, in this case a middle-aged Englishwoman, Clarissa Dalloway. Readers overhear Mrs. Dalloway's thoughts and feelings as she reflects on her life, especially her marriage. External events are indicated only through the characters' subjective impressions of them. The novel's point of view shifts among a series of characters, including Septimus Warren Smith, a shell-shocked war veteran, who functions, to a certain extent, as her alter ego.

In *To the Lighthouse*, Woolf commemorates her mother Julia Stephen, who had died in 1895. The novel explores aspects of gender and sexual difference by contrasting Mrs. Ramsay, the book's central character, with her husband, a philosopher. Another central character, Lily Briscoe, is an artist who paints a portrait of Mrs. Ramsay. As critic Lyall Gordon notes, "The artist behind her easel, the biographer behind her novel reproduce the action of the lighthouse: together they light up a woman's uncharted nature." *To the Lighthouse* is a masterpiece of literary modernism, full of the subjective experiences of a central character who is at odds with the world, and replete with poetic symbols that reveal the character's true nature.

Ernest Hemingway. One of the most imitated American writers, Ernest Hemingway (1899–1961) wrote novels and

Then & Now

ROBIN HOOD AT THE MOVIES

The adventures of Robin Hood are often retold in movies, and Robin Hood is one of the most popular screen characters of all time. When the 1938 version, *The Adventures of Robin Hood*, appeared, audiences raved about the charismatic Errol Flynn as Robin Hood and Olivia de Haviland as the demure Maid Marian.

An earlier version had been made in 1922 with Douglas Fairbanks and Mary Pickford, two of the four co-founders of United Artists. It ran 170 minutes, long for a silent film. It cost over $1.5 million—unheard of in 1922; even Warner Brothers lavished only $2 million on the Flynn remake in 1938.

The Warner Brothers version, in 1938, added sound and color, and Robin Hood came to life. Filmed in Technicolor, it contained deep blacks, dark purples, and luscious greens, and utilized stunning contrasts of light and dark that dazzled audiences. The addition of sound made it possible to speed up the pace, since a silent film required many stills of narrative and dialogue.

Perhaps the greatest contrast between the two early versions lies in the change in the country's ethos and in the studio system's effort to promote Errol Flynn as the embodiment of the hero. In the depressed 1930s, Americans needed a man who "steals from the rich to give to the poor." Flynn's flashing smile and good looks reinforced the appeal. When the film was released, newspapers and magazines covered it, radio shows dramatized parts of the story, and a paperback edition was published with Errol Flynn as Robin Hood on the cover.

Over the years, new versions have been produced. Disney created an animated feature in 1973 in which Robin Hood is a fox. Mel Brooks spoofed the legend in *Robin Hood: Men in Tights* (1993). Brooks's film parodied a previous film, *Robin Hood: Prince of Thieves* (1991), directed by Kevin Costner, in which Robin and his band of Merry Men are portrayed as politically correct rebels.

short stories in a manner that came to characterize one pole of the modern fictional idiom. His language is laconic and spare. His plots are simple. The complexity of his fiction lies in its suggestiveness, in the implications of what is said and of what is left unspoken. Hemingway believed fiction should reveal less rather than more, like an iceberg with only its tip exposed above water.

Thus Hemingway's style, tone, and manner provide the index to his literary achievement. His first significant book, *In Our Time* (1925), is a series of sketches depicting the realities of war and the violence, skill, and grace of bullfighting. The book's eighteen vignettes range in length from a paragraph to a page. The following is a typical example.

INTERCHAPTER VII

While the bombardment was knocking the trench to pieces at Fossalta, he lay very flat and sweated and prayed oh Jesus christ get me out of here. Dear Jesus please get me out. Christ please please please christ. If you'll only keep me from getting killed I'll do anything you say. I believe in you and I'll tell every one in the world that you are the only one that matters. Please please dear jesus. The shelling moved further up the line. We went to work on the trench and in the morning the sun came up and the day was hot and muggy and cheerful and quiet. The next night back at Mestre he did not tell the girl he went upstairs with at the Villa Rossa about Jesus. And he never told anybody.

Concise and direct, this sketch is remarkable for its modernist assumptions. An unglamorous pair of incidents demythologizes war, love, and religion. Instead of courage, there is fear; instead of love, a casual encounter with a prostitute. And instead of religious faith, the narrator bargains with a God he forgets once he is out of danger. In a few swift strokes, Hemingway delineates the modern attitude, so different from the past.

Franz Kafka. The fiction of Franz Kafka (1883–1924) does not form part of a school; nor does it represent a particular type of technical innovation. Kafka's fiction is so distinctive—a blend of the real and the fanciful, the ordinary and the fantastic—that a word has been coined to characterize it: *Kafkaesque.* This term also refers to nightmarish events that wheel out of control and to individuals who, driven by guilt and anxiety, experience a sense of alienation and helplessness in the face of forces they can neither explain nor control. Kafka's is a frightening universe, one in which characters suffer without cause, looking for answers they never find.

Despite the small output, Kafka's writings loom large in modern literature. His three novels, *The Trial* (1925), *The Castle* (1926), and *Amerika* (1927), were all published posthumously—against his wishes, for he had left instructions that his manuscripts be destroyed. The best known of these, *The Trial,* is the only one that contains an ending. Its beginning, one of the most frightening in modern literature, presents Joseph K., a man accused of a crime whose nature is never revealed to him. As he awaits his trial and execution one year later, Joseph K. tries to understand what has happened to him, eventually coming to believe in his guilt. He gradually realizes his guilt or innocence is immaterial, since he feels he deserves his punishment. Kafka renders a world riddled with anxiety and incomprehension, irrational, absurd, confused, lonely, and lost.

RUSSIAN FILM

SERGEI EISENSTEIN [EYE-zen-stine] (1898–1948) was a film theorist as well as a film director. His wide-ranging knowledge of history, philosophy, science, and the arts is reflected in his films. For Eisenstein, film was the most complete of the arts. It included all the various artistic expressions of conflict—the kinetic conflict of dance, the visual conflict of painting, the verbal conflict of literature and theater, and the conflicts of character essential to fiction and drama.

Eisenstein built his films shot by shot and frame by frame, calculating the dramatic tension until it finally exploded on film. Eisenstein achieved striking effects with lighting, time lapses, designs, and backgrounds in various camera shots, using narratives that were loosely structured and episodic in construction.

In his silent film *Battleship Potemkin*, first shown in 1926, Eisenstein dramatizes the mutiny on board the czarist ship *Potemkin* in 1905, and the ensuing street demonstrations in the port of Odessa. Eisenstein was commissioned to make the film as part of the twentieth anniversary celebrations of the 1905 Revolution. Eisenstein structures his film like a symphony. The first section presents the bloody mutiny and the conditions that precipitated it. The second provides a respite as the ship drops anchor in the harbor after the revolt. Following this lull, a third section focuses on the people of Odessa. Here Eisenstein creates his most brilliant editing effects, alternating between the panic-stricken and defenseless masses who support the mutinous sailors and the Cossack soldiers, armed with bayonets, who march relentlessly through the crowd, massacring those who fall in their path. The final section shows the ship returning to sea, with cheers coming from other ships in the fleet. It marks a call to action.

Eisenstein's Odessa sequence (fig. 22.24) includes a formal technique called **montage**, a set of impressions

FIGURE 22.24 These consecutive film stills from Sergei Eisenstein's *Battleship Potemkin* (1924) reveal the director's dramatic use of close-up and the contrast between human and inanimate images.

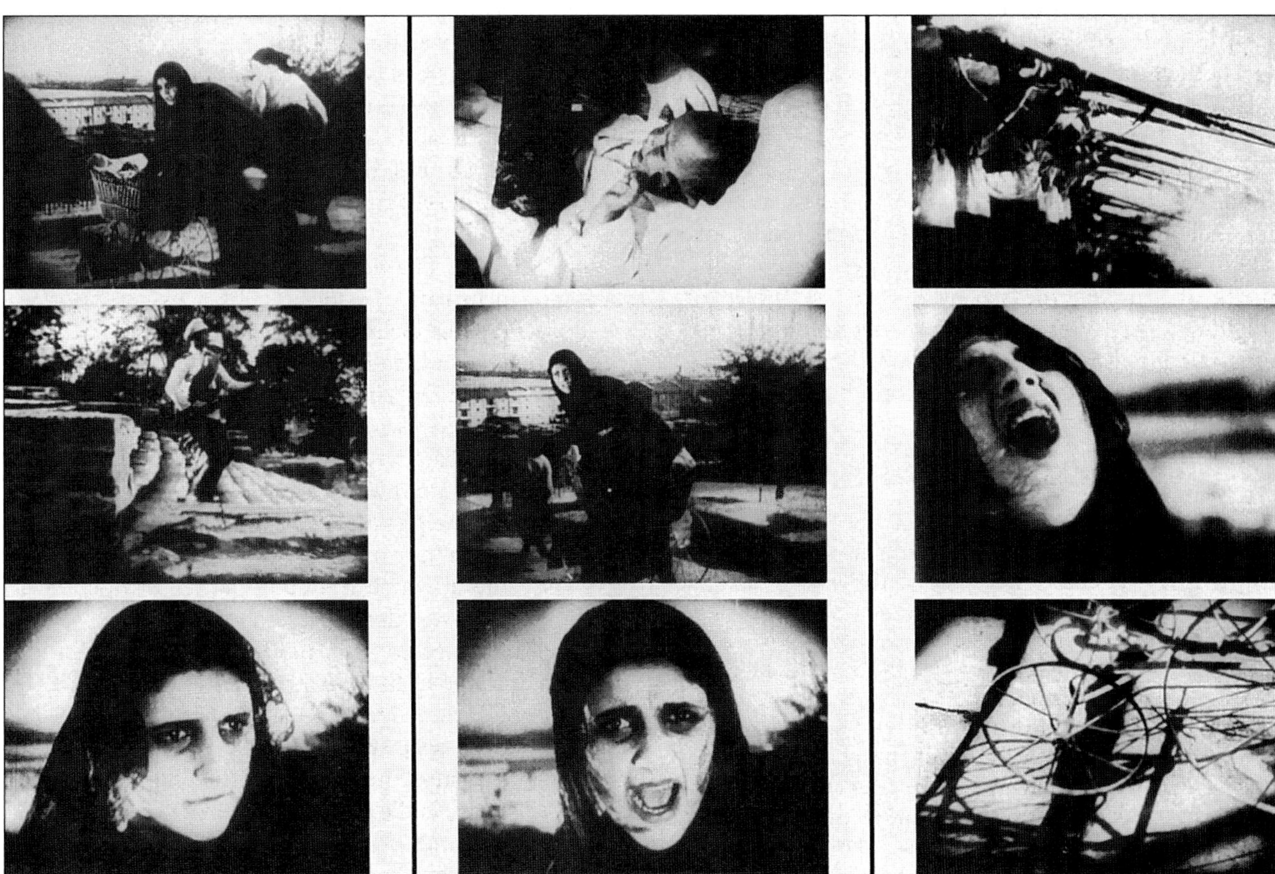

edited to achieve dramatic effect or, here, to increase tension to the point of "emotional saturation." Eisenstein believed viewer tension would find release in an emotional bonding with the victims depicted on screen. Yet, for all its innovations, the film is intentional propaganda and was made to legitimize and celebrate the revolution.

MODERN MUSIC

Music too embodied the discord and disharmony of this anxious age. Before the war, Stravinsky's *The Rite of Spring* had shaken the foundations of tonality, and hence traditional harmony. Stravinsky's use of multiple tonal centers created dissonance and harmonic disorientation. Fleeing to Switzerland during the war, and returning to Paris in 1920, Stravinsky began work on a new ballet for Diaghilev, entitled *Pulcinella.* Taking a number of sonatas by Classical composers, Stravinsky reworked their harmonies to make them dissonant, changed their phrase lengths to make them irregular, and altered their rhythms to make them lively and syncopated. "*Pulcinella,*" he would later admit, "was my discovery of the past." But his was a past thoroughly modernized.

Arnold Schoenberg. The Viennese composer ARNOLD SCHOENBERG [SHONE-berg] (1874–1951) undermined the stability of Western classical music even further by writing music that lacked a *tonal center,* or home key. **Atonality,** he called it. Much of this work was done before the war and badly received. He was convinced tonality was a "straitjacket," but also realized that atonality was structureless. Consequently, he developed a twelve-tone musical scale, as used in the *Variations for Orchestra* (1931). The twelve-tone scale was based on the traditional octave, counting all the half steps. Twelve-tone composition would "level" each tone, giving none more weight than any other, by predetermining the order in which the tones would be played. This order would be used for the entire composition, sequence after sequence.

The music is difficult to listen to for audiences accustomed to traditional harmony, but, given the proper theme, it can be moving. Jewish by birth, Schoenberg based many of his works on Jewish liturgy, including his opera *Moses und Aaron* (1923), which is based on a single twelve-tone series. For a taste of Schoenberg's actual music a decade earlier, the accompanying CD includes one of his six little piano pieces.

Schoenberg may be the most famous composer whose music hardly anyone hears. Along with Igor Stravinsky, the most influential composer of the twentieth century, Schoenberg is far less popular and considerably less appealing musically than Stravinsky. However, his fearless spirit and indomitability in the face of criticism and misunderstanding mark him as a daring artist willing to take risks in spite of the controversy his music created.

REPRESSION AND DEPRESSION: THE THIRTIES

World War I was meant to be "the war to end all wars." Instead it left a sense of disillusionment and fear that led many to crave security. Some found security in authoritarian leadership and in inflated national pride, which blamed adverse conditions on others. Although the end of the war brought a semblance of peace, it did not bring harmony. As the Russian communist experiment took hold, it threatened other nations. Workers throughout Europe looked to the Russian communists for a new vision and identity. When worldwide economic depression struck in 1929, simplistic explanations, such as blaming bankers for all economic woes, appealed to many.

FASCISM IN EUROPE

Benito Mussolini. In many respects, BENITO MUSSOLINI [moo-soh-LEE-nee] (1883–1945) is responsible for the invention of fascism, which was first established in Italy. Expelled from the Italian Socialist Party for advocating Italian entry into World War I, Mussolini formed groups of so-called *fasci* (from the Latin word for the bundle of rods that symbolize the Roman Republic). These groups consisted of young men like himself who called for Italy's entry into the war in 1915.

Mussolini's power base expanded rapidly after the war. He organized Italians who were dissatisfied with the government and who opposed the socialist cause as Bolshevik. Mussolini's fascist bands, with the support of the Italian police, openly attacked labor union offices, opposition newspapers, and antifascist politicians. Nearly two thousand people were killed between October 1920 and October 1922. Meanwhile, Mussolini gained power, and on October 29, 1922, he was named premier. By the late 1920s, the government was totally controlled by the Fascist Party, and Mussolini had become more dictator than premier, both head of the party and chief of state. He outlawed emigration, advocated the largest possible families by reducing taxes with each successive child, and taxed bachelors in an attempt to encourage them to marry. His dream was to create, in a single generation, a huge Italian army and a country thoroughly loyal to the goals of the fascist state. Education, from textbooks to professors, became a propaganda arm of the government itself. The police sought out dissenters and eliminated them.

Adolf Hitler. Meanwhile, the fascist approach to government spread to Germany, where Adolf Hitler (1889–1945) took advantage of public despair over the state of Germany's economy after World War I. In 1923, the value of the German currency decreased from a few thousand marks to the dollar to literally trillions of marks to the dollar by the end of the year. Lifetime savings were suddenly worthless. Workers found themselves earning starvation wages as even the price of bread rocketed. In Munich, Adolf Hitler created the National Socialist Party of the German Workers—the **Nazi** (abbreviation for "National Socialist") Party.

In 1921, Hitler named himself *fuhrer* (or leader) of the Nazi Party. He became chancellor of the Nazi Party in January 1933, backed by the party's new *Schutzstaffel*, or *SS* (literally, "Defense Force"), an elite honor guard, and by the *Sturmabteilung*, or *SA* (literally, "Storm Troops"), a huge private army. A month later, a fire broke out in the Reichstag, the central buildings of German government, and Hitler quickly blamed it on the communists. By noon the next day, four thousand members of the Communist Party had been arrested, and their citizenship rights had been suspended.

In August 1934, Hitler became president and chancellor of Germany. Every political party that opposed him was banned. Like Mussolini in Italy, Hitler was convinced the Bolsheviks were responsible for the catastrophic state of the German economy. The Jews became Hitler's primary target. The "Nuremberg Laws" of September 1935 defined a Jew as anyone with one Jewish grandparent. It denounced marriage between Jews and non-Jews as "racial pollution" and prohibited it. Jews were forbidden to teach in educational institutions and were banned from writing, publishing, acting, painting, and performing music. Nor were they allowed to work in hospitals or banks, bookstores or law offices. In November 1938, after a seventeen-year-old Jewish boy shot and killed the secretary of the German Embassy in Paris, mobs looted and burned Jewish shops and synagogues all over Germany. They swept through the streets, entering Jewish homes, beating the occupants, and stealing their possessions. After this night, known as *Kristallnacht* (literally, "Night of Glass"), the extent of German anti-Semitism was apparent to the world.

MAP 22.2 Left- and right-wing Europe, 1918–39.

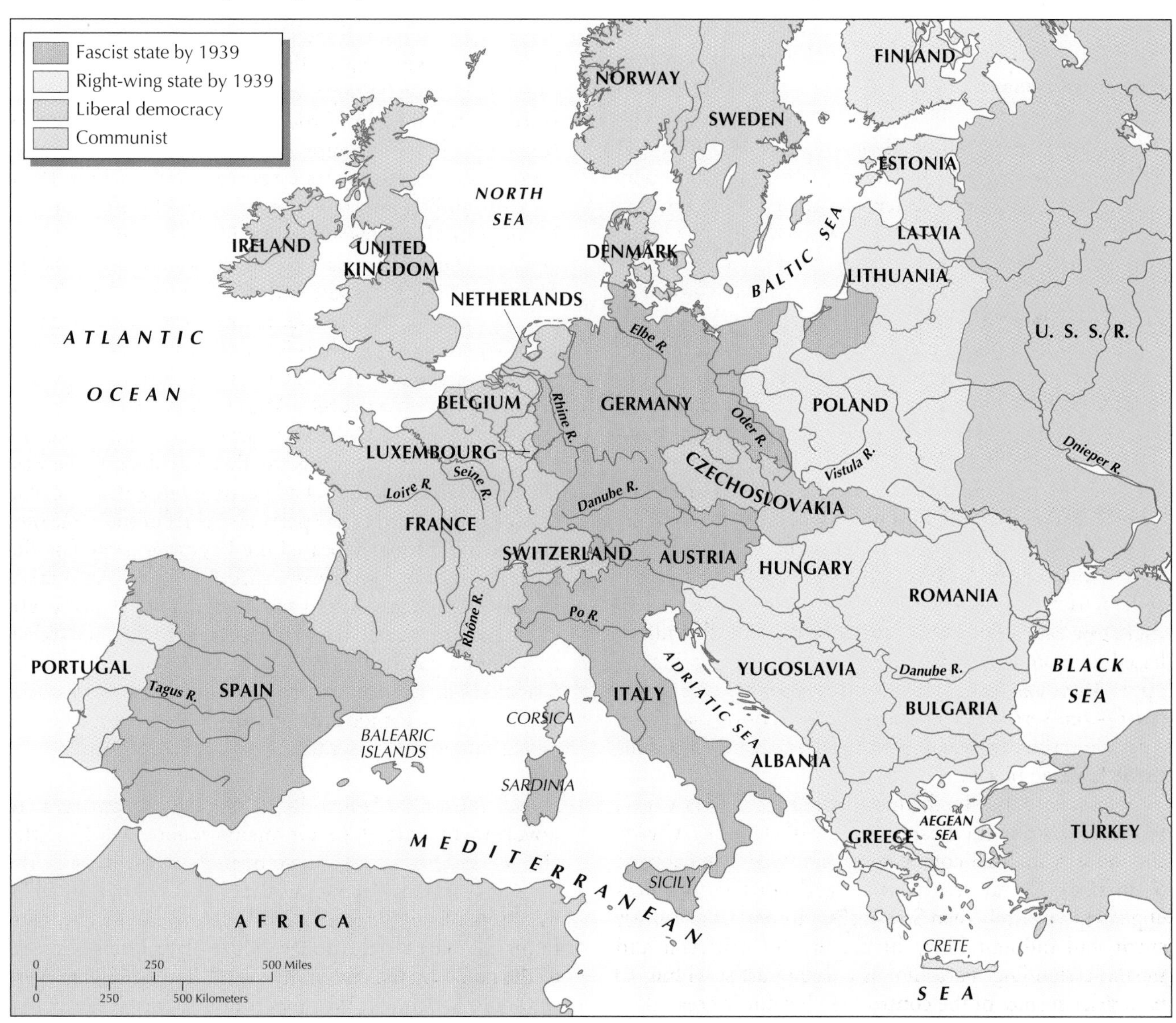

From the beginning, Hitler's Nazi Party was militaristic in its discipline, organization, and goals. Nazis were proponents of the policy of ***Lebensraum*** ("living space"), which they claimed justified the geographic expansion of the state into other countries' territories to make room for what they believed was the "superior" German race of people. By the mid-1930s, Hitler was preparing for war.

Francisco Franco. Spain had been in disarray since the king's overthrow in 1931. Spain's Popular Front, consisting of a coalition of Republicans, Socialists, labor unions, Communists, and anarchists, won an electoral victory in February 1936. Shortly thereafter, however, Spain's right formed the Falange ("Phalanx"), a coalition of monarchists, clerics (whose church schools had been closed), and the military, who desired to overthrow the new Republican government. At the Falange's head was General Francisco Franco (1892–1975), who on July 17, 1936, with his right-wing army, led a coordinated revolt in Spanish Morocco and in a number of towns in mainland Spain—Córdoba, Seville, and Burgos, among them.

The Spanish Civil War had begun. Within a few weeks, about a third of the country was under Franco's control, but Barcelona, Madrid, and Valencia remained Republican strongholds, as did the Basque provinces in the north. The Soviet Union supported the Republican cause, furnishing them with military advisers and organizing international brigades of volunteers (among them Ernest Hemingway).

Mussolini and Hitler supported Franco. Hitler even provided Franco with an air force. On April 26, 1937, Wolfram von Richthofen, the cousin of the German ace Manfred von Richthofen, the Red Baron of World War I, planned an attack on the town of Guernica in northern Spain, where Basque Republican forces were retreating. Beginning at half past four in the afternoon and lasting for three and a half hours, a strike force of thirty-three planes, each loaded with three thousand pounds of bombs, pummeled the city. By the time the fires subsided three days later, the town center had been razed to the ground—fifteen square blocks—and a thousand innocent citizens had been killed. As news of the event spread, Pablo Picasso, living in Paris, began work on a giant canvas commemorating the massacre, a disaster that foreshadowed the bombing of cities in World War II.

Guernica (fig. 22.25) is the culmination of Picasso's Surrealist style. Painted only in black, white, and grays, it contains a Pietà theme, and many elements of Surrealist dream symbolism. The horse, speared and dying in anguish, represents the fate of creativity. The entire scene is surveyed by a bull, which represents Spain and the bullfight—the struggle of life and death. The bull also represents the Minotaur, the bull-man of Greek mythology, which stands

FIGURE 22.25 Pablo Picasso, *Guernica*, 1937, oil on canvas, $11'5\frac{1}{2}'' \times 25'5\frac{1}{4}''$ (3.49 × 7.75 m). Museo Nacinal Centro de Arts Reina Sofia, Madrid, Spain. John Bigelow Taylor/Art Resource, NY. © 2007 Estate of Pablo Picasso/Artists Rights Society (ARS), NY. After Franco's victory in 1939, *Guernica* was exhibited at the Museum of Modern Art in New York where Picasso placed it on "extended loan." He did, however, affirm that the painting belonged "to the Spanish Republic," but he forbade its return to Spain until such time that democracy and "individual liberties" were restored there. With the death of Franco in 1975, the subsequent crowning of Juan Carlos as constitutional monarch in 1977, and the adoption of a democratic constitution in 1978, the painting was finally returned to Spain in 1981.

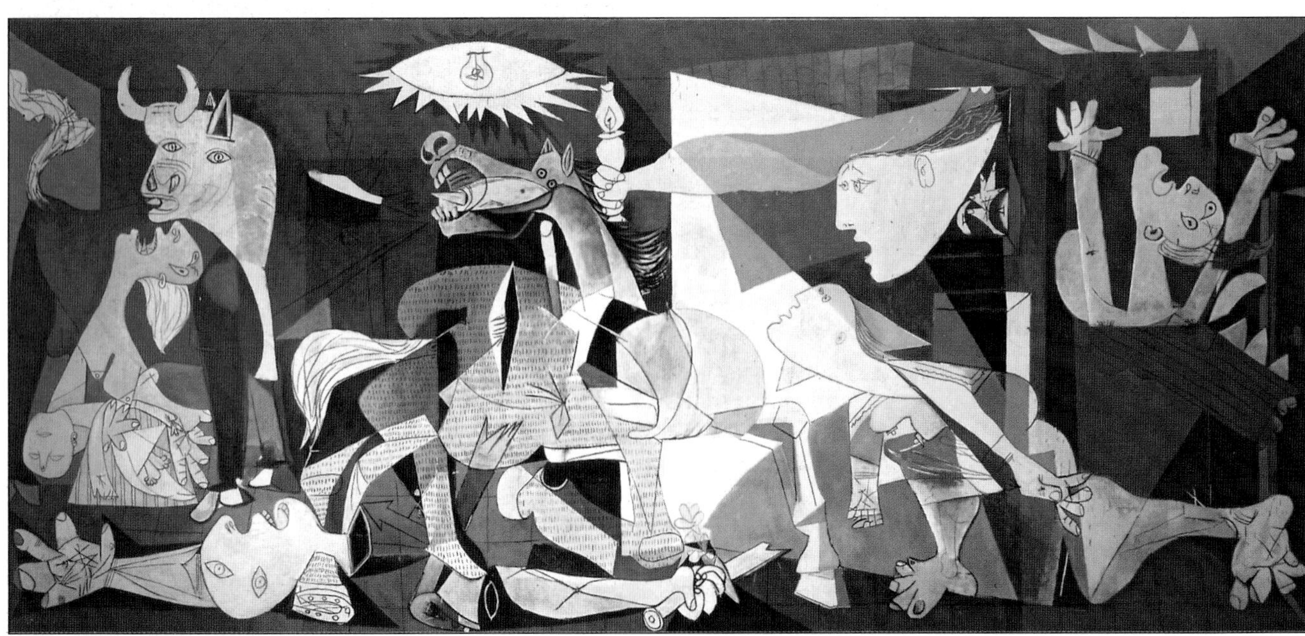

for the animalistic forces of the human psyche. The electric light bulb, at the top center of the painting, and the oil lamp, held by the woman reaching out of the window, have been much debated, and represent, on a fundamental level, old and new ways of seeing.

Franco captured the Republican strongholds of Madrid and Barcelona in 1939 and ruled Spain as a fascist dictator until his death in 1975. The attack on Guernica and other fascist victories in Spain outraged the Allies, but they proved to Hitler just how effective his military forces and tactics were. While the Spanish Civil War was winding down, Hitler sent troops into Czechoslovakia, in March 1939. Meeting with little or no resistance, shortly thereafter Hitler set his designs on Poland—and the world.

FRANKLIN DELANO ROOSEVELT AND THE NEW DEAL

Throughout the 1920s, the United States had enjoyed unprecedented prosperity, fueled by speculation on the stock market and the extraordinary expansion of the industrial infrastructure. For the first time in history, a country could define itself not as an agricultural society, nor as an industrial one, but as a consumer society. Houses, automobiles, and everyday goods were purchased on credit, in an almost unregulated economic climate. Unfortunately, this prosperity was built on a house of cards, and on October 29, 1929, it all came tumbling down in a stock market crash. Many of the wealthiest people in America were devastated, as $30 billion of assets disappeared within two weeks. Faced with massive withdrawals they could not sustain, banks closed. Families lost their life savings. By the early 1930s, over sixteen million American men were unemployed, nearly a third of the workforce. To make matters worse, whole areas of the Midwest suffered severe drought. The effect, exacerbated by overplowing, was the creation of a giant **Dust Bowl.** Whole populations left the hardest hit areas of Arkansas and Oklahoma for California, an exodus depicted by John Steinbeck in his novel *The Grapes of Wrath.*

Fearing that economic catastrophe would lead to the rise of fascism as seen in Europe, or worse, communism, the U.S. government decided to intervene. President Franklin Delano Roosevelt (1882–1945), or "FDR" as he was called, declared a bank holiday in 1933; gradually those institutions that were financially sound reopened. Roosevelt recognized that at the root of the **Depression** was a deep imbalance between the haves and the have-nots. He wanted to give the have-nots what he called a "New Deal." In 1935, a Social Security Act inaugurated unemployment insurance and old-age pensions. Tax codes were revised to increase the tax burden on wealthier Americans in an effort to close the gap. Agricultural subsidies were given to farmers to maintain agricultural production and to steady the economy. For the arts, the Works Progress Administration (WPA) was established to subsidize authors, artists, and musicians.

PHOTOGRAPHY AND THE FSA

To create a sense of national consensus for Roosevelt's social reforms, photographers were subsidized by the Farm Security Administration (FSA) to portray the plight of American farmers and sharecroppers devastated by Depression and drought.

Dorothea Lange. One of the photographers to be part of the plan was Dorothea Lange (1895–1965). Her documentary style, although seemingly objective, was driven by a social reformist impulse. Lange's most famous photograph, *Migrant Mother, Nipomo, California* (fig. 22.26), depicts a young widow with three of her ten forlorn children, migrants on the way to California, the sort that Steinbeck described. She stares into space, pensive and anxious, her glance avoiding the camera. She looks much older than her thirty-two years. Her children turn inward, seeking shelter beside their mother, who has none for herself. The picture's grainy gray tones complete the mood of resignation.

FIGURE 22.26 Dorothea Lange, *Migrant Mother; Nipomo, California*, 1936, gelatin silver print, Library of Congress, Washington, D C. Lange chose to include only three of the mother's ten children in this photograph because she did not want to add to widespread resentment in wealthier parts of American society about overpopulation among the poor.

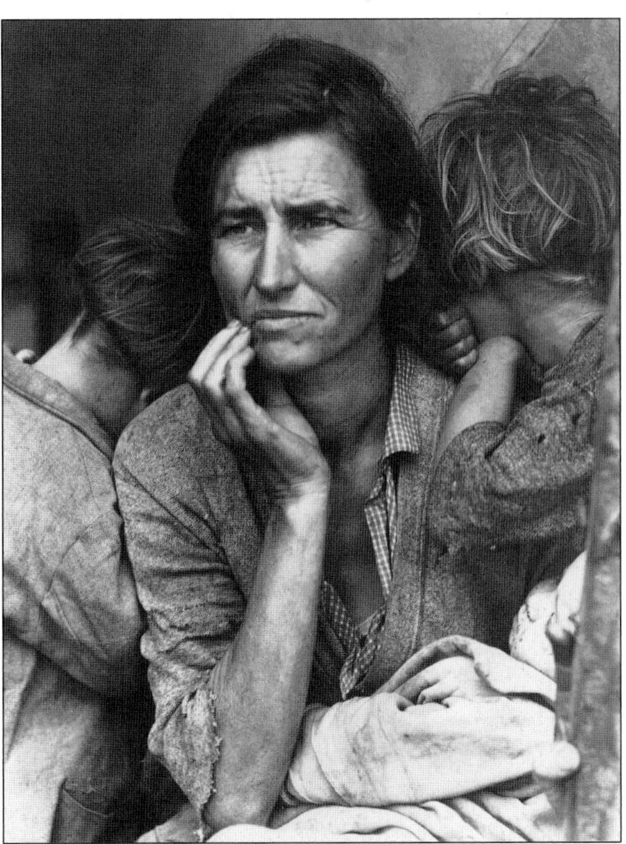

Walker Evans. Another FSA photographer, Walker Evans (1903–1975), is best known for his photographs for *Let Us Now Praise Famous Men* by James Agee published in 1941, which details Evans and Agee's life with a family of sharecroppers in Hale County, Alabama, in 1936. Agee's "famous" men are the forgotten people of poverty. He describes, for instance, the sharecroppers' house as nightfall creeps over it: "The house and all that was in it had now descended deep beneath the gradual spiral it had sunk through; it lay formal under the order of entire silence." Evans's *Washroom and Dining Area of Floyd Burroughs's Home, Hale County, Alabama* (fig. 22.27) is dominated by a grid of verticals and horizontals, punctuated by a single oval washbowl on the right and an oil lamp on the left. The work echoes Mondrian's "pure" abstractions. As it embodies the stark poverty of a sharecropper's life, Evans's photograph reveals a dignity in the clean lines of this sparse world, a dignity that also marks Agee's accompanying prose.

FIGURE 22.27 Walker Evans, *Washroom and Dining Area of Floyd Burroughs's Home, Hale County, Alabama*, 1936, photograph, Library of Congress, Washington, DC. The power of this photograph rests not only in its formal coherence, but in its stunning focus, its ability to capture the texture of wood, cloth, glass, and vinyl in a manner that makes everything almost real enough to touch.

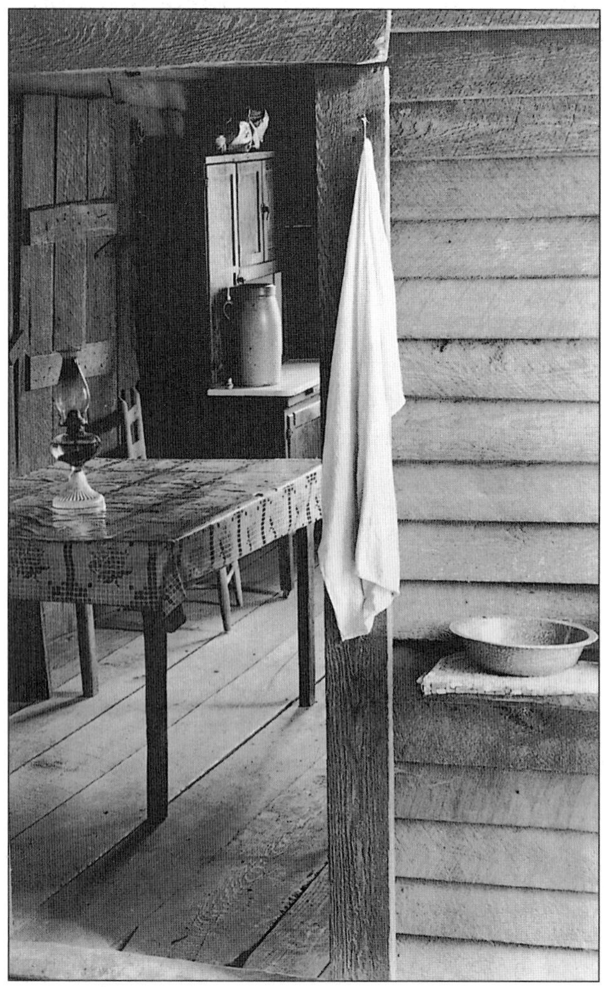

Margaret Bourke-White. One of the first photographers hired by *Life* magazine after its founding in 1936, Bourke-White (1904–1971) came to define the profession. Her photographs of the Depression depict the harsh conditions. *At the Time of the Louisville Flood* (fig. 22.28) records the aftermath of the great flood of the Ohio River in January 1937. Inundating Louisville, Kentucky, it left over nine hundred people dead or injured. On assignment for *Life*, Bourke-White arrived on the last flight before the airfield was closed, and she hitchhiked on rescue rowboats shooting photo after photo of the scene. *At the Time of the Louisville Flood* juxtaposes a soup line of African Americans displaced by disaster against the government billboard behind them.

Bourke-White worked throughout the world, covering World War II and the Korean War as a correspondent. She was the first woman photographer attached to the U.S. armed forces, and the only U.S. photographer to cover the siege of Moscow in 1941.

Louise Dahl-Wolfe. The American LOUISE DAHL-WOLFE (1895–1989), although known for her fashion photography, preferred portraiture. Her photograph of *Colette* (fig. 22.29) is among those of famous writers Dahl-Wolfe took while on staff for many years (1936–58) at the magazine *Harper's Bazaar*. This casual and intimate portrait shows Colette, the French novelist, interrupted while writing in bed, in her apartment in Paris. Known for her technical perfection, Dahl-Wolfe developed her photographs herself and was among the first

FIGURE 22.28 Margaret Bourke-White, *At the Time of the Louisville Flood*, 1937, photograph. *Life* magazine offered many photographers the opportunity to work professionally. Reacting to the arrival of *Life* magazine on the publishing scene, Bourke-White said, "I could almost feel the horizon widening and the great rush of wind sweeping in. . . . This was the kind of magazine that could be anything we chose to make it."

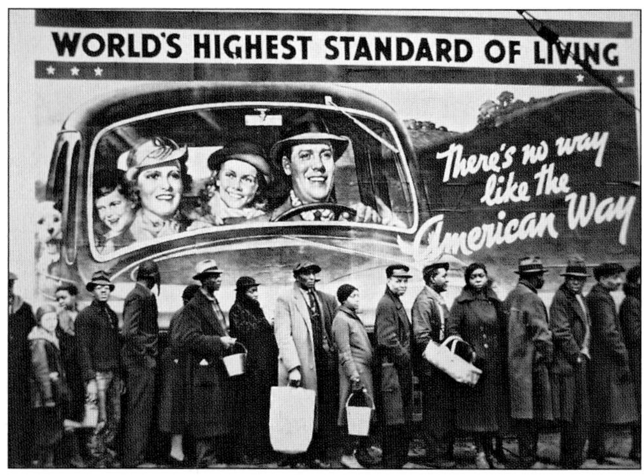

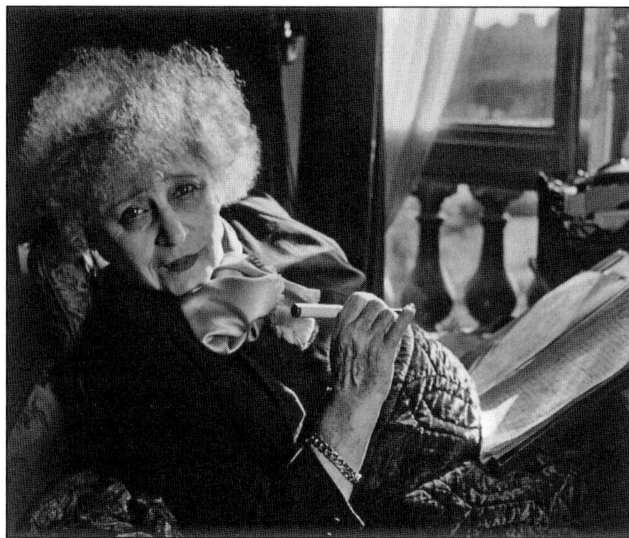

FIGURE 22.29 Louise Dahl-Wolfe, American, *Colette*, 1951, gelatin silver print, $10\frac{7}{8}'' \times 13\frac{1}{8}''$ (27.6 × 33.3 cm), National Museum of Women in the Arts, Washington, DC. Gift of Helen Cumming Ziegler. © 1989 Center for Creative Photography, Arizona Board of Regents. As Colette glances up, pen in hand, Dahl-Wolfe's photo skillfully and subtly suggests that the viewer is standing very close to the famous French author—and has disturbed her as she writes.

to work with color photography. She enjoyed her many successes during a long and productive life.

Lola Alvarez Bravo. Born Dolores (Lola) Martinez Vianda in Jalisco, Mexico, an orphan at the age of eight, Lola Alvarez Bravo (1907–1993) married the Mexican photographer Manuel Alvarez Bravo, from whom she was later divorced. Her photographs record daily life in Mexico, in the city as well as in the country, for example, *From Generation to Generation* (fig. 22.30), taken around 1950, and of the famous people as well as of the ordinary. Highly successful as a photographer, Bravo also had an art gallery in Mexico City where, in 1953, she gave Frida Kahlo a one-woman exhibition—the only one held in Mexico during Kahlo's lifetime. Bravo taught photography at the Academia de San Carlos in Mexico City.

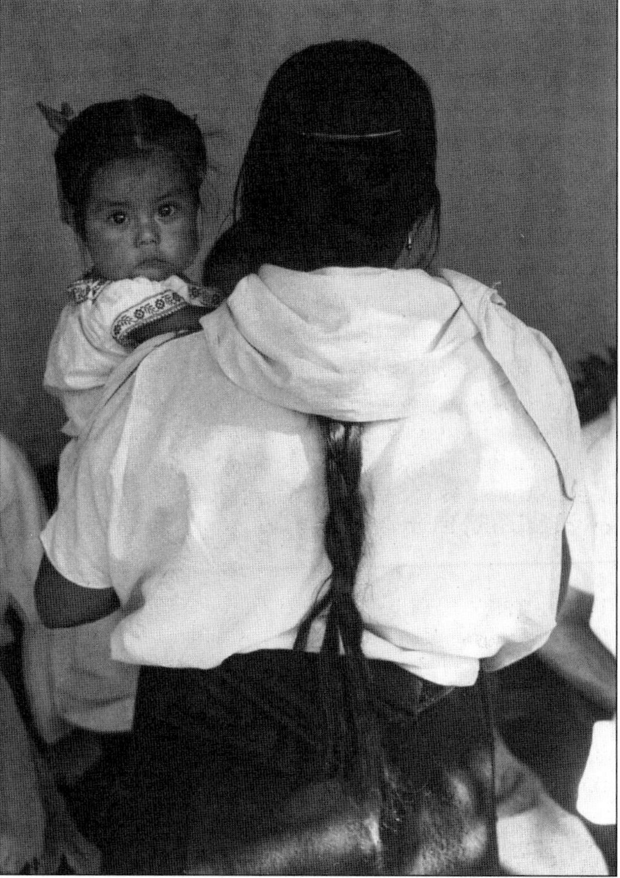

FIGURE 22.30 Lola Alvarez Bravo, *From Generation to Generation*, gelatin silver print, ca. 1950, $9'' \times 6\frac{1}{8}''$ (22.9 × 15.6 cm). National Museum of Women in the Arts, Washington, DC. Gift of the Artist. ©1995 Center for Creative Photography, The University of Arizona Foundation. In this charming photo, a wide-eyed child stares inquisitively at the viewer. Bravo created a contrast between young and old, small and large, front and back. Aesthetically striking, this could be analyzed as a carefully composed arrangement in blacks, grays, and whites.

REGIONALISM IN AMERICAN PAINTING

The success achieved by photographers working for the FSA was underpinned by the realist impulse in American culture. Many American artists, especially in the Midwest, rejected abstraction and turned instead to a more naturalistic representation of the American experience through regional scenes.

Edward Hopper. Although he had traveled to Europe several times between 1906 and 1910, for his 1933 exhibition at the Museum of Modern Art, Edward Hopper (1882–1967) wrote, "A nation's art is greatest when it most reflects the character of its people. . . . We are not French and never can be and any attempt to be so is to deny our inheritance and to try to impose upon ourselves a character that can be nothing but a veneer upon surface."

Hopper's paintings record the American scene. Its cafés, restaurants, stores, and barber-shops are his subject matter. Hopper paints places inhabited by the middle class, representing ordinary things that had previously been deemed unworthy of an artist's attention. He is adept at conveying disquieting isolation and regret. *Nighthawks* (fig. 22.31), of 1942, portrays the bleak loneliness and the alienation of city life after hours. Stark and still, few human figures appear in Hopper's paintings; often, there is no one at all.

Thomas Hart Benton. The regionalist impulse was supported by the Works Progress Administration (WPA),

Critical Thinking

Photography and Truth

A picture, it has been said, is worth a thousand words. And it has often been remarked how photographs capture the truth of a scene, rendering it as the scene exists in real life. However, we might want to ask a few questions about these commonly accepted notions.

To what extent do photographs, snapshots of a moment of time, tell the truth?

To what extent are photographs limited by the moment of their shooting? By the angle or perspective from which they are taken?

To what extent can photographs be "arranged" to suggest something that supposedly happened spontaneously, but was actually "staged" by the photographer? How would you go about deciding what was "staged" and what was unvarnished reality? And can a "staged" or "arranged" photograph convey the truth of a situation, such as a love relationship or a social situation, such as racial harmony or racial tension, for example? How would you determine if a photograph was telling the "truth," or if it was revealing only a partial, and therefore slanted, truth? How do you distinguish between photographs that portray truth and those that convey propaganda?

which initiated a mural project to decorate public buildings across the country. The murals were to represent American themes and experiences. Over two thousand murals were painted between 1935 and 1939, and among the best were those by Thomas Hart Benton (1889–1975). Benton was radically anti-European. "The fact that our art was arguable in the language of the street," he wrote, "was proof to us that we had succeeded in separating it from the hothouse atmosphere of an imported, and for our country, functionless aesthetic."

One of his most ambitious undertakings was a set of murals for the Missouri State Capitol, recording the social

FIGURE 22.31 Edward Hopper, *Nighthawks*, 1942, oil on canvas, 2′6″ × 4′8$\frac{11}{16}$″ (76.2 × 143.9 cm), Friends of American Art Collection, 1942. 1 © 1997 Art Institute of Chicago. Photograph © 2005, The Art Institute of Chicago. All Rights Reserved. Using carefully constructed compositions to depict ordinary subjects, especially the loneliness of urban life, the artist documented the American scene.

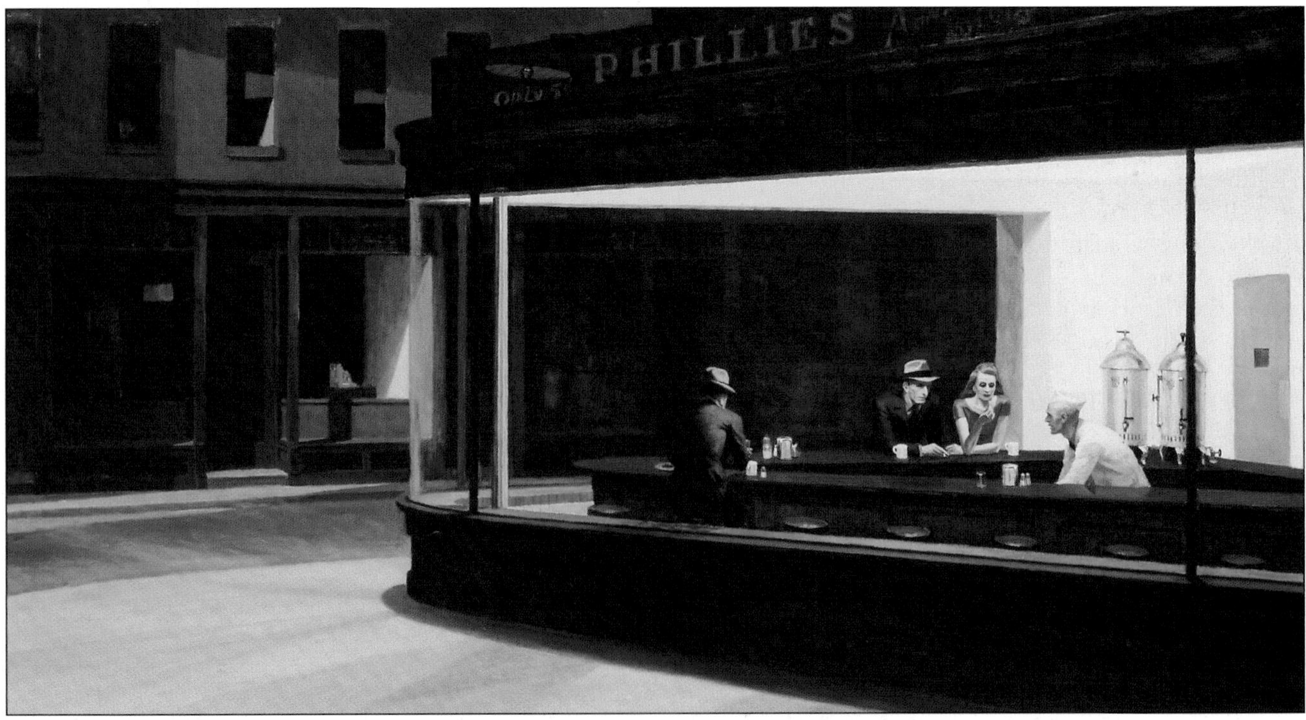

Table 22–1 IMPORTANT STYLES OF PAINTING DURING THE AGE OF ANXIETY

Style	Artist	Work and Date
Dada	Duchamp	*The Fountain*, 1917
De Stijl	Mondrian	*Composition in Red, Yellow, and Blue*, 1920
Surrealism	Miró	*Painting*, 1933
	Dali	*The Persistence of Memory*, 1931
American modernism	O'Keeffe	*Yellow Calla*, 1926
	Demuth	*Aucassin and Nicolette*, 1921
American regionalism	Hopper	*Nighthawks*, 1942
	Benton	*Missouri Mural*, 1936
	Lawrence	*They Also Found Discrimination*, 1940–41

history of Missouri (fig. 22.32). Almost every aspect of Missouri life is depicted. In a domestic scene, an old woman rolls out dough while an old man reads and a young boy drinks a glass of milk. To the left are various farming scenes; a cow is milked; pigs are fed; a farmer sits atop his tractor. To the right a lawyer argues a case before the jury in a courtroom.

Jacob Lawrence. Another, earlier migration, reminiscent of the migration of Oklahoma farmworkers, was that of African Americans after World War I. They moved steadily from the South to the North seeking employment in rapidly expanding industries. Between 1916 and 1923, the African American population in major northern cities

Figure 22.32 Thomas Hart Benton, *Missouri Mural* (section), 1936, Missouri State Capitol, Jefferson City, Missouri, oil on canvas, © T.H. Benton and R.P. Benton Testamentary Trusts/ Licensed by VAGA, New York, NY. The WPA's mural project was directly inspired by the example of the Mexican muralists, one of whom, Diego Rivera, is discussed in the Cross Currents box in this chapter, and whose efforts were supported by the Mexican government.

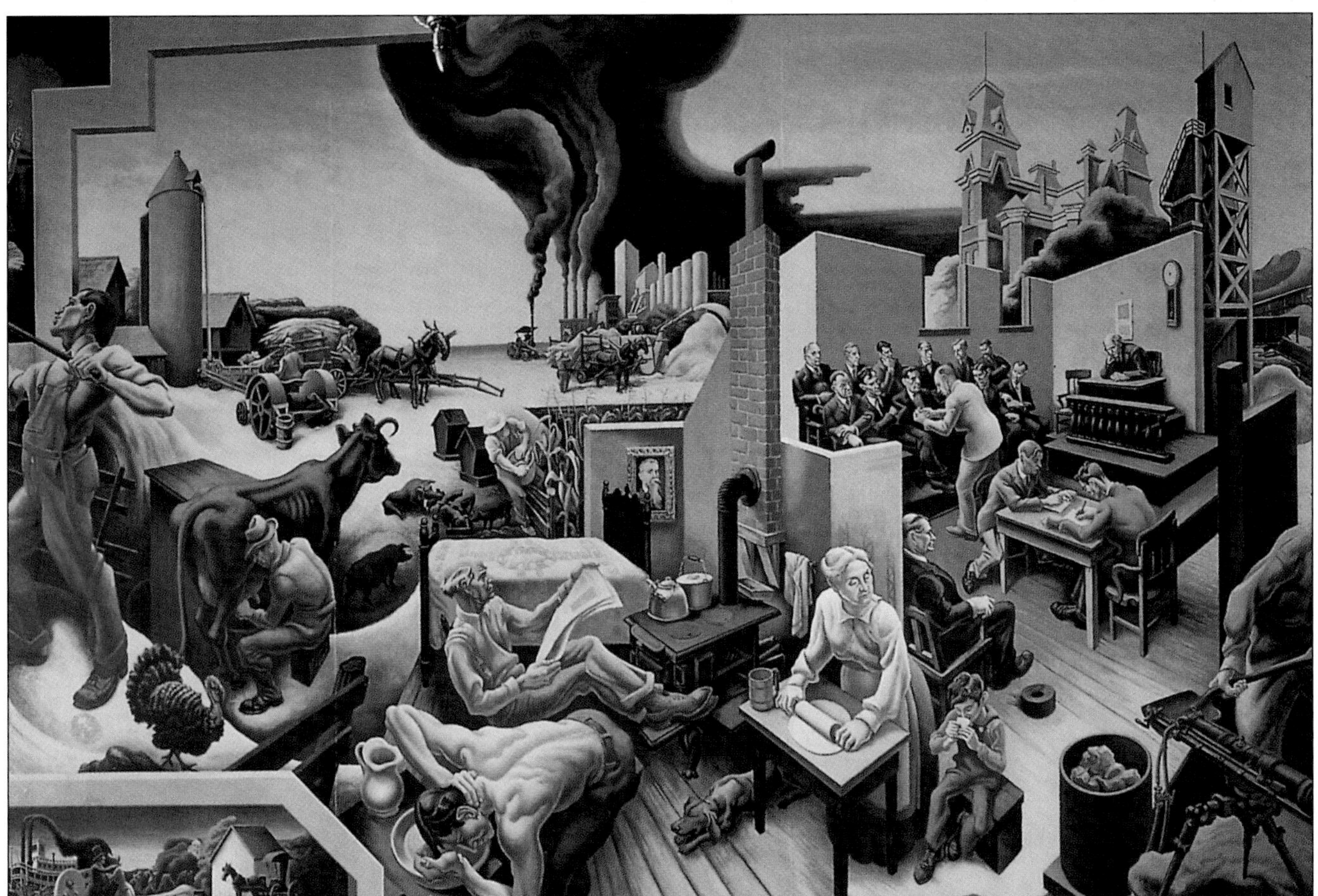

doubled. African-American artist Jacob Lawrence (1917–2000), supported by the WPA, captured this movement in a series of tempera paintings, *The Migration of the Negro*, made between 1939 and 1941.

Those who migrated first found jobs in the north because of labor shortages resulting from World War I, but as others followed, life in the north soon revealed itself to be little different from life in the south. The *Migration* series depicts the entire saga. The migrants arriving in Chicago, St. Louis, Pittsburgh, and New York encounter injustice, racism, and inadequate housing. Race riots result. In one panel, *They Also Found Discrimination* (fig. 22.33), Lawrence depicts the racial divide the African Americans encountered in the north. A subtle, yet startling effect is the facelessness of the African Americans. They are anonymous, undifferentiated, "invisible," to use the word of African American writer Ralph Ellison, who explored this experience in his classic novel, *Invisible Man.*

FIGURE 22.33 Jacob Lawrence, *They Also Found Discrimination*, from the series *The Migration of the Negro*, panel 49. 1940–41, tempera on wood, $21\frac{1}{4}'' \times 18''$ (54 × 45.7 cm), Courtesy of the Jacob and Gwendolyn Lawrence Foundation. Philips Collection, Washington, DC. When the series was exhibited in 1941, Lawrence achieved instant fame, and the series was purchased jointly by the Philips Collection and the Museum of Modern Art, in New York, who divided the panels between them. It was reassembled as a complete series in the mid-1990s when it toured the country—once again to national acclaim.

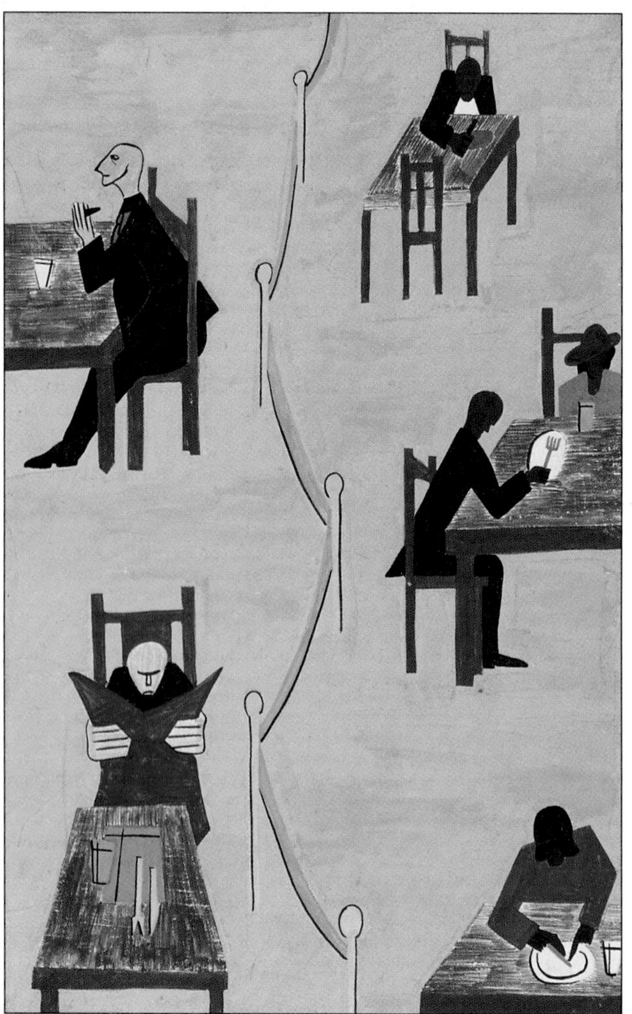

SOUTHERN REGIONALIST WRITING

Regionalism is also identifiable in American fiction between the two world wars. Especially in the South, a distinct brand of writing developed. The South's "tall-tale" tradition was enhanced by colorful dialect and usage and, in no small part, by the memory of the Civil War, which fostered a sense of hurt pride and regional identity. The writing of southern regionalists is marked by violent and grotesque characters who are often treated with colloquial humor. It is also distinguished, in particular, by a sense of place.

William Faulkner. Unlike Hemingway, who chose fictional settings in various parts of the world, William Faulkner (1897–1962) chose to remain a chronicler of the American South. Set in fictional Yoknapatawpha County—very much like his native Lafayette County, Mississippi—Faulkner's work describes the decline of local families. His work, which ranges widely in style, tone, and technique, earned him a Nobel Prize in 1950.

Faulkner novels experiment with narrative. In *The Sound and the Fury*, for instance, he tells the story of the increasing misfortunes of the Compson family from four different points of view. Each narrative perspective provides a context for the others, so the whole story becomes known through compilation. He also uses a stream of consciousness technique.

Faulkner understood that in exploring the world close to him he was also exploring ideas that resonated beyond the locales he was describing. As he himself put it, "I discovered that my own little postage stamp of native soil was worth writing about and that I would never live long enough to exhaust it." For all its experimental form and rhetorical brilliance, Faulkner's work derives its power from his depiction of characters, whose struggle to endure remains familiar and remarkable. In his Nobel Prize acceptance speech, Faulkner noted that "man will not merely endure: he will prevail . . . because he has a soul, a spirit capable of compassion and sacrifice and endurance."

Flannery O'Connor. The stories of Flannery O'Connor (1925–1964) explore humor, irony, and paradox, especially the paradox of evil and redemption. O'Connor's social satires challenge American attitudes about violence, race, and class.

Although O'Connor set her fiction in the South, she explored Christian beliefs that transcend the confines of one region. "The woods are full of regional writers," she once said, "and it is the great horror of every serious Southern writer that he will become one of them."

Several of O'Connor's stories begin with a comic protagonist who indulges in fantasies of moral or social superiority or who has a false sense of the certainty of things. The protagonist then has a traumatic encounter with other characters or with ironic situations that suggest a disturbing and incomprehensible universe. Although her stories blend comedy and tragedy, several end quite gruesomely.

THE AMERICAN SOUND

Just as American painters and writers evoked the distinct character of America's regions, a number of composers and musicians sought to convey their own sense of a distinctively American "sound." For over two centuries, people had brought their own musical customs and instruments from many different countries, and, as they settled into communities, different folk sounds developed across the land. Spirited banjo and fiddle music grew popular in the Appalachian mountains; cowboy songs thrived on the American prairie; gospel music arose in African American communities in the South; and jazz, which developed in New Orleans, spread to big cities around the country, including New York, Chicago, and Los Angeles.

Charles Ives. Charles Ives (1874–1954) was an American original, an insurance executive who was at the same time an innovative composer. While steeped in the classical music tradition, Ives wrote distinctively American music, which, like the poetry of Walt Whitman, expresses the multiplicity of American life. Ives's music echoes American folk songs, marches, fiddle tunes, spirituals, and patriotic songs while also evoking snatches of Beethoven and Brahms. Like Whitman, Ives could "hear America singing," and he captured a multitude of American voices in his collection *114 Songs*, which includes sentimental ballads, war songs, street songs, religious songs, folk tunes, cowboy songs, humorous songs, and dramatic poems.

Ives was influenced by the writings of the American Transcendentalists, especially Ralph Waldo Emerson and Henry David Thoreau. Transcendentalism's optimism, its belief in the innate goodness of human beings, its emphasis on individualism and self-reliance, and its appreciation of nature all captured Ives's imagination. These ideals find expression in Ives's songs and symphonies, and especially in his *Concord Sonata* for piano, with its movements devoted to Emerson and Thoreau, in his "Unanswered Question," subtitled philosophically "A Cosmic Landscape," and in his *Universe Symphony*, which Ives once described as "a presentation and contemplation in tones . . . of the mysterious creation of the earth and firmament, the evolution of all life in nature, in humanity to the Divine."

Aaron Copland. Born in Brooklyn, New York, AARON COPLAND [COPE-land] (1900–90) is an esteemed American composer. After his early training, Copland went to Paris for four years, where he experienced firsthand the artistic energy of Picasso, Stravinsky, Hemingway, Pound, and many other modernist writers, artists, and composers. Returning to America in the mid-1920s, Copland was determined to compose music with a distinctively American style that would appeal to a wide audience. He achieved this with a series of ballet scores that relied on American folk elements. Copland worked with two leading choreographers who were themselves striving for uniquely American dance aesthetics. Agnes de Mille choreographed the ballet *Rodeo* to Copland's music in 1942; in 1944, Martha Graham choreographed *Appalachian Spring.* De Mille went on to arrange the stage dance for several leading Broadway musicals, including *Oklahoma!* (1943) and had her own touring company for years.

Although Copland's score for the ballet *Rodeo* has been a favorite among American audiences, his *Appalachian Spring* is performed more frequently as a concert piece. The work's subject is, as he said, "a pioneer celebration in spring around a newly built farmhouse in the Pennsylvania hills" in the early nineteenth century. A bride and groom, their neighbor, and a preacher and his congregation constitute the piece's characters. Copland's music imitates American fiddle tunes and hymns, including "Simple Gifts," the traditional Shaker hymn.

Copland also had considerable success as a composer of film music. In 1939, he wrote the music for the film adaptation of John Steinbeck's novella *Of Mice and Men*, for which he received two academy award nominations. He followed this film score with music for a number of movies, including *Our Town* (1940), *The Red Pony* (1948), and *The Heiress* (1948). Copland, however, experienced another, less happy kind of notoriety, when he was listed among the fifty most notorious communist fellow travelers in the country. Although he was summoned to the hearings conducted by Senator Joseph McCarthy, Copland was not blacklisted like other artists and composers. His patriotic *A Lincoln Portrait* and *Fanfare for the Common Man*, ironically, remain two of his most popular and frequently performed compositions.

George Gershwin. Inspired by African American blues and jazz, George Gershwin (1898–1937) fused classical and jazz elements, mingling a wide range of sounds. Gershwin's work stands for the sound of the modern age, as signified by the four taxi horns in *An American in Paris* (1928), his tribute to the expatriate scene.

An accomplished jazz pianist himself, Gershwin's *Rhapsody in Blue* (1924) and his *Piano Concerto in F* (1925) were both composed with a view to taking advantage of his own skill at the keyboard, and both include long piano solos accompanied by full orchestra. Gershwin is best known for *Porgy and Bess* (1935), one of the earliest and

Connections

Art as Politics

An art as abstract as that of El Lissitzky might seem ineffectual as a political tool, but it was conceived in quite the opposite terms, as a means of bringing art to the masses. In the late nineteenth century, a number of St. Petersburg artists, calling themselves the Wanderers, sought to champion the newly emancipated peasant class by bringing art to the people through traveling exhibitions. This initiative took new form soon after the disturbances of 1905, when the Bolsheviks began to use wall posters extensively: They were inexpensive, and appealed to the mostly illiterate masses. By 1917, the poster was a major Russian art form. El Lissitzky's *Beat the Whites with the Red Wedge* (fig. 22.34), of 1919, is a perfect example. Using basic geometric shapes, the Red Army is represented by the triangle that pierces the circular form, which in turn represents the White Army. The sense of aggression, originating both figuratively and literally from "the left," is unmistakable.

Such propaganda art was soon disseminated throughout Russia, primarily by means of Agit-trains. These consisted of seven or eight railway cars sent "to establish ties between the localities and the center, to agitate, to carry out propaganda, to bring information, and to supply literature." Each was also equipped with a film projector. The peasants were fascinated by film, and Lenin quickly realized the power of the medium as propaganda. Sitting on the train, the people watched newsreels of Lenin—entertained, but also indoctrinated in the Bolshevik cause.

At first, the Agit-trains were decorated with abstract Russian art, but the peasants objected. So they were repainted with pictures of soldiers, workers, and peasants, a development that foreshadowed the fate of Russian modernist art as a whole. Abstraction did not speak to the masses after all. At the end of the first Five-Year Plan in 1932, Stalin outlawed independent artistic organizations, and in 1934 he proclaimed "Socialist Realism" as the official Soviet style. Abstraction was permanently banned in the Soviet Union.

FIGURE 22.34 El Lissitzky, *Beat the Whites with the Red Wedge*, 1919–20, lithograph, $20\frac{7}{8}'' \times 27\frac{1}{2}''$ (53 × 70 cm), Stedelijk Van Abbemuseum, Eindhoven, The Netherlands. Russian poster design would soon begin to incorporate photographic images in photomontages.

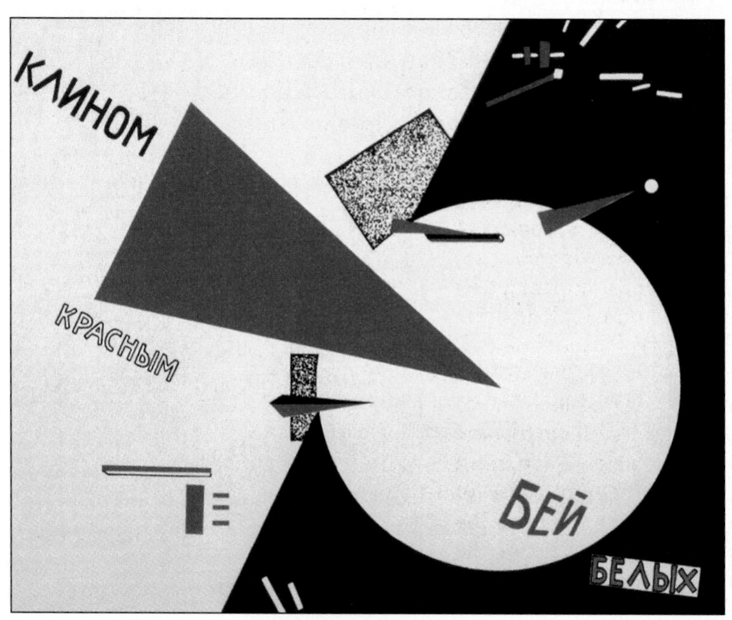

most important American operas. It addresses the lives of poor black people in Charleston, South Carolina, and contains some of the most widely heard songs of the 1930s, including the hit "Summertime." Gershwin traveled to South Carolina to familiarize himself with the local dialect and the region's performance rituals, witnessed in church services and public gatherings.

Porgy and Bess has had a difficult and somewhat fractious history. Opera companies mostly ignored the work for more than forty years, until the Houston Opera staged Gershwin's original score. Before long it came to be considered a landmark in American opera. But its depiction of African Americans caused some consternation. Because of this, a number of singers have criticized the work for perpetuating stereotypes of Black Americans. Among these critics was the opera singer Grace Bumbry, who, though she thought the role of Bess beneath her, accepted the part because she considered it to be a piece of Americana, a part of modern American history.

The Jazz Age

The origins of American **jazz** go back to the rhythms and songs of Africa. In vocal music, the call and response pattern of ritual tribal practice, in which the leader sings a phrase to which the community replies, can be heard in gospel, jazz, and even rock and roll. The jazz **riff,** a short phrase improvised over and over, often unifies the music,

Cross Currents

DIEGO RIVERA AND THE DETROIT MURALS

In the early 1920s, the Mexican government initiated a mural movement designed to give the Mexican people a sense of identity and national pride. A leading painter of this movement, Diego Rivera (1886–1957), had lived in Paris, studying the work of Picasso and Braque, and had developed a fluid Cubist style. But when confronted with the task of creating a national revolutionary art, he traveled to Italy to study the Italian fresco and immersed himself in Mexico's pre-Columbian heritage.

In 1931, Rivera was commissioned by Edsel B. Ford and the Detroit Institute of Arts to create a series of frescoes depicting Detroit for the museum's Garden Court. Being fascinated by both the promise of modern industry and the plight of industrial workers, Rivera decided to represent Detroit's industry—its famous automobile factories, pharmaceutical and chemical companies, its aviation facilities and power plants.

Working from drawings and photographs, Rivera made panels for all four walls of the court, with large panels for the north and south walls. At the top of the north panel (fig. 22.35) are depictions of two of what he regarded as the four races of humanity—the Native American and the African American. Opposite them, on the south panel, are images of the Caucasian and Asian races. The main part of the north panel depicts the assembly line of automobile manufacturing, showing people molding engine blocks, boring cylinders, and making the final touches. At the bottom left, a line of workers punch into a time clock. At the bottom right, they eat lunch. Between the two, Rivera captures the extraordinary exertion and strength required of these workers, all day, every day.

FIGURE 22.35 Diego Rivera, *Detroit Industry* (north wall), 1932–33, fresco, main panel 17′8½″ × 45′ (5.40 × 13.20 m). Detroit Institute of Arts. Gift of Edsel B. Ford. © 2003 Banco de Mexico, Diego Rivera & Frida Kahlo Museums Trust. Av. Cinco de Mayo No. 2, Col. Centro, Del. Cuauhtemoc 06059, Mexico, D.F. Reproduction authorized by the Instituto Nacional de Bellas Artes y Literatura. The Detroit Institute of Arts. At once a celebration of industry and an exposé of the workers' plight, Rivera's mural is a relatively optimistic plea for social and economic reform through, and by means of, industrial progress.

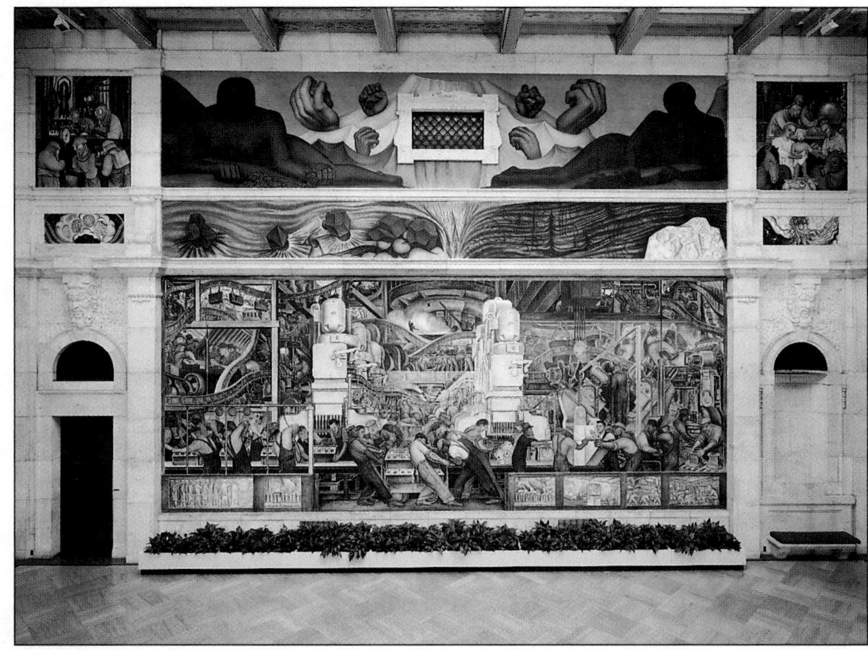

as can the so-called samples that are the basis of today's rap and hip-hop. Syncopated and offbeat rhythms, together with improvisation of a basic melody or phrase, are the characteristic features of jazz.

Scott Joplin. Scott Joplin (1868–1917) made famous **ragtime,** a type of jazz piano composition in which the left hand plays a steady beat while the right improvises on a melody in a syncopated rhythm. **Syncopation** means accenting a beat where it is not expected, in particular off beat or in between beats. Joplin, the son of a slave, began his career as the pianist at the Maple Leaf Saloon in Sedalia, Missouri. His score of the "Maple Leaf Rag," published in 1899, quickly sold hundreds of thousands of copies and ranks as one of the first pop hits.

Louis Armstrong. One of the best-loved jazz musicians of all time is Louis Armstrong (1900–1971). Also known as "Satchmo," Armstrong was a vocalist and a trumpeter. Born and raised in New Orleans, a mecca for jazz in America, Armstrong first played in a New Orleans jazz combo. A few years later, Armstrong left to play cornet in Chicago with King Oliver's Creole Jazz Band. In no time, he was recording with his own bands and secured his place as the premier jazz trumpeter.

A stunning improviser, Armstrong could take a simple melody and transform it into a singing, swinging piece by changing its rhythm and altering its pitches. He could also play the trumpet in higher registers than anyone else, and he made his music distinctive with an array of vibratos and note-altering variations.

Cultural Impact

The early Modernist spirit took root in the first years of the twentieth century when late-nineteenth-century artistic styles seemed tame in comparison with styles such as Fauvism and Cubism. Early Modernism was a time of cultural energy and artistic revolution. Braque and Picasso pushed painting toward abstraction. Severini's seemingly animate painting typified the energy of the period, as did the hard-driving propulsive music of Igor Stravinsky. Modernism celebrated the speed and energy of modern life. Literary artists, such as Joyce and Wolfe, Eliot and Pound, in their fiction and poetry, respectively, captured something of the complexity of modern life.

With the advent of Einsteinian physics and Freudian psychology, conceptions of the external world of nature and the internal world of human nature were fundamentally altered. Fixed points of reference gave way to a relativity of perspective, both physically and psychologically. Conventional explanations made way for psychological forces derived from early childhood experience and manifested in dreams. Old certainties were undermined and new forms of explanation and representation were emerging.

The greatest legacy of Modernism, perhaps, was this uprooting and upheaval of the past. Painting was no longer required to be representational. Poetry no longer required rhyme and symmetrical stanzas. Music moved past harmony and tonality into dissonance and atonality. Because of Modernism, contemporary artists, whatever their medium of expression, have a multitude of options in pursuing their art.

His gravelly voice, neither elegant nor beautiful, conveyed spirit and fire. Among his vocal techniques was **scat** singing, in which Armstrong vocalized nonsense syllables on a melody. Ella Fitzgerald, after him, was to take scat to new heights.

Duke Ellington. The great jazz pianist and arranger Edward Kennedy ("Duke") Ellington (1899–1974) was a composer and conductor of a jazz ensemble, or swing band (fig. 22.36). Unlike the New Orleans–style combo featuring improvisations by each of the five to eight members of the group, **swing** music was played by big bands of approximately fifteen musicians arranged in three groups: saxophones/clarinets, brasses (trumpets/trombones), and rhythm (piano, percussion, guitar, and bass). Although swing often included improvised solos, its music was most often arranged due to the larger size of the group. The members of the swing band did more ensemble playing, with each section taking its turn: saxes, brasses, and rhythm, playing in unison. The saxophone became a popular solo instrument during the swing era (1925–45), with percussion instruments and the piano also becoming prominent instruments of jazz expression.

Ellington composed mini-concertos within pieces. One example, his *Concerto for Cootie* (1940), showcases Ellington's trumpeter Cootie Williams, whose command of tonal color differed markedly from Louis Armstrong.

FIGURE 22.36 The Duke Ellington Orchestra in 1949. Ellington was a dynamic and creative performer. He and his band were immensely popular at the famous Cotton Club in Harlem.

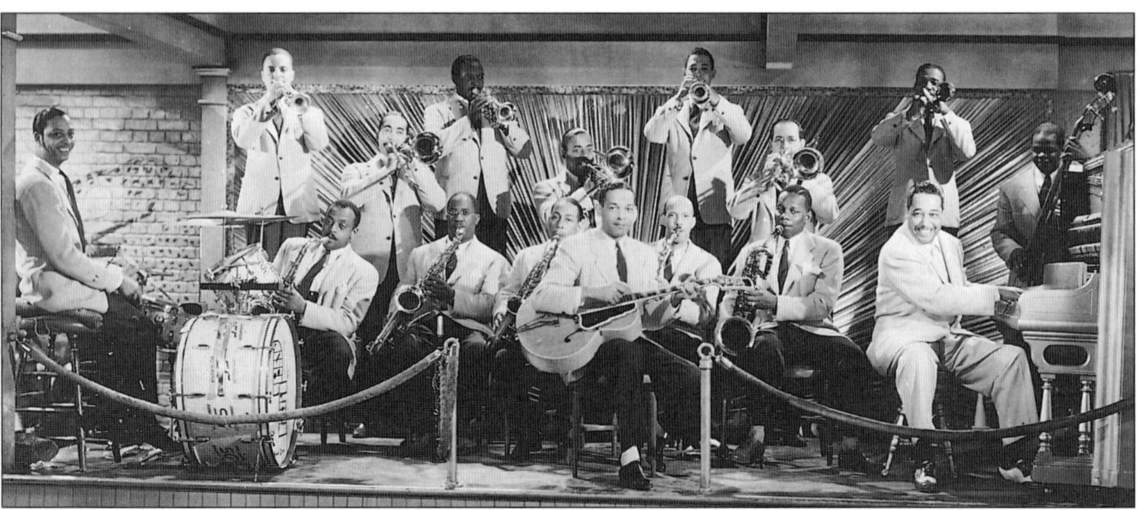

KEY TERMS

avant garde
abstraction
Fauvism
Cubism
collage
Simultanéisme
Futurism
German Expressionism
Dada
anti-art
Surrealism
automatism
De Stijl (Neo-Plasticism)
International style
Bauhaus
reinforced concrete
stream of consciousness
montage
atonality
Nazi
Lebensraum
Dust Bowl
Depression
jazz
riff
ragtime
syncopation
scat
swing

www. WEBSITES FOR FURTHER STUDY

http://artchive.com/artchive/P/picasso.html
(This is the Artchive, a website with virtually every major artist in every style from every era in art history. It is an excellent resource.)

http://collections.sfmoma.org/obj2583$12965
(Perhaps no work is more singularly identified with the transformation of art in the twentieth century than Fountain [1917] by Marcel Duchamp [1887–1968].)

http://www.mcs.csuhayward.edu/~malek/Surrealism/index.html
(An unusual but interestingly good site on Surrealism.)

http://www.masters-of-photography.com/S/stieglitz/stieglitz_equivalent_1926.html
(A good site on Stieglitz and photography in general.)

http://www.allaboutjazz.com/timeline.htm
(This site features a brief history of jazz with associated links, written by Doug Ronallo and Michael Ricci.)

http://www.artandpopularculture.com/modernist_literature
(Overview of modernism in literature, emphasizing formal and thematic characteristics. Includes Eliot, Pound, Woolf, Joyce, Hemingway, Faulkner, and many other writers.)

http://www.en.wikipedia.org/wiki/american_classical_music
(Broad overview of American classical music, including links to life and works of Copland, Ives, Gershwin, Joplin, Ellington, Armstrong, and more.)

http://www.npr.org/programs/special/milestones/991110.motm.riteofspring.html
(A National Public Radio site featuring Stravinsky's Rite of Spring, including an audio excerpt of the work.)

Chapter 23

History

1945	United States drops atomic bombs on Japan; World War II ends
1947	Marshall Plan introduced
1948	Israel founded
1949	NATO founded
1950	First shopping mall opens near Seattle
1954	Ray Kroc buys McDonald's franchise rights
1961	Berlin Wall erected
1962	Invasion of Cuba fails
1965	Major U.S. intervention in Vietnam
1965	National Endowment for the Arts and Humanities established
1965	Major buildup of U.S. troops in Vietnam
1966	National Organization for Women founded
1966	The Pill (Oral Contraceptive) becomes available in the United States
1969	*Apollo 11* lands on the moon
1973	Trial and congressional hearings on Watergate
1974	Nixon resigns

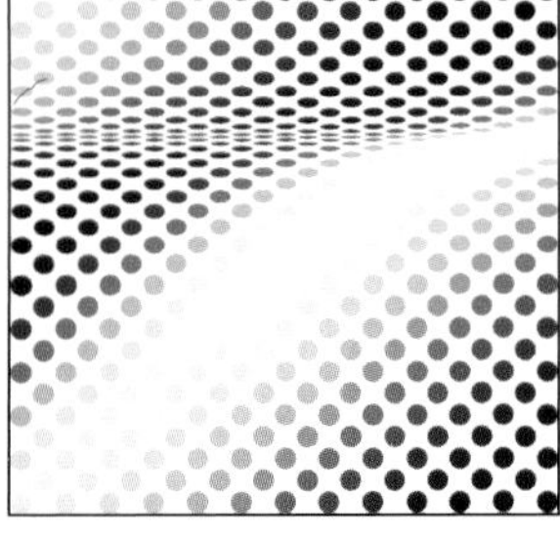

Arts and Architecture

1942–43	Wright designs Guggenheim Museum (built 1957–60)
1950	Pollock, *Autumn Rhythm*
1950–52	Mies van der Rohe, Lake Shore Drive Apartment Houses
1950–55	Le Corbusier, Notre-Dame-du-Haut
1952	Cage, *4′ 33″*
1957	Bernstein, *West Side Story*
1958	Nevelson, *Sky Cathedral*
1962	Warhol, *Marilyn Monroe Diptych*
1963	Krasner, *Flowering Limb*
1964	Kaprow, *Household Happening*
1966	Frankenthaler, *Mauve District*
1972	Jones, *Ode to Kinshasa*
1977	Piano and Rogers, Pompidou Center

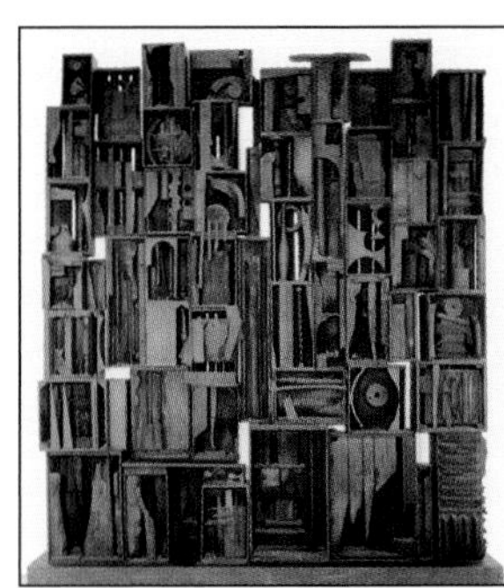

Literature and Philosophy

1943	Sartre, *Being and Nothingness*
1949	De Beauvoir, *The Second Sex*
1952	Beckett, *Waiting for Godot*
1956	Ginsberg, *Howl*
1963	Friedan, *The Feminine Mystique*

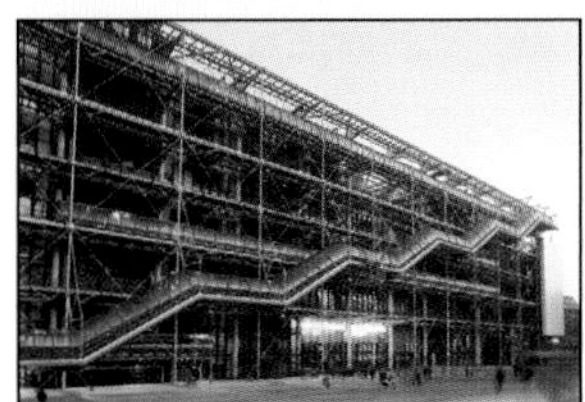

Mid-Twentieth Century and Later

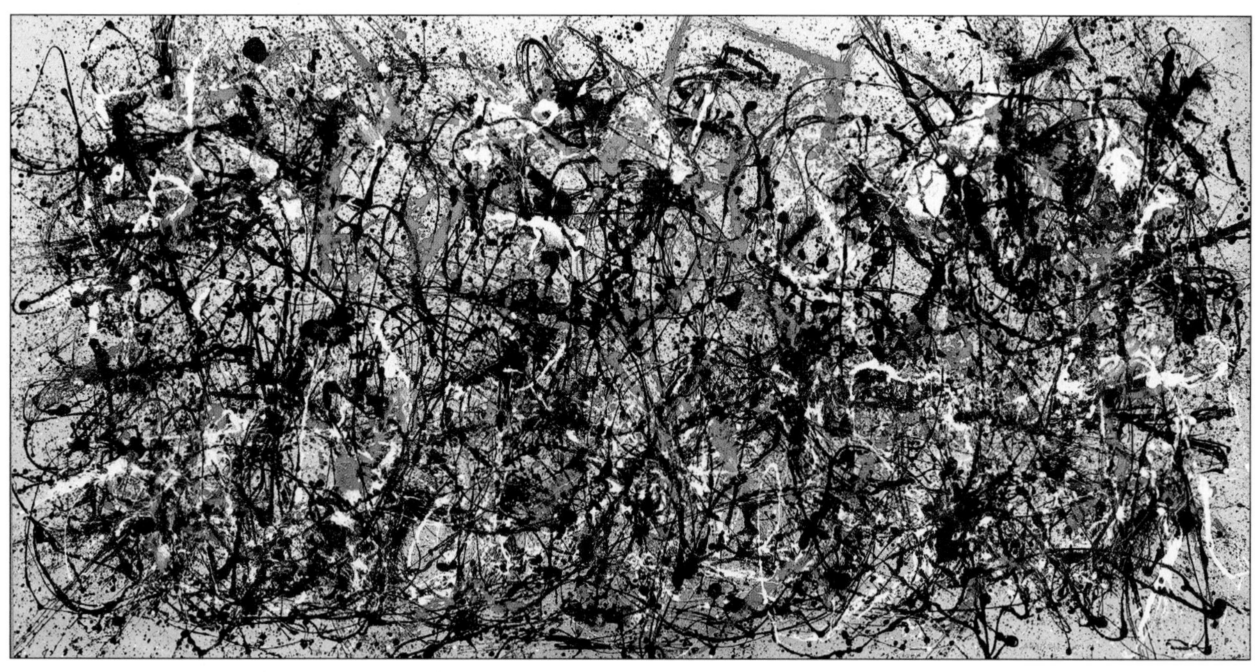

Jackson Pollock, *Autumn Rhythm: Number 30*, 1950, oil on canvas, 8′9″ × 17′3″ (2.66 × 5.25 m), George A. Hearn Fund, 1957. © 2005, ARS, NY. Metropolitan Museum of Art, NY.

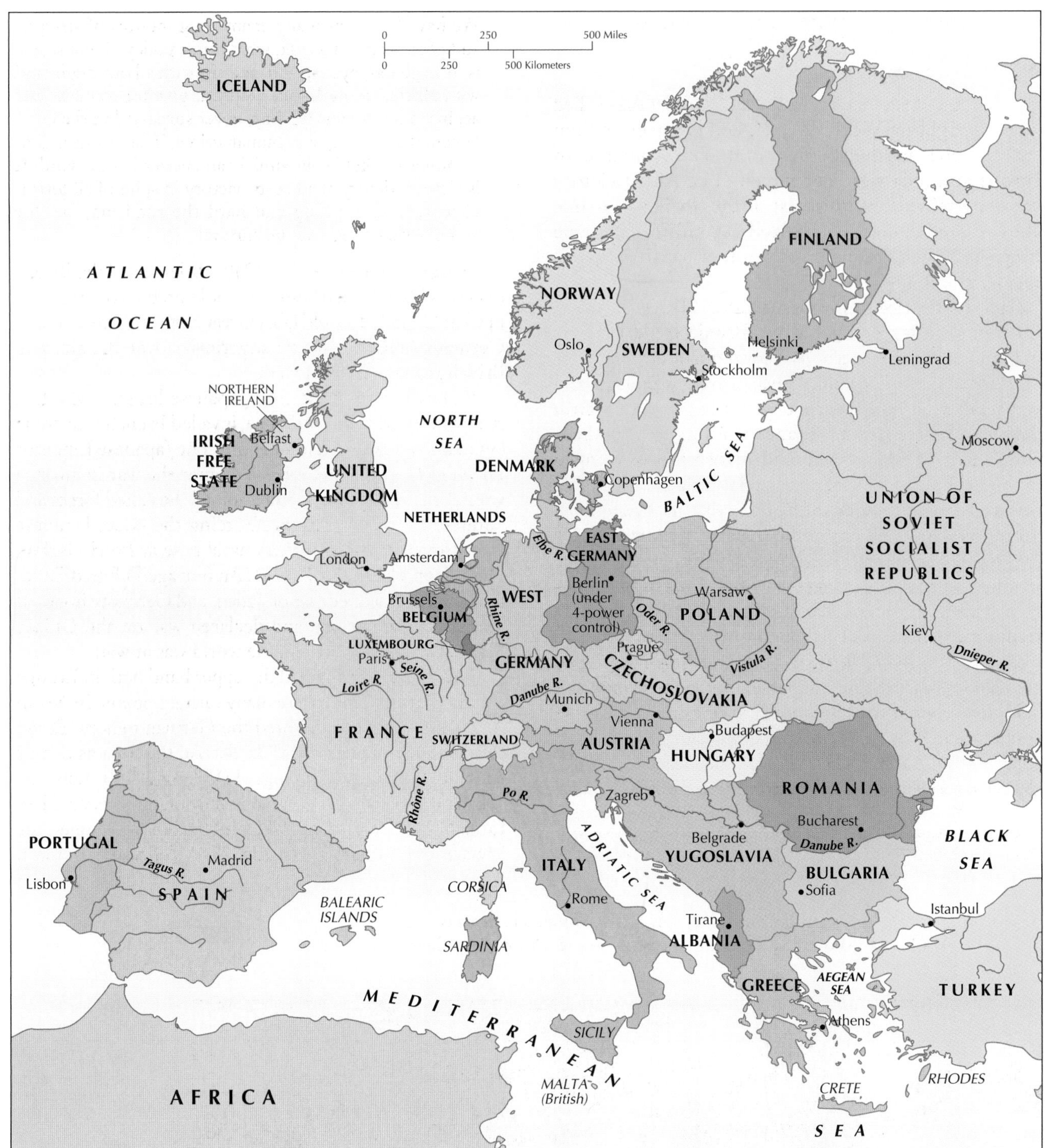

Map 23.1 Post-war Europe, 1949.

Chapter Overview

MID-TWENTIETH CENTURY AND LATER

The existential and the abstract change the face of the humanities

POP CULTURE

Modern society and art exchange ideas and influences

MID-TWENTIETH CENTURY AND LATER

MORE THAN SEVENTEEN MILLION SOLDIERS died fighting World War II, and eighteen million civilians died because of it. The economies of Europe and Asia were decimated. The Allied victory was undermined by a mistrust of the Soviets, wartime allies whose ideology demonized capitalism. Only one thing was certain: humankind was now capable of total self-destruction.

On May 10, 1940, nine months after Hitler's invasion of Poland had forced France and Britain to declare war on Germany, German troops moved north into the Low Countries. From Belgium, German troops poured into France, driving not directly to Paris but to the English Channel, thus separating France from its British allies. More than 300,000 French and British troops trapped on the beaches at Dunkirk retreated to England, and then Hitler marched on Paris. On June 13, the French declared Paris an open city and evacuated without a fight. On June 22, Marshal Henri Pétain signed an armistice with the Germans, handing over two-thirds of the country to German control, leaving himself in charge of the Mediterranean areas. His headquarters were in the small resort community of Vichy, and his government, despised as collaborators after the war, was known as Vichy France.

Hitler believed that, without France's support, Britain would give in as well, but Britain did nothing of the kind. Britain's new prime minister, Winston Churchill (1874–1965), addressed the House of Commons with these words:

> I have nothing to offer but blood, toil, tears, and sweat. We have before us an ordeal of the most grievous kind. We have before us many, many long months of struggle and of suffering. You ask, what is our policy? I will say: It is to wage war, by sea, land, and air, with all our might and with all the strength that God can give us; to make war against a monstrous tyranny, never surpassed in the dark, lamentable catalogue of human crime. That is our policy.
>
> You ask, what is our aim? I can answer in one word: It is victory, victory at all costs, victory in spite of all terror, victory, however long and hard the road may be; for without victory there is no survival.

In August and September 1940, Hitler tested the British resolve with full-scale bomber attacks on the country. But, in what Churchill would label Great Britain's "finest hour," Germany failed to win air superiority over Britain, and British resolve strengthened.

Meanwhile, in the Pacific, Japanese leaders, who had struck a deal with Vichy France, invaded French Indochina (Vietnam) and pressed into China. The Japanese Emperor Hirohito (1901–1989) agreed to enter the war in alliance with Hitler if the United States joined the Allied forces and entered the war in Europe. Forcing the issue, Japanese forces attacked the American naval base at Pearl Harbor, Hawaii, on December 7, 1941. An outraged United States immediately declared war on Japan, and Germany honored its alliance with Japan and declared war on the United States. By the end of 1941, the world was at war.

Slowly, the Allies gained the upper hand both in Europe and the Pacific. There were many turning points. In North Africa, Allied troops defeated the German general Erwin Rommel, the "Desert Fox." In Russia, the Soviets turned back the Germans at Stalingrad (Volgograd). In Italy, the Allied invasion of Sicily soon took Italy out of the war. Then came D-Day on June 6, 1944, and the Allies regained the beaches of northern France (fig. 23.1). A decisive factor in

FIGURE 23.1 Allied troops landing in Normandy. This photograph, taken two days after D-Day, on June 6, 1944, shows reinforcements arriving on French soil. The dimension of the Allied effort is evident.

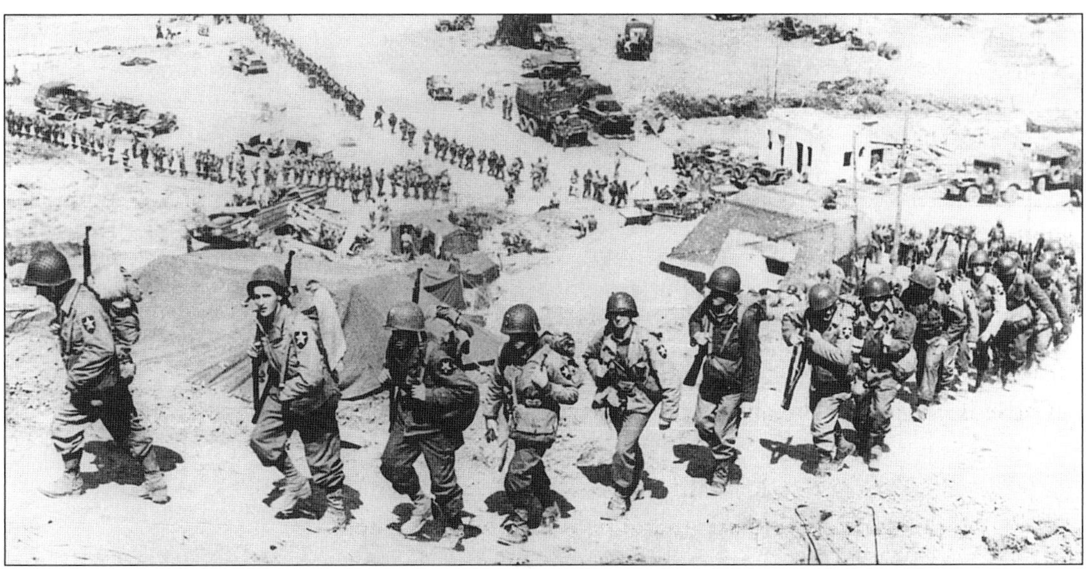

Critical Thinking

THE WEEKEND

The weekend as we know it in the West today did not always exist. Although scattered religious holidays were celebrated from the Middle Ages, and though there was, traditionally, no working on the Sabbath, the two-day weekend did not materialize until the late nineteenth century, when workers in some places took Saturday afternoons off. It did not become standardized and extended to two full days until the mid-twentieth century.

Why do you think the weekend eventually became commonplace in Western societies? Why do you think it took so long to become what it is today? And to what extent do you think new technologies like e-mail and the cell phone have begun to erode it? And, finally, do you think the weekend is a good idea, one that should be preserved? Why or why not?

defeating Germany was Allied air superiority, which demolished Germany's industrial base and oil production capabilities, halting its resupply of troops in the field.

As Allied troops overran Berlin, Hitler shot himself in defeat, having started a war that had resulted in millions of military and civilian deaths, including between six and seven million Jews in death camps such as Auschwitz, in Poland, where as many as twelve thousand Jews were executed in a single day. On May 8, 1945, Churchill and the American President, Harry S Truman (1884–1972), declared victory in Europe. The United States dropped its newly developed atom bomb on the Japanese cities of Hiroshima, on August 6, 1945, and, three days later, on Nagasaki. On September 2, 1945, Japan surrendered as well.

COLD WAR AND ECONOMIC RECOVERY

Many historians view World War II as a rekindling of unresolved hostilities from World War I. In this light, the 1920s and 1930s can be viewed as an extended truce. So devastating was the war that Europe lost its central place in world politics and culture, and Japan was left so battered that its emperor, Hirohito, referred to the situation as "the unendurable that must be endured."

The rebuilding of Europe and Japan required a huge investment. The American secretary of state, George C. Marshall (1880–1959), conceived the idea of providing economic aid to the European countries on the condition they work together for their mutual benefit. It was called the Marshall Plan, and it fostered unprecedented prosperity and affluence in Europe. In Japan, General Douglas MacArthur (1880–1964) oversaw a new democratic constitution forbidding the manufacture of arms for "land, sea, or air force . . . [and] other war potential." Japan thus became the only world power without a significant defense budget, which freed its economy.

Europe became the focal point of a struggle for world power called the Cold War, fought without open warfare between the United States and the Soviet Union. The United States had as its ally much of Western Europe while the Soviet Union dominated Eastern Europe. By 1950, the former imperial powers of Europe lost control of most of their empires overseas, and many of these countries—in Southeast Asia, Africa, and Latin America—became points of conflict in the U.S./Soviet power struggle.

Even as Western Europe lost political clout, it developed a strong economic union, the European Community, or the Common Market as it was known (it has now been renamed once more as the European Union), which brought wealth to the continent. As opposed to Eastern Europe, where shortages of food and goods remained a constant of the Soviet regime, both Western Europe and the United States enjoyed fifty years of economic expansion. Japan, too, unburdened by military expenditures in accordance with its new constitution, turned its attention to its economy, and by 1970, it led the world in the production of consumer goods. By 1996, its gross national product (GNP) was nearly four times that of France and three times that of Germany.

The period after World War II can thus be viewed as a movement from destruction and devastation to affluence and prosperity. Anything seemed possible. Visionaries speculated that one day every family might own a television. Music might be played in stereophonic sound. People might fly to the moon. Computers might interpret data, drive cars, or clean houses. More importantly, racism might end, women might achieve equality, world peace might be possible. Such were the dreams. The reality was more complicated.

THE VIETNAM WARS

Vietnam has a long history of domination by foreign powers. Throughout its history, Vietnam engaged in continued resistance, against China in the eighteenth and nineteenth centuries, and in the mid-twentieth century, against France. After the defeat of the French at Dien Bien Phu in 1945, the United States provided support to the non-Communist government of South Vietnam, which was at war with the Communist North. The United States became increasingly implicated in the war, first through supplying money and war materials, later sending American

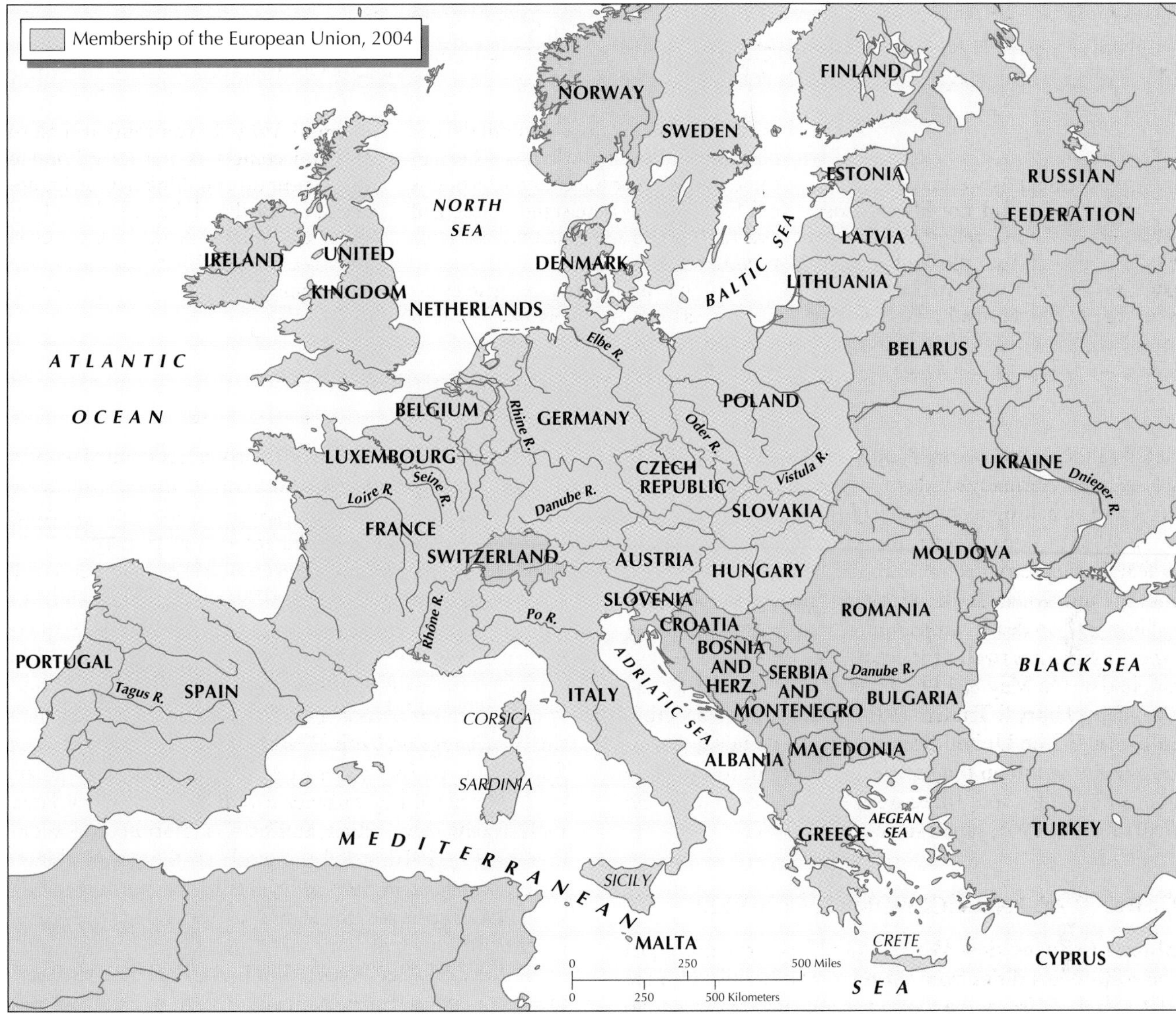

MAP 23.2

military advisors, and finally sending American soldiers to fight alongside the South Vietnamese army.

Gradually, however, due to strong political dissatisfaction with America's presence in Vietnam, U.S. forces were withdrawn and peace agreements signed in 1973. Two years, later, however, the North Vietnamese army marched on Saigon and captured the capital. One year later the country was united as the Republic of Vietnam, and Saigon was renamed Ho Chi Minh City.

THE PHILOSOPHY OF EXISTENTIALISM

The horrible reality of the German concentration camps, of "man's inhumanity to man," and, in France particularly, of the fact that thousands had collaborated with the Nazis in the Vichy government or, at the least, turned their eyes from Nazi atrocities, fueled a discourse about the individual's responsibility to make choices—**existentialism.** Its seeds lay in the ideas of the Danish philosopher SØREN KIERKEGAARD [KEAR-kah-gard] (1813–1855), who insisted on the irreducibly subjective and personal dimension of human life. Kierkegaard used the term the "existing individual" to characterize the subjective perspective, and from this the term "existential" later developed. He emphasized the essentially ethical nature of human life, with each individual responsible for making choices and commitments. Kierkegaard insisted that these choices require respect for other people, virtuous behavior on their behalf, and a faith in spiritual things that transcends the limitations and vicissitudes of material life.

For Kierkegaard, the essential choice human beings make is one between self-gratification and altruism, between selfishness and generosity toward others. This choice is less rational than existential in nature. And the choices we make existentially define who we are as individuals. We make these choices in a spirit of "Either/Or," the title of one of Kierkegaard's books, and we make them in "Fear and Trembling," the title of another. Kierkegaard's work was largely neglected in his time, but it was picked up by the French existentialists, who appreciated his antirational individualism, while ignoring the Christian religious tradition out of which Kierkegaard's thought had sprung.

Jean-Paul Sartre. Like Kierkegaard, the French philosopher JEAN-PAUL SARTRE [SAHR-truh] (1905–1980) emphasized the ethical aspect of existential thought. Unlike Kierkegaard, however, Sartre, who was an atheist, disavowed the spiritual or religious dimension. The central tenets of Sartre's philosophy begin with his idea that "existence precedes essence," which suggests that human beings defined themselves by their choices and actions. Nothing is fixed or preestablished in human nature. What is important is that human beings become what they make of themselves through their choices, decisions, and commitments, which are always in question and never finally settled.

This fundamental idea is related to another: human beings exist relative to one another; they exist in interpersonal and social situations that affect them, situations that also involve repeated decisive choices. The choices human beings make are necessary and inescapable. Those choices, moreover, not only make individuals who they are, since a person is what he or she does, but they also make people responsible for each other as well as for themselves. When people evade responsibility for themselves or for others, they exist in a state that Sartre describes as "bad faith," which results from denying their freedom to do, think, act, or be otherwise than they are.

Sartre developed his philosophy in context of World War II, including the Nazi occupation of France. During that time he came to recognize the ways one's physical freedom could be curtailed and one's life endangered. Nonetheless, he remained uncompromising in his insistence that, regardless of one's situation, one always had the conscious power to negate it and to transcend it in thought. What people make of such situations, much as what they make of themselves through the many roles they perform in life, determines who they become. It is not the situations themselves or the roles people find themselves in that fix their identities but the choices they make in response to those roles and situations.

Simone de Beauvoir. SIMONE DE BEAUVOIR [boh-VWAHR] (1908–1966) shared with Sartre ideas about the necessity for responsibility in choosing what one makes of one's life. De Beauvoir stressed more than Sartre the ambiguity that is frequently a factor in the ethical decisions people need to make.

De Beauvoir's most important contribution involves her study of women. In her groundbreaking book *The Second Sex*, she reviewed history and myth, bringing them to bear on the situation of women at midcentury. She also analyzed the biological bases of female experience, concluding that although biological differences between men and women are incontrovertible, it is social differentiation that determines their very different life experiences. De Beauvoir was especially eloquent on women's need to distinguish themselves from men, to break the pattern of being seen only in relation to them. She was ahead of her time in advancing the belief that, in a man's world, women need to band together to assert pressure for change.

ABSTRACTION IN AMERICAN ART

Existentialism became the dominant postwar philosophy, and the arts began to emphasize individual expression. In the United States, in particular, a brand of highly personal and subjective painting developed that became known as **abstract expressionism.** Although varied in style, the work of the Abstract Expressionists, was unified in its emphasis on expressive gesture and its rejection of art as representation.

During the 1930s, many artists were not working on the kind of mural painting supported by the WPA, and the government recognized this. As part of the New Deal, an easel painting project was initiated that paid artists $95 a month. Although hardly a fortune, this was a living wage, and some of the artists under this plan became the focal point of the American avant-garde of the 1940s, among them Jackson Pollock, Willem de Kooning, and Mark Rothko.

Jackson Pollock. Jackson Pollock (1912–1956) was born in Wyoming, moved to New York in the 1930s, and studied with Thomas Hart Benton, whose interest in large-scale work influenced him. By the mid-1940s, Pollock had begun developing a body of work sometimes referred to as "drip" paintings for which he was dubbed "Jack the Dripper." When he created them, he was in psychoanalysis and was interested in the role of the unconscious in art. Pollock was intrigued by the notion of psychic automatism, imported by the Surrealists who had escaped war in Europe, seeking asylum in the United States. In addition, he had been especially affected by Picasso's *Guernica* (see Chapter 21) when it was first displayed in New York in 1939.

His working method, the results of which are seen in *Autumn Rhythm: Number 30* (fig. 23.2), of 1950, was to unroll a huge canvas on the floor and throw, drip, and splatter paint onto it as he moved around it. Although Pollock said he knew what he was trying to achieve before starting on a canvas, his compositions appear accidental. There is no clear top or bottom: Pollock determined this only when he signed it. The entirety is a web of countless swirling marks, seemingly pushing and pulling one another.

Pollock's style became known as **action painting** because it conveys the artist's physical activity. Pollock swung his arms and moved his entire body when making his drip paintings. For him, the act of getting paint onto the canvas was the important part; the "work" is not so much a finished product as the process of making it.

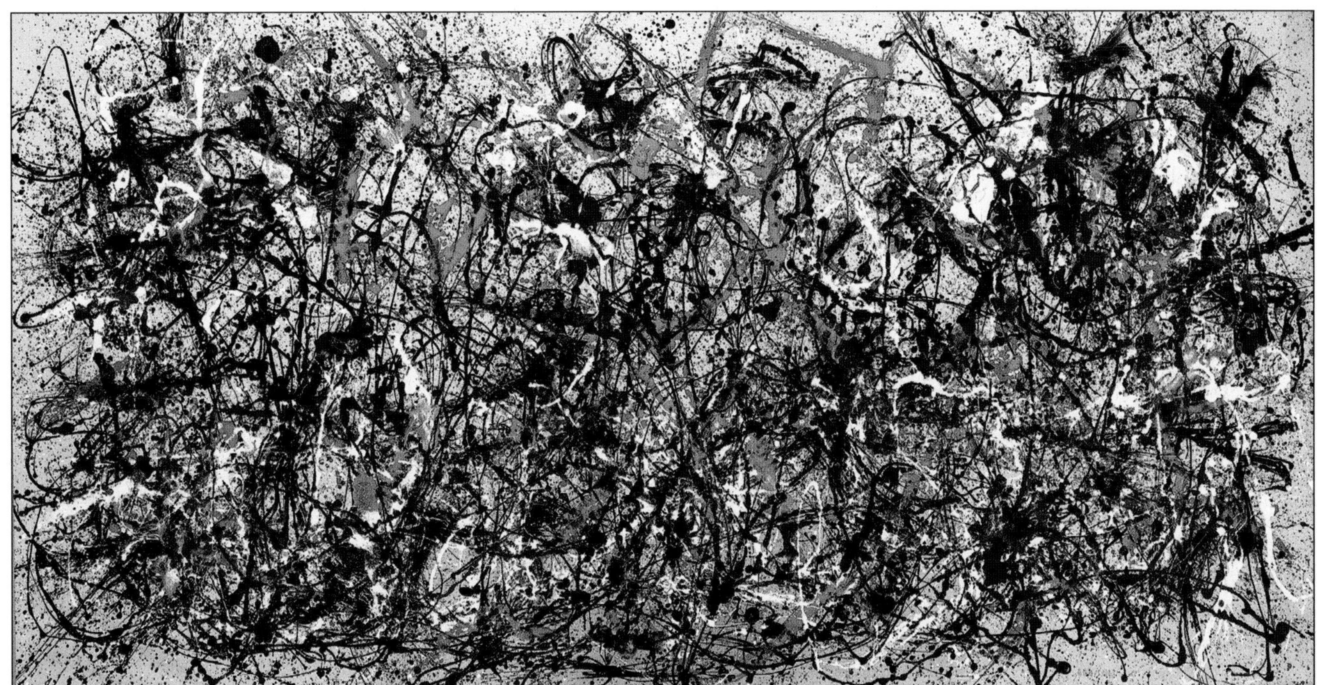

FIGURE 23.2 Jackson Pollock, *Autumn Rhythm: Number 30*, 1950, oil on canvas, 8′9″ × 17′3″ (2.66 × 5.25 m), George A. Hearn Fund, 1957. © 2005, ARS, NY. Metropolitan Museum of Art, NY. Because there is no recognizable subject, such work is referred to as "abstract expressionism." Pollock's personal technique is known as "action painting" because of the highly active physical process—he splattered, flung, and dripped paint onto canvas unrolled on the floor, the result being largely accidental.

Lee Krasner. Lee Krasner (1908–1984) was born in Brooklyn, New York, into an Orthodox Jewish family. After studying art in various New York schools, she joined the American Abstract Artists Group in 1939. She worked with Jackson Pollock in 1941 when both participated in an exhibition held in New York the following year. At this time, she was the better known of the two artists and provided him with access to the Manhattan art world. Krasner married Pollock in 1945; by the following year they were influencing each other's art.

Both worked in styles that gave visual expression to the physical energy of painting. Her *Flowering Limb* (fig. 23.3), painted in 1963, several years after Pollock's death, shows her work, by comparison, to be more controlled than his. Although her paint is applied with a brush rather than dripped onto the canvas, Krasner, too, eliminated the handcrafted quality of careful brushwork, which may be seen as an aspect of the artist's detachment from an actual subject.

Willem de Kooning. Similarly, the paintings of Willem de Kooning (1904–1997) reveal an interest not so much in representing a preconceived idea but rather in experiencing the act of painting. When de Kooning emigrated to the United States from his native Holland in 1926, he was a figure painter, albeit one deeply influenced by the Cubists. Soon, he was influenced by the Surrealists and began painting with broad, slashing strokes. In *Excavation* (fig. 23.4), of 1950, interlocking, neutral-colored shapes, simultaneously organic and geometric, arise from a multicolored ground. Identifiable items can be detected, at various points: sets of teeth, eyes, and even, in the very middle, a red, white, and blue area that suggests an American flag. De Kooning's aim was to create an afocal surface, that is, one on which the eye can never quite come to rest. For de Kooning, this disorientation, comparable to the disorientation felt by immigrants and refugees, represents the modern condition.

Mark Rothko. The **color field** abstraction of Mark Rothko (1903–1970), is characterized by an absence of a recognizable figurative subject, an absence of an illusion of space, and large areas of flat color. A Russian who moved to America, Rothko was an introspective artist whose anguish about himself and his work led to his eventual suicide in his studio in 1970. *Red, Brown, and Black* (fig. 23.5), of 1958, is characteristic of the canvases covered with rectangles of subtle, rich colors for which Rothko is best known. Working with layers of thin paint, Rothko made the edges of his rectangles fuzzy and soft, rendering the rectangles cloudlike, seemingly able to float one on top of another. These subtle color harmonies hover in an ambiguous space, sometimes advancing and sometimes receding. Rothko wished to evoke the emotions "tragic and timeless." He thought of his canvases as backdrops before which viewers experience their feelings, ranging from calm to happy to sad.

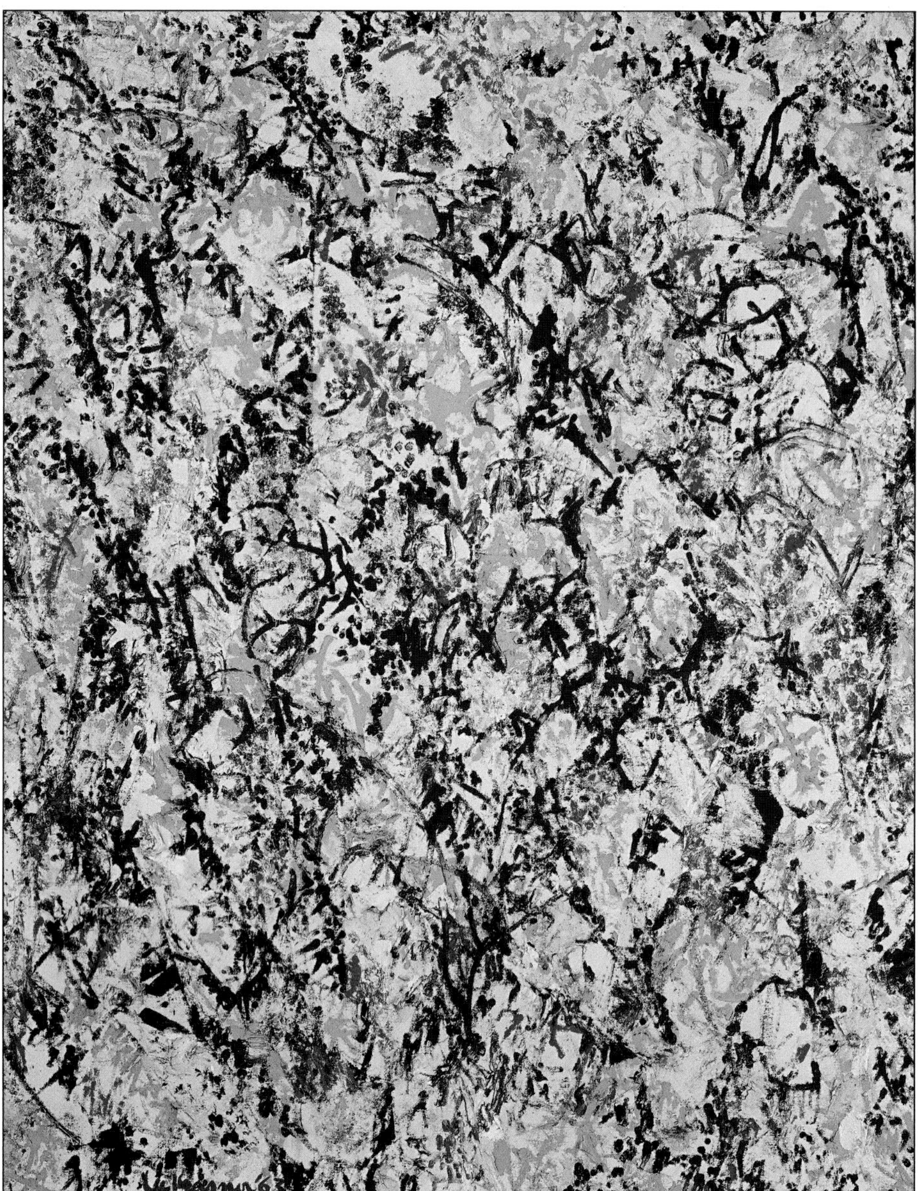

FIGURE 23.3 Lee Krasner, *Flowering Limb*, 1963, oil on canvas $57\frac{3}{4}'' \times 45\frac{3}{4}''$ (146.7 × 116.2 cm). Photograph courtesy of Robert Miller Gallery, NY. Estate of Lee Krasner © 2008 Artists Rights Society (ARS), NY. The degree of abstraction is such that the viewer is unlikely to suspect that this painting portrays a tree branch in bloom prior to reading the title. The dense pattern, almost a form of abstract calligraphy, seems to spread beyond the edges of the canvas, suggesting an ongoing expansive space.

Helen Frankenthaler. Rothko's color field painting, with its chromatic subtleties, is given freer form by the American artist Helen Frankenthaler (b. 1928), a second-generation Abstract Expressionist. Her *Mauve District* (fig. 23.6), of 1966, is an example of this nonobjective style of painting. Like Pollock, Frankenthaler worked on raw, or unprimed canvas, that is, canvas without glue and gesso (white paint) primer. Like Pollock, she worked on huge canvases laid out flat rather than placed on an easel. Unlike Pollock, however, Frankenthaler poured paint onto the canvas, soaking and staining the canvas. At first she used oil paint, thinned with turpentine until it was very fluid. Later she used acrylic paints, which are thinned with water and handled much like watercolor. Frankenthaler's experiments resulted in soft, silky biomorphic shapes in color harmonies producing floating lyrical effects with a look of ease and spontaneity. Some areas of the canvas are left unpainted, defining the painted areas abutting them.

Lois Mailou Jones. Of special interest is the black American textile designer, painter, teacher, and ambassador,

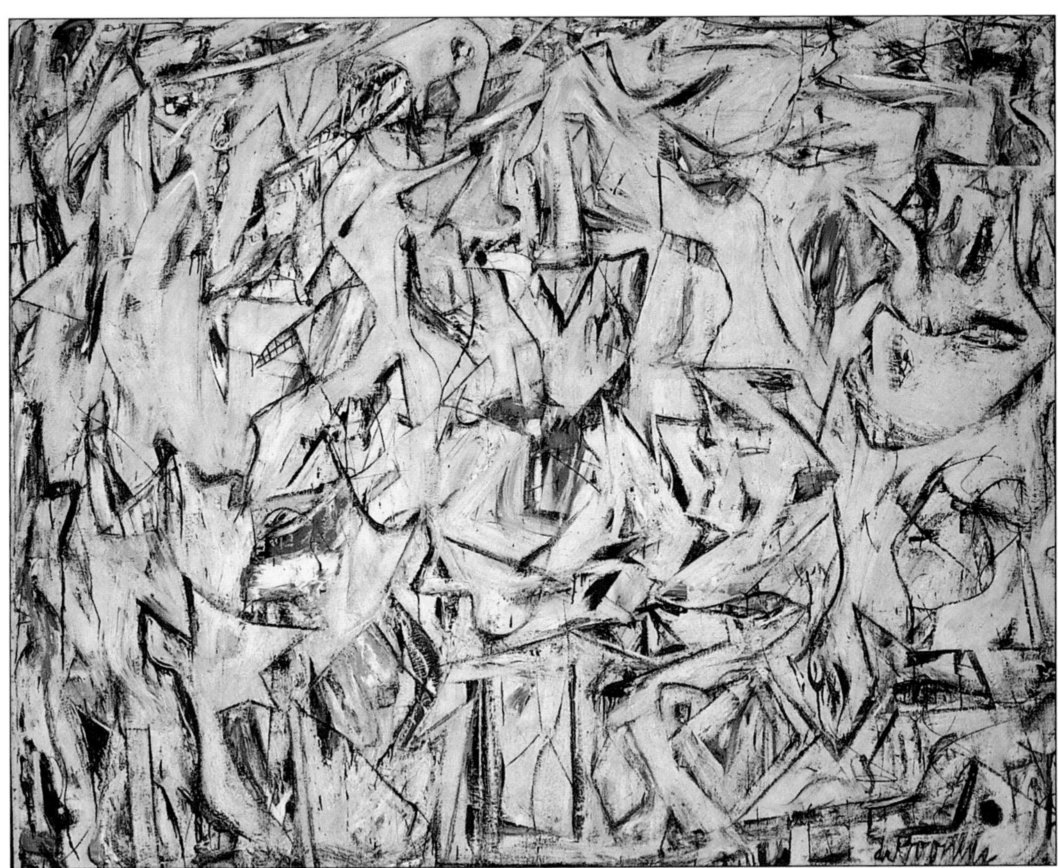

FIGURE 23.4 Willem de Kooning, *Excavation*, 1950, oil on canvas, $6'8\frac{1}{2}'' \times 8'4\frac{1}{8}''$ (2.04 × 2.54 m). Gift of Mr. and Mrs. Noah Goldowsky and Edgar Kaufmann, Jr., Mr. & Mrs. Frank G. Logan Purchase Prize, 1952. 1. Photograph © 1997, The Art Institute of Chicago. All Rights Reserved. © 2005 Artists Rights Society (ARS), NY. Fragments of human anatomy seem to reveal themselves behind, through, and across the webbed surfaces of many de Kooning paintings.

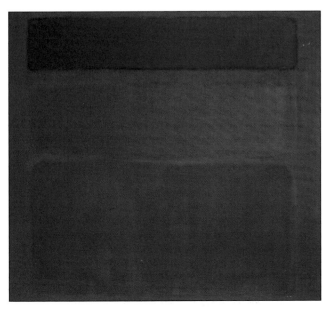

FIGURE 23.5 Mark Rothko, *Red, Brown, and Black*, 1958, oil on canvas, 8′1″ × 9′9″ (2.72 × 2.97 m), Mrs. Simon Guggenheim Fund. Museum of Modern Art, NY/ Licensed by Scala/Art Resource, NY. © ARS, NY. Working in a style known as color field painting, Rothko produced a series of paintings consisting of soft-edged rectangles of various colors that are theoretical and philosophical representations of contrasting states of emotion and discipline.

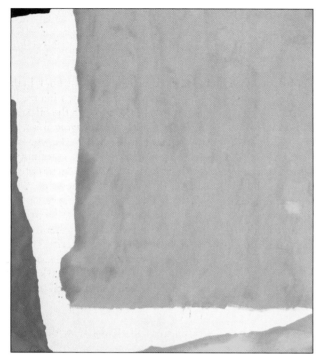

FIGURE 23.6 Helen Frankenthaler, *Mauve District*, 1966, polymer on unprimed canvas, 8′7″ × 7′11″ (2.62 × 2.41 m), Mrs. Donald Straus Fund. Museum of Modern Art/ Licensed by Scala/Art Resource, NY. © 2009 Helen Frankenthaler/Artists Rights Society (ARS), NY. Frankenthaler was deeply impressed by the work of Jackson Pollock. However, where Pollock's oil paint was thick, Frankenthaler achieved soft stained effects, similar to watercolor, by painting with thinned paint on absorbent raw canvas.

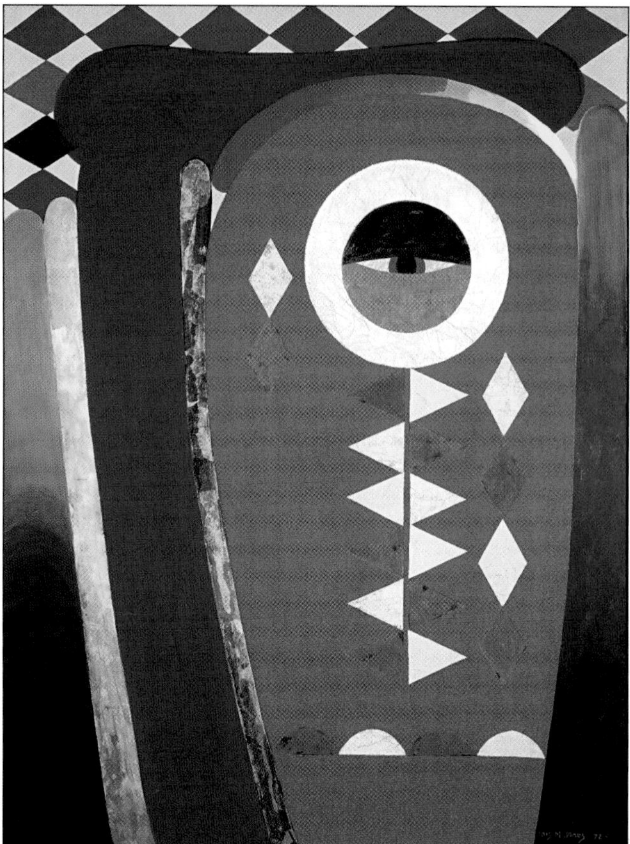

FIGURE 23.7 Lois Mailou Jones, *Ode to Kinshasa*, 1972, mixed media on canvas, 48″ × 36″ (27.9 × 20.3 cm), National Museum of Women in the Arts, Washington, DC. Gift of the artist. The title of this painting refers to the African republic of Congo (formerly Zaire), which Jones, a black American, had visited in 1970 as the United States cultural ambassador.

Lois Mailou Jones (1905–1998). She was born in Boston and graduated with honors from the School of the Museum of Fine Arts. In Washington, DC, she taught at Howard University for many years—from 1930 to 1977. In the 1930s, she began to utilize motifs from African tribal art in her painting, and was influenced also by the strong color patterns of Haitian art—her husband was Haitian. In 1970 she became the United States Information Agency's cultural ambassador to Africa. This experience is reflected in her works such as *Ode to Kinshasa* (fig. 23.7) of 1972. Simple forms, bright colors, and the various textures of the materials pasted onto the canvas are combined with both simplicity and sophistication.

ARCHITECTURE

Ludwig Mies van der Rohe. Among Walter Gropius's colleagues at the Bauhaus in Dessau was LUDWIG MIES VAN DER ROHE [mees van-duh-ROW] (1887–1969). When Hitler closed the school, Mies moved to Chicago where he concentrated his efforts on designing a new campus for the Illinois Institute of Technology. Later Mies created what we now think of as the modern skyscraper.

Typical of his work are the Lake Shore Drive Apartment Houses (fig. 23.8), built 1950–52. Mies's motto, "Less is more," is embodied in these buildings. The steel frame skeleton provides the surface pattern; ornament is avoided. The extreme simplicty approaches austerity. Solid and void are aesthetic equals.

Le Corbusier. The work of Le Corbusier was introduced in Chapter 22, with the Savoye House (fig. 22.19). He designed the church of Notre-Dame-du-Haut at Ronchamp, France (fig. 23.9), 1950–55. The name of the church refers to its location on a mountaintop. Built of masonry and sprayed concrete, the rough surfaces appear to be sheets of a soft material that has been cut with enormous scissors and bent into these concave and convex shapes. Unlike traditional religious architecture, symmetry has been abandoned. Le Corbusier does use light and stained glass, as in a Gothic cathedral (see Chapter 12), but the effect is new. Windows of different sizes and shapes are set into the thickness of the wall, and form an abstract arrangement.

Cross Currents

ABSTRACT EXPRESSIONISM IN JAPAN

In the summer of 1955, a group of young Japanese artists who called themselves the Gutai Art Association organized a thirteen-day, twenty-four-hour-a-day, outdoor exhibition in a pine grove park along the beach in Ashiya, a small town outside Osaka. Their name, Gutai, literally means "concreteness," but more importantly it derives from two separate characters, *gu*, meaning "tool" or "means," and *tai*, meaning "body" or "substance." Taking Jackson Pollock's physical approach to painting as a starting point, they approached their work with their entire bodies, literally throwing themselves into it.

They called the exhibition in Ashiya the *Experimental Outdoor Exhibition of Modern Art to Challenge the Mid-Summer Sun*. A year later, in Tokyo, Gutai held another exhibition. They applied paint to canvas with watering cans and remote control toys. Shimamato Shozo, wearing goggles and dressed for combat, threw jars of paint against rocks positioned across a canvas in a manner reminiscent of a Japanese Zen garden. The finished works were encrusted with paint and glass. Shiraga Kazuo painted on large canvases stretched across the floor, in the manner of Pollock, but used his feet as his brush as he slid through the oil paint. In a piece called *Challenging Mud*, he submerged himself half naked in a pile of dense mud. Rolling in it, squeezing it, wrestling with it, he created a sculptural version of his physical presence. Murakami Saburo built large paper screens six feet high by twelve feet wide, and then flung himself through them.

As violent as these activities were, they were also rooted in Zen. Concrete enactments of the individual's being unite the physical and spiritual in a single image.

FIGURE 23.8 Ludwig Mies van der Rohe, Lake Shore Drive Apartment Houses, Chicago, 1950–52. Modern office and apartment buildings favor simplified and standardized rectangular buildings of steel and glass, the vertical emphasized and the structural frame made obvious.

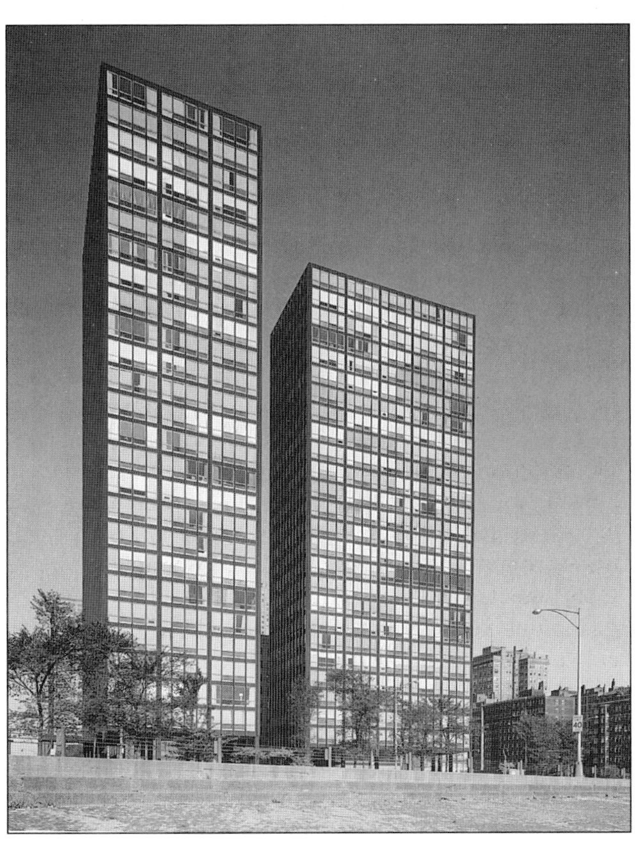

FIGURE 23.9 Le Corbusier (Charles Edouard Jenneret), Notre-Dame-du-Haut, Ronchamp, France, 1950–55. Le Corbusier turned away from the International Style and designed this extraordinary pilgrimage church. Thick masonry walls are covered with sprayed concrete to form curved sculptural surfaces that appear natural and organic rather than rigid and stiff.

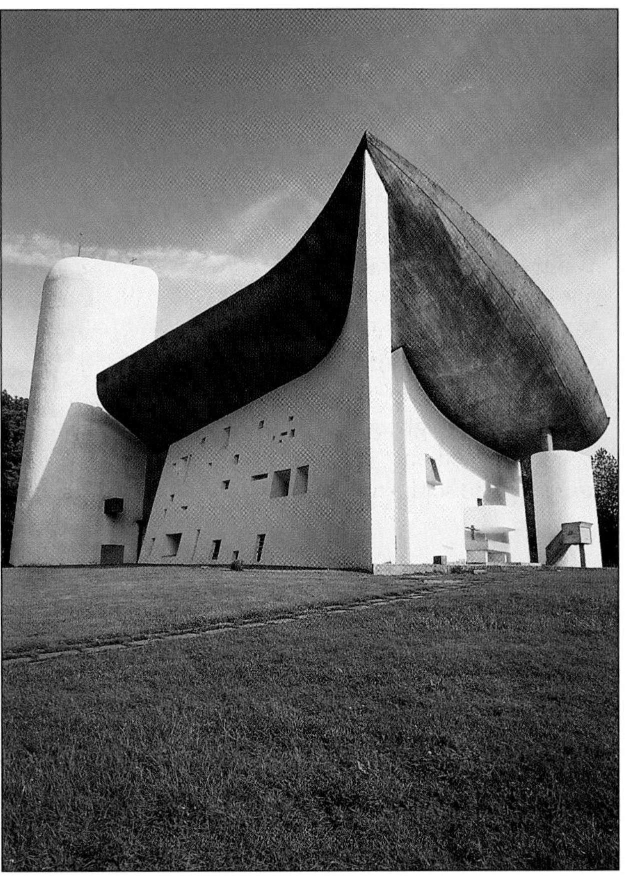

Then & Now

COFFEE: THE BEAN THAT WAKES UP THE WORLD

Coffee is one drink that people enjoy the world over. Coffee was first used by nomads in Ethiopia, where, according to legend, it was discovered by a goatherd who noticed that goats exhibited unusual energy after eating the red berries. The goatherd, named Kaldi, tried the berries himself and experienced an energy surge. A monk from a nearby monastery boiled the berries to make a drink, the ancestor of coffee as we know it today. Sometime between 1000 and 1300, coffee was made into a beverage. And although some authorities date coffee's earliest cultivation to late-sixth-century Yemen, coffee isn't mentioned in literature until the end of the first millenium.

The medicinal properties of coffee were first described by the Arabic philosopher/physician Avicenna. By the late fifteenth century, coffee had spread to the Muslim cities of Mecca and Medina, and by the seventeenth century it had been introduced to the Netherlands and to North America. During the eighteenth century, coffee became daily fare of people throughout the world, soon leading to a plethora of coffeehouses and coffee bars throughout Europe and ultimately, to the phenomenon of Starbucks and other specialty coffee merchants today.

Some highlights from the annals of coffee: Sultan Selim I introduces coffee to Constantinople in 1517; the first coffeehouses open in Venice (1645), Oxford (1650), and New York (1696); the English bring coffee cultivation to Jamaica in 1730; the New York Coffee Exchange opens in 1882; decaffeinated coffee is invented in Germany in 1910; instant coffee is invented in the United States in 1938.

Frank Lloyd Wright. Perhaps the most influential architect of the age was the American Frank Lloyd Wright whose Fallingwater was discussed in Chapter 22 (fig. 22.20).

Wright's works included not only private homes, but also public spaces, such as office buildings, churches, hotels, and museums. His Guggenheim Museum in New York City (fig. 23.10), designed 1942–43 and built 1957–60, is visually arresting. Constructed of reinforced concrete, the shape derives from the ramp inside. Visitors ride an elevator to the top and then view the art while circling down the long spiral walkway.

FIGURE 23.10 Frank Lloyd Wright, Guggenheim Museum, New York, designed 1942–43, built 1957–60. Wright believed people are greatly influenced by their architectural surroundings. Essentially an enormous concrete spiral, a sort of sculpture one can enter, the Guggenheim Museum is itself a work of art.

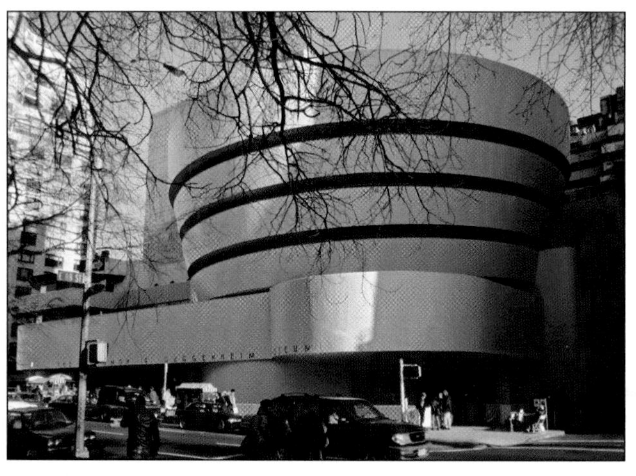

MODERN DRAMA

Modern drama begins in the nineteenth century with the plays of the Norwegian dramatist Henrik Ibsen (see Chapter 17), whose realism shocked his contemporaries and propelled the theater in new directions. Ibsen's emphasis on the psychology of his characters was developed by later playwrights to depict the new existential thought.

An existentialist sense of the absurd dominated postwar theater. A full-blown Theater of the Absurd substituted storyless action for well-contrived plots and disconnected dialogue for witty responses and grand speeches. Absurdist dramatists rejected the idea that characters can be understood or that plot should be structured, just as they rejected the order and coherence of character and action in everyday life.

The Irish-born playwright Samuel Beckett (1906–1989) is best known for *Waiting for Godot* and *Endgame.* Beckett mixes humor with pathos. Relying on the farcical gestures of vaudeville performers and circus clowns, Beckett's characters display a dark intelligence and bleakly pessimistic view of their tragicomic situation. Lacking in purpose and meaning, they wait for the inevitable.

Waiting for Godot (1952) portrays two tramps, Vladimir and Estragon, who wait for someone who never comes. As they wait, the tramps quarrel, contemplate suicide, separation, and departure. They wait until they become dependent on waiting itself. Two additional characters, a master and servant named Pozzo and Lucky, share the stage for a time with the tramps. The rich Pozzo mistreats Lucky cruelly, until Pozzo becomes blind, at which point he needs the now mute Lucky to lead him. Each pair has nothing more in life than one another. Beckett's theatrical genius lies in depicting the human will to survive, despite the direst of circumstances, in all its starkness and humor.

SCULPTURE

Alexander Calder. A new kind of sculpture was created by the American Alexander Calder (1898–1976), whose father was also a sculptor. The younger Calder first gained recognition as a toy maker in Paris in the 1930s with a miniature circus that fascinated the Surrealists, particularly Miró. By this time, Calder was already making **mobiles,** sculptural forms suspended from the ceiling that are driven by the air itself (fig. 23.11). Although many people today know what a mobile is, it was Calder who invented the form and Marcel Duchamp who gave it its name. Because a mobile moves in the faintest breeze, its form is always changing, the simple shapes constantly forming new relationships. A mobile uses color, shape, composition, motion, time, and space. The artist must be concerned with each.

Isamu Noguchi. A student of Brancusi's in Paris in the 1920s, Japanese-American sculptor ISAMU NOGUCHI [No-GOO-chee] (1904–1988) was particularly influenced by Brancusi's sense of sculpture as possessing an inherent expressive power. Noguchi drew on his own Japanese heritage in an attempt to discover in stone what the Japanese call *wabi*—the "ultimate naturalness" of an object.

Kouros (fig. 23.12) is one of Noguchi's works from the period of World War II, during which time he voluntarily entered a Japanese internment facility at Poston, Arizona, in order to help those being held there. "Kouros" is the ancient Greek term for "boy" or "young man" and refers to life-size sculptures of the nude male that began to appear in Greece in the seventh century B.C.E. (see Chapter 2). Despite the title, the form of Noguchi's work is more obviously related to that of the Surrealists, particularly Arp and Miró. The piece unites two opposing techniques for, on the one hand, it is carved while, on the other, it is constructed. When viewed from two different angles—that is, from the front and from the side—it appears to be two entirely different works of art. In other words, it induces, or indeed demands, the viewer's movement.

POP CULTURE

In the 1950s and 1960s, the material dreams of the postwar era seemed to be coming true. Society was rapidly becoming a consumer culture. In 1947, 75,000 homes in the United States were equipped with television sets. By 1967, over 55 million sets were in operation and over 95 percent of American families owned at least one. That same year, Swanson introduced the first frozen TV Dinner—turkey, mashed potatoes, and peas. In 1955, McDonald's was founded, inaugurating the fast-food industry. The growth of the automobile industry, which made fast food possible, was staggering. By 1949, Detroit was producing 5 million automobiles a year, a year later 8 million, and the number continued to grow. In response to this, shopping patterns changed. In 1950, just north of Seattle, Washington, the Northgate Shopping Center

FIGURE 23.11 Alexander Calder, *Red Gongs*, completed 1950, hanging mobile, painted aluminum, brass, steel rod and wire, overall size 4′11″ × 12′1$\frac{1}{3}$″ (1.50 × 3.70 m), Metropolitan Museum of Art, NY. Calder invented this type of hanging sculpture, called a "mobile" because its component parts, highly responsive to the environment, are moved by the faintest breeze. He also made "stabiles" out of similar thin flat shapes that did not move.

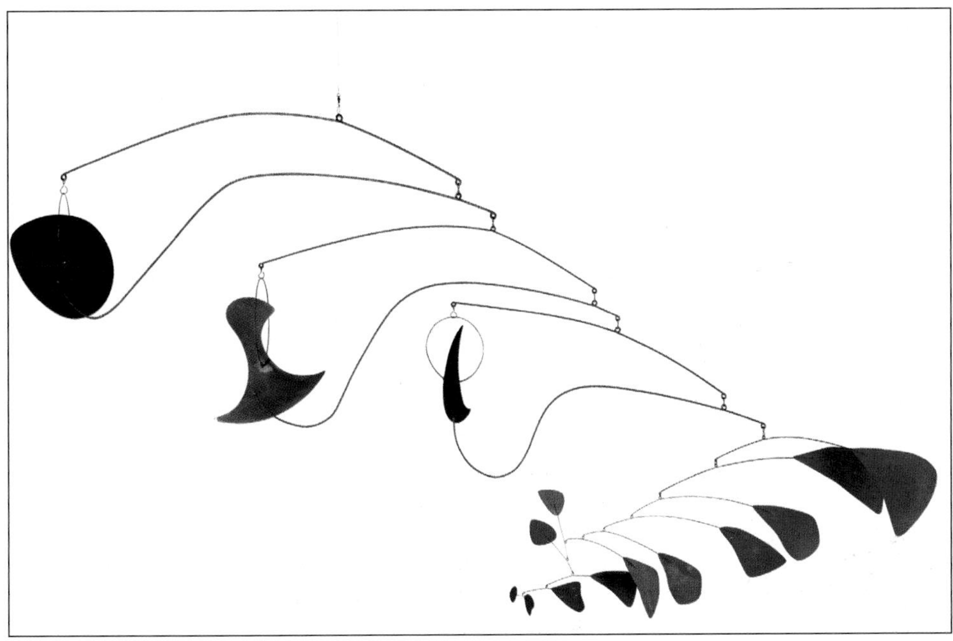

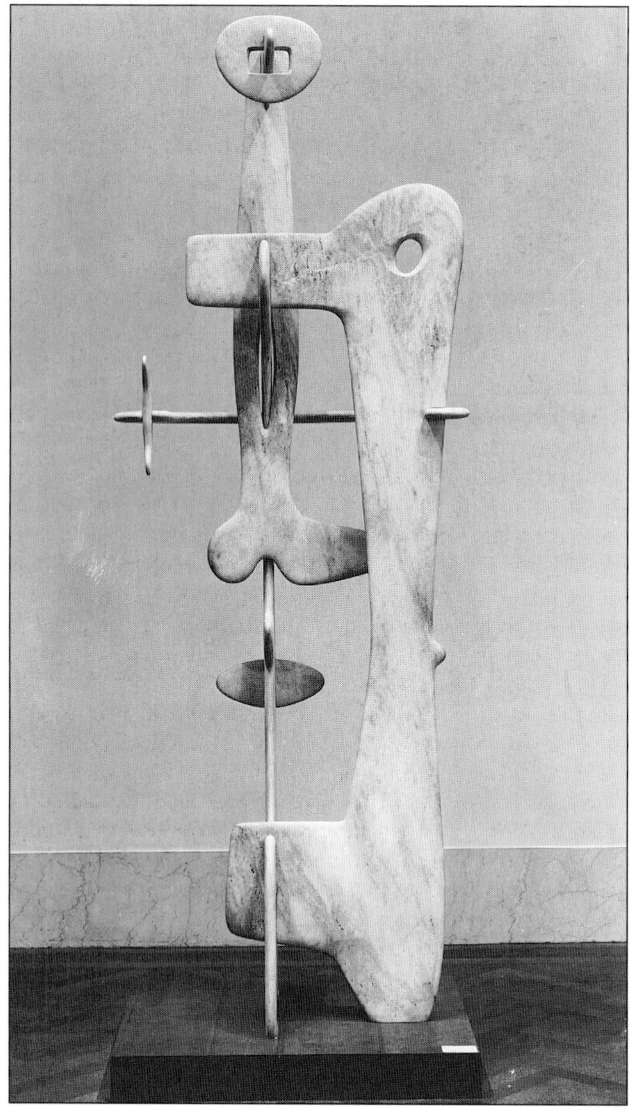

FIGURE 23.12 Isamu Noguchi, *Kouros*, 1944–45, pink Georgia marble, height 9′9″ (2.97 m), Metropolitan Museum of Art, NY, Fletcher Fund, 1953 (53.87a-i). Art Resource, NY. Noguchi turned to these flat slabs of marble because, used in the commercial building industry for facades, countertops, and the like, they were inexpensive and widely available.

opened, accessible only by car and consisting of forty shops clustered around a Bon Marché department store. Six years later, the first covered shopping mall, Southdale Center, opened in Minneapolis. In 1953, the Kinsey Report on sexual behavior in the United States was published, and by 1966, the sexual revolution had taken firm hold as an **oral contraceptive,** popularly called "the Pill," became widely available.

As consumerism increasingly preoccupied American life, artists and intellectuals turned their attention to the cycle of production, consumption, and waste that defined experience. Like the Dadaists of a previous generation, they realized that art might be almost anything.

A theoretician of this point of view was the composer John Cage (1912–1995), who first taught at Black Mountain College in North Carolina in the early 1950s, and at the New School in New York City in the late 1950s. For instance, his piece "4′3″" is four minutes and thirty-three seconds of actual silence, during which the audience becomes aware of sound in the room—"traffic sounds," in the words of one audience member at a performance at the Carnegie Recital Hall in New York, "chairs creaking, people coughing, rustling of clothes, then giggles . . . a police car with its siren running . . . the elevator in the building . . . the air conditioning going through the ducts." These sounds comprise the "music" of the piece. First performed at Woodstock, New York, on August 29, 1952, the work possesses three influential features: minimal elements—silence; commonplace chance events, which links the piece to Surrealism; uniqueness in time—two performances are never alike.

ARTISTS OF THE EVERYDAY

Robert Rauschenberg. One Black Mountain student, Robert Rauschenberg (b. 1925), influenced by Cage's composition of the everyday, began making **assemblages,** a variation on the idea of the collage (see Chapter 22), taking things one would normally discard and combining them to create "art." Creation, he said, is "the process of assemblage." *Odalisk* (fig. 23.13), made between 1955 and 1958, is compiled of a stuffed rooster, a pillow, magazine illustrations (including nude photographs), and paint, all on wood. The title is a pun, combining "odalisque" (harem girl) and "obelisk," a four-sided stone pillar capped by a small pyramid.

Like Cage, Rauschenberg brings together daily life and art. It is a messy art, an art of disorder, of chance, indeterminate, unpredictable, and multilayered. The images are not arranged neatly but are made to overlay, one intruding upon another. Rauschenberg called this work "combine painting."

Louise Nevelson. A different type of assemblage was created by Louise Nevelson (1899–1988), who was born in Kiev, Russia, and moved to Maine as a child. Nevelson studied many arts—music, dance, theater, painting, and printmaking. In her fifties, she began assembling small wooden objects, scraps and remnants that she found in furniture shops. She nailed and glued these fragments together, creating compositions within wooden boxes, which were then stacked together to create walls of a kind of large-scale relief. The entire assemblage was painted one color—black most often, or white, or gold.

Nevelson's *Sky Cathedral* (fig. 23.14), made in 1958, is painted black. According to the artist, black is the most aristocratic color and "encompasses all colors." This single color unifies what would otherwise appear

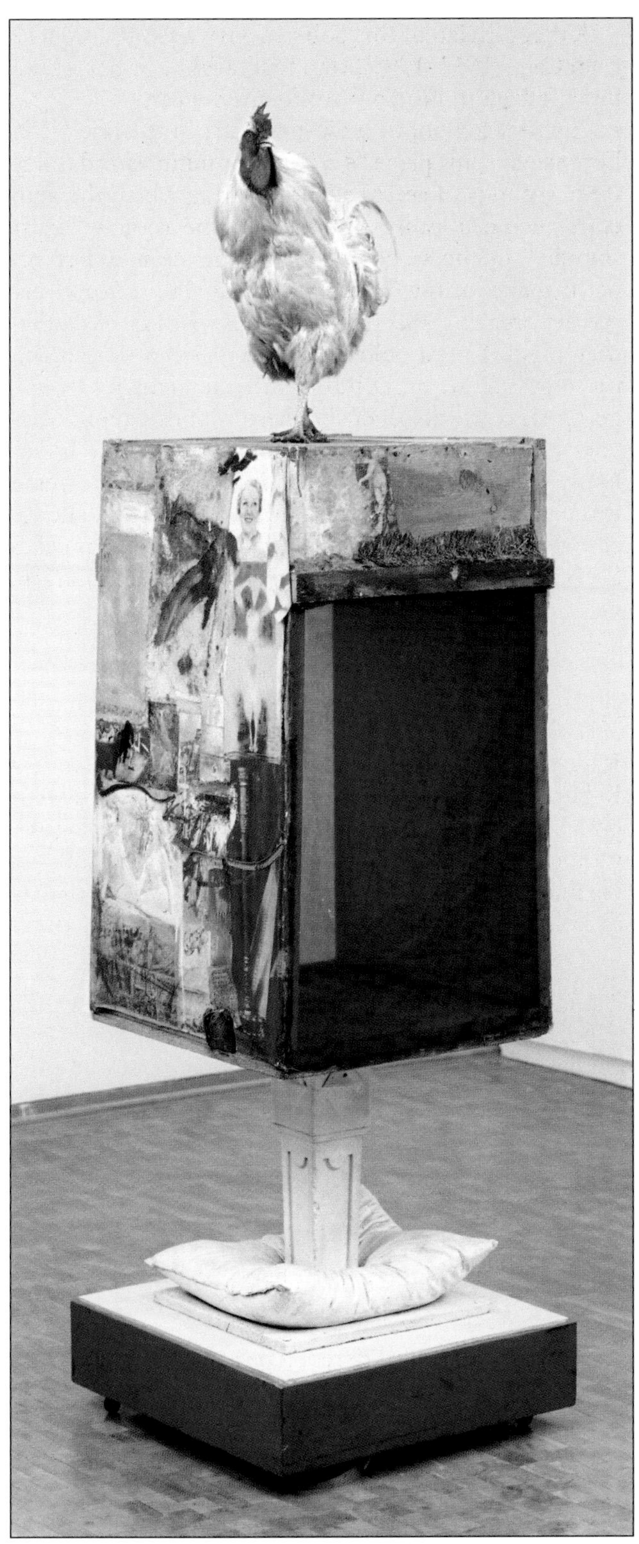

FIGURE 23.13 Robert Rauschenberg, *Odalisk*, 1955–58, assemblage, including stuffed rooster, pillow, and paint, on wood, 6′9″ × 25″ × 25″ (205.7 × 63.5 × 63.5 cm), Museum Ludwig, Koln. Rheinisches Bildarchiv, Koln. Art © Robert Rauschenberg/Licensed by VAGA, NY. This construction, or assemblage, is not carved or modeled but compiled, the materials left as found rather than transformed. Rauschenberg works with materials not traditionally used in creating fine art, materials that one would normally discard.

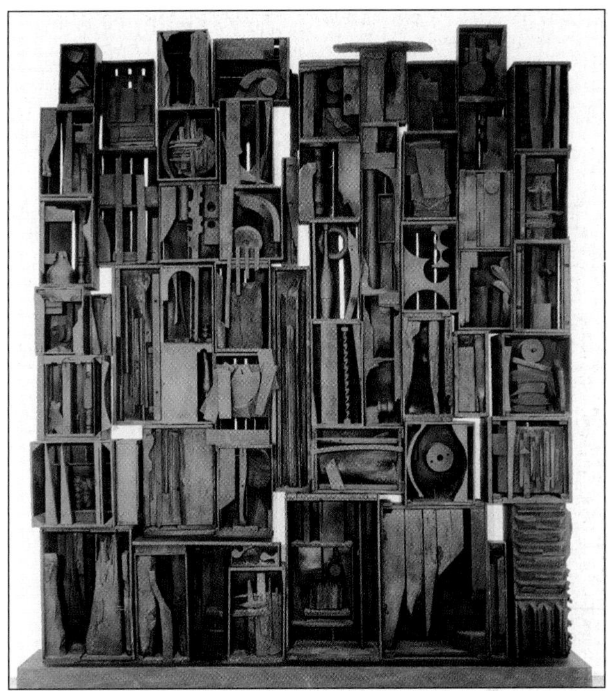

FIGURE 23.14 Louise Nevelson, *Sky Cathedral*, 1958, assemblage, wood, painted black, 11′3$\frac{1}{2}$″ × 10′$\frac{1}{4}$″ × 1′6″ (3.44 × 3.05 × 0.46 m). Digital Image © Museum of Modern Art/Licensed by SCALA/Art Resource, NY © 2008 Artists Rights Society (ARS), NY. From a series of small compositional units made of pieces of wooden furniture and furnishings, Nevelson compiled wallsize assemblages, which she unified by painting a single solid color.

fragmentary into an environment that looks like a city of many compartments, all compressed into a single plane.

Andy Warhol. The most "everyday" objects of the 1950s and 1960s were images of popular culture itself—advertising images, celebrated entertainers, product labels, and highway billboards. All of these, were "packaged," as one young artist, Andy Warhol (1928–1987), recognized. Starting in commercial art in the late 1950s, he turned his studio into what he called The Factory, where he began churning out large editions of prints, as well as unique paintings. His work mimics the world of mass production—Campbell's soup cans (fig. 23.15), Coca-Cola bottles, dollar bills, and images of Elvis Presley and Marilyn Monroe. The style was quickly labeled **Pop Art**—popular art. Warhol's images raise everyday objects and icons to artistic status; behind this lies an ironic resignation to widespread banality.

Roy Lichtenstein. The same underlying despair combines with cartoonlike presentation in the work of Roy Lichtenstein (b. 1923). Lichtenstein painted large-scale imitations of two kinds of comic strips—war comics, depicting men in battle, and romance comics, akin to television soap operas, portraying the lives of young

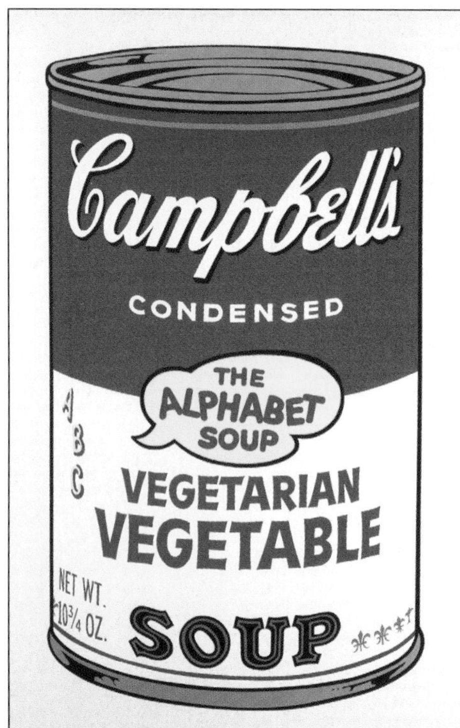

FIGURE 23.15 Andy Warhol, *Vegetarian Vegetable from Campbell Soup II*, screenprint, 1969, 35″ × 23″ (88.9 × 58.4 cm), The Metropolitan Museum of Art, NY, 1972. 724. 3. Warhol depicted common consumer items using silkscreen, itself a commercial technique. His various images of soup cans are shown singly or stacked up as in a grocery store for sale.

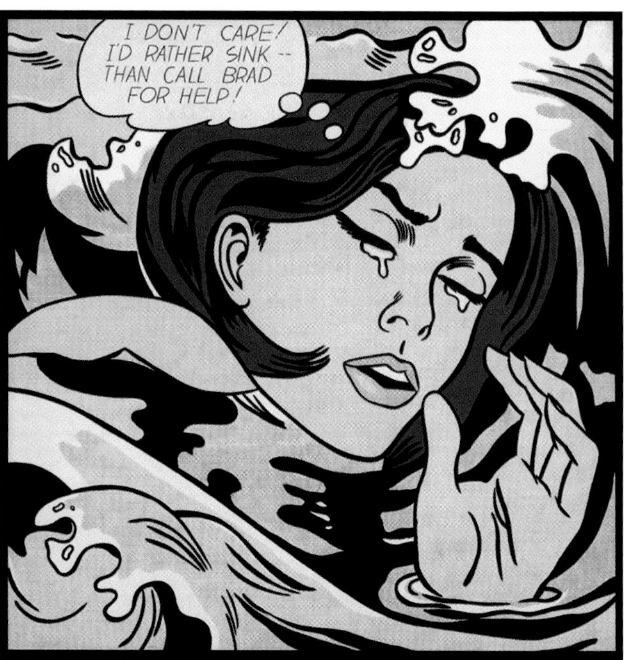

FIGURE 23.16 Roy Lichtenstein, *Drowning Girl*, 1963, oil and synthetic polymer paint on canvas, $5'7\frac{5}{8}'' \times 5'6\frac{3}{4}''$ (1.72 × 1.70 m), Museum of Modern Art/Licensed by SCALA-Art Resource, NY. Philip Johnson Fund and Gift of Mr. and Mrs. Bagley Wright. Photograph © 2005 Museum of Modern Art, NY. Lichtenstein recognized that, even though his audience might laugh at a cartoon image such as this, they would identify with the image as well.

women. *Drowning Girl* (fig. 23.16) depicts with deadpan humor an absurd relationship dilemma.

A basis of Lichtenstein's style is the printer's dot—the so-called ben-day dot—used to print color in the comic strips. The style may be seen as a parody of Seurat's pointillist technique (see Chapter 18). Lichtenstein asks us both to laugh and to take it seriously.

Claes Oldenburg. In December 1961, at 107 East Second Street in New York City, Claes Oldenburg (b. 1929), a Yale graduate and son of a Norwegian diplomat, opened an exhibition of painted plaster replicas of commodities—meat, vegetables, candy, cakes, pies, ice cream sundaes—in a shop front that he named "The Store." One replica was *Two Cheeseburgers, with Everything (Dual Hamburgers)* (fig. 23.17). At Oldenburg's store a plate of meat cost $399.98 and a sandwich $149.98. "I do things that are contradictory," Oldenburg explained. "I try to make the art look like it's part of the world around it. At the same time I take great pains to show that it doesn't function as part of the world around it." The following summer, Oldenburg recast some objects in giant scale and redid others as soft sculptures, sewn and stuffed with foam rubber. What should be soft—a hamburger, for instance—was hard plaster. What should be hard—a typewriter—was suddenly soft and sagging. Oldenburg's work jokes about audience expectations. In Oldenburg's world, consumable goods cannot be consumed, and giant versions of clothespins, spoons, electric plugs, scissors, trowels, and faucets transform the everyday into the monumental.

FIGURE 23.17 Claes Oldenburg, *Two Cheeseburgers, with Everything (Dual Hamburgers)*, 1961, burlap soaked in plaster, painted with enamel, $7'' \times 14\frac{3}{4}''$ (17.8 × 37.5 cm), Philip Johnson Fund. Museum of Modern Art, NY/Licensed by Scala/Art Resource, NY. Pop Art seems simultaneously to laud and laugh at popular culture. Should art reflect the most characteristic aspects of a culture, or strive to raise the level of culture?

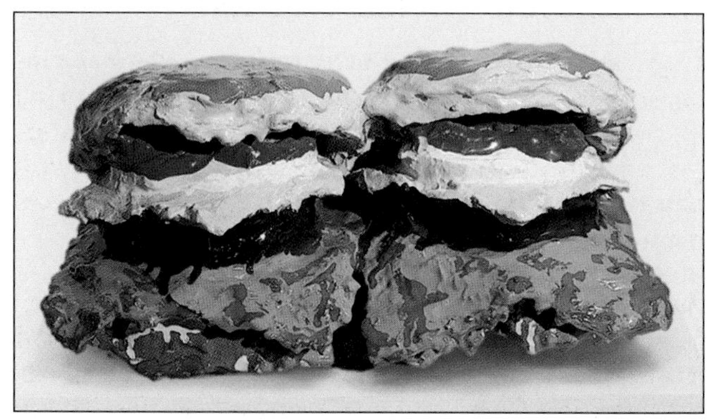

Table 23–1 IMPORTANT STYLES OF PAINTING DURING THE AGE OF AFFLUENCE

Style	Artist	Painting and Date
Abstract Expressionism	Pollock	*Autumn Rhythm,* 1950
	de Kooning	*Excavation,* 1950
	Rothko	*Red, Brown, and Black,* 1958
	Frankenthaler	*Mauve District,* 1966
Pop Art	Lichtenstein	*Drowning Girl,* 1963
	Warhol	*Vegetarian Vegetable,* 1969
Op Art	Riley	*Hesitate,* 1964

Marisol Escobar. The Pop Art sculptor MARISOL [ESCOBAR] (b. 1930) is an American who was born in Paris, although her parents were Venezuelan. She moved to Los Angeles, back to Paris, and then to Manhattan. Here, her work humorously satirizing social and political aspects of life, was well received. A well-known example is *Women and Dog* (fig. 23.18) of 1964. Here are three women, a child, and a dog, perhaps out for a stroll. Two of the women have multiple faces, suggesting that they are glancing in all directions.

Although essentially wooden sculpture, the wood is only minimally carved; the block shapes are retained. The effect depends less on carving than on painting with strong colors, the composition unified by the repetition of the pattern on a skirt and a blouse, the size and the color scheme of the pattern varied.

Happenings. Allan Kaprow (b. 1927) believed Cage's work suggested a new "total art." Kaprow's vision sprang from an "event" that Cage staged at Black Mountain College in 1952, entitled *Theater Piece #1*, that combined music, film, art, poetry, and dance. Kaprow envisaged "an assemblage of events . . . [which] unlike a stage play, may occur at a supermarket, driving along a highway, under a pile of rags, and in a friend's kitchen, either at once or sequentially." He called such a work a **Happening.** "It is art," he said, "but seems closer to life."

MINIMAL AND CONCEPTUAL ART

Cage's **minimalism** also attracted sculptors, who saw principles relevant to their work in it. First, they saw that a formal but minimal sculptural statement would be interpreted varyingly according to its situation; and, second, that the repetition of a sculptural statement, as in mass manufacture, changes the meaning of the form.

Sol LeWitt. Also working in modular units, Sol LeWitt (b. 1928) created cubic frameworks of white, baked enamel beams arranged and repeated according to various mathematical formulas. *Open Modular Cube* (fig. 23.20), for instance, appears quite straightforward. But over the course of a day, its shadows change and its appearance also changes as the viewer moves around it; thus the appearance of LeWitt's apparently stable structure is constantly changing.

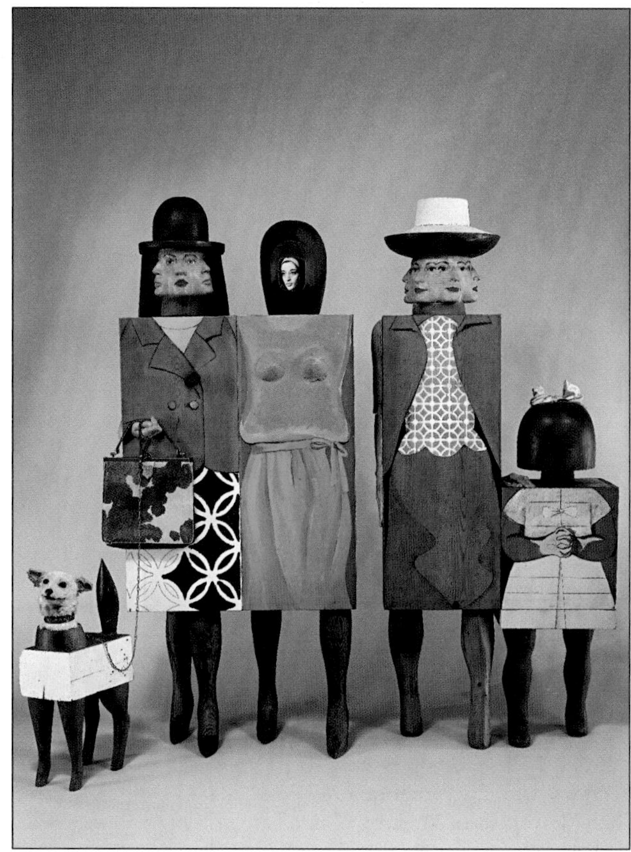

FIGURE 23.18 Marisol [Escobar], *Women and Dog*, 1964, plaster, synthetic polymer, wood, taxidermed dog head and miscellaneous items, overall: 72″ × 85″ × 48″ (182.9 × 215.9 × 121.9 cm). Whitney Museum of American Art, NY. Purchase, with funds from the Friends of the Whitney Museum of American Art 64.17 a-g. Collection of the Whitney Museum of American Art, New York. © Marisol Escobar/Licensed by VAGA, NY. Pop Art artists treat ordinary, everyday aspects of life in ways that may surprise, entertain, or even amuse the viewer—perhaps causing us to reconsider some things we tend to overlook or take for granted.

For LeWitt, a work of art is "pure information," and could exist simply *as* information rather than as an object. That is, it could exist solely as a *concept.* LeWitt soon started making verbal instructions for artworks rather than making art itself. For a wall drawing, he might say, "Draw lines from the middle of the edge to a point in the center, in each of four colors, one color for each side," and so on. Then the drawing would be executed by whomever at whatever site, each work different.

Bridget Riley. Although associated with **Op Art** (a shortening of *Optical Art*), or retinal painting, a nonrepresentational style of painting concerned with optics,

Connections

RAUSCHENBERG, CAGE, AND CUNNINGHAM

At Black Mountain College, artist Robert Rauschenberg, composer John Cage, and choreographer Merce Cunningham began a series of collaborations that lasted over three decades. At their collaboration's heart was a belief in, as one critic described Rauschenberg's combine paintings, "an aesthetics of heterogeneity." Together they trusted that, in the chance encounter of diverse materials, moments of revelation would be generated.

Both Cage and Rauschenberg were willing to admit almost anything into their work. So was Merce Cunningham, for whom the stage was an exploratory space. Cunningham took the focus off the front of the stage, where classical ballet had placed it. Instead, he treated all points on the stage as equally important, and thus, equally interesting. Cunningham dispensed with the idea that the center of the stage needed always to be the center of attention and interest. In this, he echoed the way space was treated in modern painting, in the process paying tribute to Albert Einstein's ideas about the lack of fixed points in physical space.

An example of such a dance is the 1958 *Summerspace* (fig. 23.19), with sets by Rauschenberg. "When I spoke to Bob Rauschenberg—for the decor—I said, 'One thing I can tell you about this dance is that it has no center . . .' So he made a pointillist backdrop and costumes." In another piece, *Variations V*, the dancer triggers sensors, which in turn trigger an "orchestra" of tape recorders, record players, and radio receivers containing sounds "composed" by Cage. A member of Cunningham's dance company, Gordon Mumma, describes the result as "a superbly poly: -chromatic, -genic, -phonic, -morphic, -pagic, -technic, -valent, multi-ringed circus."

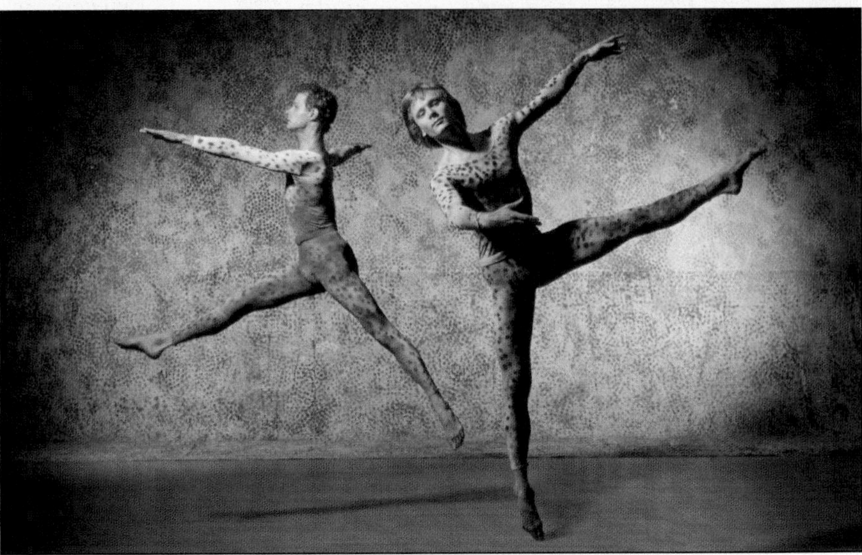

FIGURE 23.19 Merce Cunningham, *Summerspace*, 1958. Dancers: Robert Kovich and Chris Komar. Cunningham tries to devise dances in which so much is happening at once that the effect is not unlike trying to watch all three rings of a circus simultaneously.

the British painter Bridget Riley (b. 1931) explained that she never studied optics, relying instead on "empirical analyses and syntheses." Op Art is not emotional but intellectual, characterized by meticulous patterns, precisely painted, frequently in brilliant contrasting colors or in black and white.

Hesitate (fig. 23.21) is one of a group of black, gray, and white paintings Riley created in 1964. Other titles in this series include *Disturbance* and *Pause*, suggesting deeper implications. That the wavelike patterns appear to undulate and pulsate, creating illusions of three dimensions on the flat surface without using traditional methods of perspective, Riley notes "is purely fortuitous." Instead, she is concerned with polarities such as "static and active, or fast and slow," explaining that "repetition, contrast, calculated reversal and counterpoint also parallel the basis of our emotional structure."

ARCHITECTURE

Richard Rogers and Renzo Piano. Intentionally extraordinary, the Pompidou Center in Paris, built 1971–77 by Richard Rogers and Renzo Piano (fig. 23.22), is a famous—or infamous—example of modern architecture. In essence, a building turned inside out, its mechanical parts—usually hidden from view—have been oversized, put on the outside of the building, and painted bright colors according to their function: red for vertical transportation; green for water; yellow for electricity; white for ventilation, and blue for air conditioning. The

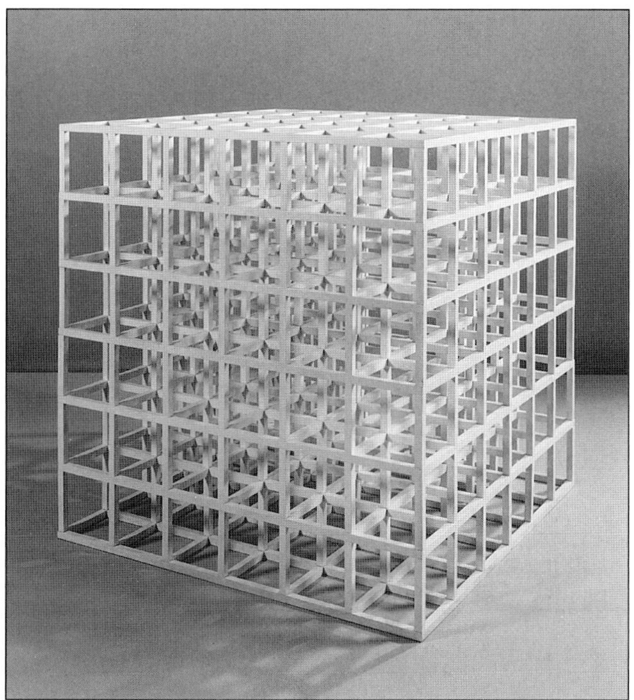

FIGURE 23.20 Sol LeWitt, *Open Modular Cube*, 1966. Painted aluminum, 5′ × 5′ × 5′ (1.52 × 1.52 × 1.52 m). © 2005 ARS, NY/Art Gallery of Ontario, Toronto. The simplest geometric shape, the square, is repeated countless times, creating a complex composition comparable to a monochromatic Mondrian in three dimensions.

FIGURE 23.21 Bridget Riley, *Hesitate*, 1964, emulsion on board, $43\frac{3}{8}'' \times 45\frac{1}{2}''$ (1.07 × 1.12 m), © Tate Gallery, London/Art Resource, NY. Tricking the eye, Op Art plays with the optical mechanics of human visual perception, the patterns appearing to vibrate and vacillate forward and backward. Riley said this effect was ancillary to her intentions, for she wanted the entire painting to be seen as a "field" rather than in individual parts, and compared it to painting a landscape.

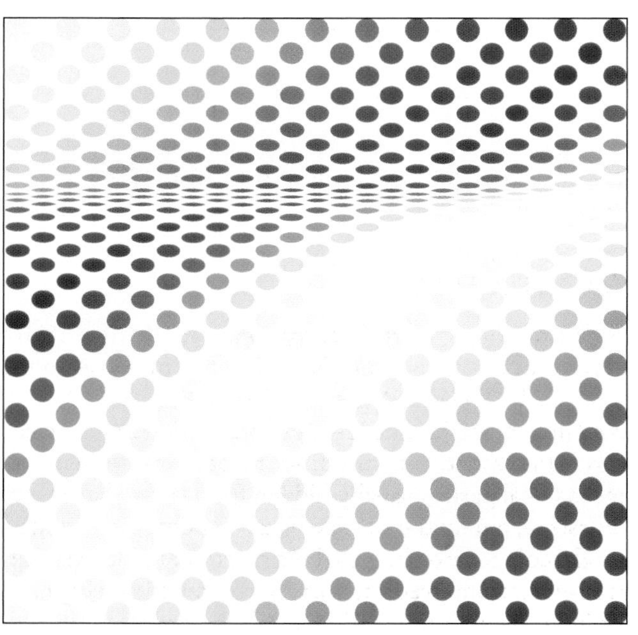

escalator looks like a huge caterpillar inching its way along the facade. The Pompidou Center emphasizes the ordinary, the everyday, the commonplace—much like Pop Art.

Likewise, in his book *Learning from Las Vegas*, the architect Robert Venturi suggests the collision of styles, signs, and symbols that marks the American commercial strip can be seen as composing a new sort of unity. On the strip, anything goes, unlike traditional architectural practice, in which the architect harmonizes the building with its environment.

LITERATURE: THE BEATS

Not everyone felt the consumer culture developing in the United States during the 1950s was such a good thing. The so-called **Beat** generation of writers saw material prosperity as leading to conformity, complacency, and oppression. Theirs was the first in a series of critiques of America after World War II, critiques that would surface again in the civil rights and anti–Vietnam War movements in the 1960s and the feminist movement in the 1970s.

Jack Kerouac. For Jack Kerouac (1922–1969), the Beats were a resurgence of the lost American type, the "wild self-believing" who had founded the country. In *On the Road*, written in 1951 and published in 1957, Kerouac reinvents the American archetype of the frontiersman and cowboy, as his narrator, Sal Paradise, a "wild yea-saying overburst of American joy," seeks to escape the confines of American civilization in Denver's skid row and Cheyenne, Wyoming's Wild West Week.

Kerouac wrote in "spontaneous prose," as he called it, with roots in the automatic writing of Surrealism and the expressive gesture of the Abstract Expressionist painters. The poet Allen Ginsberg described Kerouac's prose as "completely personal, [that] comes from the writer's own person—his person defined as his body, his breathing rhythm, his actual talk."

Allen Ginsberg. This style is, essentially, the style of Allen Ginsberg (1926–1997) himself. His long poem *Howl* (1956)—of which the first section and part of the third were drafted in one day in August 1955, in San Francisco, the rest following shortly after—is indeed a rush of language, as its title suggests. It is an outcry against a system that turns individuals into abstractions, an outcry against a world in which parents turn their children over to the ancient god Moloch (a figure standing for American culture as a whole), who consumes them. Dedicated to Carl Solomon, a patient in a mental hospital in New York—and in Ginsberg's mind, a sort of political prisoner—the poem is a celebration of madness. Madness, for Ginsberg, is a sign of salvation, a sign of rebellion against the all-consuming American Moloch. By rejecting reason, and accepting the innate rhythms of the body itself, *Howl* seeks to transcend the constrictions of civilization.

Then & Now

The Movies Past and Present

In the early twentieth century, the first films made were silent. The characters' speech was not heard; instead, music accompanied the action. Among the most important of early filmmakers was David Ward Griffith (1875–1948). Like the Russian director Sergei Eisenstein, Griffith believed that editing held the key to cinematography. In 1915, Griffith produced his first full-length film, *The Birth of a Nation*, which offered a romanticized view of the antebellum South and the struggle of white Southerners to survive the devastating effects of the Civil War. Griffith employed a full range of cinematic techniques to create suspense and human interest, including close-ups, cross-cuts, tracking, and panoramic shots, along with scenes of fast-paced suspenseful action, including just-in-time rescues.

Another master filmmaker and actor of the silent era was Charlie Chaplin (1889–1977). Chaplin became famous for the Tramp figure, who with his bowler hat, baggy pants, floppy shoes, and cane, was the supreme social outsider. In *The Tramp*, Chaplin's character saves a beautiful woman and her father from danger. But instead of being rewarded by them, he is ousted when her handsome boyfriend returns. The film ends with Chaplin's signature conclusion: The Tramp, clearly disappointed, returning to the road, walking slowly, his back to the camera, then jumping up and clicking his heels together before walking briskly away.

The silent film Chaplin wished to be remembered for was *The Gold Rush* (1925). In its most famous scene, Chaplin's Tramp character is starving and cooks his shoe, roasting and carving it as if it were a delectable piece of meat, and sucking the nails in its sole as if they were small chicken bones. He even twirls the shoelaces like spaghetti. *The Gold Rush* presents a social view that both celebrates and criticizes money and material success, suggesting that the Tramp continues to desire the very material possessions that have corrupted others.

Like the great films of the silent era, the movies of today continue to use sophisticated cinematic techniques to tell stories, portray human relationships, and offer perspectives on social issues. Like the silent films of Griffith and Chaplin, today's movies are designed to entertain audiences and to make money. Like the older films, those of today provide opportunities for audiences to escape into imagined worlds, such as the fantasy world of the *Lord of the Rings* movies. And like older films, today's connect with viewers' everyday experience to stimulate laughter, arouse emotion, awaken moral sensibility, and prompt reflection.

Other connections between the films of the past and those of the present involve their emphasis on star actors and celebrity directors, whose association with a film guarantee high production costs, large marketing campaigns, extensive distribution, and a variety of merchandising tie-ins.

Figure 23.22 Richard Rogers and Renzo Piano, Pompidou Center, Paris, 1971–77. Musée National d'Art Moderne. Reunion des Musées Nationaux/Art Resource, NY. The novelty of this museum of modern art is that the mundane mechanical parts are made the focal point, emphasized by their size, colors, and, above all, their location on the exterior rather than hidden within the walls in the usual manner. This glorification of the ordinary is the architectural equivalent of Pop Art.

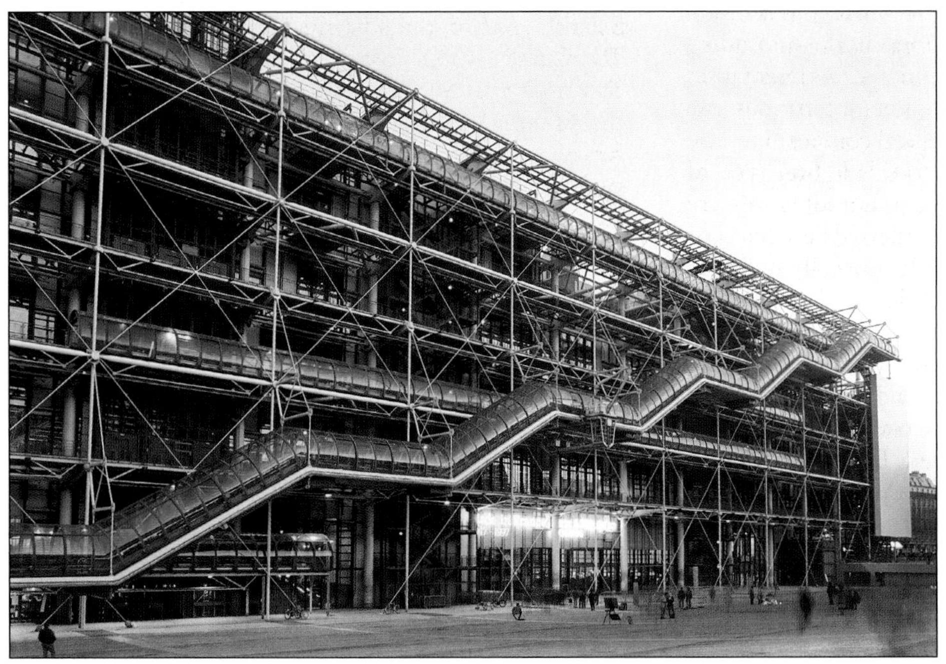

Critical Thinking

THE POPULARITY OF THE BEATLES

During the 1960s, a rock group from Britain took that country and then the United States by storm. The Beatles began their musical journey in Liverpool, a working class city, playing locally there before receiving acclaim in London and throughout England. The Beatles included four musicians, the drummer Ringo Starr, the accomplished guitarist George Harrison, and the lead singers and guitarists Paul McCartney and John Lennon, who also wrote most of the group's songs. Each of the four had a distinct personality and an individual musical identity, yet they blended into a cohesive and wonderfully identifiable group identity unlike any before in the realm of pop/rock music.

But what was it that made the Beatles the phenomenon they became? What elements combined to make them the premier pop combo of their generation not only in England and the United States, but beyond? To what extent was it the personas they created and purveyed? To what extent was it their musicianship, their originality, and their unique sound? To what extent was their popularity attributable to the musical innovations they introduced, such as the "concept album," in which all the songs on a disk were related to an overarching topical theme? To what extent was their success a function of the times in which they rose to fame? And why is it that the Beatles continue to remain popular today—in Britain, the United States, and Europe?

THE POPULARIZATION OF CLASSICAL MUSIC

The Boston Pops. In the 1950s and 1960s, in a culture defined by the consumer, music too responded to the demands of a popular audience. The Boston Pops Orchestra, led by Arthur Fiedler (1894–1979), became a national institution, famous for its concerts of folk tunes, marches such as John Philip Sousa's "Stars and Stripes Forever," and classical hits such as George Gershwin's *Rhapsody in Blue*. Bridging the gap between popular song and classical repertoire, the pops served as "the door through which young people enter into the magic domain of musical comprehension," as one critic put it.

Musical Theater. Like opera in the nineteenth century, musical theater became a popular form in the mid twentieth century. Despite the new tonalities, experimentation with rhythms and forms, and a dissonant harmony expressing the "age of anxiety" in classical composition, the music-listening public gravitated to this lighter type of musical entertainment. Unlike opera, not all words are sung in musical theater; music is interspersed between spoken dialogue. The mood of musicals is usually uplifting and the songs singable and memorable.

During the early part of the century, Victor Herbert and George M. Cohan wrote musicals about the war to entertain a popular audience. By the end of World War II, Richard Rodgers and Oscar Hammerstein had captivated audiences with *Carousel* and *Oklahoma*. By the early 1950s, Broadway had become the center of popular theatrical music in America. With the production of *West Side Story* by Leonard Bernstein in the late 1950s (see description next) the musical had matured to more complex harmonies and rhythms with libretti that were more psychological and darker than before.

Leonard Bernstein. Successful at both popularizing classical music and classicizing popular music, Leonard Bernstein (1918–1990) was a composer, conductor, pianist, and mentor. His lecture demonstrations with the New York Philharmonic Orchestra introduced a generation of children to the world of classical music and were later published as the *Young People's Guide to the Orchestra*.

Bernstein's genius for composing popular and classical music sets him apart. He is best known for his works for the musical theater: *Candide* (1956) and, especially, *West Side Story* (1957), a version of *Romeo and Juliet* in a contemporary setting with intercultural tensions. Bernstein transforms Shakespeare's warring Capulet and Montague families into two rival gangs from New York City's Spanish Harlem, the Jets and the Hispanic Sharks. Like Tchaikovsky, whose *Romeo and Juliet Fantasy Overture* was also inspired by Shakespeare's play, Bernstein writes music that is both lyrical and dramatic. Songs like "Maria," a lyrical love song, intermingle with Latin-inspired pieces such as "America" and "Tonight," set in quasi-operatic style for four voices.

Andrew Lloyd Weber. One of the most successful of contemporary composers for the musical theater has been Andrew Lloyd Weber (b. 1948), who is responsible for many hit shows produced in England and the United States. Among them are *Joseph and His Amazing Technicolor Dreamcoat* (1968), based on the story of Joseph and his brothers in the biblical book of Genesis; *Jesus Christ Superstar* (1970), a rock opera based on the last seven days of Jesus's life; *Evita* (1976), based on the life of Eva Peron, wife of an Argentinian dictator; *Cats* (1981), based on poetry by T. S. Eliot; and *Phantom of the Opera* (1986), based on a 1911 French novel by Gaston Leroux. Half of his sixteen musicals have been made into films, including

Cultural Impact

The social developments and cultural impulses that emerged at the beginning of the century continued. Automobiles, developed at the start of the century, fundamentally changed transportation, and the assembly line on which they were built revolutionized the organization of work, warfare, and consumption. Cinema, a development of photography emerged early in the century, and continued to be refined by improvements in technology. Early silent films gave way to talkies; black-and-white films were superseded by those in color; and today computer animated backgrounds and characters replace real places and actors; often, animated and real materials are combined side by side.

In music and art no single dominant style or trend has dominated. Later modernism has expanded the approaches of early modernism. Contemporary artists, in all media, benefit from the broadening of perspective and the artistic possibilities opened up by the modernists.

One legacy of the collaborations between composers and dancers working together in ballet and film was the Broadway musical, a distinctively American form of entertainment. Musicals, along with films, provide a staple of contemporary entertainment, with such long-running shows as *Cats*, *Les Miserables*, *Phantom of the Opera*, *Rent*, *Mana Mia*, and *The Lion King* on stages in the United States and around the world.

Cats, *Evita*, and *Phantom of the Opera*. Translated into nearly a dozen languages, *Cats* has played in more than twenty countries and over 250 cities, and *Phantom* has been seen by more than eighty million people in over two dozen countries, eventually surpassing *Cats* in number of performances.

Songs from his musicals have become famous worldwide, especially "Memory," from *Cats*, "The Music of the Night," from *Phantom of the Opera*, and "Don't Cry for Me, Argentina," from *Evita*. He also has the distinction of having been knighted by the Queen of England, and of having composed a *Requiem* mass, a classical work, one of whose songs, "Pie Jesu," became a popular success.

Late Modern Music

Music in the late twentieth century was influenced by the thinking of John Cage and others, who believed experimentation was the key to finding a "new voice." While elite groups tended to follow and promote this avant-garde music, the general public rejected much of this experimentation.

Returning to tonal composition, composers such as Philip Glass and Steve Reich simplified their sound by minimalizing melody, rhythm, and form. Played in simple sequences with much repetition most minimalistic music is written for the synthesizer, a machine that can replicate the tones of almost all instruments. Blending sounds of Western and Eastern music traditions, Glass's music draws the listener into a soothing state and opens the mind at a meditative level. Phillip Glass has also produced operas such as *Einstein on the Beach* and *Akhenaten*, and popular music for theater, dance, and movies. The "Dance" from *Akhenaten* given an idea of the driving repetitive rhythms of much of Glass's music.

Rock and Roll

Sometimes rock and roll music seems to be the very center of American culture. With roots in African-American rhythm and blues, rock music began as a separate form in the 1950s and has evolved into a wide variety of subtypes. The early rock of Elvis Presley and Chuck Berry appealed to the yearnings of the American teen. With the 1960s British bands such as the Beatles, rock music began to have international stature. Folk rock, and later psychedelic rock, experimented with timbres and lyrics to make antiestablishment political statements following the mood of the country. Jazz and Latin American music influenced dance music of the 1970s as well as reggae, punk rock, and rhythm and blues. The "selling of America" via advances in audiovisual technology led to a worldwide explosion on the pop rock scene in the 1980s with the advent of CDs and MTV, and two decades later with the emergence of itunes, music downloads, and YouTube.

Alternative rock bands rebelled against society with music that explored social and sexual taboos, and subcultures of heavy metal, rap, and world music gained popularity in the 1990s rock scene.

KEY TERMS

existentialism
abstract expressionism
action painting
color field
mobiles
oral contraceptive
assemblage
Pop Art
Happening
minimalism
Op Art
Beat

www. WEBSITES FOR FURTHER STUDY

http://www.tameri.com/csw/exist/
(An excellent site on existentialism with all the major philosophers and many links.)

http://www.bauhaus.de/english/bauhaus1919/architektur/
(In 1919, the Bauhaus manifesto proclaims that the ultimate aim of all creative activity is a building.)

http://www.witcombe.sbc.edu/ARTHLinks.html
(Art history resources on the Web by Chris Witcombe.)

http://www.litkicks.com/beatgen
(A site that chronicles the history of the Beat Generation and the Beat movement, with links to its primary figures, including Jack Kerouac and Allen Ginsberg.)

http://www.rockhall.com
(Site of the Rock and Roll Hall of Fame with timelines, stories, videos, and more, chronicling the story of rock music, past and present.)

http://www.guidetomusicaltheatre.com
(Site with a broad overview of all things related to musical theatre, including links to composers such as Leonard Bernstein and Andrew Lloyd Weber.)

http://www.theatrehistory.com/misc/theatre_of_the_absurd.html
(Site devoted to all aspects of theatre history, including the Theatre of the Absurd, and the life and work of Samuel Beckett.)

Chapter 24

History

1989 Berlin Wall dismantled

1991 Communism in the USSR collapses

2008 Barack Obama elected U.S. President

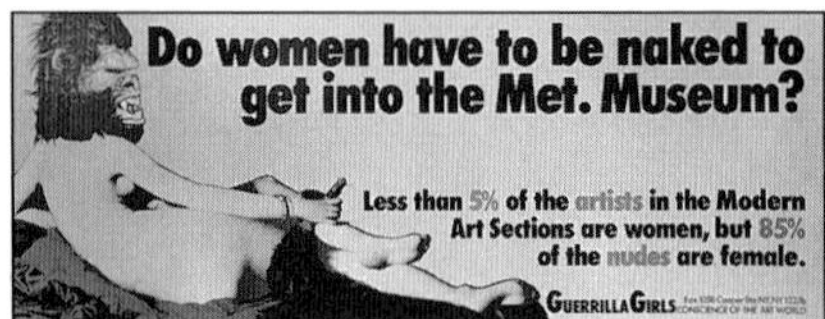

Arts and Architecture

1974–79 Chicago, *The Dinner Party*

1982 Lin, Vietnam Veterans' Memorial

1982 Basquiat, *Charles the First*

1991 Smith, *Paper Dolls for a Post-Columbian World*

1995 Fifield, *Ghost Dancers Ascending*

1999 Mori, *Dream Temple*

2005 Christo and Jeanne-Claude, Central Park Gates

2008 Dickson, Revelers

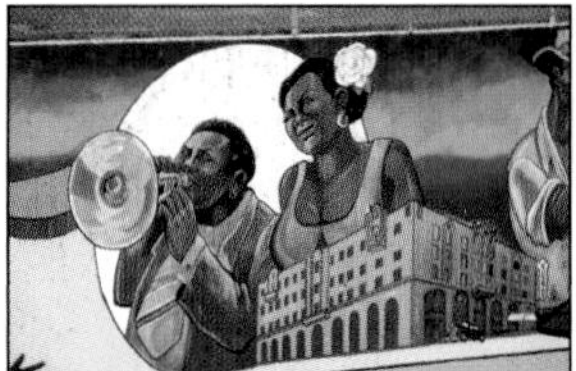

Literature and Philosophy

Late 60s Barthes, structuralism

1969 Momaday, *The Way to Rainy Mountain*

Morrison, *The Bluest Eye*

1976 Kingston, *The Woman Warrior*

1994 Cisneros, *House on Mango Street*

1988 Komunyakaa, "Facing It"

1991 Alexie, "Indian Boy Love Songs"

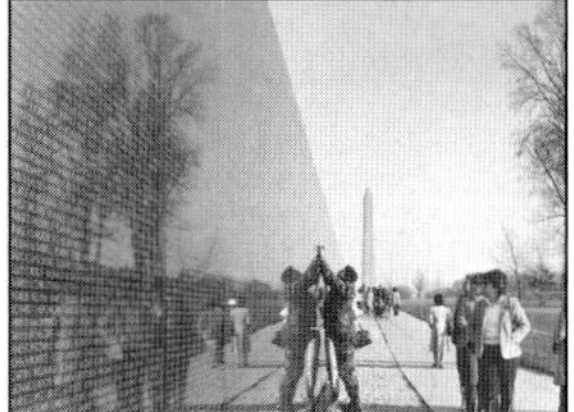

Diversity in Contemporary Life

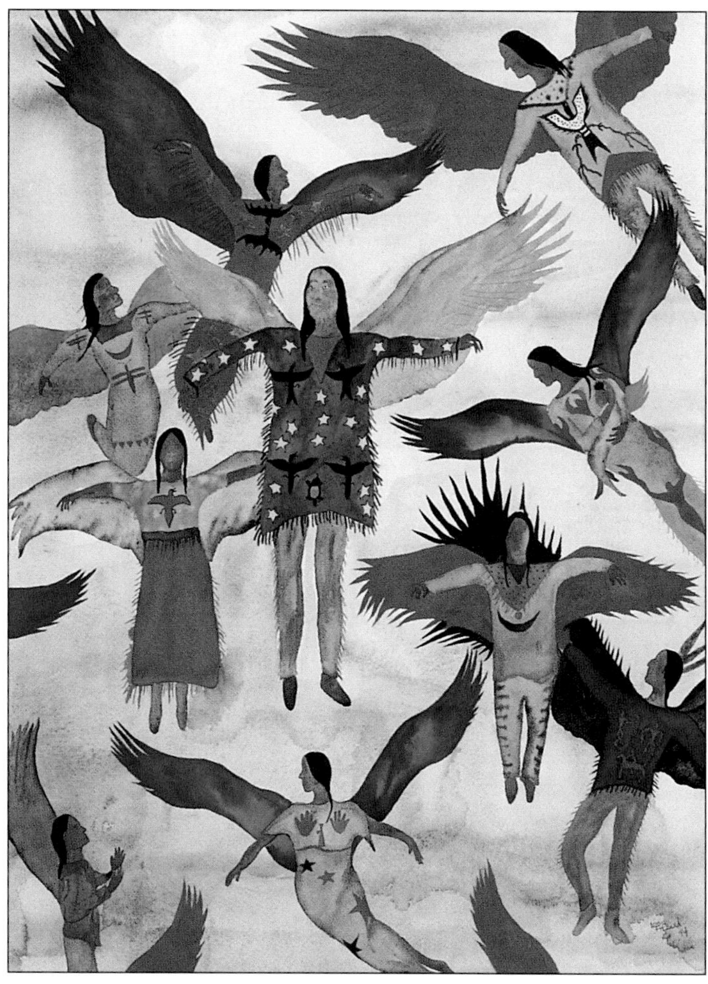

Lisa Fifield, *Ghost Dancers Ascending*, 1995, watercolor on paper, 30″ × 22″ (76.2 × 55.9 cm), private collection.

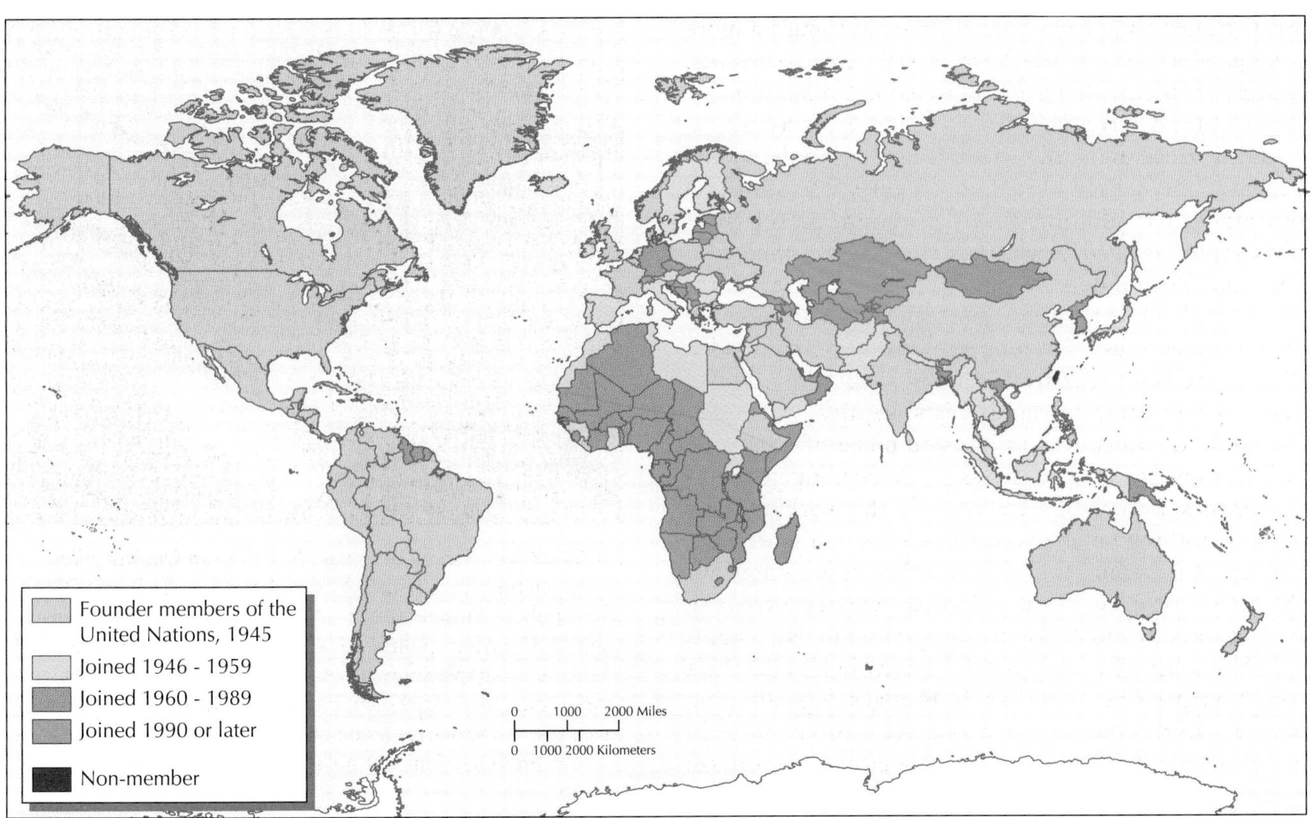

MAP 24.1 World membership of the United Nations.

CHAPTER OVERVIEW

DIVERSITY IN THE UNITED STATES

Women artists rise to prominence
The Internet connects the world

THE GLOBAL VILLAGE

Technology reaches out to all the ends of the earth, bringing humanity together

DIVERSITY IN THE UNITED STATES

THROUGHOUT THE 1960S AND INTO THE 1970s, American society underwent a profound shift in attitude. As a result of the civil rights movement, the Vietnam War, and the women's movement, Americans examined and questioned long-held customs and values. The quest for rights for African Americans and for women, especially, caused an increased awareness of the meaning and power of diversity. And in the opening decade of the twenty-first century, the first woman candidate for U.S. President, Hillary Clinton, and the first African-American man, Barack Obama, ever to become a United States President.

POSTMODERNISM

Although the term **postmodernism** is intended to represent a break from, or rejection of, the preceding modernists (the *avant-garde*), the term's meaning is imprecise and a subject of argument. Postmodernism focuses on the period between approximately 1960 (essentially post Pop Art) and the 1990s, and on the changes that occurred in politics, philosophy, art, and architecture.

Postmodernism is skeptical, even critical. In its quest for the nontraditional, it is anti-convention, anti-authority, and anti-establishment. Yet it is far from an organized, consistent, or even definable style; instead, postmodernism refers to many different ways of questioning tradition. Postmodern artists turned away from pure abstraction toward a more conceptual art that often dealt with socially conscious issues. Aspects of "postmodernism" are found in "modernism"—as in Dada and Surrealism—and in other earlier styles.

Semiotics, the study of signs and symbols, which began in the earlier twentieth century, was used as a postmodernist philosophy to propound a relativist philosophy derived from the structuralist's theory of language. Postmodernists point out that our view of reality is molded by the ways in which information about reality comes to us—for example, via commercial media. This is the key break from the modernist tradition of belief in absolutes. Postmodernists skeptically question the mode of transmission and the place of reception before they accept the message. According to postmodernists, a work of art is actually the work of many people: nothing an artist creates can be truly original, because it is based on those countless representations the artist has seen. Postmodernism encourages us to look at ways in which the meaning of symbols or signs, which consist of concepts (the "signified") and their sound images (the "signifiers"), changes depending on context, to determine ("deconstruct") the manner in which meaning is constructed. **Deconstructionism** rejects universals. Readers are free to interpret an author's words in their own way. Deconstructionists prefer written words to spoken words, intentionally seeking the obscure and complex rather than the obvious and logical.

PHOTOGRAPHY, PAINTING, AND SCULPTURE

Diverse visions have had a considerable impact in art. The single most important development in the art world in recent decades has been the rise to prominence of visions previously excluded from the mainstream. This has been, in part, a function of the art world's quest for innovative approaches to experience, but it is also true that the art world has become increasingly willing to acknowledge the "outsider's" point of view.

The photographer Cindy Sherman (b. 1954) creates a fictional persona in order to investigate different aspects of the self. Beginning in the late 1970s, Sherman photographed herself in a variety of self-portraits called *Untitled Film Stills* (fig. 24.1). In each, Sherman wears a different costume, makes herself up to look a different part, stages herself, and announces, in effect, that the "self" is a fictionalized construction. We are whoever we choose to look like. And what we choose to look like, is one or another of a series of media images. Her work undermines the very idea of an "authentic" personality behind our repertoire of selves.

Similarly critical of modernism's quest for individual innovation, Sherrie Levine "appropriated" (i.e., copied) a photo taken by Walker Evans and claimed it as her own work of art by giving it the title *After Walker Evans*, thereby both questioning and mocking art's traditional adulation of originality as, instead, an assertion of the ego.

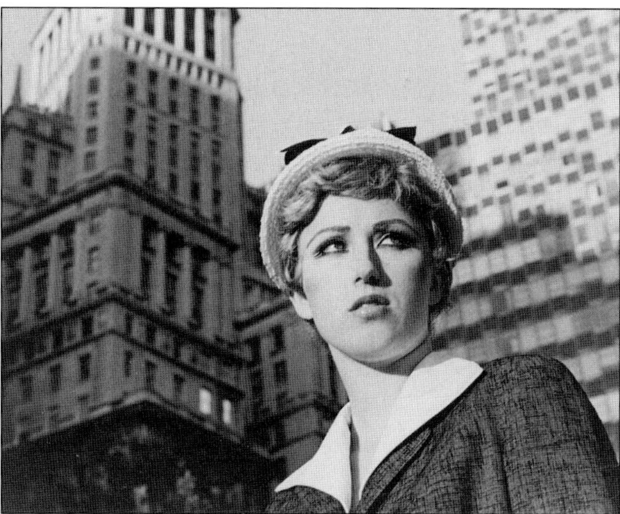

FIGURE 24.1 Cindy Sherman, *Still from an Untitled Film*, 1978, gelatin silver print, $7\frac{3}{8}'' \times 9\frac{7}{16}''$ (18.7 × 23.9 cm), The Metropolitan Museum of Art, NY, 1992. 5147. Image copyright © The Metropolitan Museum of Art / Art Resource, NY
In this photograph Sherman casts herself as the vulnerable "career girl" alone in the big city, one of the parts she plays in sixty-seven scenarios based on 1950s Hollywood movies. That is, Sherman depicts a media image, rather than a real person.

Other artists emphasized the reuse of images. Julian Schnabel's large-scale work of the early 1980s incorporated incongruent images taken from other forms of representation—from film, photography, even religious imagery. By putting the old into a new context created for these eclectic images, the unexpected and unfamiliar juxtaposition of images (recalling Dada in this regard) leaves their meaning unclear. David Salle created similar amalgamations of disparate imagery and media, intentionally seeking to challenge established assumptions about art.

The long-standing dominance of white upper-class males in the fine arts was questioned by Andreas Huyssen. Instead, he suggested that art should be more inclusive and comprehensive, based on identities, of which he defined four: national, sexual, environmental, and ethnic (non-Western). Art that focuses on these identities has traditionally been considered lesser, lower, popular art—not fine art. These identities are relevant to postmodernism, which frequently deals with political, social, and gender issues and activism—such as feminism.

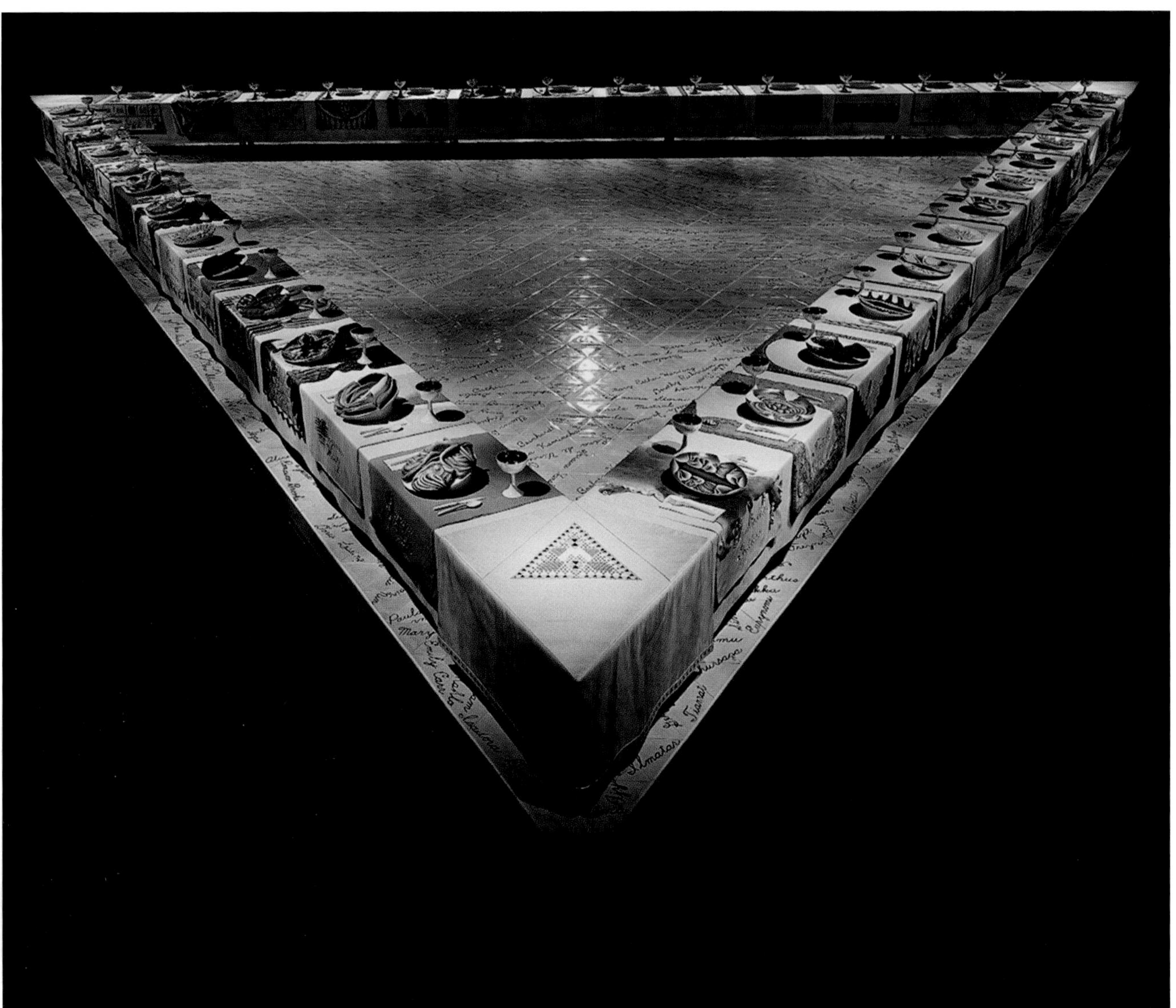

FIGURE 24.2 Judy Chicago, *The Dinner Party*, 1979, mixed media, 48′ × 48′ × 48′ (14.63 × 14.63 × 14.63 m), installed. Collection of The Brooklyn Museum of Art, NY. Gift of the Elizabeth A. Sackler Foundation. Photograph © Donald Woodman/Through the Flower. © 2005 Judy Chicago/Artists Rights Society (ARS), New York. This visually striking large-scale postmodern work is a monument to the myriad accomplishments of women through the ages.

Judy Chicago. The feminist artist Judy Chicago (b. 1939, Judy Gerowitz), working with many other women, created *The Dinner Party*, 1974–79 (fig. 24.2), a history of women's accomplishments. Each place setting at a triangular table represents a specific woman, from prehistoric and ancient Minoan goddesses to the modern novelist Virginia Woolf and the painter Georgia O'Keeffe. The thirty-nine place settings are arranged with thirteen on each side, recalling depictions of Jesus's Last Supper. The names of 999 additional women are written on the table's runner.

The Dinner Party took what had routinely been dismissed as woman's domain and transformed it into a monumental sculpture that brought public attention to women's art. Carrie Richey wrote in *Artforum* magazine in 1981 that *The Dinner Party* "is a glossary of the so-called 'lesser arts'—tatting, lace[making], weaving, making ceramic household vessels, embroidering. . . . All these crafts have been brought together. . . . *The Dinner Party* . . . proposes that the sum of the lesser arts is great art."

Guerrilla Girls. The impact of women on the art world has increased significantly in recent years. In 1970–71, only 13.5 percent of the artists exhibiting in New York were women. In the 1970s, only 10 percent of the shows devoted to living artists were one-person exhibitions by women. In 1982, the Coalition of Women's Art Organizations reported that only 2 percent of museum exhibitions by living artists were devoted to women. This

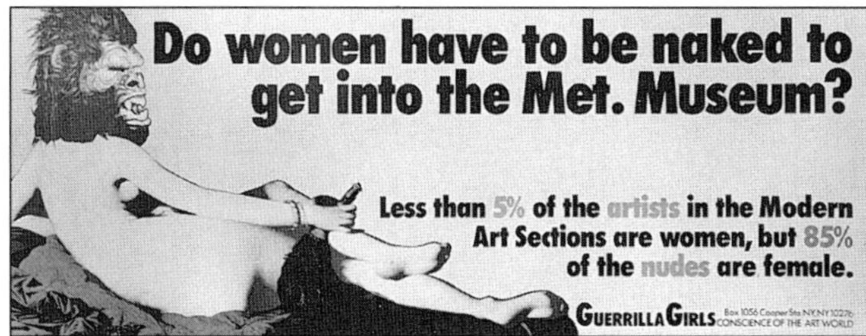

FIGURE 24.3 Guerrilla Girls, *Do Women Have to be Naked to Get into the Met. Museum?*, 1989, poster, 11″ × 28″ (27.9 × 71.1 cm), private collection. Courtesy www.querrillagirls.com. The Guerrilla Girls' posters document an art scene that was, as late as the mid-1980s, still dominated by men, where women were either excluded or underacknowledged.

imbalance was the focus of a socially active group of women known as the Guerrilla Girls, their identity hidden by their gorilla masks. Beginning in 1985, they plastered New York City with posters (fig. 24.3), publicly questioning the inequity with which women are represented, exhibited, and funded in the arts.

Eleanor Antin. Women artists have increasingly turned to new media, especially performance art. Eleanor Antin was born Eleanor Fineman in 1935 in the Bronx, NY, into a family that emigrated from Poland. Antin developed a series of characters, including Eleanora Antinova, a fictional black ballerina in Diaghilev's Ballets Russes. By playing Antinova, Antin freed herself to investigate hidden aspects of her own situation. A drawing from her memoir, *Being Antinova* (fig. 24.4), shows how removed Antinova is from the traditional Western ballet world. Not only is Antinova black, but her own sense of physical freedom contradicts the regimen and routine of ballet. Imagine, she points out, a black ballerina in *Swan Lake.* The world of ballet is, in her words, a "white machine."

Betye Saar. Artist Betye Saar (b. 1926) created the Pop Art–like construction entitled *The Liberation of Aunt Jemima* in 1972. Saar's image "converts a popular" conception of the African-American "mammy"—the smiling Aunt Jemima of pancake and syrup fame. As Aunt Jemima takes up arms, raising the fist of black power over the scene, the white baby is not merely unhappy, but terrified. "Mammy's" politics are revealed; this advertising image, once servant and slave, takes matters into her own hands. The painting announces the necessity—the actuality—of change for the African American.

FIGURE 24.4 Eleanor Antin, drawing from *Being Antinova*, 1983. Courtesy Ronald Feldman Fine Arts, NY. The physical freedom expressed by Antinova in this drawing differentiates her from other dancers in the troupe.

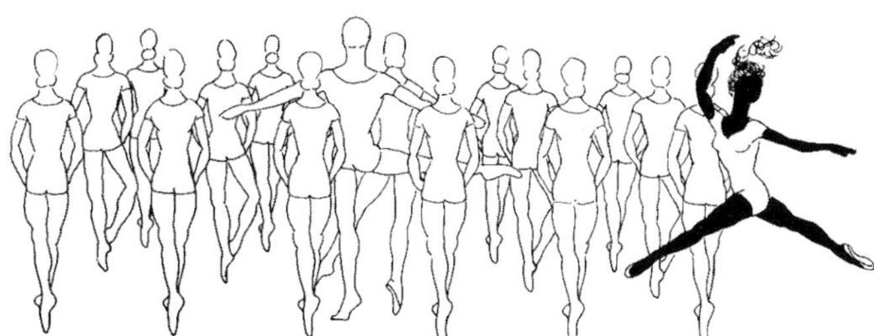

Jean-Michel Basquiat. As a teenager in New York, Jean-Michel Basquiat (1960–1988) achieved notoriety as "Samo," a graffiti artist writing on walls in Soho and Tribeca. By early 1981, gallery owners in New York, Zurich, and Milan had convinced him to apply his graffiti to canvas, and he soon became an art world media darling. The value of his paintings rose with meteoric speed. By the time he was twenty-three years old, his work had already sold at auction for $19,000. Basquiat, the son of a middle-class Haitian-born accountant and his Puerto Rican wife, possessed an authenticity—raw, direct, unmediated by tradition.

In *Charles the First* (fig. 24.5), Basquiat's homage to jazz saxophonist Charlie Parker, the immediacy of Basquiat's style is in his "mistakes." As one of Basquiat's heroes,

FIGURE 24.5 Jean-Michel Basquiat, *Charles the First*, 1982, acrylic and oilstick on canvas, triptych, 6′6″ × 5′2¼″ (1.98 × 1.58 m), © The Estate of Jean-Michel Basquiat/© 2009 Artists Rights Society (ARS), NY. The "X" crossing out elements in Basquiat's work is never entirely negative. In a book on symbols, Basquiat discovered a section on "Hobo Signs," marks left, like graffiti, by hobos to inform their brethren about the locality. In this graphic language, an "X" means "O.K. All right."

Parker is a king—hence the painting's title, the crown, and the word "Thor" (the god of Norwegian myth). At the bottom is Basquiat's admonition to kings; the word "young" is crossed out. Parker's fall from grace is everywhere in the painting: in the drips that fall from the blue field in the middle of the painting and in the way that, above the word "Cherokee" (the name of one of Parker's most important compositions), one of the feathers (Parker was known as "Bird") falls into a dollar sign.

Much of Basquiat's art protests against the exploitation of black heroes—Sugar Ray Robinson, Hank Aaron, Cassius Clay, Dizzy Gillespie, and Louis Armstrong. Basquiat identified with them, as if he knew his own meteoric rise would end in tragedy. He died, age twenty-seven, of a drug overdose.

Judith F. Baca. The mural painting of Chicana artist Judith F. Baca (b. 1948) asserts its independence from traditional approaches to painting, even as it recovers and revitalizes the Mexican mural tradition of "Los Tres Grandes"—Rivera, Orozco, and Siquieros (see Chapter 21).

In 1974, Baca inaugurated the Citywide Mural Project in Los Angeles, which completed 250 murals, 150 of which she directed herself. Since then she has continued to sponsor and direct murals through SPARC, the Social and Public Art Resource Center, which she founded. The *Great Wall of Los Angeles*, begun in 1976, is her most ambitious project. Nearly a mile long, it is located in the Tujunga Wash of the Los Angeles river, which was entirely lined in concrete as Los Angeles grew. This concrete conduit is, says Baca, "a giant scar across the land which served to further divide an already divided city. . . . Just as young Chicanos tattoo battle scars on their bodies, *Great Wall of Los Angeles* is a tattoo on a scar where the river once ran." The wall narrates a history of Los Angeles not told in textbooks. It recounts the history of indigenous peoples, immigrant minorities—Portuguese, Chinese, Japanese, Korean, and Basque, as well as Chicano—and of women from prehistory to the present. The detail reproduced here (fig. 24.6) depicts two of the major stars of Black jazz, Charlie Parker, playing the trumpet, and Billie Holiday, smiling as she sings.

FIGURE 24.6 Judith F. Baca, *Great Wall of Los Angeles* (detail: Charlie Parker and Billie Holiday), Tujunga Wash, Los Angeles, California, 1976–continuing, mural, height 13′ (3.96 m) (whole mural over a mile long). Photo © SPARC, Venice, CA. The collaborative process of making murals is, in Baca's words, "the transforming of pain . . . rage . . . and shame."

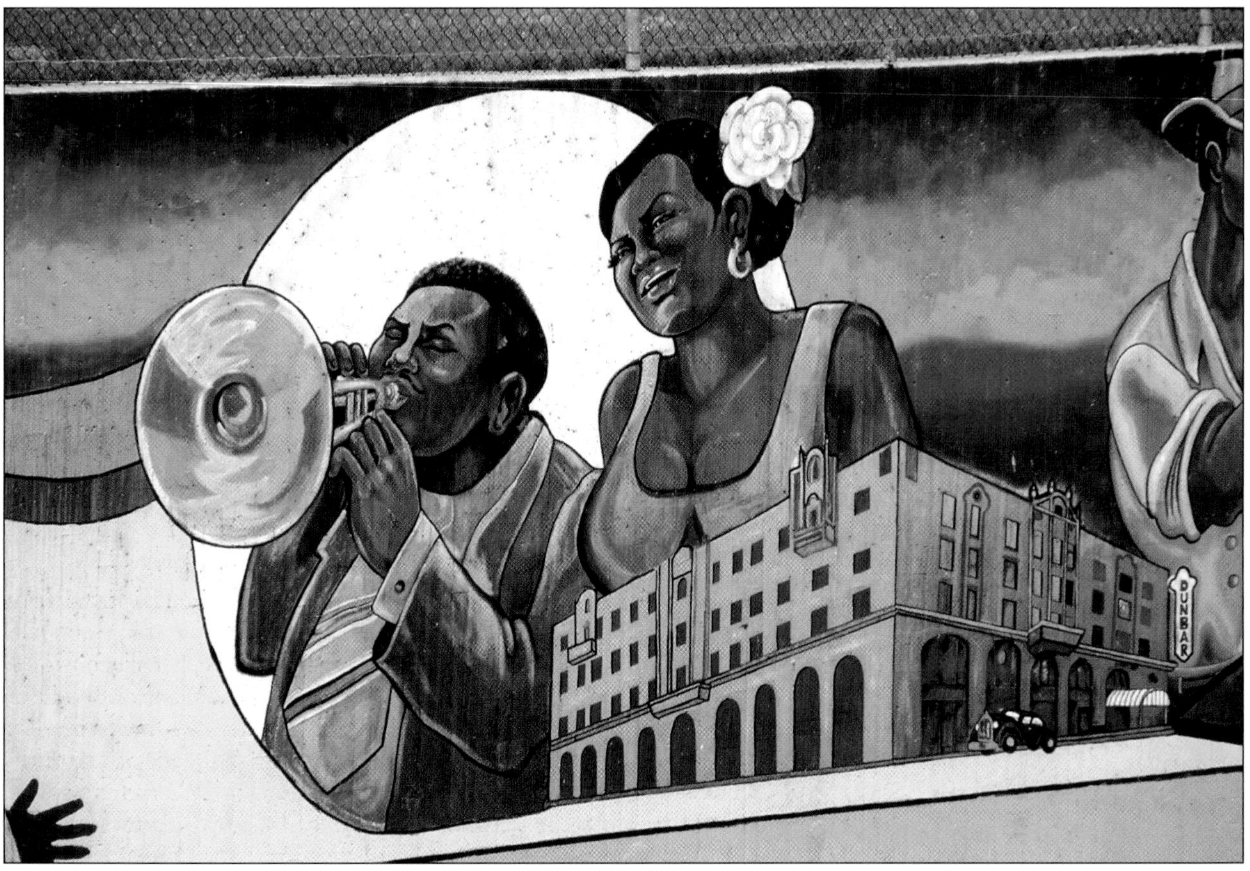

Baca worked on the *Great Wall* project as director and facilitator, but nearly four hundred inner-city youths, many from the juvenile justice system, did the actual painting and design. Rival gang members, of different races and from different neighborhoods, representing a divided city, found themselves working on the project together. For Baca, the collaborative mural process heals wounds, brings people together, and helps recreate communities for, as she said, "Collaboration is a requirement."

Lisa Fifield. Lisa Fifield (b. 1957), of Iroquois-Oneida descent, portrays the traditions and beliefs of Native American peoples. Fifield painted a series of canvases based on the slaughter at Wounded Knee, by the U.S. Army, of Native American men, women, and children. One such painting *Ghost Dancers Ascending* (fig. 24.7), depicts the spirits of the dead rising above the earth. The Plains Indians developed the Ghost Dance in the 1890s after they had lost their ancestral lands and been relegated to reservations. They danced for the return of warriors, for the return of the bison, and for the reestablishment of their former way of life. In the painting, the attire worn by the figures is based on that worn by those killed at Wounded Knee, clothing they mistakenly believed could not be pierced by bullets. With reverential spirit, Fifield depicts their spirits transcending the material fact of death in vibrant primary colors.

FIGURE 24.7 Lisa Fifield, *Ghost Dancers Ascending*, 1995, watercolor on paper, 30″ × 22″ (76.2 × 55.9 cm), private collection. Fifield depicts the spirits rising above the earth at Wounded Knee, their powerful colors and effortless floating making them seem to transcend their tragic deaths.

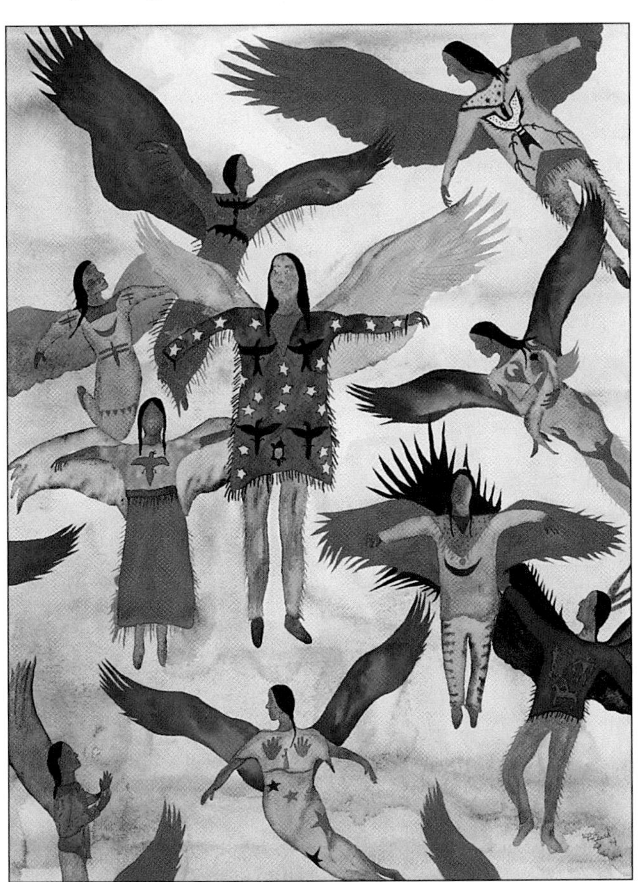

Maya Lin and the Vietnam Veterans' Memorial. The Vietnam Veterans' Memorial in Washington, DC. (fig. 24.8) was constructed and dedicated in 1982. Funded by contributions from corporations, foundations, unions, veterans, civic organizations, and nearly three million individuals, the memorial achieved the wishes of the foundation that established it, which was to begin a process of national reconciliation.

The memorial was designed by Maya Ying Lin (b. 1960), at the time a twenty-one-year-old graduate architectural student at Yale University. Lin, an American woman of Chinese descent, won a national competition that included more than 1,400 design submissions. Inscribed on the surface of the memorial's polished black granite walls are the more than 58,000 names of service-men and -women killed during the Vietnam War or missing in action. The wall is shaped like a giant V, whose vertex is set at an angle of approximately 125 degrees. The names of the casualties are listed beginning at one end of the wall in the chronological order of their deaths, encompassing the span of U.S. involvement in the war. The wall provides each name an honored place in the nation's memory. As Maya Lin said about the design, "The names would become the memorial."

Despite some dissenting voices at first, the Vietnam Veterans' War Memorial has won national approval and respect. Thousands visit the memorial every year. When looking at the names on the memorial's granite slabs, which are polished to a mirrorlike sheen, viewers can see themselves reflected in the wall's surface. Visitors are moved by the wall's profound homage and sense that here healing can begin.

NEW MEDIA

Mariko Mori. The Japanese multi-media installation artist Mariko Mori (b. 1967) was born in Tokyo and lives both there and in Manhattan. Similarly, her art consists of contrasts: Aspects of the traditional religions of Buddhism and Shintoism are combined with the most modern technology. She produces photographs, videos, and entire productions, in which she often features herself dressed in extreme costumes. Entire production crews may be employed to stage these performances.

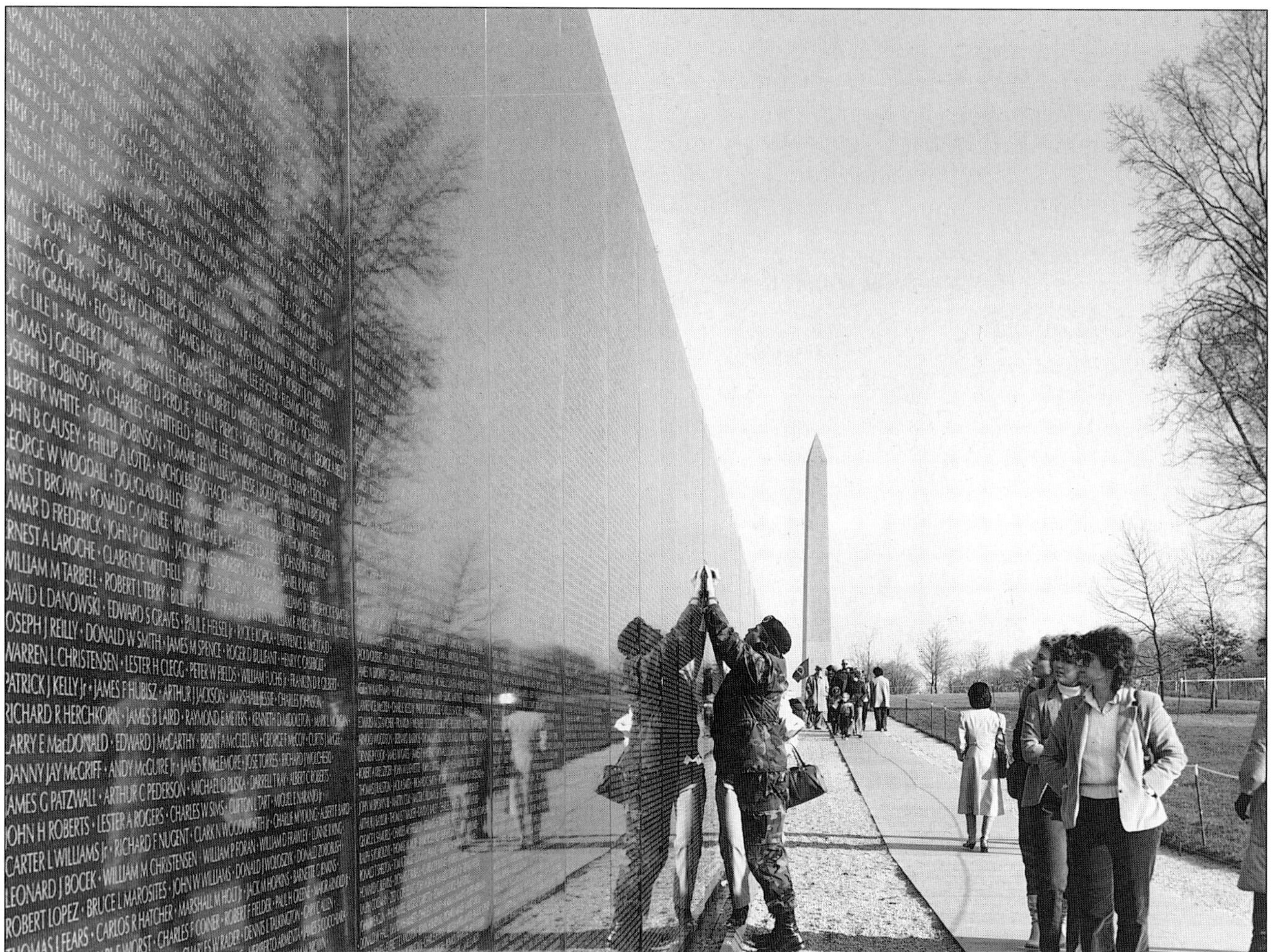

FIGURE 24.8 Maya Lin, Vietnam Veterans' Memorial, Washington, DC, 1982, black granite, length 250′ (820.21 m). Known simply as "the Wall," this memorial tribute to those killed in the Vietnam War has become a national symbol of recognition and reconciliation.

Her *Dream Temple* (fig. 24.9), 1999, creates an environment unlike anything previously created by artists and is distant from Nature's forms and materials. The visitor can literally enter into Mori's vision. The meaning of such a work derives from a fusion of religion, philosophy, and modern popular technology.

Christo and Jeanne-Claude. Large scale wrapping or drapping places temporarily in fabric is the hallmark of the site-specific artists Christo (d. 2009) and Jeanne-Claude (d. 2010), a husband and wife team, both born on the same day in 1935. He is Bulgarian and she is French.

Central Park Gates (fig. 24.10). installed in Central Park, Manhattan for several weeks, consisted of a series of large hanging banners of bright saffron-colored fabric, carefully spaced and placed along the paths of the park, delineating the curves and contours of the landscape. The many visitors walked beneath the open tunnels thus created. Jeanne-Claude and Christo said that this was to be a gift to the city of Manhattan, and indeed it was—people of all ages and ethnicities (as well as their pets) were brought together in the park to share the common experience this environment created.

The works of Christo and Jeanne-Claude are funded through the sales of their prints and preparatory drawings. To create a work such as this requires the cooperation of lawyers, government organizations, environmentalists, and many more—including the team of actual workers who were largely volunteers. Christo and Jeanne-Claude consider these procedural obstacles to be part of their controversial installations.

New Uses of Old Media

An interest in innovation seems to be an innate characteristic of contemporary artists, yet some have turned to traditional art media, which they use in new ways, to create striking results.

Dale Chihuly. The history of glass began at least as early as the fourth millennium B.C.E. in Mesopotamia or Egypt. Glass blowing began in the first century B.C.E. and reached

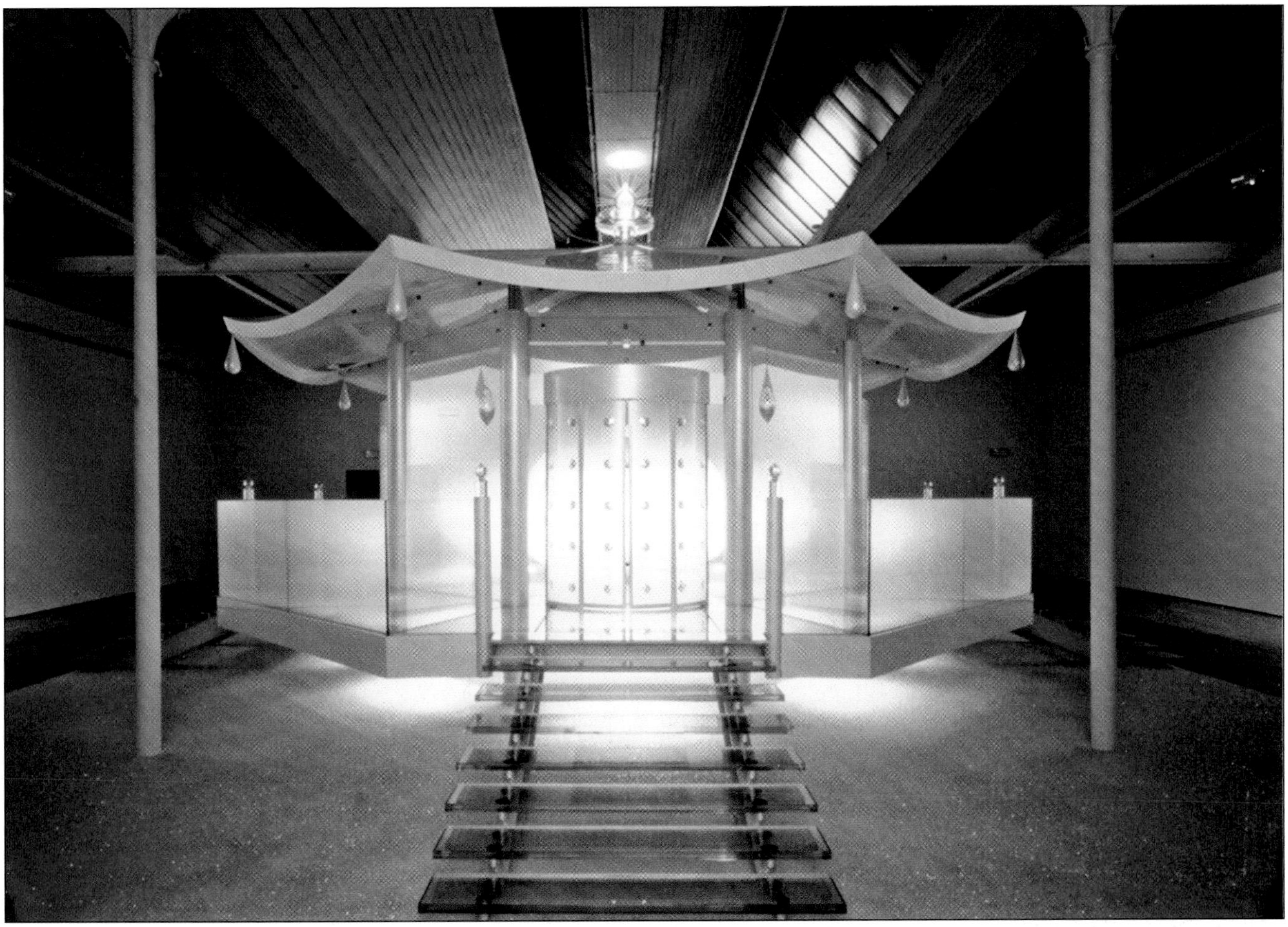

FIGURE 24.9 Mariko Mori, *Dream Temple*, 1999, audio, metal, glass, glass fiber threads, Vision Dome. 3-D semi-circular display, height 16′5″ (5 m), diameter 32′10″ (10 m). The shape of this futuristic structure derives from an eighth-century temple, although here there is no god. Mori's work has been described as "Cyborg Surrealism."

FIGURE 24.10 Christo and Jeanne-Claude, *Central Park Gates*, temporary installation, Central Park, New York City, NY, 2005. The artists "environmental art," which has included wrapping large buildings such as the Reicshstag in Berlin and the Pont Neuf in Paris, is intentionally both grand in scale and transitory, and often involves vast lengths of brightly colored fabric. The creation of a work such as the *Central Park Gates* requires the organization and cooperation of many people, the result being an event available to large numbers of visitors.

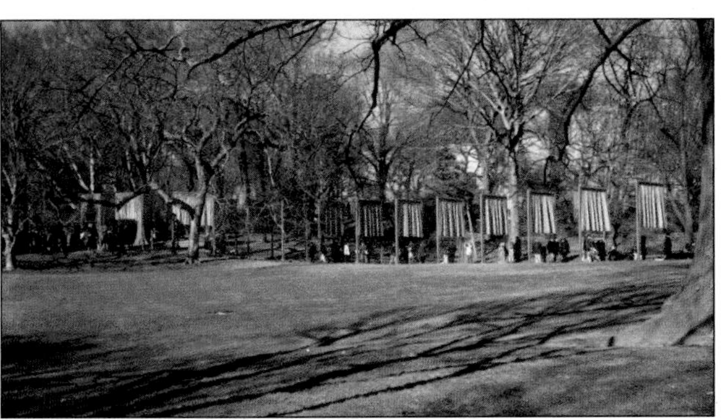

a high point in ancient Roman times when glass was used as an artistic medium, blown and shaped while hot and therefore molten, into a variety of types of hollow vessels.

The technique of blown glass was turned into a Fine Art and used to create large-scale sculpture by Dale Chihuly (b. 1941). He created the *V & A Chandelier* (fig. 24.11), as it is now known (although it was originally called *Ice Blue and Spring Green Chandelier*), in 1999, of colored transparent glass. Commissioned by the Victoria and Albert Museum, it was installed in the main entrance rotunda in 2000. This striking chandelier is compiled of many smaller pieces, all curves and coils, like plant tendrils, that appear as if they would be soft to the touch. They have a natural, organic appearance, like some sort of fish or deep-sea plant form, undulating, floating weightless, in the current. Yet this chandelier weighs 3,800 pounds.

Born in Tacoma, Washington, Chihuly holds a BA in interior design, an MS in sculpture, and an MFA. He studied glass in Venice on a Fulbright Fellowship. A car accident in 1976 left him blind in his left eye, over which he wears an

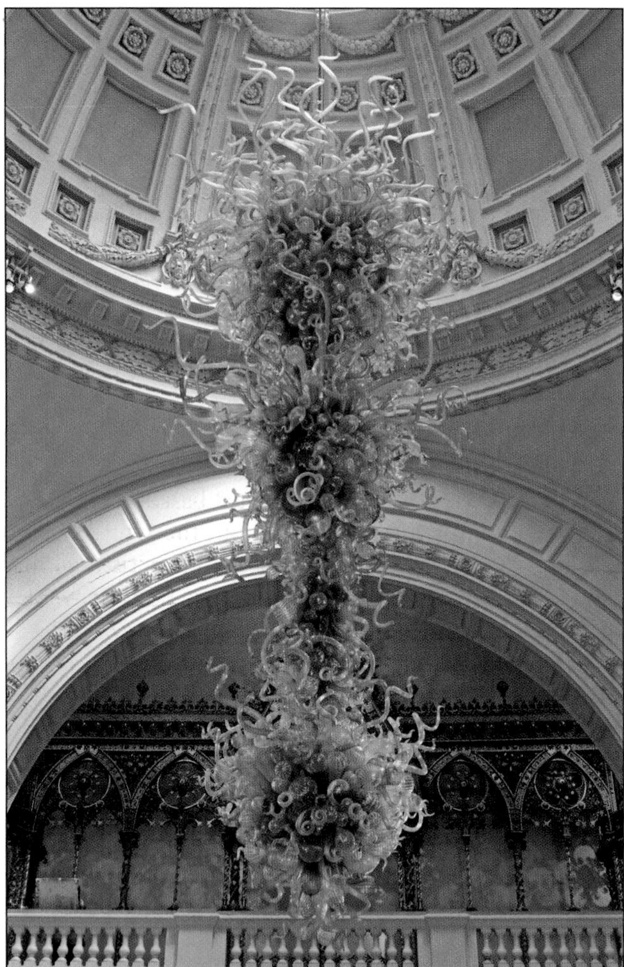

FIGURE 24.11 Dale Chihuly (b. 1941), known as the *V & A Chandelier*, originally called *Ice Blue and Spring Green Chandelier*, 1999, glass, height 30″ (9.1 m), installed 2000 in the rotunda of the main entrance of the Victoria and Albert Museum, London. Fragile, transparent blown glass is transformed into a sparkling, seemingly soft, organic life form.

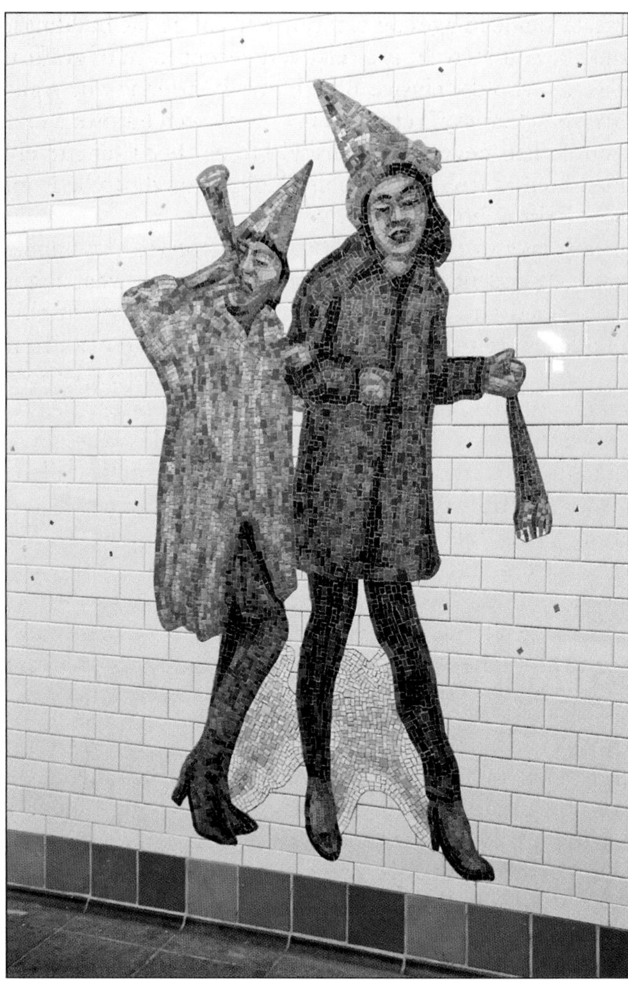

FIGURE 24.12 Jane Dickson, *The Revelers*, 2008, Murano glass mosaic, Times Square subway station, New York. Commuters rushing through the Times Square subway station in Manhattan have the company of light-hearted celebrants welcoming not only the New Year but also all who pass by.

eye patch, and a shoulder injury in 1979 left him unable to blow glass. A resourceful and effective entrepreneur, he now works by directing and supervising a team of artists.

Jane Dickson. The medium of mosaic has been used for millennia to create large-scale, durable surfaces on walls, ceilings, and floors. Mosaic was especially popular among the ancient Romans who used variously colored stones for the tesserae (the small pieces of colored material that are pressed into wet plaster). The term derives from the Greek work for "four," because of the four visible corners of the cube. In the Early Christian era, brighter and more varied colors were provided by the introduction of glass tesserae.

Jane Dickson used Murano glass for her mosaics, *The Revelers* (fig. 24.12), in Manhattan's bustling Times Square 42nd Street subway station. This extensive public art project was commissioned by the MTA (Metropolitan Transit Authority) in 2008. Sixty-seven lively, life-size figures, female and male, old and young, appear at intervals along the white wall, on which they cast shadows. As they celebrate New Year's Eve, animated and obviously enjoying themselves, equipped with horns and party hats, they seem able to elevate the moods of the actual people who hurry along the corridor.

Born in Chicago in 1952, Dickson was educated at the École des Beaux-Arts in Paris, Harvard University, and the School of the Museum of Fine Arts in Boston. Her work includes painting (often on unusual surfaces), drawing, and printing. She has been interested in public art in Times Square for many years. In 1987, she was the animator of the computer lightboard, where the famous ball is dropped each New Year's Eve.

Banksy. Stencils have long been used to decorate walls with repeat patterns, for example, in elegant Victorian homes. However, the use of stencils with spray paint to create single images on exterior walls of public buildings, quickly and secretly, is a relatively recent form of graffiti. Exactly who the elusive British graffiti artist is who signs his work "Banksy" remains uncertain. Even his own agent said he had never met Bansky! He has been tentatively identified as Robert or Robin Banks, thought to be from near Bristol, born in 1974.

Banksy's works are likely to be humorous, the humor often dependent on the location of the image—what might be termed site-specific spoofs. But the satires of this prankster are provocative and are likely to carry political opinions or moralizing messages, unconventional, perhaps controversial. Animals, especially rats, are often used to convey his ideas. The rats may act like people, wear clothing, use tools, and are even able to write on public walls—like a graffiti artist. There are philosophical rats and mischievous rats with a sense of humor, such as the *Rat with Camera* (fig. 24.13) on a wall in London. Banksy has worked on walls worldwide. At times, his wall graffiti has antagonized locals who would wash them from their walls. Yet his "off-the-wall" (so to speak) screenprints on paper sell for huge prices at auction.

Swoon. The oldest technique used to make printed images is block printing from a wood block into which the image has been incised. The technique started in China, probably during the eighth century (Tang dynasty), the woodcuts used to spread Buddhist teachings. Papercuts were also highly developed in early Asia—the oldest extant example was made in the sixth century. The importance of this technique was associated with the high value of the paper.

A large, handpainted linoleum block print and papercut called *Helena* (fig. 24.14) was created in 2008 by Swoon. The artist, who adopted this name to hide her identity in order to prevent police prosecution for the large-scale images she applied to exterior walls of public buildings, is now known to be Caledonia (Callie) Curry (b. 1978). Often called a "street artist," she creates images that are based largely on people seen on the streets, which are then wheat-pasted onto the walls of buildings on those streets. Swoon has spoken favorably about "the tying together of classical mediums and modern contexts." As her images are exposed to the natural environment, their decay is both inevitable and intentional.

FIGURE 24.13 Banksy, *Rat with Camera*, stencil and spray paint, executed on a wall in East London, 2005. The identity of the witty, satirical British graffiti artist known as Banksy has yet to be revealed. Here, a huge rat is ready to photograph the photographer. Or, perhaps he is a paparazzi rat!

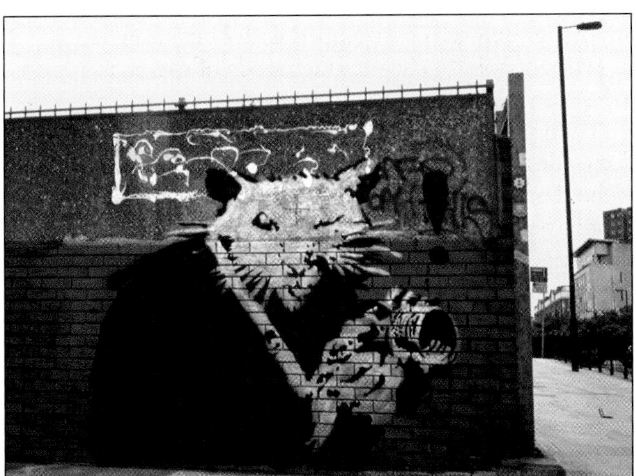

In the belief that art is provocative and experiential, using scavenged materials, she collaborated with others to create rafts on which they sailed the Mississippi River in 2006 and 2007. Seven wooden rafts sailed the Hudson River in 2008. And, using garbage from New York City to create boats, she sailed into the Venice Biennale (uninvited) with a crew of thirty in 2009.

Although she is an American artist based in Brooklyn, New York, Swoon works throughout the United States and abroad. A socially engaged, ethical artist, she has worked at a school in Zambia and is currently active in a rebuilding project in Haiti.

STRUCTURALISM AND DECONSTRUCTION

Beginning in the late 1960s, a number of French intellectuals made the case for the plurality of experience and developed strategies for challenging accepted traditions. One of these thinkers was Roland Barthes [BAR(t)] (1915–1980), whose early work was on "structural" linguistics, and whose approach to culture was thus called **structuralism.** At the heart of structural linguistics is an approach to "meaning" based on the notion of the plurality of the "sign." The "sign" is the ratio between the so-called signifier and the signified. For instance, the word "tree" is a signifier and a tree itself is the signified object. In French, the word for tree is *arbre;* in Swahili, it is *mti.* The signifier (the word) changes from language to language. In addition, the signified encompasses all possible trees. The signified is so plural and various that, on contemplation, it seems astonishing that language enables us to communicate meaningfully at all. What determines the particulars of the tree we are talking about when we say or write the word "tree" is the context of the tree. The pine tree in the backyard is different from the oak tree in the square. Context determines meaning. It follows then that when we consider any object, the object's meaning is determined not by its existence alone but by the situation in which we observe it. And this situation is always subject to change. Thus "meaning" is never absolute. It is as diverse as the situations in which it comes to exist.

What is known as "poststructuralist" thought is an application of this way of thinking, based on the assumption that speech—the meaning of which is never fully "determined"—can as easily mask reality as reveal it. The chief practitioner of poststructuralist thought is the French philosopher JACQUES DERRIDA [dare-ree-DAH] (b. 1930). Derrida's method, known as **deconstruction,**

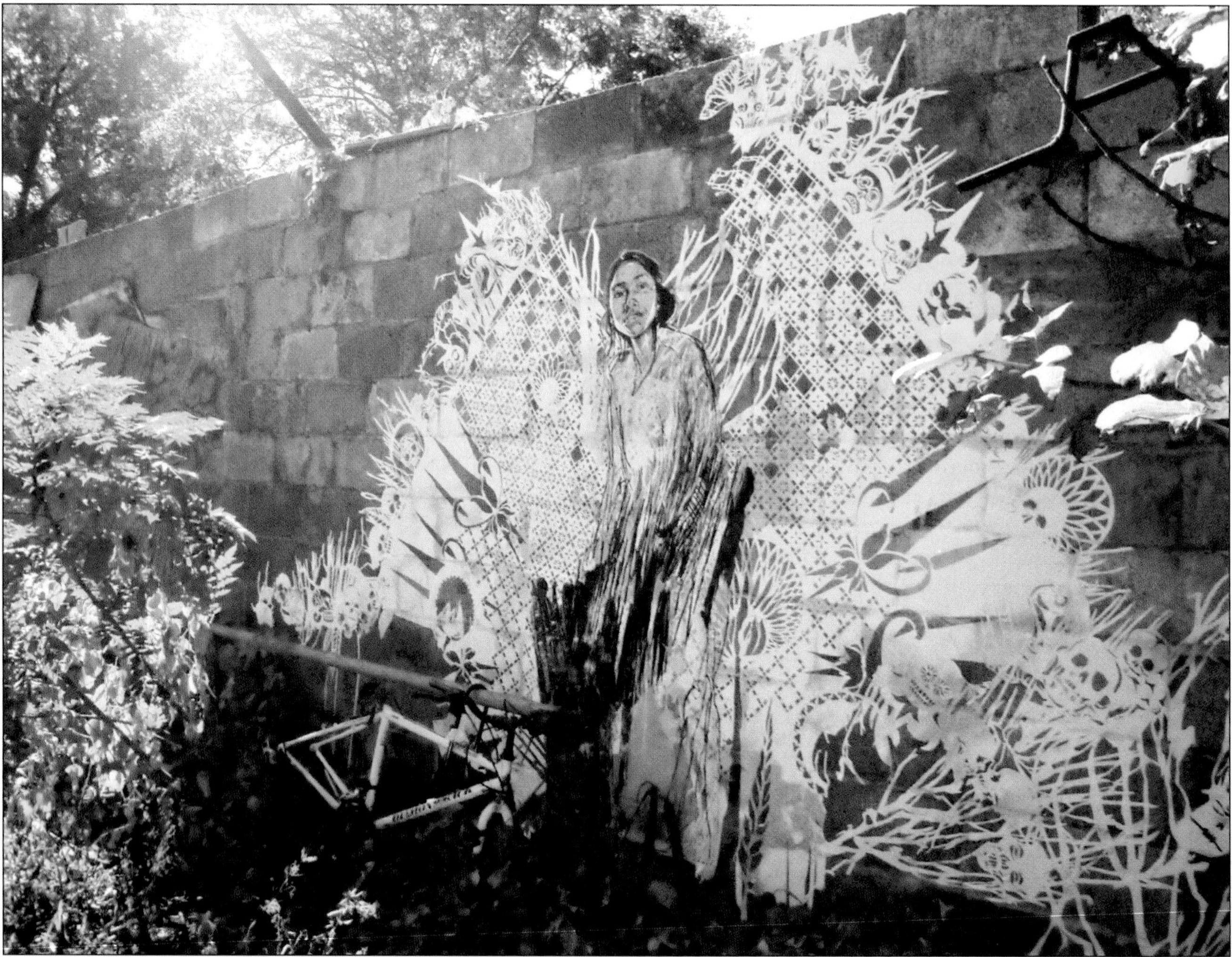

FIGURE 24.14 Swoon, *Helena*, 2008, handpainted linoleum block print and papercut, New Orleans, width ca. 15′ (4.6 m), height ca. 10′ (3 m). A street artist, Caledonia (Callie) Curry (b. 1978) initially used the alias Swoon to avoid prosecution for vandalism as she glued large-scale papercuts to public walls with wheat paste. The decay of the work is part of the artistic process.

consists of taking apart received traditions on the assumption that all thoughts include leaps in logic and inconsistencies, the revelation of which tells us more about the thought than the thought itself does. That is, in philosophy what is not said is at least as important as what is said. For Derrida, even the self is a fiction or construction, built out of unexamined assumptions, and it, too, must be deconstructed for true understanding. In sum, in the poststructuralist mind, there are no facts, only interpretations. Such a philosophical stance, which amounts to a profound skepticism, has led to a critical revision of much of Western thought.

The Diversity of American Voices

Adrienne Rich. Poet Adrienne Rich (b. 1929) was a passionate spokeswoman for feminist consciousness. Her prose and poetry, rooted in radical feminist ideology, dramatizes the freedom of self-discovery. At her best, Rich is less a polemicist and publicist than an artist who challenges preconceptions about women and their relationships to men and to one another.

In "When We Dead Awaken: Writing as Re-Vision," Rich describes how she needed to change the images that represented her ideals of both woman and poet, since her images of both had been dominated by men. She explores the concept of re-vision, which she calls "the act of looking back, of seeing with fresh eyes," as essential for writers, and as essential for women living in a male-dominated society. Re-vision, for Rich, is "an act of survival."

Maxine Hong Kingston. One characteristic of contemporary writing is the combination of elements from different genres. The autobiographical novel *The Woman Warrior* (1976), by Chinese American writer Maxine Hong Kingston (b. 1940), has been described by the author as "the book of her mother," since it is filled with stories her mother told her about her Chinese ancestors, especially the women whom Kingston describes as the ghosts of her girlhood. A second book, *China Men* (1980), is her father's book; it tells the stories of her male ancestors, including her father and grandfathers, although she learned these male stories from women, mostly from her mother. Mixing fact and fiction, autobiography and legend, Kingston's books combine family history with fictional invention. Kingston's identity as a Chinese American woman and her attempts to create images of her experience reveal her relationship to her ancestral past.

The stories Kingston recounts and invents in *The Woman Warrior* and in *China Men* derive from the Chinese "talk story," a Cantonese oral tradition kept alive mainly by woman. The books' talk-story narrators tell their stories in multiple versions, varying the amount of detail each reveals. These stories contain silences that invite the reader to engage in the imaginative world of the writer, who occasionally hints at her fictionalizing with cues such as "I wonder," "perhaps," and "may have."

By writing her mother's stories and adding variants of her own, Kingston marks the talk-story tradition with her own distinctive imprint. In the process, these stories entertain readers outside the Chinese cultural tradition. Kingston's work appeals because she gives voice to things women had spoken only in private or not at all. She also transmits her Cantonese heritage. Kingston animates a world and constructs a self that are at once strange and familiar, both "other" and inherently recognizable.

Toni Morrison. The 1996 Nobel Prize winner Toni Morrison (b. 1931) writes novels that focus on the complex balance between personal identity and social identity in African-American communities. Mixing feminist concerns with racial and cultural issues, Morrison's fiction explores the cultural inheritance of African Americans facing hardship and conflict through memory, relationships, and actions.

In her first novel, *The Bluest Eye* (1969), Morrison explores what it is like to be of mixed—white and black—descent and thus light-skinned, capturing not only the hurt of prejudices based on color but also the tragedy of unrecognized beauty. In *Sula* (1973), she portrays the family consequences of a woman achieving her own independence and freedom, and in *Song of Solomon* (1977), she portrays a black man's attempt to come to terms with his roots. The power of eroticism is the subject of *Tar Baby* (1981), and *Beloved* (1987) explores the degrading effects of slavery. Although every book is embedded in pain, Morrison's work is about survival, and her urgency to write is her quest to survive. "I think about what black writers do," she has said, "as having a quality of hunger and disturbance that never ends."

Judith Ortiz Cofer. From Puerto Rico, JUDITH ORTIZ COFER [CO-fur] (b. 1952) has published poetry and prose, in volumes such as *Silent Dancing* and *The Latin Deli*. These display Cofer's knack for conveying the experience of the lives of immigrants. Her stories, both autobiographical and fictional, show characters' conflicts with their new lives in mainland America and their memories of Puerto Rico. Elegant, lyrical, and convincing, Cofer's stories, poems, and autobiographical essays analyze and celebrate the double perspective of seeing life through the lenses of two cultures and languages.

Oscar Hijuelos. Hispanic Caribbean writer OSCAR HIJUELOS [hi-YAIL-oss] (b. 1951) captures the pre-Castro immigrant experience in the United States, particularly in New York. His novel *The Mambo Kings Play Songs of Love* won the Pulitzer Prize in 1990, the first book by a writer of Hispanic origin to win the prestigious award. In chronicling the lives of Cuban immigrants, their quest for the American dream, and their ultimate disillusionment, Hijuelos evokes the atmosphere of the 1950s. Throughout his work, Hijuelos explores the influence of Hispanic culture on American popular culture. His fascination with the diverse cultural threads woven into the fabric of contemporary American life brims over in his pages. An important influence on younger Hispanic Caribbean and Latino writers, Hijuelos captures and celebrates the spirit of place, in which his values are rooted. Hijuelos emphasizes the necessity for preserving cultural heritage, yet he also revels in the way life reflects a mosaic of cultural inflections.

N. Scott Momaday. The works of N. SCOTT MOMADAY [MOHM-ah-day] (b. 1934) were among the first by a Native American to garner a wide audience. Born in Oklahoma of Kiowa ancestry, Momaday has written poetry, fiction, and autobiography. His 1969 novel, *House Made of Dawn*, won a Pulitzer Prize. In it a young Native American man returns from military service in Vietnam to find himself without a place in either Indian society or mainstream America. Momaday's two autobiographical works, *The Way to Rainy Mountain* (1969) and *The Names* (1976), mingle Kiowa legends with American history and his family's personal experience.

Leslie Marmon Silko. Leslie Marmon Silko (b. 1948) has written poetry and prose that reflects her mixed ancestry: She is descended from the Laguna tribe but has white and Mexican ancestry as well. Her novel *Ceremony* (1978) and her collection of prose and poetry *Storyteller* (1981) both emphasize the cultural values and spirit of her Pueblo ancestors. *Ceremony* makes a connection between the shared cultural heritage of the tribal community and the experience of a Native American Indian veteran of the Vietnam War, who returns to the reservation to reclaim a sense of identity. *Storyteller*, a collection of folktales, family anecdotes, photographs, stories, and poems, reflects the intersection of the spiritual and material worlds, as well as connections between history and personal experience. The relationship between nature and culture permeates this work, emphasizing the way Native American peoples have lived in harmony with the natural world, the land being part of their identity, not merely a place to live.

Connections

Vaclav Havel, Playwright and Politician

During the 1960s and 1970s, Vaclav Havel, the first president of the post-Soviet Czech Republic, was best known as a playwright. Born in Prague, Czechoslovakia, in 1936, into a family of engineers, Havel became interested in philosophy and literature as a teenager and during the 1960s studied at the Academy of the Performing Arts. His best known plays include *The Garden Party* (1963), *The Memorandum* (1965), and *The Increased Difficulty of Concentration* (1968), which focus on political themes, especially on oppressive and threatening political environments. Havel has also written books about his political imprisonment, including *Living in Truth* (1989), *Disturbing the Peace* (1990), and *Letters to Olga* (1990).

Havel became known as a political dissident during the 1960s when he publicly criticized his country's Writer's Union for acting "as a broker between politics and literature," rather than "defending the right of literature to be literature." At that time he published an article arguing for the end of single-party rule in Czechoslovakia. The communist government responded by banning his writings.

During the 1970s, Havel helped establish an underground press to publish government-censored works. He continued to write pieces critical of the totalitarian regime, including "The Power of the Powerless," an essay on totalitarianism and dissent. Havel was arrested and imprisoned in the early 1970s and again in the early 1980s.

With the collapse of the communist system in Eastern Europe in 1991, and with the division of Czechoslovakia into separate Czech and Slovak republics in 1993, democratic government was introduced. Imprisoned again in 1989 for dissident activities, Havel was released, and by the end of the year was elected president of Czechoslovakia. In 1993, he became the first president of the new Czech Republic. Havel's political reputation grew to include that of a courageous leader, one with a vision of tolerant coexistence of people of different cultures and identities. Havel's social vision and political leadership were of a piece with the moral themes of his plays. His literary works effected social and political change, not the least of which was Havel's election to the presidency of his country.

THE GLOBAL VILLAGE

The opening of the Berlin Wall in November 1989 and, in turn, the collapse of the communist regime in the Soviet Union two years later symbolized the awakening of tolerance among diverse cultures in the contemporary world. For the first time since World War II, the citizens of East and West Germany were able to come together freely and openly. As Vaclav Havel (b. 1936), the president of the Czech Republic, put it in 1993: "All of us—whether from the west, the east, the south, or the north of Europe—can agree that the common basis of any effort to integrate Europe is the wealth of values and ideas we share. . . . All of us respect the principle of unity in diversity and share a determination to foster creative cooperation between the different nations and ethnic, religious, and cultural groups—and the different spheres of civilization—that exist in Europe." Havel's message can easily be extended to the globe as a whole. We have come to recognize and accept a worldwide imperative: we live in a pluralistic community of nearly five billion people. To survive and thrive, we need to communicate and share with one another as if we lived in a single village.

GLOBALIZATION

A major trend among the world's economies came to a head in the 1990s—the emergence of globalization, or the massive movement of information, technology, and goods across national borders. Globalization is one of a number of factors influencing changes in the general world order that present challenges to the relationships between and among nations and cultures worldwide. Fueling the fires of economic globalization are a series of technological developments, especially in communications, that have erased geographic distance and accelerated time. In addition, a number of economic agreements were made in the mid- to late-twentieth century, including the General Agreement on Free Trade and Tariffs (GATT), signed by 23 countries in 1947, and which now includes 123 signatories. In 1995 GATT gave way to the World Trade organization (WTO), with the most important recent country addition being China.

The most important practical economic development has been the emergence of global corporations, which have spread their operations around the world, as they seek business efficiencies, especially the lowest possible operating costs. The integration of world economies and the globalization of companies have been complemented by the rapid rise of Asian economies, including those of Hong Kong, Singapore, South Korea, and Taiwan, as well as those of China and India, two sleeping giants whose economies have only recently begun to awaken.

Other global economic intiatives include the North American Free Trade Agreement (NAFTA) signed by Canada, Mexico, and the United States; the Organization of Petroleum Exporting Countries (OPEC) in the Middle

Then & Now

NAVIGATING THE WEB

Perhaps no single technological development has succeeded in shrinking the globe more than the **Internet** and its network, the World Wide Web. Not only is text available on the Web, but so are images, videos, sound, and film. Over five hundred museum and gallery sites are accessible on the Web, including such sites as the A.I.R. Gallery in New York (women artists), the Andy Warhol Museum in Pittsburgh, and the Louvre in Paris, where one can view such works as Leonardo's *Mona Lisa* (see Chapter 13) and Géricault's *Raft of the Medusa* (see Chapter 17). By browsing the sites of museums and galleries around the globe, it is possible to view old and new work by artists from over fifty countries. You can browse the collection of the Ho-Am Art Museum in Seoul, Korea, viewing masterpieces from its painting, ceramics, and bronze collections, or you can tour galleries in Taipei, Taiwan.

You can watch a video clip of a war dance by the Anlo-Ewe people of Ghana, West Africa, or listen to music samples from the newest CD releases in South America. Alternatively, you could browse the current issue of *Critical Inquiry*, a scholarly journal in the United States, or check out *LIVEculture*, the online publication of the Institute for Learning Technologies at Columbia University, which focuses on contemporary art, literature, media, communications, and cultural studies. The possibilities are endless, and the availability of information about almost anything is unprecedented. The World Wide Web promises to change the way in which we think about ourselves and learn about the world around us.

East; the Association of Southeast Asian Nations (ASEAN), and the European Union (EU).

In addition to economic globalization, the late twentieth and early twenty-first centuries have seen increasing cross-cultural exchanges in ideas, arts, and cultural practices. The English language has become the world's main language of communication, especially when people of different language groups work together. The world's cultures are being brought closer together with developments in technology, including the Internet, e-mail, and the cell phone. At the same time, countries and regions struggle to preserve their own cultures, languages, and identities.

RECENT TRENDS IN INTERNATIONAL ARCHITECTURE

Globalization is especially evident in architecture. Following is a discussion of an office building in Japan designed by a French architect, a museum in Spain designed by a Canadian-American, and a sports stadium in China designed by a Swiss architectural firm.

Philippe Starck. The Asahi Beer Hall (fig. 24.15), located on the east bank of the Sumida River in Tokyo and finished in 1989, is the work of the French architect Philippe Starck. The building is striking and extremely modern, yet the company, Asahi Breweries, Ltd., was founded in 1889 and has been manufacturing beer here for more than a century. A building shaped like a beer glass with tapering sides, covered with polished black granite, supports a flame shape made of metal, hollow inside, coated in simulated gold. Referred to as the "Flame of Gold," the flame is Starck's symbol, here constructed on such a colossal scale as to have no affiliation with humility. Inside the

FIGURE 24.15 Philippe Starck, *Asahi Beer Hall*, 1989, Tokyo, Japan. Hardly intended to go unnoticed, the Beer Hall is topped by the "Flame of Gold." The headquarters of this beer company are in the taller building on the left, designed to look like a glass of beer with foam on top.

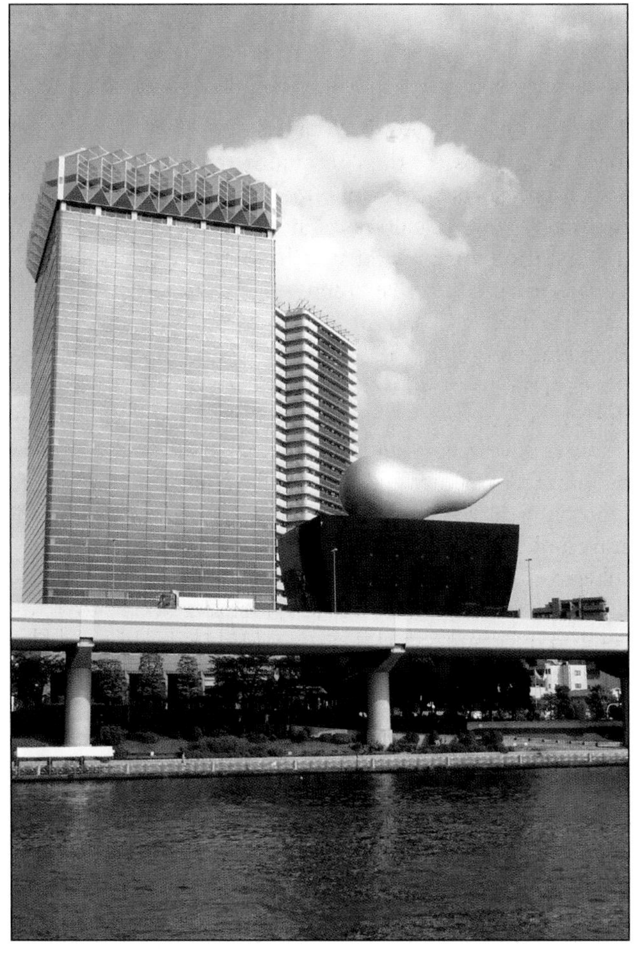

Critical Thinking

Reality TV

Reality TV is now more than a decade old—having expanded significantly since the airing of *Big Brother* in 1999. Leaving aside various kinds of game shows, documentaries, and news broadcasts, what is your opinion of, and attitude toward, reality TV? What do you think of shows such as *American Idol*, *The Bachelor* (and *The Bachelorette*), and *Survivor?* To what extent do you think reality TV shows are contrived and scripted? In using real people rather than actors as their performers, reality TV purports to present the world as it really is, events as they actually happen, and people as they truly are. What do you think about these claims? Why?

building are the beer hall and restaurants. Beside the Beer Hall is another, taller building shaped like a beer mug, with walls the color of beer, and complete with a facsimile of white foam. This building houses the company's headquarters. Designed to attract attention, this aspect of Starck's architecture has also brought criticism.

Born in Paris in 1949, Starck started his first company when he was only nineteen years old. He was originally an interior designer, creating functional items such as furniture, luggage, clothes (including a line called Starck NAKED), accessories, watches, toothbrushes, and even vehicles. An early advocate for "green" morality, Starck established an organic food company. He advocates affordable "Good Goods," which he calls "democratic ecology." The intentionally unconventional architect designs offices, restaurants, and hotels. He now lives in Paris, New York, Burano (Italy), and London.

Frank Gehry. The Guggenheim Museum Bilbao (fig. 24.16), constructed in Bilbao, Spain, in 1997, is the work of the architect Frank Gehry. The huge curving, organic planes of the walls (made of limestone, titanium, and glass) appear to have been gently bent into their present shapes. The visitor may wonder if this is sculpture as architecture, or architecture as sculpture, for here there is no longer a division between two traditionally distinct disciplines. Designed with its location just beside the Nervion River in mind, the shape of the museum intentionally recalls that of a ship and the water's waves. Further, Gehry often takes inspiration from the forms of fish; here the shiny titanium panels recall fish scales. The museum houses a permanent collection focusing on twentieth-century art and also installs temporary exhibitions of a wide range of types of art. Although the art exhibited inside attracts many visitors, the striking building is a destination in itself. The Guggenheim Museum Bilbao is one of the museums of the Solomon R. Guggenheim Foundation. Others are in New York, Venice, Berlin, and Abu Dhabi; that in Abu Dhabi was also designed by Gehry.

The Canadian-American architect Frank Gehry (b. 1929) was born Ephraim Owen Goldberg in Toronto (his first wife, Anita Snyder, suggested that he change his name to Frank Gehry). He has taught architecture at Columbia, Yale, and Harvard universities. This architect has achieved celebrity status—indeed, so famous has Gehry become that he has been dubbed a "Starchitect."

FIGURE 24.16 Frank Gehry, *Guggenheim Museum Bilbao*, Bilbao, Spain, 1997. In this extraordinary museum, forms usually reserved to the sculptor have been turned into architecture. The undulating, seemingly fluid, shiny walls relate to the museum's site close to the Nervion River.

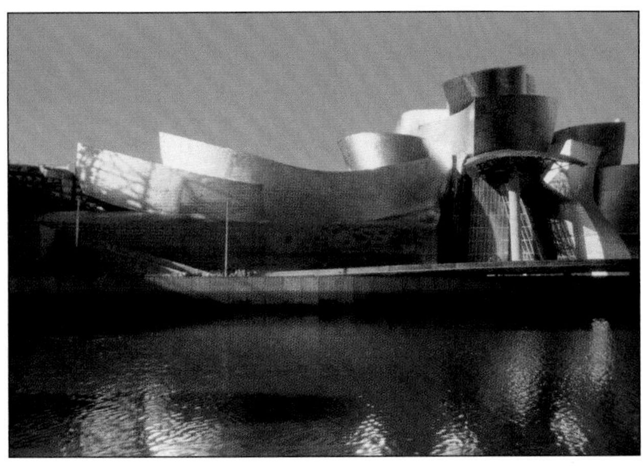

Herzog & de Meuron. The design for China's National Stadium in Beijing (fig. 24.17) was selected from thirteen submissions, each of which had to accommodate a series of requirements and specifications. The result, now widely known as the "Bird's Nest," was built 2003–08 for the 2008 Olympics. The National Stadium was intended to be what the chief architect Li Xinggang described as a "public vessel." The appearance of the stadium derives from the study of Chinese ceramics. Simple geometric forms are made complex by their multiplication. An outer frame of long steel beams surrounds a "seating bowl" formed of concrete and furnished with tiers of bright red chairs. Although giving the appearance of being a rather free-form, abstract composition, the stadium is actually almost symmetrical. After the 2008 Olympics were over,

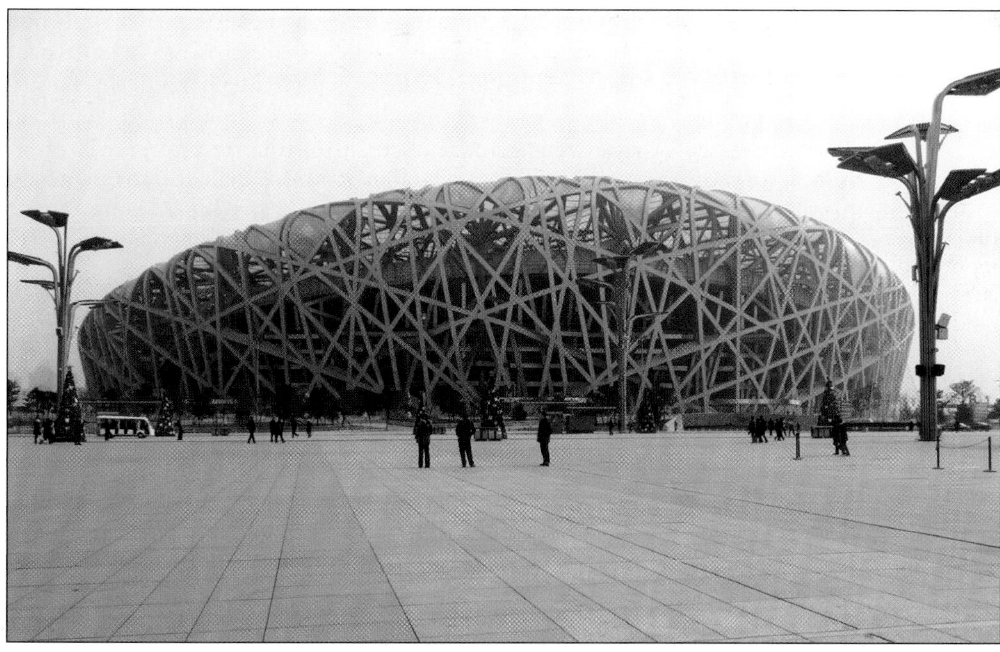

FIGURE 24.17 Herzog & de Meuron, *National Stadium*, Beijing, China, 2003–08. Descriptively dubbed "The Bird's Nest," this steel skeleton structure seats 80,000 people. Compare to the Colosseum (fig. 4.10), an ancient Roman amphitheater, built c. 80 C.E. of concrete and faced with stone, which seated over 50,000 people.

11,000 temporary seats were removed, leaving the number of seats at 80,000.

Jacques Herzog and Pierre de Meuron, both born 1950 in Basel, Switzerland, founded their architecture firm of Herzog & de Meuron there in 1978. They specialize in large public buildings, especially art museums and sports stadia.

Paul Andreu. Construction of the National Grand Theater (the literal translation of the Chinese name), in Beijing (fig. 24.18), also known as the Center for the Performing Arts, began in 2001 and the first concert was played here in 2007. The building is also known locally and colloquially by the visually descriptive name "The Egg." It generated controversy as people felt this modern building did not fit aesthetically with the Forbidden City (fig. 19.10) and other nearby buildings constructed in more traditional styles.

Constructed of titanium and glass, the dome of the National Grand Theater rises 151 feet (46 m). The building is actually an artificial island, surrounded by, and reflected in, an artificial pond shaped like a rectangle with bowed sides. Visitors enter on the north and must walk through a passageway 197 feet (60 m) long beneath the pond to gain entry. There one finds three halls: the Opera Hall, the Concert Hall, and the Theater Hall. The Opera Hall is at the center of the building, is the most important, and has the largest seating area. Total seating capacity is 5,452 people. The National Grand Theater also contains public spaces such as shops, restaurants, and seating areas. People come to see not only the performances, but also the building. Because a portion of the exterior is transparent, in the evening, when the building is lit from inside, people who pass by can look in and see the performance.

The French architect and engineer Paul Andreu, born 1938, favors simple, futuristic shapes and has designed

FIGURE 24.18 Paul Andreu, *National Grand Theater* ("The Egg"), Beijing, China, 2001–07. Indicative of an increased concern for public access to cultural events, this building contains separate halls for operas, concerts, and theatrical productions. These halls are enclosed in the simple shape of a domed oval, which is created from titanium and glass and reflects in the surrounding pool.

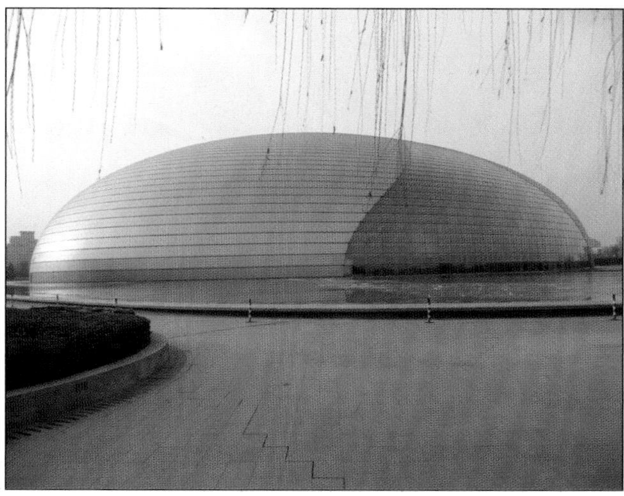

airports throughout the world. Beijing's "Egg" has also been compared to, and is said to have been inspired by, the oval shape of a drop of water; the reflection of the elliptical domed building in the surrounding water makes the shape appear to be complete.

Tom Shannon. Globalization in the visual arts is seen also in the use of related aesthetics in different art forms—such as architecture and sculpture—created contemporaneously in distant lands. Very similar to the National Grand Theater in Beijing, the shape of which was noted to have been compared to a drop of water, is Tom Shannon's sculpture, *Drop* (fig. 24.19), of 2009, which is similarly a shiny ellipse that appears to float.

The sculptor explained this illusion to the author (Benton), noting, "The water drop form hovers in equilibrium. It is balanced at its center of gravity on a point. The point is part of a counter-balancing mechanism inside the form. The mechanism enables the mirror-polished form to rise and fall slowly, spin on axis, tilt in any direction, and to glide horizontally a meter in all directions. The form always slowly returns to equilibrium." Further, the weight and movement of the three-ton sculpture is supported on a slender, mirror-polished stem that rises out of what he described as "a serious underground foundation."

The artist/inventor Tom Shannon was born in 1947. A prodigy, a work he made when he was only nineteen was included in an exhibition at the Museum of Modern Art several years later. His floating simple geometric shapes (and people), some of which are magnetically levitated, appear to defy gravity. Skillfully amalgamating art and science, his work combines the abilities of a sculptor (he is also a painter) with those of an engineer. In fact, Shannon holds patents on innovative types of telephones, television projectors, and a world clock.

FIGURE 24.19 Tom Shannon, *Drop*, 2009, stainless steel (internal counterbalance mechanism of ball bearing axles, universal joint, and massive weights), diameter 18′ (5.5 m), height 5′4″ (1.61 m), collection of the Chateau La Coste, Aix-en-Provence, France. The simple purity and sleek surfaces of Shannon's sculpture are unequaled. Combining science and art, this ellipse, its surface so shiny that its surroundings are reflected, appears to float.

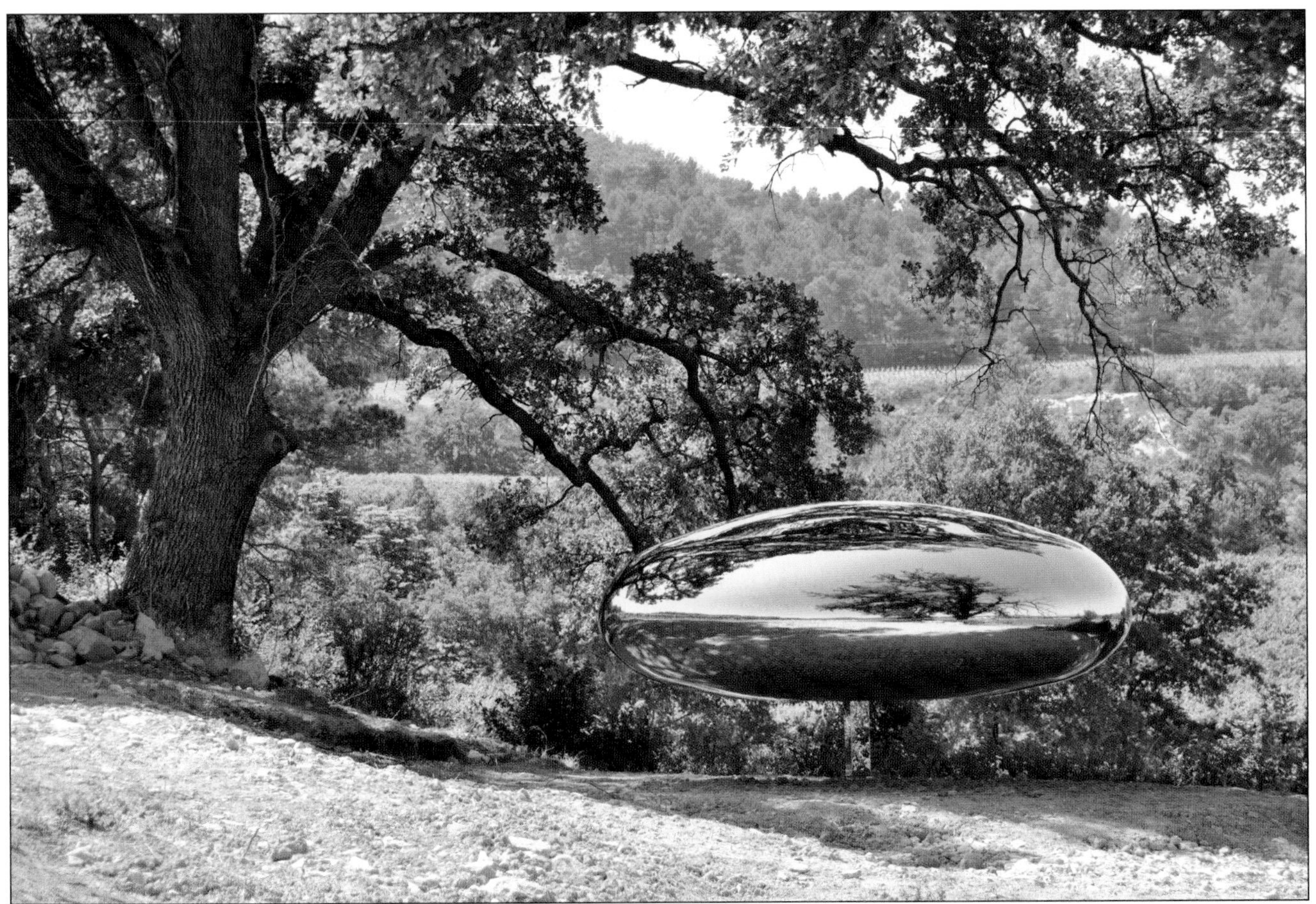

Cultural Impact

Just a few years into the twenty-first century, America continues to experience an influx of immigrants from around the world. European immigration has risen from the previous decades, partly due to the collapse of Soviet communism. Asian immigration, from India, China, Korea, and Vietnam, continues unabated, with students from Asian countries making up the majority of those studying at U.S. universities from abroad. Even larger numbers of immigrants, however, have come to the United States from the Caribbean and from Central and South America, so much so that Spanish is rapidly becoming an unofficial second language in the country.

These diverse groups of people bring a rich array of languages and cultures, which have a significant impact on the cultural life of contemporary America. African-American poets, playwrights, and novelists have altered the literary landscape. African-American musicians maintain an extensive presence and exert a powerful influence on the music of the day, from hip-hop to rock, from jazz to gospel and blues. Latin American and Caribbean musicians, performers, and composers have also made a lasting impact on American cultural life. And Latin American and Caribbean writers have left a similarly extensive legacy for the future, with works in both Spanish and in English.

The legacy of Native Americans has also recently begun to be appreciated, spurred by the renewed study of Native American history and culture in the past few decades. The popularity of Native American crafts, art, and artifacts, such as Navajo blankets and southwest Indian basketry, pottery, and jewelry, have influenced contemporary style. Native American artists and writers have had a decisive impact on contemporary attitudes toward the environment; the Native American approach to living in harmony with nature may, in fact, be the greatest of its cultural legacies.

The full force of contemporary cultural ideas can only be assessed in the future. Certain features of the contemporary landscape, however, reflect cultural values that are becoming increasingly evident. Among these are a broadening of cultural perspective and a deepening of cultural awareness to include a wider range of voices and visions than had been previously accommodated socially and artistically. Women continue to achieve greater recognition for their accomplishments. Minorities of all cultural, racial, ethnic, and linguistic backgrounds continue to have an impact on contemporary cultural and artistic values.

KEY TERMS

postmodernism
semiotics
deconstructionism
structuralism
deconstruction
Internet

www. WEBSITES FOR FURTHER STUDY

http://www.judychicago.com/
(A website on Judy Chicago, a major contemporary force in women associated with art.)

http://www.johnseed.com/basquiat.html
(An informative site on Jean-Michel Basquiat, graffiti artist-cum-master, whose meteoric fame for portraying black heroes was tragically cut short by an early death.)

http://www.greatbuildings.com/buildings/Vietnam_Veterans_Memorial.html
(GreatBuildings.com site on Maya Lin's Vietnam memorial.)

http://www.uncp.edu/home/canada/work/canam/kingston.htm
(A basic site on Maxine Hong Kingston, one of the most important woman writers of our time.)

http://www.aboriginal-art.com/desert_pages/yuendumu_thumb.html#yuendumu2
(A site on Central Australia's Western Desert Aboriginal region, featuring the art of the Yuendumu and Lajamanu communities.)

http://www.ipl.org/div/natam/
(Site contains information on contemporary Native American authors, including Leslie Silko, Sherman Alexie, and N. Scott Momaday.)

http://www.library.yale.edu/latinamerica/reference_lit.html
(A site for Yale University's Latin American collection, which includes a dictionary of Latin American authors.)

http://www.dancehelp.com
(Site devoted to dance that includes the history of dance with an overview of modern dance, dancers, and dance companies.)

Glossary

Note: Words in **boldface** indicate terms defined elsewhere in the glossary.

a cappella (ah kuh-PELL-uh) Italian for "chapel style." In music, a composition for voices only, not accompanied by any other instruments.

absolute music Instrumental composition that does not attempt to tell a story or describe a scene, but deals only with musical sound, form, tone, and color. Compare **program music.**

Abstract Expressionism Mid-twentieth-century painting style that rejected realistic representation and emphasized the artist's spontaneous and emotional interaction with the work.

abstraction Art that does not portray the actual appearance of a subject but reflects an artist's nonrepresentational conception of it.

academy Generally, a society of artists or scholars. The Academy was Plato's school for the study of philosophy.

acanthus Mediterranean plant whose leaves were copied as decoration on the **capitals** of **Corinthian** columns.

acropolis Literally meaning "high city," this was the fortified, elevated point in an ancient Greek city. The Acropolis is the specific site in Athens where the Parthenon was built.

acrylic Paint made of pigment in a solution of a synthetic resin.

Action painting Mid-twentieth-century painting style popularized by Pollock in which the artist throws, drops, or splatters paint on a canvas to convey a sense of physical activity.

adagio (uh-DAH-joe; uh-DAH-jee-oh) Musical direction for an "easy" or slow **tempo.**

aesthetic Related to the appreciation of beauty in the arts.

Afrobeat Complex pattern of musical rhythms characteristic of some forms of African music, particularly from Nigeria and Ghana, and of their influence on other musical styles.

agit-trains Trains that disseminated propaganda art in postrevolutionary Russia.

agora Meeting place in ancient Greece, especially a marketplace.

aisle A long side passageway of a church. Aisles run parallel to the central **nave.**

alap In music, an improvised prelude to an Indian **raga** composition.

alla prima (AH-la PREE-ma) To paint without making any preliminary drawing.

allegory A symbolic narrative in which a deeper, often moral meaning exists beyond the literal level of a work.

allegro Musical direction for a fast **tempo.**

altar Raised platform or table at which religious ceremonies take place. Where the Eucharist is celebrated in Christian churches.

altarpiece Painted or carved panel or panels behind or above the **altar** of a church.

alto In music, the range of the lowest female voice.

ambulatory Passageway or aisle around the interior of a church or cathedral.

amphitheater Oval or round theater with tiers of seats gradually rising from a central arena.

amphora (AM-fur-uh) Two-handled jar with a narrow neck, used by ancient Greeks and Romans to carry wine or oil.

anagnorisis In drama, the point at which a character experiences recognition or increased self-knowledge.

animal style An artistic design popular in ancient and medieval times, characterized by decorative patterns of intricate animal motifs.

anime Sophisticated Japanese animated films.

anthropomorphism The act of attributing human characteristics to non-human entities, such as gods or animals.

antiphony Vocal or instrumental music in which two or more groups sing or play in alternation.

apartheid Policy of racial segregation practiced in the Republic of South Africa, involving political, legal, and economic discrimination against nonwhites.

Apollonian Style of culture and art characterized by clarity, harmony, and restraint, and in the philosophy of Friedrich Nietzche, as embodying the power of critical reason. See also **Dionysian.**

apse Semicircular space at the end of a church sanctuary, often highly decorated; usually the location of the **altar.**

aqueduct Literally "water tube." A structure using gravity to bring water from higher sources into cities and towns below.

arcade Series of connected **arches,** supported by columns or **piers.**

arch In architecture, the curved or pointed structure spanning the top of an open space, such as a doorway.

Archaic period Greek cultural and artistic style of about 600–480 B.C.E.

Archaic smile An enigmatic facial expression, almost a half-smile, typical of early ancient Greek sculpture.

architrave Lowest horizontal portion of the **entablature,** supported by column **capitals.**

archivolt Semicircular molding outlining an **arch.**

aria (AHR-ee-ah) Section of an **opera, oratorio,** or **cantata** for a solo singer, usually with orchestral accompaniment.

Arianism Theological doctrine denying the divinity of Jesus, proclaimed by Arius (256–336 C.E.), condemned as heresy by the Roman Catholic Church.

Ars Nova Latin for New Art. Musical style of the fourteenth century that used more secular themes and more complex rhythms and harmonies than the old music of previous centuries.

Art Nouveau (art new-VOE) French for "new art." A late nineteenth- and early twentieth-century movement noted for its ornamental decoration based on the forms of nature, especially the frequent use of curvilinear and floral patterns.

art song Song in which words and music are artistically combined so the composition reflects the tone, mood, and meaning of the lyrics.

ashlar masonry Masonry of square-cut stones with right angle corners.

assonance Similarity of sound, especially the half rhyme of words with the same vowel sounds but different consonants, as in *heap* and *leak.*

atelier (AT-ul-yay) French for an artist's workshop.

atlas (plural, atlantes) Sculpted male figure that serves as an architectural support.

atmospheric (aerial) perspective See **perspective.**

atonality Lack of a home key or **tonal center** in a musical composition.

atrium Room in the center of an ancient Roman house.

automatism Surrealist artistic technique of the early twentieth century in which the artist gives up intellectual control over his or her work, allowing the subconscious to take over.

avant-garde (ah-vahnt GUARD) Literally, "advance guard" in French. Military term used to describe artists on the cutting edge, especially those vanguard artists of the early twentieth century in France who focused on **abstraction.**

avatar In **Hinduism,** an **incarnation** of a deity in human or animal form.

backbeat Steady, rhythmic background musical beat.

baldacchino (ball-dah-KEY-noh) Italian for, in architecture, a canopy placed over a sacred space, such as an altar.

ballad In poetry, a narrative poem, often of folk origin, written in four-line stanzas. In music, a song that tells a story, often about love and loss.

balustrade In architecture, a carved railing supported by small posts, or balusters, as along a staircase or roof line.

Bantu Member of any of a large number of linguistically related peoples of central and southern Africa. The word means "people" in the Bantu language.

baptistery Small building or room where baptisms are performed.

Baroque (bah-ROKE) Seventeenth-century artistic period characterized by opulence, emotionalism, theatricality, and large scale. In music, a composition style of the seventeenth and eighteenth centuries characterized by ornamentation and rigid structure.

barrel vault (tunnel vault) See drawing in Starter Kit, page xxx.

bas relief French for "low" relief. In sculpture, relief that projects only slightly from its background.

basilica Large rectangular building with a central **nave** and an **apse** at one or both ends, originally used in Rome for business and legal meetings, later adapted for early Christian churches.

bass In music, the range of the lowest male voice.

battered In architecture, sloping inward toward the top, as in a wall.

Bauhaus Early twentieth-century German art school led by Gropius that attempted to blend all forms of art, science, and technology.

bay In architecture, a spatial unit that is repeated.

beat Unit of rhythm in a musical composition, or the accent in that rhythm.

Beats Short for Beatniks; members of the Beat generation espoused unconventional attitudes, ideas, and behavior during the 1950s.

Beijing opera Chinese musical drama developed in the nineteenth century that featured fast-paced, stylized scenes based on ancient Chinese myths.

belle époque (bell-lay-PUCK) French for "beautiful age," used to refer to the era of elegance in Paris during the late nineteenth and early twentieth centuries.

Benedictines Members of the religious order founded by St. Benedict in 529.

bhakti (BUCK-tee) In Hinduism, the expression of personal devotion to a particular deity, especially in the form of poetry.

black-figure style Greek vase painting style featuring black figures painted on a red clay background with details incised to reveal the red clay below.

blank verse Unrhymed verse in iambic pentameter, frequently used in Elizabethan drama.

blind arcade Decorative **arcade** in which the **arches** and **columns** are attached to the background wall.

Bodhi In Buddhism, perfect knowledge.

bodhisattva (boe-di-SUTT-vuh) In Buddhism, an enlightened being on the brink of buddhahood who forgoes **nirvana** to help others attain salvation.

Brahmanism In Hinduism, the religious practices of ancient India as embodied in the **Vedas.**

brass instrument Musical instrument, such as a trumpet or tuba, played by blowing through a detachable brass mouthpiece.

Buddhism Religious response to **Hinduism** in East Asia that adheres to the doctrines of the Buddha, including the Four Noble Truths and the Eightfold Path.

Bunraku (boon-RAH-koo) Traditional Japanese puppet theater featuring large puppets and puppeteers on stage, and a samisen accompanist and narrator who sit just off the side of the stage.

buttress In architecture, a projecting support or reinforcement.

Byzantine (BIZ-un-teen) Artistic style of Eastern Europe in the fourth through fifteenth centuries that featured rich colors, Christian imagery, domed churches, and mosaics.

cabochon (CAB-uh-shawn) Gem that is not cut in facets but is smoothed and rounded.

caliph One of a succession of leaders who assumed religious and secular control of Islam after Muhammad's death.

call and response Style of chanting and/or singing that involves one or more leaders and a group of chanter/singers who respond with their own verses. Popular in African music.

calligraphy Beautiful handwriting.

Calvinism Theological belief system, based on John Calvin's (1509–1564) writings, that held that some individuals—the Elect—are predestined to be saved; noted for its strict moral code.

calypso Type of music that originated in the West Indies, characterized by improvised lyrics often on humorous topics.

camera obscura (ub-SKOOR-a) Crude cameralike device for verifying perspective, first used in the Renaissance. Consisted of a box with a tiny hole in one side through which a beam of light passes, projecting the scene, now inverted, on the opposite wall of the box.

campanile Italian for "bell tower."

canon In religion, the books of the Bible officially sanctioned by a church as inspired by God.

cantata From the Italian verb "to sing." Small-scale musical work for a solo singer or small group of singers and accompanying instruments. Compare **sonata.**

cantilever In architecture, a self-supporting extension from a wall.

canto Main division of a poem.

cantus firmus (CAN-tuss FURR-muss) Preexisting melody line around which a new polyphonic composition is constructed.

canzone; canzoni (can-TSOE-neh; can-TSOE-nee) A song, especially one performed by troubadours in the eleventh through thirteenth centuries and using a love poem as text.

capital In architecture, the decorative top part of a column that supports the **entablature.**

capstone Topmost stone in a **corbeled** arch or **dome.**

cartoon Full-scale preparatory drawing made on heavy paper for a large work such as a **tapestry** or **mural.**

caryatid Sculpted female figure used in place of an architectural support.

cast iron Cast alloy of iron with silicon and carbon.

catacomb Underground burial area of early Christians.

catharsis Purging of emotional tension, especially by art; originally described by Aristotle as the effect of tragic drama on the audience.

cella (SELL-uh) Inner room of a Greek or Roman temple, where the temple's cult statue was kept.

centering In architecture, a temporary wooden semicircular device used for support during construction of an **arch, vault,** or **dome.**

central plan Building having no longitudinal **axis,** such as one with a polygonal or circular floor plan.

cha-no-yu Japanese ritualistic tea ceremony.

chanson (shawn-SEWN or SHANN-sen) French for "song." A general term for a song with French lyrics, especially one performed by troubadours in the eleventh through sixteenth centuries.

chanson de geste (shawn-SAWN duh JZEST) French for "song of deeds." A medieval **epic** poem that celebrates the actions of historical figures or heroes.

chapel Small area for worship, usually found as part of a larger church or within a secular building.

château French for "castle."

chiaroscuro (key-are-oh-SKOO-roe) From the Italian *chiaro,* "clear" or "light," and *oscuro,* "obscure" or "dark." In painting, a method of modeling that uses subtle shifts of light to dark to give the impression of depth and to focus the viewer's attention.

chiton Soft clinging outer garment worn by women in ancient Greece.

chivalry System of ethical conduct of the Middle Ages based on a blend of Christian and military morals.

choir In architecture, the part of a church where the singers perform, usually between the **transept** and the **apse.**

choka A long Japanese poem.

chorale Simple Protestant hymn sung in unison by a church congregation.

chorus In ancient Greek drama, the group of actors who spoke or chanted in unison, often while moving in a stylized dance; the chorus provided a commentary on the action. Later, the term was generalized to mean a company of singers.

Christian humanism Sixteenth-century belief system that combined the ideals of classical **humanism** with biblical morality.

Cistercians Members of the austere order of monks established at Cîteaux in 1098.

Classical Artistic style of ancient Greece or Rome that emphasized balance, restraint, and quest for perfection. In music, the eighteenth-century style characterized by accessibility, balance, and clarity.

classicism Any later artistic style reminiscent of the ancient Greek or Roman **Classical** style and its values of balance, restraint, and quest for perfection.

clerestory/clearstory Story of a building with windows.

cloister Room in a monastery, square or rectangular in plan, open to the sky and containing a **garth.**

coda Repeated section of music at the end of a movement in **sonata form.**

coffers Square indentations of the underside of an **arch, vault,** or **dome.**

collage From the French word for "gluing" or "pasting." A visual art form in which bits of familiar objects, such as rope or a piece of newspaper, are glued on a surface.

colonette Small column, usually attached to a **pier** in **Gothic** cathedrals.

colonnade In architecture, a row of columns placed side by side, usually to support a roof or series of **arches.**

color field Twentieth-century abstract painting style, popularized by Rothko, that featured large rectangles of flat color intended to evoke an emotional response.

column A vertical architectural support, usually consisting of a base, **shaft,** and decorative **capital.**

comedy Amusing play or novel with a happy ending, usually including a marriage.

comic opera Light **opera,** especially of the **Classical** era, that featured simple music, an amusing plot, and spoken dialogue.

complementary colors Combination of one primary color and one secondary color formed by the two other primary colors. Red and green, blue and orange, and yellow and purple are complementary colors. See also **primary colors; secondary colors.**

composite order Combination of the volute scroll of the **Ionic** order with the acanthus leaves of the **Corinthian** order.

Conceptual art Twentieth-century artistic style whose works were conceived in the mind of the artist, often submitted in a written proposal, and did not originate in the commercial art scene.

concerto (kun-CHAIR-toe) Musical composition for solo instrument and orchestra, usually in three contrasting movements in the pattern fast–slow–fast.

concrete A hard building material made of cement, sand, and gravel; popularized by the ancient Romans.

Confucianism Chinese philosophical perspective based on the teachings of Confucius that emphasized morality, tradition, and ethical behavior.

continuous narration In art, simultaneous depiction of events that occurred sequentially.

contrapposto (CONE-truh-POSE-toe) In sculpture and painting, an asymmetrical positioning of the human body in which the weight rests on one leg, elevating the hip and opposite shoulder.

corbel In architecture, a bracket of metal, wood, or stone.

corbeled dome Dome constructed of courses of stone laid horizontally.

Corinthian Ancient Greek order of architecture characterized by a **capital** ornamented with acanthus leaves.

cornice In architecture, a horizontal molding that forms the uppermost, projecting part of an **entablature.**

cosmology Philosophical study of the evolution of the universe.

counterpoint In music, weaving two or more independent melodies into one harmonic texture.

Counter-Reformation Sixteenth-century Roman Catholic response of reform to the Protestant **Reformation.**

couplet Unit of poetry consisting of two successive rhyming lines.

covenant In theology, an agreement or contract between God and humans.

Creole Pan-African societal group in Sierra Leone, in West Africa.

crepidoma; crepis The three visible steps of a **column's platform.**

cromlech (CROM-leck) A prehistoric monument of huge stones arranged in a circle.

cross vault (groin vault) See drawing in Starter Kit, page xxv.

crossing The intersection of the **nave** and the **transept** in a cross-shaped church.

cruciform Cross shaped.

crusades Military expeditions undertaken by European Christians in the eleventh through thirteenth centuries to recover the Holy Land from Muslims.

Cubism Early twentieth-century painting and sculpture style characterized by geometric depiction of objects, and faceted multiple views of one object; leading Cubists were Picasso and Braque.

cult A community that follows special religious practices.

culture A group's way of living, including its beliefs, art, and social organization, that is transmitted from one generation to the next.

cuneiform (KYOO-nee-ah-form) Ancient Mesopotamian system of writing that uses wedge-shaped characters.

cupola (KYOO-puh-luh) In architecture, a small dome.

Cynicism Ancient Greek philosophy that held virtue is the highest good and self-control is the way to achieve it.

Dada Artistic and literary movement during and just after World War I that rejected tradition and championed the irrational and absurd.

daguerreotype (duh-GARE-oh-type) Early photograph form, produced on silver or silver-coated copper plates. Named for Daguerre, the French painter who invented the method.

daimyo Lord, in Japan, of a fortress or castle.

decadents Label that ***fin-de-siècle*** writers used for themselves to describe their moral decadence, mannered style, and fascination with morbid or perverse subject matter.

deconstruction Twentieth-century philosophical approach, especially in linguistics, of breaking apart the whole, assuming that in all systems there are gaps or inconsistencies and those gaps reveal the most about the whole system.

Deism (DEE-izm) Belief system based on the premise of a God who created the universe and then left it to run by itself.

demes Local townships in ancient Attica in Greece.

Depression Often referred to as the Great Depression, a period of drastic international economic decline in the 1930s.

Der Blaue Reiter German for "The Blue Rider." A branch of early twentieth-century German **Expressionist** art characterized by abstract forms and pure colors.

deus ex machina In Greek and Roman drama, a god lowered by stage machinery to resolve a play's plot or extricate a protagonist from a difficult situation. In later literature, the ending of a work that includes an unexpected or improbable device or event to conclude it.

dharma Hindu concept of duty or moral responsibility.

Die Brücke German for "The Bridge." A branch of early-twentieth-century German **Expressionist** art characterized by abstract forms and pure colors.

Dionysian Of an ecstatic, orgiastic, or irrational nature—after the Greek god of wine and revelry, Dionysius—in contrast to a critical and rational emphasis. See **Apollonian.**

diptych Painting or relief consisting of two panels that are hinged together and may be closed like a book.

dissonance In music, a chord or interval that sounds unfinished and seems to need resolution in a harmonious chord.

dome A hemispherical **vault.**

Doric Ancient Greek order of architecture characterized by a **capital** consisting of a square block supported by a cushion shape.

dramatic irony Type of irony in which the audience is aware of things about which a character in a play or novel is unaware.

dromos Entryway to a **tholos.**

drum In architecture, a circular wall, usually topped by a **dome,** or one of the several cylindrical stones used to construct a column.

dualism (or dualistic religion) Religious system that divides the universe into two opposing forces, good and evil (e.g., Zoroastrianism).

Duco Brand name for pyroxylin, a lacquer first developed for automobiles and commonly used as a painting medium in Mexican murals.

duplum Higher pitched of two voice parts in medieval **organum.**

earthenware Pottery made of porous clay fired at a relatively low temperature.

earthwork Large-scale artwork created by altering the land or a natural geographic area.

echinus (ee-KYE-nuhs) The cushion-shaped stone below the abacus of a **Doric capital.**

egg tempera Paint consisting of ground pigment and egg yolk.

ego Latin word for "I," designating the self as distinct from the world and others. In **psychoanalysis,** the conscious aspect of the self that relates to external reality.

emir Prince, chieftain, king, or other governing leader.

enamel Artistic technique of fusing powdered colored glass to a metal surface in a decorative pattern, or the object created by this method.

engaged column **Column** attached to a wall.

engraving Type of print made by cutting an image onto metal and inking the recesses of the image.

Enlightenment Eighteenth-century European intellectual movement that emphasized the mind's power to reason, challenged the traditional, and favored social reform.

entablature In architecture, the horizontal structure above the columns and **capitals** and below the roof.

entasis Slight bulge in the middle of a column.

epic Extended narrative poem written in a dignified style about a heroic character or characters.

Epicureanism Greek philosophy founded by Epicurus that held that pleasure, or the avoidance of pain, was the ultimate good.

epistle Book of the New Testament originally written as a letter.

ere ibeji Yoruban carvings of twins, who are believed to be gifts of the gods.

essay French for "attempt." A short literary composition, usually expressing the author's personal views.

etching Type of print made by incising an image on a waxed metal plate, corroding the exposed metal in an acid bath, removing the wax, then inking the recessed design.

etiological stories Religious myths that account for the origins of things.

étude (AY-tood) Solo musical study focusing on a particular technique.

evangelists From the Greek term for "bearer of good news." The name given to Matthew, Mark, Luke, and John, who wrote the gospel books of the New Testament; generally, one who preaches or attempts to spread the gospel.

existentialism Twentieth-century philosophy that emphasizes the uniqueness and isolation of individual experience in an indifferent world and stresses freedom of choice and responsibility for one's actions.

Expressionism Modern artistic and literary movement characterized by emotional expression, often with agitated strokes, intense colors, and themes of sexuality. See also ***Die Brücke; Der Blaue Reiter.***

facade Front face of a building.

faience High-quality glazed ceramics.

fan vaulting A decorative style of **vaulting** with **ribs** radiating like those of a fan.

fang ding Square bronze vessel with four legs, used for storing ceremonial offerings during the Chinese Shang dynasty.

feng shui The Chinese art of harmonizing people with their environment.

fête galante In Rococo painting, a depiction of an elegant outdoor party, featuring amorous conversations, graceful fashion, and social gallantry.

feudalism A medieval European political and economic system based on the holding of land and the rights and obligations of lords and vassals, respectively.

ficciones Term coined by Borges for his short puzzling fictional works that invite philosophical reflection.

fin de siècle (fan duh SYEH-cle) French for "end of the century." Describes the last years of the nineteenth century, generally noted for inventiveness, social unrest, and artistic activity.

finial Decorative part at the top of a spire, gable, lamp, or piece of furniture.

Flamboyant Late stage of Gothic architectural style of the fifteenth and sixteenth centuries, characterized by wavy, flame-like tracery and elaborate decoration.

flâneur (flah-NERR) Type of a person in ***belle époque*** Paris noted for his or her lifestyle of leisure, fine manners, elegant attire, idle strolling, and light conversation.

fluting Vertical grooves on the surface of a column.

flying buttress Characteristic of **Gothic** architecture, an arch-shaped buttress.

folio Manuscript page.

foreshortening In painting and relief sculpture, to reduce a form that is not parallel to the picture plane, thereby creating an illusion of three dimensionality.

Franciscans Members of a Christian order of monks founded by St. Francis of Assisi in 1209; noted for their emphasis on poverty and humility.

free verse Poetry that uses the natural rhythm of words and phrases instead of a consistent pattern of meter and rhyme.

fresco Painting technique in which ground pigment mixed with water is applied to wet lime plaster.

fret Ridge on the fingerboard of a stringed instrument.

friar Male member of certain Christian monastic orders.

frieze A band of ornamental carving or painting, especially the middle section of an **entablature,** between the **architrave** and **cornice.**

fugue (FYOOG) Musical composition of three or four highly independent parts in which one voice states a theme that is then imitated in succession by each of the other voices in **counterpoint.**

Functionalism Architectural theory that a building's design should be adapted to its function.

Futurism Early twentieth-century artistic movement that rejected conventional art and sought to show the fast-paced, dynamic nature of modern life and the machine age, often by portraying various views of a moving object.

gable In architecture, the triangular section at the end of a pitched roof, between the two sloping sides.

gallery In architecture, a long narrow passageway, especially found above the side aisles of a church, overlooking the **nave.**

gargoyle Gutter, carved usually in the form of a fantastic creature, the mouth serving as a waterspout. Found especially on **Gothic** churches and cathedrals.

garth The garden in a **cloister.**

geisha Professional Japanese female entertainers.

gelede Traditional Yoruban masked ritual, performed to appease "the mothers," women thought to possess special powers.

genre (JON-ruh) Category of art, music, or literature, such as portrait bust, symphony, and novel.

genre painting Scene in which the subject is taken from everyday life.

geoglyph Huge earthen design, such as the Nazca lines.

Geometric period (or Geometric style) The Greek cultural and artistic style of about 1000–700 B.C.E., noted for abstract geometric designs, especially on pottery.

glaze Thin, transparent layer of oil paint, usually applied on top of another layer or over a painted surface to achieve a glowing or glossy look. In ceramics, a glasslike surface coating.

glissando (plural, glissandi) (gli-SAHN-doe) In music, a rapid slide of a succession of adjacent tones.

Gnosticism (NOHS-tih-sizm) Dualistic doctrine of certain pagan, Jewish, and early Christian sects that redemption is achieved through an occult knowledge of God, revealed to their believers alone.

Golden Section A mathematical formula, developed in ancient Greece, for ideal proportions in fine art. The smaller of two dimensions is the same proportion to the larger as the larger is to the whole work, a ratio of about five to eight.

gospels First four books of the New Testament (Matthew, Mark, Luke, John), which describe the life and teachings of Jesus.

Gothic Style of architecture and art of the twelfth through sixteenth centuries in Western Europe and revived during the Romantic era. Characterized, especially in churches, by ribbed **vaults,** pointed **arches, flying buttresses, stained glass,** and high steep roofs.

grand opera Nineteenth-century form of **opera** that appealed to the audience because of its spectacle.

Greek cross In architecture, a floor plan of four arms of equal length. Compare to **Latin cross.**

Gregorian chant **Monophonic** liturgical chant, usually sung with no accompaniment; named after St. Gregory, who was pope from 590 to 604. Also called plainchant; plainsong.

ground bass In music, a phrase in the bass that is repeated continually throughout the composition or musical section.

guild Association of people in the same craft or trade, formed during the Middle Ages or Renaissance to give economic and political power to its members and to control the trade's standards.

hadith Islamic document containing the sayings of Muhammad and anecdotes about him.

haiku (HIGH-koo) Japanese poetry form in three lines, with seventeen syllables in the pattern five, seven, and five syllables per line; usually features imagery from nature, includes a reference to a season, and avoids rhyme.

half step In music, the distance between two adjacent keys on a piano or between two adjacent frets on a guitar.

Happening An art form of the 1960s that incorporated theater, performance, visual arts, and audience involvement.

Harlem Renaissance Mid-twentieth-century literary and artistic movement centered in the African-American community of New York City's Harlem neighborhood.

harmony In music, playing or singing two or more tones at the same time, especially when the resulting sound is pleasing to the ear; generally, the arrangement of chords.

hayashi Instruments as a group used to accompany Japanese Noh drama.

Hellenic Relating to the culture of **Classical** Greece (480–323 B.C.E.).

Hellenistic Relating to the post-**Classical** period in Greek history (after 323 B.C.E.), during which basic tenets of Classical Greek culture and thought spread throughout the Mediterranean, Middle East, and Asia.

henge A prehistoric circle of stones or posts.

hieroglyphics Writing system, such as that of the ancient Egyptians, that uses pictorial characters to convey sounds or meanings.

highlife Style of contemporary African music featuring a fusion of indigenous dance rhythms and melodies with Western marches, sea chanties, and church hymns.

Hijrah (or Hegira) (hi-JYE-ruh) Muhammad's flight from Mecca to Medina in 622 C.E. that marks the beginning of the Muslim era.

himation Rectangular piece of fabric draped over one shoulder as a garment in ancient Greece.

Hinduism Ancient religion of India characterized by a belief in reincarnation, the search for union with the divine, and liberation from earthly evils.

homophony; homophonic In music, the playing or singing of a single melodic line with harmonic accompaniment.

hôtel French for "townhouse."

huaca (WAH-cah) Pyramid made of sun-dried bricks, around which the Moche lived in Peru.

humanism Belief system, especially during the Renaissance, that stressed the worth, dignity, and accomplishments of the individual. Stemmed from renewed interest in **Classical** values of ancient Greece and Rome.

icon Religious image, such as a figure from the Bible, used as a sacred reminder of important elements of Christianity.

iconoclasm; iconoclastic controversy (eye-KON-o-KLAZ-em) Opposition to the use of religious images; the systematic destruction of religious **icons.**

iconography In visual arts, the use of symbols to communicate meaning.

iconophile A lover of artistic images, at odds with iconoclasts in the **iconoclastic controversy** of the Byzantine era.

iconostasis Panel of **icons** that typically separates the priests from the rest of the congregation in the Eastern Orthodox Church.

id Latin for "thing"; in Freudian theory the unconscious part of the psyche and the source of instinctual impulses, including sexual desires.

idée fixe (ee-day FEEKS) French for "fixed idea." In music, a recurring musical theme or idea used throughout a movement or entire composition, as in Berlioz's *Symphonie Fantastique.*

ideogram Symbol that represents an idea, not just a word or its pronunciation.

illuminated manuscript A manuscript illustrated with richly colored, gilded paintings, and ornamental lettering and borders.

illusionism Appearance of reality in art; specifically, the technique used to make a created work look like a continuation of the surrounding architecture.

imago Roman death mask.

impasto (im-POSS-toe) Paint applied thickly so an actual texture is created on the painted surface.

impost block In architecture, a block placed between the **capital** and the **arch,** used to channel the weight of the arch down onto the column.

Impressionism Late nineteenth-century artistic style that sought to portray a fleeting view of the world, usually by applying paint in short strokes of pure color. In music, a style that suggested moods and places through lush and shifting harmonies and vague rhythms.

incarnation Generally, the act of assuming a human body, especially by a god or spirit. In Christian theology, the doctrine of the birth of God in human form as Jesus Christ.

Industrial Revolution Rapid emergence of modern industrial production during the late eighteenth and early nineteenth centuries.

International style Twentieth-century architectural style focusing primarily on modern materials, especially steel and concrete, and boxlike shapes.

Intertropical Convergence Zone Climatic border zone where the cool wet air of the south Atlantic meets the warm dry air of the Sahara desert.

Ionic Ancient Greek order of architecture characterized by a capital in the shape of a curling volute scroll.

irony Language that states something different from or opposite to what is intended; **dramatic irony** puts characters in a position of ignorance about such an incongruity while keeping the audience aware of the situation.

Isis Egyptian goddess of fertility, whose cultlike worship gradually extended throughout the Roman empire.

Jainism Ascetic religion founded in sixth century B.C.E. India that affirms the immortality and the transmigration of the soul and denies the existence of a perfect or supreme being.

jamb The sides of a doorway or window.

jazz Category of music, first developed by African Americans in the early twentieth century, that usually features **syncopated** rhythms and improvisation of the melody or a phrase.

Jesuits Members of the Society of Jesus, an order of Roman Catholic priests established by St. Ignatius of Loyola in 1540.

ji Chorus for Japanese Noh drama.

ka Ancient Egyptian concept of the human soul or spirit, believed to live on after death.

kabuki (kuh-BOO-key) Japanese musical theater developed in the seventeenth century, noted for its melodramatic dancing, lively drama, and instrumental accompaniment. Traditionally performed by an all-male cast.

Kamares ware Type of Minoan ceramics characterized by curving motifs, often aquatic, painted in white and orange on a dark ground.

kami Local deities in the Japanese **Shinto** system of belief.

kana Japanese writing system.

karma **Hindu** and **Buddhist** doctrine that one's moral actions have a future consequence in determining personal destiny.

kiva (KEE-vah) Large underground ceremonial room in a Pueblo village.

koan Riddle in the form of a paradox used in **Zen** as an aid to meditation and intuitive understanding.

Kojiki Japanese ancient historical records.

Koran See **Quran.**

kore Ancient Greek statue of a standing clothed woman.

koto A Japanese stringed instrument similar to a zither.

kouros Ancient Greek statue of a standing nude man.

krater Ancient Greek vase with a large opening and two handles.

Krishna Hindu god, an **avatar** of **Vishnu,** often depicted as a handsome young man playing the flute.

lais French medieval narrative poems.

Lakshmi In **Hinduism,** a female goddess, consort of **Vishnu.**

lancet Window with a narrow **arch** shape, used frequently in **Gothic** architecture.

landscape Painting, photograph, or other visual art form that uses a natural outdoor scene as its main subject.

lantern In architecture, an open or windowed structure placed on top of a roof to allow light to enter below.

Latin cross In architecture, a floor plan with three short arms and one long one. Compare to **Greek cross.**

Lebensraum Additional territory deemed necessary to a nation, especially Nazi Germany, for its continued existence or economic well-being.

Leitmotif (LIGHT-moe-teef) German for "leading motive." In Wagnerian opera, brief fragments of melody or rhythm that trigger the audience to think of particular characters, actions, or objects.

lekythos Ancient Greek vase, small, cylindrical in shape, with a single handle.

Les Fauves; **Fauvism** (FOVE; FOVE-izm) French for "wild beasts." Early twentieth-century artistic movement characterized by violent, arbitrary colors as seen in the paintings of Matisse.

libretto Words for an opera or other textual vocal work.

Lied; Lieder (LEED; LEED-er) Romantic German **art song** designed for a vocalist and accompanist performing in a room of a home.

linear perspective See **perspective.**

lintel In architecture, a horizontal beam, as above a doorway.

literati Literary intelligentsia or leading literary figures of a country.

lithograph Type of print made when an image, drawn with a greasy substance on a stone block, is first wetted, then inked. Because the greasy areas repel water, only the image accepts the ink.

liturgy Religious rite used in public organized worship.

loggia (LOH-juh) In architecture, a covered open-air gallery.

logic Study of reasoning, or a particular system of reasoning.

lost-wax process (also known as the "cire-perdu" process) A method of metal casting in which a wax mold is coated with plaster or clay, then heated so the wax melts and runs out of vents. Molten metal is then poured into the hollow space and, when cooled, the clay or plaster mold is broken, leaving a metal core.

lozenge Ornamental diamond-shaped motif.

Lutheranism Theological belief system and denomination founded by Martin Luther (1483–1546) that holds that salvation is delivered by faith, not by personal achievement.

lyre A stringed instrument of the harp family used to accompany a singer or chanter of ancient poetry, common among the Egyptians, Assyrians, and Greeks.

lyric poetry Poems that have a songlike quality; usually emotional in nature.

madrigal **Polyphonic** music composed for a small group of singers, usually based on short **secular lyric** poems and sung with no accompaniment.

magic realism Latin American literary style that weaves together realistic events with incredible and fantastic ones to convey the often mysterious truths of life.

mandorla In religious art, an almond-shaped glory of light surrounding a sacred figure, such as Jesus.

Manicheism (MAN-i-key-izm) The religious philosophy, founded by the Persian prophet Manes in the third century C.E. and synthesized from elements of Christianity, Gnosticism, and Zoroastrianism, that divided the world between good and evil forces.

Mannerism Artistic style of the sixteenth century that rejected Renaissance aesthetic principles; noted for its obscure subject matter, unbalanced compositions, distorted bodies and poses, strange facial expressions, confusing spatial constructions, and harsh colors.

manuscript Handwritten book or document.

Manyoshu Eighth-century collection of Japanese poems.

mass Central religious ritual, principally in the Roman Catholic Church; a musical setting of this ritual.

mastaba Type of ancient Egyptian tomb, rectangular in shape with sloping walls and flat roof.

mausoleum Monumental tomb, or the building used to store one or more such tombs.

maya In **Hinduism,** the transitory, manifold appearance of the sensory world that obscures the true spiritual reality.

mazurka Lively Polish dance in triple meter.

meander Ornamental maze pattern common in Greek art.

megalith Huge stone, especially used as part of a prehistoric monument.

menhir (MEN-hear) Prehistoric monument of a single huge slab of stone, set in an upright position.

Mesoamerica Region extending south and east from central Mexico to include parts of Guatemala, Belize, Honduras, and Nicaragua. In pre-Columbian times, home to the Mayan and Olmec civilizations.

metope Part of the **entablature** of the Doric order. Metopes, squarish in shape and painted or carved, alternate with **triglyphs.**

mihrab (ME-rahb) Prayer niche in the interior wall of a mosque indicating the direction of Mecca.

millefleurs (meel-FLUHR) French for "thousand flowers." A background pattern consisting of many flowers and plants, particularly in **tapestry** designs.

minaret (min-uh-RET) In Islamic architecture, a tall slender tower attached to a **mosque,** from which a **muezzin** calls the faithful to prayer.

miniature Detailed small-scale painting, often on an **illuminated manuscript.**

Minimal art (or Minimalism) Twentieth-century artistic style featuring a small number of shapes arranged in a simple, often repeated, pattern.

minstrel Traveling entertainer of the Middle Ages, especially one who performed secular music.

minuet Slow, elegant dance in triple meter.

minuet and trio form Organizing structure for a musical work in the pattern minuet-trio-minuet. Usually the form of the third movement of a **symphony.** See also **minuet; trio.**

Mithras Persian god of light and wisdom, whose cultlike worship spread throughout the Roman empire, eventually rivaling Christianity.

mobile Sculptural form suspended from the ceiling, mechanized or moved by air currents; invented by Calder in the 1930s.

mock epic Extended narrative poem that treats a trivial incident in a heroic manner. See also **epic.**

mode Organization of musical intervals into **scales,** used in ancient and medieval music; later limited to just the major and minor scales.

model In painting, to create the illusion of depth by using light and shadow. In sculpture, to shape a pliable substance into a three-dimensional object.

Modernism; the modern Artistic and literary movement of the late nineteenth and twentieth centuries that sought to find new methods of artistic expression for the modern, dynamic world, and rejected the traditions of the past.

monastery Residence for monks.

monasticism Life of organized religious seclusion, as in a **monastery** or convent.

monolith Single slab of stone.

monophony Musical texture with a single melody and no accompaniment. Compare **polyphony.**

monotheism Belief in and worship of a single god.

montage In film, a set of abruptly edited images used for dramatic effect.

mosaic Image created by inlaying small pieces of colored glass, stone, or tile in mortar; mosaics are usually placed on floors, walls, or ceilings.

mosque Islamic house of worship.

motet In Renaissance music, a multi-voiced composition, usually based on a sacred Latin text and sung ***a cappella.***

moundbuilders Early Native American cultures in the Mississippi or Ohio river valley noted for their construction of monumental burial mounds.

mudra (moo-DRAH) Symbolic, stylized position of the body or hand in Indian art.

muezzin (myoo-EZ-in) Crier who calls the Muslim faithful to prayer five times a day.

mural A large wall painting.

music drama Musical term first used by Wagner to describe his **operas** that combined song, instrumental music, dance, drama, and poetry with no interruptions and without breaking the opera up into conventional arias or recitatives.

mystery play Medieval drama form based on biblical narratives.

myth A traditional story, usually featuring heroes, gods, or ancestors, that explains important cultural practices or beliefs.

mythology A system or collection of myths belonging to a people and expressing their origin, history, deities, ancestors, and beliefs.

Nahuatl Ancient language of the Aztecs. Also, a member of the various ancient Indian peoples of central Mexico, including the Aztecs.

narthex Entrance hall or vestibule of a church.

natural law Set of rights derived from nature and therefore superior to those established in the civil code.

natural selection The idea that nature chooses or selects organisms with natural characteristics best able to survive. Natural selection is the mechanism at the basis of Charles Darwin's theory of evolution.

naturalism Late nineteenth-century literary movement that strove to depict characters in naturalistic, objective detail, focusing on the authenticity of characters, setting, and situations; emphasized biological and cultural determinants for the behavior and fate of literary characters.

nave Long central space of a church, flanked on both sides by narrower aisles.

Nazi Member of Hitler's German National Socialist Party.

Neoclassicism Late-eighteenth-century artistic style that revived an interest in the ancient **Classical** ideals. Developed as a reaction to the more ornate Rococo style.

Neolithic The New Stone Age, about 8000 B.C.E. to 2000 B.C.E., a period characterized by the use of pottery, agriculture, development of early writing, and construction of **megalithic** structures.

Neoplatonism Revival of the philosophy of Plato, developed by Plotinus in the third century C.E. and prevalent during the Renaissance; based on the belief that the psyche is trapped within the body and philosophical thought is the only way to ascend from the material world to union with the single, higher source of existence.

neume Basic musical notation symbol used in **Gregorian chants.**

niche In architecture, a recess in a wall, often used to hold a statue or vase.

Nihongi Chronicles of Japan that continue the Kojiki.

nirvana In **Buddhism, Hinduism,** and **Jainism,** the state of ultimate bliss.

nocturne Musical composition for the night, usually melancholy in tone and for solo piano.

Noh (NO) Japanese musical theater developed in the fifteenth century, noted for its solemnity, highly poetic texts, stylized gestures, and masked actors.

nokan Japanese flute used in Noh theater.

notation In music, a symbolic method of representing tones.

novel Literary form based on social and psychological descriptions of the world and individual people, including a plot unfolded by the actions and thoughts of fictional characters. Although the novel became a dominant kind of literature in eighteenth-century England, its antecedents include *Don Quixote,* in seventeenth-century Spain, and *The Tale of Genji,* at the beginning of the second millennium, in Japan.

novella (plural, novelle) Short story, usually satirical and with a moral.

obelisk In architecture, a four-sided shaft topped by a pyramid.

octave Eight-line section of a poem, particularly the first section in a **Petrarchan sonnet;** in music, an eight-note interval.

oculus Circular window.

odalisque Harem woman.

ode Lyric poem, usually addressed to a person or object and written in a dignified style.

Oedipus complex In psychoanalysis, a subconscious sexual desire in a male child for the female parent and a sense of hostility toward the male parent.

Ogun One of the African orisa, or lesser gods who interact with humans; the god of iron.

oil paint Paint consisting of ground pigment and oil (usually linseed oil).

oinochoe A Greek wine jug with a pinched lip and curved handle.

oligarchy Form of government in which a few people rule.

olpe A Greek vase or jug with a broad lip.

Oludumare Major African god of the Yoruba, who created the world and humanity.

opera Italian for "a work." Musical form, first introduced in the **Baroque** era, that combines drama, a text set to vocal music, and orchestral accompaniment.

oracle A religious professional and prophet who interpreted the will of the gods.

orans In early Christian art, the pose of a person in prayer, with hands raised to heaven.

Oratorians Group of lay Catholics, founded in 1575 by St. Philip Neri, who met for spiritual conversation, study, and prayer.

oratories Places for prayer, such as private chapels, and associated with the Oratorians, a religious movement of priests and lay persons, founded by St. Philip Neri during the Counter-Reformation in the sixteenth century.

oratorio Sacred opera performed without costume or acting, featuring solo singers, a chorus, and an orchestra.

oratory Prayer hall.

order In architecture, a style determined by the type of column used. See also **Doric; Ionic; Corinthian.**

organum (ORE-guh-num) Early **polyphonic** music with the voices a fourth, a fifth, or an **octave** apart. The **organum duplum** is such a chant with two voices, with the lower voice holding long notes and the higher voice moving more quickly. Such a chant with three voices is an **organum triplum;** such a chant with four voices is an **organum quadruplum.**

Orientalizing period The Greek cultural and artistic style of about 700–600 B.C.E. that was influenced greatly by the Near East.

orthogonal In visual arts, a receding line perpendicular to the picture plane. In linear perspective, orthogonals converge and disappear at a **vanishing point.**

o-tsuzumi Type of hourglass drum held on the hip and used in Japanese Noh theater.

pagoda **Buddhist** temple in the shape of a tower, with many stories that each have an upward-curving roof.

Palace Style Type of Minoan ceramics characterized by plant forms painted on a pale beige background.

palaestra (plural, palaestrae) Public place in ancient Greece where young men learned to wrestle and box under the guidance of a master.

Paleolithic The Old Stone Age, about 2,000,000–10,000 B.C.E., a period characterized by hunting, fishing, the use of stone tools, the increasing dominance of *homo sapiens*, and the creation of the earliest works of art.

palette Artist's choice of colors for a particular work of art, or the surface on which such colors are placed and mixed.

pallium Ancient Roman garment made of a rectangular piece of fabric.

palmette Stylized palm leaf ornament.

Pancatantra Collection of **Sanskrit** animal fables that convey the religious principles of **Hinduism.**

pantheism Doctrine that identifies deity with the phenomena of the universe, including both animate beings and inanimate objects.

pantheon All the gods of a people, or a temple dedicated to all the gods; the Pantheon is the specific circular temple in Rome dedicated to all gods.

parables Brief stories that reveal a religious teaching, like the parables of Jesus and those of Asian traditions, including **Confucianism** and **Zen Buddhism.**

parchment Animal skin used to make manuscripts.

patrician Member of the noble family class in ancient Rome who was originally granted special civil and religious rights.

patron Person who sponsors art or artists financially.

patronage Originally, a system of **patrician** support and protection of a **plebeian** in ancient Rome; later, a system of financially sponsoring art or artists.

pediment In **Classical** architecture, a triangular space at the end of a building, formed by the **cornice** and the ends of the sloping roof.

pendentive In architecture, triangular shape used to make the transition from a square base to a circular dome.

peplos Loose outer garment worn by women in ancient Greece, hanging from the shoulders and belted at the waist.

percussion instrument Musical instrument, such as a timpani or bass drum, played by hitting or shaking.

peripteral In architecture, the adjective describing a building that is surrounded by a **peristyle.**

peristyle In architecture, a continuous row of columns, forming an enclosure around a building or courtyard.

perspective A method of creating the illusion of three-dimensional space on a two-dimensional surface. Achieved by methods such as *atmospheric perspective*, using slight variations in color and sharpness of the subject, or *linear perspective*, creating a horizon line and **orthogonals,** which meet at **vanishing points.**

Petrarchan sonnet Italian sonnet poem of an octave of eight lines, which introduces a situation or problem scene, and sestet of six lines, which expands on the scene or resolves the problem. The octave rhymes *abba abba* (or *abab abab*), and the sestet rhymes *cde cde* (or *cde ced; cde dce;* or *cd cd cd*). Devised by the poet Petrarch in the fourteenth century. See also **Shakespearean sonnet.**

phenomena (fuh-NOM-uh-nuh) In Kantian philosophy, elements as they are perceived by worldly senses, not as they really are.

philosophes (fill-uh-SOFF) Group of intellectuals of the **Enlightenment** who believed that, through reason, humans could achieve a perfect society.

pianoforte (pee-ANN-oh-FOR-tay) Literally, "soft loud" in Italian. Name originally used for the piano because of its ability to differentiate between soft and loud tones, which the harpsichord could not do.

piazza (pee-AHT-zuh) A public square in Italy.

picaresque In literature, a narrative form that originated in Spain and details the adventurous life of a *pícaro*, a rogue hero.

pictograph Picture used to represent a word or idea.

pier In architecture, a vertical support structure similar to a column, but usually square or rectangular in shape, rather than cylindrical.

pietà (pee-ay-TAH) Italian for "pity." In visual arts, a work that shows Mary mourning over her dead son Jesus in her lap.

pilaster In architecture, a flat decorative pillar attached to a wall, projecting just slightly, that may reinforce the wall.

pillar Freestanding vertical element, usually used as an architectural support.

pipa A Chinese lute.

plainchant; plainsong In music, the **monophonic,** unmetered vocal music of the early Christian church, as in **Gregorian chant.**

platform A raised horizontal surface, especially one on which **columns** sit.

Platonism Philosophy of Plato, focusing on the notion that Ideal Forms are an absolute and eternal model that all worldly phenomena strive toward.

plebeian Member of the common lower class in ancient Rome who at first lacked many of the rights **patricians** enjoyed.

plinth Slab that supports a sculpture or column.

podium In architecture, an elevated platform; often the foundation of a building, especially an ancient temple.

Pointillism Post-Impressionist technique developed by Seurat that uses an almost exact application of paint in small dots or points, intended to blend in the viewer's eyes.

polis (plural, poleis) An independent city-state in ancient Greece.

polonaise Stately, proud Polish dance in triple meter.

polyphony Simultaneous playing or singing of several independent musical lines. Compare **monophony.**

polyptych (POL-ip-tick) Painting or relief with four or more panels, often hinged so panels can be folded. See also **triptych.**

polyrhythms Multiple rhythms played or sung simultaneously within the same musical composition.

polytheism Belief in or worship of more than one god. Compare **monotheism.**

Pop Art Mid twentieth-century artistic style in which subjects were taken from everyday items from the mass media or were mass produced, such as comic strips, soup cans, or images of famous figures.

portal In architecture, an entrance or doorway.

portico In architecture, a porch or walkway covered by a roof supported by columns. Often marks an entrance to the main building.

post and lintel In architecture, vertical posts supporting a horizontal **lintel.**

potlatch Lavish ceremony among some Native Americans of northwest North America at which the host distributes gifts to guests according to their rank or status.

prelude (PRELL-yood) Short instrumental composition that usually precedes a larger musical work.

primary colors The colors red, yellow, and blue. See also **secondary colors.**

program music Instrumental composition that musically describes a scene, story, or other nonmusical situation. Popularized in the Romantic era. Compare **absolute music.**

pronaos Enclosed vestibule of a Greek or Roman temple, supported by **columns.**

propylon (plural, propylaia) Gateway to a temple or a group of buildings.

proscenium arch In theater, the framing device that separates the stage from the audience.

pseudo-peripteral Having a single row of **engaged columns** on all sides.

psychoanalysis Method of therapy originated by Sigmund Freud in which free association, dream interpretation, and analysis of resistance and transference are used to explore repressed or unconscious impulses, anxieties, and internal conflicts.

Punic Relating to ancient Carthage, its inhabitants, or their language or history.

pylon Massive gateway, especially to an Egyptian temple.

qasidah Highly formalized Arabic **ode** of 30 to 120 lines, each line ending with the same rhyme. It focuses on the poet's attempt to find his beloved.

qibla (KIB-luh) Direction facing Mecca, to which a Muslim turns when praying.

quadrivium Program of arithmetic, astronomy, geometry, and music in medieval universities.

quatrain Four-line unit of poetry.

Quran; Koran Sacred text of Islam.

radiating chapels Several chapels arranged around the **ambulatory** or **apse** of a church.

raga Indian musical composition, usually partly improvised, that attempts to convey a mood or feeling.

ragtime jazz piano composition in which the left hand plays a steady beat while the right hand improvises on a melody using a **syncopated** rhythm.

Ramadan Holy ninth month of the Islamic lunar calendar, during which Muslims must fast from sunrise to sunset.

rational humanism Philosophical belief system of the **Enlightenment** based on the idea that progress is possible only through learning and through the individual's freedom to learn.

Rayonnant (ray-on-NANT) From the French term for "to radiate." The High **Gothic** architectural style of the mid-thirteenth century, noted for its radiating **tracery** patterns and liberal use of **stained glass.**

Realism Nineteenth-century artistic and literary movement that attempted to convey to the public the realities of modern life, not just to depict the beautiful.

recitative (ress-uh-tuh-TEEV) In **opera,** a form of musically heightened speech halfway between spoken dialogue and melodic singing.

red-figure style Greek vase painting style featuring red figures surrounded by a black background, with details painted on the surface.

refectory Room in a monastery where meals are taken.

register system Method of organizing an artistic composition in horizontal bands or rows, each of which depicts a different event or idea.

regular temple Architectural plan for a temple in which the number of columns along the sides of the temple is double the number of columns on the ends plus one (e.g., an eight-by-seventeen proportion).

relic Venerated object associated with, or portion of the body of, a saint or martyr.

relief Sculpture attached to a solid background, rather than freestanding.

relieving triangle Triangular opening above a lintel, intended to relieve pressure on the **lintel.**

reliquary Decorative container for **relic.**

repoussé Metalworking technique in which the design is hammered in relief by working on the back of the metal plate.

representational Art that portrays the visual reality of an object.

requiem Mass for a deceased person and the music for such a mass.

responsorial Chant or anthem sung after a reading in a church service.

rhyton An ancient Greek drinking horn which may be shaped like an animal head.

rib In architecture, a curved, projecting **arch** used for support or decoration in a **vault.**

riff In **jazz,** a short phrase repeated frequently during improvisation.

ritornello (rit-or-NELL-low) Musical passage that will recur several times throughout a **concerto** movement.

romance Long medieval narrative form that related **chivalric** Celtic stories, especially the exploits of King Arthur and his Knights of the Round Table.

Romanesque The style of architecture and art of the eleventh and twelfth centuries in Western Europe. Characterized, especially in churches, by semicircular **arches,** barrel **vaults,** thick walls, and small windows.

rondo form Organizing structure for a musical work in which the main theme repeats itself frequently, with new, contrasting material added between each repetition. Often the form of the second or last movements of a **concerto.**

roof comb A crestlike extension along the roof of a Mayan temple that resembles the comb of a rooster.

rose window Circular "wheel" window, characteristic especially of **Gothic** architecture.

rosette A roselike ornament that is painted or sculpted.

rotunda Circular building, usually topped by a dome.

ruba'i (plural, ruba'iyat) Persian poetry form of four lines with a rhyming pattern of AABA.

sacramentary **Liturgical** book of prayers and rites of the sacraments of the Roman Catholic Church.

Salon des Refusés French for "Salon of the Rejected." Artistic **salon** established by Napoleon III in 1863 to exhibit paintings rejected by the official French Academy Salon.

salon; Salon Large reception room in a townhouse, or the social gathering held in such rooms; an annual exhibition of works of art, especially by the French Academy in the eighteenth and nineteenth centuries.

samba Brazilian dance.

samsara Hindu concept of the eternal cycle of birth and death.

samurai Ruler-warriors of Japan, especially during the feudal era.

Sanskrit Ancient Indic language; the classic language of ancient India, including Hinduism and the Vedas.

sarcophagus A stone coffin.

satire Literary or dramatic work that exposes vice or follies with ridicule or sarcasm, often in a humorous way.

satori Zen Buddhist state of enlightenment.

scale In music, an ascending or descending series of notes.

scat Method of vocal singing in nonsense syllables.

schism Break or split among factions, often religious and involving a formal breach in a church.

score Written or published version of a musical composition showing parts for all instruments and voices.

scroll In Chinese and Japanese art, a painting or text drawn on paper or silk. The scroll is conventionally kept rolled and tied except on special occasions. Some are vertical *hanging scrolls;* others are horizontal *hand scrolls.* Japanese narrative scrolls are called *emaki-mano.*

secondary colors The colors orange, green, and purple, formed when two primary colors (red, yellow, or blue) are mixed. See also **primary colors.**

secular Not sacred or religious.

serdab The cellar of an Egyptian **mastaba,** containing the **ka** statue.

sestet Six-line section of a poem, particularly the last section in a **Petrarchan sonnet.**

sestina Verse form developed by Renaissance troubadours that employs six-line stanzas and a three-line concluding envoy, with the six end words of the first **stanza** repeated throughout the other five stanzas and envoy.

sfumato (sfoo-MA-toe) The Italian word for "smoky." In painting, the intentional blurring of the outline of a figure in a hazy, almost smoky atmosphere.

shaft The vertical section of a **column** between the **capital** and the base.

Shakespearean sonnet; English sonnet Poem of three four-line stanzas and a final two-line couplet, usually rhyming *abab cdcd efef gg.* See also **Petrarchan sonnet.**

shastras Ancient Hindu texts that describe instructions for various activities, including temple building, cooking, warfare, and music.

Shi'ites Muslim sect that, along with the Sunnis, share basic theological convictions but differ strongly over the line of legitimate succession from Muhammad.

Shinto Principal and former state religion of Japan characterized by rituals and venerations for local deities and strong patriotism.

Shiva One of the principal Hindu deities, worshipped as destroyer and restorer of worlds, and often associated with two other central Hindu gods, Brahma and **Vishnu.** Shiva is often represented as a dancing figure, the Shiva Nataraja.

shogun Hereditary military dictator of Japan; originally, commander-in-chief of the **samurai.**

sitar Long-necked lute-shaped instrument from India.

skene (SKAY-nuh) In Greek theater, a building behind the acting area that functioned as a dressing room and as scenic background.

Skepticism Greek philosophical doctrine that absolute knowledge is not usually possible and inquiry must therefore be a process of doubt.

Socialist Realism Artistic style declared by Stalin in 1934 as the official Soviet style; it rejected **abstraction** and focused on images of soldiers, workers, and peasants.

soliloquy (suh-LILL-uh-kwee) In drama, a character's private reflections spoken aloud toward the audience, but not to the other characters.

sonata From the Italian verb "to sound." Musical composition for one or two instruments, usually in three or four movements. Compare **cantata.**

sonata form Organizing structure for a musical work with three main sections: exposition, development, and recapitulation, sometimes followed by a **coda.** Usually the form of the first and fourth movements of a **symphony.**

song cycle Popularized during the nineteenth century by German *Lied* composers, a group of songs based on a single theme or story.

sonnet Renaissance lyric poetic form invented by Petrarch in Italy and imitated by English Renaissance poets, including Shakespeare. A sonnet includes fourteen lines in iambic pentameter with one of two predominant structural and rhyming patterns: (1) the **Italian** or **Petrarchan sonnet** comprising an eight-line octave and six-line sestet, with a rhyme pattern of abba abba cde cde, or cd cd cd (or a variation on these); (2) the **English** or **Shakespearean sonnet**

comprising three quatrains and a concluding couplet—typically rhyming abab cdcd efef gg.

Sophists Ancient Greek philosophers and teachers, less interested in the pursuit of truth than in the use of clever rhetoric and argumentation.

soprano In music, the range of the highest voice of females or young boys.

staff In music, the five horizontal lines and four spaces used in **notation.**

stained glass Artistic technique in which many small pieces of glass are colored with internal pigment or surface paint and then held together with lead strips; used extensively in **Gothic** cathedrals.

statue in the round Sculpture that stands free of a background and is fully formed to be seen from all sides.

stele Slab of stone, set vertically.

stigmata Physical marks or scars on humans that resemble the crucifixion marks of Jesus; said to appear during states of religious ecstasy.

still life Painting or sculpture representing inanimate subjects such as flowers, fruit, or objects.

stoa In ancient Greek architecture, a long, freestanding **portico.**

Stoicism Greek and a Roman philosophy characterized by indifference to pleasure and pain and a willingness to accept what life brings with impassive equanimity.

stream of consciousness Modern literary technique that records the free flow of a character's mental impressions.

stupa Buddhist memorial monument in the shape of a mound.

Sufi Islamic mystic.

Sumo A style of Japanese wrestling in which the object is to push an opponent out of the ring or throw him down within it.

superman In the philosophy of Friedrich Nietzsche, the superior being, the over or super person who is exempt from legal and moral constraints that bind ordinary people.

Surah Chapter in the **Quran.**

Swahili People inhabiting the coast and islands of East Africa, and their language, which is widely used as a common language in that part of the continent.

swing jazz style of big bands of the 1930s and 1940s, usually fast and arranged instead of improvised.

syllogism Form of deductive reasoning consisting of a major premise, a minor premise, and a conclusion. For example, *All philosophers are mortal; Aristotle was a philosopher; Aristotle was mortal.*

Symbolists Poets of the late nineteenth century who used symbolic words and figures to express ideas, impressions, and emotions and rejected the realistic depiction of the external world.

symphony Large orchestral work, usually in four distinct movements.

syncopation Musical rhythm in which **beats** that are normally unaccented are stressed.

synoptic gospels The **gospels** of Matthew, Mark, and Luke, which are similar. The gospel of John is unique.

taiko Stick drum on a stand; used in Japanese Noh theater.

talking drum Type of African drum whose sound blurs the line between melody and rhythm.

tambura Unfretted lute used to sustain the drone chord in Indian music.

tango Popular Argentinian dance and the music affiliated with it.

tanka A short Japanese poem.

tapestry Heavy textile, the design created as the fabric is woven; a specialty of medieval and Renaissance northern Europe.

teleology In philosophy, the study of an end and how it relates to the natural processes leading up to it.

tempera (TEM-purr-uh) Paint made of egg yolk and pigment.

tenebrism Painting technique that dramatically contrasts light and dark and makes little use of middle tones.

tenor In music, the range of the highest male voice, which usually carries the melody; also, the bottom, slower line of an **organum duplum.**

Teotihuacán Major Aztec city of central Mexico, just north of present-day Mexico City.

terra cotta Italian for "baked earth." An orange-red baked clay used for pottery or sculpture.

terza rima (turr-tsah-REE-ma) Poetry form consisting of three-line stanzas in which each stanza's middle line rhymes with the first and third lines of the subsequent stanza (aba, bcb, cdc, etc.).

tessera (plural, tesserae) (TESS-ur-ah) Small cubes of stone or other material used in making a **mosaic.**

tetrarchy Area ruled by one of four rulers, or tetrarchs.

theme and variations form Organizing structure for a musical work in which a theme is presented and repeated several more times, each time in a slightly varied way. Often the form of the first and fourth movements of a **symphony.**

theocracy Political entity ruled by a religious figure or group claiming to have divine authority.

tholos Circular domed room built by **corbelled** construction.

thrust In architecture, outward or lateral pressure in a structure.

toga Ancient Roman garment.

tonal center Home key of a musical composition.

tonality In music, the arrangement of all tones of a composition in relation to the central key, or tonic.

Torah Hebrew for "instruction." The first five books of Hebrew scripture.

totem pole Post carved with animal and spirit images and erected by some Native Americans of northwest North America to memorialize the dead.

tracery Elaborate pattern of interlacing stone lines, especially in **Gothic** windows.

tragedy Serious literary or theatrical work about a central character's problems, with an unhappy ending.

Transcendentalism Romantic philosophical theory that an ideal reality transcends the material world, known only through intuition, especially in nature. See also **phenomena.**

transept In architecture, the portion of the church at a right angle to the **nave,** between the nave and the **choir,** or **apse.**

treasury Building, room, or box for storing valuables or offerings.

triclinium Dining room in an ancient Roman home, named for the three couches on which the diners reclined.

triforium In architecture, the elevated galleries above the aisles of a chuch or cathedral.

triglyphs Part of the **entablature** of **Doric** order. Triglyphs have three (tri) sections and alternate with **metopes.**

triptych Painting or relief consisting of three panels, with the side panels hinged so they can be folded over the center panel.

triumphal arch Grand freestanding gateway with a large **arch.**

trivium Program of grammar, logic, and rhetoric in medieval universities.

trompe-l'oeil (trump-LOY) French for "trick the eye." An artistic effect that creates an optical illusion of reality.

trope In music, a new word or phrase added to an existing chant as an embellishment.

troubadour (TRUE-buh-door) Poet-musician of medieval southern France.

trumeau In architecture, the vertical post supporting a **lintel** and between two doors.

tufa A porous whitish stone that is soft when cut but hardens after exposure to air.

Tuscan order Ancient Roman order, much like the Greek **Doric** order, with the addition of a base.

twelve-tone composition Musical composition style developed by Schoenberg that uses a twelve-note scale, which is the traditional octave plus all internal half steps; each tone is used equally and in a highly organized manner.

tympanum Semicircular area above a window or door.

ukiyo-e Japanese for "pictures of the floating world." Style of Japanese woodblock prints of the seventeenth and eighteenth centuries noted for their everyday subject matter.

unities In Greek drama, and in attenuated form in later Renaissance theater, the rules that a play's action should take place within a single day, at a single location, and focus on a single central plot.

vanishing point In linear perspective, a point on the horizon line at which the **orthogonals** appear to converge. See drawing in Starter Kit on p. xxvi.

vault Arched masonry roof or ceiling. A **barrel** (or tunnel) **vault,** is an uninterrupted semicircular vault made of a series of **arches.** A **cross** or **groin vault** is created by the intersection of two barrel vaults set at right angles. A *ribbed vault* is a form of groin vault in which the groins formed by the intersection of curved sides are reinforced by raised **ribs.** See drawing in Starter Kit on p. xxx.

Vedas The oldest sacred Hindu writings, composed 1500–1000 B.C.E. by the Aryans in present-day India.

vellum Thinnest, finest **parchment.**

veneer In architecture, a thin layer of high-quality material used as a surface, often covering inferior materials.

verisimilitude (ver-uh-si-MILL-uh-tude) Appearance of being true to reality.

vernacular Common language spoken in a particular country or region.

vibrato (vi-BRAHT-oh) In vocal or instrumental music, a pulsing effect achieved by slight, rapid variations in pitch.

Vishnu One of the central Hindu gods, worshipped as the protector and preserver of worlds.

volute Spiral scroll ornament, as on an **Ionic capital.**

voussoirs Wedge-shaped stones that makes up a true arch.

waltz Ballroom dance in triple meter.

warp Thick threads that run vertically on a loom and provide the structure for a piece of fabric woven of the **weft** threads.

weft Threads that run horizontally on a loom and usually form the visible pattern on a piece of woven fabric.

westwork Monumental western entryway in a Carolingian, Ottonian, or Romanesque church.

white-ground ceramics (or white-ground technique) Ancient Greek pottery ware in which a white matte slip is painted over the surface of a reddish clay vessel, with details painted on the surface with a fine brush.

whole tone; whole step In music, the **interval** between any two consecutive white keys on the piano, when a black key intervenes. A whole step is made up of two half steps.

woodcut Print made by carving a design into a wooden block, inking the raised surfaces, placing a piece of paper on the inked surface, and applying pressure to transfer the ink to the paper.

woodwind instrument Musical instrument, such as a flute or clarinet, played by blowing through a reed or mouthpiece attached to the main body of the instrument.

word painting In Renaissance music, a composition style that emphasizes the meaning of words through the accompanying music. For example, the word "weep" might be expressed by a descending melodic line.

yakshis In **Hinduism,** local nature spirits represented on temple gates in the form of shapely females.

yin and yang The Chinese **dualistic** philosophical image that represents simultaneous contrast and complement. The yin form represents the passive, negative, feminine, dark, and earthly; the yang form represents the light, masculine, positive, constructive, and heavenly. The two are in perpetual interplay.

zazen Meditation as practiced in Zen Buddhism.

Zen Buddhism Chinese and Japanese form of **Buddhism** that emphasizes enlightenment achieved by self-awareness and meditation instead of by adherence to a set religious doctrine.

ziggurat In ancient Near Eastern architecture, a monumental stepped base made of brick, to support a temple.

Credits and Further Information

Introduction
0.1 Edvard Munch (1853-1944), "The Scream", 1893. Tempera and Casin on paper. 36" x 29" (91 x 73 cm). Nasjonalgalleriet, Oslo. © 2003 The Munch Museum/The Munch-Ellingsen Group/Artists Rights Society (ARS), New York/ADAGP, Paris. J. Lathion/© Nasjonalgalleriet; 0.2 Janetta Rebold Benton, Prof of Fine Arts, Pace University; 0.3 Robert Harding World Imagery

Chapter One
1.1 AKG–Images; 1.2 © Archivo Iconografico, S.A./ CORBIS; 1.3 Douglas Mazonowicz; 1.4 Aerofilms; 1.4 Janetta Rebold Benton, Prof of Fine Arts, Pace University; 1.5 The Ancient Art & Architecture Collection Ltd.; 1.6 Fletcher Fund, 1940, (40.156). The Metropolitan Museum of Modern Art, New York, NY, U.S.A. Image copyright © The Metropolitan Museum of Art/Art Resource, NY.; 1.7 Herve Lewandowski/Musée du Louvre/Reunion Des Musées National/Art Resource, NY; 1.8 Herve Lewandowski/Musée du Louvre/Reunion Des Musées National/Art Resource, NY; 1.9 The Metropolitan Museum of Art, NY; 1.10 © The Trustees of the British Museum; 1.11 Reinhard Saczewski/Vorderasiatisches Museum/ Staatliche Museen zu Berlin, Preussischer Kulturbesitz, Vorderasiatiches Museum, Berlin/Art Resource, NY; 1.12 www.comstock.com; 1.13 Courtesy of the Oriental Institute of the University of Chicago; 1.14 Egyptian Museum, Cairo/Hirmer Fotoarchiv, Munich, Germany; 1.15 © The Trustees of the British Museum/Art Resource, NY; 1.16 Peter Wilson © Dorling Kindersley; 1.17 Geoff Brightling © Dorling Kindersley; 1.18 Alamy Images; 1.19 Harvard University–Boston Museum of Fine Arts Expedition, 11.1738 Courtesy, Museum of Fine Arts, Boston. Reproduced with permission. © 2008 Museum of Fine Arts, Boston. All Rights Reserved; 1.20 Alamy Images; 1.21 Egyptian Museum, Cairo/Hirmer Fotoarchiv, Munich, Germany; 1.22 National Geographic/ Richard Nowitz © Photolibrary; 1.23 Egyptian Tourist Authority; 1.24 © The Trustees of the British Museum/Art Resource, NY; 1.25 Robert Harding World Imagery; 1.26 © The Trustees of the British Museum/Art Resource, NY; 1.27 © The Trustees of the British Museum/Art Resource, NY; 1.28 Bildarchiv Preussischer Kulturbesitz, Berlin, Germany\ Art Resource/Bildarchiv Preussischer Kulturbesitz; 1.29 Agyptisches Museum, Staatliche Museen zu Berlin, Berlin, Germany\Art Resource/Bildarchiv Preussischer Kulturbesitz; 1.30 Superstock/Art Life Images; 1.31 Stephan Petegorsky/Smith College Museum of Art

Chapter Two
2.1 Gift of Christos G. Bastis, 1968 (68.148). The Metropolitan Museum of Art, New York, NY, U.S.A. Image copyright © The Metropolitan Museum of Art/Art Resource, NY.; 2.2 Museum of Prehistoric Thera; 2.3 The Ancient Art & Architecture Collection Ltd.; 2.4 Egyptian Tourist Authority; 2.5 Archaeological Museum of Herakleion, Crete, Greece; 2.6 Janetta Rebold Benton, Prof of Fine Arts, Pace University; 2.7 Dagli Orti/Picture Desk, Inc./Kobal Collection; 2.8 National Archeological Museum, Athens/Hirmer Fotoarchiv, Munich, Germany; 2.9 Studio Kontos Photostock; 2.10 The Metropolitan Museum of Art, Rogers Fund, 1914 (14.130.14). Photograph © 1996 The Metropolitan Museum of Art, NY; 2.11 Staatliche Museum, Berlin/Art Resource/Bildarchiv Preussischer Kulturbesitz; 2.12 © SCALA/Art Resource, NY. Museo Gregoriano Etrusco, Vatican Museums, Vatican State; 2.13 Purchase, Bequest of Joseph H. Durkee, Gift of Darius Ogden Mills and Gift of C. Ruston Love, by exchange, 1972. The Metropolitan Museum of Art New York. Art Resource, NY; 2.14 Fletcher Fund, 1932. The Metropolitan Museum of Art, NY; 2.15 Art Resource, N.Y.; 2.16 Alison Frantz Photographic Collection, American School of Classical Studies at Athens; 2.17 Art Resource, N.Y.

Chapter Three
3.1 Greek National Tourism Organization; 3.2 Janetta Rebold Benton/Robert DiYanni; 3.3 Bill Bachmann/ PhotoEdit, Inc.; 3.4 Hirmer Fotoarchiv, Munich, Germany; 3.5 Musée du Louvre, Paris. Herve Lewandowski/Reunion des Musees National/Art Resource, NY; 3.6 John Vernor-Miles, Executor for A.F. Kersting; 3.7 Rob Reichenfeld © ARF/TAP (Archaeological Receipts Fund); 3.8 Acropolis Museum/ Hirmer Fotoarchiv, Munich, Germany; 3.9 Museo Archelogico Nazionale, Naples, Italy. SCALA/Art Resource, NY; 3.10 Musei Vaticani, Rome/SCALA/Art Resource, NY; 3.11 Museo Nazionale Romano delle Terme, Rome, Italy. SCALA/Art Resource, NY; 3.12 Staatliche Antikensammlungen und Glyptothek, Munich, Germany; 3.13 ALINARI\Greek National Tourism Organization; 3.14 Museo Nacionale Romano, Rome/Hirmer Fotoarchiv, Munich, Germany; 3.15 Staatliche Antikensammlungen und Glyptothek, Munich, Germany; 3.16 Staatliche Kunstsammlungen Dresden; 3.17 Antikensammlung, Staatliche Museen zu Berlin, Germany\Art Resource/Bildarchiv Preussischer Kulturbesitz; 3.18 © The Trustees of the British Museum; 3.19 Musee du Louvre/Reunion des Musees National/Eric Lessing/Art Resource, NY; 3.20 Museo Pio Clementino/Vatican Museums, Vatican State. Scala/Art Resource, NY

Chapter Four
4.1 Tourist Organization of Greece; 4.2 SCALA/Art Resource, NY; 4.3 Robert Harding World Imagery; 4.4 Hirmer Fotoarchiv, Munich, Germany; 4.5 ALINARI/Art Resource, NY; 4.6 SCALA/Art Resource, NY; 4.7 © Gustavo Tomsich/CORBIS; 4.8 Jean-Christophe Godet\Rough Guides Dorling Kindersley; 4.9 Musei Capitolini, Rome, Italy. Photograph © SCALA/Art Resource NY; 4.10 Mike Dunning © Dorling Kindersley; 4.11 © SCALA/Art Resource, NY; 4.12 Samuel H. Kress Collection. Photograph © 2001 Board of Trustees, National Gallery of Art, Washington, DC. 1939.1.24.(135)/PA. Photo by Richard Carafelli; 4.13 Vatican Museums, Rome, Italy; 4.14 Janetta Rebold Benton; 4.15 ALINARI/Art Resource, NY; 4.16 Janetta Rebold Benton/Robert DiYanni; 4.17 ALINARI/Art Resource, NY; 4.18 Samuel D. Lee Fund. Metropolitan Museum of Art, New York. Art Resource, NY; 4.19 Janetta Rebold Benton, Prof. of Fine Arts, Pace University; 4.20 James McConnachie © Rough Guides; 4.21 Art Resource, N.Y.; 4.22 The Image Works; 4.23 SCALA\Art Resource, N.Y.; 4.24 © Scala/Art Resource, NY

Chapter Five
5.1 Canali PhotoBank; 5.2 Israel Ministry of Tourism, North America; 5.3 Janetta Rebold Benton/Robert DiYanni; 5.4 Janetta Rebold Benton/Robert DiYanni; 5.5 Janetta Rebold Benton/Robert DiYanni; 5.6 SCALA\Art Resource, N.Y.; 5.7 Janetta Rebold Benton, Prof of Fine Arts, Pace University; 5.8 ALINARI\Art Resource, N.Y.; 5.9 ALINARI\Art Resource, N.Y.; 5.10a Copyright Alinari/Art Resource, NY; 5.10b Art Resource, N.Y.; 5.11 SCALA\Art Resource, N.Y.; 5.12 Cameraphoto Arte, Venice /Art Resource, NY; 5.13 Bieber, Tim\Getty Images Inc. - Image Bank; 5.14 Janetta Rebold Benton/Robert DiYanni; 5.15 Walter. B. Denny; 5.16 Gavin Hellier\Nature Picture Library; 5.17 SuperStock, Inc.; 5.18 Picture Desk, Inc./Kobal Collection; 5.19 Andrew W. Mellon Collection Photograph © 2001 Board of Trustees, National Gallery of Art, Washington. 1937.1.1.(1)/PA

Chapter Six
6.1 Courtesy of Edinburgh University Library; 6.2 Janetta Rebold Benton/Robert DiYanni; 6.3 John Vernor-Miles, Executor for A.F. Kersting; 6.4 John Vernor-Miles, Executor for A.F. Kersting; 6.5 Janetta Rebold Benton, Prof of Fine Arts, Pace University; 6.6 Scala\Art Resource, N.Y.; 6.7 Janetta Rebold Benton, Prof of Fine Arts, Pace University; 6.8 Janetta Rebold Benton, Prof of Fine Arts, Pace University; 6.9 © The Trustees of the British Museum; 6.10 Courtesy of the Freer Gallery of Art, Smithsonian Institution, Washington, D.C.; 6.11 Francis Bartlett Donation and Picture Fund (14.692). Reproduced with permission. © 2005 Museum of Fine Arts, Boston. All Rights Reserved; 6.12 Bodleian Library, University of Oxford

Chapter Seven
7.1 The Nasli and Alice Heeramaneck Collection, Gift of Paul Mellon. Katherine Wetzel/Virginia Museum of Fine Arts, Richmond; 7.2 Archaeological Museum, Sarnath, India; 7.3 Dale Williams; 7.4 John Vernor-Miles, Executor for A.F. Kersting; 7.5 The Adolph D. and Wilkins C. Williams Fund. Katherine Wetzel/Virginia Museum of Fine Arts, Richmond; 7.6 National Museum, New Delhi; 7.7 Dinodia Picture Library Pvt Ltd; 7.8 Neil Grant\ Alamy Images; 7.9 Dinesh Khanna © Dorling Kindersley; 7.10 Von der Heydt Collection/Museum Rietberg, Zurich; 7.11 Getty Images Inc. - Hulton Archive Photos

Chapter Eight
8.1 © The Trustees of the British Museum; 8.2 © NRT-Travel/Alamy; 8.3 Janetta Rebold Benton/Robert DiYanni; 8.4 Janetta Rebold Benton, Prof of Fine Arts, Pace University; 8.5 Janetta Rebold Benton, Prof of Fine Arts, Pace University; 8.6 Werner Forman Archive Ltd; 8.7 Tokyo National Museum DNP Archives.Com Co., Ltd; 8.8 National Palace Museum, Taiwan, Republic of China; 8.9 National Palace Museum, Taiwan, Republic of China; 8.10 The Nelson-Atkins Museum of Art, Kansas City, Missouri. Purchase: William Rockhill Nelson Trust, 49-79; 8.11 The Art Archive\Picture Desk, Inc./Kobal Collection; 8.12 © Judith Miller/Dorling Kindersley/Cheffins; 8.13 National Palace Museum, Taiwan, Republic of China

Chapter Nine
9.1 © The Cleveland Museum of Art, John L. Severenance Fund, 1984.68; 9.2 Tokyo National Museum. TNM Image Archives. Source: http://TnmArchives.jp/; 9.3 Courtesy of JICC Japan Information & Cultural Center/Embassy of Japan, London; 9.4 JICC Japan Information & Cultural Center/Embassy of Japan, London.; 9.5 The Tokugawa Reimeikai Foundation; 9.6 Werner Forman\Art Resource, N.Y.; 9.7 The ArtArchive/Laurie Platt Winfrey\Picture Desk, Inc./Kobal Collection; 9.8 Tokyo National Museum, Tokyo. TNM Image Archives Source: http// TNMArchives.jp/; 9.9 Janetta Rebold Benton, Prof of Fine Arts, Pace University; 9.10 Janetta Rebold Benton, Prof of Fine Arts, Pace University; 9.11 Janetta Rebold Benton, Prof of Fine Arts, Pace University

Chapter Ten
10.1 Demetrio Carrasco © CONACULTA-INAH-MEX. Authorized reproduction by the Instituto Nacional de Antropologia e Historia.; 10.2 © Danny Lehman/ CORBIS All Rights Reserved; 10.3 George Gerster\Photo Researchers, Inc.; 10.4 Tim Draper\Rough Guides Dorling Kindersley; 10.5 South American Pictures; 10.6 © Merle Green Robertson, 1976\Howard Tilton Memorial Library; 10.7 Picture Desk, Inc./Kobal Collection; 10.8 Biblioteca Apostolica Vaticana; 10.9 George Gerster\Photo Researchers, Inc.; 10.10 Buckingham Fund, 1955.2281. Photograph © 2005, The Art Institute of Chicago. All Rights Reserved; 10.11 Linda Whitwam © Dorling Kindersley; 10.12 South American Pictures; 10.13 National Archives of Canada; 10.14 Robert Harding World Imagery; 10.15 Tony Linck\Ohio Dept. of Natural Resources; 10.16 Jack Jackson\Robert Harding World Imagery; 10.17 Kal Muller/Woodfin Camp & Associates; 10.18 Art Resource, N.Y.; 10.19 Image copyright © The Metropolitan Museum of Art/Art Resource, NY; 10.20 Werner Forman/Art Resource, NY

Chapter Eleven
11.1 © The Trustees of the British Museum/Art Resource, NY; 11.2 The Bridgeman Art Library International; 11.3 French Government Tourist Office; 11.4 Stiftsbibliothek St. Gallen; 11.5 Kunsthistorisches Museum, Vienna, Austria; 11.6 "The Bayeaux Tapestry - XIth Century" and "By special permissin of the City of Bayeux"; 11.7 Jean Dieuzaide; 11.8 Janetta Rebold Benton/Robert DiYanni; 11.9 AGE Fotostock America, Inc.; 11.10 SCALA\Art Resource, N.Y.; 11.11 David Jacobs\Robert Harding World Imagery; 11.12 SCALA\Art Resource, N.Y.; 11.13 © Achim Bednorz, Koln; 11.14 The Metropolitan Museum of Art, Gift of J. Pierpont Morgan, 1916. (1632.194) Photograph © 1999 The Metropolitan Museum of Art; 11.15 The Ancient Art & Architecture Collection Ltd.; 11.16 Courtesy of Foto Ritter, Vienna/ Klosterneuburg Abbey, Austria

Chapter Twelve
12.1 Janetta Rebold Benton/Robert DiYanni; 12.2 Hirmer Fotoarchiv, Munich, Germany; 12.3 © Scala/Art Resource, NY; 12.4 Spectrum Pictures; 12.5 Herve Champollion/ Caisse Nationale des Monuments Historique et des Sites, Paris, France; 12.6 Janetta Rebold Benton, Prof of Fine Arts, Pace University; 12.7 John Vernor-Miles, Executor for A.F. Kersting; 12.8 Sonia Halliday Photographs; 12.9 Art Resource, N.Y.; 12.10 John Vernor-Miles, Executor for A.F. Kersting; 12.11 AKG-Images; 12.12 © Guido Alberto Rossi/TIPS Images; 12.13 Janetta Rebold Benton, Prof of Fine Arts, Pace University; 12.14 Janetta Rebold Benton, Prof of Fine Arts, Pace University; 12.15 Janetta Rebold Benton, Prof of Fine Arts, Pace University; 12.16 Giraudon\Bibliotheque Nationale de France; 12.17 Janetta Rebold Benton, Prof of Fine Arts, Pace University; 12.18 Sonia Halliday Photographs; 12.19 Gift of John D. Rockefeller Jr, 1937. Cloisters Collection, Metropolitan Museum of Art, New York. Art Resource, NY; 12.20 SCALA\Art Resource, N.Y.; 12.21 SCALA\Art Resource, N.Y.; 12.22 SCALA\Art Resource, N.Y.; 12.23 SCALA\Art Resource, N.Y.; 12.24 SCALA\Art Resource, N.Y.; 12.25 SCALA\Art Resource, N.Y.; 12.26 SCALA\Art Resource, N.Y.; 12.27 By permission of The British Library

Chapter Thirteen
13.1 Galleria degli Uffizi, Florence. SCALA/Art Resource, NY; 13.2 Bodleian Library, University of Oxford; 13.3 Scala/Art Resource, N.Y.; 13.4 Janetta Rebold Benton, Prof of Fine Arts, Pace University; 13.5 Scala/Art Resource, N.Y.; 13.6 SCALA\Art Resource, N.Y.; 13.7 Museo Nazionale del Bargello, Florence. SCALA/Art Resource, NY; 13.8 Museo dell' Opera del Duomo, Florence. SCALA/Art Resource, NY; 13.9 Scala/Art Resource, N.Y.; 13.10 Galleria degli Uffizi, Florence. SCALA/ Art Resource, NY; 13.11 Galleria degli Uffizi, Florence. SCALA/Art Resource, NY; 13.12 Scala/Art Resource, N.Y.; 13.13 Galleria degli Uffizi, Florence. SCALA/Art Resource, NY; 13.14 Superstock; 13.15 Lewandowski/LeMage/Gattelet. ©Musee du Louvre/ Reunion des Musees National/Art Resource, NY; 13.16 Kunsthistorisches Museum, Vienna. Erich Lessing/Art Resource, NY; 13.17 Vatican Museums, Rome, Italy; 13.18 Scala/Art Resource, N.Y.; 13.19 Vatican Museums and Galleries, Vatican City, Italy/The Bridgeman Art Library International; 13.20 Vatican Museums, Rome, Italy; 13.21 Alinari\Art Resource, N.Y.; 13.22 Janetta Rebold Benton, Prof of Fine Arts, Pace University; 13.23 Ducal Palace, Venice. Image courtesy of Cameraphoto Arte di Codato G.P. & C.snc; 13.24 Erich Lessing/Museo Del Prado, Madrid, Spain\Art Resource, N.Y.; 13.25 Arnaudet. Musee du Louvre, Paris. Reunion des Musees National, France/Art Resource, NY; 13.26 Uffizi Gallery, Alinari, Florence, SCALA/Art Resource, NY; 13.27 ©National Gallery, London/Art Resource, NY; 13.28 San Giorgio Maggiore, Venice. SCALA/Art Resource, NY; 13.29 Archivo Fotographico Oronoz, Madrid; 13.30 Milwaukee Art Museum, Gift of the Family of Mrs. Fred Vogel, Jr., L1952.1.; 13.31 National Museum of Women in the Arts, Washington, DC. Gift of Wallace and Wilhelmina Holladay; 13.32 Kunsthistorisches Museum, Vienna, Austria; 13.33 SCALA\Art Resource, N.Y.; 13.34 SCALA\Art Resource, N.Y.; 13.35 Janetta Rebold Benton, Prof of Fine Arts, Pace University

Chapter Fourteen
14.1 The Cloisters Collection, 1956 (56.70). Metropolitan Museum of Art, New York; 14.2 © St. Baafskathedraal, Gent/ © Paul M. R. Maeyaert; 14.3 Erich Lessing / Art Resource, NY; 14.4 Monasterio de El Escorial, Spain/The Bridgeman Art Library; 14.5 Uffizi Gallery, Florence. Cranach. Scala/Art Resource, NY; 14.6 Galleria Nazionale d?Arte Antica, Rome.SCALA/Art Resource, NY; 14.7 Image copyright © The Metropolitan Museum of Art / Art Resource, NY; 14.8 Philadelphia Museum of Art, Philadelphia.; 14.9 Musée du Louvre, Paris.Reunion des Musees Nat'l/Art Resource, NY; 14.10 ©National Gallery, London; 14.11 Rogers Fund, 1919. Metropolitan Museum of Art, New York; 14.12 Erich Lessing/Art Resource, N.Y.; 14.13 ©Nils-Johan Norenlind; 14.14 Janetta Rebold Benton, Prof of Fine Arts, Pace University; 14.15 The Royal Collection ©2004 Her Majesty Queen Elizabeth II; 14.16 This item is reproduced by permission of The Huntington Library, San Marino, California; 14.17 Musee de l'Hotel Lallemant, Bourges, France/Giraudon/The Bridgeman Art Library International; 14.18 Lebrecht Authors

Chapter Fifteen
15.1 Alinari/Art Resource, N.Y.; 15.2 Janetta Rebold Benton, Prof of Fine Arts, Pace University; 15.3 Janetta Rebold Benton/Robert DiYanni; 15.4 © Gianni Dagli Orti/CORBIS; 15.5 David Sutherland © Dorling Kindersley; 15.6 Image courtesy of the Embassy of Italy; 15.7 Scala/Art Resource, N.Y.; 15.8 Galleria degli Uffizi, Florence. SCALA/Art Resource, NY; 15.9 National Museum of Women in the Arts, Washington, D.C. Gift of Wallace and Wilhelmina Holladay. Conservation funds generously provided by the Southern California State Committee of the National Museum of Women in the Arts; 15.10 Scala/Art Resource, N.Y.; 15.11 Scala/Art Resource, N.Y.; 15.12 Rijksmuseum, Amsterdam; 15.13 Nationalmuseum, Stockholm; 15.14 Rijksmuseum, Amsterdam; 15.15 ©SuperStock/Superstock; 15.16 Gift of Henry G. Marquand, 1889. Metropolitan Museum of Art, New York; 15.17 National Museum of Women in the Arts, Washington, D.C. Gift of Wallace and Wilhelmina Holladay; 15.18 Jean/Lewandowski. Musée du Louvre, Paris. Reunion des Musees Nationaux/Art Resource, NY; 15.19 Derechos reservados © Museo Nacional Del Prado – Madrid; 15.20 ©The Art Gallery Collection/Alamy; 15.21 Museo del Prado, Madrid, Spain. Erich Lessing/Art Resource, NY; 15.22 Bodleian Library, University of Oxford; 15.23 Derechos reservados © Museo Nacional Del Prado – Madrid; 15.24 Metropolitan Museum of Art, New York; 15.25 The Norton Simon Foundation; 15.26 Reunion des Musees Nationaux; 15.27 Massimo Listri\CORBIS- NY; 15.28 © Dorling Kindersley; 15.29 Girolamo Zenti. Robert Harding/Metropolitan Museum of Art, New York. Art Resource, NY; 15.30 The Crosby Brown Collection of Musical Instruments, 1889/Embassy of Mexico; 15.31 Courtesy of The Bancroft Library. University of California, Berkeley; 15.32 Courtesy of The Bancroft Library. University of California, Berkeley; 15.33 Scala/Art Resource, N.Y.

Chapter Sixteen
16.1 Gerard Blott. Musée du Louvre, Paris. Reunion des Musees National/Art Resource, NY; 16.2 Herve Lewandowski. Musée du Louvre, Paris. Reunion des Musees National/Art Resource, NY; 16.3 Copyright The Frick Collection, New York; 16.4 G. Blot/C. Jean. Louvre, Paris. Photo credit : Réunion des Musées Nationaux / Art Resource, NY; 16.5 Chateaux de Versailles et de Trianon, Versailles, France. RMN Reunion des Musees Nationaux/Art Resource, NY; 16.6 Image courtesy of Ets J. E. Bulloz; 16.7 ©National Gallery, London/Art Resource, NY; 16.8 Herve Lewandowski. Musée du Louvre, Paris. RMN Reunion des Musees National/Art Resource, NY; 16.9 Andrew W. Mellon Collection. 1937.1.95. Photograph © Board of Trustees, National Gallery of Art, Washington, D.C.; 16.10 London County Council, Kenwood House (Iveagh Bequest). English Heritage, London; 16.11 G. Blot/ C. Jean. ©Musee du Louvre/RMN Reunion des Musees Nationeux/Art Resource, NY; 16.12 Virginia Museum of Fine Arts, Richmond. The Adolph D. and Wilkins C. Williams Fund. Photo: Katherine Wetzel. © Virginia Museum of Fine Arts; 16.13 Gift of Mrs. George von Lengerke Meyer. Courtesy, Museum of Fine Arts, Boston. Reproduced with permission. © 2005 Museum of Fine Arts, Boston. All Rights Reserved; 16.14 State Capitol, Richmond, Virginia. Collection of the Commonwealth of Virginia. Photo Courtesy of the Library of Virginia; 16.15 Janetta Rebold Benton, Prof of Fine Arts, Pace University; 16.16 Image courtesy of Paul M. R. Maeyaert, Photographie; 16.17 © David R. Frazier Photolibrary, Inc.\Alamy Images; 16.18 Image courtesy of Photostage, Ltd.; 16.19 Janetta Rebold Benton/Robert DiYanni

Chapter Seventeen
17.1 Derechos reservados © Museo Nacional Del Prado – Madrid; 17.2 Musee du Louvre/RMN Reunion des Musees Nationaux, France. Bridgeman/Giraudon/Art Resource, NY; 17.3 Hervé Lewandowski. Musee du Louvre, Paris. Reunion des Musees National/Art Resource, NY; 17.4 Musée du Louvre, Paris. Reunion des Musees National. Erich Lessing/Art Resource, NY; 17.5 Fitzwilliam Museum; 17.6 ©National Gallery, London/Art Resource, NY; 17.7 Henry Lillie Pierce Fund. Courtesy, Museum of Fine Arts, Boston. Reproduced with permission. ©2005 Museum of Fine Arts, Boston. All Rights Reserved; 17.8 Lent by the Department of the Interior Museum. Smithsonian American Art Museum, Smithsonian Institution, Washington, DC. Art Resource, NY; 17.9 Arc de Triomphe, Place de l?Etoile, Paris. Image courtesy of Ets J. E. Bulloz.; 17.10 Janetta Rebold Benton, Prof of Fine Arts, Pace University; 17.11 Image courtesy of Robert Harding Picture Library Ltd; 17.12 By permission of The British Library; 17.13 ©The Trustees of the British Museum/Art Resource, NY; 17.14 ©Mary Evans Picture Library/Alamy Images; 17.15 Charles Deering Fund, 1953.530. Photograph ©2005, The Art Institute of Chicago. All Rights Reserved; 17.16 Musee d'Orsay, Paris, France. Erich Lessing/Art Resource, NY; 17.17 Musee d'Orsay, Paris, France. Photo: Herve Lewandowski. © Reunion des Musees Nationaux/Art Resource, NY; 17.18 Musee d'Orsay, Paris/Giraudon, Paris/SuperStock; 17.19 The Metropolitan Museum of Art, Gift of Mrs. Frank B. Porter, 1922. (22.207). Photograph ©1985 The Metropolitan Museum of Art, NY; 17.20 Amon Carter Museum, Purchased by the Friends of Art, Fort Worth Art Association, 1925; acquired by the Amon Carter Museum, 1990, from the Modern Art Museum of Fort Worth through grants and donations from the Amon G. Carter Foundation, the Sid W. Richardson Foundation, the Anne Burnett and Charles Tandy Foundation, Capital Cities/ABC Foundation, Fort Worth Star-Telegram, The R.D. and Joan Dale Hubbard Foundation and the people of Fort Worth; 17.21 National Museum of Women in the Arts, Washington, D.C. Gift of Wallace and Wilhelmina Holladay; 17.22 By courtesy of the National Portrait Gallery, London; 17.23 Philadelphia Museum of Art: City of Philadelphia, Trade & Convention Center, Dept. of Commerce (Commercial Museum); 17.24 Museum of Modern Art, New York/Licensed by Scala-Art Resource, NY; 17.25 National Museum of Women in the Arts, Washington, D.C. Gift of the Holladay Foundation; 17.26 © Kjell Brynildsen / istockphoto; 17.27 Smithsonian American Art Museum, DC. Art Resource, NY; 17.28 ©Ulrike Welsch

Chapter Eighteen
18.1 Painted in Le Havre, France. © Estate of Claude Monet/ARS Artists Rights Society, NY; 18.2 R. G. Ojeda. Musee d'Orsay, Paris. Reunion des Musees Nationaux/Art Resource, NY; 18.3 ©2004 Artists Rights Society (ARS), New York. Louvre Museum/Art Resource, NY; 18.4 ©National Gallery, London/Art Resource, NY; 18.5 ©National Gallery, London/Art Resource, NY; 18.6 Chester Dale Collection. Photograph © Board of Trustees, National Gallery of Art, Washington, D.C. 1963.10.94 (1758)/PA; 18.7 Jean Schormans. Musee d'Orsay, Paris. Reunion des Musees Nationaux/Art Resource, NY; 18.8 Acquired 1925. The Phillips Collection, Washington, DC; 18.9 Chester Dale Collection. Photograph © Board of Trustees, National Gallery of Art, Washington, D.C.; 18.10 Helen Birch Bartlett Memorial Collection. Photograph © 2005, The Art Institute of Chicago. All Rights Reserved; 18.11 Acquired through the Lillie P. Bliss Bequest. The Museum of Modern Art/ Licensed by Scala-Art Resource, NY; 18.12 National Museum Vincent van Gogh, Amsterdam; 18.13 A. Conger Goodyear Collection, 1965. Albright-Knox Art Gallery, Buffalo; 18.14 The Metropolitan Museum of Art, NY, Gift of Thomas F. Ryan, 1910 (11.173.9). Art Resource, NY; 18.15 ©Ramón Jimenez /Alamy; 18.16 Bayerische Staatsgemaldesammlungen, Neue Pinakothek, Munich; 18.17 Janetta Rebold Benton, Prof of Fine Arts, Pace University; 18.18 ©Art on file/ CORBIS; 18.19 © Bastin & J. Evrard; 18.20 Janetta Rebold Benton, Prof of Fine Arts, Pace University

Chapter Nineteen
19.1 National Palace Museum, Taipei, Taiwan, Republic of China; 19.2 Gift of Ruth and Bruce Dayton. The Minneapolis Institute of Arts; 19.3 The Nelson-Atkins Museum of Art, Kansas City, Missouri; 19.4 Image copyright © The Metropolitan Museum of Art / Art Resource, NY; 19.5 © The Cleveland Museum of Art, John L. Severance Fund, 1966.31.8; 19.6 Bequest of John M. Crawford Jr., 1988 (1989.363.137).The Metropolitan Museum of Art, New York, NY, U.S.A. Photo Credit: Image copyright © The Metropolitan Museum of Art / Art Resource, NY; 19.7 Hsaio Hua Collection; 19.8 The Metropolitan Museum of Art, New York, NY, U.S.A. Image copyright © The Metropolitan Museum of Art / Art Resource, NY; 19.9 Image copyright © The Metropolitan Museum of Art/Art Resource, NY; 19.10 PanoramaStock/Robert Harding; 19.11 Janetta Rebold Benton/Robert DiYanni; 19.12 Janetta Rebold Benton, Prof of Fine Arts, Pace University; 19.13 Image courtesy of Photostage, Ltd.; 19.14 © 2002 Linda Vartoogian/FrontRowPhotos. ALL RIGHTS RESERVED

Chapter Twenty
20.1 Sakamoto Manschichi Photo Research Library, Tokyo; 20.2 Chikusei Collection; 20.3 New York Public Library. Art Resource/NY; 20.4 Private Collection. Art Resource, NY; 20.5 Art Resource, N.Y.; 20.6 The Metropolitan Museum of Art, New York, NY, U.S.A. Image copyright © The Metropolitan Museum of Art / Art Resource, NY; 20.7 Image copyright © The Metropolitan Museum of Art / Art Resource, NY; 20.8 Image courtesy of the Japan National Tourist Organization; 20.9 Janetta Rebold Benton, Prof of Fine Arts, Pace University; 20.10 ©Catherine Karnow/CORBIS, Inc.; 20.11 Bill Tingrey\Arcaid; 20.12 © 2003 Jack Vartoogian/ FrontRowPhotos. ALL RIGHTS RESERVED

Chapter Twenty-One
21.1 Musee du quai Branley. Reserved Rights; 21.2 Fine Arts Museums of San Francisco, Gift of Vivian Burns, Inc., 74.8; 21.3 The Metropolitan Museum of Art, The Michael C. Rockefeller Memorial Collection, Gift of Adrian Pascal LaGamma, 1973. (1978.412.664). Art Resource, NY; 21.4 © Sandro Vannini / CORBIS; 21.5 Dennis J. Nervig/Fowler Museum of Cultural History, UCLA; 21.6 The Metropolitan Museum of Art, New York, NY, U.S.A. Image copyright © The Metropolitan Museum of Art / Art Resource, NY.; 21.7 Teepan Union Housing Project, Tlatelco, Mexico. Photo by Dr. Desmond Rochfort. Reproduction authorized by the Instituto Nacional de Bellas Artes y Literatura; 21.8 Museo Nacional de Arte Moderno, © 2001 Banco de Mexico Diego Rivera & Frida Kahlo Museums Trust/Artists Rights Society (ARS), NY. Av. Cinco de Mayo No. 2, Col. Centro, Del. Cuauhtemoc 06059,

Mexico, D.F. Reproduction authorized by the Instituto Nacional de Bellas Artes y Literatura. Bob Schalkwijk/Art Resource, NY; 21.9 Inter-American Fund. Museum of Modern Art, NY/Licensed by Scala-Art Resource, NY. ©2005 Artists Rights Society (ARS), NY; 21.10 Inter-American Fund. Museum of Modern Art, NY/ Licensed by Scala-Art Resource, NY

Chapter Twenty-Two

22.1 Bequest of Elise S. Haas. Photo: San Francisco Museum of Modern Art. ©Succession H. Matisse/Artists Rights Society (ARS), New York. Photography: Ben Blackwell; 22.2 Digital image © The Museum of Modern Art / Licensed by SCALA / Art Resource, NY. © 2003 Estate of Pablo Picasso / Artists Rights Society (ARS), New York; 22.3 Kunstmuseum, Basel, Switzerland. ©2005 Artists Rights Society (ARS), NY. © ADAGP, Paris and DACS, London 1998; 22.4 Photo: R.G. Ojeda. Musee Picasso, Paris. Reunion des Musees Nationaux. Art Resource, NY. © 2008 Estate of Pablo Picasso / Artists Rights Society (ARS), New York; 22.5 Inv. AM3307P. Musee National d'Art Moderne. Centre National d'Art et de Culture. Georges Pompidou. Philippe Migeat/Reunion des Musees Nationaux/Art Resource, NY; 22.6 Tate Gallery, London. ©2005 Artists Rights Society (ARS), NY; 22.7 Image courtesy of Stiftung Seebull Ada und Emil Nolde; 22.8 Photograph ©2005, The Art Institute of Chicago. All Rights Reserved. ©2005 Artist Rights Society (ARS), NY; 22.9 Philadelphia Museum of Art. © DACS 1998. ©2005 Artists Rights Society (ARS), NY; 22.10 Photograph by Alfred Stieglitz in "The Blind Man, no. 2, May 1917; original lost. ©Philadelphia Museum of Art: The Louise and Walter Arensberg Collection. 1998-74-1 © 2003 Artist's Rights Society (ARS), New York/ADAGP, Paris/Estate of Marcel Duchamp; 22.11 Courtesy Wadsworth Atheneum, Hartford, Connecticut. ©2005 Artist Rights Society (ARS), NY. ADAGP, Paris/DACS, London 1998; 22.12 Digital Image © The Museum of Modern Art/Licensed by SCALA/Art Resource, NY. (162.1934). Given anonymously. ©2002 Kingdom of Spain. ©2005 Salvador Dali, Gala-Salvador Dali Foundation / Artists Rights Society (ARS), New York; 22.13 Purchase. The Museum of Modern Art/ Licensed by Scala-Art Resource, NY. ©2007 ARS Artists Rights Society, NY; 22.14 Stedelijk Museum, Amsterdam. ©2011 Mondrian/Holtzman Trust c/o HCR International, Virginia; 22.15 The Museum of Modern Art/Licensed by Scala-Art Resource, NY. Given anonymously. Photograph © 2000 The Museum of Modern Art, New York. © 2000 Artists Rights Society (ARS), New York ADAGP, Paris; 22.16 Tate Gallery, London, Great Britain. Art Resource, NY © Copyright Henry Moore Foundation; 22.17 The Henry Moore Foundation/Tate Picture Gallery, London, UK; 22.18 Vanni\Art Resource, N.Y.; 22.19 Anthony Scibilia/Art Resource, NY. ©2001 Artists Rights Society (ARS), New York/ADAGP, Paris/FLC; 22.20 Janetta Rebold Benton/Robert DiYanni; 22.21 Smithsonian American Art Museum, Washington, DC. Art Resource, NY. ©2005 Artists Rights Society (ARS), NY; 22.22 Gift of Ferdinand Howald. Columbus Museum of Art, Columbus, Ohio; 22.23 © ADAGP, Paris and DACS, London 1998; 22.24 Stedelijk Van Abbemuseum, Eindhoven © DACS 1998; 22.25 Museo Nacinal Centro de Arts Reina Sofia, Madrid, Spain. John Bigelow Taylor/Art Resource, NY ©2007 Estate of Pablo Picasso/Artists Rights Society (ARS), NY; 22.26 Courtesy of the Library of Congress; 22.27 Courtesy of the Library of Congress; 22.28 Getty Images, Inc/Timepix; 22.29 National Museum of Women in the Arts, Washington, D.C. Gift of Helen Cumming Ziegler. ©1989 Center for Creative Photography, Arizona Board of Regents; 22.30 National Museum of Women in the Arts, Washington, D.C. Gift of the Artist. ©1995 Center for Creative Photography, The University of Arizona Foundation; 22.31 Friends of American Art Collection, 1942.1 ©1997 Art Institute of Chicago. Photograph ©2005, The Art Institute of Chicago. All Rights Reserved; 22.32 Missouri State Capitol, Jefferson City, Missouri. ©T.H. Benton and R.P. Benton Testamentary Trusts/Licensed by VAGA, New York, NY; 22.33 Courtesy of the Jacob and Gwendolyn Lawrence Foundation. Phillips Collection, Washington, DC; 22.34 Stedelijk Van Abbemuseum, Eindhoven, The Netherlands; 22.35 Gift of Edsel B. Ford. © 2003 Banco de Mexico Diego Rivera & Frida Kahlo Museums Trust. Av. Cinco de Mayo No. 2, Col. Centro, Del. Cuauhtemoc 06059, Mexico, D.F. Reproduction authorized by the Instituto Nacional de Bellas Artes y Literatura. The Detroit Institute of Arts; 22.36 Max Jones Archive/Courtesy of the Library of Congress

Chapter Twenty-Three

23.1 Peter Newark's American Pictures/Courtesy of the Library of Congress; 23.2 George A. Hearn Fund, 1957. ©2005 ARS, NY. Metropolitan Museum of Art, NY; 23.3 Photograph courtesy Robert Miller Gallery, New York. Estate of Lee Krasner ©2008 Artist Rights Society (ARS), New York; 23.4 Gift of Mr. & Mrs. Noah Goldowsky and Edgar Kaufmann, Jr; Mr. & Mrs. Frank G. Logan Purchase Prize, 1952.1. Photograph ©1997, The Art Institute of Chicago. All Rights Reserved. ©2005 Artists Rights Society (ARS), NY; 23.5 Mrs. Simon Guggenheim Fund. Museum of Modern Art, NY/Licensed by Scala-Art Resource, NY. © ARS, NY; 23.6 Mrs. Donald Straus Fund. Museum of Modern Art, NY/Licensed by Scala-Art Resource, NY. © 2009 Helen Frankenthaler/ Artists Rights Society (ARS), New York; 23.7 National Museum of Women in the Arts, Washington, D.C. Gift of the Artist; 23.8 Ezra Stoller ©Esto; 23.9 Image courtesy of Paul M. R. Maeyaert, Photographie; 23.10 Janetta Rebold Benton, Prof of Fine Arts, Pace University; 23.11 Image copyright ©The Metropolitan Museum of Art/Art Resource, NY; 23.12 Metropolitan Museum of Art, New York.Fletcher Fund, 1953. (53.87a-i). Art Resource, NY; 23.13 Museum Ludwig, Koln. Rheinisches Bildarchiv, Koln. Art© Robert Rauschenberg /Licensed by VAGA, New York, NY; 23.14 Digital Image © The Museum of Modern Art/Licensed by SCALA / Art Resource, NY. ©2008 Artist Rights Society (ARS), NY; 23.15 Gift of Mr. and Mrs. Peter Eider-Orley, 1972; 23.16 The Museum of Modern Art/Licensed by Scala-Art Resource, NY. Philip Johnson Fund and gift of Mr. and Mrs. Bagley Wright. Photograph ©2005 The Museum of Modern Art, New York; 23.17 Philip Johnson Fund. Museum of Modern Art, NY/Licensed by Scala-Art Resource, NY; 23.18 Whitney Museum of American Art, New York;. Purchase, with funds from the Friends of the Whitney Museum of American Art 64.17a-g. Collection of the Whitney Museum of American Art, New York. Art © Marisol Escobar/Licensed by VAGA, New York, NY; 23.19 Photo: Jack Mitchell. Cunningham Dance Foundation, DACS; 23.20 ©2005 ARS, NY/Art Gallery of Ontario, Toronto; 23.21 © Tate Gallery, London/Art Resource, NY; 23.22 De Agostini/Getty Images

Chapter Twenty-Four

24.1 Image copyright © The Metropolitan Museum of Art / Art Resource, NY; 24.2 Collection of The Brooklyn Museum of Art, Gift of the Elizabeth A. Sackler Foundation. Photograph ©Donald Woodman/Through th Flower. © 2005 Judy Chicago/Artists Rights Society (ARS), New York; 24.3 Courtesy www.guerrillagirls.com; 24.4 Courtesy Ronald Feldman Fine Arts, NY; 24.5 © The Estate of Jean-Michel Basquiat/©2009 Artists Rights Society (ARS), NY; 24.6 Image courtesy of Social and Public Art Resource Center; 24.7 Private Collection;

24.8 ©Peter Aaron/Esto; 24.9 Courtesy Fondazione Prada, Milan, Italy. Photo: Attilo Maranzano; 24.10 Janetta Rebold Benton, Prof of Fine Arts, Pace University; 24.11 ©Prisma /Superstock; 24.12 Janetta Rebold Benton, Prof of Fine Arts, Pace University; 24.13 ©Luz Martin/Alamy Images; 24.14 Janetta Rebold Benton, Prof of Fine Arts, Pace University; 24.15 Janetta Rebold Benton, Prof of Fine Arts, Pace University; 24.16 Janetta Rebold Benton, Prof of Fine Arts, Pace University; 24.17 Janetta Rebold Benton, Prof of Fine Arts, Pace University; 24.18 Janetta Rebold Benton, Prof of Fine Arts, Pace University; 24.19 Janetta Rebold Benton, Prof of Fine Arts, Pace University;

Index

E

F

G